BASIC WRITINGS OF

St. Thomas Aquinas

THE RANDOM HOUSE
Lifetime Library

BASIC WRITINGS OF
Saint
Thomas Aquinas

VOLUME TWO

Edited and Annotated, with an Introduction, by

ANTON C. PEGIS

President, Pontifical Institute of Mediaeval Studies,
Toronto

RANDOM HOUSE · NEW YORK

Twelfth Printing

NIHIL OBSTAT
ARTHUR J. SCANLAN, S.T.D.
Censor Librorum

IMPRIMATUR
✠ FRANCIS J. SPELLMAN, D.D.
Archbishop, New York

February 11, 1944.

MANUFACTURED IN THE U. S. A. BY
H. WOLFF, NEW YORK

GENERAL TABLE OF CONTENTS

Volume I

GOD AND THE ORDER OF CREATION

Summa Theologica, Part I (complete)

Volume II

MAN AND THE CONDUCT OF LIFE

Summa Contra Gentiles (III, Chapters 1-113)

Summa Theologica, First Part of the Second Part

Summa Theologica, Second Part of the Second Part

CONTENTS

Volume II

MAN AND THE CONDUCT OF LIFE

IX. THE END OF MAN.

TEXT: *Summa Contra Gentiles*, Book III, Chapters 1-63.

X. MAN AND THE PROVIDENCE OF GOD.

TEXT: *Summa Contra Gentiles,* Book III, Chapters 64-113.

XI. HUMAN ACTS.

TEXT: *Summa Theologica*, I-II, Questions 6-21.

CONTENTS

XII. HABITS, VIRTUES AND VICES.

TEXT: *Summa Theologica*, I-II, Questions 49-89.

CONTENTS

CONTENTS

XIII. LAW.

TEXT: *Summa Theologica*, I-II, Questions 90-108.

CONTENTS

XIV. GRACE.

TEXT: *Summa Theologica*, I-II, Questions 109-114.

XV. FAITH.

TEXT: *Summa Theologica*, II-II, Questions 1-7.

MAN AND THE CONDUCT OF LIFE

THE SUMMA CONTRA GENTILES

THIRD BOOK

CHAPTER I

FOREWORD

The Lord is a great God and a great King above all gods. For the Lord will not reject His people. For in His hands are all the ends of the earth and the heights of the mountains are His. For the sea is His and He made it, and His hands formed the dry land (Ps. xciv. 3 seqq.)

WE have shown in the preceding books that there is one First Being, possessing the full perfection of all being, Whom we call God, and Who, of the abundance of His perfection, bestows being on all that exists, so that He is proved to be not only the first of beings, but also the beginning of all. Moreover He bestows being on others, not through natural necessity, but according to the decree of His will, as we have shown above.[1] Hence it follows that He is the Lord of the things made by Him, since we are masters over those things that are subject to our will. Now it is a perfect dominion that He exercises over things made by Him, for in making them He needs neither the help of an extrinsic agent, nor matter as the foundation of His work. For He is the universal efficient cause of all being.

Now everything that is produced through the will of an agent is directed to an end by that agent, because the good and the end are the proper object of the will; and therefore whatever proceeds from a will must needs be directed to an end. But each thing attains its end by its own action, which action needs to be directed by him who endowed things with the principles whereby they act. Consequently God, Who in Himself is perfect in every way, and by His power endows all things with being, must needs be the Ruler of all, Himself ruled by none; nor is any thing to be excepted from His ruling, as neither is there any thing that does not owe its being to Him. Therefore, as He is perfect in being and causing, so He is perfect in ruling.

The effect of this ruling is seen to differ in different things, according to the difference of natures. For some things are so produced by God that, being intelligent, they bear a resemblance to Him and reflect His image. Hence, not only are they directed, but they direct themselves to their appointed end by their own actions. And if in thus directing themselves they

[1] *C. G.*, II, 23.

3

be subject to the divine ruling, they are admitted by that divine ruling to the attainment of their last end; but they are excluded therefrom if they direct themselves otherwise.

Others there are, lacking intelligence, which do not direct themselves to their end, but are directed by another. Of these some, being incorruptible, even as they are not subject to defect in their natural being, so neither do they wander, in their own actions, from the direction to their appointed end, but are subject, without fail, to the ruling of the supreme ruler. Such are the heavenly bodies, whose movements are invariable. Others, however, being corruptible, are subject to defects in their natural being; and yet this defect is supplied to the advantage of another, since when one thing is corrupted, another is generated. Likewise, they fail from their natural direction in their own actions, and yet this failing is compensated by some resultant good. Whence it is clear that not even those things which are seen to wander from the direction of the supreme ruling, escape from the power of the supreme ruler; for just as these corruptible bodies are created by God, so too are they perfectly subject to Him. Therefore, considering this, the Psalmist, filled with the divine spirit, in order to give us an illustration of the divine government, first describes to us the perfection of the supreme governor,—as to His nature when he says, *God;* as to His power, when he says, *a great Lord,* implying that He needs no one for His power to produce its effect; as to His authority, when he says, *A great king above all gods,* since, although there be many rulers, yet are all subject to His rule. Secondly, he describes to us the manner of this government. He describes it as regards intellectual beings, which, if they submit to His rule, receive from Him their last end which is Himself; and therefore he says, *For the Lord will not reject His people.* As regards things corruptible which, albeit at times they wander from their proper mode of action, never escape the power of the supreme ruler, he says, *Because in His hands are all the ends of the earth.* And as regards the heavenly bodies, which transcend the highest summits of the earth (that is, of corruptible bodies), and always maintain the order of the divine government, he says, *And the mountain heights are His.* Thirdly, he assigns the reason for this universal government, for the things that God made must needs be governed by Him. To this he refers when he says, *For the sea is His,* etc.

Since, then, in the First Book we have treated of the perfection of the divine nature, and, in the Second, of the perfection of the divine power, inasmuch as He is the creator and lord of all: it remains for us in this Third Book to treat of His perfect authority or dignity, inasmuch as He is the end and governor of all. We must therefore proceed in this wise, so as first to treat of Him as the end of all things; secondly of His universal government, inasmuch as He governs every creature;[1] thirdly, of that special government, whereby He governs creatures endowed with intellect.[2]

[1] Ch. 64.   [2] Ch. 111.

CHAPTER II

THAT EVERY AGENT ACTS FOR AN END

ACCORDINGLY we must first show that every agent, by its action, intends an end.

For in those things which clearly act for an end, we declare the end to be that towards which the movement of the agent tends; for when this is reached, the end is said to be reached, and to fail in this is to fail in the end intended. This may be seen in the physician who aims at health, and in a man who runs towards an appointed goal. Nor does it matter, as to this, whether that which tends to an end be endowed with knowledge or not; for just as the target is the end of the archer, so is it the end of the arrow's flight. Now the movement of every agent tends to something determinate, since it is not from any force that any action proceeds, but heating proceeds from heat, and cooling from cold; and therefore actions are differentiated by their active principles. Action sometimes terminates in something made, as for instance building terminates in a house, and healing in health; while sometimes it does not so terminate, as for instance, in the case of understanding and sensation. And if action terminates in something made, the movement of the agent tends by that action towards the thing made; while if it does not terminate in something made, the movement of the agent tends to the action itself. It follows therefore that every agent intends an end while acting, which end is sometimes the action itself, sometimes a thing made by the action.

Again. In all things that act for an end, that is said to be the last end beyond which the agent seeks nothing further; and thus the physician's action goes as far as health, and when this is attained, his efforts cease. But in the action of every agent, a point can be reached beyond which the agent does not desire to go; or else actions would tend to infinity, which is impossible, for since *it is not possible to pass through an infinite medium*,[1] the agent would never begin to act, because nothing moves towards what it cannot reach. Therefore every agent acts for an end.

Moreover. If the actions of an agent proceed to infinity, these actions must needs result either in something made, or not. If the result is something made, the being of that thing made will follow after an infinity of actions. But that which presupposes an infinity of things cannot possibly be, since *an infinite medium cannot be passed through*. Now impossibility of being argues impossibility of becoming, and that which cannot become, it is impossible to make. Therefore it is impossible for an agent to begin to make a thing for the making of which an infinity of actions is presupposed.

[1] Aristotle, *Post. Anal.*, I, 22 (82b 38).

—If, however, the result of such actions be not something made, the order of these actions must be either according to the order of active powers (for instance, if a man feels that he may imagine, and imagines that he may understand, and understands that he may will), or according to the order of objects (for instance, I consider the body that I may consider the soul, which I consider in order to consider a separate substance, which again I consider so that I may consider God). Now it is not possible to proceed to infinity, either in active powers (as neither is this possible in the forms of things, as is proved in *Metaph.* ii,[1] since the form is the principle of activity), or in objects (as neither is this possible in beings, since there is one first being, as we have proved above).[2] Therefore it is not possible for agents to proceed to infinity, and consequently there must be something, upon whose attainment the efforts of the agent cease. Therefore every agent acts for an end.

Further. In things that act for an end, whatsoever comes between the first agent and the last end, is an end in respect to what precedes, and an active principle in respect of what follows. Hence if the effort of the agent does not tend to something determinate, and if its action, as stated, proceeds to infinity, the active principles must needs proceed to infinity; which is impossible, as we have shown above. Therefore the effort of the agent must of necessity tend to something determinate.

Again. Every agent acts either by nature or by intellect. Now there can be no doubt that those which act by intellect act for an end, since they act *with* an intellectual preconception of what they attain by their action, and they act *through* such a preconception; for this is to act by intellect. Now just as in the preconceiving intellect there exists the entire likeness of the effect that is attained by the action of the intellectual being, so in the natural agent there pre-exists the likeness of the natural effect, by virtue of which the action is determined to the appointed effect; for fire begets fire, and an olive produces an olive. Therefore, even as that which acts by intellect tends by its action to a definite end, so also does that which acts by nature. Therefore every agent acts for an end.

Moreover. Fault is not found save in those things which are for an end, for we do not find fault with one who fails in that to which he is not appointed; and thus we find fault with a physician if he fail to heal, but not with a builder or a grammarian. But we find fault in things done according to art, as when a grammarian fails to speak correctly, and in things that are ruled by nature, as in the case of monstrosities. Therefore every agent, whether according to nature, or according to art, or acting of set purpose, acts for an end.

Again. Were an agent not to act for a definite effect, all effects would be indifferent to it. Now that which is indifferent to many effects does not produce one rather than another. Therefore, from that which is indifferent to

---

[1] Aristotle, *Metaph.*, I a, 2 (994, 6).   [2] *C. G.*, I, 42.

either of two effects, no effect results, unless it be determined by something to one of them. Hence it would be impossible for it to act. Therefore every agent tends to some definite effect, which is called its end.

There are, however, certain actions which would seem not to be for an end, such as playful and contemplative actions, and those which are done without attention, such as scratching one's beard, and the like. Whence some might be led to think that there is an agent that acts not for an end. —But we must observe that contemplative actions are not for another end, but are themselves an end. Playful actions are sometimes an end, when one plays for the mere pleasure of play; and sometimes they are for an end, as when we play that afterwards we may study better. Actions done without attention do not proceed from the intellect, but from some sudden act of the imagination, or some natural principle; and thus a disordered humor produces an itching sensation and is the cause of a man scratching his beard, which he does without his intellect attending to it. Such actions do tend to an end, although outside the order of the intellect. Hereby is excluded the error of certain natural philosophers of old, who maintained that all things happen by the necessity of matter, thus utterly banishing the final cause from things.[1]

CHAPTER III

THAT EVERY AGENT ACTS FOR A GOOD

HENCE we must go on to prove that every agent acts for a good.

For that every agent acts for an end clearly follows from the fact that every agent tends to something definite. Now that to which an agent tends definitely must needs be befitting to that agent, since the agent would not tend to it save because of some fittingness thereto. But that which is befitting to a thing is good for it. Therefore every agent acts for a good.

Further. The end is that wherein the appetite of the agent or mover comes to rest, as also the appetite of that which is moved. Now it is the very notion of good to be the term of appetite, since *good is the object of every appetite*.[2] Therefore all action and movement is for a good.

Again. All action and movement would seem to be directed in some way to being, either for the preservation of being in the species or in the individual, or for the acquisition of being. Now this itself, namely, being, is a good; and for this reason all things desire being. Therefore all action and movement is for a good.

Furthermore. All action and movement is for some perfection. For if the action itself be the end, it is clearly a second perfection of the agent. And if the action consist in the transformation of external matter, clearly the

[1] Cf. Aristotle, *Phys.*, II, 8 (198b 12).   [2] Aristotle, *Eth.*, I, 1 (1094a 1).

mover intends to induce some perfection into the thing moved, towards which perfection the movable also tends, if the movement be natural. Now we say that this is to be good, namely, to be perfect. Therefore every action and movement is for a good.

Also. Every agent acts according as it is actual. Now by acting it tends to something similar to itself. Therefore it tends to an act. But an act has the nature of good, since evil is not found save in a potentiality lacking act. Therefore every action is for a good.

Moreover. The intellectual agent acts for an end, as determining for itself its end; whereas the natural agent, though it acts for an end, as was proved above,[1] does not determine its end for itself, since it knows not the nature of end, but is moved to the end determined for it by another. Now an intellectual agent does not determine the end for itself except under the aspect of good; for the intelligible object does not move except it be considered as a good, which is the object of the will. Therefore the natural agent also is not moved, nor does it act for an end, except in so far as this end is a good, since the end is determined for the natural agent by some appetite. Therefore every agent acts for a good.

Again. To shun evil and to seek good are of the same nature, even as movement from below and upward are of the same nature. Now we observe that all things shun evil, for intellectual agents shun a thing for the reason that they apprehend it as evil, and all natural agents, in proportion to their strength, resist corruption which is the evil of everything. Therefore all things act for a good.

Again. That which results from the agent's action outside his intention, is said to happen by chance or luck. Now we observe in the works of nature that either always or more often that happens which is best: thus in plants the leaves are so placed as to protect the fruit; and the parts of an animal are so disposed as to conduce to the animal's safety. Therefore, if this happens outside the intention of the natural agent, it will be the result of chance or luck. But that is impossible, because things that happen always, or frequently, are not by chance or fortuitous, but those which occur seldom.[2] Therefore the natural agent tends to that which is best; and much more evidently is this so with the intellectual agent. Therefore every agent intends a good in acting.

Moreover. Whatever is moved is brought to the term of movement by the mover and agent. Therefore mover and moved tend to the same term. Now that which is moved, since it is in potentiality, tends to an act, and consequently to perfection and goodness; for by its movement it passes from potentiality to act. Therefore mover and agent by moving and acting always intend a good.

---

[1] Ch. 2.   [2] Cf. Aristotle, *Phys.*, II, 5 (196b 11).

Hence the philosophers in defining the good said: *The good is the object of every appetite;* and Dionysius says that *all things desire the good and the best.*[1]

CHAPTER IV

THAT EVIL IS UNINTENTIONAL IN THINGS

It follows from the above that evil is incidental to things beside the intention of an agent.

For when the result of an action differs from the intention of the agent, it is clear that such result occurs unintentionally. Now evil differs from good, which every agent intends. Therefore evil happens without intention.

Also. Defect in effect and action results from defect in the principles of action. Thus a monstrosity results from a defect in the seed, and limping results from a curvature of the leg. Now an agent acts according as it is possessed of active power, and not according as it suffers from defective power. And according as it acts, it intends the end. Therefore it intends an end corresponding to its power. Hence whatever follows corresponding to the defective power will be outside the agent's intention. And this is evil. Therefore evil occurs without intention.

Again. The movement of the thing moved has the same tendency as the motion of the mover. Now the thing moved tends *per se* to good, but to evil it tends accidentally and unintentionally. This is most evident in generation and corruption. For matter, while it underlies one form, is in potentiality to another form, and to the privation of the form which it has already. Thus, when it is under the form of air, it is in potentiality to the form of fire and the privation of the form of air. And the transformation of matter terminates in both at the same time: in the form of fire by reason of fire being generated, and in the privation of the form of air by reason of the air being corrupted. But the intention and appetite of matter is not towards the privation, but towards the form. For it does not tend towards the impossible, and it is impossible for matter to be alone under a privation, whereas it is possible for it to be under a form. Therefore it is unintentional that it terminate in privation; but it terminates therein in so far as it attains the form which it intends, the necessary result of which is the privation of the other form. Therefore in generation and corruption the transformation of matter is directed *per se* to the form, and privation results unintentionally. And the same must needs apply to all movements, so that in every movement there is generation and corruption in some respect. For instance, when a thing is changed from white to black, a white thing is

[1] *De Div. Nom.,* IV, 4 (PG 3, 699).

corrupted and a black one results. Now the good is according as matter is perfected by the form, and potentiality by its proper act; while evil is according as it is deprived of its proper act. Consequently, whatever is moved intends in its movement to attain some good; and it attains evil without its intention. Hence, since every agent and mover tends to the good, evil occurs without the intention of the agent.

Moreover. In those things that act by intellect or any kind of judgment, intention follows apprehension, because the intention is towards that which is apprehended as an end. Accordingly if something is attained that has no species in the apprehension, it will be outside the intention. For instance, if one were to intend to eat honey, and were to eat gall thinking that it was honey, this will be outside the intention. But every intellectual agent tends to something in so far as he considers it under the aspect of good, as we have shown above.[1] Therefore if this be not a good but an evil, it will be without intention. Therefore that which acts by intellect does not work evil except unintentionally. Therefore, since to tend to a good is common to intellectual and natural agents, evil does not ensue from the intention of an agent except without that intention. In this sense Dionysius says that *evil is unintentional and involuntary*.[2]

CHAPTERS V AND VI

ARGUMENTS THAT WOULD SEEM TO PROVE THAT EVIL IS NOT WITHOUT INTENTION [AND THEIR SOLUTION]

THERE are, however, some objections that would seem to run counter to this conclusion.

[1] For that which occurs without the intention of the agent is said to happen fortuitously, by chance and seldom. But evil is not said to happen fortuitously and by chance, nor does it occur seldom but always or frequently. For in the physical order generation is always accompanied by corruption. And in voluntary agents sin is of frequent occurrence, since *it is as difficult to behave virtuously, as to find the center of a circle*, as Aristotle states.[3] Therefore it would seem that evil is not an unintentional occurrence.

[2] Again. Aristotle says expressly that *vice is voluntary*,[4] and he proves this from the fact that a man does an injustice voluntarily (and *it is absurd to suppose that the man who does unjust actions voluntarily does not wish to be unjust, and that he who rapes voluntarily does not wish to be incontinent*), and again from the fact that legislators punish evil-doers as

---

[1] Ch. 3.   [2] *De Div. Nom.*, IV, 32; 35 (PG 3, 732; 736).   [3] *Eth.*, II, 9 (1109a 24).
[4] *Op. cit.*, III, 5 (1112b 16).

doing evil voluntarily. Therefore evil would seem not to be unintentional or involuntary.

[3] Further. Every natural movement has an end intended by nature. Now corruption is a natural movement, even as is generation. Therefore its end, which is privation having the aspect of evil, is intended by nature; even as are the form and the good, which are the end of generation.

[*Chapter VI*] In order that the solution of the arguments here given may be made clear we must observe that evil may be considered either as in a substance, or as in its action. In a substance there is evil through its lacking something natural and due to it. For that a man have not wings is not an evil to him, because it is not natural for him to have them; and again if a man have not fair hair, this is no evil, for although he may have it naturally, it is not due to him. But it is an evil if he have no hands, which are natural and due to him, if he be perfect; and yet it is not an evil to a bird. Now every privation, if we take it properly and strictly, is the lack of something natural and due; and consequently the character of evil is always in a privation thus understood.

Matter, since it is in potentiality to all forms, is adapted by nature to all of them, yet no one is due to it; since it can be actually perfect without any particular one. Nevertheless, some one of them is due to one of those things that are made of matter; for there can be no water without the form of water, nor can there be fire without the form of fire. Accordingly, the privation of such a form, in relation to matter, is not an evil to matter; but in relation to that thing of which it is the form, it is an evil (and thus the privation of the form of fire is an evil for fire). And since privations as well as habits and forms are not said to exist except inasmuch as they are in a subject, if privation be an evil in relation to the subject wherein it is, it will be an evil absolutely. Otherwise it will be the evil of something, but not absolutely. Hence that a man be deprived of a hand is an evil absolutely; but that matter be deprived of the form of air is not an evil absolutely, but an evil of the air. On the other hand, privation of order or due proportion in an action is an evil of the action. And since to every action order and proportion are due, such a privation in an action must needs be an evil absolutely.

Accordingly, taking these remarks into account, we must note that what is unintentional is not always fortuitous or by chance, as the *first argument* stated. For if that which is unintentional be always or frequently the result of that which was intended, it will not happen fortuitously or by chance. Thus if a man intends to enjoy the sweetness of wine, and becomes drunk through drinking, this will be neither fortuitous nor by chance, but it would be by chance if such a result were to occur seldom.

Therefore the evil of natural corruption, although it ensue outside the intention of the generator, follows nevertheless always, since the presence of one form is always accompanied by the privation of another. Therefore corruption does not ensue by chance, nor even seldom; although sometimes privation is not an evil absolutely, but the evil of some particular thing, as was stated above. If, however, the privation be such as to deprive the thing generated of that which is due to it, it will be by chance and an evil absolutely, as in the birth of monstrosities. For this does not follow of necessity from that which was intended, but is opposed thereto; since the agent intends the perfection of the thing generated.

Evil of action occurs in natural agents through a defect in the active power. Hence if the agent's power be defective, this evil ensues without intention; yet it will not be by chance, because it follows of necessity from such an agent (provided always that the agent in question always or frequently suffers this defect). But it will be by chance if this defect seldom accompanies this agent.

In voluntary agents the intention is directed to some particular good, if the action is to follow; for movement is not caused by universals but by singulars, among which actions are found. Hence, if the good that is intended is accompanied always or frequently by the privation of the good dictated by the reason, moral evil ensues not by chance, but either always or frequently: as in the case of a man who desires intercourse with a woman for the sake of pleasure, to which pleasure is connected the inordination of adultery: wherefore the evil of adultery is not by chance. It would, however, be a chance evil, if sin were to ensue seldom from what he intends: as in one who, while aiming at a bird, kills a man.

That anyone should intend such goods which frequently result in privation of a good dictated by the reason is due to the fact that many live according to sense; for sensible things are the more manifest to us, and move more efficaciously in a world of individual things among which operation takes place: and privation of the good dictated by the reason ensues from many goods of that kind.

Hence it follows that, although evil is without intention, it is nevertheless voluntary, as the *second argument* states, accidentally however and not *per se*. For intention is directed to the last end, which we will for its own sake. But the will is directed also to that which we will for the sake of something else, even though we would not will it absolutely. For instance, the man who throws his cargo overboard for the sake of safety, intends not the throwing of his cargo, but safety, and he wills the throwing of the cargo, not absolutely, but for the sake of safety. In like manner, for the sake of obtaining a sensible good a man wills to perform an inordinate action, neither intending the inordinateness nor willing it absolutely, but for the sake of something in particular. In the same way, therefore, sin and vice are said to be voluntary, as the throwing of a ship's cargo into the sea.

The *third objection* is solved on the same lines. For the change of corruption is never found without the change of generation; and consequently neither is the end of corruption found without the end of generation. Hence nature does not intend the end of corruption apart from the end of generation, but both at the same time. For it is not the absolute intention of nature that there be no water, but that there be air, the existence of which precludes the existence of water. Accordingly, nature intends directly that there should be air, but it does not intend that there should not be water except in so far as this is involved by the existence of air. Therefore privations are not intended by nature directly, but accidentally, whereas forms are intended directly.

From the foregoing it is clear that what is evil absolutely is utterly without intention in the operations of nature, for example, the birth of monstrosities; but which is evil, not absolutely, but relatively, is intended by nature, not directly, but accidentally.

CHAPTER VII

THAT EVIL IS NOT AN ESSENCE

FROM this it follows that no essence is evil in itself.

For evil, as we have said,[1] is nothing else but *the privation of what is connatural and due to anyone;* for the term *evil* is used in this sense by all. Now privation is not an essence, but is *the non-existence of something in a substance.*[2] Therefore evil is not a real essence.

Again. Each thing has being according to its essence. Now in so far as it has being, it has a share of good; for if *good is what all desire,* being itself must be called a good, since all things desire being. Therefore a thing is good in so far as it has an essence. But good and evil are opposed to each other. Therefore nothing is evil in so far as it has an essence. Therefore no essence is evil.

Moreover. Every thing is either an agent or something made. But evil cannot be an agent, for that which acts, acts inasmuch as it is actually existing and perfect. In like manner, neither can it be something made, since the term of every generation is a form and a good. Therefore nothing is evil as to its essence.

Again. Nothing tends to its contrary, for everything desires what is like it and becoming to it. Now everything by acting intends a good, as we proved above.[3] Therefore no being as such is evil.

Further. Every essence is natural to some thing. For if it be in the genus of substance, it is the very nature of a thing. And if it be in the genus of accident, it must needs flow from the principles of some substance, and thus will be natural to that substance; although perchance it may not be natural to some other substance. Thus heat is natural to fire, whereas it is

---

[1] Ch. 6.   [2] Aristotle, *Metaph.*, III, 2 (1004a 16).   [3] Ch. 3.

not natural to water. Now that which is evil in itself cannot be natural to a thing. For it belongs to the very nature of evil to be the privation of that which is connatural and due to a thing. Therefore evil, since it is the privation of what is natural, cannot be natural to a thing. Hence, whatever is in a thing naturally is good for that thing, and it is an evil if it be lacking. Therefore no essence is evil in itself.

Moreover. Whatever has an essence is either itself a form, or has a form, since it is by the form that each thing is placed in a genus or species. Now a form, as such, has the character of goodness, for it is the principle of action, and the end which every maker intends; and it is the act whereby whatever has a form is perfect. Therefore whatever has an essence, as such, is good. Therefore evil has not an essence.

Further. Being is divided by act and potentiality. Now act, as such, is a good, because in so far as a thing is in act, it is perfect. Again, potentiality is a good, for potentiality tends to act, as may clearly be seen in every kind of movement. Also, it is proportionate to act, and not contrary thereto. Moreover it is in the same genus as act. Furthermore privation does not apply to it save accidentally. Therefore everything that is, in whatever way it is, in so far as it is a being, is a good. Therefore evil has not an essence.

Again. It has been proved in the Second Book of this work that every being, in whatever way it is, is from God;[1] and we have shown in the First Book that God is perfect goodness.[2] Since, then, evil cannot be the effect of good, it is impossible for a being, as such, to be evil. Hence it is that it is said (*Gen.* i. 31): *God saw all the things that he had made, and they were very good;* and (*Eccles.* iii. 11): *He hath made all things good in their time;* and (*1 Tim.* iv. 4): *Every creature of God is good.*

Again, Dionysius says *that evil is not a thing that exists,* namely, *per se,* nor is it *something in things that exist,* as an accident, like whiteness or blackness.[3]

Hereby is refuted the error of the Manichees who held that there are certain things evil by their very nature.

CHAPTERS VIII AND IX

ARGUMENTS WHEREBY IT IS SEEMINGLY PROVED THAT EVIL IS A NATURE OR A THING
[AND THEIR SOLUTION]

It would seem that certain arguments militate against the aforesaid statement.

[1] For each thing derives its species from its proper difference. Now evil is a specific difference in certain genera, namely in moral habits and

---

[1] *C. G.,* II, 15.   [2] *C. G.,* I, 28 and 41.   [3] *De Div. Nom.,* IV, 20-21 (PG 3, 721).

acts; for just as virtue according to its species is a good habit, so the contrary vice is an evil habit according to its species. The same applies to virtuous and vicious acts. Therefore evil gives certain things their species. Therefore it is an essence, and is natural to certain things.

[2] Further. Each of two contraries is a nature, for if it expressed nothing, one of the contraries would be a pure privation or negation. But good and evil are said to be contraries. Therefore evil is a nature.

[3] Again. Aristotle in his *Categories* says that good and evil are *genera of contraries*.[1] Now every genus has an essence or nature, for there are no species or differences of non-being, so that what is not cannot be a genus. Therefore evil is an essence and a nature. [4] Also. Whatever is active is a thing. Now evil as such is active, for it counteracts and corrupts good. Therefore evil as such is a thing.

[5] Moreover. Whatever can be more or less must be a thing admitting of degrees, since negations and privations do not admit of being more or less. Now among evils we find one to be worse than another. Therefore, seemingly, evil must be a thing.

[6] Furthermore. *Thing* and *being* are convertible terms. Now evil exists in the world. Therefore it is a thing and a nature.

[*Chapter IX*] These objections, however, are easily solved. For evil and good in morals are said to be specific differences, as the *first argument* stated, because moral matters depend on the will; for a thing comes under the head of morals so far as it is voluntary. Now the will's object is the end and the good. Hence moral matters are specified by their end, even as natural actions are specified by the form of their active principle, for instance, the action of heating is specified by heat. Since, then, good and evil are predicated in respect of the universal direction to an end, or the privation of that direction, it follows that in morals the first differences are those of good and evil. Now for one genus there must be one first measure; and the measure in morals is reason. Consequently good and evil in moral matters must depend on the end appointed by reason. Accordingly, in morals, that which derives its species from an end that is in accord with reason is said to be specifically good; and that which derives its species from an end discordant from reason is said to be specifically bad. And yet this end, though it sets aside the end appointed by reason, is nevertheless some kind of good, such as a pleasurable object of the senses, or something similar, so that in some animals this end is good, and even in man when it is moderated by reason. Also it happens that what is evil for one is good for another. Therefore evil, so far as it is a specific difference in the moral genus, does not denote a thing essentially evil; but it rather denotes something that is good in itself, but evil for man, in so far as it removes the order of reason, which is man's good. From this it follows that evil and good are contraries according as they are applied to the moral genus. But they are

[1] *Cat.*, XI (14a 24).

not contraries in their absolute signification, as the *second objection* stated, but evil is a privation of good so far as it is evil.

In the same way we may understand the saying that evil and good, taken in the moral order, are *genera of contraries,* on which the *third objection* was based. For of all moral contraries, either both are evil, as prodigality and stinginess, or one is good and the other evil, as liberality and stinginess. Hence moral evil is both a genus and a difference, not through being the privation of a good appointed by reason (whence it is called evil), but through the nature of the action or habit that is directed to an end incompatible with the right end appointed by reason. Thus a blind man is a human individual, not as being blind, but as being this particular man; and irrational is a difference of animal, not through the privation of reason, but because of the particular nature to which privation of reason is consequent.

It may also be said that Aristotle asserts evil and good to be genera, not in his own opinion, since he does not number them among the ten first genera in each of which some contrariety is found,[1] but according to the opinion of Pythagoras, who affirmed that *good* and *evil* are supreme genera and first principles.[2] Under each of them he placed ten supreme contraries, so that we have the good which is *limited,* which is *equal,* which is *one,* which is *on the right hand,* the *male,* the *resting,* the *straight,* the *luminous,* the *square,* and lastly, the *good;* while under *evil* he placed the *unlimited,* the *unequal,* the *manifold,* the *left-hand,* the *female,* the *moving,* the *crooked,* the *darksome,* the *oblong,* and lastly, the *evil.* In the same way, and in several passages of his works on logic, he employs examples according to the opinions of other philosophers, as being probable at the time.

Moreover, this saying contains a certain amount of truth, for it is impossible that a probable statement should be utterly false. Now of all contraries one is perfect, while the other is incomplete, as containing some kind of privation. Thus, white and hot are perfect, while cold and black are imperfect, as indicating a kind of privation. Since then incompleteness and privation are a kind of evil, while every perfection and completeness comes under the head of good, it follows that in contraries one seems to be comprised under good, while the other approaches to the notion of evil. In this way good and evil seem to be genera of all contraries.

In this way too it is clear how evil is opposed to good, which was the line taken by the *fourth objection.* Because in so far as form and end, which have the aspect of good, and are the true principles of action, involve privation of a contrary form and end, the action that is consequent upon this form and end is ascribed to privation and evil; accidentally however, since privation, as such, is not a principle of action. Rightly therefore does Dionysius say that *evil does not oppose good, except by virtue of a good, and*

----

[1] Cf. *op. cit.,* IV (1b 25).   [2] Cf. *Metaph.,* I, 5 (986a 26).

in itself it is powerless and weak,[1] as not being a principle of action. Evil, however, is said to corrupt good, not only as acting by virtue of a good, as was explained, but formally by itself; even as blindness is said to corrupt the sight, through being the very corruption of sight. In the same way, whiteness is said to color the wall, because it is the very color of the wall.

A thing is said to be a greater or lesser evil by reason of its distance from the good. For thus it is that things which imply privation admit of degrees, as *inequality and unlikeness;* and thus, to be more unequal is to be more distant from equality, and to be more unlike is to go further from likeness. Therefore that is said to be more evil which is more deprived of good, as being more distant from good. But privations are subject to increase, not as having a kind of essence, as do qualities and forms, as the *fifth argument* presumed, but through the increase of the cause of privation. Thus air is more dark according as the light is impeded by the interposition of more obstacles, for thus it is further removed from a participation of light.

Again, evil is said to be in the world, not as though it had an essence, or were some thing, as the *sixth argument* supposed, but according as a thing is said to be evil with evil; even as blindness and privation of any kind is said to be, because an animal is blind with blindness. For *being* is predicated in two ways, as the Philosopher teaches.[2] First, as indicating the essence of a thing, and thus it is divided into the ten categories. In this way no privation can be called a being. Secondly, as denoting the truth of judgment. In this way evil and privation are called a being, inasmuch as a thing is said to be deprived by a privation.

CHAPTER X

THAT THE CAUSE OF EVIL IS A GOOD

WE may conclude from the foregoing that evil is not caused except by a good.

For were some evil caused by an evil, since evil does not act save by virtue of a good, as was proved above,[3] it follows that good itself is the primary cause of evil.

Again. That which is not, is not the cause of anything. Therefore every cause must be some being. Now evil is not a being, as was shown above.[4] Therefore evil cannot be the cause of anything. Hence if evil be caused by something, this must be a good.

Again. Whatever is properly and by itself the cause of something intends its proper effect. Hence, if evil by itself be the cause of something, it would intend its proper effect, namely, evil. But this is false, for it has been

---

[1] *De Div. Nom.,* IV, 29 (PG 3, 729).   [2] *Metaph.,* IV, 7 (1017a 8).—Cf. St. Thomas, *In Metaph.,* V, lect. 9.   [3] Ch. 9.   [4] Ch. 7.

shown that every agent intends a good.[1] Therefore evil by itself is not the cause of anything, but only accidentally. Now every accidental cause is reduced to a *per se* cause. But good alone can be a *per se* cause, and evil cannot be a *per se* cause. Therefore evil is caused by good.

Further. Every cause is either matter, or form, or agent, or end. But evil cannot be either matter or form, for it has been shown above that being, whether actual or potential, is a good.[2] Neither can it be an agent, since a thing acts inasmuch as it is actual and has a form. Nor again can it be an end, since it is without intention, as we have shown.[3] Therefore evil cannot be the cause of a thing, and if anything be the cause of an evil, that evil must be caused by a good.

Since, however, evil and good are opposite to each other, and one opposite cannot be the cause of the other except accidentally (thus *a cold thing causes heat,* as is stated in *Physics* viii.[4]), it follows that good cannot be the effective cause of evil except accidentally.

In the physical order, this accident may be on the part of the agent, or on the part of the effect. It is on the part of the agent, as when the agent's power is defective, with the result that the action is defective, and the effect deficient. And thus when the power of the digestive organ is defective, the result is imperfect digestion of the food and an indigested humor, which are physical evils. Now it is accidental to the agent as such that its power be defective, for it acts, not as having a defective power, but as having some power; for if it lacked power altogether, it would not act at all. Accordingly, evil is caused accidentally on the part of the agent, inasmuch as the agent's power is defective. Hence it is said that *evil has not an efficient, but a deficient, cause;* because evil does not follow from an active cause, except in so far as this cause is defective in power, and in this respect it is not effective.—And it comes to the same if defect in the action and the effect results from a defect in the instrument, or in any thing else required for the agent's action: as when the motive power causes a limp because of crookedness in the leg; for the agent acts by both its power and its instrument.

On the part of the effect, evil is caused by good accidentally, either on the part of the matter of the effect, or on the part of its form. For if the matter be indisposed to receive the impression of the agent, the effect must needs be defective. Thus a deformed offspring results from an indisposition of matter. Nor is it imputed to defect in the agent, if it fail to transform an indisposed matter to perfect actuality; for to each natural agent there is appointed a power in proportion to its nature, and if it go not beyond that power, it will not on that account fall short of its power, but only when it falls short of the measure of power due to it by nature.

On the part of the effect's form, evil occurs accidentally in so far as one form necessarily involves the privation of another; and therefore the gen-

[1] Ch. 3.   [2] Ch. 7.   [3] Ch. 4.   [4] Aristotle, *Phys.,* VIII, 1 (251a 33).

erating of one thing is necessarily followed by the corruption of another. But this evil is not an evil of the effect intended by the agent, as was made clear above,[1] but of the other thing.

Accordingly it is evident that evil is caused only accidentally by a good. —And the same applies to things produced by art, for *art, in its work, copies nature,*[2] and faults occur in both in the same way.

In morals, however, the case would seem to be different. For moral fault does not apparently follow from a defective power, since weakness of power either wholly excludes, or at least diminishes, moral fault; since weakness does not deserve punishment, which is due to guilt, but rather mercy and pardon, seeing that moral fault must be voluntary and not necessary. But if we consider the matter carefully, we shall find that there is a likeness in one respect, and unlikeness in another. There is unlikeness in that moral fault is considered in the action alone, and not in some produced effect, for moral virtues are directed not to *making* but to *doing*. But the arts are directed to making, for which reason it has been stated that faults occur in them in the same way as in nature. Therefore moral evil is considered as resulting, not from the matter or form of the effect, but only from the agent.

Now, in moral actions four active principles are to be found in due order. The first of these is the executive power, namely the motive power, whereby the members are moved to execute the will's command. Hence this power is moved by the will which is a second principle. And the will is moved by the judgment of the apprehensive power, which judges that a particular thing is good or evil, which are objects of the will, the one moving to pursuit, the other to flight. Again, the apprehensive power is moved by the thing apprehended. Hence the first active principle in moral actions is the thing apprehended; the second is the apprehensive power; the third is the will; and the fourth is the motive power, which carries out the command of reason.

Now the act of the executive power already presupposes moral good or evil. For these external acts do not belong to morals, except according as they are voluntary. Therefore if the act of the will be good, the external act will also be good, and evil, if it be evil. And there would be nothing savoring of moral evil if the defect in a defective external act has nothing to do with the will; for limping is not a moral, but a physical, evil. Therefore a defect in this executive power either wholly excuses or diminishes moral fault.—Again, the act whereby the thing moves the apprehensive power is devoid of moral fault; for the visible object moves the sight according to the natural order of things, and so too does every object move a passive power.—Again, considered in itself, the act of the apprehensive power is devoid of moral fault, since a defect therein either excuses or diminishes moral fault, in the same way as a defect in the executive power; for weakness and ignorance equally excuse or diminish sin.—It follows.

[1] Ch. 6.   [2] Aristotle, *Phys.,* II, 2 (194a 22).

then, that moral fault is found first and chiefly in the sole act of the will, and an act is properly called moral precisely because it is voluntary. Therefore the root and origin of moral fault is to be sought in the act of the will.

But there is a difficulty, seemingly, attendant upon this inquiry. For since a defective act results from a defect in the active principle, we must presuppose a defect in the will to precede the moral fault. And if this defect be natural, it will always adhere to the will, so that the will must be guilty of moral fault whenever it acts. But acts of virtue prove this to be false. But if the defect be voluntary, it is already a moral fault, whose cause will still remain to be sought; and thus the reason will carry on indefinitely. Accordingly, we must say that the defect already existing in the will is not natural, lest it follow that the will sins in every act; and that neither is it by chance or fortuitous, for then there would be no moral fault in us, since chance events are unforeseen and outside the domain of reason. Therefore it is voluntary. Yet it is not a moral fault,—lest we be forced to proceed indefinitely. How this may be, remains to be considered.

The perfection of every active principle depends on a higher active principle, since the second agent acts through the power of the first. While, therefore, the second agent remains subordinate to the first, it acts unfailingly; but it fails in acting if it happen to stray from the order of the first agent: as in the case of an instrument that falls short of the first agent's movement. Now it has been said that, in the order of moral actions, two principles precede the will, namely, the apprehensive power, and the apprehended object, which is the end. And since for each movable there is a corresponding proper motive power, every apprehensive power is not the motive force due to every appetitive power, but this one belongs to this, and another to that. Accordingly, just as the proper motive power of the sensitive appetite is the apprehensive power of the senses, so the proper motive power of the will is the reason itself.

Again, since the reason is able to apprehend many goods and many ends, and each one has its proper end, the will also must have as its end and first mover, not any, but a definite good. Hence when the will tends to its act, through being moved by the apprehension of reason presenting to it its proper good, a right action follows. But when the will breaks away at the apprehension of the sensitive power, or even of the reason which presents some good other than its proper good, there follows in the will's act a moral fault.

Consequently, the sin of action is preceded in the will by a failure of order to reason, and to its proper end: to reason, as when the will, on the sudden apprehension of a sense, tends to a good that is pleasurable to sense; —to its due end, as when, by deliberating, the reason arrives at some good which is not good either now or in some particular way, and yet the will tends to that good as though it were its proper good. Now this failure of order is voluntary, for it is in the will's power to will or not to will. Again.

it is in the will's power that the reason actually consider the matter, or cease from considering it, or that it consider this matter, or that. Nor is this failure of order a moral evil, for if the reason were to consider nothing, or to consider any good whatever, as yet there is no sin, until the will tends to an undue end; and this itself is an act of the will.

Accordingly, both in the physical and in the moral order it is clear that evil is not caused by good except accidentally.

CHAPTER XI

THAT THE SUBJECT OF EVIL IS A GOOD

FROM what we have said it can be shown that every evil resides in some good.

For evil cannot exist by itself, since it has no essence, as was proved above.[1] Therefore evil needs to be in some subject. Now every subject, as it is a substance, is a good, as is evident from what has been said.[2] Therefore every evil is in a good.

Also. Evil is a privation, as we have shown.[3] Now privation and the lacking form are in the same subject. But the subject of a form is a being in potentiality to that form, and this being is a good, for potentiality and act are in the same genus. Therefore privation, which is an evil, is in some good as its subject.

Moreover. *A thing is called evil because it injures,*[4] and this only because it injures a good, for it is good to injure evil, since the corruption of evil is good. Now it would not injure a good formally, unless it were in that good; and thus blindness is hurtful to a man in so far as it is in him. Therefore evil must be in a good.

Again. Evil is not caused except by good, and then only accidentally.[5] Now whatever is accidental is reducible to that which is *per se*. Consequently, together with the evil effect that is caused accidentally by a good, there must be some good which is the *per se* effect of that good, so as to be the foundation of that evil; because what is accidental is founded on what is *per se*.

Seeing, however, that good and evil are mutually opposed, and that one of two opposites cannot be the subject of the other, but expels it, someone at a cursory glance might think it unreasonable to state that good is the subject of evil.

And yet it is not unreasonable, if the truth be sought thoroughly. For good, even as being, is predicated universally, since every being, as such, is good, as we have shown.[6] Now it is not unreasonable that non-being

---

[1] Ch. 7.   [2] *Ibid.*   [3] Ch. 9.   [4] St. Augustine, *Enchir.,* XII (PL 40, 237).   [5] Ch. 10.   [6] Ch. 7.

should have being for its subject, for every privation is a non-being, and yet its subject is a substance, which is a being. But non-being is not in a being opposed to it as in its subject. For blindness is not universal non-being, but a particular kind of non-being, namely privation of sight; and therefore it is not in sight, as its subject, but in an animal. In like manner, evil has for its subject not the opposite good (for it is the privation of this good), but some other good. Thus moral evil is in a natural good; and an evil of nature, namely, privation of a form, is in matter, which is a good as a being in potentiality.

CHAPTER XII

THAT EVIL DOES NOT ENTIRELY DESTROY GOOD

It is clear from the foregoing that however much evil be increased it can never destroy good entirely, since there must always remain the subject of evil, as long as evil remains. Now the subject of evil is a good.[1] Therefore, some good must always remain.

But seeing that evil may be increased indefinitely, and that good is always diminished by the increase of evil, it would seem that good is decreased by evil indefinitely. Now a good that can be diminished by evil must needs be finite, because infinite good is incompatible with evil, as we proved in the First Book.[2] Seemingly, therefore, a good is sometimes wholly destroyed by evil, since if something is subtracted indefinitely from the finite, this must at length be destroyed through such subtraction.

Nor may it be said, as some say, that if the subsequent subtraction be made in the same proportion as the preceding one, and continue thus indefinitely, the good cannot be destroyed, as may be seen in the division of a continuous quantity. Thus if from a line two cubits long you subtract half, and from the remainder subtract half, and continue thus indefinitely, there will always remain something to be divided. But in this process of division that which is subtracted afterwards must always be less in quantity; for half of the whole which was subtracted at first is greater in absolute quantity than half of the half, albeit the same proportion remains. This, however, in no way applies to the diminution of good by evil. For the more a good is diminished by an evil, the weaker it becomes, and thus it will be more capable of diminution by the subsequent evil. Again, this subsequent evil may be equal to or greater than the previous one, and hence it will not happen that a smaller quantity of good will always be subsequently subtracted from the good, even if the same proportion be observed.

[1] Ch. 11.   [2] C. G., I, 39.

We must therefore find a different solution. It is clear from what has been already said that evil entirely destroys the opposite good, as blindness destroys sight,[1] and yet there must needs remain the good which is the subject of that evil. Now this subject, as such, has the aspect of a good, considered as in potentiality to the actuality of the good which is removed by the evil. Therefore, the less it is in potentiality to that good, the less good will it be. Now a subject becomes less in potentiality to a form, not indeed by the mere subtraction of some part of that subject, nor by the subtraction of some part of its potentiality, but by the fact that the potentiality is hindered by a contrary actuality from reaching to the actuality of the form; and thus according as heat is the more increased in a subject, the less is that subject potentially cold. Therefore good is diminished by evil more by the addition of its contrary than by the subtraction of good. This applies also to what we have said of evil. For we have said that evil happens outside the intention of the agent,[2] which always intends some good, the result of which is the exclusion of some other good opposed thereto. Hence the more we increase that intended good, the result of which is an evil outside the agent's intention, the more the potentiality to the contrary good will be diminished. And it is thus that the diminution of good by evil increases.

Now this diminution of good by evil cannot go on indefinitely in the physical order. Because all physical forms and powers are limited, and reach a certain term beyond which they cannot reach. Consequently neither can a contrary form, nor can the power of a contrary agent, be increased indefinitely, so as to result in the indefinite diminution of good by evil.

On the other hand, this diminution can proceed indefinitely in moral matters. For the intellect and will have no limit fixed to their actions, since the intellect can proceed indefinitely in understanding: wherefore the mathematical species of numbers and figures are infinite. In like manner, the will goes on indefinitely in willing, since he who wills to commit a theft can so will again, and so on to infinity. Now the more the will tends to unfitting ends, the more difficult is it for it to return to its proper and fitting end; as is evident in those who have acquired a vicious habit through sinning frequently. Hence the good of natural aptitude may be diminished indefinitely by moral evil; and yet it will never be entirely destroyed, and will always accompany the nature that remains.

CHAPTER XIII

THAT EVIL HAS A CAUSE OF SOME KIND

It can be shown from what precedes that although evil has no *per se* cause, yet every evil must needs have an accidental cause.

[1] Ch. 11.   [2] Ch. 4.

For whatever is in a thing as its subject must needs have a cause, since it results either from the principles of the subject, or from some external cause. Now evil is in good as its subject, as was shown above.[1] Therefore evil must have a cause.

Again. That which is in potentiality to either of two opposites is not actualized by either except by some cause, for no potentiality actualizes itself. Now evil is the privation of that which is connatural and due to anyone;[2] since it is because of this that a thing is said to be evil. Therefore evil is in a subject that is in potentiality to evil and its opposite. Therefore evil must have some cause.

Moreover. Whatever is in a thing in addition to its nature supervenes through some other cause; for whatever is natural to it is permanent, unless something else be in the way. And thus a stone is not borne upwards, unless someone throws it, and water is not heated unless something makes it hot. Now evil, in whatever subject it be, is always there in addition to the nature of that subject, since it is the privation of what is connatural and due to a thing. Therefore evil must always have a cause, either *per se* or accidental.

Further. Every evil follows upon some good;[3] and thus corruption follows upon generation. Now every good has a cause, except the First Good, in which there is no evil, as was proved in the First Book.[4] Therefore every evil has a cause, from which it results accidentally.

CHAPTER XIV

THAT EVIL IS AN ACCIDENTAL CAUSE

FROM the same premises it is clear that although evil is not a *per se* cause, it is nevertheless an accidental cause. For if A is the cause of B *per se,* whatever is accidental to A is the accidental cause of B. Thus *white,* which is accidental to the builder, is the accidental cause of the house. Now every evil is in some good,[5] and every good is in some way the cause of something. For matter is in a way the cause of form, while the converse is in a way also true; and the same applies to the agent and the end. Therefore there does not follow an indefinite sequence in causes, if each thing be the cause of something else, because the circle observed in causes and effects is composed of various kinds of cause. Therefore evil is an accidental cause.

Again. Evil is a privation, as was shown above.[6] Now privation is an accidental principle in movable things, even as matter and form are *per se* principles.[7] Therefore evil is an accidental cause of something.

[1] Ch. 11.   [2] Ch. 7.   [3] Ch. 10.   [4] *C. G.,* I, 39.   [5] Ch. 11.   [6] Ch. 7.   [7] Cf. Aristotle, *Phys.,* I, 7 (190b 26).

Moreover. From a defect in the cause there follows defect in the effect. Now defect in a cause is an evil. And yet it cannot be a *per se* cause, since a thing is not a cause in that it is defective, but in that it is a being; for were it wholly defective, it would be the cause of nothing. Therefore evil is a cause of something, not *per se,* but accidentally.

Further. If we run through all the kinds of cause, we find that evil is an accidental cause: in the species of efficient cause, because defect in effect and action results from a defect in the efficient cause; in the species of material cause, because a fault in the effect arises from indisposition in the matter; in the species of formal cause, because every form is accompanied by the privation of the opposite form; and in the species of final cause, because evil is united to an undue end, inasmuch as the due end is hindered thereby. It is therefore evident that evil is an accidental cause, and cannot be a cause *per se.*

CHAPTER XV

THAT THERE IS NO HIGHEST EVIL

IT follows from this that there cannot be a highest evil, that is the principle of all evils.

For a highest evil must needs exclude the association of all good, just as the highest good is that which is wholly disconnected from all evil. Now there cannot be an evil entirely apart from good, for it has been proved that evil resides in some good.[1] Therefore nothing is supremely evil.

Again. If anything be supremely evil, it must be essentially evil, even as the supreme good is that which is essentially good. But this is impossible, since evil has no essence, as was shown above.[2] Therefore it is impossible to suppose a supreme evil that is the principle of evils.

Also. That which is a first principle is not caused by anything. Now every evil is caused by a good, as we have proved.[3] Therefore evil is not a first principle.

Further. Evil does not act except by virtue of a good, as we have proved.[4] But a first principle acts by its own power. Therefore evil cannot be a first principle.

Moreover. Since *that which is accidental is subsequent to that which is per se,*[5] the accidental cannot be first. Now evil does not occur except accidentally and unintentionally, as we have proved.[6] Therefore evil cannot be a first principle.

Again. Every evil has an accidental cause, as we have shown.[7] But a first

---

[1] Ch. 11. [2] Ch. 7. [3] Ch. 10. [4] Ch. 9. [5] Aristotle, *Phys.,* II, 6 (198a 7). [6] Ch. 4. [7] Ch. 13.

principle has no cause, either *per se,* or accidental. Therefore evil cannot be the first cause in any genus.

Furthermore. *A per se cause precedes one that is accidental.* But evil is none but an accidental cause, as we have proved.[1] Therefore evil cannot be a first principle.

Hereby is refuted the error of the Manichees, who maintained the existence of a highest evil, that is the first principle of all evils.[2]

CHAPTER XVI

THAT THE END OF EVERYTHING IS A GOOD

ACCORDINGLY if every agent acts for some good, as we have shown above,[3] it follows that good is the end of each thing. For everything is directed by its action to some end; for either the action itself is an end, or the end of the action is also the end of the agent: and this is its good.

Again. The end of a thing is the term of its appetite. Now the appetite of a thing terminates in a good, for the philosophers define good as *the object of all appetite.*[4] Therefore the end of everything is a good.

Moreover. That toward which a thing tends while it is without it, and wherein it rests when it has it, is its end. Now anything that is without its proper perfection is moved towards it, as far as in it lies; and if it have that perfection, it rests therein. Therefore the end of a thing is its perfection. But the perfection of a thing is its good. Therefore every thing is directed to good as its end.

Further. Things that know the end and things that do not know the end are equally directed to the end; although those which know the end are moved thereto *per se,* whereas those which do not know it tend thereto as directed by another, as may be seen in the archer and the arrow. Now those that know the end are always directed to a good as their end; because the will, which is the appetite of a previously known end, does not tend towards a thing except under the aspect of good, which is its object. Therefore those things also that do not know the end are directed to a good as their end. Therefore the end of all is a good.

[1] Ch. 14.   [2] Cf. St. Augustine, *De Haeres.,* 46 (PL 42, 34).   [3] Ch. 3.   [4] *E. g.,* Aristotle, *Eth.,* I, 1 (1094a 2).

CHAPTER XVII

THAT ALL THINGS ARE DIRECTED TO ONE END, WHICH IS GOD

FROM the foregoing it is clear that all things are directed to one good as their last end.

For if nothing tends to something as its end, except in so far as this is good, it follows that good, as such, is an end. Consequently that which is the supreme good is supremely the end of all. Now there is but one supreme good, namely God, as we have shown in the First Book.[1] Therefore all things are directed to the highest good, namely God, as their end.

Again. *That which is supreme in any genus is the cause of everything in that genus.*[2] Thus fire which is supremely hot is the cause of heat in other bodies. Therefore the supreme good, namely God, is the cause of goodness in all things good. Therefore He is the cause of every end being an end, since whatever is an end is such in so far as it is good. Now *the cause that a thing is so is itself more so.*[3] Therefore God is supremely the end of all things.

Further. In every genus of causes, the first cause is more a cause than the second cause, since the second cause is not a cause save through the first. Therefore that which is the first cause in the order of final causes must needs be more the final cause of each thing than the proximate final cause. Now God is the first cause in the order of final causes, for He is supreme in the order of good things. Therefore He is the end of each thing more even than any proximate end.

Moreover. In all ordered ends the last must needs be the end of each preceding end. Thus if a potion be mixed to be given to a sick man, and is given to him that he may be purged, and he be purged that he may be lowered, and lowered that he may be healed, it follows that health is the end of the lowering, and of the purging, and of those that precede. Now all things are ordered in various degrees of goodness to the one supreme good, which is the cause of all goodness; and so, since good has the nature of an end, all things are ordered under God as preceding ends under the last end. Therefore God must be the end of all.

Furthermore. The particular good is directed to the common good as its end, for the being of the part is for the sake of the being of the whole.[4] So it is that *the good of the nation is more godlike than the good of one man.*[5] Now the supreme good, namely God, is the common good, since the good of all things depends on Him; and the good, whereby each thing is good,

---

[1] *C. G.*, I, 42. [2] Aristotle, *Metaph.*, I α, 1 (993b 22). [3] Aristotle, *Post. Anal.*, I, 2 (72a 28). [4] Aristotle, *Polit.*, I, 4 (1254a 9). [5] Aristotle, *Eth.*, I, 2 (1094b 9).

is the particular good of that thing, and of those that depend thereon. Therefore all things are directed to one good, namely God, as their end.

Again. Order among ends is consequent on the order among agents. For just as the supreme agent moves all second agents, so all the ends of second agents must be directed to the end of the supreme agent, since whatever the supreme agent does, it does for its own end. Now the supreme agent is the active principle of the actions of all inferior agents, by moving all to their actions, and consequently to their ends. Hence it follows that all the ends of second agents are ordered by the first agent to its own end. Now the first agent in all things is God, as we proved in the Second Book.[1] And His will has no other end but His own goodness, which is Himself, as we showed in the First Book.[2] Therefore all things, whether they were made by Him immediately, or by means of secondary causes, are ordered to God as their end. But this applies to all things, for, as we proved in the Second Book,[3] there can be nothing that has not its being from Him. Therefore all things are ordered to God as their end.

Moreover. The last end of every maker, as such, is himself, for what we make we use for our own sake; and if at any time a man make a thing for the sake of something else, it is referred to his own good, whether his use, his pleasure, or his virtue. Now God is the producing cause of all things: of some immediately, of others by means of other causes, as we have explained above.[4] Therefore He is the end of all things.

And again. The end holds the primary place among causes, and it is from it that all other causes derive their actual causality; since the agent does not act except for the end, as was proved.[5] Now it is due to the agent that the matter is brought to the actuality of the form, and therefore the matter is made actually the matter, and the form is made the form, of this particular thing, through the agent's action, and consequently through the end. The later end also is the cause that the preceding end is intended as an end; for a thing is not moved towards a proximate end except for the sake of the last end. Therefore the last end is the first cause of all. Now it must necessarily befit the First Being, namely God, to be the first cause of all, as we proved above.[6] Therefore God is the last end of all.

Hence it is written (*Prov.* xvi. 4): *The Lord hath made all things for himself;* and (*Apoc.* xxii. 13), *I am Alpha and Omega, the first and the last.*

---

[1] *C. G.*, II, 15. [2] *C. G.*, I, 74. [3] *C. G.*, II, 15. [4] *Ibid.* [5] Ch. 2. [6] *C. G.*, II, 15.

CHAPTER XVIII

HOW GOD IS THE END OF THINGS

IT remains to ask how God is the end of all things. This will be made clear from what has been said.

For He is the end of all things, yet so as to precede all in being.[1] Now there is an end which, though it holds the first place in causing in so far as it is in the intention, is nevertheless last in execution. This applies to any end which the agent establishes by his action. Thus the physician by his action establishes health in the sick man, which is nevertheless his end. There is also an end which, just as it precedes in causing, so also does it precede in being. Thus, that which one intends to acquire by one's motion or action is said to be one's end. For instance, fire seeks to reach a higher place by its movement, and the king seeks to take a city by fighting. Accordingly, God is the end of things as something to be obtained by each thing in its own way.

Again. God is at once the last end of things and the first agent, as we have shown.[2] Now the end effected by the agent's action cannot be the first agent, but rather is it the agent's effect. God, therefore, cannot be the end of things as though He were something effected, but only as something already existing and to be acquired.

Further. If a thing act for the sake of something already in existence, and if by its action some result ensue, then something through the agent's action must accrue to the thing for the sake of which it acts; and thus soldiers fight for the cause of their captain, to whom victory accrues, which the soldiers bring about by their actions. Now nothing can accrue to God from the action of anything whatever, since His goodness is perfect in every way, as we proved in the First Book.[3] It follows, then, that God is the end of things, not as something made or effected by them, nor as though He obtained something from things, but in this way alone, that He is obtained by them.

Moreover. The effect must tend to the end in the same way as the agent acts for the end. Now God, who is the first agent of all things, does not act as though He gained something by His action, but as bestowing something thereby; since He is not in potentiality so that He can acquire something, but solely in perfect actuality, whereby He is able to bestow. Things therefore are not ordered to God as to an end to which something will be added; they are ordered to Him to obtain God Himself from Him according to their measure, since He is their end.

[1] *C. G.*, I, 13.   [2] Ch. 17.   [3] *C. G.*, I, 37ff.

CHAPTER XIX

THAT ALL THINGS TEND TO BE LIKE UNTO GOD

FROM the fact that they acquire the divine goodness, creatures are made like unto God. Therefore, if all things tend to God as their last end, so as to acquire His goodness,[1] it follows that the last end of things is to become like unto God.

Moreover. The agent is said to be the end of the effect in so far as the effect tends to be like the agent; and hence it is that *the form of the generator is the end of the act of generation.*[2] Now God is the end of things in such wise as to be also their first producing cause. Therefore all things tend to a likeness to God, as their last end.

Again. Things give evidence that *they naturally desire to be;*[3] so that if any are corruptible, they naturally resist corruptives, and tend to where they can be safeguarded, as the fire tends upwards and earth downwards. Now all things have being in so far as they are like God, Who is self-subsistent being, since they are all beings only by participation. Therefore all things desire as their last end to be like God.

Further. All creatures are images of the first agent, namely God, since *the agent produces its like.*[4] Now the perfection of an image consists in representing the original by a likeness to it, for this is why an image is made. Therefore all things exist for the purpose of acquiring a likeness to God, as for their last end.

Again. Each thing by its movement or action tends to some good as its end, as was proved above.[5] Now a thing partakes of good in so far as it is like to the first goodness, which is God. Therefore all things, by their movements and actions, tend to a likeness to God as to their last end.

CHAPTER XX

HOW THINGS IMITATE THE DIVINE GOODNESS

FROM what has been said it is clear that the last end of all things is to become like God. Now, that which has properly the nature of an end is the good. Therefore, properly speaking, things tend to become like to God inasmuch as He is good.

Now, creatures do not acquire goodness in the way in which it is in God, even though each thing imitates the divine goodness according to its own manner. For the divine goodness is simple, being, as it were, all in one.

[1] Ch. 18. [2] Aristotle, *Phys.,* II, 7 (198a 26). [3] Aristotle, *Eth.,* IX, 7 (1168a 5); 9 (1170a 26). [4] Aristotle, *De Gener.,* I, 7 (324a 11). [5] Ch. 16.

For the divine being contains the whole fullness of perfection, as we proved in the First Book.[1] Therefore, since a thing is good so far as it is perfect, God's being is His perfect goodness; for in God, to be, to live, to be wise, to be happy, and whatever else is seen to pertain to perfection and goodness, are one and the same in God, as though the sum total of His goodness were God's very being. Again, the divine being is the substance of the existing God.[2] But this cannot be so in other things. For it was proved in the Second Book that no created substance is its own being.[3] Therefore, if a thing is good so far as it is, and if no creature is its own being, none is its own goodness, but each one is good by participating in goodness, even as by participating in being it is a being.

Also. All creatures are not placed on the same level of goodness. For in some the substance is both form and actuality: such, namely, as are competent, by the mere fact that they exist, to be actually and to be good. But in others, the substance is composed of matter and form, and such are competent to be actually and to be good, though it is by some part of their being, namely, their form. Accordingly, God's substance is His goodness, whereas a simple substance participates in goodness by the very fact that it exists, and a composite substance participates in goodness by some part of itself.

In this third degree of substances, diversity is to be found again in respect of being. For in some substances composed of matter and form, the form fills the entire potentiality of matter, in such a way that the matter retains no potentiality to another form, and consequently neither is there in any other matter a potentiality to this same form. Such are the heavenly bodies, which exhaust their entire matter.—In others, the form does not fill the whole potentiality of matter, so that the matter retains a potentiality to another form, and in another part of matter there remains potentiality to this form; for instance in the elements and their compounds. Since, then, privation is the absence in substance of what can be in substance, it is clear that, together with this form which does not fill the whole potentiality of matter, there is associated the privation of a form, which privation cannot be associated with a substance whose form fills the whole potentiality of matter, nor with that which is a form essentially, and much less with that one whose essence is its very being. And seeing that it is clear that there can be no movement where there is no potentiality to something else, for movement is *the act of that which is in potentiality,*[4] and since evil is the privation of good, it is clear that in this last order of substances, good is changeable, and has an admixture of the opposite evil; which cannot occur in the higher orders of substances. Therefore the substance answering to this last description stands lowest both in being and in goodness.

[1] *C. G.,* I, 28. [2] *C. G.,* I, 21ff. [3] *C. G.,* II, 15. [4] Aristotle, *Phys.,* III, 1 (201a 10).

We find degrees of goodness also among the parts of the substance composed of matter and form. For since matter considered in itself is being in potentiality, and since form is its act; and, again, since a composite substance has actual existence through its form, it follows that the form is, in itself, good, the composite substance is good as having its form actually, and the matter is good as being in potentiality to the form. And although a thing is good in so far as it is a being, it does not follow that matter, which is being only potentially, is only a potential good. For being is predicated absolutely, while good is founded on order, for a thing is said to be good, not merely because it is an end, or possesses the end; but even though it has not attained the end, so long as it is directed to the end, for this very reason it is said to be good. Accordingly, matter cannot be called a being absolutely, in so far as it is a potential being, whereby it is shown to have an order towards being; but this suffices for it to be called a good absolutely, because of this very order. This shows that the good, in a sense, extends further than being; for which reason Dionysius says that *the good includes both existing and non-existing things*.[1] For even non-existent things (namely, matter, considered as subject to privation) seek a good, namely, to exist. Hence it follows that matter is also good, for nothing but the good seeks the good.

In yet another way the creature's goodness falls short of that of God. For, as we have stated, God, in His very being, contains the supreme perfection of goodness. But the creature has its perfection, not in one thing but in many, because what is united in the highest is manifold in the lowest. Therefore, in respect of one and the same thing, virtue, wisdom and operation are predicated of God; but of creatures, they are predicated in respect of different things, and the further a creature is from the first goodness, the more does the perfection of its goodness require to be manifold. And if it be unable to attain to perfect goodness, it will reach to imperfect goodness in a few respects. Hence it is that, although the first and highest good is utterly simple, and although the substances nearest to it in goodness approach likewise thereto in simplicity, yet the lowest substances are found to be more simple than some that are higher. Elements, for instance, are simpler than animals and men, because they are unable to reach the perfection of knowledge and understanding, to which animals and men attain.

From what has been said, it is evident that, although God possesses His perfect and entire goodness according to the manner of His simple being, creatures nevertheless do not attain to the perfection of their goodness through their being alone, but through many things. Therefore, although each one is good inasmuch as it exists, it cannot be called good absolutely if it lack other things that are required for its goodness. Thus a man who, being despoiled of virtue, is addicted to vice, is said indeed to be good in a restricted sense, namely, as a being, and as a man; but he is not said to be

---

[1] *De Div. Nom.*, IV, 7 (PG 3, 704).

good absolutely, but rather evil. Accordingly, in every creature to be and to be good are not the same absolutely, although each one is good inasmuch as it exists; whereas in God to be and to be good are absolutely one and the same.

If, then, each thing tends to a likeness to God's goodness as its end; and if a thing is like God's goodness in respect of whatever belongs to its goodness; and if furthermore the goodness of a thing consists not merely in its being, but in whatever is required for its perfection, as we have proved: it is clear that things are directed to God as their end, not only in respect of their substantial being, but also in respect of such things as are accidental thereto and belong to its perfection, as well as in respect of their proper operation, which also belongs to a thing's perfection.

CHAPTER XXI

THAT THINGS HAVE A NATURAL TENDENCY TO BE LIKE GOD INASMUCH AS HE IS A CAUSE

It is clear from the foregoing that things have a tendency to be like God also in that they are causes of others.

For the creature tends to be like God by its operation. Now, by its operation, one thing is the cause of another. Therefore things tend to a divine likeness in this also, that they are causes of other things.

Again. Things tend to be like God in so far as He is good, as was stated above.[1] Now it is out of His goodness that God bestows being on others, for all things act inasmuch as they are actually perfect. Therefore all things seek to be like God in this respect by being causes of others.

Moreover. Order towards good is itself a good, as we have shown above.[2] Now every thing, in so far as it is the cause of another, is directed to a good; for good alone is caused *per se,* and evil is caused only by accident, as we have proved.[3] Therefore to be a cause of others is a good. Now in respect of any good to which a thing tends, that thing's tendency is to a divine likeness, since every created good is by reason of a share in the divine goodness. Therefore things tend to a divine likeness by being causes of other things.

Again. That the effect tends to be like the agent amounts to the same as that the agent causes its likeness in its effect; for the effect tends to the end towards which it is directed by the agent. Now the agent tends to assimilate the patient to itself not only in respect of its being, but also in respect of its causality; because the agent gives to its natural effect not only those natural principles whereby it subsists, but also those whereby it is a cause of other things. Thus, the animal, when begotten, receives from its

[1] Ch. 20.   [2] *Ibid.*   [3] Cb. 1a.

begetter both the power of self-nourishment, and the power of generation. Therefore the effect tends to be like the agent not only as to its species, but also as to its being the cause of other things. Now things tend to be like God, even as effects tend to be like the agent, as was proved above.[1] Therefore things have a natural tendency towards a divine likeness in this, that they are causes of other things.

Moreover. A thing is most perfect when it is able to produce its like. For that light shines perfectly which gives light to others. Now whatever tends to its own perfection tends to a divine likeness. Therefore a thing tends to a divine likeness from the very fact that it tends to be the cause of other things.

Since, however, a cause as such is higher than its effect, it is evident that to tend in this way to a divine likeness, so as to be a cause of other things, belongs to the more perfect among beings.

Furthermore. A thing is perfect in itself before being able to cause another, as we have stated already. Hence to be the cause of other things is a perfection that is last to come to a thing. Since, then, the creature tends to a divine likeness in many ways,[2] this remains last, that it seek a likeness to God by being a cause of others. Therefore Dionysius says that it is of *all things most godlike to be God's co-operator;*[3] in which sense the Apostle says (*I Cor.* iii. 9): *We are God's coadjutors.*

CHAPTER XXII

HOW THINGS ARE DIRECTED IN VARIOUS WAYS TO THEIR RESPECTIVE ENDS

IT may be shown from the foregoing that the last means whereby a thing is directed to its end is its operation; in various ways, however, according to the variety of operations. For some things have an operation whereby they move something else (*e.g., heating* and *cutting*), and some have an operation in being moved by another (*e.g., being heated* and *being cut*). Some operations are a perfection of an actually existing operator, and do not tend to the transmutation of something else: in the former respect these differ from passion and movement, and in the latter from an action which effects a transmutation on some external matter: as an instance of such an operation we have *understanding, sensation, will.* Hence it is clear that things which are set to move or operate only, without moving or making any thing themselves, tend to the divine likeness in that they are perfect in themselves; while those which make and move, as such, tend to a divine likeness in that they are causes of other things; and that those which move through being moved tend to the divine likeness in both ways.

[1] Ch. 19. [2] Ch. 20. [3] *De Cael. Hier.,* III, 2 (PG 3, 165).

The lower bodies, in so far as they are moved with natural movements, are considered to be moved only, and not to move except accidentally. For if a stone in its descent puts into motion something that stood in its path, it is an accident; and the same applies to alteration and other movements. Therefore the end of such movements is that they attain to a divine likeness in the point of their being perfect in themselves, as having their proper form and their proper place.

The heavenly bodies, however, move because they are moved; so that the end of their movement is to attain to a divine likeness in both respects. (1) As regards their own perfection this is true, inasmuch as a heavenly body may be actually *where* previously it was potentially.—Nor does it for this reason attain less to its perfection, although it retains its potentiality to be *where* it was before. For in the same way primary matter tends to its perfection by acquiring actually the form which before it had potentially, although it ceases to have the one which before it had actually. For thus matter receives successively all the forms to which it has a potentiality, so that its whole potentiality is actualized successively; which could not happen all at one time. Therefore, since a heavenly body is in potentiality to a particular *whereabouts,* even as primary matter is to a particular form, it attains to its perfection by the fact that its entire potentiality to a particular whereabouts is successively actualized, which could not happen simultaneously.

(2) Inasmuch as they move by moving, the end of their movement is the attainment of a divine likeness, in that they are causes of other things. Now they are the causes of other things by causing generation and corruption and other movements in this lower world. Accordingly the movements of heavenly bodies, in so far as they cause motion, are directed to generation and corruption in the world beneath them. And it is not unfitting that the movements of heavenly bodies conduce to the generation of these lower things, although these inferior bodies are less noble than the heavenly bodies, since the end should be of greater account than the means. For the generator's action tends to the form of the generated, and yet that which is generated is not of greater worth than the generator, but, in univocal agents, is of the same species with it. For the generator intends as its ultimate end not the form of the generated (which form is the end of generation), but the likeness to the divine Being in the perpetuation of the species, and the diffusion of His goodness, by bestowing its specific form on others, and being the cause of other things. Likewise, the heavenly bodies, although more noble than the lower bodies, nevertheless intend by means of their movements the generation of the latter bodies, and to bring to actuality the forms of things generated; not indeed as though this were their ultimate end, but as a means whereby to attain to an ultimate end, namely the divine likeness, in that they are causes of other things.

We must take note, however, that a thing, according as it participates in a likeness to God's goodness, which is the object of His will, so too has it a share in a likeness to God's will, whereby things are brought into being and preserved. The higher beings, however, participate in a likeness to the divine goodness in a more simple and universal manner; but the lower beings, in a more particular and divided way. Hence between heavenly and lower bodies we observe a likeness, not of equality, as in things belonging to the same species, but as that which is to be observed between the universal agent and a particular effect. Consequently, just as in this lower world the intention of the particular agent is confined to good of this or that species, so the intention of the celestial body is inclined to the common good of the corporeal substance, which by generation is preserved, multiplied and increased.

But since, as was already stated, everything moved tends as such towards a divine likeness in order to be perfect in itself, and since a thing is perfect in so far as it becomes actual, it follows that the intention of every thing that is in potentiality is to tend to actuality by way of movement. Hence the more an act is more final and more perfect, the more is the appetite of matter inclined to it. Therefore the appetite whereby matter seeks a form must tend towards the last and most perfect act to which matter can attain, as to the ultimate end of generation. Now certain grades are to be found in the acts of forms. For primary matter is in potentiality, first of all, to the elemental form. While under the elemental form, it is in potentiality to the form of a mixed body; and that is why elements are the matter of a mixed body. Considered as under the form of a mixed body, it is in potentiality to a vegetative soul, for the act of such a body is a soul. Again, the vegetative soul is in potentiality to the sensitive, and the sensitive to the intellective. This is proved by the process of generation, for in generation we have first the fetus living with a plant life, afterwards with animal life, and lastly with human life. After this no later or more noble form is to be found in things subject to generation and corruption. Therefore the last end of all generation is the human soul, and to this does matter tend as its ultimate form. Consequently, the elements are for the sake of the mixed body, the mixed body for the sake of living things, and of these plants are for the sake of animals, and animals for the sake of man. Therefore man is the end of all generation.

And since the same thing is the cause of generation and preservation in things, the order of the preservation of things is in keeping with the aforesaid order of their generation. Hence we find that mixed bodies are preserved by the qualities becoming to the elements; plants are nourished by mixed bodies; animals derive their nourishment from plants; and some that are more perfect and powerful from the imperfect and weak. As for man, he employs all kinds of things for his own use: some for food, some for clothing. Hence by nature he was made naked, as being able to make himself clothes from other things; even as nature provided him with no suitable nourishment except milk, so that he might supply himself with food from a variety of things. Some things also he employs as a means of transit, for he is inferior to many animals in swiftness and endurance, as though other animals were furnished for his needs. Over and above this, he employs all things endowed with a sensitive life for the perfection of his intellectual knowledge. Wherefore of man is it said in *Psalm* viii. 8, in words addressed to God: *Thou hast subjected all things under his feet.* And Aristotle says that man has a natural dominion over all animals.[1]

If, therefore, the movement of the heavens is directed to generation, and if all generation is directed to man as the last end of this genus, it is evident that the end of the movement of the heavens is directed to man as its last end in the genus of things subject to generation and movement.

Hence it is said (*Deut.* iv. 19) that God made the heavenly bodies *for the service of all the nations.*

CHAPTER XXIII

THAT THE MOVEMENT OF THE HEAVENS IS FROM AN INTELLECTIVE PRINCIPLE

It can also be shown from the foregoing that the first principle that causes the movement of the heavens is intellective.

For nothing that acts according to its own species intends a form higher than its own, since every agent intends its like. Now a heavenly body, in so far as it acts by its own movement, intends the ultimate form, which is the human intellect, which is higher than any corporeal form, as we have proved above.[2] Therefore the body of the heavens acts to the effect of generation, not in respect of its own species, as the principal agent does, but in respect of the species of some higher intellectual agent, in relation to which the body of the heavens is like an instrument in relation to a principal agent. Now the heavens acts to the effect of generation, inasmuch as it is moved. Therefore the body of the heavens is moved by some intellectual substance.

Again. Whatever is in motion must needs be moved by another, as we proved above.[3] Therefore the body of the heavens is moved by another. Now this other is either wholly separated from it, or else it is united to it, so that what is composed of the heavens and its mover is said to move itself, inasmuch as one part thereof is moved and the other is mover. If this be the case, then since whatever moves itself is living and animate, it follows that the heavens is animate. And it is animate not otherwise than with an intellectual soul, for it could not be animated with a nutritive soul, since in the body of the heavens there is no generation or corruption; nor

[1] *Polit.,* I, 5 (1254b 9).   [2] Ch. 22.   [3] *C. G.,* I, 13.

with a sensitive soul, since the body of the heavens has no variety of organs. Therefore it follows that it is moved by an intellectual soul.—If, on the other hand, it be moved by an extrinsic mover, this will be either corporeal or incorporeal. If it be corporeal, it does not cause movement without being moved, for no body moves unless it be moved, as was shown above.[1] Hence this too will require to be moved by another. But as it is not possible to have an infinite series of bodies, we must come to some incorporeal first mover. Now that which is utterly separated from a body must be intellectual, as we have shown.[2] Therefore the movement of the heavens, which is first among corporeal beings, is caused by some intellectual substance.

Moreover. Heavy and light bodies are moved by their generator and by that which removes obstacles, as is proved in *Physics* viii;[3] for it is impossible that their form be mover and the matter moved, for nothing is moved except a body. Now, as the elemental bodies are simple, and there is no composition in them, except that of matter and form, so too are the heavenly bodies simple. Hence, if they be moved in the manner of heavy and light bodies, it follows that they are moved *per se* by their generator, and accidentally by that which removes an obstacle. But this is impossible, for these bodies cannot be generated, because there is no contrariety in them, and their movements cannot be hindered. Therefore these bodies must needs be moved by beings that cause movement by a power of apprehension. This power cannot be sensitive, as we have proved. Therefore it must be an intellective power.

Further. If the principle of the movement of the heavens be nature alone, without any kind of apprehension, it follows that it must be the form of the heavenly body, as is the case with the elements; for although simple forms do not cause movement, they are principles of movements, since natural movements, like all other natural properties, follow from them. Now it is impossible that the heavenly movement follow the form of the heavenly body as its active principle. For the form is the principle of local movement inasmuch as to a particular body, in respect of its form, is due a particular place, to which it is moved by virtue of its form, which tends to that place; and because the generator gives this form, it is said to be a mover. Thus, it is due to fire, in accord with its form, to be in a higher place. Now one place is not more due to a heavenly body because of its form, than another. Therefore nature alone is not the principle of the heavenly movement; and consequently the principle of its movement must be something that moves it by apprehension.

Again. Nature always tends to one thing, and therefore things that come from nature come always in the same way, unless they be hindered, which does not happen frequently. Therefore that which is essentially varied in form cannot possibly be an end towards which nature tends. Now movement is essentially such, for that which is moved, as such, *is conditioned*

---

[1] *C. G.*, II, 20. [2] *C. G.*, I, 44. [3] *Phys.*, VIII, 4 (255b 35).

otherwise now and before.[1] Consequently nature cannot intend movement for its own sake. Therefore it intends through movement to obtain rest which is related to movement as one to many; for a thing is at rest which *is conditioned in the same way now as before.*[2] Accordingly, if the movement of the heavens were from nature alone, it would be directed to some kind of rest; whereas the contrary is the case, for movement is unceasing. Therefore the movement of the heavens is not from nature as its active principle, but from an intelligent substance.

Also. In every movement that is from nature as its active principle, if approach to a particular term be natural, recession from that term must be unnatural and contrary to nature. Thus, a heavy body naturally seeks a lower place, and recedes therefrom unnaturally. Therefore, if the movement of the heavens were natural, since it tends to the west naturally, it would be contrary to nature for it to return from the west to the east. But this is impossible, for nothing in the movement of the heavens is violent or unnatural. Consequently, it is impossible for nature to be the active principle of the movement of the heavens. Therefore its active principle is some apprehensive power, which must be an intelligence, as we have proved above. Therefore the body of the heavens is moved by an intellectual substance.

And yet we must not deny that the movement of the heavens is natural. For a movement is said to be natural, not only because of its active principle, but also because of its passive principle. This is evident in the generation of simple bodies, since such generation cannot be called natural in relation to the active principle. Because for a thing to be moved naturally by an active principle, it must have this active principle within itself, for *nature is a principle of movement in a thing in which it is;*[3] whereas the active principle in the generation of a simple body is separate. Therefore it is not natural by reason of its active principle, but only by reason of its passive principle, namely matter, wherein there is a natural appetite for its natural form. Accordingly, the movement of the heavenly body, as to its active principle, is not natural, but voluntary and intellectual, while as to its passive principle it is natural, since a heavenly body has a natural inclination for that movement.

This is made clear if we consider the relation of a heavenly body to its place. For a thing is passive and moved according as it is in potentiality, and it is active and moves according as it is in a state of actuality. Now a heavenly body, considered in its substance, is found to be potentially indifferent to any place, even as primary matter is indifferent to any form, as we have stated.[4] But it is otherwise with a heavy or light body, which, considered in itself, is not indifferent to any place, and has a definite place appointed to it by reason of its form. Therefore the nature of heavy and

[1] Aristotle, *Phys.*, V, 1 (224b 1).   [2] *Op. cit.*, V, 6 (229b 23).   [3] *Op. cit.*, II, 1 (192b 23).   [4] Ch. 22.

light bodies is the active principle of their movements, while the nature of a heavenly body is the passive principle of its movement. Consequently, we must not think that it is moved by violence, like heavy and light bodies, which are moved by us through our intellect. For heavy and light bodies have a natural aptitude for a movement contrary to that with which they are moved by us; and so they are moved by us violently, although the movement of an animal's body, whereby that body is moved by the soul, is not violent to that body as animated, although it is violent in so far as that body is something heavy. On the other hand, the heavenly bodies have no aptitude for a contrary movement, but only for that where-with they are moved by an intelligent substance. Consequently it is both voluntary, as regards its active principle, and natural, as to its passive principle.

That the movement of the heavens be voluntary in relation to its active principle is not inconsistent with the fact that it is one and uniform, as we might think from the fact that the will is indifferent to many things and is not determined to any one. For just as nature is determined to one course by its power, so is the will determined to one by its wisdom, by which the will is unerringly directed to one end.

It is evident from the foregoing that neither approach to any one place nor recession therefrom is contrary to nature. For this happens in the movement of heavy and light bodies for two reasons. First, because the intention of nature, in heavy and light bodies, is determined towards one place, and therefore just as a body tends thereto naturally, so does it recede therefrom against nature; secondly, because two movements, one of which approaches a given term and the other recedes therefrom, are contrary. If, however, we take not the last but a middle place in the movement of heavy and light bodies, both approach thereto and recession therefrom are natu-ral; for the whole movement comes under the intention of nature, and the movements are not contrary, but are one and continuous movement.

It is the same in the movement of heavenly bodies, because the inten-tion of nature is not towards one determinate place, as we have said already. Moreover, the movement with which a body moved in a circle recedes from any given place, is not contrary to the movement with which it approaches towards it, but is one and continuous movement; so that any given point in the movement of the heavens is like a middle point, and not like the term in a straight movement.

Nor does it make any difference, as to the present question, whether a heavenly body be moved by an intellectual substance united to it, which would be its soul, or by a separate substance. Nor does it make any difference whether each heavenly body be moved by God immediately, or none, and each be moved by the intermediary of created intellectual sub-stances; nor whether only the first heavenly body by God immediately, and the others through the intermediary of created substances: so long as we admit that the movement of the heavens is caused by an intellectual substance.

CHAPTER XXIV

HOW EVEN THINGS DEVOID OF KNOWLEDGE SEEK THE GOOD

IF, as we have shown,[1] the body of the heavens is moved by an intelligent substance, and if the movement of the body of the heavens is directed to generation in this lower world, it follows that the generations and movements of these lower bodies proceed from the intention of an intelligent substance. For the intention of the principal agent bears on the same thing as that of the instrument. Now the heavens is the cause of the movements of lower bodies by reason of its movement, with which it is moved by an intelligent substance. Consequently it is as an instrument of an intelligent substance. Therefore the forms and movements of lower bodies are caused by an intelligent substance and intended by it as by a principal agent, and by the body of the heavens, as by an instrument.

Now the species of things caused and intended by an intellectual agent must pre-exist in his intellect, just as the forms of the products of art pre-exist in the intellect of the craftsman and flow thence into his work. Consequently, all forms that are in these lower bodies, and all their movements, flow from intellectual forms which are in the intellect of some substance or substances. Hence Boethius says that *forms which are in matter originated in forms that are immaterial.*[2] In this respect the saying of Plato is verified, that separate Forms are the principles of forms that exist in matter;[3] although Plato held them to be *per se* subsistent, and to be the immediate cause of the forms of sensible bodies, whereas we hold them to exist in an intellect, and to cause lower forms through the movement of the heavens.

Now since whatever is moved by anything *per se,* and not accidentally, is directed thereby towards the end of its movement, and since the body of the heavens is moved by an intellectual substance; and since, furthermore the body of the heavens, by its movement, causes all movement in this lower world:—it follows of necessity that the body of the heavens is directed to the end of its movement by an intellectual substance, and consequently all lower bodies to their respective ends.

Accordingly, it is easy to understand how natural bodies devoid of knowledge are moved and act for the sake of an end. For they tend to an

---

[1] Ch. 23.   [2] *De Trin.*, II (PL 64, 1250).   [3] Cf. Aristotle, *Metaph.*, I, 6 (987b 7).

end as directed thereto by an intelligent substance, in the same way as an arrow, directed by the archer, tends to the mark. Because as the arrow receives its direction to a fixed end through the impulse of the archer, so, too, natural bodies receive an inclination to their natural ends from their natural movers, from whom they derive their forms, powers and movements.

Therefore it is also clear that every work of nature is the work of an intelligent substance, because an effect is ascribed more especially to the direction of the first mover towards the end than to the instruments which receive that direction. For this reason the operations of nature are seen to proceed to the end in an orderly manner even as do the operations of a wise man.

It is therefore evident that even things devoid of knowledge can work for an end, can desire the good with a natural appetite, and can seek a divine likeness as well as their own perfection. Nor does it matter in which way we express it, the former or the latter. Because by tending to their own perfection, they tend to a good, since a thing is good in so far as it is perfect. And according as a thing tends to be good, it tends to a divine likeness, since a thing is like God in so far as it is good. Now this or that particular good is so far appetible as it bears a likeness to the first goodness. Therefore the reason why a thing tends to its own good is because it tends to a divine likeness, and not *vice versa*. It is clear therefore that all things seek a divine likeness as their last end.

A thing's own good can be understood in several ways. First, in the sense that it is proper to that thing on the part of the individual. Thus an animal desires its own good when it desires food, whereby its existence is preserved. —Secondly, as being proper to that thing on the part of its species. Thus an animal desires its own good, in so far as it desires to beget offspring and to feed them, as well as whatever else conduces to the preservation or defense of the individuals of its species.—Thirdly, on the part of the genus. And thus an equivocal agent, for instance the heavens, desires its own good, in causing.—Fourthly, on the part of a likeness of analogy of effects to their cause. Thus God, Who is outside a genus, gives being to all things because of His own goodness.

This clearly proves that the more perfect a thing's power, and the higher its degree of goodness, the more universal is its desire for good, and the greater the range of goodness to which its appetite and operation extend. For imperfect things extend no further than their own individual good; perfect things extend to the good of the species; more perfect things, to the good of the genus; and God, Who is most perfect in goodness, to the good of all being. Therefore it is said by some, not without reason, that *good, as such, is diffusive*,[1] because the better a thing is, the further does the outpouring of its goodness extend. And since *in every genus that which is most perfect is the exemplar and measure of all that belongs to that*

---

[1] Cf. Pseudo-Dionysius, *De Div. Nom.*, IV, 1 (PG 3, 693).

genus,[1] it follows that God, Who is most perfect in goodness, and pours forth his goodness most universally, is in His outpouring the exemplar of all things that pour forth goodness. Now one thing becomes a cause of another by pouring forth its own goodness into that other. And so it is again evident that whatever tends to be the cause of something else, tends to a divine likeness, and yet tends to its own good.

Consequently, it is not unfitting to say that the movements of heavenly bodies, and the actions of their movers, are in a way for the sake of these bodies that are generated and corrupted, and less noble than they are. For they are not for the sake of these as their last end; but by intending the generation of these, they intend their own good, and the divine likeness as their last end.

CHAPTER XXV

THAT TO KNOW GOD IS THE END OF EVERY INTEL-
LECTUAL SUBSTANCE

Now, seeing that all creatures, even those that are devoid of reason, are directed to God as their last end, and that all reach this end in so far as they have some share of a likeness to Him, the intellectual creature attains to Him in a special way, namely, through its proper operation, by understanding Him. Consequently this must be the end of the intellectual creature, namely, to understand God.

For, as we have shown above,[2] God is the end of each thing, and hence, as far as it is possible to it, each thing intends to be united to God as its last end. Now a thing is more closely united to God by reaching in a way to the very substance of God; which happens when it knows something of the divine substance, rather than when it reaches to a divine likeness. Therefore the intellectual substance tends to the knowledge of God as its last end.

Again. The operation proper to a thing is its end, for it is its second perfection; so that when a thing is well conditioned for its proper operation it is said to be fit and good. Now understanding is the proper operation of the intellectual substance, and consequently is its end. Therefore, whatever is most perfect in this operation is its last end; and especially in those operations which are not directed to some product, such as understanding and sensation. And since operations of this kind take their species from their objects, by which also they are known, it follows that the more perfect the object of any such operation, the more perfect is the operation. Consequently to understand the most perfect intelligible, namely God, is the most perfect in the genus of the operation which consists in under-

---

[1] Aristotle, *Metaph.*, I a, 1 (993b 23).   [2] Ch. 17.

standing. Therefore to know God by an act of understanding is the last end of every intellectual substance.

Someone, however, might say that the last end of an intellectual substance consists indeed in understanding the best intelligible object, but that what is the best intelligible for this or that intellectual substance is not absolutely the best intelligible; and that the higher the intellectual substance, the higher is its best intelligible. So that possibly the supreme intellectual substance has for its best intelligible object that which is best absolutely, and its happiness will consist in understanding God; whereas the happiness of any lower intellectual substance will consist in understanding some lower intelligible object, which however will be the highest thing understood by that substance. Especially would it seem not to be in the power of the human intellect to understand that which is absolutely the best intelligible, because of its weakness; for it is as much adapted for knowing the supreme intelligible *as the owl's eye for seeing the sun*.[1]

Nevertheless it is evident that the end of any intellectual substance, even the lowest, is to understand God. For it has been shown above that God is the last end towards which all things tend.[2] And the human intellect, although the lowest in the order of intelligent substances, is superior to all that are devoid of understanding. Since then a more noble substance has not a less noble end, God will be the end also of the human intellect. Now every intelligent being attains to its last end by understanding it, as we have proved. Therefore the human intellect attains to God as its end, by understanding Him.

Again. Just as things devoid of intellect tend to God as their end by way of assimilation, so do intellectual substances by way of knowledge, as clearly appears from what has been said. Now, although things devoid of reason tend towards a likeness to their proximate causes, the intention of nature does not rest there, but has for its end a likeness to the highest good, as we have proved,[3] although they are able to attain to this likeness in a most imperfect manner. Therefore, however little be the knowledge of God to which the intellect is able to attain, this will be the intellect's last end, rather than a perfect knowledge of lower intelligibles.

Moreover. Everything desires most of all its last end. Now the human intellect desires, loves and enjoys the knowledge of divine things, although it can grasp but little about them, more than the perfect knowledge which it has of the lowest things. Therefore man's last end is to understand God in some way.

Further. Everything tends to a divine likeness as its own end. Therefore a thing's last end is that whereby it is most of all like God. Now the intellectual creature is especially likened to God in that it is intellectual, since this likeness belongs to it above other creatures, and includes all other likenesses. And in this particular kind of likeness it is more like God in under-

[1] Aristotle, *Metaph.*, I a, 1 (993b 9).   [2] Ch. 17.   [3] Ch. 19.

standing actually than in understanding habitually or potentially, because God is always actually understanding, as we proved in the First Book.[1] Furthermore, in understanding actually, the intellectual creature is especially like God in understanding God; for by understanding Himself God understand all other things, as we proved in the First Book.[2] Therefore the last end of every intellectual substance is to understand God.

Again. That which is lovable only because of another is for the sake of that which is lovable for its own sake alone; because we cannot go on indefinitely in the appetite of nature, since then nature's desire would be in vain, for it is impossible to pass through an infinite number of things. Now all practical sciences, arts and powers are lovable only for the sake of something else, since their end is not knowledge, but work. But speculative sciences are lovable for their own sake, for their end is knowledge itself. Nor can we find any action in human life that is not directed to some other end, with the exception of speculative consideration. For even playful actions, which seem to be done without any purpose, have some end due to them, namely that the mind may be relaxed, and that thereby we may afterwards become more fit for studious occupations; or otherwise we should always have to be playing, if play were desirable for its own sake, and this is unreasonable. Accordingly, the practical arts are directed to the speculative arts, and again every human operation, to intellectual speculation, as its end. Now, in all sciences and arts that are mutually ordered, the last end seems to belong to the one from which others take their rules and principles. Thus the art of sailing, to which belongs the ship's purpose, namely its use, provides rules and principles to the art of ship-building. And such is the relation of first philosophy to other speculative sciences, for all others depend thereon, since they derive their principles from it, and are directed by it in defending those principles; and moreover first philosophy is wholly directed to the knowledge of God as its last end, and is consequently called the *divine science*.[3] Therefore the knowledge of God is the last end of all human knowledge and activity.

Furthermore. In all mutually ordered agents and movers, the end of the first agent and mover must be the end of all, even as the end of the commander-in-chief is the end of all who are soldiering under him. Now of all the parts of man, the intellect is the highest mover, for it moves the appetite, by proposing its object to it; and the intellective appetite, or will, moves the sensitive appetites, namely the irascible and concupiscible. Hence it is that we do not obey the concupiscence, unless the will command; while the sensitive appetite, when the will has given its consent, moves the body. Therefore the end of the intellect is the end of all human actions. *Now the intellect's end and good are the true,*[4] and its last end is the first truth.

----

[1] *C. G.*, I, 56.   [2] *C. G.*, I, 49.   [3] Aristotle, *Metaph.*, I, 2 (983a 6).   [4] Aristotle, *Eth.*, VI, 2 (1139a 27).

Therefore the last end of the whole man, and of all his deeds and desires, is to know the first truth, namely, God.

Moreover. Man has a natural desire to know the causes of whatever he sees; and so through wondering at what they saw, and not knowing its cause, men first began to philosophize, and when they had discovered the cause they were at rest. Nor do they cease inquiring until they come to the first cause; and *then do we deem ourselves to know perfectly when we know the first cause*.[1] Therefore man naturally desires, as his last end, to know the first cause. But God is the first cause of all things. Therefore man's last end is to know God.

Besides. Man naturally desires to know the cause of any known effect. But the human intellect knows universal being. Therefore it naturally desires to know its cause, which is God alone, as we proved in the Second Book.[2] Now one has not attained to one's last end until the natural desire is at rest. Therefore the knowledge of any intelligible object is not enough for man's happiness, which is his last end, unless he know God also, which knowledge terminates his natural desire as his last end. Therefore this very knowledge of God is man's last end.

Further. A body that tends by its natural appetite to its place is moved all the more vehemently and rapidly the nearer it approaches its end. Hence Aristotle proves that a natural straight movement cannot be towards an indefinite point, because it would not be more moved afterwards than before.[3] Hence that which tends more vehemently to a thing afterwards than before is not moved towards an indefinite point but towards something fixed. Now this we find in the desire of knowledge, for the more one knows, the greater one's desire to know. Consequently, man's natural desire in knowledge tends to a definite end. This can be none other than the highest thing knowable, which is God. Therefore the knowledge of God is man's last end.

Now the last end of man and of any intelligent substance is called *happiness* or *beatitude*, for it is this that every intellectual substance desires as its last end, and for its own sake alone. Therefore the last beatitude or happiness of any intellectual substance is to know God.

Hence it is said (*Matt.* v. 8): *Blessed are the clean of heart, for they shall see God*; and (*Jo.* xvii. 3): *This is eternal life, that they may know thee, the only true God*. Aristotle himself agrees with this judgment when he says that man's ultimate happiness is *speculative, and this with regard to the highest object of speculation.*[4]

---

[1] Aristotle, *Metaph.*, I, 3 (983a 25).   [2] *C. G.*, II, 15.   [3] *De Caelo*, I, 8 (277a 18).
[4] *Eth.*, X, 7 (1177a 18).

CHAPTER XXVI

DOES HAPPINESS CONSIST IN AN ACT OF THE WILL?

SINCE the intellectual substance attains to God by its operation, not only by an act of understanding but also by an act of the will, through desiring and loving Him, and through delighting in Him, someone might think that man's last end and ultimate happiness consists, not in knowing God, but in loving Him, or in some other act of the will towards Him; [1] especially since the object of the will is the good, which has the nature of an end, whereas the true, which is the object of the intellect, has not the nature of an end except in so far as it also is a good. Therefore, seemingly, man does not attain to his last end by an act of his intellect, but rather by an act of his will.

[2] Further. The ultimate perfection of operation is delight, *which perfects operation as beauty perfects youth,* as the Philosopher says.[1] Hence, if the last end be a perfect operation, it would seem that it must consist in an act of the will rather than of the intellect.

[3] Again. Delight apparently is desired for its own sake, so that it is never desired for the sake of something else; for it is silly to ask of anyone why he seeks to be delighted. Now this is a condition of the ultimate end, namely, that it be sought for its own sake. Therefore, seemingly, the last end consists in an act of the will rather than of the intellect.

[4] Moreover. All agree in their desire of the last end, for it is a natural desire. But more people seek delight than knowledge. Therefore delight would seem to be the last end rather than knowledge.

[5] Furthermore. The will is seemingly a higher power than the intellect, for the will moves the intellect to its act; since when a person wills, his intellect considers by an act what he holds by a habit. Therefore, seemingly, the action of the will is more noble than the action of the intellect. Therefore, it would seem that the last end, which is beatitude, consists in an act of the will rather than of the intellect.

But this can be clearly shown to be impossible.

For since happiness is the proper good of the intellectual nature, it must needs become the intellectual nature according to that which is proper thereto. Now appetite is not proper to the intellectual nature, but is in all things, although it is found diversely in diverse things. This diversity, however, arises from the fact that things are diversely related to knowledge. For things wholly devoid of knowledge have only a natural appetite; those that have a sensitive knowledge have also a sensitive appetite, under which the irascible and concupiscible appetites are comprised; and those

---

[1] *Eth.,* X, 4 (1174b 31).

which have intellectual knowledge have also an appetite proportionate to that knowledge, namely, the will. The will, therefore, in so far as it is an appetite, is not proper to the intellectual nature, but only in so far as it is dependent on the intellect. On the other hand, the intellect is in itself proper to the intellectual nature. Therefore, beatitude or happiness consists principally and essentially in an act of the intellect, rather than in an act of the will.

Again. In all powers that are moved by their objects, the object is naturally prior to the acts of those powers, even as the mover is naturally prior to the movable being moved. Now the will is such a power, for the appetible object moves the appetite. Therefore the will's object is naturally prior to its act, and consequently its first object precedes its every act. Therefore an act of the will cannot be the first thing willed. But this is the last end, which is beatitude. Therefore beatitude or happiness cannot be the very act of the will.

Besides. In all those powers which are able to reflect on their acts, their act must first bear on some other object, and afterwards the power is brought to bear on its own act. For if the intellect understands that it understands, we must suppose first that it understands some particular thing, and that afterwards it understands that it understands; for this very act of understanding, which the intellect understands, must have an object. Hence either we must go on forever, or if we come to some first thing understood, this will not be an act of understanding, but some intelligible thing. In the same way, the first thing willed cannot be the very act of willing, but must be some other good. Now the first thing willed by an intellectual nature is beatitude or happiness; because it is for its sake that we will whatever we will. Therefore happiness cannot consist in an act of the will.

Further. The truth of a thing's nature is derived from those things which constitute its substance; for a true man differs from a man in a picture by the things which constitute man's substance. Now false happiness does not differ from true in an act of the will; because, whatever be proposed to the will as the supreme good, whether truly or falsely, it makes no difference to the will in its desiring, loving, or enjoying that good: the difference is on the part of the intellect, as to whether the good proposed as supreme be truly so or not. Therefore beatitude or happiness consists essentially in an act of the intellect rather than of the will.

Again. If an act of the will were happiness itself, this act would be an act either of desire, or love, or delight. But desire cannot possibly be the last end. For desire implies that the will is tending to what it has not yet; and this is contrary to the very notion of the last end.—Nor can love be the last end. For a good is loved not only while it is in our possession, but even when it is not, because it is through love that we seek by desire what we have not; and if the love of a thing we possess is more perfect. this arises from the fact that we possess the good we love. It is one thing, therefore, to possess the good which is our end, and another to love it; for love was imperfect before we possessed the end, and perfect after we obtained possession.—Nor again is delight the last end. For it is possession of the good that causes delight, whether we are conscious of possessing it actually, or call to mind our previous possession, or hope to possess it in the future. Therefore delight is not the last end.—Therefore no act of the will can be happiness itself essentially.

Furthermore. If delight were the last end, it would be desirable for its own sake. But this is not true. For the desirability of a delight depends on what gives rise to the delight, since that which arises from good and desirable operations is itself good and desirable, but that which arises from evil operations is itself evil and to be avoided. Therefore its goodness and desirability are from something else, and consequently it is not itself the last end or happiness.

Moreover. The right order of things agrees with the order of nature, for in the natural order things are ordered to their end without any error. Now, in the natural order delight is for the sake of operation, and not conversely. For it is to be observed that nature has joined delight with those animal operations which are clearly ordered to necessary ends: for instance, to the use of food that is ordered to the preservation of the individual, and to sexual matters, that are appointed for the preservation of the species; since were there no pleasure, animals would abstain from the use of these necessary things. Therefore delight cannot be the last end.

Again. Delight, seemingly, is nothing else than the quiescence of the will in some becoming good, just as desire is the inclining of the will towards the attaining of some good. Now just as by his will a man is inclined towards an end, and rests in it, so too natural bodies have a natural inclination to their respective ends, and are at rest when they have once attained their end. Now it is absurd to say that the end of the movement of a heavy body is not to be in its proper place, but that it is the quiescence of the inclination towards that place. For if it were nature's chief intent that this inclination should be quiescent, it would not give such an inclination; but it gives the inclination so that the body may tend towards its proper place, and when it has arrived there, as though it were its end, quiescence of the inclination follows. Hence this quiescence is not the end, but accompanies the end. Neither therefore is delight the ultimate end, but accompanies it. Much less therefore is happiness any act of the will.

Besides. If a thing have something extrinsic for its end, the operation whereby it first obtains that thing will be called its last end. Thus, for those whose end is money possession is said to be their end, but not love or desire. Now the last end of the intellectual substance is God. Hence that operation of man whereby he first obtains God is essentially his happiness or beatitude. And this is understanding, since we cannot will what we do not understand. Therefore man's ultimate happiness is essentially to know God by the intellect; it is not an act of the will.

From what has been said we can now solve the arguments that were objected in the contrary sense. For it does not necessarily follow that happiness is essentially the very act of the will, from the fact that it is the object of the will, through being the highest good, as the *first argument* reasoned. On the contrary, the fact that it is the first object of the will shows that it is not an act of the will, as appears from what we have said.

Nor does it follow that whatever perfects a thing in any way whatever must be the end of that thing, as the *second objection* argued. For a thing perfects another in two ways: first, it perfects a thing that has its species; secondly, it perfects a thing that it may have its species. Thus the perfection of a house, considered as already having its species, is that to which the species "house" is directed, namely to be a dwelling; for one would not build a house but for that purpose, and consequently we must include this in the definition of a house, if the definition is to be perfect. On the other hand, the perfection that conduces to the species of a house is both that which is directed to the completion of the species, for instance, its substantial principles; and also that which conduces to the preservation of the species, for instance, the buttresses which are made to support the building; as well as those things which make the house more fit for use, for instance, the beauty of the house. Accordingly, that which is the perfection of a thing, considered as already having its species, is its end; as the end of a house is to be a dwelling. Likewise, the operation proper to a thing, its use, as it were, is its end. On the other hand, whatever perfects a thing by conducing to its species is not the end of that thing; in fact, the thing itself is its end, for matter and form are for the sake of the species. For although the form is the end of generation, it is not the end of the thing already generated and having its species, but is required in order that the species be complete. Again, whatever preserves the thing in its species, such as health and the nutritive power, although it perfects the animal, is not the animal's end, but vice versa. And again, whatever adapts a thing for the perfection of its proper specific operations, and for the easier attainment of its proper end, is not the end of that thing, but vice versa; for instance, a man's comeliness and bodily strength, and the like, of which the Philosopher says that they *conduce to happiness instrumentally.*[1] —Now delight is a perfection of operation, not as though operation were directed thereto in respect of its species, for thus it is directed to other ends (thus, eating, in respect of its species, is directed to the preservation of the individual); but it is like a perfection that is conducive to a thing's species, since for the sake of the delight we perform more attentively and becomingly an operation we delight in. Hence the Philosopher says that

[1] *Eth.*, I, 8 (1099b 2); 9 (1099b 28).

delight perfects operation as beauty perfects youth,[1] for beauty is for the sake of the one who has youth and not *vice versa.*

Nor is the fact that men seek delight not for the sake of something else but for its own sake a sufficient indication that delight is the last end, as the *third objection* argued. Because delight, though it is not the last end, nevertheless accompanies the last end, since delight arises from the attainment of the end.

Nor do more people seek the pleasure that comes from knowledge than knowledge itself. But more there are who seek sensible delights than intellectual knowledge and the delight consequent thereto; because those things that are outside us are better known to the majority, in that human knowledge takes its beginning from sensible objects.

The suggestion put forward by the *fifth argument,* that the will is a higher power than the intellect, as being the latter's motive power, is clearly untrue. Because the intellect moves the will first and *per se,* for the will, as such, is moved by its object, which is the apprehended good; whereas the will moves the intellect accidentally as it were, in so far, namely, as the act of understanding is itself apprehended as a good, and on that account is desired by the will, with the result that the intellect understands actually. Even in this, the intellect precedes the will, for the will would never desire understanding, did not the intellect first apprehend its understanding as a good.—And again, the will moves the intellect to actual operation in the same way as an agent is said to move; whereas the intellect moves the will in the same way as the end moves, for the good understood is the end of the will. Now the agent in moving presupposes the end, for the agent does not move except for the sake of the end. It is therefore clear that the intellect is higher than the will absolutely, while the will is higher than the intellect accidentally and in a restricted sense.

CHAPTER XXVII

THAT HUMAN HAPPINESS DOES NOT CONSIST IN CARNAL PLEASURES

FROM what has been said it is clearly impossible that human happiness consist in pleasures of the body, the chief of which are pleasures of the table and of sex.

It has been shown that according to nature's order pleasure is for the sake of operation, and not conversely.[2] Therefore, if an operation be not the ultimate end, the consequent pleasure can neither be the ultimate end, nor accompany the ultimate end. Now it is manifest that the operations

[1] *Op. cit.,* X, 4 (1174b 31).   [2] Ch. 26.

which are followed by the pleasures mentioned above are not the last end; for they are directed to certain manifest ends: eating, for instance, to the preservation of the body, and carnal intercourse to the begetting of children. Therefore the aforesaid pleasures are not the last end, nor do they accompany the last end. Therefore happiness does not consist in them.

Again. The will is higher than the sensitive appetite, for it moves the sensitive appetite, as was stated above.[1] But happiness does not consist in an act of the will, as we have already proved.[2] Much less therefore does it consist in the aforesaid pleasures which are seated in the sensitive appetite.

Moreover. Happiness is a good proper to man, for it is an abuse of terms to speak of brute animals as being happy. Now these pleasures are common to man and brute. Therefore we must not assign happiness to them.

The last end is the most noble of things belonging to a reality, for it has the nature of that which is best. But the aforementioned pleasures do not befit man according to what is most noble in him, namely, the intellect, but according to the sense. Therefore happiness is not to be located in such pleasures.

Besides. The highest perfection of man cannot consist in his being united to things lower than himself, but consists in his being united to something above him; for the end is better than that which tends to the end. Now the above pleasures consist in man's being united through his senses to things beneath him, namely, certain sensible things. Therefore we must not assign happiness to such pleasures.

Further. That which is not good unless it be moderate is not good in itself, but receives its goodness from its moderator. Now the use of the aforesaid pleasures is not good for man unless it be moderate; for otherwise they would frustrate one another. Therefore these pleasures are not in themselves man's good. But the highest good is good of itself, because that which is good of itself is better than what is good through another. Therefore such pleasures are not man's highest good, which is happiness.

Again. In all *per se* predications, if A be predicated of B absolutely, an increase in A will be predicated of an increase in B. Thus if a hot thing heats, a hotter thing heats more, and the hottest thing will heat most. Accordingly, if the pleasures in question were good in themselves, it would follow that to use them very much would be very good. But this is clearly false, because it is considered sinful to use them too much; besides, it is hurtful to the body, and hinders pleasures of the same kind. Therefore they are not *per se* man's good, and human happiness does not consist in them.

Again. Acts of virtue are praiseworthy through being ordered to happiness.[3] If therefore human happiness consisted in the aforesaid pleasures, an act of virtue would be more praiseworthy in acceding to them than in abstaining from them. But this is clearly untrue, for the act of temperance

---

[1] *Ibid.*   [2] *Ibid.*   [3] Cf. Aristotle. *Eth.*, I, 12 (1101b 14).

is especially praised in abstinence from pleasures; whence that act takes its name. Therefore man's happiness is not in these pleasures.

Furthermore. The last end of everything is God, as was proved above.[1] We must therefore posit as man's last end that by which especially man approaches to God. Now man is hindered by the aforesaid pleasures from his chief approach to God, which is effected by contemplation, to which these same pleasures are a very great hindrance, since more than anything they plunge man into the midst of sensible things, and consequently withdraw him from intelligible things. Therefore human happiness is not to be placed in bodily pleasures.

Hereby is refuted the error of the Epicureans who ascribed man's happiness to pleasures of this kind. In their person Solomon says (*Eccles.* v. 17): *This therefore hath seemed good to me, that a man should eat and drink, and enjoy the fruit of his labor . . . and this is his portion*; and (*Wis.* ii. 9): *Let us everywhere leave tokens of joy, for this is our portion, and this is our lot.*

The error of the Cerinthians is also refuted. For they *pretended that*, in the state of final happiness, *after the resurrection Christ will reign for a thousand years, and men will indulge in the carnal pleasures of the table. Hence they are called 'Chiliastae,'* [2] or believers in the Millennium.

The fables of the Jews and Mohammedans are also refuted, who pretend that the reward of the righteous consists in such pleasures. For happiness is the reward of virtue.

CHAPTER XXVIII

THAT HAPPINESS DOES NOT CONSIST IN HONORS

FROM the foregoing it is also clear that neither does man's highest good, or happiness, consist in honors.

For man's ultimate end and happiness is his most perfect operation, as we have shown above.[3] But man's honor does not consist in something done by him, but in something done to him by another who shows him respect.[4] Therefore man's happiness must not be placed in honors.

Again. That which is for the sake of another good and desirable thing is not the last end. Now such is honor, for a man is not rightly honored, except because of some other good in him. For this reason men seek to be honored, as though wishing to have a voucher for some good that is in them; so that they rejoice more in being honored by the great and the wise. Therefore we must not assign man's happiness to honors.

---

[1] Ch. 17.　　[2] St. Augustine, *De Haeres.*, 8 (PL 42, 27).　　[3] Ch. 25.　　[4] Cf. Aristotle, *Eth.*, I, 5 (1095b 25).

Besides. Happiness is obtained through virtue. Now virtuous deeds are voluntary, or else they would not be praiseworthy. Therefore happiness must be a good obtainable by man through his will. But it is not in a man's power to secure honor, rather is it in the power of the man who pays honor. Therefore happiness is not to be assigned to honors.

Moreover. Only the good can be worthy of honor, and yet it is possible even for the wicked to be honored. Therefore it is better to become worthy of honor, than to be honored. Therefore honor is not man's supreme good.

Furthermore. The highest good is the perfect good. Now the perfect good is incompatible with any evil. But that which has no evil in it cannot possibly be evil. Therefore that which is in possession of the highest good cannot be evil. Yet it is possible for an evil person to receive honor. Therefore honor is not man's supreme good.

CHAPTER XXIX

THAT MAN'S HAPPINESS DOES NOT CONSIST IN GLORY

THEREFORE it is evident also that man's supreme good does not consist in glory, which is the recognition of one's good name.

For glory, according to Cicero, is *the general recognition and praise of a person's good name*,[1] and, in the words of Ambrose, consists in *being well known and praised*.[2] Now men seek praise and distinction through being famous, so that they may be honored by those whom their fame reaches. Therefore glory is sought for the sake of honor, and consequently if honor be not the highest good, much less is glory.

Again. Those goods are worthy of praise, whereby a man shows himself to be ordered to his end. Now he who is directed to his end has not yet reached his last end. Therefore praise is not bestowed on one who has reached his last end; rather does he receive honor, as the Philosopher says.[3] Therefore glory cannot be the highest good, since it consists chiefly in praise.

Besides. It is better to know than to be known, because only the higher realities know, whereas the lowest are known. Therefore man's highest good cannot be glory, which consists in a man's being known.

Further. A man does not seek to be known except in good things; in evil things he seeks to be hidden. Therefore, to be known is good and desirable, because of the good things that are known in a man. Therefore these good things are better still. Consequently glory, which consists in a man's being known, is not his highest good.

---

[1] *De Inventione*, II, 55 (p. 150b).   [2] Cf. St. Augustine, *Contra Maximin.*, II, 13 (PL 42, 770).   [3] *Eth.*, I, 12 (1101b 24).

Moreover. The highest good must needs be perfect, for it satisfies the appetite. But the knowledge of one's good name, wherein glory consists, is imperfect, for it is beset with much uncertainty and error. Therefore glory of this kind cannot be the supreme good.

Furthermore. Man's highest good must be supremely stable in human things, for it is natural to desire unfailing endurance in one's goods. Now glory, which consists in fame, is most unstable, since nothing is more changeable than human opinion and praise. Therefore such glory is not man's highest good.

CHAPTER XXX

THAT MAN'S HAPPINESS DOES NOT CONSIST IN WEALTH

HENCE it is evident that neither is wealth man's highest good. For wealth is not sought except for the sake of something else, because of itself it brings us no good, but only when we use it, whether for the support of the body or for some similar purpose. Now the highest good is sought for its own, and not for another's sake. Therefore wealth is not man's highest good.

Again. Man's highest good cannot consist in the possession or preservation of things whose chief advantage for man consists in their being spent. Now the chief advantage of wealth is in its being spent, for this is its use. Therefore the possession of wealth cannot be man's highest good.

Moreover. Acts of virtue deserve praise according as they lead to happiness. Now acts of liberality and magnificence, which are concerned with money, are deserving of praise because of money being spent rather than because of its being kept; and it is from this that these virtues derive their names. Therefore man's happiness does not consist in the possession of wealth.

Besides. Man's highest good must consist in obtaining something better than man. But man is better than wealth, since wealth is something directed to man's use. Therefore man's supreme good does not consist in wealth.

Further. Man's highest good is not subject to fortune.[1] For things that are fortuitous escape the forethought of reason, whereas man has to attain his own end by means of his reason. But fortune occupies the greatest place in the attaining of wealth. Therefore human happiness does not consist in wealth.

Moreover. This is evident from the fact that wealth is lost unwillingly; also because wealth can come into the possession of evil persons, who, of necessity, must lack the highest good. Again because wealth is unstable. Other similar reasons can be gathered from the arguments given above.[2]

[1] *Eth.*, I, 9 (1099b 24).   [2] Ch. 28ff.

CHAPTER XXXI

THAT HAPPINESS DOES NOT CONSIST IN WORLDLY POWER

In like manner, neither can worldly power be man's highest happiness, since in the achievement thereof chance can effect much. Again, it is unstable, and not subject to man's will; and it is often obtained by evil men. These are incompatible with the highest good, as was already stated.[1]

Again. Man is said to be good especially according as he approaches the highest good. But in respect to his having power, he is not said to be either good or evil, since not everyone who can do good deeds is good, nor is a person evil because he can do evil deeds. Therefore the highest good does not consist in being powerful.

Besides. Every power implies reference to something else. But the highest good is not referred to anything further. Therefore power is not man's highest good.

Moreover. Man's highest good cannot be a thing that one can use both well and ill; for the better things are those that we cannot abuse. But one can use one's power both well and ill, for *rational powers can be directed to contrary objects.*[2] Therefore human power is not man's good.

Further. If any power be man's highest good, it must be most perfect. Now human power is most imperfect, for it is based on human will and opinion, which are full of inconstancies. Also, the greater a power is reputed to be, the greater number of people does it depend on; which again conduces to its weakness, since what depends on many is in many ways destructible. Therefore man's highest good does not consist in worldly power.

Consequently man's happiness does not consist in any external good, for all external goods, which are known as *fortuitous goods,* are contained under those we have mentioned.[3]

CHAPTER XXXII

THAT HAPPINESS DOES NOT CONSIST IN GOODS OF THE BODY

Like arguments avail to prove that man's highest good does not consist in goods of the body, such as health, beauty and strength. For they are common to good and evil, they are unstable, and they are not subject to the will.

[1] Ch. 28ff.   [2] Aristotle, *Metaph.*, IX, 2 (1046b 25).   [3] Ch. 28ff.

Besides. The soul is better than the body, which neither lives nor possesses these goods without the soul. Therefore, the soul's good, such as understanding and the like, is better than the body's good. Therefore the body's good is not man's highest good.

Again. These goods are common to man and other animals, whereas happiness is a good proper to man. Therefore man's happiness does not consist in the things mentioned.

Moreover. Many animals surpass man in goods of the body, for some are fleeter than he, some more sturdy, and so on. Accordingly, if man's highest good consisted in these things, man would not excel all animals; which is clearly untrue. Therefore human happiness does not consist in goods of the body.

CHAPTER XXXIII

THAT HUMAN HAPPINESS IS NOT SEATED IN THE SENSES

BY the same arguments it is evident that neither does man's highest good consist in goods of his sensitive nature. For these goods, again, are common to man and other animals.

Again. Intellect is superior to sense. Therefore the intellect's good is better than that of the sense. Consequently man's supreme good is not seated in the senses.

Besides. The greatest sensual pleasures are those of the table and of sex, wherein the supreme good must needs be, if seated in the senses. But it does not consist in them. Therefore man's highest good is not in the senses.

Moreover. The senses are appreciated for their utility and for knowledge. Now the entire utility of the senses is referred to the goods of the body. Again, sensitive knowledge is ordered to intellectual knowledge, and hence animals devoid of intellect take no pleasure in sensation except in reference to some bodily utility, in so far as by sensitive knowledge they obtain food or sexual intercourse. Therefore, man's highest good which is happiness is not seated in the sensitive part of man.

CHAPTER XXXIV

THAT MAN'S ULTIMATE HAPPINESS DOES NOT CONSIST IN ACTS OF THE MORAL VIRTUES

IT is clear that man's ultimate happiness does not consist in moral activities.

For human happiness, if ultimate, cannot be directed to a further end. But all moral activities can be directed to something else. This is clear from a consideration of the principal among them. Because deeds of fortitude in time of war are directed to victory and peace; for it were foolish to go to war merely for its own sake.[1] Again, deeds of justice are directed to keeping peace among men, for each man possesses with contentment what is his own. The same applies to all the other virtues. Therefore man's ultimate happiness is not in moral deeds.

Again. The purpose of the moral virtues is that through them we may observe the mean in the passions within us, and in things outside us. Now it is impossible that the moderation of passions or of external things be the ultimate end of man's life, since both passions and external things can be directed to something less. Therefore it is not possible that the practice of moral virtue be man's final happiness.

Further. Since man is man through the possession of reason, his proper good, which is happiness, must needs be in accordance with that which is proper to reason. Now that which reason has in itself is more proper to reason than what it effects in something else. Seeing, then, that the good of moral virtue is a good established by reason in something other than itself, it cannot be the greatest good of man which happiness is; rather this good must be a good that is in reason itself.

Moreover. We have already proved that the last end of all things is to become like God.[2] Therefore that in which man chiefly becomes like God will be his happiness. Now this is not in terms of moral actions, since such actions cannot be ascribed to God, except metaphorically; for it is not befitting to God to have passions, or the like, with which moral virtue is concerned. Therefore man's ultimate happiness, which is his last end, does not consist in moral actions.

Furthermore. Happiness is man's proper good. Therefore that good, which of all goods is most proper to man in comparison with other animals, is the one in which we must seek his ultimate happiness. Now this is not the practice of moral virtue, for animals share somewhat either in liberality or in fortitude, whereas no animal has a share in intellectual activity. Therefore man's ultimate happiness does not consist in moral acts.

CHAPTER XXXV

THAT ULTIMATE HAPPINESS DOES NOT CONSIST IN THE ACT OF PRUDENCE

It is also evident from the foregoing that neither does man's happiness consist in the act of prudence.

For acts of prudence are solely about matters of moral virtue. But hu-

---

[1] Cf. Aristotle, *Eth.*, X, 7 (1177b 9).   [2] Ch. 19.

man happiness does not consist in the practice of moral virtue.[1] Neither therefore does it consist in the practice of prudence.

Again. Man's ultimate happiness consists in man's most excellent operation. Now man's most excellent operation, in terms of what is proper to man, is in relation to most perfect objects. But the act of prudence is not concerned with the most perfect objects of intellect or reason; for it is not about necessary things, but about contingent practical matters.[2] Therefore its act is not man's ultimate happiness.

Besides. That which is ordered to another as to its end is not man's ultimate happiness. Now the act of prudence is ordered to another as to its end, both because all practical knowledge, under which prudence is comprised, is ordered to operation, and because prudence disposes a man well in choosing means to an end, as may be gathered from Aristotle.[3] Therefore man's ultimate happiness is not in the practice of prudence.

Furthermore. Irrational animals have no share of happiness, as Aristotle proves.[4] Yet some of them have a certain share of prudence, as may be gathered from the same author.[5] Therefore happiness does not consist in an act of prudence.

CHAPTER XXXVI

THAT HAPPINESS DOES NOT CONSIST IN THE PRACTICE OF ART

It is also evident that it cannot consist in the practice of art.

For even the knowledge of art is practical, and so is directed to an end, and is not the ultimate end.

Besides. The end of the practice of art is the thing produced by art, and such a thing cannot be the ultimate end of human life, since it is rather we who are the end of those products, for they are all made for man's use. Therefore final happiness cannot consist in the practice of art.

CHAPTER XXXVII

THAT MAN'S ULTIMATE HAPPINESS CONSISTS IN CONTEMPLATING GOD

ACCORDINGLY, if man's ultimate happiness does not consist in external things, which are called goods of fortune; nor in goods of the body; nor in goods of the soul, as regards the sensitive part; nor as regards the intellec-

---

[1] Ch. 34.   [2] Cf. Aristotle, *Eth.*, VI, 5 (1104a 35).   [3] *Op. cit.*, VI, 13 (1145a 6).
[4] *Op cit.*, I, 9 (1099b 33).   [5] Aristotle, *Metaph.*, I, 1 (980a 30).

tual part, in terms of the life of moral virtue; nor in terms of the intellectual virtues which are concerned with action, namely, art and prudence:—it remains for us to conclude that man's ultimate happiness consists in the contemplation of truth.

For this operation alone is proper to man, and it is in it that none of the other animals communicates.

Again. This is not directed to anything further as to its end, since the contemplation of the truth is sought for its own sake.

Again. By this operation man is united to beings above him, by becoming like them; because of all human actions this alone is both in God and in the separate substances. Also, by this operation man comes into contact with those higher beings, through knowing them in any way whatever.

Besides, man is more self-sufficing for this operation, seeing that he stands in little need of the help of external things in order to perform it.

Further. All other human operations seem to be ordered to this as to their end. For perfect contemplation requires that the body should be disencumbered, and to this effect are directed all the products of art that are necessary for life. Moreover, it requires freedom from the disturbance caused by the passions, which is achieved by means of the moral virtues and of prudence; and freedom from external disturbance, to which the whole governance of the civil life is directed. So that, if we consider the matter rightly, we shall see that all human occupations appear to serve those who contemplate the truth.

Now, it is not possible that man's ultimate happiness consist in contemplation based on the understanding of first principles; for this is most imperfect, as being most universal, containing potentially the knowledge of things. Moreover, it is the beginning and not the end of human inquiry, and comes to us from nature, and not through the pursuit of the truth. Nor does it consist in contemplation based on the sciences that have the lowest things for their object, since happiness must consist in an operation of the intellect in relation to the most noble intelligible objects. It follows then that man's ultimate happiness consists in wisdom, based on the consideration of divine things.

It is therefore evident also by way of induction that man's ultimate happiness consists solely in the contemplation of God, which conclusion was proved above by arguments.[1]

[1] Ch. 25.

CHAPTER XXXVIII

THAT HUMAN HAPPINESS DOES NOT CONSIST IN THE KNOWL-
EDGE OF GOD WHICH IS POSSESSED GENERALLY BY THE
MAJORITY

IT remains for us to inquire in what kind of knowledge of God the ultimate happiness of an intellectual substance consists. For there is a certain
general and confused knowledge of God, which is in almost all men, whether
from the fact that, as some think, the existence of God, like other principles of demonstration, is self-evident, as we have stated in the First
Book,[1] or, as seems nearer to the truth, because by his natural reason man
is able at once to arrive at some knowledge of God. For seeing that natural
things run their course according to a fixed order, and since there cannot be
order without a cause of order, men, for the most part, perceive that there
is one who orders the things that we see. But who or of what kind this
cause of order may be, or whether there be but one, cannot be gathered
from this general consideration; just as, when we see a man in motion,
and performing other works, we perceive that in him there is some cause
of these operations which is not in other things, and we give this cause the
name of *soul*, but without knowing yet what the soul is, whether it be a
body, or how it brings about operations in question.

Now, this knowledge of God cannot possibly suffice for happiness.

For the activity of the happy man must be without any defect; but this
knowledge of God is subject to an admixture of many errors. Thus, some
believed that there was no other governor of mundane things than the
heavenly bodies; and so they said that the heavenly bodies were gods.—
Some ascribed this order to the elements and to the things generated from
them; as though they thought that their movements and natural operations
were not introduced into them by an external governor, but that the order
in other things was caused by them.—And some, deeming human acts not
to be subject to any but a human rule, declared that men who cause order
in other men were gods.—Evidently *this* knowledge of God is not sufficient
for happiness.

Moreover. Happiness is the end of human acts. But human acts are not
directed to the aforesaid knowledge as to their end; indeed, it is in everyone almost right from the very beginning. Therefore happiness does not
consist in this kind of knowledge of God.

Again. No one appears to be blamed for lacking happiness; nay, those
who lack it and seek it are praised. But he who lacks the aforesaid knowledge of God is seemingly very much to be blamed, since it is a very clear

[1] *C. G.*, I, 10.

sign of a man's dullness of perception if he fail to perceive such evident signs of God; even as a man would be deemed dull who, seeing man, understood not that he has a soul. Hence it is said in the Psalm (xiii. 1: lii. 1): *The fool hath said in his heart: There is no God.* Therefore it is not this knowledge of God which suffices for happiness.

Further. Knowledge of a thing in general only, and not in terms of what is proper to it, is most imperfect. Such is the knowledge which is had of man from the fact that he is moved; for this is a knowledge whereby a thing is known only potentially, because the proper is only potentially contained in the common. Now happiness is a perfect operation: and man's highest good must needs be in terms of what exists actually, and not in terms of what exists only potentially; since potentiality perfected by act has the character of a good. Therefore the aforesaid knowledge of God is not sufficient for our happiness.

CHAPTER XXXIX

THAT MAN'S HAPPINESS DOES NOT CONSIST IN THE KNOWLEDGE OF GOD ACQUIRED BY DEMONSTRATION

THERE is also another knowledge of God, higher than the one just mentioned, which is acquired by means of a demonstration, and which approaches nearer to a proper knowledge of Him; for by means of a demonstration many things are removed from Him, so that in consequence we understand Him as something apart from other things. For demonstration proves that God is immovable, eternal, incorporeal, utterly simple, one, and the like, as we have shown in the First Book. Now we arrive at the proper knowledge of a thing not only by affirmations, but also by negations. For just as it is proper to man to be a rational animal, so is it proper to him not to be inanimate or irrational. Yet there is this difference between these two modes of proper knowledge, that when we have proper knowledge of a thing by affirmations we know what that thing is, and how it is distinguished from others; whereas when we have proper knowledge of a thing by negations, we know that it is distinct from others, but remain ignorant of what it is. Such is the proper knowledge of God that can be obtained by demonstrations. But neither does this suffice for man's ultimate happiness.

For things belonging to one species for the most part attain to the end of that species, because nature achieves its purpose always or nearly always, and fails in a few instances because of some corruption. Now happiness is the end of the human species, since all men naturally desire it. Therefore happiness is a common good that can be attained by all men, unless some obstacle occur to some whereby they be deprived of it.[1] Few, how-

[1] Cf. Aristotle, *Eth.*, I, 9 (1099b 18).

ever, attain to the possession of the aforesaid knowledge of God by way of demonstration, because of the obstacles to this knowledge mentioned at the beginning of this work.[1] Therefore this knowledge is not essentially man's happiness.

Again. To be actual is the end of that which exists potentially, as was made clear above.[2] Therefore happiness, which is the last end, is an act free of any potentiality to a further act. Now this knowledge of God that is acquired by way of demonstration is still in potentiality to a further knowledge of God, or to the same knowledge, but by a better way: because those who came afterwards endeavored to add something to the knowledge of God besides that which they found handed down to them by those who preceded them. Therefore such knowledge is not man's ultimate happiness.

Further. Happiness excludes all unhappiness, for no man can be at the same time happy and unhappy. Now deception and error have a large place in unhappiness, since all naturally avoid them. But the aforesaid knowledge of God is subject to the admixture of many errors, as evidenced by many who knew some truths about God through demonstration, yet, following their own opinions, when they lacked proof, fell into many errors. And if there were some who by the way of demonstration discovered the truth about divine things, without any admixture of error in their opinions, it is evident that they were very few. This fact is not in keeping with happiness, which is the common end. Therefore man's ultimate happiness is not seated in such knowledge as this.

Moreover. Happiness consists in a perfect operation. Now perfect knowledge requires certitude, and that is why we cannot be said to know unless we know what cannot be otherwise, as is stated in *Post. Anal.* I.[3] But the aforesaid knowledge is beset with uncertainty, as is clear from the diversity among sciences about divine things elaborated by those who endeavored to discover something about God by the way of demonstration. Therefore ultimate happiness does not consist in such knowledge.

Besides. When the will has obtained its last end, its desire is at rest. Now the ultimate end of all human knowledge is happiness. Therefore happiness is essentially that knowledge of God the possession of which leaves no knowledge to be desired of anything knowable. Such, however, is not the knowledge which the philosophers were able to have about God by the way of demonstration; because even when we have this knowledge, we still desire to know other things—things that we do not yet know by means of this knowledge. Therefore happiness does not consist in such a knowledge of God.

Furthermore. The end of everything that exists in potentiality is that it be brought to actuality; for to this does it tend by means of the movement with which it is moved to its end. Now every potential being tends to becoming actualized as far as possible. For there are things in potentialitv

[1] *C. G.*, I, 4.   [2] Ch. 20, 22.   [3] Aristotle, *Post. Anal.*, I, 2 (72a 17).

whose whole potentiality is reducible to act: the end of such things is that
they be wholly actualized. Thus, a heavy body that is outside its medium
is in potentiality to its proper place. There are also things whose potentiality cannot be actualized all at once,—for instance primary matter: so that
by its movement it seeks actualization by various forms in succession, which
cannot be in the matter at the same time because of their diversity. Furthermore, our intellect is in potentiality to all intelligibles, as was stated in
the Second Book.[1] Now it is possible for two intelligible objects to be in
the possible intellect at the same time according to the first act which is
science, although perhaps not in respect of the second act which is *con
sideration.* Accordingly, it is clear that the whole potentiality of the possible intellect can be actualized at one time; and consequently this is required for its ultimate end, which is happiness. But the aforesaid knowledge, which can be acquired about God by the way of demonstration, does
not accomplish this, since when we have it we still are ignorant of many
things. Therefore such a knowledge of God does not suffice for ultimate
happiness.

CHAPTER XL

THAT MAN'S HAPPINESS DOES NOT CONSIST IN THE
KNOWLEDGE OF GOD BY FAITH

THERE is yet another knowledge of God, in one respect superior to the
knowledge we have been discussing, namely, that whereby God is known
by men through faith. Now this knowledge surpasses the knowledge of
God through demonstration in this respect, namely, that by faith we know
certain things about God which are so sublime that reason cannot reach
them by means of demonstration, as we have stated at the beginning of
this work.[2] But not even in this knowledge of God can man's ultimate happiness consist.

For happiness is the intellect's perfect operation, as was already declared.[3] But in knowledge by faith, the operation of the intellect is found
to be most imperfect as regards the contribution of the intellect, although
it is most perfect on the part of the object; for the intellect in believing
does not grasp the object of its assent. Therefore neither does man's happiness consist in this knowledge of God.

Again. It has been shown that ultimate happiness does not consist chiefly
in an act of the will.[4] Now in knowledge by faith, the will has the leading
place; for the intellect assents by faith to things proposed to it, because it
so wills, and not through being constrained by the evidence of their truth.
Therefore man's final happiness does not consist in this knowledge.

[1] *C. G.,* II, 47.   [2] *C. G.,* I, 5.   [3] Ch. 25.   [4] Ch. 26.

Besides. A believer assents to things proposed to him by another, but not seen by himself; so that the knowledge of faith resembles hearing rather than seeing. Now a man would not believe in what is unseen by him, and proposed to him by another, unless he thought this other to have a more perfect knowledge of the things proposed than he himself has who sees not. Either therefore the judgment of the believer is wrong, or the proposer must have more perfect knowledge of the things proposed. And if the latter also knows these things only through hearing them from another, we cannot proceed thus indefinitely, for then the assent of faith would be without foundation or certitude, since we should not come to some first principle certain in itself, to give certitude to the faith of believers. Now, in reality, it is not possible that the assent of faith be false and without foundation, as is clear from what we have said at the beginning of this work;[1] and yet if it were false and baseless, happiness could not consist in such knowledge. There is therefore some knowledge of God that is higher than the knowledge of faith, whether he who proposes faith sees the truth immediately, as when we believe Christ, or whether he receives the truth from him who sees it immediately, as when we believe the Apostles and Prophets. Since, then, man's happiness consists in the highest knowledge of God, it cannot consist in the knowledge of faith.

Moreover. Since happiness is the last end, the natural desire is set at rest thereby. But the knowledge of faith does not set the desire at rest, but inflames it; for everyone desires to see what he believes. Therefore man's ultimate happiness does not consist in the knowledge of faith.

Further. The knowledge of God has been declared to be the end inasmuch as it unites us to the last end of all, namely, God. Now the knowledge of faith does not make the thing believed to be perfectly present to the intellect, since faith is of absent, and not present, things. Hence the Apostle says (*2 Cor.* v. 6, 7) that *so long as we walk by faith, we are pilgrims from the Lord.* Yet faith makes God to be present to love, since the believer assents to God voluntarily, according to the saying of *Ephes.* iii. 17: *That Christ may dwell by faith in our hearts.* Therefore the knowledge of faith cannot be man's ultimate happiness.

CHAPTER XLI

IS IT POSSIBLE FOR MAN, IN THIS LIFE, TO UNDERSTAND SEPARATE SUBSTANCES BY THE STUDY AND INQUIRY OF THE SPECULATIVE SCIENCES?

An intellectual substance has yet another knowledge of God. For we have said in the Second Book that the separate intellectual substance, by knowing its own essence, knows both what is above it and what is below it, in a

[1] *C. G.*, I, 7.

way proportionate to its substance.[1] This must especially be the case if that which is above it be its cause, since the likeness to the cause must be found in the effect. Hence, since God is the cause of all created intellectual substances, as was proved above,[2] it follows that separate intellectual substances, by knowing their own essence, know God Himself by way of some kind of vision; for the intellect knows by way of vision the thing whose likeness is in the intellect, in the same way as the likeness of the thing seen corporeally is in the sense of the one seeing. Whatever intellect, therefore, apprehends a separate substance by knowing its essence, sees God in a higher way than He is known by any of the kinds of knowledge mentioned above.

Accordingly, since some have deemed man's ultimate happiness to be in this life, for the reason that he knows separate substances,[3] we must inquire whether in this life man be able to know separate substances. It is a point that may well be questioned. For our intellect, according to its present state, understands nothing without a phantasm, which stands in the same relation to the possible intellect, whereby we understand, as colors to the sight, as was made clear in the Second Book.[4] Hence if, through the intellectual knowledge which is acquired from phantasms it be possible for any of us to succeed in understanding separate substances, it will be possible for someone in this life to understand these same separate substances; and in consequence, by seeing these separate substances, he will participate in that mode of knowledge by which the separate substance, by understanding itself, understands God. If, on the other hand, by knowledge derived from phantasms, it be altogether unable to succeed in understanding separate substances, it will be impossible for man in the present state of life to acquire the above mode of knowing divine things.

The possibility of succeeding in understanding separate substances, through knowledge derived from phantasms, has been explained by some in various ways. Avempace maintained that by the study of the speculative sciences it is possible to arrive at a knowledge of separate substances from understanding those things which we know through phantasms.[5] For we are able by the action of the intellect to extract the quiddity of a thing which has quiddity without being its own quiddity. For the intellect is naturally adapted to know any quiddity as such, since the proper object of the intellect is *what a thing is*. Now if that which is first understood by the possible intellect is something that has a quiddity, we can, by the possible intellect, abstract the quiddity of the thing first understood; and if this quiddity has again a quiddity, it will be again possible to abstract the quiddity of this quiddity. And since we cannot go on indefinitely, we must stop somewhere. Therefore by way of analysis our intellect can arrive at know-

---

[1] *C. G.*, II, 96ff.   [2] *C. G.*, II, 15.   [3] Cf. Averroes, *In De Anima*, III, comm. 36 (VI, 175r ff).   [4] *C. G.*, II, 59 and 74.   [5] Cf. Averroes, *ibid.* (VI, 177v-178r)

ing a quiddity that has no quiddity; and such is the quiddity of a separate substance. Consequently, through its knowledge of these sensible things, acquired from phantasms, our intellect can arrive at understanding separate substances.

He goes on to prove the same conclusion by another and similar way. Thus, he lays down that that which we understand of a thing, for instance, of a horse, is multiplied in me and in you only through the multiplication of the spiritual species, which are diverse in you and me. It follows, then, that an understood thing which is not clothed with any such form is the same in you and me. Now, as we have proved, the quiddity of the understood thing, which our intellect can abstract, has no spiritual and individual species; for the quiddity of the thing understood is not the quiddity of an individual, whether corporeal or spiritual, since the thing understood, as such, is universal. Therefore our intellect has a natural aptitude to understand a quiddity of which the thing understood is one for all. Such is the quiddity of a separate substance. Therefore our intellect has a natural aptitude to know separate substances.

Yet, if we consider the matter carefully, these explanations are frivolous. For since the thing understood as such is universal, the quiddity of such a thing must be the quiddity of a universal, namely, genus or species. Now the quiddity of the genus or species in the case of sensible things, the intellectual knowledge of which we acquire through phantasms, includes both matter and form. Consequently it is quite unlike the quiddity of a separate substance, which is simple and immaterial. Therefore it is impossible to understand the quiddity of a separate substance through understanding the quiddity of a sensible thing.

Again. A form that, as to its very being, cannot be separated from a particular subject is not of the same kind as a form which, in its being, is separated from a particular subject, although both may be considered apart from that particular subject. For magnitude is not the same kind of thing as a separate substance, unless we suppose that there are separated magnitudes midway between the Forms and sensible things, as some Platonists have maintained. But the quiddity of a genus or species in the case of sensible things cannot be separated, in its very being, from a particular individual matter; unless, perhaps, as the Platonists think, we suppose the essences of things to exist separately, which Aristotle has refuted.[1] Consequently, the aforesaid quiddity is altogether different from separate substances, which are in no way in matter. Therefore it does not follow, from the fact that these quiddities are understood, that separate substances can be understood.

Moreover. If we grant that the quiddity of a separate substance is of the same kind as the quiddity of the genus or species in the case of sensible things, it cannot be said to be of the same specific kind, unless we say that

[1] *Metaph.*, I, 9 (990b 1).

the essences of these sensible things are the separate substances themselves, as the Platonists maintained. It follows that they are of the same kind only according to the nature of quiddity as quiddity, which is the common nature of genus and substance. Consequently, by means of these quiddities we shall understand nothing about separate substances except their remote genus. Now by knowing the genus, we do not therefore know the species, except potentially. Therefore it will not be possible to understand a separate substance through understanding the quiddities of these sensible things.

Besides. A separate substance differs more from sensible things than one sensible thing from another. But understanding the quiddity of one sensible thing does not suffice for understanding the quiddity of another; for a man who is born blind is quite unable, through understanding the quiddity of sound, to understand the quiddity of color. Much less, therefore, will anyone, through understanding the quiddity of a sensible substance, be able to understand the quiddity of a separate substance.

Further. If, again, we hold that separate substances move the spheres, through whose movements are caused the forms of sensible substances, even this mode of knowing separate substances through sensible things does not suffice for knowing their quiddity. Because from the effect we know a cause either in the point of likeness between cause and effect, or in so far as the effect indicates the power of the cause. In the point of likeness, we do not gather from the effect the nature of the cause, unless agent and effect be of one species; and this is not the case with separate substances and sensible things. In the point of power, it is again impossible unless the effect equal the power of the cause; since then the whole power of the cause is known from the effect, and the power of a thing indicates its substance. But this cannot apply to the situation in question, because the powers of separate substances surpass all the sensible effects that our intellect understands, even as a universal power surpasses a particular effect. It is therefore impossible, through understanding sensible things, to arrive at the understanding of separate substances.

Moreover. Whatever intelligible things we are able to come to know by means of inquiry and study belong to one or other of the speculative sciences. Accordingly, if through understanding the natures and quiddities of these sensible things we succeed in understanding separate substances, it follows that we would understand separate substances through one or another speculative science. Yet we do not find this to be the case, for no speculative science teaches *what* any separate substance is, but only the fact *that* it is. It is therefore not possible to succeed in understanding separate substances through understanding the natures of sensible things.

And if it be said that such a speculative science is possible, although it has not yet been discovered, the objection is empty, since it is not possible, from any principles known to us, to arrive at understanding the aforesaid substances. Because all the proper principles of any science whatever depend on the first indemonstrable self-evident principles, the knowledge of which we acquire from sensible things, as is stated in *Post. Anal.* ii.[1] But sensible things do not sufficiently lead to the knowledge of immaterial beings, as we have proved by the preceding arguments. Therefore no science is possible whereby one may be able to attain to the understanding of separate substances.

CHAPTER XLII

THAT IN THIS LIFE WE ARE UNABLE TO KNOW SEPARATE SUBSTANCES IN THE MANNER PROPOSED BY ALEXANDER

ALEXANDER supposed the possible intellect to be subject to generation and corruption, as being *a disposition of human nature resulting from the mixture of the elements,* as we have seen in the Second Book.[2] Now it is not possible for a power of this kind to rise above material things. And so he maintained that our possible intellect can never attain to the understanding of separate substances; but he also held that, according to our present state of life, we are nevertheless able to understand separate substances.[3]

He endeavored to prove this as follows. Whenever a thing is completed in its generation, and has reached the ultimate perfection of its substance, its proper operation, whether action or passion, will also be completed; for even as operation follows substance, so does perfection of operation follow perfection of substance. Hence an animal, when quite perfect, is able to walk by itself. Now the *habitual intellect,* which is nothing else but *the intelligible species formed by the agent intellect, and residing in the possible intellect,* has a twofold operation. One is to make things potentially understood to be actually understood,—and this operation it has through the agent intellect,—while the other is to understand what is actually understood; for it is these two things that man is able to do by an intellectual habit. Accordingly, when the generation of the habitual intellect is complete, both of these operations will be completed in it. Now whenever the intellect acquires new species it reaches the complement of its generation. And so its generation must necessarily be completed eventually, unless there be an impediment, since no generation tends to the infinite. Therefore, eventually, both operations will be completed in the habitual intellect, by its making all things potentially understood to be understood actually,—which is the complement of the first operation;—and by understanding all things intelligible, both separate and not separate.

But since, according to the opinion of Alexander (as we have stated), the possible intellect is unable to understand separate substances, he means

---

[1] Aristotle, *Post. Anal.,* II, 18 (99b 20).   [2] *C. G.,* II, 62.—Cf. Averroes, *In De Anima,* III, comm. 5 (VI, 162r-163r).   [3] Cf. Averroes, *ibid.*

that we shall understand separate substances by the habitual intellect, in so far as the agent intellect, which according to him is a separate substance, will become the form of the habitual intellect and be united to us. The result will be that we shall understand through it even as now we understand through the possible intellect. And since it is in the power of the agent intellect to make actually understood things which are potentially understandable, and to understand separate substances, in that state we shall understand separate substances, as well as all non-separate intelligible things.

According to this explanation, by this knowledge which we derive from phantasms, we attain to the knowledge of a separate substance; not as though the phantasms themselves and the things understood from them were a means for knowing separate substances, as happens in the speculative sciences, which was the position of the previous opinion,[1] but in so far as the intelligible species are in us a kind of disposition to this particular form which is the agent intellect. This is the first point of difference between these two opinions.

Consequently, when the habitual intellect becomes perfect through these intelligible species produced in us by the agent intellect, the agent intellect itself becomes a form united to us, as stated. And he calls this the *acquired intellect,* which, they say, Aristotle held to come from the outside. And so, although man's ultimate perfection is not seated in the speculative sciences, as the previous opinion maintained, yet by them man is disposed for the attainment of his ultimate perfection. This is the second point of difference between the second and first opinions.

Thirdly they differ in this, that, according to the first opinion, our understanding of the agent intellect is the cause of its union with us. Whereas, in the second opinion, the reverse is the case, since it is because it is united to us as a form that we understand it and other separate substances.

But there is no reason in these statements. For the habitual intellect, like the possible intellect, is supposed by Alexander to be subject to generation and corruption. Now, according to him, that which is eternal cannot become the form of that which can be generated and corrupted; for this is why he maintains that the possible intellect, which is united to us as a form, is subject to generation and corruption, while the agent intellect, which is incorruptible, is a separate substance. Since, then, according to Alexander, the agent intellect is supposed to be an eternal separate substance, it will be impossible for the agent intellect to become the form of the habitual intellect.

Again. The form of the intellect, as intellect, is the intelligible, just as the form of the sense is the sensible; for the intellect does not receive a thing, properly speaking, except intelligibly, as neither does the sense, except

[1] Ch. 41.

sensibly. If, then, the agent intellect cannot become an intelligible through the habitual intellect, it cannot possibly be its form.

Besides. There are three ways in which we are said to understand by means of something. First, we understand by means of the intellect, which is the power that elicits this operation. And so the intellect itself is said to understand, and the very act of the intellect in understanding becomes our act of understanding.—Secondly, we understand by means of the intelligible species. By it we are said to understand, not as though the species itself understood, but because the intellectual power is actualized by it, just as the power of sight is by the species of color.—Thirdly, as by a medium through the knowledge of which we arrive at the knowledge of something else.

If, then, man at length understands separate substances through the agent intellect, it must be in one of these ways. It is not in the third way, because Alexander does not grant that either the possible or the habitual intellect understands the agent intellect.—Nor is it in the second way, because to understand by means of an intelligible species is ascribed to the intellectual power that is informed by that species; but Alexander does not grant that either the possible or the habitual intellect understands separate substances. Consequently we cannot possibly understand separate substances by means of the agent intellect in the same way as we understand things by means of an intelligible species.—And if it is as by an intellectual power, it follows that the agent intellect's act of understanding is the man's act of understanding. Now this cannot be unless the substance of the agent intellect and the substance of the man become one in being; for it is impossible that there be identity of operation where there is diversity of substances. Hence the agent intellect will be one in being with man; but not one in being accidentally, because the agent intellect would then be, not a substance, but an accident; as for instance color added to a body makes a unity in being that is accidental. It remains, then, that the agent intellect together with man makes one being substantially. Therefore, it will be either the human soul or a part of it, and not a separate substance, as Alexander maintained. Therefore the opinion of Alexander does not explain how man can understand separate substances.

Moreover. If the agent intellect at any time becomes the form of this particular man, so that he be able to understand by means of it, for the same reason it may become the form of some other man who will likewise understand by its means. It will then follow that at the same time two men will understand through the agent intellect as through their own form. But this means that the agent intellect's act of understanding is the act of understanding of the man who understands by its means, as was already stated; and consequently two men who understand will have one act of understanding. Which is impossible.

Moreover his argument is altogether frivolous. First, because, when the generation of a genus is perfected, its operation must be perfected, yet in keeping with the mode of that genus, but not of a higher genus; for when the generation of air is perfected, it has generation and complete upward movement, yet not so as to be moved towards the place of fire. So, too, when the generation of the habitual intellect is complete, its operation, which is to understand, will be complete, according to its mode, but not according to the mode of understanding in separate substances, so as to understand separate substances. Consequently, from the generation of the habitual intellect it cannot be concluded that at some time man will understand separate substances.

Secondly, because it belongs to the same power to complete an operation and to perform it. Consequently, if the perfection of the habitual intellect's operation be to understand separate substances, it follows that the habitual intellect sometimes understands separate substances. But Alexander does not hold this; for it would follow that to understand separate substances comes to us through the speculative sciences, which are comprised under the habitual intellect.

Thirdly, those things that begin to be generated for the most part become completely generated; for all generations of things are due to determinate causes, which produce their effects either always or in the majority of cases. If, then, completeness of action follows completeness of generation, it is necessary that complete operation should follow things generated, always or most frequently. And yet those who study in order that the habitual intellect may be engendered in them do not succeed in understanding separate substances, either in most, or in all, cases. In fact no one has boasted of having attained to this point of perfection. Therefore the perfection of the habitual intellect is not to understand separate substances.

CHAPTER XLIII

THAT WE CANNOT UNDERSTAND SEPARATE SUBSTANCES, IN THIS LIFE, IN THE MANNER SUGGESTED BY AVERROES

As the greatest difficulty presented by Alexander's opinion was that he supposed the habitual intellect to be altogether corruptible, Averroes thought to offer an easier proof that at times we understand separate substances, in that he deemed the possible intellect to be incorruptible and substantially separate from us, just as the agent intellect.[1]

First, he shows the necessity of admitting that the relation of the agent intellect to those principals which we know naturally is either that of agent to instrument or that of form to matter. For the habitual intellect, whereby we understand, has for its activity not only that which consists in under-

[1] *In De Anima,* III, comm. 5 (VI, 164r).

standing, but also that which consists in producing the actually understood; for we know by experience that both are in our power. Now "to produce the actually understood" indicates more especially the habitual intellect than "to understand," because it is necessary to produce the actually understood before one understands it. Now, in us certain things are made actually understood naturally, and not by study or by choice: e.g., the first intelligible principles. But it does not belong to the habitual intellect to make these actually understood, for it belongs to it to make actually understood those things which we know by study. Rather are the first intelligibles a beginning of the habitual intellect; and so Aristotle gives the name of *understanding* to the habit of these principles.[1] They themselves are made actually understood by the agent intellect alone, but by them other things are made actually understood which we know by study. Accordingly, to make those things which are actually understood by derivation, is an act both of the habitual intellect, as to first principles, and of the agent intellect. Now one action does not proceed from two principles unless one of them be compared to the other as agent to instrument, or as form to matter. Consequently the agent intellect must be compared to the first principles of the habitual intellect either as agent to instrument, or as form to matter.

How this may be possible he explains as follows. Since the possible intellect, according to his opinion, is a separate substance,[2] it understands the agent intellect and other separate substances, as well as the first principles of speculative knowledge; and consequently it is the subject of both. Now whenever two things come together in one subject, one of them is as the form of the other; just as, since color and light are in the diaphanous body as their subject, one of them, namely light, must be the form of the other, namely color. And this is necessary when they are mutually ordered, but not when they are united accidentally in the same subject, as whiteness and music. Now the objects of speculative knowledge and the agent intellect are mutually ordered, since these understood speculative truths are made actually understood by the agent intellect. Therefore the agent intellect is related to these understood speculative truths as form to matter. Consequently, since these same truths are joined to us by phantasms, which are a kind of subject thereof, it follows that the agent intellect also is joined to us, as being the form of these truths. When, therefore, these truths are in us potentially only, the agent intellect is joined to us potentially only. When some of these truths are in us actually and some potentially, the agent intellect is joined to us actually in part, and potentially in part. Then it is said to be moved towards the above union; for the more things are made actually understood in us, the more perfectly is the agent intellect joined to us. And this progress and movement towards union is effected by study in the speculative sciences, through which we acquire true knowledge, and false opinions are put aside, which are outside the order of this movement,

---

[1] *Eth.*, VI, 6 (1141a 7).   [2] Cf. *C. G.*, II, 59.

just as monstrosities are outside the order of natural operation. Therefore men help one another towards this progress, just as they help one another in the speculative sciences. And so when all potential knowledge has become actual in us, the agent intellect will be perfectly joined to us as a form, and we shall understand perfectly by it, just as now we understand perfectly by the habitual intellect. Consequently, since it belongs to the agent intellect to understand separate substances, we shall then understand separate substances, just as now we understand speculative knowledge. This will be man's ultimate happiness, wherein man will be *as a sort of God*.[1]

That this explanation is of no account whatever is made clear enough by what we have already said; for it is based on many suppositions that have been already disproved.

First, we have shown above that the possible intellect is not a substance separate from us in being.[2] Hence it does not follow that it is the subject of separate substances; especially since Aristotle asserts that the possible intellect is the power of *becoming all things*,[3] so that seemingly it is the subject of such things only as *are made* to be understood.

Again. It has also been proved above that the agent intellect is not a separate substance, but part of the soul,[4] to which Aristotle assigns the operation of *making things to be actually understood*,[5] which lies in our power. Hence it does not follow that understanding by means of the agent intellect is the cause of our being able to understand separate substances; or else we would always understand them.

Further. If the agent intellect is a separate substance, it is not joined to us except by means of species made to be actually understood, according to his explanation; just as neither would the possible intellect be united to us, even though the possible intellect is related to those species as matter to form, while the agent intellect, on the contrary, is related to them as form to matter. Now the species which are made to be actually understood are joined to us, according to him, because of the phantasms, which stand related to the possible intellect as colors to the sight, but to the agent intellect as colors to the light, as may be gathered from the statement of Aristotle.[6] Now we cannot ascribe to a stone, in which there is color, either the action of seeing, so that it see, or the action of the sun, so that it give light. Therefore, according to this opinion, we cannot ascribe to man either the action of the possible intellect so that he understand, or the action of the agent intellect, so that he understand separate substances, or that he make things to be actually understood.

Besides. According to this opinion, the agent intellect is not supposed to be joined to us as a form, except through its being the form of the principles of understanding, whose form it is stated to be also because the agent

---

[1] *In De Anima*, III, comm. 36 (VI, 179r-180r).   [2] *C. G.*, II, 59.   [3] *De An.*, III, 5 (430a 14).   [4] *C. G.*, II, 76.   [5] *De. An.*, III, 5 (430a 15).   [6] *Ibid.* (430a 16).

intellect and these principles have an action in common, namely, to make things actually understood. Consequently, it cannot be a form to us, except in so far as the principles of knowledge have an action in common with it. But these principles have no share in the action which it has of understanding separate substances, because they are species of sensible things; unless we return to the opinion of Avempace, that the quiddities of separate substances can be known by means of what we know of the sensible world. Therefore in no way can we understand separate substances by this means.

Moreover. The agent intellect bears a different relation to the principles of knowledge, of which it is the cause, and to separate substances, of which it is not the cause, but which it only knows, according to his theory. Therefore, if it be joined to us through being the cause of the principles of knowledge, it does not follow that it is joined to us in so far as it knows separate substances. Quite the contrary, his argument clearly contains a fallacy of accident.

Again. If we know separate substances by means of the agent intellect, this is not in so far as the agent intellect is the form of this or that principle of understanding, but in so far as it becomes a form in us; for it is thus that we are able to understand by its means. Now it becomes a form in us also by means of the first principles of understanding, according to his own statement. Therefore from the very beginning man can understand separate substances by means of the agent intellect.

If, however, it be said that the agent intellect does not become a form in us perfectly by means of some principles of understanding, so that we be able to understand separate substances:—the sole reason for this is because these principles of understanding do not equal the perfection of the agent intellect in understanding separate substances. But not even all the intelligible truths combined together equal this perfection of the agent intellect in understanding separate substances; since all of them are not intelligible except in so far as they are made to be actually understood, whereas the latter are intelligible by their very nature. Therefore, although we shall know all the intelligible truths, it does not follow that the agent intellect will become a form in us so perfectly that we understand separate substances by it. Otherwise, if this be not required, we shall have to admit that by understanding anything intelligible we also understand separate substances.

CHAPTER XLIV

THAT MAN'S ULTIMATE HAPPINESS DOES NOT CONSIST IN THE KNOWLEDGE OF SEPARATE SUBSTANCES IMAGINED BY THE AFORESAID OPINIONS

But it is likewise impossible to allow that man's happiness consists in such a knowledge of separate substances as the above mentioned opinions maintained.[1]

For that is futile which is for an end that cannot be secured. Since, then, man's ultimate end is happiness, to which his natural desire tends, it is impossible to assign man's happiness to that which he cannot obtain; or else it would follow that man was made in vain, and that his natural desire is empty, which is impossible. Now it is clear from what we have said that it is impossible for man to understand separate substances, according to the above mentioned opinions. Therefore man's happiness does not consist in such a knowledge of separate substances.

Again. In order that the agent intellect be united to us as a form, in such a way that by it we may understand separate substances, it is required that the generation of the habitual intellect be complete, according to Alexander;[2] or that all the speculative truths be actualized in us, according to Averroes.[3] Both of these opinions come to the same, because the habitual intellect is engendered in us in so far as speculative truths are actualized in us. Now all the species of sensible things are understood potentially. Therefore, in order that the agent intellect be joined to a man, it is necessary that he actually understand by his speculative intellect all the natures of sensible things, and all their powers, operations and movements. But it is impossible for a man to know all this through the principles of the speculative sciences, whereby we are moved to the union with the agent intellect, as they themselves say; for it is not possible to acquire knowledge of all these things, from knowing those which come under the perception of our senses, whence the principles of the speculative sciences are derived. Therefore it is impossible for any man to arrive at this union in the way assigned by them; and consequently man's happiness cannot consist in such a union.

Besides. Granted that it be possible for man to be united to the agent intellect in the manner suggested, it is clear that such a perfection is obtainable by very few; so much so that neither they nor any others, however much they be advanced and skilled in the speculative sciences, have dared to boast of having obtained this perfection. In fact, all of them have confessed to ignorance of many things: thus Aristotle, speaking of the quadrature of a circle,[4] and of the principles of the order of the heavenly bodies.

---

[1] Cf. ch. 41ff.   [2] Ch. 42.   [3] Ch. 43.   [4] *Cat.*, VII (7b 31).

states that he can give only probable arguments;[1] and he leaves to others to decide what is necessary in these bodies and their movers.[2] Now happiness is a common good, to which many can arrive, *unless they be prevented*, as Aristotle says.[3] This is true also of any natural end of a species, namely, that it is obtained by the majority of the members of that species. Therefore man's ultimate happiness cannot consist in the aforesaid union.

It is clear that Aristotle, whose opinion the philosophers in question endeavored to follow, did not hold that man's ultimate happiness consists in a union of this kind. For he proves that man's happiness is an operation of his own according to perfect virtue.[4] That is why he had to treat specially of the virtues, which he divided into moral and intellectual. Furthermore, he proves that man's ultimate happiness consists in speculation.[5] Hence it follows that it is not seated in the act of a moral virtue, nor of prudence or art, even though these are intellectual virtues. Consequently, it must be an operation according to *wisdom*, which is the chief of the three remaining intellectual virtues, namely, *wisdom, science* and *understanding*, as he proves in *Ethics* vi.[6] For which reason he declares that the wise man is a happy man.[7] Now according to him wisdom is one of the speculative sciences, *the head of the others*; and at the beginning of the *Metaphysics* he gives the name of wisdom to the science of which he purposes to treat in that work.[9] Clearly, therefore, the opinion of Aristotle was that the ultimate happiness, which man is able to obtain in this life, is that knowledge of divine things which can be acquired through the speculative sciences. But that other way of knowing divine things, not through the speculative sciences, but by a kind of natural process of generation, was invented by some of his commentators.

CHAPTER XLV

THAT IT IS IMPOSSIBLE IN THIS LIFE TO UNDERSTAND SEPARATE SUBSTANCES

SINCE then in this life separate substances cannot be known by us in the ways mentioned above, it remains for us to inquire whether we be able to understand separate substances in this life in any way at all.

Themistius seeks to prove that this is possible by an argument *a fortiori*.[10] For separate substances are more intelligible than material things, since the latter are intelligible in so far as the agent intellect causes them to be actually understood, whereas the former are intelligible in themselves. If, there-

---

[1] *De Caelo*, II, 5 (288a 2).   [2] *Metaph.*, XI, 8 (1073b 2).   [3] *Eth.*, I, 9 (1099b 19).
[4] *Op. cit.*, I, 13 (1102a 5).   [5] *Op. cit.*, X, 7 (1177a 18).   [6] *Op. cit.*, VI, 6 (1141a 3).
[7] *Op. cit.*, X, 8 (1179a 32).   [8] *Op. cit.*, VI, 7 (1141a 16).   [9] *Metaph.*, I, 1 (981b 26).
[10] Cf. Averroes, *In De Anima*, III, comm. 36 (VI, 176v).

fore, our intellect understands these material things, much more is it adapted to understand separate substances.

This argument must be appraised in the light of the various opinions about the possible intellect. For if the possible intellect is a power independent of matter, and has its being apart from the body, as Averroes maintains, it will follow that it has no necessary relation to material things; so that the more a thing is intelligible in itself, the more will it be intelligible to the possible intellect. But then it would seem to follow, since we understand from the beginning by means of the possible intellect, that we understand separate substances from the beginning: which is clearly false. (Averroes seeks to avoid this difficulty, as we have explained above in setting forth his opinion, which we proved to be false.[1])

If, however, the possible intellect is not separate from the body in its very beginning, from the very fact that it is united in being to such a body it has a necessary relation to material things, so that only through them can it acquire knowledge of other things. Hence it does not follow, if separate substances be more intelligible in themselves, that they are more intelligible to our intellect. This is pointed out by the words of Aristotle. For he says there that *the difficulty of understanding those things is in us and not in them; because our intellect stands in relation to things most evident as the eye of the owl to the sunlight*.[2] Consequently, seeing that we cannot arrive at understanding separate substances through understanding material things, as we have proved,[3] it follows that our possible intellect can in no way understand separate substances.

This appears again from the relation of the possible to the agent intellect. For a passive power is in potentiality to those things only which are included in the range of its proper active principle; for every passive power has a corresponding active power in nature, or otherwise a passive power would be useless, since it cannot be brought to actuality, except by an active power. Hence we find that the sight is receptive only of colors, which are illumined by the light. Now the possible intellect is a power in a certain sense passive, and therefore it has its corresponding agent, namely, the agent intellect, which stands in relation to the possible intellect as light to the sight. Consequently, the possible intellect is in potentiality to those intelligible objects only which have been made so by the agent intellect. Hence Aristotle, in describing each intellect, says that *the possible intellect is the power to become all things,* while the agent intellect *is the power of making all things*:[4] so that the power in either case refers to the same objects, being active in the one and passive in the other. Since, then, separate substances are not made actually intelligible by the agent intellect, and only material things are so made, it follows that the possible intellect extends to these alone. Therefore we cannot understand separate substances through it.

---

[1] Ch. 43.   [2] *Metaph.*, I a, 1 (993b 9).   [3] Ch. 41.   [4] *De An.*, III, 5 (430a 14).

Therefore Aristotle employed a fitting example, for the owl's eye can never see the light of the sun. And yet that is why Averroes tries to weaken this example, saying that the likeness between our intellect in relation to separate substances, and the owl's eye in relation to the sun's light, is one of difficulty, not of impossibility.[1] He proves this as follows. Because if it were impossible for us to understand things intelligible in themselves, namely separate substances, they would be without purpose, just as to no purpose would a thing be visible, if it could not be seen by any sight.

Now this argument is clearly of no account. For even though these substances be never understood by us, yet they are understood by themselves; so that not without purpose would they be intelligible, as neither is the sun uselessly visible,—to continue Aristotle's comparison—because the owl cannot see it, since man and other animals can see it.

Accordingly, if we suppose the possible intellect to be united in being to the body, it cannot understand separate substances. It makes a difference, however, what we hold with regard to its substance. For if we suppose it to be a material power subject to generation and corruption, as some have maintained,[2] it follows that by its very substance it is confined to the understanding of material things. Consequently it would not in any way be able to understand separate substances, since it itself could not possibly be separate.—On the other hand, if the possible intellect, although united to the body, is incorruptible and independent of matter in its being, as we have proved above,[3] it follows that its confinement to the understanding of material things befalls it through its union with the body. And so, when the soul shall be separated from the body, the possible intellect will be able to understand things that are intelligible in themselves, namely separate substances, by the light of the agent intellect, which in the soul is like the intellectual light that is in separate substances.

This is what our Faith holds about our understanding separate substances after death, and not in this life.

CHAPTER XLVI

THAT IN THIS LIFE THE SOUL DOES NOT UNDERSTAND ITSELF BY ITSELF

A CERTAIN difficulty would seem to arise against what we have been saying, because of a passage of Augustine which must be carefully discussed. For he says: *Just as the mind gathers the knowledge of corporeal things through the senses, so does it acquire knowledge of incorporeal things through itself. Therefore it also knows itself through itself, since it is*

- Averroes, *In Metaph.*, II, comm. I (VIII, 14v).　²Cf. ch. 42.　³*C. G.*, II, 79ff.

incorporeal.[1] For it would seem to follow from these words that the soul understands itself through itself, and that, by understanding itself, it understands separate substances; and this is contrary to what we have proved. We must, accordingly, inquire how the soul understands itself through itself.

Now it cannot possibly be said that by itself it understands its own essence. Because a knowing power is made actually knowing by something in it whereby it knows. And if this be in it potentially, it knows potentially; if it be in it actually, it knows actually; and if it be in a middle way, it knows habitually. Now the soul is always actually present to itself, and never only potentially or habitually. Therefore, if the soul knows its own nature through itself, it will always understand actually what it is; and this is clearly false.

Again. If the soul, through itself, understands its own nature, since every man has a soul, every man will know *what* his soul is; which is evidently untrue.

Moreover. Knowledge that results from something implanted in us by nature is itself natural: *e.g.,* the indemonstrable principles which are known through the light of the agent intellect. Accordingly, if through the soul itself we know what the soul is, we shall know it naturally. But no one can err in things that we know naturally, for no one errs in the knowledge of indemonstrable principles. Hence no one would err about what the soul is, if the soul knew this through itself. But this is clearly false, since many have maintained the soul to be this or that body, and some, that it consisted in number or harmony.[2] Therefore the soul does not know its own nature through itself.

Besides. In every order *that which is per se precedes and causes that which is through another.*[3] Accordingly, that which is known *per se* is known before all things that are known through something else, and is the principle through which they are known: *e.g.,* first principles in comparison with conclusions. Therefore if the soul, through itself, knows its own nature, this will be known *per se,* and consequently it will be known first, and will be the principle whereby other things are known. But this is clearly false, for science does not postulate *what the soul is* as being something already known, but proposes it as a point of inquiry from other sources. Therefore the soul does not, through itself, know its own nature.

But it is clear that neither did Augustine intend this. For he says that *when the soul seeks self-knowledge, it does not seek to see itself as though it were absent, but to discern itself as present; not to know itself, as though it knew not, but in order to distinguish itself from what it knows to be something else.*[4] Whereby he gives one to understand that through itself the soul knows itself as present to itself, but not as distinct from other things. Hence he says that some erred in not distinguishing the soul from

[1] *De Trin.,* IX, 3 (PL 42, 963).   [2] Cf. *C. G.,* II, 63, 64.   [3] Aristotle, *Phys.,* VIII, 5 (257a 32).   [4] *De Trin.,* X, 9 (PL 42, 980).

things that are different from it.[1] Now through knowing what a thing is, one knows it as distinct from others. That is why a definition, which states what a thing is, distinguishes the thing defined from all others. Consequently, Augustine did not mean that the soul, through itself, knows what it is.

Neither did Aristotle mean this. He says, in fact, that *the possible intellect understands itself even as it understands other things*.[2] Because it understands itself by means of an intelligible species, by which it is brought to actual intelligibility. For, considered in itself, it is only potentially an intelligible being. Now nothing is known according as it is in potentiality, but only according as it is in act. Hence separate substances, whose substance is as something actual in the genus of intelligibles, understand through their very substances what they are; whereas our possible intellect understands what it is through the intelligible species by which it is made actually understanding. And so Aristotle shows the nature of the possible intellect from the act of understanding, namely, that it is *unmixed and incorruptible*,[3] as we explained above.[4]

Accordingly, Augustine means to say that our mind knows itself through itself inasmuch as it knows *that it is*. For, by the very fact that it perceives itself to act, it perceives that it exists; and since it acts through itself, it knows through itself that it exists.

In this way, then, the soul, by knowing itself, knows of the separate substances *that they are;* but not *what they are*, which is to understand their substance. For when either by demonstration or by faith we know about separate substances that they are certain intellectual substances, in neither way could we receive this knowledge, unless our soul derived from itself the knowledge of an intellectual being. Consequently, we must use the science about the soul's intellect as a principle on which to establish all our knowledge about separate substances.

But it does not follow, if by the speculative sciences we are able to arrive at the knowledge of what the soul is, that by means of these sciences we are able to arrive at the knowledge of what separate substances are; because our understanding, by which we arrive at the knowledge of what the soul is, is far removed from the intelligence of a separate substance. Nevertheless, through knowing what our soul is, we are able to go so far as to know some remote genus of the separate substances; but this is not the same as to understand their substance.

And just as through the soul itself we know *that* the soul is, inasmuch as we perceive its acts, and seek by a study of its acts and their objects to know *what* it is, through the principles of speculative sciences, so, too, concerning those things that are in our soul, namely its powers and habits, we know indeed *that* they are, inasmuch as we perceive their acts, but *what* they are we gather from the nature of these same acts.

[1] *Op. cit.*, X, 6 (PL 42, 978).   [2] *De An.*, III, 4 (430a 2).   [3] *Ibid.* (429a 2)
[4] *C. G.*, II, 59ff.

CHAPTER XLVII

THAT IN THIS LIFE WE ARE UNABLE TO SEE GOD IN HIS ESSENCE

IF, in this life, we are unable to understand separate substances by reason of our intellect's connatural relation to phantasms, much less can we see the divine essence in this life, since it is far above all separate substances.

We may take it as a sign of this, that the more our mind is raised to the contemplation of spiritual things, the more it is withdrawn from sensible things. Now the divine substance is the ultimate term to which contemplation can reach, and hence the mind that sees the divine substance must be wholly freed from the corporeal senses, either by death or by rapture. Therefore it is said in God's person (*Exod.* xxxiii. 20): *Man shall not see me, and live.*

If it is stated in Holy Scripture that some have seen God, we must understand this to have been either through an imaginary vision—or even a bodily vision, when the presence of the divine power is shown by corporeal species, whether appearing externally, or formed internally in the imagination, or by gathering some intellectual knowledge of God from His spiritual effects.

A difficulty, however, arises through some words of Augustine which would seem to imply that we are able to understand God in this life. For he says that *with the sight of the soul we see in the eternal truth, from which all temporal things have been made, the form according to which we are and according to which we effect something, in ourselves or in bodies, with a true and right reason; and it is from the same source that we conceive and possess a true knowledge of things.*[1] Again he says: *If we both see that what you say is true, and that what I say is true, where, I ask, do we see this? Surely, neither I in you, nor you in me, but both of us in the immutable truth itself which transcends our minds.*[2] Again, he says that *we judge of all things according to the divine truth,*[3] and again: *We must first know the truth by which other things can be known,*[4] referring, it would seem, to the divine truth. It would seem, then, from his words, that we see God Himself Who is His own truth, and that through Him we know other things.

Other words of his would seem to point to the same conclusion. In *De Trin.* xii he says: *It is the office of reason to judge of these corporeal things according to the incorporeal and eternal ideas which, unless they were above the human mind, would surely not be unchangeable.*[5] Now un-

---

[1] *De Trin.*, IX, 7 (PL 42, 967).   [2] *Confess.*, XII, 25 (PL 32, 840).   [3] *De Vera Relig.*, XXXI (PL 34, 148).   [4] *Solil.*, I, 15 (PL 32, 883).   [5] *De Trin.*, XII, 2 (PL 42, 999).

changeable and eternal ideas cannot be elsewhere than in God, since, according to the teaching of Faith, God alone is eternal. Accordingly it would seem to follow that we can see God in this life, and that, through seeing Him and the ideas of things in Him, we judge of other things.

Yet it is not to be believed that Augustine, by these words, meant that we are able in this life to see God in His essence. We must therefore inquire how, in this life, we see that *unchangeable truth,* or these *eternal ideas,* and how we judge of other things according to this truth.

Augustine allows that truth is in the soul,[1] and therefore it is that he proves the immortality of the soul from the eternity of truth. Now truth is in the soul not only in the same way as God is said to be in all things by His essence, or as He is in all things by His likeness (in so far, namely, as a thing is true according as it approaches to a likeness of God), for then the soul would not be higher than other things in this respect. It is therefore in the soul in a special way, inasmuch as the soul knows truth. Accordingly, just as the soul and other things are said to be true in their nature according as they are likened to that supreme nature, which is truth itself, since it is its own understood being, so too, that which is known by the soul is true so far as it contains a likeness to that divine truth which God knows. Therefore a *Gloss* on *Ps.* xi. 2, *Truths are decayed from among the children of men,* says that *as from one man's face many likenesses are reflected in a mirror, so many truths are reflected from the one divine truth.*[2] Now although different things are known, and different things believed to be true, by different people, yet some truths there are in which all men agree, such as the first principles both of the speculative and of the practical intellect, inasmuch as a kind of image of the divine truth is reflected in the minds of all men. Consequently, when a mind knows with certitude anything at all, and by tracing it back to the principles by which we judge of everything, comes to see it in those principles, it is said to see all such things in the divine truth or in the eternal ideas, and to judge of all things according to them. This explanation is confirmed by Augustine's words: *The speculations of the sciences are seen in the divine truth, even as these visible things are seen in the light of the sun.*[3] For it is evident that these things are not seen in the body of the sun, but by the light, which is a likeness of the solar brilliance reflected in the air, and cast upon such bodies.

Therefore, from these words of Augustine we cannot conclude that God is seen in His essence in this life, but only as in a mirror; and to this the Apostle witnesses as regards the knowledge of this life (*1 Cor.* xiii. 12): *We see now through a glass in a dark manner.*

And though this mirror, which is the human mind, reflects the likeness of God in a higher way than creatures of lower degree, yet the knowledge

---

[1] *Solil.,* II, 19 (PL 32, 901).   [2] Cf. St. Augustine, *Enarr. in Psalm,* super XI, 2 (PL 36, 138); Peter Lombard, *In Psalm,* super XI, 2 (PL 191, 155).   [3] *Solil.,* I, 8 (PL 32, 877)

of God that can be gathered from the human mind does not transcend the genus of the knowledge gathered from sensible things; since even the soul knows what it itself is through understanding the natures of sensible things, as we have already stated.[1] Consequently, even in this way God is not known in higher manner than the cause is known from its effect.

CHAPTER XLVIII

THAT MAN'S ULTIMATE HAPPINESS IS NOT IN THIS LIFE

SEEING, then, that man's ultimate happiness does not consist in that knowledge of God whereby He is known by all or many in a vague kind of opin- ion, nor again in that knowledge of God whereby He is known in the speculative sciences through demonstration, nor in that knowledge whereby He is known through faith, as we have proved above;[2] and seeing that it is not possible in this life to arrive at a higher knowledge of God in His essence, or at least so that we understand other separate substances, and thus know God through that which is nearest to Him, so to say, as we have proved;[3] and since we must place our ultimate happiness in some kind of knowledge of God, as we have shown:[4]—it is impossible for man's happiness to be in this life.

Again. Man's last end is the term of his natural appetite, so that when he has obtained it, he desires nothing more; because if he still has a movement towards something, he has not yet reached an end wherein to be at rest. Now this cannot happen in this life, since the more man understands, the more is the desire to understand increased in him (for this is natural to man), unless perhaps there be someone who understands all things. Now in this life this never did nor can happen to anyone that was a mere man, seeing that in this life we are unable to know separate substances which in themselves are most intelligible, as we have proved.[5] Therefore man's ultimate happiness cannot possibly be in this life.

Besides. Whatever is in motion towards an end has a natural desire to be established and at rest therein. Hence a body does not move away from the place towards which it has a natural movement, except by a violent movement which is contrary to that appetite. Now happiness is the last end which man naturally desires. Therefore it is his natural desire to be established in happiness. Consequently, unless together with happiness he acquires a state of immobility, he is not yet happy, since his natural desire is not yet at rest. When, therefore, a man acquires happiness, he also acquires stability and rest; so that all agree in conceiving stability as a necessary condition of happiness. Hence the Philosopher says: *We do not look*

---

[1] Ch. 45, 46. [2] Ch. 38ff. [3] Ch. 45. [4] Ch. 37. [5] Ch. 45.

upon the happy man as a kind of chameleon.[1] Now in this life there is no sure stability, since, however happy a man may be, sickness and misfortune may come upon him, so that he is hindered in the operation, whatever it be, in which happiness consists. Therefore man's ultimate happiness cannot be in this life.

Moreover. It would seem unfitting and unreasonable for a thing to take a long time in becoming, and to have but a short time in being; for it would follow that for a longer duration of time nature would be deprived of its end. Hence we see that animals which live but a short time are perfected in a short time. But if happiness consists in a perfect operation according to perfect virtue,[2] whether intellectual or moral, it cannot possibly come to man except after a long time. This is most evident in speculative matters, wherein man's ultimate happiness consists, as we have proved;[3] for hardly is man able to arrive at perfection in the speculations of science, even though he reach the last stage of life, and then, in the majority of cases, but a short space of life remains to him. Therefore man's ultimate happiness cannot be in this life.

Further. All admit that happiness is a perfect good, or else it would not bring rest to the appetite. Now perfect good is that which is wholly free from any admixture of evil; just as that which is perfectly white is that which is entirely free from any admixture of black. But man cannot be wholly free from evils in this state of life, and not only from evils of the body, such as hunger, thirst, heat, cold and the like, but also from evils of the soul. For there is no one who at times is not disturbed by inordinate passions; who sometimes does not go beyond the mean, wherein virtue consists,[4] either in excess or in deficiency; who is not deceived in some thing or another; or who at least is not ignorant of what he would wish to know, or does not feel doubtful about an opinion of which he would like to be certain. Therefore no man is happy in this life.

Again. Man naturally shuns death, and is sad about it, not only shunning it at the moment when he feels its presence, but also when he thinks about it. But man, in this life, cannot obtain not to die. Therefore it is not possible for man to be happy in this life.

Besides. Ultimate happiness consists, not in a habit, but in an operation, since habits are for the sake of actions. But in this life it is impossible to perform any action continuously. Therefore man cannot be entirely happy in this life.

Further. The more a thing is desired and loved, the more does its loss bring sorrow and pain. Now happiness is most desired and loved. Therefore its loss brings the greatest sorrow. But if there be ultimate happiness in this life, it will certainly be lost, at least by death. Nor is it certain that it will last till death, since it is possible for every man in this life to

---

[1] *Eth.,* I, 10 (1100b 5).   [2] *Op. cit.,* X, 7 (1177a 11).   [3] Ch. 37.   [4] Cf. Aristotle, *Eth.,* II, 6 (1106b 24).

encounter sickness, whereby he is wholly hindered from the operation of virtue, *e.g.*, madness and the like, which hinder the use of reason. Such happiness therefore always has sorrow naturally connected with it, and consequently it will not be perfect happiness.

But someone might say that, since happiness is a good of the intellectual nature, perfect and true happiness is for those in whom the intellectual nature is perfect, namely, in separate substances, and that in man it is imperfect, and by a kind of participation. For man can arrive at a full understanding of the truth only by a sort of movement of inquiry; and he fails entirely to understand things that are by nature most intelligible, as we have proved. Therefore neither is happiness, in its perfect nature, possible to man; but he has a certain participation of it, even in this life. This seems to have been Aristotle's opinion about happiness. Hence, inquiring whether misfortunes destroy happiness, he shows that happiness seems especially to consist in deeds of virtue, which seem to be most stable in this life, and concludes that those who in this life attain to this perfection are happy *as men,* as though not attaining to happiness absolutely, but in a human way.[1]

We must now show that this explanation does not remove the foregoing arguments. For although man is below the separate substances according to the order of nature, he is above irrational creatures, and so he attains his ultimate end in a more perfect way than they. Now these attain their last end so perfectly that they seek nothing further. Thus a heavy body rests when it is in its own proper place, and when an animal enjoys sensible pleasure, its natural desire is at rest. Much more, therefore, when man has obtained his last end, must his natural desire be at rest. But this cannot happen in this life. Therefore in this life man does not obtain happiness considered as his proper end, as we have proved. Therefore he must obtain it after this life.

Again. Natural desire cannot be empty, since *nature does nothing in vain.*[2] But nature's desire would be empty if it could never be fulfilled. Therefore man's natural desire can be fulfilled. But not in this life, as we have shown. Therefore it must be fulfilled after this life. Therefore man's ultimate happiness is after this life.

Besides. As long as a thing is in motion towards perfection, it has not reached its last end. Now in the knowledge of truth all men are always in motion and tending towards perfection; because those who follow make discoveries in addition to those made by their predecessors, as is also stated in *Metaph.* ii.[3] Therefore in the knowledge of truth man is not situated as though he had arrived at his last end. Since, then, as Aristotle himself shows,[4] man's ultimate happiness in this life consists apparently

---

[1] *Op. cit.,* I, 10 (1101a 18).   [2] Aristotle, *De Caelo,* II, 11 (291b 13).   [3] Aristotle, *Metaph.,* I a, 1 (993a 31).   [4] *Eth.,* X, 7 (1177a 18).

in speculation, whereby he seeks the knowledge of truth, we cannot possibly allow that man obtains his last end in this life.

Moreover. Whatever is in potentiality tends to become actual, so that
as long as it is not wholly actual, it has not reached its last end. Now our
intellect is in potentiality to the knowledge of all the forms of things, and
it becomes actual when it knows any one of them. Consequently, it will not
be wholly actual, nor in possession of its last end, except when it knows
all things, at least all these material things. But man cannot obtain this
through the speculative sciences, by which we know truth in this life.
Therefore man's ultimate happiness cannot be in this life.

For these and like reasons, Alexander and Averroes held that man's
ultimate happiness does not consist in that human knowledge obtained
through the speculative sciences, but in that which results from a union
with a separate substance, which union they deemed possible to man in
this life.[1] But as Aristotle realized that man has no knowledge in this life
other than that which he obtains through the speculative sciences, he
maintained that man attains to a happiness which is not perfect, but a
human one.

Hence it becomes sufficiently clear how these great minds suffered from
being so straitened on every side. We, however, shall be freed from these
straits if we hold, in accordance with the foregoing arguments, that man is
able to reach perfect happiness after this life, since man has an immortal
soul; and that in that state his soul will understand in the same way as
separate substances understand, as we proved in the Second Book.[2]

Therefore man's ultimate happiness will consist in that knowledge of
God which the human mind possesses after this life, a knowledge similar
to that by which separate substances know him. Hence our Lord promises
us a *reward . . . in heaven* (*Matt.* v. 12) and states (*Matt.* xxii. 30) that
the saints *shall be as the angels,* who always see God in heaven (*Matt.*
xviii. 10).

CHAPTER XLIX

THAT SEPARATE SUBSTANCES DO NOT SEE GOD IN HIS ESSENCE THROUGH KNOWING HIM BY THEIR OWN ESSENCES

WE must now inquire whether this same knowledge, whereby separate
substances and souls after death know God by their own essences, is sufficient for their ultimate happiness.

In order to discover the truth in this matter, we must first show that to
know God in this way is not to know His essence.

[1] Cf. ch. 42, 43.   [2] *C. G.,* II, 81.

It is possible to know a cause from its effect in several ways. First, when the effect is taken as the means of knowing the existence and character of the cause. This happens in the sciences which prove the cause from the effect.—Secondly, when the cause is seen in the effect itself, inasmuch as the likeness of the cause is reflected in the effect. Thus a man is seen in a mirror because of his likeness. This way differs from the first, because in the first there are two knowledges, of effect and of cause, of which one is the cause of the other; for the knowledge of the effect is the cause of our knowing its cause. In the second way, however, there is one sight of both, because, while seeing the effect, we see the cause therein at the same time.—Thirdly, when the very likeness of the cause in the effect is the form by which the cause is known by its effect: *e.g.*, if a box had an intellect, and were to know by its own form the art from which that very form had been produced in likeness to that art. But by none of these ways is it possible to know from its effect *what* the cause is, unless the effect be equal to the cause, and express the whole power of the cause.

Now separate substances know God by their substances in the same way as a cause is known from its effect; not however in the first way, because then their knowledge would be discursive; but in the second way, inasmuch as one of them sees God in another; and also in the third way, inasmuch as each of them sees God in itself. Yet none of them is an effect equalling God's power, as we have shown in the Second Book.[1] Therefore they cannot see the divine essence by this kind of knowledge.

Besides. The intelligible likeness, whereby a thing is understood in its substance, must be of the same species, in fact it must be its species; even as the form of the house, which is in the architect's mind, is of the same species as the form of the house which exists in matter, or rather it is its species. For we do not understand what an ass is, or what a horse is, through the species of a man. But the nature of a separate substance is not of the same species as the divine nature, indeed, not even of the same genus, as we showed in the First Book.[2] Therefore a separate substance cannot possibly understand God through its own nature.

Further. Every created thing is limited to a certain genus or species. But the divine essence is infinite, comprising within itself the entire perfection of all being, as we proved in the First Book.[3] Therefore the divine substance cannot be seen through anything created.

Moreover. Every intelligible species, through which the quiddity or essence of a thing is understood, comprehends that thing in representing it. And so the words signifying what a thing is are called *terms* and *definitions*. But no created likeness can possibly represent God thus, since every created likeness belongs to some determinate genus, whereas God does not, as was proved in the First Book.[4] Therefore it is not possible to understand the divine substance through a created likeness.

[1] *C. G.*, II, 22.   [2] *C. G.*, I, 25.   [3] *C. G.*, I, 28, 43.   [4] *C. G.*, I, 25.

Further. It was proved in the First Book that God's substance is His being.[1] But the being of a separate substance is distinct from its substance, as we proved in the Second Book.[2] Therefore the essence of a separate substance is not a sufficient means whereby God may be seen in His essence.

And yet the separate substance, through its own substance, knows of God that He is, that He is the cause of all things, that He is above all and far removed from all, not only from the things that are, but even from those that can be conceived by the created mind. This knowledge about God we also are able somewhat to obtain, because from His effects we know of God that He is, and that He is the cause of other things, surpassing all and remote from all. And this is the limit and the highest point of our knowledge in this life in which, as Dionysius says, *we are united to God as to something unknown.*[3] This happens when we know of Him *what He is not,* while *what He is* remains utterly unknown. Hence, in order to indicate the ignorance of this most sublime knowledge, it is said of Moses (*Exod.* xx. 21) that he *went to the dark cloud wherein God was.*

Since, however, the lower nature in its summit attains only to what is lowest in the higher nature, it follows that this same knowledge is more sublime in separate substances than in us. This can be shown as to each way of attaining to this knowledge. For if the cause be known by its effect, the nearer that effect is, and the clearer its resemblance to its cause, the more evident does it make the existence of that cause. Now separate substances, that know God by themselves, are nearer effects and bear a clearer resemblance to God, than the effects through which we know God. Therefore separate substances know more certainly and more clearly than we that God exists.—Again. Since by negations we come by any way whatever to a proper knowledge of a thing, as was stated above,[4] the more things one knows to be removed from God, and the greater their propinquity, the nearer does one approach to a proper knowledge of Him; just as he who knows that man is neither inanimate nor insensible approaches nearer to a proper knowledge of man than one who knows only that he is not inanimate, although neither of them knows what man is. Now separate substances know more things than we do, and things that are nearer to God; and consequently by their intellect they remove from God more things and things nearer to God than we do. Therefore they approach nearer to a proper knowledge of God than we; although neither do they, through understanding themselves, see the divine substance.

Again. The higher the persons over whom one knows a man to be placed, the better the knowledge one has of his eminence. Thus, although a peasant may know that the king is the highest in the land, yet since he knows only some of the lowest officials of the kingdom, with whom he has business, he does not realize the king's exalted position, as one who knows the dignity of all the great men of the kingdom, over whom he knows the king

---

[1] *C. G.,* I, 22.   [2] *C. G.,* II, 52.   [3] *De Myst. Theol.,* I, 1 (PG 3, 997).   [4] Ch. 39

to be placed; although neither of them may comprehend the height of the kingly rank. Now we know none but the lowest things, and consequently, although we know that God is far above all, we do not know the divine supereminence as the separate substances do, since they know the highest orders of things, and also that God is higher than them all.

Again. It is clear that the causality and power of a cause are all the better known, according as more and greater effects of it are known. Therefore it evidently follows that separate substances know the divine causality and power better than we, even though we know God to be the cause of all.

CHAPTER L

THAT THE NATURAL DESIRE OF THE SEPARATE SUBSTANCES IS NOT SET AT REST IN THE NATURAL KNOWLEDGE THEY HAVE OF GOD

Now it is not possible that the natural desire of a separate substance rest in such a knowledge of God.

For whatever is imperfect in a species seeks to acquire the perfection of that species. Thus, whoso has an opinion about a matter, and therefore an imperfect knowledge about it, for this very reason is spurred to the desire for certain knowledge about it. Now the aforesaid knowledge which separate substances have about God, which does not include a knowledge of His substance, is an imperfect kind of knowledge; for we do not deem ourselves to know a thing if we do not know its substance. Hence, the chief point in knowing a thing is to know *what it is*. Therefore this knowledge, which the separate substances have about God, does not set their appetite at rest, but spurs it on to the vision of the divine substance.

Again. The knowledge of effects is an incitement to know the cause. Therefore it was that men began to philosophize because they sought the causes of things.[1] Therefore the desire for knowledge naturally implanted in all intellectual substances does not rest unless, having acquired the knowledge of the substance of the effects, they know also the substance of their cause. Consequently, since separate substances know that God is the cause of all the things whose substances they see, their natural desire does not rest, unless they see God's substance also.

Besides. As knowing *why* a thing is so [*propter quid*] is related to knowing *whether* it is so [*quia*], so knowing *what* a thing is [*quid est*] is related to knowing *whether* it is [*an est*]. For the question *why* a thing is so seeks the means of demonstrating *that* a thing is so, *e.g.*, that the moon is in eclipse. So, too, the question *what* a thing is seeks a means of demonstrating *whether* a thing is so. Such is the teaching of *Post. Anal.* ii.[2] Now we observe that those who know *that* a thing is so naturally seek to

[1] Cf. Aristotle, *Metaph.*, I, 2 (982b 12).   [2] Aristotle, *Post. Anal.*, II, 1 (89b 22).

know the why of its being so. Therefore those who know *that* a thing exists naturally seek to know *what* it is; and this is to know its essence. Therefore the natural desire for knowledge is not set at rest by that knowledge of God whereby it is known that He exists.

Further. Nothing finite can set the intellect's desire at rest. This is proved from the fact that the intellect, given any finite thing, strives to go beyond it; so that, given a finite line of any length, it strives to apprehend a longer. So, too, in the case of numbers. This is the reason why we can add indefinitely to numbers and mathematical lines. Now the excellence and power of any created substance is finite. Therefore the intellect of a separate substance is not satisfied with knowing separate substances, however excellent they be, but still tends by its natural desire to understand the substance which is of an infinite excellence, as we proved in the First Book concerning the divine substance.[1]

Moreover. Just as there is a natural desire for knowledge in all intellectual natures, so there is in them a natural desire to rid themselves of ignorance or nescience. Now separate substances, as has been stated,[2] know in the manner already mentioned that God's substance is above them, and above everything that they understand; and therefore they know that the divine substance is unknown to them. Therefore their natural desire tends to understand the divine substance.

Besides. The nearer a thing is to its end, the greater the desire with which it tends to that end. Hence we see that the natural movement of bodies is increased towards the end. Now the intellects of separate substances are nearer to the knowledge of God than ours, and consequently they desire to know God more intensely than we do. And however much we know that God is, and other things mentioned above,[3] we still go on desiring and seek to know Him in His essence. Much more therefore do separate substances desire this naturally; and consequently their natural desire is not satisfied with the above-mentioned knowledge of God.

Hence we conclude that the ultimate happiness of a separate substance does not consist in the knowledge whereby it knows God by its own substance, since its desire still leads it on to the substance of God.

It also clearly follows from this that ultimate happiness is to be sought nowhere else but in an operation of the intellect, since no desire leads us so high as the desire of knowing the truth. For all our desires, whether of pleasure or of anything else that man wants, can be satisfied with other things; whereas the aforesaid desire does not rest until it has reached God, the supreme cause and maker of all. Hence Wisdom fittingly says (*Ecclus.* xxiv. 7): *I dwell in the highest places, and my throne is in a pillar of a cloud.* It is also written (*Prov.* ix. 3) that *Wisdom by her maids inviteth to the tower.* They should blush, then, who seek man's happiness in the lowest things, when it is placed on such a height.

[1] *C. G.*, I, 43.   [2] Ch. 49.   [3] *Ibid.*

CHAPTER LI

HOW GOD MAY BE SEEN IN HIS ESSENCE

SINCE, then, it is impossible for a natural desire to be empty (and it would be, were it impossible to arrive at understanding the divine substance, for all minds desire this naturally), we must conclude that it is possible for the divine substance to be seen through the intellect, both by separate intellectual substances, and by our souls.

It is sufficiently clear, from what has been said, what manner of vision this is. For we have proved that the divine substance cannot be seen by the intellect by means of any created species.[1] Therefore, if God's essence is to be seen at all, it must be that the intellect sees it through the divine essence itself; so that in that vision the divine essence is both the object and the medium of vision.

Since, however, the intellect is unable to understand any particular substance unless it be actualized by a species informing it, which is the likeness of the thing understood, someone might deem it impossible for a created intellect to see the very substance of God through the divine essence as an intelligible species. For the divine essence is self-subsistent, and we have proved in the First Book that God cannot be the form of anything.[2]

In order to understand this truth, we must note that a self-subsisting substance is either a form alone, or a composite of matter and form. Accordingly, that which is composed of matter and form cannot be the form of something else, because the form therein is already confined to that matter, so that it cannot be the form of another thing. But that which so subsists that it is yet a form alone, can be the form of something else, provided its being be such that some other thing can participate in it, as we have proved concerning the human soul in the Second Book.[3] If, however, its being cannot be participated in by another, it cannot be the form of anything, because by its very being it is determined in itself, just as material things are determined by their matter. Now we must consider this as being the case not only with regard to substantial or natural being, but also as regards intelligible being. For, since truth is the perfection of the intellect, that intelligible which is truth itself will be a pure form in the genus of intelligible things. This applies solely to God, for, since truth is consequent upon being,[4] that alone is its own truth, which is its own being; and this belongs to God alone, as we have proved in the Second Book.[5] Consequently, other subsistent intelligibles are not pure forms in the genus of intelligible things, but have a form in a subject; for each of them is a true

---

[1] Ch. 49.   [2] C. G., I, 26ff.   [3] C. G., II. 68.   [4] Cf. Aristotle, Metaph., I a, 1 (993b 30).   [5] C. G., II, 15.

thing, but not the truth, even as it is a being, but not being itself. It is therefore clear that the divine essence can be compared to the created intellect as an intelligible species by which it understands; which cannot be said of the essence of any separate substance. And yet it cannot be the form of another thing through its natural being. For it would follow that, once united to another being, it would constitute one nature; which is impossible, since the divine essence is in itself perfect in its own nature. But an intelligible species, in its union with the intellect, does not constitute a nature, but perfects the intellect for understanding; and this is not inconsistent with the perfection of the divine essence.

This immediate vision of God is promised to us in Holy Scripture (*1 Cor.* xiii. 12): *We see now through a glass in a dark manner; but then face to face.* It would be impious to understand this in a material way, and imagine a material face in the Godhead; for we have proved that God is not a body.[6] Nor is it possible for us to see God with a bodily face, since the eyes of the body, which are situated in the face, can see only bodily things. Thus then shall we see God face to face, because we shall see Him immediately, even as a man whom we see face to face.

It is through this vision that we become most like God, and participators of His blessedness, since God understands His substance through His essence, and this is His blessedness. Therefore it is said (*1 John* iii. 2): *When He shall appear, we shall be like to Him; because we shall see Him as He is.* Again, our Lord said (*Luke* xxii. 29, 30): *I dispose to you, as My Father hath disposed to Me, a banquet, that you may eat and drink at My table in My kingdom.* Now these words cannot be understood as referring to bodily food and drink, but to that which is taken from the table of Wisdom, of which Wisdom says (*Prov.* ix. 5): *Eat my bread and drink the wine which I have mingled for you.* Accordingly, to eat and drink at God's table is to enjoy the same blessedness as that which makes God happy, and to see God as He sees Himself.

CHAPTER LII

THAT NO CREATED SUBSTANCE CAN BY ITS NATURAL POWER ARRIVE AT SEEING GOD IN HIS ESSENCE

HOWEVER, it is not possible for any created substance to attain, by its own power, to this way of seeing God.

For that which is proper to the higher nature cannot be acquired by a lower nature, except through the action of the higher nature to which it properly belongs. Thus water cannot become hot except through the action of heat. Now to see God through His essence is proper to the divine nature,

[1] *C. G.*, I, 27.

since to operate through his own form is proper to each operator. Therefore no intellectual substance can see God through the divine essence, unless God Himself bring this about.

Again. A form proper to A does not become B's except through A's agency, because an agent produces its like by communicating its form to another. Now it is impossible to see the divine substance unless the divine essence itself become the form by which the intellect understands, as we have proved.[1] Therefore no created substance can attain to that vision, except through the divine agency.

Besides. If any two things have to be united together so that one be formal and the other material, their union must be completed by an action on the part of the one that is formal, and not by the action of the one that is material; for the form is the principle of action, whereas matter is the passive principle. Now in order that the created intellect see God's substance, the divine essence itself must be united to the intellect as an intelligible form, as we have proved. Therefore no created intellect can attain to this vision except through the divine agency.

Further. *What is so of itself is the cause of what is so through another.*[2] Now the divine intellect sees through itself the divine substance, for the divine intellect is the divine essence itself, by means of which God's substance is seen, as we proved in the First Book.[3] But the created intellect sees the divine substance through the divine essence as through something other than itself. Therefore this vision cannot be acquired by the created intellect, except through the action of God.

Moreover. Whatever exceeds the limits of a given nature, cannot be acquired by that nature except through the agency of another; and thus water does not flow upwards unless it be moved by something else. Now it is beyond the limits of any created nature to see God's substance, because it is proper to every created intellectual nature to understand according to the mode of its substance. But the divine substance cannot be thus understood, as we proved above.[4] Therefore no created intellect can possibly attain to a vision of the divine substance except by the agency of God, Who surpasses all creatures.

Hence it is said (*Rom.* vi. 23): *The grace of God is life everlasting.* For we have proved that man's happiness consists in seeing God, which is called life everlasting.[5] Now we are said to obtain this by God's grace alone, because that vision surpasses the ability of every creature, and it is impossible to attain thereto except by God's gift; and when such things are obtained by a creature, it is put down to God's grace. And so our Lord says (*Jo.* xiv. 21): *I will manifest myself to him.*

---

[1] Ch. 51.   [2] Cf. Aristotle, *Phys.*, VIII, 5 (257a 31).   [3] *C. G.*, I, 45.   [4] Ch. 49.
[5] Ch. 50.

CHAPTER LIII

THAT THE CREATED INTELLECT NEEDS THE ASSISTANCE OF THE DIVINE LIGHT IN ORDER TO SEE GOD IN HIS ESSENCE

To so sublime a vision the created intellect needs to be raised by some kind of outpouring of the divine goodness. For it is impossible that the proper form of anything become the form of another, unless this other bear some resemblance to the thing to which that form properly belongs. Thus light does not actualize a body which has nothing in common with the diaphanous. Now the divine essence is the proper intelligible form of the divine intellect, and is proportionate to it; for these three, *understanding, means of understanding* and *object understood* are one in God. Therefore that same essence cannot become the intelligible form of a created intellect, except because the created intellect participates in some divine likeness. Therefore this participation in a divine likeness is necessary in order that the divine substance be seen.

Again. Nothing can receive a higher form unless it be raised through some disposition to the capacity for this form; for every act is realized in its proper potency. Now the divine essence is a higher form than any created intellect. Therefore, in order that the divine essence become the intelligible species of a created intellect, which is requisite in order that the divine substance be seen, the created intellect needs to be raised to that capacity by some higher disposition.

Besides. If two things, after not being united, become united, this must be either because both are changed, or only one. Now if we suppose that some created intellect begins to see the divine essence, it follows, from what we have said,[1] that the divine essence comes to be united to that intellect as an intelligible species. But it is impossible that the divine essence be changed, as we have proved.[2] Therefore this union must begin through a change in the created intellect, and this change can consist only in the fact that the created intellect acquires some new disposition.—The same conclusion follows if we suppose some created intellect to be endowed from the outset of its creation with such a vision. For if, as we have proved,[3] this vision exceeds the ability of nature, it is possible to conceive any created intellect as complete in the species of its nature without its seeing God's substance. Consequently, whether it see God from the beginning, or begin to see Him afterwards, its nature needs something to be added to it.

Further. Nothing can be raised to a higher operation except through its power being strengthened. Now a power may be strengthened in two ways

[1] Ch. 51.   [2] *C. G.*, I, 13.   [3] Ch. 52.

First, by a mere intensifying of its power. Thus, the active power of a hot thing is increased by the intensity of the heat, so that it is capable of a more vehement action of the same species. Secondly, by the addition of a new form. Thus the power of a diaphanous body is strengthened so that it can give light, through its being made actually lucid by receiving the form of light anew. This increase of power is necessary in order to accomplish an operation of another species. Now the natural power of the created intellect is not sufficient for the vision of the divine substance, as we have shown.[1] Therefore its power needs to be increased in order that it attain to that vision. But increase through intensification of the natural power is insufficient, because that vision is not of the same kind as the natural vision of the created intellect; which is clear from the distance separating the things seen. Therefore there must be an increase of the intellectual power through its receiving a new disposition.

Now, owing to the fact that we derive our knowledge of intelligible beings from sensible things, we transfer the terms employed in sensible knowledge to our intellectual knowledge; especially those terms that pertain to the sight, which of all the senses is the highest and most spiritual, and therefore most akin to the intellect. It is for this reason that intellectual knowledge is called *sight* [*visio*]. And because bodily sight is not effected without light, those things which serve for the perfection of intellectual vision are called *light;* and so Aristotle compares the agent intellect to light, because the agent intellect makes things actually intelligible, even as light somehow makes things to be actually visible.[2] Accordingly, the disposition whereby the created intellect is raised to the intellectual vision of the divine substance is rightly called the *light of glory;* not indeed because it makes the object actually intelligible, as the light of the agent intellect does, but because it makes the intellect able to understand actually.

This is the light of which it is said (*Ps.* xxxv. 10): *In Thy light we shall see light,* i.e., the light of the divine substance. Again it is said (*Apoc.* xxii. 5 [cf. xxi. 23]): *The city,* namely of the Blessed, *hath no need of the sun, nor of the moon . . . for the glory of God hath enlightened it.* Again it is said (*Isa.* lx. 19): *Thou shalt no more have the sun for thy light by day, neither shall the brightness of the moon enlighten thee; but the Lord shall be unto thee for an everlasting light, and thy God for thy glory.*—For this reason, too, since in God to be is the same as to understand, and because He is to all the cause of their understanding, He is said to be *the light (Jo.* i. 9): *That was the true light which enlighteneth every man that cometh into this world;* and (*1 John* i. 5): *God is light.* Again (*Ps.* ciii. 2): *Thou . . . art clothed with light as with a garment.*—For this reason, too, both God and the angels are described in Holy Scripture in figures of fire, because of the splendor of fire (*Exod.* xxiv. 17; *Acts* ii. 3; *Ps.* ciii. 4).

[1] *Ibid.*   [2] *De An.,* III, 5 (430a 15).

CHAPTER LIV

ARGUMENTS THAT WOULD SEEM TO PROVE THAT GOD CANNOT BE SEEN IN HIS ESSENCE, AND THEIR SOLUTION

SOMEONE will object against the foregoing:

[1] No additional light can help the sight to see things that surpass the natural ability of corporeal sight, since the sight can see only colored things. Now the divine substance surpasses every capacity of a created intellect, more even than the intellect surpasses the senses' capacity. Therefore no additional light can raise the created intellect to see the divine substance.

[2] Again. This light, that is received into the created intellect, is something created. Therefore it also is infinitely distant from God, and consequently such a light cannot help the created intellect to see the divine substance.

[3] Besides. If the aforesaid light can do this for the reason that it is a likeness of the divine substance, since every intellectual substance, for the very reason that it is intellectual, bears a likeness to God, the nature itself of an intellectual substance will suffice for it to see God.

[4] Further. If this light is created, since there is no reason why that which is created should not be connatural to some creature, there might possibly be a creature that would see the divine substance through its connatural light. But the contrary of this has been proved.[1]

[5] Moreover. *The infinite, as such, is unknown.*[2] Now we proved in the First Book that God is infinite.[3] Therefore the divine substance cannot be seen through the light in question.

[6] Again. There should be a proportion between the one understanding and the thing understood. But there is no proportion between the created intellect, even perfected by this light, and the divine substance; for there still remains an infinite distance between them. Therefore the created intellect cannot be raised by any light to see the divine substance.

By these and like arguments some have been induced to maintain that the divine substance is never seen by a created intellect. This opinion both destroys the rational creature's true happiness, which can consist in nothing but the vision of the divine substance, as we have proved,[4] and is contrary to the authority of Holy Scripture, as appears from what we have said.[5] Therefore it should be rejected as false and heretical.

Now it is not difficult to answer the above arguments. For the divine substance is not so outside the range of the created intellect, as to be absolutely beyond its reach, as sound is to the sight, or an immaterial substance to the senses. For the divine substance is the first intelligible, and the prin-

---

[1] Ch. 52.   [2] Aristotle, *Phys.*, I, 4 (187b 7).   [3] *C. G.*, I, 43.   [4] Ch. 50.   [5] Ch. 51.

ciple of all intellectual knowledge. Rather, it is outside the range of the created intellect as exceeding its power, just as the highest sensibles are outside the range of the senses. Therefore the Philosopher says that *our intellect stands in relation to the most evident things as the owl's eye does in relation to the sun.*[1] Therefore the created intellect needs to be strengthened by some divine light in order to be able to see the divine substance. This solves the *first argument*.

Moreover, this light raises the created intellect to the vision of God, not because of its affinity to the divine substance, but because of the power which it receives from God to produce such an effect; even though in its being it is infinitely distant from God, as the *second argument* stated. For this light unites the created intellect to God, not in being, but only in understanding.

Since, however, it belongs to God Himself to understand His substance perfectly, the light in question is a likeness of God in this that it perfects the intellect for seeing the divine substance. Now no intellectual substance can be like God in this way. For since no created substance's simplicity is equal to the divine simplicity, it is impossible for the created substance to have its entire perfection in one subject: for this is proper to God, as we proved in the First Book,[2] Who is *being, understanding* and *blessed* in respect of the same reality. Consequently, in the intellectual substance, the created light through which it is raised to the beatific vision of God differs from any light whereby it is perfected in its specific nature and understands proportionately to its substance. Hence the reply to the *third argument* is clear.

The *fourth argument* is solved thus. The vision of the divine substance surpasses all natural power, as was shown. Consequently the light whereby the created intellect is perfected in order to see the divine substance must needs be supernatural.

Nor can the fact that God is infinite be an obstacle to the vision of the divine substance, as the *fifth objection* argued. For He is not said to be infinite by way of privation, as is quantity. The infinite of this kind is quite logically unknown, because it is like matter devoid of form, which is the principle of knowledge. But God is said to be infinite negatively, as a *per se* subsistent form that is not limited by being received into matter. Therefore, that which is infinite in this way is in itself most knowable.

There is, furthermore, a proportion between the created intellect and understanding God, a proportion not of a common measure, but of a relation of one thing to another, such as of matter to form, or cause to effect. In this way there is no reason against there being in the creature a proportion to God, consisting in the relation of the one understanding to the thing understood, as well as of an effect to its cause. Therefore the solution of the *sixth objection* is clear.

[1] *Metaph.,* I a, 1 (993b 9).   [2] *C. G.,* I, 28.

CHAPTER LV

THAT THE CREATED INTELLECT DOES NOT COMPREHEND THE DIVINE SUBSTANCE

THE mode of any action whatever depends on the efficacity of its active principle, for that which has the stronger heat imparts greater heat. Hence it is that the mode of knowledge also must depend on the efficacity of the principle of knowledge.

Now the light mentioned above is a principle of knowing God,[1] since thereby the created intellect is raised to the vision of the divine substance. Accordingly, the mode of the divine vision must be commensurate with the power of this same light. But this light is far short in strength of the clarity of the divine intelligence. Therefore it is impossible that the divine substance be seen through the aforesaid light as perfectly as it is seen by the divine intellect. Now the divine intellect sees this substance as perfectly as it is perfectly visible, because the truth of the divine substance and the clarity of the divine intellect are equal, nay more, are one. Therefore the created intellect cannot possibly by the aforesaid light see the divine substance as perfectly as it is perfectly visible. Now whoever knows a thing so as to comprehend it, knows it as perfectly as it is knowable. For whoever knows that a triangle has three angles equal to two right angles, as a matter of opinion based on probable reasons, because wise men say so, does not yet comprehend it; but only he does who knows it as a scientific conclusion, through the means that cause that conclusion. Therefore the created intellect cannot possibly comprehend the divine substance.

Again. A finite power cannot in its operation rise to the level of an infinite object. Now the divine substance is something infinite in comparison with every created intellect, since every created intellect is limited to a certain species. Therefore the vision of a created intellect cannot possibly rise to the level of the divine substance in seeing it, namely, by seeing the divine substance as perfectly as it is visible. Therefore no created intellect comprehends it.

Further. Every agent acts perfectly so far as it perfectly participates in the form that is the principle of action. Now the intelligible form by which the divine substance is seen is the divine essence itself; and although it becomes the intelligible form of the created intellect, the created intellect does not grasp it as much as it can be grasped. Therefore it does not see it as perfectly as it can be seen. Therefore it is not comprehended by the created intellect.

Besides. Nothing comprehended goes beyond the limits of the one com-

[1] Ch. 53.

prehending. Consequently if the created intellect were to comprehend the divine substance, this would not exceed the limits of the created intellect; which is impossible. Therefore the created intellect cannot possibly comprehend the divine substance.

We do not however say that the divine substance is seen, yet not comprehended by a created intellect, as though something of it were seen and something not seen; for the divine substance is utterly simple. But we say it because it is not seen as perfectly by the created intellect as it is visible, even as one who holds a demonstrated conclusion as an opinion is said to know it but not to comprehend it, because he does not know it perfectly, that is, scientifically, although there be no part of it that he does not know.

CHAPTER LVI

THAT NO CREATED INTELLECT, IN SEEING GOD, SEES ALL THAT CAN BE SEEN IN HIM

HENCE it is clear that, though the created intellect may see the divine substance, it does not know all that can be seen in the divine substance.

For then alone does it necessarily follow that, if one principle be known, all its effects are known through it, when that principle is comprehended by the intellect; because a principle is then known as to its whole power, when all its effects are known from it. Now other things are known through the divine essence as effects are known from their cause. Consequently, since the created intellect cannot know the divine substance so as to comprehend it, it does not follow that, because it sees it, it sees also all that can be known through it.

Again. The higher the intellect the more it knows,—either a greater number of things, or at least more about the same things. Now the divine intellect surpasses every created intellect, and consequently it knows more things than any created intellect. Yet it does not know things except through knowing its own essence, as we have proved in the First Book.[1] Therefore more things are knowable through the divine essence than any created intellect can see through it.

Besides. The measure of a power is according to what it can do. Consequently, to know all that a power can do is the same as to comprehend that power. But, since the divine power is infinite, no created intellect can comprehend it any more than it can comprehend its essence, as we have proved above.[2] Neither, therefore, can a created intellect know all that the divine power can do. Yet all the things that the divine power can do are knowable through the divine essence, because God knows them all, and not otherwise

---

[1] *C.G.*, I, 49.   [2] Ch. 56

than through His essence. Therefore a created intellect, by seeing the divine essence, does not see all that can be seen in the divine substance.

Moreover. No cognitive power knows a thing except under the aspect of its own proper object; and thus by sight we do not know a thing except as colored. Now the proper object of the intellect is *what a thing is,* namely, the substance of a thing, as is stated in *De Anima* iii.[1] Consequently whatever the intellect knows of a thing, it knows it through the knowledge of its substance, so that whenever by demonstration we become acquainted with the proper accidents of a thing, we take as principle *what that thing is,* as is stated in *Post. Anal.* i.[2] On the other hand, if the intellect knows the substance through the accidents (according to the statement in *De Anima* i, that *accidents are a great help in knowing what a thing is*[3]) this is accidental, in so far as the knowledge of the intellect arises from the senses, and so by knowing the accidents as perceived by the senses we need to arrive at knowing the substance. For this reason this does not occur in mathematics, but only in physics. Consequently, whatever cannot be known in a thing by knowing its substance must remain unknown to the intellect. Now by knowing the substance of one who wills, we cannot arrive at knowing what he wills, because the will does not tend altogether naturally to that which it wills; and for which reason *will* and *nature* are said to be two active principles. Therefore the intellect cannot know what a person wills, except perhaps from certain effects; and thus if we see a person working willingly, we know what he willed. Or again from a cause; and thus God knows what we will, as also other of His effects, in that He is the cause of our willing. Or again by someone indicating his will to another, as when by speaking he makes known his likes and dislikes. Since, then, many things depend on God's simple will, as we have partly shown above,[4] and will show yet more clearly further on,[5] although the created intellect may see the divine essence, it does not know all the things that God sees through His substance.

Someone may object to what has been said, that God's substance is something greater than all the things He can do, or understand, or will, except Himself; and therefore if the created intellect can see God's substance, much more can it know all that God either understands, or wills, or can do, except Himself.

But if we consider carefully, to know a thing in itself is not the same as to know it in its cause, since there are things which are easy to know in themselves, but not easy to know in their causes. It is true, then, that to know God in Himself is more than to know anything else besides Him, if this can be known in itself. But it belongs to a more perfect knowledge to know the divine substance and to see its effects therein, than to know the

---

[1] Aristotle, *De An.,* III, 4 (429b 10).—Cf. St. Thomas, *In De An.,* III, lect. 8.
[2] Aristotle, *Post. Anal.,* I, 4 (73a 37).   [3] Aristotle, *De An.,* I, 1 (402b 21).   [4] *C. G.,* I, 81.   [5] Ch. 64ff.

divine substance without seeing its effects in it. Now it is possible to see the divine substance without comprehending it. But it is not possible to know all that can be known in that substance without comprehending it, as we have proved.

CHAPTER LVII

THAT EVERY INTELLECT OF ANY DEGREE CAN PARTICIPATE IN THE DIVINE VISION

SINCE, as we have proved,[1] the created intellect is raised by a kind of supernatural light to the vision of the divine substance, there is no created intellect of so low a degree in its nature that cannot be raised to this vision.

For we have proved that this light cannot be connatural to any creature,[2] but surpasses every created nature in its power. Now that which is done by a supernatural power is not hindered by any diversity of nature, since the divine power is infinite; and so in the miraculous healing of a sick man, it matters not whether he ail much or little. Consequently, the diversity of degrees in the intellectual nature does not prevent the lowest in that nature from being raised by the aforesaid light to that vision.

Again. The highest intellect in the order of nature is infinitely distant from God in perfection and goodness, whereas its distance from the lowest intellect is finite; for there cannot be an infinite distance between one finite thing and another. Consequently the distance between the lowest created intellect and the highest is as nothing in comparison with the distance between the highest created intellect and God. Now that which is as nothing cannot cause an appreciable variation. Thus, the distance between the center of the earth and the human eye is as nothing in comparison with the distance between the human eye and the eighth sphere, compared with which the earth occupies the space of a mere point; for which reason no appreciable variation arises from the fact that astronomers use the human eye as the center of the earth in their demonstrations. It makes no difference, therefore, what intellect be raised by the aforesaid light to the vision of God, whether it be of the highest, or of the lowest, or of a middle degree.

Besides. It was proved above that every intellect desires naturally to see the divine substance.[3] Now natural desire cannot be empty. Therefore every created intellect can arrive at the vision of the divine substance, without any obstacle arising from the lowliness of its nature.

Hence it is that (*Matt.* xxii., 30) our Lord promises men the glory of the angels: *They shall be,* He says, speaking of men, *like the angels of God in heaven.* Again, (*Apoc.* xx [cf. xxi. 17]) it is stated that *the measure of a man* is that *of an angel.* For this reason nearly everywhere in Holy Scripture

[1] Ch. 53.   [2] *Ibid.*   [3] Ch. 50

angels are described in the form of men, either wholly, as the angels who appeared to Abraham in the likeness of men (*Gen.* xviii. 2), or in part, as may be seen in the animals (*Ezech.* i. 8) of which it is said that they had the *hands of a man under their wings.*

Hereby is removed the error of those who said that, however much the human soul be raised, it cannot attain to an equality with the higher intellects.

CHAPTER LVIII

THAT IT IS POSSIBLE FOR ONE TO SEE GOD MORE PERFECTLY THAN ANOTHER

BECAUSE the mode of operation follows from the form that is the principle of operation, and the aforesaid light is a principle of the vision whereby the created intellect sees the divine substance, as we have proved,[1] it follows that the mode of the divine vision is in keeping with the mode of this light. Now it is possible that there be various degrees of participation in this light, so that one be more perfectly illumined than another. Therefore it is possible that, of those who see God, one may see Him more perfectly than another, even though both see His substance.

Again. In whatever genus there is one thing higher than the others, we shall find degrees according as these others approach more or less to that thing; and thus things are more or less hot according as they approach to fire which is supremely hot. Now God sees His own substance most perfectly, inasmuch as He alone comprehends it, as we have proved above.[2] Therefore, of those who see Him, one sees His substance more perfectly than another, according to their greater or lesser approach to Him.

Besides. The light of glory raises one to the divine vision for the reason that it is a likeness of the divine intellect, as we have stated.[3] Now a thing may be more or less like to God. Therefore it is possible for one to see the divine substance more or less perfectly.

Further. Since there is proportion between the end and things directed to the end, it follows that things directed differently to an end participate in that end differently. Now the vision of the divine substance is the last end of every intellectual substance, as we have shown.[4] But intellectual substances are not all equally prepared for that end, for some are more virtuous, some less; and virtue is the way to happiness. Consequently, there must be diversity in the divine vision, in that some see the divine substance more perfectly, some less perfectly. Hence, in order to indicate this difference in happiness, our Lord says (*Jo.* xiv. 2): *In my Father's house there are many mansions.*

[1] Ch. 53.   [2] Ch. 55.   [3] Ch. 53.   [4] Ch. 50.

Hereby too is excluded the error of those who say that all rewards are equal.

Again, just as the mode of vision indicates a diversity of degrees among the blessed, so the object of the vision shows that their glory is the same; for each one's happiness consists in his seeing God's substance, as we have proved. The same thing then makes them all happy, but they do not all derive an equal happiness therefrom. Hence it does not stand in the way of what has been said that our Lord declares (*Matt.* xx. 10) the laborers in the vineyard to have received the same wage, namely, *a penny*, although they did not work equally; because the same thing is appointed as a reward to be seen and enjoyed, namely, God.

Wherein it must also be observed that corporeal and spiritual movements are somewhat contrary to each other. For all corporeal movements have the identically same first subject, but their ends are diverse; whereas spiritual movements, namely intellectual apprehensions and acts of the will, have various first subjects, but one identical end.

CHAPTER LIX

HOW THOSE WHO SEE THE DIVINE SUBSTANCE SEE ALL THINGS

Now since the vision of the divine substance is the last end of every intellectual substance, as we have proved,[1] and since the appetite of everything that has obtained its last end is at rest, it follows that the natural appetite of the intellectual substance that sees the divine substance must be entirely at rest. Now the natural desire of the intellect is to know all the genera, species and powers of things, and the whole order of the universe; as is evident from the fact of man's pursuit of all these things. Therefore everyone that sees the divine substance knows all the things mentioned above.

Again. Intellect and sense differ, as is clear from *De Anima* iii,[2] in that sense is destroyed or weakened by powerful sensibles, so that afterwards it cannot perceive weaker objects, whereas the intellect, through not being destroyed or weakened by its object, but only perfected thereby, after it has understood a higher intelligible, is not less but more able to understand other intelligibles. Now the highest in the genus of intelligibles is the divine substance. Consequently, the intellect which by the divine light is raised to see the substance of God is *a fortiori* perfected by the same light so as to see all other intelligibles in the universe.

Besides. Intelligible being is not of less, but may be of greater, extent than physical being; for the intellect is naturally adapted to understand all the things in the universe, as well as things that have no physical being, such as negations and privations. Consequently, anything required for the

[1] Ch. 50.   [2] Aristotle, *De An.*, III, 4 (429a 14).

perfection of physical being, that and even more is required for the perfection of intelligible being. Now the perfection of intelligible being is realized when the intellect has reached its last end, even as the perfection of physical being consists in the very making of a thing. Therefore God makes known to the intellect, which sees Him, all the things that He has made for the perfection of the universe.

Moreover. Although of those who see God one sees him more perfectly than another, as we have shown,[1] yet each one sees Him so perfectly that all his natural capacity is filled; indeed, the vision itself surpasses all natural capacity, as was proved above.[2] Therefore everyone that sees the divine substance must needs know in the divine substance all the things to which his natural capacity extends. Now the natural capacity of every intellect extends to the knowledge of all genera and species, and the order of things. Therefore everyone that sees God will know these things in the divine substance.

Hence the Lord's answer to Moses' request to see the divine substance (*Exod.* xxxiii. 19): *I will show thee all good*; and Gregory says: *What know they not who know Him that knows all?*[3]

If we consider carefully the foregoing, it is clear that those who see the divine substance in one sense see all things, and in another sense do not. For if by *all* we understand those things that belong to the perfection of the universe, it is evident from what has been said that those who see God see all things, as the arguments just adduced prove. For as the intellect is, in a sense, all things,[4] whatever belongs to the perfection of nature belongs also to the perfection of intelligible being; and for this reason, according to Augustine, all things made by the Word of God that they might subsist in their respective natures, were made likewise in the angelic intelligence so as to be understood by the angels.[5] Now, to the perfection of natural being belong specific natures, their properties and powers, because the intention of nature is directed to the specific natures, since individuals are for the sake of the species. Consequently, it belongs to the perfection of an intellectual substance to know the nature, powers and proper accidents of every species; and therefore it will obtain this in the final beatitude through the vision of the divine essence.—Moreover, through its knowledge of natural species, the individuals contained in these species are also known by the intellect that sees God, as may be gathered from what has been already said of the divine and angelic knowledge.[6]

On the other hand, if by *all* we understand all that God knows by seeing His essence, no created intellect sees all things in the divine substance, as we have shown.[7]

This may be considered in respect of several things.

---

[1] Ch. 58. [2] Ch. 52. [3] St. Gregory, *Dial.*, II, 33 (PL 66, 194). [4] *De An.*, III, 5 (430a 14). [5] *De Genesi ad Litt.*, II, 8 (PL 34, 269). [6] *C. G.*, I, 69; II, 96ff. [7] Ch. 56.

First, as to those things which God can make, but neither has made nor ever will make. For all such things cannot be known without comprehending His power, which is impossible for any created intellect, as we have proved.[1] Hence it is said (*Job.* xi. 7, *seqq.*): *Peradventure thou wilt understand the steps of God, and wilt find out the Almighty perfectly? He is higher than heaven, and what wilt thou do? He is deeper than hell, and how wilt thou know? The measure of Him is longer than the earth, and broader than the sea.* For these things are said, not as though God were great in dimensive quantity, but because His power is not limited to all that are seen to be great, so that He be unable to make greater still.

Secondly, as to the reasons of things made, which reasons cannot all be known by an intellect without its comprehending the divine goodness. Because the reason for every thing made is taken from the end which the maker has in view. Now the end of all things made by God is the divine goodness, and therefore the reason for things made is that the divine goodness may be diffused in things. Hence, a man would know all the reasons of created things, if he knew every good that can accrue to things according to the order of divine wisdom; and this would be to comprehend the divine goodness and wisdom, which is impossible to any created intellect. Therefore it is said (*Eccles.* viii. 17): *I understood that man can find no reason of all those works of God.*

Thirdly, as to the things which depend on God's will alone, such as predestination, election and justification, and whatever belongs to the creature's sanctification. Hence it is said (*1 Cor.* ii. 11): *No man knoweth the things of a man, but the spirit of a man that is in him. So the things also that are of God, no man knoweth but the Spirit of God.*

CHAPTER LX

THAT THOSE WHO SEE GOD SEE ALL IN HIM AT ONCE

SINCE we have shown that the created intellect, which sees the divine substance, sees therein all the species of things;[2] and since whatever is seen in one species must needs be seen at once and by one vision, because vision must correspond to the principle of vision, it follows that the intellect which sees the divine substance sees all things, not successively, but at once.

Again. The supreme and perfect happiness of the intellectual nature consists in seeing God, as was proved above.[3] Now happiness results, not from a habit, but from an act, since it is the ultimate perfection and last end. Consequently, whatever we see in the beatific vision of the divine substance is all seen by us actually, and therefore not one thing after another.

[1] Ch. 55   [2] Ch. 59.   [3] Ch. 50.

Besides. Whenever a thing arrives at its last end, it is at rest, since all movement is toward the attainment of an end. Now the last end of the intellect is the vision of the divine substance, as was shown above.[1] Therefore the intellect that sees the divine substance does not pass from one intelligible thing to another. Therefore whatsoever it knows in this vision, it considers it all actually.

Moreover. In the divine substance the intellect knows all the species of things, as we have proved.[2] Now of some genera there are an infinite number of species, for instance of numbers, figures and proportions. Therefore the intellect sees an infinite number of things in the divine substance. But it would not see them all unless it saw them at one time, because *it is not possible to pass through the infinite.*

Consequently all the intellect sees in the divine substance, it sees at once.

Hence Augustine says: *Our thoughts will not then be unstable, going to and fro from one thing to another, but we shall see all we know by one glance.*[3]

CHAPTER LXI

THAT BY SEEING GOD A MAN IS MADE A PARTAKER OF
ETERNAL LIFE

IT follows that by the aforesaid vision the created intellect is made a partaker of eternal life.

For eternity differs from time in that the latter has its being in a kind of succession, whereas the former is all simultaneously.[4] Now it has already been proved that there is no succession in the vision in question,[5] and that whatsoever is seen in it, is seen at once and at a glance. Therefore this vision takes place in a kind of participation of eternity. Moreover this vision is a kind of life, because the act of the intellect is a kind of life.[6] Therefore by that vision the created intellect becomes a partaker of eternal life.

Again. Actions take their species from their objects. Now the object of the aforesaid vision is the divine substance in its very being, and not in some created likeness, as we have shown.[7] But the being of the divine substance is in eternity, or rather is eternity itself. Therefore the aforesaid vision consists in a participation of eternity.

Besides. If an action takes place in time, this is either because the principle of the action is in time (for instance, the actions of natural things are temporal), or because of the term of the action (for instance, the actions which spiritual substances, which are above time, exercise on things subject to time). Now the vision in question is not subject to time on the

---

[1] *Ibid.*   [2] Ch. 59.   [3] *De Trin.*, XV, 16 (PL 42, 1079).   [4] Cf. Boethius, *De Consol.*, V, prose 6 (PL 63, 858).   [5] Ch. 60.   [6] *Eth.*, IX, 9 (1170a 18).   [7] Ch. 50.

part of the thing seen, since this is an eternal substance; nor on the part of the medium of vision, which is also the eternal substance; nor on the part of the seer, namely the intellect, whose being is independent of time because it is incorruptible, as we have proved.[1] Therefore this vision is according to a participation of eternity, as altogether transcending time.

Further. The intellectual soul is created *on the border line between eternity and time,* as is stated in the *Book of Causes,*[2] and was explained above,[3] because it is the last in order among intellects, and yet its substance stands above corporeal matter, and is independent thereof. On the other hand, its action, in respect of which it comes into conjunction with lower and temporal things, is itself temporal. Consequently, its action, by reason of which it comes into conjunction with higher things that are above time, partakes of eternity. Especially does this apply to the vision in which it sees the divine substance. Therefore by this vision it enters into a participation of eternity; and for the same reason, so too does any other created intellect that sees God.

For this reason our Lord says (*Jo.* xvii. 3): *This is eternal life, that they may know Thee, the only true God.*

CHAPTER LXII

THAT THOSE WHO SEE GOD WILL SEE HIM FOREVER

IT follows from what has been said that those who obtain ultimate happiness from the divine vision never fall away from it. Because *whatever at one time is, and at another time is not, is measured by time,* as is stated in *Physics* iv.[4] Now the vision in question, which makes intellectual creatures happy, is not in time but in eternity.[5] Therefore no one, having once become a partaker thereof, can lose it.

Again. The intellectual creature does not arrive at its last end except until its natural desire is at rest. Now just as it naturally desires happiness, so does it desire perpetuity of happiness; for, since it is perpetual in its substance, that which it desires for its own sake and not for the sake of something else, it desires to have always. Consequently happiness would not be its last end unless it endured forever.

Besides. Whatever is possessed with love causes sorrow if it be known that at length it will be lost. Now since the vision in question, which makes the possessor happy, is supremely enjoyable and desirable, it is supremely loved by those who possess it. Therefore they could not but be sorrowful if they knew that they would lose it some time. But if it were not perpetual, they would know this, for it has been shown that in seeing the divine sub-

---

[1] *C. G.,* II, 55, 79.   [2] *De Causis,* II (p. 162).   [3] *C. G.,* II, 68.   [4] Aristotle, *Phys.,* IV, 12 (221b 28).   [5] Ch. 61.

stance, they know also other things that exist naturally;[1] and hence much more do they know the conditions of that vision, whether it be perpetual or about to cease eventually. Therefore they would not possess that vision without sorrow. Consequently it would not be true happiness, which should insure man from all evil, as we have proved.[2]

Moreover. That which is naturally moved towards a thing as the end of its movement, is not moved away from it except by violence; as a heavy body, when it is projected upwards. Now it is clear from what has been said that every intellectual substance tends to that vision with a natural desire.[3] Therefore it cannot fall away from it except by violence. But nothing is taken away by violence unless the power of him who takes it exceeds that of him who caused it. Now the cause of the divine vision is God, as we have proved.[4] Consequently, as no power exceeds God's, it is impossible for that vision to be taken away by violence. Therefore it will last forever.

Further. If a man ceases to see what he saw hitherto, this will be either because he loses the ability to see—as when a man dies, or becomes blind, or is hindered in some other way; or because he wishes no longer to see,—as when we turn our eyes away from a thing we saw before; or because the object is withdrawn. And this is invariably true, whether we speak of sensitive or of intellective vision. Now the intellectual substance that sees God cannot lose the ability to see God, either through ceasing to exist, since it is immortal, as we proved above;[5] or through failure of the light by which it sees God, since that light is received incorruptibly, on the part both of the recipient and of the giver. Nor can it lack the will to enjoy that vision, for it knows its ultimate happiness to consist in that vision, even as it cannot but desire to be happy. Nor will it cease to see through the withdrawal of the object, because that object, which is God, is unchangeable, nor does He withdraw Himself more than we withdraw from Him. Therefore it is impossible for this beatific vision ever to cease.

Again. It is impossible for a man to wish to give up a good which he is enjoying, except because of some evil that he thinks to be attached to the enjoyment of that good, which enjoyment, at least, is an obstacle to a greater good; for just as the appetite desires nothing except under the aspect of a good, so does it shun nothing except as an evil. But in the enjoyment of that vision there cannot be any evil, since it is the greatest good to which the intellectual creature can attain. Nor is it possible that one who enjoys that vision deem any evil to be in it, or anything to be better than it, because the vision of that Supreme Truth excludes all false opinion. Therefore it is impossible that the intellectual substance which sees God ever desire to lose that vision.

Moreover. The reason why we become weary of what we enjoyed hitherto is that it causes some kind of change, by destroying or diminishing one's power. Hence fatigue is incidental to the exercise of the sensitive powers

----

[1] Ch. 59.　　[2] Ch. 48.　　[3] Ch. 50.　　[4] Ch. 53.　　[5] *C. G.*, II, 55.

through the action of the sensible objects on the bodily organ (in fact, the power may be altogether destroyed by too powerful an object) and after a time they are loth to enjoy that which hitherto had been a pleasant sensation. For the same reason we become weary in mind after long or concentrated thought, because powers that employ organs of the body are subject to fatigue, and in this life it is not possible to give the intellect to thought without employing those organs. Now the divine substance does not corrupt but, more than anything, perfects the intellect. Nor does any action performed by a corporeal organ concur in the vision of God. Therefore it is impossible for anyone to be weary of seeing Him, when they have once enjoyed the sight of Him.

Further. Nothing can be wearisome that is wonderful to him that looks on it, because as long as we wonder at it, it still moves our desire. Now the created intellect always looks with wonder on the divine substance, since no created intellect can comprehend it. Therefore the intellectual substance cannot possibly become weary of that vision; and consequently it cannot, of its own choice, desist from it.

Besides. If two things were united before, and afterwards become separated, this must be the result of a change in one of them; because just as a relationship does not begin except through a change in one of the relatives, so does it not cease except through a fresh change in one of them. Now the created intellect sees God through being, in some way, united to Him, as was proved above.[1] Consequently, if that vision cease, through the cessation of that union, this must result from a change either in the divine substance or in the intellect of the one who sees it. But neither of these is possible, since the divine substance is unchangeable, as we proved in the First Book;[2] and the intellectual substance is raised above all changes, when it sees the divine substance. Therefore it is impossible to lapse from the happiness of seeing God.

Furthermore. The nearer a thing is to God, Who is utterly unchangeable, the less changeable and the more enduring is it; so that certain bodies, *through being far distant from God,* cannot last for ever, as is stated in *De Gener.* ii.[3] But no creature can come nearer to God than one who sees His substance. Therefore the intellectual creature that sees the divine substance becomes, in a very high degree, unchangeable. Therefore it can never fall away from that vision. Hence it is said (*Ps.* lxxxiii. 5): *Blessed are they that dwell in Thy house, O Lord: they shall praise Thee for ever and ever;* and elsewhere (*Ps.* cxxiv. 1): *He shall not be moved for ever that dwelleth in Jerusalem.* Again (*Isa.* xxxiii. 21): *Thy eyes shall see Jerusalem, a rich habitation, a tabernacle that cannot be removed: neither shall the nails thereof be taken away for ever, neither shall any of the cords thereof be broken, because only there our Lord is magnificent;* and (*Apoc.* iii. 12):

---

[1] Ch. 51.   [2] *C. G.,* I, 13.   [3] Aristotle, *De Gener.,* II, 10 (336b 30).

He that shall overcome, I will make him a pillar in the temple of my God, and he shall go out no more.

Hereby is excluded the error of the Platonists who said that souls after being separated from the body, and obtaining ultimate happiness, begin to desire reunion with the body, and that when the happiness of that life is ended, they are plunged once more into this life of unhappiness; and again that of Origen, who maintained that souls and angels can return from blessedness to unhappiness.[1]

CHAPTER LXIII

HOW IN THAT ULTIMATE HAPPINESS MAN'S EVERY DESIRE IS FULFILLED

It is evident, from what has been said, that in this happy state, which results from the divine vision, man's every desire is fulfilled (according to *Ps.* cii. 5, *Who satisfieth thy desire with good things*) and his every end achieved. This is clear to anyone who considers man's various desires in the particular.

There is a desire in man, as an intellectual being, to *know the truth,* and men pursue this desire by the pursuit of the contemplative life. And this will be most clearly fulfilled in that vision, when the intellect, by gazing on the First Truth, will know all that it naturally desires to know, as we have proved above.[2]

There is also a desire in man as a rational being capable of regulating things beneath him, and he pursues this desire in the occupations of the active and civic life. The chief object of this desire is that man's entire life be regulated in accord with reason, namely, that he may *live according to virtue;* because the end of every virtuous man in all his actions is the good of his own virtue,—that of the brave man, for instance, that he may act bravely. Now this desire will then be wholly fulfilled, because the reason will be in the full flood of its power, being enlightened with the very light of God lest it stray from righteousness.

Consequent to his life as a citizen, there are also certain goods that man needs for his civic actions. Such is *a position of honor,* through inordinate desire of which men become proud and ambitious. Now by this vision men are raised to the highest position of honor, because, in a way, they are united to God, as we have proved above.[3] Hence, even as God Himself is the *King of ages,* so the Blessed united to Him are said to be kings (*Apoc.* xx. 6): *They shall reign with Christ.*

There is another desirable thing consequent to the civic life, and this is

[1] Origen, *Peri Archon,* II, 3 (PG 11, 242-243).   [2] Ch. 59.   [3] Ch. 51.

to be well known, through inordinate desire of which men are said to be desirous of vain glory. Now by this vision the Blessed become well known, not in the opinion of men, who can both deceive and be deceived, but in the most true knowledge both of God and of all the Blessed. Hence this happiness is many times described as *glory* in Holy Scripture. Thus it is said in the *Psalm* (cxlix. 5): *The saints shall rejoice in glory.*

There is yet another desirable thing in the civic life, and this is *riches,* through inordinate desire of which men become illiberal and unjust. Now in that happy state there is a sufficiency of all goods, inasmuch as the Blessed enjoy Him Who contains the perfection of all goods. Hence it is said (*Wis.* vii. 11): *All good things came to me together with her;* and again (*Ps.* cxi. 3): *Glory and wealth shall be in his house.*

There is a third desire in man, common to him and other animals, namely the desire for *the enjoyment of pleasure,* and this men pursue especially by leading a voluptuous life, and through lack of moderation become intemperate and incontinent. Now in that blessedness there is the most perfect pleasure, all the more perfect than the pleasure of sense, which brute animals can enjoy, as the intellect is above the senses; and also as the good, in which we shall delight surpasses all sensible good, is more penetrating, and more continuously delightful; and as that pleasure is freer from all alloy of sorrow, or trouble of anxiety, of which it is said (*Ps.* xxxv. 9): *They shall be inebriated with the plenty of Thy house, and Thou shalt make them drink of the torrent of Thy pleasure.*

There is also the natural desire, common to all things, whereby all seek to be preserved in their being, as far as possible; and through lack of moderation in this desire, men become timorous, and spare themselves overmuch from strenuous work. This desire will be altogether fulfilled when the Blessed obtain perfect immortality, and security from all evil, according to *Isa.* xlix. 10 and *Apoc.* xxi. 4 [cf. vii. 16]: *They shall no more hunger or thirst, neither shall the sun fall on them, nor any heat.*

It is therefore evident that intellectual substances by seeing God attain to true beatitude, when their every desire is satisfied, and when there is a sufficiency of all good things, as is required for happiness, according to Aristotle.[1] Hence Boethius says that happiness is *a state of life made perfect by the accumulation of all goods.*[2]

In this life there is nothing so like this ultimate and perfect happiness as the life of those who contemplate the truth, as far as that is possible in this life. Hence the philosophers who were unable to obtain full knowledge of that final beatitude placed man's ultimate happiness in that contemplation which is possible during this life.[3] For this reason, too, Holy Scripture commends the contemplative rather than other forms of life, when our Lord said (*Luke* x. 42): *Mary hath chosen the better part,* namely the contem-

---

[1] *Eth.,* X, 7 (1177a 24).   [2] *De Consol.,* III, prose 2 (PL 63, 724).   [3] Cf. Aristotle, *Eth.,* X, 7 (1177a 18).

plation of truth, *which shall not be taken from her*. For the contemplation of truth begins in this life, but will be consummated in the life to come; while the active and civic life does not transcend the limits of this life.

CHAPTER LXIV

THAT GOD GOVERNS THINGS BY HIS PROVIDENCE

FROM what has been laid down in the preceding chapters, it has been sufficiently proved that God is the end of all things; and from this we may further conclude that by His providence He governs or rules all things.

For whenever certain things are ordered to a certain end, they are all subject to the disposal of the one to whom chiefly that end belongs. This may be seen in an army, since all the parts of the army, and their actions, are directed to the good of the general, namely, victory, as their ultimate end; for which reason the government of the whole army belongs to the general. In the same way, that art which is concerned with the end dictates and gives laws to the art which is concerned with things directed to the end: thus, statecraft rules the military art, and this directs the art of horsemanship; and the art of sailing directs the art of ship-building. Since, then, all things are directed to the divine goodness as their last end, as we have shown above,[1] it follows that God to Whom that goodness belongs chiefly as being substantially possessed, understood and loved, must be the governor of all things.

Again. Whoever makes a thing for the sake of an end makes use of it for that end. Now it has been shown above that whatsoever has being in any way is an effect of God,[2] and that God makes all things for an end which is Himself.[3] Therefore He uses everything by directing it to its end. But this is to govern. Therefore God, by His providence, is the governor of all.

Besides. It has been shown that God is the first unmoved mover.[4] Now the first mover moves no less than do second movers; more so, indeed, because without Him they do not move other things. But all things that are moved, are moved for an end, as was shown above.[5] Therefore God moves each thing to its end. Moreover He moves them by His intellect. for it has been proved above that He acts, not by natural necessity, but by intellect and will.[6] Now to rule and govern by providence is nothing else but to move certain things to their end by one's intellect. Therefore God by His providence governs and rules all things that are moved to their end, whether they be moved corporeally, or spiritually, as the seeker is said to be moved by the object desired.

[1] Ch. 17. [2] *C. G.,* II, 15. [3] *C. G.,* I, 75. [4] *C. G.,* I, 13. [5] Ch. 2. [6] *C. G.,* I, 81; II, 23ff.

Moreover. It was proved that natural bodies are moved and work towards an end, although they have no knowledge of an end, from the fact that always or nearly always that which is best happens to them, nor would they be made otherwise if they were made by art.[1] Now it is impossible that things without knowledge of an end should act for an end, and attain to that end in an orderly manner, unless they be moved to that end by one who has knowledge of the end; just as the arrow is directed to the mark by the archer. Therefore the whole operation of nature must be directed by some knowledge. This must be traced back to God mediately or immediately; because every subordinate art and knowledge must take its principles from a higher one, as may be seen in the speculative and practical sciences. Therefore God governs the world by His providence.

Further. Things distinct in their nature do not converge into one order, unless they be brought together by one controller. Now the universe is composed of things distinct from one another and of contrary natures; and yet they all converge into one order, with some things acting on others, and some helping or directing others. Therefore there must be one ordainer and governor of the universe.

Moreover. Natural necessity cannot be alleged as the reason for the various phenomena to be observed in the movements of the heavenly bodies; for the movements of some are more numerous than, and wholly different from, the movements of others. Therefore the ordering of their movements must come from some providence, and consequently so must the ordering of all those movements and operations, here below, that are ordered by the movements of the heavens.

Besides. The nearer a thing is to its cause the greater share it has in the effect. Therefore if we observe that a thing is the more perfectly shared by certain individuals, according as these are nearer to a certain thing, this is a sign that this thing is the cause of that which is shared in various degrees; and thus, if certain things are hotter according as they are nearer fire, this shows that fire is the cause of their heat. Now we see that things are all the more perfectly ordered according as they are nearer to God. For in the lower bodies, which are farthest removed from God by unlikeness of nature, we sometimes find defects from the ordinary course of nature, as in monstrosities and in other chance happenings; whereas this never happens in the heavenly bodies, although they are changeable in a certain degree, nor in the separate intellectual substances. Therefore God is the cause of the entire order of things, and consequently He is the governor of the whole universe by His providence.

Further. As we proved above, God brought all things into being, not by natural necessity, but by His intellect and will. Now His intellect and will can have no other ultimate end but His goodness, that is, to bestow His

[1] Ch. 3.

goodness on things, as was shown above.[1] Now things partake of the divine goodness by way of likeness, in being themselves good. But the greatest good in the things made by God is the good consisting in the order of the universe, which is most perfect, as the Philosopher says,[2] with whom divine Scripture also agrees (*Gen.* i. 31): *God saw all the things He had made, and they were very good;* whereas of each single work it was said simply that *they were good.* Consequently, that which is chiefly willed and caused by God is the good consisting in the order of the things of which He is the cause. But to govern things is nothing else but to impose order on them. Therefore God by His intellect and will governs all things.

Moreover. Whoever has an end in view cares more for what is nearest to the last end, because the other ends are directed to this. Now the last end of God's will is His goodness, the nearest thing to which among created things is the good consisting in the order of the universe; because every particular good of this or that thing is ordered to it as to its end, just as the less perfect is ordered to that which is more perfect, even as each part is for the sake of its whole. Consequently that which God cares for most in created things is the order of the universe; and therefore He governs it.

Again. Every created thing attains its ultimate perfection by its proper operation, because a thing's ultimate end and perfection must be either an operation or the term or effect of an operation (the form, whereby a thing is, is its *first* perfection, as it is stated in *De Anima* ii [3]). Now the order among effects, according to distinction and grades among natures, issues from divine wisdom, as we showed in the Second Book.[4] Therefore, so, too, does the order also among the operations, whereby things approach nearer to their ultimate end. But to direct the actions of things to their end is to govern them. Therefore God, by the providence of His wisdom, governs and rules things.

Hence Holy Scripture acclaims God as Lord and King, according to *Psalm* xcix. 2: *The Lord, He is God,* and *Psalm* xlvi. 8: *God is the King of all the earth;* because the king and lord is he whose office it is to rule and govern subjects. Therefore Holy Scripture ascribes the course of events to the divine command (*Job* ix. 7): *Who commandeth the sun, and it riseth not, and shutteth up the stars, as it were under a seal;* and (*Ps.* cxlviii. 6): *He hath made a decree and it shall not pass away.* Hereby is refuted the error of the ancient naturalists, who held that everything happens from the necessity of matter; whence it followed that all things happen by chance, and not by the ordinance of Providence.

---

[1] *C. G.,* I, 75ff.　　[2] *Metaph.,* XI, 10 (1075a 12).　　[3] Aristotle, *De An.,* II, 1 (412a 28).　　[4] *C. G.,* II, 45.

CHAPTER LXV

THAT GOD PRESERVES THINGS IN BEING

FROM the fact that God governs things by His providence, it follows that He preserves them in being.

For whatever is required in order that certain things obtain their end belongs to the government of those things, because things are said to be governed or ruled according as they are directed to their end. Now things are directed to the ultimate end intended by God, namely, the divine goodness, not only in that they operate, but also in the very fact that they exist. For inasmuch as they exist they bear a likeness to the divine goodness, which is the end of all things, as we have proved.[1] Therefore it belongs to divine providence that things be preserved in being.

Again. The cause of a thing must needs be the same as the cause of its preservation, because preservation is nothing else than its continued being. Now we have shown above that God is the cause of being for all things by His intellect and will.[2] Therefore by His intellect and will He preserves things in being.

Besides. No particular univocal agent can be absolutely the cause of its species. Thus an individual man cannot be the cause of the human species, for then he would be the cause of every man, and consequently of himself, which is impossible. But, properly speaking, the individual is the cause of the individual. Now this individual man exists inasmuch as human nature is in this particular matter which is the principle of individuation. Therefore the individual man is not the cause of a man except in so far as he is the cause of the human form being in this particular matter. Now this is to be the principle of the generation of this particular man. It is consequently evident that neither the individual man, nor any other natural univocal agent, is a cause except of the generation of an individual. Now there must needs be some *per se* active cause of the human species; as is evidenced by his composite nature, and the order of his parts, which is always the same, unless it be hindered accidentally. The same applies to all other species of natural things. This cause is God, either mediately or immediately: for it has been shown that He is the first cause of all things.[3] Consequently He must stand in relation to the species of things in the same way as in nature the individual generator to generation, of which He is the *per se* cause. But generation ceases when the generator's action ceases. Therefore all the species of things would cease, were the divine operation to cease. Therefore by His operation He preserves things in being.

[1] Ch. 19.   [2] *C. G.*, II, 23ff.   [3] *C. G.*, I, 13; II, 15.

Moreover. Although movement may affect an existing thing, it is something additional to the thing's being. Now nothing corporeal is the cause of any thing except in so far as it is moved, because no body acts except through movement, as Aristotle proves.[1] Therefore no body is the cause of a thing's being, as such; but it is the cause of a thing's being moved towards being, that is, of its becoming. Now the being of a thing is participated being, since no thing is its own being, save God, as we have proved above.[2] Consequently, God, Who is His own being, must be first and essentially the cause of all being. Accordingly, the divine operation stands in the same relation to the being of things as the movement of a corporeal mover to the *being made* and the *being moved* of things made or moved. Now it is impossible that a thing continue to be made or to be moved if the movement of the mover cease. Therefore a thing cannot possibly continue to exist except through the divine operation.

Further. As the operation of art presupposes the operation of nature, so the operation of nature presupposes the creative operation of God. For art takes its matter from nature, and nature receives its matter from God through creation. Now the products of art are preserved in being by virtue of the products of nature; a house, for instance, by the solidity of the stones. Therefore all natural things continue to exist only by the power of God.

Again. The impression of the agent does not remain in the effect after the action of the agent has ceased, unless it become part of the nature of the effect. For the forms of generated things, and their properties, remain in them to the end after generation, since they become natural to them. In like manner, the reason why habits are hard to remove is that they become part of nature, whereas dispositions and passions, whether in the body or in the soul, remain for a time after the action of the agent, but not for always, because they are in their subject as preparing a way to nature. On the other hand, that which belongs to the nature of a higher genus in no way remains after the action of the agent; and thus light does not remain in the diaphanous body after the cause of light has been removed. Now being is not the nature or essence of any created thing, but of God alone, as was proved in the First Book.[3] Therefore nothing could continue to remain in being, if the divine operation were to cease.

Further. There are two explanations of the origin of things. One is that proposed by faith, that things were first brought into being by God; the other is that of certain philosophers holding that things emanated from God from eternity.[4] According to either explanation it is necessary to say that things are preserved in being by God. For if things were brought into being by God after not being, their being as well as their non-being must result from the divine will; because He permitted things not to be when

[1] *Phys.*, VII, 2 (243a 3).   [2] *C. G.*, I, 22; II, 15.   [3] *C. G.*, I, 22.   [4] Cf. *C. G.*, II, 31ff; *De Pot.*, I, 5; III, 1; III, 4-5; *S. T.*, I, q. 44, a. 2.

He so willed, and caused them to be when He so willed. Therefore they exist so long as He wills them to exist. Therefore His will is the preserver of things.—If, on the other hand, things emanated from God from eternity, we cannot assign a time or an instant when they first emanated from God. Either, therefore, they were never produced by God, or their being is always emanating from God, as long as they exist. Therefore He preserves things in being by His operation.

Hence it is said (*Heb.* i. 3): *Upholding all things by the word of His power.* Augustine, too, says: *The power of the Creator, and the strength of the Almighty and All-upholder, is the cause of every creature's subsistence. If this ruling power were withdrawn from His creatures, their form would cease at once, and all nature would collapse. When a man is building a house, and goes away, the building remains after he has ceased to work and has gone; whereas the world would not stand for a single instant, if God withdrew His support.*[1]

Hereby is refuted the position of certain Moslem theologians,[2] who in order to be able to maintain that the world needs to be preserved by God, held that all forms are accidents, and that no accident lasts for two instants, so that things would always be in the process of formation; as though a thing did not need an active cause except while in the process of being made.—And so some of them are stated to have maintained that the indivisible bodies of which, they say, all substances are composed, and which alone, according to them, have any permanency, would be able for a time to remain in being, if God were to withdraw His government from things. —Some of these even say that things would not cease to exist unless God caused in them the accident of *ceasing-to-be.*—All of which is plainly absurd.

CHAPTER LXVI

THAT NOTHING GIVES BEING EXCEPT IN SO FAR AS IT ACTS BY GOD'S POWER

It is evident from what has gone before that all inferior agents do not give being except in so far as they act by God's power.

Nothing gives being except in so far as it is a being in act. Now God preserves things in being by His providence, as we have proved.[3] Therefore it is by God's power that a thing causes being.

Again. When several different agents are subordinate to one agent, the effect that proceeds from them in common must needs be ascribed to them in so far as they are united together in partaking of the movement and power of that agent; for many things do not make up what is one, except in

[1] *De Genesi ad Litt.,* IV, 12 (PL 34, 304).   [2] Cf. Maimonides, *Guide,* I, 73 (p. 124).
[3] Ch. 65.

so far as they are one. Thus it is clear that all the men in an army work in order to bring about victory; and this effect they bring about inasmuch as they are subordinate to the general, whose proper effects the victory is. Now it was shown in the First Book that the first agent is God.[1] Since, then, being is the effect common to all agents, for every agent makes a thing to be actually, it follows that they produce this effect in so far as they are subordinate to the first agent, and act by its power.

Besides. In all ordered active causes, the last thing in the order of generation and the first in the intention is the proper effect of the first cause. Thus the form of a house, which is the proper effect of the builder, comes into being after the cement, stones and timber have prepared the way, which is the work of the subordinate workmen who are subject to the builder. Now in every action actual being is the chief thing intended, and is the last thing in the order of generation; because, when it is obtained, the agent ceases to act, and the passive principle ceases to be acted upon. Therefore being is the proper effect of the first cause, namely God, and whatever gives being does so in so far as it acts by the power of God.

Moreover. Among the things that can be reached by the power of a secondary agent, the limit in goodness and perfection is that which comes within its range through the power of the first agent; because the secondary agent's power receives its complement from the first agent. Now the most perfect of all effects is being, since every nature and form is perfected through being actually, and is compared to being actually as potency to act itself. Therefore being is what secondary agents produce by the power of the first agent.

Besides. The order of effects is according to the order of causes. Now the first of all effects is being, for all others are determinations of being. Therefore being is the proper effect of the first agent, and all other agents produce it by the power of the first agent. Furthermore secondary agents which, as it were, particularize and determine the action of the first agent, produce, as their proper effects, the other perfections which determine being.

Furthermore. That which is such by its essence is the proper cause of that which is such by participation. Thus fire is the cause of all things that are afire. Now God alone is being by His essence, while all other things are beings by participation; for in God alone being is His essence. Therefore the being of every existing thing is His proper effect, so that whatever brings a thing into being does so in so far as it acts by God's power.

Therefore it is said (*Wis.* i. 14): *God created, that all things might be;* and in several passages of Holy Scripture it is stated that God makes all things.—Again, in the *Book of Causes* it is said that not even an intelligence gives being except *in so far as it is something divine,*[2] *i.e.,* in so far as it acts by God's power.

[1] *C. G.,* I, 13.   [2] *De Causis,* I (p. 162).

CHAPTER LXVII

THAT IN ALL THINGS THAT OPERATE GOD IS THE CAUSE OF THEIR OPERATING

HENCE it is clear that in all things that operate God is the cause of their operating. For everything that operates is in some way a cause of being, either of substantial or of accidental being. But nothing is a cause of being except in so far as it acts by God's power, as has been shown.[1] Therefore everything that operates acts by God's power.

Again. Every operation consequent upon a certain power is ascribed to the giver of that power as effect to cause. Thus the natural movement of heavy and light bodies is consequent upon their form, whereby they are heavy or light; and hence the cause of their movement is said to be the generating agent, which gave them their form. Now all the power of any agent whatsoever is from God as from the first principle of all perfection. Therefore, since all operation is consequent upon some power, it follows that God is the cause of every operation.

Moreover. It is clear that every action that cannot continue after the influence of a given agent has ceased is from that agent. Thus, the visibility of colors cannot continue after the action of the sun has ceased to illumine the air, and therefore without doubt it is the cause of the visibility of colors. The same applies to violent motion, which ceases when the violence of the impelling force has ceased. Now since God not only gave being to things when they first began to exist, but also causes being in them as long as they exist, by preserving them in being, as we have proved,[2] so not only did He give them active powers when He first made them, but is always causing these powers in them. Consequently, if the divine influence were to cease, all operation would come to an end. Therefore every operation of a thing is reduced to Him as to its cause.

Besides. Whatever applies an active power to action is said to be the cause of that action; for the craftsman, when he applies the forces of nature to an action, is said to be the cause of that action,—as the cook is the cause of cooking, which is done by fire. Now every application of power to action is chiefly and primarily from God. For active powers are applied to their proper operations by some movement of the body or of the soul. Now the first principle of either movement is God. For He is the first mover, wholly immovable, as we have proved above.[3] Likewise every movement of the will, whereby certain powers are applied to action, is reduced to God as to the first object of appetite, and to the first willing cause. There-

[1] Ch. 66.   [2] Ch. 65.   [3] *C. G.*, I, 13.

fore every operation should be ascribed to God as to its first and principal agent.

Further. In all ordered active causes, the causes that follow must always act by the power of the first. Thus, in natural things the lower bodies act by the power of the heavenly bodies; and in voluntary things all the subordinate craftsmen act in accordance with the direction of the master craftsman. Now, in the order of active causes, God is the first cause, as we proved in the First Book.[1] Consequently all the lower active causes act by His power. But the cause of an action is the thing by whose power it is done, more even than that which does it; just as the principal agent is more the cause of an action than the instrument. Therefore God is more the cause of every action than even secondary active causes.

Further. Every operator is directed through its operation to its ultimate end, since either the operation itself is its last end, or the thing done, namely, the effect of the operation. Now it belongs to God Himself to direct things to their end, as we have proved.[2] Therefore we must conclude that every agent acts by the power of God, and consequently it is He who causes the actions of all things.

Hence it is said (*Isa.* xxvi. 12): *Lord, Thou hast wrought all our works in us*; and (*Jo.* xv. 5): *Without Me you can do nothing*; so, too (*Philip.* ii. 13): *It is God who worketh in us both to will and to accomplish, according to His good will.* For this reason Holy Scripture often ascribes natural effects to the divine operation, because it is He Who works in every agent, natural or voluntary, as it is written in *Job* x. 10. 11: *Hast Thou not milked me as milk, and curdled me like cheese? Thou hast clothed me with skin: Thou hast put me together with bones and sinews;* and again in *Psalm* xvii. 14: *The Lord thundered from heaven, and the highest gave His voice: hail and coals of fire.*

CHAPTER LXVIII

THAT GOD IS EVERYWHERE

FROM this it is evident that God must be everywhere and in all things.

For the mover and the thing moved must be simultaneous, as the Philosopher proves.[3] Now God moves all things to their actions, as we have proved.[4] Therefore He is in all things.

Again. Whatever is in a place, or in anything whatsoever, is in some way in contact with it; for a body is located somewhere by contact of dimensive quantity, while an incorporeal thing is said to be somewhere by contact of its power, since it lacks dimensive quantity. Accordingly, an incorporeal being stands in relation to being somewhere by its power, as a body to

[1] *Ibid.* [2] Ch. 64. [3] *Phys.*, VII, 2 (243a 3). [4] Ch. 67.

being somewhere by dimensive quantity. And if there were a body having infinite dimensive quantity, it would of necessity be everywhere. Consequently, if there be an incorporeal being with infinite power, it must needs be everywhere. Now we proved in the First Book that God has infinite power.[1] Therefore He is everywhere.

Besides. As an individual cause is to an individual effect, so a universal cause is to a universal effect. Now the individual cause must needs be present to its proper effect. Thus fire by its substance gives out heat, and the soul by its essence gives life to the body. Since, then, God is the universal cause of all being, as we proved in the Second Book,[2] it follows that wherever being is to be found, there also God is present.

Furthermore. If an agent be present to but one of its effects, its action cannot extend to other things except through that one, because agent and patient must be simultaneous. Thus the motive power moves the various members of the body not otherwise than through the heart. Consequently, if God were present to but one of His effects, such as the *primum mobile*, which is moved by Him immediately, it would follow that His action could not extend to other things except through that first effect. But this is incongruous. For if the action of an agent cannot extend to other things except through some first effect, the latter must be equal to the agent as regards the agent's whole power, or else the agent could not use its whole power. And so we see that all the movements which the motive power is able to cause can be performed by the heart. Now there is no creature through which can be done everything that the divine power is capable of doing; for the divine power surpasses infinitely every created thing, as we proved in the First Book.[3] Consequently it is incongruous to say that the divine action does not extend to other things except through some first thing. Therefore He is present, not in one effect only, but in all His effects. —For it would amount to the same if someone were to say that He is in some, and not in all; because no matter how many divine effects we take, they will not suffice to carry into effect the execution of the divine power.

Moreover. The active cause must needs be joined together with its proximate and immediate effect. Now in each thing there is a proximate and immediate effect of God. For we proved in the Second Book that God alone can create.[4] Now in each thing there is something caused by creation: in bodies, there is primary matter; in incorporeal beings there is their simple essence. This is clear from what we have said in the Second Book.[5] Accordingly, God must be present in all things at the same time, especially since those things which He called into being from non-being are continually preserved in being by Him, as we have proved.[6]

Therefore it is said (*Jer.* xxiii. 24): *I fill heaven and earth*; and (*Ps.* cxxxviii. 8): *If I ascend into heaven, Thou art there: if I descend into hell, Thou art present.*

[1] *C. G.*, I, 43.   [2] *C. G.*, II, 15.   [3] *C. G.*, I, 43.   [4] *C. G.*, II, 21.   [5] *C. G.*, II, 15ff.   [6] Ch. 65.

Hereby is removed the error of some who said that God is in a definite part of the world, for instance in the first heaven, and in the eastern portion, so that He is the principle of the heavenly movement.—Yet this statement of theirs might be upheld, if rightly understood; so that the meaning be, not that God is confined to some particular part of the world, but that according to the order of nature all corporeal movement begins in one particular part under the divine motion. For this reason Holy Scripture specially describes God as being in heaven, according to *Isa.* lxvi. 1: *Heaven is My throne,* and *Ps.* cxiii. 16: *The heaven of heavens is the Lord's,* etc.—However, the fact that God works in the lowest bodies some effect outside the ordinary course of nature, which cannot be wrought by the power of a heavenly body, shows clearly that God is immediately present not only to the heavenly body but also to the lowest things.

But we must not think that God is everywhere in such a way as to be distributed throughout local space, with one part of Him here, another there; for God is everywhere wholly, since, being utterly simple, He has no parts.

Nor is He simple in the way that a point is simple. For a point is the term of a continuous quantity, and consequently occupies a definite place therein; so that one point cannot be elsewhere than in one indivisible place. But God is indivisible as existing altogether outside the genus of continuous quantity. Consequently He is not necessitated by His essence to a definite place, great or small, as though He needed to be in some place; for He was from eternity before there was any place. Yet by the immensity of His power He reaches all things that are in a place, because He is the universal cause of being, as we have stated. Accordingly, He is wholly wheresoever He is, because He reaches to all things by His simple power.

And yet again we must not think that He is in things as though mingled with them; for we proved in the First Book that He is neither the matter nor the form of anything.[1] But He is in all things after the manner of an agent.

CHAPTER LXIX

CONCERNING THE OPINION OF THOSE WHO WITHDRAW FROM NATURAL THINGS THEIR PROPER ACTIONS

THIS conclusion was an occasion of error to some who thought that no creature has an active part in the production of natural effects; so that, for example, fire would not heat, but God would cause heat at the presence of fire. They maintain the like in the case of all other natural effects.[2]

They have endeavored to confirm this error with arguments, by show-

---

[1] *C. G.,* I, 17, 27.   [2] Cf. Averroes, *In Metaph.,* IX, comm. 7; XII, comm. 18 (VIII, 109r; 143v).

ing that no form, whether substantial or accidental, is brought into being except by the way of creation. Because forms and accidents cannot be made out of matter, since matter is not a part of them. Hence, if they be made, they must be made out of nothing, and this is to be created. And since creation is the act of God alone, as we proved in the Second Book,[1] it would seem to follow that God alone produces both the substantial and accidental forms in nature.

The opinion of certain philosophers agreed in part with this position. For, seeing that whatever is not *per se* must result from that which is *per se*, it would seem that the forms of things, which do not exist by themselves but in matter, result from forms that are by themselves without matter; which would mean that forms existing in matter were participations of forms that are without matter. For this reason Plato held that the species of sensible things are certain separate Forms, which are causes of being for the things of sense, in so far as these partake of the Forms.[2]

Avicenna maintained that all substantial forms emanate from the *agent intellect*.[3] But as to accidental forms, he held them to be dispositions of matter, resulting from the action of lower agents disposing the matter; and in this he avoided the absurdity of the previous opinion. A sign of this apparently was that no active power can be found in these bodies except an accidental form, active and passive qualities, for instance; and these would not seem capable of causing substantial forms.

Moreover in this sublunary world we find certain things that are not generated from their like: animals caused through putrefaction, for instance. Therefore, apparently, the forms of these are caused by higher principles. And in like manner other forms, some of which are much more perfect.

Some, too, find proof of this in the inadequacy of natural bodies for action. Because the form of every natural body is joined to quantity. Now quantity is an obstacle to action and movement, a sign of which they see in the fact that the more we add to the quantity of a body, the heavier it becomes, and the slower its movement. Whence they conclude that no body is active, but that all bodies are purely passive.

They also attempt to prove this from the fact that every patient is recipient to the agent, and that every agent, save the first which creates, requires a subject inferior to itself. But no substance is inferior to a body. Therefore seemingly no body is active.

They add also that corporeal substance is the most removed from the first agent, and therefore they do not see how the active power can reach as far as corporeal substance. They maintain, therefore, that, as God is purely active, so corporeal substance, being the lowest thing of all, is purely passive. For these reasons, then, Avicebron held in the *Fount of Life* that

---

[1] *C. G.*, II, 21.   [2] Cf. Aristotle, *Metaph.*, I, 9 (990a 34).   [3] *Metaph.*, IX, 5 (fol. 105rv).

no body is active, but that the power of a spiritual substance pervading through bodies produces the actions which seem to be performed by bodies.[1]

Moreover certain Moslem theologians are said to have argued that even accidents are not the result of corporeal activity, because an accident does not pass from one subject to another. Hence they deem it impossible for heat to pass from a hot body into another body so as to heat it. What they say is that all such accidents are created by God.[2]

However, many absurdities arise from the foregoing positions. For if no inferior cause, above all a body, is active, and if God works alone in all things, then, since God is not changed through working in various things, no diversity will follow among the effects through the diversity of the things in which God works. Now this is evidently false to the senses, for from the application of a hot body there follows, not cooling, but only heating, and from human seed only a man is generated. Therefore the causing of inferior effects is not to be ascribed to the divine power in such a way as to withdraw the causality of inferior agents.

Again. It is contrary to the notion of wisdom that anything should be done in vain in the works of a wise man. But if creatures did nothing at all towards the production of their effects, and God alone wrought everything immediately, other things would be employed by Him in vain for the production of those effects. Therefore the above position is incompatible with divine wisdom.

Besides. He who gives something essential, gives whatever accompanies it; and thus, the cause that gives gravity to an element, gives it downward movement. Now to make something actual results from being actual, as we see to be the case in God; for He is pure act, and is also the first cause of being in all things, as we proved above.[3] If therefore He bestowed His likeness on others in respect of being, in so far as He brought things into being, it follows that He also bestowed on them His likeness in respect of being causes, so that creatures too should have their proper actions.

Further. The perfection of the effect indicates the perfection of the cause, since a greater power produces a more perfect effect. Now God is the most perfect agent. Therefore things created by Him must needs receive perfection from him. Consequently to detract from the creature's perfection is to detract from the perfection of the divine power. But if no creature exercises an action for the production of an effect, much is detracted from the perfection of the creature; because it is due to the abundance of its perfection that a thing is able to communicate to another the perfection that it has. Therefore this opinion detracts from the divine power.

Moreover. Just as it belongs to the good to produce a good, so it belongs to the highest good to make a thing best. Now God is the highest good, as

[1] *Fons Vitae,* II, 9 (p. 41); III, 44, 45 (p. 177, 179-180). [2] Cf. Maimonides, *Guide,* I, 73 (p. 125). [3] *C. G.,* II, 15.

we proved in the First Book.[1] Therefore it belongs to Him to make all things best. Now it is better that the good bestowed on someone should be common to many than that it should be proper to one: since *the common good is always considered more godlike than the good of one only*.[2] But the good of one becomes common to many if it flows from the one to the others, and this can be only when the one, by its own action, communicates it to them; but if it has not the power to transmit it to others, that good remains its own property. Accordingly, God communicated His goodness to His creatures in such wise that one thing can communicate to another the good it has received. Therefore it is derogatory to the divine goodness to deny to things their proper operations.

Again. To take order away from creatures is to deny them the best thing they have, because, though each one is good in itself, together they are very good because of the order of the universe; for the whole is always better than the parts, and is their end. Now if we take away action from things, the order among things is withdrawn; because things differing in nature are not bound together in the unity of order, except through the fact that some are active and some passive. Therefore it is unfitting to say that things have not their proper actions.

Besides. If effects be produced not by the act of creatures but only by the act of God, the power of a created cause cannot possibly be manifested by its effect, since the effect is no indication of the cause's power, except by reason of the action which proceeds from the power and terminates in the effect. Now the nature of a cause is not known from its effect except in so far as this is an indication of its power which results from its nature. Consequently if creatures have no action for the production of effects, it will follow that the nature of a creature can never be known from its effect: so that all knowledge in the philosophy of nature would be denied us, for it is there that demonstrations from effects are chiefly employed.

Further. By induction it can be proved that *like produces like*. Now that which is produced in lower things is not a mere form, but a composite of matter and form; because every generation is out of something, namely, *matter,* and to something, namely, *form.* Therefore the generating cause must be, not a mere form, but composed of matter and form. Therefore the cause of forms which exist in matter is not the separate species of things, as the Platonists maintained, nor the agent intellect, as Avicenna said, but an individual composed of matter and form.

Again. If action is consequent upon being actual, it is unreasonable that the more perfect act be deprived of action. Now the substantial form is a more perfect act than the accidental. Consequently, if the accidental forms in corporeal things have their proper actions, much more has the substantial form an operation proper to it. But this action does not consist in disposing matter, because this is effected by alteration, for which acci-

[1] *C. G.,* I, 41.   [2] Aristotle, *Eth.,* I, 2 (1094b 9).

dental forms suffice. Therefore the substantial form of the generating cause is the principle of the action whereby the substantial form is introduced into the thing generated.

The arguments they adduce are easily solved.

For since a thing is made that it may be, just as a form is called a being, not as though it itself had being, but because by it the composite is, so neither is the form made, properly speaking, but it begins to be through the fact that the composite is brought from potentiality to the act which is the form.

Nor is it necessary that whatever has a form by way of participation receive it from that which is a form essentially; for it may receive it immediately from something having a like form in a like manner, namely, by participation (though it may act in the power of that separate form, if there be any such); and thus like agent produces like effect.

Nor does it follow, because every action of inferior bodies is effected through active or passive qualities, which are accidents, that nothing, save accidents, results from those actions; for even as those accidental forms are caused by the substantial form, which together with matter is the cause of all the proper accidents, so do they act by virtue of the substantial form. Now that which acts by virtue of another produces an effect like not only to itself, but also, and more, to that by virtue of which it acts. Thus the action of the instrument reproduces in the work done the likeness of the art. Hence the action of accidental forms produces substantial forms, inasmuch as they act instrumentally in the power of substantial forms. As to animals generated from putrefaction, the substantial form is caused in them through the agency of a body, namely, a heavenly body, and that is the first principle of alteration; consequently in this lower sphere whatever acts dispositively to a form must act by virtue of that body. That is why the power of the heavenly body suffices, without an univocal agent, for the production of certain imperfect forms; whereas for the production of more perfect forms, such as the souls of perfect animals, a univocal agent is required besides the celestial agent. For such animals are not produced otherwise than by seed, and hence Aristotle says that *man and the sun generate man.*[1]

Again, it is untrue that quantity is an obstacle to a form's activity, except accidentally, namely, in so far as all continuous quantity is in matter. Now a form which exists in matter, through being less actual, has less active power; so that the body which has less matter and more form, fire, for instance, is more active. But if we suppose the measure of action of which a form existing in matter is capable, then quantity favors an increase rather than a decrease of action. For the greater the fiery body, supposing the heat to be equally intense, the more heat does it give; and supposing an equally intense gravity, the greater a heavy body is, the more rapid will be

[1] *Phys.*, II, 2 (194b 14).

its natural movement, and for the same reason the slower will its non-natural movement be. Accordingly, the fact that heavy bodies are slower in their non-natural movements, through being of greater quantity, is no proof that quantity is an obstacle to action, but rather that it is a help to its increase.

Again, it does not follow that all bodies must be without action, because, in the order of things, corporeal substance is of the lowest kind; since even among bodies one is higher, more formal and more active than another, as fire in comparison with lower bodies, and yet not even the lowest body is excluded from activity. For it is clear that a body cannot be wholly active, since it is composed of matter, which is being potentially, and form which is act. For a thing acts according as it is actual, and therefore every body acts according to its form, to which the other body, namely, the recipient, is compared, according to its matter, as subject, inasmuch as its matter is in potentiality to the form of the agent. If, on the other hand, the matter of the active body be in potentiality to the form of the passive body, they will be mutually agent and recipient, as in the case of two elementary bodies; or else, one will be purely active and the other purely passive in relation to it, as a heavenly body compared to the elementary body. Accordingly, a body acts on a subject, not by reason of its entirety, but by reason of the form by which it works.

Nor is it true that bodies are most removed from God. For as God is pure act, things are more or less distant from Him according as they are more or less in act or potentiality. Hence, of all things that is most distant from God which is pure potentiality, namely, primary matter, which is therefore purely passive and in no way active. On the other hand, bodies, being composed of matter and form, approach to a likeness to God inasmuch as they have a form, which Aristotle calls a divine thing;[1] and therefore they act inasmuch as they have a form, and are passive inasmuch as they have matter.

Again, it is absurd to say that a body is not active because accidents do not pass from one subject to another. For when we say that a hot body gives heat, we do not mean that the identical heat which is in the heater passes into the heated body; but that by virtue of the heat in the heater, another heat, individually distinct, which previously had been in it potentially, becomes actual in the heated body. For the natural agent does not transmit its own form into another subject, but reduces the receptive subject from potentiality to act. Consequently, we do not deny creatures their proper actions, although we ascribe all the effects of creatures to God, as operating in all things.

---

[1] *Phys.*, I, 9 (192a 16).

CHAPTER LXX

HOW THE SAME EFFECT IS FROM GOD AND FROM THE NATURAL AGENT

SOME find it difficult to understand how the effects of nature are ascribed to God and to the natural agent.

For it would seem impossible that one action should proceed from two agents. Hence if the action productive of a natural effect proceeds from a natural body, it does not proceed from God.

Again. If a thing can be done adequately by means of one, it is superfluous to do it by means of several; for we observe that nature does not employ two instruments where one suffices. Since, then, the divine power suffices to produce natural effects, it is superfluous to employ, for the production of the same effects, the powers of nature also; or, if the forces of nature suffice, it is superfluous for the divine power to work for the same effect.

Besides. If God produces the whole natural effect, nothing of the effect is left for the natural agent to produce. Therefore, it seems impossible that God produce the same effects as natural things.

However, these arguments offer no difficulty if we consider what has been already said. For two things may be considered in every agent, namely, the thing itself that acts, and the power whereby it acts. Thus fire by its heat makes a thing hot. Now the power of the lower agent depends on the power of the higher agent, in so far as the higher agent gives the lower agent the power whereby it acts, or preserves that power, or applies it to action. Thus the craftsman applies the instrument to its proper effect, although sometimes he does not give the instrument the form whereby it acts, nor preserves that form, but merely puts it into motion. Consequently, the action of the lower agent must not only proceed from the lower agent through the agent's own power, but also through the power of all the higher agents, for it acts by the power of them all. Now just as the lowest agent is found to be immediately active, so the power of the first agent is found to be immediate in the production of the effect; because the power of the lowest agent does not of itself produce this effect, but by the power of the proximate higher agent, and this by the power of a yet higher agent, so that the power of the supreme agent is found to produce the effects of itself, as though it were the immediate cause, as may be seen in the principles of demonstration, the first of which is immediate. Accordingly, just as it is not unreasonable that one action be produced by an agent and by the power of that agent, so is it not unreasonable that the same effect be produced by the inferior agent and by God, and by both immediately, though in a different way.

It is also evident that there is nothing superfluous if a natural thing produce its proper effect and God also produce it, since a natural thing does not produce it except by God's power.

Nor is it superfluous, if God can produce all natural effects by Himself, that they should be produced by certain other causes; because this is not owing to the insufficiency of His power, but to the immensity of His goodness, by which it was His will to communicate His likeness to things not only in the point of their being, but also in the point of their being causes of other things. For it is in these two ways that all creatures in common have the divine likeness bestowed on them, as we proved above.[1]—In this way, too, the beauty of order is made evident in creatures.

It is also clear that the same effect is ascribed to a natural cause and to God, not as though part were effected by God and part by the natural agent; but the whole effect proceeds from each, yet in different ways, just as the whole of one and the same effect is ascribed to the instrument, and again the whole is ascribed to the principal agent.

CHAPTER LXXI

THAT THE DIVINE PROVIDENCE DOES NOT ENTIRELY EXCLUDE EVIL FROM THINGS

FROM the foregoing it is also clear that the divine providence, which governs things, does not prevent corruption, defects and evil from being in the world.

For the divine government whereby God works among things does not exclude the operation of second causes, as we have already shown.[2] Now, a defect may occur in an effect through a defect in the secondary active cause, without there being any defect in the first agent. Thus there may be a defect in the work of a craftsman, who is perfect in his craft, because of some defect in the instrument; even so, a man with a healthy locomotive power may limp, through no fault in the locomotive power, but because his leg is not straight. Accordingly, in the things moved and governed by God, defect and evil may be found because of defects in the secondary agents, even though there is no defect in God Himself.

Moreover. Perfect goodness would not be found in things unless there were degrees of goodness, so that, namely, there be some things better than others; or else all the possible degrees of goodness would not be fulfilled, nor would any creature be found like to God in the point of being better than others. Moreover, this would do away with the chief beauty in things if the order resulting from distinction and disparity were abolished; and, what is more, the absence of inequality in goodness would involve the elimi-

[1] Ch. 20, 21.   [2] Ch. 69ff.

nation of multitude, since it is because things differ from one another that one is better than another: *e.g.*, the animate than the inanimate, and the rational than the irrational. Consequently, if there were absolute equality among things, there would be but one created good; which is clearly derogatory to the goodness of the creature. Now the higher degree of goodness is that a thing be good and unable to fail from goodness; and the lower degree is of that which can fail from goodness. Therefore the perfection of the universe requires both degrees of goodness. Now it belongs to the providence of the governor to preserve and not to diminish perfection in the things governed. Therefore it does not belong to the providence of God to exclude from things completely the possibility of failing from goodness. But evil results from this possibility, because that which can fail, at times does fail; and this very failure is evil, as we have proved.[1] Therefore it does not belong to the divine providence to remove evil entirely from things.

Again. In every government the best thing is that provision be made for the things governed according to their mode, for in this consists the justice of the régime. Consequently, even as it would be contrary to the nature of human rule, if the governor of a state were to forbid men to act according to their various duties,—except perhaps for a time, because of some particular urgency,—so it would be contrary to the notion of God's government, if He did not allow creatures to act in accordance with the mode of their respective natures. Now because things thus act according to the mode of their natures, corruption and evil result in things; since by reason of the contrariety and incompatibility that exist in things, one thing is corruptive of another. Therefore it does not belong to the divine providence to exclude evil from things altogether.

Besides. An agent cannot possibly produce an evil, except by reason of its intending some good, as we proved above.[2] Now it does not belong to the providence of one who is the cause of all good to exclude from creatures all intention of any particular good; for thus many goods would be banished from the universe. And so, if fire were deprived of the intention of producing its like, a consequence of which is the evil of the burning of combustible things, the good consisting in the generation of fire and its preservation in its species would be done away. Therefore it is not part of the divine providence to exclude evil altogether from things.

Further. There are in the world many good things which would have no place unless there were evils. Thus there would be no patience of the righteous, if there were no ill-will of the persecutors; nor would there be any place for a vindicating justice, were there no crimes; and even in the physical order there would be no generation of one thing, unless there were corruption of another. Consequently, if evil were entirely excluded from the universe by the divine providence, it would be necessary to lessen the great number of good things. This ought not to be, since good is more

[1] Ch. 7.   [2] Ch. 3, 4.

powerful in goodness than evil is in malice, as was shown above.[1] Therefore evil should not be utterly excluded from things by the divine providence.

Again. The good of the whole is of more account than the good of the
part. Therefore it belongs to a prudent governor to overlook a lack of
goodness in a part, that there may be an increase of goodness in the whole.
Thus the builder hides the foundation of a house underground, that the
whole house may stand firm. Now if evil were taken away from certain
parts of the universe, the perfection of the universe would be much diminished, since its beauty results from the ordered unity of good and evil
things, seeing that evil arises from the failure of good, and yet certain
goods are occasioned from those very evils through the providence of the
governor, even as the silent pause gives sweetness to the chant. Therefore
evil should not be excluded from things by the divine providence.

Further. Other things, especially those of lower degree, are directed to
man's good as their end. But if there were no evils in the world, man's good
would be lessened considerably, both in his knowledge, and in his desire
or love of the good. For his knowledge of the good is increased by comparison with evil, and through suffering evil his desire of doing good is kindled;
and thus the sick know best what a great good health is, and they, too,
are more keen about it than those who have it. Therefore it does not belong to the divine providence to exclude evil from the world altogether.

Hence it is said (*Isa.* xlv. 7): *I make peace and create evil*; and (*Amos*
iii. 6): *Shall there be evil in the city, which the Lord hath not done?*

Hereby is refuted the error of those who, through observing the presence
of evil in the world, said that there is no God. Thus Boethius introduces a
philosopher who asks: *If there be a God, whence comes evil?*[2] On the
contrary, he should have argued: *If there is evil, there is a God.* For there
would be no evil, if the order of good were removed, the privation of which
is evil; and there would be no such order, if there were no God.

Moreover, by what has been laid down, an occasion of erring is removed
from those who denied that the divine providence extends to this corruptible
world, because they observed that many evils occur in it. They said that
incorruptible things alone are subject to God's providence, because no defects and no evils are to be found in them.

So, too, there is also removed an occasion of error from the Manicheans,
who posited two first active principles, good and evil, as though evil could
have no place under the providence of a good God.

The doubt, also, of some is solved, namely, whether evil deeds are from
God. For since we proved that every agent produces its action in so far as
it acts by the power of God,[3] and that therefore God is the cause of all
effects and actions; and since, again, we proved that evil and defect in
things ruled by the divine providence result from the condition of the sec-

---

[1] Ch. 11, 12.   [2] *De Consol.*, I, prose 4 (PL 63, 625).   [3] Ch. 66.

ondary causes, which may be themselves defective, it is evident that evil deeds, considered as defective, are not from God, but from their defective proximate causes. But in so far as they possess activity and entity, they must be from God; even as a limp is from the locomotive power in so far as it has movement, but in so far as it has a defect it is from the crookedness of the leg.

CHAPTER LXXII

THAT THE DIVINE PROVIDENCE DOES NOT EXCLUDE CONTINGENCY FROM THINGS

JUST as the divine providence does not altogether banish evil from the world, so neither does it exclude contingency, nor impose necessity on things.

For we have already proved that the operation of providence, whereby God operates in the world, does not exclude secondary causes, but is fulfilled by them inasmuch as they act by God's power.[1] Now certain effects are said to be necessary or contingent in relation to their proximate, not to their remote, causes. Thus, for a plant to bear fruit is a contingent effect because of the proximate cause, which is the power of germination, that can be hindered and fail; although a remote cause, namely the sun, is a cause that acts of necessity. Since, then, among proximate causes there are many that can fail, not all the effects subject to the divine providence will be necessary, but many of them will be contingent.

Again. It belongs to the divine providence that the possible degrees of being be fulfilled, as was made evident above.[2] Now being is divided into contingent and necessary, and this is an essential division of being. Therefore, if the divine providence excluded all contingency, not all the degrees of being would be preserved.

Besides. The nearer things are to God, the more they partake of a likeness to Him; and the further they are from Him, the more they fail in their likeness to Him. Now those things that are nearest to God are altogether immovable. Such are the separate substances which approach nearest to a likeness to God, Who is utterly immovable. On the other hand, such beings as are nearest to them and are immediately moved by those that are unchangeable retain a certain degree of immobility in that they are always moved in the same way (for instance, the heavenly bodies). Consequently, those beings that come after the foregoing, and are moved by them, are further removed from the divine immobility, so that they are not always moved in the same way; and in this the beauty of order is evident. But every necessary being, as such, never varies. Therefore it would be

[1] Ch. 6off.   [2] Ch. 71.

incompatible with the divine providence, to which it belongs to establish and preserve order among things, if all things happened of necessity.

Moreover. That which is of necessity is always. Now nothing corruptible is always. Therefore, if the divine providence requires all things to be necessary, it would follow that nothing in the world is corruptible, and consequently neither is anything generable. Hence the whole realm of things subject to generation and corruption would be withdrawn from the world. Now this detracts from the perfection of the universe.

Further. In every movement there is some generation and corruption, since in a thing that is moved, something begins to be, and something ceases to be. Consequently, if all generation and corruption were banished, through the elimination of all contingent things, as we have just proved, all movement and all movable things would as a result be taken away.

Besides. If the power of a substance be weakened, or if it be hindered by a contrary agent, this argues some change in that power. Consequently, if the divine providence does not banish movement from things, it will prevent neither the weakening of their power nor the impediment arising from the resistance of another agent. Now it is because that power is sometimes weakened and hindered that nature does not always work in the same way, but sometimes fails in that which belongs to a thing according to its nature, so that natural effects do not follow of necessity. Therefore it does not belong to the divine providence to impose necessity on the things governed.

Moreover. In things that are fittingly ruled by providence, there should be nothing in vain. Since, therefore, it is evident that some causes are contingent, seeing that they can be hindered from producing their effects, it is clearly inconsistent with providence that all things should happen of necessity. Therefore the divine providence does not impose necessity on things, by excluding contingency from them altogether.

CHAPTER LXXIII

THAT THE DIVINE PROVIDENCE DOES NOT EXCLUDE THE LIBERTY OF CHOICE

HENCE it is also clear that providence does not exclude the liberty of the will.

For the government of any prudent governor is directed to the perfection of the things governed, whether it be to attain it, or increase it, or preserve it. Therefore whatever pertains to perfection is to be safeguarded by providence rather than what is part of imperfection and defect. Now in inanimate beings, contingency in causes arises from imperfection and deficiency, because by their nature they are determined to one effect, which they always produce, unless there be an impediment due either to weakness of power, or to some extrinsic agency, or to the indisposition of matter. For this reason natural causes are not indifferent to one or other result, but generally produce their effect in the same way, and seldom fail. On the other hand, it is owing to the perfection of the will that it is a contingent cause, because its power is not limited to one effect; indeed, the will has it in its power to produce this or that effect, and consequently is undetermined to either. Therefore it belongs to the divine providence to preserve the liberty of the will, more than contingency in natural causes.

Moreover. It belongs to the divine providence to use things according to their mode. But the mode of a thing's action is in keeping with its form, which is the principle of action. Now the form through which a voluntary agent acts is not determined, because the will acts through a form apprehended by the intellect, since it is the apprehended good that moves the will as its object. Now, precisely, the intellect has not one determinate form of the effect, but is of such a nature as to understand a multitude of forms. That is why the will is able to produce manifold effects. Therefore it does not belong to the divine providence to exclude the liberty of the will.

Again. The things governed are brought to a fitting end by the government of providence; and so Gregory of Nyssa says of the divine providence that it is *God's will from which all existing things receive a fitting end.*[1] Now the last end of every creature is to attain to God's likeness, as we proved above.[2] It would therefore be inconsistent with the divine providence if any thing were deprived of that whereby it attains to a likeness to God. But the voluntary agent attains to God's likeness in that he acts freely, for we have proved that there is free choice in God.[3] Therefore providence does not deprive the will of liberty.

Besides. Providence multiplies good things among the subjects of its government. Therefore whatever would deprive things of many goods does not belong to providence. Now if the will were deprived of liberty, many goods would be done away, for no praise would be given to human virtue, since virtue would be as nothing if man did not act freely; there would be no justice in rewarding or punishing, if man were not free in acting well or ill; and there would be no prudence in taking counsel, which would be of no use if things occurred of necessity. Therefore it would be against the nature of providence to deprive the will of liberty.

Hence it is said (*Ecclus.* xv. 14): *God made man from the beginning and left him in the hand of his own counsel*; and again (*ibid.*, 18): *Before man is life and death, good and evil, that which he shall choose shall be given him.*

Hereby is removed the opinion of the Stoics who held that all things happen of necessity according to the order of infallible causes, which order the Greeks called εἱμαρμένη.[4]

[1] Nemesius, *De Nat. Hom.*, XLIII (PG 40, 792).   [2] Ch. 19.   [3] *C. G.*, I, 88.
[4] Nemesius, *De Nat. Hom.*, XXXVII (PG 40, 752).

CHAPTER LXXIV

THAT THE DIVINE PROVIDENCE DOES NOT EXCLUDE FORTUNE AND CHANCE

It is also evident from what has been said that the divine providence does not remove from the world fortune and chance.

Fortune and chance are said of things that happen seldom. If nothing happened seldom, all things would happen of necessity; because those things that happen more frequently than not differ from necessary things in this alone, that they may possibly fail in a few instances. Now it would be against the nature of the divine providence if all things happened of necessity, as we proved above.[1] Therefore it would also be against the nature of the divine providence if nothing happened in the world fortuitously and by chance.

Again. It would be against the nature of providence if things subject to providence were not to act for an end, since it is the part of providence to direct all things to their end. Furthermore, it would be contrary to the perfection of the universe, were there nothing corruptible, nor any power subject to failure, as we proved above.[2] Now it is owing to the fact that an agent acting for the sake of some end fails to attain that end, that certain things happen by chance. Therefore it would be against the nature of providence, and the perfection of the world, if nothing happened by chance.

Besides. The number and diversity of causes result from the ordering of divine providence and disposition. Now given a diversity of causes, it must happen sometimes that one concurs with another, so that one is either hindered or assisted in producing its effect. But chance occurrences are due to the concurrence of two or more causes, when some end which was not intended happens from the concurrence of some cause. For instance, the finding of his debtor by one who went to market to buy something happened because the debtor also went to market. Therefore it is not against the divine providence that there be fortuitous and chance happenings in the world.

Moreover. That which is not, cannot be the cause of any thing. Therefore a thing must stand in relation to *being a cause* in the same way as to *being.* Hence the diversity of order in causes must be in keeping with diversity of order among things. Now it belongs to the perfection of the world that there should be in it not only substances, but also accidents. Because things which have not their ultimate perfection in their substance must needs acquire some perfection by means of accidents, which accidents will be all the more numerous, as the things themselves are more distant from God's

[1] Ch. 72.   [2] Ch. 71.

simplicity. Now if a subject has many accidents, it follows that it is a being accidentally, since subject and accident, or two accidents in one subject, are *one* and *being* accidentally: *e.g.*, a *white man*, and a *musical white thing*. Therefore the perfection of the world requires that there should also be accidental causes. But that which results accidentally from a cause is said to occur by chance or fortuitously. Therefore it is not against the nature of providence that some things happen by chance or fortune.

Further. It belongs to the order of the divine providence that there be an order and a gradation among causes. Now the higher a cause is above its effect, the greater its power, so that its causality extends to a greater number of things. But the intention of a natural cause never extends further than its power, for such an intention would be in vain. Consequently the intention of a particular cause cannot possibly extend to all possible contingencies. Now it is because things happen outside the intention of the agent that things occur by chance or fortuitously. Therefore the order of the divine providence requires the presence of chance and fortune in the world.

Hence it is said (*Eccles.* ix. 11): *I saw that . . . the race is not to the swift, etc., but time and chance in all,* namely, here below.

CHAPTER LXXV

THAT THE DIVINE PROVIDENCE IS CONCERNED WITH SINGULAR CONTINGENTS

FROM what we have proved it is evident that the divine providence reaches to each individual among things subject to generation and corruption.

For the only reason for excluding such things from providence would seem to be their contingent nature, and the fact that many of them are chance or fortuitous occurrences; for in this alone do they differ from incorruptible realities and from the universals of corruptible things, with which it is said that providence is concerned. Now providence is not inconsistent with contingency, chance and fortune, as neither is it with voluntary action, as we have proved.[1] There is no reason, therefore, why providence should not be about such things, even as it is about incorruptibles and universals.

Besides. If God's providence does not extend to these singular things, this is either because He does not know them, or because He is unable or unwilling to care for them. But it cannot be said that God does not know singulars, since we have proved that He has knowledge of them.[2] Nor can it be said that God is unable to care for them, since His power is infinite,

[1] Ch. 72ff. [2] *C. G.,* I, 65.

as we proved above.[1] Nor, again, can it be said that these singulars are incapable of being governed, since we see them to be governed by the efforts of reason, as is evident in man, or by natural instinct, as is evident in bees and many brute animals, which are governed by a kind of natural instinct. Nor, finally, can it be said that God is unwilling to govern them, since His will is the universal cause of all good, and the good of things governed consists chiefly in the order of government. Therefore it cannot be said that God has no care for these singulars.

Besides. Every secondary cause, by the mere fact of its being a cause, attains to a likeness to God, as was proved above.[2] Now it is to be universally observed that things which are productive have the care of the things they produce; and thus, animals naturally nourish their offspring. Therefore God has care of the things of which He is the cause. Now He is the cause even of these singulars, as was proved above.[3] Therefore He has care of them.

Further. It was proved above that God acts in created things, not from natural necessity, but by His will and intellect.[4] But things that are done by will and intellect are subject to providence, which seems to consist in ruling things by the intellect. Consequently the things done by God are subject to His providence. But it has been proved that God works in all second causes, and that all their effects are to be referred to God as their cause, so that whatever is done in these individuals is His own work.[5] Consequently, these individual things, their movements and operations, are subject to the divine providence.

Again. A man's providence is foolish if he cares not for those things without which the things he cares for cannot be. Now it is clear that if all individuals ceased to exist, their universals would likewise cease. Therefore if God cares only for universals, and neglects these individuals altogether, His providence will be foolish and imperfect.

If, however, someone say that God cares for these individuals so far as to preserve them in existence, but no further, this is quite impossible, since whatever happens to individuals concerns their preservation or their corruption. Consequently, if God cares for individuals as to their preservation, He cares also for whatever happens to them.

Yet someone can say that the mere care of universals suffices for the preservation of individuals in being, since each species is provided with the means of self-preservation for every individual of that species. Thus animals were given organs for taking and digesting food, and horns for self-protection; and the usefulness of these organs does not fail except in a few cases, since that which is of nature produces its effect either always or more frequently. Hence all the individuals could not cease to exist, although some might.

[1] *C. G.*, II, 22.   [2] Ch. 21.   [3] *C. G.*, II, 15.   [4] *C. G.*, II, 23ff.   [5] Ch. 67.

But, according to this way of reasoning, whatever happens to individuals will be subject to providence, even as is their preservation in being; for nothing can happen to the individual member of a species that cannot in some way be referred to the principles of that species. Accordingly, individuals are not more subject to the divine providence as to their preservation in being than they are in other matters.

Moreover. The order of things in relation to the end is such that accidents are for the sake of substances, in order that the latter may be perfected by them. And in substances, matter is for the sake of the form, since it is through the form that matter has a participation in the divine goodness, for the sake of which all things were made, as we proved above.[1] Hence it is evident that the individual is for the sake of the universal nature. A sign of this is that where the universal nature can be preserved in one individual, there are not many individuals of one species: *e.g.,* the moon and sun. Now since providence has the ordering of things to their end, it follows that to providence belong both the end and the things directed to the end. Therefore, not only universals, but also individuals, are subject to the divine providence.

Again. The difference between speculative and practical knowledge is that speculative knowledge and what is connected with it is perfected in the universal, whereas what pertains to practical knowledge is perfected in the particular. For the end of speculative knowledge is truth, which consists first and of its very nature in the immaterial and universal; whereas the end of practical knowledge is operation, which is about individual things. Hence the physician does not heal a universal man, but this particular man, and the whole of medical science is directed to this. Now it is clear that providence belongs to practical knowledge, since it directs things to their end. Therefore God's providence would be most imperfect if it extended no further than universals and did not reach individuals.

Besides. Speculative knowledge is perfected in the universal rather than in the particular, because universals are known better than individuals; and that is why the knowledge of the most universal principles is common to all. Yet the more perfect in speculative knowledge is he who possesses not only a universal, but also a proper, knowledge of things; since he who knows a thing only universally knows it only potentially. For this reason the disciple is led from the universal knowledge of principles to the proper knowledge of conclusions by the teacher, who is possessed of both knowledges, just as a thing is brought from potentiality to act by that which is in act. *A fortiori,* therefore, the more perfect in practical knowledge is he who directs things to actuality not only universally but also in particular. Consequently, the divine providence, being supremely perfect, extends to individuals.

---

[1] Ch. 17.

Moreover. Since God is the cause of being as being, as we proved above,[1] it follows that His providence must care for being as being, since He governs things inasmuch as He is their cause. Therefore, whatever exists, no matter in what way it exists, is subject to His providence. Now individuals are beings, and more so than universals, because universals do not exist by themselves, but only in individuals. Therefore the divine providence is also concerned about individuals.

Further. Creatures are subject to the divine providence as being directed thereby to their end, which is the divine goodness. Therefore participation in the divine goodness by creatures is the work of the divine providence. But even contingent singulars participate in the divine goodness. Therefore the divine providence must extend also to them.

Hence it is said (*Matt.* x. 29): *Are not two sparrows sold for a farthing: and not one of them shall fall on the ground without your Father,* etc.; again (*Wis.* viii. 1): *She reacheth . . . from end to end mightily,* that is, from the highest creatures to the lowest. Moreover, the opinion is refuted of some who said (*Ezech.* ix. 9): *The Lord hath forsaken the earth, and the Lord seeth not,* and of those who asserted (*Job* xxii. 14): *He doth not consider our things, and He walketh about the poles of heaven.*

Hereby is refuted the opinion of some who maintained that the divine providence does not extend to these individual things,—an opinion ascribed by some to Aristotle, although it cannot be gathered from his words.

CHAPTER LXXVI

THAT GOD'S PROVIDENCE CARES FOR ALL INDIVIDUALS IMMEDIATELY

Now some have granted that the divine providence reaches to these individual things, but through certain intermediary causes. For Plato, according to Gregory of Nyssa,[2] posited a threefold providence. The first is that of the *supreme God,* who cares first and foremost for His own, *i.e.* spiritual and intellectual beings, and then for the whole world, as regards genera, species and the universal causes, *i.e.,* the heavenly bodies. The second consists in the care of individual animals and plants and other things subject to generation and corruption, in the matter of their generation, corruption and other changes. This providence Plato ascribed to the *gods* who circulated in the heavens, while Aristotle ascribes the causality of such things to the *oblique circle.*[3] The third providence he places over things pertaining to human life, and he ascribes it to *certain demons who dwell in the neighborhood of the earth* and, according to him, are in charge of human

---

[1] *C. G.,* II, 15.   [2] Nemesius, *De Nat. Hom.,* XLIV (PG 40, 793).   [3] *De Gener.,* I[I]. 10 (336a 32).

actions. However, according to Plato, the second and third providence depend on the first, because *the supreme God appointed those of the second and third class as governors.*

This opinion accords with the Catholic Faith in so far as it refers universal providence to God as its first author. But it seems contrary to the Faith in that it denies that every individual thing is immediately subject to the divine providence. This may be proved from what has been already laid down.

For God has immediate knowledge of individuals as knowing them, not merely in their causes, but also in themselves, as we proved in the First Book.[1] Now it seems incongruous if, knowing individuals, He did not desire their order, wherein the chief good of things consists, since His will is the source of all goodness. Consequently, just as He knows individuals immediately, so He establishes order among them immediately.

Again. The order established by providence in the things governed is derived from the order conceived in the mind of the governor; just as the art-form that is produced in matter is derived from that which is in the mind of the craftsman. Now where there are several in charge, one subordinate to another, the higher must deliver to the inferior the order he has conceived, just as a subordinate art receives its principles from the higher. Accordingly, supposing the governors of the second and third rank to be under the chief governor who is the supreme God, it follows that they must receive from the supreme God the order to be established among things. But this order cannot be more perfect in them than in the supreme God; in fact, all perfections proceed from Him into other things in descending order, as we proved above.[2] And the order of things must be in the governors of the second rank, not only in general, but also as to the individual; or else they would be unable to establish order in individuals by their providence. Much more, therefore, is the order of individuals under the control of the divine providence.

Besides. In things ruled by human providence, it is to be observed that someone is placed at the head, who has charge of general matters of great importance, and by himself devises what arrangements to make with regard to them; while he himself does not devise the order of minor affairs, but leaves this to others lower than himself. Now this is owing to a defect on his part, inasmuch as he is ignorant of the conditions of particular matters of less importance, or is himself incompetent to decide the order of every thing because of the labor and delay required for the purpose. But such defects are far removed from God, for He knows all individual things, nor does He require labor or time in order to understand them, since by understanding Himself, He knows all other things, as we proved above.[3] Therefore He Himself devises the order of all individuals, and consequently His providence extends to all individuals immediately.

[1] *C. G.,* I, 65ff.   [2] *C. G.,* I, 38ff.   [3] *C. G.,* I, 46.

Moreover. In human affairs, lesser officials by their own skill devise the ordering of the things committed to their government by the chief governor. This skill they do not receive from the chief, nor its use, for if they received it from the chief, the ordering would be done by the superior, and they would no longer be devisers of this ordering, but executors. Now from what has been said it is clear that all wisdom and understanding is caused in every intelligent being by the supreme God;[1] nor can any intellect understand anything except by God's power, even as neither does any agent act except in so far as it acts by God's power. Therefore God Himself cares for all things immediately by His providence, and whoever is said to govern under Him is the executor of His providence.

Further. The higher providence gives rules to the lower providence, even as the statesman gives rules and laws to the commander in chief of the army, who in turn gives rules and laws to the captains and generals. Consequently, if there be other providences subordinate to the highest providence of the supreme God, God must give the second and third governors the rules of their office. Either, therefore, He gives universal rules and laws or particular. If He gives them universal rules, since universal rules are not always applicable to particular cases, especially in matters that are subject to movement and change, it would be necessary for these governors of the second or third rank to go beyond the rules given them in deciding about matters confided to their care. Consequently, they would exercise judgment on the rules given to them, as to when to act according to them, and when it would be necessary to disregard them. Now this is impossible, because such a judgment belongs to the superior, since the interpretation of laws and the dispensation from their observance belong to Him Who made the law. Accordingly, judgment concerning universal rules that have been given must be pronounced by the governor in chief; and this would not be possible unless He concerned Himself immediately with the ordering of individuals. Therefore, on this supposition, He should be the immediate governor of such things.—If, on the other hand, the governors of the second or third rank receive particular rules and laws from the supreme governor, it is clear that then the ordering of these individual matters comes immediately from the divine providence.

Moreover. The higher governor always has the right to judge of the arrangements made by the lower governors, as to whether they be fitting or not. Consequently, if the second or third governors are subordinate to God the chief governor, it follows that God judges of the arrangements made by them; which would be impossible if God did not consider the ordering of these individual matters. Therefore He personally cares for individuals by Himself.

Again. If God does not care for these lower individuals immediately by

---

[1] Ch. 67.

Himself, this is either because He despises them or, as some say,[1] lest His dignity should be besmirched by them. But this is absurd. For there is more dignity in providing for and planning the ordering of things, than in operating in them. Consequently, if God works in all things, as was proved above,[2] and if, far from being derogatory to His dignity, on the contrary, this belongs to His all-pervading and supreme power, it is in no way contemptible in Him, nor does it besmirch His dignity, if His providence extends to these individual things immediately.

Further. Every wise man, who uses his power providently, moderates that use in his actions, by directing the purpose and extent of that use; or else his power would not be subject to his wisdom. Now it is clear from what has been said that the divine power, in its operations, extends to the lowest things.[3] Consequently, divine wisdom directs *which* and *how many* effects are to result from its power, and *how* they are to result therefrom, even in the very lowest of things. Therefore God Himself, by His providence, immediately plans the ordering of all things.

Hence it is said (*Rom.* xiii. 1): *Those that are, are ordained of God*; and again (*Judith* ix. 4): *Thou hast done the things of old, and hast devised one thing after another, and what thou hast designed hath been done.*

CHAPTER LXXVII

THAT THE EXECUTION OF THE DIVINE PROVIDENCE IS CARRIED OUT BY SECONDARY CAUSES

It must be observed that two things are required for providence, an *order* and an *execution* of the order. The first is the work of the cognitive power, and so those that are more perfect in knowledge are said to order others. *For it belongs to the wise man to order.*[4] The second is the work of the operative power. Now these two are in inverse proportion to each other. For the ordering is the more perfect according as it extends to the smallest things, whereas the execution of the least things belongs to a lower power, proportionate to the effect. In God we find the highest perfection as to both, since in Him is the most perfect wisdom for ordering, and the most perfect power for operation. Consequently, He it is Who by His wisdom disposes all things even the very least in their order; but He executes the least or lowest things by means of other inferior powers, through which He operates, as a universal and higher power through an inferior and particular power. It is fitting, therefore, that there should be inferior active powers to execute the divine providence.

[1] Cf. Averroes, *In Metaph.*, XII, comm. 37; 52 (VIII, 150v; 158v).   [2] Ch. 67ff.
[3] *Ibid.*   [4] Aristotle, *Metaph.*, I, 2 (982a 18).

Again. It was proved above that the divine operation does not exclude the operations of secondary causes.[1] But whatever is effected by the operations of secondary causes is subject to the divine providence, since God directs all individual things by Himself, as was proved above.[2] Therefore secondary causes execute the divine providence.

Besides. The stronger the power of an agent, the further does its operation extend; and thus, the greater the fire, the more distant things does it heat. But this is not the case with an agent that does not act through an intermediary, because everything on which it acts is close to it. Since, then, the power of the divine providence is supreme, it must bring its operation to bear on the most distant things through certain intermediaries.

Further. It belongs to the dignity of a ruler to have many ministers and various executors of his rule, for the greater the number of his subordinates of various degrees, the more complete and extensive is his dominion shown to be. But no government can compare with the divine in point of dignity. Therefore it is fitting that the execution of the divine providence be committed to agents of various degrees.

Moreover. Suitable order is a proof of perfect providence, for order is the proper effect of providence. Now suitable order implies that nothing be allowed to be out of order. Consequently, the perfection of the divine providence requires that it should reduce the excess of certain things over others to a suitable order. Now this is done by allowing those who have less to benefit from the superabundance of others. Since, then, the perfection of the universe requires that some share more abundantly in the divine goodness, as we proved above,[3] the perfection of the divine providence demands that the execution of the divine government be fulfilled by those beings which have the larger share of divine goodness.

Again. The order of causes excels the order of effects, even as the cause excels the effect consequently it is a greater witness to the perfection of providence. Now if there were no intermediary causes to execute the divine providence, there would be no order of causes in the world, but of effects only. Therefore the perfection of the divine providence requires intermediary causes for its fulfillment. Hence it is written (*Ps.* cii. 21): *Bless the Lord, all ye His hosts: you ministers of His who do His will*; and (*Ps.* cxlviii. 8): *Fire, hail, snow, ice, stormy winds, which fulfill His word.*

[1] Ch. 69ff.   [2] Ch. 76.   [3] *C. G.*, II, 45.

CHAPTER LXXVIII

THAT BY MEANS OF INTELLECTUAL CREATURES OTHER CREATURES ARE RULED BY GOD

SINCE it belongs to the divine providence that order be preserved in the world, and since suitable order consists in a proportionate descent from the highest to the lowest, it is proper that the divine providence should reach the most distant things according to a certain proportion. This proportion consists in this, that just as the highest creatures are subject to God and governed by Him, so the lower creatures are subject to, and are governed by, the higher. Now of all creatures the highest is the intellectual, as was proved above.[1] Therefore, the very nature of the divine providence demands that the remaining creatures be ruled by rational creatures.

Again. Whatever creature executes the order of the divine providence, does so in so far as it shares in the power of the supreme providence; just as the instrument has no movement except in so far as, through being moved, it shares in the power of the principal agent. Accordingly, those things which have a larger share in the power of the divine providence are the executors of the divine providence in regard to those whose share is smaller. Now intellectual creatures have a greater share in this power than others, because, while providence requires both the disposition of order, which is effected by a cognitive power, and execution, which is the work of the operative power, rational creatures share in both powers, whereas other creatures have only the latter. Therefore, all other creatures are ruled, under the divine providence, by rational creatures.

Moreover. To whomsoever God gives a power, it is given in relation to the effect of that power; for then are all things disposed in the best way, when each one is directed to all the goods that it has a natural aptitude to produce. Now the intellectual power by its very nature is a directive and governing power. Hence we see that when they are united in the one subject, the operative power follows the rule of the intellectual power: e.g., in man the members of the body move at the will's command. The same may also be seen if they be in different subjects; since those men who excel in the operative power need to be directed by those who excel in the intellectual power. Therefore the nature of the divine providence requires that other creatures be ruled by intellectual creatures.

Again. Particular powers are naturally adapted to be moved by universal powers, as may be seen both in art and in nature. Now it is evident that the intellectual power is more universal than any other operative power because it contains universal forms, whereas all operative powers proceed only from

[1] C. G., II, 46.

a form belonging to the operator. Therefore all other creatures must be moved and ruled by intellectual powers.

Moreover. In all ordered powers, that one is directive of another which has the better knowledge about the plan to be followed. Thus we may observe in the arts that the art which is concerned with the end (whence is taken the entire plan of the work to be produced) directs and governs the art that is immediately productive of that work: for instance, the art of sailing governs the art of shipbuilding, and the art which gives the form governs the art which prepares the material. On the other hand, the instruments, through having no knowledge of any plan, are governed only. Since, then, intellectual creatures alone are able to know the plan of the ordering of creatures, it belongs to them to rule and govern all other creatures.

Further. That which is through itself is the cause of that which is by another. Now intellectual creatures alone act through themselves, since they are masters of their own actions through the choice of their wills; whereas other creatures act through natural necessity, as being moved by another. Therefore intellectual creatures by their operations move and rule other creatures.

CHAPTER LXXIX

THAT LOWER INTELLECTUAL SUBSTANCES ARE RULED BY THE HIGHER

SINCE some intellectual creatures are higher than others, as we have shown,[1] the lower intellectual natures must needs be governed by the higher.

Again. The more universal powers move the particular powers, as was already stated.[2] But the higher intellectual natures have more universal forms, as we have proved.[3] Therefore they rule the lower intellectual natures.

Besides. The intellectual power that is nearer to the principle is always found to be the ruler of the intellectual power that is more distant from the principle. This is evident both in the speculative and in the practical sciences. For the speculative science that receives its principles of demonstration from another is said to be subalternate to it, and the practical science that is nearer to the end, which is the principle in practical matters, is the master science in comparison with the more distant. Since, then, some intellectual substances are nearer to the first principle, namely, God, as we have shown,[4] they will be the rulers of the others.

Moreover. The higher intellectual substances receive the influence of the divine wisdom more perfectly, since each one receives something according to its mode. Now all things are governed by the divine wisdom, so that

[1] *C. G.*, II, 91, 95.   [2] Ch. 78.   [3] *C.G.*, II, 98.   [4] *C. G.*, II, 95.

those which have the greater share of divine wisdom govern those which have the smaller share. Therefore the lower intellectual substances are governed by the higher.

Therefore the higher spirits are called both *angels,* inasmuch as they direct the lower spirits, by annunciation as it were, for angels are so called as being messengers; and *ministers,* inasmuch as by their operation they execute, even in corporeal things, the order of the divine providence, because a minister *is like an animate instrument,* according to the Philosopher.[1] And so it is said (*Ps.* ciii. 4): *Who makest thy angels spirits, and thy ministers a burning fire.*

CHAPTER LXXX

THE ORDERING OF THE ANGELS TOWARDS ONE ANOTHER

SINCE corporeal beings are governed by spiritual beings, as we have proved,[2] and since there is an order among corporeal things, it follows that the higher bodies are governed by the higher intellectual substances, and the lower bodies by the lower intellectual substances. Now the higher a substance is, the more universal is its power. But the power of an intellectual substance is more universal than the power of a body. Therefore the higher intellectual substances have powers entirely independent of any corporeal power, and consequently are not united to bodies, whereas the lower intellectual substances have limited powers which depend on certain corporeal instruments for their work, and consequently need to be united to bodies.

And just as the higher intellectual substances have a more universal power, so too they receive from God more perfectly the divine disposition of things, in that they are acquainted with the plan of the order, even as regards individuals, by receiving it from God. This manifestation of the divine governance, made by God, reaches to the lowest intellectual substances. As it is said (*Job* xxv. 3): *Is there any numbering of his soldiers? and upon whom shall not his light arise?* On the other hand, the lower intellects do not receive this manifestation so perfectly as to be able to know thereby every detail of the order of the divine providence left to their execution, but only in a general way; and the lower their position, the less detailed knowledge of the divine government do they receive through this first manifestation received from above; so much so, that the human intellect, which is the lowest in point of natural knowledge, has a knowledge of only certain most universal things.

Accordingly, the higher intellectual substances receive immediately from God the perfection of the knowledge in question. This perfection the other lower intellectual substances need to receive through them; just as we have

[1] *Polit.,* I, 4 (1253b 29).   [2] Ch. 78.

said above that the universal knowledge of the disciple is brought to perfection by means of the specific knowledge of the teacher.[1] Hence it is that
Dionysius, speaking of the highest intellectual substances which he assigns
to the *first hierarchy* or *holy sovereignty*, says that *they are not sanctified
by means of other substances, but that they are placed by God Himself
immediately around Him, and as far as possible close to His immaterial
and invisible beauty on which they gaze, and in which they contemplate the
intelligible models of His works*; and by these, he says, *the inferior ranks
of heavenly substances are instructed*.[2] Hence the higher intellects receive
their perfection from a higher source of knowledge.

Now in every disposition of providence, the ordering itself among effects
is derived from the form of the agents, since the effect must needs proceed
from its cause in some kind of likeness. But it is for the sake of an end that
the cause communicates the likeness of its form to the effect. Hence the first
principle in the disposition of providence is the end; the second is the form
of the agent; the third is the appointment of the order of the effects. Consequently, in the ordination of the intellect the most important thing is that
the nature of order be considered *in the end*; the second thing is that the nature of order be considered *in the form*; while the third thing is that the disposition itself of the order be known *in itself* and not in a higher principle.
Therefore the art which considers the end governs the art which considers
the form, just as the art of sailing governs the art of shipbuilding; and the
art which considers the form governs the art which considers only the order
of movements preparing the way for the form, just as the art of ship-
building governs the handiwork of the builders.

Consequently, there is a certain order among the intellects which take
from God Himself an immediate and perfect knowledge of the order of the
divine providence. The first and highest perceive the nature of the providential order in the last end itself which is the divine goodness. Some of
them, however, perceive more clearly than others; and these are called
Seraphim, *i.e., fiery* or *setting on fire*, because fire is used to designate the
intensity of love or desire, which are about the end. Hence Dionysius says
that this name indicates both their *fervent and intent activity towards God,
and their leading of lower things to God as their end*.[3]

The second place belongs to those that know perfectly the nature of the
providential order in the divine form; and these are called *Cherubim*, which
signifies *fullness of knowledge*, for knowledge is made complete through the
form of the thing known. Therefore Dionysius says that *their name indicates that they contemplate the highest operative power of the divine
beauty*.[4]

The third grade is of those that contemplate the disposition of divine
judgments in itself; and they are called *Thrones*, because the throne is sig-

---

[1] Ch. 75.   [2] *De Cael. Hier.*, VII, 2 (PG 3, 208).   [3] *Op. cit.*, VII, 1 (PG 3, 205).
[4] *Ibid.*

nificative of judicial power, according to *Ps.* ix. 5: *Thou hast sat on the throne, who judgest justice.* Hence Dionysius says that this name signifies that they are *God-bearers and ready for the obedient fulfillment of all divine undertakings.*[1]

What has been said, however, must not be understood as though the divine goodness, the divine essence and the divine knowledge of the disposition of things were three distinct things, but in the sense that there is a different consideration of God according to these different attributes.

Again. There must be order among even the lower spirits who receive from the higher spirits a perfect knowledge of the divine order to be fulfilled by them. Because the higher ones among them are also of a more universal power of understanding, so that they acquire their knowledge of the order of providence from more universal principles and causes; but those beneath them, from more particular causes, for a man who could consider the entire physical order in the heavenly bodies would be of a higher intellect than one who needed to turn his mind to lower things in order to perfect his knowledge. Accordingly, those spirits that are able to know perfectly the order of providence from the universal causes which stand midway between God, the supremely universal cause, and particular causes, are themselves between those who are able to consider the nature of the aforesaid order in God Himself and those who need to consider it in particular causes. Dionysius assigns these to the middle hierarchy which, according to him, governs the lowest hierarchy, just as it is governed by the highest.[2]

Again. Among these intellectual substances also there must be some kind of order, since the universal disposition of providence is distributed, first of all, among many executors. This work belongs to the order of *Dominations,* because to command what others execute belongs to one having dominion. Hence Dionysius says that domination signifies a *certain liberty free from servile condition and any subjection.*[3] Secondly, it is distributed by the operator and executor in reference to many effects. This is done by the order of *Virtues,* whose names, as Dionysius says in the same passage, designates *a certain strength and virility in carrying out the divine operations, without so much as swerving, through weakness, from the divine movement.* Hence it is evident that the principle of universal operation belongs to this order: so that apparently the movement of the heavenly bodies belongs to this order also, from which as from universal causes particular effects ensue in nature. That is why they are called *powers of heaven* in *Luke* xxi. 26, where it is said: *The powers of heaven shall be moved.* To the same spirits seems to belong the execution of those divine works which are done outside the order of nature. For these are the highest of God's ministries, and hence Gregory says that the *Virtues are those spirits through which miracles are frequently wrought.*[4] And if there be

[1] *Ibid.*   [2] *Op. cit.,* VIII. 1 (PG 3, 237).   [3] *Ibid.*   [4] *In Evang.,* hom. 34 (PL 76, 1251).

anything else of a universal and prominent nature in the fulfillment of the divine ministry, it is fittingly ascribed to this order.

Thirdly, the universal order of providence, once established in its effects, is guarded from confusion by curbing the things which might disturb that order. This belongs to the order of *Powers*. Therefore Dionysius says in the same place that the name *Powers* implies *a well-established order, without confusion, in the divine undertakings*; and so Gregory says that it belongs to this order *to check contrary powers*.[1]

The lowest of superior intellectual substances are those that receive from God the knowledge of the order of the divine providence as knowable in relation to particular causes. These are placed in immediate authority over human affairs. Of them Dionysius says: *This third rank of spirits presides, in consequence, over the human hierarchy*.[2] By human affairs we must understand all lower natures and particular causes that are subordinated to man and serve for his use, as we have already explained.[3]

Among these also there is a certain order. For in human affairs there is a common good, namely, the good of the city or of the nation,[4] and this seems to belong to the order of *Principalities*. Hence Dionysius says in the same chapter that the name *Principality* indicates *leadership in a sacred order*. Hence mention is made (*Dan.* x. 12-20) of *Michael the Prince of the Jews, of a Prince of the Persians, and of a Prince of the Greeks*. And thus the government of kingdoms, and the change of supremacy from one nation to another, must belong to the ministry of this order. It would also seem part of their office to instruct those men who are in positions of authority in matters pertaining to the administration of their office.

There is also a human good, not common to many, but belonging to an individual by himself, yet useful not to one only, but to many: *e.g.*, those things which all and each one must believe and observe, such as the articles of faith, the divine worship, and the like. This belongs to the *Archangels*, of whom Gregory says that *they announce the highest things*.[5] Thus we call Gabriel an *Archangel*, because he announced the Incarnation of the Word to the Virgin, which is an article of faith for all.

There is also a human good that belongs to each one singly. This pertains to the order of *Angels*, of whom Gregory says that they *announce minor matters*.[6] Hence they are called *guardian angels* according to *Ps.* xc. 11: *He hath given His angels charge over thee, to keep thee in all thy ways*. Therefore Dionysius says that the Archangels are between the Principalities and the Angels, because they have something in common with both: with the Principalities, *inasmuch as they lead the lower angels*, and rightly so, because in human affairs matters of restricted interest must be regulated according to those that are of common interest; and with the Angels, because *they announce to the Angels, and through the Angels, to us*, for it

---

[1] *Ibid.*   [2] *De Cael. Hier.*, IX, 2 (PG 3, 260).   [3] Ch. 71.   [4] Cf. Aristotle, *Eth.*, I, 2 (1094b 8).   [5] *In Evang.*, hom. 34 (PL 76, 1250).   [6] *Ibid.*

is the duty of the latter to announce to men *what concerns each individual*.[1] For this reason the lowest order has received as proper the name common to all, because, that is to say, its duty is to announce to us immediately. And so the name Archangel is, as it were, composed of both, since Archangel means a *Principal Angel*.

Gregory, however, assigns the ordering of the heavenly spirits differently.[2] For he places the Principalities among the spirits of the second rank, immediately after the Dominations, and the Virtues among the lowest, above the Archangels. But to one who considers the matter carefully, the difference is but small. For, according to Gregory, the Principalities are not placed over nations but *over good spirits*, as holding the principal place in the execution of the divine ministry. For, says he, *to be principal is to stand in a higher place than others*.[3] According to the explanation given above, we said that this belonged to the Virtues.—As for the Virtues, according to Gregory they are assigned to certain particular operations when, in some special case, outside the usual order of things, miracles have to be wrought. In this way they are fittingly numbered among the lowest angels.

Both explanations have the authority of the Apostle. For he says (*Ephes.* i. 20, 21): *Setting Him*, namely Christ, *on his right hand in heavenly places, above all principality, and power, and virtue, and dominion*, where it is clear that in the ascending order he places the Powers above the Principalities, and the Virtues above these, and the Dominations above the last named. This is the order adopted by Dionysius. But speaking of Christ to the Colossians (i. 16), he says: *Whether thrones or dominations or principalities or powers, all things were created by Him and in Him*. Here we see that beginning with the Thrones, in a descending order, he places the Dominations under them, beneath these the Principalities, and lower still the Powers. This is the order adopted by Gregory.

Mention is made of the Seraphim in *Isa.* vi. 2, 6; of the Cherubim, *Ezech.* i. 3; of the Archangels, in the canonical epistle of Jude (9): *When Michael the archangel, disputing with the devil*, etc.; and of the Angels, in the *Psalms*, as was already observed.

In all ordered powers there is this in common, that the lower all work by the power of the higher. Hence what we have stated as belonging to the order of Seraphim, all the lower angels accomplish by the power of the Seraphim; and the same applies to the other orders.

---

[1] *De Cael. Hier.*, IX, 2 (PG 3, 257).   [2] *In Evang.*, hom. 34 (PL 76, 1249).   [3] *Ibid.* (PL 76, 1251).

CHAPTER LXXXI

ON THE ORDERING OF MEN TO ONE ANOTHER AND TO OTHER THINGS

IN comparison with other intellectual substances, the human soul holds the lowest place, because, as we have already stated,[1] when it is first created it receives the knowledge of the order of the divine providence only in a general way; whereas, in order to acquire a perfect knowledge of that order in the particular, it needs to start from things themselves, in which the order of the divine providence is already established in detail. Consequently the human soul needs bodily organs, so as to be able to receive knowledge from corporeal things. But because of the weakness of its intellectual light, it is unable to acquire from things a perfect knowledge of what concerns man without the help of higher spirits; for God so disposes that the lower spirits reach perfection through the higher, as we have already proved.[2] Since, however, man has some share of intellectual light, brute animals, which have none at all, are subject to man according to the order of the divine providence. Hence it is said (*Gen.* i. 26): *Let us make man to our own image and likeness,* that is to say, inasmuch as he is an intelligent being, *and let him have dominion over the fishes of the sea, and the fowls of the air, and the beasts of the earth.*

Brute animals, though bereft of intellect, yet, since they have some kind of knowledge, are placed by the order of the divine providence above plants and other things devoid of knowledge. Hence it is said (*Gen.* i. 29-30): *Behold I have given you every herb bearing seed upon the earth, and all trees that have in themselves seed of their own kind, to be your meat, and to all the beasts of the earth.*

Among those that are wholly bereft of knowledge, one thing is placed before another according as one is more capable of action than another. For they have no share in the disposition of providence, but only in the execution.

And since man has both intellect and sense, and bodily power, these are ordered to one another, according to the disposition of the divine providence, in likeness to the order to be observed in the universe. For bodily power is subject to the powers of sense and intellect, as carrying out their commands; and the sensitive power is subject to the intellectual power, and is controlled by its rule.

In the same way, we find order among men. For those who excel in intellect are naturally rulers, whereas those who are less intelligent, but strong in body, seem made by nature for service, as Aristotle says in his *Politics.*[3]

[1] Ch. 80.   [2] Ch. 79.   [3] *Polit.,* I, 5 (1254b 25).

The statement of Solomon (*Prov.* xi. 29) is in agreement with this: *The fool shall serve the wise*; as also the words of *Exodus* (xviii. 21, 22): *Provide out of all the people wise men such as fear God . . . who may judge the people at all times.*

And just as in the works of one man there is disorder because the intellect is obsequious to the sensual power, while the sensual power, through the indisposition of the body, is drawn to the movement of the body, as is evident in those who limp: so, too, in human government disorder results when a man is set in authority, not because of his excelling in intellect, but because he has usurped the government by bodily force, or because he has been appointed to rule through motives of sensual desire. Nor does Solomon omit to mention this disorder, for he says (*Eccles.* x. 5, 6): *There is an evil that I have seen under the sun, as it were by an error proceeding from the face of the prince; a fool set in high dignity.* Now the divine providence is not denied by a disorder of this kind. For it results, by God's permission, from a defect in the lower agents, just as we have said of other evils.[1] Nor is the natural order wholly perverted by such a disorder, for the government of fools is weak, unless it be strengthened by the counsels of the wise. Hence it is said (*Prov.* xx. 18): *Designs are strengthened by counsels, and wars are to be arranged by governments*; and (xxiv. 5, 6): *A wise man is strong, and a knowing man, stout and valiant: because war is managed by due ordering, and there shall be safety when there are many counsels.* And since the counsellor rules him who receives his counsel, and, in a sense, governs him, it is said (*Prov.* xvii. 2) that *a wise servant shall rule over foolish sons.*

It is therefore evident that the divine providence imposes order on all things, and thus the Apostle says truly (*Rom.* xiii. 1) that *the things which are of God are well ordered.*

CHAPTER LXXXII

THAT THE INFERIOR BODIES ARE RULED BY GOD BY MEANS OF THE HEAVENLY BODIES

JUST as in intellectual substances some are of higher and some of lower degree, so too in corporeal substances. Now intellectual substances are governed by higher substances, so that the disposition of the divine providence may reach down proportionately to the lowest things, as we have already said.[2] Therefore, in like manner, bodies of lower degree are ruled by those of a higher.

Again. The higher a body is as regards its place, the more formal it is; and hence it is reasonably the place of a lower body, because form con-

[1] Ch. 71.　　[2] Ch. 78ff

tains even as place does. Thus water is more formal than earth, air than water, fire than air. Now the heavenly bodies have a higher place than all others. Therefore they are more formal and consequently more active than all other bodies. Therefore they act on lower bodies, and consequently the latter are ruled by them.

Besides. That which in its nature is perfected without contrariety is of more universal power than that which in its nature is not perfected without contrariety. For contrariety arises from differences which determine and contract the genus, and therefore in the conception of the intellect, inasmuch as it is universal, the species of contraries are not contrary to one another, since they coexist in the intellect. Now the heavenly bodies are perfected in their respective natures without any contrariety, for they are neither light nor heavy, neither hot nor cold, whereas lower bodies are not perfected in their respective natures without any contrariety. This is proved by their movements, for there is no contrary to the circular movement of the heavenly bodies, so that there can be nothing violent in them; whereas there are movements contrary to that of the lower bodies: *e.g.,* downward movement is contrary to upward movement. Therefore the heavenly bodies have a more universal power than lower bodies. Now universal powers move particular powers, as we have proved.[1] Therefore the heavenly bodies move and govern lower bodies.

Moreover. We have shown that all other things are ruled by intellectual substances.[2] Now the heavenly bodies resemble the intellectual substances more than other bodies do, inasmuch as they are incorruptible. Moreover, they are nearer to them, inasmuch as they are moved by them immediately, as we have shown above.[3] Therefore lower bodies are ruled by them.

Further. The first principle of movement must be something unmoved. Consequently, things that approach nearest to immobility must be the movers of others. Now the heavenly bodies approach nearer to the immobility of a first principle than do lower bodies, for they have but one species of movement, namely local, whereas other bodies have all manner of movements. Therefore the heavenly bodies move and rule the lower bodies.

Again. In each genus the first is the cause of that which comes after. Now the movement of the heavens is the first of all movements. *First,* because local movement precedes all others.—It precedes time, because it alone can be everlasting, as is proved in *Physics* viii.[4] It precedes in nature, because without it there could be no other, since a thing cannot be increased without a previous alteration, whereby that which was dissimilar is transformed and assimilated; nor can there be alteration without a previous change of place, since in order that there be alteration, the cause of alternation must become nearer to the subject altered than it was before.— And it precedes in perfection, because local movement does not cause a thing to vary in respect of something inherent, but only in respect of some-

---

[1] Ch. 78.   [2] *Ibid.*   [3] Ch. 80.   [4] Aristotle, *Phys.,* VIII, 7 (260b 29).

thing extrinsic; and for this reason it belongs to a thing already perfect.

Secondly, because, even among local movements, circular movement holds the first place. It is first in time, because it alone can be everlasting, as is proved in *Physics* viii.[1] It is first by nature, because it excels in simplicity and unity, since it is not divided into beginning, middle and end, but is all middle, as it were. And it is first in perfection, because it returns to its principle.

Thirdly, because only the movement of the heavens is always regular and uniform, since in the movements of heavy and light bodies the speed increases towards the end if the movement be natural, and decreases if the movement be violent.

Therefore the movement of the heavens must be the cause of all other movements.

Further. As that which is absolutely immovable is in comparison with movement absolutely, so is that which is immovable in respect of a particular kind of movement, in comparison with that particular movement. Now that which is absolutely immovable is the principle of all movement, as we have proved.[2] Therefore that which is immovable in respect of alteration is the principle of all alteration. But of all corporeal things the heavenly bodies alone are unalterable, and this is proved by their disposition, which is always the same. Therefore the body of the heavens is the cause of alteration in all alterable things. But in this lower world alteration is the principle of all movement, because alteration leads to augmentation and generation, and the generator is an essential mover in the local movement of heavy and light bodies. Consequently, the heavens must be the cause of all movement in these lower bodies.

Therefore it is evident that lower bodies are governed by God by means of the heavenly bodies.

CHAPTER LXXXIII

CONCLUSION OF THE FOREGOING

FROM all that has been proved hitherto, we are able to conclude that, as regards the design of the order to be imposed on things, God governs all things by Himself.[3] Therefore Gregory, commenting on *Job* xxxiv. 13 (*What other hath He appointed over the earth?*) says: *He who created the world by Himself governs it by Himself;*[4] and Boethius says: *God rules all things by Himself alone.*[5] As to the execution, however, He governs the lower by means of the higher things:—bodily things by means of spiritual things,[6] and hence Gregory says: *In this visible world nothing*

---

[1] *Op. cit.,* VIII, 8 (261b 27).   [2] *C. G.,* I, 13.   [3] Ch. 77.   [4] *Moral.,* XXIV, 20 (PL 76, 314).   [5] *De Consol.,* III, prose 12 (PL 63, 777).   [6] Ch. 78.

can be ruled except by means of the invisible creature;[1]—the lower spirits by the higher,[2] and hence Dionysius says that *the intelligent heavenly substances first of all shed forth the divine enlightenment on themselves, and bestow on us manifestations which surpass our capacity;*[3]—and the lower bodies by the higher,[4] and hence Dionysius says that *the sun contributes to the generation of visible bodies, as also to life itself, by means of nourishment, growth and perfection, by cleansing and renewing them.*[5]

Of all these together Augustine says: *As the grosser and lower bodies are ruled in a certain orderly way by bodies of greater subtlety and power, so all bodies are ruled by the rational spirit of life, and the sinful rational spirit by the righteous rational spirit.*[6]

CHAPTER LXXXIV

THAT THE HEAVENLY BODIES DO NOT ACT ON OUR INTELLECTS

FROM what has been said it is at once clear that the heavenly bodies cannot be the causes of what belongs to the intellect. For it has already been shown that the order of divine providence requires lower things to be ruled and moved by the higher.[7] Now the intellect, according to the order of nature, surpasses all bodies, as we have already proved.[8] Consequently, the heavenly bodies cannot act directly on the intellect. Therefore they cannot be the direct cause of what belongs to the intellect.

Again. No body acts except through movement, as is proved in *Physics* viii.[9] Now things that are immovable are not caused by movement, because nothing is the result of the movement of an agent except when the agent, while in motion, moves the patient. Consequently, things that are wholly outside movement cannot be caused by the heavenly bodies. But what belongs to the intellect is, properly speaking, wholly outside movement, as the Philosopher states.[10] In fact, *the soul becomes prudent and wise through being free from movement*, as he says in the same place. It is not possible, therefore, that the heavenly bodies be the direct cause of what belongs to the intellect.

Besides. If nothing be caused by a body except in so far as the body causes movement through being moved, it follows that whatever receives an impression from a body must be moved. Now nothing is moved except a body, as is proved in *Physics* vi.[11] Therefore whatever receives an impression from a body must be either a body or a bodily power. But it was proved in the Second Book that the intellect is neither a body nor a bodily power.[12] Therefore the heavenly bodies cannot directly act on the intellect.

[1] *Dial.*, IV, 6 (PL 77, 329).   [2] Ch. 79.   [3] *De Cael. Hier.*, IV, 2 (PG 3, 180).
[4] Ch. 82.   [5] *De Div. Nom.*, IV, 4 (PG 3, 697, 700).   [6] *De Trin.*, III, 4 (PL 42, 873).
[7] Ch. 78ff.   [8] *C. G.*, II, 49ff.   [9] Aristotle, *Phys.*, VIII, 6 (259b 7).   [10] *Op. cit.*,
VII, 3 (247b 1).   [11] *Op. cit.*, VI, 4 (234b 10).   [12] *C. G.*, II, 49ff.

Further. Whatever is moved by a thing is reduced by it from potentiality to act. Now nothing is reduced from potentiality to act except by something in act. Therefore every agent and mover must be, in some way, in act with regard to those things to which the passive or moved subject is in potentiality. But the heavenly bodies are not actually intelligible because they are singular sensibles. Since, then, our intellect is not in potentiality except to what is actually intelligible, it is impossible for the heavenly bodies to act directly on the intellect.

Moreover. A thing's proper operation follows its nature, which generated things acquire by generation, together with their proper operation. This may be seen in heavy and light things, which have their proper movement as soon as they are generated, unless there be an obstacle; and for this reason the generator is said to be a mover. Consequently, that which, as regards the cause of its nature, is not subject to the action of the heavenly bodies, cannot be subject to them in respect of its operation. Now the intellectual part of man is not caused by any bodily principles, but is entirely from an extrinsic source, as we proved above.[1] Therefore the operation of the intellect is not directly subject to the heavenly bodies.

Again. Things caused by the heavenly movements are subject to time, which is *the measure of the first heavenly movement.*[2] Therefore those things that wholly abstract from time are not subject to heavenly movements. Now the intellect in its operation abstracts from time, as also from place; for it considers the universal which abstracts from here and now. Hence the operation of the intellect is not subject to heavenly movements.

Further. Nothing acts outside its species. Now the act of understanding transcends the species and form of any corporeal agent, since every corporeal form is material and individuated; whereas the act of understanding is informed by its object which is universal and immaterial. Consequently, no body can understand by means of its corporeal form. Much less, therefore, can any body whatsoever cause in another the act of understanding.

Besides. A thing is not subject to that which is beneath it in respect of that by which it is united to things above it. Now our soul, inasmuch as it is intelligent, is united to intellectual substances, which in the order of nature are above heavenly bodies; because our soul cannot understand except in so far as it derives its intellectual light from those substances. Therefore the intellectual operation cannot be directly subject to the heavenly movements.

Moreover. We shall find a confirmation of this if we consider what philosophers have said in the matter. The natural philosophers of old, *e.g.,* Democritus, Empedocles and others, held that intellect does not differ from sense, as is stated in *Metaph.* iv[3] and *De Anima* iii.[4] Hence it followed that, as sense is a corporeal power resulting from a corporeal transmuta-

---

[1] *C. G.*, II, 86 ff.   [2] Aristotle, *Phys.*, IV, 14 (223b 17).   [3] Aristotle, *Metaph.*, IV, 5 (1009b 13).   [4] Aristotle, *De An.*, III, 3 (427a 21).

tion, so likewise was the intellect. Therefore they said, as the transmutation of the lower bodies follows transmutation of the higher bodies, that intellectual operation follows the movements of the heavenly bodies. In the words of Homer: *The intellect of gods and men on earth is even as their day, which comes from the father of men and gods,*[1]—namely, the sun, or rather Jupiter, whom they called the supreme god, understanding by this the whole heavens, as Augustine says.[2]

Hence, too, followed the opinion of the Stoics who said that intellectual knowledge is caused by images of bodies being imprinted on the mind, just as a mirror, or a page, receives the imprinted characters without any action on its part, as Boethius relates.[3] According to this opinion, it followed that our intellectual notions were chiefly the result of impressions received from heavenly bodies; and consequently it was chiefly the Stoics who held that man's life was bound by a kind of fatal necessity.—This opinion, however, is shown to be false, as Boethius says in the same reference, by the fact that the intellect is capable of composing and dividing, compares the highest with the lowest, and knows universals and simple forms,—none of which is within the capacity of bodies. Consequently, it is evident that the intellect does not merely receive the images of bodies, but is possessed of a power that transcends bodies; for the external senses, which receive only images of bodies, do not extend to the things mentioned above.

All subsequent philosophers, however, distinguished intellect from sense, and assigned, not bodies, but immaterial things as the cause of our knowledge. Thus Plato ascribed this to the *Forms* and Aristotle to the *agent intellect*.

From all this we may gather that to say that the heavenly bodies are the cause of our knowledge is a sequel to the opinion of those who held that intellect does not differ from sense, as Aristotle also observes.[4] Now it is evident that this opinion is false. Therefore, manifestly false is likewise the opinion of those who maintained that the heavenly bodies are the direct cause of our knowledge.

For this reason Holy Scripture assigns as the cause of our knowledge, not a body, but God (*Job* xxxv. 10, 11): *Where is God who made me; who hath given songs in the night; who teacheth us more than the beasts of the earth, and instructeth us more than the fowls of the air?* Again (*Ps.* xciii. 10): *He that teacheth man knowledge.*

Nevertheless, we must observe that, although the heavenly bodies cannot be the direct cause of our knowledge, they can contribute something indirectly towards it. For though the intellect is not a power of the body, yet in us the operation of the intellect cannot be exercised without the operation of bodily powers, namely, the imagination, the memory and the cogita-

---

[1] *Odyssey*, XVIII, 136ff.   [2] *De Civit. Dei*, IV, 11 (PL 41, 121).   [3] *De Consol.*, V, verse 4 (PL 63, 850).   [4] *De An.*, III, 3 (427a 21).

tive power, as we have already shown.[1] Hence it is that when the activity of these powers is hampered by some bodily indisposition, the activity of the intellect is also hampered, as may be seen in cases of frenzy, lethargy and the like. For the same reason, goodness of disposition in a man's body fits him to understand easily, inasmuch as these bodily powers are strengthened by such a disposition. Therefore it is said in *De Anima* ii, that *it is to be observed that men of soft flesh are of quick intelligence*.[2] Now the disposition of the human body is subject to the heavenly movements. For Augustine says that *it is not altogether absurd to ascribe the mere differences between bodies to the influence of the stars*;[3] and Damascene says that *the various planets produce in us various temperaments, habits and dispositions*.[4] Consequently, the heavenly bodies contribute indirectly to the goodness of our understanding. Thus, even as physicians are able to judge of a man's intellect from his bodily temperament, as a proximate disposition thereto, so too can an astrologer, from the heavenly movements, as being a remote cause of this disposition. In this sense we can approve of the saying of Ptolemy: *When Mercury is in one of Saturn's regions at the time of a man's birth, and he is waxing, he bestows on him a quick intelligence of the inner nature of things*.[5]

CHAPTER LXXXV

THAT THE HEAVENLY BODIES ARE NOT THE CAUSE OF OUR WILLING AND CHOOSING

IT is also evident from the foregoing that the heavenly bodies are not the cause of our willing and choosing.

For the will is in the intellectual part of the soul, according to the Philosopher.[6] Therefore, if the heavenly bodies cannot make a direct impression on our intellect, as we have proved,[7] neither will they be able to influence the will directly.

Moreover. All choice and actual willing in us is caused immediately through an intellectual apprehension, for the apprehended good is the object of the will.[8] Therefore there cannot ensue perverseness of choice, unless the judgment of the intellect err in the particular object of choice, as the Philosopher states.[9] But the heavenly bodies are not the cause of our intellectual apprehension. Therefore neither can they be the cause of our choice.

Further. Whatever takes place in this lower world, through the influence

[1] *C. G.*, II, 68.　[2] Aristotle, *De An.*, II, 9 (421a 26).　[3] *De Civit. Dei*, V, 6 (PL 41, 146).　[4] *De Fide Orth.*, II, 7 (PG 94, 893).　[5] Ptolemy, *Centiloquium*, verbum 38.　[6] *De An.*, III, 9 (432b 6).　[7] Ch. 84.　[8] Aristotle, *De An.*, III, 10 (433a 16).　[9] *Eth.*, VII, 3 (1147a 1).

of heavenly bodies, happens naturally, since the things here below are naturally subordinate to them. If, therefore, the heavenly bodies have any influence on our choice, this must happen naturally; so that, in fact, man naturally chooses to perform his actions, even as brute animals perform theirs
from natural instinct, and as inanimate bodies are moved naturally. Consequently, there will not be two active principles, namely, the free and the
natural, but only one, namely, nature. But Aristotle proves the contrary.[1]
Therefore it is untrue that the influence of the heavenly bodies is the cause of
our choice.

Besides. Things that happen naturally are brought to their end by determinate means. Hence they always happen in the same way, for nature is
determined to uniformity. But man's choice tends to the end in various
ways, both in morals and in things made by art. Therefore man's choosing
does not come from nature.

Again. Things which are done naturally, for the most part are done
rightly, since nature fails but seldom. Consequently, if man chose by nature, his choice would be right for the most part; which is clearly false.
Therefore man does not choose naturally, although this would be the case
if his choice were subject to the influence of the heavenly bodies.

Further. Things of the same species do not differ in those natural operations which result from the specific nature. Hence each swallow makes its
nest in the same way, and every man equally understands the first principles which are known naturally. Now choosing is an operation that results from the human species. Consequently, if man chose naturally, all
men would choose in the same way; and this is evidently untrue, both in
morals and in things made by art.

Moreover. Virtue and vice are proper principles of choice, because the
virtuous and the vicious man differ through choosing contraries. Now
political virtues and vices are not in us by nature but by habituation. The
Philosopher proves this from the fact that we acquire the habit of those
operations to which we are accustomed, especially from childhood.[2] Our
choosing therefore does not come from nature, and consequently, it is not
caused by the influence of the heavenly bodies, whose effects happen
naturally.

Again. The heavenly bodies make no direct impression except on bodies,
as we have shown.[3] Consequently, if they are the cause of our choosing,
this will be by an impression made either on our bodies or on external
bodies. Yet in neither way can they be a sufficient cause of our choosing.
For the objective presentation of some corporeal thing cannot be the sufficient cause of our choice, since it is clear that when a man meets with
something that pleases him, be it meat or woman, the temperate man is
not moved to choose these things, whereas the intemperate is. Again, no
possible change wrought in our bodies by an impression of the heavenly

---

[1] *Phys.*, II, 5 (196b 16).   [2] *Eth.*, II, 1 (1103a 19).   [3] Ch. 84.

bodies can suffice to cause us to make a choice. For all that results there-from are certain passions, more or less violent, and passions, however violent, are not a sufficient cause of choosing, since the same passions lead the incontinent to follow them by choice, and fail to induce the continent man. Therefore it cannot be said that the heavenly bodies cause our choice.

Further. No power is bestowed on a being without a purpose. Now man has the power of judging and of taking counsel about all matters relative to his own actions, whether in the use of externals, or in giving a loose or a tight rein to his internal passions. But this would be of no use, if our choice were the result of the heavenly bodies and not in our own power. Therefore the heavenly bodies are not the cause of our choice.

Besides. *Man is naturally a political or social animal.*[1] This is evident from the fact that one man does not suffice for himself if he live alone, because the things are few wherein nature makes adequate provision for man, since she gave him his reason by means of which he might provide himself with all necessaries of life, such as food, clothes and so forth, for the production of which one man is not enough. Therefore man has a natural inclination to live in society. Now the order of providence does not deprive a thing of what is natural to it; rather is each thing provided for according to its nature, as we have said above.[2] Therefore man is not so made by the order of providence as to be deprived of social life. Yet he would be deprived of it, were our choice to proceed from the influence of the heavenly bodies, like the natural instinct of other animals.

Moreover. Laws and precepts of conduct would be useless were man not the master of his own choice; and useless, too, would be punishments and rewards for the good and the wicked, if it were not in our power to choose this or that. And yet, if there were not such things, there would be at once an end to society. Consequently, man is not so made according to the order of providence that his choice should result from the movements of the heavenly bodies.

Again. A man's choice is of good and evil things. Hence, if our choosing were the result of the movements of the stars, it would follow that the stars are the essential cause of wicked deeds. But that which is evil has no natural cause, since evil results from a defect in a cause, and has no essential cause, as we have proved.[3] Therefore it is impossible that our choice be the direct and essential effect of the heavenly bodies.

Someone, however, might endeavor to meet this argument by saying that every evil choice results from the desire of some particular good, as we have proved above.[4] Thus the choice of the lustful man arises from his desire for a good consisting in sexual pleasure; and some star causes movement to this general good. In fact, this is necessary for the generating of animals; and this common good was not to be omitted because of the

---

[1] Aristotle, *Eth.*, I, 7 (1097b 11)   [2] Ch. 71.   [3] Ch. 4ff.   [4] Ch. 5 and 6.

particular evil of an individual who, through this instigation, chooses an evil.

But this reply is not sufficient if we suppose the heavenly bodies to be the essential cause of our choice by making direct impressions on our intellect and will. For the impression made by a universal cause is received in a thing according to that thing's mode. Consequently, the effect of a star, which causes a movement towards pleasure connected in an ordinate manner with generation, will be received into a thing according to the mode proper thereto. Thus we see that various animals have various ways and various times of coming together, as becomes their nature, as Aristotle remarks.[1] Hence the intellect and will receive the impression of that star according to their mode. Now when a thing is desired according to the mode of the intellect and reason, there is no sin in the choice, which is always evil through not being according to right reason. Therefore if the heavenly bodies were the cause of our choice, we should never make an evil choice.

Further. No active power extends to things above the species and nature of the agent, because every agent acts through its form. Now, to will, as also to understand, transcends every corporeal species; for just as our intellect understands the universal, so our will tends to the universal: *e.g., we dislike every kind of thief,* as the Philosopher says.[2] Therefore the act of the will is not caused by a heavenly body.

Besides. Things directed to an end are proportioned to that end. Now, our choice is directed to happiness as to the last end. And this does not consist in bodily goods, but in the union of our soul, through the intellect, with divine things. This was proved above to be the case both according to the teaching of Faith and according to the teaching of the philosophers.[3] Therefore the heavenly bodies cannot be the cause of our choice.

Hence it is said (*Jer.* x. 2, 3): *Be not afraid of the signs of heaven which the heathens fear; for the laws of people are vain.*

Thus is refuted the opinion of the Stoics,[4] who held that all our actions, even our every choice, are governed by the heavenly bodies.—This is also said to have been the opinion of the Pharisees among the Jews of old.[5]— And the Priscillianists were also guilty of this error, as is stated in *De Haeresibus.*[6]

This was also the opinion of the ancient physicists, who held that intellect does not differ from sense.[7] Therefore Empedocles, as quoted by Aristotle,[8] said that *the will of man, like that of other animals, is strengthened presently,* i.e., according to the present moment, by the movement of the heavens which is the cause of time.

We must observe, however, that although the heavenly bodies are not the

[1] *De Hist. Anim.,* V, 8 (542a 1).   [2] *Rhetor.,* II, 4 (1382a 6).   [3] Ch. 25ff.   [4] Cf. ch. 84.   [5] Josephus, *Antiquities,* XIII, 5, 9 (VII, 310, 312).   [6] St. Augustine, *De Haeres.,* 70 (PL 42, 44).   [7] Cf. ch. 84.   [8] *De An.,* III, 3 (427a 22).

direct cause of our choosing, by making a direct impression on our will, nevertheless indirectly they do occasion our choice, through making an impression on bodies. This happens in two ways. First, the impression made by a heavenly body on bodies other than our own may be an occasion of our making a particular choice. Thus, when through the action of the heavenly bodies the air becomes intensely cold, we choose to warm ourselves by the fire, or to do something similarly befitting the moment. Secondly, they may make impressions on our own body. Now when the body is affected, movements of the passions arise, either because such impressions make us liable to certain passions (for instance, the bilious are prone to anger), or because they produce in us a bodily disposition that occasions a particular choice (thus, when we are ill, we choose to take medicine).—Sometimes, too, the heavenly bodies are a cause of human acts, when through an indisposition of the body a person goes out of his mind, and loses the use of reason. Such persons are not capable of choosing, properly speaking, but they are moved by a natural instinct, like brute animals.

It is evident, however, and we know by experience, that such occasions, whether exterior or interior, are not a necessary cause of choice; since man can use his reason to reject or obey them. But those who follow their natural bent are in the majority, and few, namely, the wise alone, are those who avoid the occasions of ill-doing and who follow not the impulse of nature. Hence Ptolemy says that *the soul of the wise man assists the work of the stars*;[1] and that the astrologer *cannot read the stars unless he knows well the bent of the mind and the natural temperament*; and that *the astrologer should not express himself in detail but only in general terms*.[2] For the majority do not resist their bodily disposition, and so the impression of the stars takes effect in them; but not always in this or that individual who, it may happen, uses his reason to resist that inclination.

CHAPTER LXXXVI

THAT CORPOREAL EFFECTS IN THIS LOWER WORLD DO NOT RESULT OF NECESSITY FROM THE ACTION OF THE HEAVENLY BODIES

NOT only are the heavenly bodies unable to necessitate man's choice, but even corporeal effects do not proceed from them of necessity.

For the impressions of universal causes are received by their effects according to the mode of the recipient. Now the things of this lower world are fluctuating and changeable, both by reason of matter, which is in po-

---

[1] Ptolemy, *Centiloquium*, verbum 8. [2] *Op. cit.*, verbum 1.

tentiality to several forms, and because of the contrariety of forms and powers. Therefore the impressions of the heavenly bodies are not received with necessity by these lower bodies.

Again. A remote cause does not lead to a necessary result, unless the middle cause be also necessary. In a syllogism, for instance, if the major premise be a *necessary* proposition, and the minor a *contingent* proposition, the conclusion that follows is not *necessary*. Now the heavenly bodies are remote causes, and the proximate causes of the effects here below are the active and passive powers in the bodies of this lower world; and these are not necessary, but contingent, causes, for they can fail in a few instances. Therefore the heavenly bodies do not produce necessary effects in these lower bodies.

Besides. The heavenly bodies are always moved in the same way. Consequently, if the heavenly bodies produced a necessary effect on these lower bodies, there would be no variety in the things that happen in this world. Now, they are not always the same, but only for the most part. Therefore they do not happen necessarily.

Moreover. Many contingents do not make one necessary thing, since, just as each one of them by itself may fail in its effect, so too may all of them together. Now it is evident that in these lower bodies each thing that happens through the influence of the heavenly bodies is contingent. Therefore the things that happen here below through the influence of heavenly bodies are not necessarily connected with necessity, since it is evident that each one of them may be hindered.

Further. The heavenly bodies are natural agents and therefore require matter on which to act. Consequently, their action does not remove what is required by matter. Now the matter on which the heavenly bodies act is the bodies of this lower world. And since these are by nature corruptible, they can fail in action just as they can fail in being, so that their nature requires that they should produce their effects without necessity. Therefore the effects of the heavenly bodies on the bodies of this lower world do not result of necessity.

Perhaps someone will say that the effects of the heavenly bodies must necessarily follow, and yet potentiality is not therefore removed from this lower world, because each effect is in potentiality before it comes into being, and is then said to be possible; but when it is in act, it passes from potentiality to necessity. The whole of this process is subject to the heavenly movements, and consequently a given effect is not prevented from being at some time possible, although it is necessary that it be at length produced. In fact, Albumasar tries to defend the *possible* along these lines in the First Book of his *Introductorium*.

But the *possible* cannot be defended in this way. For there is one kind of *possible* which *follows from that which is necessary*. Because that which must be necessarily, is possible; since what cannot possibly be, is impossible, and that which is impossible, necessarily is not. Consequently [if what is necessary is not possible] what must necessarily be, must necessarily not be: which is impossible. Hence it is impossible that the same thing should be necessarily, and yet that at the same time it should be impossible for it to be. Therefore the possible follows from the necessary.

But it is not this kind of *possible* that we need defend against the contention that effects result of necessity; we must rather defend the *possible which is contrary to the necessary*, in the sense in which we say that that is possible *which can be and not be*. Now a thing is not said to be possible or contingent merely because it is at one time potential and at another time actual, as the foregoing reply supposes; since thus, even in the heavenly movements there is possibility and contingency. For the sun and moon are not always actually in conjunction or opposition, but sometimes actually and sometimes potentially: and yet these are necessary phenomena, since such matters are subject to demonstration. But the possible or contingent that is contrary to the necessary is of such a nature that there is no necessity for it to be, when it is not. And the reason for this is that it does not follow necessarily from its cause. Thus we say that it is contingent that Socrates will sit, whereas it is necessary that he will die, because the latter results from its cause necessarily, but not the former. Consequently, if it follows necessarily from the movements of the heavenly bodies that their effects will result at some time, there will be nothing possible or contingent contrary to that which is necessary.

We must observe, however, that Avicenna, having a mind to prove that the effects of the heavenly bodies result of necessity, offers the following argument.[1] If an effect of the heavenly bodies is hindered, this must be due to some cause either voluntary or natural. Now every cause, whether voluntary or natural, is reducible to some heavenly principle. Therefore even the impediment to the heavenly bodies' effect results from some heavenly principles. Consequently, if we take the whole heavenly order at once, it is impossible for its effect ever to fail. Whence he concludes that the heavenly bodies must necessarily produce effects in this lower world, both voluntary and natural.

This argument, as Aristotle observes,[2] was employed by some of the ancients who denied the existence of chance and fortune, for the reason that every effect has its determinate cause, and that given the cause the effect follows of necessity; so that, since everything happens necessarily, nothing can be referred to chance and fortune.

He solves this argument by denying the two propositions on which it is based.[3] One is that *given any cause whatsoever, the effect must follow of necessity*. For this is not true of every cause, since even the essential, proper and sufficient cause of a certain effect may be hindered through the

[1] *Metaph.*, X, 1 (fol. 108ra).   [2] *Phys.*, II, 4 (195b 36).   [3] Aristotle, *Metaph.*, V, 3 (1027a 8).

entrance of another cause, so that it fails to produce that effect.—The other proposition which Aristotle denies is that *not everything that exists in any way whatever has a per se cause, but only that which exists per se; and things which exist accidentally have no cause at all*. For instance, that a man be musical is to be ascribed to a cause, but that he be musical as well as white is not due to any cause. Because whatever things concur because of some cause are mutually related by reason of that cause; whereas accidental things are not mutually related, and consequently they are not the result of a *per se* active cause, but are merely an accidental result. Thus it is accidental to the teacher of music that his pupil be a white man, since it is outside his intention, for his intention is to teach one who is receptive of instruction.

Accordingly, given any particular effect, we shall say that it had a cause from which it did not necessarily result, because it might have been hindered by the accidental concurrence of another cause. And although we may trace that concurrent cause to some higher cause, we cannot ascribe to any cause the concurrence itself that proved to be a hindrance. Consequently, we cannot say that the hindrance to this or that effect is to be traced to some heavenly principle. Therefore we cannot say that the effects of heavenly bodies happen of necessity in this lower world.

Hence Damascene says in the Second Book that *the heavenly bodies do not cause the generation of things that are made, nor the corruption of things that are destroyed;*[1] because, that is to say, their effects do not follow of necessity.

Aristotle likewise says that *many things betokened by corporeal things, even heavenly bodies, by water for instance or wind, do not happen. For if a stronger movement arise than that which presaged the future, the latter fails in its effect; even so, we often renounce our first intent, though it be well conceived, because of other and better beginnings.*[2]

Ptolemy also says: *Again, we must not think that the things which occur through the influence of higher beings are inevitable, like those which happen by divine decree and are altogether unavoidable, and such as do actually and necessarily occur.*[3] He says again in the *Centiloquium: These principles which I give you are midway between the necessary and the possible.*[4]

---

[1] *De Fide Orth.*, II, 7 (PG 94, 893).   [2] Cf. *De Divin. per Somn.*, II (463b 23).
[3] Ptolemy, *Quadripartitum*, I, 2.   [4] Ptolemy, *Centiloquium*, verbum 1.

CHAPTER LXXXVII

THAT THE MOVEMENT OF A HEAVENLY BODY IS NOT THE CAUSE OF OUR CHOOSING BY VIRTUE OF ITS SOUL MOVING US, AS SOME SAY

WE must observe, however, that Avicenna also holds that the movements of the heavenly bodies are the causes of our choice, not merely by being its occasion, but even as a *per se* cause.[1] For he holds the heavenly bodies to be animate, and hence, since the movement of the heavens proceeds from its soul, and is the movement of a body, it follows that just as, inasmuch as it is a body's movement, it must have the power to transform bodies, so, inasmuch as it comes from a soul, it must have the power to make impressions on our souls. Hence the movement of the heavens is the cause of our acts of will and choice. The position of Albumasar would seem to come to the same, according to the First Book of his *Introductorium*.[2]

But this position is unreasonable. Because any effect that is caused by an agent through an instrument, must be proportionate to the instrument as well as to the agent; for we do not employ any instrument for any effect. Consequently, it is not possible to produce by means of an instrument an effect which is utterly outside the scope of its action. Now it is altogether beyond the scope of a body's action to affect the intellect or will, as was proved above,[3] except perhaps indirectly by making an impression on the body, as we have said.[4] Therefore it is impossible for the soul of a heavenly body, if it have one, to make an impression on the intellect and will by means of the movement of that heavenly body.

Moreover. The particular active cause, while acting, bears a resemblance to the universal active cause, and imitates it. Now if a human soul were to make an impression on another human soul through an action of the body, as when it reveals its mind by means of vocal signs, the bodily action that proceeds from the one soul does not reach the other soul except by means of the body; for the vocal sounds affect the organ of hearing, and thus, being perceived by the sense, its meaning reaches the understanding. Consequently, if the celestial soul makes an impression on our soul by means of a corporeal movement, its action will not reach our soul except through a change effected in our body. But this does not cause our choice, but only occasions it, as we have shown above.[5] Therefore the movement of the heavens is not the cause, but only the occasion, of our choice.

Again. Since mover and moved must be simultaneous, as is proved in

---

[1] *Metaph.*, X, 1 (fol. 108rb).   [2] Cf. P. Duhem, *Le système du monde*, II, pp. 374-376.   [3] Ch. 84ff.   [4] *Ibid.*   [5] *Ibid.*

Physics vii,[1] it follows that movement must come from the first mover to the last thing moved in a certain order, so that, namely, the mover moves that which is distant through that which is nearest. Now our body is nearer to the body of the heavens, which is supposed to be moved by the soul united to it, than our soul, which is not related to the body of the heavens except through its own body. This is proved by the fact that separated intellects are not related to the body of the heavens, except perhaps as a mover to that which it moves. Therefore the impression of a heavenly body that originates in its soul does not reach our soul save through our body. But our soul is not moved in response to the movement of the body, except accidentally, nor does choice result from an impression made on the body except as occasioned thereby, as we have said. Therefore the movement of the heavens cannot be the cause of our choice on the hypothesis that it is from the soul of the heavens.

Besides. According to the opinion of Avicenna and certain other philosophers, the agent intellect is a separate substance which acts on our souls in so far as it makes what is potentially intelligible to be understood actually.[2] Now this is the result of abstraction from all material conditions, as is clear from what we have said in the Second Book.[3] Consequently, that which acts directly on the soul does so, not by means of a corporeal movement, but rather by abstraction of everything corporeal. Therefore the soul of the heavens, if it have a soul, cannot be, through the movement of the heavens, the cause of our acts of choosing or understanding.

By the same arguments it can be proved that the movement of the heavens is not the cause of our choice by the power of a separate substance, if anyone suppose the heaven not to be animate, but to be moved by a separate substance.

CHAPTER LXXXVIII

THAT CREATED SEPARATE SUBSTANCES CANNOT BE THE DIRECT CAUSES OF OUR ACTS OF CHOOSING AND WILLING, BUT GOD ALONE

WE must not think, however, that the souls of heavenly bodies, if there be any,[4] or any separate intellectual substances, can directly impel our will or cause our choice.

For the actions of all creatures are subordinate to the divine providence; so that they are unable to act outside its laws. Now it is a law of providence that everything is moved immediately by its proximate cause. Consequently, unless this order be observed, the higher created cause can neither

---

[1] Aristotle, *Phys.*, VII, 2 (243a 3).   [2] Cf. *C. G.*, II, 76.   [3] *C. G.*, II, 50, 59.
[4] *C. G.*, II, 70.

move nor act. But the proximate moving cause of the will is the apprehended good, which is its object, and the will is moved by it as sight is by color. Therefore no created substance can move the will except by means of the apprehended good—in so far, namely, as it shows it that a particular thing is good to do; and this is *to persuade*. Therefore no created substance can act on the will, or cause our choice, except by way of persuasion.

Again. A thing is naturally moved by, and passive to, that agent by whose form it can be reduced to act; since every agent acts by its form. Now the will is made actual by the appetible object, which satisfies the movement of its desire. But the will's desire is satisfied by the divine good alone as its last end, as we have proved above.[1] Therefore God alone can move the will as an agent.

Besides. The natural inclination (which we call the *natural appetite*) of inanimate things for their proper end is like the will or intellectual appetite in intellectual substances. Now a natural inclination cannot be given except by the maker of nature. Therefore the will cannot be inclined to anything except by the maker of the intellectual nature. But this belongs to God alone, as we have proved above.[2] Therefore He alone can incline our will to anything.

Moreover. As is stated in *Ethics* iii, a violent action *is one in which the principle is external, and the one who suffers violence contributes nothing.*[3] Consequently, if the will be moved by an external principle, its movement will be violent;—and I speak of being moved by an external principle that moves *as an agent,* and not *as an end.* Now the violent is opposed to the voluntary. Therefore it is impossible that the will be moved by an external principle as an agent, but every movement of the will must come from within. But no created substance is united to the intellectual soul in its inmost being except God alone, Who alone is the cause and sustainer of its being. Therefore the movement of the will can be caused by none but God alone.

Further. *Violent* movement is contrary to *natural* and *voluntary* movement, because both of these must be from an internal principle. But an external agent does not cause a natural movement except in so far as it causes an internal principle of movement to be in the movable thing. Thus, the generator, that gives the form of gravity to the generated heavy body, gives it a natural downward movement. And nothing else external can move a natural body without violence, except perhaps indirectly, as that which removes an obstacle, for such a thing makes use of natural movement or action rather than causes it. Therefore that agent alone can cause a movement of the will without violence which causes the internal principle of that movement, namely, the power itself of the will. And this is God, Who alone creates the soul, as we proved in the Second Book.[4] Therefore God alone can move the will, as an agent, without violence.

[1] Ch. 37.   [2] *C. G.*, II, 87.   [3] Aristotle, *Eth.*, III, 1 (1110b 1).   [4] *C. G.*, II, 87.

This is expressed in the words of *Prov.* xxi. 1: *The heart of the King is in the hand of the Lord, whithersoever He will He shall turn it*; and *Philip.* ii. 13: *It is God who worketh in us both to will and to accomplish, according to His good will.*

CHAPTER LXXXIX

THAT THE MOVEMENT OF THE WILL, AND NOT ONLY THE POWER OF THE WILL, IS CAUSED BY GOD

SOME, nevertheless, unable to understand how God can cause in us the movement of the will without prejudice to the liberty of the will, have tried to give a false exposition to the authorities quoted.[1] They say, in fact, that God causes in us *to will and to accomplish*, by causing in us the power to will, and not by causing us to will this or that. This is the exposition of Origen who defended free choice in a sense contrary to the aforesaid authorities.[2]

Apparently this was the source of the opinion of some who maintained that providence does not regard things subject to free choice, namely, our elections, but only external happenings. For he who chooses to get or do something, for instance, to build or get rich, is not always able to succeed; and so the outcome of our actions is not subject to our free choice, but is ordained by providence.

But the authority of Scripture is in manifest opposition to all this. For it is said (*Isa.* xxvi. 12): *O Lord, Thou hast wrought all our works in us.* Hence we receive from God not only the power to will, but also our very operations.

Further. The very words of Solomon, *Whithersoever He will He shall turn it,* show that the divine causality extends not only to the will, but also to its act.

Again. Not only does God give things their powers, but it is also true that nothing can act by its own power, unless it act by His power, as we proved above.[3] Therefore man cannot use the power of will given to him, except in so far as he acts by God's power. Now that by whose power the agent acts, is the cause not only of the power but also of the act. This is apparent in the craftsman, by whose power the instrument acts, even though it may not have received its own form from the craftsman in question, and is merely applied by him to action. Therefore God is the cause not only of our will but also of our willing.

Further. Order in spiritual beings is more perfect than in corporeal beings. Now in corporeal beings every movement is caused by the first

---

[1] Cf. end of ch. 88.   [2] *Peri Archon*, III, 1 (PG 11, 293).   [3] Ch. 67 and 70.

movement. Therefore in spiritual beings every movement of the will must be caused by the first will, which is God's.

Besides. We proved above that God is the cause of every action, and that He works in every agent.[1] Therefore He is the cause of the movements of the will.

Again. Aristotle argues in the same sense as follows [2] There must be some cause which explains the fact that a person understands, takes counsel, chooses and wills, because everything new must have a cause. Now if the cause of these acts was another act of counsel and another act of will, since in such things we cannot proceed to infinity, we must come at length to something first. And this first thing must be something better than the reason. Now nothing but God is better than the intellect and the reason. Therefore God is the first principle of our acts of counsel and will.

CHAPTER XC

THAT HUMAN CHOICE AND WILL ARE SUBJECT TO DIVINE PROVIDENCE

HENCE it follows that human will and choice are subject to divine providence.

For whatsoever God does, He does according to the order of His providence. Therefore, since He is the cause of our choice and will, these are subject to divine providence.

Moreover. All corporeal beings are governed by means of spiritual beings, as we have shown above.[3] Now spiritual beings act on corporeal beings by their will. Consequently, if the acts of choice and the movements of the will in intellectual substances are not the concern of God's providence, it follows that corporeal beings also are withdrawn from His providence, so that there will be no providence at all.

Besides. The higher a thing is placed in the universe, the more must it participate in the order in which the good of the universe consists. Hence Aristotle reproaches the ancient philosophers for admitting chance and fortune in the scheme of the heavenly bodies, but not in the things of the lower world.[4] Now intellectual substances hold a higher place than corporeal substances. Therefore if corporeal substances, as regards their essence and operation, are included in the order of providence, much more so are intellectual substances.

Again. Those things which are nearest to the end are more subject to the order whereby things are directed to the end, since by their means even other things are ordered to the end. Now the actions of intellectual sub-

[1] *Ibid.*   [2] *Eth. Eudem.*, VII, 14 (1248a 18).   [3] Ch. 78.   [4] *Phys.*, II, 4 (196a 25).

stances are more intimately ordered to God as their end than the actions
of other things, as we have proved above.[1] Therefore the actions of intellectual substances come under the order of providence, whereby God directs all things to Himself, more than the actions of other things.

Further. The government of providence proceeds from God's love for
the things created by Him; for love consists chiefly in this, that *the lover
desires the good of the beloved.*[2] Consequently, the more God loves a thing,
the more it comes under His providence. This is the teaching of Holy Scripture, *Ps.* cxliv. 20, where it is said: *The Lord keepeth all them that love
Him*; and the Philosopher also says that God cares most for those who
love the intellect, as being His friends.[3] From this we may again conclude
that He loves intellectual substances most of all. Therefore their acts of
will and choice are the object of His providence.

Moreover. Man's interior goods, which depend on his will and action,
are more proper to man than external goods, such as acquiring wealth, and
the like. Hence a man is said to be good in respect of the former and not
of the latter. Consequently, if human choice and the movements of man's
will do not come under divine providence, but only external happenings,
it will be truer to say that human affairs are not the concern of providence
than that they are. But the former saying is put into the mouth of blas-
phemers (*Job* xxii. 14): *He doth not consider our things, and he walketh
about the poles of heaven*; and (*Ezech.* ix. 9): *The Lord hath forsaken
the earth, and the Lord seeth not*; and (*Lament.* iii. 37): *Who is he that
hath commanded a thing to be done, when the Lord commandeth it not?*

Some passages in Holy Scripture might seem to give utterance to that
opinion. Thus it is said (*Ecclus.* xv. 14): *God made man from the beginning and left him in the hand of his own counsel*; and further on (17, 18):
*He hath set water and fire before thee: stretch forth thy hand to which
thou wilt. Before man is life and death, good and evil; that which he shall
choose shall be given him.* Again (*Deut.* xxx. 15): *Consider that I have
set before thee this day life and good, and on the other hand death and
evil.*—But these words indicate that man has free choice, not that his
choice is withdrawn from divine providence.

Likewise the statement of Gregory of Nyssa, in his book *On Man:
Providence regards those things that are not in our power, and not those
that are,*[4] and the saying of Damascene, who followed him, in the Second
Book, that *God preknows but does not predetermine the things which are
in our power,*[5] are to be understood as meaning that the things which are
in our power are not subject to the divine predetermination in such a way
as to be necessitated thereby.

---

[1] Ch. 25 and 78.   [2] Aristotle, *Rhetor.*, II, 4 (1380b 35).   [3] *Eth.*, X, 8 (1179a 29).
[4] Nemesius, *De Nat. Hom.*, XLIV (PG 40, 813).   [5] *De Fide Orth.*, II, 30 (PG 94, 972)

CHAPTER XCI

HOW HUMAN AFFAIRS MAY BE REFERRED TO HIGHER CAUSES

FROM what has been proved we are able to gather how human affairs are to be referred to higher causes, and do not happen by chance.

For acts of choice and movements of will are under the immediate governance of God.[1] Human knowledge, however, as pertaining to the intellect, is directed by God through angelic intermediaries;[2] while things pertaining to the body, whether internal or external, and adapted to man's use, are governed by God by means of the angels and heavenly bodies.[3]

There is one general reason for this. Because every thing that is multiform, changeable and defectible must be referred to a principle that is uniform, unchangeable and indefectible. Now everything connected with us is multiform, changeable and defectible.

For it is clear that our choice is made in many different ways, since different people choose different things in different circumstances. Again, our choice is changeable, both through the instability of the soul, which is not firmly fixed on the last end, and because things themselves surrounding us change. That man's choice is defectible is proved by his sins. On the other hand, the divine will is uniform, since by willing one thing God wills all things, and is unchangeable and indefectible, as we proved in the First Book.[4] Therefore all movements of will and choice must be reduced to the divine will, and not to any other cause, because God alone is the cause of our willing and choosing.

In like manner, our understanding is manifold, since from many sensible things we gather into one, as it were, the intelligible truth. It is also changeable, since by movement it passes from one thing to another discursively, proceeding from the known to the unknown. Again, it is defectible, through admixture of imagination and sense, as the errors of men testify.—On the other hand, the knowledge of the angels is uniform, because they receive the knowledge of truth from the one fount of truth, namely, God.[5] It is also unchangeable, because they see the truth about things, not by proceeding discursively from effects to cause or vice versa, but by simple intuition.[6] It is also indefectible, since they see intuitively the very natures or quiddities of things in themselves, about which the intellect cannot err, as neither can the senses about their proper sensible objects; whereas we figure out the nature of a thing from its accidents and effects. Therefore, our intellectual knowledge must be ruled by the knowledge of the angels.

[1] Ch. 85ff.   [2] Ch. 79.   [3] Ch. 78 and 82.   [4] *C. G.*, I, 13 and 75.   [5] Ch. 80.
[6] *C. G.*, II, 96ff.

Again. As to human bodies and the external things of which men make use, it is evident that they are blended together and contrary to one another in many ways, that they are not always moved in the same way, because their movements cannot be continual, and that they are defectible by alteration and corruption.—But the heavenly bodies are uniform, being simple and devoid of all contrariety. Also, their movements are uniform, continual and unchangeable. Nor can there be corruption or alteration in them. Consequently, our bodies, and whatever else serves for our use, must be ruled by the movements of the heavenly bodies.

CHAPTER XCII

HOW A MAN MAY BE SAID TO BE FORTUNATE, AND HOW HE IS ASSISTED BY HIGHER CAUSES

It may be seen from what has been said how a man is said to be fortunate.

For a man is said to have good fortune *when something good happens to him outside his intention*:[1] e.g., when a man, while digging in a field, finds a treasure which he was not seeking. Now a man, while working, may do something outside his own intention, yet not outside the intention of someone above him: e.g., if a master sends a servant to a place whither he had already sent another servant without the knowledge of the former, the finding of the latter is unintentional to the former, but not to the master who sent him; and therefore, although in relation to this servant the meeting is fortuitous and by chance, it is not so in relation to the master, but is intentional. Since, then, man, as to his body, is subordinate to the heavenly bodies, as to his intellect, to the angels, and as to his will, to God, it is possible for something to happen outside the intention of man, which is nevertheless according to the order of the heavenly bodies, or the influence of the angels, or even of God. And although God's action alone has a direct bearing on man's choice, nevertheless, the angel's action has a certain bearing on man's choice by way of persuasion; and the action of a heavenly body by way of disposition, inasmuch as the corporeal impressions of the heavenly bodies on our bodies dispose us to choose in certain ways. Accordingly, when, through the influence of higher causes, in the aforesaid manner, a man is led to choose such things as turn to his profit without his being aware of their utility by his own reason; and when, besides this, his understanding is enlightened from the light of intellectual substances to the effect of doing those same things; and when, too, through the divine operation his will is inclined so as to choose that which is profitable to him, without knowing why it is so,—he is said to be *fortunate*. On the contrary, he is said to be *unfortunate* when, through the influence

[1] Aristotle, *Magna Moralia*, II, 8 (1207a 28).

of higher causes, his choice is inclined to contrary things; as it is said of someone (*Jer.* xxii. 30): *Write this man barren, a man that shall not prosper in his days.*

Yet herein we must observe a difference. For the impressions of the heavenly bodies on our bodies cause in us natural dispositions of the body. Consequently, from the disposition left in our body by a heavenly body, one is said not only to be fortunate or unfortunate, but also to have a good or a bad natural disposition, in which sense the Philosopher says that to be fortunate is to have a good natural disposition.[1] For it is inconceivable that the fact of one person choosing what is useful and another what is hurtful, without their knowing it, be due to any difference in understanding, since the nature of the intellect and the will is the same in all; because a formal diversity would cause a specific diversity, whereas a material diversity causes a diversity according to number. Consequently, in so far as the human intellect is enlightened for the purpose of operation, or the will instigated by God, a man is not said to be well disposed by nature, but to be *well guarded* or *well governed.*

Again. Another difference is to be observed here. For the operation of an angel and of a heavenly body merely *disposes* a man to choose, whereas the operation of God gives *accomplishment* to his choice. And since the disposition arising from a quality affecting the body, or from the persuasion of the intellect, does not necessitate his choice, man does not always choose what his guardian angel intends, nor that to which the heavenly body inclines him; whereas he always chooses in accord with God's operation in his will. Hence the guardianship of the angels is sometimes frustrated, according to *Jer.* li. 9: *We would have cured Babylon, but she is not healed,* and much more so the influence of the heavenly bodies; whereas divine providence never fails.

Yet another difference must be observed. For a heavenly body does not dispose a man to choose, except in so far as it affects our bodies, so that a man is influenced in his choice in the same way as he is led by his passions to choose; and hence every disposition towards choosing, resulting from the influence of the heavenly bodies, is in the manner of a passion, as when one is led to make a certain choice through hate, love, or anger and the like.—On the other hand, a man is disposed by an angel to make a certain choice by way of intellectual consideration, without passion. And this happens in two ways. Sometimes man's understanding is enlightened by an angel so as to know only that a certain thing is good to do, without being instructed as to the reason for its being good, which depends on the end. Consequently sometimes a man thinks it good to do a certain thing, *and yet were he asked why, he would answer that he did not know.*[2] Hence when he achieves the useful end, to which he had given no thought, it will be fortuitous for him. Sometimes, however, he is instructed by the angel

[1] *Ibid.* (1207a 35).   [2] *Ibid.* (1207b 1).

who enlightens him, both as to the goodness of a thing to be done, and as to the reason why it is good, which depends on the end. And so, when he achieves the end to which he looked forward, it will not be fortuitous.— It must also be noted that the active power of a spiritual nature surpasses that of a corporeal nature in being wider in its scope even as it is higher in its kind. Consequently, the disposition caused by a heavenly body does not extend to all those things that come under the scope of man's choice.

Again. The power of the human soul or even of an angel is restricted in comparison with the divine power, which extends universally to all beings. Hence some good can happen to a man both outside his intention, and outside the influence of heavenly bodies, and also outside the angelic enlightenment, but not outside divine providence which is the governor, even as it is the maker, of being *qua* being, and hence must hold all things in its power. Consequently, some good or evil may happen to a man by chance both in relation to himself, and in relation to heavenly bodies, and in relation to the angels, but not in relation to God. For in relation to God, not only in human affairs but in all things whatsoever, there then can be nothing fortuitous or unforeseen.

But since fortuitous things are those which are unintentional, and since moral goods cannot be unintentional, because they are founded on choice, in relation to them no man can be described as fortunate or unfortunate, although one may say that in relation toward goods he has by nature a good or evil disposition, when through the natural dispositions of his body he is inclined to the choice of virtue or vice. With regard to external goods, which can accrue to man outside his intention, he may be described *both as having a natural disposition for them*, and *as having good fortune*, and *as governed by God*, and *as guarded by the angels*.

Man receives yet another assistance from higher causes, with regard to the performance of his actions. For whereas man has the power to choose and to pursue what he has chosen, in either case he is sometimes helped by higher causes, and sometimes hindered: with regard to his choice, as we have said, in so far as a man is either disposed to choose a certain thing through the influence of heavenly bodies, or enlightened as it were through the guardianship of angels, or inclined through the operation of God;— with regard to the execution, in so far as man receives from some higher cause the strength and the efficacy to accomplish his choice. These things may come not only from God and the angels, but even from heavenly bodies, in so far as the said efficacy resides in a body. For it is evident that even inanimate bodies receive certain forces and abilities from the heavenly bodies, even besides those which result from the active and passive qualities of the elements (which qualities themselves, without any doubt, are subject to the heavenly bodies). Thus that the magnet attracts iron is due to the power of a heavenly body, and in the same way certain stones and plants have other hidden powers. Therefore there is no reason why one man should not receive, through the influence of a heavenly body, a certain efficacy for certain corporeal effects, that is not possessed by another man: *e.g.*, a physician for healing, a farmer for planting, a soldier for fighting. But this efficacy is bestowed on men by God much more perfectly for the purpose of accomplishing their works. Accordingly, as regards the first kind of assistance, which man receives in choosing, God is said to *direct* him; as to the second, He is said to *strengthen* him. These two assistances are indicated in the *Psalms* (xxvi. 1), where it is said, in reference to the first: *The Lord is my light and my salvation, whom shall I fear?* and in reference to the second: *The Lord is the protector of my life, of whom shall I be afraid?*

There is, however, a twofold difference between these two assistances. The first is that man is assisted by the first both in things subject to his power, and in others; whereas the second assistance extends only to those things for which man's power is adequate. Thus, if a man, while digging a grave, find a treasure, this does not result from any power of his; and hence with a view to such a result a man may be assisted through being instigated to seek where the treasure is, but not by receiving the power for finding treasures. But that a physician heal, or that a soldier conquer in battle, may result both from assistance received in the choice of means adapted to the end, and from the power received from a higher cause for the success of their actions. Hence the first assistance is more universal.— The other difference is that the second assistance is given for the purpose of accomplishing what one intends to do. Therefore, since the fortuitous is unintentional, a man cannot, properly speaking, be said to be fortunate through receiving such assistance, as he can through receiving the former kind of assistance, as we have shown above.

Now, a man is fortunate or unfortunate sometimes when he acts alone, as when he finds a hidden treasure while he is digging; and sometimes through the concurrent action of another cause, as when a man, while going to market intent on buying, meets a debtor whom he did not expect to meet. In the first instance, the man was assisted to his good fortune solely in that he was directed in the choice of something to which a profit was accidentally attached outside his intention. In the second instance, both agents need to be directed to choose an action or movement resulting in their mutual encounter.

There is yet another observation to be made about the foregoing. For it has been said that the happening of good or bad fortune to a man is from God, and may be from a heavenly body, inasmuch as man is led by God to choose a thing to which some advantage or disadvantage is attached which the chooser had not expected, and in so far as he is disposed by a heavenly body to make such a choice. This advantage or disadvantage, in reference to man's choice, is fortuitous; in reference to God, it is not fortuitous; whereas it is so in reference to the heavenly body. This is proved as follows. An event does not cease to be fortuitous until it is referred to a *per se* cause. Now the power of a heavenly body is an active cause, not by way of understanding or choosing, but by way of nature; and it is proper to nature to tend to one thing. Accordingly, if a certain effect is not one thing, no natural power can be its *per se* cause. Now when two things are united together accidentally, they are one, not really, but only accidentally. Therefore no natural cause can be the *per se* cause of such a conjunction. Suppose, then, that the man in question is led through the impression of a heavenly body, as by a passion, as we said before, to dig a grave. Now the grave and the place of the treasure are not one thing save accidentally, because they have no mutual connection. Consequently, the power of the heavenly body cannot cause an inclination *per se* to this effect, considered as a whole, namely, that the man in question should dig a grave and a place where a treasure is. But one that acts through the intellect can cause an inclination to this whole, because it belongs to an intelligent being to direct many things to one. It is also plain that a man who knew the treasure to be there might send another, who knew it not, to dig a grave in the same place, so that he might find the treasure unintentionally. Accordingly, such fortuitous events, when referred to the divine causality, cease to be fortuitous, but not when they are referred to a heavenly body.

The same argument shows that a man cannot be fortunate in every possible way through the influence of a heavenly body, but only in this or that respect. When I say *in every way,* I mean that a man is not by nature such that, through the influence of a heavenly body, he chooses always or nearly always those particular things to which some advantage or disadvantage is accidentally connected. For nature is directed to one thing only, and the things in regard to which man is fortunate or unfortunate are not reducible to something one, but are indeterminate and infinite in number, as the Philosopher says,[1] and is evident to the sense. Therefore it is impossible for anyone to be of such a nature as invariably to choose those things which have some advantage incidental to them. But one may be inclined by a heavenly body to choose something to which an incidental advantage is attached, and by some other inclination, to choose something else, and by yet a third inclination, to choose yet another thing, but not by one inclination to choose them all. But man can be directed to all things by one divine disposition.

[1] *Phys.,* II, 5 (196b 28).

CHAPTER XCIII

IS THERE SUCH A THING AS FATE, AND WHAT IS IT?

WE may gather from the foregoing what we should think about fate.

For observing that many things happen in this world accidentally, if particular causes be taken into consideration, some have maintained that such things are not subject even to any superior causes. According to this opinion, there is no such thing as fate.

Others, however, have tried to refer such things to certain higher causes, from which, according to some plan, they proceed in an orderly way. These held that there is *fate,* as though things which appear to happen by chance were *effata,* that is, *foretold* or preordained by someone to be.

Some of these pretended to ascribe all contingent occurrences of this world to the causality of heavenly bodies, not excluding human elections, and they held that all such things are subject to the directing force of the stars, which force they called *fate.* This opinion is impossible and contrary to faith, as we have already shown.[1]

Others, however, wished to assign to the direction of divine providence all such things as appear to happen by chance in this lower world. Hence they maintained that all these things are subject to *fate,* for this was the name given by them to the disposition which divine providence causes to be in things. Hence Boethius says that *fate is a disposition inherent in changeable things, by which providence connects each one with its proper order.*[2] In this definition *disposition* stands for *order*; the words *inherent in things* are included to differentiate fate from providence, because the order as existing in the divine mind and not yet impressed on things is *providence,* but as already expressed in things, is called *fate; changeable* is added to show that the order of providence does not deprive things of contingency and changeableness, as some maintained.

In this sense, to deny fate is to deny divine providence. Since, however, we should not use even names in common with unbelievers, lest use of the same expressions be the occasion of error, the faithful should not use the word *fate,* lest they seem to agree with those who, having false notions about fate, subject all things to a necessity imposed by the stars. Hence Augustine says: *If anyone gives the name of fate to God's will or power, let him keep his opinion, but hold his tongue;*[3] and Gregory says to the same effect: *Far be it from the minds of the faithful to think that fate is anything real.*[4]

[1] Ch. 84ff. [2] *De Consol.,* IV, prose 6 (PL 63, 815). [3] *De Civit. Dei,* V, 1 (PL 41, 141). [4] *In Evang.,* I, hom. 10 (PL 76, 1112).

CHAPTER XCIV

OF THE CERTAINTY OF THE DIVINE PROVIDENCE

A DIFFICULTY, however, arises from what has been said. For if all, even the contingent, happenings of this lower world are subject to the divine providence, it would follow, apparently, that either providence is uncertain, or all happenings necessary.

[1] For the Philosopher proves that if we suppose every effect to have a *per se* cause, and again that given any *per se* cause, we must of necessity grant the effect, it will follow that all future events happen of necessity.[1] For if every effect has a *per se* cause, every effect will be reducible to some cause either present or past. Thus, if it be asked whether a certain man will be killed by robbers, this effect is preceded by a cause which is his being met by the robbers; and this effect is again preceded by another cause, namely, that he went out; and this again was preceded by another cause, namely, that he went to fetch some water; and this by another cause, namely, that he was thirsty; and this was caused by his partaking of salt meat; which he is either eating now or has already eaten. Accordingly, if, given the cause, we must necessarily grant the effect, if he eats the salt meat, he is of necessity thirsty; if he thirsts, it is necessary that he wish to seek water; and if he wish to seek water, that he leave his house; and if he go out, that the robbers meet him; and if they meet him, that they kill him. Therefore from first to last, it is necessary that this eater of salt meat be killed by robbers. The Philosopher concludes, then, that it is untrue that, given the cause, the effect must of necessity be also granted, since some of these causes may be ineffective. Nor again is it true that every effect has a *per se* cause; because that which is accidental, namely, that the man who wants water should meet some robbers, has no cause.

This argument proves, then, that all effects reducible to a *per se* cause, whether present or past, from which, if it is posited, the effect follows of necessity, happen themselves of necessity. Either, therefore, we must say that not all effects are subject to the divine providence (and thus providence would not extend to all things, contrary to what was proved above[2]), or we must say that, granted providence, it is not necessary for its effects to follow (and then providence will not be certain), or that all things must needs happen of necessity. For providence is not only in the present and the past, but from eternity, since nothing can be in God that is not eternal.

[2] Further. If the divine providence is certain, this conditional proposition must be true: *If God foresaw this, it will be.* Now the antecedent of this proposition is necessary, for it is eternal. Therefore the consequent is

---

[1] *Metaph.*, V, 3 (1027a 29).   [2] Ch. 64.

necessary, because whenever the antecedent of a conditional proposition is necessary, the consequent is likewise necessary; so that the consequent is like a conclusion of the antecedent. Now whatever follows from the necessary is itself necessary. Accordingly, if the divine providence is certain, all things must happen of necessity.

[3] Moreover. Supposing a thing to be foreseen by God, for instance, that so and so will be king. Either then it is possible for it to happen that he does not reign, or it is not possible. If it is not possible for him not to reign, then it is impossible; and therefore it is necessary that he will reign. On the other hand, if it is possible that he will not reign, then, since *given a possibility nothing impossible follows*, it remains that it is not impossible for the divine providence to fail; for we are here saying that the divine providence does fail. Consequently, it follows, if all things are foreseen by God, that either the divine providence is uncertain, or that all things happen of necessity.

[4] Again. Tully argues thus:[1] If all things are foreseen by God, the order of causes is certain. If this be true, then all things are subject to fate. If all things are subject to fate, nothing is subject to our power, and the choice of the will is non-existent. Therefore, if the divine providence is certain, there is no free choice. And it will also follow that there is no such thing as a contingent cause.

[5] Besides. The divine providence does not exclude intermediary causes, as we have proved.[2] But some causes are contingent and defectible. Therefore an effect of the divine providence may fail. Therefore God's providence is uncertain.

In order to solve these difficulties, we must recall some points already laid down, so as to make it clear that nothing escapes the divine providence; that the order of the divine providence is utterly unchangeable; and that, notwithstanding, it does not follow that whatever results from the divine providence must happen of necessity.

First, we must observe that as God is the cause of all existent things, by giving them their very being, the order of His providence must needs include all things; because to those things to which He has given being, He must grant a continuance of being, and He must grant perfection in the last end.[3]

Now in everyone that exercises providence there are two points for consideration,[4] namely, forethought about the order of things, and establishment of the premeditated order in the things subject to providence. The former pertains to the cognitive power, and the latter to the operative power. There is this difference between them, that in the forethought given to the order, providence is so much the more perfect, as its order is more able to reach the most minute things. For it is owing to our defective knowledge, which cannot comprise all individual things, that we are unable to

---

[1] *De Divinat.*, II, 7 (p. 71ᵇ).   [2] Ch. 77.   [3] Ch. 64ff.   [4] Ch. 77

arrange beforehand all the particulars in those matters that are subject to
our direction. Now a man is considered more fit to make provision according as his foresight extends to more particulars; but one whose foresight
extends only to general considerations has but a small share of prudence.
The same may be observed in all productive arts. On the other hand, as
regards the causing of the premeditated order to be in things, the providence of the governor is the higher in order and perfection, according
as it is more universal, and brings about the realization of its forethought through more ministers; for the organization itself of the subordinate ministers has a large place in the order of providence.—Now
God's providence must be supremely perfect because He is absolutely
and universally perfect, as we proved in the First Book.[1] Consequently, in
His providence He orders all things, even the most trivial, by the eternal
forethought of His wisdom: and whatsoever things operate, do so as instruments moved by Him,[2] and serve Him obediently, so as to bring forth into
the world the order of providence excogitated, as it were, from eternity.—
And if all things that are capable of action must needs act as His ministers, it is impossible that any agent hinder the execution of the divine providence by acting contrary thereto. Nor, again, is it possible for the divine
providence to be hindered through a defect in any agent or patient, since
every power, active or passive, is caused in things according to God's disposition.[3] Again, it is impossible for the execution of the divine providence
to be prevented through a change in the author of providence, since God
is utterly unchangeable, as we have proved.[4] It follows, therefore, that the
divine providence cannot possibly fail.

Secondly, it must be observed that every agent aims at a good, and at a
greater good so far as it is able, as we have proved.[5] Now, *good* and *better*
are not the same as considered in the whole and as considered in the parts.[6]
For in the whole, the good consists in the integrity which results from the
order and composition of the parts. Consequently, for the whole it is better
that there be disparity of parts, which is necessary for the order and perfection of the whole, than that all the parts be equal, with each part on a
level with the most excellent part; whereas each part of inferior degree
would be better, considered in itself, if it were on the same level as a higher
part. Take, as an example, the human body. The foot would be a more
excellent part if it possessed the beauty and power of the eye; but the
whole body would be more imperfect, if it were deprived of the service of
the foot. Accordingly, the intention of the particular agent differs from
that of the universal agent; for the particular agent aims at the good of
the part absolutely, and makes it as good as it can, whereas the universal
agent aims at the good of the whole. Consequently, a defect is outside the
intention of the particular agent, but according to the intention of the
universal agent. Thus the generation of a female is clearly outside the

[1] *C. G.*, I, 28.   [2] Ch. 67.   [3] Ch. 70.   [4] *C. G.*, I, 13.   [5] Ch. 3.   [6] Ch. 71.

intention of a particular nature, namely, of this particular force in this particular seed, the tendency of which is to make the embryo as perfect as possible; on the other hand, it is the purpose of universal nature, namely, of the power of the universal cause of generation in inferior beings, that a female be generated, which is a necessary condition for the generation of many animals. In like manner, corruption, diminution and every defect is in the purpose of universal nature, but not of the particular nature; because each particular thing shuns defect and, for its own part, aims at perfection. It is clear, then, that the particular agent aims at the greatest possible perfection of its effect in its kind; while the universal nature aims at a particular perfection in a particular effect, for instance, the perfection of a male in one effect, that of a female in another.

Among the parts of the whole universe, the first distinction to be observed is between the contingent and the necessary.[1] For the higher beings are necessary, incorruptible and unchangeable, and the lower a thing is, the more it falls short of this condition; so that the lowest are corruptible in their very being, changeable in their disposition, and produce their effects, not of necessity, but contingently. Therefore every agent that is a part of the universe has a tendency to persist in its being and natural disposition, and to establish its effect; while God, Who governs the universe, intends to establish some of His effects by way of necessity, and others by way of contingency. Accordingly, He adapts various causes to those effects, to some necessary, to others contingent causes. Therefore it belongs to the order of the divine providence, not only that such and such an effect be produced, but that it be caused necessarily, and that some other effect be produced contingently. Consequently, some of the things subject to the divine providence are necessary, and some contingent; they are not all necessary.—It is therefore evident that, though the divine providence is the *per se* cause of a particular future effect, and though it is present and past, yet more truly eternal, it does not follow, as the *first argument* pretended, that this particular effect necessarily will be; for the divine providence is the *per se* cause that this particular effect will happen contingently. And this cannot fail.

Hence it is also clear that this conditional proposition is true: *If God foresaw that this would happen, it will be so,* as the second argument stated. But it will be as God foresaw that it would be. Now, He foresaw that it would happen contingently. It follows infallibly, then, that it will be contingently and not of necessity.

It is also clear that if this thing, which we suppose to be foreseen by God as future, be of a contingent nature, it will be possible for it not to happen considered in itself; for it is foreseen in such a way as to be contingent, and possible not to be. Yet the order of the divine providence cannot fail to enable this future thing to happen contingently. Thus the *third argument* is solved. Consequently, we may say that the man in question will not

[1] Ch. 72.

reign if we consider the statement in itself, but not if we consider it as foreseen.

Again. The argument advanced by Tully appears of small account in the light of what we have said. For seeing that not only effects but also causes and modes of being are subject to the divine providence, as is clear from the foregoing, it does not follow, if all things are ruled by the divine providence, that nothing is under our control; for they are so foreseen by God as to be freely done by us.

Nor can the defectibility of second causes, by means of which the effects of providence are produced, deprive the divine providence of certainty, as the *fifth objection* argued. For God Himself works in all things according to the decree of His will, as we proved above.[1] Consequently, it belongs to His providence sometimes to allow defectible causes to fail, and sometimes to preserve them from failing.

Such arguments as might be used to prove the necessity of things foreseen by God from the certitude of His knowledge were solved above when we were treating of the divine knowledge.[2]

CHAPTERS XCV AND XCVI

THAT THE UNCHANGEABLENESS OF THE DIVINE PROVIDENCE DOES NOT EXCLUDE THE USEFULNESS OF PRAYER

WE must also observe that, as the unchangeableness of providence does not impose necessity on things foreseen, so neither does it exclude the usefulness of prayer. For we do not pray that the eternal disposition of His providence may be changed, since this is impossible, but that He may grant what we desire.

For it is fitting that God should assent to the holy desires of the rational creature; not that our desires have the effect of changing a God Who is unchangeable, but as an effect befitting His goodness in granting our desires. Because, since all things naturally desire the good, as we have proved,[3] and since it belongs to the supereminence of the divine goodness to bestow being and well-being on all things in a certain order, it follows that He fulfills, according to His goodness, the holy desires of which our prayers are the expression.

Again. He who causes a thing to move should lead that thing to the end. Hence a thing is moved to its end, attains to that end and rests therein through one and the same nature. Now every desire is a movement to a good, and it cannot be in a thing except it come from God, Who is good in His essence, and the source of goodness; for every mover moves to its like. Therefore it belongs to God, according to His goodness, to bring to a fitting

[1] Ch. 67; *C. G.*, II, 23.   [2] *C. G.*, I, ch. 63ff.   [3] Ch. 3.

issue the fitting desires which are expressed by means of one's prayers.

Besides. The nearer things are to their mover, the more effectively do they receive the mover's impression. Thus things which are nearer to a fire are more heated thereby. Now intellectual substances are nearer to God than inanimate natural substances. Consequently, the impression of the divine motion is more efficacious in intellectual substances than in other natural substances. Now natural bodies participate in the divine motion to the extent that they receive therefrom a natural appetite for the good, as well as the fulfillment of that appetite, which is realized when they attain to their respective ends. Much more therefore do intellectual substances attain to the fulfillment of their desires which are proffered to God in their prayers.

Moreover. It is essential to friendship that the lover wish the desire of the beloved to be fulfilled, inasmuch as he seeks his good and perfection. Hence it has been said that *friends have but one will*.[1] Now we have proved that God loves His creature,[2] and so much the more as it has a greater share of His goodness, which is the first and chief object of His love.[3] Hence He wills the desires of the rational creature to be fulfilled, since of all creatures it participates most perfectly in the divine goodness. Now His will is perfective of things, because He is the cause of things through His will, as was proved above.[4] Therefore it belongs to God's goodness to fulfill the rational creature's desires, as laid before Him in prayer.

Besides. The creature's good flows from the divine goodness, according to a certain likeness. Now it is a most praiseworthy trait in a man if he grant the request of those whose petition is just, since for this reason he is said to be liberal, clement, merciful and kind. Therefore it belongs in a special manner to the divine goodness to grant holy prayers.

Therefore it is said in the *Psalm* (cxliv. 19): *He will do the will of them that fear Him, and He will hear their prayers and save them*; so too our Lord says (*Matt.* vii. 8): *Every one that asketh receiveth: and he that seeketh, findeth; and to him that knocketh, it shall be opened.*

[*Chapter XCVI*] And yet it is not unfitting that sometimes the petitions of those who pray be not granted by God.

For it was proved that God fulfills the desires of the rational creature inasmuch as the good is the object of the creature's desire. Sometimes, however, it happens that what we seek is not a true good but an apparent one, and is, absolutely speaking, evil. Such a prayer, therefore, cannot be granted by God; and hence it is said (*Jas.* iv. 3): *You ask and you receive not, because you ask amiss.*

Again. It was shown to be fitting that God fulfills our desires, because He moves us to desire. Now the thing moved is not brought to the end of its movement by the mover unless the movement continue. Accordingly, if the

---

[1] Sallust, *Catiline*, XX (ed. A. Ahlberg, Leipsig: B. G. Teubner, 1919), p. 16. [2] *C. G.*, I, 75. [3] *C. G.*, I, 74. [4] *C. G.*, II, 23ff.

movement of desire be not continued by repeated prayer, it is not unfitting that the prayer be ineffectual. Thus our Lord says (*Luke* xviii. 1) *that we ought always to pray and not to faint*; and (*1 Thess*. v. 17) the Apostle says: *Pray without ceasing.*

Further. We proved that God fittingly fulfills the desire of the rational creature inasmuch as the creature approaches to Him. Now a man approaches to God by contemplation, devout affection, and humble and firm resolution. A prayer, therefore, that lacks these conditions in its approach to God does not deserve to be granted by Him. Hence it is said in the *Psalm* (ci. 18): *He hath had regard to the prayer of the humble*; and (*Jas* i. 6): *Let him ask in faith, nothing wavering.*

Moreover. We have proved that God grants the prayers of the devout on the score of friendship. Consequently, if a man rejects God's friendship, his prayer is unworthy of being granted. Hence it is said (*Prov.* xxviii. 9): *He that turneth away his ears from hearing the law, his prayer shall be an abomination*; and (*Isa.* i. 15): *When you multiply prayer, I will not hear, for your hands are full of blood.*

It is on the same principle that sometimes a friend of God is not heard when he prays for those who are not God's friends. Thus it is said (*Jer.* vii. 16): *Therefore do not thou pray for this people, nor take to thee praise and supplication for them; and do not withstand me, for I will not hear thee.*

It happens, too, sometimes that through friendship a man refuses his friend's request, because he knows it to be hurtful to him, or the contrary to be better for him; even as a physician will sometimes refuse a sick man what he asks, knowing that it is not good for regaining his health. Therefore, since it has been proved that God, for love of the rational creature, fulfills the desires set forth in his prayers, we must not be surprised if sometimes He does not fulfill the prayers of those even who are most dear to Him, that He may accomplish what is best for the welfare of the suppliant. That is why He did not remove from Paul the thorn in his flesh, though thrice he prayed for this, because He foresaw that this would be good for him by keeping him humble, as is related in *2 Cor.* xii. 8, 9. Hence also our Lord said to some (*Matt.* xx. 22): *You know not what you ask*; and (*Rom.* viii. 26) it is said: *For we know not what we should pray for as we ought.* For this reason Augustine says: *The Lord is good, for often He grants not what we want, that He may give what we want more.*[1]

It is clear, then, from what has been said, that prayers and holy desires are the cause of some of the things done by God. Now it has been shown that God's providence does not exclude other causes;[2] rather indeed does He dispose of them so that the order appointed by His providence may be established in things. Consequently, second causes are not opposed to providence; in fact, they accomplish the effect of providence. Accordingly,

---

[1] *Epist.* XXXI, 1 (PL 33, 121).   [2] Ch. 77.

prayers are efficacious before God; yet they do not upset the unchangeable order of the divine providence, since even the granting of each suppliant's prayer is included within the order of the divine providence. To say, therefore, that we must not pray that we may obtain something from God, because the order of His providence is unchangeable, is like saying that we must not walk in order to arrive at a place, nor eat that we may have nourishment; all of which is clearly absurd.

By the foregoing there is removed a twofold error about prayer. For some have said that prayer has no fruit. This was asserted both by those who, like the Epicureans, utterly denied the divine providence, and by those who, like certain Peripatetics, withdrew human affairs from the providence of God;[1] and again by those who with the Stoics contended that all things subject to providence happen of necessity.[2] For it follows from all these opinions that prayer produces no fruit, and that consequently all worship of the Godhead is in vain. There is an allusion to this error in *Malach.* iii. 14: *You have said: He laboreth in vain that serveth God. And what profit is it that we have kept His ordinances, and that we have walked sorrowful before the Lord of hosts?*

On the other hand, some have contended that the divine ordinance can be changed by our prayers. Thus the Egyptians said that fate was averted by prayers, certain images, incensings or incantations. Certain passages in Holy Scripture would seem at the first glance to admit of being taken in this sense. For it is related (*Isa.* xxxviii. 1-5) that Isaias, at God's command, said to King Ezechias: *Thus saith the Lord: Take order with thy house, for thou shalt die, and shalt not live*; and that after Ezechias had prayed, *the word of the Lord came to Isaias saying: Go and say to Ezechias . . . I have heard thy prayer . . . behold I will add to thy days fifteen years.*—Again (*Jer.* xviii. 7, 8) it is said in the name of God: *I will suddenly speak against a nation, and against a kingdom, to root out, to pull down and to destroy it. If that nation against which I have spoken shall repent of their evil, I also will repent of the evil that I have thought to do to them.* And (*Joel* ii. 13, 14): *Turn to the Lord your God; for He is gracious and merciful. . . . Who knoweth but He will return and forgive?*

These passages, if taken in their superficial sense, lead to an incongruous result. For, in the first place, it follows that God's will is changeable. Also, that God acquires something in the course of time. Further, that things happening in time to creatures cause something that is in God. These are all impossible, as appears evidently from what has already been laid down.[3]

They are also contrary to Holy Scripture which contains the expression of infallible truth. For it is said (*Num.* xxiii. 19): *God is not as a man that He should lie, nor as the son of man that He should be changed. Hath He said then, and will He not do? Hath He spoken, and will He not fulfill?*

---

[1] Cf. the end of ch. 75.　　[2] Cf. the end of ch. 73.　　[3] *C. G.,* I, 13ff.

Again (*1 Kings* xv. 29): *The triumpher in Israel will not spare, and will not be moved to repentance; for He is not a man that He should repent.* And (*Malach.* iii. 6): *I am the Lord and I change not.*

Now it suffices to consider carefully what we have said above for one to realize that every error occurring in the present matter is due to one's overlooking the difference between the universal and the particular orders. For, since all effects are ordered one to another, inasmuch as they have one common cause, this order must needs be the more universal as the cause is more universal. Hence the order appointed by the universal cause, which is God, must of necessity include all things. There is nothing therefore to prevent a particular order being changed through prayer or in some other manner; because there is outside that order something that can change it. Therefore it is not strange that the Egyptians, who reduced the ordering of human affairs to the heavenly bodies, held that fate, having its origin in the stars, can be changed by certain prayers and rites; because outside and above the heavenly bodies there is God, Who can hinder the heavenly bodies from producing the effect which was to have taken place in this lower world as a result of their influence.—But outside that order which includes all things, it is not possible to assign a thing whereby the order depending on the universal cause can be subverted. For this reason the Stoics, who reduced the ordering of all things to God as the universal cause, held that the order appointed by God is utterly unchangeable. But these again failed to consider the universal order, in that they held prayers to be altogether useless, thus implying that man's volitions and desires, which lead him to pray, are not included in that universal order. For, when they say that, whether we pray or not, the result is the same because of the universal order of things, it is clear that they exclude the suppliant's prayers from that order. For if they were contained in that order, effects would follow through the divine ordinance from ⁺hese prayers in the same way as they follow through other causes. Accordingly, to deny the efficacy of prayer is to deny the efficacy of all other causes. And if the unchangeableness of the divine order does not deprive other causes of their efficacy, neither does it destroy the efficacy of prayer. Therefore prayers have value, not as though they bring about a change in the order appointed from eternity, but as included in that very order.

On the other hand, there is no reason why the particular order of an inferior cause should not be changed by God through the efficacy of prayer; for He transcends all causes, so that He is not bound by the order of any cause, but on the contrary all necessity imposed by the order of a lower cause is subject to Him, because it originated from Him. Accordingly, when some change is brought about by prayer in the order of inferior causes established by God, God is said *to return* or *to repent*; not that His eternal ordinance is changed, but that some effect of His is changed. Hence Gregory says that God *changes not His mind, although at times He changes*

His judgment,[1] not that judgment, mark you, which expresses His eternal decree, but that which expresses the order of lower causes, in keeping with which Ezechias was to die, and a nation was to be exterminated for its sins. Such a change of judgment is described metaphorically as *repentance* in God, inasmuch as He behaves like a penitent, who shows himself penitent by changing his behavior. In the same way, He is said figuratively *to be angry*, inasmuch as by punishing He does what an angry man does.[2]

CHAPTER XCVII

HOW THE DISPOSITION OF PROVIDENCE IS ACCORDING TO A PLAN

FROM what has been said, one can see clearly that things are arranged by divine providence according to a plan.

For we have proved that God, by His providence, directs all things to His goodness as their end;[3] not indeed as though His goodness gains anything from the things that are made, but in order that the likeness of His goodness may be impressed on things as far as possible.[4] But since every created substance must needs fall short of the perfection of the divine goodness, it was necessary, in order that the divine goodness might the more perfectly be bestowed on things, that there should be diversity among them, so that what could not be perfectly represented by one individual thing might be more perfectly represented in various ways by things of various kinds. Thus when man finds that he cannot adequately express an idea by one word, he uses several words so as to express his idea in several ways. In this too we are able to consider the eminence of the divine perfection, since perfect goodness, which in God exists in a united and simple manner, cannot be in creatures otherwise than in many ways and many subjects. Now things are diversified through having diverse forms whence they derive their species. Consequently, the reason for diversity in the forms of things is taken from the end.

But the plan of the order in things is taken from the diversity of forms. Because, as it is from the form that a thing has its being, and as a thing, in so far as it has being, approaches to a likeness to God, Who is His own simple being, it follows of necessity that the form is nothing else than a divine likeness existing by participation in things. Therefore Aristotle, speaking of the form, rightly says that it is *something godlike and desirable*.[5] Now a likeness to one simple thing cannot be diversified except because the resemblance is more or less close, or more or less distant. Now the closer a thing approaches to the divine likeness, the more perfect

[1] *Moral.*, XVI, 10 (PL 76, 1127). [2] Cf. *C. G.*, I, 91. [3] Ch. 64. [4] Ch. 18ff.
[5] *Phys.*, I, 9 (192a 17).

it is. Consequently, a difference in forms must be according as one is more perfect than another; for which reason Aristotle likens definitions, whereby the natures and forms of things are indicated, to numbers among which species are diversified by addition or subtraction of unity.[1] We are thus given to understand that diversity of forms requires a diverse degree of perfection. This is evident to anyone who studies the natures of things. For, if he consider carefully he will find that the diversity of things is made up of degrees, since above inanimate bodies he will find plants, and above these irrational animals, above these intelligent substances, and in each one of these he will find diversity according as some are more perfect than others; so much so, that the highest members of a lower genus appear to be close to the higher genus, and conversely: *e.g.*, animals that cannot move are like plants. Hence Dionysius says that *divine wisdom has joined together the last things of higher degree to the first things of lower degree.*[2] Therefore it is clear that the diversity of things requires that all be not equal, but that there be order and degrees in the universe.

From the diversity of forms, whence things derive their specific differences, there follows also the difference of operations. For since things act according as they are actual (because those things that are in potentiality, as such, are devoid of action), and since a thing is actual by its form, a thing's operation must needs follow its form. Accordingly, if there be diverse forms, these must have diverse operations.

Furthermore, since each thing attains to its proper end by its proper action, it follows that there must be diverse proper ends in things, although there is one common end of all.

Moreover. From the diversity of forms there results a diversity in the relation of matter to things. For since forms are diverse according as some are more perfect than others, some of them are perfect to the extent of being subsistent and complete in themselves, having no need of the assistance of matter. Whereas some are unable to subsist perfectly by themselves, and require matter to uphold them, so that what subsists is not a form only, nor matter only—which by itself is not an actual being—but something composed of both.

Now matter and form would be unable to concur in making one thing unless they were mutually proportionate. But if they need to be proportionate, it follows that diverse matters correspond to diverse forms. Consequently, certain forms require simple, while others require composite, matter; and to diverse forms there must correspond a diverse composition of parts, in keeping with the species and operation of the form.

From the diverse relation to matter there results diversity of agents and patients. For since a thing acts by reason of its form, and is receptive by reason of its matter, it follows that things which have more perfect and

[1] *Metaph.*, VII, 3 (1043b 34).   [2] *De Div. Nom.*, VII, 3 (PG 3, 872).

less material forms, act on those that are more material and have more imperfect forms.

Again. From the diversity of forms, matters and agents there results diversity of properties and accidents. For since substance is the cause of accident, as the perfect of the imperfect, it follows that diverse proper accidents must result from diverse substantial principles. Moreover, since diverse agents produce diverse impressions on patients, it follows that a diversity of agents must result in a diversity of accidents proceeding from their activity.

From what has been said, then, it is clear that it is not without reason that the divine providence has appointed to creatures diverse accidents, actions, passions and orders. Therefore Holy Scripture ascribes the formation and government of things to the divine wisdom and prudence. Thus it is said (*Prov.* iii. 19, 20): *The Lord by wisdom hath founded the earth: He hath established the heavens by prudence. By His wisdom the depths have broken out, and the clouds grow thick with dew.* Again (*Wis.* viii. 1) it is said that divine wisdom *reacheth from end to end mightily, and ordereth all things sweetly*; and (xi. 21): *Thou hast ordered all things in measure, and number, and weight,* where by *measure* we are to understand the quantity, mode, or degree of perfection in each thing; by *number,* the multitude and diversity of species resulting from the various degrees of perfection; and by *weight* the various inclinations of things to their respective ends and operations, as well as the agents and patients, and such accidents as result from a diversity of species.

In this same order wherein we find the plan of the divine providence, we have stated that the first place must be assigned to the divine goodness, as being the last end, which is the first principle in practical matters; and after this comes the multiplicity of things, the establishment of which needs a diversity of grades in forms and matters, agents and patients, actions and accidents. Accordingly, as the fundamental principle of the divine providence, absolutely speaking, is the divine goodness, so the fundamental principle in creatures is their multitude, to the making and preservation of which all other things are seen to be subordinated. In this sense Boethius, it would seem, fittingly said that *number seems to have been the aim of nature in the original formation of things.*[1]

We must, however, observe that the practical and speculative reasons partly agree and partly differ. They agree in this, that as speculative reason starts from a principle and employs means to reach the intended conclusion, so the practical reason begins from some first principle and through certain means arrives at the intended operation or product of operation. In speculative matters, the principle is the form and the essence; whereas in practical matters it is the end, which sometimes is a form, at other times something else. Moreover, the principle in speculative

[1] *Arith.,* I, 2 (PL 63, 1083).

matters must always be necessary, whereas in practical matters it is some-times necessary and sometimes not. Thus it is necessary that man desire happiness as his end, but it is not necessary that he desire to build a house. Likewise in demonstrations, that which follows is always a necessary se-quel to that which precedes, but in practical matters not always, but only when the end cannot be obtained except by the way indicated. Thus he who would build a house must needs get some wood; but it depends on his absolute will, and not on his will to build a house, that he gets pine.

Accordingly, that God loves His own goodness is something necessary, but it does not necessarily follow from this that it should be embodied in creatures, since the divine goodness is perfect without this. Consequently, although the divine goodness is the reason why creatures were originally brought into being, yet this depends on the absolute will of God.—Sup-posing, however, that God wishes to communicate His goodness to His creatures by way of likeness as far as it is possible, this is the reason why creatures are of diverse kinds; although there is no necessity for this di-versity being according to this or that degree of perfection, or this or that number of things.—And supposing it to be God's will to establish a par-ticular number in things, and to bestow on each thing a particular measure of perfection, this is the reason why a particular thing has such and such a form and such and such matter; and so on in like manner.

It is therefore clear that the dispensations of providence are according to a certain plan, and yet this plan presupposes the divine will.

Accordingly a twofold error is refuted by what we have said. First, there is the error of those who maintain that all things are the result of God's absolute will without any plan. This is the error of the Moslem theologians, as Rabbi Moses relates,[1] according to whom the sole reason why fire heats rather than chills is because God so wills. Secondly, there is included the error of those who assert that the ordering of causes pro-ceeds from the divine providence by way of necessity.[2] Both of these views are false, as is clear from what has been said.

There are, however, certain expressions of Scripture that would seem to ascribe all things to God's absolute will. But such things are said, not to remove any plan from the dispensations of providence, but to show that God's will is the first cause of all things, as we have already shown. Such are the words of the *Psalm* (cxxxiv. 6): *Whatsoever the Lord pleased, He hath done,* and of *Job* ix. 12: *Who can say: Why dost Thou so?* and of *Rom.* ix. 19: *Who resisteth His will?* Augustine likewise says: *God's will alone is the first cause of health and sickness, reward and punishment, grace and retribution.*[3]

Accordingly, if we be asked the *wherefore* of a particular natural effect, we can assign the reason to some proximate cause, provided, however, that

---

[1] Maimonides, *Guide,* III, 25 (p. 308).   [2] Cf. ch. 72ff; ch. 94.   [3] *De Trin.,* III, 3; 4 (PL 42, 872; 873).

we refer all things to the divine will as their first cause. Thus if it be asked: *Why was the wood heated in the presence of fire?* we reply: *Because to heat is the natural action of fire,* and this *because heat is its proper accident*; and this results from its proper form—and so on until we come to the divine will. Hence if we reply to the question *Why was the wood made hot?* by saying: *Because God so willed,* we shall answer rightly, if we intend to trace the question back to its first cause, but incorrectly if we intend to exclude all other causes.

CHAPTER XCVIII

HOW IT IS POSSIBLE, AND HOW IT IS IMPOSSIBLE, FOR GOD TO DO SOMETHING OUTSIDE THE ORDER OF HIS PROVIDENCE

FROM what has been said we are able to consider a twofold order: the one, dependent on the first cause of all things, and hence embracing all; the other, a particular order, dependent on some created cause, and comprising such things as are subordinate to that cause. The latter order is manifold, in accordance with the diversity of causes to be found among creatures. Yet one such order is subordinate to another, even as one cause is subordinate to another. Consequently, all particular orders of causes are comprised under, and are derived from, that universal order found in things in so far as they are dependent on the first cause. We have an example of this in political affairs. For there is a certain order among all the members of a household according as they are subject to the head of the house; again, the head of the house and all the other heads of houses in the same city have a certain order among themselves, and in relation to the governor of the city; and he again, together with all the other governors in the kingdom, is subordinate to the king.

This universal order, according to which all things are ruled by the divine providence, may be considered in two ways: namely, with regard to the things subject to that order, and with regard to the plan of the order, which depends on the principle of the order.

Now we proved in the Second Book that the things themselves, which are ordered by God, do not proceed from Him as from an agent that is necessitated by nature or by anything else, but rather proceed from His absolute will, especially as regards the original establishment of things.[1] Consequently, there are other things that God can do besides those which are comprised under the order of divine providence, since His power is not limited to them.

On the other hand, if we consider the aforesaid order with respect to the plan that depends on the principle, then it is not possible for God to do

[1] *C. G.,* II, 23ff.

anything outside that order. For this order, as we have proved,[1] proceeds from the knowledge and will of God directing all things to His goodness as their end. Now, it is not possible that God do anything that is not willed by Him, since creatures proceed from Him, not by nature, but because He wills them to, as we have proved. Nor is it possible for anything to be done by Him that is not included in His knowledge, since nothing can be willed that is not known. Nor, again, is it possible for Him to do anything as regards creatures, that is not directed to His goodness as its end, since His goodness is the proper object of His will. Likewise, since God is utterly unchangeable, He cannot possibly will that which He did not previously will, or begin to know something anew, or direct it to His goodness. Therefore God can do nothing but what is comprised in the order of His providence, even as He can do only what is subject to His operation. And yet, if we consider His power absolutely, He can do other things besides those that are subject to His providence or operation; but He cannot do what has not been eternally contained in the order of His providence, because He is unchangeable.

Through failing to observe this distinction some have fallen into various errors. Some, in an endeavor to extend to things themselves the unchangeableness of the divine order, said that all things must of necessity be as they are; so much so, that some declared that God is able to do only what He does.[2] Against this we have the words of *Matt.* xxvi. 53: *Cannot I ask my Father, and he will give me presently more than twelve legions of angels?*

Others, however, thinking in their carnal wisdom that God, like carnal man, is inconstant of will, ascribed the changeableness of things subject to the divine providence to changeableness in the divine providence itself. Against this it is said (*Num.* xxiii. 19): *God is not as a man that he should lie; nor as the son of man that He should be changed.*

Others again withdrew contingent things from the divine providence. Against these it is said (*Lament.* iii. 37): *Who is he that hath commanded a thing to be done, when the Lord commandeth it not?*

CHAPTER XCIX

THAT GOD CAN WORK OUTSIDE THE ORDER IMPOSED ON THINGS, BY PRODUCING EFFECTS WITHOUT THEIR PROXIMATE CAUSES

IT remains to be proved that God can act outside the order imposed on things by Himself.

---

[1] Ch. 97.   [2] Cf. St. Thomas, *De Pot.*, q. 1, a. 5.

For the order imposed on things by God is that lower things be moved by the higher, as was shown above.[1] Now God can act independently of this order. In other words, He can by Himself produce an effect in inferior things, without a higher agent doing anything towards that effect. For the agent that works by natural necessity differs from the agent that acts by will in this, that the effect cannot result from the former except according to the mode of its active power. Hence the agent which has very great power cannot produce immediately a small effect, but produces an effect proportionate to its power. In this effect, however, there will sometimes be less power than in its cause, so that at length through many intermediaries a small effect results from the highest cause. But it is not so in the agent that acts by its will. Because the agent that acts by its will can at once, without any intermediary, produce any effect that does not surpass its power. Thus the most perfect craftsman can produce a work such as an imperfect craftsman would produce. Now God works by His will, and not by necessity of nature, as we proved above.[2] Therefore He can produce lesser effects, that are produced by inferior causes, immediately without their proper causes.

Again. The divine power is compared to all active powers as a universal power to particular powers, as is clear from what has been said above.[3] Now an active universal power may be determined to the production of a particular effect in two ways. First, by a particular intermediary cause. Thus, the active power of a heavenly body is determined to the effect which is the begetting of a man by the particular power seated in the semen; just as the power of a universal proposition in a syllogism is determined to a particular conclusion by the assumption of a particular proposition. Secondly, by an intellect which apprehends a particular form and produces it in the effect. Now the divine intellect knows not only its own essence, which is like a universal active power, nor only universal and first causes, but also all particular causes, as we have proved above.[4] Therefore God can produce immediately every effect that is produced by any particular agent.

Further. Since accidents accompany the substantial principles of a thing, it follows that he who is the immediate cause of the substance is able to produce in a thing whatever accompanies the substance; for the generator, which gives the form, gives likewise all the resultant properties and movements. Now we have shown that God, in the original production of things, brought all things into being immediately by creation.[5] Therefore He can move any being to a given effect independently of intermediate causes.

Besides. The order of things comes from God into things according as it is preknown in His intellect. So, too, in human affairs we see that the head of the state imposes on the citizens the order preconceived by him. Now

---

[1] Ch. 83 and 88.   [2] *C. G.*, II, 23ff.   [3] Ch. 67.   [4] *C. G.*, I, 50.   [5] *C. G.*, II, 21.

the divine intellect is not necessarily limited to this particular order, so as to be unable to conceive any other, since even we are able by our intellect to apprehend another order; for it is intelligible to us that God might make a man of earth and not of seed. Therefore God can produce an effect without the inferior causes to which that effect is proper.

Moreover. Although the order imposed on things by the divine providence reflects the divine goodness in its own particular way, yet it does not reflect it perfectly, since the creature's goodness does not reach to an equality with the goodness of God. Now, that which is not perfectly represented by one copy can be represented again in some other way. Now the representation of the divine goodness in things is the end of their production by God, as was above stated.[1] Therefore God's will is not confined to this particular order of causes and effects, as though He could not choose to produce an effect in lower things immediately and independently of other causes.

Further. All creatures are more subject to God than man's body is to his soul; for the soul is proportionate to the body as its form, whereas God surpasses all proportion to the creature. Now sometimes, when the soul imagines a thing and is strongly drawn towards it, there results a change in the body in the direction of health or sickness, independently of any action on the part of those bodily principles whose natural function is to cause sickness or health in the body. Much more, therefore, by the divine will can an effect be produced in creatures independently of the causes which in the course of nature produce that effect naturally.

Further. According to the order of nature, the active powers of the elements are subordinate to the active powers of the heavenly bodies. Now the power of a heavenly body sometimes produces an effect proper to elemental powers without the action of an element. Thus the sun heats without the action of fire. Much more, therefore, can the power of God produce the effects of created causes without any action on their part.

If, however, anyone were to say that, since God has implanted this order in things, He cannot produce in them effects apart from their proper causes without a change in Himself, he can be answered by referring to the very nature of things. For the order imposed on things by God is in terms of that which is wont to occur in things for the most part, but it is not everywhere in terms of what always occurs, because many natural causes produce their effects in the same way usually, but not always; since sometimes (though seldom) it happens otherwise, whether because of a defect in the power of the agent, or through indisposition of the matter, or by reason of a stronger agency: as when nature produces a sixth finger in a man. Yet the order of providence does not therefore fail or change, because the fact itself that the natural order, established according to what happens for the most part, may at times fail, is subject to the divine provi-

[1] Ch. 19.

dence. Therefore, if it be possible for the natural order to be changed by a created power from that which is of frequent to that which is of rare occurrence, without any change in the divine providence, much more can the divine power at times work apart from the order assigned by God to nature, without prejudice to His providence. In fact, He does this sometimes in order to manifest His power. For by no other means can it better be made manifest that all nature is subject to the divine will, than by the fact that He sometimes works independently of the order of nature; for this shows that the order of things proceeded from Him, not through natural necessity, but through His free will.

Nor should it be deemed a slight argument that God should produce something in nature in order to manifest Himself to the minds of men, since it was shown above that all corporeal creatures are in some way directed to the intellectual nature as their end,[1] while the end of the intellectual creature itself is the knowledge of God, as we have proved.[2] It is not strange, then, if some change be wrought in a corporeal substance, in order to bring the intellectual nature to the knowledge of God.

CHAPTER C

THAT WHAT GOD DOES OUTSIDE THE ORDER OF NATURE IS NOT CONTRARY TO NATURE

It would seem, however, necessary to observe that, although God sometimes does something outside the order assigned to things, yet He does nothing contrary to nature.

For since God is pure act, whereas all other things have some admixture of potentiality, it follows that God must be compared to all things as the mover to the thing moved, and as the active to the potential. Now, when that which in the natural order is in potentiality with regard to a certain agent, is acted upon by that agent, this is not contrary to nature absolutely, although sometimes it is contrary to that particular form which is corrupted by such action. Thus when fire is generated, and air is corrupted through the action of the fire, both generation and corruption are natural. Consequently, whatever is done by God in created things is not contrary to nature, although it may seem to be contrary to the order proper to a particular nature.

Again. Since God is the first agent, as we have proved,[3] all subsequent agents are as His instruments. Now the purpose of an instrument is to serve the action of the principal agent while it is being moved by it. Hence the matter and form of an instrument must be such as to be suitable for the action intended by the principal agent. Hence it is not contrary, but most

---

[1] Ch. 22.   [2] Ch. 25.   [3] *C. G.*, I, 13.

becoming, to the nature of an instrument to be moved by the principal agent. Neither, therefore, is it contrary to nature that creatures be moved by God in any way whatsoever, since they were made that they might serve Him.

Further. Even in corporeal agents we observe that the movements resulting in inferior bodies from the influence of higher bodies are neither violent nor unnatural, although they may seem unsuited to the natural movement which the inferior body has as proper to its form. For we do not say that the ebb and flow of the sea is a violent movement just because it results from the influence of a heavenly body, even though the natural movement of water is only in one direction, namely, toward the center. Much less, therefore, can whatsoever God does in any creature be described as violent or unnatural.

Besides. The first measure of every essence and nature is God, just as He is the first being, which is the cause of being in all other things. Since, then, we judge of everything by its measure, we must regard as natural to a thing that whereby it is conformed to its measure. Hence, whatever is implanted in a thing by God is natural to that thing. Therefore, if something else be implanted by God in that same thing, it will not be unnatural.

Moreover. All creatures are compared to God as works of art are compared to the artist, as appears from what we have already said.[1] Hence all nature is the work of the divine art. Now it is not inconsistent with a work of art that the artist make some alteration in his work, even after giving it its first form. Neither, therefore, is it contrary to nature if God does something in natural things other than that which occurs in the ordinary course of nature. Therefore Augustine says: *God, the creator and author of all natures, does nothing unnatural; because, to each thing that is natural which is caused by Him from whom is all measure, number and order in nature.*[2]

CHAPTER CI

ON MIRACLES

THESE works, however, that are sometimes done by God outside the usual order assigned to things are wont to be called *miracles*, because we are astonished [*admiramur*] at a thing when we see an effect without knowing the cause. And since at times one and the same cause is known to some and unknown to others, it happens that, of several who see an effect, some are astonished and some not. Thus an astronomer is not astonished when he sees an eclipse of the sun, for he knows the cause; whereas one who is ignorant of this science must needs wonder, since he knows not the cause.

[1] *C. G.*, II, 24.   [2] *Contra Faust.*, XXVI, 3 (PL 42, 480).

Therefore it is wonderful to the latter but not to the former. Accordingly, a thing is wonderful absolutely when its cause is hidden absolutely. This is what we mean by a *miracle*, something, namely, that is *wonderful in itself* and not only in respect of this person or that. Now God is the cause which is absolutely hidden from every man. For we have proved above that in this state of life no man can comprehend Him by his intellect.[1] Therefore, properly speaking, miracles are works done by God outside the order usually observed in things.

Of these miracles there are various degrees and orders. The highest degree in miracles comprises those works wherein something is done by God that nature can never do. For instance, that two bodies occupy the same place, that the sun recede or stand still, that the sea be divided and make way to passers by. Among these also there is a certain order. For the greater the work done by God, and the further it is removed from the capability of nature, the greater the miracle. Thus it is a greater miracle that the sun recede than that the waters be divided.

The second degree in miracles belongs to those whereby God does something that nature can do, but not in the same order. Thus it is a work of nature that an animal live, see and walk; but that an animal live after being dead, see after being blind, walk after being lame, this nature cannot do, but God does these things sometimes by a miracle. Among these miracles, also, there are degrees, according as the thing done is further removed from the power of nature.

In the third degree of miracles God does what is wont to be done by the operation of nature, but without the operation of the natural principles: *e.g.*, when by the power of God a man is cured of a fever that nature is able to cure; or when it rains without the operation of the principles of nature.

CHAPTER CII

THAT GOD ALONE WORKS MIRACLES

From what has been said it can be shown that God alone can work miracles.

For whatever is entirely subject to an order cannot do anything above that order. Now every creature is placed under the order established in things by God. Therefore no creature can do anything above that order (which is to work miracles).

Again. When a finite power produces the proper effect to which it is limited, it is not a miracle although it may be wonderful to one who does not understand that power. Thus to an ignorant person it is wonder-

[1] Ch. 47.

ful that the magnet attracts iron, or that a small fish should stop a ship. Now every creature's power is limited to one definite effect, or to a few. Therefore, whatever is done by the power of any creature whatsoever cannot properly be described as a miracle, although it may be wonderful to one who does not understand the power of that creature. But that which is done by the power of God, which, being infinite, is incomprehensible, is truly a miracle.

Moreover. Every creature requires in its action a subject on which to act; for it belongs to God alone to make something out of nothing, as we proved above.[1] Now that which requires a subject in its action can do only those things to which that subject is in potentiality; for the agent acts on the subject in order to bring it from potentiality to act. Therefore, just as a creature cannot create, so neither can it do in a thing save what is in the potentiality of that thing. But in many miracles wrought by God, something is done in a thing that is not in that thing's capacity; for instance, that the dead live again, that the sun recede, that two bodies occupy the same place. Therefore such miracles cannot be wrought by any created power.

Further. The subject acted upon is ordered both to the agent that reduces it from potentiality to act, and to the act to which it is reduced. Accordingly, just as any particular subject is in potentiality to some determinate act, and not to any act, so it cannot be brought from potentiality to a determinate act except by some determinate agent; for agents must needs differ according as they introduce different acts. Thus, whereas air is potentially fire or water, one agent makes it to be actually fire, and another makes it to be actually water. Likewise it is clear that corporeal matter is not brought to a perfect actuality by the sole action of a universal power, but there must be some proper agent by which the action of the universal power is determined to a particular effect. Nevertheless, corporeal matter can be brought to a less perfect actuality by the universal power alone, without a particular agent. Thus perfect animals are not formed by the power of a heavenly body alone, but determinate seed is necessary; whereas the power of a heavenly body, without any seed, suffices for the generation of certain imperfect animals. Accordingly, effects produced among these lower things, if they be of a nature to be wrought by universal higher causes, without the action of particular inferior causes, can be produced in this way without any miracle. Thus it is not a miracle that animals be formed from putrefaction without seed. But if they be not of a nature to be produced by superior causes alone, then particular inferior causes are required for their perfect formation. Now there is no miracle if an effect be produced by a higher cause by means of its proper principles. Therefore it is altogether impossible for miracles to be wrought by the power of the higher creatures.

[1] *C. G.*, II, 16 and 21.

Moreover. Seemingly these amount to the same:—the production of a work out of a subject;—the production of that to which the subject is in potentiality;—and the orderly production of something through definite intermediary stages. Because a subject is not in proximate potentiality to the ultimate effect, until it has arrived at the middle stage. Thus food is not in immediate potentiality flesh, but only when it is changed into blood. Now every creature needs a subject in order to produce something, nor can it produce other than that to which the subject is in potentiality, as we have shown. Therefore it cannot produce anything without bringing the subject to actuality through definite intervening stages. Therefore miracles, which consist in something being done without observing the order in which it is naturally feasible, cannot be worked by the power of a creature.

Also. There is a natural order to be observed in the various kinds of movement. The first is local movement, and hence it is the cause of other movements, because in every genus that which is first is the cause of all that follows in that genus. Now every effect that is produced in this lower world must needs result from some generation or alteration. Consequently, it must be caused through something that is moved locally, if it be the effect of an incorporeal agent which, properly speaking, is incapable of local movement. But no effect that is caused by incorporeal substances through corporeal instruments is a miracle, since bodies have no operation that is not natural. Therefore, created incorporeal substances cannot work miracles by their own power; and much less corporeal substances, whose every action is natural.

Therefore it belongs to God alone to work miracles. For He is above the order which contains all things, as one from whose providence the whole of this order is derived. Moreover, His power, being absolutely infinite, is not determined to any special effect, nor to the producing of its effect in any particular way or order.

Therefore it is said of God in the *Psalm* (cxxxv. 4): *Who alone doth great wonders.*

CHAPTER CIII

HOW SPIRITUAL SUBSTANCES DO WONDERS WHICH, HOWEVER, ARE NOT TRULY MIRACLES

Now it was the opinion of Avicenna that matter is more obedient to separate substances in the production of an effect than to contrary agents in matter. Hence he states that sometimes, at the apprehension of the aforesaid substances, an effect ensues in this lower world, such as rain, or the healing of a sick person, without any corporeal agent intervening.

He regarded as a sign of this the fact that when our soul is of strong imagination, the body is affected by mere thought alone.[1] Thus a man, while walking on a plank at a height, easily falls, because through fear he imagines himself to fall; whereas he would not fall, were the plank placed on the ground, so that he would not fear to fall. It is also clear that the body is heated at a mere apprehension of the soul, for instance in lustful or angry persons; or again, becomes cold, as happens in those who are seized with fear. Sometimes, too, through a strong apprehension, it is inclined to some illness, for instance fever or even leprosy. In this way, says he, if the soul be pure and not subject to the passions of the body, and strong of apprehension, not only its own body is obedient to its apprehension, but even external bodies; so much so that a sick man is healed, or something similar occurs, at its mere apprehension. He holds this to be the cause of fascination, namely, because a certain person's soul, being deeply affected with malevolence, exercises a baneful influence on someone, especially on a child, who by reason of the softness of the body is most impressionable. Hence he maintains that much more, without the action of a corporeal agent, do certain effects result in these lower bodies, at the apprehension of the separate substances, which he considers to be the souls or movers of the spheres.

This theory is consistent enough with other opinions of his.[2] For he holds that all substantial forms emanate from a separate substance into these lower bodies, and that corporeal agents merely dispose matter to receive the impression of the separate agent. But this is untrue according to the teaching of Aristotle, who proves that the forms which are in matter do not come from separate forms, but from forms in matter; for thus it is that we find a likeness between the maker and the thing made.[3]

Moreover. The comparison with the soul's impression on the body does not advance his theory very much. For no impression is made on the body as a result of an apprehension, unless united to the apprehension there be some emotion, as of joy, fear, desire, or of some other passion. Now these passions are accompanied by a certain definite movement of the heart, from which there results a change in the entire body, either in terms of local motion, or in terms of some alteration. Hence it still remains that the apprehension of a spiritual substance does not affect the body, except by means of local movement.

As to his remark about fascination, this does not happen because the apprehension of one affects immediately the body of another; but because the apprehension affects the conjoined body through the movement of the heart, the influence of which reaches even to the eye, which is able to work evil on an external object, especially if it be easily impressionable,—as the eye of a woman in her menses infects a mirror.[4]

[1] Avicenna, *De An.*, IV, 4 (fol. 20vb).   [2] Avicenna, *Metaph.*, IX, 5 (fol. 105rv).
[3] *Metaph.*, VI, 8 (1033b 26).   [4] *De Somno*, II (459b 29).

Accordingly, except through the local movement of a body, a created spiritual substance cannot, by its own power, induce any form into corporeal matter, as though matter, obedient to it, were to assume the act of some form. For it is in the power of a created spiritual substance that a body should be obedient to it in respect of local movement. Now by moving a particular body locally, it applies certain natural forces to the production of certain effects; just as the art of the smith applies fire to make the iron malleable. But this is not miraculous, properly speaking. It follows, therefore, that created spiritual substances do not work miracles by their own power.

And I say *by their own* power, because nothing prevents these substances from working miracles in so far as they work by divine power. This indeed may be seen from the fact that, as Gregory states, one order of angels is especially deputed to the working of miracles.[1] He also says that certain saints sometimes *work miracles by power,* and not merely by intercession.[2]

We must observe, however, that when angels or demons apply natural things in order to produce certain definite effects, they employ them as instruments, just as a physician uses certain herbs as instruments for the purpose of healing. Now from an instrument there proceeds an effect, not only in proportion to its power, but also in excess thereof, inasmuch as it acts by the power of the principal agent. Thus a saw or an axe could not produce a bedstead except through being applied by craftsmanship for that particular effect; nor could natural heat produce flesh, except by the power of the vegetative soul that employs it as an instrument. It is therefore fitting that certain higher effects should result from these same natural things as a consequence of the fact that spiritual substances employ them as instruments.

Accordingly, although such effects cannot be called miracles absolutely, since they result from natural causes, yet they are wonderful to us in two ways. First, because these causes are applied for the production of their proper effects by spiritual substances in a way that is strange to us; even so the works of skillful craftsmen seem wonderful to others who do not see how the work is done.—Secondly, because the natural causes employed for the production of certain effects are invested with a certain power through serving as instruments of spiritual substances; and this comes nearer to the nature of a miracle.

[1] Cf. ch. 80.   [2] *Dial.,* II, 31 (PL 66, 190).

CHAPTER CIV

THAT THE WORKS OF MAGICIANS DO NOT RESULT ONLY FROM THE INFLUENCE OF HEAVENLY BODIES

THERE were some who said that such works as seem wonderful to us, being wrought by the magic art, are done, not by certain spiritual substances, but by the power of the heavenly bodies. This would seem to be indicated by the fact that those who practice works of this kind observe the position of the stars. They are also assisted by the employment of certain herbs and other corporeal things, for the purpose, as it were, of preparing matter of lower degree to receive the influence of the celestial power.

But this is in contradiction with the apparitions [in the works of magicians]. For as it is impossible that an intellect be formed from corporeal principles, as we proved above,[1] it is impossible for effects that are caused exclusively by the intellectual nature to be produced by the power of a heavenly body. Now in these works of magicians, things appear that are exclusively the work of a rational nature; for instance, answers are given about stolen goods, and the like, and this could not be done except through an intellect. Therefore it is not true that all such effects are caused by the mere power of a heavenly body.

Further. Speech is an act proper to the rational nature. Now in these works people appear speaking to men and reasoning about various matters. Therefore such things cannot be done by the mere power of heavenly bodies.

If, however, someone say that these apparitions are present, not according to the external sense, but only according to the imagination:—this is, in the first place, evidently untrue. For imaginary forms do not appear to anyone to be actual things unless he is alienated from his external senses; since it is not possible for a person to look on a likeness as a reality, except the natural judgments of the senses be fettered. Now these conversations and apparitions are addressed to those who have free use of their external senses. Therefore these apparitions and speeches cannot be imaginary.

Besides. No imaginary forms can lead a person to intellectual knowledge beyond the natural or acquired capability of his intellect. This is evident in dreams, since even if they contain some indication of the future, it is not every dreamer that understands the meaning of his dreams. Now in these apparitions and speeches that occur in the works of magicians, it frequently happens that a person obtains knowledge of things surpassing the capability of his intellect, such as the discovery of hidden treasure, the manifestation of the future, and sometimes true answers are given in mat-

[1] Ch. 84.

ters of science. Either, therefore, these apparitions or speeches are not purely imaginary, or at least this is the work of some higher intellect, and not only of a heavenly body, that a person obtain the aforesaid knowledge through these imaginings.

Again. That which is done by the power of heavenly bodies is a natural effect, since it is natural forms that are caused in this lower world by the powers of heavenly bodies. Hence that which cannot be natural to any-thing, cannot be caused by the power of the heavenly bodies. And yet some such things are stated to be caused by the aforesaid works. For instance, it is averred that at the mere presence of a certain person all doors are un-locked, that a certain man becomes invisible, and many like occurrences are related. Therefore this cannot be done by the power of the heavenly bodies.

Further. The reception, through the power of the heavenly bodies, of that which follows, implies the reception of what precedes. Now movement of its very nature follows from having a soul, since it is proper to animate things to move themselves. Therefore it is impossible for an inanimate being to be moved by itself, through the power of a heavenly body. Yet it is stated that by the magic art a statue is made to move of itself, or to speak. Therefore it is not possible for the effects of the magic art to be caused by the power of a heavenly body.

And if it be said that the statue in question is endowed with some vital principle by the power of the heavenly bodies, this is impossible. For the principle of life in all living things is the substantial form, because, as the Philosopher says, *in living things to be is to live*.[1] Now it is impossible for anything to receive anew a substantial form, unless it lose the form which it had previously, since *the generation of one thing is the corruption of an-other*.[2] But in the making of a statue no substantial form is discarded, and there is only a change of shape, which is an accident, since the form of copper or something of the kind remains. Therefore the statue in question cannot possibly be endowed with some vital principle.

Further. If anything is moved by a principle of life, it is necessarily en-dowed with sense, for the principle of movement is sensation or under-standing. But understanding is not found without sensation in generable and corruptible things. Now there cannot be sense where there is not touch, nor touch, without an organ of mean temperature. Such a temperature, how-ever, is not found in the stone or wax or metal out of which the statue is made. It is not possible, therefore, that statues of this sort should be moved by a principle of life.

Besides. Perfect living beings are generated not only by a celestial power, but also from seed, for *man and the sun generate man*;[3] and such as are generated by a celestial power alone without seed, are animals formed by putrefaction, belonging to a lower grade than the others. Ac-cordingly, if these statues be endowed with a vital principle by a celestial

---

[1] *De An.*, II, 4 (415b 13).   [2] Aristotle. *Phys.*, III. 8 (208a 10).   [3] *Ob. cit.*, II. 2 (104b 14).

power alone, so as to move themselves, it follows that they belong to the lowest grade of animals. And yet this would be false if they worked by an intrinsic principle of life, since among their operations some are of a high degree, for they give answers about hidden things. Therefore it is not possible that their operations and movements proceed from a principle of life.

Again. We sometimes find a natural effect produced by the power of the heavenly bodies without the operation of art. Thus, although one may try to produce frogs, or something of the kind, by means of some artifice, frogs do happen to be produced without any artifice. Consequently, if these statues, that are made by necromancy, are endowed with a vital principle by the power of heavenly bodies, it will be possible for them to be formed without the operation of art. But this is not the case. Therefore it is evident that such statues have not a principle of life, nor are they moved by the power of the heavenly bodies.

Hereby is removed the opinion of Hermes who, according to Augustine, expressed himself thus: *As God is the cause of the heavenly gods, so man fashions the gods that reside in temples, satisfied to live near men. I refer to those animated statues, endowed with sense and spirit, that do great and wonderful things, statues gifted with knowledge of the future, and that foretell by dreams and many other things; who afflict men with ailments and heal them, who bring sorrow and joy to them according to their merits.*[1]

This opinion is also refuted by divine authority. For it is said in the *Psalm* (cxxxiv. 15 *seqq.*): *The idols of the Gentiles are silver and gold, the works of men's hands. They have a mouth but they speak not . . . neither is there any breath in their mouths.*

Yet we must not absolutely deny the possibility of some kind of efficacy being in these things through the power of the heavenly bodies; but only for such effects as some lower bodies are able to cause by the power of the heavenly bodies.

CHAPTER CV

WHENCE THE WORKS OF MAGICIANS DERIVE THEIR
EFFICACY

It remains for us to inquire whence the magic arts derive their efficacy: a question that will present no difficulty if we consider their mode of operation.

For in the practice of their art they make use of certain significative words in order to produce certain definite effects. Now, words, in so far as

---

[1] *De Civit. Dei*, VIII, 23 (PL 41, 247).

they signify something, have no power except as derived from some intellect,—either of the speaker, or of the person to whom they are spoken: from the intellect of the speaker, as when an intellect is of such great power that it can cause things by its mere thought, which the voice serves to convey, as it were, to the things that are to be produced; from the intellect of the person to whom the words are addressed, as when the hearer is induced to do some particular thing when his intellect receives the signification of those words. Now it cannot be said that these significative words uttered by magicians derive any efficacy from the intellect of the speaker. For since power follows essence, diversity of power indicates diversity of essential principles. But man's intellect is invariably of such a disposition that its knowledge is caused by things, rather than that it is able by its mere thought to cause things. Consequently, if there be any men that are able of their own power to transform things by words expressive of their thoughts, they will belong to another species, and it would be an equivocation to call them *men*.

Further. By learning we acquire, not the *power to do* a thing, but the *knowledge of how to do* it. Yet some, by learning, are rendered able to perform these magic works. Therefore they must have only knowledge, and not the power, to produce these effects.

But suppose someone were to say that these men, by the influence of the stars, are born with the aforesaid power, while others are excluded from it; so that however much the others, who are born without this power, may be instructed, they cannot succeed in performing these works. To this we must reply, first that, as was shown above,[1] the heavenly bodies cannot make an impression on the intellect. Therefore a man's intellect cannot, through the influence of the stars, receive a power whereby the vocal expression of its thoughts is productive of something.

And if it be said that the imagination likewise produces an effect in the utterance of significative words, and that the heavenly bodies can act on the imagination, since its operation is performed by a bodily organ:— this does not apply to all the results produced by this art. For we have shown that these effects cannot all be produced by the power of the stars.[2] Neither, therefore, can anyone by the power of the stars receive the power to produce these effects.

Consequently, it follows that these effects are accomplished by an intellect to whom the discourse of the person uttering these words is addressed. We have an indication of this in the fact that the significative words employed by the magician are *invocations, supplications, adjurations,* or even *commands,* as though he were addressing another.

Again. Certain characters and definite figures are employed in the observances of this art. Now a figure cannot be the principle of either action or passion, or else, mathematical bodies would be active and passive. There-

[1] Ch. 84. [2] Ch. 104.

fore matter cannot, by definite figures, be disposed to receive a certain natural effect. Therefore magicians do not employ figures as dispositions. It remains, then, that they employ them only as signs, for there is no third solution. But we make signs only to other intelligent beings. Therefore the magic arts derive their efficacy from another intelligent being, to whom the magician's words are addressed.

And if someone were to say that certain figures are appropriated to certain heavenly bodies, and hence that the lower bodies are determined by certain figures to receive the impressions of certain heavenly bodies:— this does not seem to be a reasonable statement. For the patient is not directed to receive the impression of the agent, except through being in potentiality. Hence those things alone determine it to receive a particular impression, that cause it to be somehow in potentiality. Now figures do not cause matter to be in potentiality to any particular form, because a figure, as such, abstracts from all matter and sensible forms, since it is something mathematical. Therefore a body is not determined by figures or characters to receive the influence of a heavenly body.

Besides. Certain figures are appropriated to the heavenly bodies as their effects, for the figures of the lower bodies are caused by heavenly bodies. Now, the aforesaid arts do not use characters or figures as produced by the heavenly bodies; in fact, they are produced by the man practicing the art. Therefore the appropriation of figures to certain heavenly bodies has nothing to do with the question.

Further. As we have shown, matter is in no way disposed to form by means of figures. Hence the bodies on which these figures are impressed are as capable of receiving the influence of heavenly bodies as are other bodies of the same species. Now, that an agent act on one rather than another of several equally disposed things, by reason of something appropriated to be found in it, is a mark of its operating, not by natural necessity, but by choice. Hence it is clear that these arts which employ figures in order to produce certain effects derive their efficacy, not from something that acts by nature, but from some intellectual substance that acts through its intellect.

This is also proved by the very name *character* which they apply to these figures; for a character is a sign. Thereby we are given to understand that they employ these figures merely as signs shown to some intellectual nature.

Since, however, in the products of art, figures are like specific forms, someone might say that there is no reason why, through the influence of a heavenly body, some power should not shape the figure that gives an image its species, not indeed as a figure, but as specifying the product of art, which acquires this power from the stars. But as to the letters that form an inscription on a statue, and other characters, nothing else can be said of them, but that they are signs. Therefore they are directed to only some intellect.—This is also proved by the sacrifices, prostrations and other similar practices, which can be nothing else than signs of reverence shown to an intellectual nature.

CHAPTER CVI

THAT THE INTELLECTUAL SUBSTANCE WHICH GIVES EFFICACY TO THE PRACTICES OF MAGIC IS NOT GOOD ACCORDING TO VIRTUE

WE must furthermore inquire what is this intellectual nature by whose power these works are done.

And in the first place it is plain that it is not good and praiseworthy. For it is the mark of an ill-disposed intellect to countenance things contrary to virtue. Now this is what happens in these arts, for they are often employed in order to further adultery, theft, murder and like malefices; and therefore those who practice these arts are called *malefics*. Therefore the intellectual nature on whose assistance these arts depend is not well disposed according to virtue.

Again. It is not the mark of an intellect well disposed according to virtue, to befriend and assist men of evil life, rather than any upright man. Now those who practice these arts are generally men of evil life. Therefore the intellectual nature from whose assistance these arts derive their efficacy is not well disposed according to virtue.

Further. It is the mark of a well disposed intellect to guide men towards those goods that are proper to man, namely, the goods of reason. Consequently, to lead men away from these, and to draw men to goods of the least worth, shows a mind of evil disposition. Now by these arts men progress, not in the goods of reason, which are the sciences and the virtues, but in goods of least account, such as the discovery of stolen goods, the capture of thieves, and so forth. Therefore the intellectual substances, whose assistance these arts employ, are not well disposed according to virtue.

Moreover. There is a certain deception and irrationality in the works of these arts; for they require a man indifferent to lustful pleasure, whereas they are frequently employed to further lustful intercourse. But there is nothing irrational or contradictory in the work of a well-disposed intellect. Therefore these arts do not employ the assistance of an intellect that is well disposed as to virtue.

Besides. It is an ill-disposed intellect that is incited by the commission of crime to lend his assistance to another. But this is done in these arts for we read of innocent children being slain by those who practice them

Therefore the persons by whose assistance such things are done have an evil intellect.

Again. The proper good of the intellect is truth. Since, therefore, it belongs to good to lead others to good, it belongs to any well-disposed intellect to lead others to truth. In the works of the magicians, however, many things are done by which men are mocked and deceived. The intellect whose help they use, therefore, is not morally well disposed.

Further. A well-disposed intellect is allured by truth in which it takes delight, but not by lies. The magicians, however, in their invocations make use of various lies, whereby they allure those whose help they employ. For they threaten certain impossible things, as for instance that, unless the one who is called upon gives help, he who invokes him will shatter the heavens or displace the stars, as Porphyry narrates in his *Letter to Anebontes*.[1] Those intellectual substances, therefore, with whose help the works of the magicians are performed, do not seem to be intellectually well disposed.

Moreover. That a superior should be subject as an inferior to one that commands him, or that an inferior should allow himself to be invoked as a superior, would seem to indicate a person of an ill-disposed intellect. Now, magicians call upon those whose assistance they employ, as though these were their superiors, and as soon as they appear they command them as inferiors. In no way therefore do they appear to be of a well-disposed intellect.

Hereby is removed the error of the pagans, who ascribed these works to the gods.

CHAPTER CVII

THAT THE INTELLECTUAL SUBSTANCE WHOSE ASSISTANCE IS EMPLOYED IN THE MAGIC ARTS IS NOT EVIL IN ITS NATURE

IT is impossible that there be natural malice in the intellectual substances whose assistance is employed in the practice of the magic arts.

For if a being tends to something by its nature, it tends to it not accidentally but essentially, as a heavy body tends downwards. Now if these intellectual substances are evil essentially, they tend to evil naturally and, consequently, not accidentally but essentially. But this is impossible, for we have proved that all things tend essentially to good, and nothing tends to evil except accidentally.[2] Therefore these intellectual substances are not naturally evil.

Again. Everything that exists must be either cause or caused, or other-

---

[1] Cf. St. Augustine, *De Civit. Dei*, X, 11 (PL 41, 290).   [2] Ch. 3ff.

wise there would be no order between it and other things. Hence the sub-stances in question are either causes only, or are also caused. If they be causes, since evil cannot cause a thing save accidentally, as was proved above,[1] and since whatever is accidental must be traced to something es-sential, it follows that there must be in them something preceding their malice, whereby they are causes. Now in each thing it is the nature and essence that comes first. Therefore these substances are not evil by nature.

The same follows if they be caused. For no agent acts except by intend-ing some good. Therefore evil cannot be the effect of a cause except acci-dentally. Now that which is caused only by accident cannot exist naturally, since every nature has a definite mode of coming into being. Therefore it is impossible for the substances in question to be evil by nature.

Besides. Every being has its own being according to the mode of its nature. Now *to be*, as such, is good, a sign of which is that all things desire being. Consequently, if these substances were evil by nature, they would have no being.

Moreover. We have proved that nothing can exist that does not have being from the first being;[2] and that the first being is the highest good.[3] Since then every agent, as such, produces its like, whatever proceeds from the first being must be good. Therefore the aforesaid substances, in so far as they exist, and have a certain nature, cannot be evil.

Further. There cannot possibly exist a thing that is altogether deprived of a participation in good; for since the good and the appetible are the same, if a thing were utterly without a share in good, there would be noth-ing appetible in it. But its own being is appetible to each thing. Conse-quently, if anything be described as evil in its nature, this must be, not be-cause it is absolutely evil, but because it is evil to *this* being, or in *some* respect. Thus poison is not evil absolutely, but to one to whom it is harm-ful; and hence one man's poison is another man's meat. Now this happens because the particular good that is proper to one is contrary to the par-ticular good that is proper to another; and thus heat, which is the good of fire, is contrary to cold, which is the good of water, and destroys it. Accordingly, that which by its nature is directed, not to this or that good, but to good absolutely, cannot possibly, even in this way, be called evil by its nature. Now such is every intellect, because its good is in its own opera-tion, the object of which is the universal, and things that exist absolutely. Therefore no intellect can be evil in its nature, either absolutely or in rela-tion to something else.

Again. In every intellectual subject, the intellect moves the appetite, according to the order of nature, because the proper object of the will is the understood good. Now the good of the will consists in its following the intellect. Thus, in man, the good is that which is according to reason, and whatever is outside this is evil. It is according to a natural order, there-

[1] Ch. 14.   [2] *C. G.*, II, 15.   [3] *C. G.*, I, 41.

fore, that an intellectual substance wills the good. Consequently, it is impossible that the intellectual substances, whose assistance is employed by magical arts, be naturally evil.

Besides. Since the will tends naturally to the understood good, as its proper object and end, it is impossible for an intellectual substance to have a will naturally evil, unless its intellect err naturally in its judgment of good. Now there can be no such intellect, because false judgments in the acts of the intellect are like monstrosities in natural things, for they are not according to, but outside, nature; since the good and natural end of the intellect is the knowledge of truth. Therefore there cannot be an intellect that is naturally deceived in its judgment of truth. Neither, consequently, is it possible for an intellectual substance to have a will naturally evil.

Further. No cognitive power fails in the knowledge of its object, save because of being defective or corrupted, since by its very nature it is directed to the knowledge of that object. Thus the sight does not fail in the perception of color, unless the sight itself be injured. Now every defect and corruption is outside nature, because nature aims at the being and perfection of a thing. Therefore no cognitive power can fail in the right judgment of its object. Now the proper object of the intellect is the true. Therefore there cannot be an intellect that errs naturally in the knowledge of truth. Neither, therefore, can any will fall away naturally from the good.

This is confirmed by the authority of Scripture. For it is said (*1 Tim.* iv. 4): *Every creature of God is good*; and (*Gen.* i. 31): *God saw all the things that He had made, and they were very good.*

Hereby also is removed the error of the Manicheans who held that these intellectual substances, which we are wont to call *demons* or *devils*, are naturally evil.

There is also removed the error described by Porphyry in his *Letter to Anebontes*, where he says that *some are of the opinion that there is a genus of spirits, to whom it belongs to grant the prayers of magicians, spirits naturally deceitful, appearing under all kinds of forms, pretending to be gods, or demons, or souls of the departed. It is they who cause all these effects that seem either good or evil. As to those effects that are really good, they give no assistance; in fact, they know nothing about them. But they counsel evil, and impugn and sometimes hinder those who are intent on leading a virtuous life; they are full of presumption and arrogance; they delight in vanities, and are fascinated by flattery.*[1] These words of Porphyry indicate clearly enough the malice of the demons, whose assistance the magic arts employ. In this alone are his words reprehensible that he states this malice to be natural to the demons.

[1] Cf. St. Augustine, *De Civit. Dei*, X, 11 (PL 41, 289).

CHAPTER CVIII

ARGUMENTS THAT WOULD SEEM TO PROVE THAT THERE CAN BE NO SIN IN THE DEMONS

SINCE malice in the demons is not natural to them, and since it has been proved that they are evil,[1] it follows of necessity that the evil in them is voluntary. Accordingly, we must inquire how this can be, for it would seem altogether impossible.

[1] For we proved in the Second Book that no intellectual substance is naturally united to a body, except the human soul [2] (or according to some, the souls of the heavenly bodies,[3] which it is unfitting to deem evil, since the movement of heavenly bodies is most orderly, and, in a sense, is the principle of the entire natural order). Now every other cognitive power, except the intellect, employs animate corporeal organs. Therefore the substances in question cannot have any cognitive power besides the intellect. Therefore whatever they know they understand. Now one does not err in what one understands, since all error results from lack of understanding. Therefore there can be no error in the knowledge of such substances. But there can be no sin in the will without error, because the will always tends to the apprehended good; so that unless there be error in the apprehension of good, there cannot be sin in the will. Therefore it seems that there can be no sin of the will in those substances.

[2] Again. In man, sin occurs in the will about matters of which we have true knowledge in general, through the fact that the judgment of the reason is hindered by a passion that shackles the reason in a particular instance. But there can be no such passions in the demons, because passions belong to the sensitive part of the soul, which exercises no operation without a corporeal organ. Consequently, if these separate substances have a right knowledge in general, it is impossible for their will to tend to evil through defective knowledge in a particular matter.

[3] Moreover. No cognitive power is deceived about its proper object, but only about one that is extraneous. Thus, the sight is not deceived in its judgment about colors; whereas deception may occur if a man judge by sight of taste, or of the species of a thing. Now the proper object of the intellect is the quiddity of a thing. Consequently, there can be no deception in the knowledge of the intellect, if it were to apprehend the mere quiddities of things; but all deception of the intellect would seem to occur through its apprehending the forms of things mingled with phantasms, as is the case with man. But this mode of knowledge is not in intellectual substances that are not united to bodies, since there can be no phantasms apart

---

[1] Ch. 106.   [2] C. G., II, 90.   [3] C. G., I, 70.

from a body. Therefore there can be no error in the knowledge of separate substances, and consequently neither can there be sin in the will.

[4] Besides. In man, falsehood occurs in the work of the intellect composing and dividing, because the intellect does not apprehend the quiddity of a thing absolutely, but composes something with the apprehended thing. Now in the operation whereby the intellect apprehends the essence, falsehood does not occur except accidentally, in so far as, in this operation also, there is a certain mixture of the work of composing and dividing by the intellect. This happens because our intellect attains to the knowledge of the quiddity of a thing, not at once, but in a certain order of inquiry. Thus, at first we apprehend *animal*, then we divide it by opposite differences, and setting one of these aside, add the other to the genus, until we come to the definition of the species. In this process there may be falsehood, if we take as a difference of the genus one that is not a difference of the genus. Now, to proceed thus to the knowledge of the essence of a thing belongs to an intellect that proceeds discursively from one thing to another by reasoning; but it is not becoming to separate intellectual substances, as we proved above.[1] Seemingly, therefore, there can be no error in the knowledge of such substances. Consequently, neither can there be sin in their will.

[5] Moreover. Since nothing desires other than its own good, it would seem impossible for that which has but one single good, to err in its appetite. For this reason, although faults happen in natural things through some defect occurring in the execution of the appetite, they never happen in the natural appetite. For a stone always tends to a lower place, whether it reach it or be hindered. Now, in man, sin happens in the act of appetite, because, as our nature is composed of spiritual and corporeal elements, there is more than one good in man; for one thing is his good in relation to the intellect, another is his good in relation to the senses, or even in relation to the body. But among these various things that are man's goods, there is an order, so that what is of less account must be subordinate to that which is of more account. Hence, sin of the will occurs in man when, in defiance of this order, he desires that which is good for him in a restricted sense in preference to that which is good absolutely. But this composition and diversity of goods is not in separate substances. In fact, their every good is in relation to the intellect. Therefore, seemingly, no sin of the will is possible in them.

[6] Again. In man, sin of the will results from excess or deficiency, between which virtue stands. Consequently, in matters that do not admit of excess and deficiency, but only of the mean, the will cannot sin. Hence no man can sin in desiring justice, since justice itself is a kind of mean. Now separate substances cannot desire other than intellectual goods, for it is absurd to say that beings by nature incorporeal desire corporeal goods, or

[1] *C. G.,* II, 101.

that those which have no senses desire sensible goods. But in intellectual goods there can be no excess, for by their very nature they are a mean between excess and deficiency. Thus the truth is a mean between two errors, one of which is on the side of excess, the other on that of deficiency (and that is why sensible and corporeal goods are in the mean in so far as they are according to reason). Therefore, seemingly, separate intellectual substances cannot sin through the will.

[7] Moreover. An incorporeal substance is, seemingly, more remote from defects than a corporeal substance. Now no defect can occur in those corporeal substances that are remote from contrariety, namely, the heavenly bodies. Much less, therefore, can any sin occur in separate substances that are remote both from contrariety, and from matter, and from movement, which seem to be the sources of any possible defect.

CHAPTER CIX

THAT THERE CAN BE SIN IN THE DEMONS, AND HOW THIS IS POSSIBLE

THAT sin of the will is in the demons is clear from the authority of Scripture. For it is said (*1 John* iii. 8) that *the devil sinneth from the beginning*; again it is said (*Jo.* viii. 44) that *the devil is a liar, and the father of lies,* and that *he was a murderer from the beginning*; and it is also said (*Wis.* ii. 24) that *by the envy of the devil, death came into the world.*

If anyone chose to follow the opinions of the Platonists,[1] he would easily explain the above arguments. For they assert that the demons are *living beings with a body composed of air*; and so, since they have a body united to them, there can be a sensitive part in them. Hence they ascribe to them passions which in us are a cause of sin, namely, anger, hate and the like. That is why Apuleius says that they *are susceptive in mind.*

Moreover. Independently of their being united to bodies, as the Platonists hold, perhaps yet another kind of knowledge might be assigned to them besides that of the intellect. For, according to Plato, the sensitive soul also is incorruptible,[2] so that it must have an operation in which the body does not concur. Consequently, nothing prevents the operation of the sensitive soul, and therefore the passions, from being in an intellectual substance, even though it be not united to a body. Hence the same source of sin is found in them as in us.

But both of these explanations are impossible. For it has been proved above that, with the exception of human souls, no other intellectual substances are united to bodies.[3] And that the operations of the sensitive soul

---

[1] Cf. St. Augustine, *De Civit. Dei,* VII, 14ff. (PL 41, 239).   [2] Cf. *C. G.,* II, 82.
[3] *C. G.,* II, 90.

are impossible apart from a body is clear from the fact that when a sensorial organ is destroyed, one operation of sense is destroyed. Thus sight ceases with the loss of an eye. For this reason, as soon as the organ of touch, which is necessary to the constitution of the animal,[1] is destroyed, the animal must die.

In order to solve the question proposed,[2] then, we must observe that, just as there is order among active causes, so too among final causes; so that, namely, the secondary end depends on the principal end, even as the secondary agent depends on the principal agent. Now a fault occurs in active causes when the secondary agent departs from the order of the principal agent; just as, when the leg fails to accomplish the movement commanded by the appetitive power through being crooked, the result is a limping gait. In the same way, therefore, in final causes also, when the secondary end is not subordinate to the principal end, there is sin in the will, the object of which is *the good and the end*.

Now every will naturally desires that which is the proper good of the one willing, namely, perfect being, nor can it will anything contrary to this. Accordingly, no sin of the will can occur in anyone willing whose proper good is the ultimate end, which is not subordinate to any other end, and to which all other ends are subordinate. Such a willing being is God, whose being is the highest good, which is the ultimate end. Therefore in God there can be no sin of the will.

But in every other voluntary being, whose proper good must needs be subordinate to another good, sin of the will can occur, if we consider such a voluntary being in his nature. For, though there be a natural inclination of the will in every voluntary being to will and love his own perfection, so that he cannot will anything contrary thereto, yet it is not naturally implanted in him so that he directs his perfection to another end unfailingly; since the higher end is not his proper end, but that of the superior nature. Therefore it is left to his choice to direct his own perfection to a higher end. For beings endowed with a will differ from those which are not so endowed, in that the former direct themselves and what is theirs to an end, and are therefore said to have free choice; whereas the latter do not direct themselves to an end, but are directed by a higher agent, being, as it were, moved to the end by another's action, and not by their own.

Hence there could be sin in the will of a separate substance, from the fact that he did not direct his own good and perfection to his last end, but adhered to his own good as his end. And since rules of action must needs be taken from the end, the consequence is that, through making himself his own end, he pretended to submit other things to his rule, and that his will was not subject to another higher than himself. But this belongs to God alone. In this sense then we are to understand that *he desired to be equal to God* [*Isa.* xiv. 14]; not that his good might be equal to the divine

---

[1] Aristotle, *De An.*, II, 2 (413b 4). [2] *I.e.*, the question in ch. 108.

good, because such a thing could not come into his mind, and because by desiring it he would be desiring not to be, since the distinction of species is according to the various degrees of things, as is clear from what has been said above.[1]—Now, the will to rule others, and the refusal to submit one's will to the ruling of a superior, is the will to be supreme and, so to say, not to be subject; which is the sin of pride. Hence it is fittingly said that the demon's first sin was *pride*.—But as from one error concerning a principle various and manifold errors result, so from the first disorder in the demon's will, there arose all manner of sins in his will: both of hate towards God as resisting his pride and most justly punishing his fault; and of envy towards man; and of many such sins.

We must also observe that, as the proper good of a thing is subordinate to several higher goods, he who wills is free to depart from the order of one superior, and not from the order of another that is either higher or lower than the former. Thus, a soldier who is subordinate both to his king and to his general, can direct his will to the good of the general, and not that of the king, or *vice versa*. But if the general depart from the order of the king, the will of the soldier will be good, if he depart from the will of his general, and direct his own will to his king; and the will of the soldier who obeys the will of his general against the will of his king will be evil, because the order of the lower principle depends on the order of the higher. Now, separate substances are not only subordinate to God, but one of them is subordinate to another, from the first to the last, as we proved in the Second Book.[2] And since in every voluntary being under God there can be sin of the will, if such a being be considered in his nature, it was possible for one of the higher separate substances, or even the highest of all, to sin in his will. And this indeed is not improbable, for he would not have rested in his good as his end unless that good were very perfect. Possibly, then, some of the lower separate substances, of their own will, directed their good to him, thus departing from the divine order, and so sinned even as he did; while others, adhering by the movement of their will to the divine order, rightly departed from the order of the one who sinned, although he was higher than they according to the order of nature. In the Fourth Book we shall show how in either case their wills persevere in goodness or malice unchangeably.[3] For this regards the punishments or rewards of the good or wicked.

There is, however, this difference between a man and a separated substance, that in one man there are several appetitive powers which are subordinated one to the other. But this is not the case with separate substances, although one substance is subordinated to another. Now sin occurs in the will whenever the inferior appetite rebels. Just as sin, therefore, would be brought about in a separate substance either by its being turned aside from the divine order or because an inferior substance is turned aside

[1] Ch. 97.   [2] *C. G.*, II, 95.   [3] *C. G.*, IV, 92ff.

from its order to a superior one (which latter remains under the divine order), so in a man sin occurs in two ways. It occurs in one way from the fact that the human will does not direct its proper good to God; and this sin is common both to man and to separate substances. It occurs in another way from the fact that the good of the lower appetite is not regulated with regard to the higher, as for instance when we will the delights of the flesh, towards which the concupiscible appetite tends, not in accordance with the rule of reason. This kind of sin is not found in separate substances.

CHAPTER CX

SOLUTION OF THE AFORESAID ARGUMENTS

CONSEQUENTLY it is not difficult to solve the objections that have been raised.[1]

[1-4] For we are not forced to say that there was error in the intellect of the separate substance because he judged a good not to be good; the error consisted rather in not considering the higher good to which his own good should have been referred. For his will, through being intent on his own good, could be the cause of this lack of consideration, since it is free to the will to turn to this or that.[2]

[5] It is also clear that he desired but one good, and that was his own good; but his sin consisted in his disregarding the higher good, to which his own should have been directed. For just as in us there is sin through our desiring inferior goods, those, namely, of the body, outside the order of reason, so in the devil was there sin through his not referring his own good to the divine.

[6] It is also clear that he ignored the mean of virtue, inasmuch as he did not submit to the order of his superior. Thus he gave to himself more than his due, and to God less than was due to Him as the sovereign rule to whose order all things should be subject. Consequently, it is evident that in this sin the mean was not missed through excess of passion, but merely through inequality of justice, which is concerned with operations. For in separate substances there can be operations, but passions not at all.

[7] Nor does it follow that, because in the higher bodies there can be no defects, there can be no sin in separate substances. Because bodies and all irrational beings are acted upon, and do not put themselves in action, for they have no dominion over their actions. Therefore they cannot escape the first rule that puts them in action and moves them, unless they be unable to receive adequately the rectitude of the supreme rule, owing to an indisposition of matter. Therefore the higher bodies, in which there cannot be any indisposition of matter, can never fall from the rectitude of the

[1] Ch. 108.   [2] Cf. St. Thomas, *De Malo*, q. 1, a. 3.

first rule. But rational or intellectual substances are not only acted upon, but also move themselves to their own actions. And this applies to them all the more, according as their nature is the more perfect, since the more perfect a thing's nature, the more perfect is its power for action. Consequently, the perfection of their nature does not prevent the possibility of sin in them in the manner explained above, namely, through adhering to themselves, and disregarding the order of the superior agent.

CHAPTER CXI

THAT RATIONAL CREATURES ARE SUBJECT TO THE DIVINE PROVIDENCE IN A SPECIAL MANNER

FROM what has been proved up to now,[1] it is evident that the divine providence extends to all things. And yet there must be some special aspect of providence to found in the case of intellectual and rational creatures, over and above other creatures. For they surpass other creatures both in the perfection of their nature, and in the excellence of their end: in the perfection of their nature, because the rational creature alone has dominion over its action, since it moves itself freely to act, whereas other crea-- tures are moved to their proper actions rather than act themselves, as was proved above;[2] in the excellence of their end, because the intellectual creature alone by its own operation attains to the last end of the universe, namely, by knowing and loving God, whereas other creatures cannot attain to the last end except by a certain participation of His likeness. Now, actions vary in kind according to the diversity of end and of their subject matter. Thus in art the operations vary according to the difference of end and matter; for a physician acts differently to expel sickness, and to confirm health; and differently, again, in bodies of different temperament. In like manner, in the government of a state, a different kind of order must be observed according to the different status of the subjects, and according to the different ends to which they are directed; for there must be a different rule for soldiers to make them ready to fight, and for craftsmen that they may be able to work. Accordingly, there is one kind of order whereby rational creatures are subject to the divine providence, and another whereby other creatures are subject to it.

[1] Ch. 64ff.　　[2] Ch. 47.

CHAPTER CXII

THAT RATIONAL CREATURES ARE GOVERNED FOR THEIR OWN SAKE, AND OTHER CREATURES AS DIRECTED TO THEM

IN the first place, then, the very condition of the rational creature, as having dominion over its actions, requires that the care of providence should be bestowed on it for its own sake; whereas the condition of other things, that have no dominion over their actions, shows that they are cared for, not for their own sake, but as being directed to other things. For that which acts only when moved by another is like an instrument, whereas that which acts by itself is like a principal agent. Now an instrument is required, not for its own sake, but that the principal agent may use it. Hence, whatever is done for the care of instruments must be referred to the principal agent as its end; whereas any action directed to the principal agent as such, either by the agent itself or by another, is for the sake of the same principal agent. Accordingly, intellectual creatures are ruled by God as though He cared for them for their own sake, while other creatures are ruled as being directed to rational creatures.

Again. That which has dominion over its own act is free in its action, because *he is free who is his own master*,[1] whereas that which by some kind of necessity is moved by another to act is subject to slavery. Therefore every other creature is naturally under slavery; the intellectual nature alone is free. Now, in every government provision is made for the free for their own sake; but for slaves that they may be useful to the free. Accordingly, the divine providence makes provision for the intellectual creature for its own sake, but for other creatures for the sake of the intellectual creature.

Moreover. Whenever things are directed to a certain end, if any of them are unable of themselves to attain to the end, they must needs be directed to those that attain to the end, which are directed to the end for their own sake. Thus the end of the army is victory, which the soldiers obtain by their own action in fighting, and they alone in the army are required for their own sake; whereas all others, to whom other duties are assigned, such as the care of horses, the preparing of arms, are requisite for the sake of the soldiers of the army. Now it is clear from what has been said that God is the last end of the universe,[2] Whom the intellectual nature alone obtains in Himself, namely, by knowing and loving Him, as was proved above.[3] Therefore the intellectual nature alone is requisite for its own sake in the universe, and all others for its sake.

[1] Aristotle, *Metaph.*, I, 2 (982b 26).   [2] Ch. 17.   [3] Ch. 25ff.

Further. In every whole, the principal parts are requisite on their own account for the establishment of the whole, while the others are required for the preservation or betterment of the former. Now, of all the parts of the universe, intellectual creatures hold the highest place, because they approach nearest to the divine likeness. Therefore the divine providence provides for the intellectual nature for its own sake, and for all others for its sake.

Besides. It is clear that all the parts are directed to the perfection of the whole, since the whole is not for the sake of the parts, but the parts for the sake of the whole. Now intellectual natures are more akin to the whole than other natures; because, in a sense, the intellectual substance is all things, inasmuch as by its intellect it is able to comprehend all things, whereas every other substance has only a particular participation of being. Consequently, God fittingly cares for other things for the sake of intellectual substances.

Besides. Whatever happens to a thing in the course of nature happens to it naturally. Now we see that in the course of nature the intellectual substance uses all others for its own sake: either for the perfection of the intellect, which sees the truth in them as in a mirror; or for the execution of its power and the development of its knowledge, in the same way as a craftsman develops the conception of his art in corporeal matter; or, again, to sustain the body that is united to the intellectual soul, as is the case in man. It is clear, therefore, that God cares for all things for the sake of intellectual substances.

Moreover. If a man seeks something for its own sake, he seeks it always, because *what is per se, is always*; whereas if he seek a thing for the sake of something else, he does not of necessity seek it always but only in reference to that for the sake of which he seeks it. Now, as we proved above, things derive their being from the divine will.[1] Therefore whatever is always is willed by God for its own sake; and what is not always is willed by God, not for its own sake, but for another's. Now intellectual substances approach nearest to being always, since they are incorruptible. They are, moreover, unchangeable, except in their choice. Therefore, intellectual substances are governed as it were for their own sake, while others for the sake of intellectual substances.

The fact that all the parts of the universe are directed to the perfection of the whole is not in contradiction with the foregoing conclusion, since all the parts are directed to the perfection of the whole, in so far as one part serves another. Thus in the human body, it is clear that the lungs belong to the body's perfection, in that they serve the heart; and hence there is no contradiction in the lungs being for the sake of the heart, and for the sake of the whole animal. In like manner, that other natures are for the sake of the intellectual is not contrary to their being for the perfection of

[1] *C. G.*, II, 23.

the universe; for without the things required for the perfection of the intellectual substance, the universe would not be complete.

Nor again does the fact that individuals are for the sake of the species
argue against what has been said. Because, through being directed to their
species, they are directed also to the intellectual nature. For a corruptible
thing is directed to man, not for the sake of only one individual man, but
for the sake of the whole human species. Yet a corruptible thing could not
serve the whole human species, except in terms of its own entire species.
Hence the order whereby corruptible things are directed to man requires
that individuals be directed to the species.

When we assert that intellectual substances are directed by the divine
providence for their own sake, we do not mean that they are not also referred to God and to the perfection of the universe. Accordingly, they are
said to be provided for for their own sake, and others for them, because the
goods bestowed on them by the divine providence are not given them for
another's profit. Whereas those bestowed on others are in the divine plan
intended for the use of intellectual substances.

Hence it is said (*Deut.* iv. 19): *Lest thou see the sun and the moon and
the other stars, and being deceived by error, thou adore and serve them,
which the Lord thy God created for the service of all the nations that are
under heaven*; and (*Ps.* viii. 8): *Thou hast subjected all things under his
feet, all sheep and oxen; moreover, the beasts also of the field*; again
(*Wis.* xii. 18): *Thou, being master of power, judgest with tranquillity,
and with great favor disposest of us.*

Hereby is refuted the error of those who said it is sinful for a man to kill
brute animals; for by the divine providence they are intended for man's use
according to the order of nature. Hence it is not wrong for man to make
use of them, either by killing or in any other way whatever. For this
reason the Lord said to Noe (*Gen.* ix. 3): *As the green herbs I have delivered all flesh to you.*

And if any passages of Holy Scripture seem to forbid us to be cruel to
brute animals, for instance to kill a bird with its young [*Deut.* xxii. 6],
this is either to remove man's thoughts from being cruel to other men,
lest through being cruel to animals one become cruel to human beings; or
because injury to an animal leads to the temporal hurt of man, either of the
doer of the deed, or of another; or because of some signification, as the
Apostle expounds [*1 Cor.* ix. 9] the prohibition against *muzzling the ox
that treadeth the corn* [*Deut.* xxv. 4].

CHAPTER CXIII

THAT THE RATIONAL CREATURE IS DIRECTED TO ITS ACTIONS BY GOD NOT ONLY IN WHAT BEFITS THE SPECIES, BUT ALSO IN WHAT BEFITS THE INDIVIDUAL

HENCE it is clear that the rational creature alone is directed to its actions by God, not only in what befits the species, but also in what befits the individual. For everything is for the sake of its operation, since operation is the ultimate perfection of a thing. Therefore each thing is directed to its action by God, according as it is subject to the divine providence. Now the rational creature is subject to the divine providence as being for its own sake governed and cared for, and not, as other corruptible creatures, for the sake of the species only. For the individual that is governed only for the sake of the species is not governed for its own sake, whereas the rational creature is governed for its own sake, as we have made clear.[1] Accordingly, rational creatures alone are directed by God to their actions for the sake, not only of the species, but also of the individual.

Besides. Things that are directed in their actions only so far as these refer to the species, have not the power to act or not to act; since whatever results from the species is common and natural to all the individuals contained in the species, and we have no choice about what is natural. Hence, if man were directed in his actions only in reference to what befits the species, he would not have the power to act or not to act, but he would have to follow the natural inclination common to the whole species, as is the case with all irrational creatures. It is therefore clear that rational creatures are directed in their actions, not only in accord with what befits the species, but also in accord with what befits the individual.

Moreover. As we have proved above, the divine providence extends to every single thing, even the least.[2] Therefore whatever things have actions outside the inclination of the species, must in such actions receive from the divine providence a direction beyond that which pertains to the species. But many actions are found in the rational creature, for which the inclination of the species is not sufficient; and a sign of this is that they are not the same in all, but differ in different subjects. Therefore the rational creature must be directed to its actions by God, not only in accord with what befits the species, but also in accord with what befits the individual.

Again. God provides for every nature according to its capacity. For He made each creature such that He knew it to be adapted to obtain its end through His government. Now the rational creature alone is capable of being directed to its actions, not only in accord with what befits the species,

---

[1] Ch. 112.   [2] Ch. 75ff.

but also in accord with what befits the individual. For it has intellect and reason, and hence is able to perceive the different ways in which a certain thing is good or evil in relation to various persons, times and places. Therefore the rational creature alone is directed by God to its actions, not only in accord with what befits the species, but also in accord with what befits the individual.

Besides. The rational creature is subject to the divine providence in such a way, that not only is it governed thereby, but is able to know something of the nature of providence; so that it is capable of exercising providence and government in relation to others. This is not the case with other creatures, for they participate in providence only by being subject to it. Now through being capable of providence, a man can direct and govern his own actions also. Therefore the rational creature participates in the divine providence not only in being governed, but also in governing; for it governs itself in its own actions, and also other things. Now every lower providence is subject to the divine providence as to the highest providence. Therefore the government of a rational creature's acts, as personal acts, belongs to the divine providence.

Again. The personal acts of a rational creature are properly those that proceed from the rational soul. Now the rational soul is capable of perpetuity, not only in respect of the species, like other creatures, but also in respect of the individual. Therefore the acts of a rational creature are directed by the divine providence, not only in so far as they belong to the species, but also inasmuch as they are personal.

Hence it is that, though all things are subject to the divine providence, yet Holy Scripture ascribes the care of men to it in a special manner, according to *Ps.* viii. 5: *What is man that thou art mindful of him?* and *1 Cor.* ix. 9: *Doth God take care of oxen?* These things are said because God watches over man's actions not only as belonging to the species, but also as personal acts.

THE SUMMA THEOLOGICA

FIRST PART OF THE SECOND PART

Question VI

ON THE VOLUNTARY AND THE INVOLUNTARY
(*In Eight Articles*)

Since therefore happiness is to be gained by means of certain acts, we must as a consequence consider human acts in order to know by what acts we may obtain happiness, and by what acts we are prevented from obtaining it. But because operations and acts are concerned with what is singular, consequently, all practical knowledge is incomplete unless it take account of things in the particular. The study of Morals, therefore, since it treats of human acts, should consider, first, what is universal; and, secondly, what pertains to the particular.[1]

In treating of what is universal in human acts, the points that offer themselves for our consideration are (1) human acts themselves; (2) their principles.[2] Now of human acts some are proper to man, while others are common to man and animals. And since happiness is man's proper good, those acts which are proper to man have a closer connection with happiness than have those which are common to man and the other animals. First, then, we must consider those acts which are proper to man; secondly, those acts which are common to man and the other animals, and are called passions of the soul.[3] The first of these points offers a twofold consideration: (1) What makes a human act? (2) What distinguishes human acts? [4]

And since those acts are properly called human which are voluntary, because the will is the rational appetite, which is proper to man, we must consider acts in so far as they are voluntary.

First, then, we must consider the voluntary and involuntary in general; secondly, those acts which are voluntary, as being elicited by the will, and as issuing from the will immediately;[5] thirdly, those acts which are voluntary, as being commanded by the will, which issue from the will through the medium of the other powers.[6]

Furthermore, because voluntary acts have certain circumstances, according to which we form our judgment concerning them, we must first

[1] *S. T.,* II-II. [2] Q. 49. [3] Q. 22. [4] Q. 18. [5] Q. 8. [6] Q. 17.

consider the voluntary and the involuntary, and afterwards, the circumstances of those acts which are found to be voluntary or involuntary.[7] Under the first head there are eight points of inquiry: (1) Whether there is anything voluntary in human acts? (2) Whether in irrational animals? (3) Whether there can be voluntariness without any act? (4) Whether violence can be done to the will? (5) Whether violence causes involuntariness? (6) Whether fear causes involuntariness? (7) Whether concupiscence causes involuntariness? (8) Whether ignorance causes involuntariness?

First Article

WHETHER THERE IS ANYTHING VOLUNTARY IN HUMAN ACTS?

We proceed thus to the First Article:—

Objection 1. It would seem that there is nothing voluntary in human acts. For that is voluntary *which has its principle within itself,* as Gregory of Nyssa,[8] Damascene[9] and Aristotle[10] declare. But the principle of human acts is not in man himself, but outside him, since man's appetite is moved to act by the appetible object which is outside him, and which is as a *mover unmoved.*[11] Therefore there is nothing voluntary in human acts.

Obj. 2. Further, the Philosopher proves that in animals no new movement arises that is not preceded by another and exterior motion.[12] But all human acts are new, since none is eternal. Consequently, the principle of all human acts is from outside man, and therefore there is nothing voluntary in them.

Obj. 3. Further, he that acts voluntarily can act of himself. But this is not true of man, for it is written (*Jo.* xv. 5): *Without Me you can do nothing.* Therefore there is nothing voluntary in human acts.

On the contrary, Damascene says that *the voluntary is an act consisting in a rational operation.*[13] Now such are human acts. Therefore there is something voluntary in human acts.

I answer that, There must needs be something voluntary in human acts. In order to make this clear, we must take note that the principle of some acts is within the agent, or in that which is moved; whereas the principle of some movements or acts is outside. For when a stone is moved upwards, the principle of this movement is outside the stone; whereas, when it is moved downwards, the principle of this movement is in the stone. Now of those things that are moved by an intrinsic principle, some move themselves, some not. For since every agent or thing moved acts or is moved for an end, as was stated above,[14] those are perfectly moved by an intrinsic principle whose intrinsic principle is one not only of movement but of move-

---

[7] Q. 7.   [8] Cf. Nemesius, *De Nat. Hom.,* XXXII (PG 40, 728).   [9] *De Fide Orth.,* II, 24 (PG 94, 953).   [10] *Eth.,* III, 1 (1111a 23).   [11] Aristotle, *De An.,* III, 10 (433b 11).   [12] *Phys.,* VIII, 2 (253a 11).   [13] *De Fide Orth.,* II, 24 (PG 94, 953). [14] Q. 1, a. 2.

ment for an end. Now in order that a thing be done for an end, some knowledge of the end is necessary. Therefore, whatever so acts or is so moved by an intrinsic principle that it has some knowledge of the end, has within itself the principle of its act, so that it not only acts, but acts for an end. On the other hand, if a thing has no knowledge of the end, even though it have an intrinsic principle of action or movement, nevertheless, the principle of acting or being moved for an end is not in that thing, but in something else, by which the principle of its action towards an end is imprinted on it. Therefore such things are not said to move themselves, but to be moved by others. But those things which have a knowledge of the end are said to move themselves because there is in them a principle by which they not only act but also act for an end. And, consequently, since both are from an intrinsic principle, *i.e.*, that they act and that they act for an end, the movements and acts of such things are said to be voluntary; for the term *voluntary* signifies that their movements and acts are from their own inclination. Hence it is that, according to the definitions of Aristotle,[15] Gregory of Nyssa[16] and Damascene,[17] the voluntary is defined not only as having *a principle within* the agent, but also as implying *knowledge*. Therefore, since man especially knows the end of his work, and moves himself, in his acts especially is the voluntary to be found.

Reply Obj. 1. Not every principle is a first principle. Therefore, although it is of the nature of the voluntary act that its principle be within the agent, nevertheless, it is not contrary to the nature of the voluntary act that this intrinsic principle be caused or moved by an extrinsic principle; for it is not of the nature of the voluntary act that its intrinsic principle be a first principle.—Nevertheless, it must be observed that a principle of movement may happen to be first in a genus, but not first absolutely. Thus, in the genus of things subject to alteration, the first principle of alteration is the body of the heavens, which nevertheless is not the first mover absolutely, but is moved locally by a higher mover. And so the intrinsic principle of the voluntary act, *i.e.*, the cognitive and appetitive power, is the first principle in the genus of appetitive movement, although it is moved by an extrinsic principle according to other species of movement.

Reply Obj. 2. New movements in animals are indeed preceded by a motion from without; and this in two respects. First, in so far as by means of an extrinsic motion an animal's senses are confronted with something sensible, which, on being apprehended, moves the appetite. Thus a lion, on seeing the approach of the stag through its movement, begins to be moved towards the stag.—Secondly, in so far as some extrinsic motion produces a physical change in an animal's body, for example, through cold or heat; and when the body is thus affected by the motion of an exterior body, the sensitive appetite likewise, which is the power of a bodily organ, is moved

[15] *Eth.*, III, 1 (1111a 23).   [16] Cf. Nemesius, *De Nat. Hom.*, XXXII (PG 40, 728).
[17] *De Fide Orth.*, II, 24 (PG 94, 953).

accidentally. Thus, it happens that through some alteration in the body the appetite is roused to the desire of something. But this is not contrary to the nature of voluntariness, as was stated above, for such movements caused by an extrinsic principle are of another genus of movement.

Reply Obj. 3. God moves man to act, not only by proposing the appetible to the senses, or by effecting a change in his body, but also by moving the will itself; for every movement both of the will and of nature proceeds from God as the First Mover. And just as it is not incompatible with nature that the movement of nature be from God as the First Mover, inasmuch as nature is an instrument of God moving it, so it is not contrary to the character of a voluntary act that it proceed from God, inasmuch as the will is moved by God. Nevertheless, both natural and voluntary movements have this in common, that it belongs to the nature of both that they should proceed from a principle within the agent.

Second Article

WHETHER THERE IS ANYTHING VOLUNTARY IN IRRATIONAL ANIMALS?

We proceed thus to the Second Article:—

Objection 1. It would seem that there is nothing voluntary in irrational animals. For *voluntary* is so called from *voluntas* [*will*]. Now since the will is in the reason,[18] it cannot be in irrational animals. Therefore neither is there anything voluntary in them.

Obj. 2. Further, according as human acts are voluntary, man is said to be master of his actions. But irrational animals are not masters of their actions; for *they act not, but rather are they acted upon*, as Damascene says.[19] Therefore there is no voluntary act in irrational animals.

Obj. 3. Further, Damascene says that *voluntary acts lead to praise and blame*.[20] But neither praise nor blame befits the acts of irrational animals. Therefore such acts are not voluntary.

On the contrary, The Philosopher says that *both children and irrational animals participate in the voluntary*.[21] The same is said by Gregory of Nyssa[22] and Damascene.[23]

I answer that, As was stated above, it is of the nature of a voluntary act that its principle be within the agent, together with some knowledge of the end. Now knowledge of the end is twofold, perfect and imperfect. Perfect knowledge of the end consists in not only apprehending the thing which is the end, but also in knowing it under the aspect of end, and the relationship of the means to that end. And such a knowledge of the end belongs to none but the rational nature.—But imperfect knowledge of

---

[18] Aristotle, *De An.*, III, 9 (432b 5).   [19] *De Fide Orth.*, II, 27 (PG 94, 960). [20] *Op. cit.*, II, 24 (PG 94, 953).   [21] *Eth.*, III, 2 (1111b 8).   [22] Cf. Nemesius. *De Nat. Hom.*, XXXII (PG 40, 729).   [23] *De Fide Orth.*, II, 24 (PG 94, 956).

the end consists in a mere apprehension of the end, without knowing it under the aspect of end, or the relationship of an act to the end. Such a knowledge of the end is exercised by irrational animals, through their senses and their natural estimative power.

Consequently, perfect knowledge of the end is accompanied by the voluntary in its perfect nature, inasmuch as, having apprehended the end, a man can, from deliberating about the end and the means thereto, be moved, or not, to gain that end.—But imperfect knowledge of the end is accompanied by the voluntary in its imperfect nature, inasmuch as the agent apprehends the end, but does not deliberate, and is moved to the end at once. Therefore the voluntary in its perfection belongs to none but the rational nature, whereas the imperfect voluntary belongs also to irrational animals.

Reply Obj. 1. The will is the name of the rational appetite, and consequently it cannot be in beings devoid of reason. But the term *voluntary* is derived from *voluntas* [*will*], and can be extended to those things in which there is some participation of will, by way of likeness thereto. It is thus that voluntary action is attributed to irrational animals, in so far as they are moved to an end, through some kind of knowledge.

Reply Obj. 2. The fact that man is master of his actions is due to his being able to deliberate about them; for since the deliberating reason is indifferently disposed to opposites, the will can proceed to either. But it is not thus that voluntariness is in irrational animals, as was stated above.

Reply Obj. 3. Praise and blame attach to the voluntary act according to the perfect notion of the voluntary, which is not to be found in irrational animals.

Third Article

WHETHER THERE CAN BE VOLUNTARINESS WITHOUT ANY ACT?

We proceed thus to the Third Article:—

Objection 1. It would seem that voluntariness cannot be without any act. For that is voluntary which proceeds from the will. But nothing can proceed from the will, except through some act, at least an act of the will itself. Therefore there cannot be voluntariness without act.

Obj. 2. Further, just as one is said to will by an act of the will, so when the act of the will ceases, one is said not to will. But not to will causes involuntariness, which is contrary to voluntariness. Therefore there can be nothing voluntary when the act of the will ceases.

Obj. 3. Further, knowledge is part of the nature of the voluntary, as was stated above. But knowledge involves an act. Therefore voluntariness cannot be without some act.

On the contrary. The term *voluntary* is applied to that of which we are masters. Now we are masters in respect of to act and not to act, to will and not to will. Therefore, just as to act and to will are voluntary, so also are not to act and not to will.

I answer that, Voluntary is what proceeds from the will. Now one thing proceeds from another in two ways. First, directly, in which sense something proceeds from another inasmuch as this other acts: *e.g.,* heating from heat. Secondly, indirectly, in which sense something proceeds from another through the fact that this other does not act. Thus the sinking of a ship is attributed to the helmsman, from his having ceased to steer.—But we must take note that the cause of what follows from the failure to act is not always the agent as not acting, but only then when the agent can and ought to act. For if the helmsman were unable to steer the ship, or if the ship's helm were not entrusted to him, the sinking of the ship would not be attributed to him, although it might be due to his absence from the helm.

Since, then, by willing and acting, the will is able, and sometimes ought, to hinder not-willing and not-acting, this not-willing and not-acting is imputed to the will as though proceeding from it. And thus it is that we can have the voluntary without an act, and this sometimes without an outward act, but with an interior act, for instance, when one wills not to act, and sometimes without even an interior act, as when one does not will to act.

Reply Obj. 1. We apply the term *voluntary* not only to that which proceeds from the will directly, as from its agent, but also to that which proceeds from it indirectly as from its non-agent.

Reply Obj. 2. *Not to will* is said in two senses. First, as though it were one word, and the infinitive of *I-do-not-will*. Consequently, just as when I say *I do not will to read,* the sense is, *I will not to read,* so *not to will to read* is the same as *to will not to read;* and in this sense *not to will* causes involuntariness.—Secondly it is taken as a sentence, and then no act of the will is affirmed. And in this sense *not to will* does not cause involuntariness.

Reply Obj. 3. Voluntariness requires an act of knowledge in the same way as it requires an act of will, namely, in order that it be in one's power to consider, to will and to act. And then, just as not to will and not to act, when it is time to will and to act, is voluntary, so is it voluntary not to consider.

Fourth Article

WHETHER VIOLENCE CAN BE DONE TO THE WILL?

We proceed thus to the Fourth Article:—

Objection 1. It would seem that violence can be done to the will. For everything can be compelled by that which is more powerful. But there is something, namely, God, that is more powerful than the human will. Therefore it can be compelled, at least by Him.

Obj. 2. Further, every passive subject is compelled by its active principle, when it is changed by it. But the will is a passive power, for it is a *moved mover.*[24] Therefore, since it is sometimes moved by its active principle, it seems that it is sometimes compelled.

Obj. 3. Further, violent movement is that which is contrary to nature. But the movement of the will is sometimes contrary to nature, as is clear of the will's movement to sin, which is contrary to nature, as Damascene says.[25] Therefore the movement of the will can be compelled.

On the contrary, Augustine says that what is done voluntarily is not done of necessity.[26] Now whatever is done under compulsion is done of necessity, and consequently what is done by the will cannot be compelled. Therefore the will cannot be compelled to act.

I answer that, The act of the will is twofold: one is its immediate act, as it were, elicited by it, namely, *to will;* the other is an act of the will commanded by it, and put into execution by means of some other power: *e.g., to walk* and *to speak,* which are commanded by the will to be executed by means of the power of locomotion.

As regards the commanded acts of the will, then, the will can suffer violence, in so far as violence can prevent the exterior members from executing the will's command. But as to the will's own proper act, violence cannot be done to the will. The reason for this is that the act of the will is nothing else than an inclination proceeding from an interior knowing principle, just as the natural appetite is an inclination proceeding from an interior principle without knowledge. Now what is compelled or violent is from an exterior principle. Consequently, it is contrary to the nature of the will's own act that it should be subject to compulsion or violence; just as it is also contrary to the nature of the natural inclination or the movement of a stone to be moved upwards. For a stone may have an upward movement from violence, but that this violent movement be from its natural inclination is impossible. In like manner, a man may be dragged by force, but it is contrary to the very notion of violence that he be thus dragged of his own will.

Reply Obj. 1. God, Who is more powerful than the human will, can move the will of man, according to *Prov.* xxi. 1: *The heart of the king is in the hand of the Lord; whithersoever He will He shall turn it.* But if this were by compulsion, it would no longer be by an act of the will, nor would the will itself be moved, but something else against the will.

Reply Obj. 2. It is not always a violent movement when a passive subject is moved by its active principle, but only then when this is done against the interior inclination of the passive subject. Otherwise, every alteration and generation of simple bodies would be unnatural and violent; whereas they are natural by reason of the natural interior aptitude

---

[24] Aristotle, *De An.,* III, 10 (433a 9; b 16).   [25] *De Fide Orth.,* IV, 20 (PG 94, 1196).   [26] *De Civit. Dei,* V, 10 (PL 41, 152).

of the matter or subject to such a disposition. In like manner, when the will is moved, according to its own inclination, by the appetible object, this movement is not violent but voluntary.

Reply Obj. 3. That to which the will tends by sinning, although in reality it is evil and contrary to the rational nature, is nevertheless apprehended as something good and suitable to nature, in so far as it is suitable to man by reason of some pleasurable sensation or some vicious habit.

Fifth Article

WHETHER VIOLENCE CAUSES INVOLUNTARINESS?

We proceed thus to the Fifth Article:—

Objection 1. It would seem that violence does not cause involuntariness. For we speak of voluntariness and involuntariness in terms of the will. But violence cannot be done to the will, as was shown above. Therefore violence cannot cause involuntariness.

Obj. 2. Further, that which is done involuntarily is done with grief, as Damascene[27] and the Philosopher[28] say. But sometimes a man suffers compulsion without being grieved thereby. Therefore violence does not cause involuntariness.

Obj. 3. Further, what is from the will cannot be involuntary. But some violent actions proceed from the will, for instance, when a man with a heavy body goes upwards, or when a man contorts his members in a way contrary to their natural flexibility. Therefore violence does not cause involuntariness.

On the contrary, The Philosopher[29] and Damascene[30] say that *things done under compulsion are involuntary.*

I answer that, Violence is directly opposed to the voluntary, as likewise to the natural. For the voluntary and the natural have this in common, that both are from an intrinsic principle, whereas the violent is from an extrinsic principle. And for this reason, just as in things devoid of knowledge violence effects something against nature, so in things endowed with knowledge it effects something against the will. Now that which is against nature is said to be *unnatural,* and, in like manner, that which is against the will is said to be *involuntary.* Therefore violence causes involuntariness.

Reply Obj. 1. The involuntary is opposed to the voluntary. Now it has been said that not only the act which proceeds immediately from the will is called voluntary, but also the act commanded by the will. Consequently, as to the act which proceeds immediately from the will, violence cannot be done to the will, as was stated above. But as to the commanded act, the will can suffer violence, and consequently in this respect violence causes involuntariness.

---

[27] *De Fide Orth.,* II, 24 (PG 94, 953). [28] *Eth.,* III, 1 (1111a 20). [29] *Ibid.* (1109b 35). [30] *De Fide Orth.,* II, 24 (PG 94, 953).

Reply Obj. 2. Just as that is said to be natural which is according to the inclination of nature, so that is said to be voluntary which is according to the inclination of the will. Now a thing is said to be natural in two ways. First, because it is from nature as from an active principle: *e.g.*, it is natural for fire to produce heat. Secondly, according to a passive principle, because, namely, there is in nature an inclination to receive an action from an extrinsic principle. Thus, the movement of the heavens is said to be natural by reason of the natural aptitude in the body of the heavens to receive such movement, although the cause of that movement is a voluntary agent. In like manner, an act is said to be voluntary in two ways. First, in regard to action, for instance, when one wills to act; secondly, in regard to passion, as when one wills to receive an action from another. Hence, when action is inflicted by an extrinsic agent, as long as the will to suffer that action remains in the passive subject, this is not violent absolutely; for although the patient does nothing by way of action, he does something by being willing to suffer. Consequently this cannot be called involuntary.

Reply Obj. 3. As the Philosopher says,[31] the movement of an animal, whereby at times an animal is moved against the natural inclination of the body, although it is not natural to the body, is nevertheless in a way natural to the animal, to which it is natural to be moved according to its appetite. Accordingly this is violent, not absolutely, but relatively.—The same remark applies in the case of one who contorts his members in a way that is contrary to their natural disposition. For this is violent relatively, *i.e.*, as to that particular member; but not absolutely, *i.e.*, as to the man himself.

Sixth Article

WHETHER FEAR CAUSES WHAT IS INVOLUNTARY ABSOLUTELY?

We proceed thus to the Sixth Article:—

Objection 1. It would seem that fear causes what is involuntary absolutely. For just as violence regards that which is contrary to the will in the present, so fear regards a future evil which is repugnant to the will. But violence causes what is involuntary absolutely. Therefore fear too causes what is involuntary absolutely.

Obj. 2. Further, that which is of itself such, remains such, whatever be added to it. Thus what is of itself hot, as long as it remains, is still hot, whatever be added to it. But that which is done through fear is involuntary in itself. Therefore, even with the addition of fear it is involuntary.

Obj. 3. Further, that which is such, subject to a condition, is such in a certain respect; whereas what is such, without any condition, is such absolutely. Thus, what is necessary, subject to a condition, is necessary in some

[31] *Phys.*, VIII, 4 (254b 14).

respect, but what is necessary without qualification is necessary absolutely. But that which is done through fear is involuntary absolutely; and it is not voluntary, save under a condition, namely, in order that the evil feared may be avoided. Therefore that which is done through fear is involuntary absolutely.

On the contrary, Gregory of Nyssa[32] and the Philosopher[33] say that such things as are done through fear are *voluntary rather than involuntary.*

I answer that, As the Philosopher says,[34] and likewise Gregory of Nyssa in his book *On Man,*[35] such things as are done through fear *are of a mixed character,* being partly voluntary and partly involuntary. For that which is done through fear, considered in itself, is not voluntary; but it becomes voluntary in this particular case, in order, namely, to avoid the evil feared.

But if the matter be considered rightly, such things are voluntary rather than involuntary; for they are voluntary absolutely, but involuntary in a certain respect. For a thing is said to be absolutely according as it is in act; but according as it is only in the apprehension, it is not so absolutely, but in a certain respect. Now that which is done through fear, is in act in so far as it is done. For, since acts are concerned with singulars, and since the singular, as such, is here and now, that which is done is in act in so far as it is here and now and under other individuating circumstances. Hence that which is done through fear is voluntary, inasmuch as it is here and now, that is to say, in so far as, under the circumstances, it hinders a greater evil which was feared; and thus, the throwing of the cargo into the sea becomes voluntary during the storm, through fear of danger, and so it is clear that it is voluntary absolutely. And hence it is that what is done out of fear has the nature of what is voluntary, because its principle is within.—But if we consider what is done through fear, as outside this particular case, and inasmuch as it is repugnant to the will, this exists only according to our consideration of things; and consequently it is involuntary, considered in that respect, that is to say, outside the actual circumstances of this or that particular case.

Reply Obj. 1. Things done through fear and compulsion differ not only according to present and future time, but also in this, that the will does not consent, but is moved entirely counter to that which is done through compulsion; whereas what is done through fear becomes voluntary because the will is moved towards it, although not for its own sake, but because of something else, that is, in order to avoid an evil which is feared. For the conditions of a voluntary act are satisfied, if it be done because of something else voluntary; since the voluntary is not only what we will for its own sake as an end, but also what we will for the sake of something else as an end. It is clear therefore that in what is done from compulsion, the will does nothing inwardly, whereas in what is done through fear, the will

[32] Cf. Nemesius, *De Nat. Hom.,* XXX (PG 40, 721).   [33] *Eth.,* III, 1 (1110a 12). [34] *Ibid.*   [35] Cf. Nemesius, *De Nat. Hom.,* XXX (PG 40, 721).

does something. Accordingly, as Gregory of Nyssa says,[36] in order to exclude things done through fear, a violent action is defined not only as one *whose principle is from the outside,* but with the addition, *in which he that suffers violence concurs not at all;* for the will of him that is in fear does concur somewhat in that which he does through fear.

Reply Obj. 2. Things that are such absolutely, remain such, whatever be added to them: *e.g.,* a cold thing, or a white thing; but things that are such relatively vary according as they are compared with different things. For what is big in comparison with one thing is small in comparison with another. Now a thing is said to be voluntary, not only for its own sake, as it were, absolutely; but also for the sake of something else, as it were, relatively. Accordingly, nothing prevents a thing, which was not voluntary in comparison with one thing, from becoming voluntary when compared with another.

Reply Obj. 3. That which is done through fear is voluntary without any condition, that is to say, according as it is actually done; but it is involuntary under a certain condition, that is to say, if such a fear were not threatening. Consequently, this argument proves rather the opposite.

Seventh Article

WHETHER CONCUPISCENCE CAUSES INVOLUNTARINESS?

We proceed thus to the Seventh Article:—

Objection 1. It would seem that concupiscence causes involuntariness. For just as fear is a passion, so is concupiscence. But fear causes involuntariness to a certain extent. Therefore concupiscence does so too.

Obj. 2. Further, just as the timid man through fear acts counter to that which he proposed, so does the incontinent, through concupiscence. But fear causes involuntariness to a certain extent. Therefore concupiscence does so also.

Obj. 3. Further, knowledge is necessary for voluntariness. But concupiscence impairs knowledge, for the Philosopher says that *delight,* or the lust of pleasure, *destroys the judgment of prudence.*[37] Therefore concupiscence causes involuntariness.

On the contrary, Damascene says: *The involuntary act deserves mercy or indulgence, and is done with regret.*[38] But neither of these can be said of that which is done out of concupiscence. Therefore concupiscence does not cause involuntariness.

I answer that, Concupiscence does not cause involuntariness, but, on the contrary, makes something to be voluntary. For a thing is said to be voluntary from the fact that the will is moved to it. Now concupiscence inclines the will to desire the object of concupiscence. Therefore the effect of con-

---

[36] *Ibid.* (PG 40, 720).   [37] *Eth.,* VI, 5 (1140b 12).   [38] *De Fide Orth.,* II, 24 (PG 94, 953).

cupiscence is to make something to be voluntary rather than involuntary.

Reply Obj. 1. Fear has reference to evil, but concupiscence has reference to good. Now evil of itself is counter to the will, whereas good harmonizes with the will. Therefore fear has a greater tendency than concupiscence to cause involuntariness.

Reply Obj. 2. He who acts from fear retains the repugnance of the will to that which he does, considered in itself. But he that acts from concupiscence, *e.g.*, an incontinent man, does not retain his former will whereby he repudiated the object of his concupiscence; rather his will is changed so that he desires that which previously he repudiated. Accordingly, that which is done out of fear is involuntary, to a certain extent, but that which is done from concupiscence is in no way involuntary. For the man who yields to concupiscence acts counter to that which he purposed at first, but not counter to that which he desires now; whereas the timid man acts counter to that which in itself he desires now.

Reply Obj. 3. If concupiscence were to destroy knowledge altogether, as happens with those whom concupiscence has rendered mad, it would follow that concupiscence would take away voluntariness. And yet, properly speaking, it would not make the act involuntary, because in beings bereft of reason there is neither voluntary nor involuntary. But sometimes in those actions which are done from concupiscence, knowledge is not completely destroyed, because the power of knowing is not taken away entirely, but only the actual consideration in some particular possible act. Nevertheless, this itself is voluntary, according as by voluntary we mean that which is in the power of the will, for example, *not to act* or *not to will*, and in like manner *not to consider;* for the will can resist the passion, as we shall state later on.[39]

Eighth Article

WHETHER IGNORANCE CAUSES INVOLUNTARINESS?

We proceed thus to the Eighth Article:—

Objection 1. It would seem that ignorance does not cause involuntariness. For *the involuntary act deserves pardon,* as Damascene says.[40] But sometimes that which is done through ignorance does not deserve pardon, according to *1 Cor.* xiv. 38: *If any man know not, he shall not be known.* Therefore ignorance does not cause involuntariness.

Obj. 2. Further, every sin implies ignorance, according to *Prov.* xiv. 22: *They err, that work evil.* If, therefore, ignorance causes involuntariness, it would follow that every sin is involuntary; which is opposed to the saying of Augustine, that *every sin is voluntary.*[41]

Obj. 3. Further, *involuntariness is not without sadness,* as Damascene

---

[39] Q. 10, a. 3; q. 77, a. 7. [40] *De Fide Orth.,* II, 24 (PG 94, 953). [41] *De Vera Relig.,* XIV (PL 34, 133).

says.[42] But some things are done out of ignorance, but without sadness. For instance, a man may kill a foe, whom he wishes to kill, thinking at the time that he is killing a stag. Therefore ignorance does not cause involuntariness.

On the contrary, Damascene[43] and the Philosopher[44] say that *what is done through ignorance is involuntary.*

I answer that, If ignorance cause involuntariness, it is in so far as it deprives one of knowledge, which is a necessary condition of voluntariness, as was declared above. But it is not every ignorance that deprives one of this knowledge. Accordingly, we must take note that ignorance has a three-fold relationship to the act of the will: in one way, *concomitantly;* in another, *consequently*; in a third way, *antecedently. Concomitantly,* when there is ignorance of what is done, but so that even if it were known, it would be done. For then ignorance does not induce one to will this to be done, but it just happens that a thing is at the same time done and not known. Thus, in the example given, a man did indeed will to kill his foe, but killed him in ignorance, thinking to kill a stag. And ignorance of this kind, as the Philosopher states,[45] does not cause involuntariness, since it is not the cause of anything that is repugnant to the will; but it causes *non-voluntariness,* since that which is unknown cannot be actually willed.

Ignorance is *consequent* to the act of the will, in so far as ignorance itself is voluntary; and this happens in two ways in accordance with the two aforesaid modes of the voluntary. First, because the act of the will is brought to bear on the ignorance, as when a man wills not to know, that he may have an excuse for sin, or that he may not be withheld from sin, according to *Job* xxi. 14: *We desire not the knowledge of Thy ways.* And this is called *affected ignorance.*—Secondly, ignorance is said to be voluntary, when it regards that which one can and ought to know, for in this sense *not to act* and *not to will* are said to be voluntary, as was stated above. And ignorance of this kind happens either when one does not actually consider what one can and ought to consider (this is called *ignorance of evil choice,* and arises from some passion or habit), or when one does not take the trouble to acquire the knowledge which one ought to have; in which sense, ignorance of the general principles of law, which one ought to know, is voluntary, as being due to negligence.

Accordingly, if in either of these ways ignorance is voluntary, it cannot cause what is involuntary absolutely. Nevertheless it causes involuntariness in a certain respect, inasmuch as it precedes the movement of the will towards the act, which movement would not be, if there were knowledge.

Ignorance is *antecedent* to the act of the will when it is not voluntary, and yet is the cause of man's willing what he would not will otherwise.

---

[42] *De Fide Orth.,* II, 24 (PG 94, 953).   [43] *Ibid.*   [44] *Eth.,* III, 1 (1110a 1).
[45] *Ibid.* (1110b 25).

Thus a man may be ignorant of some circumstance of his act, which he was not bound to know, with the result that he does that which he would not do if he knew of that circumstance. For instance, a man, after taking proper precaution, may not know that someone is coming along the road, so that he shoots an arrow and slays a passer-by. Such ignorance causes what is involuntary absolutely.

From this may be gathered the solution of the objections. For the first objection deals with ignorance of what a man is bound to know. The second, with ignorance of choice, which is voluntary to a certain extent, as was stated above. The third, with that ignorance which is concomitant with the act of the will.

ON THE CIRCUMSTANCES OF HUMAN ACTS
(*In Four Articles*)

WE must now consider the circumstances of human acts, under which head there are four points of inquiry: (1) What is a circumstance? (2) Whether a theologian should take note of the circumstances of human acts? (3) How many circumstances are there? (4) Which are the most important of them?

First Article

WHETHER A CIRCUMSTANCE IS AN ACCIDENT OF A HUMAN ACT?

We proceed thus to the First Article:—

Objection 1. It would seem that a circumstance is not an accident of a human act. For Tully says that a circumstance is that from *which an orator adds authority and strength to his argument.*[1] But oratorical arguments are derived principally from things pertaining to the substance of a thing, such as the definition, the genus, the species and the like, from which also Tully declares that an orator should draw his arguments.[2] Therefore a circumstance is not an accident of a human act.

Obj. 2. Further, *to be in* is proper to an accident. But that which surrounds [*circumstat*] is rather *out* than in. Therefore the circumstances are not accidents of human acts.

Obj. 3. Further, an accident has no accident. But human acts themselves are accidents. Therefore the circumstances are not accidents of acts.

On the contrary, The particular conditions of any singular thing are called its individuating accidents. But the Philosopher calls the circumstances particular things,[3] *i.e.*, the particular conditions of each act. Therefore the circumstances are individual accidents of human acts.

I answer that, Since, according to the Philosopher,[4] names are the signs of our concepts, it must needs be that in naming things we follow the process of intellectual knowledge. Now our intellectual knowledge proceeds from the more known to the less known. Accordingly, with us, names of more known things are transferred so as to signify less known things. Hence it is that, as is stated in *Metaph.* x.,[5] the notion of distance has been transferred from things that are apart locally to all kinds of opposition;

---

[1] *De Invent.,* I, 24 (p. 31ᵇ).　　[2] Cicero, *Topica,* III (pp. 427-428).　　[3] *Eth.,* III, 1 (1110b 33).　　[4] *Perih.,* I (16a 3).　　[5] Aristotle, *Metaph.,* IX, 4 (1055a 9).

and, in like manner, names that signify local movement are employed to designate all other movements, because bodies, which are circumscribed by place, are best known to us. And hence it is that the name *circumstance* has passed from located things to human acts.

Now in located things, that is said to surround something which is outside it, but touches it, or is placed near it. Accordingly, whatever conditions are outside the substance of an act, and yet in some way touch the human act, are called circumstances. But what is outside a thing's substance, while it belongs to that thing, is called its accident. Therefore the circumstances of human acts should be called their accidents.

Reply Obj. 1. The orator gives strength to his argument, in the first place, from the substance of the act; and, secondly, from the circumstances of the act. So, too, a man becomes indictable, first, through being guilty of murder; secondly, through having done it fraudulently, or from motives of greed, or at a holy time or place, and so forth. And so in the passage quoted it is said pointedly that the orator *adds strength to his argument*, as though this were something secondary.

Reply Obj. 2. A thing is said to be an accident of something in two ways. First, from being in that thing; and thus, whiteness is said to be an accident of Socrates. Secondly, because it is together with that thing in the same subject; thus, whiteness is an accident of the musical inasmuch as they meet in the same subject, so as to touch one another, as it were. And in this sense circumstances are said to be the accidents of human acts.

Reply Obj. 3. As was stated above, an accident is said to be the accident of an accident from the fact that they meet in the same subject. But this happens in two ways. First, in so far as two accidents are both related to the same subject, without any relation to one another: *e.g.,* whiteness and music in Socrates. Secondly, when such accidents are related to one another, as when the subject receives one accident by means of the other: for instance, a body receives color by means of its surface. And thus also is one accident said to be in another, for we speak of color as being in the surface.

Accordingly, circumstances are related to acts in both these ways. For some circumstances, that have a relation to acts, belong to the agent otherwise than through the act: *e.g.,* place and condition of person; whereas others belong to the agent by reason of the act: *e.g.,* the manner in which the act is done.

Second Article

WHETHER THEOLOGIANS SHOULD TAKE NOTE OF THE CIRCUMSTANCES OF HUMAN ACTS?

We proceed thus to the Second Article:—

Objection 1. It would seem that theologians should not take note of the circumstances of human acts. For theologians do not consider human acts otherwise than according to their quality of good or evil. But it seems that circumstances cannot give quality to human acts, for a thing is never qualified, formally speaking, by that which is outside it, but by that which is in it. Therefore theologians should not take note of the circumstances of acts.

Obj. 2. Further, circumstances are the accidents of acts. But one thing may be subject to an infinity of accidents, and so the Philosopher says that *no art or science considers accidental being, except only the art of sophistry.*[6] Therefore the theologian has not to consider circumstances.

Obj. 3. Further, the consideration of circumstances belongs to the orator. But oratory is not a part of theology. Therefore it is not a theologian's business to consider circumstances.

On the contrary, Ignorance of circumstances causes an act to be involuntary, according to Damascene[7] and Gregory of Nyssa.[8] But involuntariness excuses from sin, the consideration of which belongs to the theologian. Therefore circumstances also should be considered by the theologian.

I answer that, Circumstances come under the consideration of the theologian, for a threefold reason. First, because the theologian considers human acts inasmuch as man is thereby directed to happiness. Now everything that is directed to an end should be proportioned to that end. But acts are proportioned to an end by means of a certain commensurateness, which results from the due circumstances. Hence the theologian has to consider the circumstances.—Secondly, because the theologian considers human acts according as they are found to be good or evil, better or worse; and this diversity depends on circumstances, as we shall see further on.[9]— Thirdly, because the theologian considers human acts under the aspect of merit and demerit, which is proper to human acts; and for this it is requisite that they be voluntary. Now a human act is deemed to be voluntary or involuntary according to knowledge or ignorance of circumstances, as was stated above.[10] Therefore the theologian has to consider circumstances.

Reply Obj. 1. The good that is directed to the end is said to be useful, and this implies some kind of relation; and so the Philosopher says that *the good in the genus 'relation' is the useful.*[11] Now, in the genus of *relation* a thing is denominated not only according to that which is inherent in the thing, but also according to that which is extrinsic to it; as may be seen in the expressions *right* and *left, equal* and *unequal,* and the like. Accordingly, since the goodness of acts consists in their utility to the end, nothing hinders their being called good or bad according to their proportion to things that attend them extrinsically.

[6] *Op. cit.,* V, 2 (1026b 3).   [7] *De Fide Orth.,* II, 24 (PG 94, 953).   [8] Cf. Nemesius, *De Nat. Hom.,* XXXI (PG 40, 724).   [9] Q. 18, a. 10 and 11; q. 73, a. 7. [10] Q. 6, a. 8.   [11] *Eth.,* I, 6 (1096a 26).

Reply Obj. 2. Accidents which are altogether accidental are neglected by every art, by reason of their uncertainty and infinity. But such accidents are not what we call circumstances; because circumstances, although, as we have stated above, they are extrinsic to the act, nevertheless are in a kind of contact with it, by being related to it. Proper accidents, however, come under the consideration of art.

Reply Obj. 3. The consideration of circumstances belongs to the moralist, the statesman and the orator. To the moralist, in so far as with respect to circumstances we find or lose the mean of virtue in human acts and passions. To the statesman and to the orator, in so far as circumstances make acts to be worthy of praise or blame, of excuse or indictment. In different ways, however, because where the orator persuades, the statesman judges. To the theologian this consideration belongs in all the aforesaid ways, since to him all the other arts are subservient; for he has to consider virtuous and vicious acts, just as the moralist does; and with the orator and statesman he considers acts according as they are deserving of reward or punishment.

Third Article

WHETHER THE CIRCUMSTANCES ARE PROPERLY SET FORTH IN THE THIRD BOOK OF THE *ETHICS*?

We proceed thus to the Third Article:—

Objection 1. It would seem that the circumstances are not properly set forth in *Ethics* iii.[12] For a circumstance of an act is described as something outside the act. Now time and place answer to this description. Therefore there are only two circumstances, namely, *when* and *where*.

Obj. 2. Further, we judge from the circumstances whether a thing is well or ill done. But this belongs to the mode of an act. Therefore all the circumstances are included under one, which is the *mode of acting*.

Obj. 3. Further, circumstances are not part of the substance of an act. But the causes of an act seem to belong to its substance. Therefore no circumstance should be taken from the cause of the act itself. Accordingly, neither *who*, nor *why*, nor *about what*, are circumstances, since *who* refers to the efficient cause, *why* to the final cause, and *about what* to the material cause.

On the contrary is the authority of the Philosopher in *Ethics* iii.[13]

I answer that, In his *Rhetoric*[14] Tully gives seven circumstances, which are contained in this verse:

> *Quis, quid, ubi, quibus auxiliis, cur, quomodo, quando—*
> *Who, what, where, by what aids, why, how, and when.*

[12] *Op. cit.*, III, 1 (1111a 3). [13] *Ibid.* [14] *De Invent.*, I, 24 (p. 32ᵇ).

For in acts we must take note of *who* did it, *by what aids* or *instruments* he did it, *what* he did, *where* he did it, *why* he did it, *how* and *when* he did it. But Aristotle in *Ethics* iii.[15] adds yet another, namely, *about what*, which Tully includes in the circumstance *what*.

The reason for this enumeration may be considered as follows. For a circumstance is described as something outside the substance of the act, and yet in a way touching it. Now this happens in three ways: first, inasmuch as it touches the act itself; secondly, inasmuch as it touches the cause of the act; thirdly, inasmuch as it touches the effect. It touches the act itself, either as a measure, as *time* and *place*, or by qualifying the act, as the *mode of acting*. It touches the effect when we consider *what* is done. It touches the cause of the act, as to the final cause, by the circumstance *why*; as to the material cause, or object, in the circumstance *about what*; as to the principal efficient cause, in the circumstance *who*; and as to the instrumental efficient cause, in the circumstance *by what aids*.

Reply Obj. 1. Time and place surround [*circumstant*] the act as a measure; but the others surround the act by touching it in any other way according as they are extrinsic to the substance of the act.

Reply Obj. 2. The mode *well* or *ill* is not a circumstance, but results from all the circumstances. But the mode which refers to a quality of the act is a special circumstance: *e.g.*, that a man walks fast or slowly, that he strikes hard or gently, and so forth.

Reply Obj. 3. That condition of the cause on which the substance of the act depends is not a circumstance; it must be an additional condition. Thus, in regard to the object, it is not a circumstance of theft that the object is another's property, for this belongs to the substance of the act; but that it be great or small. And the same applies to the other circumstances which are considered in reference to the other causes. For the end that specifies the act is not a circumstance, but some additional end. Thus, that a valiant man act *valiantly for the sake of* the good of the virtue of fortitude, is not a circumstance; but it is if he act valiantly for the sake of the delivery of the state, or of Christendom, or some such purpose. The same is to be said with regard to the circumstance *what*; for that a man by pouring water on someone should happen to wash him, is not a circumstance of the washing; but that in doing so he give him a chill, or scald him, heal him or harm him, these are circumstances.

Fourth Article

WHETHER THE MOST IMPORTANT CIRCUMSTANCES ARE WHY AND *IN WHAT THE ACT CONSISTS*?

We proceed thus to the Fourth Article:—

Objection 1. It would seem that these are not the most important cir-

[15] *Eth.*, III, 1 (1111a 4).

cumstances, namely, the circumstances *why* and *in which the act is,* as is stated in *Ethics* iii.[16] For place and time seem to be the circumstances *in which the act is,* and these do not seem to be the most important of the circumstances, since, of them all, they are the most extrinsic to the act. Therefore those things in which the act is are not the most important circumstances.

Obj. 2. Further, the end of a thing is extrinsic to it. Therefore it is not the most important circumstance.

Obj. 3. Further, that which holds the foremost place in regard to each thing, is its cause and its form. But the cause of an act is the person that does it, while the form of an act is the manner in which it is done. Therefore these two circumstances seem to be of the greatest importance.

On the contrary, Gregory of Nyssa says that *the most important circumstances* are *why it is done* and *what is done.*[17]

I answer that, As we have stated above, acts are properly called human inasmuch as they are voluntary.[18] Now, the motive and object of the will is the end. Therefore that circumstance is the most important of all which touches the act on the part of the end, viz., the circumstance *why;* and the second in importance is that which touches the very substance of the act, viz., the circumstance *what he did.* As to the other circumstances, they are more or less important, according as they more or less approach to these.

Reply Obj. 1. By those things *in which the act is* the Philosopher does not mean time and place, but those circumstances that are affixed to the act itself.[19] Therefore Gregory of Nyssa, as though he were explaining the dictum of the Philosopher, instead of the latter's term, *in which the act is,* substitutes, *what is done.*[20]

Reply Obj. 2. Although the end is not part of the substance of the act, yet it is the most important cause of the act, inasmuch as it moves the agent to act. Therefore the moral act is specified chiefly by the end.

Reply Obj. 3. The person that does the act is the cause of that act, inasmuch as he is moved thereto by the end; and it is chiefly in this respect that he is directed to the act. But the other conditions of the person have not such an important relation to the act.—As to the mode, it is not the substantial form of the act, for in an act the substantial form depends on the object and term or end; but it is, as it were, a certain accidental quality of the act.

[16] *Ibid.* (1111a 18).   [17] Cf. Nemesius, *De Nat. Hom.,* XXXI (PG 40, 728).
[18] Q. 1, a. 1.   [19] *Eth.,* III, 1 (1111a 18).   [20] Cf. Nemesius, *De Nat. Hom.,* XXXI (PG 40, 728).

ON THE WILL, IN REGARD TO WHAT IT WILLS
(*In Three Articles*)

WE must now consider the different acts of the will, and in the first place, those acts which belong to the will itself immediately, as being elicited by the will; secondly, those acts which are commanded by the will.[1]

Now the will is moved to the end, and to the means to the end. We must therefore consider (1) those acts of the will whereby it is moved to the end; and (2) those whereby it is moved to the means.[2] And since it seems that there are three acts of the will in reference to the end: viz., *volition, enjoyment* and *intention*, we must consider (1) volition; (2) enjoyment;[3] (3) intention.[4]—Concerning the first, three things must be considered: (1) Of what things is the will? (2) By what is the will moved?[5] (3) How is it moved?[6]

Under the first head there are three points of inquiry: (1) Whether the will is of good only? (2) Whether it is of the end only, or also of the means? (3) If in any way it be of the means, whether it be moved to the end and to the means by the same movement?

First Article

WHETHER THE WILL IS OF GOOD ONLY?

We proceed thus to the First Article:—

Objection 1. It would seem that the will is not of good only. For the same power is related to opposites, for instance, sight to white and black. But good and evil are opposites. Therefore the will is not only of good, but also of evil.

Obj. 2. Further, rational powers can be directed to opposite courses, according to the Philosopher.[7] But the will is a rational power, since it is *in the reason,* as is stated in *De Anima* iii.[8] Therefore the will can be directed to opposites; and consequently it is not confined to good, but extends to evil.

Obj. 3. Further, good and being are convertible. But the will is directed not only to beings, but also to non-beings. For sometimes we will *not to walk,* or *not to speak*; and, again, at times we will future things, which are not actual beings. Therefore the will is not of good only.

[1] Q. 17.　[2] Q. 13.　[3] Q. 11.　[4] Q. 12.　[5] Q. 9.　[6] Q. 10.　[7] *Metaph.,* VIII, 2 (1046b 8).　[8] Aristotle, *De An.,* III, 9 (432b 5).

On the contrary, Dionysius says that *evil is outside the scope of the will,* and that *all things desire good.*[9]

I answer that, The will is a rational appetite. Now every appetite is only of something good. The reason for this is that the appetite is nothing else than the inclination of a being desirous of a thing towards that thing. Now every inclination is to something like and suitable to the thing inclined. Since, therefore, everything, inasmuch as it is being and substance, is a good, it must needs be that every inclination is to something good. And hence it is that the Philosopher says that *the good is that which all desire.*[10]

But it must be noted that, since every inclination results from a form, the natural appetite results from a form existing in the nature of things, while the sensitive appetite, as also the intellectual or rational appetite, called the *will,* follows from an apprehended form. Therefore, just as the natural appetite tends to good existing in a thing, so the animal or the voluntary appetite tends to the apprehended good. Consequently, in order that the will tend to anything, it is requisite, not that this be good in very truth, but that it be apprehended as good. Therefore the Philosopher says that *the end is a good, or an apparent good.*[11]

Reply Obj. 1. The same power is related to opposites, but it is not referred to them in the same way. Accordingly, the will is referred both to good and to evil, but to good, by desiring it, and to evil, by shunning it. Therefore the actual desire of good is called *will* [*volition*], meaning thereby the *act* of the will; for it is in this sense that we are now speaking of will. On the other hand, the shunning of evil is better described as *nolition;* and so just as volition is of good, so nolition is of evil.

Reply Obj. 2. A rational power is not directed to all opposites but to those which are contained under its proper object; for no power seeks other than its proper object. Now the object of the will is the good. Therefore the will can be directed to such opposites as are contained under good, such as to be moved or to be at rest, to speak or to be silent, and the like; for the will can be directed to either under the aspect of good.

Reply Obj. 3. That which is not a being in nature is considered as a being in the reason, and so negations and privations are said to be *beings of reason.* In this way, too, future things, in so far as they are apprehended, are beings. Accordingly, in so far as such are beings, they are apprehended under the aspect of good, and it is thus that the will is directed to them. Therefore the Philosopher says that *to lack evil has the nature of a good.*[12]

---

[9] *De Div. Nom.,* IV, 32 (PG 3, 732); cf. *op. cit.,* IV, 10 (PG 3, 708).   [10] *Eth.,* I, 1 (1094a 3).   [11] *Phys.,* II, 3 (195a 26).   [12] *Eth.,* V, 1 (1129b 8).

Second Article

WHETHER VOLITION IS OF THE END ONLY, OR ALSO OF THE MEANS?

We proceed thus to the Second Article:—

Objection 1. It would seem that volition is not of the means, but of the end only. For the Philosopher says that *volition is of the end, while choice is of the means.*[13]

Obj. 2. Further, *For objects differing in genus there are corresponding different powers of the soul.*[14] Now the end and the means are in different genera of good, because the end, which is a good either of rectitude or of pleasure, is in the genus *quality*, or *action*, or *passion*; whereas the good which is useful, and is directed to an end, is in the genus *relation.*[15] Therefore, if volition is of the end, it is not of the means.

Obj. 3. Further, habits are proportioned to powers, since they are their perfections. But in those habits which are called practical arts, the end belongs to one, and the means to another art. Thus the use of a ship, which is its end, belongs to the art of the helmsman; whereas the building of the ship, which is directed to the end, belongs to the art of the shipwright. Therefore, since volition is of the end, it is not of the means.

On the contrary, In natural things, it is by the same power that a thing passes through the middle ground and arrives at the terminus. But the means are a kind of middle ground through which one arrives at the end or terminus. Therefore, if volition is of the end, it is also of the means.

I answer that, The term *voluntas* [*will*] sometimes designates the power of the will, sometimes its act [*volition*]. Accordingly, if we speak of the will as a power, thus it extends both to the end and to the means. For every power extends to those things in which the nature of its object may be found in any way whatever. Thus the sight extends to all things whatsoever that are in any way colored. Now the nature of good, which is the object of the power of will, may be found not only in the end, but also in the means.

If, however, we speak of will in so far as it is properly the name of an act, then, strictly speaking, it is of the end only. For every act denominated from a power designates the simple act of that power. Thus, *to understand* designates the simple act of the understanding. Now the simple act of a power is referred to that which is in itself the object of that power. But that which is good and willed in itself is the end. Therefore volition, properly speaking, is of the end itself. On the other hand, the means are good and willed, not in themselves, but as referred to the end. Therefore the will is directed to them only in so far as it is directed to the

---

[13] *Op. cit.,* III, 2 (1111b 26).   [14] *Op. cit.,* VI, 1 (1139a 8).   [15] *Op. cit.,* I, 6 (1096a 26).

end; so that what it wills in them, is the end. So, too, to understand is properly directed to things that are known in themselves, *i.e.*, first principles; but we do not speak of understanding with regard to things known through first principles, except in so far as we see the principles in those things. Now in morals the end is what principles are in speculative matters.[16]

Reply Obj. 1. The Philosopher is speaking of the will as signifying the simple act of the will, not as signifying the power of the will.[17]

Reply Obj. 2. There are different powers for objects that differ in genus and are mutually independent. For instance, sound and color are different genera of sensibles, to which are referred hearing and sight. But the useful and the righteous are not mutually independent, but are as that which is of itself and that which is in relation to another. Now such objects are always referred to the same power. For instance, the power of sight perceives both color and the light by which color is seen.

Reply Obj. 3. Not everything that diversifies habits diversifies the powers, since habits are certain determinations of powers to certain special acts. Moreover, every practical art considers both the end and the means. For the art of the helmsman does indeed consider the end, as that which it effects; and the means, as that which it commands. On the other hand, the ship-building art considers the means as that which it effects; but it considers that which is the end as that to which it refers what it effects. And again, in every practical art there is an end proper to it and the means that belong properly to that art.

Third Article

WHETHER THE WILL IS MOVED BY THE SAME ACT TO THE END AND TO THE MEANS?

We proceed thus to the Third Article:—

Objection 1. It would seem that the will is moved by the same act to the end and to the means. For according to the Philosopher, *where one thing is for the sake of another, there is only one.*[18] But the will does not will the means save for the sake of the end. Therefore it is moved to both by the same act.

Obj. 2. Further, the end is the reason for willing the means, just as light is the reason of seeing colors. But light and colors are seen by the same act. Therefore it is the same movement of the will whereby it wills the end and the means.

Obj. 3. Further, it is one and the same natural movement which tends through the middle ground to the terminus. But the means are in comparison to the end as the middle ground is to the terminus. Therefore it is

---

[16] *Op. cit.,* VII, 8 (1151a 16).   [17] *Op. cit.,* III, 2 (1111b 26).   [18] *Top.,* III, 2 (117a 18)

the same movement of the will whereby it is directed to the end and to the means.

On the contrary, Acts are diversified according to their objects. But the end is a different species of good from the means, which are a useful good. Therefore the will is not moved to both by the same act.

I answer that, Since the end is willed in itself, whereas the means, as such, are willed only for the end, it is evident that the will can be moved to the end without being moved to the means; whereas it cannot be moved to the means, as such, unless it is moved to the end. Accordingly, the will is moved to the end in two ways: first, absolutely and in itself; secondly, as the reason for willing the means. Hence it is evident that the will is moved, by one and the same movement, to the end, as the reason for willing the means, and to the means themselves. But it is another act by which the will is moved to the end absolutely. Sometimes, too, this act precedes the other in time, for example, when a man first wills to have health, and afterwards, deliberating by what means to be healed, he wills to send for the doctor to heal him. The same happens in regard to the intellect, for at first a man understands the principles in themselves, but afterwards he understands them in the conclusions, inasmuch as he assents to the conclusions because of the principles.

Reply Obj. 1. This argument holds according as the will is moved to the end as the reason for willing the means.

Reply Obj. 2. Whenever color is seen, by the same act the light is seen; but the light can be seen without the color being seen. In like manner, whenever a man wills the means, by the same act he wills the end; but not conversely.

Reply Obj. 3. In the execution of a work, the means are as the middle ground, and the end as the terminus. Therefore, just as natural movement sometimes stops on the way and does not reach the terminus, so sometimes one is busy with the means, without gaining the end. But in willing it is the reverse, for it is through [willing] the end that the will comes to will the means; just as the intellect arrives at the conclusions through the principles which are called means. Hence it is that sometimes the intellect understands a means and does not proceed thence to the conclusion. And in like manner the will sometimes wills the end, and yet does not proceed to will the means.

The solution to the argument in the contrary sense is clear from what has been said above. For the useful and the righteous are not species of good in an equal degree, but are as that which is for its own sake and that which is for the sake of something else; and so the act of the will can be directed to one and not to the other, but not conversely.

ON THAT WHICH MOVES THE WILL

(In Six Articles)

WE must now consider what moves the will, and under this head there are six points of inquiry: (1) Whether the will is moved by the intellect? (2) Whether it is moved by the sensitive appetite? (3) Whether the will moves itself? (4) Whether it is moved by an extrinsic principle? (5) Whether it is moved by a heavenly body? (6) Whether the will is moved by God alone as by an extrinsic principle?

First Article

WHETHER THE WILL IS MOVED BY THE INTELLECT?

We proceed thus to the First Article:—

Objection 1. It would seem that the will is not moved by the intellect. For Augustine says on *Ps.* cxviii. 20 (*My soul hath coveted to long for Thy justifications*): *The intellect flies ahead, the desire follows sluggishly or not at all; we know what is good, but deeds delight us not.*[1] But it would not be so, if the will were moved by the intellect; for the movement of the movable results from the motion of the mover. Therefore the intellect does not move the will.

Obj. 2. Further, the intellect in presenting the appetible object to the will, stands in relation to the will as the imagination in representing the appetible object to the sensitive appetite. But the imagination, in presenting the appetible object, does not move the sensitive appetite; indeed sometimes our imagination affects us no more than what is set before us in a picture, and moves us not at all.[2] Therefore neither does the intellect move the will.

Obj. 3. Further, the same is not mover and moved in respect of the same thing. But the will moves the intellect, for we exercise the intellect when we will. Therefore the intellect does not move the will.

On the contrary, The Philosopher says that *the appetible is a mover not moved, whereas the will is a mover moved.*[3]

I answer that, A thing requires to be moved by something in so far as it is in potentiality to several things. For that which is in potentiality needs to be reduced to act by something actual; and to do this is to move. Now a power of the soul is found to be in potentiality to different things in two

---

[1] *Enarr. in Psalm.*, super CXVIII, 20, serm. VIII (PL 37, 1552).　　[2] Aristotle, *De An.*, III, 3 (427b 23).　　[3] *Op. cit.*, III, 6 (433b 10; b 16).

ways: first, with regard to acting and not acting; secondly, with regard to this or that action. Thus, the sight sometimes sees actually, and sometimes sees not; and sometimes it sees white, and sometimes black. It needs therefore a mover in two respects: viz., as to the exercise or use of the act, and as to the determination of the act. The first of these is on the part of the subject, which is sometimes acting, sometimes not acting; while the other is on the part of the object, by reason of which the act is specified.

The motion of the subject itself is due to some agent. And since every agent acts for an end, as was shown above,[4] the principle of this motion lies in the end. Hence it is that the art, which is concerned with the end, by its command moves the art which is concerned with the means; just as the *art of sailing commands the art of shipbuilding*.[5] Now the good in general, which has the nature of an end, is the object of the will. Consequently, in this respect, the will moves the other powers of the soul to their acts, for we make use of the other powers when we will. For the ends and the perfections of every other power are included under the object of the will as particular goods; and the art or power, to which the universal end belongs, always moves to their acts the arts or powers to which belong the particular ends included in the universal end. Thus the leader of an army, who intends the common good—*i.e.*, the order of the whole army—by his command moves one of the captains, who intends the order of one company.

On the other hand, the object moves, by determining the act, after the manner of a formal principle, whereby in natural things actions are specified, as heating by heat. Now the first formal principle is universal *being* and *truth*, which is the object of the intellect. And therefore by this kind of motion the intellect moves the will, as presenting its object to it.

Reply Obj. 1. The passage quoted proves, not that the intellect does not move, but that it does not move of necessity.

Reply Obj. 2. Just as the imagination of a form without estimation of fitness or harmfulness does not move the sensitive appetite, so neither does the apprehension of the true without the aspect of goodness and desirability. Hence it is not the speculative intellect that moves, but the practical intellect.[6]

Reply Obj. 3. The will moves the intellect as to the exercise of its act, since even the true itself, which is the perfection of the intellect, is included in the universal good as a particular good. But as to the determination of the act, which the act derives from the object, the intellect moves the will; for the good itself is apprehended under a special aspect as contained in the universal true. It is therefore evident that the same is not mover and moved in the same respect.

[4] Q. 1, a. 2.   [5] Aristotle, *Phys.*, II, 2 (194b 5).   [6] Aristotle, *De An.*, III, 9 (432b 26); 10 (433a 17).

Second Article

WHETHER THE WILL IS MOVED BY THE SENSITIVE APPETITE?

We proceed thus to the Second Article:—
Objection 1. It would seem that the will cannot be moved by the sensi-tive appetite. For *to move and to act is more excellent than to be passive,* as Augustine says.[7] But the sensitive appetite is less excellent than the will whïch is the intellectual appetite, just as sense is less excellent than intel-lect. Therefore, the sensitive appetite does not move the will.

Obj. 2. Further, no particular power can produce a universal effect. But the sensitive appetite is a particular power, because it follows the particular apprehension of sense. Therefore, it cannot cause the movement of the will, which movement is universal, as following the universal apprehension of the intellect.

Obj. 3. Further, as is proved in *Physics* viii., the mover is not moved by that which it moves, in such a way that there be reciprocal motion.[8] But the will moves the sensitive appetite, inasmuch as the sensitive appetite obeys the reason. Therefore the sensitive appetite does not move the will.

On the contrary, It is written (*Jas.* i. 14): *Every man is tempted by his own concupiscence, being drawn away and allured.* But man would not be drawn away by his concupiscence, unless his will were moved by the sensitive appetite, wherein concupiscence resides. Therefore the sensitive appetite moves the will.

I answer that, As we have stated above, that which is apprehended un-der the nature of what is good and befitting moves the will as an object. Now that a thing appear to be good and fitting happens from two causes, namely, from the condition either of the thing proposed, or of the one to whom it is proposed. For fitness is spoken of by way of relation, and hence it depends on both extremes. And hence it is that taste, according as it is variously disposed, takes to a thing in various ways, as being fitting or un-fitting. Therefore as the Philosopher says: *According as a man is, such does the end seem to him.*[9]

Now it is evident that according to a passion of the sensitive appetite man is changed to a certain disposition. Therefore, according as man is affected by a passion, something seems to him fitting, which does not seem so when he is not so affected; and thus that seems good to a man when angered, which does not seem good when he is calm. It is in this way that the sensitive appetite moves the will, on the part of the object.

Reply Obj. 1. Nothing hinders that which is better absolutely and in itself from being less excellent in a certain respect. Accordingly, the will is absolutely more excellent than the sensitive appetite; but in respect of the

[7] *De Genesi ad Litt.,* XII, 16 (PL 34, 467).   [8] Aristotle, *Phys.,* VIII, 5 (257b 23).
[9] *Eth.,* III, 5 (1114a 32).

man in whom a passion is predominant, in so far as he is subject to that passion, the sensitive appetite is more excellent.

Reply Obj. 2. Men's acts and choices are concerned singulars. Therefore, from the very fact that the sensitive appetite is a particular power, it has great influence in disposing man so that something seems to him such or otherwise, in particular cases.

Reply Obj. 3. As the Philosopher says,[10] the reason, in which resides the will, moves the irascible and concupiscible powers by its command, not, indeed, *by a despotic rule,* as a slave is moved by his master, but by a *royal and political rule,* as free men are ruled by their governor, and can nevertheless act counter to his commands. Hence both the irascible and concupiscible parts can move counter to the will, and, accordingly, nothing hinders the will from being moved by them at times.

Third Article

WHETHER THE WILL MOVES ITSELF?

We proceed thus to the Third Article:—

Objection 1. It would seem that the will does not move itself. For every mover, as such, is in act, whereas what is moved is in potentiality; for *movement is the act of that which is in potentiality, in so far as it is in potentiality.*[11] Now the same is not in potentiality and in act in respect of the same. Therefore nothing moves itself. Neither, therefore, can the will move itself.

Obj. 2. Further, the movable is moved when the mover is present. But the will is always present to itself. If, therefore, it moved itself, it would always be moved, which is clearly false.

Obj. 3. Further, the will is moved by the intellect, as was stated above. If, therefore, the will moves itself, it would follow that the same thing is at once moved immediately by two movers; which seems unreasonable. Therefore the will does not move itself.

On the contrary, The will is mistress of its own act, and to it belongs to will and not to will. But this would not be so, had it not the power to move itself to will. Therefore it moves itself.

I answer that, As was stated above, it belongs to the will to move the other powers, by reason of the end which is the will's object. Now, as we have stated above, the end is in the order of appetibles what a principle is in the order of intelligibles.[12] But it is evident that the intellect, through its knowledge of a principle, reduces itself from potentiality to act as to its knowledge of conclusions; and thus it moves itself. And, in like manner, the will, through its volition of the end, moves itself to will the means.

Reply Obj. 1. It is not in the same respect that the will moves itself and is moved, and so neither is it in act and in potentiality in the same respect.

[10] *Polit.,* I, 2 (1254b 5).   [11] Aristotle, *Phys.,* III, 1 (201a 10).   [12] Q. 8, a. 2.

But in so far as it actually wills the end, it reduces itself from potentiality to act concerning the means, so as to will them actually.

Reply Obj. 2. The power of the will is always actually present to itself; but the act of the will, by which it wills an end, is not always in the will. But it is by this act that it moves itself. Accordingly, it does not follow that it is always moving itself.

Reply Obj. 3. The will is moved in the same way by the intellect and by itself. By the intellect it is moved on the part of the object, whereas it is moved by itself, as to the exercise of its act, in respect of the end.

Fourth Article

WHETHER THE WILL IS MOVED BY AN EXTERIOR PRINCIPLE?

We proceed thus to the Fourth Article:—

Objection 1. It would seem that the will is not moved by anything exterior. For the movement of the will is voluntary. But it is of the nature of the voluntary act that it be from an intrinsic principle, just as it is of the nature of the natural act. Therefore the movement of the will is not from anything exterior.

Obj. 2. Further, the will cannot suffer violence, as was shown above.[13] But the violent act is one *the principle of which is outside the agent.*[14] Therefore the will cannot be moved by anything exterior.

Obj. 3. Further, that which is sufficiently moved by one mover needs not to be moved by another. But the will moves itself sufficiently. Therefore it is not moved by anything exterior.

On the contrary, The will is moved by the object, as was stated above. But the object of the will can be something exterior, offered to the sense. Therefore the will can be moved by something exterior.

I answer that, As far as the will is moved by the object, it is evident that it can be moved by something exterior. But in so far as it is moved in the exercise of its act, we must likewise hold it to be moved by some exterior principle. For everything that is at one time an agent actually, and at another time an agent in potentiality, needs to be moved by a mover. Now it is evident that the will begins to will something, which previously it did not will. Therefore it must, of necessity, be moved by something to will it. And, indeed, it moves itself, as was stated above, in so far as through willing the end it reduces itself to the act of willing the means. Now it cannot do this without the aid of counsel. For when a man wills to be healed, he begins to reflect how this can be attained, and through this reflection he comes to the conclusion that he can be healed by a physician; and this he wills. But since he did not always actually will to have health, he must, of necessity, have begun, through something moving him, to will to be

[13] Q. 6, a. 4.   [14] Aristotle, *Eth.,* III, 1 (1110a 1).

healed. And if the will moved itself to will this, it must, of necessity, have done this with the aid of counsel following some previous volition. But this process could not go on to infinity. Therefore we must, of necessity, suppose that the will advanced to its first movement in virtue of the instigation of some exterior mover, as Aristotle concludes in a chapter of the *Eudemian Ethics*.[15]

Reply Obj. 1. It is of the nature of the voluntary act that its principle be within the agent; but it is not necessary that this inward principle be a first principle unmoved by another. Therefore, though the voluntary act has an inward proximate principle, nevertheless, its first principle is from the outside. Thus, too, the first principle of natural movement, namely, that which moves nature, is from the outside.

Reply Obj. 2. For an act to be violent it is not enough that its principle be extrinsic, but we must add, *without the concurrence of him that suffers violence*. This does not happen when the will is moved by an exterior principle; for it is the will that wills, though moved by another. But this movement would be violent, if it were counter to the movement of the will; which in the present case is impossible, since then the will would will and not will the same thing.

Reply Obj. 3. The will moves itself sufficiently in one respect, and in its own order, that is to say, as a proximate agent; but it cannot move itself in every respect, as we have shown. Therefore it needs to be moved by another as first mover.

Fifth Article

WHETHER THE WILL IS MOVED BY A HEAVENLY BODY?

We proceed thus to the Fifth Article:—

Objection 1. It would seem that the human will is moved by a heavenly body. For all various and multiform movements are reduced, as to their cause, to a uniform movement which is that of the heavens, as is proved by *Physics* viii.[16] But human movements are various and multiform, since they begin to be, when previously they were not. Therefore they are reduced, as to their cause, to the movement of the heavens, which is uniform according to its nature.

Obj. 2. Further, according to Augustine *the lower bodies are moved by the higher*.[17] But the movements of the human body, which are caused by the will, could not be reduced to the movement of the heavens, as to their cause, unless the will too were moved by the heavens. Therefore the heavens move the human will.

---

[15] *Eth. Eudem.*, VII, 14 (1248a 14).   [16] Aristotle, *Phys.*, VIII, 9 (265a 27); cf *op. cit.*, IV, 14 (223b 18).   [17] *De Trin.*, III, 4 (PL 42, 873).

Obj. 3. Further, by observing the heavenly bodies astrologers foretell the truth about future human acts, which are caused by the will. But this would not be so if the heavenly bodies could not move man's will. Therefore the human will is moved by a heavenly body.

On the contrary, Damascene says that *the heavenly bodies are not the causes of our acts.*[18] But they would be, if the will, which is the principle of human acts, were moved by the heavenly bodies. Therefore the will is not moved by the heavenly bodies.

I answer that, It is evident that the will can be moved by the heavenly bodies in the same way as it is moved by its exterior object, that is to say, in so far as exterior bodies, which move the will through being offered to the senses, and also the organs themselves of the sensitive powers, are subject to the movements of the heavenly bodies.

But some have maintained that heavenly bodies have an influence directly on the human will, in the same way as some exterior agent moves the will, as to the exercise of its act.[19] But this is impossible. For the *will,* as is stated in *De Anima* iii., *is in the reason.*[20] Now the reason is a power of the soul not bound to a bodily organ, and so it follows that the will is a power absolutely incorporeal and immaterial. But it is evident that no body can act on what is incorporeal, but rather the reverse; for things incorporeal and immaterial have a power that is more formal and more universal than any corporeal things. Therefore it is impossible for a heavenly body to act directly on the intellect or the will. For this reason Aristotle ascribed to those who held that intellect differs not from the sense,[21] the theory that *such is the will of men, as is the day which the father of men and of gods brings on*[22] (referring to Jupiter, by whom they understand the entire heavens). For all the sensitive powers, since they are acts of bodily organs, can be moved accidentally by the heavenly bodies— *i.e.,* when those bodies are moved, whose acts they are.

But since it has been stated that the intellectual appetite is moved, in a fashion, by the sensitive appetite, the movements of the heavenly bodies have an indirect bearing on the will, in so far, namely, as the will happens to be moved by the passions of the sensitive appetite.

Reply Obj. 1. The multiform movements of the human will are reduced to some uniform cause, which, however, is above the intellect and will. This can be said, not of any body, but of some superior immaterial substance. Therefore there is no need for the movement of the will to be reduced to the movement of the heavens as to its cause.

Reply Obj. 2. The movements of the human body are reduced, as to their cause, to the movement of a heavenly body, in so far as the disposition suitable to a particular movement is somewhat due to the in-

---

[18] *De Fide Orth.,* II, 7 (PG 94, 893).   [19] Cf. H. Denifle, *Chartularium,* no. 432, error 4 (I, 487).   [20] Aristotle, *De An.,* III, 9 (432b 5).   [21] *E.g.,* Empedocles: cf. Aristotle, *De An.,* III, 3 (427a 21).   [22] *Ibid.* (427a 25).—Homer, *Odyss.,* XVIII, 136.

fluence of heavenly bodies;—also, in so far as the sensitive appetite is stirred by the influence of heavenly bodies;—and again, in so far as exterior bodies are moved in accordance with the movement of heavenly bodies, at whose presence, the will begins to will or not to will something: e.g., when the body is chilled, we begin to wish to make the fire. But this movement of the will is on the part of the object offered from the outside, not on the part of an inward instigation.

Reply Obj. 3. As was stated above, the sensitive appetite is the act of a bodily organ.[23] Therefore there is no reason why man should not be prone to anger or concupiscence, or some like passion, by reason of the influence of heavenly bodies, just as by reason of his natural temperament. Now the majority of men are led by the passions, which the wise alone resist. Consequently, in the majority of cases predictions about human acts, gathered from the observation of the heavenly bodies, are fulfilled. Nevertheless, as Ptolemy says, *the wise man governs the stars,*[24] as though to say that by resisting his passions, he opposes his will, which is free and in no way subject to the movement of the heavens, to such effects of the heavenly bodies.

Or, as Augustine says: *We must confess that when the truth is foretold by astrologers, this is due to some most hidden inspiration, to which the human mind is subject without knowing it. And since this is done in order to deceive man, it must be the work of the lying spirits.*[25]

Sixth Article

WHETHER THE WILL IS MOVED BY GOD ALONE, AS EXTERIOR PRINCIPLE?

We proceed thus to the Sixth Article:—

Objection 1. It would seem that the will is not moved by God alone as exterior principle. For it is natural that the inferior be moved by its superior; and thus the lower bodies are moved by the heavenly bodies. But there is something which is higher than the will of man and below God, namely, the angel. Therefore man's will can be moved by an angel also, as exterior principle.

Obj. 2. Further, the act of the will follows the act of the intellect. But man's intellect is reduced to act, not by God alone, but also by the angel who illumines it, as Dionysius says.[26] For the same reason, therefore, the will also is moved by an angel.

Obj. 3. Further, God is not cause of other than good things, according to *Gen.* i. 31: *God saw all the things that He had made, and they were very good.* If, therefore, man's will were moved by God alone, it would never be

---

[23] *S.T.,* I, q. 84, a. 6 and 7.   [24] *Centiloquium,* verba 4-8.—Cf. also St. Albert, *In II Sent.,* d. xv, a. 4 (XXVII, 276).   [25] *De Genesi ad Litt.,* II, 17 (PL 34, 278). [26] *De Cael. Hier.,* IV, 2 (PG 3, 180).

moved to evil; and yet it is the will by which *we sin and by which we do the right,* as Augustine says.[27]

On the *contrary,* It is written (*Phil.* ii. 13): *It is God Who worketh in us both to will and to accomplish.*

I answer that, The movement of the will is from within, as is also natural movement. Now although it is possible for something to move a natural thing, without being the cause of the nature of the thing moved, yet that alone which is in some way the cause of a thing's nature can cause a natural movement in that thing. For a stone is moved upwards by a man, who is not the cause of the stone's nature, but this movement is not natural to the stone; but the natural movement of the stone is caused by none other than the cause of its nature. Therefore it is said in *Physics* viii. that the generator moves locally heavy and light things.[28] Accordingly, man endowed with a will is sometimes moved by something that is not his cause; but that his voluntary movement be from an exterior principle which is not the cause of his will, is impossible.

But the cause of the will can be none other than God. And this is evident for two reasons. First, because the will is a power of the rational soul, which is caused by God alone through creation, as was stated in the First Part.[29] Secondly, it is evident from the fact that the will is ordained to the universal good. Therefore nothing else can be the cause of the will, except God Himself, Who is the universal good, while every other good is good by participation, and is some particular good; and a particular cause does not give a universal inclination. Hence, neither can primary matter, which is in potentiality to all forms, be created by some particular agent.

Reply Obj. 1. An angel is not above man in such a way as to be the cause of his will, as the heavenly bodies are the causes of natural forms, from which result the natural movements of natural bodies.

Reply Obj. 2. Man's intellect is moved by an angel, on the part of the object, which by the power of the angelic light is proposed to man's knowledge. And in this way the will also can be moved by a creature from the outside, as was stated above.

Reply Obj. 3. God moves man's will, as the Universal Mover, to the universal object of the will, which is the good. And without this universal motion man cannot will anything. But man determines himself by his reason to will this or that, which is a true or apparent good. Nevertheless, sometimes God moves some specially to the willing of something determinate, which is good; as in the case of those whom He moves by grace, as we shall state later on.[30]

---

[27] *Retract.,* I, 9 (PL 32, 596).   [28] Aristotle, *Phys.,* VIII, 4 (255b 35).   [29] *S. T.,* I, q. 90, a. 2 and 3.   [30] Q. 109, a. 2.

ON THE MANNER IN WHICH THE WILL IS MOVED
(*In Four Articles*)

WE must now consider the manner in which the will is moved. Under this head there are four points of inquiry: (1) Whether the will is moved to anything naturally? (2) Whether it is moved of necessity by its object? (3) Whether it is moved of necessity by the lower appetite? (4) Whether it is moved of necessity by the exterior mover which is God?

First Article

WHETHER THE WILL IS MOVED TO ANYTHING NATURALLY?

We proceed thus to the First Article:—

Objection 1. It would seem that the will is not moved to anything naturally. For the natural agent is co-divided with the voluntary agent, as is stated at the beginning of *Physics* ii.[1] Therefore the will is not moved to anything naturally.

Obj. 2. Further, that which is natural is in a thing always, as *being hot* is in fire. But no movement is always in the will. Therefore no movement is natural to the will.

Obj. 3. Further, nature is determined to one thing, whereas the will is related to opposites. Therefore the will wills nothing naturally.

On the contrary, The movement of the will follows the act of the intellect. But the intellect understands some things naturally. Therefore the will, too, wills some things naturally.

I answer that, As Boethius says,[2] and the Philosopher also,[3] the term *nature* is used in a manifold sense. For sometimes it stands for the intrinsic principle in movable things. In this sense, nature is either matter or the material form, as is stated in *Physics* ii.[4] In another sense, nature stands for any substance, or even for any being. And in this sense, that is said to be natural to a thing which befits it according to its substance; and this is what is in a thing essentially. Now whatever does not belong to a thing essentially is reduced to something, which belongs to that thing essentially, as to its principle. Therefore, taking nature in this sense, it is necessary that the principle of whatever belongs to a thing be a natural principle. This is evident in regard to the intellect, for the principles of intellectual knowl-

---

[1] Aristotle, *Phys.*, II, 1 (192b 8); 5 (196b 21).   [2] *De Duab. Nat.*, I (PL 64, 1341).
[3] *Metaph.*, IV, 4 (1014b 16).   [4] Aristotle, *Phys.*, II, 1 (193a 28).

edge are naturally known. In like manner, the principle of voluntary movements must be something naturally willed.

Now this is the good in general, namely, that to which the will tends naturally, in the same way as each power tends to its object; and again it is the last end, which stands in the same relation to things appetible, as the first principles of demonstration to things intelligible; and, speaking generally, it is all those things which belong to the one willing according to his nature. For it is not only things pertaining to the will that the will desires, but also that which pertains to each power, and to the entire man. Therefore man wills naturally not only the object of the will, but also other things that are appropriate to the other powers, such as the knowledge of truth, which befits the intellect, and to be and to live and other like things which regard his natural well-being,—all of which are included in the object of the will as so many particular goods.

Reply Obj. 1. The will is distinguished from nature as one kind of cause from another, for some things happen naturally and some are done voluntarily. There is, however, another manner of causing that is proper to the will, which is mistress of its act, besides the manner proper to nature, which is determined to one thing. But since the will is founded in some nature, it is necessary that the movement proper to nature be shared by the will, to some extent; just as what belongs to a prior cause is shared by a subsequent cause. For in every thing, being itself, which is from nature, precedes volition, which is from the will. And hence it is that the will wills something naturally.

Reply Obj. 2. In the case of natural things, that which is natural, as consequent upon form only, is always in them actually, as heat is in fire. But that which is natural, as a result of matter, is not always in them actually, but sometimes only in potentiality; for form is act, whereas matter is potentiality. Now movement is *the act of that which is in potentiality.*[5] Therefore that which belongs to, or results from, movement, in the case of natural things, is not always in them. Thus fire does not always move upwards, but only when it is outside its own place. And in like manner, it is not necessary that the will (which is reduced from potentiality to act, when it wills something), should always be in the act of volition; but only when it is in a certain determinate disposition. But God's will, which is pure act, is always in the act of volition.

Reply Obj. 3. Something one always corresponds to nature, proportioned to it. For to that which is nature generically there corresponds that which is one in genus; to nature considered in the species there corresponds that which is one in species; and to individuated nature there corresponds something that is individually one. Since, therefore, the will, like the intellect, is an immaterial power, there corresponds to it naturally a common unity, namely, *the good;* just as to the intellect likewise there corresponds a com-

[5] *Op. cit.,* III, 1 (201a 10).

mon unity, namely, *the true,* or *being,* or *essence.* Now under the good which is common there are contained many particular goods, to none of which is the will determined.

Second Article

WHETHER THE WILL IS MOVED OF NECESSITY BY ITS OBJECT?

We proceed thus to the Second Article:—

Objection 1. It seems that the will is moved of necessity by its object. For the object of the will is compared to the will as mover to the movable, as is stated in *De Anima* iii.[6] But a mover, if it be sufficient, moves the movable of necessity. Therefore the will can be moved of necessity by its object.

Obj. 2. Further, just as the will is an immaterial power, so is the intellect; and both powers are ordained to a universal object, as was stated above. But the intellect is moved of necessity by its object. Therefore the will also is moved of necessity by its object.

Obj. 3. Further, whatever one wills is either the end, or something ordained to the end. But, it would seem, one wills an end necessarily, because it is like a principle in speculative matters, to which one assents of necessity. Now the end is the reason for willing the means; and so it seems that we likewise will the means necessarily. Therefore the will is moved of necessity by its object.

On the contrary, Rational powers, according to the Philosopher, are directed to opposites.[7] But the will is a rational power, since it is in the reason, as is stated in *De Anima* iii.[8] Therefore the will is directed to opposites. Therefore it is not moved, of necessity, to either of the opposites.

I answer that, The will is moved in two ways: first, as to the exercise of its act; secondly, as to the specification of its act, derived from the object. As to the first way, no object moves the will necessarily, for no matter what the object be, it is in man's power not to think of it, and consequently not to will it actually. But as to the second manner of motion, the will is moved by one object necessarily, by another not. For in the movement of a power by its object, we must consider under what aspect the object moves the power. For the visible moves the sight under the aspect of color actually visible. Therefore, if color be offered to the sight, it moves the sight necessarily, unless one turns one's eyes away; which belongs to the exercise of the act. But if the sight were confronted with something not in all respects colored actually, but only so in some respects, and in other respects not, the sight would not of necessity see such an object: for it might look at that part of the object which is not actually colored, and thus would not see it.

---

[6] Aristotle, *De An.,* III, 10 (433b 10; b 16).   [7] *Metaph.,* VIII, 2 (1046b 8).
[3] Aristotle, *De An.,* III, 9 (432b 5).

Now just as the actually colored is the object of sight, so good is the object of the will. Therefore if the will be offered an object which is good universally and from every point of view, the will tends to it of necessity, if it wills anything at all; since it cannot will the opposite. If, on the other hand, the will is offered an object that is not good from every point of view, it will not tend to it of necessity.—And since the lack of any good whatever is a non-good, consequently, that good alone which is perfect and lacking in nothing is such a good that the will cannot not-will it; and this is happiness. But any other particular goods, in so far as they are lacking in some good, can be regarded as non-goods; and, from this point of view, they can be set aside or approved by the will, which can tend to one and the same thing from various points of view.

Reply Obj. 1. The sufficient mover of a power is none other than that object that in every respect possesses the nature of the mover of that power. If, on the other hand, it is lacking in any respect, it will not move of necessity, as was stated above.

Reply Obj. 2. The intellect is moved, of necessity, by an object which is such as to be always and necessarily true; but not by that which may be either true or false, viz., by that which is contingent, as we have said of the good.

Reply Obj. 3. The last end moves the will necessarily, because it is the perfect good; so does whatever is ordained to that end, and without which the end cannot be attained, such as *to be* and *to live,* and the like. But other things, without which the end can be gained, are not necessarily willed by one who wills the end; just as he who assents to a principle does not necessarily assent to the conclusions without which the principles can still be true.

Third Article

WHETHER THE WILL IS MOVED OF NECESSITY BY THE LOWER APPETITE?

We proceed thus to the Third Article:—

Objection 1. It would seem that the will is moved of necessity by a passion of the lower appetite. For the Apostle says (*Rom.* vii. 19): *The good which I will I do not, but the evil which I will not, that I do;* and this is said by reason of concupiscence, which is a passion. Therefore the will is moved of necessity by a passion.

Obj. 2. Further, as is stated in *Ethics* iii., *according as a man is, such does the end seem to him.*[9] But it is not in man's power to cast aside a passion at once. Therefore it is not in man's power not to will that to which the passion inclines him.

---

[9] Aristotle, *Eth.,* III, 5 (1114a 32).

Obj. 3. Further, a universal cause is not applied to a particular effect, except by means of a particular cause; and so the universal reason does not move save by means of a particular estimation, as is stated in *De Anima* iii.[10] But as the universal reason is to the particular estimation, so is the will to the sensitive appetite. Therefore the will is not moved to will something particular, except through the sensitive appetite. Therefore, if the sensitive appetite happens to be disposed to something, by reason of a passion, the will cannot be moved in a contrary sense.

On the contrary, It is written (*Gen.* iv. 7): *Thy lust shall be under thee, and thou shalt have dominion over it.* Therefore man's will is not moved of necessity by the lower appetite.

I answer that, As we have stated above, the passion of the sensitive appetite moves the will in so far as the will is moved by its object[11]—inasmuch as, namely, through being disposed in such and such a way by a passion, a man judges something to be fitting and good, which he would not judge thus were it not for the passion. Now this influence of passion on man occurs in two ways. First, so that his reason is wholly bound, so that he has not the use of reason: as happens in those who, through violent anger or concupiscence, become mad or insane, just as they may from some other bodily disorder; for such passions do not take place without some change in the body. And of such men the same is to be said as of irrational animals, which follow of necessity the impulse of their passions; for in them there is neither movement of reason, nor, consequently, of will.

Sometimes, however, the reason is not entirely engrossed by the passion, so that the judgment of reason retains, to a certain extent, its freedom; and thus the movement of the will remains in a certain degree. Accordingly, in so far as the reason remains free, and not subject to the passion, the will's movement, which also remains, does not tend of necessity to that whereto the passion inclines it. Consequently, either there is no movement of the will in man, and the passion alone holds its sway, or if there be a movement of the will, it does not necessarily follow passion.

Reply Obj. 1. Although the will cannot prevent the movement of concupiscence from arising (of which the Apostle says [*Rom.* vii. 19]: *The evil which I will not, that I do*—i.e., I desire), yet it is in the power of the will not to will to desire, or not to consent to concupiscence. And thus it does not necessarily follow the movement of concupiscence.

Reply Obj. 2. Although there is in man a twofold nature, intellectual and sensitive, sometimes man is entirely disposed in one way throughout his whole soul, and this either because the sensitive part is wholly subject to his reason, as in the virtuous, or because reason is entirely engrossed by passion, as in madmen. But sometimes, although reason is clouded by passion, yet something of the reason remains free. And in respect of this, man can either repel the passion entirely, or at least hold himself in check so as not to be

[10] Aristotle, *De An.*, III, 11 (434a 19).   [11] Q. 9, a. 2.

led away by the passion. For when thus disposed, since man is variously affected according to the various parts of the soul, a thing appears to him otherwise according to his reason, than it does according to a passion.

Reply Obj. 3. The will is moved not only by the universal good apprehended by the reason, but also by the good apprehended by sense. Therefore he can be moved to some particular good independently of a passion of the sensitive appetite. For we will and do many things without passion, and through choice alone, as is most evident in those cases wherein reason resists passion.

Fourth Article

WHETHER THE WILL IS MOVED OF NECESSITY BY THE EXTERIOR MOVER WHICH IS GOD?

We proceed thus to the Fourth Article:—

Objection 1. It would seem that the will is moved of necessity by God. For every agent that cannot be resisted moves of necessity. But God cannot be resisted, because His power is infinite; and so it is written (*Rom.* ix. 19): *Who resisteth His will?* Therefore God moves the will of necessity.

Obj. 2. Further, the will is moved of necessity to whatever it wills naturally, as was stated above. But *whatever God does in a thing is what is natural to it,* as Augustine says.[12] Therefore the will wills of necessity everything to which God moves it.

Obj. 3. Further, a thing is possible, if nothing impossible follows from its being supposed. But something impossible follows from the supposition that the will does not will that to which God moves it, because in that case God's operation would be ineffectual. Therefore it is not possible for the will not to will that to which God moves it. Therefore it wills it of necessity.

On the contrary, It is written (*Ecclus.* xv. 14): *God made man from the beginning, and left him in the hand of his own counsel.* Therefore He does not of necessity move man's will.

I answer that, As Dionysius says, *it belongs to the divine providence, not to destroy, but to preserve the nature of things.*[13] Therefore it moves all things in accordance with their conditions, in such a way that from necessary causes, through the divine motion, effects follow of necessity, but from contingent causes effects follow contingently. Since, therefore, the will is an active principle that is not determined to one thing, but having an indifferent relation to many things, God so moves it that He does not determine it of necessity to one thing, but its movement remains contingent and not necessary, except in those things to which it is moved naturally.

Reply Obj. 1. The divine will extends not only to the doing of something by the thing which He moves, but also to its being done in a way which is

---

[12] *Contra Faust.,* XXVI, 3 (PL 42, 480).   [13] *De Div. Nom.,* IV, 33 (PG 3, 733).

fitting to the nature of that thing. Hence, it would be more repugnant to the divine motion for the will to be moved of necessity, which is not fitting to its nature, than for it to be moved freely, which is becoming to its nature.

Reply Obj. 2. That is natural to a thing, which God so works in it that it may be natural to it; for thus is something becoming to a thing, according as God wills it to be becoming. Now He does not will that whatever He works in things should be natural to them, for instance, that the dead should rise again. But this He does wish to be natural to each thing, that it be subject to the divine power.

Reply Obj. 3. If God moves the will to anything, it is incompatible with this supposition that the will be not moved thereto. But it is not impossible absolutely. Consequently, it does not follow that the will is moved by God necessarily.

ON ENJOYMENT, WHICH IS AN ACT OF THE WILL
(*In Four Articles*)

We must now consider enjoyment [*fruitio*], concerning which there are four points of inquiry: (1) Whether to enjoy is an act of the appetitive power? (2) Whether it belongs to the rational creature alone, or also to irrational animals? (3) Whether enjoyment is only of the last end? (4) Whether it is only of the end possessed?

First Article

WHETHER *TO ENJOY* IS AN ACT OF THE APPETITIVE POWER?

We proceed thus to the First Article:—

Objection 1. It would seem that *to enjoy* does not belong only to the appetitive power. For to enjoy [*frui*] seems nothing else than to receive the fruit [*fructum capere*]. But it is the intellect, in whose act happiness consists, as was shown above[1] that receives the fruit of human life, which is happiness. Therefore to enjoy is not an act of the appetitive power, but of the intellect.

Obj. 2. Further, each power has its proper end, which is its perfection. Thus the end of sight is to know the visible, of the hearing, to perceive sounds; and so forth. But the end of a thing is its fruit. Therefore to enjoy belongs to each power, and not only to the appetite.

Obj. 3. Further, enjoyment implies a certain delight. But sensible delight belongs to sense, which delights in its object; and for the same reason, intellectual delight belongs to the intellect. Therefore enjoyment belongs to the apprehensive power, and not to the appetitive power.

On the contrary, Augustine says: *To enjoy is to adhere lovingly to something for its own sake.*[2] But love belongs to the appetitive power. Therefore to enjoy likewise is an act of the appetitive power.

I answer that, Fruitio [enjoyment] and *fructus* [fruit] seem to refer to the same thing, one being derived from the other; but which was derived from which matters not for our purpose, though it seems probable that the one which is more clearly known, was first named. Now those things are most manifest to us which appeal most to the senses; and that is why it seems that the term *fruition* is derived from sensible fruits. Now sensible

---

[1] Q. 3, a. 4.   [2] *De Doct. Christ.*, I, 4 (PL 34, 20); *De Trin.*, X, 10; 11 (PL 42, 981; 982).

fruit is that which we expect the tree to produce last, and in which a certain sweetness is to be perceived. Hence fruition seems to have relation to love, or to the delight which one has in realizing the longed-for term, which is the end. But the end and the good is the object of the appetitive power. Therefore it is evident that fruition [enjoyment] is an act of the appetitive power.

Reply Obj. 1. Nothing hinders one and the same thing from belonging, under different aspects, to different powers. Accordingly, the vision of God, as vision, is an act of the intellect, but as a good and an end, is the object of the will. It is therefore as a good that the vision of God is enjoyed. Hence, the intellect attains this end as the executive power, but the will as the motive power, moving towards the end and enjoying the end attained.

Reply Obj. 2. The perfection and end of every other power is contained in the object of the appetitive power, as the proper is contained in the common, as was stated above.[3] Hence the perfection and end of each power, in so far as it is a good, belongs to the appetitive power. Therefore the appetitive power moves the other powers to their ends, and itself realizes the end, when each of them reaches the end.

Reply Obj. 3. In delight there are two things, the perception of what is befitting, which belongs to the apprehensive power, and satisfaction with what is offered as befitting, which belongs to the appetitive power, in which the nature of delight is fulfilled.

Second Article

WHETHER *TO ENJOY* BELONGS TO THE RATIONAL CREATURE ALONE, OR ALSO TO IRRATIONAL ANIMALS?

We proceed thus to the Second Article:—

Objection 1. It would seem that to enjoy belongs to human beings alone. For Augustine says that *it is given to us men to enjoy and to use.*[4] Therefore other animals cannot enjoy.

Obj. 2. Further, to enjoy relates to the last end. But irrational animals cannot obtain the last end. Therefore it is not for them to enjoy.

Obj. 3. Further, just as the sensitive appetite is beneath the intellectual appetite, so the natural appetite is beneath the sensitive. If, therefore, to enjoy belongs to the sensitive appetite, it seems that for the same reason it can belong to the natural appetite. But this is evidently false, since the latter cannot delight in anything. Therefore the sensitive appetite cannot enjoy, and accordingly enjoyment is not possible for irrational animals.

On the contrary, Augustine says: *It is not so absurd to suppose that even beasts enjoy their food and any bodily pleasure.*[5]

I answer that, As was stated above, to enjoy is not the act of the power that achieves the end as executor, but of the power that commands the

---

[3] Q. 9, a. 1.   [4] *De Doct. Christ.,* I, 22 (PL 34, 25).   [5] *Lib. 83 Quaest.,* q. 30 (PL 40, 19).

achievement; for it has been said to belong to the appetitive power. Now things devoid of reason have indeed a power of achieving an end by way of execution, *e.g.*, that by which a heavy body has a downward tendency, and a light body has an upward tendency. Yet the power of command in respect of the end is not in them, but in some higher nature, which moves all nature by its command, just as in things endowed with knowledge the appetite moves the other powers to their acts. Therefore, it is clear that things devoid of knowledge, although they attain an end, have no enjoyment of the end; but this is for those only that are endowed with knowledge.

Now knowledge of the end is twofold: perfect and imperfect. Perfect knowledge of the end is that by which we know not only what it is that is the end and the good, but also the universal nature of the end and the good; and such knowledge belongs to the rational nature alone. On the other hand, imperfect knowledge is that by which the end and the good are known in the particular. Such knowledge is to be found in irrational animals, whose appetitive powers do not command with freedom, but are moved according to a natural instinct to whatever they apprehend. Consequently, enjoyment, in its perfect nature, belongs to the rational nature; to irrational animals, imperfectly; and to other creatures, not at all.

Reply Obj. 1. Augustine is speaking there of perfect enjoyment.

Reply Obj. 2. Enjoyment need not be of the last end absolutely, but it can be of that which each one chooses for his last end.

Reply Obj. 3. The sensitive appetite follows some knowledge; not so the natural appetite, especially in things void of knowledge.

Reply Obj. 4. Augustine is speaking there of imperfect enjoyment.[6] This is clear from his manner of speaking, for he says that *it is not so absurd to suppose that even beasts enjoy*, that is, as it would be, if one were to say that they *use*.

Third Article

WHETHER ENJOYMENT IS ONLY OF THE LAST END?

We proceed thus to the Third Article:—

Objection 1. It would seem that enjoyment is not only of the last end. For the Apostle says (*Philem.* 20): *Yea, brother, may I enjoy thee in the Lord*. But it is evident that Paul had not placed his last end in man. Therefore to enjoy is not only of the last end.

Obj. 2. Further, What we enjoy is the fruit. But the Apostle says (*Gal.* v. 22): *The fruit of the Spirit is charity, joy, peace* and other like things, which have not the nature of the last end. Therefore enjoyment is not only of the last end.

Obj. 3. Further, the acts of the will reflect on themselves; for I will to will, and I love to love. But to enjoy is an act of the will, since *it is the will*

[6] *Ibid.*

with which we enjoy, as Augustine says.[7] Therefore a man enjoys his enjoyment. But the last end of man is not enjoyment, but the uncreated good alone, which is God. Therefore enjoyment is not only of the last end.

On the contrary, Augustine says: *A man does not enjoy that which he desires for the sake of something else.*[8] But the last end alone is that which man does not desire for the sake of something else. Therefore enjoyment is of the last end alone.

I answer that, As we have stated above, the notion of fruit implies two things: first, that it should come last; second, that it should calm the appetite with a certain sweetness and delight. Now a thing is last either absolutely or relatively. It is last absolutely if it be referred to nothing else; relatively, if it is the last in a particular series. Therefore, that which is last absolutely, and in which one delights as in the last end, is properly called fruit; and this it is what one is properly said to enjoy.—But that which is delightful, not in itself, but is desired only as referred to something else, *e.g.,* a bitter potion for the sake of health, can in no way be called fruit.—And that which has something delightful about it, to which a number of preceding things are referred, can indeed be called fruit in a certain sense; but we cannot be said to enjoy it properly or as though it answered perfectly to the notion of fruit. Hence Augustine says that *we enjoy what we know, when the delighted will is at rest therein.*[9] But its rest is not absolute save in the last end; for as long as something is looked for, the movement of the will remains in suspense, even though it has reached some good. So, too, in local movement, although any point between the two terms is a beginning and an end, yet it is not considered as an actual end, except when the movement stops there.

Reply Obj. 1. As Augustine says, *if he had said, 'May I enjoy thee,' without adding 'in the Lord,' he would seem to have set the end of his love in him. But since he added 'in the Lord,' he signified that he set his end in the Lord, and also his enjoyment in Him.*[10] In effect he said that he enjoyed his brother not as a term but as a means.

Reply Obj. 2. Fruit has one relation to the tree that bears it, and another to man that enjoys it. To the tree that bears it, it is compared as effect to cause; to the one enjoying it, as the final object of his longing and the consummation of his delight. Accordingly, these fruits mentioned by the Apostle are so called because they are certain effects of the Holy Ghost in us (and this is why they are called *fruits of the Spirit*); but not as though we are to enjoy them as our last end. Or we may say with Ambrose that they are called fruits because *we should desire them for their own sake;*[11]

---

[7] *De Trin.,* X, 10 (PL 42, 981).   [8] *Op. cit.,* X, 11 (PL 42, 983).   [9] *Op. cit.,* X, 10 (PL 42, 981).   [10] *De Doct. Christ.,* I, 33 (PL 34, 33).   [11] Cf. *Glossa interl.,* super *Gal.,* V, 22 (VI, 87v); Peter Lombard, *In Gal.,* super V, 22 (PL 192, 160); *Sent.,* I, i, 3 (I, 19).—Cf. also St. Ambrose, *In Gal.,* super V, 22 (PL 17, 389).

not indeed as though they were not ordained to beatitude, but because they are such that we ought to find pleasure in them.

Reply Obj. 3. As we have stated above, we speak of an end in a twofold sense: first, as being the thing itself; secondly, as the attainment thereof.[12] These are not, of course, two ends, but one end, considered in itself, and in its relation to something else. Accordingly, God is the last end, as that which is ultimately sought for; while the enjoyment is the last end as the attainment of this last end. And so, just as God is not one end, and the enjoyment of God, another, so it is the same enjoyment whereby we enjoy God, and whereby we enjoy our enjoyment of God. And the same applies to created happiness which consists in enjoyment.

Fourth Article

WHETHER ENJOYMENT IS ONLY OF THE END POSSESSED?

We proceed thus to the Fourth Article:—

Objection 1. It would seem that enjoyment is only of the end possessed. For Augustine says that *to enjoy is to use joyfully, with the joy, not of hope, but of possession.*[13] But so long as a thing is not had, there is joy, not of possession, but of hope. Therefore enjoyment is only of the end possessed.

Obj. 2. Further, as was stated above, enjoyment is properly only of the last end, because this alone gives rest to the appetite. But the appetite has no rest save in the possession of the end. Therefore enjoyment, properly speaking, is only of the end possessed.

Obj. 3. Further, to enjoy is to lay hold of the fruit. But one does not lay hold of the fruit until one is in possession of the end. Therefore enjoyment is only of the end possessed.

On the contrary, To enjoy is to adhere lovingly to something for its own sake, as Augustine says.[14] But this is possible even in regard to a thing which is not in our possession. Therefore it is possible to enjoy the end even though it be not possessed.

I answer that, To enjoy implies a certain relation of the will to the last end, according as the will possesses something as a last end. Now an end is possessed in two ways, perfectly and imperfectly. Perfectly, when it is possessed not only in intention but also in reality; imperfectly, when it is possessed in intention only. Perfect enjoyment, therefore, is of the end already possessed; but imperfect enjoyment is also of the end possessed, not really, but only in intention.

Reply Obj. 1. Augustine speaks there of perfect enjoyment.

Reply Obj. 2. The will is hindered in two ways from being at rest. First, on the part of the object, namely, when it is not the last end, but is ordained to something else; secondly, on the part of the one who desires the end, by

[12] Q. 1, a. 8; q. 2, a. 7.   [13] *De Trin.*, X, 11 (PL 42, 982).   [14] *De Doct. Christ.*, I, 4 (PL 34, 20).

reason of his not being yet in possession of it. Now it is the object that specifies an act; but on the agent depends the manner of acting, so that the act be perfect or imperfect, as compared with the actual circumstances of the agent. Therefore, the enjoyment of anything but the last end is not enjoyment properly speaking, as falling short of the nature of enjoyment. But the enjoyment of the last end, when it is not yet possessed, is enjoyment properly speaking, but imperfect, because of the imperfect way in which it is possessed.

Reply Obj. 3. One is said to lay hold of or to have an end, not only in reality, but also in intention, as was stated above.

ON INTENTION
(*In Five Articles*)

WE must now consider intention, concerning which there are five points of inquiry: (1) Whether intention is an act of the intellect or of the will? (2) Whether it is only of the last end? (3) Whether one can intend two things at the same time? (4) Whether the intention of the end is the same act as the volition of the means to the end? (5) Whether intention befits irrational animals?

First Article

WHETHER INTENTION IS AN ACT OF THE INTELLECT OR OF THE WILL?

We proceed thus to the First Article:—

Objection 1. It would seem that intention is an act of the intellect, and not of the will. For it is written (*Matt.* vi. 22): *If thy eye be single, thy whole body shall be lightsome,* where, according to Augustine, the eye signifies intention.[1] But since the eye is the organ of sight, it signifies the apprehensive power. Therefore intention is not an act of the appetitive power, but of the apprehensive power.

Obj. 2. Further, Augustine says that Our Lord spoke of intention as a light, when He said (*Matt.* vi. 23): *If the light that is in thee be darkness,* etc.[2] But light pertains to knowledge. Therefore intention does too.

Obj. 3. Further, intention signifies a kind of ordaining to an end. But to ordain is an act of reason. Therefore intention belongs, not to the will, but to the reason.

Obj. 4. Further, an act of the will is either of the end or of the means. But the act of the will in respect of the end is called volition, or enjoyment, and with regard to the means, it is called choice. Intention is distinct from these. Therefore it is not an act of the will.

On the contrary, Augustine says that *the intention of the will unites the sight to the seen body; and likewise it unites an image existing in the memory to the gaze of the soul thinking within itself.*[3] Therefore intention is an act of the will.

I answer that, Intention, as the very term denotes, signifies, *to tend to*

---

[1] *De Serm. Dom.,* II, 13 (PL 34, 1289).   [2] *Ibid.*   [3] *De Trin.,* XI, 4; 8; 9 (PL 42, 990; 994; 996).

something. Now both the action of the mover and the movement of the thing moved tend to something. But that the movement of the thing moved tends to anything is due to the action of the mover. Consequently, intention belongs first and principally to that which moves to the end; and so we say that an architect, or anyone who is in authority, moves others by his command to that which he intends. Now it is the will that moves all the other powers of the soul to the end, as was shown above.[4] Therefore it is evident that intention, properly speaking, is an act of the will.

Reply Obj. 1. The eye designates intention figuratively, not because intention has reference to knowledge, but because it presupposes knowledge, which proposes to the will the end to which the latter moves. So, too, we see ahead with the eye whither we should tend with our bodies.

Reply Obj. 2. Intention is called a light because it is manifest to him who intends. Therefore works are called darkness because a man knows what he intends, but knows not what the result may be, as Augustine expounds in the same reference.

Reply Obj. 3. The will does not ordain, but tends to something according to the order of reason. Consequently, this term *intention* indicates an act of the will, presupposing the act by which the reason orders something to the end.

Reply Obj. 4. Intention is an act of the will in relation to the end. Now the will stands in a threefold relation to the end. First, absolutely, and thus we have *volition,* by which we will absolutely to have health and so forth. Secondly, it considers the end as its place of rest, and thus *enjoyment* regards the end. Thirdly, it considers the end as the term towards which something is ordained; and thus *intention* regards the end. For when we speak of intending to have health, we mean not only that we will to have it, but that we will to reach it by means of something else.

Second Article

WHETHER INTENTION IS ONLY OF THE LAST END?

We proceed thus to the Second Article:—

Objection 1. It would seem that intention is only of the last end. For it is said in the book of Prosper's *Sentences: The intention of the heart is a cry to God.*[5] But God is the last end of the human heart. Therefore intention always regards the last end.

Obj. 2. Further, intention regards the end as the terminus, as was stated above. But a terminus is something last. Therefore intention always regards the last end.

Obj. 3. Further, just as intention regards the end, so does enjoyment. But enjoyment is always of the last end. Therefore intention is too.

On the contrary, There is but one last end of human volition, viz., hap-

---

[4] Q. 9, a. 1.   [5] Prosper of Aquitaine, *Sent.* C (PL 51, 441).

piness, as was stated above.[6] If, therefore, intentions were only of the last end, men would not have different intentions; which is evidently false.

I answer that, As we have stated above, intention regards the end as a terminus of the movement of the will. Now a terminus of movement may be taken in two ways. First, the very last terminus, when the movement comes to a stop; and this is the terminus of the whole movement. Secondly, some point midway, which is the beginning of one part of the movement and the end or terminus of the other. Thus, in the movement from A to C through B, C is the last terminus, while B is a terminus, but not the last. And intention can be of both. Consequently, though intention is always of the end, it need not always be of the last end.

Reply Obj. 1. The intention of the heart is called a cry to God, not because God is always the object of intention, but because He sees our intention.—Or because, when we pray, we direct our intention to God, which intention has the force of a cry.

Reply Obj. 2. A terminus is something last, not always in respect of the whole, but sometimes in respect of a part.

Reply Obj. 3. Enjoyment signifies rest in the end; and this belongs to the last end alone. But intention signifies movement towards an end, not rest. Therefore the comparison does not hold.

Third Article

WHETHER ONE CAN INTEND TWO THINGS AT THE SAME TIME?

We proceed thus to the Third Article:—

Objection 1. It would seem that one cannot intend several things at the same time. For Augustine says that man's intention cannot be directed at the same time to God and to bodily benefits.[7] Therefore, for the same reason, neither to any other two things.

Obj. 2. Further, intention designates a movement of the will towards a terminus. Now there cannot be several termini in the same direction of one movement. Therefore the will cannot intend several things at the same time.

Obj. 3. Further, intention presupposes an act of the reason or of the intellect. But *it is not possible to understand several things at the same time,* according to the Philosopher.[8] Therefore, neither is it possible to intend several things at the same time.

On the contrary, Art imitates nature. Now nature intends two purposes by means of one instrument. Thus *the tongue* is *for the purpose of taste and speech.*[9] Therefore, for the same reason, art or reason can at the same time

[6] Q. 1, a. 7.   [7] *De Serm. Dom.,* II, 14; 17 (PL 34, 1290; 1294).   [8] *Top.,* II, 10 (114b 35).   [9] Aristotle, *De An.,* II, 8 (420b 18).

direct one thing to two ends; so that one can intend several ends at the same time.

I answer that, Two things may be taken in two ways, namely, as related to one another, or as unrelated. And if they be related to one another, it is evident, from what has been said, that a man can intend several things at the same time. For intention is not only of the last end, as was stated above, but also of an intermediary end. Now a man intends, at the same time, both the proximate and the last end: *e.g.,* the mixing of a medicine and the giving of health.

But if we take two things that are not related to one another, thus also a man can intend several things at the same time. This is evident from the fact that a man prefers one thing to another because it is the better of the two. Now one of the reasons for which one thing is better than another is that it is available for more purposes; and so one thing can be chosen in preference to another because of the greater number of purposes for which it is available; so that evidently a man can intend several things at the same time.

Reply Obj. 1. Augustine means to say that man cannot at the same time direct his intention to God and to bodily benefits, as to two last ends; for, as was stated above, one man cannot have several last ends.[10]

Reply Obj. 2. There can be several termini of the same movement and in the same direction, if one is related to the other; but there cannot be two unrelated termini of the same movement and in the same direction. At the same time, it must be observed that what is not one in reality may be taken as one by the reason. Now intention is a movement of the will to something already ordained by the reason, as was stated above. Therefore, where we have many things in reality, we may take them as one term of intention, in so far as the reason takes them as one; and this either because two things concur in the integrity of one whole, as a proper measure of heat and cold conduce to health, or because two things are included in one which may be intended. For instance, the acquiring of wine and clothing is included in wealth, as in something common to both; and so nothing hinders the man who intends to acquire wealth from intending both the others.

Reply Obj. 3. As was stated in the First Part, it is possible to understand several things at the same time in so far as, in some way, they are one.[11]

Fourth Article

WHETHER THE INTENTION OF THE END IS THE SAME ACT AS THE VOLITION OF THE MEANS TO THE END?

We proceed thus to the Fourth Article:—

Objection 1. It would seem that the intention of the end and the volition of the means to the end are not one and the same movement. For Augustine

[10] Q. 1, a. 5.   [11] *S. T.,* I, q. 12, a. 10; q. 58, a. 2; q. 85, a. 4.

says that *the will to see the window has for its end the seeing of the window, and is another act from the will to see, through the window, the passers-by.*[12] But that I should will to see the passers-by, through the window, belongs to the intention; whereas that I will to see the window belongs to the volition of the means. Therefore, the intention of the end and the willing of the means are distinct movements of the will.

Obj. 2. Further, acts are distinguished according to their objects. But the end and the means are diverse objects. Therefore, the intention of the end and the willing of the means are distinct movements of the will.

Obj. 3. Further, the willing of the means is called choice. But choice and intention are not the same. Therefore, the intention of the end and the willing of the means are not the same movement of the will.

On the contrary. The means to the end are related to the end as the midground to the terminus. Now, in the realm of natural things, it is all the same movement that passes through the mid-ground to the terminus. Therefore, in things pertaining to the will, the intention of the end is likewise the same movement as the willing of the means.

I answer that, The movement of the will to the end and to the means to the end can be considered in two ways. First, according as the will is moved to each of them absolutely and in itself. And thus there are absolutely two movements of the will to them. Secondly, it may be considered according as the will is moved to the means for the sake of the end; and thus the movement of the will to the end and its movement to the means are one and the same thing. For when I say: *I wish to take medicine for the sake of health,* I signify no more than one movement of my will, and this is because the end is the reason for willing the means to the end. Now the object, and that by reason of which it is an object, come under the same act; and thus it is the same act of sight that perceives color and light, as was stated above.[13] The same applies to the intellect. For if it considers principle and conclusion absolutely, it considers each by a distinct act; but when it assents to the conclusion because of the principles, there is but one act of the intellect.

Reply Obj. 1. Augustine is speaking of seeing the window and of seeing, through the window, the passers-by, according as the will is moved to either absolutely.

Reply Obj. 2. The end, considered as a thing, and the means to that end are distinct objects of the will. But in so far as the end is the reason for willing the means, they are one and the same object.

Reply Obj. 3. A movement which is in one subject may differ, according to our way of looking at it, as to its beginning and end, as in the case of ascent and descent.[14] Accordingly, in so far as the movement of the will is to the means, as ordained to the end, it is called *choice;* but the movement of the will to the end, as acquired by the means, is called *intention.* A sign of this

[12] *De Trin.,* XI, 6 (PL 42, 992). [13] Q. 8, a. 3, ad 2. [14] Aristotle, *Phys.,* III 3 (202a 19).

is that we can have an intention of the end without having determined the means to the end, which are the object of choice.

Fifth Article

WHETHER INTENTION BEFITS IRRATIONAL ANIMALS?

We proceed thus to the Fifth Article:—

Objection 1. It would seem that irrational animals intend the end. For in beings devoid of reason, nature is farther removed from the rational nature than is the sensitive nature which is found in irrational animals. But nature intends the end even in beings devoid of reason, as is proved in *Physics* ii.[15] Much more, therefore, do irrational animals intend the end.

Obj. 2. Further, just as intention is of the end, so is enjoyment. But enjoyment befits irrational animals, as was stated above.[16] Therefore intention does too.

Obj. 3. Further, to intend an end belongs to one who acts for an end, since to intend is nothing else than to tend to something. But irrational animals act for an end, for an animal is moved either to seek food, or to do something of the kind. Therefore irrational animals intend an end.

On the contrary, The intention of an end signifies the ordering of something to the end; and this is the work of reason. Since, therefore, irrational animals are devoid of reason, it seems that they do not intend an end.

I answer that, As we have stated above, to intend is to tend to something, and this belongs both to the mover and to the moved. According, therefore, as that which is moved to an end by another is said to intend the end, so nature is said to intend an end, as being moved to its end by God, as the arrow is moved by the archer. In this way, too, irrational animals intend an end, inasmuch as they are moved to something by natural instinct.—The other way of intending an end belongs to the mover, according as he ordains the movement of something, either his own or another's, to an end. This belongs to reason alone. Therefore, irrational animals do not intend an end in this way, which is to intend properly and principally, as we have stated above.

Reply Obj. 1. This argument takes intention as belonging to the being that is moved to an end.

Reply Obj. 2. Enjoyment does not signify the ordaining of one thing to another, as intention does, but absolute repose in the end.

Reply Obj. 3. Irrational animals are moved to an end, not as though they recognize that they can gain the end by this movement (this belongs properly to the intending being); but through desiring the end by natural instinct, they are moved to the end, as it were, moved by another, like other things that are moved naturally.

[15] *Op. cit.,* II, 8 (199b 30).   [16] Q. 11, a. 2.

ON CHOICE, WHICH IS AN ACT OF THE WILL IN RELATION TO THE MEANS TO THE END

(*In Six Articles*)

WE must now consider the acts of the will which are related to the means to the end. There are three of them: *to choose, to consent* and *to use*. Now choice is preceded by counsel. First of all, then, we must consider choice; secondly, counsel;[1] thirdly, consent;[2] fourthly, use.[3]

Concerning choice there are six points of inquiry: (1) Of what power is it the act, whether of the will or of the reason? (2) Whether choice is to be found in irrational animals? (3) Whether choice is only of the means to the end, or sometimes also of the end? (4) Whether choice is only of things that we do ourselves? (5) Whether choice is only of possible things? (6) Whether man chooses of necessity or freely?

First Article

WHETHER CHOICE IS AN ACT OF THE WILL OR OF THE REASON?

Objection 1. It would seem that choice is an act, not of the will, but of the reason. For choice expresses a certain comparison, whereby one thing is preferred to another. But to compare is an act of reason. Therefore choice is an act of reason.

Obj. 2. Further, it belongs to the same power to form a syllogism and to draw the conclusion. But, in practical matters, it is the reason that forms syllogisms. Since, therefore, choice is a kind of conclusion in practical matters, as is stated in *Ethics* vii.,[4] it seems that it is an act of reason.

Obj. 3. Further, ignorance does not belong to the will but to the cognitive power. Now there is an *ignorance attending choice*, as is stated in *Ethics* iii.[5] Therefore it seems that choice does not belong to the will but to the reason.

On the contrary, The Philosopher says that choice is *the desire of things which are in our power*.[6] But desire is an act of will. Therefore choice is too.

I answer that, The term *choice* expresses something belonging to the reason or intellect, and something belonging to the will; for the Philosopher says that choice is either *intellect influenced by appetite or appetite in-*

---

[1] Q. 14. [2] Q. 15. [3] Q. 16. [4] Cf. Aristotle, *Eth.*, III, 3 (1113a 4; a 11). [5] *Op. cit.*, III, 1 (1110b 31). [6] *Op. cit.*, III, 3 (1113a 9).

fluenced by intellect.[7] Now whenever two things concur to make one, one of them is as a form in relation to the other. Hence Gregory of Nyssa says that choice *is neither desire only, nor counsel only, but a combination of the two. For just as we say that an animal is composed of soul and body, and that it is neither only the body, nor only the soul, but both, so is it with choice.*[8]

Now we must observe, as regards the acts of the soul, that an act belonging essentially to some power or habit receives its form or species from a higher power or habit, according as the inferior is ordered by the superior. For if a man were to perform an act of fortitude for the love of God, that act is materially an act of fortitude, but formally, an act of charity. Now it is evident that, in a sense, reason precedes the will and directs its act, namely, in so far as the will tends to its object according to the order of reason; for the apprehensive power presents to the appetite its object. Accordingly, that act whereby the will tends to something proposed to it as being good, through being ordained to the end by the reason, is materially an act of the will, but formally an act of the reason. Now in such matters, the substance of the act is as the matter in comparison to the order imposed by the higher power. Therefore, choice is substantially, not an act of the reason, but of the will; for choice is accomplished in a certain movement of the soul towards the good which is chosen. Consequently, it is evidently an act of the appetitive power.

Reply Obj. 1. Choice implies a previous comparison, but not that it consists in the comparison itself.

Reply Obj. 2. It is quite true that it is for the reason to draw the conclusion of a practical syllogism; and it is called *a decision* or *judgment*, to be followed by *choice*. And for this reason the conclusion seems to belong to the act of choice, as to that which results from it.

Reply Obj. 3. In speaking *of ignorance attending choice*, we do not mean that choice itself is a sort of knowledge, but that there is ignorance of what ought to be chosen.

Second Article

WHETHER CHOICE IS TO BE FOUND IN IRRATIONAL ANIMALS?

Objection 1. It would seem that irrational animals are able to choose. For choice *is the desire of certain things because of an end,* as stated in *Ethics* iii.[9] But irrational animals desire something because of an end, since they act for an end, and from desire. Therefore choice is in irrational animals.

Obj. 2. Further, the very term *electio* [*choice*] seems to signify the taking of something in preference to others. But irrational animals take something

[7] *Op. cit.,* VI, 2 (1139b 4).   [8] Cf. Nemesius, *De Nat. Hom.,* XXXIII (PG 40, 733).
[9] Aristotle, *Eth.,* III, 2 (1111b 27); 3 (1113a 11).

in preference to others; and thus we can easily see for ourselves that a sheep will eat one grass and refuse another. Therefore choice is in irrational animals.

Obj. 3. Further, according to *Ethics* vi., *it is from prudence that a man makes a good choice of means.*[10] But prudence is found in irrational animals: hence it is said in the beginning of the *Metaphysics* that *those animals which, like bees, cannot hear sounds are prudent without acquiring it by learning.*[11] We see this plainly in wonderful cases of sagacity manifested in the works of various animals, such as bees, spiders and dogs. For a hound in following a stag, on coming to a cross road, tries by scent whether the stag has passed by the first or the second road; and if he finds that the stag has not passed there, being thus assured, takes to the third road without trying the scent, as though he were reasoning by way of exclusion, arguing that the stag must have passed by this way, since he did not pass by the others, and there is no other road. Therefore, it seems that irrational animals are able to choose.

On the contrary, Gregory of Nyssa says that *children and irrational animals act willingly but not from choice.*[12] Therefore choice is not in irrational animals.

I answer that, Since choice is the taking of one thing in preference to another, it must of necessity be in respect of several things that can be chosen. Consequently, in those things which are altogether determined to one course there is no place for choice. Now the difference between the sensitive appetite and the will is that, as we have stated above,[13] the sensitive appetite is determined to one particular thing according to the order of nature; whereas the will, although determined to one thing in general, viz., the good, according to the order of nature, is nevertheless undetermined in respect of particular goods. Consequently choice belongs properly to the will, and not to the sensitive appetite which is all that irrational animals have. Therefore, irrational animals are not endowed with choice.

Reply Obj. 1. Not every desire of a thing because of an end is called choice; there is also required a certain discrimination of one thing from another. And this cannot be except when the appetite can be moved to several things.

Reply Obj. 2. An irrational animal takes one thing in preference to another because its appetite is naturally determined to that thing. Therefore, as soon as an animal, whether by its sense or by its imagination, is offered something to which its appetite is naturally inclined, it is moved to that alone, without making any choice. So, too, fire is moved upwards and not downwards, without its making any choice.

Reply Obj. 3. As is stated in *Physics* iii., *movement is the act of the mov-*

able, caused by a mover.[14] Therefore the power of the mover appears in the movement of that which it moves. Accordingly, in all things moved by reason, the order of reason which moves them is evident, although the things themselves are without reason; for through the motion of the archer the arrow goes straight towards the target, as though it were endowed with reason to direct its course. The same may be seen in the movements of clocks and all devices put together by the art of man. Now as artificial things are in comparison to human art, so are all natural things in comparison to the divine art. Accordingly, order is to be seen in things moved by nature, just as in things moved by reason, as is stated in *Physics* ii.[15] And thus it is that in the works of irrational animals we notice certain marks of sagacity, in so far as they have a natural inclination to set about their actions in a most orderly manner through being ordained by the supreme art. For which reason, too, certain animals are called prudent or sagacious; and not because they reason or exercise any choice about things. This is clear from the fact that all that share in one nature invariably act in the same way.

Third Article

WHETHER CHOICE IS ONLY OF THE MEANS TO THE END OR SOMETIMES ALSO OF THE END?

We proceed thus to the Third Article:—

Objection 1. It would seem that choice is not only of the means to the end. For the Philosopher says that *virtue makes us choose rightly; but it is not the part of virtue, but of some other power, to direct rightly those things which are to be done for its sake.*[16] But that for the sake of which something is done is the end. Therefore choice is of the end.

Obj. 2. Further, choice signifies preference of one thing to another. But just as there can be preference of means, so can there be preference of ends. Therefore choice can be of ends, just as it can be of means.

On the contrary, The Philosopher says that *volition is of the end, but choice of the means.*[17]

I answer that, As we have already stated, choice follows the decision or judgment which is, as it were, the conclusion of a practical syllogism. Hence that which is the conclusion of a practical syllogism is the matter of choice. Now in practical things the end stands in the position of a principle, not of a conclusion, as the Philosopher says.[18] Therefore the end, as such, is not a matter of choice.

But just as in speculative matters nothing hinders the principle of one demonstration or of one science from being the conclusion of another demonstration or science (although the first indemonstrable principle can-

---

[14] *Phys.*, III, 3 (202a 13).   [15] *Op. cit.*, II, 5 (196b 17).   [16] *Eth.*, VI, 12 (1144a 20).   [17] *Op. cit.*, III, 2 (1111b 26).   [18] *Phys.*, II, 9 (200a 20).

not be the conclusion of any demonstration or science), so, too, that which is the end in one operation may be ordained to something as an end. And in this way it is a matter of choice. Thus in the work of a physician health is the end, and so it is not a matter of choice for a physician, but a matter of principle. But the health of the body is ordained to the good of the soul, and, consequently, with one who has charge of the soul's health, health or sickness may be a matter of choice; for the Apostle says (*2 Cor.* xii. 10): *For when I am weak, then am I powerful.* But the last end is in no way a matter of choice.

Reply Obj. 1. The proper ends of the virtues are ordained to happiness as to their last end. And thus it is that they can be a matter of choice.

Reply Obj. 2. As was stated above, there is but one last end.[19] Accordingly, wherever there are several ends, they can be the subject of choice, in so far as they are ordained to a further end.

Fourth Article

WHETHER CHOICE IS OF THOSE THINGS ONLY THAT ARE DONE BY US?

We proceed thus to the Fourth Article:—

Objection 1. It would seem that choice is not only in respect of human acts. For choice is of the means. Now, not only acts, but also the organs, are means.[20] Therefore choice is not only concerned with human acts.

Obj. 2. Further, action is distinct from contemplation. But choice has a place even in contemplation, in so far, namely, as one opinion is preferred to another. Therefore choice is not concerned with human acts alone.

Obj. 3. Further, men are chosen for certain posts, whether secular or ecclesiastical, by those who exercise no action in their regard. Therefore choice is not concerned with human acts alone.

On the contrary, The Philosopher says that *no man chooses save what he thinks he can do himself.*[21]

I answer that, Just as intention regards the end, so choice regards the means. Now the end is either an action or a thing. And when the end is a thing, some human action must intervene, and this either in so far as man produces the thing which is the end, as the physician produces health (and so the production of health is said to be the end of the physician), or in so far as man, in some fashion, uses or enjoys the thing which is the end: *e.g.*, for the miser, money or the possession of money is the end. The same is to be said of the means. For the means must needs be either an action, or a thing, with some action intervening whereby man either makes the thing which is the means, or puts it to some use. And thus it is that choice is always in regard to human acts.

[19] Q. 1, a. 5.   [20] Aristotle, *Phys.* II, 3 (195a 1).   [21] *Eth.*, III, 2 (1111b 25).

Reply Obj. 1. The organs are ordained to the end inasmuch as man makes use of them for the sake of the end.

Reply Obj. 2. In contemplation itself there is the act of the intellect assenting to this or that opinion. It is exterior action that is put in contradistinction to contemplation.

Reply Obj. 3. When a man chooses someone for a bishopric or some high position in the state, he chooses to name that man to that post. Otherwise, if he had no right to act in the appointment of the bishop or prince, he would have no right to choose. Likewise, whenever we speak of one thing being chosen in preference to another, it is in conjunction with some action of the chooser.

Fifth Article

WHETHER CHOICE IS ONLY OF POSSIBLE THINGS?

We proceed thus to the Fifth Article:—

Objection 1. It would seem that choice is not only of possible things. For choice is an act of the will, as was stated above. Now *there is a willing of the possible and the impossible.*[22] Therefore there is also a choice of them.

Obj. 2. Further, choice is of things done by us, as was stated above. Therefore it matters not, as far as the act of choosing is concerned, whether one choose that which is impossible in itself, or that which is impossible to the chooser. Now it often happens that we are unable to accomplish what we choose, so that this proves to be impossible to us. Therefore choice is of the impossible.

Obj. 3. Further, to try to do a thing is to choose to do it. But the Blessed Benedict says that, if the superior command what is impossible, it should be attempted.[23] Therefore choice can be of the impossible.

On the contrary, The Philosopher says that *there is no choice of the impossible.*[24]

I answer that, As was stated above, our choice is always concerned with our actions. Now whatever is done by us is possible to us. Therefore we must needs say that choice is only of possible things.

Moreover, the reason for choosing a thing is that we may gain the end through it, or that it conduces to an end. But what is impossible cannot conduce to an end. A sign of this is that when men, in taking counsel together, come to something that is impossible to them, they depart, as being unable to proceed with the business.

Again, this is evident if we examine the preceding process of the reason. For the means, which are the object of choice, are to the end as the conclusion is to the principle. Now it is clear that an impossible conclusion does not follow from a possible principle. Therefore an end cannot be possible

---

[22] *Ibid.* (1111b 22).   [23] *Reg. ad Mon.,* LXVIII (PL 66, 917).   [24] *Eth.,* III, 3 (1111b 20).

unless the means be possible. Now no one is moved to the impossible. Consequently, no one would tend to the end, save for the fact that the means appear to be possible. Therefore the impossible is not the object of choice.

Reply Obj. 1. The will stands between the intellect and the external action; for the intellect proposes to the will its object, and the will causes the external action. Hence the principle of the movement in the will is to be found in the intellect, which apprehends something as a universal good; but the term or perfection of the will's act is to be observed in its relation to the action by which a man tends to the attainment of a thing, for the movement of the will is from the soul to the thing. Consequently, the perfection of the act of the will is in respect of something that is good for one to do. Now this cannot be something impossible. Therefore, perfect willing is only in respect of what is possible and good for him that wills. But imperfect willing is in respect of the impossible; and by some it is called *velleity*, because, namely, one would will [*vellet*] such a thing, were it possible. But choice is an act of the will already fixed on something to be done by the chooser. And therefore it is by no means of anything but what is possible.

Reply Obj. 2. Since the object of the will is the apprehended good, we must judge of the object of the will according as it is apprehended. And so, just as sometimes the will tends to something which is apprehended as good, and yet is not really good, so choice is sometimes made of something apprehended as possible to the chooser, and yet impossible to him.

Reply Obj. 3. The reason for this is that the subject should not rely on his own judgment to decide whether a certain thing is possible; but in each case should stand by his superior's judgment.

Sixth Article

WHETHER MAN CHOOSES OF NECESSITY OR FREELY?

We proceed thus to the Sixth Article:—

Objection 1. It would seem that man chooses of necessity. For the end stands in relation to the object of choice as principles to what follows from them, as is declared in *Ethics* vii.[25] But conclusions follow of necessity from their principles. Therefore the end moves a man necessarily to choose.

Obj. 2. Further, as was stated above choice follows the reason's judgment of what is to be done. But reason judges of necessity about some things, because of the necessity of the premises. Therefore it seems that choice also follows of necessity.

Obj. 3. Further, if two things are absolutely equal, man is not moved to one more than to the other. Thus, if a hungry man, as Plato says,[26] be confronted on either side with two portions of food equally appetizing and at an equal distance, he is not moved towards one more than to the other; and

---

[25] *Op. cit.*, VII, 8 (1151a 16).   [26] Cf. Averroes, *In De Caelo*, comm. 90 (V, 73v).

he finds the reason of this in the immobility of the earth in the middle of the world as it is said in *De Caelo*.[27] Now, if that which is equally [eligible] with something else cannot be chosen, much less can that be chosen which appears as less [eligible]. Therefore if two or more things are available, of which one appears to be more [eligible], it is impossible to choose any of the others. Therefore that which appears to be best is chosen of necessity. But every act of choosing is in regard to something that seems in some way better. Therefore every choice is made necessarily.

On the contrary, Choice is an act of a rational power, and such a power, according to the Philosopher, stands in relation to opposites.[28]

I answer that, Man does not choose of necessity. And this is because that which is possible not to be, is not of necessity. Now the reason why it is possible not to choose, or to choose, may be gathered from a twofold power in man. For man can will and not will, act and not act; and again, he can will this or that, and do this or that. The reason for this is to be found in the very power of the reason. For the will can tend to whatever the reason can apprehend as good. Now the reason can apprehend as good not only this, viz., *to will* or *to act*, but also this, viz., *not to will* and *not to act*. Again, in all particular goods, the reason can consider the nature of some good, and the lack of some good, which has the nature of an evil; and in this way, it can apprehend any single one of such goods as to be chosen or to be avoided. The perfect good alone, which is happiness, cannot be apprehended by the reason as an evil, or as lacking in any way. Conse- quently, man wills happiness of necessity, nor can he will not to be happy, or to be unhappy. Now since choice is not of the end, but of the means, as was stated above, it is not of the perfect good, which is happiness, but of other and particular goods. Therefore, man chooses, not of necessity, but freely.

Reply Obj. 1. The conclusion does not always of necessity follow from the principles, but only when the principles cannot be true if the conclusion is not true. In like manner, the end does not always necessitate in man the choosing of the means to the end, because the means are not always such that the end cannot be gained without them; or, if they be such, they are not always considered in that light.

Reply Obj. 2. The reason's decision or judgment of what is to be done is about things that are contingent actions that are possible to us. In such mat- ters, the conclusions do not follow of necessity from principles that are abso- lutely necessary, but from such as are so conditionally: *e.g., If he runs, he is in motion.*

Reply Obj. 3. If two things be proposed as equal under one aspect, nothing hinders us from considering in one of them some particular point of superiority, so that the will is turned towards that one rather than to- wards the other.

---

[27] Aristotle, *De Caelo*, II, 13 (295b 12; b 25).—Cf. St. Thomas, *In De Caelo*, II, lect. 25.   [28] *Metaph.*, VIII, 2 (1046b 8).

Question XIV

ON COUNSEL, WHICH PRECEDES CHOICE

(*In Six Articles*)

WE must now consider counsel, concerning which there are six points of inquiry: (1) Whether counsel is an inquiry? (2) Whether counsel is of the end or only of the means? (3) Whether counsel is only of things that we do? (4) Whether counsel is of all things that we do? (5) Whether counsel proceeds by way of resolution? (6) Whether the process of counsel is without end?

First Article

WHETHER COUNSEL IS AN INQUIRY?

We proceed thus to the First Article:—

Objection 1. It would seem that counsel is not an inquiry. For Damascene says that counsel is *an [inquiring] appetite*.[1] But inquiry is not an act of the appetite. Therefore counsel is not an inquiry.

Obj. 2. Further, inquiry is a discursive act of the intellect; for which reason it is not found in God, Whose knowledge is not discursive, as was shown in the First Part.[2] But counsel is ascribed to God, for it is written (*Ephes.* i. 11) that *He worketh all things according to the counsel of His will.* Therefore counsel is not an inquiry.

Obj. 3. Further, inquiry is of doubtful matters. But counsel is given in matters that are with certainty good; and thus the Apostle says (*1 Cor.* vii. 25): *Now concerning virgins I have no commandment of the Lord; but I give counsel.* Therefore, counsel is not an inquiry.

On the contrary, Gregory of Nyssa says: *Every counsel is an inquiry; but not every inquiry is a counsel.*[3]

I answer that, Choice, as we have stated above, follows the judgment of the reason in matters of action.[4] Now there is much uncertainty in matters of action, because actions are concerned with contingent singulars which, by reason of their variability, are uncertain. Now in things doubtful and uncertain, the reason does not pronounce judgment without previous inquiry. Therefore the reason must of necessity institute an inquiry before deciding on what is to be chosen; and this inquiry is called counsel. Hence

---

[1] *De Fide Orth.*, II, 22 (PG 94, 945). [2] *S.T.*, I, q. 14, a. 7. [3] Cf. Nemesius, *De Nat. Hom.*, XXXIV (PG 40, 736). [4] Q. 13, a. 1, ad 2; a. 3.

the Philosopher says that choice is the *desire of what has been already counselled.*[5]

Reply Obj. 1. When the acts of two powers are ordered to one another, in each of them there is something belonging to the other power; and consequently each act can be denominated from either power. Now it is evident that the act of the reason giving direction as to the means, and the act of the will tending to these means according to the reason's direction, are ordered to one another. Consequently, there is to be found something of the reason, viz., order, in the act of the will which is choice; and in counsel, which is an act of reason, something is found of the will, both as matter (since counsel is of what man wills to do), and as motive (because it is from willing the end that man is moved to take counsel in regard to the means). And, therefore, just as the Philosopher says that choice is *intellect influenced by appetite,*[6] thus pointing out that both concur in the act of choosing, so Damascene says that counsel is *appetite based on inquiry,*[7] so as to show that counsel belongs, in a way, both to the will, on whose behalf and by whose impulsion the inquiry is made, and to the reason that pursues the inquiry.

Reply Obj. 2. The things that we say of God must be understood without any of the defects which are to be found in us; and thus in us science is of conclusions derived by reasoning from causes to effects, but science, when said of God, means sure knowledge of all effects in the First Cause, without any reasoning process. In like manner we ascribe counsel to God, as to the certainty of His decision or judgment, which in us arises from the inquiry of counsel. But such inquiry has no place in God, and so in this respect it is not ascribed to God; in which sense Damascene says: *God takes not counsel, for those only take counsel who lack knowledge.*[8]

Reply Obj. 3. It may happen that things which are most certainly good in the opinion of wise and spiritual men are not certainly good in the opinion of the many, or at least of carnal men. Consequently, in such things counsel may be given.

Second Article

WHETHER COUNSEL IS OF THE END, OR ONLY OF THE MEANS TO THE END?

We proceed thus to the Second Article:—

Objection 1. It would seem that counsel is not only of the means but also of the end. For whatever is doubtful can be the subject of inquiry. Now in things to be done by man there happens sometimes a doubt as to the end and not only as to the means. Since, therefore, inquiry as to what is to be done is counsel, it seems that counsel can be of the end.

---

[5] *Eth.,* III, 3 (1113a 11); 2 (1112a 15).   [6] *Op. cit.,* VI, 2 (1139b 4).   [7] *De Fide Orth.,* II, 22 (PG 94, 945).   [8] *Ibid.*

Obj. 2. Further, the matter of counsel is human actions. But some human actions are ends, as is stated in *Ethics* i.[9] Therefore counsel can be of the end.

On the contrary, Gregory of Nyssa says that *counsel is not of the end, but of the means.*[10]

I answer that, The end is the principle in practical matters, because the nature of the means is taken from the end. Now the principle cannot be called in question, but must be presupposed in every inquiry. Since, therefore, counsel is an inquiry, it is not of the end, but only of the means to the end. Nevertheless, it may happen that what is the end in regard to some things is ordained to something else; just as also what is the principle of one demonstration is the conclusion of another. Consequently, that which is looked upon as the end in one inquiry may be looked upon as the means in another; and thus it will become an object of counsel.

Reply Obj. 1. That which is looked upon as an end is already fixed. Consequently, as long as there is any doubt about it, it is not looked upon as an end. Therefore, if counsel is taken about it, it will be counsel, not about the end, but about the means to the end.

Reply Obj. 2. Counsel is about operations in so far as they are ordered to some end. Consequently, if any human act be an end, it will not, as such, be the matter of counsel.

Third Article

WHETHER COUNSEL IS ONLY OF THINGS THAT WE DO?

We proceed thus to the Third Article:—

Objection 1. It would seem that counsel is not only of things that we do. For counsel signifies some kind of comparison. But it is possible for many to compare things that are not subject to movement, and are not the result of our actions, such as the natures of various things. Therefore counsel is not only of things that we do.

Obj. 2. Further, men sometimes seek counsel about things that are laid down by law; and so there are men called counsellors-at-law. And yet those who seek such counsel have nothing to do in making the laws. Therefore, counsel is not only of things that we do.

Obj. 3. Further, some are said to take consultation about future events; which, however, are not in our power. Therefore, counsel is not only of things that we do.

Obj. 4. Further, if counsel were only of things that we do, no one would take counsel about what another does. But this is clearly untrue. Therefore, counsel is not only of things that we do.

[9] Aristotle, *Eth.,* I, 1 (1094a 4).   [10] Cf. Nemesius, *De Nat. Hom.,* XXXIV (PG 40, 740).

On the contrary, Gregory of Nyssa says: *We take counsel of things that are within us and that we are able to do.*[11]

I answer that, Counsel signifies a conference held among several. The term [*consilium*] denotes this, for it means a sitting together [*considium*], from the fact that many sit together in order to confer with one another. Now we must take note that, in contingent particulars, in order that anything be known with certainty, it is necessary to take several conditions or circumstances into consideration, which it is not easy for one to do; but these are considered by several with greater certainty, since what one takes note of escapes the notice of another. In necessary and universal matters, however, our consideration is more absolute and more simple, so that one man by himself can be sufficient to consider these matters. Therefore, the inquiry of counsel is concerned, properly speaking, with contingent singulars. Now the knowledge of the truth in such matters does not rank so high as to be desirable of itself, as is the knowledge of what is universal and necessary; but it is desired as being useful towards action, because actions bear on contingent singulars. Consequently, properly speaking, counsel is about things done by us.

Reply Obj. 1. Counsel signifies conference, not of any kind, but about what is to be done, for the reason given above.

Reply Obj. 2. Although that which is laid down by the law is not due to the action of him who seeks counsel, nevertheless it directs him in his action; for the mandate of the law is one reason for doing something.

Reply Obj. 3. Counsel is not only about actions but also about whatever is related to actions. And for this reason we speak of consulting about future events, in so far as man is induced to do or omit something through the knowledge of future events.

Reply Obj. 4. We seek counsel about the actions of others in so far as they are, in some way, one with us; and this either by union of affection (thus a man is solicitous about what concerns his friend, as though it concerned himself), or after the manner of an instrument, for the principal agent and the instrument are, in a way, one cause, since one acts through the other (thus the master takes counsel about what he would do through his servant).

Fourth Article

WHETHER COUNSEL IS ABOUT ALL THINGS THAT WE DO?

We proceed thus to the Fourth Article:—

Objection 1. It would seem that counsel is about all things that we have to do. For choice is the *desire of what is counselled,* as was stated above. But choice is about all things that we do. Therefore counsel is too.

Obj. 2. Further, counsel signifies the reason's inquiry. But whenever we

[11] Cf. *ibid.* (PG 40, 737).

do not act through the impulse of passion, we act in virtue of the reason's inquiry. Therefore, there is counsel about everything that we do.

Obj. 3. Further, the Philosopher says that *if it appears that something can be done by more means than one, we take counsel by inquiring whereby it may be done most easily and best; but if it can be accomplished by one means, how it can be done by this.*[12] But whatever is done, is done by one means or by several. Therefore counsel takes place in all things that we do.

On the contrary, Gregory of Nyssa says that *counsel has no place in things that are done according to science or art.*[13]

I answer that, Counsel is a kind of inquiry, as we have stated above. Now we are wont to inquire about things that admit of doubt, and so the process of inquiry, which is called an argument, *is a reason that attests something that admitted of doubt.*[14] Now that something in relation to human acts admits of no doubt, arises from a twofold source. First, because certain determinate ends are gained by certain determinate means, as happens in the arts which are governed by certain fixed rules of action; and thus a person writing does not take counsel how to form his letters, for this is determined by art. Secondly, from the fact that it matters little whether it is done this or that way; and this occurs in small matters, which help or hinder but little with regard to the end aimed at. Now reason looks upon small things as mere nothings. Hence there are two things about which we do not take counsel, although they conduce to the end, as the Philosopher says,[15] namely, small things, and those which have a fixed way of being done, as in works produced by art, with the exception of those arts that admit of conjecture, such as medicine, commerce and the like, as Gregory of Nyssa says.[16]

Reply Obj. 1. Choice presupposes counsel because of its judgment or decision. Consequently, when the judgment or decision is evident without inquiry, there is no need for the inquiry of counsel.

Reply Obj. 2. In matters that are evident, the reason makes no inquiry, but judges at once. Consequently, there is no need of counsel in all that is done by reason.

Reply Obj. 3. When a thing can be accomplished by one means, but in different ways, doubt may arise, just as when it can be accomplished by several means; and hence the need of counsel. But when not only the means, but also the way of using the means, is fixed, then there is no need of counsel.

---

[12] *Eth.,* III, 3 (1112b 16). [13] Cf. Nemesius, *De Nat. Hom.,* XXXIV (PG 40, 740). [14] Cf. Cicero, *De Invent.,* I, 34 (p. 45^b^). [15] *Eth.,* III, 3 (1112b 9). [16] Cf. Nemesius, *ibid.*

Fifth Article

WHETHER COUNSEL PROCEEDS BY WAY OF RESOLUTION?

We proceed thus to the Fifth Article:—

Objection 1. It would seem that counsel does not proceed by way of resolution. For counsel is about things that we do. But our operations do not proceed by resolution, but rather by composition, viz., from the simple to the composite. Therefore, counsel does not always proceed by way of resolution.

Obj. 2. Further, counsel is an inquiry of the reason. But reason proceeds from things that precede to things that follow, according to the more appropriate order. Since, then, the past precedes the present, and the present precedes the future, it seems that in taking counsel one should proceed from the past and present to the future; which is not by way of resolution. Therefore, counsel does not proceed by way of resolution.

Obj. 3. Further, counsel is only of such things as are possible to us, according to *Ethics* iii.[17] But the question as to whether a certain thing is possible to us depends on what we are able or unable to do, in order to gain such and such an end. Therefore, the inquiry of counsel should begin from things present.

On the contrary, The Philosopher says that *he who takes counsel seems to proceed by inquiry and resolution.*[18]

I answer that, In every inquiry one must begin from some principle. And if this principle precedes both in knowledge and in being, the process is not by way of resolution, but by way of composition; for to proceed from cause to effect is to proceed in a composite way, since causes are more simple than effects. But if that which precedes in knowledge is later in the order of being, the process is one of resolution, as when our judgment deals with known effects, which we reduce to their simple causes. Now the principle in the inquiry of counsel is the end, which precedes in intention but comes afterwards into realization. Hence the inquiry of counsel must needs be one of resolution, beginning, that is to say, from that which is intended in the future, and continuing until it arrives at that which is to be done at once.

Reply Obj. 1. Counsel is indeed about action. But actions take their nature from the end; and consequently the order of reasoning about actions is contrary to the order of actions.

Reply Obj. 2. Reason begins with that which is first according to reason; but not always with that which is first in point of time.

Reply Obj. 3. We should not want to know whether something to be done for an end be possible, if it were not suitable for gaining that end. Hence

---

[17] Aristotle, *Eth.*, III, 3 (1112b 26; b32).   [18] *Ibid.* (1112b 20).

we must first inquire whether it be conducive to the end, before considering whether it be possible.

WHETHER THE PROCESS OF COUNSEL IS WITHOUT END?

We proceed thus to the Sixth Article:—

Objection 1. It would seem that the process of counsel is without end. For counsel is an inquiry about the singular things with which action is concerned. But singulars are infinite. Therefore the process of counsel is without end.

Obj. 2. Further, the inquiry of counsel has to consider not only what is to be done, but how to avoid obstacles. But every human action can be hindered, and an obstacle can be removed by some human reason. Therefore the inquiry about removing obstacles can go on without end.

Obj. 3. Further, the inquiry of demonstrative science does not go on without end, because one can come to principles that are self-evident, which are absolutely certain. But such certainty is not to be had in contingent singulars, which are variable and uncertain. Therefore the inquiry of counsel goes on without end.

On the contrary, No one is moved to that which he cannot possibly reach.[19] But it is impossible to pass through the infinite. If, therefore, the inquiry of counsel is infinite, no one would begin to take counsel. Which is clearly untrue.

I answer that, The inquiry of counsel is actually finite on both sides, namely, on that of its principle and on that of its term. For a twofold principle is available in the inquiry of counsel. One is proper to it, and belongs to the very genus of things pertaining to operation; and this is the end, which is not the matter of counsel, but is accepted in counsel as its principle, as was stated above. The other principle is taken from another genus, so to speak, just as in the demonstrative sciences one science postulates certain things from another, without inquiring into them. Now these principles which are accepted in the inquiry of counsel are any facts received through the senses: *e.g.,* that this is bread or iron, and also any principles known in a universal way either through a speculative or through a practical science: *e.g.,* that adultery is forbidden by God, or that man cannot live without suitable nourishment. Of such things counsel makes no inquiry.—But the term of inquiry is that which we are able to do at once. For just as the end has the nature of a principle, so the means have the nature of a conclusion. Therefore, that which presents itself as first to be done holds the position of an ultimate conclusion whereat the inquiry comes to an end.—Nothing however prevents counsel from being without end potentially, according as

[19] Aristotle. *De Caelo*, I, 7 (274b 17).

an infinite number of things may present themselves to be inquired into by means of counsel.

Reply Obj. 1. Singulars are infinite, not actually, but only potentially.

Reply Obj. 2. Although human action can be hindered, the hindrance is not always at hand. Consequently, it is not always necessary to take counsel about removing the obstacle.

Reply Obj. 3. In contingent singulars, something may be taken for certain, not absolutely, indeed, but for the time being, as far as it concerns the work to be done. Thus, that Socrates is sitting is not necessary; but that he is sitting, as long as he continues to sit, is necessary; and this can be known with certainty.

ON CONSENT, WHICH IS AN ACT OF THE WILL IN RELATION TO THE MEANS

(*In Four Articles*)

WE must now consider consent, concerning which there are four points of inquiry: (1) Whether consent is an act of the appetitive or of the apprehensive power? (2) Whether it is to be found in irrational animals? (3) Whether it is directed to the end or to the means? (4) Whether consent to an act belongs only to the higher part of the soul?

First Article

WHETHER CONSENT IS AN ACT OF THE APPETITIVE OR OF THE APPREHENSIVE POWER?

We proceed thus to the First Article:—

Objection 1. It would seem that consent belongs only to the apprehensive part of the soul. For Augustine ascribes consent to the higher reason.[1] But the reason is an apprehensive power. Therefore consent belongs to an apprehensive power.

Obj. 2. Further, consent is *co-sense*. But sense is an apprehensive power. Therefore consent is the act of an apprehensive power.

Obj. 3. Further, just as assent is an application of the intellect to something, so is consent. But assent belongs to the intellect, which is an apprehensive power. Therefore consent also belongs to an apprehensive power.

On the contrary, Damascene says that *if a man judge without affection for that of which he judges, there is no decision,*[2] *i.e.,* consent. But affection belongs to the appetitive power. Therefore consent does also.

I answer that, Consent expresses the application of sense to something. Now it is proper to sense to take cognizance of things present. For the imagination apprehends the likenesses of corporeal things, even in the absence of the things of which they bear the likeness; while the intellect apprehends universal notions, which it can apprehend indifferently, whether the singulars be present or absent. And since the act of an appetitive power is a kind of inclination to the thing itself, the application of the appetitive power to the thing, in so far as it cleaves to it, acquires by a kind of likeness the name of sense, since, as it were, it acquires an experience of the thing to which it cleaves, in so far as it finds satisfaction in it. Hence it is written

[1] *De Trin.,* XII, 12 (PL 42, 1007).   [2] *De Fide Orth.,* II, 22 (PG 94, 945).

(*Wis.* i. 1): *Think of* [*Sentite*] *the Lord in goodness.* And on these grounds consent is an act of the appetitive power.

Reply Obj. 1. As is stated in *De Anima* iii., *the will is in the reason.*[3] Hence, when Augustine ascribes consent to the reason, he takes reason as including the will.

Reply Obj. 2. *To sense,* properly speaking, belongs to the apprehensive power; but by way of likeness, as being a certain experience, it belongs to the appetitive power, as was stated above.

Reply Obj. 3. *Assentire* [*to assent*] is, so to speak, *ad aliud sentire* [*to sense towards something else*]; and thus it implies a certain distance from that to which assent is given. But *consentire* [*to consent*] is *to sense with*, and this implies a certain union to the object of consent. Hence the will, to which it belongs to tend to the thing itself, is more properly said to consent; whereas the intellect, whose act does not consist in a movement towards the thing, but rather the reverse, as we have stated in the First Part,[4] is more properly said to assent, although one term is wont to be used for the other. We may also say that the intellect assents in so far as it is moved by the will.

Second Article

WHETHER CONSENT IS TO BE FOUND IN IRRATIONAL ANIMALS?

We proceed thus to the Second Article:—

Objection 1. It would seem that consent is to be found in irrational animals. For consent expresses a determination of the appetite to one thing. But the appetite of irrational animals is determined to one course of action. Therefore consent is to be found in irrational animals.

Obj. 2. Further, if you remove what is first, you remove what follows. But consent precedes the accomplished act. If, therefore, there were no consent in irrational animals, there would be no act accomplished; which is clearly false.

Obj. 3. Further, men are sometimes said to consent to do something through some passion, *e.g.*, through desire or anger. But irrational animals act through passion. Therefore they have consent.

On the contrary, Damascene says that *after judging, man approves and embraces the judgment of his counselling, and this is called the decision,*[5] *i.e.*, consent. But counsel is not in irrational animals. Therefore neither is consent.

I answer that, Consent, properly speaking, is not in irrational animals. The reason for this is that consent implies an application of the appetitive movement to something that is to be done. Now to apply the appetitive movement to the doing of something belongs to the subject in whose power it is

---

[3] Aristotle, *De An.*, III, 9 (432b 5).   [4] *S.T.*, I, q. 16, a. 1; q. 27, a. 4; q. 59, a. 2.
[5] *De Fide Orth.*, II, 22 (PG 94, 945).

to move the appetite; and thus to touch a stone is an action suitable to a stick, but to apply the stick so that it touch the stone belongs to one who has the power of moving the stick. But irrational animals have not the command of the appetitive movement, for this is in them through natural instinct. Hence in the irrational animal there is indeed the movement of appetite, but it does not apply that movement to some particular thing. And hence it is that the irrational animal is not properly said to consent; this is rather proper to the rational nature, which has the command of the appetitive movement, and is able to apply or not to apply it to this or that thing.

Reply Obj. 1. In irrational animals, the determination of the appetite to a particular thing is merely passive; whereas consent expresses a determination of the appetite, which is active rather than merely passive.

Reply Obj. 2. If the first be removed, then what follows is removed, provided that, properly speaking, it follow from that only. But if something can follow from several things, it is not removed by the fact that one of them is removed; and thus, if hardening is the effect of heat and of cold (since bricks are hardened by fire, and frozen water is hardened by the cold), then by removing heat it does not follow that there is no hardening. Now the accomplishment of an act follows not only from consent, but also from the impulse of the appetite, such as is found in irrational animals.

Reply Obj. 3. The man who acts through passion is able not to follow the passion, whereas irrational animals have not that power. Hence the comparison fails.

Third Article

WHETHER CONSENT IS DIRECTED TO THE END OR TO THE MEANS TO THE END?

We proceed thus to the Third Article:—

Objection 1. It would seem that consent is directed to the end. For that because of which a thing is such is still more such. But it is because of the end that we consent to the means. Therefore, still more do we consent to the end.

Obj. 2. Further, the act of the intemperate man is his end, just as the act of the virtuous man is his end. But the intemperate man consents to his own act. Therefore consent can be directed to the end.

Obj. 3. Further, the desire of the means is choice, as was stated above.[6] If, therefore, consent were directed only to the means, it would in no way differ from choice. And this is proved to be false by the authority of Damascene who says that *after the approval*, which he calls *the decision, comes the choice*.[7] Therefore consent is not directed only to the means.

On the contrary, Damascene says that the *decision, i.e.,* the consent, takes

---

[6] Q. 13, a. 1.   [7] *De Fide Orth.,* II, 22 (PG 94, 945).

place *when man approves and embraces the judgment of his counsel.*[8] But counsel is only about the means. Therefore the same applies to consent.

I answer that, Consent is the application of the appetitive movement to something that is already in the power of him who causes the application. Now the order of action is this. First, there is the apprehension of the end; then, the desire of the end; then, the counsel about the means; then, the desire of the means. Now the appetite tends to the last end naturally, and hence the application of the appetitive movement to the apprehended end has not the nature of consent, but of simple volition. But as to those things which come under consideration after the last end, in so far as they are directed to the end, they come under counsel; and so consent can be applied to them, in so far as the appetitive movement is applied to what has been judged through counsel. But the appetitive movement to the end is not applied to counsel; it is rather counsel that is applied to it, because counsel presupposes the appetite of the end. On the other hand, the appetite of the means presupposes the decision of counsel. Hence, the application of the appetitive movement to the resolution of counsel is consent, properly speaking. Consequently, since counsel is only about the means, consent, properly speaking, is of nothing else but the means.

Reply Obj. 1. Just as the knowledge of conclusions through the principles is science, whereas the knowledge of the principles is not science, but something higher, namely, understanding, so our consent to the means is because of the end, in respect of which our act is not consent but something greater, namely, volition.

Reply Obj. 2. Delight in his act, rather than the act itself, is the end of the intemperate man, and for sake of this delight he consents to that act.

Reply Obj. 3. Choice includes something that consent has not, namely, a certain relation to something to which something else is preferred; and therefore after consent there still remains a choice. For it may happen that by aid of counsel several means have been found conducive to the end, and since each of these meets with approval, consent has been given to each; but after approving of many, we have given our preference to one by choosing it. But if only one meets with approval, then consent and choice do not differ in reality, but only in our way of looking at them; so that we call it consent, according as we approve of doing that thing, but choice, according as we prefer it to those that do not meet with our approval.

Fourth Article

WHETHER CONSENT TO THE ACT BELONGS ONLY TO THE HIGHER PART OF THE SOUL?

We proceed thus to the Fourth Article:—

Objection 1. It would seem that consent to the act does not always belong to the higher reason. For *delight follows action, and perfects it, just as*

[8] *Ibid.*

beauty perfects youth.[9] But consent to delight belongs to the lower reason, as Augustine says.[10] Therefore consent to the act does not belong only to the higher reason.

Obj. 2. Further, an act to which we consent is said to be voluntary. But it belongs to many powers to produce voluntary acts. Therefore the higher reason is not alone in consenting to the act.

Obj. 3. Further, *the higher reason is that which is intent on the contemplation and consultation of things eternal,* as Augustine says.[11] But man often consents to an act, not for eternal, but for temporal reasons, or even because of some passion of the soul. Therefore consent to an act does not belong to the higher reason alone.

On the contrary, Augustine says: *It is impossible for man to make up his mind to commit a sin, unless that intention of the mind which has the sovereign power of urging his members to, or restraining them from, act, yield to the evil deed and become its slave.*[12]

I answer that, The final decision belongs to him who holds the highest place, and to whom it belongs to judge of the others; for as long as judgment about some matter remains to be pronounced, the final decision has not been given. Now it is evident that it belongs to the higher reason to judge of all; for it is by the reason that we judge of sensible things, and of things pertaining to human principles we judge according to divine principles, which is the function of the higher reason. Therefore, as long as a man is uncertain whether he should resist or not, according to divine principles, no judgment of the reason can be considered as a final decision. Now the final decision of what is to be done is the consent to the act. Therefore, consent to the act belongs to the higher reason, but in the sense in which the reason includes the will, as we have stated above.

Reply Obj. 1. Consent to delight in the work done belongs to the higher reason, as also does consent to the work; but consent to delight in thought belongs to the lower reason, just as to the lower reason it belongs to think. Nevertheless, the higher reason exercises judgment on the fact of thinking or not thinking, considered as an action; and in like manner on the consequent delight. But in so far as the act of thinking is considered as ordered to a further act, it belongs to the lower reason. For that which is ordered to something else belongs to a lower art or power than does the end to which it is ordered; and hence it is that the art which is concerned with the end is called the architectonic or principal art.

Reply Obj. 2. Since actions are called voluntary from the fact that we consent to them, it does not follow that consent is an act of every power, but of the will, which is in the reason, as was stated above, and from which the voluntary act is named.

Reply Obj. 3. The higher reason is said to consent not only because it always moves to act according to the eternal exemplars, but also because it does not dissent according to these same exemplars.

---

[9] Aristotle, *Eth.,* X, 4 (1174b 31; 1175a 5).   [10] *De Trin.,* XII, 12 (PL 42, 1007).
[11] *Op. cit.,* XII, 7 (PL 42, 1005).   [12] *Op. cit.,* XII, 12 (PL 42, 1008).

ON USE, WHICH IS AN ACT OF THE WILL IN RELATION TO THE MEANS TO THE END

(In Four Articles)

WE must now consider use, concerning which there are four points of inquiry: (1) Whether use is an act of the will? (2) Whether it is to be found in irrational animals? (3) Whether it concerns only the means, or also the end? (4) The relation of use to choice.

First Article

WHETHER USE IS AN ACT OF THE WILL?

We proceed thus to the First Article:—

Objection 1. It would seem that use is not an act of the will. For Augustine says that *to use is to refer that which is the object of use to the obtaining of something else.*[1] But *to refer* something to another is an act of the reason, to which it belongs to compare and to direct. Therefore use is an act of the reason and not of the will.

Obj. 2. Further, Damascene says that man *goes forward to operation, and this is called impulse; then he makes use [of the powers], and this is called use.*[2] But operation belongs to the executive power, and the act of the will does not follow the act of the executive power, but on the contrary execution comes last. Therefore use is not an act of the will.

Obj. 3. Further, Augustine says: *All things that were made were made for man's use, because the reason, with which man is endowed, uses all things by its judgment of them.*[3] But judgment of things created by God belongs to the speculative reason, which seems to be altogether distinct from the will, which is the principle of human acts. Therefore use is not an act of the will.

On the contrary, Augustine says: *To use is to apply something to the purpose of the will.*[4]

I answer that, The use of a thing signifies the application of that thing to an operation; and hence the operation to which we apply a thing is called its use: *e.g.*, the use of a horse is to ride, and the use of a stick is to strike. Now we apply to an operation not only the interior principles of action, viz., the powers of the soul or the members of the body (*e.g.*, the

---

[1] *De Doct. Christ.,* I, 4 (PL 34, 20).   [2] *De Fide Orth.,* II, 22 (PG 94, 945).
[3] *Lib. 83 Quaest.,* q. 30 (PL 40, 20).   [4] *De Trin.,* X, 11 (PL 42, 982).

intellect, to understand, and the eye, to see), but also external things, as a stick, to strike. But it is evident that we do not apply external things to an operation save through the intrinsic principles which are either the powers of the soul, or the habits of those powers, or the organs which are parts of the body. Now it has been shown above that it is the will which moves the soul's powers to their acts; and this is to apply them to operation.[5] Hence it is evident that, first and principally, use belongs to the will as first mover; to the reason, as directing; and to the other powers as executing the operation, which powers are compared to the will, which applies them to act, as the instruments are compared to the principal agent. Now action is properly ascribed, not to the instrument, but to the principal agent, as building is ascribed to the builder, but not to his tools. Hence it is evident that use is, properly speaking, an act of the will.

Reply Obj. 1. Reason does indeed refer one thing to another; but the will tends to that which is referred by the reason to something else. And in this sense to use is to refer one thing to another.

Reply Obj. 2. Damascene is speaking of use in so far as it belongs to the executive powers.

Reply Obj. 3. Even the speculative reason is applied by the will to the act of understanding or judging. Consequently, the speculative reason is said to use, in so far as it is moved by the will, in the same way as the other powers.

Second Article

WHETHER USE IS TO BE FOUND IN IRRATIONAL ANIMALS?

We proceed thus to the Second Article:—

Objection 1. It would seem that use is to be found in irrational animals. For it is better to enjoy than to use, because, as Augustine says, *we use things by referring them to something else which we are to enjoy.*[6] But enjoyment is to be found in irrational animals, as was stated above.[7] Much more, therefore, is it possible for them to have use.

Obj. 2. Further, to apply the members to action is to use them. But irrational animals apply their members to action: *e.g.,* their feet, to walk; their horns, to strike. Therefore, it is possible for irrational animals to use.

On the contrary, Augustine says: *None but a rational animal can make use of a thing.*[8]

I answer that, As we have stated above, to use is to apply an active principle to action; and thus to consent is to apply the appetitive movement to the desire of something, as was stated above.[9] Now he alone who has the disposal of a thing can apply it to something else; and this belongs to him

---

[5] Q. 9, a. 1.   [6] *De Trin.,* X, 10 (PL 42, 981).   [7] Q. 11, a. 2.   [8] *Lib. 83 Quaest.,* q. 30 (PL 40, 19).   [9] Q. 15, a. 1, 2 and 3.

alone who knows how to refer it to something else, which is an act of the reason. And therefore none but a rational animal consents and uses.

Reply Obj. 1. *To enjoy* signifies the absolute movement of the appetite to the appetible, whereas *to use* signifies a movement of the appetite to something as directed to something else. If, therefore, we compare use and enjoyment in relation to their objects, enjoyment is better than use, because that which is appetible absolutely is better than that which is appetible only as directed to something else. But if we compare them in relation to the apprehensive power that precedes them, greater excellence is required on the part of use; for to direct one thing to another is an act of reason, whereas to apprehend something absolutely is within the competence even of sense.

Reply Obj. 2. Animals by means of their members do something from natural instinct, not through knowing the relation of their members to these operations. Therefore, properly speaking, they do not apply their members to action, nor do they use them.

Third Article

WHETHER USE CAN APPLY ALSO TO THE LAST END?

We proceed thus to the Third Article:—

Objection 1. It would seem that use can apply also to the last end. For Augustine says: *Whoever enjoys, uses.*[10] But man enjoys the last end. Therefore he uses the last end.

Obj. 2. Further, *to use is to apply something to the purpose of the will.*[11] But the last end, more than anything else, is the object of the will's application. Therefore it can be the object of use.

Obj. 3. Further, Hilary says that *Eternity is in the Father, Likeness in the Image, i.e.,* in the Son, *Use in the Gift, i.e.,* in the Holy Ghost.[12] But the Holy Ghost, since He is God, is the last end. Therefore the last end can be the object of use.

On the contrary, Augustine says: *No one rightly uses God.*[13] But God alone is the last end. Therefore we cannot use the last end.

I answer that, Use, as was stated above, signifies the application of one thing to another. Now that which is applied to another is regarded in the light of a means to an end; and consequently use always applies to the means. For this reason, things that are adapted to a certain end are said to be *useful*; in fact, their very usefulness is sometimes called use.

It must, however, be observed that the last end may be taken in two ways: first, absolutely; secondly, in relation to an individual. For since the end, as was stated above,[14] signifies sometimes the thing itself, and sometimes the attainment or possession of that thing (thus the miser's end is either money or the possession of it), it is evident that, absolutely speaking,

---

[10] *De Trin.*, X, 11 (PL 42, 982).   [11] *Ibid.*   [12] *De Trin.*, II (PL 10, 51).
[13] *Lib. 83 Quaest.*, q. 30 (PL 40, 20).   [14] Q. 1, a. 8; q. 2, a. 7.

the last end is the thing itself; for the possession of money is good only inasmuch as there is some good in money. But in relation to the individual, the obtaining of money is the last end; for the miser would not seek for money, save that he might have it. Therefore, absolutely and properly speaking, a man enjoys money because he places his last end therein; but in so far as he seeks to possess it, he is said to use it.

Reply Obj. 1. Augustine is speaking of use in general, in so far as it implies the relation of an end to the enjoyment which a man seeks in that end.

Reply Obj. 2. The end is applied to the purpose of the will, that the will may find rest in it. Consequently, this rest in the end, which is the enjoyment thereof, is in this sense called the use of the end. But the means are applied to the will's purpose, not only in being used as means, but as being ordered to something else in which the will finds rest.

Reply Obj. 3. The words of Hilary refer to use as applicable to rest in the last end; just as, speaking in a general sense, one may be said to use the end for the purpose of attaining it, as was stated above. Hence Augustine says that *this love, delight, felicity, or happiness is called use by him.*[15]

Fourth Article

WHETHER USE PRECEDES CHOICE?

We proceed thus to the Fourth Article:—

Objection 1. It would seem that use precedes choice. For nothing follows after choice, except execution. But use, since it belongs to the will, precedes execution. Therefore it precedes choice also.

Obj. 2. Further, the absolute precedes the relative. Therefore, the less relative precedes the more relative. But choice implies two relations: one, of the thing chosen, in relation to the end; the other, of the thing chosen, in relation to that to which it is preferred; whereas use implies relation to the end only. Therefore, use precedes choice.

Obj. 3. Further, the will uses the other powers in so far as it moves them. But the will moves itself too, as was stated above.[16] Therefore it uses itself, by applying itself to act. But it does this when it consents. Therefore, there is use in consent. But consent precedes choice, as was stated above.[17] Therefore use does also.

On the contrary, Damascene says that *the will, after choosing, has an impulse to the operation, and afterwards it uses [the powers].*[18] Therefore use follows choice.

I answer that, The will has a twofold relation to the thing willed. One, according as the thing willed is, in a way, in the willing subject, by a kind of proportion or order to the thing willed. Therefore, those things that are naturally proportioned to a certain end are said to desire that end

---

[15] *De Trin.,* VI, 10 (PL 42, 932).   [16] Q. 9, a. 3.   [17] Q. 15, a. 3, ad 3.   [18] *De Fide Orth.,* II, 22 (PG 94, 945).

naturally. Yet to have an end thus is to have it imperfectly. Now every imperfect thing tends to perfection. Therefore, both the natural and the voluntary appetite tend to possess the end in reality; and this is to possess it perfectly. This is the second relation of the will to the thing willed.

Now the thing willed is not only the end, but also the means. And the last act that belongs to the first relation of the will to the means is choice; for there the will becomes fully proportioned by willing the means fully. Use, on the other hand, belongs to the second relation of the will, in respect of which it tends to the realization of the thing willed. Therefore it is evident that use follows choice; provided, of course, that by use we mean the will's use of the executive power in moving it. But since the will, in a way, moves the reason also, and uses it, we may take the use of the means as consisting in the consideration of the reason, whereby it refers the means to the end. In this sense use precedes choice.

Reply Obj. 1. The motion of the will to the execution of the work precedes execution, but follows choice. And so, since use belongs to that very motion of the will, it stands between choice and execution.

Reply Obj. 2. What is essentially relative is subsequent to what is absolute; but the thing to which relation is referred need not be subsequent. Indeed, the more a cause precedes, the more numerous the effects to which it has relation.

Reply Obj. 3. Choice precedes use, if they be referred to the same object. But nothing prevents the use of one thing from preceding the choice of another. And since the acts of the will reflect on themselves, in each act of the will we can find consent and choice and use; so that we may say that the will consents to choose, and consents to consent, and uses itself in consenting and choosing. And such acts as are ordained to that which precedes, precede also.

ON THE ACTS COMMANDED BY THE WILL

(*In Nine Articles*)

WE must now consider the acts commanded by the will, under which head there are nine points of inquiry: (1) Whether command is an act of the will or of the reason? (2) Whether command belongs to irrational animals? (3) Of the order between command and use. (4) Whether command and the commanded act are one act or distinct? (5) Whether the act of the will is commanded? (6) Whether the act of the reason is commanded? (7) Whether the act of the sensitive appetite is commanded? (8) Whether the act of the vegetative soul is commanded? (9) Whether the acts of the external members are commanded?

First Article

WHETHER COMMAND IS AN ACT OF THE REASON OR OF THE WILL?

We proceed thus to the First Article:—

Objection 1. It would seem that command is not an act of the reason but of the will. For command is a kind of motion, because Avicenna says that there are four ways of moving, *by perfecting, by disposing, by commanding and by counselling*.[1] But it belongs to the will to move all the other powers of the soul, as was stated above.[2] Therefore command is an act of the will.

Obj. 2. Further, just as to be commanded belongs to that which is subject, so to command seems to belong to that which is most free. But the root of liberty is especially in the will. Therefore to command belongs to the will.

Obj. 3. Further, command is followed at once by act. But the act of the reason is not followed at once by act, for he who judges that a thing should be done does not do it at once. Therefore command is not an act of the reason, but of the will.

On the contrary, Gregory of Nyssa[3] and the Philosopher[4] say that *the appetite obeys reason*. Therefore command is an act of the reason.

I answer that, Command is an act of the reason, presupposing, however, an act of the will. In proof of this, we must take note that, since the acts of

---

[1] *Suffic.*, I, 10 (19ra).   [2] Q. 9, a. 1.   [3] Cf. Nemesius, *De Nat. Hom.*, XVI (PG 40, 672).   [4] *Eth.*, I, 13 (1102b 26).

the reason and of the will can be brought to bear on one another, in so far as the reason reasons about willing, and the will wills to reason, it follows that the act of the reason precedes the act of the will, and conversely. And since the power of the preceding act continues in the act that follows, it happens sometimes that there is an act of the will in so far as it retains in itself something of the act of the reason, as we have stated in reference to use[5] and choice;[6] and conversely, that there is an act of the reason in so far as it retains in itself something of the act of the will.

Now, command is essentially indeed an act of the reason, for the commander orders the one commanded to do something, by way of intimation or declaration. Now to order thus by intimating or declaring is an act of the reason. But the reason can intimate or declare something in two ways. First, absolutely, and this intimation is expressed by a verb in the indicative mood, as when one person says to another: *This is what you should do.* Sometimes, however, the reason intimates something to a man by moving him thereto; and this intimation is expressed by a verb in the imperative mood; as when it is said to someone: *Do this.* Now the first mover, among the powers of the soul, to the doing of an act is the will, as was stated above.[7] Since, therefore, the second mover does not move save in the power of the first mover, it follows that the very fact that the reason moves by commanding, is due to the power of the will. Consequently, it follows that command is an act of the reason, presupposing an act of the will, in virtue of which the reason, by its command, moves to the execution of the act.

Reply Obj. 1. To command is to move, not anyhow, but by intimating and declaring to another; and this is an act of the reason.

Reply Obj. 2. The root of liberty is the will as the subject thereof; but it is the reason as its cause. For the will can tend freely towards various objects precisely because the reason can have various notions of good. Hence philosophers define free choice as being *a free judgment arising from reason,*[8] implying that reason is the cause of liberty.

Reply Obj. 3. This argument proves that command is an act of reason, not absolutely, but with a kind of motion, as was stated above.

Second Article

WHETHER COMMAND BELONGS TO IRRATIONAL ANIMALS?

We proceed thus to the Second Article:—

Objection 1. It would seem that command belongs to irrational animals. For, according to Avicenna, *the power that commands movement is the appetite; and the power that executes movement is in the muscles and nerves.*[9] But both powers are in irrational animals. Therefore command is to be found in irrational animals.

---

[5] Q. 16, a. 1.   [6] Q. 13, a. 1.   [7] Q. 9, a. 1; *S. T.,* I, q. 82, a. 4.   [8] Boethius, *Maior Comm. in De Interpret. Arist.,* III, Prol. (PL 64, 492).   [9] *De An.,* I, 5 (4vb).

Obj. 2. Further, the condition of a slave is that of one who receives commands. But the body is compared to the soul as a slave to his master, as the Philosopher says.[10] Therefore the body is commanded by the soul, even in irrational animals, since they are composed of soul and body.

Obj. 3. Further, by commanding, man has an impulse towards an action. But impulse to action is to be found in irrational animals, as Damascene says.[11] Therefore command is to be found in irrational animals.

On the contrary, Command is an act of reason, as was stated above. But in irrational animals there is no reason. Neither, therefore, is there command.

I answer that, To command is nothing else than to direct someone to do something, by a certain motion of intimation. Now to direct is the proper act of the reason. Therefore it is impossible that irrational animals should command in any way, since they are devoid of reason.

Reply Obj. 1. The appetitive power is said to command movement in so far as it moves the commanding reason. But this is only in man. But in irrational animals the appetitive power is not, properly speaking, a commanding power, unless command be taken loosely for motion.

Reply Obj. 2. The body of the irrational animal is competent to obey, but its soul is not competent to command, because it is not competent to direct. Consequently, there is not in the animal the nature of commander and commanded, but only of mover and moved.

Reply Obj. 3. Impulse to action is in irrational animals otherwise than in man. For the impulse of man to action arises from the directing reason, and so his impulse has the nature of command. On the other hand, the impulse of the irrational animal arises from natural instinct, because, as soon as they apprehend the fitting or the unfitting, their appetite is moved naturally to pursue or to avoid. Therefore, they are directed by another to act, and they themselves do not direct themselves to act. Consequently, there is impulse in them but not command.

Third Article

WHETHER USE PRECEDES COMMAND?

We proceed thus to the Third Article:—

Objection 1. It would seem that use precedes command. For command is an act of the reason presupposing an act of the will, as was stated above. But, as we have already shown,[12] use is an act of the will. Therefore use precedes command.

Obj. 2. Further, command is one of the things that are directed to the end. But use is of those things that are directed to the end. Therefore it seems that use precedes command.

---

[10] *Polit.*, I, 2 (1254b 4).   [11] *De Fide Orth.*, II, 22 (PG 94, 945).   [12] Q. 16, a. 1.

Obj. 3. Further, every act of a power moved by the will is called use, be-cause the will uses the other powers, as was stated above.[13] But command is an act of the reason as moved by the will, as was stated above. Therefore command is a kind of use. Now the common precedes the proper. Therefore use precedes command.

On the contrary, Damascene says that impulse to action precedes use.[14] But impulse to operation is given by command. Therefore command precedes use.

I answer that, Use of that which is directed to the end, in so far as it is in the reason referring this to the end, precedes choice, as was stated above.[15] Therefore still more does it precede command. On the other hand, the use of that which is directed to the end, in so far as it is subject to the executive power, follows command; because use in the user is united to the act of the thing used, for one does not use a stick before doing something with the stick. But command is not simultaneous with the act of the thing to which the command is given; for it naturally precedes its fulfillment, some-times, indeed, by priority of time. Consequently, it is evident that command precedes use.

Reply Obj. 1. Not every act of the will precedes the act of the reason which is command; but an act of the will precedes, viz., choice, and an act of the will follows, viz., use. For after the decision of counsel, which is reason's judgment, the will chooses; and after choice, the reason commands that power which has to do what was chosen; and then, last of all, some-one's will begins the act of use, by executing the command of reason (some-times it is another's will, when one commands another; sometimes it is the will of the one that commands, when he commands himself to do some-thing).

Reply Obj. 2. Just as act ranks before power, so the object ranks before the act. Now the object of use is that which is directed to the end. Conse-quently, from the fact that command is directed to the end one should con-clude that command precedes, rather than that it follows, use.

Reply Obj. 3. Just as the act of the will, in using the reason for the pur-pose of command, precedes the command, so also we may say that this act, whereby the will uses the reason, is preceded by a command of reason; for the acts of these powers react on one another.

Fourth Article

WHETHER COMMAND AND THE COMMANDED ACT ARE ONE ACT, OR DISTINCT?

We proceed thus to the Fourth Article:—

Objection 1. It would seem that the commanded act is not one with the

---

[13] *Ibid.*   [14] *De Fide Orth.,* II, 22 (PG 94, 945).—Cf. St. Albert, *Summa de Creatur.,* II, q. 69, a. 2 (XXXV, 567).   [15] Q. 16, a. 4.

command itself. For the acts of different powers are themselves distinct. But the commanded act belongs to one power, and the command to another, since one is the power that commands, and the other is the power that receives the command. Therefore the commanded act is not one with the command.

Obj. 2. Further, whatever things can be separate from one another, are distinct; for nothing is severed from itself. But sometimes the commanded act is separate from the command, for sometimes the command is given, and the commanded act follows not. Therefore command is a distinct act from the commanded act.

Obj. 3. Further, whatever things are related to one another as precedent and consequent are distinct. But command naturally precedes the commanded act. Therefore they are distinct.

On the contrary, The Philosopher says that *where one thing is by reason of another, there is but one.*[16] But there is no commanded act unless by reason of the command. Therefore they are one.

I answer that, Nothing prevents certain things from being many in one respect, and one in another respect. Indeed, every multitude is one in some respect, as Dionysius says.[17] But a difference is to be observed in this, that some are many absolutely, and one in a particular respect, while with others it is the reverse. Now *one* is predicated in the same way as *being.* Substance is being absolutely, whereas an accident, or even logical being, is a being only in a certain respect. Therefore, those things that are one in substance are one absolutely, though many in a certain respect. Thus, in the genus substance, the whole composed of its integral or essential parts is one absolutely; for the whole is being and substance absolutely, but the parts are beings and substances in the whole. But those things which are distinct in substance, and one according to an accident, are distinct absolutely, and one in a certain respect. Thus, many men are one people, and many stones are one heap; which is unity of composition or order. In like manner, also, many individuals that are one in genus or species are many absolutely, and one in a certain respect; for to be one in genus or species is to be one according to the consideration of the reason.

Now just as in the genus of natural things a whole is composed of matter and form (*e.g.*, man, who is one natural being, though he has many parts, is composed of soul and body), so in human acts, the act of a lower power is as matter in relation to the act of a higher power, in so far as the lower power acts in virtue of the higher power moving it; for thus also the act of the first mover is as the form in relation to the act of its instrument. Hence it is evident that command and the commanded act are one human act, just as a whole is one, yet, in its parts, many.

Reply Obj. 1. If the different powers are not ordered to one another, their acts are absolutely diverse. But when one power is the mover of the

---

[16] *Top.,* III, 2 (117a 18).　　[17] *De Div. Nom.,* XIII, 2 (PG 3, 977).

other, then their acts are, in a way, one; for *the act of the mover and the act of the thing moved are one act.*[18]

Reply Obj. 2. The fact that command and the commanded act can be separated from one another shows that they are many in their parts. For the parts of a man can be separated from one another, and yet they form one whole.

Reply Obj. 3. In those things that are many in their parts, but one as a whole, nothing hinders one part from preceding another. Thus the soul, in a way, precedes the body; and the heart, the other members.

Fifth Article

WHETHER THE ACT OF THE WILL IS COMMANDED?

We proceed thus to the Fifth Article:—

Objection 1. It would seem that the act of the will is not commanded. For Augustine says: *The mind commands the mind to will, and yet it does not.*[19] But to will is the act of the will. Therefore the act of the will is not commanded.

Obj. 2. Further, to receive a command belongs to one who can understand the command. But the will cannot understand the command, for the will differs from the intellect, to which it belongs to understand. Therefore the act of the will is not commanded.

Obj. 3. Further, if one act of the will is commanded, for the same reason all are commanded. But if all the acts of the will are commanded, we must needs proceed to infinity, because the act of the will precedes the act of reason commanding, as was stated above; for if that act of the will be also commanded, this command will be preceded by another act of the reason, and so on to infinity. But to proceed to infinity is not possible. Therefore the act of the will is not commanded.

On the contrary, Whatever is in our power is subject to our command. But the acts of the will, most of all, are in our power, since all our acts are said to be in our power in so far as they are voluntary. Therefore the acts of the will are commanded by us.

I answer that, As was stated above, command is nothing else than the act of the reason directing, with a certain motion, something to act. Now it is evident that the reason can direct the act of the will; for just as it can judge it to be good to will something, so it can direct by commanding man to will. From this it is evident that an act of the will can be commanded.

Reply Obj. 1. As Augustine says, when the mind commands itself perfectly to will, then already it wills; but that sometimes it commands and wills not is due to the fact that it commands imperfectly. Now imperfect command arises from the fact that the reason is moved by opposite motives

---

[18] Aristotle, *Phys.*, III, 3 (202a 18; b 20).   [19] *Confess.*, VIII, 9 (PL 32, 758).

to command or not to command; with the result that it fluctuates between the two, and fails to command perfectly.

Reply Obj. 2. Just as each of the members of the body works, not for itself alone, but for the whole body (thus, it is for the whole body that the eye sees), so is it with the powers of the soul. For the intellect understands, not for itself alone, but for all the powers, and the will wills not only for itself, but for all the powers too. Therefore man, in so far as he is endowed with intellect and will, commands the act of the will for himself.

Reply Obj. 3. Since command is an act of the reason, that act is commanded which is subject to reason. Now the first act of the will is not due to the direction of the reason but to the instigation of nature, or of a higher cause, as we have stated above.[20] Therefore there is no need to proceed to infinity.

Sixth Article

WHETHER THE ACT OF THE REASON IS COMMANDED?

We proceed thus to the Sixth Article:—

Objection 1. It would seem that the act of the reason cannot be commanded. For it seems unfitting for a thing to command itself. But it is the reason that commands, as was stated above. Therefore the act of the reason is not commanded.

Obj. 2. That which is what it is essentially is distinct from that which is what it is by participation. But the power whose act is commanded by reason is rational by participation, as is stated in *Ethics* i.[21] Therefore the act of that power which is essentially rational is not commanded.

Obj. 3. Further, that act is commanded which is in our power. But to know and judge the truth, which is an act of reason, is not always in our power. Therefore the act of the reason cannot be commanded.

On the contrary, That which we do with free choice can be done by our command. But the acts of the reason are accomplished through free choice, for Damascene says that *by his free choice man inquires, considers, judges, approves.*[22] Therefore the acts of the reason can be commanded.

I answer that, Since the reason acts reflexively on itself, hence, just as it directs the acts of other powers, so it can direct its own act. Consequently, its act can be commanded.

But we must take note that the act of the reason may be considered in two ways. First, as to the exercise of the act. And considered thus, the act of the reason can always be commanded, as when one is told to be attentive, and to use one's reason. Secondly, as to the object, in respect of which two acts of the reason have to be noticed. One is the act whereby it apprehends the truth about something. This act is not in our power, because it hap-

---

[20] Q. 9, a. 4.   [21] Aristotle, *Eth.*, I, 13 (1102b 13; b 26).   [22] *De Fide Orth.*, II, 22 (PG 94, 945).

pens in virtue of a light, whether natural or supernatural. Consequently, in this respect, the act of the reason is not in our power, and cannot be commanded. The other act of the reason is that by which it assents to what it apprehends. If, therefore, that which the reason apprehends is such that it naturally assents thereto, *e.g.*, first principles, it is not in our power to assent to it or to dissent. For in such cases, assent follows naturally, and consequently, properly speaking, is not subject to our command. But some things which are apprehended do not convince the intellect to such an extent as not to leave it free to assent or dissent, or at least suspend its assent or dissent because of some cause or other; and in such things, assent or dissent is in our power, and is subject to our command.

Reply Obj. 1. Reason commands itself, just as the will moves itself, as was stated above,[23] that is to say, in so far as both powers act reflexively on their own act, and from one thing tend to another.

Reply Obj. 2. Because of the diversity of the objects subject to the act of the reason, nothing prevents the reason from participating in itself; and thus the knowledge of principles is participated in the knowledge of the conclusions.

The reply to the third objection is evident from what has been said.

Seventh Article

WHETHER THE ACT OF THE SENSITIVE APPETITE IS COMMANDED?

We proceed thus to the Seventh Article:—

Objection 1. It would seem that the act of the sensitive appetite is not commanded. For the Apostle says (*Rom.* vii. 15): *For I do not that good which I will;* and the *Gloss* explains this by saying that man lusts, although he wills not to lust.[24] But to lust is an act of the sensitive appetite. Therefore the act of the sensitive appetite is not subject to our command.

Obj. 2. Further, corporeal matter obeys God alone, so far as a change in form is concerned, as was shown in the First Part.[25] But the act of the sensitive appetite is accompanied by a formal change in the body, consisting in heat or cold. Therefore the act of the sensitive appetite is not subject to man's command.

Obj. 3. Further, the proper motive principle of the sensitive appetite is something apprehended by sense or imagination. But it is not always in our power to apprehend something by sense or imagination. Therefore the act of the sensitive appetite is not subject to our command.

On the contrary, Gregory of Nyssa says: *That which obeys reason is twofold, the concupiscible and the irascible,*[26] which belong to the sensitive

---

[23] Q. 9, a. 3.   [24] *Glossa ordin.*, super *Rom.*, VII, 15 (VI, 17B).—St. Augustine, *Contra Iulian.*, III, 26 (PL 44, 734).   [25] *S. T.*, I, q. 65, a. 4; q. 91, a. 2; q. 110, a. 2.
[26] Cf. Nemesius, *De Nat. Hom.*, XVI (PG 40, 672).

appetite. Therefore the act of the sensitive appetite is subject to the command of reason.

I answer that, An act is subject to our command in so far as it is in our power, as we have stated above. Consequently, in order to understand in what manner the act of the sensitive appetite is subject to the command of reason, we must consider in what manner it is in our power. Now it must be observed that the sensitive appetite differs from the intellectual appetite, which is called the will, in the fact that the sensitive appetite is a power of a corporeal organ, whereas the will is not. But every act of a power that uses a corporeal organ depends not only on a power of the soul, but also on the disposition of that corporeal organ. Thus, the act of vision depends on the power of sight, and on the condition of the eye, which condition is a help or a hindrance to that act. Consequently, the act of the sensitive appetite likewise depends not only on the appetitive power, but also on the disposition of the body.

Now in so far as an act proceeds from a power of the soul, it follows apprehension. Furthermore, the apprehension of the imagination, being a particular apprehension, is regulated by the apprehension of reason, which is universal; just as a particular active power is regulated by a universal active power. Consequently, in this respect, the act of the sensitive appetite is subject to the command of reason.—On the other hand, the condition and disposition of the body is not subject to the command of reason, and consequently, in this respect, the movement of the sensitive appetite is hindered from being wholly subject to the command of reason.

Moreover, it happens sometimes that the movement of the sensitive appetite is aroused suddenly in consequence of an apprehension of the imagination or sense. And then such a movement occurs without the command of reason, although reason could have prevented it, had it foreseen it. Hence the Philosopher says that the reason governs the irascible and concupiscible, not by a *despotic rule,* which is that of a master over his slave, but by a *political and royal rule,*[27] whereby the free are governed, who are not wholly subject to command.

Reply Obj. 1. That a man lusts, although he wills not to lust, is due to a disposition of the body, whereby the sensitive appetite is hindered from perfect compliance with the command of reason. Hence the Apostle adds: *I see another law in my members, fighting against the law of my mind* (*Rom.* vii. 23).—This may also happen through a sudden movement of concupiscence, as was stated above.

Reply Obj. 2. The condition of the body stands in a twofold relation to the act of the sensitive appetite. First, as preceding it, according as a man may be disposed in one way or another, in his body, to this or that passion. Secondly, as consequent to it, according as a man becomes heated through anger. Now the condition that precedes is not subject to the command of

[27] *Polit.,* I, 2 (1254b 5).

reason, since it is due either to nature or to some previous movement which cannot cease at once. But the condition that is consequent follows the command of reason, since it results from the local movement of the heart, which has various movements according to the various acts of the sensitive appetite.

Reply Obj. 3. Since the external sensible thing is necessary for the apprehension of the senses, it is not in our power to apprehend anything by the senses, unless the sensible be present; and this presence of the sensible is not always in our power. For it is then that man can use his senses if he will so to do, unless there be some obstacle on the part of the organ.—On the other hand, the apprehension of the imagination is subject to the ordering of reason, in proportion to the strength or weakness of the imaginative power. For that a man is unable to imagine the things that reason considers is either because they cannot be imagined, such as incorporeal things, or because of the weakness of the imaginative power, produced by some organic indisposition.

Eighth Article

WHETHER THE ACT OF THE VEGETATIVE SOUL IS COMMANDED?

We proceed thus to the Eighth Article:—

Objection 1. It would seem that the acts of the vegetative soul are subject to the command of reason. For the sensitive powers are of higher rank than the vegetative powers. But the powers of the sensitive soul are subject to the command of reason. Much more, therefore, are the powers of the vegetative soul.

Obj. 2. Further, man is called a *microcosm*,[28] because the soul is in the body as God is in the world.[29] But God is in the world in such a way that everything in the world obeys His command. Therefore all that is in man, even the powers of the vegetative soul, obey the command of reason.

Obj. 3. Further, praise and blame are awarded only to such acts as are subject to the command of reason. But in the acts of the nutritive and generative power, there is room for praise and blame, and virtue and vice: *e.g.*, in the case of gluttony and lust, and their contrary virtues. Therefore the acts of these powers are subject to the command of reason.

On the contrary, Gregory of Nyssa says that *the nutritive and generative powers are that over which the reason has no control.*[30]

I answer that, Some acts proceed from the natural appetite, others from the animal, or from the intellectual appetite; for every agent desires the

---

[28] Aristotle, *Phys.*, VIII, 2 (252b 26).   [29] For this interpretation, cf. St. Albert, *Summa de Creatur.*, II, q. 3, a. 1 (XXXV, 28); St. Bonaventure, *In III Sent.*, d. ii. a. 1, q. 2 (III, 40). For a source, cf. Alcher of Clairvaux, *De Spir. et An.*, XXXV (PL 40, 805).—Cp. St. Thomas Aquinas, *S.T.*, I-II, q. 110, a. 1, ad. 2.   [30] Cf. Nemesius, *De Nat. Hom.*, XXII (PG 40, 692).

end in some way. Now the natural appetite does not follow from some apprehension, as do the animal and the intellectual appetite. But the reason commands as an apprehensive power. Therefore, those acts that proceed from the intellectual or the animal appetite can be commanded by the reason; but not those acts that proceed from the natural appetite. And such are the acts of the vegetative soul; and so Gregory of Nyssa says that *generation and nutrition belong to what are called natural powers.*[31] Consequently, the acts of the vegetative soul are not subject to the command of reason.

Reply Obj. 1. The more immaterial an act is, the more noble it is, and the more is it subject to the command of reason. Hence, the very fact that the acts of the vegetative soul do not obey reason shows that they rank lowest.

Reply Obj. 2. The comparison holds in a certain respect, namely, because as God moves the world, so the soul moves the body. But it does not hold in every respect, for the soul did not create the body out of nothing, as God created the world; for which reason the world is wholly subject to His command.

Reply Obj. 3. Virtue and vice, praise and blame, are not due the acts themselves of the nutritive or the generative power, *i.e.*, digestion and the formation of the human body; but they are due the acts of the sensitive part which are ordered to the acts of generation and nutrition: *e.g.*, the desire for pleasure in the act of taking food or in the act of generation, and the right or wrong use thereof.

Ninth Article

WHETHER THE ACTS OF THE EXTERNAL MEMBERS ARE COMMANDED?

We proceed thus to the Ninth Article:—

Objection 1. It would seem that the members of the body do not obey reason as to their acts. For it is evident that the members of the body are more distant from the reason than are the powers of the vegetative soul. But the powers of the vegetative soul do not obey reason, as was stated above. Therefore much less do the members of the body obey.

Obj. 2. Further, the heart is the principle of animal movement. But the movement of the heart is not subject to the command of reason, for Gregory of Nyssa says that *the pulse is not controlled by reason.*[32] Therefore the movement of the bodily members is not subject to the command of reason.

Obj. 3. Further, Augustine says that *the movement of the genital members is sometimes inopportune and not desired; sometimes when sought it*

[31] Cf. *ibid.*   [32] Cf. *ibid.* (PG 40, 693).

fails, and whereas the heart is warm with desire, the body remains cold.[33] Therefore the movements of the members are not obedient to reason.

On the contrary, Augustine says: *The mind commands a movement of the hand, and so ready is the hand to obey, that scarcely can one discern obedience from command.*[34]

I answer that, The members of the body are organs of the soul's powers. Consequently, according as the powers of the soul are disposed towards obedience to reason, so are the members of the body disposed. Since, then, the sensitive powers are subject to the command of reason, whereas the natural powers are not, therefore all movements of members that are moved by the sensitive powers are subject to the command of reason; whereas those movements of members that arise from the natural powers are not subject to the command of reason.

Reply Obj. 1. The members do not move themselves, but are moved through the powers of the soul; of which powers, some are nearer to the reason than are the powers of the vegetative soul.

Reply Obj. 2. In what pertains to intellect and will, that which is according to nature stands first, whence all other things are derived; and thus from the knowledge of principles naturally known is derived knowledge of the conclusions, and from volition of the end naturally desired is derived the choice of the means. So also in bodily movements the principle is according to nature. Now the principle of bodily movements begins with the movement of the heart. Consequently, the movement of the heart is according to nature, and not according to the will; for, like a proper accident, it results from life, which follows from the union of soul and body. So, too, the movement of heavy and light things results from their substantial form; and for this reason they are said to be moved by their generator, as the Philosopher states.[35] Therefore this movement is called *vital.* For which reason Gregory of Nyssa says that, just as the movement of generation and nutrition does not obey reason, so neither does the pulse which is a vital movement.[36] By the pulse he means the movement of the heart, which is indicated by the pulse veins.

Reply Obj. 3. As Augustine says,[37] it is in punishment of sin that the movement of these members does not obey reason. That is to say, the soul is punished for its rebellion against God by the insubmission of that member whereby original sin is transmitted to posterity.

But because, as we shall state later on,[38] the effect of the sin of our first parent was that his nature was left to itself, through the withdrawal of the supernatural gift which God had bestowed on man, we must consider the natural cause of this particular member's insubmission to reason. This is stated by Aristotle who says that *the movements of the heart and of the*

---

[33] *De Civit. Dei,* XIV, 16 (PL 41, 425).   [34] *Confess.,* VIII, 9 (PL 32, 758). [35] *Phys.,* VIII, 4 (255b 35).   [36] Cf. Nemesius, *De Nat. Hom.,* XXII (PG 40, 693). [37] *De Civit. Dei,* XIV, 17; 20 (PL 41, 425; 428).   [38] Q. 85, a. 1, ad 3.

organs of generation are involuntary,[39] and that the reason for this is as follows. These members are stirred at the occasion of some apprehension; in so far as the intellect and imagination represent such things as arouse the passions of the soul, of which passions these movements are a consequence. But they are not moved at the command of the reason or intellect, because these movements are conditioned by a certain natural change, namely, of heat and cold, which is not subject to the command of reason. This is the case with these two organs in particular, because each is as it were a separate animal being, in so far as it is a principle of life; and the principle is virtually the whole. For the heart is the principle of the senses; and from the organ of generation proceeds the seminal principle, which is virtually the entire animal. Consequently, they have their proper movements naturally, because principles must needs be natural, as was stated above.

[39] *De Mot. Anim.,* XI (703b 5).

ON THE GOODNESS AND MALICE OF HUMAN ACTS, IN GENERAL

(In Eleven Articles)

WE must now consider the goodness and malice of human acts. First, we must consider how a human act is good or evil; secondly, what results from the goodness or malice of a human act, as merit or demerit, sin and guilt.[1]

Under the first head there will be a threefold consideration: the first will be of the goodness and malice of human acts, in general; the second, of the goodness and malice of internal acts;[2] the third, of the goodness and malice of external acts.[3]

Concerning the first there are eleven points of inquiry: (1) Whether every human action is good, or are there evil actions? (2) Whether the good or evil of a human act is derived from its object? (3) Whether it is derived from a circumstance? (4) Whether it is derived from the end? (5) Whether a human action is good or evil in its species? (6) Whether an act has the species of good or evil from its end? (7) Whether the species derived from the end is contained under the species derived from the object, as under its genus, or conversely? (8) Whether any act is indifferent in its species? (9) Whether an individual act can be indifferent? (10) Whether a circumstance places a moral act in a species of good or evil? (11) Whether every circumstance that makes an act better or worse places the moral act in a species of good or evil?

First Article

WHETHER EVERY HUMAN ACTION IS GOOD, OR ARE THERE EVIL ACTIONS?

We proceed thus to the First Article:—

Objection 1. It would seem that every human action is good, and that none is evil. For Dionysius says that evil acts not, save by the power of the good.[4] But no evil is done by the power of the good. Therefore no action is evil.

Obj. 2. Further, nothing acts except in so far as it is in act. Now a thing is evil, not according as it is in act, but according as its potentiality is deprived of act; whereas in so far as its potentiality is perfected by act, it is

---

[1] Q. 21.   [2] Q. 19.   [3] Q. 20.   [4] *De Div. Nom.*, IV, 20 (PG 3, 717).

good, as is stated in *Metaph.* ix.[5] Therefore nothing acts in so far as it is evil, but only according as it is good. Therefore every action is good, and none is evil.

Obj. 3. Further, evil cannot be a cause, save accidentally, as Dionysius declares.[6] But every action has some effect which is proper to it. Therefore no action is evil, but every action is good.

On the contrary, Our Lord said (*Jo.* iii. 20): *Every one that doth evil, hateth the light.* Therefore some actions of man are evil.

I answer that, We must speak of good and evil in actions as of good and evil in things, because such as everything is, such is the act that it produces. Now in things, each one has so much good as it has being, for good and being are convertible, as was stated in the First Part.[7] But God alone has the whole fullness of His Being in a manner which is one and simple, whereas every other thing has its proper fullness of being in a certain multiplicity. Therefore it happens with some things, that they have being in some respect, and yet they are lacking in the fullness of being due to them. Thus the fullness of human being requires a composite of soul and body, having all the powers and instruments of knowledge and movement; and so if any man be lacking in any of these, he is lacking in something due to the fullness of his being. Hence, as much as he has of being, so much has he of goodness, while so far as something is lacking in the fullness of its being, so far does this fall short of goodness, and is said to be evil. Thus a blind man is possessed of goodness inasmuch as he lives, and of evil, inasmuch as he lacks sight. That, however, which has nothing of being or goodness, could not be said to be either evil or good. But since this same fullness of being is of the very notion of good, if a thing be lacking in its due fullness of being, it is not said to be good absolutely, but in a certain respect, inasmuch as it is a being; although it can be called a being absolutely, and a non-being in a certain respect, as was stated in the First Part.[8]

We must therefore say that every action has goodness in so far as it has being, whereas it is lacking in goodness in so far as it is lacking in something that is due to its fullness of being; and thus it is said to be evil, for instance, if it lacks the measure determined by reason, or its due place, or something of the kind.

Reply Obj. 1. Evil acts in the power of a deficient good. For if there were nothing of good there, there would be neither being nor possibility of action. On the other hand, if good were not deficient, there would be no evil. Consequently, the action done is a deficient good, which is good in a certain respect, but evil absolutely.

Reply Obj. 2. Nothing hinders a thing from being in act in a certain respect, so that it can act, and in a certain respect deficient in act, so as to cause a deficient act. Thus, a blind man has actually the power of walking,

---

[5] Aristotle, *Metaph.*, VIII, 9 (1051a 4; a 29). [6] *De Div. Nom.*, IV, 20; 32 (PG 3, 717; 732). [7] *S. T.*, I, q. 5, a. 1 and 3; q. 17, a. 4, ad 2. [8] *S. T.*, I, q. 5, a. 1, ad 1.

whereby he is able to walk; but inasmuch as he is deprived of sight, he suffers a defect in walking by stumbling when he walks.

Reply Obj. 3. An evil action can have a proper effect, according to the goodness and being that it has. Thus, adultery is the cause of human generation, inasmuch as it implies union of male and female, but not inasmuch as it lacks the order of reason.

Second Article

WHETHER THE GOOD OR EVIL OF A MAN'S ACTION IS
DERIVED FROM ITS OBJECT?

We proceed thus to the Second Article:—

Objection 1. It would seem that the good or evil of an action is not derived from its object. For the object of any action is a thing. But *evil is not in things, but in the sinner's use of them,* as Augustine says.[9] Therefore the good or evil of a human action is not derived from its object.

Obj. 2. Further, the object is compared to the action as its matter. But the goodness of a thing is not from its matter, but rather from the form, which is an act. Therefore good and evil in actions is not derived from their object.

Obj. 3. Further, the object of an active power is compared to the action as effect to cause. But the goodness of a cause does not depend on its effect; rather is it the reverse. Therefore good or evil in actions is not derived from their object.

On the contrary, It is written (*Osee* ix. 10): *They became abominable as those things which they loved.* Now man becomes abominable to God because of the malice of his action. Therefore the malice of his action is according to the evil objects that man loves. And the same applies to the goodness of his action.

I answer that, As was stated above, the good or evil of an action, as of other things, depends on its fullness of being or its lack of that fullness. Now the first thing that belongs to the fullness of being seems to be that which gives a thing its species. And just as a natural thing has its species from its form, so an action has its species from its object, just as does movement from its term. Therefore, just as the primary goodness of a natural thing is derived from its form, which gives it its species, so the primary goodness of a moral action is derived from its suitable object; and so some call such an action *good in its genus,*[10] e.g., to make use of what is one's own. And just as, in natural things, the primary evil is when a generated thing does not realize its specific form (for instance, if instead of a man, something else be generated), so the primary evil in moral actions is that which is from the object, for instance, *to take what belongs to another.* Furthermore,

[9] *De Doct. Christ.,* III, 12 (PL 34, 73).   [10] Cf. Peter Lombard, *Sent.,* II, xxxvi, 6 (I, 504).

this action is said to be *evil in its genus* (genus here stands for species, just as we apply the term *mankind* [*humanum genus*] to the whole human species).

Reply Obj. 1. Although external things are good in themselves, nevertheless, they have not always a due proportion to this or that action. And so, inasmuch as they are considered as objects of such actions, they have not the nature of a good.

Reply Obj. 2. The object is not the matter *out of which*, but the matter *about which*, and stands in relation to the act as its form, as it were, through giving it its species.

Reply Obj. 3. The object of human action is not always the object of an active power. For the appetitive power is in a way passive, in so far as it is moved by the appetible object; and yet it is a principle of human actions. —Nor again have the objects of the active powers always the nature of an effect, but only when they are already transformed. Thus food, when transformed, is the effect of the nutritive power, whereas food, before being transformed, stands in relation to the nutritive power as the matter about which it exercises its operation. Now since the object is in some way the effect of the active power, it follows that it is the term of its action, and consequently that it gives it its form and species, since movement derives its species from its terms.—Moreover, although the goodness of an action is not caused by the goodness of its effect, yet an action is said to be good from the fact that it can produce a good effect. Consequently, the very proportion of an action to its effect is the measure of its goodness.

Third Article

WHETHER MAN'S ACTION IS GOOD OR EVIL FROM A CIRCUMSTANCE?

We proceed thus to the Third Article:—

Objection 1. It would seem that an action is not good or evil from a circumstance. For circumstances stand around [*circumstant*] an action, as being outside it, as was stated above.[11] But *good and evil are in things themselves*, as is stated in *Metaph.* vi.[12] Therefore an action does not derive goodness or malice from a circumstance.

Obj. 2. Further, the goodness or malice of an action is considered principally in the doctrine of morals. But since circumstances are accidents of actions, it seems that they are outside the scope of an art, because *no art takes notice of what is accidental*.[13] Therefore the goodness or malice of an action is not taken from a circumstance.

Obj. 3. Further, that which belongs to a thing through its substance is not attributed to it through an accident. But good and evil belong to an action in its substance, for an action can be good or evil in its genus, as was

[11] Q. 7, a. 1.   [12] Aristotle, *Metaph.*, V, 4 (1027b 25).   [13] *Op. cit.*, V, 2 (1026b 4).

stated above. Therefore an action is not good or evil from a circumstance.

On the contrary, the Philosopher says that a virtuous man acts as he should, and when he should, and so on, according to the other circumstances.[14] Therefore, on the other hand, the vicious man, in the matter of each vice, acts when he should not, or where he should not, and so on with the other circumstances. Therefore human actions are good or evil according to circumstances.

I answer that, In natural things, it is to be noted that the whole fullness of perfection due to a thing is not from the mere substantial form, that gives it its species, for a thing derives much from supervening accidents, as man does from shape, color and the like; and if any one of these accidents be out of due proportion, evil is the result. So it is with action. For the fullness of its goodness does not consist wholly in its species, but also in certain additions which accrue to it by reason of certain accidents; and such are its due circumstances. Therefore, if something be wanting that is requisite as a due circumstance, the action will be evil.

Reply Obj. 1. Circumstances are outside an action inasmuch as they are not part of its essence; but they are in an action as its accidents. So, too, accidents in natural substances are outside the essence.

Reply Obj. 2. Every accident is not accidentally in its subject; for some are proper accidents, and of these every art takes notice. And thus it is that the circumstances of actions are considered in the doctrine of morals.

Reply Obj. 3. Since good and being are convertible, according as being is predicated substantially and accidentally, so good is predicated of a thing both in respect of its essential being, and in respect of its accidental being; and this, both in natural things and in moral actions.

Fourth Article

WHETHER A HUMAN ACTION IS GOOD OR EVIL FROM ITS END?

We proceed thus to the Fourth Article:—

Objection 1. It would seem that the good and evil in human actions are not from the end. For Dionysius says that *nothing acts with a view to evil.*[15] If, therefore, an action were good or evil from its end, no action would be evil. Which is clearly false.

Obj. 2. Further, the goodness of an action is something in the action. But the end is an extrinsic cause. Therefore an action is not said to be good or evil according to its end.

Obj. 3. Further, a good action may happen to be ordered to an evil end, as when a man gives an alms from vainglory; and conversely, an evil action

---

[14] *Eth.,* II, 3 (1104b 26).   [15] *De Div. Nom.,* IV, 19; 31 (PG 3, 716; 732).

may happen to be ordered to a good end, as a theft committed in order to give something to the poor. Therefore an action is not good or evil from its end.

On the contrary, Boethius says that *if the end is good, the thing is good,* and if the end be evil, the thing also is evil.[16]

I answer that, The disposition of things as to goodness is the same as their disposition as to being. But in some things the being does not depend on another, and in these it suffices to consider their being absolutely. But there are things the being of which depends on something else, and hence concerning them we must consider their being in its relation to the cause on which it depends. Now just as the being of a thing depends on the agent and the form, so the goodness of a thing depends on its end. Hence in the divine Persons, Whose goodness does not depend on another, the measure of goodness is not taken from the end. But human actions, and other things, the goodness of which depends on something else, have a measure of goodness from the end on which they depend, in addition to that goodness which is in them absolutely.

Accordingly, a fourfold goodness may be considered in a human action First, that goodness which, as an action, it derives from its genus; since, as much as it has of action and being, so much has it of goodness, as was stated above. Secondly, it has goodness according to its species, which is derived from its befitting object. Thirdly, it has goodness from its circumstances,—its accidents, as it were. Fourthly, it has goodness from its end, to which it is compared as to the cause of its goodness.

Reply Obj. 1. The good in view of which one acts is not always a true good; but sometimes it is a true good, sometimes an apparent good. And in the latter event, an evil action results from the end in view.

Reply Obj. 2. Although the end is an extrinsic cause, nevertheless, a due proportion to the end and a relation to it are inherent in the action.

Reply Obj. 3. Nothing hinders an action that is good in one of the ways mentioned above from lacking goodness in another way. And thus it may happen that an action which is good in its species or in its circumstances is ordained to an evil end, or vice versa. However, an action is not good absolutely, unless it is good in all those ways; for *evil results from any single defect, but good from the complete cause,* as Dionysius says.[17]

Fifth Article

WHETHER A HUMAN ACTION IS GOOD OR EVIL
IN ITS SPECIES?

We proceed thus to the Fifth Article:—

Objection 1. It would seem that good and evil in moral actions do not make a difference of species. For the existence of good and evil in actions is

[16] *De Differ. Top.,* II (PL 64, 1189).   [17] *De Div. Nom.,* IV, 30 (PG 3, 729).

in conformity with their existence in things, as was stated above. But good and evil do not make a specific difference in things, for a good man is specifically the same as a bad man. Therefore neither do they make a specific difference in actions.

Obj. 2. Further, since evil is a privation, it is a non-being. But non-being cannot be a difference, according to the Philosopher.[18] Since, therefore, the difference constitutes the species, it seems that an action is not constituted in a species through being evil. Consequently, good and evil do not diversify the species of human actions.

Obj. 3. Further, acts that differ in species produce different effects. But the same specific effect results from a good and from an evil action; and thus a man is born of adulterous or of lawful wedlock. Therefore good and evil actions do not differ in species.

Obj. 4. Further, actions are sometimes said to be good or bad from a circumstance, as was stated above. But since a circumstance is an accident, it does not give an action its species. Therefore human actions do not differ in species because of their goodness or malice.

On the contrary, According to the Philosopher, *like habits produce like actions.*[19] But a good and a bad habit differ in species, as liberality and prodigality. Therefore good and evil actions likewise differ in species.

I answer that, Every action derives its species from its object, as we have stated above. Hence it follows that a difference of object causes a diversity of species in our actions. Now it must be observed that a difference of objects causes a diversity of species in our actions according as our actions are referred to one active principle, which does not cause a difference in actions, according as they are referred to another active principle. For nothing accidental constitutes a species, but only that which is essential; and a difference of object may be essential in reference to one active principle, and accidental in reference to another. Thus, to know color and to know sound differ essentially in reference to sense, but not in reference to the intellect.

Now in human actions, good and evil are predicated in relation to the reason, because, as Dionysius says, the good of man is to be in accordance with reason, *and evil is to be against reason.*[20] For that is good for a thing which suits it according to its form; and evil, that which is against the order of its form. It is therefore evident that the difference of good and evil, considered in reference to the object, is an essential difference in relation to reason, *i.e.,* according as the object is suitable or unsuitable to reason. Now certain actions are called human or moral inasmuch as they proceed from the reason. Consequently, it is evident that good and evil diversify the species in human actions, since essential differences cause a diversity in species.

[18] *Metaph.,* II, 3 (998b 22).   [19] *Eth.,* II, 1 (1103b 21).   [20] *De Div. Nom.,* IV, 32 (PG 3, 732).

Reply Obj. 1. Even in natural things, good and evil, inasmuch as something is according to nature, and something against nature, diversify the natural species; for a dead body and a living body are not of the same species. In like manner, good, inasmuch as it is in accord with reason, and evil, inasmuch as it is against reason, diversify the moral species.

Reply Obj. 2. Evil signifies privation, not an absolute one, but one affecting some potentiality. For an action is said to be evil in its species, not because it has no object at all, but because it has an object in disaccord with reason, for instance, to appropriate another's property. Therefore, in so far as the object is something positive, it can constitute the species of an evil act.

Reply Obj. 3. The conjugal act and adultery, as compared to reason, differ specifically and have effects specifically different; for the one deserves praise and reward, the other, blame and punishment. But as compared to the generative power, they do not differ in species, and thus they have one specific effect.

Reply Obj. 4. A circumstance is sometimes taken as the essential difference of the object, according as it is related to the reason; and then it can specify a moral act. And it must needs be so whenever a circumstance transforms an action from good to evil, for a circumstance would not make an action evil, except through being repugnant to reason.

Sixth Article

WHETHER AN ACT HAS THE SPECIES OF GOOD OR EVIL
FROM ITS END?

We proceed thus to the Sixth Article:—

Objection 1. It would seem that the good and evil which are from the end do not diversify the species of acts. For acts derive their species from the object. But the end is outside the nature of the object. Therefore the good and evil which are from the end do not diversify the species of an act.

Obj. 2. Further, that which is accidental does not constitute the species, as was stated above. But it is accidental to an act to be ordained to some particular end, for instance, to give alms from vainglory. Therefore acts are not diversified in species, according to the good and evil which are from the end.

Obj. 3. Further, acts that differ in species can be ordained to the same end; and thus to the end of vainglory, actions of various virtues and vices can be ordained. Therefore the good and evil which are taken from the end do not diversify the species of action.

On the contrary, It has been shown above that human acts derive their species from the end.[21] Therefore good and evil in respect of the end diversify the species of acts.

I answer that, Certain acts are called human inasmuch as they are

[21] Q. 1, a. 3.

voluntary, as we have stated above.[22] Now, in a voluntary act, there is a twofold act, viz., the interior act of the will, and the external act; and each of these acts has its object. The end is properly the object of the interior act of the will, while the object of the external action is that on which the action is brought to bear. Therefore, just as the external act takes its species from the object on which it bears, so the interior act of the will takes its species from the end, as from its own proper object.

Now that which is on the part of the will is as form in relation to that which is on the part of the external act, because the will uses the members to act as its instruments; nor have external acts any measure of morality, save in so far as they are voluntary. Consequently, the species of a human act is considered formally with regard to the end, but materially with regard to the object of the external action. Hence the Philosopher says that *he who steals that he may commit adultery is, strictly speaking, more adulterer than thief.*[23]

Reply Obj. 1. The end also has the nature of an object, as we have stated above.

Reply Obj. 2. Although it is accidental to the external act to be ordered to some particular end, it is not accidental to the interior act of the will, which is compared to the external act as form to matter.

Reply Obj. 3. When many acts, differing in species, are ordered to the same end, there is indeed a diversity of species on the part of the external acts; but there is a unity of species on the part of the interior act.

Seventh Article

WHETHER THE SPECIES DERIVED FROM THE END IS CON-
TAINED UNDER THE SPECIES DERIVED FROM THE OBJECT
AS UNDER ITS GENUS OR CONVERSELY?

We proceed thus to the Seventh Article:—

Objection 1. It would seem that the species of goodness derived from the end is contained under the species of goodness derived from the object as a species is contained under its genus: *e.g.,* when a man wills to steal in order to give an alms. For an act takes its species from its object, as was stated above. But it is impossible for a thing to be contained under another species, if this species be not contained under the proper species of that thing; for the same thing cannot be contained in different species if there is no subalternation among them. Therefore the species which is taken from the end is contained under the species which is taken from the object.

Obj. 2. Further, the last difference always constitutes the lowest species. But the difference derived from the end seems to come after the difference derived from the object, because the end is something last. Therefore the

---

[22] Q. 1, a. 1.   [23] *Eth.,* V, 2 (1130a 24).

species derived from the end is contained under the species derived from the object as its lowest species.

Obj. 3. Further, the more formal a difference is, the more specific it is, because difference is compared to genus as form to matter. But the species derived from the end is more formal than that which is derived from the object, as was stated above. Therefore the species derived from the end is contained under the species derived from the object as the lowest species is contained under the subaltern genus.

On the contrary, Each genus has its determinate differences. But an act of one and the same species, on the part of its object, can be ordered to an infinite number of ends: *e.g.,* theft can be ordered to an infinite number of good and bad ends. Therefore the species derived from the end is not contained under the species derived from the object as under its genus.

I answer that, The object of the external act can stand in a twofold relation to the end of the will: first, as being essentially ordered to it: *e.g.,* to fight well is of itself ordained to victory; secondly, as being ordained to it accidentally: *e.g.,* to take what belongs to another is ordered accidentally to the giving of alms. Now the differences that divide a genus and constitute the species of that genus must, as the Philosopher says, divide that genus essentially.[24] But if they divide it accidentally, the division is incorrect. Such would be the case if one were to say: *Animals are divided into rational and irrational, and the irrational into animals with wings and animals without wings;* for *winged* and *wingless* are not essential determinations of *irrational.* But the following division would be correct: *Some animals have feet, some have no feet, and of those that have feet, some have two feet, some four, some many;* for these are essential determinations of the prior difference. Accordingly, when the object is not essentially ordered to the end, the specific difference derived from the object is not an essential determination of the species derived from the end, nor is the reverse the case. Hence one of these species is not under the other; but then the moral action is contained under two species that are disparate, as it were. Consequently, we say that he that commits theft for the sake of adultery is guilty of a twofold malice in one action.—On the other hand, if the object be essentially ordered to the end, one of these differences is an essential determination of the other. Therefore one of these species will be contained under the other.

It remains to be considered which of the two is contained under the other. In order to make this clear, we must first of all observe that the more particular the form is from which a difference is taken, the more specific is the difference; secondly, that the more universal an agent is, the more universal a form does it cause; thirdly, that the more remote an end is, the more universal the agent to which it corresponds (*e.g.,* victory, which is the last end of the army, is the end intended by the commander in chief,

---

[24] *Metaph.,* VI, 12 (1038a 9).

while the right ordering of this or that regiment is the end intended by one of the lower officers). From all this it follows that the specific difference derived from the end is more general; and that the difference derived from an object which is essentially ordered to that end is a specific difference in relation to the former. For the will, the proper object of which is the end, is the universal mover in respect of all the powers of the soul, the proper objects of which are the objects of their particular acts.

Reply Obj. 1. One and the same thing, considered in its substance, cannot be in two species, one of which is not subordinate to the other. But in respect of those things which are superadded to the substance, one thing can be contained under diverse species. Thus, one and the same fruit, as to its color, is contained under one species, *i.e.,* a white thing; and, as to its odor, under the species of sweet-smelling things. In like manner, an act which, as to its substance, is in one natural species, considered in respect to the moral conditions that are added to it can belong to two species, as was stated above.[25]

Reply Obj. 2. The end is last in execution, but first in the intention of the reason, according to which moral actions receive their species.

Reply Obj. 3. Difference is compared to genus as form to matter, inasmuch as it actualizes the genus. On the other hand, the genus is considered as more formal than the species, inasmuch as it is something more absolute and less contracted. So, too, the parts of a definition are reduced to the genus of formal cause, as is stated in the *Physics.*[26] And in this sense the genus is the formal cause of the species; and so much the more formal, as it is more universal.

Eighth Article

WHETHER ANY ACT IS INDIFFERENT IN ITS SPECIES?

We proceed thus to the Eighth Article:—

Objection 1. It would seem that no action is indifferent in its species. For evil is the privation of good, according to Augustine.[27] But privation and habit are immediate contraries, according to the Philosopher.[28] Therefore, there is no such thing as an action that is indifferent in its species, as though it were between good and evil.

Obj. 2. Further, human acts derive their species from their end or object, as was stated above.[29] But every end and every object is either good or evil. Therefore every human act is good or evil according to its species. None, therefore, is indifferent in its species.

Obj. 3. Further, as was stated above, an act is said to be good when it has its due complement of goodness, and evil, when it lacks that complement. But every act must needs either have the entire fullness of its

---

[25] Q. 1, a. 3, ad 3.   [26] Aristotle, *Phys.,* II, 3 (194b 26).   [27] *Enchir.,* XI (PL 40, 236).   [28] *Cat.,* X (12a 2; b 27).   [29] A. 6; q. 1, a. 3.

goodness, or lack it in some respect. Therefore every act must needs be either good or evil in its species, and none is indifferent.

On the contrary, Augustine says that *there are certain deeds of a middle kind, which can be done with a good or evil mind,* of which it is rash to form a judgment.[30] Therefore some acts are indifferent according to their species.

I answer that, As we have stated above, every act takes its species from its object, and the human act, which is called the moral act, takes its species from the object as related to the principle of human acts, which is the reason. Therefore, if the object of an act includes something in accord with the order of reason, it will be a good act according to its species (for instance, to give alms to a person in want). On the other hand, if it includes something repugnant to the order of reason. it will be an evil act according to its species (for instance, to steal, which is to appropriate what belongs to another). But it may happen that the object of an act does not include something pertaining to the order of reason (for instance, to pick up a straw from the ground, to walk in the fields, and the like), and such acts are indifferent according to their species.

Reply Obj. 1. Privation is twofold. One is privation *as a result* [*privatum esse*], and this leaves nothing, but takes all away: *e.g.,* blindness takes away sight altogether; darkness, light; and death, life. Between this privation and the contrary habit, there can be no medium in respect of the proper subject.—The other is privation *in process* [*privari*]: *e.g.,* sickness is privation of health; not that it takes health away altogether, but that it is a kind of road to the entire loss of health, brought about by death. And since this sort of privation leaves something, it is not always the immediate contrary of the opposite habit. It is in this way that evil is a privation of good, as Simplicius says in his commentary on the *Categories*;[31] for it does not take away all good, but leaves some. Consequently, there can be something intermediate between good and evil.

Reply Obj. 2. Every object or end has some goodness or malice, at least that of its nature; but an object or an end does not always imply moral goodness or malice, which is considered in relation to the reason, as we have stated above. And it is of this that we are here treating.

Reply Obj. 3. Not everything belonging to an act belongs also to its species. Therefore, although according to the nature of its species an act may not contain all that belongs to the full complement of its goodness, it is not therefore an act specifically bad; nor is it specifically good. Thus, man, according to his species, is neither virtuous nor vicious.

---

[30] *De Serm. Dom.,* II, 18 (PL 34, 1296).   [31] *In Cat.,* X (p. 388[7]).

Ninth Article

WHETHER AN INDIVIDUAL ACT CAN BE INDIFFERENT?

We proceed thus to the Ninth Article:—

Objection 1. It seems that an individual act can be indifferent. For there is no species that does not, or cannot, contain an individual. But an act can be indifferent in its species, as was stated above. Therefore an individual act can be indifferent.

Obj. 2. Further, individual acts are the causes of like habits, as is stated in *Ethics* ii.[32] But a habit can be indifferent, for the Philosopher says that those who are of an even temper and prodigal disposition are not evil;[33] and yet it is evident that they are not good, since they depart from virtue. And thus, they are indifferent in respect of a habit. Therefore some individual acts are indifferent.

Obj. 3. Further, moral good belongs to virtue, while moral evil belongs to vice. But it happens sometimes that a man fails to ordain a specifically indifferent act to a vicious or virtuous end. Therefore an individual act may happen to be indifferent.

On the contrary, Gregory says in a homily: *An idle word is one that lacks either the usefulness of rectitude or the motive of just necessity or pious utility.*[34] But an idle word is an evil, because *men . . . shall render an account of it in the day of judgment* (*Matt.* xii. 36); while if it does not lack the motive of just necessity or pious utility, it is good. Therefore every word is either good or evil. For the same reason, every other act is either good or evil. Therefore no individual act is indifferent.

I answer that, It sometimes happens that an act is indifferent in its species, which yet is good or evil, considered in the individual. And the reason for this is because a moral act, as we have stated above, derives its goodness not only from the object which specifies it, but also from the circumstances, which are its accidents, as it were. So, too, something belongs to a man by reason of his individual accidents, which does not belong to him by reason of his species. And every individual act must needs have some circumstance that makes it good or evil, at least in respect of the intention of the end. For since it belongs to the reason to direct, if an act that proceeds from deliberate reason be not directed to the due end, it is, by that fact alone, repugnant to reason, and has the character of evil. But if it be directed to a due end, it is in accord with the order of reason, and hence it has the character of good. Now it must needs be either directed or not directed to a due end. Consequently, every human act that proceeds from deliberate reason, if it be considered in the individual, must be good or evil.

If, however, it does not proceed from deliberate reason, but from some

---

[32] Aristotle, *Eth.*, II, 1 (1103b 21). [33] *Op. cit.*, IV, 1 (1121a 26). [34] *In Evang.*, I, hom. 6 (PL 76, 1098).

act of the imagination, as when a man strokes his beard, or moves his hand or foot, such an act, properly speaking, is not moral or human, since an act has the character of being moral or human from the reason. Hence it will be indifferent, as standing outside the genus of moral acts.

Reply Obj. 1. For an act to be indifferent in its species can happen in several ways. First, in such a way that its species demands that it remain indifferent; and the objection proceeds on this line. But no act can be specifically indifferent thus, since no object of a human act is such that it cannot be directed to good or evil, either through its end or through a circumstance.—Secondly, the specific indifference of an act may be due to the fact that, as far as its species is concerned, it is neither good nor evil. Therefore it can be made good or evil by something else. In the same way, man, as far as his species is concerned, is neither white nor black, nor is it a condition of his species that he should not be black or white; but blackness or whiteness can be superadded to man by other principles than those of his species.

Reply Obj. 2. The Philosopher states that a man is evil, properly speaking, if he is injurious to others.[35] Accordingly, he says that the prodigal is not evil, because he injures none save himself.[36] And the same applies to all others who are not injurious to other men. But here we are calling evil, in general, all that is repugnant to right reason. And in this sense every individual act is either good or evil, as we have stated above.

Reply Obj. 3. Whenever an end is intended by deliberate reason, it belongs either to the good of some virtue, or to the evil of some vice. Thus, if a man's act is directed to the support or repose of his body, it is also directed to the good of virtue, provided he direct his body itself to the good of virtue. The same clearly applies to other acts.

Tenth Article

WHETHER A CIRCUMSTANCE PLACES A MORAL ACT IN A SPECIES OF GOOD OR EVIL?

We proceed thus to the Tenth Article:—

Objection 1. It would seem that a circumstance cannot place a moral act in a species of good or evil. For the species of an act is taken from its object. But circumstances differ from the object. Therefore circumstances do not give an act its species.

Obj. 2. Further, circumstances are as accidents in relation to the moral act, as was stated above.[37] But an accident does not constitute a species. Therefore a circumstance does not constitute a species of good or evil.

Obj. 3. Further, one thing is not in several species. But one act has several circumstances. Therefore a circumstance does not place a moral act in a species of good or evil.

[35] *Eth.,* IV, 1 (1121a 29).   [36] *Ibid* (1121a 26).   [37] Q. 7, a. 1.

On the contrary, Place is a circumstance. But place makes a moral act to be in a certain species of evil; for theft of a thing from a holy place is a sacrilege. Therefore a circumstance places a moral act in some species of good or evil.

I answer that, Just as the species of natural things are constituted by their natural forms, so the species of moral acts are constituted by forms as conceived by the reason, as is evident from what was said above. But since nature is determined to one course of action, and a process of nature cannot go on to infinity, there must needs be some ultimate form, giving a specific difference, after which no further specific difference is possible. Hence it is that, in natural things, that which is accidental to a thing cannot be taken as a difference constituting the species. But the process of reason is not fixed to one particular term, for at any point it can still proceed further. Consequently that which, in one act, is taken as a circumstance added to the object that specifies the act, can again be taken, by the directing reason, as the principal condition of the object that determines the species of the act. Thus, to appropriate another's property is specified by the character of being *another's,* for this is why it is placed in the species of theft; and if we further consider the notion of place or time, then this will be an additional circumstance. But since the reason can direct as to place, time, and the like, it may happen that the condition as to place, in relation to the object, is considered as being in disaccord with reason: for instance, reason forbids damage to be done to a holy place. Consequently, to steal from a holy place has an additional repugnance to the order of reason. And thus place, which was first of all considered as a circumstance, is considered here as the principal condition of the object, and as itself repugnant to reason. In this way, whenever a circumstance has a special relation to reason, either for or against, it must needs specify the moral act, whether good or evil.

Reply Obj. 1. A circumstance, in so far as it specifies an act, is considered as a condition of the object, as we have stated above, and as being, as it were, a specific difference of the object.

Reply Obj. 2. A circumstance, so long as it is but a circumstance, does not specify an act, since thus it is a mere accident; but when it becomes a principal condition of the object, then it does specify the act.

Reply Obj. 3. It is not every circumstance that places the moral act in a species of good or evil, for not every circumstance implies accord or disaccord with reason. Consequently, although one act may have many circumstances, it does not follow that it is in many species. Nevertheless, there is no reason why one act should not be in several, even disparate, moral species, as we have said above.[38]

[38] A. 7, ad 1; q. 1, a. 3, ad 3.

Eleventh Article

WHETHER EVERY CIRCUMSTANCE THAT MAKES AN ACT BET-
TER OR WORSE PLACES A MORAL ACTION IN A SPECIES
OF GOOD OR EVIL?

We proceed thus to the Eleventh Article:—

Objection 1. It would seem that every circumstance relating to good or evil specifies an act. For good and evil are specific differences in moral acts. Therefore, that which causes a difference in the goodness or malice of a moral act causes a specific difference, which is the same as to make it differ in species. Now that which makes an act better or worse makes it differ in goodness and malice. Therefore it causes it to differ in species. Therefore every circumstance that makes an act better or worse constitutes a species.

Obj. 2. Further, an additional circumstance either has in itself some character of goodness or malice, or it has not. If not, it cannot make the act better or worse, because what is not good, cannot make a greater good, and what is not evil cannot make a greater evil. But if it has in itself the char- acter of good or evil, for this very reason it has a certain species of good or evil. Therefore, every circumstance that makes an action better or worse constitutes a new species of good or evil.

Obj. 3. Further, according to Dionysius, *evil is caused by each single defect.*[39] Now every circumstance that increases malice has a special defect. Therefore every such circumstance adds a new species of sin. And for the same reason, every circumstance that increases goodness seems to add a new species of goodness; just as every unity added to a number makes a new species of number, for the good consists in number, weight and measure.

On the contrary, *More*-and-*less* does not change a species. But *more*-and-*less* is a circumstance of additional goodness or malice. Therefore, not every circumstance that makes a moral act better or worse, places it in a species of good or evil.

I answer that, As we have stated above, a circumstance gives the species of good or evil to a moral act in so far as it refers to a special order of rea- son. Now it happens sometimes that a circumstance does not refer to a special order of reason in respect of good or evil, except on the supposition of another previous circumstance, from which the moral act takes its spe- cies of good or evil. Thus, to take something in a large or small quantity does not concern the order of reason in respect of good or evil, except a cer- tain other condition be presupposed, from which the act takes its malice or goodness. Suppose, for instance, that what is taken belongs to another, which makes the act to be discordant with reason. Therefore, to take what belongs to another in a large or small quantity does not change the species

[39] *De Div. Nom.,* IV, 30 (PG 3, 729).

of the sin. Nevertheless it can aggravate or diminish the sin. The same applies to other evil or good acts. Consequently, not every circumstance that makes a moral act better or worse changes its species.

Reply Obj. 1. In things which can be more or less intense, the difference of more or less does not change the species. Thus, by differing in whiteness through being more or less white, a thing is not changed in its species of color. In like manner, that which makes an act to be more or less good or evil does not make the act differ in species.

Reply Obj. 2. A circumstance that aggravates a sin or adds to the goodness of an act sometimes has no goodness or malice in itself, but in relation to some other condition of the act, as was stated above. Consequently, it does not add a new species, but adds to the goodness or malice derived from this other condition of the act.

Reply Obj. 3. A circumstance does not always involve a distinct defect of its own; sometimes it causes a defect in reference to something else. In like manner, a circumstance does not always add further perfection, except in reference to something else. And, in so far as it does, although it may add to the goodness or malice, it does not always change the species of good or evil.

ON THE GOODNESS AND MALICE OF THE INTERIOR ACT OF THE WILL

(*In Ten Articles*)

WE must now consider the goodness of the interior act of the will, under which head there are ten points of inquiry: (1) Whether the goodness of the will depends on the object? (2) Whether it depends on the object alone? (3) Whether it depends on the reason? (4) Whether it depends on the eternal law? (5) Whether erring reason binds? (6) Whether the will is evil if it follows the erring reason against the law of God? (7) Whether the goodness of the will in regard to the means depends on the intention of the end? (8) Whether the degree of goodness or malice in the will depends on the degree of good or evil in the intention? (9) Whether the goodness of the will depends on its conformity to the divine will? (10) Whether it is necessary for the human will, in order to be good, to be conformed to the divine will as regards the thing willed?

First Article

WHETHER THE GOODNESS OF THE WILL DEPENDS ON THE OBJECT?

We proceed thus to the First Article:—

Objection 1. It would seem that the goodness of the will does not depend on the object. For the will cannot be directed otherwise than to what is good, since *evil is outside the scope of the will*, as Dionysius says.[1] If, therefore, the goodness of the will depended on the object, it would follow that every act of the will is good, and none bad.

Obj. 2. Further, the good is first of all in the end, and so the goodness of the end, as such, does not depend on any other. But, according to the Philosopher, *goodness of action is the end, but goodness of making is never the end*;[2] for the latter is always ordained to the thing made as to its end. Therefore the goodness of the act of the will does not depend on any object.

Obj. 3. Further, such as a thing is, such does it make another to be. But the object of the will is good with the goodness of nature. Therefore it cannot give moral goodness to the will. Therefore the moral goodness of the will does not depend on the object.

On the contrary, The Philosopher says that justice is that habit *through*

[1] *De Div. Nom.*, IV, 32 (PG 3, 732).   [2] *Eth.*, VI, 5 (1140b 6).

which men wish for just things;[3] and, similarly, virtue is a habit through which men wish for good things. But a good will is one which is in accordance with virtue. Therefore the goodness of the will is from the fact that a man wills that which is good.

I answer that, Good and evil are essential differences of the act of the will. For good and evil pertain essentially to the will; just as truth and falsehood pertain to the reason, the act of which is distinguished essentially by the difference of truth and falsehood (according as we say that an opinion is true or false). Consequently, good and evil volition are acts differing in species. Now the specific difference in acts is according to objects, as was stated above.[4] Therefore good and evil in the acts of the will is derived properly from the objects.

Reply Obj. 1. The will is not always directed to what is truly good, but sometimes to the apparent good; and this has indeed some measure of good, but not of a good that is suitable absolutely to be desired. Hence it is that the act of the will is not always good, but sometimes evil.

Reply Obj. 2. Although an act can, in a certain way, be man's last end, nevertheless such an act is not an act of the will, as was stated above.[5]

Reply Obj. 3. Good is presented to the will as its object by the reason; and in so far as it is in accord with reason, it enters the moral order, and causes moral goodness in the act of the will, for the reason is the principle of human and moral acts, as we have stated above.[6]

Second Article

WHETHER THE GOODNESS OF THE WILL DEPENDS
ON THE OBJECT ALONE?

We proceed thus to the Second Article:—

Objection 1. It would seem that the goodness of the will does not depend on the object alone. For the end has a closer relationship to the will than to any other power. But the acts of the other powers derive goodness not only from the object but also from the end, as we have shown above.[7] Therefore the act of the will likewise derives goodness not only from the object but also from the end.

Obj. 2. Further, the goodness of an act is derived not only from the object but also from the circumstances, as was stated above.[8] But according to the diversity of circumstances there may be diversity of goodness and malice in the act of the will: *e.g.,* if a man will, when he ought, where he ought, as much as he ought, and how he ought, or if he will as he ought not. Therefore the goodness of the will depends not only on the object, but also on the circumstances.

---

[3] *Op. cit.,* V, 1 (1129a 9).   [4] Q. 18, a. 5.   [5] Q. 1, a. 1, ad 2.   [6] Q. 18, a. 5.
[7] Q. 18, a. 4.   [8] Q. 18, a. 3.

Obj. 3. Furth⟨v⟩r, ignorance of circumstances excuses the malice of the will, as was stated above.[9] But it would not be so, unless the goodness or malice of the will depended on the circumstances. Therefore the goodness and malice of the will depend on the circumstances, and not only on the object.

On the contrary, An action does not take its species from the circumstances as such, as was stated above.[10] But good and evil are specific differences of the act of the will, as we have stated above. Therefore the goodness and malice of the will depend, not on the circumstances, but on the object alone.

I answer that, In every genus, the more a thing is first, the more simple it is, and the fewer the principles of which it consists. Thus, primary bodies are simple. Hence it is to be observed that the first things in every genus are in some way simple and consist of one principle. Now the principle of the goodness and malice in human acts is taken from the act of the will. Consequently, the goodness and malice of the act of the will depend on some one thing, while the goodness and malice of other acts may depend on several things.

Now that one thing which is the principle in each genus is not something accidental to that genus, but something essential to it; for whatever is accidental is reduced to something essential as to its principle. Therefore, the goodness of the will's act depends on that one thing alone, which essentially causes goodness in the act; and that one thing is the object, and not the circumstances, which are simply accidents of the act.

Reply Obj. 1. The end is the object of the will, but not of the other powers. Hence, in regard to the act of the will, the goodness derived from the object does not differ from that which is derived from the end, as is the case in the acts of the other powers (except perhaps accidentally, in so far as one end depends on another, and one act of the will on another).

Reply Obj. 2. Given that the act of the will is fixed on some good, no circumstance can make that act evil. Consequently, when it is said that a man wills a good when he ought not, or where he ought not, this can be understood in two ways. First, so that this circumstance is referred to the thing willed. According to this, the act of the will is not fixed on something good, since to will to do something when it ought not to be done is not to will something good. Secondly, so that the circumstance is referred to the act of willing. According to this, it is impossible to will something good when one ought not to, because one ought always to will what is good; except, perhaps, accidentally, in so far as a man, by willing some particular good, is prevented from willing at the same time another good which he ought to will at that time. And then evil results, not from his willing that particular good, but from his not willing the other. The same applies to the other circumstances.

[9] Q. 6, a. 8.   [10] Q. 18, a. 10, ad 2.

Reply Obj. 3. Ignorance of the circumstances excuses the malice of the will in so far as the circumstance affects the thing willed, that is to say, in so far as a man is ignorant of the circumstances of the act which he wills.

Third Article

WHETHER THE GOODNESS OF THE WILL DEPENDS ON REASON?

We proceed thus to the Third Article:—

Objection 1. It would seem that the goodness of the will does not depend on reason. For what comes first does not depend on what follows. But the good belongs to the will before it belongs to the reason, as is clear from what has been said above.[11] Therefore the goodness of the will does not depend on reason.

Obj. 2. Further, the Philosopher says that the goodness of the practical intellect is *a truth that is in conformity with right appetite.*[12] But right appetite is a good will. Therefore the goodness of the practical reason depends on the goodness of the will, rather than conversely.

Obj. 3. Further, the mover does not depend on that which is moved, but *vice versa.* But the will moves the reason and the other powers, as was stated above.[13] Therefore the goodness of the will does not depend on reason.

On the contrary, Hilary says: *It is an unruly will that persists in its desires in opposition to reason.*[14] But the goodness of the will consists in not being unruly. Therefore the goodness of the will depends on its being subject to reason.

I answer that, As we have stated above, the goodness of the will depends properly on its object. Now the will's object is proposed to it by the reason. For the understood good is the proportioned object of the will, while the sensible or imaginary good is proportioned, not to the will, but to the sensitive appetite; for the will can tend to the universal good, which reason apprehends, whereas the sensitive appetite tends only to the particular good, apprehended by a sensitive power. Therefore the goodness of the will depends on the reason in the same way as it depends on its object.

Reply Obj. 1. The good considered under the notion of good, *i.e.,* as appetible, pertains to the will before pertaining to the reason. But it pertains to the reason considered under the notion of the true before pertaining to the will under the notion of good; for the will cannot desire a good that is not previously apprehended by reason.

Reply Obj. 2. The Philosopher speaks there of the practical intellect in so far as it counsels and reasons about the means to the end; for in this respect it is perfected by prudence. Now in regard to the means, the rectitude of the reason depends on its conformity with the appetite of a due

---

[11] Q. 9, a. 1.   [12] *Eth.,* VI, 2 (1139a 29).   [13] Q. 9, a. 1.   [14] *De Trin.,* X (PL 10, 344).

end; and yet the very appetite of the due end presupposes a right apprehension of the end, which is the work of the reason.

Reply Obj. 3. The will moves the reason in one way: the reason moves
the will in another, viz., on the part of the object, as we have stated above.[15]

Fourth Article

WHETHER THE GOODNESS OF THE WILL DEPENDS ON THE ETERNAL LAW?

We proceed thus to the Fourth Article:—

Objection 1. It would seem that the goodness of the human will does not
depend on the eternal law. For to one thing there is one rule and one measure. But the rule of the human will, on which its goodness depends, is right
reason. Therefore the goodness of the will does not depend on the eternal
law.

Obj. 2. Further, *a measure is homogeneous with the thing measured.*[16]
But the eternal law is not homogeneous with the human will. Therefore the
eternal law cannot be the measure on which the goodness of the human will
depends.

Obj. 3. Further, a measure should be most certain. But the eternal law is
unknown to us. Therefore it cannot be the measure on which the goodness
of our will depends.

On the contrary, Augustine says that *sin is a deed, word or desire against
the eternal law.*[17] But malice of the will is the root of sin. Therefore, since
malice is contrary to goodness, the goodness of the will depends on the
eternal law.

I answer that, Wherever a number of causes are ordered to one another,
the effect depends more on the first than on the second cause, since the second cause acts only in the power of the first. Now it is from the eternal
law, which is the divine reason, that human reason is the rule of the human
will, from which the human will derives its goodness. Hence it is written
(*Ps.* iv. 6, 7): *Many say: Who showeth us good things? The light of Thy
countenance, O Lord, is signed upon us*; as though to say: 'The light of
our reason is able to show us good things, and guide our will, in so far as it
is the light of (*i.e.,* derived from) Thy countenance.' It is therefore evident
that the goodness of the human will depends on the eternal law much more
than on the human reason; and when the human reason fails, we must
have recourse to the eternal reason.

Reply Obj. 1. For one thing there are not several proximate measures;
but there can be several measures if one is subordinate to the other.

Reply Obj. 2. A proximate measure is homogeneous with the thing measured; a remote measure is not.

---

[15] Q. 9, a. 1.   [16] Aristotle, *Metaph.*, IX, 1 (1053a 24).   [17] *Contra Faust.*, XXII,
27 (PL 42, 418).

Reply Obj. 3. Although the eternal law is unknown to us according as it is in the divine mind, nevertheless, it becomes somewhat known to us either by the natural reason, which is derived from it as its proper image, or by some sort of additional revelation.

Fifth Article

WHETHER THE WILL IS EVIL WHEN IT IS AT VARIANCE WITH ERRING REASON?

We proceed thus to the Fifth Article:—

Objection 1. It would seem that the will is not evil when it is at variance with erring reason. For the reason is the rule of the human will, in so far as it is derived from the eternal law, as was stated above. But erring reason is not derived from the eternal law. Therefore erring reason is not the rule of the human will. Therefore the will is not evil if it be at variance with erring reason.

Obj. 2. Further, according to Augustine, the command of a lower authority does not bind if it be contrary to the command of a higher authority:[18] *e.g.*, if a provincial governor command something that is forbidden by the emperor. But erring reason sometimes proposes what is against the command of a higher power, namely, God, Whose power is supreme. Therefore the decision of an erring reason does not bind. Consequently, the will is not evil if it be at variance with erring reason.

Obj. 3. Further, every evil will is reducible to some species of malice. But the will that is at variance with erring reason is not reducible to some species of malice. For instance, if a man's reason err in telling him to commit fornication, his will, in not willing to do so, cannot be reduced to any species of malice. Therefore the will is not evil when it is at variance with erring reason.

On the contrary, As we have stated in the First Part, conscience is nothing else than the application of knowledge to some action.[19] Now knowledge is in the reason. Therefore when the will is at variance with erring reason, it is against conscience. But every such will is evil, for it is written (*Rom.* xiv. 23): *All that is not of faith—i.e.,* all that is against conscience *—is sin.* Therefore the will is evil when it is at variance with erring reason.

I answer that, Since conscience is a kind of dictate of the reason (for it is an application of knowledge to action, as was stated in the First Part)[20] to inquire whether the will is evil when it is at variance with erring reason is the same as to inquire whether an erring conscience binds. On this matter, some distinguished three kinds of acts;[21] for some are good of their nature;

---

[18] *Serm.* LXII, 8 (PL 38, 421).   [19] *S. T.,* I, q. 79, a. 13.   [20] *Ibid.*   [21] St. Bonaventure, *In II Sent.,* d. xxxix, a. 1, q. 3 (II, 906).—Cf. Alex. of Hales, *Summa Theol.,* II-II, no. 388 (III, 388).

some are indifferent, some are evil of their nature. And they say that if reason or conscience tell us to do something which is of its nature good, there is no error; and the same thing is true, if it tell us not to do something which is evil of its nature, since it is the same reason that prescribes what is good and forbids what is evil. On the other hand, if a man's reason or conscience tell him that he is bound by precept to do what is in itself evil, or that what is in itself good is forbidden, then his reason or conscience errs. In like manner, if a man's reason or conscience tell him that what is in itself indifferent, for instance, to lift a straw from the ground, is forbidden or commanded, his reason or conscience errs. They say, therefore, that reason or conscience, when erring in matters of indifference, either by commanding or by forbidding them, binds; so that the will which is at variance with that erring reason is evil and sinful. But when reason or conscience errs in commanding what is evil in itself, or in forbidding what is good in itself and necessary for salvation, it does not bind; and so in such cases the will which is at variance with erring reason or conscience is not evil.

But this is unreasonable. For in matters of indifference, the will that is at variance with erring reason or conscience is evil in some way because of the object on which the goodness or malice of the will depends; not indeed because of the object according as it is in its own nature, but according as it is accidentally apprehended by reason as something evil to do or to avoid. And since the object of the will is that which is proposed by the reason, as we have stated above, from the very fact that a thing is proposed by the reason as being evil, the will by tending thereto becomes evil. And this is the case not only in indifferent matters, but also in those that are good or evil in themselves. For it is not only indifferent matters that can receive the character of goodness or malice accidentally; but likewise that which is good can receive the character of evil, or that which is evil can receive the character of goodness, because of the reason apprehending it as such. For instance, to refrain from fornication is good, and yet the will does not tend to this good except in so far as it is proposed by the reason. If, therefore, the erring reason propose it as an evil, the will tends to it as to something evil. Consequently, the will is evil because it wills evil, not indeed that which is evil in itself, but that which is evil accidentally, through being apprehended as such by the reason. In like manner, to believe in Christ is good in itself, and necessary for salvation; but the will does not tend thereto, except inasmuch as it is proposed by the reason. Consequently, if it be proposed by the reason as something evil, the will tends to it as to something evil; not as if it were evil in itself, but because it is evil accidentally, through the apprehension of the reason. Hence the Philosopher says that, *properly speaking, the incontinent man is one who does not follow right reason; but accidentally, he is also one who does not follow false reason.*[22] We must there-

---

[22] *Eth.,* VII, 9 (1151a 33).

fore conclude that, absolutely speaking, every will at variance with reason, whether right or erring, is always evil.

Reply Obj. 1. Although the judgment of an erring reason is not derived from God, yet the erring reason puts forward its judgment as being true, and consequently as being derived from God, from Whom is all truth.

Reply Obj. 2. The saying of Augustine holds good when it is known that the inferior authority prescribes something contrary to the command of the higher authority. But if a man were to believe the command of the proconsul to be the command of the emperor, in scorning the command of the proconsul he would scorn the command of the emperor. In like manner, if a man were to know that human reason was dictating something contrary to God's commandment, he would not be bound to abide by reason; but then reason would not be entirely erroneous. But when erring reason proposes something as being commanded by God, then, to scorn the dictate of reason is to scorn the commandment of God.

Reply Obj. 3. Whenever reason apprehends something as evil, it apprehends it under some species of evil; *e.g.*, as being something contrary to a divine precept, or as giving scandal, or for some such reason. And then that evil is reduced to that species of malice.

Sixth Article

WHETHER THE WILL IS GOOD WHEN IT ABIDES BY ERRING REASON?

We proceed thus to the Sixth Article:—

Objection 1. It would seem that the will is good when it abides by erring reason. For just as the will, when at variance with the reason, tends to that which reason judges to be evil, so, when in accord with the reason, it tends to what reason judges to be good. But the will is evil when it is at variance with reason, even when erring. Therefore even when it abides by erring reason, the will is good.

Obj. 2. Further, the will is always good when it abides by the commandment of God and the eternal law. But the eternal law and God's commandment are proposed to us by the apprehension of the reason, even when it errs. Therefore the will is good even when it abides by erring reason.

Obj. 3. Further, the will is evil when it is at variance with erring reason. If, therefore, the will is evil also when it abides by erring reason, it seems that the will is always evil when in conjunction with erring reason; so that in such a case a man would be in a dilemma, and of necessity would sin, which is unreasonable. Therefore the will is good when it abides by erring reason.

On the contrary, The will of those who slew the apostles was evil. And yet it was in accord with their erring reason, according to *John* xvi. 2: *The hour cometh, that whosoever killeth you, will think that he doth a service to God.* Therefore the will can be evil when it abides by erring reason.

I answer that, Whereas the previous question is the same as inquiring whether an erring conscience binds, this question is the same as inquiring whether an erring conscience excuses. Now this question depends on what has been said above about ignorance. For it was said that ignorance sometimes causes an act to be involuntary, and sometimes not.[23] And since moral good and evil consist in an act in so far as it is voluntary, as was stated above, it is evident that when ignorance causes an act to be involuntary, it takes away the character of moral good and evil; but not, when it does not cause the act to be involuntary. Again, it has been stated above that when ignorance is in any way willed, either directly or indirectly, it does not cause the act to be involuntary.[24] And I call that ignorance *directly* voluntary to which the act of the will tends, and that, *indirectly* voluntary, which is due to negligence, because a man does not wish to know what he ought to know, as we have stated above.[25]

If, therefore, reason or conscience err with an error that is voluntary, either directly or through negligence, so that one errs about what one ought to know, then such an error of reason or conscience does not excuse the will, which abides by that erring reason or conscience, from being evil. But if the error arise from the ignorance of some circumstance, and without any negligence, so that it cause the act to be involuntary, then that error of reason or conscience excuses the will, which abides by that erring reason, from being evil. For instance, if erring reason tell a man that he should go to another man's wife, the will that abides by that erring reason is evil, since this error arises from ignorance of the divine law, which he is bound to know. But if a man's reason errs in mistaking another for his wife, and if he wish to give her her right when she asks for it, his will is excused from being evil; for this error arises from ignorance of a circumstance, which ignorance excuses, and causes the act to be involuntary.

Reply Obj. 1. As Dionysius says, *good results from the entire cause, evil from each particular defect.*[26] Consequently, in order that the thing to which the will tends be called evil, it suffices, either that it be evil according to its nature or that it be apprehended as evil. But in order for it to be good, it must be good in both ways.

Reply Obj. 2. The eternal law cannot err, but human reason can. Consequently, the will that abides by human reason is not always right, nor is it always in accord with the eternal law.

Reply Obj. 3. Just as in syllogistic arguments, granted one absurdity, others must needs follow, so in moral matters, given one absurdity, others must follow too. Thus suppose a man to seek vainglory, he will sin, whether he does his duty for vainglory or whether he omit to do it. Nor is he in a dilemma about the matter, because he can put aside his evil intention. In

---

[23] Q. 6, a. 8.   [24] *Ibid.*   [25] *Ibid.*   [26] *De Div. Nom.,* IV, 30 (PG 3, 729).

like manner, suppose a man's reason or conscience to err through inexcusable ignorance, then evil must needs result in the will. Nor is this man in a dilemma, because he can lay aside his error, since his ignorance is vincible and voluntary.

Seventh Article

WHETHER THE GOODNESS OF THE WILL, AS REGARDS THE MEANS, DEPENDS ON THE INTENTION OF THE END?

We proceed thus to the Seventh Article:—

Objection 1. It would seem that the goodness of the will does not depend on the intention of the end. For it has been stated above that the goodness of the will depends on the object alone. But as regards the means, the object of the will is one thing, and the end intended is another. Therefore, in such matters, the goodness of the will does not depend on the intention of the end.

Obj. 2. Further, to wish to keep God's commandment belongs to a good will. But this can be referred to an evil end, for instance, to vainglory or covetousness, by willing to obey God for the sake of temporal gain. Therefore the goodness of the will does not depend on the intention of the end.

Obj. 3. Further, just as good and evil diversify the will, so do they diversify the end. But the malice of the will does not depend on the malice of the end intended, since a man who wills to steal in order to give alms has an evil will, although he intends a good end. Therefore neither does the goodness of the will depend on the goodness of the end intended.

On the contrary, Augustine says that God rewards the intention.[27] But God rewards a thing because it is good. Therefore the goodness of the will depends on the intention of the end.

I answer that, The intention may stand in a twofold relation to the act of the will: first, as preceding it, secondly as following it. The intention precedes the act of the will causally, when we will something because we intend a certain end. And then the order to the end is considered as the reason of the goodness of the thing willed, *e.g.,* when a man wills to fast for God's sake, because the act of fasting is specifically good from the very fact that it is done for God's sake. Therefore, since the goodness of the will depends on the goodness of the thing willed, as we have stated above, it must, of necessity, depend on the intention of the end.

On the other hand, intention follows the act of the will when it is added to a preceding act of the will. For instance, a man may will to do something, and may afterwards refer it to God. In such a case, the goodness of the previous act of the will does not depend on the subsequent intention, except in so far as that act is repeated with the subsequent intention.

Reply Obj. 1. When the intention is the cause of the act of willing, the

[27] Cf. *Confess.,* XIII, 26 (PL 32, 863).

order to the end is considered as the reason of the goodness of the object, as was stated above.

Reply Obj. 2. The act of the will cannot be said to be good, if an evil intention is the cause of willing. For when a man wills to give an alms for the sake of vainglory, he wills that which is good in itself, under a species of evil; and therefore, as willed by him, it is evil. Therefore his will is evil. If, however, the intention is subsequent to the act of the will, then the latter may be good; and the intention does not spoil that act of the will which preceded, but that which is repeated.

Reply Obj. 3. As we have already stated, *evil results from each particular defect, but good from the whole and entire cause.* Hence, whether the will tend to what is evil in itself, even under the species of good, or to the good under the species of evil, it will be evil in either case. But in order that the will be good, it must tend to the good under the species of good; in other words, it must will the good for the sake of the good.

Eighth Article

WHETHER THE DEGREE OF GOODNESS OR MALICE IN THE WILL DEPENDS ON THE DEGREE OF GOOD OR EVIL IN THE INTENTION?

We proceed thus to the Eighth Article:—

Objection 1. It would seem that the degree of goodness in the will depends on the degree of good in the intention. For on *Matt.* xii. 35 (*A good man out of the good treasure of his heart bringeth forth that which is good*) the *Gloss* says: *A man does as much good as he intends.*[28] But the intention gives goodness not only to the external action, but also to the will, as was stated above. Therefore the goodness of a man's will is according to the goodness of his intention.

Obj. 2. Further, if you add to the cause, you add to the effect. But the goodness of the intention is the cause of the good will. Therefore a man's will is good, according as his intention is good.

Obj. 3. Further, in evil actions, a man sins in proportion to his intention; for if a man were to throw a stone with a murderous intention, he would be guilty of murder. Therefore, for the same reason, in good actions, the will is good in proportion to the good intended.

On the contrary, The intention can be good, while the will is evil. Therefore, for the same reason, the intention can be better, and the will less good.

I answer that, In regard to both the act and the intention of the end, we may consider a twofold quantity: one, on the part of the object, in so far as a man wills or does a good that is greater; the other, taken from the intensity of the act, according as a man wills or acts intensely; and this is greater on the part of the agent.

---

[28] *Glossa interl.* (V, 43r).

If, then, we speak of these respective quantities from the point of view of the object, it is evident that the quantity in the act does not depend on the quantity in the intention. With regard to the external act, this may happen in two ways. First, because the object that is ordained to the intended end is not proportioned to that end: *e.g.*, if a man were to give ten pounds, he could not realize his intention, if he intended to buy a thing worth a hundred pounds. Secondly, because of the obstacles that may supervene in regard to the exterior action, which we are unable to remove: *e.g.*, a man intends to go to Rome, and encounters obstacles, which prevent him from going.—On the other hand, with regard to the interior act of the will, this happens in only one way, because the interior acts of the will· are in our power, whereas the external acts are not. But the will can will an object that is not proportioned to the intended end, and thus the will that tends to that object, considered absolutely, is not as good as the intention. Yet because the intention also belongs, in a way, to the act of the will, inasmuch, namely, as it is the principle of the act, it happens that the quantity of goodness in the intention redounds upon the act of the will; that is to say, in so far as the will wills some great good for an end, although that by which it wills to gain so great a good is not proportioned to that good.

But if we consider the quantity in the intention and in the act according to their respective intensity, then the intensity of the intention redounds upon the interior act and the exterior act of the will; for the intention stands in relation to both of them as a form, as is clear from what was said above.[29] And yet considered materially, while the intention is intense, the interior or exterior act may be not so intense, materially speaking: *e.g.*, when a man does not will with as much intensity to take medicine as he wills to regain health. Nevertheless, the very fact of intending health intensely redounds, as a formal principle, upon the intense volition of medicine.

We must observe, however, that the intensity of the interior or exterior act may be referred to the intention as its object: *e.g.*, when a man intends to will intensely, or to do something intensely. And yet it does not follow that he wills or acts intensely, because the quantity of goodness in the interior or exterior act does not depend on the quantity of the good intended, as we have said above. Hence it is that a man does not merit as much as he intends to merit, because the quantity of merit is measured by the intensity of the act, as we shall show later on.[30]

Reply Obj. 1. The *Gloss* quoted speaks of good as in the estimation of God, Who considers principally the intention of the end. Therefore another *Gloss* says on the same passage that *the treasure of the heart is the intention, according to which God judges our works.*[31] For the goodness of the intention, as we have stated above, redounds in a way upon the goodness

---

[29] Q. 12, a. 4; q. 18, a. 6.   [30] Q. 20, a. 4; q. 114, a. 4.   [31] *Glossa ordin.*, super *Matt.*, XII, 35 (V, 43A).—Cf. Rhabanus Maurus, *In Matt.*, IV, super XII, 35 (PL 107, 931).

of the will, which makes even the external act to be meritorious in God's sight.

Reply Obj. 2. The goodness of the intention is not the whole cause of a good will. Hence the argument does not hold.

Reply Obj. 3. The mere malice of the intention suffices to make the will evil; and therefore the will is as evil as the intention is evil. But the same reasoning does not apply to goodness, as we have stated above.

Ninth Article

WHETHER THE GOODNESS OF THE WILL DEPENDS ON
ITS CONFORMITY TO THE DIVINE WILL?

We proceed thus to the Ninth Article:—

Objection 1. It would seem that the goodness of the human will does not depend on its conformity to the divine will. For it is impossible for man's will to be conformed to the divine will, as appears from the word of *Isaias* (lv. 9): *As the heavens are exalted above the earth, so are My ways exalted above your ways, and My thoughts above your thoughts.* If, therefore, the goodness of the will depended on its conformity to the divine will, it would follow that it is impossible for man's will to be good. Which is inadmissible.

Obj. 2. Further, just as our wills arise from the divine will, so does our knowledge flow from the divine knowledge. But our knowledge does not require to be conformed to God's knowledge, since God knows many things that we know not. Therefore there is no need for our will to be conformed to the divine will.

Obj. 3. Further, the will is a principle of action. But our action cannot be conformed to God's. Therefore neither can our will be conformed to His.

On the contrary, It is written (*Matt.* xxvi. 39): *Not as I will, but as Thou wilt*; which words He said because *He wishes man to be upright and to tend to God,* as Augustine expounds in the *Enchiridion.*[32] But the rectitude of the will is its goodness. Therefore the goodness of the will depends on its conformity to the divine will.

I answer that, As we have stated above, the goodness of the will depends on the intention of the end. Now the last end of the human will is the highest good, namely, God, as was stated above.[33] Therefore the goodness of the human will requires it to be ordained to the highest good. Now this Good is primarily and essentially compared to the divine will as its proper object. Now that which is first in any genus is the measure and rule of all that belongs to that genus. But everything attains to rectitude and goodness in so far as it is in accord with its proper measure. Therefore, in order that man's will be good it needs to be conformed to the divine will.

Reply Obj. 1. The human will cannot be conformed to the will of God so

---

[32] Cf. *Enarr. in Psalm.,* super XXXII, 1 (PL 36, 278).   [33] Q. 1, a. 8; q. 3, a. 1.

as to equal it, but only so as to imitate it. In like manner, human knowledge is conformed to the divine knowledge in so far as it knows truth, and human action is conformed to the divine in so far as it is becoming to the agent,—and this by way of imitation, not by way of equality.

From the above may be gathered the replies to the Second and Third Objections.

Tenth Article

WHETHER IT IS NECESSARY FOR THE HUMAN WILL, IN ORDER TO BE GOOD, TO BE CONFORMED TO THE DIVINE WILL AS REGARDS THE THING WILLED?

We proceed thus to the Tenth Article:—

Objection 1. It would seem that the human will need not always ·be conformed to the divine will as regards the thing willed. For we cannot will what we do not know, since the apprehended good is the object of the will. But in many things we do not know what God wills. Therefore the human will cannot be conformed to the divine will as to the thing willed.

Obj. 2. Further, God wills to damn the man whom He foresees about to die in mortal sin. If, therefore, man were bound to conform his will to the divine will, in the point of the thing willed, it would follow that a man is bound to will his own damnation. Which is inadmissible.

Obj. 3. Further, no one is bound to will what is against filial piety. But if man were to will what God wills, this would sometimes be contrary to filial piety. For instance, when God wills the death of a father, if his son were to will it also, it would be against filial piety. Therefore man is not bound to conform his will to the divine will, as to the thing willed.

On the contrary, [1] On *Ps.* xxxii. 1 (*Praise becometh the upright*) the *Gloss* says: *That man has an upright heart who wills what God wills.*[34] But everyone is bound to have an upright heart. Therefore everyone is bound to will what God wills.

[2] Moreover, the will takes its form from the object, as does every act. If, therefore, man is bound to conform his will to the divine will, it follows that he is bound to conform it as to the thing willed.

[3] Moreover, opposition of wills arises because men will different things. But whoever has a will in opposition to the divine will, has an evil will. Therefore whoever does not conform his will to the divine will, as to the thing willed, has an evil will.

I answer that, As is evident from what has been said above, the will tends to its object according as it is proposed by the reason. Now a thing may be considered in various ways by the reason, so as to appear good from one point of view, and not good from another point of view. Therefore, if a

---

[34] *Glossa ordin.* (III, 130A); Peter Lombard, *In Psalm.,* super XXXII, 1 (PL 191, 325).—St. Augustine, *Enarr. in Psalm.,* super XXXII, 1 (PL 36, 277).

man's will wills a thing to be according as it appears to be good, his will is good; and the will of another man, who wills that thing not to be, according as it appears evil, is also good. Thus a judge has a good will in willing a thief to be put to death, because this is just; while the will of another (*e.g.*, the thief's wife or son) who wishes him not to be put to death, inasmuch as killing is a natural evil, is also good.

Now since the will follows the apprehension of the reason or intellect, the more universal the nature of the apprehended good, the more universal the good to which the will tends. This is evident in the example given above, because the judge has care of the common good, which is justice, and therefore he wishes the thief's death, which has the nature of good in relation to the common welfare; whereas the thief's wife has to consider the private good of the family, and from this point of view she wishes her husband, the thief, not to be put to death. Now the good of the whole universe is that which is apprehended by God, Who is the Maker and Governor of all things. Hence, whatever He wills, He wills it under the nature of the common good; and this is His own Goodness, which is the good of the whole universe. On the other hand, the apprehension of a creature, according to its nature, is of some particular good, proportioned to that nature. Now a thing may happen to be good under a particular aspect, and yet not good under a universal aspect, or *vice versa*, as stated above. And therefore it happens that a certain will is good from willing something considered under a particular aspect, which yet God does not will under a universal aspect, and *vice versa*. And hence, too, it is that various wills of various men can be good in respect of opposite things, inasmuch as, under various aspects, they wish a particular thing to be or not to be.

But a man's will is not right in willing a particular good, unless he refer it to the common good as an end, since even the natural appetite of each part is ordained to the common good of the whole. Now it is the end that supplies the formal reason, as it were, of willing whatever is directed to the end. Consequently, in order that a man will some particular good with a right will, he must will that particular good materially, and the divine and universal good, formally. Therefore the human will is bound to be conformed to the divine will, as to that which is willed formally, for it is bound to will the divine and universal good; but not as to that which is willed materially, for the reason given above.

At the same time, in both these respects the human will is conformed to the divine will in a certain degree. For, inasmuch as it is conformed to the divine will in the common nature of the thing willed, it is conformed thereto in the point of the last end. But inasmuch as it is not conformed to the divine will in the thing willed materially, it is conformed to that will considered as the efficient cause; for the proper inclination consequent upon nature, or upon the particular apprehension of some particular thing, comes to a thing from God as its efficient cause. Hence it is customary to say that, in this respect, a man's will is conformed to the divine will, because it wills what God wills him to will.

There is yet another kind of conformity in respect of the formal cause, consisting in man's willing something from charity, as God wills it. And this conformity is also reduced to the formal conformity, that is based on the relation to the last end, which is the proper object of charity.

Reply Obj. 1. We can know in a general way what God wills. For we know that whatever God wills, He wills it under the aspect of good. Consequently, whoever wills a thing under any aspect of good, has a will conformed to the divine will, as to the nature of the thing willed. But we do not know what God wills in particular, and in this respect we are not bound to conform our will to the divine will.

But in the state of glory, every one will see in each thing that he wills the relation of that thing to what God wills in that particular matter. Consequently, he will conform his will to God in all things not only formally, but also materially.

Reply Obj. 2. God does not will the damnation of a man, considered precisely as damnation, nor a man's death, considered precisely as death, because, *He wills all men to be saved* (*1 Tim.* ii. 4); but He wills such things under the nature of justice. Therefore, in regard to such things it suffices for man to will the upholding of God's justice and of the natural order.

Therefore the reply to the Third Objection is evident.

To the first argument advanced in a contrary sense, it should be said that a man who conforms his will to God's, with reference to the reason for the thing willed, wills what God wills, more than the man who conforms his will to God's, with reference to the very thing willed; because the will tends more to the end than to that which is for the sake of the end.

To the second, it must be replied that the species and form of an act is taken from the object considered formally, rather than from the object considered materially.

To the third, it must be said that there is no opposition of wills when several people desire different things, but not under the same aspect; but there is opposition of wills when, under one and the same aspect, one man wills a thing which another wills not. But there is no question of this here.

ON THE GOODNESS AND MALICE OF EXTERNAL HUMAN ACTS

(In Six Articles)

WE must next consider goodness and malice as to external acts, under which head there are six points of inquiry: (1) Whether goodness and malice are first in the act of the will, or in the external act? (2) Whether the whole goodness or malice of the external act depends on the goodness of the will? (3) Whether the goodness and malice of the interior act are the same as those of the external act? (4) Whether the external act adds any goodness or malice to that of the interior act? (5) Whether the consequences of an external act increase its goodness or malice? (6) Whether one and the same external act can be both good and evil?

First Article

WHETHER GOODNESS OR MALICE IS FIRST IN THE ACT OF THE WILL, OR IN THE EXTERNAL ACT?

We proceed thus to the First Article:—

Objection 1. It would seem that good and evil are in the external act prior to being in the act of the will. For the will derives goodness from its object, as was stated above.[1] But the external act is the object of the interior act of the will, for a man is said to will to commit a theft, or to will to give an alms. Therefore good and evil are in the external act, prior to being in the act of the will.

Obj. 2. Further, good belongs first to the end, since what is directed to the end has the nature of good from its relation to the end. Now whereas the act of the will cannot be an end, as was stated above,[2] the act of another power can be an end. Therefore good is in the act of some other power prior to being in the act of the will.

Obj. 3. Further, the act of the will is related as a form to the external act, as was stated above.[3] But that which is formal is subsequent, since form is something added to matter. Therefore good and evil are in the external act prior to being in the act of the will.

On the contrary, Augustine says that *it is by the will that we sin, and that we behave rightly.*[4] Therefore moral good and evil are first in the will.

[1] Q. 19, a. 1 and 2.   [2] Q. 1, a. 1, ad 2.   [3] Q. 18, a. 6.   [4] *Retract.,* I, 9, (PL 32, 596).

I answer that, External acts may be said to be good or evil in two ways. First, in regard to their genus, and the circumstances connected with them. Thus, the giving of alms, if the required conditions be observed, is said to be good. Secondly, a thing is said to be good or evil from its relation to the end; and thus the giving of alms for vainglory is said to be evil. Now, since the end is the will's proper object, it is evident that the nature of good or evil, which the external act derives from its relation to the end, is to be found first of all in the act of the will, whence it passes to the external act. On the other hand, the goodness or malice which the external act has of itself, in that it is about due matter and is attended by due circumstances, is not derived from the will, but rather from the reason. Consequently, if we consider the goodness of the external act in so far as it comes from reason's ordination and apprehension, it is prior to the goodness of the act of the will; but if we consider it in so far as it is in the execution of the act done, it is subsequent to the goodness of the will, which is its principle.

Reply Obj. 1. The exterior act is the object of the will inasmuch as it is proposed to the will by the reason as a good apprehended and ordained by the reason; and thus it is prior to the good in the act of the will. But inasmuch as it is found in the execution of the act, it is an effect of the will, and is subsequent to the will.

Reply Obj. 2. The end precedes in the order of intention, but follows in the order of execution.

Reply Obj. 3. A form, as received into matter, is subsequent to matter in the order of generation, although it precedes it in the order of nature; but inasmuch as it is in the active cause, it precedes in every way. Now the will is compared to the exterior act as its efficient cause. Therefore the goodness of the act of the will, as existing in the active cause, is the form of the exterior act.

Second Article

WHETHER THE WHOLE GOODNESS AND MALICE OF THE EXTER-
NAL ACT DEPEND ON THE GOODNESS OF THE WILL?

We proceed thus to the Second Article:—

Objection 1. It would seem that the whole goodness and malice of the external act depends on the goodness of the will. For it is written (*Matt.* vii. 18): *A good tree cannot bring forth evil fruit, neither can an evil tree bring forth good fruit.* But, according to the *Gloss,* the tree signifies the will, and fruit signifies works.[5] Therefore, it is impossible for the interior act of the will to be good, and the external act evil, or *vice versa.*

Obj. 2. Further, Augustine says that there is no sin without the will.[6] If, therefore, there is no sin in the will, there will be none in the external

---

[5] *Glossa ordin.,* super *Matt.,* VII, 18 (V, 29B).—St. Augustine, *Contra Iulian.,* I, 8 (PL 44, 667).   [6] *Retract.,* I, 9 (PL 32, 596).

act. And so the whole goodness or malice of the external act depends on the will.

Obj. 3. Further, the good and evil of which we are speaking now are differences of the moral act. Now differences make an essential division in a genus, according to the Philosopher.[7] Since, therefore, an act is moral from being voluntary, it seems that goodness and malice in an act are derived from the will alone.

On the contrary, Augustine says that *there are some actions which neither a good end nor a good will can make good.*[8]

I answer that, As we have stated above, we may consider a twofold goodness or malice in the external act: one, according to due matter and circumstances, the other, according to the order to the end. And that which is according to the order to the end depends entirely on the will, while that which is according to due matter or circumstances depends on the reason; and on this goodness depends the goodness of the will, in so far as the will tends towards it.

Now it must be observed, as was noted above,[9] that for a thing to be evil, one single defect suffices, whereas for it to be good absolutely, it is not enough for it to be good in one point only, it must be good in every respect. If, therefore, the will be good both from its proper object and from its end, it follows that the external act is good. But if the will be good from its intention of the end, this is not enough to make the external act good; and if the will be evil either by reason of its intention of the end, or by reason of the act willed, it follows that the external act is evil.

Reply Obj. 1. If the good tree be taken to signify a good will, it must be in so far as the will derives goodness from the act willed and from the end intended.

Reply Obj. 2. A man sins by his will, not only when he wills an evil end, but also when he wills an evil act.

Reply Obj. 3. Voluntariness applies not only to the interior act of the will, but also to external acts, inasmuch as they proceed from the will and the reason. Consequently, the difference of good and evil is applicable to both the interior and external act.

Third Article

WHETHER THE GOODNESS AND MALICE OF THE EXTERNAL ACT ARE THE SAME AS THOSE OF THE INTERIOR ACT?

We proceed thus to the Third Article:—

Objection 1. It would seem that the goodness and malice of the interior act of the will are not the same as those of the external act. For the principle of the interior act is the interior apprehensive or appetitive power of

---

[7] *Metaph.,* VI, 12 (1038a 9).   [8] *Contra Mendacium.,* VII (PL 40, 528).   [9] Q. 19, a. 6, ad 1.

the soul; whereas the principle of the external act is the power that accomplishes the movement. Now where the principles of action are different, the acts themselves are different. But it is the act which is the subject of goodness or malice; and the same accident cannot be in different subjects. Therefore the goodness of the interior act cannot be the same as that of the external act.

Obj. 2. Further, *A virtue makes that which has it to be good, and renders its action good also.*[10] But the intellectual virtue in the commanding power is distinct from the moral virtue in the power commanded, as is declared in *Ethics* ii.[11] Therefore the goodness of the interior act, which belongs to the commanding power, is distinct from the goodness of the external act, which belongs to the power commanded.

Obj. 3. Further, the same thing cannot be cause and effect, since nothing is its own cause. But the goodness of the interior act is the cause of the goodness of the external act, or *vice versa,* as was stated above. Therefore it is not the same goodness in each.

On the contrary, It was shown above that the act of the will is as the form of the external act.[12] Now that which results from the material and formal elements is one thing. Therefore there is but one goodness of the internal and external act.

I answer that, As we have stated above, the interior act of the will and the external act, considered morally, are one act.[13] Now it happens sometimes that one and the same individual act has several aspects of goodness or malice, and sometimes that it has but one. Hence we must say that sometimes the goodness or malice of the interior act is the same as that of the external act, and sometimes not. For, as we have already said, these two goodnesses or malices, of the internal and external acts, are ordered to one another. Now it may happen, in things that are subordinate to something else, that a thing is good merely from being subordinate: *e.g.,* a bitter draught is good merely because it procures health. Therefore there are not two goodnesses, one the goodness of health, and the other the goodness of the draught; but one and the same. On the other hand, it happens sometimes that that which is subordinate to something else has some aspect of goodness in itself, besides the fact of its being subordinate to some other good: *e.g.,* a palatable medicine can be considered as a pleasurable good, besides being conducive to health.

We must, therefore, say that when the external act derives goodness or malice only from its relation to the end, then there is but one and the same goodness of the act of the will which of itself refers to the end, and of the external act, which refers to the end through the medium of the act of the will. But when the external act has goodness or malice of itself, *i.e.,* according to its matter and circumstances, then the goodness of the exter-

---

[10] Aristotle, *Eth.* II, 6 (1106a 15).   [11] Cf. *op. cit.,* I, 13 (1103a 3).   [12] Q. 18, a. 6.   [13] Q. 17, a. 4.

nal act is distinct from the goodness of the will derived from the end; yet so that the goodness of the end passes into the external act, and the goodness of the matter and circumstances passes into the act of the will, as we have stated above.

Reply Obj. 1. This argument proves that the internal and external act are different as realities; yet distinct as they are in that respect, they combine to form one thing in the moral order, as we have stated above.[14]

Reply Obj. 2. As is stated in *Ethics* vi.,[15] a moral virtue is ordered to the act of that virtue, which act is the end, as it were, of that virtue; whereas prudence, which is in the reason, is ordered to things directed to the end. For this reason, various virtues are necessary. But right reason in regard to the very end of a virtue has no other goodness than the goodness of that virtue, in so far as the goodness of the reason is participated in each virtue.

Reply Obj. 3. When a thing is derived by one thing from another as from a univocal efficient cause, then it is not the same in both; and thus, when a hot thing heats, the heat of the heater is distinct from the heat of the thing heated, although it be the same specifically. But when a thing is derived by one thing from another according to analogy or proportion, then it is one and the same in both; and thus, the healthiness which is in medicine or urine is derived from the healthiness of the animal's body; nor is health, as applied to urine and medicine, distinct from health as applied to the body of an animal, of which health medicine is the cause, and urine the sign. It is in this way that the goodness of the external action is derived from the goodness of the will, and *vice versa*, viz., according to the order of one to the other.

Fourth Article

WHETHER THE EXTERNAL ACT ADDS ANY GOODNESS OR MALICE TO THAT OF THE INTERIOR ACT?

We proceed thus to the Fourth Article:—

Objection 1. It would seem that the external act does not add any goodness or malice to that of the interior act. For Chrysostom says: *It is the will that is rewarded for doing good, or punished for doing evil.*[16] Now works are the witnesses of the will. Therefore God seeks for works not on His own account, in order to know how to judge, but for the sake of others, that all may understand how just He is. But good or evil is to be estimated according to God's judgment rather than according to the judgment of man. Therefore the external act adds no goodness or malice to that of the interior act.

Obj. 2. Further, the goodness and malice of the interior and external

---

[14] *Ibid.*   [15] Aristotle, *Eth.*, VI, 12 (1144a 8).   [16] *In Matt.*, hom. XIX (PG 57, 274).

acts are one and the same, as was stated above. But increase is the addition of one thing to another. Therefore the external act does not add to the goodness or malice of the interior act.

Obj. 3. Further, the entire goodness of created things does not add to the divine goodness, because it is entirely derived therefrom. But sometimes the entire goodness of the external act is derived from the goodness of the interior act, and sometimes conversely, as was stated above. Therefore, neither of them adds to the goodness or malice of the other.

On the contrary, Every agent intends to attain good and avoid evil. If, therefore, by the external act no further goodness or malice be added, it is to no purpose that he who has a good or an evil will does a good deed or refrains from an evil deed. Which is unreasonable.

I answer that, If we speak of the goodness which the external act derives from the will tending to the end, then the external act adds nothing to this goodness, unless it happens that the will in itself is made better in good things, or worse in evil things. This, it seems, may happen in three ways. First in point of number. If, for instance, a man wishes to do something with a good or an evil end in view, and does not do it then, but afterwards wills and does it, the act of his will is doubled, and a double good or a double evil is the result.—Secondly, in point of extension. Suppose, for instance, that a man wishes to do something for a good or an evil end, and is hindered by some obstacle, whereas another man perseveres in the movement of the will until he accomplish it in deed. In such a case, it is evident that the will of the latter is more lasting in good or evil, and, in this respect, is better or worse.—Thirdly, in point of intensity. For there are certain external acts which, in so far as they are pleasurable or painful, are such as naturally to make the will more intense or less so; and it is evident that the more intensely the will tends to good or evil, the better or worse it is.

On the other hand, if we speak of the goodness which the external act derives from its matter and due circumstances, thus it stands in relation to the will as its term and end. And in this way it adds to the goodness or malice of the will, because every inclination or movement is perfected by attaining its end or reaching its term. Therefore the will is not perfect, unless it be such that, given the opportunity, it realizes the operation. But if this prove impossible, as long as the will is perfect, so as to realize the operation if it could, the lack of the perfection derived from the external action is absolutely involuntary. Now just as the involuntary deserves neither punishment nor reward in the accomplishment of good or evil deeds, so neither does it lessen reward or punishment, if a man through absolute involuntariness fail to do good or evil.

Reply Obj. 1. Chrysostom is speaking of the case where a man's will is completed and does not refrain from the act save through the impossibility of achievement.

Reply Obj. 2. This argument applies to that goodness which the external act derives from the will as tending to the end. But the goodness which the external act takes from its matter and circumstances is distinct from that which it derives from the end; but it is not distinct from that which it has from the very act willed, to which it stands in the relation of measure and cause, as was stated above.

From this the reply to the Third Objection is evident.

Fifth Article

WHETHER THE CONSEQUENCES OF THE EXTERNAL ACT INCREASE ITS GOODNESS OR MALICE?

We proceed thus to the Fifth Article:—

Objection 1. It would seem that the consequences of the external act increase its goodness or malice. For the effect pre-exists virtually in its cause. But the consequences result from the act as an effect from its cause. Therefore they pre-exist virtually in the acts. Now a thing is judged to be good or bad according to its virtue, since a virtue *makes that which has it to be good.*[17] Therefore the consequences increase the goodness or malice of an act.

Obj. 2. Further, the good acts of his hearers are consequences resulting from the words of a preacher. But such goods as these redound to the merit of the preacher, as is evident from *Phil.* iv. 1: *My dearly beloved brethren, my joy and my crown.* Therefore the consequences of an act increase its goodness or malice.

Obj. 3. Further, punishment is not increased unless the fault increases; and so it is written (*Deut.* xxv. 2): *According to the measure of the sin shall the measure also of the stripes be.* But the punishment is increased because of the consequences, for it is written (*Exod.* xxi. 29): *But if the ox was wont to push with his horn yesterday and the day before, and they warned his master, and he did not shut him up, and he shall kill a man or a woman, then the ox shall be stoned, and his owner also shall be put to death.* But he would not have been put to death, if the ox, although he had not been shut up, had not killed a man. Therefore the consequences increase the goodness or malice of an act.

Obj. 4. Further, if a man do something which may cause death, by striking, or by sentencing, and if death does not ensue, he does not contract irregularity; but he would if death were to ensue. Therefore the consequences of an act increase its goodness or malice.

On the contrary, The consequences do not make an act that was evil, to be good; nor one that was good, to be evil. For instance, if a man give an alms to a poor man who makes bad use of the alms by committing a sin, this does not undo the good done by the giver; and, in like manner,

[17] Aristotle, *Eth.*, II, 6 (1106a 15).

if a man bear patiently a wrong done to him, the wrongdoer is not thereby excused. Therefore the consequences of an act do not increase its goodness or malice.

I answer that, The consequences of an act are either foreseen or not. If they are foreseen, it is evident that they increase the goodness or malice. For when a man foresees that many evils may follow from his act, and yet does not therefore desist from it, this shows his will to be all the more inordinate.

But if the consequences are not foreseen, we must make a distinction. For if they follow from the nature of the action, and in the majority of cases, in this respect the consequences increase the goodness or malice of that action; for it is evident that an action is of its nature better, if better results can follow from it, and of its nature worse, if it is of a nature to produce worse results. On the other hand, if the consequences follow by accident and seldom, then they do not increase the goodness or malice of the act; for we do not judge of a thing according to that which belongs to it by accident, but only according to that which belongs to it essentially.

Reply Obj. 1. The virtue of a cause is measured by its essential effect, not by its accidental effects.

Reply Obj. 2. The good acts done by the hearers result from the preacher's words as an essential effect. Hence they redound to the merit of the preacher, and especially so when such is his intention.

Reply Obj. 3. The consequences for which that man is ordered to be punished both follow from the nature of the cause, and are supposed to be foreseen. For this reason they are reckoned as punishable.

Reply Obj. 4. This argument would hold good if irregularity were the result of a fault. But it is not the result of a fault, but of a fact, because of an impediment to the sacrament.

Sixth Article

WHETHER ONE AND THE SAME EXTERNAL ACT CAN BE BOTH GOOD AND EVIL?

We proceed thus to the Sixth Article:—

Objection 1. It would seem that one and the same external act can be both good and evil. For *movement, if continuous, is one and the same.*[18] But one continuous movement can be both good and bad: *e.g.,* a man may go to Church continuously, intending at first vainglory, and afterwards the service of God. Therefore one and the same act can be both good and evil.

Obj. 2. Further, according to the Philosopher, action and passion are one act.[19] But the passion may be good, as Christ's was; and the action evil, as that of the Jews. Therefore one and the same act can be both good and evil.

[18] Aristotle, *Phys.,* V, 4 (228a 20).   [19] *Op. cit.,* III, 3 (202a 18).

Obj. 3. Further, since a servant is an instrument, as it were, of his master, the servant's action is his master's, just as the action of a tool is the workman's action. But it may happen that the servant's action results from his master's good will, and is therefore good: and from the evil will of the servant, and is therefore evil. Therefore the same act can be both good and evil.

On the contrary, The same thing cannot be the subject of contraries. But good and evil are contraries. Therefore the same act cannot be both good and evil.

I answer that, Nothing hinders a thing from being one, in so far as it is in one genus, and manifold, in so far as it is referred to another genus. Thus a continuous surface is one, considered as in the genus of quantity; and yet it is manifold, considered as to the genus of color, if it be partly white and partly black. Accordingly, nothing hinders an act from being one, considered in its reality, whereas it is not one, considered in the moral order; and *vice versa,* as we have stated above.[20] For continuous walking is one act, considered in its reality, but it may resolve itself into many acts, considered in the moral order, if a change take place in the walker's will; for the will is the principle of moral acts. If, therefore, we consider one act in the moral order, it is impossible for it to be morally both good and evil. Whereas if it be one as to its reality and not as to its moral constitution, it can be both good and evil.

Reply Obj. 1. This continual movement which proceeds from various intentions, although it is one in its reality, is not one in the point of moral unity.

Reply Obj. 2. Action and passion belong to the moral order in so far as they are voluntary. Therefore, in so far as they are voluntary in relation to diverse wills, they are two distinct things, and good can be in one of them while evil is in the other.

Reply Obj. 3. The act of the servant, in so far as it proceeds from the will of the servant, is not the master's act; but only in so far as it proceeds from the master's command. Therefore the evil will of the servant does not make the act evil in this respect.

[20] Q. 18, a. 7, ad 1.

ON THE CONSEQUENCES OF HUMAN ACTS BY REASON OF THEIR GOODNESS AND MALICE

(*In Four Articles*)

WE have now to consider the consequences of human acts by reason of their goodness and malice; and under this head there are four points of inquiry: (1) Whether a human act is right or sinful by reason of its being good or evil? (2) Whether it thereby deserves praise or blame? (3) Whether, accordingly, it is meritorious or demeritorious? (4) Whether it is, accordingly, meritorious or demeritorious before God?

First Article

WHETHER A HUMAN ACT IS RIGHT OR SINFUL IN SO FAR AS IT IS GOOD OR EVIL?

We proceed thus to the First Article:—

Objection 1. It seems that a human act is not right or sinful, in so far as it is good or evil. For *monsters are the sins of nature.*[1] But monsters are not acts, but things engendered outside the order of nature. Now things that are produced according to art and reason imitate the things that are produced according to nature.[2] Therefore an act is not sinful by reason of its being inordinate and evil.

Obj. 2. Further, as is stated in *Physics* ii., sin occurs in nature and art, when the end intended by nature or art is not attained.[3] But the goodness or malice of a human act depends, before all, on the intention of the end, and on its achievement. Therefore it seems that the malice of an act does not make it sinful.

Obj. 3. Further, if the malice of an act makes it sinful, it follows that wherever there is evil, there is sin. But this is false, since punishment is not a sin, although it is an evil. Therefore an act is not sinful by reason of its being evil.

On the contrary, As was shown above,[4] the goodness of a human act depends principally on the eternal law, and consequently its malice consists in its being in disaccord with the eternal law. But this is the very nature of sin, for Augustine says that *sin is a word, deed or desire in*

---

[1] Aristotle, *Phys.*, II, 8 (199b 4). [2] *Ibid.* (199a 16). [3] *Ibid.* (199a 33).
[4] Q. 19, a. 4.

opposition to the eternal law.[5] Therefore a human action is sinful by reason of its being evil.

I answer that, Evil is more comprehensive than sin, as also is good than right. For every privation of good, in whatever subject, is an evil, whereas sin consists properly in an act done for a certain end, and lacking due order to that end. Now the due order to an end is measured by some rule. In things that act according to nature, this rule is the power itself of nature that inclines them to that end. When, therefore, an act proceeds from a natural power, in accord with the natural inclination to an end, then the act is said to be right; for the mean does not exceed its limits, viz., the action does not swerve from the order of its active principle to the end. But when an act strays from this rectitude, it comes under the notion of sin.

Now in those things that are done by the will, the proximate rule is the human reason, while the supreme rule is the eternal law. When, therefore, a human act tends to the end according to the order of reason and of the eternal law, then that act is right; but when it turns aside from that rectitude, then it is said to be a sin. Now it is evident, from what has been said,[6] that every voluntary act that turns aside from the order of reason and of the eternal law is evil, and that every good act is in accord with reason and the eternal law. Hence it follows that a human act is right or sinful by reason of its being good or evil.

Reply Obj. 1. Monsters are called sins, inasmuch as they result from a sin in nature's act.

Reply Obj. 2. The end is twofold, namely, the last end, and the proximate end. In the sin of nature, the act does indeed fail in respect of the last end, which is the perfection of the thing generated, but it does not fail in respect of any proximate end whatever; for when nature works it forms something. In like manner, the sin of the will always fails as regards the last end intended, because no voluntary evil action can be ordained to happiness, which is the last end, even though it does not fail in respect of some proximate end intended and achieved by the will. Hence, since the very intention of this end is ordained to the last end, this same intention can contain the nature of rectitude or of sin.

Reply Obj. 3. Each thing is ordered to its end by its act, and therefore sin, which consists in deviating from the order to the end, consists properly in an act. On the other hand, punishment refers to the person of the sinner, as was stated in the First Part.[7]

---

[5] *Contra Faust.,* XXII, 27 (PL 42, 418).   [6] Q. 19, a. 3 and 4.   [7] *S. T.,* I, q. 48, a. 5, ad 4; a. 6, ad 3.

Second Article

WHETHER A HUMAN ACT DESERVES PRAISE OR BLAME, BY REASON OF ITS BEING GOOD OR EVIL?

We proceed thus to the Second Article:—

Objection 1. It would seem that a human act does not deserve praise or blame by reason of its being good or evil. For *sin happens even in things done by nature,*[8] and yet natural things are not deserving of praise or blame.[9] Therefore a human act does not deserve blame by reason of its being evil or sinful, and, consequently, neither does it deserve praise by reason of its being good.

Obj. 2. Further, just as sin occurs in moral acts, so does it happen in the productions of art; because, as it is stated in *Physics* ii., *it is a sin in a grammarian to write badly, and in a doctor to give the wrong medicine.*[10] But the artist is not blamed for making something bad, because the artist's work is such that he can produce a good or a bad thing, just as he pleases. Therefore it seems that neither is there any reason for blaming a moral act on the ground that it is evil.

Obj. 3. Further, Dionysius says that evil is *weak and incapable.*[11] But weakness or inability either takes away or diminishes guilt. Therefore a human act does not incur guilt from being evil.

On the contrary, The Philosopher says that *virtuous deeds deserve praise, while deeds that are opposed to virtue deserve censure and blame.*[12] But good acts are virtuous, because *virtue makes that which has it good, and makes its action good;*[13] and hence acts opposed to virtue are evil. Therefore a human act deserves praise or blame through being good or evil.

I answer that, Just as evil is more comprehensive than sin, so is sin more comprehensive than guilt [*culpa*]. For an act is said to deserve praise or blame [*culpabilis*] from its being imputed to the agent, since to praise or to blame means nothing else than to impute to someone the malice or goodness of his act. Now an act is imputed to an agent when it is in his power, so that he has dominion over it; and this is the case in all voluntary acts, because it is through his will that man has dominion over his acts, as was made clear above.[14] Hence it follows that, in voluntary acts alone, good and evil constitute the nature of praise or blame; and in such acts, evil, sin and guilt are one and the same thing.

Reply Obj. 1. Natural acts are not in the power of the natural agent, since the act of nature is determined to one course of action. And, therefore, although there may be sin in natural acts, there is no blame.

Reply Obj. 2. Reason stands in different relations to the productions of

---

[8] Aristotle, *Phys.,* II, 8 (199a 33).   [9] Aristotle, *Eth.,* III, 5 (1114a 23).   [10] Aristotle, *Phys.,* II, 8 (199a 33).   [11] *De Div. Nom.,* IV, 31 (PG 3, 732).   [12] *Eth.,* III, 1 (1109b 31); IV, 5 (1127b 4); cf. *De Virt. et Vit.,* I (1249a 28).   [13] Aristotle, *Eth.,* II 6 (1106a 15).   [14] Q. 1, a. 1 and 2.

art, and to moral acts. In matters of art, reason is directed to a particular end, which is something devised by reason; whereas in moral matters, it is directed to the universal end of all human life. Now a particular end is directed to the universal end. Since, therefore, sin is a departure from the order to the end, as was stated above, sin may occur in two ways in the operation of art. First, by a departure from the particular end intended by the artist, and this sin will be proper to the art: *e.g.*, if an artist produce a bad thing, while intending to produce something good, or produce something good, while intending to produce something bad. Secondly, by a departure from the universal end of human life, and then he will be said to sin if he intend to produce a bad work, and does so in effect, so that another is deceived by it. But this sin is not proper to the artist as an artist, but as a man. Consequently, for the former sin the artist is blamed as an artist, while for the latter he is blamed as a man.—On the other hand, in moral matters, where we take into consideration the order of reason to the universal end of human life, sin and evil are always due to a departure from the order of reason to the universal end of human life. Therefore man is blamed for such a sin, both as man and as a moral being. Hence the Philosopher says that *in art, he who sins voluntarily is preferable; but in prudence, as in the moral virtues,* which prudence directs, *he is the reverse.*[15]

Reply Obj. 3. The weakness that occurs in voluntary evils is subject to man's power, and so it neither takes away nor diminishes guilt.

Third Article

WHETHER A HUMAN ACT IS MERITORIOUS OR DEMERITORIOUS IN SO FAR AS IT IS GOOD OR EVIL?

We proceed thus to the Third Article:—

Objection 1. It would seem that a human act is not meritorious or demeritorious because of its goodness or malice. For we speak of merit or demerit in relation to retribution, which has no place save in matters relating to another person. But good or evil acts are not all related to another person, for some are related to the person of the agent. Therefore not every good or evil human act is meritorious or demeritorious.

Obj. 2. Further, no one deserves punishment or reward for doing as he chooses with that of which he is master. Thus, if a man destroys what belongs to him, he is not punished, as if he had destroyed what belongs to another. But man is master of his own acts. Therefore a man does not merit punishment or reward through putting his act to a good or evil purpose.

Obj. 3. Further, if a man acquire some good for himself, he does not on that account deserve to be benefited by another man; and the same ap-

[15] *Eth.*, VI, 5 (1140b 22).

plies to evil. Now a good act is itself a good and a perfection of the agent, while an inordinate act is an evil for him. Therefore a man does not merit or demerit, from the fact that he performed a good or an evil act.

On the contrary, It is written (*Isa.* iii. 10, 11): *Say to the just man that it is well; for he shall eat the fruit of his doings. Woe to the wicked unto evil; for the reward of his hands shall be given him.*

I answer that, We speak of merit and demerit in relation to retribution, rendered according to justice. Now, retribution according to justice is rendered to a man by reason of his having done something to another's advantage or hurt. It must, moreover, be observed that every individual member of a society is, in a fashion, a part and member of the whole society. Therefore, any good or evil done to a member of a society redounds to the whole society. So, too, who hurts the hand, hurts the man. When, therefore, anyone does good or evil to another individual, there is a twofold measure of merit or demerit in his act: first, in respect of the retribution owed to him by the individual to whom he has done good or harm; secondly, in respect of the retribution owed to him by the whole of society.—Now when a man orders his act directly to the good or evil of the whole society, retribution is owed to him, before and above all, by the whole society; secondarily, by all the parts of society. Whereas when a man does that which conduces to his own benefit or disadvantage, then again is retribution owed to him, in so far as this too affects the community, according as he is a part of society; although retribution is not due to him in so far as it conduces to the good or harm of an individual, who is identical with the agent (unless, perhaps, he owe retribution to himself, by a sort of resemblance, in so far as a man is said to be just to himself).

It is therefore evident that a good or evil act deserves praise or blame in so far as it is in the power of the will; that it is right or sinful according as it is ordered to the end; and that its merit or demerit depends on the recompense for justice or injustice towards another.

Reply Obj. 1. A man's good or evil acts, although not ordered to the good or evil of another individual, are nevertheless ordered to the good or evil of another, *i.e.,* the community itself.

Reply Obj. 2. Man is master of his actions, and yet, in so far as he belongs to another, *i.e.,* the community, of which he forms part, he merits or demerits inasmuch as he disposes his acts well or ill; just as if he were to dispense well or ill other belongings of his, in respect of which he is bound to serve the community.

Reply Obj. 3. This very good or evil which a man does to himself by his act, redounds to the community, as was stated above.

Fourth Article

WHETHER A HUMAN ACT IS MERITORIOUS OR DEMERITORIOUS BEFORE GOD ACCORDING AS IT IS GOOD OR EVIL?

We proceed thus to the Fourth Article:—

Objection 1. It would seem that man's acts, good or evil, are not meritorious or demeritorious in the sight of God. For, as was stated above, merit and demerit imply a relation to retribution for good or harm done to another. But a man's act, good or evil, does no good or harm to God; for it is written (*Job* xxxv. 6, 7): *If thou sin, what shalt thou hurt Him? . . . And if thou do justly, what shalt thou give Him?* Therefore a human act, good or evil, is not meritorious or demeritorious in the sight of God.

Obj. 2. Further, an instrument acquires no merit or demerit in the sight of him that uses it, because the entire action of the instrument belongs to the user. Now when man acts, he is the instrument of the divine power which is the principal cause of his act; and so it is written (*Isa.* x. 15): *Shall the axe boast itself against him that cutteth with it? Or shall the saw exalt itself against him by whom it is drawn?* Here man as an agent is evidently being compared to an instrument. Therefore, man merits or demerits nothing in God's sight by good or evil acts.

Obj. 3. Further, a human act acquires merit or demerit through being ordered to someone else. But not all human actions are ordered to God. Therefore, not every good or evil act acquires merit or demerit in God's sight.

On the contrary, It is written (*Eccles.* xii. 14): *All things that are done, God will bring into judgment . . . whether it be good, or evil.* Now judgment implies retribution, in respect of which we speak of merit and demerit. Therefore, every human act, both good and evil, acquires merit or demerit in God's sight.

I answer that, A human act, as we have stated above, acquires merit or demerit through being ordered to someone else, either by reason of himself, or by reason of the community; and in both ways our acts, good and evil, acquire merit or demerit in the sight of God. On the part of God Himself, inasmuch as He is man's last end; and it is our duty to refer all our acts to the last end, as was stated above.[16] Consequently, whoever does an evil deed, not referable to God, does not give God the honor due to Him as our last end.—On the part of the whole community of the universe, because, in every community, he who governs the community cares especially for the common good; and hence it is his business to award retribution for such things as are done well or ill in the community. Now God is the governor and ruler of the whole universe, as we have stated in the First Part,[17] and especially of rational creatures. Consequently, it is evident that human

---

[16] Q. 19, a. 10.   [17] *S. T.,* I, q. 103, a. 5.

acts acquire merit or demerit in relation to Him; or otherwise it would follow that God did not have care over human acts.

Reply Obj. 1. God in Himself neither gains nor loses anything by the act of man; but man, for his part, takes something from God, or offers something to Him, when he observes or does not observe the order instituted by God.

Reply Obj. 2. Man is so moved as an instrument by God, that, at the same time, he moves himself by his free choice, as was explained above.[18] Consequently, by his act, he acquires merit or demerit in God's sight.

Reply Obj. 3. Man is not ordained to the body politic according to all that he is and has; and so it does not follow that every act of his acquires merit or demerit in relation to the body politic. But all that man is, and can, and has, must be referred to God; and therefore every act of man, whether good or bad, acquires merit or demerit in the sight of God from the fact of the act itself.

[18] Q. 9, a. 6, ad 3.

FIRST PART OF THE SECOND PART

TREATISE ON HABITS

Question XLIX

ON HABITS IN GENERAL, AS TO THEIR SUBSTANCE
(*In Four Articles*)

AFTER treating of human acts and passions, we now pass on to the consideration of the principles of human acts. And first we must consider intrinsic principles; secondly, the extrinsic principles.[1] The intrinsic principle is power and habit, but as we have treated of powers in the First Part,[2] it remains for us to consider habits. We shall first consider them in general; in the second place we shall consider virtues and vices and other like habits, which are the principles of human acts.[3]

Concerning habits in general there are four points to be considered: First, the substance of habits; second, their subject;[4] third, the cause of their generation, increase and corruption;[5] fourth, how they are distinguished from one another.[6]

Under the first head, there are four points of inquiry: (1) Whether habit is a quality? (2) Whether it is a distinct species of quality? (3) Whether habit implies an order to an act? (4) The necessity of habit.

First Article

WHETHER HABIT IS A QUALITY?

We proceed thus to the First Article:—

Objection 1. It would seem that habit is not a quality. For Augustine says: *This term 'habit' is derived from the verb 'to have.'*[7] But *to have* belongs not only to quality, but also to the other categories, for we speak of ourselves as *having* quantity and money and other like things. Therefore habit is not a quality.

Obj. 2. Further, habit is reckoned as one of the predicaments, as may be clearly seen in the *Categories*.[8] But one predicament is not contained under another. Therefore habit is not a quality.

Obj. 3. Further, *every habit is a disposition,* as is stated in the *Cate-*

---

[1] Q. 90. [2] QQ. 77-83. [3] Q. 55. [4] Q. 50. [5] Q. 51. [6] Q. 54. [7] *Lib. 83 Quaest.*, q. 73 (PL 40, 84). [8] Aristotle, *Cat.*, VIII (8b 27).

gories.[9] Now disposition is *the order of that which has parts,* as is stated in *Metaph.* v.[10] But this belongs to the predicament *Position.* Therefore habit is not a quality.

On the contrary, The Philosopher says, in the *Categories,* that *habit is a quality which it is difficult to change.*[11]

I answer that, The term *habitus* [*habit*] is derived from *habere* [*to have*]. Now habit is taken from this word in two ways: in one way, inasmuch as man, or any other being, is said to *have* something; in another way, inasmuch as something is disposed in a particular way either in regard to itself or in regard to something else.

Concerning the first, we must observe that *to have,* as said in regard to anything that is *had,* is common to the various predicaments. And so the Philosopher puts *to have* among the post-predicaments,[12] so-called because they result from the various predicaments, as, for instance, opposition, priority, posteriority and the like. Now among things which are had, there seems to be this distinction, that there are some in which there is no medium between the one having and that which is had; as, for instance, there is no medium between the subject and quality or quantity. Then there are some in which there is a medium, but only a relation, as, for instance, a man is said to have a companion or a friend. And, further, there are some in which there is a medium, not indeed an action or a passion, but something after the manner of action or passion. Thus, for instance, something adorns or covers, and something else is adorned or covered. Hence the Philosopher says that *a habit is said to be, as it were, an action of the haver and that which is had;*[13] as is the case in those things which we have about ourselves. And therefore these constitute a special genus of things, called the predicament of *habit.* Of this the Philosopher says that *between the clothing which is had and the man who has it, there is a having.*[14]

But if *to have* be taken according as a thing is disposed in a certain way in regard to itself or to something else, in that case habit is a quality, since this mode of having is in respect of some quality. Of this the Philosopher says that *habit is a disposition whereby that which is disposed is disposed well or ill, and this, either in regard to itself or in regard to another. Thus health is a habit.*[15] It is in this sense that we speak of habit now. Therefore we must say that habit is a quality.

Reply Obj. 1. This argument takes *to have* in the general sense; for thus it is common to many predicaments, as we have said.

Reply Obj. 2. This argument takes habit in the sense in which we understand it to be a medium between the haver and that which is had; and in this sense it is a predicament, as we have said.

Reply Obj. 3. Disposition does, indeed, always imply an order of that

---

[9] *Ibid.* (9a 10).   [10] Aristotle, *Metaph.,* IV, 19 (1022b 1).   [11] *Cat.,* VIII (9a 3; a 10).   [12] *Op. cit.,* XI (15b 17).   [13] *Metaph.,* IV, 20 (1022b 4).   [14] *Ibid.* (1022b 7).   [15] *Ibid.* (1022b 10).

which has parts, but this happens in three ways, as the Philosopher goes on at once to say: namely, *either as to place, or as to power, or as to species.*[16] *In saying this,* as Simplicius observes in his *Commentary on the Categories, he includes all dispositions:—bodily dispositions, when he says 'as to place'* and this belongs to the predicament *Position,* which is the order of parts in a place; *when he says 'as to power,' he includes all those dispositions which are in course of formation and not yet arrived at perfect usefulness,* such as inchoate science and virtue; *and when he says, 'as to species,' he includes perfect dispositions, which are called habits,*[17] such as perfected science and virtue.

Second Article

WHETHER HABIT IS A DISTINCT SPECIES OF QUALITY?

We thus proceed to the Second Article:—

Objection 1. It would seem that habit is not a distinct species of quality. Because, as we have said, habit, in so far as it is a quality, is a *disposition whereby that which is disposed is disposed well or ill.* But this happens in regard to any quality, for a thing happens to be well or ill disposed in regard also to shape, and in like manner, in regard to heat and cold, and in regard to all such things. Therefore habit is not a distinct species of quality.

Obj. 2. Further, the Philosopher says in the *Categories* that heat and cold are dispositions or habits, just as sickness and health.[18] But heat and cold are in the third species of quality. Therefore habit or disposition is not distinct from the other species of quality.

Obj. 3. Further, *difficult to change* is not a difference belonging to the predicament of quality, but rather to movement or passion. Now no genus is contracted to a species by a difference of another genus; but *differences should be proper to a genus,* as the Philosopher says in *Metaph.* vii.[19] Therefore, since habit is *a quality difficult to change,* it does not seem to be a distinct species of quality.

On the contrary, The Philosopher says in the *Categories* that *one species of quality is habit and disposition.*[20]

I answer that, The Philosopher in the *Categories* reckons disposition and habit as the first of four species of quality.[21] Now Simplicius, in his *Commentary on the Categories,* explains the difference of these species as follows. He says *that some qualities are natural, and are in their subject in virtue of its nature, and are always there; but some are adventitious, being caused from without, and these can be lost. Now the latter (i.e.,* those which are adventitious) *are habits and dispositions, differing in the point of being*

[16] *Op. cit.,* IV, 19 (1022b 1).   [17] *In Cat.,* VIII (p. 240²⁹⁻³⁴).   [18] *Cat.,* VIII (8b 36).   [19] *Metaph.,* VI, 12 (1038a 9).   [20] Aristotle, *Cat.,* VIII (9a 3; a 10). [21] *Ibid.* (8b 27)

easily or with difficulty lost. As to natural qualities, some belong to a thing in so far as a thing is in a state of potentiality, and thus we have the second species of quality; while others belong to a thing in so far as it is in act, and this either deeply rooted therein or only on its surface. If deeply rooted, we have the third species of quality; if on the surface, we have the fourth species of quality, as shape, and form, which is the shape of an animated being.[22] But this distinction of the species of quality seems unsuitable. For there are many shapes, and passible qualities, which are not natural but adventitious; and there are also many dispositions which are not adventitious but natural, as health, beauty and the like. Hence, it does not suit the order of the species, since that which is the more natural is always prior.

Therefore we must explain otherwise the distinction of dispositions and habits from other qualities. For quality, properly speaking, implies a certain mode of substance. Now mode, as Augustine says, *is that which a measure determines,*[23] and therefore it implies a certain determination according to a certain measure. Therefore, just as that in accordance with which the potentiality of matter is determined to its substantial being is called the quality which is a difference affecting substance, so that in accordance with which the potentiality of the subject is determined to its accidental being is called an accidental quality, which is also a kind of difference, as is clear from the Philosopher.[24]

Now the mode or the determination of the subject according to accidental being may be taken in relation to the very nature of the subject, or according to the action and passion resulting from its natural principles, which are matter and form; or, again, according to quantity. If we take the mode or determination of the subject according to quantity, we shall then have the fourth species of quality. And because quantity, considered in itself, is without movement, and without the character of good or evil, therefore it does not concern the fourth species of quality whether a thing be well or ill disposed, or quickly or slowly moving.

But the mode or determination of the subject according to action and passion is considered in the second and third species of quality. And therefore in both, we take into account whether a thing be done with ease or difficulty; whether it be transitory or lasting. But we do not consider in them anything pertaining to the notion of good or evil, because movements and passions have not the nature of an end, whereas good and evil are said in relation to an end.

On the other hand, the mode or determination of the subject in relation to the nature of a thing belongs to the first species of quality, which is habit and disposition; for the Philosopher says, when speaking of habits of the soul and of the body, that they are *dispositions of the perfect to the best; and by perfect I mean that which is disposed in accordance with its na-*

[22] *In Cat.*, VIII (p. 228[19-33]).   [23] *De Genesi ad Litt.*, IV, 3 (PL 34, 299).
[24] *Metaph.*, IV, 14 (1020a 33).

ture.[25] And since the form itself and the nature of a thing is the end and the cause why a thing is made,[26] therefore, in the first species we consider both evil and good, and also changeableness, whether easy or difficult, inasmuch as a certain nature is the end of generation and movement. And so the Philosopher defines habit as *a disposition whereby someone is disposed, well or ill;*[27] and in *Ethics* ii. he says that by *habits we are directed well or ill in reference to the passions*.[28] For when the mode is suitable to the thing's nature, it has the nature of good, and when it is unsuitable, it has the nature of evil. And since nature is the first object of consideration in anything, for this reason habit is reckoned as the first species of quality.

Reply Obj. 1. Disposition implies a certain order, as was stated above. Therefore a man is not said to be disposed by some quality except in relation to something else. And if we add *well or ill*, which belongs to the nature of habit, we must consider the quality's relation to the nature, which is the end. So in regard to shape, or heat, or cold, a man is not said to be well or ill disposed, except by reason of a relation to the nature of a thing, with regard to its suitability or unsuitability. Consequently even shapes and passible qualities, in so far as they are considered to be suitable or unsuitable to the nature of a thing, belong to habits or dispositions. For shape and color, according to their suitability to the nature of a thing, concern beauty; while heat and cold, according to their suitability to the nature of a thing, concern health. In this way, heat and cold are put by the Philosopher in the first species of quality.[29] Therefore it is clear how to answer the second objection; though some give another solution, as Simplicius says in his *Commentary on the Categories*.[30]

Reply Obj. 3. This difference, *difficult to change,* does not distinguish habit from the other species of quality, but from disposition. Now disposition may be taken in two ways: in one way, as the genus of habit, for disposition is included in the definition of habit;[31] in another way, according as it is divided against habit. Now disposition, properly so called, can be divided against habit in two ways. First, as perfect and imperfect within the same species. Thus we call it a disposition, retaining the name of the genus, when it is had imperfectly, so as to be easily lost; whereas we call it a habit, when it is had perfectly, so as not to be lost easily. And thus a disposition becomes a habit, just as a boy becomes a man. Secondly, they may be distinguished as diverse species of the one subaltern genus, so that we call dispositions, those qualities of the first species which by reason of their very nature are easily lost because they have changeable causes, *e.g.*, sickness and health; whereas we call habits those qualities which, by reason of their very nature, are not easily changed, in that they have unchange-

---

[25] *Phys.*, VII, 3 (246a 13). [26] *Op. cit.*, II, 7 (198b 3). [27] *Metaph.*, IV, 20 (1022b 10). [28] *Eth.*, II, 5 (1105b 25). [29] *Cat.*, VIII (8b 36). [30] *In Cat.*, VIII (pp. 233[10]; 256[16]). [31] Aristotle, *Metaph.*, IV, 20 (1022b 4).

able causes, *e.g.*, the sciences and the virtues. In this sense, a disposition does not become a habit.

The latter explanation seems more in keeping with the intention of Aristotle.[32] For, in order to confirm this distinction, he adduces the common mode of speaking, according to which, when a quality, by reason of its nature, is easily changeable, and through some accident becomes with difficulty changeable, then it is called a habit; while the contrary happens in regard to qualities which, by reason of their nature, are with difficulty changeable. For supposing a man to have a science imperfectly, so as to be liable to lose it easily, we say that he is disposed to that science, rather than that he has the science. From this it is clear that the term *habit* implies a certain lastingness, while the term *disposition* does not.

Nor does it matter that in this *to be easy* and *difficult to change* are specific differences [of a quality], although they belong to passion and movement, and not to the genus of quality. For these differences, though apparently accidental to quality, nevertheless designate differences which are proper and essential to quality. In the same way, in the genus of substance we often take accidental instead of substantial differences, in so far as by the former essential principles are designated.

Third Article

WHETHER HABIT IMPLIES ORDER TO AN ACT?

We proceed thus to the Third Article:—

Objection 1. It would seem that habit does not imply order to an act. For everything acts according as it is in act. But the Philosopher says that *when one is become knowing by habit, one is still in a state of potentiality, but otherwise than before learning.*[33] Therefore habit does not imply the relation of a principle to an act.

Obj. 2. Further, that which is put in the definition of a thing belongs to it essentially. But to be a principle of action is put in the definition of a power, as we read in *Metaph.* v.[34] Therefore to be the principle of an act belongs to a power essentially. Now that which is essential is first in every genus. If, therefore, habit also is a principle of an act, it follows that it is posterior to power. And so habit or disposition will not be the first species of quality.

Obj. 3. Further, health is sometimes a habit, and so are leanness and beauty. But these do not indicate relation to an act. Therefore it is not essential to habit to be a principle of an act.

On the contrary, Augustine says that *habit is that whereby something is*

---

[32] Aristotle, *Cat.*, VIII (8b 27).   [33] *De An.*, III, 4 (429b 6).   [34] Aristotle, *Metaph.*, IV, 12 (1019a 15).

done when necessary.[35] And the Commentator says that *habit is that whereby we act when we will.*[36]

I answer that, To have relation to an act may belong to a habit both according to the nature of habit, and according to the subject in which the habit is. Now according to the nature of habit, it belongs to every habit to have relation to an act. For it is essential to habit to imply some relation to a thing's nature, in so far as it is suitable or unsuitable to it. But a thing's nature, which is the end of generation, is further ordained to another end, which is either an operation, or some product of operation, to which one attains by means of operation. Therefore habit implies relation, not only to the very nature of a thing, but also, consequently, to operation, inasmuch as this is the end of nature, or conducive to the end. And so it is also stated in the definition of habit, that it is *a disposition whereby that which is disposed, is well or ill disposed either in regard to itself,* that is, to its nature, *or in regard to something else,* that is, to the end.[37]

But there are some habits which, even on the part of the subject in which they are, imply primarily and principally a relation to an act. For, as we have said, habit primarily and of itself implies a relation to the nature of a being. If, therefore, the nature of the thing in which the habit is consists in this very relation to an act, it follows that the habit principally implies relation to an act. Now it is clear that the nature and character of power is that it should be a principle of act. Therefore every habit whose subject is a power implies principally a relation to an act.

Reply Obj. 1. Habit is an act in so far as it is a quality, and in this respect it can be a principle of operation. It is, however, in a state of potentiality in respect to operation. Therefore habit is called first act, and operation, second act, as is explained in *De Anima* ii.[38]

Reply Obj. 2. It is not of the essence of habit to refer to a power, but to refer to a nature. And as nature precedes action, to which power refers, therefore habit is put before power as a species of quality.

Reply Obj. 3. Health is said to be a habit, or a habitual disposition, in relation to nature, as was stated above. But in so far as nature is the principle of an act, it consequently implies a relation to an act. Therefore the Philosopher says that man, or one of his members, is called healthy *when he can perform the operation of a healthy man.*[39] And the same applies to other habits.

Fourth Article

WHETHER HABITS ARE NECESSARY?

We proceed thus to the Fourth Article:—

Objection 1. It would seem that habits are not necessary. For by habits

---

[35] *De Bono Coniug.,* XXI (PL 40, 390).   [36] Averroes, *In De Anima,* III, comm. 18 (VI, 169v).   [37] Aristotle, *Metaph.,* IV, 20 (1022b 10).   [38] Aristotle, *De An.,* II, 1 (412a 22).   [39] *Hist. Anim.,* X, 1 (633b 23).

we are well or ill disposed in respect of something, as was stated above. But a thing is well or ill disposed by its form, for it is according to its form that a thing is good, even as it is a being. Therefore there is no necessity for habits.

Obj. 2. Further, habit implies relation to an act. But power implies sufficiently a principle of act, for even the natural powers, without any habits, are principles of acts. Therefore there was no necessity for habits.

Obj. 3. Further, as power is related to good and evil, so also is habit, and as power does not always act, so neither does habit. Given, therefore, the powers, habits become superfluous.

On the contrary, Habits are perfections.[40] But perfection is of the greatest necessity to a thing, since it is in the nature of an end. Therefore it was necessary that there should be habits.

I answer that, As we have said above, habit implies a disposition in relation to a thing's nature, and to its operation or end, by reason of which disposition a thing is well or ill disposed thereto. Now for a thing to need to be disposed to something else, three conditions are necessary. The first condition is that that which is disposed should be distinct from that to which it is disposed, and that it should be related to it as potentiality is to act. Whence, if there is a being whose nature is not composed of potentiality and act, whose substance is its own operation, and which exists for itself, we can find no room in such a thing for habit and disposition, as is clearly the case in God.

The second condition is, that that which is in a state of potentiality in regard to something else, be capable of determination in several ways and to various things. Whence, if something be in a state of potentiality in regard to something else, but in regard to that only, we find no room in such a thing for disposition and habit; for such a subject has of its own nature a proper relation to such an act. Therefore if a heavenly body be composed of matter and form, since that matter is not in a state of potentiality to another form, as we said in the First Part,[41] there is no need for disposition or habit in relation to form, or even in relation to operation, since the nature of the heavenly body is not in a state of potentiality to more than one fixed movement.

The third condition is that in disposing the subject to one of those things to which it is in potentiality, several things should occur, capable of being adjusted in various ways, so as to dispose the subject well or ill to its form or to its operation. Therefore the simple qualities of the elements, which suit the natures of the elements in one single fixed way, are not called dispositions or habits, but *simple qualities.* But we call dispositions or habits such things as *health, beauty,* and so forth, which imply the adjustment of several things which may vary in their relative adjustability. For this rea-

---

[40] Aristotle, *Phys.,* VII, 3 (246a 11).   [41] *S. T.,* I, q. 66, a. 2.

son the Philosopher says that *habit is a disposition*,[42] and *disposition is the order of that which has parts either as to place, or as to potentiality, or as to species*,[43] as we have said above. Therefore, since there are many things for whose natures and operations several things must concur which may vary in their relative adjustability, it follows that habit is necessary.

Reply Obj. 1. By the form the nature of a thing is perfected; yet the subject needs to be disposed in regard to the form itself by some disposition. But the form itself is further ordained to operation, which is either the end, or a means to the end. And if the form is limited to one fixed operation, no further disposition, besides the form itself, is needed for the operation. But if the form be such that it can operate in diverse ways, as is the soul, it needs to be disposed to its operations by means of habits.

Reply Obj. 2. Power sometimes has a relation to many things, and then it needs to be determined by something else. But if a power has not a relation to many things, it does not need a habit to determine it, as we have said. For this reason natural forces do not perform their operations by means of habits, because they are of themselves determined to one mode of operation.

Reply Obj. 3. The same habit has not a relation to good and evil, as will be made clear further on,[44] but the same power has a relation to good and evil. Hence it is that habits are necessary that powers be determined to good.

[42] *Metaph.*, IV, 20 (1022b 10).   [43] *Op. cit.*, IV, 19 (1022b 1).   [44] Q. 54, a. 3.

ON THE SUBJECT OF HABITS
(*In Six Articles*)

WE consider next the subjects of habits. Under this head there are six points of inquiry: (1) Whether there is a habit in the body? (2) Whether the soul is a subject of habit according to its essence or according to its power? (3) Whether in the powers of the sensitive part there can be a habit? (4) Whether there is a habit in the intellect? (5) Whether there is a habit in the will? (6) Whether there is a habit in separate substances?

First Article

WHETHER THERE IS A HABIT IN THE BODY?

We proceed thus to the First Article:—

Objection 1. It would seem that there is not a habit in the body. For, as the Commentator says, *a habit is that whereby we act when we will.*[1] But bodily actions are not subject to the will, since they are natural. Therefore there can be no habit in the body.

Obj. 2. Further, all bodily dispositions are easy to change. But habit is a quality difficult to change. Therefore no bodily disposition can be a habit.

Obj. 3. Further, all bodily dispositions are subject to alteration. But alteration can be only in the third species of quality, which is distinguished from habit. Therefore there is no habit in the body.

On the contrary, The Philosopher says in the *Categories* that health of the body and incurable disease are called habits.[2]

I answer that, As we have said above,[3] habit is a disposition in a subject which is in potentiality either to form or to operation. Therefore, in so far as habit implies disposition to operation, no habit is principally in the body as its subject. For every operation of the body proceeds either from a natural quality of the body or from the soul moving the body. Consequently, as to those operations which are natural, the body is not disposed by a habit, because the natural powers are determined to one mode of operation; and we have already said that it is when the subject is in potentiality to many things that a habitual disposition is required.[4] As to the operations which proceed from the soul through the body, they belong principally to the soul, and secondarily to the body. Now habits are propor-

---

[1] Averroes, *In De Anima*, III, comm. 18 (VI, 169v).   [2] *Cat.*, VIII (9a 14).
[3] Q. 49, a. 2, 3 and 4.   [4] Q. 49, a. 4.

tioned to their operations. Whence *by like acts like habits are formed.*[5]
Therefore the dispositions to such operations are principally in the soul.
But they can be secondarily in the body, namely, in so far as the body is
disposed and enabled with promptitude to help in the operations of the soul.

If, however, we speak of the disposition of the subject to form, thus a
habitual disposition can be in the body, which is related to the soul as a
subject is to its form. And in this way *health* and *beauty* and the like are
called habitual dispositions. Yet they have not the nature of habit perfectly, because their causes, of their very nature, are easily changeable.

On the other hand, as Simplicius reports in his *Commentary on the
Categories,*[6] Alexander denied absolutely that habits or dispositions of the
first species are in the body, and held that the first species of quality belonged to the soul alone. He held also that Aristotle mentions health and
sickness in the *Categories,* not as though they belonged to the first species
of quality, but by way of example.[7] So his meaning would be that, just as
health and sickness may be easy or difficult to change, so also are all the
qualities of the first species, which are called habits and dispositions. But
this is clearly contrary to the intention of Aristotle, both because he speaks
in the same way of health and sickness, as examples, as of virtue and
science; and because in *Physics* vii.[8] he expressly mentions beauty and
health among habits.

Reply Obj. 1. This objection concerns habit as a disposition to operation, and those actions of the body which are from nature; but it does not
concern those actions which proceed from the soul, and the principle of
which is the will.

Reply Obj. 2. Bodily dispositions are not, absolutely, difficult to change
because of the changeableness of their bodily causes. But they may be
difficult to change by comparison to such and such a subject, because,
namely, as long as such a subject endures, they cannot be removed; or because they are difficult to change, by comparison to other dispositions. But
qualities of the soul are, absolutely, difficult to change because of the
unchangeableness of the subject. And therefore Aristotle does not say that
health which is difficult to change is a habit absolutely, but that it is *as a
habit,* as we read in the Greek.[9] On the other hand, the qualities of the soul
are called habits absolutely.

Reply Obj. 3. Bodily dispositions, which are in the first species of quality,
as some maintained,[10] differ from qualities of the third species in this, that
the qualities of the third species consist in becoming and movement, as
it were, and therefore they are called passions or passible qualities. But
when they have attained to perfection (specific perfection, so to speak),
they have then passed into the first species of quality. But Simplicius in

---

[5] Aristotle, *Eth.,* II, 1 (1103b 21).   [6] *In Cat.,* VIII (pp. 233[16]; 241[27]).   [7] *Cat.,*
VIII (8b 36).   [8] *Phys.,* VII, 3 (246b 4).   [9] Aristotle, *Cat.,* VIII (9a 3).   [10] Cf.
Simplicius, *In Cat.,* VIII (pp. 233[22]; 234[11]).

his *Commentary* disapproves of this.[11] For in this view heating would be in the third species, and heat in the first species of quality; whereas Aristotle puts heat in the third.

Therefore Porphyry, as Simplicius reports,[12] says that passion, or passion-like quality, and disposition and habit differ in bodies by way of intensity and remission. For when a thing receives heat only in this, that it is being heated, and not so as to be able to give heat, then we have passion, if it is temporary; or passion-like quality if it is permanent. But when it has been brought to the point that it is able to heat something else, then it is a disposition; and if it goes so far as to be firmly fixed and to become difficult to change, then it will be a habit; so that disposition would be a certain intensity or perfection of passion or passion-like quality, and habit an intensity or perfection of disposition. But Simplicius disapproves of this, for such intensity and remission do not imply diversity on the part of the form itself, but on the part of the diverse participation in it by the subject; so that there would thus be no diversity among the species of quality.[13]

And therefore we must conclude otherwise. We must say that, as was explained above,[14] the adjustment of the passion-like qualities themselves, according to their suitability to nature, has the nature of disposition; and so, when a change takes place in these same passion-like qualities, which are heat and cold, moisture and dryness, there results a change as to sickness and health. But alteration does not occur, primarily and directly, in regard to such habits and dispositions.

Second Article

WHETHER THE SOUL IS THE SUBJECT OF HABIT ACCORDING TO ITS ESSENCE OR ACCORDING TO ITS POWER?

We proceed thus to the Second Article:—

Objection 1. It would seem that habit is in the soul according to its essence rather than according to its powers. For we speak of dispositions and habits in relation to nature, as was stated above.[15] But nature is considered according to the essence of the soul rather than the powers, because it is according to its essence that the soul is the nature of such a body and the form thereof. Therefore habits are in the soul according to its essence and not according to its powers.

Obj. 2. Further, accident is not the subject of accident. Now habit is an accident. But the powers of the soul are in the genus of accident, as we have said in the First Part.[16] Therefore habit is not in the soul in respect of its powers.

---

[11] *Ibid.* (p. 234[11]).   [12] *Ibid.* (p. 234[30]).   [13] *Ibid.* (p. 234[6]).   [14] Q. 49, a. 2, ad 1.
[15] Q. 49, a. 2.   [16] *S. T.,* I, q. 77, a. 1, ad 5.

Obj. 3. Further, the subject is prior to that which is in the subject. But since habit belongs to the first species of quality, it is prior to power, which belongs to the second species. Therefore habit is not in a power of the soul as its subject.

On the contrary, The Philosopher puts various habits in the various parts of the soul.[17]

I answer that, As we have said above,[18] habit implies a certain disposition in relation to nature or to operation. If, therefore, we take habit as having a relation to nature, it cannot be in the soul—that is, if we speak of human nature; for the soul itself is the form completing human nature. Hence, regarded in this way, habit or disposition is rather to be found in the body by reason of its relation to the soul, than in the soul by reason of its relation to the body.—But if we speak of a higher nature, of which man may become a partaker (according to *2 Peter* i. 4, *that we may be partakers of the divine nature*), thus nothing hinders some habit, namely, grace, from being in the soul according to its essence, as we shall state later on.[19]

On the other hand, if we take habit in its relation to operation, it is chiefly thus that habits are found in the soul, in so far as the soul is not determined to one operation, but is indifferent to many. This indifference is a condition required for a habit, as we have said above.[20] And since the soul is the principle of operation through its powers, therefore, regarded in this sense, habits are in the soul according to its powers.

Reply Obj. 1. The essence of the soul belongs to human nature, not as a subject requiring to be disposed to something further, but as a form and nature to which someone is disposed.

Reply Obj. 2. Accident is not of itself the subject of accident. But since among accidents themselves there is a certain order, the subject, according as it is under one accident, is conceived as the subject of a further accident. In this way we say that one accident is the subject of another. Thus a surface is the subject of color. In this sense power is the subject of habit.

Reply Obj. 3. Habit precedes power according as it implies a disposition to nature, whereas power always implies a relation to operation, which is posterior, since nature is the principle of operation. But the habit whose subject is a power does not imply relation to nature, but to operation. Therefore it is posterior to power. Or, we may say that habit precedes power as the complete precedes the incomplete, and as act precedes potentiality. For act is naturally prior to potentiality, though potentiality is prior in the order of generation and time, as is stated in *Metaph.* vii. and ix.[21]

[17] *Eth.,* I, 13 (1103a 3).   [18] Q. 49, a. 2 and 3.   [19] Q. 110, a. 4.   [20] Q. 49, a. 4.
[21] Aristotle, *Metaph.,* VI, 3 (1029a 5); VIII, 8 (1049b 4).

Third Article

WHETHER THERE CAN BE ANY HABITS IN THE POWERS OF THE SENSITIVE PART?

We proceed thus to the Third Article:—

Objection 1. It would seem that there cannot be any habits in the powers of the sensitive part. For as the nutritive power is an irrational part, so is the sensitive power. But there can be no habits in the powers of the nutritive part. Therefore we ought not to put any habit in the powers of the sensitive part.

Obj. 2. Further, the sensitive parts are common to us and the brutes. But there are not any habits in brutes; for in them there is no will, which is included in the definition of habit, as we have said above.[22] Therefore there are no habits in the sensitive powers.

Obj. 3. Further, the habits of the soul are sciences and virtues; and just as science is related to the apprehensive power, so virtue is related to the appetitive power. But in the sensitive powers there are no sciences, since science is of universals, which the sensitive powers cannot apprehend. Therefore, neither can there be habits of virtue in the sensitive part.

On the contrary, The Philosopher says that *some virtues,* namely, temperance and fortitude, *belong to the irrational parts.*[23]

I answer that, The sensitive powers can be considered in two ways: first, according as they act from natural instinct; secondly, according as they act at the command of reason. According as they act from natural instinct, they are ordained to one thing, even as nature is. Therefore, just as there are no habits in the natural powers, so likewise there are none in the sensitive powers in so far as they act from natural instinct. But according as they act at the command of reason, they can be ordained to various things. And thus there can be habits in them, by which they are well or ill disposed in regard to something.

Reply Obj. 1. The powers of the nutritive part have not an inborn aptitude to obey the command of reason, and therefore there are no habits in them. But the sensitive powers have an inborn aptitude to obey the command of reason, and therefore habits can be in them; for in so far as they obey reason, in a certain sense they are said to be rational, as is stated in *Ethics* i.[24]

Reply Obj. 2. The sensitive powers of brute animals do not act at the command of reason. But if they are left to themselves, such animals act from natural instinct, and so there are in them no habits ordained to operations. There are in them, however, certain dispositions in relation to nature, as health and beauty. But whereas by man's reason brutes are disposed by a sort of conditioning to do things in this or that way, so in this sense,

---

[22] Q. 49, a. 3.   [23] *Eth.,* III, 10 (1117b 23).   [24] *Op. cit.,* I, 13 (1102b 25; b 13).

to a certain extent, we can admit the existence of habits in brute animals. Therefore Augustine says: *We find the most untamed beasts deterred, by fear of pain, from that wherein they take the keenest pleasure; and when this has become a custom in them, we say that they are tame and gentle.*[25] But the habit is incomplete, as to the use of the will, for they have not that power of using or of refraining, which seems to belong to the notion of habit: and therefore, properly speaking, there can be no habits in them.

Reply Obj. 3. The sensitive appetite has an inborn aptitude to be moved by the rational appetite, as is stated in *De Anima* iii.[26] But the rational powers of apprehension have an inborn aptitude to receive from the sensitive powers. And therefore it is more suitable that habits should be in the powers of sensitive appetite than in the powers of sensitive apprehension, since in the powers of sensitive appetite habits do not exist except according as they act at the command of the reason. And yet even in the interior powers of sensitive apprehension, we may admit of certain habits whereby man has a facility of memory, cogitation or imagination. So, too, the Philosopher says that *custom conduces much to a good memory.*[27] The reason for this is that these powers also are moved to act at the command of the reason.

On the other hand, the exterior apprehensive powers, as sight, hearing and the like, are not susceptive of habits, but are ordained to their fixed acts, according to the disposition of their nature; just as are the members of the body, for there are no habits in them, but rather in the powers which command their movements.

Fourth Article

WHETHER THERE IS ANY HABIT IN THE INTELLECT?

We proceed thus to the Fourth Article:—

Objection 1. It would seem that there are no habits in the intellect. For habits are in conformity with operations, as was stated above. But the operations of man are common to soul and body, as is stated in *De Anima* i.[28] Therefore so are habits. But the intellect is not an act of the body.[29] Therefore the intellect is not the subject of a habit.

Obj. 2. Further, whatever is in a thing is there according to the mode of that in which it is. But that which is form without matter is act only, whereas what is composed of form and matter has potentiality and act at the same time. Therefore nothing at the same time potential and actual can be in that which is form only, but only in that which is composed of matter and form. Now the intellect is form without matter. Therefore

[25] *Lib. 83 Quaest.,* q. 36 (PL 40, 25).   [26] Aristotle, *De An.,* III, 11 (434a 12). [27] *De Memor.,* II (452a 28).   [28] Aristotle, *De An.,* I, 1 (403a 8); 4 (408b 8). [29] *Op. cit.,* III, 4 (429a 24).

habit, which has potentiality as well as act, being, as it were, intermediate between the two, cannot be in the intellect, but only in the composite which is made up of soul and body.

Obj. 3. Further, *habit is a disposition whereby we are well or ill disposed in regard to something, as it is said in Metaph. v.*[30] But that anyone should be well or ill disposed to an act of the intellect is due to some disposition of the body. Hence it is also stated that *we observe men with soft flesh to be quick witted.*[31] Therefore the habits of knowledge are not in the intellect, which is separate, but in some power which is the act of some part of the body.

On the contrary, The Philosopher puts *science, wisdom* and *understanding,* which is the habit of first principles, in the intellective part of the soul.[32]

I answer that, Concerning habits of knowledge there have been various opinions. Some, supposing that there was only one possible intellect for all men, were bound to hold that habits of knowledge are not in the intellect itself, but in the interior sensitive powers.[33] For it is manifest that men differ in habits; and so it was impossible to put the habits of knowledge directly in that which, being only one, would be common to all men. Therefore, if there were but one single possible intellect of all men, the habits of the sciences, in which men differ from one another, could not be in the possible intellect as their subject, but would be in the interior sensitive powers, which are multiplied in diverse men.

Now, in the first place, this supposition is contrary to the mind of Aristotle. For it is manifest that the sensitive powers are rational, not by their essence, but only by participation.[34] Now the Philosopher puts the intellectual virtues, which are *wisdom, science* and *understanding,* in that which is rational by its essence.[35] Therefore they are not in the sensitive powers, but in the intellect itself. Moreover, he says expressly that when the possible intellect *thus becomes each thing,* that is, when it is reduced to act in respect of singulars by the intelligible species, *then it is said to be in act, as the knower is said to be in act; and this happens when the intellect can act of itself,* i.e., by considering. *And even then it is in potentiality in a sense; but not in the same way as before learning and discovering.*[36] Therefore the possible intellect itself is the subject of the habit of science, by which the intellect, even though it be not actually considering, is able to consider.

In the second place, this supposition is contrary to the truth. For just as to whom belongs the operation, belongs also the power to operate, so to whom belongs the operation, belongs also the habit. But to understand and

---

[30] Aristotle, *Metaph.,* IV, 20 (1022b 10).   [31] Aristotle, *De An.,* II, 9 (421a 26).   [32] *Eth.,* VI, 3 (1139b 16).   [33] Averroes, *In De Anima,* III, comm. 5 (VI, 164r).   [34] Aristotle, *Eth.,* I, 13 (1102b 13).   [35] *Op. cit.,* VI, 3 (1139b 16).   [36] *De An.,* III, 4 (429b 6).

to consider is the proper act of the intellect. Therefore also the habit whereby one considers is properly in the intellect itself.

Reply Obj. 1. Some said, as Simplicius reports in his *Commentary on the Categories*,[37] that, since every operation of man is to a certain extent an operation of the composite, as the Philosopher holds,[38] therefore no habit is in the soul only, but in the composite. And from this it follows that no habit is in the intellect, for the intellect is separate, according to the argument reported above.[39] But the argument is not cogent. For habit is not a disposition of the object towards the power, but rather a disposition of the power towards the object. Therefore the habit needs to be in that power which is principle of the act, and not in that which is compared to the power as its object.

Now the act of understanding is not said to be common to soul and body, except in respect of the phantasm, as is stated in *De Anima* i.[40] But it is clear that the phantasm is compared as object to the possible intellect.[41] Whence it follows that the intellective habit is chiefly on the part of the intellect itself, and not on the part of the phantasm, which is common to soul and body. And therefore we must say that the possible intellect is the subject of habit. For that is a competent subject of habit, which is in potentiality to many; and this belongs, above all, to the possible intellect. Therefore the possible intellect is the subject of intellectual habits.

Reply Obj. 2. As potentiality to sensible being belongs to corporeal matter, so potentiality to intelligible being belongs to the possible intellect. Therefore nothing forbids habit to be in the possible intellect, for it is midway between pure potentiality and perfect act.

Reply Obj. 3. Because the apprehensive powers inwardly prepare the proper object for the possible intellect, therefore it is by the good disposition of these powers, to which disposition the good disposition of the body contributes, that man is rendered apt to understand. And so in a secondary way an intellective habit can be in these powers. But principally it is in the possible intellect.

Fifth Article

WHETHER ANY HABIT IS IN THE WILL?

We proceed thus to the Fifth Article:—

Objection 1. It would seem that there is not a habit in the will. For it is the intelligible species, by means of which the intellect actually understands, which are the habit that is in the intellect. But the will does not act by means of species. Therefore the will is not the subject of any habit.

Obj. 2. Further, no habit is allotted to the agent intellect, as there is to

<hr>

[37] *In Cat.*, VIII (p. 233²²). [38] *De An.*, I, 1 (403a 8); 4 (408b 8). [39] Cf. Simplicius, *In Cat.*, VIII (p. 241²³). [40] Aristotle, *De An.*, I, 1 (403a 5). [41] *Op. cit.*, III, 7 (431a 14).

the possible intellect, because the former is an active power. But the will is above all an active power, because it moves all the powers to their acts, as was stated above.[42] Therefore there is no habit in the will.

Obj. 3. Further, in the natural powers there is no habit, because, by reason of their nature, they are determined to one thing. But the will, by reason of its nature, is ordained to tend to the good which reason directs. Therefore there is no habit in the will.

On the contrary, Justice is a habit. But justice is in the will, for it is *a habit whereby men will and do that which is just.*[43] Therefore the will is the subject of a habit.

I answer that, Every power which may be variously directed to act needs a habit whereby it is well disposed to its act. Now since the will is a rational power, it may be variously directed to act. And therefore in the will we must admit the presence of a habit whereby it is well disposed to its act. Moreover, from the very nature of habit it is clear that it is principally related to the will, inasmuch as habit *is that which one uses when one wills,* as was stated above.

Reply Obj. 1. Even as in the intellect there is a species which is the likeness of the object, so in the will, and in every appetitive power, there must be something by which the power is inclined to its object; for the act of the appetitive power is nothing but a certain inclination, as we have said above.[44] And therefore towards those things to which it is inclined sufficiently by the nature of the power itself, the power needs no quality to incline it. But since it is necessary, for the end of human life, that the appetitive power be inclined to something fixed, to which it is not inclined by the nature of the power, which has a relation to many and various things, therefore it is necessary that, in the will and in the other appetitive powers, there be certain qualities to incline them, and these are called habits.

Reply Obj. 2. The agent intellect is active only, and in no way passive. But the will, and every appetitive power, is both mover and moved.[45] Therefore the comparison between them does not hold, for to be susceptible of habit belongs to that which is somehow in potentiality.

Reply Obj. 3. The will from the very nature of the power is inclined to the good of the reason. But because this good is varied in many ways, the will needs to be inclined, by means of a habit, to some fixed good of the reason in order that action may follow more promptly.

Sixth Article

WHETHER THERE ARE HABITS IN THE ANGELS?

We proceed thus to the Sixth Article:—

Objection 1. It would seem that there are no habits in the angels. For

---

[42] Q. 9, a. 1.   [43] Aristotle, *Eth.,* V, 1 (1129a 7).   [44] Q. 6, a. 4.   [45] Aristotle, *De An.,* III, 10 (433b 16).

Maximus, the commentator of Dionysius, says: *It is not proper to suppose that there are intellectual* (i.e., spiritual) *powers in the divine intelligences* (i.e., in the angels) *after the manner of accidents, as in us, as though one were in the other as in a subject; for accident of any kind is foreign to them.*[46] But every habit is an accident. Therefore there are no habits in the angels.

Obj. 2. Further, as Dionysius says: *The holy dispositions of the heavenly essences participate, above all other things, in God's goodness.*[47] But that which is of itself is prior to and more powerful than that which is by another. Therefore the angelic essences are perfected of themselves unto conformity with God, and therefore not by means of habits. And this seems to have been the reasoning of Maximus, who in the same passage adds: *For if this were the case, surely their essence would not remain in itself, nor could it have been as far as possible deified of itself.*[48]

Obj. 3. Further, *habit is a disposition.*[49] But disposition, as is said in the same book, is *the order of that which has parts.*[50] Since, therefore, angels are simple substances, it seems that there are no dispositions and habits in them.

On the contrary, Dionysius says that the angels of the first hierarchy are called: *Fire-bearers and Thrones and Out-pouring of Wisdom, by which is indicated the godlike nature of their habits.*[51]

I answer that, Some have thought that there are no habits in the angels, and that whatever is said of them, is said essentially. Whence Maximus, after the words which we have quoted, says: *Their dispositions and the powers which are in them are essential, through the absence of matter in them.*[52] And Simplicius says the same in his *Commentary on the Categories: Wisdom which is in soul is a habit, but that which is in intellect is its substance. For everything divine is sufficient of itself, and exists in itself.*[53]

Now this opinion contains some truth, and some error. For it is manifest, from what we have said, that only a being in potentiality is the subject of habit.[54] So the above-mentioned commentators considered that angels are immaterial substances, and that there is no material potentiality in them; and on that account they excluded from them habit and every kind of accident. Yet since, though there is no material potentiality in angels, there is still some potentiality in them (for to be pure act belongs to God alone), therefore, as far as potentiality is found to be in them, so far may habits be found in them. But because the potentiality of matter and the potentiality of intellectual substance are not of the same kind, so neither are the respective habits of the same kind. Whence, Simplicius says

---

[46] *In De Cael. Hier.,* VII, 1 (PG 4, 65).　　[47] *De Cael. Hier.,* IV, 2 (PG 3, 180). [48] *In De Cael. Hier.,* VII, 1 (PG 4, 65).　　[49] Aristotle, *Metaph.,* IV, 20 (1022b 10). [50] *Op. cit.,* IV, 19 (1022b 1).　　[51] *De Cael. Hier.,* VII, 1 (PG 3, 205).　　[52] *In De Cael. Hier.,* VII, 1 (PG 4, 65).　　[53] *In Cat.,* VIII (p. 241[30-31]).　　[54] Q. 49, a. 4.

in his *Commentary on the Categories* that: *The habits of an intellectual substance are not like the habits here below; rather are they like simple and immaterial species which it contains in itself.*[55]

However, the angelic intellect and the human intellect differ with regard to this habit. For the human intellect, being the lowest in the intellectual order, is in potentiality as regards all intelligible things, just as primary matter is as regards all sensible forms; and therefore for the understanding of all things, it needs some habit. But the angelic intellect is not as a pure potentiality in the order of intelligible beings, but as an act. Not indeed as pure act (for this belongs to God alone), but with an admixture of some potentiality; and the higher it is, the less potentiality it has. And therefore, as we said in the First Part,[56] so far as it is in potentiality, so far is it in need of habitual perfection by means of intelligible species in regard to its proper operation; but so far as it is in act, through its own essence it can understand some things, at least itself, and other things according to the mode of its substance, as is stated in the *Book of Causes*;[57] and the more perfect it is, the more perfectly will it understand.

But since no angel attains to the perfection of God, but all are infinitely distant from Him, for this reason, in order to attain to God Himself through intellect and will, the angels need some habits, being as it were in potentiality in regard to that Pure Act. Therefore Dionysius says that *their habits are godlike,*[58] that is to say, that by them they are made like to God.

But those habits that are dispositions to natural being are not in angels, since they are immaterial.

Reply Obj. 1. This saying of Maximus must be understood of material habits and accidents.

Reply Obj. 2. As to that which belongs to angels by their essence, they do not need a habit. But as they are not so far beings of themselves, as not to partake of divine wisdom and goodness, therefore, so far as they need to partake of something from without, so far do they need to have habits.

Reply Obj. 3. In angels there are no essential parts, but there are potential parts, in so far as their intellect is perfected by several species, and in so far as their will has a relation to several things.

---

[55] *In Cat.*, VIII (p. 241[27-29]).   [56] Q. 55, a. 1.   [57] *De Causis*, VIII (p. 168).
[58] *De Cael. Hier.*, VII, 1 (PG 3, 205).

ON THE CAUSE OF HABITS, AS TO THEIR FORMATION
(*In Four Articles*)

WE must next consider the cause of habits. And firstly, as to their formation; secondly, as to their increase;[1] thirdly, as to their diminution and corruption.[2] Under the first head there are four points of inquiry: (1) Whether any habit is from nature? (2) Whether any habit is caused by acts? (3) Whether a habit can be generated by one act? (4) Whether any habits are infused in man by God?

First Article
WHETHER ANY HABIT IS FROM NATURE?

We proceed thus to the First Article:—

Objection 1. It would seem that no habit is from nature. For the use of those things which are from nature does not depend on the will. But habit *is that which we use when we will,* as the Commentator says on *De Anima* iii.[3] Therefore habit is not from nature.

Obj. 2. Further, nature does not employ two where one is sufficient. But the powers of the soul are from nature. If, therefore, the habits of the powers were from nature, habit and power would be one.

Obj. 3. Further, nature does not fail in the necessaries. But habits are necessary in order to act well, as we have stated above.[4] If, therefore, any habits were from nature, it seems that nature would not fail to cause all necessary habits. But this is clearly false. Therefore habits are not from nature.

On the contrary, In *Ethics* vi.[5] among other habits place is given to the *understanding of first principles,* which habit is from nature. Hence, too, first principles are said to be known naturally.[6]

I answer that, One thing can be natural to another in two ways. First, in respect of the specific nature, as the ability to laugh is natural to man, and to have an upward tendency is natural to fire. Secondly, in respect of the individual nature, as it is natural to Socrates or Plato to be prone to sickness or inclined to health, in accordance with their respective temperaments.—Again, in respect of both natures, something may be called natu-

---

[1] Q. 52.   [2] Q. 53.   [3] Averroes, *In De Anima*, III, comm. 18 (VI, 169v).
[4] Q. 49, a. 4.   [5] Aristotle, *Eth.*, VI, 6 (1141a 5).   [6] Cf. a text of St. Albert, *Summa de Bono,* quoted by O. Lottin, *Le droit naturel,* p. 117.

ral in two ways: first, because it is entirely from the nature; secondly, because it is partly from nature, and partly from an extrinsic principle. For
instance, when a man is healed by himself, his health is entirely from
nature; but when a man is healed by means of medicine, health is partly
from nature, partly from an extrinsic principle.

Therefore, if we speak of habit as a disposition of the subject in relation
to form or nature, it may be natural in either of the foregoing ways. For
there is a certain natural disposition demanded by the human species, so
that no man can be without it. And this disposition is natural in respect
of the specific nature. But since such a disposition has a certain latitude,
it happens that different grades of this disposition are becoming to different men in respect of the individual nature. And this disposition may be
either entirely from nature, or partly from nature, and partly from an
extrinsic principle, as we have said of those who are healed by means of
art.

But the habit which is a disposition to operation, and whose subject
is a power of the soul, as was stated above,[7] may be natural both in respect
of the specific nature and in respect of the individual nature:—in respect
of the specific nature, on the part of the soul itself, which, since it is the
form of the body, is the specific principle; but in respect of the individual
nature, on the part of the body, which is the material principle. Yet in
neither way does it happen that there are natural habits in man, so that
they be entirely from nature. In the angels, indeed, this does happen, since
they have intelligible species naturally impressed on them; which does
not belong to human nature, as we said in the First Part.[8]

There are, therefore, in man certain natural habits, owing their existence
partly to nature, and partly to some extrinsic principle. They exist in one
way, indeed, in the apprehensive powers; in another, in the appetitive
powers. For in the apprehensive powers there may be a natural habit by
way of a beginning, both in respect of the specific nature and in respect
of the individual nature. This happens with regard to the specific nature,
on the part of the soul itself. Thus the *understanding of first principles* is
called a natural habit.[9] For it is owing to the very nature of the intellectual
soul that man, having once grasped what is a whole and what is a part,
should at once perceive that every whole is larger than its part. And the
same is the case in like manner with regard to other such instances. Yet
what is a whole, and what is a part, this he cannot know except through
the intelligible species which he has received from phantasms. For this
reason, the Philosopher at the end of the *Posterior Analytics* shows that
the knowledge of principles comes to us from the senses.[10]

[7] Q. 50, a. 2.   [8] *S.T.*, I, q. 55, a. 2; q. 84, a. 3.   [9] For the opinions of Alexander of
Hales and John of Rochelle on the "understanding of first principles," cf. O. Lottin, "La
syndérèse chez les premiers maîtres franciscains de Paris" (*Revue néoscolastique de
philosophie*, XXIX [1927], pp. 269, 273, 277).   [10] *Post. Anal.*, II. 15 (100a 3).

But in respect of the individual nature, a habit of knowledge is natural as to its beginning, in so far as one man, from the disposition of his organs of sense, is more apt than another to understand well, since we need the sensitive powers for the operation of the intellect.

In the appetitive powers, however, no habit is natural in its beginning, on the part of the soul itself, as to the substance of the habit; but only as to certain of its principles, as, for instance, the principles of common law are called *the seeds of the virtues.*[11] The reason for this is because the inclination to its proper objects, which seems to be the beginning of a habit, does not belong to the habit, but rather to the very nature of the powers.

But on the part of the body, in respect of the individual nature, there are some appetitive habits by way of natural beginnings. For some are disposed from their own bodily temperament to chastity or meekness or the like.

Reply Obj. 1. This objection takes nature as divided against reason and will; whereas reason itself and will belong to the nature of man.

Reply Obj. 2. Something may be added even naturally to the nature of a power, although it cannot belong to the power itself. For instance, with regard to the angels, it cannot belong to the intellective power itself to be of itself capable of knowing all things; for thus it would have to be the act of all things, which belongs to God alone. Evidently, that by which something is known must needs be the actual likeness of the thing known. Hence, if the power of the angel knew all things by itself, it would follow that it was the likeness and act of all things. Therefore there must needs be added to the angels' intellective power some intelligible species, which are likenesses of things understood; for it is by participation in the divine wisdom, and not by their own essence, that their intellects can be actually those things which they understand. And so it is clear that not everything belonging to a natural habit can belong to the power.

Reply Obj. 3. Nature is not equally inclined to cause all the various kinds of habits, since some can be caused by nature, and some not, as we have said above. And so it does not follow that, because some habits are natural, therefore all are natural.

Second Article

WHETHER ANY HABIT IS CAUSED BY ACTS?

We proceed thus to the Second Article:—

Objection 1. It would seem that no habit is caused by acts. For habit is a quality, as we have said above.[12] Now every quality is caused in a subject according as the subject is receptive of something. Since, then, the

---

[11] Cf. the texts of St. Albert, *Summa de Bono,* as quoted by O. Lottin, *Le droit naturel,* p. 117.   [12] Q. 49, a. 1.

agent, inasmuch as it acts, does not receive but rather gives, it seems impossible for a habit to be caused in an agent by its own acts.

Obj. 2. Further, the thing wherein a quality is caused is moved to that quality, as may be clearly seen in that which is heated or cooled; whereas that which produces the act that causes the quality, moves, as may be seen in that which heats or cools. If, therefore, habits were caused in anything by its own act, it would follow that the same would be mover and moved, active and passive; which is impossible, as is stated in *Physics* vii.[13]

Obj. 3. Further, the effect cannot be more noble than its cause. But a habit is more noble than the act which precedes the habit, as is clear from the fact that habit makes an act to be more perfect. Therefore a habit cannot be caused by an act which precedes the habit.

On the contrary, The Philosopher teaches that habits of virtue and vice are caused by acts.[14]

I answer that, In the agent there is sometimes only the active principle of its act. For instance, in fire there is only the active principle of heating. In such an agent a habit cannot be caused by its own act; for which reason natural things cannot become accustomed or unaccustomed, as is stated in *Ethics* ii.[15] But there is an agent in which there is both the active and the passive principle of its act, as we see in human acts. For the acts of the appetitive power proceed from that same power according as it is moved by the apprehensive power presenting the object; and further, the intellective power, according as it reasons about conclusions, has, as it were, an active principle in a self-evident proposition. Therefore by such acts habits can be caused in their agents; not indeed with regard to the first active principle, but with regard to that principle of the act which is a moved mover. For everything that is passive and moved by another is disposed by the action of the agent; and therefore if the acts be multiplied, a certain quality is formed in the power which is passive and moved, which quality is called a habit; just as the habits of the moral virtues are caused in the appetitive powers, according as they are moved by the reason, and as the habits of science are caused in the intellect, according as it is moved by first propositions.

Reply Obj. 1. The agent, as agent, does not receive anything. But in so far as it moves through being moved by another, it receives something from that which moves it; and thus a habit is caused.

Reply Obj. 2. The same thing, and in the same respect, cannot be mover and moved; but nothing prevents a thing from being moved by itself as to different respects, as is proved in *Physics* viii.[16]

Reply Obj. 3. The act which precedes the habit, in so far as it comes from an active principle, proceeds from a more excellent principle than is the habit caused thereby; just as the reason is a more excellent principle

---

[13] Aristotle, *Phys.*, VII, 1 (241b 24).   [14] *Eth.*, II, 1 (1103a 31).   [15] *Ibid.* (1103a 19).   [16] Aristotle, *Phys.*, VIII, 5 (257a 31).

than the habit of moral virtue produced in the appetitive power by repeated acts, and as the understanding of first principles is a more excellent
principle than the science of conclusions.

Third Article

WHETHER A HABIT CAN BE CAUSED BY ONE ACT?

We proceed thus to the Third Article:—

Objection 1. It would seem that a habit can be caused by one act. For
demonstration is an act of reason. But science, which is the habit of one
conclusion, is caused by one demonstration. Therefore habit can be caused
by one act.

Obj. 2. Further, as acts happen to increase by multiplication, so do they
happen to increase by intensity. But a habit is caused by multiplication of
acts. So, too, if an act be very intense, it can be the generating cause of
a habit.

Obj. 3. Further, health and sickness are habits. But it happens that a
man is healed or becomes ill by one act. Therefore one act can cause a
habit.

On the contrary, The Philosopher says: *As neither does one swallow nor
one day make spring, so neither does one day nor a short time make a man
blessed and happy.*[17] But *happiness is an operation according to a habit
of perfect virtue.*[18] Therefore a habit of virtue, and for the same reason,
other habits, is not caused by one act.

I answer that, As we have said already, habit is caused by act, in so far
as a passive power is moved by an active principle. But in order that some
quality be caused in that which is passive, the active principle must entirely
overcome the passive. Whence we see that because fire cannot at once overcome the combustible, it does not enkindle it at once, but gradually expels
contrary dispositions, so that, by overcoming it entirely, it may impress its
likeness on it. Now it is clear that the active principle which is reason cannot entirely overcome the appetitive power in one act. For the appetitive
power is inclined variously, and to many things, while the reason judges, in
a single act, what should be willed in the light of various conditions and
circumstances. Therefore the appetitive power is not thereby entirely overcome, so as to be inclined naturally to the same thing in the majority of
cases; which inclination belongs to the habit of virtue. Therefore a habit of
virtue cannot be caused by one act, but only by many.

But in the apprehensive powers, we must observe that there are two passive principles: one is the possible intellect itself; the other is the intellect
which Aristotle calls *passive,*[19] and is the particular reason, that is, the cogitative power, with memory and imagination.[20] With regard then to the

---

[17] *Eth.,* I, 7 (1098a 18).   [18] *Ibid.* (1098a 16); 13 (1102a 5).   [19] *De An.,* III, 5
(430a 24).   [20] Cf. *S. T.,* I, q. 78. a. 4.

former passive principle, it is possible for a certain active principle to overcome entirely, by one act, the power of its passive principle. Thus one self-evident proposition convinces the intellect, so that it gives a firm assent to the conclusion; but a probable proposition cannot do this. Therefore a habit of opinion needs to be caused by many acts of the reason, even on the part of the possible intellect; whereas a habit of science can be caused by a single act of the reason, so far as the possible intellect is concerned. But with regard to the lower apprehensive powers, the same acts need to be repeated many times for anything to be firmly impressed on the memory. And so the Philosopher says that *meditation strengthens memory*.[21] Bodily habits, however, can be caused by one act, if the active principle is of great power. Sometimes, for instance, a powerful medicine restores health at once.

Hence the solutions to the objections are clear.

Fourth Article

WHETHER ANY HABITS ARE INFUSED IN MAN BY GOD?

We proceed thus to the Fourth Article:—

Objection 1. It would seem that no habit is infused in man by God. For God treats all equally. If, therefore, He infuses habits into some, He would infuse them into all; which is clearly untrue.

Obj. 2. Further, God works in all things according to the mode which is suitable to their nature; for *it belongs to the divine providence to preserve nature*, as Dionysius says.[22] But habits are naturally caused in man by acts, as we have said above. Therefore God does not cause habits to be in man except by acts.

Obj. 3. Further, if any habit be infused into man by God, man can by that habit perform many acts. But *from those acts a like habit is caused*.[23] Consequently, there will be two habits of the same species in the same man, one acquired, the other infused. Now this seems impossible, for two forms of the same species cannot be in the same subject. Therefore a habit is not infused into man by God.

On the contrary, it is written (*Ecclus.* xv. 5): *God filled him with the spirit of wisdom and understanding*. Now wisdom and understanding are habits. Therefore some habits are infused into man by God.

I answer that, Some habits are infused by God into man, for two reasons. The first reason is because there are some habits by which man is disposed to an end which exceeds the proportion of human nature, namely, the ultimate and perfect happiness of man, as was stated above.[24] And since habits need to be in proportion with that to which man is disposed by them, therefore it is necessary that those habits, which dispose to this end, likewise

---

[21] *De Memor.*, I (451a 12).   [22] *De Div. Nom.*, IV, 33 (PG 3, 733).   [23] Aristotle, *Eth.*, II, 1 (1103b 21).   [24] Q. 5. a. 5.

exceed the proportion of human nature. Therefore such habits can never be in man except by divine infusion, as is the case with all gratuitous virtues.

The other reason is, because God can produce the effects of second causes without second causes themselves, as we have said in the First Part.[25] Just as, therefore, in order to show His power, God sometimes causes health, without its natural cause, but which nature could have caused, so also, at times, for the manifestation of His power, He infuses into man even those habits which can be caused by a natural power. Thus He gave to the apostles the science of the Scriptures and of all tongues, which men can acquire by study or by custom, though not so perfectly.

Reply Obj. 1. God, considered in His nature, is the same to all; but, considered according to the order of His wisdom, for some fixed motive, He gives certain things to some, which He does not give to others.

Reply Obj. 2. That God works in all according to their mode, does not hinder God from doing what nature cannot do; rather it follows from this that He does nothing contrary to that which is suitable to nature.

Reply Obj. 3. Acts produced by an infused habit do not cause a habit, but strengthen an already existing habit; just as the remedies of medicine given to a man who is naturally healthy do not cause a kind of health, but give new strength to the health he had before.

[25] *S. T.*, I, q. 105, a. 6.

Question LII

ON THE INCREASE OF HABITS
(*In Three Articles*)

WE have now to consider the increase of habits, under which head there are three points of inquiry: (1) Whether habits increase? (2) Whether they increase by addition? (3) Whether each act increases a habit?

First Article

WHETHER HABITS INCREASE?

We proceed thus to the First Article:—

Objection 1. It would seem that habits cannot increase. For increase concerns quantity.[1] But habits are not in the genus quantity, but in that of quality. Therefore there can be no increase of habits.

Obj. 2. Further, *habit is a perfection.*[2] But since perfection conveys a notion of end and term, it seems that it cannot be subject to more or less. Therefore a habit cannot increase.

Obj. 3. Further, those things which can be more or less are subject to alteration; for that which, from being less hot becomes more hot, is said to be altered. But in habits there is no alteration, as is proved in *Physics* vii.[3] Therefore habits cannot increase.

On the contrary, Faith is a habit, and yet it increases. So it was that the disciples said to our Lord (*Luke* xvii. 5): *Lord, increase our faith.* Therefore habits increase.

I answer that, Increase, like other things pertaining to quantity, is transferred from bodily quantities to spiritual and intellectual realities because of the natural connection of the human intellect with corporeal things, which come under the imagination. Now in corporeal quantities, a thing is said to be great according as it reaches the perfection of quantity due to it; and so a certain quantity is reputed great in man, which is not reputed great in an elephant. So, too, in forms, we say a thing is great because it is perfect. And since the good has the nature of what is perfect, therefore *in things which are great, but not in quantity, to be greater is the same as to be better,* as Augustine says.[4]

Now the perfection of a form may be considered in two ways: first, according to the form itself: secondly, according to the participation in the

---

[1] *Phys.,* V, 2 (226a 30). [2] *Op. cit.,* VII, 3 (246a 13). [3] *Ibid.* (246a 10).
[4] *De Trin.,* VI, 8 (PL 42, 929).

393

form by its subject. In so far as we consider the perfections of a form according to the form itself, thus the form is said to be *little* or *great*: for instance, great or little health or science. But in so far as we consider the perfection of a form according to the participation in it by the subject, it is said to be *more* or *less*: for instance, more or less white or healthy. Now this distinction is not to be understood as implying that the form has a being outside its matter or subject, but that it is one thing to consider the form according to its specific nature, and another to consider it according as it is participated in a subject.

In this way, then, there were four opinions among philosophers concerning the intensity and remission of habits and forms, as Simplicius relates in his *Commentary on the Categories.*[5] For Plotinus[6] and the other Platonists held that qualities and habits themselves were susceptible of more and less, for the reason that they were material, and so had a certain indetermination because of the infinity of matter.[7] Others, on the contrary, held that qualities and habits of themselves were not susceptible of more and less; but that the things affected by them are said to be more and less, according to a diversity in participation: that, for instance, justice is not more or less, but the just thing.[8] Aristotle alludes to this opinion in the *Categories.*[9] The third opinion was that of the Stoics, and lies between the two preceding opinions. For they held that some habits are of themselves susceptible of more and less, for instance, the arts; and that some are not, as the virtues.[10] The fourth opinion was held by some who said that qualities and immaterial forms are not susceptible of more and less, but that material forms are.[11]

In order that the truth in this matter be made clear, we must observe that, that according to which a thing receives its species, must be something fixed and permanent, and as it were indivisible; for whatever attains to it is contained under the species, and whatever recedes from it, more or less, belongs to another species, more or less perfect. Therefore the Philosopher says that *the species of things are like numbers,*[12] in which addition or subtraction changes the species. If, therefore, a form, or anything at all, receives through itself, or through something belonging to it, the nature of a species, it is necessary that, considered in itself, it should possess a definite nature, which can be neither more nor less. Such are heat, whiteness and other like qualities which are not denominated from a relation to something else; and much more so, substance, which is *per se* being. But those things which receive their species from something to which they are related can be diversified, in themselves, according to more or less, and none the less they remain in the same species, because of the oneness of that to which

[5] *In Cat.*, VIII (p. 284[12]).   [6] Cf. Plotinus, *Enneads, VI*, III. 20 (VI, 149).
[7] Simplicius, *In Cat.*, VIII (p. 284[13-17]).   [8] *Ibid.* (p. 284[17-32]).   [9] *Cat.*, VIII (10b 30).   [10] Simplicius, *In Cat.*, VIII (p. 284[32-35]).   [11] *Ibid.* (p. 285[1-5]).   [12] *Metaph.*, VII, 3 (1043b 33).

they are related, and from which they receive their species. For example, movement is in itself more intense or more remitted, and yet it remains in the same species because of the oneness of the term by which it is specified. We may observe the same thing in health; for a body attains to the charac- ter of health according as it has a disposition suitable to an animal's nature, to which various dispositions may be suitable; which disposition is there- fore variable as regards more or less, and yet the character of health remains. Whence the Philosopher says: *Health itself may be more or less, for the measure is not the same in all, nor is it always the same in one indi- vidual; but down to a certain point it may decrease and still remain health.*[13] Now these various dispositions and measures of health are by way of excess and defect. Therefore if the name of health were given to the most perfect measure, then we should not speak of health as greater or less.—Thus, therefore, it is clear how a quality or form may increase or de- crease in itself, and how it cannot.

But if we consider a quality or form according to its participation by the subject, thus again we find that some qualities and forms are susceptive of more or less, and some not. Now Simplicius assigns the cause of this di- versity to the fact that substance in itself cannot be susceptible of more or less, because it is *per se* being.[14] Hence every form which is participated substantially by its subject cannot vary in intensity and remission; and therefore in the genus of substance nothing is predicated according to more or less. And because quantity is near to substance, and because shape fol- lows on quantity, therefore it is that neither in these can there be such a thing as more or less. Whence the Philosopher says that when a thing re- ceives form and shape, it is not said to be altered, but to become.[15] But other qualities which are further removed from quantity, and are con- nected with passions and actions, are susceptible of more or less, accord- ing to the participation by the subject.

Now it is possible to explain yet further the reason for this diversity. For, as we have said, that from which a thing receives its species must re- main fixed and constant in something indivisible. Therefore in two ways it may happen that a form cannot be participated according to more or less. First, because the participator has its species through that form. And for this reason no substantial form is participated according to more or less. Therefore the Philosopher says that, *as a number cannot be more or less, so neither can that which is in the species of substance,* that is, in respect of its participation in the specific form: *but in so far as substance may be with matter, i.e.,* in respect of material dispositions, *more and less are found in substance.*[16]

Secondly, this may happen from the fact that the form is essentially indi-

[13] *Eth.*, X, 3 (1173a 24).   [14] *In Cat.*, VIII (p. 285[27-28]).   [15] *Phys.*, VII, 3 (246a 1).   [16] *Metaph.*, VII, 3 (1044a 9).

visible. Hence, if anything participate that form, it must needs participate it according to the nature of its indivisibility. For this reason we do not speak of the species of number as varying in respect of more and less; because each species of number is constituted by an indivisible unity. The same is to be said of the species of continuous quantity, which are denominated from numbers, as two-cubits-long, three-cubits-long, and of relations of quantity, as double and treble, and of figures of quantity, as triangle and tetragon.

This same explanation is given by Aristotle in the *Categories,* where, in explaining why figures are not susceptible of more or less, he says: *Things which are given the nature of a triangle or a circle are accordingly triangles and circles.*[17] For indivisibility is essential to the nature of such, and hence whatever participates their nature must participate it in its indivisibility.

It is clear, therefore, that since we speak of habits and dispositions according to a relation to something,[18] intensity and remission may be observed in habits and dispositions in two ways. First, according to the habit itself: thus, for instance, we speak of greater or less health, or greater or less science, which extends to more or fewer things. Secondly, according to participation by the subject, namely, in so far as equal science or health is participated more in one than in another, according to a diverse aptitude arising either from nature, or from custom. For habit and disposition do not give species to the subject, nor again do they essentially imply indivisibility.

We shall say further on how it is with virtue.[19]

Reply Obj. 1. As the name *great* is taken from corporeal quantities and applied to the intelligible perfections of forms, so also is the name *growth,* the term of which is something great.

Reply Obj. 2. Habit is indeed a perfection, but not a perfection which is the term of its subject, for instance, a term giving the subject its specific being. Nor again does the nature of a habit include the notion of term, as do the species of numbers. Therefore there is nothing to hinder it from being susceptive of more or less.

Reply Obj. 3. Alteration is primarily indeed in the qualities of the third species; but secondarily it may be in the qualities of the first species. For, supposing an alteration as to hot and cold, there follows in an animal an alteration as to health and sickness. In like manner, if an alteration take place in the passions of the sensitive appetite, or the sensitive powers of apprehension, an alteration follows as to the sciences and the virtues.[20]

---

[17] *Cat.,* VIII (11a 7).   [18] Aristotle, *Phys.,* VII, 3 (246b 3; 247a 1).   [19] Q. 66, a. 1.   [20] Aristotle, *Phys.,* VII, 3 (247a 6; 248a 6).

Second Article

WHETHER HABIT INCREASES BY ADDITION?

We proceed thus to the Second Article:—

Objection 1. It would seem that the increase of habits is by way of addition. For the name *increase,* as we have said, is transferred to forms from corporeal quantities. But in corporeal quantities there is no increase without addition; and therefore it is said that *increase is an addition to a magnitude already existing.*[21] Therefore in habits also there is no increase without addition.

Obj. 2. Further, a habit is not increased except by means of some agent. But every agent does something in the receiving subject. For instance, that which heats causes heat in that which is heated. Therefore there is no increase without addition.

Obj. 3. Further, as that which is not white is in potentiality to be white, so that which is less white is in potentiality to be more white. But that which is not white is not made white except by the addition of whiteness. Therefore that which is less white is not made more white, except by an added whiteness.

On the contrary, The Philosopher says: *That which is hot is made hotter, without making in the matter something hot, that was not hot when the thing was less hot.*[22] Therefore, in like manner, neither is any addition made in other forms when they increase.

I answer that, The solution of this question depends on what we have said above. For we said that increase and decrease in forms which are capable of intensity and remission happen, in one way, not on the part of the form itself considered in itself, but through a diverse participation in it by the subject. Therefore such increase of habits and other forms is not caused by an addition of form to form, but by the subject participating, more or less perfectly, in one and the same form. And just as, by an agent which is in act, something is made actually hot, beginning, as it were, to participate a form, not as though the form itself were made (as is proved in *Metaph.* vii.[23]), so by an intense action of the agent, something is made more hot, as it were participating in the form more perfectly, not as though something were added to the form.

For if this increase in forms were understood to be by way of addition, this could be only either in the form itself or in the subject. If it be understood of the form itself, it has already been stated that such an addition or subtraction would change the species; even as the species of color is changed when a thing from being yellow becomes white.—If, on the other hand, this addition be understood as applying to the subject, this could be only

[21] Aristotle, *De Gener.,* I, 5 (320b 30).   [22] *Phys.,* IV, 9 (217a 34).   [23] Aristotle. *Metaph.,* VI, 8 (1033b 5); 9 (1034b 7).

either because one part of the subject receives a form which it had not previously (thus we may say that cold increases in a man who, after being cold in one part of his body, is cold in several parts), or because some other subject is added sharing in the same form (as when a hot thing is added to another, or one white thing to another). But in either of these two ways we have not a more white or a more hot thing, but a greater white or hot thing.

Since, however, as was stated above, certain accidents are of themselves susceptible of more or less, in some of these we may find increase by addition. For movement increases by an addition either to the time it lasts, or to the course it follows; and yet the species remains the same because of the oneness of the terminus. Furthermore, movement increases in intensity through the participation of its subject, *i.e.*, in so far as the same movement can be executed more or less speedily or readily.—In like manner, science likewise can increase in itself by addition. Thus when anyone learns several conclusions of geometry, the same specific habit of science increases in that man. Yet a man's science increases in intensity, as to the subject's participation in it, in so far as one man is quicker and readier than another in considering the same conclusions.

As to bodily habits, it is difficult to see that they receive increase by way of addition. For an animal is not said to be healthy or beautiful absolutely, unless it be such in all its parts. And if it be brought to a more perfect measure, this is the result of a change in the simple qualities, which are not susceptible of increase save in intensity on the part of the subject partaking of them.

How this question affects virtues we shall state further on.[24]

Reply Obj. 1. Even in bodily bulk increase is twofold. First, by addition of one subject to another: such is the increase of living things. Secondly, by mere intensity, without any addition at all: such is the case with things subject to rarefaction, as is stated in *Physics* iv.[25]

Reply Obj. 2. The cause that increases a habit always effects something in the subject, but not a new form. Rather it causes the subject to partake more perfectly of a pre-existing form, or it makes the form to extend further.

Reply Obj. 3. What is not already white is potentially white, as not yet possessing the form of whiteness. Hence the agent causes a new form in the subject. But that which is less hot or white is not in potentiality to a form, since it already has it actually; but it is in potentiality to a perfect mode of participation, and this it receives through the agent's action.

[24] Q. 66, a. 1.   [25] Aristotle, *Phys.*, IV, 7 (214b 2); 9 (217b 8).

Third Article

WHETHER EVERY ACT INCREASES ITS HABIT?

We proceed thus to the Third Article:—

Objection 1. It would seem that every act increases its habit. For when the cause is increased the effect is increased. Now acts are causes of habits, as was stated above.[26] Therefore a habit increases when its acts are multiplied.

Obj. 2. Further, of like things a like judgment should be formed. But all the acts proceeding from one and the same habit are alike.[27] Therefor ; if some acts increase a habit, every act should increase it.

Obj. 3. Further, like is increased by like. But any act is like the habit whence it proceeds. Therefore every act increases its habit.

On the contrary, Opposite effects do not result from the same cause. But according to *Ethics* ii., some acts lessen the habit whence they proceed, for instance, if they be done carelessly.[28] Therefore it is not every act that increases a habit.

I answer that, Like acts cause like habits.[29] Now things are like or unlike not only according to the sameness or diversity of their quality, but also according to the same or a diverse mode of participation. For it is not only black that is unlike white, but also the less white is unlike the more white; since movement likewise takes place from the less white to the more white, as from one opposite to another, as is stated in *Physics* v.[30]

But since the use of habits depends on the will, as was shown above,[31] just as one who has a habit may fail to use it or may act contrary to it, so he may happen to use the habit by performing an act that is not in proportion to the intensity of the habit. Accordingly, if the intensity of the act be in proportion to the intensity of the habit, or even surpass it, every such act either increases the habit or disposes to its increase, if we may speak of the increase of habits as we do of the increase of an animal. For not every morsel of food actually increases the animal's size, as neither does every drop of water hollow out the stone; but the multiplication of food results at last in an increase of the body. So, too, repeated acts cause a habit to grow.—If, however, the act falls proportionately short of the intensity of the habit, such an act does not dispose to an increase of that habit, but rather to its lessening.

From this it is clear how to solve the objections.

[26] Q. 51, a. 2.   [27] Aristotle, *Eth.*, II, 2 (1104a 29).   [28] *Ibid.* (1104a 18).   [29] *Op cit.*, II, 1 (1103b 21).   [30] Aristotle, *Phys.*, V, 5 (229b 14).   [31] Q. 50, a. 5.

HOW HABITS ARE CORRUPTED AND DIMINISHED·
(*In Three Articles*)

WE must now consider how habits are lost and weakened. Under this head there are three points of inquiry: (1) Whether a habit can be corrupted? (2) Whether it can be diminished? (3) How are habits corrupted and diminished?

First Article

WHETHER A HABIT CAN BE CORRUPTED?

We proceed thus to the First Article:—

Objection 1. It would seem that a habit cannot be corrupted. For habit is within its subject as a kind of nature, and that is why it is pleasant to act from habit. Now so long as a thing is, its nature is not corrupted. Therefore neither can a habit be corrupted so long as its subject remains.

Obj. 2. Further, whenever a form is corrupted, this is due either to corruption of its subject, or to its contrary. Thus, sickness ceases through corruption of the animal, or through the advent of health. But science, which is a habit, cannot be lost through corruption of its subject, since *the intellect,* which is its subject, *is a substance that is incorruptible.*[1] In like manner, neither can it be lost through the action of its contrary, since intelligible species are not contrary to one another.[2] Therefore the habit of science can in no way be lost.

Obj. 3. Further, all corruption results from some movement. But the habit of science, which is in the soul, cannot be corrupted by a direct movement of the soul itself, since the soul is not moved directly. It is, however, moved indirectly through the movement of the body. But no bodily change seems capable of corrupting the intelligible species residing in the intellect, since the intellect, independently of the body, is the proper abode of the species; for which reason it is held that habits are not lost either through old age or through death. Therefore science cannot be corrupted. For the same reason neither can habits of virtue be corrupted, since they also are in the rational soul, and, as the Philosopher declares, *virtue is more lasting than learning.*[3]

On the contrary, The Philosopher says that *forgetfulness and deception*

---

[1] Aristotle, *De An.,* I, 4 (408b 18).   [2] Aristotle, *Metaph.,* VI, 7 (1032b 2),
[3] *Eth.,* I, 10 (1100b 14).

are the corruption of science.[4] Moreover, by sinning a man loses a habit of virtue; and again, virtues are engendered and corrupted by contrary acts.[5]

I answer that, A form is said to be corrupted directly by its contrary; indirectly, through its subject being corrupted. When, therefore, a habit has a corruptible subject, and a cause that has a contrary, it can be corrupted both ways. This is clearly the case with bodily habits—for instance, health and sickness. But those habits that have an incorruptible subject cannot be corrupted indirectly. There are, however, some habits which, while residing chiefly in an incorruptible subject, nevertheless reside secondarily in a corruptible subject. Such is the habit of science which is chiefly indeed in the possible intellect, but secondarily in the sensitive powers of apprehension, as was stated above.[6] Consequently the habit of science cannot be corrupted indirectly, on the part of the possible intellect, but only on the part of the lower sensitive powers.

We must therefore inquire whether habits of this kind can be corrupted directly. Now if there be a habit having a contrary, either on the part of itself or on the part of its cause, it can be corrupted directly; but if it has no contrary, it cannot be corrupted directly. But it is evident that an intelligible species residing in the possible intellect has no contrary; nor can the agent intellect, which is the cause of that species, have a contrary. Therefore, if in the possible intellect there be a habit caused immediately by the agent intellect, such a habit is incorruptible both directly and indirectly. Such are the habits of first principles, both speculative and practical, which cannot be corrupted by any forgetfulness or deception whatever; even as the Philosopher says about prudence that it cannot be lost by being forgotten.[7]—There is, however, in the possible intellect a habit caused by the reason, namely, the habit of conclusions, which is called science, to the cause of which something may be contrary in two ways. First, on the part of those very propositions which are the starting-point of the reason; for the assertion *Good is not good* is contrary to the assertion *Good is good.*[8] Secondly, on the part of the process itself of reasoning, in so far as a sophistical syllogism is contrary to a dialectic or demonstrative syllogism. Therefore it is clear that a false reason can corrupt the habit of a true opinion or even of science. Hence the Philosopher, as was stated above, says that *deception is the corruption of science.*[9]

As to virtues, some of them are intellectual, residing in the reason itself, as is stated in *Ethics* vi.;[10] and to these applies what we have said of science and opinion.—Some, however, viz., the moral virtues, are in the appetitive part of the soul; and the same may be said of the contrary vices. Now the habits of the appetitive part are caused therein because it is natural to it

[4] *De Long. et Brev. Vitae,* II (465a 23).   [5] Aristotle, *Eth.,* II, 1 (1103b 7); 3 (1105a 15).   [6] Q. 50, a. 3, ad 3.   [7] *Eth.,* VI, 5 (1140b 29).   [8] *Perih.,* II, 14 (24a 2).   [9] *De Long. et Brev. Vitae,* II (465a 23).   [10] Aristotle, *Eth.,* VI, 1 (1139a 1); 2 (1139b 12).

to be moved by the reason. Therefore a habit either of virtue or of vice may be corrupted by a judgment of reason, whenever its motion is contrary to such vice or virtue, whether through ignorance, passion or deliberate choice.

Reply Obj. 1. As is stated in *Ethics* vii., a habit is like nature, and yet it falls short of it.[11] And so it is that while the nature of a thing cannot in any way be taken away from a thing, a habit is removed, though with difficulty.

Reply Obj. 2. Although there is no contrary to intelligible species, yet there can be a contrary to assertions and to the process of reason, as was stated above.

Reply Obj. 3. Science is not taken away by movement of the body, if we consider the root itself of the habit, but only as it may prove an obstacle to the act of science, in so far as the intellect has need in its operation of the sensitive powers, which are impeded by corporal transmutation. But the intellectual movement of the reason can corrupt the habit of science, even as regards the very root of the habit. In like manner a habit of virtue can be corrupted.—Nevertheless, when it is said that *virtue is more lasting than learning,*[12] this must be understood, not of the subject or cause, but of the act; because the use of virtue continues through the whole of life, whereas the use of learning does not.

Second Article

WHETHER A HABIT CAN DIMINISH?

We proceed thus to the Second Article:—

Objection 1. It would seem that a habit cannot diminish. Because a habit is a simple quality and form. Now a simple thing is possessed either wholly or not at all. Therefore, although a habit can be lost, it cannot diminish.

Obj. 2. Further, if a thing is befitting an accident, this is by reason either of the accident or of its subject. Now a habit does not become more or less intense by reason of itself, or else it would follow that a species might be predicated of its individuals according to more and less. Now if it can become less intense through the participation of its subject, it would follow that some property befell the habit, which was not common to the habit and its subject. Now whenever a form has something proper to it besides its subject, that form can be separate, as is stated in *De Anima* i.[13] Hence it follows that a habit is a separable form; which is impossible.

Obj. 3. Further, the very notion and nature of a habit, as of any accident, is inherence in a subject; and therefore any accident is defined with reference to its subject. Therefore, if a habit does not become more or less

[11] *Op. cit.,* VII, 10 (1152a 31).   [12] *Op. cit.,* I, 10 (1100b 14).   [13] Aristotle, *De An.,* I, 1 (403a 10).

intense in itself, neither can it be diminished in its inherence in its subject; and consequently it will be in no way less intense.

On the contrary, It is natural for contraries to be applicable to the same thing. Now increase and decrease are contraries. Since, therefore, a habit can increase, evidently it can also diminish.

I answer that, Habits diminish, just as they increase, in two ways, as we have already explained.[14] And since they increase through the same cause as that which engenders them, so too they diminish by the same cause as that which corrupts them; for the diminishing of a habit is the road which leads to its corruption, even as, on the other hand, the engendering of a habit is a foundation of its increase.

Reply Obj. 1. A habit, considered in itself, is a simple form. It is not thus that it is subject to decrease, but according to the different ways in which its subject participates in it. This is due to the fact that the subject's potentiality is indeterminate, through its being able to participate in a form in various ways, or to extend to a greater or a smaller number of things.

Reply Obj. 2. This argument would hold if the essence itself of a habit were in no way subject to decrease. This we do not hold, but that a certain decrease in the essence of a habit has its origin, not in the habit, but in its subject.

Reply Obj. 3. No matter how we take an accident, its very notion implies dependence on a subject, but in different ways. For if we take an accident in the abstract, it implies relation to a subject, which relation begins in the accident and terminates in the subject; for whiteness is that whereby a thing is white. Accordingly, in defining an accident in the abstract, we do not put the subject as though it were the first part of the definition, viz., the genus; but we give it the second place, which is that of the difference: thus, we say that snubness is a *curvature of the nose.* But if we take accidents in the concrete, the relation begins in the subject and terminates at the accident; for *a white thing* is *something that has whiteness.* Accordingly, in defining this kind of accident, we place the subject as the genus, which is the first part of a definition; for we say that the snub is a *curved nose.* Accordingly, whatever is befitting an accident on the part of the subject, but is not of the very essence of the accident, is ascribed to that accident, not in the abstract, but in the concrete. Such are increase and decrease in certain accidents. Hence to be more or less white is not ascribed to whiteness but to a white thing. The same applies to habits and other qualities; save that certain habits increase or diminish by a kind of addition, as we have already explained.[15]

---

[14] Q. 52, a. 1.   [15] Q. 52, a. 2.

Third Article

WHETHER A HABIT IS CORRUPTED OR DIMINISHED THROUGH MERE CESSATION FROM ACT?

We proceed thus to the Third Article:—

Objection 1. It would seem that a habit is not corrupted or diminished through mere cessation from act. For habits are more lasting than passion-like qualities, as we have explained above.[16] But passion-like qualities are neither corrupted nor diminished by cessation from act; for whiteness is not lessened through not affecting the sight, nor heat through ceasing to make something hot. Therefore neither are habits diminished or corrupted through cessation from act.

Obj 2. Further, corruption and diminution are changes. Now nothing is changed without a moving cause. Since, therefore, cessation from act does not imply a moving cause, it does not appear how a habit can be diminished or corrupted through cessation from act.

Obj. 3. Further, the habits of science and virtue are in the intellectual soul, which is above time. Now those things that are above time are neither destroyed nor diminished by length of time. Neither, therefore, are such habits destroyed or diminished through length of time, if one should fail for long to exercise them.

On the contrary, The Philosopher says that not only *deception,* but also *forgetfulness, is the corruption of science.*[17] Moreover he says that *want of communication has dissolved many a friendship.*[18] In like manner, other habits of virtue are diminished or destroyed through cessation from act.

I answer that, As stated in *Physics* viii., a thing is a cause of movement in two ways.[19] First, directly, and such a thing causes movement by reason of its own form: thus, fire causes heat. Secondly, indirectly: for instance, that which removes an obstacle. It is in this latter way that the destruction or diminution of a habit results through cessation from act, in so far, namely, as we cease from exercising an act which removed the causes that destroyed or weakened that habit. For it has been stated that habits are destroyed or diminished directly through some contrary agent. Consequently, all habits that are gradually undermined by contrary agents which need to be counteracted by acts proceeding from those habits, are diminished or even destroyed altogether by long cessation from act, as is clearly seen in the case both of science and of virtue. For it is evident that a habit of moral virtue makes a man ready to choose the mean in deeds and passions. And when a man fails to make use of his virtuous habit in order to moderate his own passions or deeds, the necessary result is that many passions and deeds fail to observe the norm of virtue, by reason of the in-

---

[16] Q. 49, a. 2, ad 3; q. 50, a. 1.   [17] *De Long. et. Brev. Vitae,* II (465a 23).
[18] Aristotle, *Eth.,* VIII, 5 (1157b 13).   [19] Aristotle, *Phys.,* VIII, 4 (254b 7).

clination of the sensitive appetite and of other and external causes. Therefore virtue is destroyed or lessened through cessation from act.—The same
applies to the intellectual habits, which render a man ready to judge
rightly of those things that are pictured by his imagination. Hence when a
man ceases to make use of his intellectual habits, strange fancies, sometimes
in opposition to them, arise in his imagination; so that unless those fancies
be, as it were, cut off or kept back by frequent use of his intellectual habits,
a man becomes less fit to judge rightly, and sometimes is even wholly disposed to the contrary. And thus the intellectual habit is diminished or even
wholly destroyed by cessation from act.

Reply Obj. 1. Even heat would be destroyed through ceasing to give
heat, if, for this same reason, cold, which is destructive of heat, were to
increase.

Reply Obj. 2. Cessation from act is a moving cause conducive to corruption or diminution, by removing the obstacles thereto, as was explained
above.

Reply Obj. 3. The intellectual part of the soul, considered in itself, is
above time; but the sensitive part is subject to time, and therefore in the
course of time it undergoes change as to the passions of the sensitive part,
and also as to the powers of apprehension. Hence the Philosopher says that
time makes us forget.[20]

[20] *Phys.* IV, 12 (221a 32); 13 (222b 16).

ON THE DISTINCTION OF HABITS
(*In Four Articles*)

WE have now to consider the distinction of habits. Under this head there are four points of inquiry: (1) Whether many habits can be in one power? (2) Whether habits are distinguished by their objects? (3) Whether habits are divided into good and bad? (4) Whether one habit may be made up of many habits?

First Article

WHETHER MANY HABITS CAN BE IN ONE POWER?

We proceed thus to the First Article:—

Objection 1. It would seem that there cannot be many habits in one power. For when several things are distinguished in the same respect, if one of them be multiplied, the others are too. Now habits and powers are distinguished in the same respect, viz., their acts and objects. Therefore they are multiplied in like manner. Therefore there cannot be many habits in one power.

Obj. 2. Further, a power is a simple force. Now in one simple subject there cannot be diversity of accidents, for the subject is the cause of its accidents, and it does not appear how diverse effects can proceed from one simple cause. Therefore there cannot be many habits in one power.

Obj. 3. Further, just as the body is informed by its shape, so is a power informed by a habit. But one body cannot be informed at the same time by various shapes. Therefore neither can a power be informed at the same time by many habits. Therefore many habits cannot be at the same time in one power.

On the contrary, The intellect is one power, wherein, nevertheless, are the habits of various sciences.

I answer that, As was stated above, habits are dispositions of a thing that is in potentiality to something, either to nature, or to operation, which is the end of nature.[1] As to those habits which are dispositions to nature, it is clear that several can be in one same subject; for in one subject we may consider *parts* in various ways, and according to the various dispositions of these parts there are various habits. Thus, if we take the humors as parts of the human body, according to their disposition in human nature, we

[1] Q. 49, a. 4.

have the habit or disposition of health; if we take like parts, such as nerves, bones and flesh, the disposition of these in respect of nature is strength or weakness; and if we take the members, *i.e.*, the hands, feet, and so on, the disposition of these which befits nature is beauty. Thus there are several habits or dispositions in the same subject.

If, however, we speak of those habits that are dispositions to operation, and belong properly to the powers, thus, again, there may be several habits in one power. The reason for this is that the subject of a habit is a passive power, as was stated above;[2] for it is only an active power that cannot be the subject of a habit, as was shown above.[3] Now a passive power is compared to the determinate act of any species as matter to form. For, just as matter is determined to one form by one agent, so, too, a passive power is determined by the nature of one active object to an act specifically one. Therefore, just as several objects can move one passive power, so can one passive power be the subject of several acts or perfections specifically diverse. Now habits are qualities or forms adhering to a power, and inclining that power to acts of a determinate species. Consequently, several habits, even as several specifically different acts, can belong to one power.

Reply Obj. 1. Even as in natural things diversity of species is according to the form, and diversity of genus according to matter, as is stated in *Metaph.* v.[4] (since things that differ in matter belong to different genera), so, too, a generic diversity of objects entails a distinction of powers (and so the Philosopher says in *Ethics* vi. that *those things that differ generically belong to different parts of the soul*);[5] while a specific difference of objects entails a specific difference of acts, and consequently also of habits. Now things that differ in genus differ in species, but not vice versa. Therefore the acts and habits of different powers differ in species; but it does not follow that different habits are in different powers, for several can be in one power. And even as several genera may be included in one genus, and several species be contained in one species, so does it happen that there are several species of habits and powers.

Reply Obj. 2. Although a power is simple as to its essence, it is multiple virtually, inasmuch as it extends to many specifically different acts. Consequently, there is nothing to prevent many superficially different habits from being in one power.

Reply Obj. 3. A body is informed by its shape as by its own terminal boundaries; whereas a habit is not the terminal boundary of a power, but the disposition of a power to an act as to its ultimate term. Consequently, one and the same power cannot have several acts at the same time, except in so far as perchance one act is comprised in another; just as neither can a body have several shapes, save in so far as one shape enters into another, as

---

[2] Q. 51, a. 2.   [3] *Ibid.*   [4] Aristotle, *Metaph.*, IV, 28 (1024b 9); cf. *op. cit.*, IX, 3 (1054b 26).   [5] *Eth.*, VI, 1 (1139a 8).

a three-sided in a four-sided figure. For the intellect cannot understand several things at the same time *actually*; and yet it can know several things at the same time *habitually*.

Second Article

WHETHER HABITS ARE DISTINGUISHED BY THEIR OBJECTS?

We proceed thus to the Second Article:—

Objection 1. It would seem that habits are not distinguished by their objects. For contraries differ in species. Now the same habit of science regards contraries. Thus medicine regards the healthy and the unhealthy. Therefore habits are not distinguished by objects specifically distinct.

Obj. 2. Further, different sciences are different habits. But the same scientific truth belongs to different sciences. Thus, both the natural philosopher and the astronomer prove the earth to be round, as is stated in *Physics* ii.[6] Therefore habits are not distinguished by their objects.

Obj. 3. Further, wherever the act is the same, the object is the same. But the same act can belong to different habits of virtue, if it be directed to different ends. Thus, to give money to anyone, if it be done for God's sake, is an act of charity; while, if it be done in order to pay a debt, it is an act of justice. Therefore the same object can also belong to different habits. Therefore diversity of habits does not follow diversity of objects.

On the contrary, Acts differ in species according to the diversity of their objects, as was stated above.[7] But habits are dispositions to acts. Therefore habits also are distinguished according to the diversity of objects.

I answer that, A habit is both a form and a habit. Hence the specific distinction of habits may be taken in the ordinary way in which forms differ specifically, or according to that mode of distinction which is proper to habits. Now forms are distinguished from one another in reference to the diversity of their active principles, since every agent produces its like in species. Habits, however, imply order to something, and all things that imply order to something are distinguished according to the distinction of the things to which they are ordained. Now a habit is a disposition implying a twofold order: viz., to nature, and to an operation consequent to nature. Accordingly, habits are specifically distinct in respect of three things. First, in respect of the active principles of such dispositions; secondly, in respect of nature; thirdly, in respect of specifically different objects, as will appear from what follows.

Reply Obj. 1. In distinguishing powers, or also habits, we must consider the object, not in its material aspect, but in its formal aspect, which may differ in species or even in genus. And though the distinction between specific contraries is a real distinction, yet they are both known under one

---

[6] Aristotle, *Phys.*, II, 2 (193b 25).   [7] Q. 18, a. 5.

aspect, since one is known through the other. And, consequently, in so far as they concur in the one aspect of cognoscibility, they belong to one cognitive habit.

Reply Obj. 2. The natural philosopher proves the earth to be round by one means, the astronomer by another. For the latter proves this by means of mathematics, *e.g.*, by the shapes of eclipses, or something of the sort; while the former proves it by means of physics, *e.g.*, by the movement of heavy bodies towards the center, and so forth. Now the whole force of a demonstration, which is *a syllogism producing science,* as is stated in *Posterior Analytics* i.,[8] depends on the means. And consequently various means are as so many active principles according to which the habits of science are distinguished.

Reply Obj. 3. As the Philosopher says, the end is, in practical matters, what a principle is in demonstrative matters.[9] Consequently, a diversity of ends demands a diversity of virtues, even as a diversity of active principles does.—Moreover, the ends are objects of the internal acts, with which, above all, the virtues are concerned, as is evident from what has been said.[10]

Third Article

WHETHER HABITS ARE DIVIDED INTO GOOD AND BAD?

We proceed thus to the Third Article:—

Objection 1. It would seem that habits are not divided into good and bad. For good and bad are contraries. Now the same habit regards contraries, as was stated above. Therefore habits are not divided into good and bad.

Obj. 2. Further, good is convertible with being, so that, since it is common to all, it cannot be accounted a specific difference, as the Philosopher declares.[11] Again, evil, since it is a privation and a non-being, cannot differentiate any being. Therefore habits cannot be specifically divided into good and evil.

Obj. 3. Further, there can be different evil habits about one and the same object: for instance, intemperance and insensibility about matters of concupiscence; and in like manner there can be several good habits: for instance, human virtue and heroic or godlike virtue, as the Philosopher clearly states.[12] Therefore, habits are not divided into good and bad.

On the contrary, A good habit is contrary to a bad habit, as virtue to vice. Now contraries are distinct specifically. Therefore habits are divided specifically into good and bad habits.

I answer that, As was stated above, habits are specifically distinct not only in respect of their objects and active principles, but also in their rela-

---

[8] Aristotle, *Post. Anal.,* I, 2 (71b 18).   [9] *Phys.,* II, 9 (200a 15); *Eth.,* VII, 8 (1151a 16).   [10] Q. 18, a. 6; q. 19, a. 2, ad 1; q. 34, a. 4.   [11] *Top.,* IV, 6 (127a 26).   [12] *Eth.,* VII, 1 (1145a 15).

tion to nature. Now this happens in two ways. First, by reason of their suitableness or unsuitableness to nature. In this way a good habit is specifically distinct from a bad habit. For a good habit is one which disposes to an act suitable to the agent's nature, while a bad habit is one which disposes to an act unsuitable to nature. Thus, acts of virtue are suitable to human nature, since they are according to reason, whereas acts of vice are opposed to human nature, since they are against reason. Hence it is clear that habits are distinguished specifically by the difference of good and bad.

Secondly, habits are distinguished in relation to nature from the fact that one habit disposes to an act that is suitable to a lower nature, while another habit disposes to an act befitting a higher nature. And thus human virtue, which disposes to an act befitting human nature, is distinct from godlike or heroic virtue, which disposes to an act befitting some higher nature.

Reply Obj. 1. The same habit may be about contraries in so far as contraries agree in one common aspect. Never, however, does it happen that contrary habits are in one species, since contrariety of habits follows contrariety of aspect. Accordingly, habits are divided into good and bad, namely, inasmuch as one habit is good, and another bad; but not because one habit is about something good, and another about something bad.

Reply Obj. 2. It is not the good which is common to every being that is a difference constituting the species of a habit; it is rather some determinate good, by reason of a suitability to some determinate, viz., human, nature. In like manner, the evil that constitutes a difference of habits is not a pure privation, but something determinate repugnant to a determinate nature.

Reply Obj. 3. Several good habits about one and the same specific thing are distinguished according to their suitability to various natures, as was stated above. But several bad habits in respect of one action are distinguished according to their diverse repugnance to that which is in keeping with nature. Thus, various vices about one and the same matter are contrary to one virtue.

Fourth Article

WHETHER ONE HABIT IS MADE UP OF MANY HABITS?

We proceed thus to the Fourth Article:—

Objection 1. It would seem that one habit is made up of many habits. For whatever is engendered, not at once, but little by little, seems to be made up of several parts. But a habit is engendered, not at once, but little by little, out of several acts, as was stated above.[13] Therefore one habit is made up of several.

---

[13] Q. 51, a. 3.

Obj. 2. Further, a whole is made up of its parts. Now many parts are assigned to one habit. Thus Tully assigns many parts of fortitude, temperance and the other virtues.[14] Therefore one habit is made up of several.

Obj. 3. Further, one conclusion suffices both for an act and for a habit of scientific knowledge. But many conclusions belong to but one science, to geometry, for instance, or to arithmetic. Therefore one habit is made up of many.

On the contrary, A habit, since it is a quality, is a simple form. But nothing simple is made up of many. Therefore one habit is not made up of many.

I answer that, A habit directed to operation, such as we are chiefly concerned with at present, is a perfection of a power. Now every perfection is proportioned to that which it perfects. Hence, just as a power, while it is one, extends to many things in so far as they have something in common (*i.e.,* some general objective aspect), so also a habit extends to many things in so far as they are related to one thing, for instance, to some specific objective aspect, or to one nature, or to one principle, as was stated above.

If, then, we consider a habit from the standpoint of the things to which it extends, we shall find a certain multiplicity in it. But since this multiplicity is directed to something one, on which the habit is chiefly intent, hence it is that a habit is a simple quality, not composed of several habits, even though it extend to many things. For a habit does not extend to many things save in relation to something one, whence it derives its unity.

Reply Obj. 1. That a habit is engendered little by little is due, not to one part being engendered after another, but to the fact that the subject does not acquire all at once a firm and with difficulty changeable disposition; and also to the fact that it begins by being imperfectly in the subject, and is gradually perfected. The same applies to other qualities.

Reply Obj. 2. The parts which are assigned to each cardinal virtue are not integral parts that combine to form a whole, but subjective or potential parts, as we shall explain further on.[15]

Reply Obj. 3. In any science, he who acquires by demonstration a scientific knowledge of one conclusion has the habit indeed, yet imperfectly. And when he obtains by demonstration the scientific knowledge of another conclusion, no additional habit is engendered in him, but the habit which was in him previously is made more perfect, in so far as it extends to more things. For the conclusions and demonstrations of one science are mutually ordered, and one flows from another.

---

[14] *De Invent.,* II, 54 (p. 149ᵇ).   [15] Q. 57, a. 6, ad 4; II-II, q. 48.

ON THE VIRTUES, AS TO THEIR ESSENCE
(*In Four Articles*)

WE come now to a particular consideration of habits. And since habits, as we have said, are divided into good and bad,[1] we must speak in the first place of good habits, which are virtues, and of other matters connected with them, namely, the Gifts, Beatitudes and Fruits;[2] in the second place, of bad habits, namely, of vices and sins.[3] Now five things must be considered about virtues: (1) the essence of virtue; (2) its subject;[4] (3) the division of the virtues;[5] (4) the cause of virtue;[6] (5) certain properties of virtue.[7]

Under the first head, there are four points of inquiry: (1) Whether human virtue is a habit? (2) Whether it is an operative habit? (3) Whether it is a good habit? (4) The definition of virtue.

First Article

WHETHER HUMAN VIRTUE IS A HABIT?

We proceed thus to the First Article:—

Objection 1. It would seem that human virtue is not a habit. For virtue is *the peak of power.*[8] But the peak of anything is reducible to the genus of that of which it is the peak, as a point is reducible to the genus of line. Therefore virtue is reducible to the genus of power, and not to the genus of habit.

Obj. 2. Further, Augustine says that *virtue is good use of free choice.*[9] But use of free choice is an act. Therefore virtue is not a habit, but an act.

Obj. 3. Further, we do not merit by our habits, but by our actions, or otherwise a man would merit continually, even while asleep. But we do merit by our virtues. Therefore virtues are not habits, but acts.

Obj. 4. Further, Augustine says that *virtue is the order of love,*[10] and that *the ordering which is called virtue consists in enjoying what we ought to enjoy, and using what we ought to use.*[11] Now order, or ordering, denominates either an action or a relation. Therefore virtue is not a habit, but an action or a relation.

---

[1] Q. 54, a. 3.   [2] Q. 68.   [3] Q. 71.   [4] Q. 56.   [5] Q. 57.   [6] Q. 63.   [7] Q. 64.
[8] Aristotle, *De Caelo,* I, 11 (281a 14; a 18).—Cf. St. Thomas, *In De Caelo,* I, lect. 25.
[9] *De Lib. Arb.,* II, 19 (PL 32, 1268); *Retract.,* I, 9 (PL 32, 598).   [10] *De Mor. Eccl.,* I, 15 (PL 32, 1322).   [11] *Lib. 83 Quaest.,* q. 30 (PL 40, 19).

Obj. 5. Further, just as there are human virtues, so there are natural virtues. But natural virtues are not habits, but powers. Neither therefore are human virtues habits.

On the contrary, The Philosopher says that *science and virtue are habits.*[12]

I answer that, Virtue denotes a certain perfection of a power. Now a thing's perfection is considered chiefly in relation to its end. But the end of power is act. Therefore power is said to be perfect according as it is determined to its act. Now there are some powers which of themselves are determined to their acts, for instance, the active natural powers. And therefore these natural powers are in themselves called virtues. But the rational powers, which are proper to man, are not determined to one particular action, but are inclined indifferently to many; but they are determined to acts by means of habits, as is clear from what we have said above.[13] Therefore human virtues are habits.

Reply Obj. 1. Sometimes we give the name of a virtue to that to which the virtue is directed, namely, either to its object or to its act. For instance, we give the name faith to that which we believe, or to the act of believing, as also to the habit by which we believe. When therefore we say that *virtue is the peak of power,* virtue is taken for the object of virtue. For the highest point to which a power can reach is said to be its virtue: for instance, if a man can carry a hundredweight and not more, his virtue [*i.e.,* his strength] is put at a hundredweight, and not at sixty. But the objection takes virtue as being essentially the peak of power.

Reply Obj. 2. Good use of free choice is said to be a virtue in the same sense as above, that is to say, because it is that to which virtue is directed as to its proper act. For an act of virtue is nothing else than the good use of free choice.

Reply Obj. 3. We are said to merit by something in two ways. First, as by merit itself, just as we are said to run by running; and thus we merit by acts. Secondly, we are said to merit by something as by the principle whereby we merit, as we are said to run by the power of locomotion; and thus are we said to merit by virtues and habits.

Reply Obj. 4. When we say that virtue is the order or ordering of love, we refer to the end to which virtue is ordered; because in us love is set in order by virtue.

Reply Obj. 5. Natural powers are of themselves determined to one act; not so the rational powers. Hence there is no comparison, as we have said.

---

[12] *Cat.,* VIII (8b 29). [13] Q. 49, a. 4.

Second Article

WHETHER HUMAN VIRTUE IS AN OPERATIVE HABIT?

We proceed thus to the Second Article:—

Objection 1. It would seem that it is not essential to human virtue to be an operative habit. For Tully says that as health and beauty belong to the body, so virtue belongs to the soul.[14] But health and beauty are not operative habits. Therefore neither is virtue.

Obj. 2. Further, in natural things we find virtue not only in reference to act, but also in reference to being, as is clear from the Philosopher,[15] for some things have a virtue to be always, while others have a virtue to be, not always, but at some definite time. Now as natural virtue is in natural things, so human virtue is in rational beings. Therefore human virtue is referred not only to act, but also to being.

Obj. 3. Further, the Philosopher says that virtue *is the disposition of that which is perfect to that which is best.*[16] Now the best thing to which man needs to be disposed by virtue is God Himself, as Augustine proves,[17] to Whom the soul is disposed by being made like to Him. Therefore it seems that virtue is a quality of the soul in reference to God, likening it, as it were, to Him; and not in reference to operation. It is not, therefore, an operative habit.

On the contrary, The Philosopher says that *the virtue of a thing is that which makes its work good.*[18]

I answer that, Virtue, from the very nature of the name, implies some perfection of power, as we have said above. Therefore, since potency is of two kinds, namely, potency in reference to being, and potency in reference to act, the perfection of both these potencies is called virtue. But potency in reference to being is on the part of matter, which is potential being, whereas potency in reference to act [or *power*] is on the part of the form, which is the principle of action, since everything acts in so far as it is in act.

Now man is so constituted that the body holds the place of matter, the soul that of form. The body, indeed, man has in common with other animals; and the same is to be said of the powers which are common to the soul and body; and only those powers which are proper to the soul, namely, the rational powers, belong to man alone. Therefore, human virtue, of which we are speaking now, cannot belong to the body, but belongs only to that which is proper to the soul. Therefore human virtue does not imply reference to being, but rather to act. Consequently it is essential to human virtue to be an operative habit.

[14] *Tusc. Disp.,* IV, 13 (pp. 375-376).   [15] *De Caelo,* I, 12 (281a 28).   [16] *Phys.,* VII, 3 (246b 23).—Cf. *ibid.* (246a 13).   [17] *De Mor. Eccl.,* II, 3 (PL 32, 1347).   [18] *Eth.,* II, 6 (1106a 15).

Reply Obj. 1. The mode of action follows on the disposition of the agent; for such as a thing is, such is its act. And therefore, since virtue is the principle of some kind of operation, there must needs pre-exist in the operator, in respect of virtue, some corresponding disposition. Now virtue causes an ordered operation. Therefore virtue itself is an ordered disposition of the soul, in so far as, namely, the powers of the soul are in some way ordered to one another, and to that which is outside. Hence virtue, inasmuch as it is a suitable disposition of the soul, is like health and beauty, which are suitable dispositions of the body. But this does not hinder virtue from being also a principle of operation.

Reply Obj. 2. Virtue which is referred to being is not proper to man; but only that virtue which is referred to works of reason, which are proper to man.

Reply Obj. 3. As God's substance is His act, the highest likeness of man to God is in respect of some operation. Therefore, as we have said above, happiness or beatitude, by which man is made most perfectly conformed to God, and which is the end of human life, consists in an operation.[19]

Third Article

WHETHER HUMAN VIRTUE IS A GOOD HABIT?

We proceed thus to the Third Article:—

Objection 1. It would seem that it is not essential to virtue that it should be a good habit. For sin is always taken in a bad sense. But there is a virtue even of sin, according to *1 Cor.* xv. 56: *The virtue* [Douay, *strength*] *of sin is the Law.* Therefore virtue is not always a good habit.

Obj. 2. Further, Virtue corresponds to power. But power is not referred only to good, but also to evil, according to *Isa.* v. 22: *Woe to you that are mighty to drink wine, and stout men at drunkenness.* Therefore virtue also is referred to good and evil.

Obj. 3. Further, according to the Apostle (*2 Cor.* xii. 9): *Virtue* [Douay, *Power*] *is made perfect in infirmity.* But infirmity is an evil. Therefore virtue is referred not only to good, but also to evil.

On the contrary, Augustine says: *No one can doubt that virtue makes the soul exceeding good;*[20] and the Philosopher says: *Virtue is that which makes its possessor good, and his work good likewise.*[21]

I answer that, As we have said above, virtue implies a perfection of power, and therefore the virtue of a thing is fixed by the peak of its power.[22] Now the peak of any power must needs be good, for all evil implies defect. Hence Dionysius says that every evil is a weakness.[23] And for this reason the virtue of a thing must be regarded in reference to good.

---

[19] Q. 3, a. 2.   [20] *De Mor. Eccl.,* I, 6 (PL 32, 1314).   [21] *Eth.,* II, 6 (1106a 15).
[22] Aristotle, *De Caelo,* I, 11 (281a 14; a 18).   [23] *De Div. Nom.,* IV, 32 (PG 3, 732).

Therefore human virtue, which is an operative habit, is a good habit, productive of good works.

Reply Obj. 1. Just as bad things are said metaphorically to be perfect, so are they said to be good; for we speak of a perfect thief or robber, and of a good thief or robber, as the Philosopher explains.[24] In this way, therefore, virtue is applied to evil things. And thus it is that the *virtue of sin* is said to be the *law,* in so far as occasionally sin is aggravated through the law, so as to attain to the limit of its possibility.

Reply Obj. 2. The evil of drunkenness and excessive drink consists in a falling away from the order of reason. Now it happens that, together with this falling away from reason, some lower power is perfect in reference to that which belongs to its own kind, even in direct opposition to reason, or in defection from it. But the perfection of that power, since it is accompanied by a defection from reason, cannot be called a human virtue.

Reply Obj. 3. Reason is shown to be so much the more perfect according as it is able to overcome or endure more easily the weakness of the body and of the lower powers. And that is why human virtue, which is attributed to reason, is said to be *made perfect in infirmity,* not indeed in an infirmity of the reason, but of the body and of the lower powers.

Fourth Article

WHETHER VIRTUE IS SUITABLY DEFINED?

We proceed thus to the Fourth Article:—

Objection 1. It would seem that the definition usually given of virtue (namely, *Virtue is a good quality of the mind, by which we live righteously, of which no one can make bad use, which God works in us without us*[25]) is not suitable. For virtue is man's goodness, since it is virtue that makes its subject good. But goodness does not seem to be good, as neither is whiteness white. It is therefore unsuitable to describe virtue as a *good quality*.

Obj. 2. Further, no difference is more common than its genus, since it is that which divides the genus. But *good* is more common than quality, since it is convertible with being. Therefore *good* should not be put in the definition of virtue, as a difference of quality.

Obj. 3. Further, as Augustine says: *When we come across anything that is not common to us and the beasts of the field, it is something pertaining to the mind.*[26] But there are virtues even of the irrational parts, as the Philosopher says.[27] Every virtue, therefore, is not a good quality *of the mind*.

Obj. 4. Further, righteousness seems to belong to justice; whence the righteous are called just. But justice is a species of virtue. It is therefore

[24] *Metaph.,* IV, 16 (1021b 17).   [25] Cf. Peter Lombard, *Sent.,* II, xxvii, 5 (I, 446).
[26] *De Trin.,* XII, 8 (PL 42, 1005).   [27] *Eth.,* III, 10 (1117b 23).

unsuitable to put *righteous* in the definition of virtue, when it is said that virtue is that *by which we live righteously.*

Obj. 5. Further, whoever is proud of a thing, makes bad use of it. But many are proud of virtue, for Augustine says in his *Rule,* that *pride lies in wait for good works in order to slay them.*[28] It is untrue, therefore, *that no one can make bad use of virtue.*

Obj. 6. Further, man is justified by virtue. But Augustine, commenting on *Jo.* xiv. 12 (*He shall do greater things than these*) says: *He who created thee without thee will not justify thee without thee.*[29] It is therefore unsuitable to say that *God works virtue in us without us.*

On the contrary, We have the authority of Augustine, from whose words this definition is gathered, and principally in *De Libero Arbitrio* ii.[30]

I answer that, This definition comprises perfectly the whole essential notion of virtue. For the perfect nature of anything is gathered from all its causes. Now the above definition comprises all the causes of virtue. For the formal cause of virtue, as of everything, is gathered from its genus and difference, when it is defined as *a good quality;* for *quality* is the genus of virtue, and the difference, *good.* To be sure, the definition would be more suitable if for *quality* we substitute *habit,* which is the proximate genus.

Now virtue has no matter *out of which* it is formed, as neither has any other accident; but it has the matter *about which* it is concerned, and the matter *in which* it exists, namely, the subject. The matter about which virtue is concerned is its object, and this could not be included in the above definition because the object fixes the virtue to a certain species, and here we are giving the definition of virtue in general. And so for the material cause we have the subject, which is mentioned when it is said that virtue is a good quality *of the mind.*

The end of virtue, since it is an operative habit, is operation itself. But it must be observed that some operative habits are always referred to evil, as are vicious habits. Others are sometimes referred to good, sometimes to evil. For instance, opinion is referred both to the true and to the untrue. But virtue is a habit which is always referred to good. Hence the distinction of virtue from those habits which are always referred to evil is expressed in the words *by which we live righteously*; and its distinction from those habits which are sometimes directed to good, and sometimes to evil, is expressed in the words, *of which no one makes bad use.*

Lastly, God is the efficient cause of infused virtue, to which this definition applies; and this is expressed in the words *which God works in us without us.* If we omit this phrase, the remainder of the definition will apply to all virtues in general, whether acquired or infused.

Reply Obj. 1. That which first falls in the intellect is *being,* and there-

---

[28] *Epist.* CCXI (PL 33, 960). [29] *Serm.* CLXIX, 11 (PL 38, 923); *Tract.* LXXII super *Ioann.*, XIV, 12 (PL 35, 1823). [30] *De Lib. Arb.,* II, 19 (PL 32, 1268).

fore everything that we apprehend we consider as being, and consequently as *one,* and as *good,* which are convertible with being. Hence we say that *essence is being* and *one* and *good*; and that *oneness is being* and *one* and *good*; and in like manner *goodness.* But this is not the case with specific forms, as whiteness and health, for everything that we apprehend is not apprehended with the notion of white and healthy. We must, however, observe that, as accidents and non-subsistent forms are called beings, not as if they themselves had being, but because things are by them, so also are they called good or one, not by some distinct goodness or oneness, but because by them something is good or one. So also is virtue called good, because by it something is good.

Reply Obj. 2. The good which is put in the definition of virtue is not the good in general which is convertible with being, and which extends further than quality, but the good as fixed by reason, with regard to which Dionysius says *that the good of the soul is to be in accord with reason.*[31]

Reply Obj. 3. Virtue cannot be in the irrational part of the soul, except in so far as this participates in the reason.[32] Therefore reason, or the mind, is the proper subject of virtue.

Reply Obj. 4. Justice has a righteousness of its own by which it puts those outward things right which come into human use, and which are the proper matter of justice, as we shall show further on.[33] But the righteousness which denotes order to a due end and to the divine law, which is the rule of the human will, as was stated above,[34] is common to all virtues.

Reply Obj. 5. One can make bad use of a virtue considered as an object, for instance, by having evil thoughts about it, *e.g.,* by hating it, or by being proud of it; but one cannot make bad use of virtue as principle of action, so that an act of virtue be evil.

Reply Obj. 6. Infused virtue is caused in us by God without any action on our part, but not without our consent. This is the sense of the words, *which God works in us without us.* As to those things which are done by us, God causes them in us, yet not without action on our part, for He works in every will and in every nature.

---

[31] *De Div. Nom.,* IV, 32 (PG 3, 733).   [32] Aristotle, *Eth.,* I, 13 (1102b 13; 1103 a 3).   [33] Q. 60, a. 2; II-II, q. 58, a. 8.   [34] Q. 19, a. 4.

ON THE SUBJECT OF VIRTUE
(*In Six Articles*)

WE have now to consider the subject of virtue, about which there are six points of inquiry: (1) Whether virtue is in a power of the soul as in a subject? (2) Whether one virtue can be in several powers? (3) Whether the intellect can be a subject of virtue? (4) Whether the irascible and concupiscible powers can be a subject of virtue? (5) Whether the sensitive powers of apprehension can be a subject of virtue? (6) Whether the will can be a subject of virtue?

First Article

WHETHER VIRTUE IS IN A POWER OF THE SOUL AS IN A SUBJECT?

We proceed thus to the First Article:—

Objection 1. It would seem that the subject of virtue is not a power of the soul. For Augustine says that *virtue is that by which we live righteously.*[1] But we live by the essence of the soul, and not by a power of the soul. Therefore virtue is not in a power, but in the essence of the soul.

Obj. 2. Further, the Philosopher says that *virtue is that which makes its possessor good, and his work good likewise.*[2] But as a work is established by a power, so he that has a virtue is established by the essence of the soul. Therefore virtue does not belong to the power, any more than to the essence of the soul.

Obj. 3. Further, power is in the second species of quality. But virtue is a quality, as we have said above,[3] and quality is not the subject of quality. Therefore a power of the soul is not the subject of virtue.

On the contrary, Virtue is the peak of power.[4] But the peak is in that of which it is the peak. Therefore virtue is in a power of the soul.

I answer that, It can be proved in three ways that virtue belongs to a power of the soul. First, from the very nature of virtue, which implies the perfection of a power; for perfection is in that which it perfects.—Secondly, from the fact that virtue is an operative habit, as we have said above.[5] Now all operation proceeds from the soul through a power.—

---

[1] *De Lib. Arb.*, II, 19 (PL 32, 1268).   [2] *Eth.*, II, 6 (1106a 15).   [3] Q. 55, a. 4.
[4] Aristotle, *De Caelo*, I, 11 (281a 14; a 18).—Cf. St. Thomas, *In De Caelo*, I, lect. 25.
[5] Q. 55, a. 2.

Thirdly, from the fact that virtue disposes to that which is best; and the best is the end, which is either a being's operation, or something acquired by an operation proceeding from the being's power. Therefore a power of the soul is the subject of virtue.

Reply Obj. 1. *To live* may be taken in two ways. Sometimes it is taken for the very being of the living thing, and thus it belongs to the essence of the soul, which is the principle of being in the living thing. But sometimes *to live* is taken for the operation of the living thing, and in this sense we live righteously by virtue inasmuch as by virtue we perform righteous actions.

Reply Obj. 2. Good is either the end, or something referred to the end. Therefore, since the good of the worker consists in the work, this fact also, that virtue makes the worker good, is referred to the work, and consequently, to the power.

Reply Obj. 3. One accident is said to be the subject of another, not as though one accident could uphold another, but because one accident inheres in a substance by means of another, as color in a body by means of the surface; so that surface is said to be the subject of color. In this way a power of the soul is said to be the subject of virtue.

Second Article

WHETHER ONE VIRTUE CAN BE IN SEVERAL POWERS?

We proceed thus to the Second Article:—

Objection 1. It would seem that one virtue can be in two powers. For habits are known by their acts. But one act proceeds in various ways from several powers. Thus walking proceeds from the reason as directing, from the will as moving, and from the power of locomotion as executing. Therefore also one habit can be in several powers.

Obj. 2. Further, the Philosopher says that three things are required for virtue, namely: *to know, to will, and to work steadfastly.*[6] But *to know* belongs to the intellect, and *to will* belongs to the will. Therefore virtue can be in several powers.

Obj. 3. Further, prudence is in the reason, since it is *the right reason of things to be done.*[7] And it is also in the will, for it cannot exist together with a perverse will.[8] Therefore one virtue can be in two powers.

On the contrary, The subject of virtue is a power of the soul. But the same accident cannot be in several subjects. Therefore one virtue cannot be in several powers of the soul.

I answer that, It happens in two ways that one thing is in two subjects. First, so that it is in both on an equal footing. In this way it is impossible

[6] *Eth.,* II, 4 (1105a 31).   [7] *Op. cit.,* VI, 5 (1140b 4; b 20); 13 (1144b 27).
[8] *Op. cit.,* VI, 12 (1144a 36).

for one virtue to be in two powers, since diversity of powers follows the generic conditions of the objects, while diversity of habits follows their specific conditions; and so wherever there is diversity of powers, there is diversity of habits, but not vice versa. In another way, one thing can be in two or more subjects, not on an equal footing, but in a certain order. And thus one virtue can belong to several powers, so that it is in one chiefly, while it extends to others by a kind of diffusion, or by way of a disposition, in so far as one power is moved by another, and one power receives from another.

Reply Obj. 1. One act cannot belong to several powers equally, and in the same degree; but only in different ways, and in various degrees.

Reply Obj. 2. To know is a condition required for moral virtue, inasmuch as moral virtue works according to right reason. But moral virtue is essentially in the appetite.

Reply Obj. 3. Prudence is really in the reason as in its subject; but it presupposes as its principle the rectitude of the will, as we shall see further on.[9]

Third Article

WHETHER THE INTELLECT CAN BE A SUBJECT OF VIRTUE?

We proceed thus to the Third Article:—

Objection 1. It would seem that the intellect is not a subject of virtue. For Augustine says that all virtue is love.[10] But the subject of love is not the intellect, but the appetitive power alone. Therefore no virtue is in the intellect.

Obj. 2. Further, virtue is related to good, as is clear from what has been said above.[11] Now good is not the object of the intellect, but of the appetitive power. Therefore the subject of virtue is not the intellect, but the appetitive power.

Obj. 3. Further, virtue is that *which makes its possessor good,* as the Philosopher says.[12] But the habit which perfects the intellect does not make its possessor good, since a man is not said to be a good man because of his science or his art. Therefore the intellect is not a subject of virtue.

On the contrary, It is the intellect which is most especially called *mind.* But the subject of virtue is the mind, as is clear from the above given definition of virtue.[13] Therefore the intellect is a subject of virtue.

I answer that, As we have said above, virtue is a habit by which we work well.[14] Now a habit may be directed to a good act in two ways. First, in so far as by the habit a man acquires an aptness for a good act. For instance, by the habit of grammar man has the aptness to speak correctly. But gram-

---

[9] A. 3; q. 57, a. 4.   [10] *De Mor. Eccl.,* I, 15 (PL 32, 1322).   [11] Q. 55, a. 3.   [12] *Eth.,* II, 6 (1106a 15).   [13] Q. 55, a. 4.   [14] Q. 55, a. 3.

mar does not make a man always to speak correctly, for a grammarian may be guilty of a barbarism or a solecism; and the case is the same with other sciences and arts. Secondly, a habit may confer not only aptness to act, but also the right use of that aptness. For instance, justice not only gives man the prompt will to do just actions, but also makes him act justly.

And since a thing is not said absolutely to be good or a being in so far as it is potentially, but in so far as it is actually, therefore it is from having habits of the latter sort that man is said absolutely to do good, and to be good; for instance, because he is just, or temperate. And the same is true as regards other such virtues. And since virtue is that *which makes its possessor good, and his work good likewise,* these latter habits are called virtues absolutely, because they make the work to be actually good, and the subject good absolutely. But habits of the first kind are not called virtues absolutely, because they do not make the work good except in regard to a certain aptness, nor do they make their possessor good absolutely. For through being gifted in science or art, a man is said to be good, not absolutely but relatively; for instance, a good grammarian, or a good smith. And for this reason, science and art are often distinguished from virtue, while at other times they are called virtues.[15]

Hence the subject of a habit which is called a virtue in a relative sense can be the intellect, and not only the practical intellect, but also the speculative, without any reference to the will. For thus the Philosopher holds that science, wisdom and understanding, and also art, are intellectual virtues.[16] But the subject of a habit which is called a virtue absolutely can be only the will, or some power in so far as it is moved by the will. And the reason for this is, that the will moves to their acts all those other powers that are in some way rational, as we have said above.[17] Therefore, if man do well actually, this is because he has a good will. Therefore, the virtue which makes a man to do well actually, and not merely to have the aptness to do well, must be either in the will itself, or in some power as moved by the will.

Now it happens that the intellect is moved by the will, just as are the other powers; for a man considers something actually because he wills to do so. Hence the intellect, in so far as it is subordinate to the will, can be the subject of virtue absolutely so called. And in this way the speculative intellect, or the reason, is the subject of faith; for the intellect is moved by the command of the will to assent to what is of faith: for *no man believeth, unless he will.*[18] But the practical intellect is the subject of prudence. For since prudence is the right reason of things to be done, it is a condition thereof that man be rightly disposed in regard to the principles of this reason of things to be done, that is, in regard to their ends; and to these

---

[15] Aristotle, *Eth.,* VI, 3 (1139b 16); 2 (1139b 13).   [16] *Op. cit.,* VI, 3 (1139b 16). [17] Q. 9, a. 1; q. 17, a. 1 and 5; I, q. 82, a. 4.   [18] St. Augustine, *Tract.* XXVI, super *Ioann.,* VI, 44 (PL 35, 1607).

man is rightly disposed by the rectitude of the will, just as to the principles of speculative truth he is rightly disposed by the natural light of the agent intellect. Therefore, just as the subject of science, which is the right reason of speculative truths, is the speculative intellect in relation to the agent intellect, so the subject of prudence is the practical intellect in relation to a right will.

Reply Obj. 1. The saying of Augustine is to be understood of virtue absolutely so called; not that every such virtue is love absolutely, but that it depends in some way on love, in so far as it depends on the will, whose first movement consists in love, as we have said above.[19]

Reply Obj. 2. The good of each thing is its end: and therefore, as truth is the end of the intellect, so to know truth is the good act of the intellect. Whence the habit which perfects the intellect in regard to the knowledge of truth, whether speculative or practical, is a virtue.

Reply Obj. 3. This objection considers virtue absolutely so called.

Fourth Article

WHETHER THE IRASCIBLE AND CONCUPISCIBLE POWERS ARE A SUBJECT OF VIRTUE?

We proceed thus to the Fourth Article:—

Objection 1. It would seem that the irascible and concupiscible powers cannot be a subject of virtue. For these powers are common to us and brute animals. But we are now speaking of virtue as proper to man, since for this reason it is called human virtue. It is therefore impossible for human virtue to be in the irascible and concupiscible powers, which are parts of the sensitive appetite, as we have said in the First Part.[20]

Obj. 2. Further, the sensitive appetite is a power which makes use of a corporeal organ. But the good of virtue cannot be in man's body, for the Apostle says (*Rom.* vii. 18): *I know that good does not dwell in my flesh.* Therefore the sensitive appetite cannot be a subject of virtue.

Obj. 3. Further, Augustine proves that virtue is not in the body but in the soul, for the reason that the body is ruled by the soul; and so it is entirely due to his soul that a man makes good use of his body: *For instance, if my coachman, through obedience to my orders, guides well the horses which he is driving, this is all due to me.*[21] But just as the soul rules the body, so also does the reason rule the sensitive appetite. Therefore, that the irascible and concupiscible powers are rightly ruled is entirely due to the rational part. Now *virtue is that by which we live rightly,* as we have said above.[22] Therefore virtue is not in the irascible and concupiscible powers, but only in the rational part.

---

[19] Q. 25, a. 1, 2 and 3; q. 27, a. 4; I, q. 20, a. 1.   [20] *S. T.,* I, q. 81, a. 2.   [21] *De Mor. Eccl.,* I, 5 (PL 32, 1314).   [22] Q. 55, a. 4.

Obj. 4. Further, *the principal act of moral virtue is choice.*[23] Now choice is not an act of the irascible and concupiscible powers, but of the reason, as we have said above.[24] Therefore moral virtue is not in the irascible and concupiscible powers, but in the reason.

On the contrary, Fortitude is assigned to the irascible power, and temperance to the concupiscible power. Whence the Philosopher says that *these virtues belong to the irrational parts of the soul.*[25]

I answer that, The irascible and concupiscible powers can be considered in two ways. First, in themselves, in so far as they are parts of the sensitive appetite; and in this way they are not competent to be the subject of virtue. Secondly, they can be considered as participating in the reason, because it belongs to their nature to obey the reason. And thus the irascible or the concupiscible power can be the subject of human virtue; for, in so far as it participates in the reason, it is the principle of a human act. And to these powers we must needs assign virtues.

For it is clear that there are some virtues in the irascible and concupiscible powers. Because an act which proceeds from one power, according as it is moved by another power, cannot be perfect unless both powers be well disposed to the act; for instance, the act of a craftsman cannot be successful unless both the craftsman and his instrument be well disposed to act. Therefore, in the case of the objects of the operations of the irascible and concupiscible powers, according as they are moved by reason, there must needs be, not only in the reason, but also in the irascible and concupiscible powers, some habit aiding for the work of acting well. And since the good disposition of the power which moves through being moved depends on its conformity with the power that moves it, therefore the virtue which is in the irascible and concupiscible powers is nothing else but a certain habitual conformity of these powers to reason.

Reply Obj. 1. The irascible and concupiscible powers considered in themselves, as parts of the sensitive appetite, are common to us and brute animals. But in so far as they are rational by participation, as obeying reason, they are proper to man. And in this way they can be a subject of human virtue.

Reply Obj. 2. Just as human flesh has not of itself the good of virtue, but is made the instrument of a virtuous act, inasmuch as, being moved by reason, we *yield our members to serve justice (Rom.* vi. 19), so, also, the irascible and concupiscible powers, of themselves indeed, have not the good of virtue, but rather the infection of the 'fomes'; whereas, inasmuch as they are in conformity with reason, the good of reason is begotten in them.

Reply Obj. 3. The body is ruled by the soul, and the irascible and concupiscible powers by the reason, but in different ways. For the body obeys

---

[23] Aristotle, *Eth.,* VIII, 13 (1163a 22).   [24] Q. 13, a. 2.   [25] *Eth.,* III, 10 (1117b 23).

the soul instantly, without any contradiction, in those things in which it has a natural aptitude to be moved by the soul. Hence the Philosopher says that the *soul rules the body with a despotic rule*,[26] as the master rules his slave; and that is why the entire movement of the body is referred to the soul. For this reason virtue is not in the body, but in the soul. But the irascible and concupiscible powers do not obey the reason instantly. On the contrary, they have their own proper movements, by which, at times, they go against reason; and hence the Philosopher says that the *reason rules the irascible and concupiscible powers by a political rule*,[27] such as that by which free men are ruled, who have in some respects a will of their own. And for this reason also there must be some virtues in the irascible and concupiscible powers, by which these powers may be well disposed for operation.

Reply Obj. 4. In choice there are two things, namely, the intention of the end, which belongs to moral virtue, and the preferential selection of the means to the end, which belongs to prudence.[28] But that the election has a right intention of the end in regard to the passions of the soul is due to the good disposition of the irascible and concupiscible powers. Hence, the moral virtues concerned with the passions are in the irascible and concupiscible powers, but prudence is in the reason.

Fifth Article

WHETHER THE SENSITIVE POWERS OF APPREHENSION ARE A SUBJECT OF VIRTUE?

We proceed thus to the Fifth Article:—

Objection 1. It would seem that it is possible for virtue to be in the interior sensitive powers of apprehension. For the sensitive appetite can be a subject of virtue, in so far as it obeys reason. But the interior sensitive powers of apprehension obey reason, for the powers of imagination, of cogitation and of memory act at the command of reason. Therefore there can be virtue in these powers.

Obj. 2. Further, just as the rational appetite, which is the will, can be hindered or helped in its act by the sensitive appetite, so also can the intellect or reason be hindered or helped by the powers mentioned above. Just as, therefore, there can be virtue in the interior powers of appetite, so also can there be virtue in the interior powers of apprehension.

Obj. 3. Further, prudence is a virtue, of which Cicero says that memory is a part.[29] Therefore in the power of memory also there can be a virtue; and in like manner, in the other interior sensitive powers of apprehension.

On the contrary, All virtues are either intellectual or moral.[30] Now all the

---

[26] *Polit.,* I, 2 (1254b 4).   [27] *Ibid.* (1254b 5).   [28] Aristotle, *Eth.,* VI, 12 (1144a 6).
[29] *De Invent.,* II, 53 (p. 147ᵇ).   [30] Aristotle, *Eth.,* II, 1 (1103a 14).

moral virtues are in the appetite, while the intellectual virtues are in the intellect or reason, as is clear from *Ethics* vi.[31] Therefore there is no virtue in the interior sensitive powers of apprehension.

I answer that, In the interior sensitive powers of apprehension there are some habits. And this is made clear principally from what the Philosopher says, that *in remembering one thing after another, we become accustomed to it; and custom is a sort of nature.*[32] Now a habit from custom is nothing else than a habit acquired by custom, which is like a nature. Therefore Tully says of virtue in his *Rhetoric* that *it is a habit after the manner of a nature, in accord with reason.*[33] Yet, in man, that which he acquires by custom, in his memory and other sensitive powers of apprehension, is not a habit properly so called, but something annexed to the habits of the intellectual parts of the soul, as we have said above.[34]

Nevertheless, even if there be habits in such powers, they cannot be called virtues. For virtue is a perfect habit, by which it never happens that anything but good is done; and so virtue must needs be in that power which completes a good act. But the knowledge of truth is not completed in the sensitive powers of apprehension, for such powers prepare the way to intellectual knowledge. Therefore in such powers there are none of the virtues by which we know truth; these are rather in the intellect or reason.

Reply Obj. 1. The sensitive appetite is related to the will, which is a rational appetite, as being moved by it. Hence the work of the appetitive power is completed in the sensitive appetite, and for this reason the sensitive appetite is a subject of virtue. But the sensitive powers of apprehension are related to the intellect rather as moving it, for the phantasms are related to the intellectual soul as colors to sight.[35] Hence the work of knowledge is terminated in the intellect, and for this reason the cognitive virtues are in the intellect itself, or the reason.

And thus is made clear the Reply to the second objection.

Reply Obj. 3. Memory is not a part of prudence, as species is of a genus, as though memory were a virtue properly so called. The point is rather that one of the conditions required for prudence is a good memory; so that, in a fashion, it is related to prudence after the manner of an integral part.

Sixth Article

WHETHER THE WILL CAN BE A SUBJECT OF VIRTUE?

We proceed thus to the Sixth Article:—

Objection 1. It would seem that the will is not a subject of virtue. Because no habit is required for that which belongs to a power by reason of its very nature. But since the will is *in the reason,* according to the Philoso-

---

[31] *Op. cit.,* VI, 1 (1138b 35). [32] *De Memor.,* II (452a 27). [33] *De Invent., ibid.* [34] Q. 50, a. 4, ad 3. [35] Aristotle, *De An.,* III, 7 (431a 14).

pher, it is of the very essence of the will to tend to that which is good according to reason.[36] And to this good every virtue is ordered, since everything naturally desires its own good; for virtue, as Tully says in his *Rhetoric*, is a *habit after the manner of a nature, in accord with reason*.[37] Therefore the will is not a subject of virtue.

Obj. 2. Further, every virtue is either intellectual or moral.[38] But intellectual virtue is in the intellect and reason as in its subject, and not in the will; while moral virtue finds its subject in the irascible and concupiscible powers, which are rational by participation. Therefore no virtue is in the will as in its subject.

Obj. 3. Further, all human acts, to which virtues are ordained, are voluntary. If, therefore, there is a virtue in the will in respect of some human acts, in like manner there will be a virtue in the will in respect of all human acts. Either, therefore, there will be no virtue in any other power, or there will be two virtues ordained to the same act; which seems unreasonable. Therefore the will cannot be a subject of virtue.

On the contrary, Greater perfection is required in the mover than in the moved. But the will moves the irascible and concupiscible powers. Much more therefore should there be virtue in the will than in the irascible and concupiscible powers.

I answer that, Since the habit perfects the power in reference to act, then does the power need a habit perfecting it for doing well (this habit is a virtue) when the power's own proper nature does not suffice for the purpose. Now the proper nature of a power is seen in its relation to its object. Since, therefore, as we have said above, the object of the will is the good of reason proportioned to the will, in respect of this the will does not need a virtue perfecting it.[39] But if man's will is confronted with a good that exceeds its capacity, whether as regards the whole human species, such as the divine good, which transcends the limits of human nature, or as regards the individual, such as the good of one's neighbor, then it is that the will needs virtue. And therefore such virtues as those which direct man's affections to God or to his neighbor, as charity, justice and the like, have the will as their subject.

Reply Obj. 1. This objection is true of that virtue which is ordained to the good belonging to the one willing, *e.g.*, temperance and fortitude, which are concerned with human passions, and the like, as is clear from what we have said.[40]

Reply Obj. 2. Not only the irascible and concupiscible powers are rational by participation, but *the appetitive power altogether, i.e.*, in its entirety.[41] Now the will is included in the appetitive power. And therefore

---

[36] *Op. cit.*, III, 9 (432b 5).   [37] *De Invent.*, II, 53 (p. 147[b]).   [38] Aristotle, *Eth.*, I, 13 (1103a 4); II, 1 (1103a 14).   [39] Q. 19, a. 3.   [40] Q. 25, a. 6, ad 3; I, q. 21, a. 1, ad 1; q. 59, a. 4, ad 3.   [41] Aristotle, *Eth.*, I, 13 (1102b 30).

whatever virtue is in the will must be a moral virtue, unless it be a theological one, as we shall see later on.[42]

Reply Obj. 3. Some virtues are directed to the good of moderated passion,
which is the proper good of this or that man, and in these cases there is no
need for virtue in the will, for the nature of the power suffices for the
purpose, as we have said. This need exists only in the case of those virtues
which are directed to some extrinsic good.

[42] Q. 62, a. 3.

ON THE DISTINCTION OF THE INTELLECTUAL VIRTUES
(*In Six Articles*)

WE now have to consider the distinction of the virtues, which are (1) the intellectual virtues; (2) the moral virtues;[1] (3) the theological virtues.[2] Concerning the first there are six points of inquiry: (1) Whether the habits of the speculative intellect are virtues? (2) Whether they are three, namely, *wisdom, science* and *understanding*? (3) Whether the intellectual habit *art* is a virtue? (4) Whether *prudence* is a virtue distinct from art? (5) Whether prudence is a virtue necessary to man? (6) Whether *eubulia, synesis* and *gnome* are virtues annexed to prudence?

First Article

WHETHER THE HABITS OF THE SPECULATIVE INTELLECT ARE VIRTUES?

We proceed thus to the First Article:—

Objection 1. It would seem that the habits of the speculative intellect are not virtues. For virtue is an operative habit, as we have said above.[3] But speculative habits are not operative, for what is speculative is distinguished from the practical, *i.e.,* the operative. Therefore the habits of the speculative intellect are not virtues.

Obj. 2. Further, virtue is about those things by which man is made happy or blessed; for *happiness is the reward of virtue.*[4] Now intellectual habits do not consider human acts or other human goods by which man acquires happiness, but rather things pertaining to nature or to God. Therefore such habits cannot be called virtues.

Obj. 3. Further, science is a speculative habit. But science and virtue are distinguished from one another as genera which are not related subalternately, as the Philosopher proves in *Topics* iv.[5] Therefore speculative habits are not virtues.

On the contrary, The speculative habits alone consider necessary things which cannot be otherwise than they are. Now the Philosopher places certain intellectual virtues in that part of the soul which considers necessary things that cannot be otherwise than they are.[6] Therefore the habits of the speculative intellect are virtues.

---

[1] Q. 58.   [2] Q. 62.   [3] Q. 55, a. 2.   [4] Aristotle, *Eth.,* I, 9 (1099b 16).   [5] *Top.,* IV, 2 (121b 34).   [6] *Eth.,* VI, 1 (1139a 7).

I answer that, Since every virtue is ordained to some good, as was stated above,[7] a habit, as we have already observed,[8] may be called a virtue for two reasons: first, because it confers aptness for doing good; secondly, because, besides aptness, it confers the right use of it. The latter condition, as above was stated,[9] belongs to those habits alone which affect the appetitive part of the soul, since it is the soul's appetitive power that puts all the powers and habits to their respective uses.

Since, then, the habits of the speculative intellect do not perfect the appetitive part, nor affect it in any way, but only the intellective part, they may indeed be called virtues in so far as they confer aptness for a good work, viz., the consideration of truth (since this is the good work of the intellect); yet they are not called virtues in the second way, as though they conferred the right use of a power or habit. For if a man possess the habit of a speculative science, it does not follow that he is inclined to make use of it, but he is made able to consider the truth in those matters of which he has scientific knowledge. That he make use of the knowledge which he has, however, is due to the motion of his will. Consequently, a virtue which perfects the will, as charity or justice, confers the right use of these speculative habits. And in this way, too, there can be merit in the acts of these habits, if they be done out of charity. Thus, Gregory says that the *contemplative life has greater merit than the active life.*[10]

Reply Obj. 1. Work is of two kinds, exterior and interior. Accordingly, the *practical* or *operative,* which is distinguished from the *speculative,* is concerned with exterior work, to which a speculative habit is not ordained. But it is ordained to the interior work of the intellect, which is to consider the truth. And in this way it is an operative habit.

Reply Obj. 2. Virtue is *about* certain things in two ways. In the first place, a virtue is about its objects. In this sense, these speculative virtues are not about those things whereby man is made happy, except, perhaps, in so far as the word *whereby* indicates the efficient cause or the object of complete happiness, *i.e.,* God, Who is the supreme object of contemplation. —Secondly, a virtue is said to be about its acts, and in this sense the intellectual virtues are about those things whereby a man is made happy, both because the acts of these virtues can be meritorious, as was stated above, and also because they are a kind of beginning of perfect beatitude, which consists in the contemplation of truth, as we have already stated.[11]

Reply Obj. 3. Science is contrasted with virtue taken in the second sense, according to which virtue belongs to the appetitive power.

[7] Q. 55, a. 3.   [8] Q. 56, a. 3.   [9] *Ibid.*   [10] *Moral.,* VI, 37 (PL 75, 764). [11] Q. 3, a. 7.

Second Article

WHETHER THERE ARE ONLY THREE HABITS OF THE SPECULA-
TIVE INTELLECT, VIZ., *WISDOM, SCIENCE* AND *UNDER-
STANDING?*

We proceed thus to the Second Article:—

Objection 1. It would seem unfitting to distinguish three virtues of the speculative intellect, viz., *wisdom, science* and *understanding.* For a species should not be co-divided with its genus. But wisdom is a science, as is stated in *Ethics* vi.[12] Therefore wisdom should not be co-divided with science among the intellectual virtues.

Obj. 2. Further, in differentiating powers, habits and acts in respect of their objects, we consider chiefly the formal aspect of these objects, as we have already explained.[13] Therefore habits are diversified, not according to their material objects, but according to the formal aspect of their objects. Now the principle of a demonstration is the cause of having a science of conclusions. Therefore the understanding of principles should not be set down as a habit or virtue distinct from the science of conclusions.

Obj. 3. Further, an intellectual virtue is one which resides in the essentially rational part of the soul. Now even the speculative reason employs the dialectical syllogism in its reasoning, just as it employs the demonstrative syllogism. Therefore, just as science, which is the result of a demonstrative syllogism, is considered to be an intellectual virtue, so also should opinion be.

On the contrary, The Philosopher reckons these three alone as being intellectual virtues, viz., *wisdom, science* and *understanding.*[14]

I answer that, As has already been stated, the virtues of the speculative intellect are those which perfect the speculative intellect for the consideration of truth; for this is its good work. Now truth is subject to a twofold consideration, namely, as known in itself, and as known through another. What is known in itself is as a *principle,* and is at once understood by the intellect; and that is why the habit that perfects the intellect for the consideration of such truth is called *understanding,* which is the *habit of principles.*

On the other hand, a truth which is known through another is understood by the intellect, not at once, but by means of the reason's inquiry, and is as a *term.* This may happen in two ways: first, so that it is the last in some particular genus; secondly, so that it is the ultimate term of all human knowledge. And, since *things that are later knowable in relation to us are knowable first and chiefly in their nature,*[15] hence it is that that which is last with respect to all human knowledge is that which is know-

---

[12] Aristotle, *Eth.,* VI, 7 (1141a 19).   [13] Q. 54, a. 2, ad 1; I, q. 77, a. 3.   [14] *Eth.,* VI, 7 (1141a 19); 3 (1139b 16).   [15] Aristotle, *Phys.,* I, 1 (184a 18).

able first and chiefly in its nature. And about these truths is *wisdom,* which considers the highest causes, as is stated in *Metaph.* i.[16] Therefore it rightly judges and orders all truths, because there can be no perfect and universal judgment except by resolution to first causes.—But in regard to that which is last in this or that genus of knowable truths, it is *science* that perfects the intellect. Therefore, according to the diverse genera of knowable truths, there are diverse habits of the sciences; whereas there is but one wisdom.

Reply Obj. 1. Wisdom is a science, in so far as it has that which is common to all the sciences: viz., to demonstrate conclusions from principles. But since it has something proper to itself above the other sciences, inasmuch as it judges of them all, not only as to their conclusions, but also as to their first principles, therefore it is a more perfect virtue than science.

Reply Obj. 2. When the formal aspect of the object is referred to a power or habit by one and the same act, there is no distinction of habit or power in relation to the formal aspect and the material object. Thus, it belongs to the same power of sight to see both color and light, which is the formal aspect under which color is seen, and is seen at the same time as the color. On the other hand, the principles of demonstration can be considered by themselves, without the conclusion being considered at all. They can also be considered together with the conclusions, in so far as the principles are extended to lead to the conclusions. Accordingly, to consider principles in this second way belongs to *science,* which considers the conclusions also; while to consider principles in themselves belongs to *understanding.*

Consequently, if we consider the point rightly, these three virtues are not distinguished as being on a par with one another, but in a certain order. The same is to be observed in potential wholes, wherein one part is more perfect than another: *e.g.,* the rational soul is more perfect than the sensitive soul, and the sensitive, than the vegetative soul. For it is thus that *science* depends on *understanding* as on a virtue of higher degree. So, too, both of these depend on *wisdom* as obtaining the highest place; for it contains beneath itself both understanding and science, as judging both of the conclusions of sciences and of the principles on which they are based.

Reply Obj. 3. As was stated above, a virtuous habit has a fixed relation to good, and is in no way referable to evil.[17] Now the good of the intellect is truth, and falsehood is its evil. Therefore those habits alone are called intellectual virtues, whereby we express the truth and never a falsehood. But opinion and surmise can be about both truth and falsehood; and so, as is stated in *Ethics* vi.,[18] they are not intellectual virtues.

---

[16] Aristotle, *Metaph.,* I, 1 (981b 28); 2 (982b 9).   [17] Q. 55, a. 3 and 4.   [18] Aristotle, *Eth.,* VI, 3 (1139b 17).

Third Article

WHETHER THE INTELLECTUAL HABIT *ART* IS A VIRTUE?

We proceed thus to the Third Article:—

Objection 1. It would seem that art is not an intellectual virtue. For Augustine says that *no one makes bad use of virtue*.[19] But one may make bad use of art, for a craftsman can work badly according to the science of his art. Therefore art is not a virtue.

Obj. 2. Further, there is no virtue of a virtue. But *there is a virtue of art*, according to the Philosopher.[20] Therefore art is not a virtue.

Obj. 3. Further, the liberal arts excel the mechanical arts. But just as the mechanical arts are practical, so the liberal arts are speculative. Therefore, if art were an intellectual virtue, it would have to be reckoned among the speculative virtues.

On the contrary, The Philosopher says that art is a virtue.[21] However, he does not reckon it among the speculative virtues, which, according to him, reside in the scientific part of the soul.

I answer that, Art is nothing else but *the right reason about certain works to be made.* And yet the good of these things depends, not on the disposition of man's appetite, but on the goodness of the work done. For a craftsman as such is commendable, not for the will with which he does a work, but for the quality of the work. Art, therefore, properly speaking, is an operative habit. And yet it has something in common with the speculative habits, since the disposition of the things considered by them is a matter of concern to the speculative habits also, although they are not concerned with the disposition of the appetite towards their objects. For as long as the geometrician demonstrates the truth, it matters not how his appetite is disposed, whether he be joyful or angry; even as neither does this matter in a craftsman, as we have observed. And so art has the nature of a virtue in the same way as the speculative habits, in so far, namely, as neither art nor a speculative habit makes a good work as regards the use of the habit, which is distinctive of a virtue that perfects the appetite, but only as regards the ability to work well.

Reply Obj. 1. When anyone endowed with an art produces bad workmanship, this is not the work of that art; in fact, it is contrary to the art. In the same way, when a man lies, while knowing the truth, his words are not in accord with what he knows, but contrary thereto. Therefore, just as science has always a relation to good, as was stated above, so it is with art; and it is for this reason that it is called a virtue. And yet it falls short of being a perfect virtue, because it does not make its possessor to use it well; for which purpose something further is requisite, even though there cannot be a good use without the art.

[19] *De Lib. Arb.,* II, 18; 19 (PL 32, 1267; 1268).   [20] Aristotle, *Eth.,* VI, 5 (1140b 22).   [21] *Op. cit.,* VI, 3 (1139b 16); 7 (1141a 19).

Reply Obj. 2. In order that a man may make good use of the art he has, he needs a good will, which is perfected by moral virtue; and for this reason the Philosopher says that there is a virtue of art, namely, a moral virtue, in so far as the good use of art requires a moral virtue. For it is evident that a craftsman is inclined by justice, which rectifies his will, to do his work faithfully.

Reply Obj. 3. Even in speculative matters there is something by way of work: *e.g.*, the making of a syllogism or of a fitting speech, or the work of counting or measuring. Hence whatever habits are ordained to such works of the speculative reason are, by a kind of comparison, called arts indeed, but *liberal* arts, in order to distinguish them from those arts that are ordained to works done by the body; for these arts are, in a fashion, servile, inasmuch as the body is in servile subjection to the soul, and man, as regards his soul, is free [*liber*]. On the other hand, those sciences which are not ordained to any such work are called sciences absolutely, and not arts. Nor, if the liberal arts be more excellent, does it follow that the notion of art is more applicable to them.

Fourth Article

WHETHER PRUDENCE IS A DISTINCT VIRTUE FROM ART?

We proceed thus to the Fourth Article:—

Objection 1. It would seem that prudence is not a distinct virtue from art. For art is right reason about certain works. But diversity of works does not make a habit cease to be an art, since there are various arts about works widely different. Since, therefore, prudence is also right reason about works, it seems that it too should be reckoned an art.

Obj. 2. Further, prudence has more in common with art than the speculative habits have, for they are both *about contingent matters that may be otherwise than they are.*[22] Now some speculative habits are called arts. Much more, therefore, should prudence be called an art.

Obj. 3. Further, it belongs to prudence *to be of good counsel.*[23] But counselling takes place in certain arts also, as is stated in *Ethics* iii.,[24] *e.g.*, in the arts of warfare, of seamanship and of medicine. Therefore prudence is not distinct from art.

On the contrary, The Philosopher distinguishes prudence from art.[25]

I answer that, Where the nature of virtue differs, there is a different kind of virtue. Now it has been stated above that some habits have the nature of virtue, through merely conferring ability for a good work; while some habits are virtues, not only through conferring ability for a good work, but also through conferring the use.[26] But art confers the mere ability for good

---

[22] Aristotle, *Eth.*, VI, 6 (1140b 35).   [23] *Op. cit.*, VI, 5 (1140a 25).   [24] *Op. cit.*, III, 3 (1112b 3).   [25] *Op. cit.*, VI, 3 (1139b 16); 5 (1140b 2; b 21).   [26] A. 1; q. 56, a. 3.

work, since it does not regard the appetite, whereas prudence confers not only ability for a good work, but also the use, for it regards the appetite, since it presupposes the rectitude of the appetite.

The reason for this difference is that art is the *right reason of things to be made,* whereas prudence is the *right reason of things to be done.* Now *making* and *doing* differ, as is stated in *Metaph.* ix.,[27] in that *making* is an action passing into external matter, *e.g., to build, to saw,* and so forth; whereas *doing* is an action abiding in the agent, *e.g., to see, to will,* and the like. Accordingly, prudence stands in the same relation to such human actions, consisting in the use of powers and habits, as art does to external makings; since each is the perfect reason about the things with which it is concerned. But perfection and rectitude of reason in speculative matters depend on the principles from which reason argues; just as we have said above that science depends on and presupposes understanding, which is the habit of principles. *Now in human acts ends are what principles are in speculative matters,* as is stated in *Ethics* vii.[28] Consequently, it is requisite for prudence, which is right reason about things to be done, that man be well disposed with regard to ends; and this depends on the rectitude of his appetite. Therefore, for prudence there is need of moral virtue, which rectifies the appetite. On the other hand, the good of things made by art is not the good of man's appetite, but the good of the artificial things themselves, and hence art does not presuppose rectitude of the appetite. The consequence is that more praise is given to a craftsman who is at fault willingly, than to one who is unwillingly; whereas it is more contrary to prudence to sin willingly than unwillingly; since rectitude of the will is essential to prudence, but not to art.—Accordingly, it is evident that prudence is a virtue distinct from art.

Reply Obj. 1. The various kinds of things made by art are all external to man, and therefore there is no diversification in the nature of virtue. But prudence is right reason about human acts themselves, and hence it is a distinct kind of virtue, as was stated above.

Reply Obj. 2. Prudence has more in common with art than a speculative habit has, if we consider their subject and matter; for they are both in the part of the soul that does not deal with necessary truths, as well as about things that may be otherwise than they are. But if we consider them as virtues, then art has more in common with the speculative habits than with prudence, as is clear from what has been said.

Reply Obj. 3. Prudence is of good counsel about matters regarding man's entire life, and the last end of human life. But in some arts there is counsel about matters concerning the ends proper to those arts. Hence some men, in so far as they are good counsellors in matters of warfare, or seamanship, are said to be prudent officers or pilots, but not prudent absolutely; for only

[27] Aristotle, *Metaph.,* VIII, 8 (1050a 30).   [28] Aristotle, *Eth.,* VII, 8 (1151a 16).

those are prudent absolutely who give good counsel about what concerns man's entire life.

Fifth Article

WHETHER PRUDENCE IS A VIRTUE NECESSARY TO MAN?

We proceed thus to the Fifth Article:—

Objection 1. It would seem that prudence is not a virtue necessary for a good life. For as art is to things that are made, of which it is the right reason, so prudence is to things that are done, in respect of which we judge of a man's life; for prudence is the right reason about these things, as is stated in *Ethics* vi.[29] Now art is not necessary in things that are made, save in order that they be made, but not after they have been made. Neither, therefore, is prudence necessary to man for a good life, after he has become virtuous, but perhaps only in order that he may become virtuous.

Obj. 2. Further, *It is by prudence that we are of good counsel,* as is stated in *Ethics* vi.[30] But man can act not only from his own good counsel, but also from another's. Therefore a man does not need prudence for a good life, but it is enough that he follow the counsels of prudent men.

Obj. 3. Further, an intellectual virtue is one by which one always expresses the truth, and never what is false. But this does not seem to be the case with prudence, for it is not human never to err in taking counsel about what is to be done, since human actions are about things that may be otherwise than they are. Hence it is written (*Wis.* ix. 14): *The thoughts of mortal men are fearful, and our counsels uncertain.* Therefore it seems that prudence should not be reckoned an intellectual virtue.

On the contrary, It is reckoned with other virtues necessary for human life, when it is written (*Wis.* viii. 7) of divine Wisdom: *She teacheth temperance and prudence and justice and fortitude, which are such things as men can have nothing more profitable in life.*

I answer that, Prudence is a virtue most necessary for human life. For a good life consists in good deeds. Now in order to do good deeds, it matters not only what a man does, but also how he does it; in other words, it matters that he do it from right choice and not merely from impulse or passion. Now since choice is about means to the end, rectitude of choice requires two things, namely, the due end, and that which is suitably ordained to that due end. Now man is suitably directed to his due end by a virtue which perfects the soul in the appetitive part, the object of which is the good and the end. But to that which is suitably ordained to the due end man needs to be rightly disposed by a habit in his reason, because counsel and choice, which are about means ordained to the end, are acts of the reason. Consequently an intellectual virtue is needed in the reason, to perfect the reason

[29] *Op. cit.,* VI, 5 (1140b 3). [30] *Ibid.,* (1140a 25); 7 (1141b 9).

and make it suitably affected towards means ordained to the end; and this virtue is prudence. Consequently prudence is a virtue necessary for a good life.

Reply Obj. 1. The good of an art is to be found, not in the craftsman, but in the product of the art, since art is right reason about things to be made. For, since making passes into external matter, it is not a perfection of the maker, but of the thing made, even as movement is the act of the thing moved. Now art is concerned with the making of things. On the other hand, the good of prudence is in the agent himself, whose perfection consists in action itself; for prudence is right reason about things to be done, as was stated above. Consequently, art does not require of the craftsman that his act be a good act, but that his work be good. Rather would it be necessary for the thing made to act well (*e.g.,* that a knife should carve well, or that a saw should cut well), if it were proper to such things to act, rather than to be acted on, because they have not dominion over their actions. Therefore the craftsman needs art, not that he may live well, but that he may produce a good work of art, and an enduring one; whereas prudence is necessary to man that he may lead a good life, and not merely that he may become a good man.

Reply Obj. 2. When a man does a good deed, not of his own counsel, but moved by that of another, his operation is not yet quite perfect, as regards his reason in directing him and his appetite in moving him. Therefore, if he do a good deed, he does not do well absolutely; and yet this is required in order that he may lead a good life.

Reply Obj. 3. As is stated in *Ethics* vi.,[31] truth is not the same for the practical as for the speculative intellect. For the truth of the speculative intellect depends on the conformity of the intellect to the thing. And since the intellect cannot be infallibly in conformity with things in contingent matters, but only in necessary matters, therefore no speculative habit about contingent things is an intellectual virtue, but only such as is about necessary things.—On the other hand, the truth of the practical intellect depends on conformity with right appetite. This conformity has no place in necessary matters, which are not effected by the human will, but only in contingent matters which can be effected by us, whether they be matters of interior action or the products of external work. Hence it is only about contingent matters that an intellectual virtue is assigned to the practical intellect, viz., *art,* as regards things to be made, and *prudence,* as regards things to be done.

[31] Aristotle, *Eth.,* VI, 2 (1139a 26).

Sixth Article

WHETHER *EUBULIA, SYNESIS* AND *GNOME* ARE VIRTUES
ANNEXED TO PRUDENCE?

We proceed thus to the Sixth Article:—

Objection 1. It would seem that εὐβουλία, σύνεσις and γνώμη are unfittingly assigned as virtues annexed to prudence. For εὐβουλία [*eubulia*] is *a habit whereby we take good counsel.*[32] Now it *belongs to prudence to take good counsel,* as is stated in the same place.[33] Therefore εὐβουλία is not a virtue annexed to prudence, but rather is prudence itself.

Obj. 2. Further, it belongs to the higher to judge of the lower. The highest virtue would therefore seem to be the one whose act is judgment. Now σύνεσις [*synesis*] enables us to judge well. Therefore σύνεσις is not a virtue annexed to prudence, but rather is a principal virtue.

Obj. 3. Further, just as there are various matters to pass judgment on, so there are different points on which one has to take counsel. But there is one virtue referring to all matters of counsel. Therefore, in order to judge well of what has to be done, there is no need, besides σύνεσις, of the virtue of γνώμη [*gnome*].

Obj. 4. Further, Cicero mentions three other parts of prudence; viz., *memory of the past, understanding of the present and foresight of the future.*[34] Moreover, Macrobius mentions yet others: viz., *caution, docility* and the like.[35] Therefore it seems that the above are not the only virtues annexed to prudence.

On the contrary stands the authority of the Philosopher, who assigns these three virtues as being annexed to prudence.[36]

I answer that, Wherever several powers are ordered in relation to one another, that power is the highest which is ordered to the highest act. Now there are three acts of reason in respect of anything to be done by man: the first of these is counsel; the second, judgment; the third, command. The first two correspond to the acts of the speculative intellect which are inquiry and judgment, for counsel is a kind of inquiry; but the third is proper to the practical intellect in so far as the practical intellect is ordained to operation, for reason does not have to command in things that man cannot do. Now it is evident that in things done by man the chief act is that of command, to which all the rest are subordinate. Consequently, that virtue which excels in commanding, viz., prudence, as obtaining the highest place, has other secondary virtues annexed to it, viz., εὐβουλία, which perfects counsel; and σύνεσις and γνώμη, which are parts of prudence in relation to judgment, and of whose distinction we shall speak further on.

Reply Obj. 1. Prudence makes us be of good counsel, not as though its

---

[32] *Op. cit.,* VI, 9 (1142b 16). [33] *Op. cit.,* VI, 5 (1140a 25); 7 (1141b 9). [34] *De Invent.,* II, 53 (pp. 147ᵇ-148ᵇ). [35] *In Somn. Scipion.,* I, 8 (p. 518). [36] *Eth.,* VI, 11 (1143a 25).

immediate act consisted in being of good counsel, but because it perfects the latter act by means of a subordinate virtue, viz., εὐβουλία.

Reply Obj. 2. Judgment about what is to be done is directed to something further; for it may happen in some matter of action that a man's judgment is sound, while his execution is wrong. The whole process does not attain its perfection until reason commands with rightness on what ought to be done.

Reply Obj. 3. The judgment of anything should be based on that thing's proper principles. But inquiry does not reach to the proper principles, because, if we were in possession of these, we should need no more to inquire, for the truth would be already discovered. Hence only one virtue is directed to being of good counsel, whereas there are two virtues for good judgment, because distinction is based not on common but on proper principles. Consequently, in speculative matters, likewise, there is one science of dialectics, which inquires about all matters; whereas demonstrative sciences, which pronounce judgment, differ according to their different objects.—Σύνεσις and γνώμη are distinguished according to the different rules on which judgment is based; for σύνεσις judges of actions according to the common law, while γνώμη bases its judgment on the natural law, in those cases where the common law fails to apply, as we shall explain further on.[37]

Reply Obj. 4. Memory, understanding and foresight, as also caution and docility and the like, are not virtues distinct from prudence; they are, as it were, integral parts thereof, in so far as they are all requisite for perfect prudence.—There are, moreover, subjective parts or species of prudence, *e.g.*, domestic and political economy, and the like. But the three first named are, in a fashion, potential parts of prudence, because they are subordinate thereto, as secondary virtues to a principal virtue. We shall speak of them later.[38]

[37] *S. T.*, II-II, q. 51, a. 4.   [38] *S. T.*, II-II, q. 48.

Question LVIII

ON THE DIFFERENCE BETWEEN MORAL AND INTELLECTUAL VIRTUES

(*In Five Articles*)

WE must now consider the moral virtues. We shall speak (1) of the difference between them and the intellectual virtues; (2) of their distinction, one from another, in respect of their proper matter;[1] (3) of the difference between the chief or cardinal virtues and the others.[2]

Under the first head there are five points of inquiry: (1) Whether every virtue is a moral virtue? (2) Whether moral virtue differs from intellectual virtue? (3) Whether virtue is adequately divided into moral and intellectual virtue? (4) Whether there can be moral virtue without intellectual virtue? (5) Whether, on the other hand, there can be intellectual virtue without moral virtue?

First Article

WHETHER EVERY VIRTUE IS A MORAL VIRTUE?

We proceed thus to the First Article:—

Objection 1. It would seem that every virtue is a moral virtue. For moral virtue is so called from the Latin *mos, i.e.,* custom. Now, we can accustom ourselves to the acts of all the virtues. Therefore every virtue is a moral virtue.

Obj. 2. Further, the Philosopher says that moral virtue is *a habit of choosing the rational mean.*[3] But every virtue is a habit of choosing, since the acts of any virtue can be done from choice. And, moreover, every virtue consists in following the rational mean in some way, as we shall explain further on.[4] Therefore every virtue is a moral virtue.

Obj. 3. Further, Cicero says that *virtue is a habit after the manner of a nature, in accord with reason.*[5] But since every human virtue is directed to man's good, it must be in accord with reason; for man's good *consists in being in accord with reason,* as Dionysius states.[6] Therefore every virtue is a moral virtue.

On the contrary, The Philosopher says: *When we speak of a man's morals, we do not say that he is wise or intelligent, but that he is gentle or sober.*[7] Accordingly, then, wisdom and understanding are not moral virtues;

---

[1] Q. 59.　　[2] Q. 61.　　[3] *Eth.,* II, 6 (1106b 36).　　[4] Q. 64, a. 1, 2 and 3.　　[5] *De Invent.,* II, 53 (p. 147[b]).　　[6] *De Div. Nom.,* IV, 32 (PG 3, 733).　　[7] *Eth.,* I, 13 (1103a 7).

and yet they are virtues, as was stated above.[8] Therefore, not every virtue is a moral virtue.

I answer that, In order to answer this question clearly, we must consider the meaning of the Latin word *mos,* for thus we shall be able to discover what *moral* virtue is. Now *mos* has a twofold meaning. For sometimes it means custom, in which sense we read (*Acts* xv. 1): *Except you be circumcised after the manner [morem] of Moses, you cannot be saved;* sometimes it means a natural or quasi-natural inclination to do some particular action, in which sense the word is applied to brute animals. Thus we read (*2 Macc.* xi. 11) that *rushing violently upon the enemy, like lions [leonum more], they slew them.* The word is used in the same sense in *Ps.* lxvii. 7, where we read: *Who maketh men of one manner [moris] to dwell in a house.* For both these significations there is but one word in Latin; but in Greek there is a distinct word for each, for the word *ethos,* which signifies the same as the Latin *mos,* is written sometimes with a long *e,* and is written η, and sometimes with a short *e,* and is written ε.

Now *moral* virtue is so called from *mos* in the sense of a natural or quasi-natural inclination to do some particular action. And the other meaning of *mos,* i.e., *custom,* is akin to this, because custom somehow becomes a nature, and produces an inclination similar to a natural one. But it is evident that inclination to an action belongs properly to the appetitive power, whose function it is to move all the powers to their acts, as was explained above.[9] Therefore not every virtue is a moral virtue, but only those that are in the appetitive power.

Reply Obj. 1. This argument takes *mos* in the sense of *custom.*

Reply Obj. 2. Every act of virtue can be done from choice, but no virtue makes us choose rightly, save that which is in the appetitive part of the soul; for it has been stated above that choice is an act of the appetitive part.[10] Therefore a habit of choosing, *i.e.,* a habit which is the principle whereby we choose, is that habit alone which perfects the appetitive power; although the acts of other habits also may be a matter of choice.

Reply Obj. 3. *Nature is the principle of movement.*[11] Now to move to act is the proper function of the appetitive power. Consequently, to become like nature in the point of consenting to the reason is proper to those virtues which are in the appetitive power.

Second Article

WHETHER MORAL VIRTUE DIFFERS FROM INTELLECTUAL VIRTUE?

We proceed thus to the Second Article:—

Objection 1. It would seem that moral virtue does not differ from intel

[8] Q. 57, a. 2.   [9] Q. 9, a. 1.   [10] Q. 13, a. 1.   [11] Aristotle, *Phys.,* II, 1 (192b 21).

lectual virtue. For Augustine says that *virtue is the art of living rightly*.[12] But art is an intellectual virtue. Therefore moral and intellectual virtue do not differ.

Obj. 2. Further, some authors put science in the definition of the moral virtues. Thus some define perseverance as a *science or habit regarding those things to which we should hold or not hold*; and holiness as *a science which makes man to be faithful and to do his duty to God*.[13] Now science is an intellectual virtue. Therefore moral virtue should not be distinguished from intellectual virtue.

Obj. 3. Further, Augustine says that *virtue is the rectitude and perfection of reason*.[14] But this belongs to intellectual virtue, as is stated in *Ethics* vi.[15] Therefore moral virtue does not differ from intellectual virtue.

Obj. 4. Further, a thing does not differ from that which is included in its definition. But intellectual virtue is included in the definition of moral virtue; for the Philosopher says that *moral virtue is a habit of choosing the mean appointed by reason as a prudent man would appoint it*.[16] Now this right reason, that fixes the mean of moral virtue, belongs to intellectual virtue, as is stated in *Ethics* vi.[17] Therefore moral virtue does not differ from intellectual virtue.

On the contrary, It is stated in *Ethics* i. that *there are two kinds of virtue: some we call intellectual, some, moral*.[18]

I answer that, Reason is the first principle of all human acts, and whatever other principles of human acts may be found, they obey reason in some way, but diversely. For some obey reason instantaneously and without any contradiction whatever. Such are the members of the body, provided they be in a healthy condition, for as soon as reason commands, the hand or the foot proceeds to action. Hence the Philosopher says that *the soul rules the body with a despotic rule*,[19] *i.e.*, as a master rules his slave, who has no right to rebel. Accordingly, some held that all the active principles in man are subordinate to reason in this way. If this were true, for a man to act well it would suffice that his reason be perfect. Consequently, since virtue is a habit perfecting man in view of his doing good actions, it would follow that virtue existed only in the reason, so that there would be none but intellectual virtues. This was the opinion of Socrates, who said *every virtue is a kind of prudence*, as is stated in *Ethics* vi.[20] Hence he maintained that as long as a man was in possession of knowledge, he could not sin, and that every one who sinned did so through ignorance.[21]

---

[12] *De Civit. Dei,* IV, 21 (PL 41, 128).   [13] Cf. St. Thomas, *S. T.,* II-II, q. 137, a. 1, sed contra, and for Andronicus, cf. J. von Arnim, *Stoicorum Veterum Fragmenta,* III, p. 66.   [14] *Solil.,* I, 6 (PL 32, 876).   [15] Aristotle, *Eth.,* VI, 13 (1144b 21). [16] *Op. cit.,* II, 6 (1106b 36).   [17] *Op. cit.,* VI, 13 (1144b 21).   [18] *Op. cit.,* I, 13 (1103a 3).   [19] *Polit.,* I, 2 (1254b 4).   [20] Aristotle, *Eth.,* VI, 13 (1144b 19). [21] Cf. *op. cit.,* VII, 2 (1145b 23).— Cf. also Plato, *Protag.* (pp. 352B; 355A; 357B).

Now this is based on a false supposition. For the appetitive part obeys the reason, not instantaneously, but with a certain power of opposition; and so the Philosopher says that *reason commands the appetitive part by a political rule*,[22] whereby a man rules over subjects that are free, having a certain right of opposition. Hence Augustine says on *Ps.* cxviii. that *sometimes the intellect marks the way, while desire lags, or follows not at all;*[23] so much so, that sometimes the habits or passions of the appetitive part cause the use of reason to be impeded in some particular action. And in this way, there is some truth in the saying of Socrates that so long as a man is in possession of knowledge he does not sin: provided, however, that this knowledge is made to include the use of reason in this individual act of choice.

Accordingly, for a man to do a good deed, it is requisite not only that his reason be well disposed by means of a habit of intellectual virtue, but also that his appetite be well disposed by means of a habit of moral virtue. And so moral differs from intellectual virtue, even as the appetite differs from the reason. Hence, just as the appetite is the principle of human acts, in so far as it partakes of reason, so moral habits are to be considered human virtues in so far as they are in conformity with reason.

Reply Obj. 1. Augustine usually applies the term *art* to any form of right reason; in which sense art includes prudence, which is the right reason about things to be done, even as art is the right reason about things to be made. Accordingly, when he says that *virtue is the art of right conduct,* this applies to prudence essentially; but to other virtues by participation, in so far as they are directed by prudence.

Reply Obj. 2. All such definitions, by whomsoever given, have been based on the Socratic theory, and should be explained according to what we have said about art.

The same applies to the Third Objection.

Reply Obj. 4. Right reason in matters of prudence is included in the definition of moral virtue, not as part of its essence, but as something belonging by way of participation to all the moral virtues, in so far as they are all under the direction of prudence.

Third Article

WHETHER VIRTUE IS ADEQUATELY DIVIDED INTO MORAL AND INTELLECTUAL?

We proceed thus to the Third Article:—

Objection 1. It would seem that virtue is not adequately divided into moral and intellectual. For prudence seems to be intermediate between moral and intellectual virtue, since it is reckoned among the intellectual

---

[22] *Polit.*, I, 5 (1254b 4).   [23] *Enarr. in Psalm.*, serm. VIII, super *Ps.* CXVIII, 20 (PL 37, 1522).

virtues;[24] and again is placed by all among the four cardinal virtues, which are moral virtues, as we shall show further on.[25] Therefore virtue is not adequately divided into intellectual and moral, as though these were essentially distinct parts of virtue.

Obj. 2. Further, continency, perseverance and patience are not reckoned to be intellectual virtues. Yet neither are they moral virtues, since they do not reduce the passions to a mean, and are consistent with an abundance of passion. Therefore virtue is not adequately divided into intellectual and moral.

Obj. 3. Further, faith, hope and charity are virtues. Yet they are not intellectual virtues, for there are only five of these, viz., science, wisdom, understanding, prudence and art, as was stated above.[26] Neither are they moral virtues, since they are not about the passions, which are the chief concern of moral virtue. Therefore virtue is not adequately divided into intellectual and moral.

On the contrary, The Philosopher says that *virtue is twofold, intellectual and moral.*[27]

I answer that, Human virtue is a habit perfecting man for the purpose of acting well. Now in man there are but two principles of human actions, viz., the intellect or reason and the appetite: for these are the two principles of movement in man, as is stated in *De Anima* iii.[28] Consequently every human virtue must needs be a perfection of one of these principles. Accordingly, if it perfects man's speculative or practical intellect in order that his action may be good, it will be an intellectual virtue; whereas if it perfects his appetite, it will be a moral virtue. It follows therefore that every human virtue is either intellectual or moral.

Reply Obj. 1. Prudence is essentially an intellectual virtue. But considered on the part of its matter, it has something in common with the moral virtues, for it is right reason about things to be done, as was stated above.[29] It is in this sense that it is reckoned with the moral virtues.

Reply Obj. 2. Continence and perseverance are not perfections of the sensitive appetite. This is clear from the fact that unruly passions abound in the continent and persevering man, which would not be the case if his sensitive appetite were perfected by a habit making it conformable to reason. Continence and perseverance are, however, perfections of the rational part, which withstand the passions lest reason be led astray. But they fall short of being virtues, since intellectual virtue, which makes reason to conduct itself well in respect of moral matters, presupposes a right appetite of the end, so that it may hold itself with rectitude in respect of principles, *i.e.,* the ends, from which its reasoning begins; and this is wanting in the continent and persevering man.—Nor again can an action proceeding from

---

[24] Aristotle, *Eth.,* VI, 3 (1139b 16); 5 (1140b 28).   [25] Q. 61, a. 1.   [26] Q. 57, a. 2, 3 and 5.   [27] *Eth.,* II, 1 (1103a 14).   [28] Aristotle, *De An.,* III, 10 (433a 9; a 21).   [29] Q. 57, a. 4.

two principles be perfect, unless each principle be perfected by the habit corresponding to that operation; and thus, however perfect be the principal agent employing an instrument, it will produce an imperfect effect if the instrument be not well disposed also. Hence if the sensitive appetite, which is moved by the rational part, is not perfect, however perfect the rational part may be, the resulting action will be imperfect, and consequently the principle of that action will not be a virtue.—And for this reason, continence, desisting from pleasures, and perseverance in the midst of pains, are not virtues, but something less than a virtue, as the Philosopher maintains.[30]

Reply Obj. 3. Faith, hope and charity are above the virtues, for they are virtues of man as sharing in the grace of God.

Fourth Article

WHETHER THERE CAN BE MORAL VIRTUE WITHOUT INTELLECTUAL VIRTUE?

We proceed thus to the Fourth Article:—

Objection 1. It would seem that moral virtue can be without intellectual virtue. For moral virtue, as Cicero says, is *a habit after the manner of a nature, in accord with reason.*[31] Now, though nature may be in accord with some higher reason that moves it, there is no need for that reason to be united to nature in the same subject, as is evident of natural things devoid of reason. Therefore in a man there may be a moral virtue after the manner of a nature, inclining him to consent to his reason, even though his reason is not perfected by an intellectual virtue.

Obj. 2. Further, by means of intellectual virtue a man obtains perfect use of reason. But it happens at times that men are virtuous and acceptable to God without being vigorous in the use of reason. Therefore it seems that moral virtue can be without intellectual virtue.

Obj. 3. Further, moral virtue makes us inclined to do good works. But some, without depending on the judgment of reason, have a natural inclination to do good works. Therefore moral virtues can be without intellectual virtues.

On the contrary, Gregory says *unless the other virtues perform with prudence what they seek, they cannot be real virtues.*[32] But prudence is an intellectual virtue, as was stated above.[33] Therefore the moral virtues cannot be without the intellectual virtues.

I answer that, Moral virtue can be without some of the intellectual virtues, viz., wisdom, science and art; but not without understanding and prudence. Moral virtue cannot be without prudence, because moral virtue

---

[30] *Eth.,* VII, 1 (1145b 1); 9 (1151b 32).   [31] *De Invent.,* II, 53 (p. 147^b).
[32] *Moral.* XXII, 1 (PL 76, 212).   [33] A. 3, ad 1; q. 57, a. 5.

is a habit of choosing, *i.e.,* making us choose well. Now in order that a choice be good, two things are required. First, that the intention be directed to a due end; and this is done by moral virtue, which inclines the appetitive power to the good that is in accord with reason, which is a due end. Secondly, that man choose rightly those things which are means to the end; and this he cannot do unless his reason counsel, judge and command rightly, which is the function of prudence and the virtues annexed to it, as was stated above.[34] Therefore there can be no moral virtue without prudence, and consequently neither can there be without understanding. For it is by the virtue of understanding that we know naturally known principles both in speculative and in practical matters. Consequently, just as right reason in speculative matters, in so far as it proceeds from naturally known principles, presupposes the understanding of principles, so also does prudence, which is the right reason about things to be done.

Reply Obj. 1. The inclination of nature in things devoid of reason is without choice, and hence such an inclination does not of necessity require reason. But the inclination of moral virtue is with choice, and consequently, in order that it may be perfect, it requires that reason be perfected by intellectual virtue.

Reply Obj. 2. A man may be virtuous without having full use of reason as to everything, provided he have it with regard to those things which have to be done virtuously. In this way all virtuous men have full use of reason. Hence even those who seem to be simple, through lack of worldly shrewdness, can be prudent. In the words of *Matt.* x. 16: *Be ye therefore prudent* [Douay, *wise*] *as serpents, and simple as doves.*

Reply Obj. 3. The natural inclination to the good of virtue is a kind of beginning of virtue; but it is not perfect virtue. For the stronger this inclination is, the more perilous it can prove to be, unless it be accompanied by right reason, which rectifies the choice of fitting means towards the due end. Thus, if a running horse be blind, the faster it runs the more heavily will it fall, and the more grievously will it be hurt. And consequently, although moral virtue is not right reason, as Socrates held,[35] yet not only is it *according to right reason,* in so far as it inclines man to that which is according to right reason, as the Platonists maintained,[36] but it also needs to be *joined with right reason,* as Aristotle declares.[37]

Fifth Article

WHETHER THERE CAN BE INTELLECTUAL VIRTUE WITHOUT MORAL VIRTUE?

We proceed thus to the Fifth Article:—

Objection 1. It would seem that there can be intellectual virtue without

---

[34] Q. 57, a. 5 and 6. [35] Cf. Aristotle, *Eth.,* VI, 13 (1144b 19). [36] Cf. *ibid.* (1144b 21). [37] *Ibid.*

moral virtue. For the perfection of what precedes does not depend on the perfection of what follows. Now reason precedes and moves the sensitive appetite. Therefore intellectual virtue, which is a perfection of the reason, does not depend on moral virtue, which is a perfection of the appetitive part. Hence it can be without moral virtue.

Obj. 2. Further, morals are the matter of prudence, even as makable things are the matter of art. Now art can be without its proper matter, as a smith without iron. Therefore prudence can be without the moral virtues, even though, of all the intellectual virtues, it seems most akin to the moral virtues.

Obj. 3. Further, prudence is *a virtue whereby we are of good counsel.*[38] Now many are of good counsel without having the moral virtues. Therefore prudence can be without moral virtue.

On the contrary, To wish to do evil is directly opposed to moral virtue; and yet it is not opposed to anything that can be without moral virtue. Now it is contrary to prudence *to sin willingly.*[39] Therefore prudence cannot be without moral virtue.

I answer that, Other intellectual virtues can, but prudence cannot, be without moral virtue. The reason for this is that prudence is right reason about things to be done, and this not merely in general, but also in the particular, where action takes place. Now right reason demands principles from which reason proceeds. But when reason is concerned with the particular, it needs not only universal principles, but also particular ones. For as to universal principles of action, a man is rightly disposed by the natural understanding of principles, by which he knows that he should do no evil; or, again, he may be rightly disposed by some practical science. But this is not enough in order that a man may reason rightly about particular cases. For it happens sometimes that the aforesaid universal principle, known by means of understanding or science, is destroyed in a particular case by a passion. Thus, to one who is swayed by concupiscence, when he is overcome thereby, the object of his desire seems good, although it is opposed to the universal judgment of his reason. Consequently, just as by the habit of natural understanding or of science, a man is made to be rightly disposed in regard to the universal principles, so, in order that he be rightly disposed with regard to the particular principles of action, viz., the ends, he needs to be perfected by certain habits, whereby it becomes connatural to man, as it were, to judge rightly about the end. This is done by moral virtue, for the virtuous man judges rightly of the end of virtue, because *such as a man is, such does the end seem to him.*[40] Consequently the right reason about things to be done, viz., *prudence,* requires man to have moral virtue.

---

[38] *Op. cit.,* VI, 5 (1140a 25); 7 (1141b 10).   [39] *Op. cit.,* VI, 5 (1140b 22).   [40] *Op. cit.,* III, 5 (1114a 32).

Reply Obj. 1. Reason, as apprehending the end, precedes the appetite for the end; but the appetite for the end precedes the reason in so far as it deliberates about the choice of the means, which is the concern of prudence. Even so, in speculative matters, the understanding of principles is the starting point of reason in its work of syllogizing.

Reply Obj. 2. It does not depend on the disposition of our appetite whether we judge well or ill of the principles of art, as it does, when we judge of the end which is the principle in moral matters; in the former case our judgment depends on reason alone. Hence art does not require a virtue perfecting the appetite, as prudence does.

Reply Obj. 3. Prudence not only helps us to be of good counsel, but also to judge and command well. This is not possible unless the impediment of the passions, destroying the judgment and the command of prudence, be removed; and this is done by moral virtue.

Question LIX

THE DISTINCTION OF THE MORAL VIRTUES IN RELATION TO THE PASSIONS

(*In Five Articles*)

WE must now consider the difference of one moral virtue from another. And since the moral virtues which are about the passions differ according to the differences of the passions, we must consider (1) the general relation of virtue to passion; (2) the different kinds of moral virtue in relation to the passions.[1] Under the first head there are five points of inquiry: (1) Whether moral virtue is a passion? (2) Whether there can be moral virtue with passion? (3) Whether sorrow is compatible with moral virtue? (4) Whether every moral virtue is about a passion? (5) Whether there can be moral virtue without passion?

First Article

WHETHER MORAL VIRTUE IS A PASSION?

We proceed thus to the First Article:—

Objection 1. It would seem that moral virtue is a passion. For the mean is of the same genus as the extremes. But moral virtue is a mean between passions. Therefore moral virtue is a passion.

Obj. 2. Further, virtue and vice, being contrary to one another, are in the same genus. But some passions are reckoned to be vices, such as envy and anger. Therefore some passions are virtues.

Obj. 3. Further, pity is a passion, since it is sorrow for another's ills, as was stated above.[2] Now *Cicero the renowned orator did not hesitate to call pity a virtue,* as Augustine states in *De Civitate Dei* ix.[3] Therefore a passion may be a moral virtue.

On the contrary, It is stated in *Ethics* ii. that *passions are neither virtues nor vices.*[4]

I answer that, Moral virtue cannot be a passion. This is clear for three reasons. First, because a passion is a movement of the sensitive appetite, as was stated above,[5] whereas moral virtue is not a movement, but rather a principle of the movement of the appetite; for it is a habit. Secondly, because passions are not in themselves good or evil. For man's good or evil is in terms of the reason, and hence the passions, considered in themselves, are

[1] Q. 60. [2] Q. 35, a. 8. [3] *De Civit. Dei,* IX, 5 (PL 41, 261). [4] Aristotle, *Eth.,* II, 5 (1105b 28). [5] Q. 22, a. 3.

open to both good and evil, according as they are in agreement or disagreement with reason. Now nothing of this sort can be a virtue, since virtue is related only to good, as was stated above.[6] Thirdly, because, granted that some passions are, in some way, related only to good, or only to evil, even then the movement of passion, as passion, begins in the appetite, and ends in the reason, since the appetite tends to conformity with reason. On the other hand, the movement of virtue is the reverse, for it begins in the reason and ends in the appetite, inasmuch as the latter is moved by reason. Hence the definition of moral virtue states that it is *a habit of choosing the mean appointed by reason as a prudent man would appoint it.*[7]

Reply Obj. 1. Virtue is a mean between passions, not by reason of its essence, but because of its effect; because, namely, it establishes the mean between passions.

Reply Obj. 2. If by vice we understand a habit of doing evil deeds, it is evident that no passion is a vice. But if vice is taken to mean sin, which is a vicious act, nothing hinders a passion from being a vice, or, on the other hand, from concurring in an act of virtue (according as a passion is either opposed to reason or in agreement with reason).

Reply Obj. 3. Pity is said to be a virtue, *i.e.*, an act of virtue, in so far as *that movement of the soul is obedient to reason*; viz., *when pity is bestowed without violating justice, as when the poor are relieved, or the penitent forgiven,* as Augustine says.[8] But if by pity we understand a habit perfecting man so that he bestows pity reasonably, nothing hinders pity, in this sense, from being a virtue. The same applies to similar passions.

Second Article

WHETHER THERE CAN BE MORAL VIRTUE WITH PASSION?

We proceed thus to the Second Article:—

Objection 1. It would seem that moral virtue cannot be with passion. For the Philosopher says that *a gentle man is one who is not passionate; but a patient man is one who is passionate but does not give way.*[9] The same applies to all the moral virtues. Therefore all moral virtues are without passion.

Obj. 2. Further, virtue is a right disposition of the soul, as health is of the body, as is stated *Physics* vii.;[10] and therefore *virtue is a kind of health of the soul,* as Cicero says.[11] But the soul's passions are *the soul's diseases,* as he says in the same book.[12] Now health is incompatible with disease. Therefore neither is passion compatible with virtue.

Obj. 3. Further, moral virtue requires perfect use of reason even in par-

---

[6] Q. 55, a. 3.   [7] Aristotle, *Eth.*, II, 6 (1106b 36).   [8] *De Civit. Dei*, IX, 5 (PL 41, 261).   [9] *Top.*, IV, 5 (125b 22).   [10] Aristotle, *Phys.*, VII, 3 (246b 2; 247a 2).   [11] *Tusc. Disp.*, IV, 13 (pp. 375-376).   [12] *Op. cit.*, IV, 10 (p. 372).

ticular matters. But the passions are an obstacle to this, for the Philosopher says that *pleasures destroy the judgment of prudence*;[13] and Sallust says that *when they*, i.e., the soul's passions, *interfere, it is not easy for the mind to grasp the truth*.[14] Therefore passion is incompatible with moral virtue.

On the contrary, Augustine says: *If the will is perverse, these movements*, viz., the passions, *are perverse also; but if it is upright, they are not only blameless, but even praiseworthy*.[15] But nothing praiseworthy is incompatible with moral virtue. Therefore moral virtue does not exclude the passions, but can co-exist with them.

I answer that, The Stoics and Peripatetics disagreed on this point, as Augustine relates.[16] For the Stoics held that the soul's passions cannot be in a wise or virtuous man, whereas the Peripatetics, who were founded by Aristotle, as Augustine says,[17] maintained that the passions are compatible with moral virtue, if they be reduced to the mean.

This difference, as Augustine observes, was one of words rather than of opinions. For the Stoics, through not distinguishing between the intellectual appetite, *i.e.*, the will, and the sensitive appetite, which is divided into irascible and concupiscible, did not (as the Peripatetics did) distinguish the passions from the other affections of the human soul in the point of their being movements of the sensitive appetite, whereas the other affections of the soul, which are not passions, are movements of the intellectual appetite or will; but they distinguished the passions only to the extent of considering them to be any affections in disaccord with reason. These affections could not be in a wise or virtuous man if they arose deliberately, while it would be possible for them to be in a wise man if they arose suddenly; because, in the words of Aulus Gellius, quoted by Augustine, *it is not in our power to call up the visions of the soul, known as its fancies; and when they arise from awesome things, they must needs disturb the mind of a wise man, so that he is somewhat startled by fear, or depressed with sorrow, as though these passions forestall the use of reason without his approving of such things or consenting thereto*.[18]

Accordingly, if, as the Stoics held, the passions be taken for inordinate affections, they cannot be in a virtuous man, so that he consent to them deliberately. But if the passions be taken for any movements of the sensitive appetite, they can be in a virtuous man, in so far as they are subordinate to reason. Hence Aristotle says that *some describe virtue as being a kind of freedom from passion and disturbance: this is incorrect, because the assertion should be qualified*; they should have said virtue is freedom from those passions *that are not as they should be as to manner and time*.[19]

Reply Obj. 1. The Philosopher quotes this, as well as many other examples in his logical works, in order to illustrate, not his own mind, but

---

[13] *Eth.*, VI, 5 (1140b 12).   [14] *In Coniurat. Catil.*, LI (p. 47).   [15] *De Civit. Dei*, XIV, 6 (PL 41, 407).   [16] *Op. cit.*, IX, 4 (PL 41, 258).   [17] *Ibid.*   [18] *Ibid.* (PL 41, 259).   [19] *Eth.*, II, 3 (1104b 24).

that of others. It was the opinion of the Stoics that the passions of the soul were incompatible with virtue.[20] The Philosopher rejects this opinion when he says that virtue is not freedom from passion.[21]—It may be said, however, that when he says that *a gentle man is not passionate,* we are to understand this of inordinate passion.

Reply Obj. 2. This and all similar arguments which Tully brings forward, in the *Tusculan Disputations,* take the passions in the sense of inordinate affections.

Reply Obj. 3. When a passion forestalls the judgment of reason, so as to prevail on the soul to give its consent, it hinders counsel and the judgment of reason. But when it follows that judgment, as though being commanded by reason, it helps towards the execution of reason's command.

Third Article

WHETHER SORROW IS COMPATIBLE WITH MORAL VIRTUE?

We proceed thus to the Third Article:—

Objection 1. It would seem that sorrow is incompatible with virtue. For the virtues are effects of wisdom, according to *Wis.* viii. 7: *She, i.e.,* divine wisdom, *teacheth temperance, and prudence, and justice and fortitude.* Now the *conversation* of wisdom *hath no bitterness,* as we read further on (*verse* 16). Therefore sorrow is incompatible with virtue also.

Obj. 2. Further, sorrow is a hindrance to work, as the Philosopher states.[22] But a hindrance to good works is incompatible with virtue. Therefore sorrow is incompatible with virtue.

Obj. 3. Further, Tully calls sorrow a disease of the soul.[23] But disease of the soul is incompatible with virtue, which is a good disposition of the soul. Therefore sorrow is opposed to virtue and is incompatible with it.

On the contrary, Christ was perfect in virtue. But there was sorrow in Him, for He said (*Matt.* xxvi. 38): *My soul is sorrowful even unto death.* Therefore sorrow is compatible with virtue.

I answer that, As Augustine says,[24] the Stoics held that in the soul of the wise man there are three εὐπάθειαι, *i.e., three good passions,* in place of the three disturbances: viz., instead of covetousness, *desire,* instead of mirth, *joy,* instead of fear, *caution.* But they denied that anything corresponding to sorrow could be in the soul of a wise man, for two reasons.

First, because sorrow is for an evil that is already present. Now they held that no evil can happen to a wise man, for they thought that, just as man's only good is virtue, and bodily goods are no good to man, so man's only evil is vice, which cannot be in a virtuous man. But this is unreasona-

---

[20] Cf. Cicero, *Tusc. Disp.,* III, 4 (p. 320).　[21] *Eth.,* II, 3 (1104b 24).　[22] *Op. cit.,* VII, 13 (1153b 2); X, 5 (1175b 17).　[23] *Tusc. Disp.,* III, 7 (p. 325).　[24] *De Civit. Dei,* XIV, 8 (PL 41, 411).

ble. For, since man is composed of soul and body, whatever conduces to preserve the life of the body is some good to man; yet not his supreme good,
because he can abuse it. Consequently the evil which is contrary to this
good can be in a wise man, and can cause him moderate sorrow.—Again,
although a virtuous man can be without grave sin, yet no man is to be
found to live without committing slight sins, according to *1 John* i. 8: *If we
say that we have no sin, we deceive ourselves.*—A third reason is because a
virtuous man, though not actually in a state of sin, may have been so in the
past. And he is to be commended if he sorrow for that sin, according to *2
Cor.* vii. 10: *The sorrow that is according to God worketh penance steadfast
unto salvation.*—Fourthly, because he may praiseworthily sorrow for another's sin. Therefore sorrow is compatible with moral virtue in the same
way as the other passions are when moderated by reason.

Their second reason for holding this opinion was that sorrow is about
present evil, whereas fear is for evil to come, even as pleasure is about a
present good, while desire is for a future good. Now the enjoyment of a
good possessed, or the desire to have a good that one possesses not, or
even the concern to avoid some future evil, may be consistent with virtue;
but depression of the soul resulting from sorrow for a present evil is altogether contrary to reason, and hence it is incompatible with virtue. But
this is unreasonable. For there is an evil which can be present to the virtuous man, as we have just stated, and this evil reason loathes. Therefore
the sensitive appetite follows reason's loathing by sorrowing for that evil;
yet moderately, according as reason dictates. Now it pertains to virtue that
the sensitive appetite be conformed to reason, as was stated above. Therefore moderated sorrow for an object which ought to make us sorrowful is a
mark of virtue; as also the Philosopher says.[25]—Moreover, this proves
useful for avoiding evil, since, just as good is more readily sought for the
sake of pleasure, so evil is more undauntedly shunned because of sorrow.

Accordingly we must allow that sorrow for things that befit virtue is
incompatible with virtue, since virtue rejoices in its own. On the other
hand, virtue sorrows moderately for all that thwarts virtue, no matter how.

Reply Obj. 1. The passage quoted proves that the wise man is not made
sorrowful by wisdom. Yet he sorrows for anything that hinders wisdom.
Consequently there is no room for sorrow in the blessed, in whom there
can be no hindrance to wisdom.

Reply Obj. 2. Sorrow hinders the work that makes us sorrowful; but it
helps us to do more readily whatever banishes sorrow.

Reply Obj. 3. Immoderate sorrow is a disease of the soul, but moderate
sorrow is the mark of a well-disposed soul, according to the present state of
life.

[25] *Eth.*, II, 6 (1106b 20).

Fourth Article

WHETHER ALL THE MORAL VIRTUES ARE ABOUT THE PASSIONS?

We proceed thus to the Fourth Article:—

Objection 1. It would seem that all the moral virtues are about the passions. For the Philosopher says that *moral virtue is about pleasure and sorrow.*[26] But pleasure and sorrow are passions, as was stated above.[27] Therefore all the moral virtues are about the passions.

Obj. 2. Further, the subject of the moral virtues is that which is rational by participation, as the Philosopher states.[28] But the passions are in this part of the soul, as was stated above.[29] Therefore every moral virtue is about the passions.

Obj. 3. Further, some passion is to be found in every moral virtue, and so either all are about the passions, or none are. But some are about the passions, as fortitude and temperance, as is stated in *Ethics* iii.[30] Therefore all the moral virtues are about the passions.

On the contrary, Justice, which is a moral virtue, is not about the passions, as is stated in *Ethics* v.[31]

I answer that, Moral virtue perfects the appetitive part of the soul by directing it to the good of reason. The good of reason is that which is moderated or directed by reason. Consequently, there are moral virtues about all matters that are subject to reason's direction and moderation. Now reason directs not only the passions of the sensitive appetite, but also the operations of the intellectual appetite, *i.e.*, the will, which is not the subject of a passion, as was stated above.[32] Therefore not all the moral virtues are about passions, but some are about passions, some about operations.

Reply Obj. 1. The moral virtues are not all about pleasures and sorrows, as about their proper matter, but as about something resulting from their proper acts. For every virtuous man rejoices in acts of virtue, and sorrows for the contrary. Hence the Philosopher, after the words already quoted, adds: *if virtues are about actions and passions, and every action and passion is followed by pleasure or sorrow, it follows that virtue is about pleasures and sorrows,*[33] viz., as about something that results from virtue.

Reply Obj. 2. Not only the sensitive appetite, which is the subject of the passions, is rational by participation, but also the will, in which there are no passions, as was stated above.

---

[26] *Op. cit.,* II, 3 (1104b 8).   [27] Q. 23, a. 4; q. 31, a. 1; q. 35, a. 1 and 2. [28] Aristotle, *Eth.,* I, 13 (1103a 1).   [29] Q. 22, a. 3.   [30] Aristotle, *Eth.,* III, 5 (1115a 6); 10 (1117b 25).   [31] *Op. cit.,* V, 1 (1129a 4).   [32] Q. 22, a. 3.   [33] *Eth.,* II, 3 (1104b 13).

Reply Obj. 3. Some virtues have passions as their proper matter, but some virtues not. Hence the comparison does not hold for all cases, as will be shown later on.[34]

Fifth Article

WHETHER THERE CAN BE MORAL VIRTUE WITHOUT PASSION?

We proceed thus to the Fifth Article:—

Objection 1. It would seem that moral virtue can be without passion. For the more perfect moral virtue is, the more does it overcome the passions. Therefore, at its highest point of perfection it is altogether without passion.

Obj. 2. Further, then is a thing perfect, when it is removed from its contrary and from whatever inclines to its contrary. Now the passions incline us to sin which is contrary to virtue, and hence they are called *passions of sins (Rom.* vii. 5). Therefore perfect virtue is altogether without passion.

Obj. 3. Further, it is by virtue that we are conformed to God, as Augustine declares.[35] But God does all things without passion. Therefore the most perfect virtue is without any passion at all.

On the contrary, No man is just who rejoices not in just deeds, as is stated in *Ethics* i.[36] But joy is a passion. Therefore justice cannot be without passion; and still less can the other virtues.

I answer that, If we take the passions as being inordinate affections, as the Stoics did, it is evident that in this sense perfect virtue is without the passions.—But if by passions we understand any movement of the sensitive appetite, it is plain that moral virtues, which are about the passions as about their proper matter, cannot be without passions. The reason for this is that otherwise it would follow that moral virtue would make the sensitive appetite altogether inert; whereas it is not the function of virtue to deprive the powers subordinate to reason of their proper activities, but to make them execute the commands of reason by exercising their proper acts. Therefore just as virtue directs the bodily members to their appointed external acts, so does it direct the sensitive appetite to its own regulated movements.

Those moral virtues, however, which are not about the passions, but about operations, can be without passions. Such a virtue is justice, because it applies the will to its proper act, which is not a passion. Nevertheless, joy results from an act of justice, at least in the will, in which case it is not a passion. And if this joy be increased through the perfection of justice, it will overflow into the sensitive appetite, in so far as the lower powers follow the movement of the higher, as was stated above.[37] Therefore by reason of this kind of overflow, the more perfect a virtue is, the more does it cause passion.

---

[34] Q. 60, a. 2.   [35] *De Mor. Eccl.,* I, 6; 11; 13 (PL 32, 1315; 1319, 1321).
[36] Aristotle, *Eth.,* I, 8 (1099a 17).   [37] Q. 17, a. 7; q. 24, a. 3.

Reply Obj. 1. Virtue overcomes inordinate passion, and it produces ordinate passion.

Reply Obj. 2. It is inordinate, not ordinate, passion that leads to sin.

Reply Obj. 3. The good of anything depends on the condition of its nature. Now there is no sensitive appetite in God and the angels, as there is in man. Consequently good operation in God and the angels is altogether without passion, as it is without a body; whereas a good operation of man is with passion, even as it is produced with the body's help.

HOW THE MORAL VIRTUES ARE DISTINGUISHED FROM ONE ANOTHER

(*In Five Articles*)

WE must now consider how the moral virtues are distinguished from one another. Under this head there are five points of inquiry: (1) Whether there is only one moral virtue? (2) Whether those moral virtues which are about operations are distinguished from those which are about passions? (3) Whether there is but one moral virtue about operations? (4) Whether there are different moral virtues about different passions? (5) Whether the moral virtues are distinguished according to the various objects of the passions?

First Article

WHETHER THERE IS ONLY ONE MORAL VIRTUE?

We proceed thus to the First Article:—

Objection 1. It would seem that there is only one moral virtue. For just as the direction of moral actions belongs to reason, which is the subject of the intellectual virtues, so their inclination belongs to the appetitive power, which is the subject of moral virtues. But there is only one intellectual virtue to direct all moral acts, viz., prudence. Therefore, there is also but one moral virtue to give all moral acts their respective inclinations.

Obj. 2. Further, habits differ, not in respect of their material objects, but according to the formal aspects of their objects. Now the formal aspect of the good to which moral virtue is directed is one, viz., the mean defined by reason. Therefore it appears that there is but one moral virtue.

Obj. 3. Further, moral matters are specified by the end, as was stated above.[1] Now there is but one common end of all the moral virtues, viz., happiness, while the proper and proximate ends are infinite in number. But the moral virtues themselves are not infinite in number. Therefore it seems that there is but one.

On the contrary, One habit cannot be in several powers, as was stated above.[2] But the subject of the moral virtues is the appetitive part of the soul, which is distinguished into several powers, as was stated in the First Part.[3] Therefore there cannot be only one moral virtue.

I answer that, As was stated above, the moral virtues are habits of the

---

[1] Q. 1, a. 3.   [2] Q. 56, a. 2.   [3] *S. T.,* I, q. 80, a. 2; q. 81, a. 2.

appetitive part of the soul.[4] Now habits differ specifically according to the specific differences of their objects, as was stated above.[5] Now the species of the object of appetite, as of anything, depends on its specific form which it receives from the agent. But we must observe that the matter of the receptive subject bears a twofold relation to the agent. For sometimes it receives the form of the agent in the same manner as the agent has that form, as happens with all univocal agents, so that if the agent be one specifically, the matter must of necessity receive a form that is specifically one. Thus, the univocal effect of fire is of necessity something in the species of fire.—Sometimes, however, the matter receives the form from the agent, but not in the same manner as the agent, as is the case with non-univocal causes of generation. Thus an animal is generated by the sun. In this case, the forms received into matter from one and the same agent are not of one species, but vary according to the adaptability of the matter to receive the action of the agent. For instance, we see that owing to the one action of the sun, animals of various species are produced by putrefaction according to the various adaptability of matter.

Now it is evident that in moral matters the reason holds the place of commander and mover, while the appetitive power is commanded and moved. But the appetite does not receive the action of reason univocally, so to say; for it is rational, not essentially, but by participation.[6] Consequently, appetible objects are established in various species according to the movement of reason, by having various relations to reason; so that it follows that moral virtues are of various species and are not one only.

Reply Obj. 1. The object of the reason is the true. Now in all moral matters, which are contingent matters of action, there is but one kind of truth. Consequently, there is but one virtue to direct all such matters, viz. prudence.—On the other hand, the object of the appetitive power is the appetible good, which varies in kind according to its various relations to reason, the directing power.

Reply Obj. 2. This formal element is one generically because of the unity of the agent; but it varies in species because of the various relations of the receiving subjects, as was explained above.

Reply Obj. 3. Moral matters do not receive their species from the last end, but from their proximate ends; and these, although they be infinite in number, are not infinite in species.

Second Article

WHETHER MORAL VIRTUES ABOUT OPERATIONS ARE DIFFERENT FROM THOSE THAT ARE ABOUT PASSIONS?

We proceed thus to the Second Article:—
Objection 1. It would seem that moral virtues are not divided into those

---

[4] Q. 58, a. 1, 2 and 3. [5] Q. 54, a. 2. [6] Aristotle, *Eth.*, I, 13 (1102b 13; b 26).

which are about operations and those which are about passions. For the Philosopher says that moral virtue is *an operative habit whereby we do what is best in matters of pleasure or sorrow*.[7] Now pleasure and sorrow are passions, as was stated above.[8] Therefore the same virtue which is about passions is also about operations, since it is an operative habit.

Obj. 2. Further, the passions are principles of external action. If, therefore, some virtues regulate the passions, they must, as a consequence, regulate operations also. Therefore the same moral virtues are about both passions and operations.

Obj. 3. Further, the sensitive appetite is moved well or ill towards every external operation. Now the movements of the sensitive appetite are passions. Therefore the same virtues that are about operations are also about the passions.

On the contrary, The Philosopher reckons justice to be about operations; and temperance, fortitude and gentleness about passions.[9]

I answer that, Operation and passion stand in a twofold relation to virtue. First, as its effects, and in this way every moral virtue has some good operations as its product, as well as a certain pleasure or sorrow, which are passions, as was stated above.[10]

Secondly, operation may be compared to moral virtue as the matter about which virtue is concerned, and in this sense those moral virtues which are about operations must needs differ from those which are about passions. The reason for this is that good and evil, in certain operations, is taken from the very nature of those operations, no matter how man may be affected towards them: viz., in so far as good and evil in them depends on the nature of their relationship to something else. In operations of this kind there needs to be some power to regulate the operations in themselves. Such is the case with buying and selling, and with all operations in which there is an element of something due or undue to another. For this reason justice and its parts are properly about operations as their proper matter.— On the other hand, in some operations good and evil depends only on relationship with the agent. Consequently, good and evil in these operations depends on how well or ill man is affected towards them. And for this reason in such operations virtue must needs be chiefly about internal affections, which are called passions of the soul, as is evidently the case with temperance, fortitude and the like.

It happens, however, in operations which are directed to another, that the good of virtue is neglected by reason of some inordinate passion of the soul. In such cases, justice is destroyed in so far as the due measure of the external act is destroyed; while some other virtue is destroyed in so far as the internal passions exceed their due measure. Thus, when through anger

---

[7] *Op. cit.,* II, 3 (1104b 27).   [8] Q. 31, a. 1; q. 35, a. 1.   [9] *Eth.,* V, 1 (1129a 4); 5 (1133b 32).   [10] Q. 59, a. 4, ad 1.

one man strikes another, justice is destroyed in the undue blow; while gentleness is destroyed by immoderate anger. The same may be clearly applied to other virtues.

This suffices for the Replies to the Objections. For the first considers operations as the effect of virtue, while the other two consider operation and passion as concurring in the same effect. But in some cases virtue is chiefly about operations, in others, about passions, for the reason given above.

Third Article

WHETHER THERE IS ONLY ONE MORAL VIRTUE ABOUT OPERATIONS?

We proceed thus to the Third Article:—

Objection 1. It would seem that there is but one moral virtue about operations. For the rectitude of all external operations seems to belong to justice. Now justice is but one virtue. Therefore there is but one virtue about operations.

Obj. 2. Further, those operations seem to differ most which are directed on the one side to the good of the individual, and on the other to the good of the many. But this diversity does not cause diversity among the moral virtues, for the Philosopher says that legal justice, which directs the acts of men to the common good, does not differ, save logically, from the virtue which directs a man's actions to one man only.[11] Therefore diversity of operations does not cause a diversity of moral virtues.

Obj. 3. Further, if there were various moral virtues about various operations, the diversity of moral virtues would needs follow the diversity of operations. But this is clearly untrue, for it is the function of justice to establish rectitude in various kinds of commutations, and again in distributions, as is set down in *Ethics* v.[12] Therefore there are not different virtues about different operations.

On the contrary, Religion is a moral virtue distinct from piety, yet both of these are about operations.

I answer that, All the moral virtues that are about operations agree in the one general notion of justice, which is measured by what is due to another; but they differ according to their special natures. The reason for this is that in external operations, the order of reason is established, as we have stated, not according to how a man is affected towards such operations, but according to the becomingness of the thing itself; from which becomingness we derive the notion of something due, which is the formal aspect of justice. For it evidently pertains to justice that a man give another his due. Therefore all such virtues as are about operations bear, in some

[11] *Eth.,* V, 1 (1130a 12).   [12] *Op. cit.,* V, 2 (1130b 30).

way, the character of justice.—But the thing due is not of the same kind in all these virtues; for something is due to an equal in one way, to a superior, in another way, and to an inferior, in yet another; and the nature of a debt differs according as it arises from a contract, a promise, or a favor already conferred. And corresponding to these various kinds of debt there are various virtues: *e.g., religion,* whereby we pay our debt to God; *piety,* whereby we pay our debt to our parents or to our country; *gratitude,* whereby we pay our debt to our benefactors, and so forth.

Reply Obj. 1. Justice, properly so called, is one special virtue, whose object is the perfect due, which can be paid in the equivalent. But the name of justice is extended also to all cases in which something due is rendered. In this sense it is not a special virtue.

Reply Obj. 2. That justice which seeks the common good is another virtue from that which is directed to the private good of an individual; and so public law differs from private law, and Tully reckons as a special virtue *piety* which directs man to the good of his country.[13]—But that justice which directs man to the common good is a general virtue through its act of command; for it directs all the acts of the virtues to its own end, viz., the common good. And the virtues, in so far as they are commanded by that justice, receive the name of justice; and in this sense virtue does not differ from legal justice, save logically, just as there is only a logical difference between a virtue that is active of itself, and a virtue that is active through the command of another virtue.

Reply Obj. 3. There is the same notion of debt in all the operations belonging to special justice. Consequently, there is one and the same virtue of justice, especially in regard to commutations. For it may be that distributive justice is of another species from commutative justice; but about this we shall inquire later on.[14]

Fourth Article

WHETHER THERE ARE DIFFERENT MORAL VIRTUES ABOUT DIFFERENT PASSIONS?

We proceed thus to the Fourth Article:—

Objection 1. It would seem that there are not different moral virtues about different passions. For there is but one habit about things that concur in their principle and end, as is evident especially in the case of the sciences. But the passions all concur in one principle, viz., love; and they all terminate in the same end, viz., joy or sorrow, as we stated above.[15] Therefore there is but one moral virtue about all the passions.

Obj. 2. Further, if there were different moral virtues about different passions, it would follow that there are as many moral virtues as passions.

[13] *De Invent.,* II, 53 (p. 148ᵇ).   [14] *S. T.,* II-II, q. 61, a. 1.   [15] Q. 25, a. 1, 2 and 4; q. 27, a. 4.

But this clearly is not the case, since there is one moral virtue about contrary passions: *e.g.,* fortitude, about fear and daring; temperance, about pleasure and sorrow. Therefore there is no need for different moral virtues about different passions.

Obj. 3. Further, love, desire and pleasure are passions of different species, as was stated above.[16] Now there is but one virtue about all these three, viz., temperance. Therefore there are not different moral virtues about different passions.

On the contrary, Fortitude is about fear and daring, temperance about concupiscence, meekness about anger, as is stated in *Ethics* iii. and iv.[17]

I answer that, It cannot be said that there is only one moral virtue about all the passions, since some passions are not in the same power as other passions; for some belong to the irascible, others to the concupiscible power, as was stated above.[18]

On the other hand, neither does every diversity among the passions necessarily suffice for a diversity of moral virtues. First, because some passions are in contrary opposition to one another, such as joy and sorrow, fear and daring, and so on. About passions which are in this sort of opposition to one another there must needs be one and the same virtue. Because, since moral virtue consists in a kind of mean, the mean in contrary passions is established according to the same norm, even as in material things there is but one mean between contraries, *e.g.,* between black and white.—Secondly, because there are different passions opposing reason in the same manner, *e.g.* by impelling to that which is contrary to reason, or by withdrawing from that which is in accord with reason. Therefore the different passions of the concupiscible power do not require different moral virtues, because their movements follow one another in a certain order, as being directed to one and the same thing, viz., the attainment of some good or the avoidance of some evil. Thus, from love proceeds concupiscence, and from concupiscence we arrive at pleasure; and it is the same with the opposite passions, for hatred leads to avoidance or dislike, and this leads to sorrow. —On the other hand, the irascible passions are not all of one order, but are directed to different things; for daring and fear are about some great danger, hope and despair are about some difficult good, while anger seeks to overcome something contrary which has wrought harm. Consequently, there are different virtues about such passions: *e.g.,* temperance, about the concupiscible passions; fortitude, about fear and daring; magnanimity, about hope and despair; meekness, about anger.

Reply Obj. 1. All the passions concur in one common principle and end, but not in one proper principle or end; and so this does not suffice for the oneness of moral virtue.

Reply Obj. 2. Just as in the physical order the same principle causes

---

[16] Q. 23, a. 4.   [17] Aristotle, *Eth.,* III, 5 (1115a 6); 10 (1117b 25); IV, 5 (1125b 26).   [18] Q. 23, a. 1.

movement from one extreme and movement towards the other, and just as in the intellectual order contraries have one common notion, so too between contrary passions there is but one moral virtue, which, after the manner of a nature, consents to reason's dictates.

Reply Obj. 3. Those three passions are directed to the same object in a certain order, as was stated above, and so they belong to the same virtue.

Fifth Article

WHETHER THE MORAL VIRTUES ARE DISTINGUISHED ACCORDING TO THE VARIOUS OBJECTS OF THE PASSIONS?

We proceed thus to the Fifth Article:—

Objection 1. It would seem that the moral virtues are not distinguished according to the objects of the passions. For just as there are objects of passions, so are there objects of operations. Now those moral virtues that are about operations are not distinguished according to the objects of the operations; for the buying and selling either of a house or of a horse belong to one and the same virtue of justice. Therefore neither do those moral virtues that are about passions differ according to the objects of those passions.

Obj. 2. Further, the passions are acts or movements of the sensitive appetite. Now it needs a greater difference to diversify habits than acts. Hence diverse objects which do not diversify the species of passion, do not diversify the species of moral virtue; so that there is but one moral virtue about all objects of pleasure, and the same applies to the other passions.

Obj. 3. Further, more and less do not change a species. Now various objects of pleasure differ only by reason of being more or less pleasurable. Therefore all objects of pleasure belong to one species of virtue; and for the same reason so do all fearful objects, and the same applies to others. Therefore moral virtue is not diversified according to the objects of the passions.

Obj. 4. Further, virtue hinders evil, even as it produces good. But there are various virtues about the desires for good things. Thus temperance is about desires for the pleasure of touch, and wittiness about pleasures in games. Therefore there should be different virtues about fears of evils.

On the contrary, Chastity is about sexual pleasures, abstinence about pleasures of the table, and wittiness about pleasures in games.

I answer that, The perfection of virtue depends on the reason, whereas the perfection of passion depends on the sensitive appetite. Consequently, the virtues must needs be differentiated according to their relation to reason, but the passions according to their relation to the appetite. Hence the objects of the passions, according as they are variously related to the sensitive appetite, cause the different species of passions; while according as they are related to reason they cause the different species of virtues.

Now the movement of the reason is not the same as that of the sensitive appetite. Therefore nothing hinders a difference of objects from causing diversity among the passions, without causing a diversity among the virtues, as when one virtue is about several passions, as was stated above; and again, nothing hinders a difference of objects from causing a diversity among the virtues, without causing a diversity among the passions, since several virtues are directed towards one passion, *e.g.,* pleasure.

And because diverse passions, belonging to diverse powers, always belong to diverse virtues, as was stated above, therefore a diversity of objects that corresponds to a diversity of powers always causes a specific difference among virtues,—for instance, the difference between that which is good absolutely speaking, and that which is good and difficult to obtain. Moreover, the reason rules man's lower powers with a certain order, and even extends to outward things. For this reason, therefore, one single object of the passions, according as it is apprehended by sense, imagination, or reason, and again, according as it belongs to the soul, body, or external things, has various relations to reason, and consequently is of a nature to diversify the virtues. Consequently, man's good, which is the object of love, concupiscence and pleasure, may be taken as referred either to a bodily sense, or to the inner apprehension of the soul; and this whether it be directed to man's good in himself, either in his body or in his soul, or to man's good in relation to other men. And every such diversity diversifies virtue because of the diverse relation to reason.

Accordingly, if we take a good, and it be something apprehended by the sense of touch, and something pertaining to the upkeep of human life either in the individual or in the species, such as the pleasures of the table or of sex, it will belong to the virtue of *temperance.* As regards the pleasures of the other senses, they are not intense, and so they do not present much difficulty to the reason. Hence there is no virtue corresponding to them, for virtue, *like art, is about difficult things.*[19]

On the other hand, a good that is apprehended, not by the senses, but by an inner power, and belonging to man in himself, is like money and honor: the former, by its very nature, is employable for the good of the body, while the latter is based on the apprehension of the soul. These goods, again, may be considered either absolutely, in which way they concern the concupiscible power, or as being difficult to obtain, in which way they belong to the irascible power. This distinction, however, has no place in pleasurable objects of touch, since such are very lowly, and are becoming to man in so far as he has something in common with irrational animals. Accordingly, in reference to money, considered as a good absolutely as an object of concupiscence, pleasure or love, there is *liberality*; but if we consider this good as difficult to get, and as being the object of our hope, there is *magnificence.* With regard to that good which we call honor, taken absolutely, as the ob-

---

[19] Aristotle, *Eth.,* II, 3 (1105a 9).

ject of love, we have a virtue called *philotimia*,[20] *i.e., love of honor*; while
if we consider it as hard to attain, and as an object of hope, then we have
magnanimity. Therefore *liberality* and *philotimia* seem to be in the concupiscible part, while *magnificence* and *magnanimity* are in the irascible.

As regards man's good in relation to other men, it does not seem hard to
obtain, but is considered absolutely as the object of the concupiscible passions. This good may be pleasurable to a man in his behavior towards another either in some serious matter (in actions, namely, that are directed
by reason to a due end) or in playful actions (viz., in actions that are done
for mere pleasure, and which do not stand in the same relation to reason
as the former). Now one man behaves towards another, in serious matters,
in two ways. First, as being pleasant in his regard, by becoming speech and
deeds; and this belongs to a virtue which Aristotle calls *friendship*,[21] and
may be rendered *affability*. Secondly, one man behaves towards another by
being frank with him, in words and deeds; and this belongs to another
virtue which he calls *truthfulness*.[22] For frankness is more akin to the reason than pleasure, and to serious matters more than to play. Hence there is
another virtue about the pleasures of games, which the Philosopher calls
wittiness.[23]

It is therefore evident that, according to Aristotle,[24] there are ten moral
virtues about the passions, viz., fortitude, temperance, liberality, magnificence, magnanimity, love of honor, gentleness, friendship, truthfulness and
wittiness. All of them are distinguished according to their diverse matter,
passions or objects; so that if we add *justice*, which is about operations,
there will be eleven in all.

Reply Obj. 1. All objects of the same specific operation have the same
relation to reason; not so all the objects of the same specific passion, because operations do not thwart reason as the passions do.

Reply Obj. 2. Passions are not diversified by the same rule as virtues are,
as was stated above.

Reply Obj. 3. More and less do not diversify a species unless there be a
diverse relation to reason.

Reply Obj. 4. Good is a more potent mover than evil, because evil does
not cause movement, save by the power of good, as Dionysius states.[25]
Hence an evil does not force reason to seek the aid of virtue, unless it be an
excelling evil; and there seems to be one such evil corresponding to each
kind of passion. Hence there is but one virtue, meekness, for every form of
anger; and, again, but one virtue, fortitude, for all forms of daring.—On
the other hand, good exerts a pressure that requires the aid of virtue, even
if it be not a great good in that particular kind of passion. Consequently,
there are various moral virtues about desires, as was stated above.

[20] Aristotle, *op. cit.*, II, 7 (1107b 32).   [21] *Ibid.* (1108a 28).   [22] *Ibid.* (1108a 20)
[23] *Ibid.* (1108a 24).   [24] *Ibid.* (1107a 32).   [25] *De Div. Nom..* IV, 31 (PG 3, 732).

THE CARDINAL VIRTUES

(*In Five Articles*)

WE must now consider the cardinal virtues. Under this head there are five points of inquiry: (1) Whether the moral virtues should be called cardinal or principal virtues? (2) Of their number. (3) Which are they? (4) Whether they differ from one another? (5) Whether they are fittingly divided into political, perfecting, perfect, and exemplar virtues?

First Article

WHETHER THE MORAL VIRTUES SHOULD BE CALLED CARDINAL OR PRINCIPAL VIRTUES?

We proceed thus to the First Article:—

Objection 1. It would seem that moral virtues should not be called cardinal or principal virtues. For *the opposed members of a division are by nature simultaneous*,[1] so that one is not principal rather than another. Now all the virtues are opposed members of the division of the genus *virtue*. Therefore none of them should be called principal.

Obj. 2. Further, the end is superior to the means. But the theological virtues are about the end, while the moral virtues are about the means. Therefore the theological virtues, rather than the moral virtues, should be called principal or cardinal.

Obj. 3. Further, that which is essentially so is superior to that which is so by participation. But the intellectual virtues belong to that which is essentially rational, whereas the moral virtues belong to that which is rational by participation, as was stated above.[2] Therefore the intellectual virtues are principal, rather than the moral virtues.

On the contrary, Ambrose, in explaining the words *Blessed are the poor in spirit* (*Luke* vi. 20) says: *We know that there are four cardinal virtues, viz., temperance, justice, prudence and fortitude.*[3] But these are moral virtues. Therefore the moral virtues are cardinal virtues.

I answer that, When we speak without qualification of virtue, we are understood to speak of human virtue. Now human virtue, as was stated above, is virtue according to its perfect nature if it requires the rectitude of the appetite;[4] for such a virtue not only confers the ability to do well, but

---

[1] Aristotle, *Cat.*, XIII (14b 33).   [2] Q. 56, a. 6, ad 2; q. 58, a. 3; q. 59, a. 4, obj. 2.
[3] *In Luc.*, V, super VI, 20 (PL 15, 1738).   [4] Q. 56, a. 3.

also causes the use of the good work. On the other hand, a virtue is so called according to the imperfect notion of virtue, when it does not require rectitude of the appetite, because it merely confers the ability of doing well without causing the use of the good work. Now it is evident that the perfect is principal as compared to the imperfect; and so those virtues which contain rectitude of the appetite are called principal virtues. Such are the moral virtues, and among the intellectual virtues prudence alone is such, for it is also in a way a moral virtue with respect to its subject matter, as was shown above.[5] Consequently, those virtues which are called principal or cardinal are fittingly found among the moral virtues.

Reply Obj. 1. When a univocal genus is divided into its species, the members of the division are on a par in the point of the generic notion; although considered according to reality, one species may surpass another in rank and perfection, as man surpasses the other animals. But when we divide an analogous notion, which is applied to several things, but to one before it is applied to another, nothing hinders one from ranking before another, even with respect to the common notion; as the notion of being is applied to substance more principally than to accident. Such is the division of virtue into the various genera of virtue, since the good defined by reason is not found in the same way in all things.

Reply Obj. 2. The theological virtues are above man, as was stated above.[6] Hence they should properly be called not human, but *super-human* or divine virtues.

Reply Obj. 3. Although the intellectual virtues, except prudence, rank before the moral virtues, in the point of their subject, they do not rank before them according to the nature of virtue; for a virtue, as such, has reference to the good, which is the object of the appetite.

Second Article

WHETHER THERE ARE FOUR CARDINAL VIRTUES?

We proceed thus to the Second Article:—

Objection 1. It would seem that there are not four cardinal virtues. For prudence is the directing principle of the other moral virtues, as is clear from what has been said above.[7] But that which directs others ranks before them. Therefore prudence alone is a principal virtue.

Obj. 2. Further, the principal virtues are, in a way, moral virtues. Now we are directed to moral works both by the practical reason and by a right appetite, as is stated in *Ethics* vi.[8] Therefore there are only two cardinal virtues.

Obj. 3. Further, even among the other virtues one ranks higher than another. But in order that a virtue be principal, it need not rank above

---

[5] Q. 57, a. 4.   [6] Q. 58, a. 3, ad 3.   [7] Q. 58, a. 4.   [8] Aristotle, *Eth.*, VI, 2 (1139a 24).

all the others, but above some. Therefore it seems that there are many more principal virtues.

On the contrary, Gregory says: *The entire structure of good works is built on four virtues.*[9]

I answer that, Things may be numbered either in respect of their formal principles, or according to the subjects in which they are; and in either way we find that there are four cardinal virtues.

For the formal principle of the virtue of which we speak now is the good as defined by reason. This good can be considered in two ways. First, as existing in the consideration itself of reason, and thus we have one principal virtue called *prudence.*—Secondly, according as the reason puts its order into something else, and this either into operations, and then we have *justice,* or into passions, and then we need two virtues. For the need of putting the order of reason into the passions is due to their thwarting reason; and this occurs in two ways. First, when the passions incite to something against reason, and then they need a curb, which we thus call *temperance;* secondly, when the passions withdraw us from following the dictate of reason, *e.g.,* through fear of danger or toil, and then man needs to be strengthened for that which reason dictates, lest he turn back, and to this end there is *fortitude.*

In like manner, we find the same number if we consider the subjects of virtue. For there are four subjects of the virtue of which we now speak, viz., the power which is rational in its essence, and this is perfected by *prudence;* and that which is rational by participation, and is threefold, the will, subject of *justice,* the concupiscible power, subject of *temperance,* and the irascible power, subject of *fortitude.*

Reply Obj. 1. Prudence is absolutely the principal of all the virtues. The others are principal, each in its own genus.

Reply Obj 2. That part of the soul which is rational by participation is threefold, as was stated above.

Reply Obj. 3. All the other virtues, among which one ranks before another, are reducible to the above four, both as to the subject and as to the formal principles.

Third Article

WHETHER ANY OTHER VIRTUES SHOULD BE CALLED PRINCIPAL RATHER THAN THESE?

We proceed thus to the Third Article:—

Objection 1. It would seem that the other virtues should be called principal rather than these. For the greatest is clearly the principal in any

---

[9] *Moral.,* II, 49 (PL 75, 592).

genus. Now *magnanimity has a great influence on all the virtues*.[10] Therefore, magnanimity should, more than any, be called a principal virtue.

Obj. 2. Further, that which strengthens the other virtues should above
all be called a principal virtue. But such is humility, for Gregory says that
*he who gathers the other virtues without humility is as one who carries
straw against the wind*.[11] Therefore humility seems above all to be a principal virtue.

Obj. 3. Further, that which is most perfect seems to be principal. But
this applies to patience, according to *Jas.* i. 4: *Patience hath a perfect
work*. Therefore, patience should be reckoned a principal virtue.

On the contrary, Cicero reduces all other virtues to these four.[12]

I answer that, As was stated above, these four are reckoned as cardinal
virtues according to the four formal principles of virtue as we understand it
here. These principles are found chiefly in certain acts and passions. Thus
the good which exists in the act of reason is found chiefly in reason's command, but not in its counsel or its judgment, as was stated above.[13] Again,
good as defined by reason, and put into our operations as something right
and due, is found chiefly in commutations and distributions in relation to
another person, and on a basis of equality. The good of curbing the passions is found chiefly in those passions which are most difficult to curb, viz.,
in the pleasures of touch. The good of being firm in holding to the good
defined by reason, against the impulse of passion, is found chiefly in perils
exposing us to death, which are most difficult to withstand.

Accordingly, the above four virtues may be considered in two ways. First,
according to their common formal principles. In this way, they are called
principal, being general, as it were, in comparison with all the virtues; so
that, for instance, any virtue that causes good in reason's act of consideration may be called prudence; every virtue that causes the good of rectitude
and the due in operations, be called justice; every virtue that curbs and re-
presses the passions, be called temperance; and every virtue that strengthens
the soul against any passions whatever, be called fortitude. Many, both holy
doctors,[14] as also philosophers,[15] speak about these virtues in this sense. It
is in this way that the other virtues are contained under them.—Therefore
all the objections fail.

Secondly, they may be considered according as each one of them is
named from that which is foremost in its respective matter, and thus they
are specific virtues, co-divided with the others. Yet they are called principal in comparison with the other virtues because of the importance of
their matter. Thus, prudence is the virtue which commands; justice, the

---

[10] Aristotle, *Eth.*, IV, 3 (1123b 30).   [11] *In Evang.*, I, hom. 7 (PL 76, 1103).
[12] *De Invent.*, II, 53 (p. 147ᵇ).   [13] Q. 57, a. 6.   [14] St. Ambrose, *De Off. Ministr.*,
I, 36 (PL 16, 82); St. Augustine, *De Mor. Eccl.*, I, 15 (PL 32, 1322); St. Gregory,
Moral., XXII, 1 (PL 76, 212).   [15] Seneca, *Ad Lucilium Epistulae Morales*, Epist.
LXVII, ed. R. M. Gummere (New York: G. P. Putnam's Sons), vol. II (1920),
pp. 36, 38.

virtue which is about due actions between equals; temperance, the virtue which suppresses desires for the pleasures of touch; and fortitude, the virtue which strengthens against dangers of death.—Thus again do the objections fail; because the other virtues may be principal in some other way, but these are called principal by reason of their matter, as was stated above.

Fourth Article

WHETHER THE FOUR CARDINAL VIRTUES DIFFER FROM ONE ANOTHER?

We proceed thus to the Fourth Article:—

Objection 1. It would seem that the above four virtues are not diverse and distinct from one another. For Gregory says: *There is no true prudence unless it be just, temperate and brave; no perfect temperance that is not brave, just and prudent; no sound fortitude that is not prudent, temperate and just; no real justice without prudence, fortitude and temperance.*[16] But this would not be so, if the above four virtues were distinct from one another, since the different species of one genus do not denominate one another. Therefore the aforesaid virtues are not distinct from one another.

Obj. 2. Further, among things distinct from one another what belongs to one is not attributed to another. But what belongs to temperance is attributed to fortitude, for Ambrose says: *Rightly do we call it fortitude when a man conquers himself, and is not weakened and bent by any enticements.*[17] And of temperance he says that it *safeguards the manner and order in all things that we decide to do and say.*[18] Therefore it seems that these virtues are not distinct from one another.

Obj. 3. Further, the Philosopher says that the necessary conditions of virtue are, first of all, *that a man should have knowledge; secondly, that he should exercise choice for a particular end; thirdly, that he should possess the habit and act with firmness and steadfastness.*[19] But the first of these seems to belong to prudence, which is right reason in things to be done; the second, *i.e.,* choice, belongs to temperance, whereby a man, holding his passions in check, acts, not from passion but from choice; the third, that a man should act for the sake of a due end, implies a certain rectitude, which appears to belong to justice; while the last, viz., firmness and steadfastness, belongs to fortitude. Therefore each of these virtues is general in comparison to other virtues. Therefore they are not distinct from one another.

On the contrary, Augustine says that *there are four virtues, corresponding to the various affections of love,*[20] and he applies this to the four virtues mentioned above. Therefore the above four virtues are distinct from one another.

---

[16] *Moral.,* XXII, 1 (PL 76, 212).　　[17] *De Off. Ministr.,* I, 36 (PL 16, 82).　　[18] *Op. cit.,* I, 24 (PL 16, 62).　　[19] *Eth.,* II, 4 (1105a 31).　　[20] *De Mor. Eccl.,* XV (PL 32, 1322).

I answer that, As was stated above, these four virtues are understood in two ways by various writers. For some[21] take them as signifying certain general conditions of the human soul to be found in all the virtues. This would mean that prudence is merely a certain rectitude of discernment in any actions or matters whatever; justice, a certain rectitude of the soul whereby man does what he ought in any matters; temperance, a disposition of the soul moderating any passions or operations, so as to keep them within bounds; and fortitude, a disposition whereby the soul is strengthened for that which is in accord with reason, against any assaults of the passions, or the toil involved by any operations. To distinguish these four virtues in this way does not imply that justice, temperance and fortitude are distinct virtuous habits; because it is fitting that every moral virtue, from the fact that it is a *habit,* should be accompanied by a certain firmness so as not to be moved by its contrary. This, we have said, belongs to fortitude. Moreover, inasmuch as it is a *virtue,* it is directed to good, which involves the notion of right and due; and this, we have said, belongs to justice. Again, owing to the fact that it is a *moral virtue* partaking of reason, it observes the limit imposed by reason in all things, and does not exceed its bounds, which has been stated to belong to temperance. It is only in the point of having discernment, which we ascribed to prudence, that there seems to be a distinction from the other three, inasmuch as discernment belongs essentially to reason; whereas the other three imply a certain share of reason by way of a kind of application to passions or operations. According to this explanation, then, prudence would be distinct from the other three virtues, but these would not be distinct from one another; for it is evident that one and the same virtue is both habit, and virtue, and moral virtue.

Others,[22] however, with better reason, take these four virtues, according as they have their special determinate matter; for each is determined to one matter, in which that general condition is singled out from which the virtue's name is taken, as was stated above. In this way, it is clear that the aforesaid virtues are distinct habits, differentiated in respect of their diverse objects.

Reply Obj. 1. Gregory is speaking of the four virtues in the first sense given above.—It may also be said that these four virtues qualify one another by a kind of overflow. For the qualities of prudence overflow into the other virtues in so far as they are directed by prudence. And each of the others overflows into the rest, for the reason that whoever can do what is more difficult, can do what is less difficult. Therefore whoever can curb his desires for the pleasures of touch, so that they keep within bounds, which is a very hard thing to do, for this very reason is more able to check his daring in dangers of death, so as not to go too far, which is much easier; and in this sense fortitude is said to be temperate. Again, temperance is

---

[21] Cf. O. Lottin, in *Mélanges Mandonnet* (II, 252).   [22] Aristotle, *Eth.,* II, 7 (1107a 33); St. Albert, in O. Lottin, *loc. cit.* (II, 258).

said to be brave because fortitude overflows into temperance. This is true in so far as he whose soul is strengthened by fortitude against dangers of death, which is a matter of very great difficulty, is more able to remain firm against the onslaught of pleasures; for, as Cicero says, *it would be inconsistent for a man to be unbroken by fear, and yet vanquished by cupidity, or that he should be conquered by lust, after showing himself to be unconquered by toil.*[23]

From this the Reply to the Second Objection is clear. For temperance observes the mean in all things, and fortitude keeps the soul unbent by the enticements of pleasures,—either in so far as these virtues are taken to denote certain general conditions of virtue, or in the sense that they overflow into one another, as explained above.

Reply Obj. 3. These four general conditions of virtue set down by the Philosopher are not proper to the aforesaid virtues. They may, however, be appropriated to them, in the way stated above.

Fifth Article

WHETHER THE CARDINAL VIRTUES ARE FITTINGLY DIVIDED INTO POLITICAL VIRTUES, PERFECTING, PERFECT, AND EXEMPLAR VIRTUES?

We proceed thus to the Fifth Article:—

Objection 1. It would seem that these four virtues are unfittingly divided into exemplar virtues, perfecting virtues, perfect virtues, and political vir-ues. For as Macrobius says, *the exemplar virtues are such as exist in the mind of God.*[24] Now the Philosopher says that *it is absurd to ascribe justice, fortitude, temperance and prudence to God.*[25] Therefore these virtues cannot be exemplar.

Obj. 2. Further, the *perfect* virtues are those which are without any passion. For Macrobius says that *in a soul that is cleansed, temperance has not to check worldly desires, but to forget them completely*; and *to fortitude it belongs to be ignorant of the passions, not to conquer them.*[26] Now it was stated above that the aforesaid virtues cannot be without passions.[27] Therefore there is no such thing as *perfect* virtue.

Obj. 3. Further, Macrobius says that the *perfecting* virtues are those of the man *who flies from human affairs and devotes himself exclusively to the things of God.*[28] But it seems wrong to do this, for Cicero says: *I think that it is not only unworthy of praise, but wicked for a man to say that he despises what most men admire, viz., power and office.*[29] Therefore there are no *perfecting* virtues.

[23] *De Off.*, I, 20 (p. 33).   [24] *In Somn. Scipion.*, I, 8 (p. 519).   [25] *Eth.*, X, 8 (1178b 10).   [26] *In Somn. Scipion.*, ibid.   [27] Q. 59, a. 5.   [28] *In Somn. Scipion.*, ibid.   [29] *De Off.*, I, 21 (p. 34).

Obj. 4. Further, Macrobius says that the *political* virtues are those *whereby good men work for the good of their country and for the safety of the city.*[30] But it is only legal justice that is directed to the common weal, as the Philosopher states.[31] Therefore other virtues should not be called *political.*

On the contrary, Macrobius says: *Plotinus, together with Plato foremost among teachers of philosophy, says: 'The four kinds of virtue are fourfold. In the first place there are political virtues; secondly, there are perfecting virtues; thirdly, there are perfect virtues; and fourthly, there are exemplar virtues.'* [32]

I answer that, As Augustine says, *the soul needs to follow something in order to give birth to virtue. This something is God, and if we follow Him, we shall live the good life.*[33] Consequently the exemplar of human virtue must needs pre-exist in God, just as in Him pre-exist the exemplars of all things. Accordingly, virtue may be considered as existing originally in God, and thus we speak of *exemplar* virtues, so that in God the divine mind itself may be called prudence; while temperance is the turning of God's gaze on Himself, even as in us temperance is that which conforms concupiscence to reason. God's fortitude is His unchangeableness, and His justice is the observance of the Eternal Law in His works, as Plotinus states.[34]

Again, since man by his nature is a political animal, these virtues, in so far as they are in him according to the condition of his nature, are called *political* virtues; since it is by reason of them that man deports himself well in the conduct of human affairs. It is in this sense that we have been speaking of these virtues until now.

But since it belongs to man to do his utmost to strive onward to divine things, as the Philosopher also declares in *Ethics* x.,[35] and as Scripture often admonishes us (for instance: *Be ye . . . perfect, as your heavenly Father is perfect* [*Matt.* v. 48]), we must needs place some virtues between the political virtues, which are human virtues, and the exemplar virtues, which are divine. Now these intermediate virtues are distinguished by reason of a difference of movement and term. Thus, some are virtues of men who are on their way and tending towards the divine similitude, and these are called *perfecting* virtues. Thus prudence, by contemplating the things of God, counts as nothing all things of the world, and directs all the thoughts of the soul to God alone; temperance, so far as nature allows, neglects the needs of the body; fortitude prevents the soul from being afraid of neglecting the body and rising to heavenly things; and justice consists in the soul's giving a whole-hearted consent to follow the way thus proposed.—Besides these there are the virtues of those who have already attained to the divine

---

[30] *In Somn. Scipion.,* I, 8 (p. 518).   [31] *Eth.,* V, 1 (1129b 15).   [32] *In Somn. Scipion.,* I, 8 (pp. 517-518).   [33] *De Mor. Eccl.,* I, 6 (PL 32, 1314).   [34] Cf. Macrobius, *In Somn. Scipion., ibid* (p. 519).   [35] *Eth.,* X, 7 (1177b 26).

likeness, these are called the *perfect virtues* [literally, *virtues of a now cleansed soul*]. Thus, prudence now sees nought else but the things of God; temperance knows no earthly desires; fortitude has no knowledge of passion; and justice, by imitating the divine mind, is united thereto by an everlasting covenant. Such are the virtues attributed to the blessed, or, in this life, to some who are at the summit of perfection.

Reply Obj. 1. The Philosopher is speaking of these virtues according as they relate to human affairs: for instance, of justice in relation to buying and selling, of fortitude in relation to fears, of temperance in relation to desires. Now in this sense it is absurd to attribute them to God.

Reply Obj. 2. Human virtues, that is to say, virtues of men living together in this world, are about the passions. But the virtues of those who have attained to perfect beatitude are without passions. Hence Plotinus says that *the political virtues check the passions, i.e.,* they bring them to the mean; *the second kind,* viz., the perfecting virtues, *uproot them; the third kind,* viz., the perfect virtues, *forget them; while it is impious to mention them in connection with virtues of the fourth kind,*[36] viz., the exemplar virtues.—It may also be said that here he is speaking of passions as denoting inordinate movements.

Reply Obj. 3. To neglect human affairs when necessity forbids is wicked. Otherwise it is virtuous. Hence Cicero said a little before this: *Perhaps one should make allowances for the lack of interest in public affairs on the part of those who by reason of their exceptional talents have devoted themselves to learning; as also for those who have retired from public life because of failing health, or for some other yet weightier motive, when such men yielded to others the power and renown of authority.*[37] This agrees with what Augustine says: *The love of truth demands a hallowed leisure; charity necessitates that we undertake just works. If no one lays this burden on us, we may devote ourselves to the experience and contemplation of truth; but if the burden is laid on us, it is to be taken up under the pressure of charity.*[38]

Reply Obj. 4. Legal justice alone regards the common weal directly; but, by commanding the other virtues, it draws them all into the service of the common weal, as the Philosopher declares.[39] For we must note that it concerns the political virtues, as we understand them here, to do well not only towards the community, but also towards the parts of the community, viz., towards the household, or even towards one individual.

---

[36] Cf. Macrobius, *In Somn. Scipion.*, I, 8 (pp. 519-520).   [37] *De Off.*, I, 21 (p. 34).   [38] *De Civit. Dei,* XIX, 19 (PL 41, 647).   [39] *Eth.*, V, 1 (1129b 31).

THE THEOLOGICAL VIRTUES
(*In Four Articles*)

WE must now consider the Theological Virtues. Under this head there are four points of inquiry: (1) Whether there are theological virtues? (2) Whether the theological virtues are distinguished from the intellectual and moral virtues? (3) How many, and which are they? (4) Of their order.

First Article

WHETHER THERE ARE THEOLOGICAL VIRTUES?

We proceed thus to the First Article:—

Objection 1. It would seem that there are not any theological virtues. For according to *Physics* vii., *virtue is the disposition of a perfect thing to that which is best; and by perfect I mean that which is disposed according to nature.*[1] But that which is divine is above man's nature. Therefore the theological virtues are not the virtues of a man.

Obj. 2. Further, theological virtues are quasi-divine virtues. But the divine virtues are exemplars, as was stated above,[2] which are not in us but in God. Therefore the theological virtues are not the virtues of man.

Obj. 3. Further, the theological virtues are so called because they direct us to God, Who is the first cause and last end of all things. But by the very nature of his reason and will, man is directed to his first cause and last end. Therefore there is no need for any habits of theological virtue to direct the reason and the will to God.

On the contrary, The precepts of law are about acts of virtue. But the divine law contains precepts about the acts of faith, hope and charity: for it is written (*Ecclus.* ii. 8, *seqq.*): *Ye that fear the Lord believe Him,* and again, *hope in Him,* and again, *love Him.* Therefore faith, hope and charity are virtues directing us to God. Therefore they are theological virtues.

I answer that, Man is perfected by virtue for those actions by which he is directed to happiness, as was explained above.[3] Now man's happiness or felicity is twofold, as was also stated above.[4] One is proportioned to human nature, a happiness, namely, which man can obtain by means of the principles of his nature. The other is a happiness surpassing man's nature, and

---

[1] Aristotle, *Phys.*, VII, 3 (246b 23).—Cf. *ibid.* (246a 13). [2] Q. 61, a. 5.
[3] Q. 5, a. 7. [4] Q. 5, a. 5.

which man can obtain by the power of God alone, by a kind of participation of the Godhead; and thus it is written (*2 Pet.* i. 4) that by Christ we are made *partakers of the divine nature.* And because such happiness surpasses the power of human nature, man's natural principles, which enable him to act well according to his power, do not suffice to direct man to this same happiness. Hence it is necessary for man to receive from God some additional principles, by which he may be directed to supernatural happiness, even as he is directed to his connatural end by means of his natural principles, albeit not without the divine assistance. Such principles are called *theological virtues.*[5] They are so called, first, because their object is God, inasmuch as they direct us rightly to God; secondly, because they are infused in us by God alone; thirdly, because these virtues are not made known to us, save by divine revelation, contained in Holy Scripture.

Reply Obj. 1. A certain nature may be ascribed to a certain thing in two ways. First, essentially, and thus these theological virtues surpass the nature of man. Secondly, by participation, as kindled wood partakes of the nature of fire, and thus, after a fashion, man becomes a partaker of the divine nature, as was stated above. Hence these virtues befit man according to the nature of which he is made a partaker.

Reply Obj. 2. These virtues are called divine, not as though God were virtuous by reason of them, but because by them God makes us virtuous, and directs us to Himself. Hence they are not exemplar virtues but copies.

Reply Obj. 3. The reason and the will are naturally directed to God, inasmuch as He is the cause and the end of nature, but according to the ability of nature. But the reason and the will, according to their nature, are not sufficiently directed to Him in so far as He is the object of supernatural happiness.

Second Article

WHETHER THE THEOLOGICAL VIRTUES ARE DISTINGUISHED FROM THE INTELLECTUAL AND MORAL VIRTUES?

We proceed thus to the Second Article:—

Objection 1. It would seem that the theological virtues are not distinguished from moral and intellectual virtues. For the theological virtues, if they be in a human soul, must needs perfect it either as to the intellectual part or as to the appetitive part. Now the virtues which perfect the intellectual part are called intellectual, and the virtues which perfect the appetitive part are called moral. Therefore the theological virtues are not distinguished from the moral and intellectual virtues.

Obj. 2. Further, the theological virtues are those which direct us to God. Now among the intellectual virtues there is one which directs us to God,

---

[5] Cf. William of Auxerre, *Summa Aurea,* III, tr. 2, ch. 2 (fol. 130ra).

namely, wisdom, which is about divine things, since it considers the highest cause. Therefore the theological virtues are not distinguished from the intellectual virtues.

Obj. 3. Further, Augustine shows how the four cardinal virtues are the *order of love.*[6] Now love is charity, which is a theological virtue. Therefore the moral virtues are not distinct from the theological.

On the contrary, That which is above man's nature is distinguished from that which is according to his nature. But the theological virtues are above man's nature, while the intellectual and moral virtues are proportioned to his nature, as was shown above.[7] Therefore they are distinguished from one another.

I answer that, As was stated above, habits are distinguished specifically from one another according to the formal difference of their objects.[8] Now the object of the theological virtues is God Himself, Who is the last end of all, as surpassing the knowledge of our reason. On the other hand, the object of the intellectual and moral virtues is something comprehensible to human reason. Therefore the theological virtues are distinguished specifically from the moral and intellectual virtues.

Reply Obj. 1. The intellectual and moral virtues perfect man's intellect and appetite according to the power of human nature; the theological virtues, supernaturally.

Reply Obj. 2. The wisdom which the Philosopher reckons as an intellectual virtue considers divine things so far as they are open to the investigation of human reason.[9] Theological virtue, on the other hand, is about these same things so far as they surpass human reason.

Reply Obj. 3. Though charity is love, yet love is not always charity. When, then, it is stated that every virtue is the *order of love,* this can be understood either of love in the general sense, or of the love of charity. If it be understood of love commonly so called, then each virtue is stated to be the order of love in so far as each cardinal virtue requires an ordered affection. Now love is the root and cause of every affection, as was stated above.[10] If, however, it be understood of the love of charity, it does not mean that every other virtue is charity essentially, but that all other virtues depend on charity in some way, as we shall show further on.[11]

Third Article

WHETHER FAITH, HOPE AND CHARITY ARE FITTINGLY RECKONED AS THEOLOGICAL VIRTUES?

We proceed thus to the Third Article:—

Objection 1. It would seem that faith, hope and charity are not fittingly

[6] *De Mor. Eccl.,* I, 15 (PL 32, 1322).   [7] Q. 58, a. 3.   [8] Q. 54, a. 2, ad 1
[9] *Eth.,* VI, 3 (1139b 17).   [10] Q. 27, a. 4; q. 28, a. 6, ad 2; q. 41, a. 2, ad 1.
[11] Q. 65, a. 2 and 4; II-II, q. 23, a. 7.

reckoned as three theological virtues. For the theological virtues are in relation to divine happiness just as the inclination of nature is in relation to the connatural end. Now among the virtues directed to the connatural end there is but one natural virtue, viz., the understanding of principles. Therefore there should be but one theological virtue.

Obj. 2. Further, the theological virtues are more perfect than the intellectual and moral virtues. Now faith is not reckoned among the intellectual virtues, but is something less than a virtue, since it is imperfect knowledge. Likewise, hope is not reckoned among the moral virtues, but is something less than a virtue, since it is a passion. Much less therefore should they be reckoned as theological virtues.

Obj. 3. Further, the theological virtues direct man's soul to God. Now man's soul cannot be directed to God save through the intellectual part, in which are intellect and will. Therefore there should be only two theological virtues, one perfecting the intellect, the other, the will.

On the contrary, The Apostle says (*1 Cor.* xiii. 13): *Now there remain faith, hope, charity, these three.*

I answer that, As was stated above, the theological virtues direct man to supernatural happiness in the same way as by the natural inclination man is directed to his connatural end. Now the latter direction happens in two respects. First, according to the reason or intellect, in so far as it contains the first universal principles which are known to us through the natural light of the intellect, and which are reason's starting-point, both in speculative and in practical matters. Secondly, through the rectitude of the will tending naturally to the good as defined by reason.

But these two fall short of the order of supernatural happiness, according to *1 Cor.* ii. 9: *The eye hath not seen, nor ear heard, neither hath it entered into the heart of man, what things God hath prepared for them that love Him.* Consequently, in relation to both intellect and will, man needed to receive in addition something supernatural to direct him to a supernatural end. First, as regards the intellect, man receives certain supernatural principles, which are held by means of a divine light; and these are the things which are to be believed, about which is *faith.*—Secondly, the will is directed to this end, both as to the movement of intention, which tends to that end as something attainable,—this pertains to *hope*—and as to a certain spiritual union, whereby the will is, in a way, transformed into that end—and this belongs to *charity.* For the appetite of a thing is naturally moved and tends towards its connatural end and this movement is due to a certain conformity of the thing with its end.

Reply Obj. 1. The intellect requires intelligible species whereby to understand, and consequently there is need of a natural habit in addition to the power. But the very nature of the will suffices for it to be directed naturally to the end, both as to the intention of the end and as to its conformity with the end. But in relation to the things which are above nature, the nature itself of the power is insufficient. Consequently there was need for an additional supernatural habit in both respects.

Reply Obj. 2. Faith and hope imply a certain imperfection, since faith is of things unseen, and hope of things not possessed. Hence to have faith and hope in things that are subject to human power falls short of the nature of virtue. But to have faith and hope in things which are above the ability of human nature surpasses every virtue that is proportioned to man, according to *1 Cor.* i. 25: *The weakness of God is stronger than men.*

Reply Obj. 3. Two things pertain to the appetite, viz., movement to the end, and conformity with the end by means of love. Hence there must needs be two theological virtues in the human appetite, namely, hope and charity.

Fourth Article

WHETHER FAITH PRECEDES HOPE, AND HOPE CHARITY?

We proceed thus to the Fourth Article:—

Objection 1. It would seem that the order of the theological virtues is not that faith precedes hope, and hope charity. For the root precedes that which grows from it. Now charity is the root of all virtues, according to *Ephes.* iii. 17: *Being rooted and founded in charity.* Therefore charity precedes the others.

Obj. 2. Further, Augustine says: *A man cannot love what he does not believe to exist. But if he believes and loves, by doing good works he ends in hoping.*[12] Therefore it seems that faith precedes charity, and charity hope.

Obj. 3. Further, love is the principle of all our affections, as was stated above. Now hope is a kind of affection, since it is a passion, as was stated above.[13] Therefore charity, which is love, precedes hope.

On the contrary, The Apostle enumerates them thus (*1 Cor.* xiii. 13): *Now there remain faith, hope, charity.*

I answer that, There is a twofold order, namely, that of generation, and that of perfection. According to the order of generation, in which matter precedes form, and the imperfect precedes the perfect, in one and the same subject faith precedes hope, and hope charity, as to their acts; for the habits are infused together. For the movement of the appetite cannot tend to anything, either by hoping or loving, unless that thing be apprehended by the sense or by the intellect. Now it is by faith that the intellect apprehends what it hopes for and loves. Hence, in the order of generation, faith must precede hope and charity. In like manner, a man loves a thing because he apprehends it as his good. Now from the very fact that a man hopes to be able to obtain some good from someone, he looks on the man in whom he hopes as a good of his own. Hence, for the very reason that a man bases his hopes in

---

[12] *De Doct. Christ.,* I, 37 (PL 34, 35).   [13] Q. 23, a. 4.

someone, he proceeds to love him; so that in the order of generation, hope precedes charity as regards their respective acts.

But in the order of perfection, charity precedes faith and hope, because both faith and hope are quickened by charity, and receive from charity their full complement as virtues. For thus charity is the mother and the root of all the virtues, inasmuch as it is the form of them all, as we shall state further on.[14]

This suffices for the Reply to the First Objection.

Reply Obj. 2. Augustine is speaking of that hope by which a man hopes to obtain beatitude through the merits which he has already; and this belongs to hope quickened by, and following, charity. But it is possible for a man, before having charity, to hope through merits not already possessed, but which he hopes to possess.

Reply Obj. 3. As was stated above in treating of the passions, hope has reference to two things.[15] One is its principal object, viz., the good hoped for. With regard to this, love always precedes hope, for a good is never hoped for unless it be desired and loved.—Hope also regards the person from whom a man hopes to be able to obtain some good. With regard to this, hope precedes love at first, though afterwards hope is increased by love. Because, from the fact that a man thinks that he can obtain a good through someone, he begins to love him; and from the fact that he loves him, he then hopes all the more in him.

[14] *S. T.*, II-II, q. 23, a. 8.   [15] Q. 40, a. 7.

Question LXIII

THE CAUSE OF THE VIRTUES

(*In Four Articles*)

WE must now consider the cause of the virtues. Under this head there are four points of inquiry: (1) Whether virtue is in us by nature? (2) Whether any virtue is caused in us by habituation from our acts? (3) Whether any moral virtues are in us by infusion? (4) Whether virtue acquired by habituation is of the same species as infused virtue?

First Article

WHETHER VIRTUE IS IN US BY NATURE?

We proceed thus to the First Article:—

Objection 1. It would seem that virtue is in us by nature. For Damascene says: *Virtues are natural to us and are equally in all of us.*[1] And Anthony says in a sermon to the monks: *If the will contradicts nature, it is perverse, if it follow nature, it is virtuous.*[2] Moreover, the *Gloss* on *Matt.* iv. 23 (*Jesus went about,* etc.) says: *He taught them natural virtues, i.e., chastity, justice, humility, which man possesses naturally.*[3]

Obj. 2. Further, the good of virtue is to be in accord with reason, as was shown above.[4] But that which is in accord with reason is natural to man, since reason is man's nature. Therefore virtue is in man by nature.

Obj. 3. Further, that which is in us from birth is said to be natural to us. Now virtues are in some from birth, for it is written (*Job* xxxi. 18): *From my infancy mercy grew up with me, and it came out with me from my mother's womb.* Therefore virtue is in man by nature.

On the contrary, Whatever is in man by nature is common to all men, and is not taken away by sin, since even in the demons natural gifts remain, as Dionysius states.[5] But virtue is not in all men, and is cast out by sin. Therefore it is not in man by nature.

I answer that, With regard to corporeal forms, it has been maintained by some that they are wholly from within. It was so held, for instance, by those who upheld the theory of *latent forms.*[6] Others held that forms are entirely from the outside, those, for instance, who thought that corporeal forms originated from some separate cause.[7] Others, however, esteemed that they

---

[1] *De Fide Orth.,* III, 14 (PG 94, 1045).   [2] Cf. St. Athanasius, *Vita S. Antonii.* trans. Evagrius (PG 26, 873).   [3] *Glossa ordin.* (V. 17E).   [4] Q. 55, a. 4, ad 2.   [5] *De Div. Nom.,* IV, 23 (PG 3, 725).   [6] Cf. *S. T.,* I, q. 45, a. 8.   [7] Cf. *ibid.*

are partly from within, in so far as they pre-exist potentially in matter, and partly from the outside, in so far as they are reduced to act by an agent.[8]

In like manner, with regard to the sciences and the virtues, some held that they are wholly from within,[9] so that all virtues and sciences pre-exist in the soul naturally, but that the hindrances to science and virtue, which befall the soul because of the burden of the body, are removed by study and practice, even as iron is made bright by being polished. This was the opinion of the Platonists. Others said that they are wholly from the outside, being due to the action of the agent intellect, as Avicenna maintained.[10] Others, again, said that the sciences and the virtues are in us by nature, so far as we possess the ability to acquire them, but not in their perfection. This is the teaching of the Philosopher,[11] and is nearer the truth.

To make this clear, it must be observed that there are two ways in which something is said to be natural to a man. One is according to his specific nature, the other according to his individual nature. And, since each thing derives its species from its form, and its individuation from matter; furthermore, since the form of man is the rational soul, while the matter is the body, hence it is that whatever belongs to man according to the rational soul is natural to him according to his specific nature, while whatever belongs to him according to the particular temperament of his body is natural to him according to his individual nature. For whatever is natural to man because of his body, considered as part of his species, in a way is to be referred to the soul, in so far as this particular body is proportioned to this particular soul.

In both these ways virtue is natural to man inchoately. It is natural to man according to the specific nature, in so far as in man's reason there are to be found naturally present certain naturally known principles of both knowledge and action, which are the seeds of intellectual and moral virtues, and in so far as there is in the will a natural appetite for the good which is in accord with reason. Again, it is natural to man according to the individual nature, in so far as, by reason of a disposition in the body, some are disposed either well or ill to certain virtues. This happens according as certain sensitive powers are acts of certain parts of the body, whose disposition helps or hinders these powers in the exercise of their acts, and, in consequence, the rational powers also, which such sensitive powers assist. In this way, one man has a natural aptitude for science, another for fortitude, another for temperance. This is the manner in which both the intellectual and the moral virtues are in us naturally, namely, according to an inchoateness which consists in our ability to acquire them. But their completion is not present naturally, since nature is determined to one course of action, while the completion of these virtues does not depend on one particular mode of action; rather does the completion vary according to the

---

[8] Cf. *ibid.*   [9] Cf. *S. T.*, I, q. 84, a. 3, obj. 3.   [10] *De An.*, V, 5 (25 rb).   [11] *Eth.*, II, 1 (1103a 25).

various matters which constitute the sphere of action of the virtues, and according to the variety of circumstances.

It is therefore evident that all virtues are in us by nature aptitudinally and inchoately, but not according to perfection, except the theological virtues, which are entirely from the outside.

This suffices for the Replies to the Objections. For the first two argue about the seeds of virtue which are in us by nature, inasmuch as we are rational beings.—The third objection must be taken in the sense that, owing to the natural disposition which the body has from birth, one has an aptitude for pity, another for living temperately, another for some other virtue.

Second Article

WHETHER ANY VIRTUE IS CAUSED IN US BY HABITUATION FROM OUR ACTS?

We proceed thus to the Second Article:—

Objection 1. It would seem that virtues cannot be caused in us by habituation from our acts. For the *Gloss* of Augustine, commenting on *Rom.* xiv. 23 (*All that is not of faith is sin*) says: *The whole life of an unbeliever is a sin, and there is no good without the highest good. Where knowledge of the truth is lacking, virtue is a mockery even in the most excellent behavior.*[12] Now faith cannot be acquired by means of works, but is caused in us by God, according to *Ephes.* ii. 8: *By grace you are saved through faith.* Therefore no virtue can be acquired by us through habituation from our acts.

Obj. 2. Further, sin and virtue are contraries, so that they are incompatible. Now man cannot avoid sin except by the grace of God, according to *Wis.* viii. 21: *I knew that I could not otherwise be continent, except God gave it.* Therefore neither can any virtues be caused in us by habituation from our acts, but only by the gift of God.

Obj. 3. Further, actions which are without virtue lack the perfection of virtue. But an effect cannot be more perfect than its cause. Therefore a virtue cannot be caused by actions that precede it.

On the contrary, Dionysius says that good is more efficacious than evil.[13] But vicious habits are caused by evil acts. Much more, therefore, can virtuous habits be caused by good acts.

I answer that, We have spoken already in a general way about the generation of habits from acts.[14] Speaking now in a special way of this matter in relation to virtue, we must take note that, as was stated above, man's virtue perfects him in relation to good.[15] But since the notion of good consists in *mode, species and order,* as Augustine states,[16] or in *number, weight and measure,* according to *Wis.* xi. 21, man's good must needs be

---

[12] *Glossa ordin.* (VI, 30B).   [13] *De Div. Nom.,* IV, 20; 32 (PG 3, 717; 732).
[14] Q. 51, a. 2 and 3.   [15] Q. 55, a. 3 and 4.   [16] *De Nat. Boni,* III (PL 42, 553).

appraised with respect to some rule. Now this rule is twofold, as was stated above, viz., human reason and divine law.[17] And since divine law is the higher rule, it extends to more things, so that whatever is ruled by human reason is ruled by the divine law too; but the converse does not hold.

It follows that human virtue, directed to the good which is defined according to the rule of human reason, can be caused by human acts; for such acts proceed from reason, by whose power and rule the good in question is established. On the other hand, virtue which directs man to good as defined by the divine law, and not by human reason, cannot be caused by human acts, whose principle is reason, but is produced in us by the divine operation alone. Hence Augustine, in giving the definition of this virtue, inserts the words, *which God works in us without us*.[18] It is also of this virtue that the First Objection holds good.

Reply Obj. 2. Mortal sin is incompatible with divinely infused virtue, especially if this virtue be considered in its perfect nature. But actual sin, even mortal, is compatible with humanly acquired virtue, because the use of a habit in us is subject to our will, as was stated above,[19] and one sinful act does not destroy a habit of acquired virtue, since it is not an act but a habit that is directly contrary to a habit. Therefore, though man cannot avoid mortal sin without grace, so as never to sin mortally, yet he is not hindered from acquiring a habit of virtue, whereby he may abstain from evil in the majority of cases, and chiefly in matters most opposed to reason. —There are also certain mortal sins which man can in no way avoid without grace, those, namely, which are directly opposed to the theological virtues, which are in us through the gift of grace. This, however, will be more fully explained later.[20]

Reply Obj. 3. As was stated above, certain seeds or principles of the acquired virtues pre-exist in us by nature.[21] These principles are more excellent than the virtues acquired through their power. Thus, the understanding of speculative principles is more excellent than the science of conclusions, and the natural rectitude of the reason is more excellent than the rectification of the appetite which takes place through participation in the reason. This rectification belongs to moral virtue. Accordingly, human acts, in so far as they proceed from higher principles, can cause acquired human virtues.

Third Article

WHETHER ANY MORAL VIRTUES ARE IN US BY INFUSION?

We proceed thus to the Third Article:—

Obj. 1. It would seem that no virtues besides the theological virtues are

---

[17] Q. 19, a. 3 and 4.   [18] Cf. above, q. 55, a. 4, obj. 1.   [19] Q. 49, a. 3.   [20] Q. 109, a. 4.   [21] A. 1; q. 51, a. 1.

infused in us by God. For God does not do by Himself, save perhaps some-times miraculously, those things that can be done by second causes; be-cause, as Dionysius says, *it is God's rule to bring about extremes through the mean*.[22] Now intellectual and moral virtues can be caused in us by our acts, as was stated above. Therefore it is not fitting that they should be caused in us by infusion.

Obj. 2. Further, much less superfluity is found in God's works than in the works of nature. But the theological virtues suffice to direct us to the supernatural good. Therefore there are no other supernatural virtues re-quiring to be caused in us by God.

Obj. 3. Further, nature does not employ two means where one suffices. Much less does God. But God sowed the seeds of virtue in our souls, ac-cording to the *Gloss* on *Heb.* i. 6.[23] Therefore it is unfitting for Him to cause in us other virtues by means of infusion.

On the contrary, It is written (*Wis.* viii. 7): *She teacheth temperance and prudence and justice and fortitude.*

I answer that, Effects must needs be proportioned to their causes and principles. Now all virtues, intellectual and moral, that are acquired by our actions, arise from certain natural principles pre-existing in us, as was stated above.[24] In the place of these natural principles, God bestows on us the theological virtues, by which we are directed to a supernatural end, as was stated above.[25] Therefore we need to receive from God other habits annexed proportionately to the theological virtues, which are to the theo-logical virtues what the moral and intellectual virtues are to the natural principles of the virtues.

Reply Obj. 1. Some moral and intellectual virtues can be caused in us by our actions, but they are not proportioned to the theological virtues. There-fore it was necessary for us to receive, from God immediately, others that are proportioned to those virtues.

Reply Obj. 2. The theological virtues direct us sufficiently to our super-natural end in an inchoate way, that is, in so far as it is to God Himself im-mediately. But the soul needs further to be perfected by infused virtues in regard to other things, yet in relation to God.

Reply Obj. 3. The power of those naturally instilled principles does not extend beyond the capability of nature. Consequently man needs in addi-tion to be perfected by other principles in relation to his supernatural end.

---

[22] *De Cael. Hier.*, IV, 3 (PG 3, 181).   [23] *Glossa ordin.* (VI, 79E).   [24] A. 1; q. 51, a. 1.   [25] Q. 62, a. 1.

Fourth Article

WHETHER VIRTUE ACQUIRED BY HABITUATION FROM OUR
ACTS BELONGS TO THE SAME SPECIES AS INFUSED VIRTUE?

We proceed thus to the Fourth Article:—

Objection 1. It would seem that the infused virtues do not differ in
species from the acquired virtues. For acquired and infused virtues, according to what has been said, do not seem to differ save in relation to the last
end. Now human habits and acts are specified, not by their last end, but
by their proximate end. Therefore the infused moral or intellectual virtues
do not differ specifically from the acquired virtues.

Obj. 2. Further, habits are known by their acts. But the act of infused
and acquired temperance is the same, viz., to moderate desires of touch.
Therefore they do not differ in species.

Obj. 3. Further, acquired and infused virtue differ as that which is
wrought by God immediately, and that which is wrought by a creature.
But the man whom God made is of the same species as a man begotten
naturally; and the eye which He gave to the man born blind, as one produced by the power of generation. Therefore it seems that acquired and
infused virtue belong to the same species.

On the contrary, Any change introduced into the difference expressed in
a definition involves a difference of species. But the definition of infused
virtue contains the words, *which God works in us without us,* as was stated
above.[26] Therefore acquired virtue, to which these words cannot apply, is
not of the same species as infused virtue.

I answer that, There is a twofold specific difference among habits. The
first, as was stated above, is taken from the special and formal aspects of
their objects.[27] Now the object of every virtue is a good considered as in
that virtue's proper matter. Thus, the object of temperance is a good in
relation to the pleasures connected with the concupiscence of touch. The
formal aspect of this object is from reason, which fixes the mean in these
concupiscences; while the material element is something on the part of the
concupiscences. Now it is evident that the mean that is appointed, in such
concupiscences, according to the rule of human reason is of a different
nature than the mean which is fixed according to the divine rule. For instance, in the consumption of food, the mean fixed by human reason is that
food should not harm the health of the body, nor hinder the use of reason;
whereas, according to the divine rule, it behooves man to *chastise* his *body,
and bring it into subjection* (*1 Cor.* ix. 27), by abstinence in food, drink
and the like. It is therefore evident that infused and acquired temperance
differ in species; and the same applies to the other virtues.

The other specific difference among habits is taken from the things to

[26] A. 2; q. 55, a. 4.   [27] Q. 54, a. 2; q. 56, a. 2; q. 60, a. 1.

which they are directed. For the health of a man and a horse is not of the same species, because of the diverse natures to which the health of the man and the health of the horse are directed. In the same sense, the Philosopher says that citizens have diverse virtues according as they are well directed to diverse forms of government.[28] In the same way, too, those infused moral virtues, by which men behave well in relation to their being *fellow-citizens with the saints, and of the household of God* (*Ephes*. ii. 19), differ from the acquired virtues by which man behaves well in relation to human affairs.

Reply Obj. 1. Infused and acquired virtue differ not only in relation to the ultimate end, but also in relation to their proper objects, as has been said.

Reply Obj. 2. Both acquired and infused temperance moderate desires for pleasures of touch, but for different reasons, as was stated, and therefore their respective acts are not identical.

Reply Obj. 3. God gave the man born blind an eye for the same act as the act for which other eyes are formed naturally, and consequently it was of the same species. It would be the same if God wished to give a man miraculously virtues such as those that are acquired by acts. But the case is not so in the question before us, as has been said.

[28] *Polit.*, III, 2 (1276b 31).

ON THE MEAN OF VIRTUE

(In Four Articles)

WE must now consider the properties of virtues. We must consider (1) the mean of virtue; (2) the connection among the virtues;[1] (3) the equality of the virtues;[2] (4) the duration of the virtues.[3] Under the first head there are four points of inquiry: (1) Whether the moral virtues consist in a mean? (2) Whether the mean of moral virtue is a real mean or a mean of reason? (3) Whether the intellectual virtues consist in a mean? (4) Whether the theological virtues do?

First Article

WHETHER THE MORAL VIRTUES CONSIST IN A MEAN?

We proceed thus to the First Article:—

Objection 1. It would seem that moral virtue does not consist in a mean. For the nature of a mean is incompatible with that which is extreme. Now the nature of virtue is to be something extreme; for it is stated in *De Caelo* i. that *virtue is the peak of power.*[4] Therefore moral virtue does not consist in a mean.

Obj. 2. Further, the maximum is not a mean. Now some moral virtues tend to a maximum: for instance, magnanimity to very great honors, and magnificence to very large expenditures, as is stated in *Ethics* iv.[5] Therefore not every moral virtue consists in a mean.

Obj. 3. Further, if it is essential to a moral virtue to consist in a mean, it follows that a moral virtue is not perfected, but on the contrary corrupted, through tending to something extreme. Now some moral virtues are perfected by tending to something extreme. Thus virginity, which abstains from all sexual pleasure, observes the extreme, and is the most perfect chastity. In the same way, to give all to the poor is the most perfect mercy or liberality. Therefore it seems that it is not essential to moral virtue that it should consist in a mean.

On the contrary, The Philosopher says that *moral virtue is an elective habit consisting in the mean.*[6]

I answer that, As has already been explained, the nature of virtue is

---

[1] Q. 65. [2] Q. 66. [3] Q. 67. [4] Aristotle, *De Caelo*, I, 11 (281a 11; a 18).—Cf. St. Thomas, *In De Caelo*, I, lect. 25. [5] Aristotle, *Eth.*, IV, 2 (1122a 18); 3 (1123a 34). [6] *Op. cit.*, II, 6 (1106b 36).

that it should direct man to good.[7] Now moral virtue is properly a perfection of the appetitive part of the soul in regard to some determinate matter; and the measure and rule of the appetitive movement in relation to appetible objects is the reason. But the good of that which is measured or ruled consists in its conformity with its rule; and, thus, the good of things made by art is that they follow the rule of art. Consequently, in things of this sort, evil consists in discordance from their rule or measure. Now this may happen either by their exceeding the measure or by their falling short of it; as we may clearly observe in all things ruled or measured. Hence it is evident that the good of moral virtue consists in conformity with the rule of reason. Now it is clear that between excess and deficiency the mean is equality or conformity. Therefore it is evident that moral virtue consists in a mean.

Reply Obj. 1. Moral virtue derives its goodness from the rule of reason, while its matter consists in passions or operations. If, therefore, we compare moral virtue to reason, then, if we look at that which it has of reason, it holds the position of one extreme, viz., conformity; while excess and defect take the position of the other extreme, viz., deformity. But if we consider moral virtue in respect of its matter, then it has the nature of a mean, in so far as it makes the passion conform to the rule of reason. Hence the Philosopher says that *virtue, as to its essence, is a mean,* in so far as the rule of virtue is imposed on its proper matter; *but it is an extreme in reference to the "best" and "the excellent,"* viz., as to its conformity with reason.[8]

Reply Obj. 2. In actions and passions, the mean and the extremes depend on various circumstances. Hence nothing hinders something from being extreme in a particular virtue according to one circumstance, while the same thing is a mean according to other circumstances, through its conformity with reason. This is the case with magnanimity and magnificence. For if we look at the absolute quantity of the respective objects of these virtues, we shall call it an extreme and a maximum; but if we consider the quantity in relation to other circumstances, then it has the character of a mean, since these virtues tend to this maximum in accordance with the rule of reason, *i.e., where* it is right, *when* it is right, and for an *end* that is right. There will be excess, if one tends to this maximum *when* it is not right, or *where* it is not right, or for an undue *end*; and there will be deficiency if one fails to tend thereto *where* one ought, and *when* one ought. This agrees with the saying of the Philosopher that the *magnanimous man observes the extreme in quantity, but the mean in the right mode of his action.*[9]

Reply Obj. 3. The same is to be said of virginity and poverty as of magnanimity. For virginity abstains from all sexual matters, and poverty from all wealth, for a right end, and in a right manner, *i.e.,* according to God's

---

[7] Q. 55, a. 3.   [8] *Eth.,* II, 6 (1107a 7).   [9] *Op. cit.,* IV, 3 (1123b 13).

commandment, and for the sake of eternal life. But if this be done in an undue manner, *i.e.*, out of unlawful superstition, or again for vainglory, it will be in excess. And if it be not done when it ought to be done, or as it ought to be done, it is a vice by deficiency; as for instance, in those who break their vows of virginity or poverty.

Second Article

WHETHER THE MEAN OF MORAL VIRTUE IS A REAL MEAN,
OR A MEAN OF REASON?

We proceed thus to the Second Article:—

Objection 1. It would seem that the mean of moral virtue is not the mean of reason, but a real mean. For the good of moral virtue consists in a mean. Now good, as is stated in *Metaph.* vi, is in things themselves.[10] There fore the mean of moral virtue is a real mean.

Obj. 2. Further, the reason is a power of apprehension. But moral virtue does not observe a mean between apprehensions, but rather a mean between operations and passions. Therefore the mean of moral virtue is not the mean of reason, but a real mean.

Obj. 3. Further, a mean that is observed according to arithmetical or geometrical proportion is a real mean. Now such is the mean of justice, as is stated in *Ethics* v.[11] Therefore the mean of moral virtue is not the mean of reason, but a real mean.

On the contrary, The Philosopher says that *moral virtue observes the mean in relation to us, that is set by reason.*[12]

I answer that, The mean of reason can be understood in two ways. First, according as the mean is found in the act itself of reason, as though the very act of reason were reduced to a mean. In this sense, since moral virtue perfects, not the act of reason, but the act of the appetitive power, the mean of moral virtue is not the mean of reason. Secondly, the mean of reason may be considered as that which the reason establishes in some particular matter. In this sense, every mean of moral virtue is a mean of reason; for, as was stated above, moral virtue is said to consist in a mean through conformity with right reason.

But it happens sometimes that the mean of reason is also a real mean, and in that case the mean of moral virtue is the real mean (for instance, in justice). On the other hand, sometimes the mean of reason is not the real mean, but is established in relation to us. Such is the mean in all the other moral virtues. The reason for this is that justice is about operations, which deal with external things, wherein the right has to be established absolutely and in itself, as was stated above.[13] Hence the mean of reason in justice is

---

[10] Aristotle, *Metaph.*, VI, 4 (1027b 26).   [11] Aristotle, *Eth.*, V, 4 (1132a 2); 3 (1131b 13): II. 6 (1106a 28).   [12] *Op. cit.*, II, 6 (1106b 36).   [13] Q. 60, a. 2.

the same as the real mean, in so far, namely, as justice gives to each one his due, neither more nor less. But the other moral virtues deal with interior passions, wherein the right cannot be established in the same way, since men vary in their relations to their passions. Hence the rectitude of reason has to be established in the passions with reference to us, who are influenced through the passions.

This suffices for the Replies to the Objections. For the first two arguments take the mean of reason as being in the very act of reason, while the third argues from the mean of justice.

Third Article

WHETHER THE INTELLECTUAL VIRTUES CONSIST IN A MEAN?

We proceed thus to the Third Article:—

Objection 1. It would seem that the intellectual virtues do not consist in a mean. For the moral virtues observe the mean by conforming to the rule of reason. But the intellectual virtues are in the reason itself, so that they seem to have no higher rule. Therefore the intellectual virtues do not consist in a mean.

Obj. 2. Further, the mean of moral virtue is fixed by an intellectual virtue; for it is stated in *Ethics* ii. that *virtue consists in a mean appointed by reason, as a prudent man would appoint it.*[14] If, therefore, intellectual virtues also consist in a mean, this mean will have to be appointed for them by another virtue, so that there would be an infinite series among the virtues.

Obj. 3. Further, a mean, properly speaking, is between contraries, as the Philosopher explains.[15] But there seems to be no contrariety in the intellect, since contraries themselves, as they are in the intellect, are not in opposition to one another, but are understood together, as white and black, healthy and sick. Therefore there is no mean in the intellectual virtues.

On the contrary, Art is an intellectual virtue,[16] and yet there is a mean in art.[17] Therefore, intellectual virtue likewise consists in a mean.

I answer that, The good of anything consists in a mean, according to which it is conformed to a rule or measure which it is possible to overstep or to fail to reach, as was stated above. Now intellectual virtue, like moral virtue, is directed to the good, as we have already said.[18] Hence the good of an intellectual virtue consists in a mean, in so far as it is subject to a measure. Now the good of intellectual virtue is the true: in the case of contemplative virtue, it is the true taken absolutely;[19] in the case of practical virtue, it is the true in conformity with a right appetite.

[14] Aristotle, *Eth.*, II, 6 (1106b 36).   [15] *Metaph.*, IX, 7 (1057a 30).   [16] Aristotle, *Eth.*, VI, 3 (1139b 16).   [17] *Op. cit.*, II, 6 (1106b 13).   [18] Q. 56, a. 3.   [19] Aristotle, *Eth.*, VI, 2 (1139a 29).

Now truth apprehended by our intellect, if we consider it absolutely, is as something measured by things, since things are the measure of our intellect, as is stated in *Metaph.* x.[20] For there is truth in what we think or say according as the thing is so or not. Accordingly, the good of speculative intellectual virtue consists in a certain mean, by way of conformity with things themselves, in so far as the intellect expresses that what is, is, and what is not, is not. In this consists the nature of the true. There will be excess if something false is affirmed, as though something were, which in reality is not; and there will be deficiency if something is falsely denied, and declared not to be, whereas in reality it is.

The truth of practical intellectual virtue, however, if we consider it in relation to things, has the nature of that which is measured. Hence, both in the practical and in the speculative intellectual virtues, the mean consists in conformity with things.—But if we consider it in relation to the appetite, it has the nature of a rule and measure. Consequently, the rectitude of reason is the mean of moral virtue, and also the mean of prudence:—of prudence, as ruling and measuring; of moral virtue, as ruled and measured by that mean. In like manner, the difference between excess and deficiency is to be applied in both cases.

Reply Obj. 1. Intellectual virtues also have their measure, as we have stated, and they observe the mean according as they conform to that measure.

Reply Obj. 2. There is no need for an infinite series among the virtues, because the measure and rule of intellectual virtue is not another kind of virtue, but things themselves.

Reply Obj. 3. The things themselves that are contrary have no contrariety in the soul, because one is the reason for knowing the other. Nevertheless, there is in the intellect contrariety of affirmation and negation, which are contraries, as is stated at the end of the *De Interpretatione*.[21] For though *to be* and *not to be* are not in contrary, but in contradictory, opposition to one another, so long as we consider what they signify as existing in things themselves (for the one is *being* and the other is absolutely *non-being*), yet if we refer them to the act of the soul, both posit something. Hence *to be* and *not to be* are contradictory; but the opinion stating that *good is good* is contrary to the opinion stating that *good is not good*. It is between two such contraries that intellectual virtue is a mean.

Fourth Article

WHETHER THE THEOLOGICAL VIRTUES CONSIST IN A MEAN?

We proceed thus to the Fourth Article:—

Objection 1. It would seem that theological virtue consists in a mean.

[20] Aristotle, *Metaph.*, IX, 1 (1053a 33).   [21] Aristotle, *Perih.*, XIV (23a 27).

For the good of the other virtues consists in a mean. Now theological virtue surpasses the others in goodness. Therefore much more does theological virtue consist in a mean.

Obj. 2. Further, the mean of moral virtue depends on the appetite being ruled by reason, while the mean of intellectual virtue consists in the intellect being measured by things. Now theological virtue perfects both the intellect and the appetite, as was stated above.[22] Therefore theological virtue also consists in a mean.

Obj. 3. Further, hope, which is a theological virtue, is a mean between despair and presumption. Likewise, faith holds a middle course between contrary heresies, as Boethius states.[23] Thus, by confessing one Person and two natures in Christ, we observe the mean between the heresy of Nestorius, who maintained the existence of two persons and two natures, and the heresy of Eutyches, who held to one person and one nature. Therefore theological virtue consists in a mean.

On the contrary, Wherever virtue consists in a mean, it is possible to sin by excess as well as by deficiency. But there is no sinning by excess against God, Who is the object of theological virtue; for it is written (*Ecclus.* xliii. 33): *Blessing the Lord, exalt Him as much as you can; for He is above all praise.* Therefore theological virtue does not consist in a mean.

I answer that, As was stated above, the mean of virtue depends on conformity with its rule or measure, in so far as one may exceed or fall short of that rule. Now the measure of theological virtue may be twofold. One is taken from the very nature of virtue, and thus the measure and rule of theological virtue is God Himself. For our faith is ruled according to divine truth; charity, according to His goodness; hope, according to the immensity of His omnipotence and loving kindness. This measure surpasses all human power, so that never can we love God as much as He ought to be loved, nor believe and hope in Him as much as we should. Much less, therefore, can there be excess in such things. Accordingly the good of such virtues does not consist in a mean, but increases the more we approach to the summit.

The other rule or measure of theological virtue is by comparison with us: for although we cannot be borne towards God as much as we ought, yet we should approach Him by believing, hoping and loving, according to the measure of our condition. Consequently, it is possible to find a mean and extremes in theological virtue, accidentally and in reference to us.

Reply Obj. 1. The good of the intellectual and the moral virtues consists in a mean through a conformity with a measure that may be exceeded: whereas, absolutely speaking, this is not so in the case of theological virtue, as was stated above.

Reply Obj. 2. Moral and intellectual virtues perfect our intellect and

---

[22] Q. 62, a. 3.   [23] *De Duab. Nat.,* VII (PL 64, 1352).

appetite in relation to a created measure and rule; whereas the theological virtues perfect them in relation to an uncreated rule and measure. Therefore the comparison fails.

Reply Obj. 3. Hope observes the mean between presumption and despair, in relation to us, in so far, namely, as a man is said to be presumptuous through hoping to receive from God a good in excess of his condition, or to despair through failing to hope for that which according to his condition he could hope for. But there can be no excess of hope in comparison with God, Whose goodness is infinite. In like manner, faith holds a middle course between contrary heresies, not by comparison with its object, which is God, in Whom we cannot believe too much, but in so far as human opinion itself takes a middle position between contrary opinions, as was explained above.

THE CONNECTION OF THE VIRTUES

(In Five Articles)

WE must now consider the connection of the virtues. Under this head there are five points of inquiry: (1) Whether the moral virtues are connected with one another? (2) Whether the moral virtues can be without charity? (3) Whether charity can be without them? (4) Whether faith and hope can be without charity? (5) Whether charity can be without them?

First Article

WHETHER THE MORAL VIRTUES ARE CONNECTED WITH ONE ANOTHER?

We proceed thus to the First Article:—

Objection 1. It would seem that the moral virtues are not connected necessarily with one another. For the moral virtues are sometimes caused by the exercise of acts, as is proved in *Ethics* ii.[1] But man can exercise himself in the acts of one virtue, without exercising himself in the acts of some other virtue. Therefore it is possible to have one moral virtue without another.

Obj. 2. Further, magnificence and magnanimity are moral virtues. Now a man may have other moral virtues without having magnificence or magnanimity. For the Philosopher says that *a poor man cannot be magnificent,*[2] and yet he may have other virtues; and that *he who is worthy of small things, and so accounts his worth, is modest, but not magnanimous.*[3] Therefore the moral virtues are not connected with one another.

Obj. 3. Further, as the moral virtues perfect the appetitive part of the soul, so do the intellectual virtues perfect the intellectual part. But the intellectual virtues are not mutually connected, since we may have one science without having another. Neither, therefore, are the moral virtues connected with one another.

Obj. 4. Further, if the moral virtues are mutually connected, this can be only because they are united together in prudence. But this does not suffice to connect the moral virtues together. For, evidently, one may be prudent about things to be done which pertain to one virtue without being prudent in those that concern another. So, too, one may have the art of making

---

[1] Aristotle, *Eth.,* II, 1 (1103a 31).   [2] *Op. cit.,* IV, 2 (1122b 26).   [3] *Op. cit.,* IV, 3 (1123b 5).

certain things without the art of making certain others. Now prudence is
right reason about things to be done. Therefore the moral virtues are not
necessarily connected with one another.

On the contrary, Ambrose says on *Luke* vi. 20: *The virtues are connected
and linked together, so that whoever has one, is seen to have several.*[4] Likewise, Augustine says that *the virtues that reside in the human soul are
quite inseparable from one another.*[5] And Gregory says that *one virtue without the other is either of no account whatever, or very imperfect.*[6] So, too,
Cicero says: *If you confess to not having one particular virtue, it must
needs be that you will have none at all.*[7]

I answer that, Moral virtue may be considered either as perfect or as imperfect. An imperfect moral virtue, temperance, for instance, or fortitude,
is nothing but an inclination in us to do some sort of good deed, whether
such an inclination be in us by nature or by habituation. If we take the
moral virtues in this way, they are not connected, since we find men who, by
natural temperament or by being so accustomed, are prompt in doing deeds
of liberality, but not prompt in doing deeds of chastity.

But a perfect moral virtue is a habit that inclines us to do a good deed
well; and if we take the moral virtues in this way, we must say that they are
connected, as nearly all are agreed in saying. For this two reasons are given,
corresponding to the different ways of assigning the distinction of the
cardinal virtues. For, as we stated above, some distinguish them according
to certain general properties of the virtues;[8] as, for instance, by saying that
discernment belongs to prudence, rectitude to justice, moderation to temperance, and strength of soul to fortitude, in whatever matter we consider
these properties. According to this, the reason for the connection is evident,
for strength of soul is not commended as virtuous, if it be without moderation or rectitude or discretion; and so forth. This, too, is the reason assigned for the connection by Gregory, who says that *a virtue cannot be
perfect* as a virtue, *if isolated from the others*; for *there can be no true
prudence without temperance, justice and fortitude.*[9] And he goes on to
speak in like manner of the other virtues. Augustine also gives the same
reason.[10]

Others, however, differentiate these virtues according to their subject
matter,[11] and it is in this way that Aristotle assigns the reason for their
connection.[12] For, as was stated above,[13] no moral virtue can be had without prudence, since it is proper to moral virtue to make a right choice,
because it is an elective habit. Now right choice requires not only the inclination to a due end, which inclination is the direct outcome of moral
virtue, but also a correct choice of means to the end; and this is done by

---

[4] *In Luc.,* V, super VI, 20 (PL 15, 1738).   [5] *De Trin.,* VI, 4 (PL 42, 927).
[6] *Moral.,* XXII, 1 (PL 76, 212).   [7] *Tusc. Disp.,* II, 14 (p. 296).   [8] Q. 61, a. 3 and 4.
[9] *Moral.,* XXII, 1 (PL 76, 212).   [10] *De Trin.,* VI, 4 (PL 42, 927).   [11] Cf. above,
q. 61, a. 4.   [12] *Eth.,* VI, 13 (1144b 36).   [13] Q. 58, a. 4.

prudence, that counsels, judges and commands the means to the end. In like manner, one cannot have prudence unless one has the moral virtues, since prudence is *right reason about things to be done,* and the starting-point of reason is the end of the thing to be done, to which end man is rightly disposed by moral virtue. Hence, just as we cannot have speculative science unless we have the understanding of principles, so neither can we have prudence without the moral virtues. From this it follows clearly that the moral virtues are connected with one another.

Reply Obj. 1. Some moral virtues perfect man according to his general state, in other words, with regard to those things which have to be done in every kind of human life. Hence man needs to exercise himself at the same time in the matters of all moral virtues. And if he exercise himself, by good deeds, in all such matters, he will acquire the habits of all the moral virtues. But if he exercise himself by good deeds in regard to one matter, but not in regard to another, for instance, by behaving well in matters of anger, but not in matters of concupiscence, he will indeed acquire a certain habit of restraining his anger; but this habit will lack the nature of virtue, through the absence of prudence, which is wanting in matters of concupiscence. In the same way, natural inclinations fail to have the complete character of virtue if prudence be lacking.

But there are some moral virtues which perfect man with regard to some eminent state, such as magnificence and magnanimity. And because it does not happen to all in common to be exercised in the matter of such virtues, it is possible for a man to have the other moral virtues without actually having the habits of these virtues—provided we speak of acquired virtue. Nevertheless, when once a man has acquired the other virtues, he possesses these in proximate potentiality. For when, by practice, a man has acquired liberality in small gifts and expenditure, if he were to come into the possession of a large sum of money, he would acquire the habit of magnificence with but little practice; even as a geometrician, by dint of little study, acquires scientific knowledge about some conclusion which he had never before considered. Now we are said to have a thing when we can easily have it, according to the saying of the Philosopher: *That which is scarcely lacking is not lacking at all.*[14]

This suffices for the Reply to the Second Objection.

Reply Obj. 3. The intellectual virtues are about diverse matters having no relation to one another, as is clearly the case with the various sciences and arts. Hence we do not observe in them the connection that is to be found among the moral virtues, which are about passions and operations, that are clearly related to one another. For all the passions have their rise in certain primal passions, viz., love and hatred, and terminate in certain others, viz., pleasure and sorrow. In like manner, all the operations that are the matter of moral virtue are related to one another, and to the pas

[14] *Phys.,* II, 5 (197a 29).

sions. Hence the whole matter of the moral virtues falls under the one rule of prudence.

Nevertheless, all intelligibles are related to first principles. And in this way, all the intellectual virtues depend on the understanding of principles, even as prudence depends on the moral virtues, as we have stated. On the other hand, the universal principles which are the object of the understanding of principles do not depend on the conclusions, which are the objects of the other intellectual virtues. The situation of the moral virtues is different, for they depend on prudence, because the appetite in a way moves the reason, and the reason the appetite, as we have stated above.[15]

Reply Obj. 4. Those things to which the moral virtues incline are related to prudence as principles, whereas the products of art are not the principles but the matter of art. Now it is evident that, though reason may be right in one part of the matter, and not in another, yet in no way can it be called right reason if it be deficient in any principle whatever. Thus, if a man were wrong about the principle, *A whole is greater than its part,* he could not acquire the science of geometry, because he would have to depart much from the truth in his future steps.—Moreover, things *done* are related to one another, but not things *made,* as was stated above. Consequently, the lack of prudence in one part of things to be done would result in a deficiency affecting other things to be done; whereas this does not occur in things to be made.

Second Article

WHETHER THE MORAL VIRTUES CAN BE WITHOUT CHARITY?

We proceed thus to the Second Article:—

Objection 1. It would seem that the moral virtues can be without charity. For it is stated in the *Sentences* of Prosper that *every virtue save charity may be common to the good and bad.*[16] But *charity can be in none except the good,* as is stated in the same reference. Therefore the other virtues can be had without charity.

Obj. 2. Further, the moral virtues can be acquired by means of human acts, as it is said in *Ethics* ii.,[17] whereas charity cannot be had otherwise than by infusion, according to *Rom.* v. 5: *The charity of God is poured forth in our hearts by the Holy Ghost Who is given to us.* Therefore it is possible to have the other virtues without charity.

Obj. 3. Further, the moral virtues are connected together, through depending on prudence. But charity does not depend on prudence; indeed, it surpasses prudence, according to *Ephes.* iii. 19: *The charity of Christ, which surpasseth all knowledge.* Therefore the moral virtues are not connected with charity, but can be without it.

[15] Q. 9, a. 1; q. 58, a. 5, ad 1.   [16] Prosper of Aquitaine, *Sent.,* VII (PL 51, 428).
[17] Aristotle, *Eth.,* II, 1 (1103a 31).

On the contrary, It is written (*1 John* iii. 14): *He that loveth not, abideth in death.* Now the spiritual life is perfected by the virtues, since it is *by them* that *we lead a good life,* as Augustine states.[18] Therefore they cannot be without the love of charity.

I answer that, As we have stated above, it is possible by means of human works to acquire the moral virtues, in so far as they produce good works that are directed to an end not surpassing the natural ability of man.[19] And when they are acquired thus; they can be without charity, even as they were in many of the pagans. But in so far as they produce good works in relation to a supernatural last end, thus they have the character of virtue, truly and perfectly, and cannot be acquired by human acts, but are infused by God. Such moral virtues cannot be without charity. For it has been stated above [20] that the other moral virtues cannot be without prudence, and that prudence cannot be without the moral virtues, because they make man well disposed to certain ends, from which prudence takes its nature. Now for the true character of prudence it is much more necessary that man be well disposed towards his ultimate end, which is the effect of charity, than that he be well disposed in respect of other ends, which is the effect of the moral virtues; just as in speculative matters right reason has greatest need of the first indemonstrable principle that *contradictories cannot both be true at the same time.* It is therefore evident that neither can infused prudence be without charity, nor, consequently, the other moral virtues, since they cannot be without prudence.

It is therefore clear from what has been said that only the infused virtues are perfect, and deserve to be called virtues absolutely, since they direct man well to the absolutely ultimate end. But the other virtues, those, namely, that are acquired, are virtues in a restricted sense, but not absolutely, for they direct man well in respect of the last end in some particular genus of action, but not in respect of the last end absolutely. Hence, on the words, *All that is not of faith is sin* (*Rom.* xiv. 23), the *Gloss* of Augustine says: *He that fails to acknowledge the truth, has no true virtue, even if his conduct be good.*[21]

Reply Obj. 1. Virtue, in the words quoted, denotes imperfect virtue. Else, if we take moral virtue in its perfect state, *it makes its possessor good,* and consequently cannot be in the wicked.

Reply Obj. 2. This argument holds good of the acquired virtues.

Reply Obj. 3. Though charity surpasses science and prudence, yet prudence depends on charity, as we have stated; and consequently so do all the infused moral virtues.

---

[18] *De Lib. Arb.,* II, 19 (PL 32, 1268).   [19] Q. 63, a. 2.   [20] A. 1; q. 58, a. 4 and 5.
[21] *Glossa ordin.* (VI, 30 B).—Cf. Prosper of Aquitaine, *Sent.,* CVI (PL 51, 441).

Third Article

WHETHER CHARITY CAN BE WITHOUT THE MORAL VIRTUES?

We proceed thus to the Third Article:—

Objection 1. It would seem possible to have charity without the moral virtues. For when one thing suffices for a certain purpose, it is superfluous to employ others. Now charity alone suffices for the fulfillment of all the works of virtue, as is clear from *1 Cor.* xiii. 4, *seqq.: Charity is patient, is kind,* etc. Therefore it seems that if one has charity, other virtues are superfluous.

Obj. 2. Further, he that has a habit of virtue easily performs the works of that virtue, and those works are pleasing to him for their own sake; and hence *pleasure taken in a work is a sign of habit.*[22] Now many have charity, being free from mortal sin, and yet they find it difficult to do works of virtue; nor are these works pleasing to them for their own sake, but only for the sake of charity. Therefore many have charity without the other virtues.

Obj. 3. Further, charity is to be found in every saint, and yet there are some saints who are without certain virtues. For Bede says that the saints are more humbled because of their not having certain virtues, than rejoiced at the virtues they have.[23] Therefore, if a man has charity, it does not follow of necessity that he has all the moral virtues.

On the contrary, The whole Law is fulfilled through charity, for it is written (*Rom.* xiii. 8): *He that loveth his neighbor, hath fulfilled the Law.* Now it is not possible to fulfill the whole Law without having all the moral virtues, since law contains precepts about all the acts of virtue, as is stated in *Ethics* v.[24] Therefore, he that has charity has all the moral virtues. Moreover, Augustine says in one of his letters that charity contains all the cardinal virtues.[25]

I answer that, All the moral virtues are infused together with charity. The reason for this is that God operates no less perfectly in the works of grace than in the works of nature. Now, in the works of nature we find that whenever a thing contains a principle of certain works, it has also whatever is necessary for their execution. Thus, animals are provided with organs whereby to perform the actions that their souls have the power to do. But it is evident that charity, inasmuch as it directs man to his last end, is the principle of all the good works that are directed to the last end. Therefore all the moral virtues must needs be infused together with charity, since it is through them that man performs each different kind of good work.

It is therefore clear that the infused moral virtues are connected, not only through prudence, but also because of charity; and, again, that

---

[22] Aristotle, *Eth.,* II, 3 (1104b 3).   [23] St. Bede, *In Luc.,* V, super XVII, 10 (PL 92, 541).   [24] Aristotle, *Eth.,* V, 1 (1129b 23).   [25] *Epist.* CLXVII (PL 33, 738).

whoever loses charity through mortal sin forfeits all the infused moral virtues.

Reply Obj. 1. In order that the act of a lower power be perfect, not only must there be perfection in the higher, but also in the lower, power; for if the principal agent were well disposed, perfect action would not follow if the instrument also were not well disposed. Consequently, in order that man work well in things that are means to the end, he needs not only a virtue disposing him well to the end, but also those virtues which dispose him well to whatever is a means to the end. For the virtue which regards the end is the chief and moving principle in relation to those things which are means to the end. Therefore it is necessary to have the moral virtues together with charity.

Reply Obj. 2. It sometimes happens that a man who has a habit finds it difficult to act in accordance with the habit, and consequently feels no pleasure and satisfaction in the act, because of some impediment entering from the outside. Thus, a man who has a habit of science finds it difficult to understand, through being sleepy or unwell. In like manner, sometimes the habits of the infused moral virtues experience difficulty in their works, by reason of certain contrary dispositions surviving from previous acts. This difficulty does not occur in the acquired moral virtues, because the repeated acts by which they are acquired remove also the contrary dispositions.

Reply Obj. 3. Certain saints are said not to have certain virtues in so far as they experience difficulty in the acts of those virtues, for the reason stated; although they have the habits of all the virtues.

Fourth Article

WHETHER FAITH AND HOPE CAN BE WITHOUT CHARITY?

We proceed thus to the Fourth Article:—

Objection 1. It would seem that faith and hope are never without charity. Because, since they are theological virtues, they seem to be more excellent than even the infused moral virtues. But the infused moral virtues cannot be without charity. Neither therefore can faith and hope be without charity.

Obj. 2. Further, *no man believes unwillingly,* as Augustine says.[26] But charity is in the will as a perfection thereof, as was stated above.[27] Therefore faith cannot be without charity.

Obj. 3. Further, Augustine says that *there can be no hope without love.*[28] But love is charity; for it is of this love that he speaks. Therefore hope cannot be without charity.

On the contrary, The *Gloss* on *Matt.* i. 2 says that *faith begets hope, and hope, charity.*[29] Now the begetter precedes the begotten, and can be

---

[26] *Tract.* XXVI, super *Ioann.*, VI, 44 (PL 35, 1607). [27] Q. 62, a. 3. [28] *Enchir.*, VIII (PL 40, 235). [29] *Glossa interl.*, super *Matt.*, I, 2 (V, 5r).

without it. Therefore faith can be without hope; and hope, without charity.

I answer that, Faith and hope, like the moral virtues, can be considered in two ways: first, in an inchoate state; secondly, as complete virtues. For since virtue is directed to the doing of good works, perfect virtue is that which gives the ability of doing a perfectly good work, and this consists in not only doing what is good, but also in doing it well. Otherwise, if what is done is good, but not well done, it will not be perfectly good; and therefore neither will the habit that is the principle of such an act have the perfect character of virtue. For instance, if a man do what is just, what he does is good, but it will not be the work of perfect virtue unless he do it well, *i.e.,* by choosing rightly, which is the result of prudence; for which reason justice cannot be a perfect virtue without prudence.

Accordingly, faith and hope can in a way exist without charity, but they have not the perfect character of virtue without charity. For, since the work of faith is to believe in God, and since to believe is to assent to someone of one's own free will, hence, to will not as one ought, will not be a perfect work of faith. To will as one ought is caused by charity, which perfects the will; for every right movement of the will proceeds from a right love, as Augustine says.[30] Hence, faith may be without charity, but not as a perfect virtue; just as temperance or fortitude can be without prudence. The same applies to hope. For the act of hope consists in looking to God for future beatitude. This act is perfect if it is based on the merits which we have; and this cannot be without charity. But to expect future beatitude through merits which one has not yet, but which one proposes to acquire at some future time, will be an imperfect act; and this is possible without charity. Consequently, faith and hope can be without charity; yet, without charity, they are not virtues properly so called, because the nature of virtue requires that by it we should not only do what is good, but also that we should do it well.[31]

Reply Obj. 1. Moral virtue depends on prudence, and not even infused prudence has the character of prudence without charity; for this involves the absence of due order to the first principle, viz., the ultimate end. On the other hand, faith and hope, as such, do not depend either on prudence or charity; so that they can be without charity, although they are not virtues without charity, as we have stated.

Reply Obj. 2. This argument is true of faith considered as a perfect virtue.

Reply Obj. 3. Augustine is speaking here of that hope whereby we look to gain future beatitude through merits which we have already; and this is not without charity.

[30] *De Civit. Dei,* XIV, 9 (PL 41, 413).   [31] Aristotle, *Eth.,* II, 6 (1106a 23).

Fifth Article

WHETHER CHARITY CAN BE WITHOUT FAITH AND HOPE?

We proceed thus to the Fifth Article:—

Objection 1. It would seem that charity can be without faith and hope. For charity is the love of God. But it is possible for us to love God naturally, without already having faith or hope in future beatitude. Therefore charity can be without faith and hope.

Obj. 2. Further, charity is the root of all the virtues, according to *Ephes.* iii. 17: *Rooted and founded in charity.* Now the root is sometimes without branches. Therefore charity can sometimes be without faith and hope, and the other virtues.

Obj. 3. Further, there was perfect charity in Christ. And yet He had neither faith nor hope, because He was a perfect comprehensor, as we shall explain further on.[32] Therefore charity can be without faith and hope.

On the contrary, The Apostle says (*Heb.* xi. 6): *Without faith it is impossible to please God;* and this evidently belongs most to charity, according to *Prov.* viii. 17: *I love them that love me.* Again, it is by hope that we are brought to charity, as was stated above.[33] Therefore it is not possible to have charity without faith and hope.

I answer that, Charity signifies not only the love of God, but also a certain friendship with Him; which implies, besides love, a certain mutual return of love, together with mutual communion, as is stated in *Ethics* viii.[34] That this belongs to charity is evident from *1 John* iv. 16: *He that abideth in charity, abideth in God, and God in him,* and from *1 Cor.* i. 9, where it is written: *God is faithful, by Whom you are called unto the fellowship of His Son.* Now this fellowship of man with God, which consists in a certain familiar colloquy with Him, is begun here, in this life, by grace, but will be perfected in the future life by glory; and both of these things we hold by faith and hope. Therefore, just as friendship with a person would be impossible, if one disbelieved in, or despaired of, the possibility of their fellowship or familiar colloquy; so too, friendship with God, which is charity, is impossible without faith, so as to believe in this fellowship and colloquy with God, and to hope to attain to this fellowship. Therefore charity is quite impossible without faith and hope.

Reply Obj. 1. Charity is not any kind of love of God, but that love of God, by which He is loved as the object of beatitude, to which we are directed by faith and hope.

Reply Obj. 2. Charity is the root of faith and hope in so far as it gives them the perfection of virtue. But faith and hope as such are presupposed

---

[32] *S. T.,* III, q. 7, a. 3 and 4. [33] Q. 62, a. 4. [34] Aristotle, *Eth.,* VIII, 2 (1155b 28); 12 (1161b 11).

to charity, as we have stated above,[35] and so charity is impossible without them.

Reply Obj. 3. In Christ there was neither faith nor hope, because of the imperfection they contain. But instead of faith, He had manifest vision, and instead of hope, full comprehension; so that in Him there was perfect charity.

[35] Q. 62, a. 4.

ON EQUALITY AMONG THE VIRTUES

(In Six Articles)

WE must now consider equality among the virtues. Under this head there are six points of inquiry: (1) Whether one virtue can be greater or less than another? (2) Whether all the virtues existing together in one subject are equal? (3) The moral virtues in comparison with the intellectual virtues. (4) The moral virtues as compared with one another. (5) The intellectual virtues in comparison with one another. (6) The theological virtues in comparison with one another.

First Article

WHETHER ONE VIRTUE CAN BE GREATER OR LESS THAN ANOTHER?

We proceed thus to the First Article:—

Objection 1. It would seem that one virtue cannot be greater or less than another. For it is written (*Apoc.* xxi. 16) that the sides of the city of Jerusalem are equal, and the *Gloss* says that the sides denote the virtues.[1] Therefore all the virtues are equal, and consequently one cannot be greater than another.

Obj. 2. Further, a thing that by its nature consists in a maximum cannot be more or less. But the nature of virtue consists in a maximum, for virtue is *the peak of power,* as the Philosopher states.[2] And Augustine says that *the virtues are very great goods, and no one can use them to evil purpose.*[3] Therefore it seems that one virtue cannot be greater or less than another.

Obj. 3. Further, the quantity of an effect is measured by the power of the agent. But perfect, viz., infused virtues, are from God, Whose power is uniform and infinite. Therefore it seems that one virtue cannot be greater than another.

On the contrary, Wherever there can be increase and greater abundance, there can be inequality. Now virtues admit of greater abundance and increase, for it is written (*Matt.* v. 20): *Unless your justice abound more than that of the Scribes and Pharisees, you shall not enter into the kingdom of heaven;* and (*Prov.* xv. 5): *In abundant justice there is the greatest*

---

[1] *Glossa ordin.* (VI, 272 E).   [2] *De Caelo,* I, 11 (281a 11; a 18).   [3] *De Lib. Arb.,* II, 18 (PL 32, 1267).

strength [*virtus*]. Therefore it seems that a virtue can be greater or less than another.

I answer that, When it is asked whether one virtue can be greater than another, the question can be taken in two senses. First, as applying to virtues of different species. In this sense it is clear that one virtue is greater than another, since a cause is always more excellent than its effect, and among effects, those nearer to the cause are the more excellent. Now it is clear from what has been said that the cause and root of human good is the reason.[4] Hence prudence, which perfects the reason, surpasses in goodness the other moral virtues which perfect the appetitive power, in so far as it partakes of reason. And among the moral virtues, likewise, one is better than another according as it approaches nearer to the reason. Consequently, justice, which is in the will, is superior to the remaining moral virtues; and fortitude, which is in the irascible part, stands before temperance, which is in the concupiscible part, which has a smaller share of reason, as is stated in *Ethics* vii.[5]

The question can be taken in another way, as referring to virtues of the same species. In this way, according to what was said above, when we were treating of the intensity of habits,[6] virtue may be said to be greater or less in two ways: first, in itself; secondly, with regard to the subject that partakes of it. If we consider it in itself, we shall call it great or little according to the things to which it extends. Now whoever has a virtue, *e.g.,* temperance, has it in relation to everything to which temperance extends. But this does not apply to science and art, for every grammarian does not know everything relating to grammar. In this sense, the Stoics said rightly, as Simplicius states in his *Commentary on the Categories,*[7] that virtue cannot be more or less, as science and art can; for the nature of virtue consists in a maximum.

If, however, we consider virtue on the part of the subject, it may then be greater or less, either in relation to different times, or in different men. For one man is better disposed than another to attain to the mean of virtue which is defined by right reason; and this, because of either greater habituation, or a better natural disposition, or a more discerning judgment of reason, or again a greater gift of grace, which is given to each one *according to the measure of the giving of Christ,* as is stated in *Ephes.* iv. 7. —And here the Stoics erred, for they held that no man should be deemed virtuous unless he were, in the highest degree, disposed to virtue.[8] Because the nature of virtue does not require that a man should reach the mean of right reason as though it were an indivisible point, as the Stoics thought; but it is enough that he should approach the mean, as is stated in *Ethics* ii.[9] Moreover, one and the same indivisible mark is reached more nearly and

---

[4] Q. 18, a. 5; q. 61, a. 2.   [5] Aristotle, *Eth.,* VII, 6 (1149b 1).   [6] Q. 52, a. 1.
[7] *In Cat.,* VIII (pp. 284[32-35]; 237[30-32]).   [8] Cf. St. Augustine, *Epist.* CLXVII, 3 (PL 33, 738).   [9] Aristotle, *Eth.,* II, 9 (1109b 18).

more readily by one than by another; as may also be seen when several archers aim at a fixed target.

Reply Obj. 1. This equality is not one of absolute quantity, but of proportion; because all virtues increase in a man proportionately, as we shall see further on.

Reply Obj. 2. This *peak* which belongs to virtue can have the character of something *more* or *less* good in the ways explained above; since, as we have stated, it is not an indivisible limit.

Reply Obj. 3. God does not work by necessity of nature, but according to the order of His wisdom, by which He bestows on men various measures of virtue, according to *Ephes.* iv. 7: *To every one of you is given grace according to the measure of the giving of Christ.*

Second Article

WHETHER ALL THE VIRTUES, THAT ARE TOGETHER IN ONE MAN, ARE EQUAL?

We proceed thus to the Second Article:—

Objection 1. It would seem that the virtues in one and the same man are not all equally intense. For the Apostle says (*1 Cor.* vii. 7): *Everyone hath his proper gift from God; one after this manner, and another after that.* Now one gift would not be more individual than another to a man, if God infused all the virtues equally into each man. Therefore it seems that the virtues are not all equal in one and the same man.

Obj. 2. Further, if all the virtues were equally intense in one and the same man, it would follow that whoever surpasses another in one virtue would surpass him in all the others. But this is clearly not the case, since various saints are specially praised for different virtues: *e.g.,* Abraham for faith (*Rom.* iv. 1), Moses for his meekness (*Num.* xii. 3), Job for his patience (*Job* ii. 12). This is why of each Confessor the Church sings: *There was not found his like in keeping the law of the most High,*[10] since each one was remarkable for some virtue or other. Therefore the virtues are not all equal in one and the same man.

Obj. 3. Further, the more intense a habit is, the greater one's pleasure and readiness in making use of it. Now experience shows that a man is more pleased and ready to make use of one virtue than of another. Therefore the virtues are not all equal in one and the same man.

On the contrary, Augustine says that *those who are equal in fortitude are equal in prudence and temperance,*[11] and so on. Now this would not be so unless all the virtues in one man were equal. Therefore all virtues are equal in one man.

I answer that, As was explained above, the comparative greatness of

---

[10] Cf. the Epistle in the Mass *Statuit* (Dominican Missal), and cp. *Ecclus.*, XLIV, 20.
[11] *De Trin.*, VI, 4 (PL 42, 927).

virtues can be understood in two ways. First, as referring to their specific nature, and in this way there is no doubt that in a man one virtue is greater than another, for example, charity, than faith and hope. Secondly, it may be taken as referring to the degree of participation by the subject, according as a virtue becomes intense or weak in its subject. In this sense, all the virtues in one man are equal with an equality of proportion, in so far as their increase in man is equal. Thus the fingers are unequal in size, but equal in proportion, since they grow in proportion to one another.

Now the nature of this equality is to be explained in the same way as the connection of virtues, for equality among the virtues is their connection as to greatness. Now it has been stated above[12] that a twofold principle in the connection of virtues may be assigned. The first is according to the opinion of those who understand these four virtues to be four general properties of virtues, each of which is found together with the other in any matter.[13] In this way, the virtues cannot be said to be equal in any matter unless they have all these properties equal. Augustine alludes to this kind of equality when he says: *If you say these men are equal in fortitude, but that one is more prudent than the other, it follows that the fortitude of the latter is less prudent. Consequently, they are not really equal in fortitude, since the former's fortitude is more prudent. You will find that this applies to the other virtues if you run over them all in the same way.*[14]

The other kind of connection among virtues followed the opinion of those who hold these virtues to have their own proper respective matters.[15] In this way, the principle in the connection among moral virtues is taken from prudence, and, as to the infused virtues, from charity, and not from the inclination which is found in the subject, as was stated above.[16] Accordingly, the nature of the equality among virtues can also be considered according to prudence, with reference to that which is formal in all the moral virtues; for in one and the same man, so long as his reason has the same degree of perfection, the mean must be proportionately defined according to right reason in each matter of virtue.

But in regard to that which is material in the moral virtues, viz., the inclination to the virtuous act, one may be readier to perform the act of one virtue than the act of another virtue, and this either from nature, or from habituation, or again by the grace of God.

Reply Obj. 1. This saying of the Apostle may be taken to refer to the gifts of gratuitous grace, which are not common to all, nor all equal in one and the same subject.—We might also say that it refers to the measure of sanctifying grace, by reason of which one man has all the virtues in greater abundance than another man, because of his greater abundance of prudence, or also of charity, in which all the infused virtues are connected.

---

[12] Q. 65, a. 1.   [13] Cf. above, q. 61, a. 4.   [14] *De Trin.*, VI, 4 (PL 42, 927).
[15] Q. 65. a. 1 and 2.   [16] *Ibid.*

Reply Obj. 2. One saint is praised chiefly for one virtue, another saint for another virtue, because of his more perfect readiness for the act of one virtue than for the act of another.

This suffices for the Reply to the Third Objection.

Third Article

WHETHER THE MORAL VIRTUES ARE BETTER THAN THE INTELLECTUAL VIRTUES?

We proceed thus to the Third Article:—

Objection 1. It would seem that the moral virtues are better than the intellectual. For that which is more necessary, and more lasting, is better. Now the moral virtues are *more lasting even than the sciences,*[17] which are intellectual virtues; and, moreover, they are more necessary for human life. Therefore they are preferable to the intellectual virtues.

Obj. 2. Further, virtue is defined as *that which makes its possessor good.* Now man is said to be good in respect of moral virtue, and not in respect of intellectual virtue, except perhaps in respect of prudence alone. Therefore moral virtue is better than intellectual virtue.

Obj. 3. Further, the end is more excellent than the means. But according to *Ethics* vi. *moral virtue gives a right intention of the end; whereas prudence gives the right choice of the means.*[18] Therefore moral virtue is more excellent than prudence, which is the intellectual virtue that regards moral matters.

On the contrary, Moral virtue is in that part of the soul which is rational by participation, while intellectual virtue is in the essentially rational part, as is stated in *Ethics* i.[19] Now the rational by essence is more excellent than the rational by participation. Therefore intellectual virtue is better than moral virtue.

I answer that, A thing may be said to be greater or less in two ways: first, absolutely; secondly, relatively. For nothing hinders something from being better absolutely, *e.g., learning than riches,* and yet not better relatively, *i.e., for one who is in want.*[20] Now to consider a thing absolutely is to consider it in its proper specific nature. Accordingly, a virtue takes its species from its object, as was explained above.[21] Hence, speaking absolutely, that virtue is more excellent which has the more excellent object. Now it is evident that the object of the reason is more excellent than the object of the appetite, since the reason apprehends things in the universal, while the appetite tends to things themselves, whose being is restricted to the particular. Consequently, speaking absolutely, the intellectual virtues, which perfect the reason, are more excellent than the moral virtues, which perfect the appetite.

---

[17] Aristotle, *Eth.,* I, 10 (1100b 14).   [18] *Op. cit.,* VI, 12 (1144a 8).   [19] *Op. cit.,* I, 13 (1103a 1).   [20] Aristotle, *Top.,* III, 2 (118a 10).   [21] Q. 54, a. 2; q. 60, a. 1.

But if we consider virtue in its relation to act, then moral virtue, which perfects the appetite, whose function it is to move the other powers to act (as was stated above[22]) is more excellent. And since virtue is so called from its being a principle of action, for it is the perfection of a power, it follows also that the nature of virtue agrees more with moral virtue than with intellectual virtue, though the intellectual virtues are more excellent habits, absolutely speaking.

Reply Obj. 1. The moral virtues are more lasting than the intellectual virtues, because they are practiced in matters pertaining to everyday life. Yet it is evident that the objects of the sciences, which are necessary and invariable, are more lasting than the objects of the moral virtues, which are certain particular matters of action.—That the moral virtues are more necessary for human life proves that they are more excellent, not absolutely, but relatively. Indeed, the speculative intellectual virtues, from the very fact that they are not directed to something else, as a useful thing is referred to an end, are more excellent. The reason for this is that in them we have a kind of beginning of that happiness which consists in the knowledge of truth, as we have stated above.[23]

Reply Obj. 2. The reason why a man is said to be good absolutely in relation to moral virtue, but not in relation to intellectual virtue, is because the appetite moves the other powers to their acts, as was stated above.[24] Therefore this argument, too, proves merely that moral virtue is better relatively.

Reply Obj. 3. Prudence directs the moral virtues not only in the choice of the means, but also in appointing the end. Now the end of each moral virtue is to attain the mean in the matter proper to that virtue; and this mean is appointed according to the right reason of prudence, as it is said in *Ethics* ii. and vi.[25]

Fourth Article

WHETHER JUSTICE IS THE CHIEF OF THE MORAL VIRTUES?

We proceed thus to the Fourth Article:—

Objection. 1. It would seem that justice is not the chief of the moral virtues. For it is better to give of one's own than to pay what is due. Now the former belongs to liberality, the latter to justice. Therefore liberality is apparently a greater virtue than justice.

Obj. 2. Further, that is most important in a thing which is most perfect in it. Now, according to *James* i. 4, *Patience hath a perfect work.* Therefore it would seem that patience is greater than justice.

Obj. 3. Further, *Magnanimity has a great influence on every virtue,* as

[22] Q. 9, a. 1. [23] Q. 3, a. 6. [24] Q. 56, a. 3. [25] Aristotle, II, 6 (1107a 1); VI, 13 (1144b 21).

is stated in *Ethics* iv.[26] Therefore it magnifies even justice. Therefore it is greater than justice.

On the contrary, The Philosopher says that *justice is the most excellent of the virtues.*[27]

I answer that, A virtue, considered in its species, may be greater or less, either absolutely or relatively. A virtue is said to be greater absolutely when a greater good of reason shines forth, as was stated above. In this way justice is the most excellent of all the moral virtues, as being most akin to reason. This is made evident by considering its subject and its object: its subject, because this is the will, and the will is the rational appetite, as we have stated above;[28] its object or matter, because it is about operations, whereby man is set in order not only in himself, but also in regard to another. Hence *justice is the most excellent of virtues.*[29]—Among the other moral virtues, which are about the passions, the more excellent the matter in which the appetitive movement is subjected to reason, so much the more does the good of reason shine forth in each. Now in things affecting man, the chief of all is life, on which all other things depend. Consequently fortitude, which subjects the appetitive movement to reason in matters of life and death, holds the first place among those moral virtues that are about the passions; but it is subordinate to justice. Hence the Philosopher says that *those virtues must needs be greatest which receive the most praise, since virtue is a power of doing good. Hence the brave man and the just man are honored more than others, because the former, i.e., fortitude, is useful in war, and the latter, i.e.,* justice, *both in war and in peace.*[30] After fortitude comes temperance, which subjects the appetite to reason in matters directly relating to life, in one individual or in the one species, viz.. in matters of food and of sex.—And so these three virtues, together with prudence, are called principal virtues also in dignity.

A virtue is said to be greater relatively, by reason of its helping or adorning a principal virtue. So, too, substance is more excellent absolutely than accident, and yet relatively some particular accident is more excellent than substance, in so far as it perfects substance in some accidental mode of being.

Reply Obj. 1. The act of liberality needs to be founded on an act of justice, for *a man is not liberal in giving, unless he gives of his own.*[31] Hence there could be no liberality apart from justice, which discerns between *mine* and *thine*; whereas justice can be without liberality. Hence justice is, absolutely, greater than liberality, as being more universal, and as being its foundation; while liberality is greater relatively, since it is an ornament and an addition to justice.

Reply Obj. 2. Patience is said to have *a perfect work* by enduring evils,

[26] *Op. cit.,* IV, 3 (1123b 30).   [27] *Op. cit.,* V, 1 (1129b 27).   [28] Q. 8, a. 1; q. 26, a. 1.   [29] Aristotle, *Eth.,* V, 1 (1129b 27).   [30] *Rhetor.,* I, 9 (1366b 3).   [31] Aristotle, *Polit.,* II, 2 (1263b 13).

wherein it excludes not only unjust revenge, which is also excluded by justice; not only hatred, which is also suppressed by charity; nor only anger, which is calmed by gentleness; but also inordinate sorrow, which is the root of all the above. Therefore it is more perfect and excellent because it extirpates the very root of this matter. It is not, however, more perfect absolutely than all the other virtues. Because fortitude not only endures trouble without being disturbed, but also fights against it if necessary. Hence whoever is brave is patient; but the converse does not hold, for patience is a part of fortitude.

Reply Obj. 3. There can be no magnanimity without the other virtues, as is stated in *Ethics* iv.[32] Hence it is compared to them as their ornament, so that, relatively, it is greater than all the others, but not absolutely.

Fifth Article

WHETHER WISDOM IS THE GREATEST OF THE INTELLECTUAL VIRTUES?

We proceed thus to the Fifth Article:—

Objection 1. It would seem that wisdom is not the greatest of the intellectual virtues. Because the commander is greater than the one commanded. Now prudence seems to command wisdom, for it is stated in *Ethics* i. that political science, which belongs to prudence,[33] *orders that sciences should be cultivated in states, and to which of these each individual should devote himself, and to what extent.*[34] Since, then, wisdom is one of the sciences, it seems that prudence is greater than wisdom.

Obj. 2. Further, it belongs to the nature of virtue to direct man to happiness, because virtue is *the disposition of a perfect thing to that which is best,* as is stated in *Physics* vii.[35] Now prudence is *right reason about things to be done,* by which man is brought to happiness, whereas wisdom is not concerned with human acts, by which man attains happiness. Therefore prudence is a greater virtue than wisdom.

Obj. 3. Further, the more perfect knowledge is, the greater it seems to be. Now we can have a more perfect knowledge of human affairs, which are the subject matter of science, than of divine things, which are the subject matter of wisdom (according to the distinction given by Augustine[36]), because divine things are incomprehensible, according to *Job* xxxvi. 26: *Behold God is great, exceeding our knowledge.* Therefore science is a greater virtue than wisdom.

Obj. 4. Further, a knowledge of principles is more excellent than a knowledge of conclusions. But wisdom draws conclusions from indemonstrable principles, which are the object of the virtue of understanding, even

---

[32] Aristotle, *Eth.,* IV, 3 (1124a 2). [33] *Op. cit.,* VI, 8 (1141b 20). [34] *Op. cit.,* I, 2 (1094a 28). [35] *Phys.,* VII, 3 (246b 23). [36] *De Trin.,* XII, 14 (PL 42, 1009).

as other sciences do. Therefore understanding is a greater virtue than wisdom.

On the contrary, The Philosopher says that wisdom is *the head* among the intellectual virtues.[37]

I answer that, As was stated above, the greatness of a virtue, as to its species, is taken from its object. Now the object of wisdom surpasses the objects of all the intellectual virtues, because wisdom considers the highest cause, which is God, as is stated at the beginning of the *Metaphysics.*[38] And since it is by the cause that we judge of an effect, and by the higher cause that we judge of the lower effects, hence it is that wisdom exercises judgment over all the other intellectual virtues, directs them all, and is architectonic among them all.

Reply Obj. 1. Since prudence is about human affairs, and wisdom about the highest cause, it is impossible for prudence to be a greater virtue than wisdom, *unless,* as is stated in *Ethics* vi., *man were the greatest thing in the world.*[39] Therefore we must say, as is stated in the same book, that prudence does not command wisdom, but vice versa,[40] because *the spiritual man judgeth all things, and he himself is judged of no man* (*1 Cor.* ii. 15). For prudence has no business with highest matters which are the subject matter of wisdom; but its command covers things directed to wisdom, viz., how men are to obtain wisdom. Therefore prudence, or political science, is, in this way, the servant of wisdom; for it leads to wisdom, preparing the way for her, as the doorkeeper for the king.

Reply Obj. 2. Prudence considers the means of acquiring happiness, but wisdom considers the very object of happiness, viz., the highest intelligible. And if indeed the consideration of wisdom were perfect in respect of its object, there would be perfect happiness in the act of wisdom; but since, in this life, the act of wisdom is imperfect in respect of its principal object, which is God, it follows that the act of wisdom is a beginning or participation of future happiness; so that wisdom is nearer than prudence to happiness.

Reply Obj. 3. As the Philosopher says, *one knowledge is preferable to another, either because it is about a higher object, or because it is more certain.*[41] Hence if the subjects be equally good and sublime, that virtue will be the greater which possesses more certain knowledge. But a virtue which is less certain about a higher and better thing is preferable to that which is more certain about a thing of inferior degree. Therefore the Philosopher says that *it is a great thing to be able to know something about celestial things, though it be based on weak and probable reasoning;*[42] and again that *it is better to know a little about sublime things than much*

---

[37] *Eth.,* VI, 7 (1141a 19). [38] Aristotle, *Metaph.,* I, 1 (981b 28); 2 (982b 9; 983a 7). [39] Aristotle, *Eth.,* VI, 7 (1141a 21). [40] *Op. cit.,* VI, 13 (1145a 6). [41] *De An.,* I, 1 (402a 2). [42] *De Caelo,* II, 12 (291b 27).

about mean things.[43] Accordingly wisdom, to which knowledge about God pertains, is beyond the reach of man, especially in this life, so as to be his possession; for this *belongs to God alone.*[44] But yet this little knowledge about God which we can have through wisdom is preferable to all other knowledge.

Reply Obj. 4. The truth and knowledge of indemonstrable principles depend on the meaning of the terms; for as soon as we know what is a whole, and what is a part, we know at once that every whole is greater than its part. Now to know the meaning of being and non-being, of whole and part, and of other things consequent to being, which are the terms of which indemonstrable principles are constituted, is the function of wisdom; since universal being is the proper effect of the highest cause, which is God. And so wisdom makes use of indemonstrable principles, which are the object of understanding, not only by drawing conclusions from them, as other sciences do. but also by passing its judgment on them, and by vindicating them against those who deny them. Hence it follows that wisdom is a greater virtue than understanding.

Sixth Article

WHETHER CHARITY IS THE GREATEST OF THE
THEOLOGICAL VIRTUES?

We proceed thus to the Sixth Article:—

Objection 1. It would seem that charity is not the greatest of the theological virtues. Because, since faith is in the intellect, while hope and charity are in the appetitive power, as we have already said, it seems that faith is compared to hope and charity as intellectual to moral virtue. Now intellectual virtue is greater than moral virtue, as was made evident above.[45] Therefore faith is greater than hope and charity.

Obj. 2. Further, when two things are added together, the result is greater than either one. Now hope is by way of addition to charity, for it presupposes love, as Augustine says,[46] and it adds a certain movement of striving towards the beloved. Therefore hope is greater than charity.

Obj. 3. Further, a cause is more noble than its effect. Now faith and hope are the cause of charity, for the *Gloss* on *Matt.* i. 2 says that *faith begets hope, and hope, charity.*[47] Therefore faith and hope are greater than charity.

On the contrary, The Apostle says (*1 Cor.* xiii. 13): *Now there remain faith, hope, charity, these three; but the greatest of these is charity.*

I answer that, As we have stated above, the greatness of a virtue, as to its species, is taken from its object. Now, since the three theological virtues

---

[43] *De Part. Anim.,* I, 5 (644b 31).   [44] Aristotle, *Metaph.,* I, 2 (982b 28).   [45] Q. 62, a. 3.   [46] *Enchir.,* VIII (PL 40, 235).   [47] *Glossa interl.,* super *Matt.,* I, 2 (V, 5r).

concern God as their proper object, it cannot be said that any one of them is greater than another by reason of its having a greater object, but only from the fact that it approaches nearer than another to that object; and in this way charity is greater than the others. Because the others, in their very nature, imply a certain distance from the object, since faith is of what is not seen, and hope is of what is not possessed. But the love of charity is of that which is already possessed, since the beloved is, in a manner, in the lover, and, again, the lover is drawn by desire to union with the beloved. Hence it is written (*1 John* iv. 16): *He that abideth in charity abideth in God, and God in him.*

Reply Obj. 1. Faith and hope are not related to charity in the same way as prudence to moral virtue; and for two reasons. First, because the theological virtues have an object surpassing the human soul, whereas prudence and the moral virtues are about things beneath man. Now in things that are above man, to love them is more excellent than to know them. Because knowledge is perfected by the known being in the knower, whereas love is perfected by the lover being drawn to the beloved. Now that which is above man is more excellent in itself than in man, since a thing is in another according to the mode of the being in which it is. But it is the other way about in things beneath man. Secondly, because prudence moderates the appetitive movements pertaining to the moral virtues, whereas faith does not moderate the appetitive movement tending to God, which belongs to the theological virtues; it only shows the object. And this appetitive movement towards its object surpasses human knowledge, according to *Ephes.* iii. 19: *The charity of Christ which surpasseth all knowledge.*

Reply Obj. 2. Hope presupposes love of that which a man hopes to obtain; and such love is love of concupiscence, by which he who desires good loves himself rather than something else. On the other hand, charity implies love of friendship, to which we are led by hope, as was stated above.[48]

Reply Obj. 3. An efficient cause is more noble than its effect, but not a disposing cause. For otherwise the heat of fire would be more noble than the soul, to which the heat disposes the matter. It is in this way that faith begets hope, and hope, charity; in the sense, namely, that one is a disposition to the other.

[48] Q. 62, a. 4.

ON THE DURATION OF THE VIRTUES AFTER THIS LIFE
(*In Six Articles*)

WE must now consider the duration of virtues after this life, under which head there are six points of inquiry: (1) Whether the moral virtues remain after this life? (2) Whether the intellectual virtues remain? (3) Whether faith remains? (4) Whether hope remains? (5) Whether anything remains of faith or hope? (6) Whether charity remains.

First Article

WHETHER THE MORAL VIRTUES REMAIN AFTER THIS LIFE?

We proceed thus to the First Article:—

Objection 1. It would seem that the moral virtues do not remain after this life. For in the future state of glory men will be like angels, according to *Matt.* xxii. 30. But it is absurd to put moral virtues in the angels, as is stated in *Ethics* x.[1] Therefore neither in man will there be moral virtues after this life.

Obj. 2. Further, moral virtues perfect man in the active life. But the active life does not remain after this life, for Gregory says: *The works of the active life pass away with the body.*[2] Therefore the moral virtues do not remain after this life.

Obj. 3. Further, temperance and fortitude, which are moral virtues, are in the irrational parts of the soul, as the Philosopher states.[3] Now the irrational parts of the soul are corrupted when the body is corrupted, since they are acts of bodily organs. Therefore it seems that the moral virtues do not remain after this life.

On the contrary, It is written (*Wis.* i. 15) that *justice is perpetual and immortal.*

I answer that, As Augustine says, Cicero held that the cardinal virtues do not remain after this life, and that, as Augustine adds, *in the other life men are made happy by the mere knowledge of that nature, than which nothing is better or more lovable, that nature, namely, which created all others.*[4] Afterwards he himself concludes that these four virtues remain in the future life, but after a different manner.

---

[1] Aristotle, *Eth.*, X, 8 (1178b 8). [2] *Moral.*, VI, 37 (PL 75, 764). [3] *Eth.*, III, 10 (1117b 23). [4] *De Trin.*, XIV, 9 (PL 42, 1046).

In order to make this evident, we must note that in these virtues there is a formal element, and a quasi-material element. The material element in these virtues is a certain inclination of the appetitive part to the passions and operations according to a certain mode; and since this mode is fixed by reason, hence the formal element in all the virtues is precisely this order of reason.

Accordingly, we must say that these moral virtues do not remain in the future life, as regards their material element. For in the future life there will be no concupiscences and pleasures in matters of food and sex, nor fear and daring about dangers of death, nor distributions and commutations of things employed in this present life. But, as regards the formal element, they will remain most perfectly after this life in the blessed inasmuch as each one's reason will have most perfect rectitude in regard to things concerning him according to that state of life, and his appetitive power will be moved entirely according to the order of reason, in things pertaining to that same state. Hence Augustine says that *prudence will be there without any danger of error; fortitude, without the anxiety of bearing with evil; temperance, without the rebellion of the desires. Hence prudence will neither prefer nor equal any good to God; fortitude will adhere to Him most steadfastly; and temperance will delight in Him Who knows no imperfection.*[5] As to justice, it is yet more evident what will be its act in that life, viz., *to be subject to God,* because even in this life subjection to a superior is part of justice.

Reply Obj. 1. The Philosopher is speaking there of these moral virtues as to their material element. Thus he speaks of justice, as regards *commutations and distributions*; of fortitude, as to *matters of terror and danger*; of temperance, in respect of *lewd desires.*[6]

The same applies to the Second Objection. For those things that concern the active life belong to the material element of the virtues.

Reply Obj. 3. There is a twofold state after this life: one before the resurrection, during which the soul will be separate from the body; the other, after the resurrection, when the souls will be reunited to their bodies. In this state of resurrection, the irrational powers will be in the bodily organs, just as they now are. Hence it will be possible for fortitude to be in the irascible, and temperance in the concupiscible part, in so far as each power will be perfectly disposed to obey the reason. But in the state preceding the resurrection, the irrational parts will not be in the soul actually, but only radically in its essence, as has been stated in the First Part.[7] Therefore, neither will these virtues be actually, but only in their root, *i.e.,* in the reason and will, wherein are certain seeds of these virtues, as we have stated above.[8] Justice, however, will remain because it is in the will. Hence, of justice is it specially said that it is *perpetual and immortal,*

---

[5] *Ibid.*   [6] *Eth.*, X, 8 (1178b 10).   [7] *S. T.,* I, q. 77, a. 8.   [8] Q. 63, a. 1.

both by reason of its subject, since the will is incorruptible, and because its act will not change, as was said above.

Second Article

WHETHER THE INTELLECTUAL VIRTUES REMAIN AFTER THIS LIFE?

We proceed thus to the Second Article:—

Objection 1. It would seem that the intellectual virtues do not remain after this life. For the Apostle says (*1 Cor.* xiii. 8, 9) that *knowledge shall be destroyed,* and he states the reason to be because *we know in part.* Now just as the knowledge of science is in part, *i.e.,* imperfect, so also is the knowledge of the other intellectual virtues, as long as this life lasts. Therefore all the intellectual virtues will cease after this life.

Obj. 2. Further, the Philosopher says that since science is a habit, it is a quality difficult to remove;[9] for it is not easily lost, except by reason of some great change or sickness. But no bodily change is so great as that of death. Therefore science and the other intellectual virtues do not remain after death.

Obj. 3. Further, the intellectual virtues perfect the intellect so that it may perform its proper act well. Now there seems to be no act of the intellect after this life, since *the soul understands nothing without a phantasm;*[10] but after this life, phantasms do not remain, since their only subject is an organ of the body. Therefore the intellectual virtues do not remain after this life.

On the contrary, The knowledge of what is universal and necessary is more constant than that of particular and contingent things. Now the knowledge of contingent particulars remains in man after this life, for instance, the knowledge of what one has done or suffered, according to *Luke* xvi. 25: *Son, remember that thou didst receive good things in thy lifetime, and likewise Lazarus evil things.* Much more, therefore, does the knowledge of universal and necessary things remain, which belong to science and the other intellectual virtues.

I answer that, As we have stated in the First Part,[11] some have held that the intelligible species do not remain in the possible intellect except when it actually understands;[12] and that so long as actual consideration ceases, the species are not preserved save in the sensitive powers which are acts of bodily organs, viz., in the powers of imagination and memory. Now these powers cease when the body is corrupted. Consequently, according to this opinion, neither science nor any other intellectual virtue will remain after this life when once the body is corrupted.

---

[9] *Cat.,* VIII (8b 29).   [10] Aristotle, *De An.,* III, 7 (431a 16).   [11] *S. T.,* I, q. 79, a. 6.   [12] Avicenna, *De An.,* V, 6 (26rb).

But this opinion is contrary to the doctrine of Aristotle, who states that *the possible intellect is in act when it becomes each thing as knowing it; and yet, even then, it is in potentiality to consider it actually.*[13] It is also contrary to reason, because intelligible species are contained by the possible intellect immovably, according to the mode of their recipient. Hence the possible intellect is called *the abode of species,*[14] because it preserves the intelligible species.

And yet the phantasms, by turning to which man understands in this life by applying the intelligible species to them, as we have stated in the First Part,[15] cease as soon as the body is corrupted. Hence, so far as the phantasms are concerned, which are the quasi-material element in the intellectual virtues, the intellectual virtues cease when the body is destroyed; but as regards the intelligible species, which are in the possible intellect, the intellectual virtues remain. Now the species are the quasi-formal element of the intellectual virtues. Therefore these remain after this life, as regards their formal element, but not as regards their material element, just as we have stated concerning the moral virtues.

Reply Obj. 1. The saying of the Apostle is to be understood as referring to the material element in science, and to the mode of understanding; because, namely, neither do the phantasms remain when the body is destroyed, nor will there be the use of science by turning to the phantasms.

Reply Obj. 2. Sickness destroys the habit of science as to its material element, viz., the phantasms, but not as to the intelligible species, which are in the possible intellect.

Reply Obj. 3. As we have stated in the First Part,[16] the separated soul has a mode of understanding other than by turning to the phantasms. Consequently, science remains, yet not as to the same mode of operation, as we have likewise stated concerning the moral virtues.

Third Article

WHETHER FAITH REMAINS AFTER THIS LIFE?

We proceed thus to the Third Article:—

Objection 1. It would seem that faith remains after this life. Because faith is more excellent than science. Now science remains after this life, as was stated above. Therefore faith remains also.

Obj. 2. Further, it is written (*1 Cor.* iii. 11): *Other foundation no man can lay, but that which is laid; which is Christ Jesus, i.e.,* faith in Jesus Christ. Now if the foundation is removed, that which is built upon it remains no more. Therefore, if faith remains not after this life, no other virtue would remain.

---

[13] *De An.,* III, 4 (429b 6).   [14] *Ibid.* (429a 27).   [15] *S. T.,* I, q. 84, a. 7; q. 85, a. 1, ad 5.   [16] *S. T.,* I, q. 89, a. 1.

Obj. 3. Further, the knowledge of faith and the knowledge of glory differ as perfect from imperfect. Now imperfect knowledge is compatible with perfect knowledge. Thus in an angel there can be *evening* and *morning* knowledge; and a man can have science through a demonstrative syllogism, together with opinion through a probable syllogism, about one and the same conclusion. Therefore after this life faith also is compatible with the knowledge of glory.

On the contrary, The Apostle says (*2 Cor.* v. 6, 7): *While we are in the body, we are absent from the Lord: for we walk by faith and not by sight.* But those who are in glory are not absent from the Lord, but present to Him. Therefore after this life faith does not remain in the life of glory.

I answer that, Opposition is of itself the proper cause of one thing being excluded from another, in so far, namely, as wherever two things are opposite to one another, we find opposition of affirmation and negation. Now in some things we find opposition according to contrary forms. Thus, in colors we find white and black. In others, we find opposition according to perfect and imperfect. Therefore in alterations, more and less are considered to be contraries, as when a thing from being less hot is made more hot.[17] And since perfect and imperfect are opposed to one another, it is impossible for perfection and imperfection to affect the same thing at the same time.

Now we must note that imperfection sometimes belongs to a thing's very nature, and pertains to its species; and thus, lack of reason belongs to the specific nature of a horse and an ox. And since a thing, so long as it remains the same identically, cannot pass from one species to another, it follows that if such an imperfection be removed, the species of that thing is changed. Thus, it would no longer be an ox or a horse, were it to be rational. Sometimes, however, the imperfection does not belong to the specific nature, but is accidental to the individual by reason of something else; and thus, sometimes lack of reason is accidental to a man, because he is asleep, or because he is drunk, or for some like reason. Now it is evident that if such an imperfection be removed, the thing remains substantially.

It is clear, however, that imperfect knowledge belongs to the very nature of faith, for it is included in its definition, since faith is defined as *the substance of things to be hoped for, the evidence of things that appear not* (*Heb.* xi. 1). Therefore Augustine says: *What is faith? Believing without seeing.*[18] But it belongs to the imperfection of knowledge that it be of things unapparent or unseen. Consequently, imperfect knowledge belongs to the very nature of faith. Therefore it is clear that the knowledge of faith cannot be perfect and remain identically the same.

But we must also consider whether it is compatible with perfect knowledge, for there is nothing to prevent some kind of imperfect knowledge

---

[17] Aristotle, *Phys.,* V, 2 (226b 2).   [18] *Tract.* XL, super *Ioann.,* VIII, 32 (PL 35, 1690).

from being sometimes with perfect knowledge. Accordingly, we must observe that knowledge can be imperfect in three ways: first, on the part of the knowable object; secondly, on the part of the means; thirdly, on the part of the subject. The difference of perfect and imperfect knowledge on the part of the knowable object is seen in the *morning* and *evening* knowledge of the angels. For the *morning* knowledge is about things according to the being which they have in the Word, while the *evening* knowledge is about things according as they have being in their own natures, which being is imperfect in comparison with the First Being.—On the part of the means, perfect and imperfect knowledge are exemplified in the knowledge of a conclusion through a demonstrative means, and through a probable means.—On the part of the subject, the difference of perfect and imperfect knowledge applies to opinion, faith and science. For it is essential to opinion that we assent to one of two opposite assertions with fear of the other, so that our adhesion is not firm; to science it is essential to have firm adhesion with intellectual vision, for science possesses certitude which results from the understanding of principles; while faith holds a middle place, for it surpasses opinion in so far as its adhesion is firm, but falls short of science in so far as it lacks vision.

Now it is evident that a thing cannot be perfect and imperfect in the same respect; yet the things which differ as perfect and imperfect can be together in the same respect in one and the same other thing. Accordingly, knowledge which is perfect on the part of the object is quite incompatible with imperfect knowledge about the same object; but they are compatible with one another in respect of the same means or the same subject. For nothing hinders a man from having, at one and the same time, through one and the same means, perfect and imperfect knowledge about two things, one perfect, the other imperfect, *e.g.*, about health and sickness, good and evil. In like manner, knowledge that is perfect on the part of the means is incompatible with imperfect knowledge through one and the same means; but nothing hinders them being about the same object or in the same subject. For one man can know the same conclusions through a probable and through a demonstrative means.—Again, knowledge that is perfect on the part of the subject is incompatible with imperfect knowledge in the same subject. Now faith, of its very nature, contains an imperfection on the part of the subject, viz., that the believer sees not what he believes; whereas beatitude, of its very nature, implies perfection on the part of the subject, viz., that the blessed see that which makes them happy, as we have stated above.[19] Hence it is manifest that faith and beatitude are incompatible in one and the same subject.

Reply Obj. 1. Faith is more excellent than science, on the part of the object, because its object is the First Truth. Yet science has a more perfect

[19] Q. 3, a. 8.

mode of knowing its object, which, unlike faith, is not incompatible with the perfection of happiness, namely, vision.

Reply Obj. 2. Faith is the foundation inasmuch as it is knowledge. Consequently, when this knowledge is perfected, the foundation will be perfected also.

The Reply to the Third Objection is clear from what has been said.

Fourth Article

WHETHER HOPE REMAINS, AFTER DEATH, IN THE STATE OF GLORY?

We proceed thus to the Fourth Article:—

Objection 1. It would seem that hope remains, after death, in the state of glory. Because hope perfects the human appetite in a more excellent manner than the moral virtues. But the moral virtues remain after this life, as Augustine clearly states.[20] Much more then does hope remain.

Obj. 2. Further, fear is opposed to hope. But fear remains after this life: —in the blessed, filial fear, which abides forever—in the lost, the fear of punishment. Therefore, in a like manner, hope can remain.

Obj. 3. Further, just as hope is of future good, so is desire. But in the blessed there is desire for future good, both for the glory of the body, which the souls of the blessed desire, as Augustine declares,[21] and for the glory of the soul, according to *Ecclus.* xxiv. 29: *They that eat me, shall yet hunger, and they that drink me, shall yet thirst*; and *1 Pet.* i. 12: *On Whom the angels desire to look.* Therefore it seems that there can be hope in the blessed after this life is past.

On the contrary, The Apostle says (*Rom.* viii. 24): *What a man seeth, why doth he hope for?* But the blessed see that which is the object of hope, viz., God. Therefore they do not hope.

I answer that, As was stated above, that which, in its very nature, implies imperfection in its subject is incompatible with the opposite perfection in that subject. Thus, it is evident that movement of its very nature implies imperfection in its subject, since it is *the act of that which is in potentiality in so far as it is such*; so that as soon as this potentiality is brought into act, the movement ceases, for a thing does not continue to become white when once it is made white. Now hope denotes a movement towards that which is not possessed, as is clear from what we have said above about the passion of hope.[22] Therefore, when we possess that which we hope for, viz., the enjoyment of God, it will no longer be possible to have hope.

Reply Obj. 1. Hope surpasses the moral virtues as to its object, which is

[20] *De Trin.,* XIV, 9 (PL 42, 1045).   [21] *De Genesi ad Litt.,* XII, 35 (PL 34, 183).
[22] Q. 40, a. 1 and 2.

God. But the acts of the moral virtues are not incompatible with the perfection of happiness, as the act of hope is; except perhaps, as regards their matter, in respect of which they do not remain. For moral virtue perfects the appetite, not only in respect of what is not yet possessed, but also as regards something which is in our actual possession.

Reply Obj. 2. Fear is twofold, servile and filial, as we shall state further on.[23] Servile fear regards punishment, and will be impossible in the life of glory, since there will no longer be the possibility of being punished. Filial fear, on the other hand, has two acts: one is an act of reverence to God, and with regard to this act, it remains; the other is an act of fear lest we be separated from God, and as regards this act, it does not remain. Because separation from God is in the nature of an evil, and no evil will be feared there, according to *Prov.* i. 33: *He . . . shall enjoy abundance without fear of evils.* Now fear is opposed to hope by opposition of good and evil, as we have stated above,[24] and therefore the fear which will remain in glory is not opposed to hope. In the lost there can be fear of punishment, more than hope of glory is possible in the blessed. Because in the lost there will be a succession of punishments, so that the notion of something future remains there, which is the object of fear; but the glory of the saints has no succession, by reason of its being a kind of participation of eternity, wherein there is neither past nor future, but only the present.—And yet, properly speaking, neither in the lost is there fear. For, as we have stated above, fear is never without some hope of escape;[25] and the lost will have no such hope. Consequently, neither will there be fear in them, except speaking in a general way, in so far as any expectation of future evil is called fear.

Reply Obj. 3. As to the glory of the soul, there can be no desire in the blessed, in so far as desire looks for something future, for the reason already given. Yet hunger and thirst are said to be in them because they never weary, and for the same reason desire is said to be in the angels. With regard to the glory of the body, there can be desire in the souls of the saints, but not hope, properly speaking. Hope is possible neither as a theological virtue, for thus its object is God, and not a created good, nor in its general signification. For the object of hope is something difficult, as was stated above,[26] while a good whose unfailing cause we already possess is not compared to us as something difficult. Hence he that has money, properly speaking, is not said to hope for what he can buy at once. In like manner, those who have the glory of the soul are not, properly speaking, said to hope for the glory of the body, but only to desire it.

---

[23] *S. T.*, II-II, q. 19, a. 2. [24] Q. 23, a. 2; q. 40, a. 1. [25] Q. 42, a. 2. [26] Q. 40, a. 1.

Fifth Article

WHETHER ANYTHING OF FAITH OR HOPE REMAINS IN GLORY?

We proceed thus to the Fifth Article:—

Objection 1. It would seem that something of faith and hope remains in glory. For when that which is proper to a thing is removed, there remains what is common. Thus, it is stated in the *Book of Causes* that *if you take away rational, there remains living, and when you remove living, there remains being.*[27] Now in faith there is something that it has in common with beatitude, viz., knowledge; and there is something proper to it, viz., obscurity, for faith is knowledge in an obscure manner. Therefore, when the obscurity of faith is removed, the knowledge of faith still remains.

Obj. 2. Further, faith is a spiritual light of the soul, according to *Ephes.* i. 17, 18: *The eyes of your heart enlightened . . . in the knowledge of God;* yet this light is imperfect in comparison with the light of glory, of which it is written (*Ps.* xxxv. 10): *In Thy light we shall see light.* Now an imperfect light remains when a perfect light supervenes; for a candle is not extinguished when the sun's rays appear. Therefore it seems that the light of faith itself remains with the light of glory.

Obj. 3. Further, the substance of a habit does not cease through the withdrawal of its matter; for a man may retain the habit of liberality, though he have lost his money, but he cannot exercise the act. Now the object of faith is the First Truth as unseen. Therefore when this ceases, when the First Truth is seen, the habit of faith can still remain.

On the contrary, Faith is a simple habit. Now a simple thing is either withdrawn entirely, or remains entirely. Since, therefore, faith does not remain entirely, but is taken away, as we have stated above, it seems that it is withdrawn entirely.

I answer that, Some have held that hope is taken away entirely, but that faith is taken away in part, viz., as to its obscurity, and remains in part, viz., as to the substance of its knowledge.[28] And if this be understood to mean that it remains the same, not identically, but generically, it is absolutely true; since faith is of the same genus (viz., knowledge) as the beatific vision. On the other hand, hope is not of the same genus as heavenly beatitude, because it is compared to the enjoyment of beatitude as movement is to rest in the term of movement.

But if it be understood to mean that in heaven the knowledge of faith remains identically the same, this is absolutely impossible. Because, when you remove a specific difference, the substance of the genus does not remain identically the same. Thus, if you remove the difference constituting whiteness, the substance of color does not remain identically the same, as

---

[27] *De Causis,* I (p. 161).   [28] William of Auxerre, *Summa Aurea,* III, tr. 5, q. 5 (fol. 138 va); St. Albert, *In III Sent.,* d. xxxi, a. 7 (XXVIII, 586).

though the identical color were at one time whiteness, and, at another, blackness. The reason is that genus is not related to difference as matter to form, so that the substance of the genus remain identically the same when the difference is removed, in the same way as the substance of matter remains identically the same when the form is changed; for genus and difference are not the parts of a species, or otherwise they would not be predicated of the species. But even as the species signifies *a whole, i.e.,* the composite of matter and form in material things, so does the difference, and likewise the genus: the genus denotes the whole by signifying it from that which is as matter; the difference, by signifying it from that which is as form; the species, by signifying both. Thus, in man, the sensitive nature is as matter to the intellectual nature, and animal is predicated of that which has a sensitive nature, rational of that which has an intellectual nature, and man of that which has both. So that one and the same whole is denoted by these three, but not under the same aspect.

It is therefore evident that, since the signification of the difference is confined to the genus, if the difference be removed, the substance of the genus cannot remain the same; for the same animal nature does not remain, if another kind of soul constitute the animal. Hence it is impossible for the identical knowledge, which was previously obscure, to become clear vision. It is therefore evident that, in heaven, nothing remains of faith either identically or specifically the same, but only generically.

Reply Obj. 1. If *rational* be withdrawn, the remaining *living* thing is the same, not identically, but generically, as we have stated.

Reply Obj. 2. The imperfection of candle-light is not opposed to the perfection of sunlight, since they do not regard the same subject; whereas imperfection of faith and the perfection of glory are opposed to one another and regard the same subject. Consequently they are incompatible with one another, just as light and darkness in the air.

Reply Obj. 3. He that loses his money does not lose the possibility of having money, and therefore it is fitting for the habit of liberality to remain. But in the state of glory, not only is the object of faith, which is the unseen, removed actually, but even its possibility, by reason of the unchangeableness of heavenly beatitude; and so such a habit would remain to no purpose.

Sixth Article

WHETHER CHARITY REMAINS, AFTER THIS LIFE, IN GLORY?

We proceed thus to the Sixth Article:—

Objection 1. It would seem that charity does not remain, after this life, in glory. Because according to *1 Cor.* xiii. 10, *when that which is perfect is come, that which is in part, i.e.,* that which is imperfect, *shall be done away.* Now the charity of the wayfarer is imperfect. Therefore it will be done away when the perfection of glory is attained.

Obj. 2. Further, habits and acts are differentiated by their objects. But the object of love is the apprehended good. Since therefore the apprehension of the present life differs from the apprehension of the life to come, it seems that charity is not the same in both cases.

Obj. 3. Further, things of the same nature can advance from imperfection to perfection by continuous increase. But the charity of the wayfarer can never attain to equality with the charity of heaven, however much it be increased. Therefore it seems that the charity of the wayfarer does not remain in heaven.

On the contrary, The Apostle says (*1 Cor.* xiii. 8): *Charity never falleth away.*

I answer that, As we have stated above, when the imperfection of a thing does not belong to its specific nature, there is nothing to hinder the identical thing from passing from imperfection to perfection, even as man is perfected by growth, and whiteness by intensity. Now charity is love, the nature of which does not include imperfection, since it may relate to an object either possessed or not possessed, either seen or not seen. Therefore charity is not removed by the perfection of glory, but remains identically the same.

Reply Obj. 1. The imperfection of charity is accidental to it, because imperfection is not included in the nature of love. Now although that which is accidental to a thing be withdrawn, the substance remains. Hence when the imperfection of charity is removed charity itself is not done away.

Reply Obj. 2. The object of charity is not knowledge itself, for if it were, the charity of the wayfarer would not be the same as the charity of heaven; its object is, rather, the thing known, which remains the same, viz., God Himself.

Reply Obj. 3. The reason why the charity of the wayfarer cannot attain to the perfection of the charity of heaven is a difference on the part of the cause; for vision is the cause of love, as is stated in *Ethics* ix.,[29] and the more perfectly we know God, the more perfectly we love Him.

[29] Aristotle, *Eth.,* IX, 5 (1167a 4).

Question LXVIII

ON THE GIFTS
(In Eight Articles)

WE now come to consider the Gifts, under which head there are eight points of inquiry: (1) Whether the Gifts differ from the virtues? (2) Of the necessity of the Gifts. (3) Whether the Gifts are habits? (4) Which, and how many are they? (5) Whether the Gifts are connected? (6) Whether they remain in heaven? (7) Of their comparison with one another. (8) Of their comparison with the virtues.

First Article

WHETHER THE GIFTS DIFFER FROM THE VIRTUES?

We proceed thus to the First Article:—

Objection 1. It would seem that the gifts do not differ from the virtues. For Gregory, commenting on *Job* i. 2 (*There were born to him seven sons*) says: *Seven sons are born to us when through the conception of heavenly thought, the seven virtues of the Holy Ghost take birth in us;*[1] and he quotes the words of *Isaias* (xi. 2, 3): *And the Spirit . . . of understanding . . . shall rest upon him*, etc. where the seven gifts of the Holy Ghost are enumerated. Therefore the seven gifts of the Holy Ghost are virtues.

Obj. 2. Further, Augustine, commenting on *Matt.* xii. 45 (*Then he goeth and taketh with him seven other spirits*, etc), says: *The seven vices are opposed to the seven virtues of the Holy Ghost, i.e., to the seven gifts.*[2] Now the seven vices are opposed to the seven virtues, commonly so called. Therefore the gifts do not differ from the virtues, commonly so called.

Obj. 3. Further, things whose definition is the same are themselves the same. But the definition of virtue applies to the gifts, for each gift is *a good quality of the mind, whereby we lead a good life*, etc. Likewise the definition of a gift can apply to the infused virtues, for a gift is *an unreturnable giving*, according to the Philosopher.[3] Therefore the virtues and gifts do not differ from one another.

Obj. 4. Several of the things mentioned among the gifts are virtues. For, as we have stated above, wisdom, understanding and science are intellectual virtues, counsel pertains to prudence, piety is a species of justice,

---

[1] *Moral.*, I, 27 (PL 75, 544). [2] *Quaest. Evang.*, I, 8, super *Matt.*, XII, 45 (PL 35, 1325). [3] *Top.*, IV, 4 (125a 18).

and fortitude is a moral virtue.[4] Therefore it seems that the gifts do not differ from the virtues.

On the contrary, Gregory distinguishes the seven gifts, which he states to be denoted by the seven sons of Job, from the three theological virtues, which, he says, are signified by Job's three daughters.[5] He also distinguishes the same seven gifts from the four cardinal virtues, which he says were signified by the four corners of the house.[6]

I answer that, If we speak of *gift* and *virtue* with regard to the notion of each name, there is no opposition between them. Because the term *virtue* conveys the notion that it perfects man in relation to well-doing,[7] while the term *gift* refers to the cause from which it proceeds. Now there is no reason why that which proceeds from one as a gift should not perfect another in well-doing, especially since we have already stated that some virtues are infused into us by God.[8] Therefore in this respect we cannot differentiate gifts from virtues. Consequently, some have held that the gifts are not to be distinguished from the virtues.[9] But there remains no less a difficulty for them to solve, for they must explain why some virtues are called gifts and some not; and why among the gifts there are some, fear, for instance, that are not reckoned virtues.

Hence it is that others have said that the gifts should be distinguished from the virtues.[10] But they have not assigned a suitable reason for this distinction, a reason, namely, which would apply either to all the virtues, and to none of the gifts, or vice versa. For, having seen that of the seven gifts four belong to the reason, viz., wisdom, science, understanding and counsel, and three to the appetite, viz., fortitude, piety and fear, they held that the gifts perfect free choice according as it is an ability of the reason, while the virtues perfect it as an ability of the will. They did this because they found only two virtues in the reason or intellect, viz., faith and prudence, while the others were in the appetitive power or the affections.[11] If this distinction were true, all the virtues would have to be in the appetite, and all the gifts in the reason.

Others, observing that Gregory says that *the gift of the Holy Ghost, by coming into the soul, endows it with prudence, temperance, justice, and fortitude, and at the same time strengthens it against every kind of temptation by His sevenfold gift,*[12] said that the virtues are given to us that we may do good works, and the gifts, that we may resist temptation.[13] But neither is this distinction sufficient. For the virtues also resist those temp-

---

[4] Q. 57, a. 2.   [5] *Moral.,* I, 27 (PL 75, 544).   [6] *Op. cit.,* II, 49 (PL 75, 592). [7] Q. 55, a. 3 and 4.   [8] Q. 63, a. 3.   [9] On this problem, cf. the study and texts published by O. Lottin, "Les dons du Saint-Ésprit chez les théologiens depuis P. Lombard jusqu'à s. Thomas d'Aquin" (*Recherches de théologie ancienne et médiévale.* I, 1929, pp. 41-97).—For the present opinion, cf. Peter Lombard, *Sent.,* III, xxxiv, 2 (II, 699), and O. Lottin, *art. cit.,* pp. 41-46.   [10] Philip the Chancellor: cf. O. Lottin, *art. cit.,* pp. 46, 79.   [11] Praepositinus: cf. O. Lottin, *art. cit.,* pp. 42, 66. [12] *Moral.,* II, 49 (PL 75, 592).   [13] Philip the Chancellor: cf. O. Lottin, *art. cit.,* pp. 35, 76.

tations which lead to the sins that are contrary to the virtues; for every-thing naturally resists its contrary, as is especially clear with regard to charity, of which it is written (*Cant.* viii. 7): *Many waters cannot quench charity.*

Others, again, seeing that these gifts are set down in Holy Scripture as having been in Christ, according to *Isa.* xi. 2, 3, said that the virtues are intended absolutely that we may do good works, but the gifts, in order to conform us to Christ, chiefly with regard to His Passion, for it was then that these gifts shone with the greatest splendor.[14] Yet neither does this appear to be a satisfactory distinction. Because Our Lord Himself espe-cially wished us to be conformed to Him in humility and meekness (ac-cording to *Matt.* xi. 29: *Learn of Me, because I am meek and humble of heart*) and in charity (according to *John* xv. 12: *Love one another, as I have loved you*). Moreover, these virtues were especially resplendent in Christ's Passion.

Accordingly, in order to differentiate the gifts from the virtues, we must be guided by the way in which Scripture expresses itself, for we find there that the term employed is *spirit* rather than *gift*. For thus it is written (*Isa.* xi. 2, 3): *The spirit . . . of wisdom and of understanding . . . shall rest upon him,* etc. From these words we are clearly given to understand that these seven are there set down as being in us by divine inspiration. Now inspiration denotes motion from the outside. For it must be noted that in man there is a twofold principle of movement, one within him, viz., the reason, the other extrinsic to him, viz., God, as we have stated above.[15] Moreover the Philosopher says the same thing in the chapter *On Good Fortune.*[16]

Now it is evident that whatever is moved must be proportioned to its mover; and the perfection of what is moved, as such, consists in a disposi-tion whereby it is disposed to be well moved by its mover. Hence, the more exalted the mover, the more perfect must be the disposition whereby that which is moved is proportioned to its mover. Thus we see that a disciple needs a more perfect disposition in order to receive a higher teaching from his master. Now it is manifest that human virtues perfect man according as it is natural for him to be moved by his reason in his interior and ex-terior actions. Consequently, man needs yet higher perfections whereby to be disposed to be moved by God. These perfections are called gifts, not only because they are infused by God, but also because by them man is disposed to become amenable to the divine inspiration, according to *Isa.* l. 5: *The Lord . . . hath opened my ear, and I do not resist; I have not gone back.* The Philosopher likewise says in the chapter *On Good Fortune* that for those who are moved by divine instigation there is no need to take

---

[14] Philip the Chancellor: cf. O. Lottin, *art. cit.,* p. 80.   [15] Q. 9, a. 4 and 6.
[16] Cf. *Eth. Eudem.,* VII, 14 (1248a 14).

counsel according to human reason, but only to follow their inner prompt-ings, since they are moved by a principle higher than human reason.[17] And this is what some say, viz., that the gifts perfect man for acts which are higher than acts of virtue.[18]

Reply Obj. 1. Sometimes these gifts are called *virtues* in the broad sense of the term. Nevertheless, they have something over and above the virtues understood in this broad way, in so far as they are divine virtues perfecting man as moved by God. Hence the Philosopher places above virtue, com-monly so called, a kind of *heroic* or *divine* virtue, in respect of which some men are called *divine*.[19]

Reply Obj. 2. The vices are opposed to the virtues in so far as they are opposed to the good as appointed by reason; but they are opposed to the gifts inasmuch as they are opposed to the divine instigation. For the same thing is opposed both to God and to reason, whose light comes from God.

Reply Obj. 3. This definition applies to virtue taken in its general sense. Consequently, if we wish to restrict it to virtue as distinguished from the gifts, we must explain the words, *whereby we lead a good life,* as referring to the rectitude of life which is measured by the rule of reason. Likewise the gifts, as distinct from infused virtue, may be defined as something given by God in relation to His motion; something, namely, that makes man to follow well the promptings of God.

Reply Obj. 4. Wisdom is called an intellectual virtue in so far as it proceeds from the judgment of reason; but it is called a gift according as its work proceeds from the divine instigation. The same applies to the other virtues.

Second Article

WHETHER THE GIFTS ARE NECESSARY TO MAN FOR SALVATION?

We proceed thus to the Second Article:—

Objection 1. It would seem that the gifts are not necessary to man for salvation, because they are ordained to a perfection surpassing the ordinary perfection of virtue. Now it is not necessary for man's salvation that he should attain to a perfection surpassing the ordinary standard of virtue; for such a perfection falls, not under the precept, but under a counsel. Therefore the gifts are not necessary to man for salvation.

Obj. 2. Further, it is enough for man's salvation that he behave well in matters concerning God and in matters concerning man. Now man's be-havior to God is sufficiently directed by the theological virtues, and his

---

[17] Cf. *ibid.* (1248a 32).   [18] St. Albert, *In III Sent.,* d. xxxiv, a. 1 (XXVIII, 616); St. Bonaventure, *In III Sent.,* d. xxxiv, a. 1, q. 1 (III, 735).   [19] *Eth.,* VII, 1 (1145a 20).

behavior towards men, by the moral virtues. Therefore the gifts are not necessary to man for salvation.

Obj. 3. Further, Gregory says that *the Holy Ghost gives wisdom against folly, understanding against dullness, counsel against rashness, fortitude against fear, science against ignorance, piety against hardness of heart, and fear against pride.*[20] But a sufficient remedy for all these things is to be found in the virtues. Therefore the gifts are not necessary to man for salvation.

On the contrary, Of all the gifts, wisdom seems to be the highest, and fear the lowest. But both of these are necessary for salvation, since of wisdom it is written (*Wis.* vii. 28): *God loveth none but him that dwelleth with wisdom*; and of fear (*Ecclus.* i. 28): *He that is without fear cannot be justified.* Therefore the other gifts that are placed between these are also necessary for salvation.

I answer that, As we have stated above, the gifts are certain perfections of man by which he is disposed to follow promptly the divine instigation. Therefore, in those matters where the instigation of reason is not sufficient, and there is need for the instigation of the Holy Ghost, there is consequently need for a gift.

Now man's reason is perfected by God in two ways: first, with its natural perfection, namely, the natural light of reason; secondly, with a supernatural perfection, namely, the theological virtues, as we have stated above.[21] And, though this latter perfection is greater than the former, yet the former is possessed by man in a more perfect manner than the latter; because man has the former in his full possession, whereas he possesses the latter imperfectly, since we love and know God imperfectly. Now it is evident that anything that has a nature, or a form, or a virtue perfectly, can work through itself according to it. (This does not, however, exclude the operation of God, Who works inwardly in every nature and in every will.) On the other hand, that which has a nature, or form, or virtue imperfectly, cannot work through itself unless it be moved by another. Thus, the sun, which possesses light perfectly, can shine by itself; whereas the moon, which has the nature of light imperfectly, sheds only a borrowed light. Again, a physician, who knows the medical art perfectly, can work by himself; but his pupil, who is not yet fully instructed, cannot work by himself, but needs to receive instructions from him.

Accordingly, in matters subject to human reason, and directed to man's connatural end, man can work through the judgment of his reason. If, however, even in these things man is aided by a special instigation from God, this will be out of God's superabundant goodness. Hence, according to the philosophers, not every one that had the acquired moral virtues had also the heroic or divine virtues.[22] But in matters directed to the super-

---

[20] *Moral.*, II, 49 (PL 75, 592).　　[21] Q. 62, a. 1.　　[22] Aristotle. *Eth.*, VII, 1 (1145a 20)

natural last end, to which man's reason moves him according as it is, in a manner and imperfectly, informed by the theological virtues, the motion of reason does not suffice, unless it receive in addition the instigation or motion of the Holy Ghost, according to *Rom.* viii. 14, 17: *Whosoever are led by the Spirit of God, they are the sons of God . . . and if sons, heirs also*; and *Ps.* cxlii. 10: *Thy good Spirit shall lead me into the right land.* For none can receive the inheritance of that land of the blessed, except he be moved and led thither by the Holy Ghost. Therefore, in order to reach this end, it is necessary for man to have the gift of the Holy Ghost.

Reply Obj. 1. The gifts surpass the ordinary perfection of the virtues, not as regards the kind of works (this is the way in which the counsels surpass the commandments), but as regards the manner of working, according as man is moved by a higher principle.

Reply Obj. 2. By the theological and moral virtues man is not so perfected in relation to his last end as not to stand in continual need of being moved by the yet higher instigation of the Holy Ghost, for the reason already given.

Reply Obj. 3. Whether we consider human reason as perfected in its natural perfection, or as perfected by the theological virtues, it does not know all things, nor are all things possible to it. Consequently, it is unable under all circumstances to avoid folly and other like things mentioned in the objection. God, however, to Whose knowledge and power all things are subject, by His motion safeguards us from all folly, ignorance, dullness of mind and hardness of heart, and the rest. Consequently, the gifts of the Holy Ghost, which make us amenable to His instigation, are said to be given as remedies to these defects.

Third Article

WHETHER THE GIFTS OF THE HOLY GHOST ARE HABITS?

We proceed thus to the Third Article:—

Objection 1. It would seem that the gifts of the Holy Ghost are not habits. For a habit is a quality abiding in man, being defined as *a quality difficult to remove,* as is stated in the *Categories*.[23] Now it is proper to Christ that the gifts of the Holy Ghost rest in Him, as is stated in *Isa.* xi. 2, 3. Moreover, it is written (*Jo.* i. 33): *He upon Whom thou shalt see the Spirit descending and remaining upon Him, He it is that baptizeth;* on which words Gregory comments as follows: *The Holy Ghost comes upon all the faithful, but, in a singular way, He dwells always in the Mediator alone*.[24] Therefore the gifts of the Holy Ghost are not habits.

Obj. 2. Further, the gifts of the Holy Ghost perfect man according as he is moved by the Spirit of God, as we have stated above. But in so far as

---

[23] Aristotle, *Cat.*, VIII (8b 30).   [24] *Moral.*, II, 56 (PL 75, 598).

man is moved by the Spirit of God, he is somewhat like an instrument in His regard. Now to be perfected by a habit is befitting, not an instrument, but a principal agent. Therefore the gifts of the Holy Ghost are not habits.

Obj. 3. Further, as the gifts of the Holy Ghost are due to divine inspiration, so is the gift of prophecy. Now prophecy is not a habit, for *the spirit of prophecy does not always reside in the prophets,* as Gregory states.[25] Neither, therefore, are the gifts of the Holy Ghost habits.

On the contrary, Our Lord, in speaking of the Holy Ghost, said to His disciples (*Jo.* xiv. 17): *He shall abide with you, and shall be in you.* Now the Holy Ghost is not in men without His gifts. Therefore His gifts abide in men. Therefore they are not merely acts or passions, but abiding habits.

I answer that, As was stated above, the gifts are certain perfections of man by which he becomes amenable to the instigation of the Holy Ghost. Now it is evident from what has been already said that the moral virtues perfect the appetitive power according as it partakes somewhat of the reason, in so far, namely, as it has a natural aptitude to be moved by the command of reason.[26] Accordingly, the gifts of the Holy Ghost are related to man in his relation to the Holy Ghost as the moral virtues are related to the appetitive power in its relation to reason. Now the moral virtues are certain habits by which the powers of appetite are disposed to obey reason promptly. Therefore the gifts of the Holy Ghost are habits by which man is perfected to obey readily the Holy Ghost.

Reply Obj. 1. Gregory solves this objection by saying that *by those gifts without which one cannot obtain life, the Holy Ghost ever abides in all the elect, but not by His other gifts.*[27] Now the seven gifts are necessary for salvation, as we have stated above. Therefore, with regard to them, the Holy Ghost always abides in the saints.

Reply Obj. 2. This argument holds in the case of an instrument which has no power of action, but only of being acted upon. But man is not an instrument of that kind; for he is so acted upon by the Holy Ghost, that he also acts himself, in so far as he has free choice. Therefore he needs a habit.

Reply Obj. 3. Prophecy is one of those gifts which are for the manifestation of the Holy Ghost, not for the necessity of salvation. Hence the comparison fails.

Fourth Article

WHETHER THE SEVEN GIFTS OF THE HOLY GHOST ARE SUITABLY ENUMERATED?

We proceed thus to the Fourth Article:—

Objection 1. It would seem that the seven gifts of the Holy Ghost are unsuitably enumerated. For in that enumeration four are set down cor-

---

[25] *In Ezech.,* hom. 1 (PL 76, 788).   [26] Q. 58, a. 2.   *Moral.,* II, 56 (PL 75, 598).

responding to the intellectual virtues, viz., wisdom, understanding, science and counsel, which corresponds to prudence; whereas nothing is set down corresponding to art, which is the fifth intellectual virtue. Moreover, something is included corresponding to justice, viz., piety, and something corresponding to fortitude, viz., the gift of fortitude; while there is nothing to correspond to temperance. Therefore the gifts are enumerated insufficiently.

Obj. 2. Further, piety is a part of justice. But no part of fortitude is assigned to correspond thereto, but fortitude itself. Therefore justice itself, and not piety, ought to have been set down.

Obj. 3. Further, the theological virtues, more than any, direct us to God. Since, then, the gifts perfect man according as he is moved by God, it seems that some gifts, corresponding to the theological virtues, should have been included.

Obj. 4. Further, just as God is an object of fear, so is He of love, of hope, and of joy. Now love, hope and joy are passions co-divided against fear. Therefore, just as fear is set down as a gift, so ought the other three.

Obj. 5. Further, wisdom is added in order to direct understanding; counsel, to direct fortitude; science, to direct piety. Therefore, some gift should have been added for the purpose of directing fear. Therefore the seven gifts of the Holy Ghost are unsuitably enumerated.

On the contrary stands the authority of Holy Scripture (*Isa.* xi. 2, 3).

I answer that, As we have stated above, the gifts are habits perfecting man so that he be ready to follow the instigations of the Holy Ghost, even as the moral virtues perfect the appetitive powers so that they obey the reason. Now just as it is natural for the appetitive powers to be moved by the command of reason, so it is natural for all the powers in man to be moved by the instigation of God, as by a superior power. Therefore whatever powers in man can be the principles of human actions, can also be the subjects of gifts, even as they are of virtues; and such powers are the reason and appetite.

Now the reason is speculative and practical, and in both we find the apprehension of truth, which pertains to the discovery of truth and to the judgment concerning the truth. Accordingly, for the apprehension of truth, the speculative reason is perfected by *understanding*; the practical reason, by *counsel*. In order to judge rightly, furthermore, the speculative reason is perfected by *wisdom*; the practical reason by *science*.—The appetitive power, in matters touching a man's relations to another, is perfected by *piety*; in matters touching himself, it is perfected by *fortitude* against the fear of dangers, and against inordinate lust for pleasures, by *fear,* according to *Prov.* xv. 27: *By the fear of the Lord every one declineth from evil,* and *Ps.* cxviii. 120: *Pierce Thou my flesh with Thy fear: for I am afraid of Thy judgments.*—Hence it is clear that these gifts extend to all those things to which both the intellectual and moral virtues extend.

Reply Obj. 1. The gifts of the Holy Ghost perfect man in matters concerning a good life, whereas art is not directed to such matters, but to external things that can be made, since art is the right reason, not about things to be done, but about things to be made.[28] However, we may also say that, as regards the infusion of the gifts, art is on the part of the Holy Ghost, Who is the principal mover, and not on the part of men, who are His organs when He moves them. The gift of fear corresponds, in a manner, to temperance; for just as it belongs to temperance, properly speaking, to restrain man from evil pleasures for the sake of the good appointed by reason, so does it belong to the gift of fear to withdraw man from evil pleasures through fear of God.

Reply Obj. 2. Justice is so called from the rectitude of the reason, and so it is more suitably called a virtue than a gift. But the name of piety denotes the reverence which we give to our father and to our country. And since God is the Father of all, the worship of God is also called piety, as Augustine observes.[29] Therefore the gift whereby a man, through reverence for God, works good to all is fittingly called piety.

Reply Obj. 3. The soul of man is not moved by the Holy Ghost unless in some way it be united to Him; even as the instrument is not moved by the craftsman unless there be contact or some other kind of union between them. Now the primal union of man with God is by faith, hope and charity, and, consequently, these virtues are presupposed to the gifts, as being their roots. Therefore all the gifts correspond to these three virtues, as being derived from them.

Reply Obj. 4. Love, hope and joy have good for their object. Now God is the highest good. Therefore the names of these passions are transferred to the theological virtues which unite man to God. On the other hand, the object of fear is evil, which can in no way apply to God. Hence fear does not denote union with God, but rather withdrawal from certain things through reverence for God. Hence it does not give its name to a theological virtue, but to a gift, which withdraws us from evil for higher motives than moral virtue does.

Reply Obj. 5. Wisdom directs both the intellect and the affections of man. Hence two gifts are set down as corresponding to wisdom as their directing principle: on the part of the intellect, the gift of understanding; on the part of the affections, the gift of fear. For the principal reason for fearing God is taken from a consideration of the divine excellence, with which wisdom is concerned.

---

[28] Aristotle, *Eth.*, VI, 4 (1140a 10; a 17).   [29] *De Civit. Dei*, X, 1 (PL 41, 279).

Fifth Article

WHETHER THE GIFTS OF THE HOLY GHOST ARE CONNECTED?

We proceed thus to the Fifth Article:—

Objection 1. It would seem that the gifts are not connected, for the Apostle says (*1 Cor.* xii. 8): *To one . . . by the Spirit, is given the word of wisdom, and to another, the word of knowledge [science], according to the same Spirit.* Now wisdom and science are reckoned among the gifts of the Holy Ghost. Therefore the gifts of the Holy Ghost are given to diverse men, and are not connected together in the same man.

Obj. 2. Further, Augustine says that *many of the faithful have not science, though they have faith.*[30] But some of the gifts, at least the gift of fear, accompany faith. Therefore it seems that the gifts are not necessarily connected together in one and the same man.

Obj. 3. Further, Gregory says that wisdom *is of small account if it lack understanding, and understanding is wholly useless if it be not based upon wisdom. . . . Counsel is worthless, when the strength of fortitude is lacking thereto, . . . and fortitude is very weak if it be not supported by counsel. . . . Science is nought if it hath not the use of piety, . . . and piety is very useless if it lack the discernment of science, . . . and assuredly, unless it has these virtues with it, fear itself rises up to the doing of no good action.*[31] From this it seems that it is possible to have one gift without another. Therefore the gifts of the Holy Ghost are not connected.

On the contrary, Gregory prefaces the passage above quoted with the following remark: *It is worthy of note, in this feast of Job's sons, that by turns they feed one another.*[32] Now the sons of Job, of whom he is speaking, denote the gifts of the Holy Ghost. Therefore the gifts of the Holy Ghost are connected together by strengthening one another.

I answer that, The true answer to this question is easily gathered from what has been already set down. For it has been stated that, just as the powers of appetite are disposed by the moral virtues in relation to the governance of reason, so all the powers of the soul are disposed by the gifts to the motion of the Holy Ghost. Now the Holy Ghost dwells in us by charity, according to *Rom.* v. 5: *The charity of God is poured forth in our hearts by the Holy Ghost, Who is given to us,* even as our reason is perfected by prudence. Therefore, just as the moral virtues are united together in prudence, so the gifts of the Holy Ghost are connected together in charity; so that whoever has charity has all the gifts of the Holy Ghost, none of which can be possessed without charity.

Reply Obj. 1. Wisdom and science can be considered in one way as gratuitous graces, in so far, namely, as man so far abounds in the science of things divine and human, that he is able both to instruct the believers and

---

[30] *De Trin.,* XIV, 1 (PL 42, 1037).   [31] *Moral.,* I, 32 (PL 75, 547).   [32] *Ibid.*

confound the unbelievers. It is in this sense that the Apostle speaks, in this passage, about wisdom and science. Hence he mentions pointedly the *word* of wisdom and the *word* of science. They may be taken in another way for the gifts of the Holy Ghost; and thus wisdom and science are nothing else but perfections of the human mind, rendering it amenable to the instigation of the Holy Ghost in the knowledge of things divine and human. Consequently it is clear that these gifts are in all who are possessed of charity.

Reply Obj. 2. Augustine is speaking there of science in connection with his exposition of the passage of the Apostle quoted above. Hence he is speaking of science, in the sense already explained, as a gratuitous grace. This is clear from the context which follows: *For it is one thing to know only what a man must believe in order to gain the happy life, which is none other than eternal life; and another, to know how to impart this to godly souls, and to defend it against the ungodly, which latter the Apostle seems to have styled by the proper name of science.*[33]

Reply Obj. 3. Just as the connection of the cardinal virtues is proved in one way from the fact that one is, in a manner, perfected by another, as we have stated above,[34] so Gregory wishes to prove the connection of the gifts in the same way from the fact that one cannot be perfect without the other. Hence he had already observed that *each particular virtue is to the last degree destitute, unless one virtue lends its support to another.*[35] We are therefore not to understand that one gift can be without another, but that if understanding were without wisdom, it would not be a gift; even as temperance, without justice, would not be a virtue.

Sixth Article

WHETHER THE GIFTS OF THE HOLY GHOST REMAIN IN HEAVEN?

We proceed thus to the Sixth Article:—

Objection 1. It would seem that the gifts of the Holy Ghost do not remain in heaven. For Gregory says that by means of His sevenfold gift the *Holy Ghost instructs the mind against all temptations.*[36] Now there will be no temptations in heaven, according to *Isa.* xi. 9: *They shall not hurt, nor shall they kill in all My holy mountain.* Therefore there will be no gifts of the Holy Ghost in heaven.

Obj. 2. Further, the gifts of the Holy Ghost are habits, as was stated above. But habits are of no use where their acts are impossible. Now the acts of some gifts are not possible in heaven; for Gregory says that *understanding . . . penetrates the truths heard, . . . counsel . . . stays us from acting rashly, . . . fortitude . . . has no fear of adversity, . . .*

---

[33] *De Trin.,* XIV, 1 (PL 42, 1037). [34] Q. 65, a. 1. [35] *Moral.,* I, 32 (PL 75, 547).
[36] *Op. cit.,* II, 49 (PL 75, 592).

piety satisfies the inmost heart with deeds of mercy,[37] all of which are incompatible with the heavenly state. Therefore these gifts will not remain in the state of glory.

Obj. 3. Further, some of the gifts perfect man in the contemplative life, *e.g.*, wisdom and understanding, and some in the active life, *e.g.*, piety and fortitude. Now the active life ends with the present life, as Gregory states.[38] Therefore not all the gifts of the Holy Ghost will be in the state of glory.

On the contrary, Ambrose says: *The city of God, the heavenly Jerusalem, is not washed with the waters of an earthly river; it is the Holy Ghost, of Whose outpouring we but taste, Who, proceeding from the Fount of life, seems to flow more abundantly in those celestial spirits, a seething torrent of sevenfold heavenly virtue.*[39]

I answer that, We may speak of the gifts in two ways. First, as to their essence, and thus they will be most perfectly in heaven, as may be gathered from the passage of Ambrose just quoted. The reason for this is that the gifts of the Holy Ghost render the human mind amenable to the motion of the Holy Ghost; which will be especially realized in heaven, where God will be *all in all* (*1 Cor.* xv. 28), and man will be entirely subject to Him. Secondly, they may be considered as regards the matter about which their operations are, and thus in the present life they have an operation about things concerning which they will have no operation in the state of glory. Considered in this way, they will not remain in the state of glory; just as we have stated to be the case with regard to the cardinal virtues.[40]

Reply Obj. 1. Gregory is speaking there of the gifts according as they belong to the present state,[41] for it is thus that they afford us protection against evil temptations. But in the state of glory, where all evil will have ceased, we shall be perfected in good by the gifts of the Holy Ghost.

Reply Obj. 2. Gregory, in almost every gift, includes something that passes away with the present state, and something that remains in the future state. For he says that *wisdom strengthens the mind with the hope and certainty of eternal things,*[42] of which two hope passes, and certainty remains.—Of understanding he says *that it penetrates the truths heard, refreshing the heart and enlightening its darkness,* of which hearing passes away, since *they shall teach no more every man . . . his brother* (*Jer.* xxxi. 34); but the enlightening of the mind remains.—Of counsel he says that it *prevents us from being impetuous,* which is necessary in the present life; and also that *it makes the mind full of reason,* which is necessary even in the future state.—Of fortitude he says that it *fears not adversity,* which is necessary in the present life; and further, that it *sets before us the viands of confidence,* which remains also in the future life.—With regard to science he mentions only one thing, viz., that *she overcomes the void of ignorance,*

---

[37] *Op. cit.,* I, 32 (PL 75, 547).   [38] *Op. cit.,* VI, 37 (PL 75, 764).   [39] *De Spir. Sancto,* XVI (PL 16, 770).   [40] Q. 67, a. 1.   [41] *Moral.,* II, 49 (PL 75, 592).   [42] *Op. cit.,* I, 32 (PL 75, 547).

which refers to the present state. When, however, he adds *in the womb of the mind,* this may refer figuratively to the fullness of knowledge, which belongs to the future state.—Of piety he says that *it satisfies the inmost heart with deeds of mercy.* These words taken literally refer only to the present state, yet the close love of neighbor, signified by *the inmost heart,* belongs also to the future state, when piety will achieve, not works of mercy, but a fellowship of joy.—Of fear he says that *it oppresses the mind, lest it pride itself in present things,* which refers to the present state, and that *it strengthens it with the meat of hope for the future,* which also belongs to the present state, as regards hope, but may likewise refer to the future state, as regards being *strengthened* for things we hope for here, and obtain there.

Reply Obj. 3. This argument considers the gifts as to their matter. For the matter of the gifts will not be works of the active life; but all the gifts will have their respective acts about things pertaining to the contemplative life, which is the life of heavenly beatitude.

Seventh Article

WHETHER THE GIFTS ARE SET DOWN BY ISAIAS IN THEIR ORDER OF DIGNITY?

We proceed thus to the Seventh Article:—

Objection 1. It would seem that the gifts are not set down by Isaias in their order of dignity. For the principal gift is evidently that which, more than the others, God requires of man. Now God requires of man fear, more than the other gifts, for it is written (*Deut.* x. 12): *And now, Israel, what doth the Lord thy God require of thee, but that thou fear the Lord thy God?* and (*Malach.* i. 6): *If . . . I be a master, where is My fear?* Therefore it seems that fear, which is mentioned last, is not the lowest but the greatest of the gifts.

Obj. 2. Further, piety seems to be a universal good, since the Apostle says (*1 Tim.* iv. 8): *Piety is profitable to all things.* Now a universal good is preferable to particular goods. Therefore piety, which is given the last place but one, seems to be the most excellent gift.

Obj. 3. Further, science perfects man's judgment, while counsel pertains to inquiry. But judgment is more excellent than inquiry. Therefore science is a more excellent gift than counsel, and yet it is set down as being below it.

Obj. 4. Further, fortitude pertains to the appetitive power, while science belongs to reason. But reason is a more excellent power than the appetite. Therefore science is a more excellent gift than fortitude, and yet the latter is given precedence. Therefore the gifts are not set down in their order of dignity.

On the contrary, Augustine says: *It seems to me that the sevenfold operation of the Holy Ghost, of which Isaias speaks, agrees in degrees and expression with these* (of which we read in *Matt.* v. 3); *but there is a difference of order, for there* (viz., in *Isaias*) *the enumeration begins with the more excellent gifts, here, with the lower gifts.*[43]

I answer that, The excellence of the gifts can be measured in two ways: first, absolutely, viz., by comparison with their proper acts in so far as these proceed from their principles; secondly, relatively, viz., by comparison with their matter. If we consider the excellence of the gifts absolutely, they follow the same rule as the virtues, as to their comparison one with another; because the gifts perfect man for all the acts of the soul's powers, even as the virtues do, as we have stated above. Hence, just as the intellectual virtues have precedence over the moral virtues, and among the intellectual virtues, the contemplative are preferable to the active, viz., wisdom, understanding and science to prudence and art (yet so that wisdom stands before understanding, and understanding before science, and prudence and synesis before eubulia), so also among the gifts, wisdom, understanding, science and counsel are more excellent than piety, fortitude and fear; and among the latter, piety excels fortitude, and fortitude, fear, even as justice surpasses fortitude, and fortitude, temperance.—But in regard to their matter, fortitude and counsel precede science and piety, because fortitude and counsel are concerned with difficult matters, whereas piety and science regard ordinary matters.—Consequently, the excellence of the gifts corresponds with the order in which they are enumerated; but, so far as wisdom and understanding are given the preference to the others, their excellence is considered absolutely, while, so far as counsel and fortitude are preferred to science and piety, it is considered with regard to their matter.

Reply Obj. 1. Fear is chiefly required as being in a way the foundation of the perfection of the other gifts, for *the fear of the Lord is the beginning of wisdom* (*Ps.* cx. 10; *Ecclus.* i. 16), and not as though it were more excellent than the others. Because, in the order of generation, man departs from evil because of fear (*Prov.* xvi. 16) before doing good works (which result from the other gifts).

Reply Obj. 2. In the words quoted from the Apostle, piety is not compared with all God's gifts, but only with *bodily exercise,* of which he had said that it *is profitable to little.*

Reply Obj. 3. Although science stands before counsel by reason of its judgment, yet counsel is more excellent by reason of its matter; for counsel is concerned only with matters of difficulty,[44] whereas the judgment of science embraces all matters.

Reply Obj. 4. The directive gifts which pertain to the reason are more excellent than the executive gifts, if we consider them in relation to their acts in so far as these proceed from their powers; for reason transcends the appetite as a rule transcends the thing ruled. But on the part of the matter,

---

[43] *De Serm. Dom.,* I, 4 (PL 34, 1234).   [44] Aristotle, *Eth.,* III, 3 (1112b 9).

counsel is united to fortitude as the directive power to the executive, and so is science united to piety; because counsel and fortitude are concerned with matters of difficulty, while science and piety are concerned with ordinary matters. Hence counsel and fortitude, by reason of their matter, are given the preference to science and piety.

Eighth Article

WHETHER THE VIRTUES ARE MORE EXCELLENT THAN THE GIFTS?

We proceed thus to the Eighth Article:—

Objection 1. It would seem that the virtues are more excellent than the gifts. For Augustine says while speaking of charity: *No gift of God is more excellent than this. It is this alone which divides the children of the eternal kingdom from the children of eternal damnation. Other gifts are bestowed by the Holy Ghost, but, without charity, they avail nothing.*[45] But charity is a virtue. Therefore a virtue is more excellent than the gifts of the Holy Ghost.

Obj. 2. Further, that which is naturally prior seems to be more excellent. Now the virtues precede the gifts of the Holy Ghost, for Gregory says that *the gift of the Holy Ghost, in the mind it works on, forms first of all justice, prudence, fortitude, temperance . . . and doth afterwards give it a temper in the seven virtues* (viz., the gifts), *so as against folly to bestow wisdom; against dullness, understanding; against rashness, counsel; against fear, fortitude; against ignorance, science; against hardness of heart, piety; against pride, fear.*[46] Therefore the virtues are more excellent than the gifts.

Obj. 3. Further, Augustine says that *the virtues cannot be used to evil purpose.*[47] But it is possible to make evil use of the gifts, for Gregory says: *We offer up the sacrifice of prayer . . . lest wisdom may make us proud; or understanding, while it runs nimbly, deviate from the right path; or counsel, while it multiplies itself, grow into confusion; that fortitude, while it gives confidence, may not make us rash; lest science, while it knows and yet loves not, may swell the mind; lest piety, while it swerves from the right line, may become distorted; and lest fear, while it is unduly alarmed, may plunge us into the pit of despair.*[48] Therefore the virtues are more excellent than the gifts of the Holy Ghost.

On the contrary, The gifts are bestowed to assist the virtues and to remedy certain defects, as is shown in the passage quoted, so that they seem to accomplish what the virtues cannot. Therefore the gifts are more excellent than the virtues.

I answer that, As was shown above, there are three kinds of virtues; for

[45] *De Trin.,* XV, 18 (PL 42, 1082).   [46] *Moral.,* II, 49 (PL 75, 592).   [47] *De Lib. Arb.,* II, 18; 19 (PL 32, 1267; 1268).   [48] *Moral.,* I, 35 (PL 75, 549).

some are theological, some intellectual, and some moral.[49] The theological virtues are those whereby man's mind is united to God; the intellectual virtues are those whereby reason itself is perfected; and the moral virtues are those which perfect the powers of appetite for obedience to the reason. On the other hand, the gifts of the Holy Ghost dispose all the powers of the soul to be amenable to the divine motion.

Accordingly, the gifts seem to be compared to the theological virtues, by which man is united to the Holy Ghost his Mover, in the same way as the moral virtues are compared to the intellectual virtues, which perfect the reason, the moving principle of the moral virtues. Therefore, just as the intellectual virtues are more excellent than the moral virtues and control them, so the theological virtues are more excellent than the gifts of the Holy Ghost and regulate them. Hence Gregory says that *the seven sons, i.e.,* the seven gifts, *never attain the perfection of the number ten, unless all that they do be done in faith, hope, and charity.*[50]

But if we compare the gifts to the other virtues, intellectual and moral, then the gifts have precedence over the virtues. Because the gifts perfect the soul's powers in relation to the Holy Ghost their Mover, whereas the virtues perfect either the reason itself, or the other powers in relation to reason. Now it is evident that the more exalted the mover, the more excellent the disposition whereby the thing moved requires to be disposed. Therefore the gifts are more perfect than the virtues.

Reply Obj. 1. Charity is a theological virtue, and such we grant to be more perfect than the gifts.

Reply Obj. 2. There are two ways in which one thing precedes another. One is according to the order of perfection and dignity, as the love of God precedes the love of neighbor; and in this way the gifts precede the intellectual and moral virtues, but are less perfect than the theological virtues. The other is the order of generation or disposition, and thus the love of one's neighbor precedes the love of God, as regards the act. And in this way, the moral and intellectual virtues precede the gifts, since man, through being well ordered in relation to his own reason, is disposed to be rightly ordered in relation to God.

Reply Obj. 3. Wisdom, understanding and the like are gifts of the Holy Ghost, according as they are quickened by charity, which *dealeth not perversely* (*1 Cor.* xiii. 4). Consequently wisdom, understanding and the like cannot be used to evil purpose, in so far as they are gifts of the Holy Ghost. But, lest they depart from the perfection of charity, they assist one another. This is what Gregory means to say.

[49] Q. 58, a. 3; q. 62, a. 1.   [50] *Moral.,* I, 27 (PL 75, 544).

Question LXIX

ON THE BEATITUDES

(*In Four Articles*)

WE must now consider the beatitudes, under which head there are four points of inquiry: (1) Whether the beatitudes differ from the gifts and virtues? (2) The rewards of the beatitudes: whether they belong to this life? (3) The number of the beatitudes. (4) The fittingness of the rewards ascribed to the beatitudes.

First Article

WHETHER THE BEATITUDES DIFFER FROM THE VIRTUES AND GIFTS?

We thus proceed to the First Article:—

Objection 1. It would seem that the beatitudes do not differ from the virtues and gifts. For Augustine assigns the beatitudes recited by Matthew (v. 3, *seqq.*) to the gifts of the Holy Ghost;[1] and Ambrose in his commentary on *Luke* vi. 20, *seqq.*, ascribes the beatitudes mentioned there to the four cardinal virtues.[2] Therefore the beatitudes do not differ from the virtues and gifts.

Obj. 2. Further, there are but two rules of the human will, namely, the reason and the eternal law, as was stated above.[3] Now the virtues perfect man in relation to reason, while the gifts perfect him in relation to the eternal law of the Holy Ghost, as is clear from what has been said.[4] Therefore there cannot be anything else pertaining to the rectitude of the human will besides the virtues and gifts. Therefore the beatitudes do not differ from them.

Obj. 3. Further, among the beatitudes are included meekness, justice and mercy, which are said to be virtues. Therefore the beatitudes do not differ from the virtues and gifts.

On the contrary, Certain things are included among the beatitudes that are neither virtues nor gifts, *e.g.,* poverty, mourning and peace. Therefore the beatitudes differ from the virtues and gifts.

I answer that, As we have stated above, happiness is the last end of human life.[5] Now one is said to possess the end already when one hopes to possess it; and therefore the Philosopher says that *children are said to be*

---

[1] *De Serm. Dom.,* I, 4 (PL 34, 1234).   [2] *In Luc.,* V, super VI, 20 (PL 15, 1734).
[3] Q. 19, a. 3 and 4; q. 21, a. 1.   [4] Q. 68, a. 1 and 3.   [5] Q. 2, a. 7; q. 3, a. 1.

happy because they are full of hope;[6] and the Apostle says (*Rom.* viii. 24): *We are saved by hope.* Again, we hope to obtain an end because we are suitably moved towards that end and approach thereto; and this takes place through some action. Now a man is moved towards the end which is happiness, and approaches to it by works of virtue, and above all by the works of the gifts, if we speak of eternal happiness, for which our reason is not sufficient, since we need to be moved by the Holy Ghost, and to be perfected with His gifts that we may obey and follow him. Consequently, the beatitudes differ from the virtues and gifts, not as habit from habit, but as an act from a habit.

Reply Obj. 1. Augustine and Ambrose assign the beatitudes to the gifts and virtues in the way that acts are ascribed to habits. But the gifts are more excellent than the cardinal virtues, as we have stated above.[7] Therefore Ambrose, in explaining the beatitudes propounded to the throng, assigns them to the cardinal virtues, whereas Augustine, who is explaining the beatitudes delivered to the disciples on the mountain, and so to those who were more perfect, ascribes them to the gifts of the Holy Ghost.

Reply Obj. 2. This argument proves that no other habits, besides the virtues and gifts, rectify human life.

Reply Obj. 3. Meekness is to be taken as denoting the act of meekness; and the same applies to justice and mercy. And though these might seem to be virtues, they are nevertheless ascribed to the gifts, because the gifts perfect man in all matters wherein the virtues perfect him, as was stated above.[8]

Second Article

WHETHER THE REWARDS ASSIGNED TO THE BEATITUDES BELONG TO THIS LIFE?

We proceed thus to the Second Article:—

Objection 1. It would seem that the rewards assigned to the beatitudes do not belong to this life. Because some are said to be happy because they hope for a reward, as we have stated above. Now the object of hope is future happiness. Therefore these rewards belong to the life to come.

Obj. 2. Further, certain punishments are set down in opposition to the beatitudes in *Luke* vi. 25, where we read: *Woe to you that are filled, for you shall hunger. Woe to you that now laugh, for you shall mourn and weep.* Now these punishments do not belong to this life, because frequently men are not punished in this life, according to *Job* xxi. 13: *They spend their days in wealth.* Therefore neither do the rewards of the beatitudes belong to this life.

Obj. 3. Further, the kingdom of heaven which is set down as the reward

[6] *Eth.,* I, 9 (1100a 3).   [7] Q. 68, a. 8.   [8] Q. 68, a. 2.

of poverty is the happiness of heaven, as Augustine says.[9] Again, abundant fullness is not to be had save in the life to come, according to *Ps.* xvi. 15: *I shall be filled when Thy glory shall appear.*—Again, it is only in the future life that we shall see God, and that our divine sonship will be made manifest, according to *1 John* iii. 2: *We are now the sons of God; and it hath not yet appeared what we shall be. We know that, when He shall appear, we shall be like to Him, because we shall see Him as He is.* Therefore these rewards belong to the future life.

On the contrary, Augustine says: *These promises can be fulfilled in this life, as we believe them to have been fulfilled in the apostles. For no words can express that complete change into the likeness even of an angel, which is promised to us after this life.*[10]

I answer that, The interpreters of Holy Scripture are not agreed in speaking of these rewards. For some hold, with Ambrose, that all these rewards refer to the life to come;[11] while Augustine holds them to refer to the present life;[12] and Chrysostom in his homilies says that some refer to the future life, and some to the present life.[13]

In order to make the matter clear we must note that hope of future happiness may be in us for two reasons. First, by reason of our having a preparation for, or a disposition to, future happiness, and this is by way of merit; secondly, by a kind of imperfect inchoation of future happiness in holy men, even in this life. For it is one thing to hope that the tree will bear fruit, when the leaves begin to appear, and another, when we see the first signs of the fruit.

Accordingly, those things which are set down as merits in the beatitudes are a kind of preparation for, or disposition to, happiness, either perfect or inchoate; while those that are assigned as rewards may be either perfect happiness itself, and thus refer to the future life, or some beginning of happiness, such as is found in those who have attained perfection, in which case they refer to the present life. For when a man begins to make progress in the acts of the virtues and the gifts, it is to be hoped that he will arrive at perfection, both as a wayfarer and as a citizen of the heavenly kingdom.

Reply Obj. 1. Hope regards future happiness as the last end; and yet it may also regard the assistance of grace as that which leads to the end, according to *Ps.* xxvii. 7: *In Him hath my heart hoped, and I have been helped.*

Reply Obj. 2. Although the wicked sometimes do not undergo temporal punishment in this life, yet they suffer spiritual punishment. Hence Augustine says: *Thou hast decreed, and it is so, Lord, that the disordered soul should be its own punishment.*[14] The Philosopher, too, says of the wicked

---

[9] *De Civit. Dei*, XVII, 7 (PL 41, 539); *De Serm. Dom.*, I, 1 (PL 34, 1231).   [10] *De Serm. Dom.*, I, 4 (PL 34, 1235).   [11] *In Luc.*, V, super VI, 20 (PL 15, 1738).   [12] *De Serm. Dom.*, I, 4 (PL 34, 1234).   [13] *In Matt.*, hom. XV (PG 57, 223).   [14] *Confess.*, I, 12 (PL 32, 670).

that *their soul is divided against itself,* . . . *one part pulls this way, another that;*[15] and afterwards he concludes, saying: *If wickedness makes a man so miserable, he should strain every nerve to avoid vice.*[16]—In like manner, although, contrariwise, the good sometimes do not receive material rewards in this life, yet they never lack spiritual rewards, even in this life, according to *Matt.* xix. 29, and *Mark* x. 30: *Ye shall receive a hundred times as much* even *in this time.*

Reply Obj. 3. All these rewards will be fully consummated in the life to come; but meanwhile they are, in a manner, begun, even in this life. For the *kingdom of heaven,* as Augustine says, can denote the beginning of perfect wisdom, in so far as *the spirit* begins to reign in men.[17]—The *possession* of the land denotes the well-ordered affections of the soul that rests, by its desire, on the solid foundation of the eternal inheritance, signified by *the land.*—They are *comforted* in this life, by receiving the Holy Ghost, Who is called the *Paraclete, i.e.,* the Comforter.[18]—They *have their fill,* even in this life, of that food of which Our Lord said (*Jo.* iv. 34): *My meat is to do the will of Him that sent Me.*—Again, in this life, men *obtain* God's *mercy.*—Again, when the eye is cleansed by the gift of understanding, we can, so to speak, *see God.*—Likewise, in this life, those who are the *peacemakers* of their own movements, approach to a likeness to God, and are called *the children of God.*—Nevertheless, these things will be more perfectly fulfilled in heaven.

Third Article

WHETHER THE BEATITUDES ARE SUITABLY ENUMERATED?

We proceed thus to the Third Article:—

Objection 1. It would seem that the beatitudes are unsuitably enumerated. For the beatitudes are assigned to the gifts, as has been stated above. Now some of the gifts, viz., wisdom and understanding, belong to the contemplative life; and yet no beatitude is assigned to the act of contemplation, for all are assigned to matters connected with the active life. Therefore the beatitudes are insufficiently enumerated.

Obj. 2. Further, not only do the executive gifts belong to the active life, but also some of the directive gifts, *e.g.,* science and counsel; and yet none of the beatitudes seems to be directly connected with the acts of science or counsel. Therefore the beatitudes are insufficiently indicated.

Obj. 3. Further, among the executive gifts connected with the active life, fear is said to be connected with poverty, while piety seems to correspond to the beatitude of mercy; and yet nothing is included directly connected with justice. Therefore the beatitudes are insufficiently enumerated.

Obj. 4. Further, many other beatitudes are mentioned in Holy Scripture.

---

[15] *Eth.,* IX, 4 (1166b 19).   [16] *Ibid.* (1166b 27).   [17] *De Serm. Dom.,* I, 4 (PL 34, 1235).   [18] Cf. St. Jerome, *In Isaiam,* XI, super XL, 1 (PL 24, 414).

Thus, it is written (*Job* v. 17): *Blessed is the man whom God correcteth*; and (*Ps.* i. 1): *Blessed is the man who hath not walked in the counsel of the ungodly*; and (*Prov.* iii. 13): *Blessed is the man that findeth wisdom.* Therefore the beatitudes are insufficiently enumerated.

Obj. 5. *On the other hand,* it seems that too many are mentioned. For there are seven gifts of the Holy Ghost, whereas eight beatitudes are indicated.

Obj. 6. Further, only four beatitudes are indicated in the sixth chapter of *Luke* (vi. 20). Therefore the seven or eight mentioned in *Matt.* (v. 3) are too many.

I answer that, These beatitudes are most suitably enumerated. To make this evident, it must be observed that beatitude has been held to consist in one of three things;[19] for some have ascribed it to a sensual life, some, to an active life, and some, to a contemplative life. Now these three kinds of happiness stand in different relations to future beatitude, by hoping for which we are said to be happy. For sensual happiness, being false and contrary to reason, is an obstacle to future beatitude, while the happiness of the active life is dispositive towards future beatitude; and contemplative happiness, if perfect, is the very essence of future beatitude, and, if imperfect, is a beginning thereof.

And so Our Lord placed, in the beginning, certain beatitudes as removing the obstacle of sensual happiness. For a life of pleasure consists of two things. First, in the affluence of external goods, whether riches or honors. From these a man is withdrawn by virtue, so that he uses them in moderation; and by a gift, in a more excellent way, so that he despises them altogether. Hence the first beatitude is: *Blessed are the poor in spirit,* which may refer either to the contempt of riches or to the contempt of honors, which results from humility. Secondly, the sensual life consists in following the bent of one's passions, whether irascible or concupiscible. From following the irascible passions, a man is withdrawn by a virtue, so that they are kept within the bounds appointed by the rule of reason; and by a gift, in a more excellent manner, so that, according to God's will, a man is altogether undisturbed by them. Hence the second beatitude is: *Blessed are the meek.* From following the concupiscible passions, a man is withdrawn by virtue, so that man uses these passions in moderation; and by a gift, so that, if necessary, he casts them aside altogether—nay more, so that, if need be, he makes a deliberate choice of sorrow. Hence the third beatitude is: *Blessed are they that mourn.*

The active life, on the other hand, consists chiefly in man's relations with his neighbor, either by way of duty or by way of spontaneous gratuity. To the former we are disposed by virtue, so that we do not refuse to do our duty to our neighbor, which pertains to justice; and by a gift, so that we

[19] Cf. Aristotle, *Eth.,* I, 5 (1095b 16).

do the same much more heartily, by accomplishing works of justice with an ardent desire, even as a hungry and thirsty man desires food and drink with eager appetite. Hence the fourth beatitude is: *Blessed are they that hunger and thirst after justice.* With regard to spontaneous favors, we are perfected by a virtue, so that we give where reason dictates we should give, *e.g.,* to our friends or others united to us, which pertains to the virtue of liberality; and by a gift, so that, through reverence for God, we consider only the needs of those on whom we bestow our gratuitous bounty. Hence it is written (*Luke* xiv. 12, 13): *When thou makest a dinner or supper, call not thy friends, nor thy brethren,* etc. . . . *but* . . . *call the poor, the maimed,* etc.; which, properly, is to have mercy. Hence the fifth beatitude is: *Blessed are the merciful.*

Those things which concern the contemplative life are either final beatitude itself, or some beginning thereof; and therefore they are included in the beatitudes, not as merits, but as rewards. Yet the effects of the active life, which dispose man for the contemplative life, are included as merits in the beatitudes. Now the effect of the active life, as regards those virtues and gifts by which man is perfected in himself, is the cleansing of man's heart, so that it is not defiled by the passions. Hence the sixth beatitude is: *Blessed are the clean of heart.* But as regards the virtues and gifts by which man is perfected in relation to his neighbor, the effect of the active life is peace, according to *Isaias* xxxii. 17: *The work of justice shall be peace.* Hence the seventh beatitude is: *Blessed are the peacemakers.*

Reply Obj. 1. The acts of the gifts which belong to the active life are indicated in the merits themselves, but the acts of the gifts pertaining to the contemplative life are indicated in the rewards, for the reason given above. For to *see God* corresponds to the gift of understanding; and to be like God, by being adopted *children of God,* corresponds to the gift of wisdom.

Reply Obj. 2. In things pertaining to the active life, knowledge is not sought for its own sake, but for the sake of operation, as also the Philosopher states.[20] Therefore, since beatitude implies something ultimate, the beatitudes do not include the acts of those gifts which direct man in the active life—such acts, namely, as are elicited by those gifts, as, *e.g.,* to counsel is the act of counsel, and to judge, the act of science; but, on the other hand, they include those operative acts of which the gifts have the direction, as, *e.g.,* mourning in respect of science, and mercy in respect of counsel.

Reply Obj. 3. In applying the beatitudes to the gifts, we may consider two things. One is likeness of matter. In this way, all the first five beatitudes may be assigned to science and counsel as to their directing principles. But they must be distributed among the executive gifts, so that, namely, hunger and thirst for justice, and mercy, too, correspond to piety, which perfects

---

[20] *Eth.,* II, 2 (1103b 27).

man in his relations to others; meekness to fortitude, for Ambrose says on *Luke* vi. 22: *It is the business of fortitude to conquer anger, and to curb indignation*,[21] since fortitude is concerned with the irascible passions; poverty and mourning to the gift of fear, whereby man withdraws from the lusts and pleasures of the world.

Secondly, we may consider the motives of the beatitudes, and, in this way, some of them will have to be assigned differently in some respects. Because the principal motive for meekness is reverence for God, which belongs to piety. The chief motive for mourning is science, whereby man knows his failings and those of worldly things, according to *Eccles.* i. 18: *He that addeth knowledge* [*scientia*], *addeth also sorrow* [Vulg., *labor*]. The principal motive for hungering after the works of justice is fortitude of the soul; and the chief motive for being merciful is God's counsel, according to *Dan.* iv. 24: *Let my counsel be acceptable to the king; and redeem thou thy sins with alms, and thy iniquities with works of mercy to the poor.*—It is thus that Augustine assigns them.[22]

Reply Obj. 4. All the beatitudes mentioned in Holy Scripture must be reduced to these, either as to merits or as to rewards; because they must all belong either to the active life or to the contemplative life. Accordingly, when we read, *Blessed is the man whom the Lord correcteth,* we must refer this to the beatitude of mourning; when we read, *Blessed is the man that hath not walked in the counsel of the ungodly,* we must refer it to cleanness of the heart; and when we read, *Blessed is the man that findeth wisdom,* this must be referred to the reward of the seventh beatitude. The same applies to all others that can be adduced.

Reply Obj. 5. The eighth beatitude is a confirmation and declaration of all those that precede. For, from the very fact that a man is confirmed in poverty of spirit, meekness and the rest, it follows that no persecution will induce him to renounce them. Hence the eighth beatitude corresponds, in a way, to all the preceding seven.

Reply Obj. 6. Luke relates Our Lord's sermon as addressed to the multitude (vi. 17). Hence he sets down the beatitudes according to the capacity of the multitude, who know no other happiness than pleasure, temporal and earthly. Therefore by these four beatitudes Our Lord excludes four things which seem to belong to such happiness. The first of these is abundance of external goods, which he sets aside by saying: *Blessed are ye poor.*—The second is that man be well off as to his body, in food and drink and so forth, and this he excludes by saying in the second place: *Blessed are ye that hunger.* The third is that it should be well with man as to joyfulness of heart, and this he puts aside by saying: *Blessed are ye that weep now.* The fourth is the outward favor of man, and this he excludes, saying, fourthly: *Blessed shall you be, when men shall hate you.*

---

[21] *In Luc.,* V, super VI, 22 (PL 15, 1739).   [22] *De Serm. Dom.,* I, 4 (PL 34, 1234).

And, as Ambrose says on *Luke* vi. 20, *poverty corresponds to temperance, which is unmoved by delights; hunger, to justice, since he who hungers is compassionate and, through compassion, gives; mourning, to prudence, which deplores perishable things; endurance of men's hatred belongs to fortitude.*[23]

Fourth Article

WHETHER THE REWARDS OF THE BEATITUDES ARE SUITABLY ENUMERATED?

We proceed thus to the Fourth Article:—

Objection 1. It would seem that the rewards of the beatitudes are unsuitably enumerated. For the kingdom of heaven, which is eternal life, contains all good things. Therefore, once given the kingdom of heaven, no other rewards should be mentioned.

Obj. 2. Further, the kingdom of heaven is assigned as the reward both of the first and of the eighth beatitude. Therefore, on the same ground, it should have been assigned to all.

Obj. 3. Further, the beatitudes are arranged in an ascending order, as Augustine remarks;[24] whereas the rewards seem to be placed in a descending order, since to *possess the land* is less than to possess *the kingdom of heaven*. Therefore these rewards are unsuitably enumerated.

On the contrary stands the authority of Our Lord Who propounded these rewards (*Matt.* v. 3; *Luke* vi. 20).

I answer that, These rewards are most suitably assigned, considering the nature of the beatitudes in relation to the three kinds of happiness posited above. For the first three beatitudes concerned the withdrawal of man from those things in which sensual happiness consists; which happiness man desires by seeking the object of his natural desire, not where he should seek it, viz., in God, but in temporal and perishable things. Therefore the rewards of the first three beatitudes correspond to the things which some men seek to find in earthly happiness. For men seek in external things, viz., in riches and honors, a certain excellence and abundance, both of which are contained in the kingdom of heaven, whereby man attains to excellence and abundance of good things in God. Hence Our Lord promised the kingdom of heaven to the poor in spirit. Again, cruel and pitiless men seek by wrangling and fighting to destroy their enemies so as to gain security for themselves. Hence Our Lord promised the meek a secure and peaceful possession of the land of the living, whereby the solid reality of eternal goods is denoted. Again, men seek consolation for the toils of the present life in the lusts and pleasures of the world. Hence Our Lord promises comfort to those that mourn.

Two other beatitudes belong to the works of active happiness, which are

[23] *In Luc.*, V, super VI, 20 (PL 15, 1739).   [24] *De Serm. Dom.*, I, 4 (PL 34, 1234).

the works of virtues directing man in his relations to his neighbor; from which operations some men withdraw through inordinate love of their own good. Hence Our Lord assigns to these beatitudes rewards in correspondence with the motives for which men recede from them. For there are some who recede from acts of justice, and instead of rendering what is due, lay hands on what is not theirs, that they may abound in temporal goods. Therefore Our Lord promised those who hunger after justice that they shall have their fill. Some, again, recede from works of mercy, lest they be busied with other people's misery. Hence Our Lord promised the merciful that they should obtain mercy, by which they shall be delivered from all misery.

The last two beatitudes belong to contemplative happiness or beatitude. Hence the rewards are assigned in correspondence with the dispositions included in the merit. For cleanness of the eye disposes one to see clearly, and hence the clean of heart are promised that they shall see God.— Again, to make peace, either in oneself or among others, shows a man to be a follower of God, Who is a God of unity and peace. Hence, as a reward, he is promised the glory of the divine sonship, consisting in perfect union with God through consummate wisdom.

Reply Obj. 1. As Chrysostom says,[25] all these rewards are one in reality, viz., eternal happiness, which the human intellect cannot grasp. Hence it was necessary to describe it by means of various goods known to us, while observing their fittingness in relation to the merits to which those rewards are assigned.

Reply Obj. 2. Just as the eighth beatitude is a confirmation of all the beatitudes, so it deserves all the rewards of the beatitudes. Hence it returns to the first, that we may understand all the other rewards to be attributed consequently to it. Or else, according to Ambrose,[26] the kingdom of heaven is promised to the poor in spirit, as regards the glory of the soul; but to those who suffer persecution in their bodies, it is promised as regards the glory of the body.

Reply Obj. 3. The rewards are also arranged in ascending order. For it is more to possess the land of the heavenly kingdom than simply to have it, since we have many things without possessing them firmly and peacefully. Again, it is more to be comforted in the kingdom than to have and possess it, for there are many things the possession of which is accompanied by sorrow. Again, it is more to have one's fill than simply to be comforted, because fullness implies abundance of comfort. And mercy surpasses satiety, for thereby man receives more than he merited or was able to desire. And yet more is it to see God, even as he is a greater man who not only dines at court, but also sees the king's countenance. Lastly, the highest place in the royal palace belongs to the king's son.

[25] *In Matt.*, hom. XV (PG 57, 228).   [26] *In Luc.*, V, super VI, 20 (PL 15, 1737).

ON THE FRUITS OF THE HOLY GHOST

(*In Four Articles*)

WE must now consider the Fruits of the Holy Ghost, under which head there are four points of inquiry: (1) Whether the fruits of the Holy Ghost are acts? (2) Whether they differ from the beatitudes? (3) Of their number. (4) Of their opposition to the works of the flesh.

First Article

WHETHER THE FRUITS OF THE HOLY GHOST WHICH THE APOSTLE ENUMERATES IN THE EPISTLE TO THE GALATIANS ARE ACTS?

We proceed thus to the First Article:—

Objection 1. It would seem that the fruits of the Holy Ghost, enumerated by the Apostle (*Gal.* v. 22, 23), are not acts. For that which bears fruit should not itself be called a fruit, else we should go on indefinitely. But our actions bear fruit, for it is written (*Wis.* iii. 15): *The fruit of good labor is glorious,* and (*Jo.* iv. 36): *He that reapeth receiveth wages, and gathereth fruit unto life everlasting.* Therefore our actions are not to be called fruits.

Obj. 2. Further, as Augustine says, *we enjoy [fruimur] the things we know, when the will rests by rejoicing in them.*[1] But our will should not rest in our actions for their own sake. Therefore our actions should not be called fruits.

Obj. 3. Further, among the fruits of the Holy Ghost, the Apostle numbers certain virtues, viz., charity, meekness, faith and chastity. Now the virtues are not actions but habits, as we have stated above.[2] Therefore the fruits are not actions.

On the contrary, It is written (*Matt.* xii. 33): *By the fruit the tree is known.* That is to say, man is known by his works, as holy men explain the passage.[3] Therefore human actions themselves are called fruits.

I answer that, The name *fruit* has been transferred from the material to the spiritual. Now fruit, among material things, is the product of a plant when it comes to perfection, and has a certain sweetness. This fruit has a twofold relation, namely, to the tree that produces it, and to the man who

---

[1] *De Trin.,* X, 10 (PL 42, 981).   [2] Q. 55, a. 1.   [3] *Glossa ordin.* (V, 29B).—Cf. below, q. 73, a. 6.

gathers the fruit from the tree. Accordingly, in spiritual matters, we may take the name *fruit* in two ways: first, so that the fruit of man, who is likened to the tree, is that which he produces; secondly, so that man's fruit is what he gathers.

Yet not all that man gathers is fruit, but only that which is last and gives pleasure. For a man has both a field and a tree, and yet these are not called fruits, but that only which is last, namely, that which man intends to derive from the field and from the tree. In this sense man's fruit is his last end, which is intended for his enjoyment.

If, however, by man's fruit we understand a product of man, then human actions are called fruits. For operation is the second act of the operator, and gives pleasure if it is suitable to him. If, then, man's operation proceeds from man according to the ability of his reason, it is said to be the fruit of his reason; but if it proceeds from him according to a higher power, which is the power of the Holy Ghost, then man's operation is said to be the fruit of the Holy Ghost, as of a divine seed; for it is written (*1 John* iii. 9): *Whosoever is born of God committeth no sin, for His seed abideth in him.*

Reply Obj. 1. Since fruit is something last and final, nothing hinders one fruit bearing another fruit, even as one end is subordinate to another. And so our works, in so far as they are produced by the Holy Ghost working in us, are fruits; but, in so far as they are directed to the end which is eternal life, they should rather be called flowers. Hence it is written (*Ecclus.* xxiv. 23): *My flowers are the fruits of honor and riches.*

Reply Obj. 2. When the will is said to delight in a thing for its own sake, this may be understood in two ways. First, so that the expression *for the sake of* be taken to designate the final cause; and in this way, man delights in nothing for its own sake, except the last end. Secondly, so that it express the formal cause; and in this way a man may delight in anything that is delightful by reason of its form. Thus it is clear that a sick man delights in health for its own sake, as in an end; in a pleasant medicine, not as in an end, but as in something tasty; and in a bitter medicine, in no way for its own sake, but only for the sake of something else.—Accordingly, we must say that a man must delight in God for His own sake, as being his last end, and in virtuous deeds, not as being his end, but for the sake of their inherent goodness, which is delightful to the virtuous. Hence Ambrose says that virtuous deeds are called fruits because *they refresh those that have them, with a holy and genuine delight.*[4]

Reply Obj. 3. Sometimes the names of the virtues are applied to their actions. Thus Augustine writes: *Faith is to believe what thou seest not;*[5] and: *Charity is the movement of the soul towards loving God and neighbor.*[6] It is thus that the names of the virtues are used in reckoning the fruits.

[4] *De Parad.*, XIII (PL 14, 325).   [5] *Tract.* XL, super *Ioann.* VIII, 32 (PL 35, 1690).   [6] *De Doct. Christ.*, III, 10 (PL 34, 71).

Second Article

WHETHER THE FRUITS DIFFER FROM THE BEATITUDES?

We proceed thus to the Second Article:—

Objection 1. It would seem that the fruits do not differ from the beatitudes. For the beatitudes are assigned to the gifts, as we have stated above.[7] But the gifts perfect man in so far as he is moved by the Holy Ghost. Therefore the beatitudes themselves are the fruits of the Holy Ghost.

Obj. 2. Further, as the fruit of eternal life is to future beatitude, which is that of actual possession, so the fruits of the present life are related to the beatitudes of the present life, which are based on hope. Now the fruit of eternal life is future beatitude itself. Therefore the fruits of the present life are the beatitudes.

Obj. 3. Further, fruit is essentially something ultimate and delightful. Now this is the very nature of beatitude, as we have stated above.[8] Therefore fruit and beatitude have the same nature, and consequently should not be distinguished from one another.

On the contrary, Things divided into different species, differ from one another. But fruits and beatitudes are divided into different parts, as is clear from the way in which they are enumerated. Therefore the fruits differ from the beatitudes.

I answer that, More is required for a beatitude than for a fruit. For it is sufficient for a fruit to be something ultimate and delightful; whereas for a beatitude, it must be something perfect and excellent. Hence all the beatitudes may be called fruits, but not *vice versa*. For the fruits are any virtuous deeds in which one delights, whereas the beatitudes are none but perfect works, and which, by reason of their perfection, are assigned to the gifts rather than to the virtues, as we have already stated.[9]

Reply Obj. 1. This argument proves the beatitudes to be fruits, but not that all the fruits are beatitudes.

Reply Obj. 2. The fruit of eternal life is absolutely ultimate and perfect. Hence it differs in no way from future beatitude. On the other hand, the fruits of the present life are not absolutely ultimate and perfect; and therefore not all the fruits are beatitudes.

Reply Obj. 3. More is required for the nature of beatitude than for that of fruit, as has been stated.

Third Article

WHETHER THE FRUITS ARE SUITABLY ENUMERATED BY THE APOSTLE?

We proceed thus to the Third Article:—

Objection 1. It would seem that the fruits are unsuitably enumerated by

[7] Q. 69, a. 1, ad 1. [8] Q. 3, a. 1; q. 4, a. 1. [9] Q. 69, a. 1, ad 1.

the Apostle (*Gal.* v. 22, 23). Because he says elsewhere that there is only one fruit of the present life. Thus *Rom.* vi. 22: *You have your fruit unto sanctification.* Moreover it is written (*Isa.* xxvii. 9): *This is all the fruit . . . that the sin . . . be taken away.* Therefore we should not reckon twelve fruits.

Obj. 2. Further, fruit is the product of a spiritual seed, as has been stated. But Our Lord mentions (*Matt.* xiii. 23) a threefold fruit as growing from a spiritual seed in a good ground, viz., *hundredfold, sixtyfold* and *thirtyfold.* Therefore one should not reckon twelve fruits.

Obj. 3. Further, the very nature of fruit is to be something ultimate and delightful. But this does not apply to all the fruits mentioned by the Apostle, for patience and long-suffering seem to imply a painful object, while faith is not something ultimate, but rather something primary and fundamental. Therefore too many fruits are enumerated.

Obj. 4. *On the other hand,* It seems that they are enumerated insufficiently and incompletely. For it has been stated that all the beatitudes may be called fruits, and yet not all are mentioned here. Nor is there anything corresponding to the acts of wisdom, and of many other virtues. Therefore it seems that the fruits are insufficiently enumerated.

I answer that, The number of the twelve fruits enumerated by the Apostle is suitable. There is possibly a reference to them in the twelve fruits of which it is written (*Apoc.* xxii. 2): *On both sides of the river was the tree of life bearing twelve fruits.* Since, however, a fruit is something that proceeds from a source as from a seed or root, the difference among these fruits must be gathered from the various ways in which the Holy Ghost proceeds in us. This process consists in this, that the mind of man is set in order, first of all, in regard to itself; secondly, in regard to things that are near it; thirdly, in regard to things that are below it.

Accordingly, man's mind is then well disposed in regard to itself when it has a good disposition towards good things and towards evil things. Now the first disposition of the human mind towards the good is effected by love, which is the first of our affections and the root of them all, as we have stated above.[10] Therefore, among the fruits of the Holy Ghost, we reckon *charity* first, in which the Holy Ghost is given in a special manner, as in His own likeness, since He Himself is love. Hence it is written (*Rom.* v. 5): *The charity of God is poured forth in our hearts by the Holy Ghost, Who is given to us.*—The necessary result of the love of charity is joy, because every lover rejoices at being united to the beloved. Now charity has always present the God Whom it loves, according to *1 John* iv. 16: *He that abideth in charity, abideth in God, and God in Him*; and therefore the sequel of charity is *joy*. Now the perfection of joy is peace, and this in two respects. First, as regards freedom from outward disturbance, for it is

---

[10] Q. 27, a. 4; q. 28, a. 6, ad 2; q. 41, a. 2, ad 1.

impossible to rejoice perfectly in the beloved good, if one is disturbed in the enjoyment thereof; and again, if a man's heart is perfectly at peace in one object, he cannot be disquieted by any other, since he accounts all others as nothing. Hence it is written (*Ps.* cxviii. 165): *Much peace have they that love Thy Law, and to them there is no stumbling-block,* because, namely, external things do not disturb them in their enjoyment of God. Secondly, as regards the subsiding of restless desire, for he does not perfectly rejoice, who is not satisfied with the object of his joy. Now peace implies these two things, namely, that we be not disturbed by external things, and that our desires rest altogether in one object. Therefore after charity and joy, *peace* is given the third place.—In evil things the mind has a good disposition, in respect of two things. First, by not being disturbed whenever evil threatens, which pertains to *patience*; secondly, by not being disturbed, whenever good things are delayed, which belongs to *long-suffering,* since *to lack good is a kind of evil.*[11]

Man's mind is well disposed as regards what is near him, viz., his neighbor, first, as to the will to do good, and to this belongs *goodness*; secondly, as to the execution of well-doing, and to this belongs *benignity,* for the benign are those in whom the salutary flame of love has enkindled the desire to do good to their neighbor; thirdly, as to his suffering with equanimity the evils his neighbor inflicts on him, and to this belongs *meekness,* which curbs anger; fourthly, in the point of our refraining from doing harm to our neighbor not only through anger, but also through fraud or deceit, and to this pertains *faith,* if we take it as meaning fidelity. But if we take it for the faith whereby we believe in God, then man is directed thereby to that which is above him, so that he subject his intellect and, consequently, all that is his to God.

Man is well disposed in respect of that which is below him, as regards external action, by *modesty,* whereby we observe the *mode* in all our words and deeds; as regards internal desires, by *continence* and *chastity* (whether these two differ because chastity withdraws man from unlawful desires, continence also from lawful desires, or because the continent man is subject to concupiscence, but is not led away, whereas the chaste man is neither subject to, nor led away by, them).

Reply Obj. 1. Sanctification is effected by all the virtues, by which also sins are taken away. Consequently, fruit is mentioned there in the singular because it is generically one, though divided into many species which are spoken of as so many fruits.

Reply Obj. 2. The hundredfold, sixtyfold and thirtyfold fruits do not differ as various species of virtuous acts, but as various degrees of perfection, even in the same virtue. Thus continence of the married state is said to be signified by the thirtyfold fruit; the continence of widowhood, by the

[11] Cf. Cicero, *Tusc. Disp.,* I, 36 (p. 262); Aristotle. *Eth.,* V, 3 (1131b 21).

sixtyfold; and virginal continence, by the hundredfold fruit.[12] There are, moreover, other ways in which holy men distinguish three evangelical fruits according to the three degrees of virtue;[13] and they speak of three degrees, because the perfection of anything is considered with respect to its beginning, its middle and its end.

Reply Obj. 3. The fact of not being disturbed by painful things is something to delight in.—And as to faith, if we consider it as the foundation, it has the aspect of being ultimate and delightful, inasmuch as it contains certainty. Hence the *Gloss* explains: *Faith, which is certainty about the unseen.*[14]

Reply Obj. 4. As Augustine says on *Gal.* v. 22, 23, *the Apostle had no intention of teaching us how many works of the flesh, or fruits of the Spirit there are; but to show how the former should be avoided, and the latter sought after.*[15] Hence, either more or fewer fruits might have been mentioned. Nevertheless, all the acts of the gifts and virtues can be reduced to these by a certain kind of fittingness, in so far as all the virtues and gifts must needs direct the mind in one of the above-mentioned ways. Therefore the acts of wisdom, and of any gifts directing to good, are reduced to charity, joy and peace. The reason why he mentions these rather than others is that these imply either enjoyment of good things, or relief from evils, which things seem to belong to the notion of fruit.

Fourth Article

WHETHER THE FRUITS OF THE HOLY GHOST ARE
CONTRARY TO THE WORKS OF THE FLESH?

We proceed thus to the Fourth Article:—

Objection 1. It would seem that the fruits of the Holy Ghost are not contrary to the works of the flesh, which the Apostle enumerates (*Gal.* v. 19, *seqq.*). For contraries are in the same genus. But the works of the flesh are not called fruits. Therefore the fruits of the Spirit are not contrary to them.

Obj. 2. Further, one thing has one contrary. Now the Apostle mentions more works of the flesh than fruits of the Spirit. Therefore the fruits of the Spirit and the works of the flesh are not contrary to one another.

Obj. 3. Further, among the fruits of the Spirit, the first place is given to charity, joy and peace, to which fornication, uncleanness and immodesty, which are the first of the works of the flesh, are not opposed. Therefore the fruits of the Spirit are not contrary to the works of the flesh.

On the contrary, The Apostle says (*ibid.* 17) that *the flesh lusteth against the spirit, and the spirit against the flesh.*

---

[12] St. Jerome, *Adv. Iovin.*, I, 3 (PL 23, 223).   [13] Cf. St. Augustine, *Quaest. Evang.*, I, 9, super *Matt.*, XIII, 13 (PL 35, 1325).   [14] *Glossa interl.*, super *Gal.*, V, 23 (VI, 87v).   [15] *In Gal.*, super V, 22 (PL 35, 2141).

I answer that, The works of the flesh and the fruits of the Spirit may be taken in two ways. First, in general, and in this way the fruits of the Holy Ghost, considered in general, are contrary to the works of the flesh. For the Holy Ghost moves the human mind to that which is in accord with reason, or rather to that which surpasses reason; whereas the appetite of the flesh, viz., the sensitive appetite, draws man to sensible goods which are beneath him. Therefore, since upward and downward are contrary movements in the physical order, so in human actions the works of the flesh are contrary to the fruits of the Spirit.

Secondly, both fruits and carnal works as enumerated may be considered singly, each according to its specific nature. And in this way they are not of necessity contrary each to each, because, as was stated above, the Apostle did not intend to enumerate all the works, whether spiritual or carnal.—However, by a kind of adaptation, Augustine, commenting on *Gal.* v. 22, 23, contrasts the fruits with the carnal works, each to each. Thus *to fornication, which is the love of satisfying lust outside lawful wedlock, we may contrast charity, whereby the soul is wedded to God, wherein also is true chastity. By uncleanness we must understand whatever disturbances arise from fornication, and to these the joy of tranquillity is opposed. Idolatry, by reason of which war was waged against the Gospel of God, is opposed to peace. Against witchcrafts, enmities, contentions, emulations, wraths and quarrels, there is long-suffering, which helps us to bear the evils inflicted on us by those among whom we dwell, while kindness helps us to cure those evils, and goodness, to forgive them. In contrast to heresy there is faith; to envy, mildness; to drunkenness and revellings, continence.*[16]

Reply Obj. 1. That which proceeds from a tree, against the tree's nature, is not called its fruit, but rather its corruption. And since works of virtue are connatural to reason, while works of vice are contrary to reason, therefore it is that works of virtue are called fruits, but not so works of vice.

Reply Obj. 2. *Good happens in one way, evil in all manner of ways,* as Dionysius says.[17] Hence, to one virtue many vices are contrary. Consequently, we must not be surprised if the works of the flesh are more numerous than the fruits of the spirit.

The Reply to the Third Objection is clear from what has been said.

[16] *In Gal.,* super V, 22 (PL 35, 2141).   [17] *De Div. Nom.,* IV, 31 (PG 3, 732).

Question LXXI

ON VICE AND SIN, CONSIDERED IN THEMSELVES

(*In Six Articles*)

WE have in the next place to consider vice and sin, about which six points have to be considered: (1) Vice and sin considered in themselves; (2) their distinction;[1] (3) their comparison with one another;[2] (4) the subject of sin;[3] (5) the cause of sin;[4] (6) the effect of sin.[5]

Under the first head there are six points of inquiry: (1) Whether vice is contrary to virtue? (2) Whether vice is contrary to nature? (3) Which is worse, a vice or a vicious act? (4) Whether a vicious act is compatible with virtue? (5) Whether every sin includes some act? (6) On the definition of sin proposed by Augustine: *Sin is a word, deed or desire against the eternal law.*[6]

First Article

WHETHER VICE IS CONTRARY TO VIRTUE?

We proceed thus to the First Article:—

Objection 1. It would seem that vice is not contrary to virtue. For one thing has one contrary, as is proved in *Metaph.* x.[7] Now sin and malice are contrary to virtue. Therefore vice is not contrary to ·it, since vice applies also to an undue disposition of bodily members or of any things whatever.

Obj. 2. Further, virtue denotes a certain perfection of a power. But vice does not denote anything relative to a power. Therefore vice is not contrary to virtue.

Obj. 3. Further, Cicero says that *virtue is the soul's health.*[8] Now sickness or disease, rather than vice, is opposed to health. Therefore vice is not contrary to virtue.

On the contrary, Augustine says that *vice is a quality according to which the soul is evil.*[9] But *virtue is a quality which makes its subject good,* as was shown above.[10] Therefore vice is contrary to virtue.

I answer that, Two things may be considered in virtue, namely, the essence of virtue, and that to which virtue is ordained. In the essence of virtue we may consider something directly, and we may consider something consequently. Virtue implies *directly* a disposition whereby the sub-

---

[1] Q. 72. [2] Q. 73. [3] Q. 74. [4] Q. 75. [5] Q. 85. [6] *Contra Faust.*, XXII, 27 (PL 42, 418). [7] Aristotle, *Metaph.*, IX, 4 (1055a 19); 5 (1055b 30). [8] *Tusc. Disp.*, IV, 13 (pp. 375-376). [9] *De Perfect. Iust.*, II (PL 44, 294). [10] Q. 55, a. 3 and 4.

ject is well disposed according to the mode of its nature; and hence the Philosopher says that *virtue is a disposition of a perfect thing to that which is best; and by perfect I mean that which is disposed according to its nature.*[11] That which virtue implies *consequently* is that it is a kind of goodness, because the goodness of a thing consists in its being well disposed according to the mode of its nature. Now that to which virtue is directed is a good act, as was shown above.[12]

Accordingly, three things are found to be contrary to virtue. One of these is *sin,* which is opposed to virtue in respect of that to which virtue is ordained; for, properly speaking, sin denotes an inordinate act, even as an act of virtue is an ordered and due act. In respect of that which virtue implies consequently, viz., that it is a kind of goodness, the contrary of virtue is *malice;* while in respect of that which belongs to the essence of virtue directly, its contrary is *vice,* because the vice of a thing seems to consist in its not being disposed in a way befitting its nature. Hence Augustine says: *Whatever is lacking for a thing's natural perfection may be called a vice.*[13]

Reply Obj. 1. These three things are contrary to virtue, but not in the same respect; for sin is opposed to virtue according as the latter is productive of a good work; malice, according as virtue is a kind of goodness; while vice is opposed to virtue properly as virtue.

Reply Obj. 2. Virtue signifies not only the perfection of a power which is the principle of action, but also the due disposition of its subject. The reason for this is because a thing operates according as it is in act; so that a thing needs to be well disposed if it has to produce a good work. It is in this respect that vice is contrary to virtue.

Reply Obj. 3. As Cicero says, *disease and sickness are vicious qualities,* for in speaking of the body he calls it disease *when the whole body is infected,* for instance, with fever or the like; he calls it sickness *when the disease is attended with weakness;* and vice *when the parts of the body are not well compacted together.*[14] And although at times there may be disease in the body without sickness, for instance, when a man has a hidden complaint without being hindered outwardly from his wonted occupations, *yet in the soul,* as he says, *these two things are indistinguishable, except in thought.*[15] For whenever a man is ill-disposed inwardly, through some inordinate affection, he is rendered thereby unfit for fulfilling his duties, since *a tree is known by its fruit, i.e.,* a man by his works, according to *Matt.* xii. 33. But *vice of the soul,* as Cicero says, *is a habit or affection of the soul discordant and at war with itself throughout life;* and this is to be found even without disease and sickness, *e.g.,* when a man sins from weakness or passion. Consequently, vice is of wider extent than sickness or

---

[11] *Phys.,* VII, 3 (246a 13).   [12] Q. 56, a. 3.   [13] *De Lib. Arb.,* III, 14 (PL 32, 1291).
[14] *Tusc. Disp.,* IV, 13 (p. 375).   [15] *Ibid.*

disease; even as virtue extends to more things than health, for health itself is reckoned a kind of virtue.[16] Consequently, vice is reckoned as contrary to virtue more fittingly than sickness or disease.

Second Article

WHETHER VICE IS CONTRARY TO NATURE?

We proceed thus to the Second Article:—

Objection 1. It would seem that vice is not contrary to nature. For vice is contrary to virtue, as we have stated above. Now virtue is in us, not by nature, but by infusion or habituation, as was stated above.[17] Therefore vice is not contrary to nature.

Obj. 2. Further, it is impossible to become habituated to that which is contrary to nature. Thus *a stone never becomes habituated to upward movement.*[18] But some men become habituated to vice. Therefore vice is not contrary to nature.

Obj. 3. Further, anything contrary to a nature is not found in the greater number of individuals possessed of that nature. Now vice is found in the greater number of men; for it is written (*Matt.* vii. 13): *Broad is the way that leadeth to destruction, and many there are who go in thereat.* Therefore vice is not contrary to nature.

Obj. 4. Further, sin is compared to vice as act to habit, as was stated above. Now sin is defined as *a word, deed or desire contrary to the law of God,* as Augustine shows.[19] But the law of God is above nature. Therefore we should say that vice is contrary to the Law, rather than to nature.

On the contrary, Augustine says: *Every vice, simply because it is a vice, is contrary to nature.*[20]

I answer that, As we have stated above, vice is contrary to virtue. Now the virtue of a thing consists in its being well disposed in a manner befitting its nature, as was stated above. Hence the vice of any thing consists in its being disposed in a manner not befitting its nature, and for this reason that thing is *vituperated,*—a term which is derived from *vice,* according to Augustine.[21]

But it must be observed that the nature of a thing is chiefly the form from which that thing derives its species. Now man derives his species from his rational soul, and consequently whatever is contrary to the order of reason is, properly speaking, contrary to the nature of man, as man; while whatever is in accord with reason is in accord with the nature of man, as man. Now *man's good is to be in accord with reason, and his evil is to be against reason,* as Dionysius states.[22] Therefore human virtue,

---

[16] Aristotle, *Phys.,* VII, 3 (246b 4).   [17] Q. 63, a. 1, 2 and 3.   [18] Aristotle, *Eth.,* II, 1 (1103a 20).   [19] *Contra Faust.,* XXII, 27 (PL 42, 418).   [20] *De Lib. Arb.,* III, 13 (PL 32, 1290).   [21] *Op. cit.,* III, 14 (PL 32, 1291).   [22] *De Div. Nom.,* IV, 32 (PG 3, 733).

which makes a man good, and his work good, is in accord with man's nature in so far as it accords with his reason; while vice is contrary to man's nature in so far as it is contrary to the order of reason.

Reply Obj. 1. Although the virtues are not caused by nature according to their perfect being, yet they incline us to that which accords with nature, *i.e.*, with the order of reason. For Cicero says that *virtue is a habit in accord with reason, after the manner of a nature;*[23] and it is in this sense that virtue is said to be in accord with nature, and, on the other hand, that vice is contrary to nature.

Reply Obj. 2. The Philosopher is speaking there of a thing as being against nature in so far as *being against nature* is contrary to *being from nature,* and not in so far as *being against nature* is contrary to *being in accord with nature,* in which latter sense virtues are said to be in accord with nature, inasmuch as they incline us to that which is suitable to nature.

Reply Obj. 3. There is a twofold nature in man, rational and sensitive. And since it is through the operation of his senses that man arrives at acts of reason, hence there are more who follow the inclinations of the sensitive nature, than who follow the order of reason; because more reach the beginning of a thing than achieve its completion. Now the presence of vices and sins in man is owing to the fact that he follows the inclination of his sensitive nature against the order of his reason.

Reply Obj. 4. Whatever is contrary to the nature of a work of art is likewise contrary to the nature of the art which produced that work. Now the eternal law is compared to the order of human reason as art to a work of art. Therefore it amounts to the same that vice and sin are against the order of human reason, and that they are contrary to the eternal law. Hence Augustine says that *every nature, as such, is from God; and is a vicious nature, in so far as it fails from the divine art whereby it was made.*[24]

Third Article

WHETHER VICE IS WORSE THAN A VICIOUS ACT?

We proceed thus to the Third Article:—

Objection 1. It would seem that vice, *i.e.*, a bad habit, is worse than a sin, *i.e.*, a bad act. For, as the more lasting a good is, the better it is, so the longer an evil lasts, the worse it is. Now a vicious habit is more lasting than vicious acts, that pass forthwith. Therefore a vicious habit is worse than a vicious act.

Obj. 2. Further, several evils are more to be shunned than one. But a bad habit is virtually the cause of many bad acts. Therefore a vicious habit is worse than a vicious act.

---

[23] *De Invent.*, II, 53 (p. 147b).   [24] *De Lib. Arb.*, III, 15 (PL 32, 1291).

Obj. 3. Further, a cause is more potent than its effect. But a habit produces its actions both as to their goodness and as to their badness. Therefore a habit is more potent than its act, both in goodness and in badness.

On the contrary, A man is justly punished for a vicious act, but not for a vicious habit, so long as no act ensues. Therefore a vicious action is worse than a vicious habit.

I answer that, A habit stands midway between power and act. Now it is evident that, both in good and in evil, act is better than potency, as is stated in *Metaph.* ix.[25] For it is better to do well than to be able to do well, and, in like manner, it is more blameworthy to do evil, than to be able to do evil. Whence it also follows that, both in goodness and in badness, habit stands midway between power and act, so that, namely, even as a good or evil habit stands above the corresponding power in goodness or in badness, so does it stand below the corresponding act. This is also made clear from the fact that a habit is not called good or bad, save in so far as it induces to a good or bad act; and hence a habit is called good or bad by reason of the goodness or badness of its act. Therefore, an act surpasses its habit in goodness or badness, since *the cause that a thing is such, is yet more so.*

Reply Obj. 1. Nothing hinders one thing from standing above another absolutely, and below it in some respect. Now a thing is deemed above another absolutely, if it surpasses it in a point which is proper to both; while it is deemed above it in a certain respect, if it surpasses it in something which is accidental to both. Now it has been shown from the very nature of act and habit, that act surpasses habit both in goodness and in badness. But the fact that habit is more lasting than act, is accidental to them, and is due to the fact that they are both found in a nature such that it cannot always be in action, and whose action consists in a transient movement. Consequently, act excels absolutely in goodness and badness, but habit excels in a certain respect.

Reply Obj. 2. A habit is several acts, not absolutely, but in a certain respect, *i.e.,* virtually. Therefore this does not prove that habit precedes act absolutely, both in goodness and in badness.

Reply Obj. 3. Habit causes act by way of efficient causality, but act causes habit by way of final causality, in respect of which we consider the nature of good and evil. Consequently, act surpasses habit both in goodness and in badness.

Fourth Article

WHETHER SIN IS COMPATIBLE WITH VIRTUE?

We proceed thus to the Fourth Article:—

Objection 1. It would seem that a vicious act, *i.e.,* sin, is incompatible

---

[25] Aristotle, *Metaph.,* VIII, 9 (1051a 4).

with virtue. For contraries cannot be together in the same subject. Now sin is, in a way, contrary to virtue, as was stated above. Therefore sin is incompatible with virtue.

Obj. 2. Further, sin is worse than vice, *i.e.,* an evil act than evil habit. But vice cannot be in the same subject with virtue. Neither, therefore, can sin.

Obj. 3. Further, sin occurs in natural things, even as in voluntary matters.[26] Now sin never happens in natural things, except through some corruption of a natural power. Thus monsters are due to a corruption of some elemental force in the seed, as is stated in *Physics* ii.[27] Therefore no sin occurs in voluntary matters, except through the corruption of some virtue in the soul; so that sin and virtue cannot be together in the same subject.

On the contrary, The Philosopher says that *virtue is engendered and corrupted by contrary causes.*[28] Now one virtuous act does not cause a virtue, as was stated above;[29] and, consequently, one sinful act does not corrupt virtue. Therefore they can be together in the same subject.

I answer that, Sin is compared to virtue as an evil act to a good habit. Now the position of a habit in the soul is not the same as that of a form in a natural thing. For the form of a natural thing produces, of necessity, an operation befitting itself, and therefore a natural form is incompatible with the act of a contrary form. Thus, heat is incompatible with the act of cooling, and lightness with downward movement (unless perhaps violence be used by some extrinsic mover). But the habit that resides in the soul does not, of necessity, produce its operation, but is used by man when he wills. Consequently man, while possessing a habit, may either fail to use the habit, or produce a contrary act; and so a man having a virtue may produce an act of sin. And this sinful act, so long as there is but one, cannot corrupt virtue, if we compare the act to the virtue itself as a habit: since, just as a habit is not engendered by one act, so neither is it destroyed by one act, as was stated above.[30] But if we compare the sinful act to the cause of the virtues, then it is possible for some virtues to be destroyed by one sinful act. For every mortal sin is contrary to charity, which is the root of all the infused virtues, as virtues; and, consequently, when charity is banished by one act of mortal sin, it follows that all the infused virtues are expelled as virtues. And this I say for the sake of faith and hope, whose habits remain unquickened after mortal sin, so that they are no longer virtues. On the other hand, since venial sin is neither contrary to charity, nor banishes it, neither does it, as a consequence, expel the other virtues. As to the acquired virtues, they are not destroyed by one act of any kind of sin.

Accordingly, mortal sin is incompatible with the infused virtues, but is

---

[26] Aristotle, *Phys.,* II, 8 (199a 33).   [27] *Ibid.* (199b 4).   [28] *Eth.,* II, 3 (1105a 14).
[29] Q. 51, a. 3.   [30] Q. 63, a. 2, ad 2.

consistent with the acquired virtues; while venial sin is compatible with virtues, whether infused or acquired.

Reply Obj. 1. Sin is contrary to virtue, not by reason of itself, but by reason of its act. Hence sin is incompatible with the act, but not with the habit, of virtue.

Reply Obj. 2. Vice is directly contrary to virtue, even as sin to a virtuous act; and so vice excludes virtue, just as sin excludes an act of virtue.

Reply Obj. 3. The natural powers act of necessity, and hence so long as the power is unimpaired, no sin can be found in the act. On the other hand, the virtues of the soul do not produce their acts of necessity. Hence the comparison fails.

Fifth Article

WHETHER EVERY SIN INCLUDES SOME ACT?

We proceed thus to the Fifth Article:—

Objection 1. It would seem that every sin includes some act. For as merit is compared with virtue, even so is sin compared with vice. Now there can be no merit without some act. Neither, therefore, can there be sin without some act.

Obj. 2. Further, Augustine says: *So true is it that every sin is voluntary, that, unless it be voluntary, it is no sin at all.*[31] Now nothing can be voluntary save through an act of the will. Therefore every sin implies some act.

Obj. 3. Further, if sin could be without some act, it would follow that a man sins as soon as he ceases doing what he ought. Now he who never does something that he ought to do, ceases continually doing what he ought. Therefore it would follow that he sins continually; and this is untrue. Therefore there is no sin without some act.

On the contrary, It is written (*Jas.* iv. 17): *To him . . . who knoweth to do good, and doth it not, to him it is a sin.* Now *not to do* does not signify some act. Therefore sin can be without an act.

I answer that, The reason for urging this question has reference to the sin of omission, about which there have been various opinions. For some[32] say that in every sin of omission there is some act, either interior or exterior: interior, as when a man wills *not to go to church,* when he is bound to go; exterior, as when a man, at the very hour that he is bound to go to church (or even before), occupies himself in such a way that he is hindered from going. This seems, in a way, to amount to the same as the first, for whoever wills one thing that is incompatible with this other, wills, consequently, to go without this other; unless, perchance, it does not occur to him that what he wishes to do will hinder him from that which he is bound to do, in which case he might be deemed guilty of negligence. On the other

---

[31] *De Lib. Arb.,* III, 18 (PL 32, 1295); *De Vera Relig.,* XIV (PL 34, 133).
[32] Anonymously reported by Peter Lombard, *Sent.,* II, xxxv, 3 (I, 495).

hand, others[33] say, that a sin of omission does not necessarily suppose an act; for the mere fact of not doing what one is bound to do is a sin.

Now each of these opinions has some truth in it. For if in the sin of omission we look merely at that in which the notion of the sin consists, the sin of omission will be sometimes with an interior act, as when a man wills *not to go to church*; while sometimes it will be without any act at all, whether interior or exterior, as when a man, at the time that he is bound to go to church, does not think of going or not going to church.

If, however, in the sin of omission we consider also the causes or occasions of the omission, then the sin of omission must of necessity include some act. For there is no sin of omission, unless we omit what we can do or not do. Now that we turn aside so as not to do what we can do or not do, must needs be due to some cause or occasion, either united with the omission or preceding it. If this cause be not in man's power, the omission will not be sinful, as when someone omits going to church because of sickness. But if the cause or occasion be subject to the will, the omission is sinful; and then such a cause, in so far as it is voluntary, must needs always include some act, at least the interior act of the will. Now this act sometimes bears directly on the omission, as when a man wills *not to go to church,* because it is too much trouble; and in this case the act, of its very nature, belongs to the omission, because the volition of any sin whatever pertains, of itself, to that sin, since voluntariness is essential to sin. Sometimes, however, the act of the will bears directly on something else, which hinders a man from doing what he ought, whether this something else be united with the omission (as when a man wills to play at the time he ought to go to church) or precede the omission (as when a man wills to sit up late at night, with the result that he does not go to church in the morning). In this case the act, interior or exterior, is accidental to the omission, since the omission follows outside the intention. Now that which is outside the intention is said to be accidental.[34] Therefore it is evident that then the sin of omission has indeed an act united with, or preceding, the omission, but that this act is accidental to the sin of omission.

Now in judging about things, we must be guided by that which is essential, and not by that which is accidental; and consequently it is truer to say that a sin can be without any act, or else circumstantial acts and occasions would be essential to other actual sins.

Reply Obj. 1. More things are required for good than for evil, since *good results from a whole and entire cause, whereas evil results from each single defect,* as Dionysius states.[35] Hence, sin may arise when a man does what he ought not, or by his not doing what he ought. But there can be no merit unless a man do willingly what he ought to do, and therefore there can be no merit without an act, whereas there can be sin without an act.

[33] Cf. St. Albert, *In II Sent.,* d. xxxv, a. 3 (XXVII, 565).   [34] Aristotle, *Phys.,* II, 5 (196b 23).   [35] *De Div. Nom.,* IV, 30 (PG 3, 729).

Reply Obj. 2. The term *voluntary* is applied not only to that on which the act of the will is brought to bear, but also to that which we have the power to do or not to do, as is stated in *Ethics* iii.[36] Hence even *not to will* may be called voluntary, in so far as man has it in his power to will and not to will.

Reply Obj. 3. The sin of omission is contrary to an affirmative precept which binds always, but not for always. Hence, by omitting to act, a man sins only for the time at which the affirmative precept binds him to act.

Sixth Article

WHETHER SIN IS FITTINGLY DEFINED AS *A WORD, DEED OR DESIRE CONTRARY TO THE ETERNAL LAW?*

We proceed thus to the Sixth Article:—

Objection 1. It would seem that sin is unfittingly defined by saying: *Sin is a word, deed, or desire, contrary to the eternal law.*[37] Because *word, deed* and *desire* imply an act, whereas not every sin implies an act, as was stated above. Therefore, this definition does not include every sin.

Obj. 2. Further, Augustine says: *Sin is the will to retain or obtain what justice forbids.*[38] Now will is comprised under desire, in so far as desire denotes generally any act of the appetite. Therefore it was enough to say: *Sin is a desire contrary to the eternal law,* nor was there need to add *word* or *deed.*

Obj. 3. Further, sin appears to consist properly in aversion from the end, for good and evil are measured chiefly with regard to the end, as was explained above.[39] Therefore Augustine defines sin in reference to the end, by saying that *sin is nothing else than to neglect eternal things, and seek after temporal things;*[40] and again he says that *all human wickedness consists in using what we should enjoy, and in enjoying what we should use.*[41] Now the definition in question contains no mention of aversion from our due end, and therefore it is an insufficient definition of sin.

Obj. 4. Further, a thing is said to be forbidden because it is contrary to law. Now not all sins are evil through being forbidden, but some are forbidden because they are evil. Therefore sin in general should not be defined as being against the law of God.

Obj. 5. Further, a sin denotes an evil human act, as was explained above.[42] Now man's evil is to be against reason, as Dionysius states.[43] Therefore it would have been better to say that sin is against reason than to say that it is contrary to the eternal law.

On the contrary, the authority of Augustine suffices.[44]

---

[36] Aristotle, *Eth.,* III, 5 (1113b 20).   [37] St. Augustine, *Contra Faust.,* XXII, 27 (PL 42, 418).   [38] *De Duab. An.,* XI (PL 42, 105).   [39] Q. 18, a. 6.   [40] *De Lib. Arb.,* I, 11 (PL 32, 1233).   [41] *Lib. 83 Quaest.,* q. 30 (PL 40, 19).   [42] A. 1; q. 21, a. 1.   [43] *De Div. Nom.,* IV, 32 (PG 3, 733).   [44] *Contra Faust.,* XXII, 27 (PL 42, 418).

I answer that, As was shown above, sin is nothing else than an evil human act. Now an act is a human act because it is voluntary, as was stated above,[45] whether it be voluntary, as being elicited by the will, *e.g.,* to will or to choose, or as being commanded by the will, *e.g.,* the exterior actions of speech or operation. Again, a human act is evil through lacking conformity with its due measure. Now the conformity of measure in a thing depends on a rule, from which if that thing depart, it is without measure. But there are two rules of the human will: one is proximate and homogeneous, viz., the human reason; the other is the first rule, viz. the eternal law, which is God's reason, so to speak. Accordingly, Augustine includes two things in the definition of sin: one, pertaining to the substance of a human act, and which is, as it were, the matter of sin, when he says, *word, deed or desire;* the other, pertaining to the nature of evil, and which is the form, as it were, of sin, when he says, *contrary to the eternal law.*

Reply Obj. 1. Affirmation and negation are reduced to one and the same genus: *e.g.,* in divine things, begotten and unbegotten are reduced to the genus of *relation,* as Augustine observes.[46] Hence *word* and *deed* denote equally what is said and what is not said, what is done and what is not done.

Reply Obj. 2. The first cause of sin is in the will, which commands all voluntary acts, in which alone sin is to be found; and hence it is that Augustine sometimes defines sin in reference to the will alone. But since external acts themselves also belong to the substance of sin, because they are evil of themselves, as we have stated,[47] it was necessary in defining sin to include something referring to external acts.

Reply Obj. 3. The eternal law first and foremost directs man to his end, and, in consequence, makes man to be well disposed in regard to things which are directed to the end. Hence, when he says, *contrary to the eternal law,* he includes aversion from the end and all other forms of lack of order.

Reply Obj. 4. When it is said that not every sin is evil on the ground that it is forbidden, this must be understood of prohibition by positive law. If, however, the prohibition be referred to the natural law, which is contained primarily in the eternal law, but secondarily in the natural tribunal of the human reason, then every sin is evil through being prohibited; since it is contrary to natural law precisely because it is lacking in order.

Reply Obj. 5. The theologian considers sin chiefly as an offense against God, and the moral philosopher, as something contrary to reason. Hence Augustine defines sin more fittingly with reference to its being *contrary to the eternal law* than with reference to its being contrary to reason; the more so as the eternal law directs us in many things that surpass human reason, *e.g.,* in matters of faith.

[45] Q. 1, a. 1.   [46] *De Trin.,* V, 6; 7 (PL 42, 914; 915).   [47] Q. 20, a. 1, 2 and 3.

ON THE DISTINCTION OF SINS
(*In Nine Articles*)

WE must now consider the distinction of sins or vices, under which head there are nine points of inquiry: (1) Whether sins are distinguished specifically by their objects? (2) The distinction between spiritual and carnal sins. (3) Whether sins differ in reference to their causes? (4) Whether they differ with respect to those who are sinned against? (5) Whether sins differ in relation to the debt of punishment? (6) Whether they differ in regard to omission and commission? (7) Whether they differ according to their various stages? (8) Whether they differ in respect of excess and deficiency? (9) Whether they differ according to their various circumstances?

First Article

WHETHER SINS DIFFER IN SPECIES ACCORDING TO THEIR OBJECTS?

We proceed thus to the First Article:—

Objection 1. It would seem that sins do not differ in species according to their objects. For acts are said to be good or evil chiefly in relation to their end, as was shown above.[1] Since, then, sin is nothing else than an evil human act, as was stated above,[2] it seems that sins should differ specifically according to their ends rather than according to their objects.

Obj. 2. Further, evil, being a privation, differs specifically according to the different species of opposites. Now sin is an evil in the genus of human acts. Therefore sins differ specifically according to their opposites rather than according to their objects.

Obj. 3. Further, if sins differed specifically according to their objects, it would be impossible to find the same specific sin with diverse objects; and yet such sins are to be found. For pride is about things spiritual and material, as Gregory says,[3] and avarice is about different kinds of things. Therefore sins do not differ in species according to their objects.

On the contrary, Sin is a word, deed or desire against God's law.[4] Now words, deeds and desires differ in species according to their various objects, since acts differ by their objects, as was stated above.[5] Therefore sins also differ in species according to their objects.

[1] Q. 18, a. 6.   [2] Q. 21, a. 1; q. 71, a. 1.   [3] *Moral.*, XXXIV, 23 (PL 76, 744).
[4] St. Augustine, *Contra Faust.*, XXII, 27 (PL 42, 418).   [5] Q. 18, a. 5; I, q. 77, a. 3

I answer that, As we have stated above, two things concur in the nature of sin, viz., the voluntary act, and its lack of order, which consists in departing from God's law.[6] Of these two, one is referred essentially to the sinner, who intends such and such an act in such and such a matter; the other, viz., the lack of order in the act, is referred accidentally to the intention of the sinner, for *no one acts intending evil,* as Dionysius declares.[7] Now it is evident that a thing derives its species from that which is essential and not from that which is accidental; for what is accidental is outside the specific nature. Consequently, sins differ specifically on the part of the voluntary acts rather than of the lack of order inherent in sin. Now voluntary acts differ in species according to their objects, as was proved above.[8] Therefore, it follows that sins are properly distinguished in species by their objects.

Reply Obj. 1. The end has primarily the nature of a good, and therefore the end stands in the relation of object to the act of the will which is at the root of every sin. Consequently, it amounts to the same whether sins differ by their objects or by their ends.

Reply Obj. 2. Sin is not a pure privation but an act deprived of its due order. Hence, sins differ specifically according to the objects of their acts rather than according to their opposites, although, even if they were distinguished in reference to the opposite virtues, it would come to the same; since the virtues differ specifically according to their objects, as was stated above.[9]

Reply Obj. 3. In various things differing in species or genus, nothing hinders our finding one formal aspect of the object, from which aspect sin receives its species. It is thus that pride seeks excellence in reference to various things, and avarice seeks an abundance of things adapted to human use.

Second Article

WHETHER SPIRITUAL SINS ARE FITTINGLY DISTINGUISHED FROM CARNAL SINS?

We proceed thus to the Second Article:—

Objection 1. It would seem that spiritual sins are unfittingly distinguished from carnal sins. For the Apostle says (*Gal.* v. 19): *The works of the flesh are manifest, which are fornication, uncleanness, immodesty, luxury, idolatry, witchcrafts,* etc., from which it seems that all the genera of sins are works of the flesh. Now carnal sins are called works of the flesh. Therefore carnal sins should not be distinguished from spiritual sins.

Obj. 2. Further, whosoever sins, walks according to the flesh, as is stated in *Rom.* viii. 13: *If you live according to the flesh, you shall die.*

---

[6] Q. 71, a. 6.   [7] *De Div. Nom.,* IV, 19; 31 (PG 3, 716; 732).   [8] Q. 18, a. 5.   [9] Q. 60, a. 5.

But if by the spirit you mortify the deeds of the flesh, you shall live. Now to live or walk according to the flesh seems to pertain to the nature of carnal sin. Therefore carnal sins should not be distinguished from spiritual sins, since all sins are carnal.

Obj. 3. Further, the higher part of the soul, which is the mind or reason, is called the spirit, according to *Ephes.* iv. 23: *Be renewed in the spirit of your mind,* where spirit stands for reason, according to the *Gloss.*[10] Now every sin, which is committed in accordance with the flesh, flows from the reason by its consent; for consent in a sinful act belongs to the higher reason, as we shall state further on.[11] Therefore the same sins are both carnal and spiritual, and consequently they should not be distinguished from one another.

Obj. 4. Further, if some sins are specifically carnal, this, seemingly, should apply chiefly to those sins whereby man sins against his own body. But, according to the Apostle (*1 Cor.* vi. 18), *every sin that a man doth is without the body; but he that committeth fornication, sinneth against his own body.* Therefore fornication would be the only carnal sin, whereas the Apostle reckons covetousness with the carnal sins (*Ephes.* v. 3.).

On the contrary, Gregory says that *of the seven capital sins five are spiritual, and two carnal.*[12]

I answer that, As we have stated above, sins take their species from their objects. Now every sin consists in the desire for some mutable good, for which man has an inordinate desire, and the possession of which gives him inordinate pleasure. But, as was explained above, pleasure is two-fold.[13] One belongs to the soul, and is consummated in the mere apprehension of a thing possessed in accordance with desire; and this can also be called spiritual pleasure, *e.g.,* when one takes pleasure in human praise or the like. The other pleasure is bodily or natural, and is realized in bodily touch, and this can also be called carnal pleasure.

Accordingly, those sins which consist in spiritual pleasure are called spiritual sins; while those which consist in carnal pleasure are called carnal sins, *e.g.,* gluttony, which consists in the pleasures of the table, and lust, which consists in sexual pleasures. Hence the Apostle says (*2 Cor.* vii. 1): *Let us cleanse ourselves from all defilement of the flesh and of the spirit.*

Reply Obj. 1. As the *Gloss* says on the same passage, these vices are called works of the flesh, but not as though they consisted in carnal pleas-ure.[14] Rather flesh here denotes man, who is said to live according to the flesh when he lives according to himself, as Augustine also says.[15] The rea-son for this is, because every failing in the human reason is due in some way to the carnal sense.

---

[10] *Glossa ordin.* (VI, 94 F); *Glossa interl.* (VI, 94v). [11] Q. 74, a. 7. [12] *Moral.,* XXXI, 45 (PL 76, 621). [13] Q. 31, a. 3. [14] *Glossa ordin.,* super *Gal.,* V, 19 (VI, 87E); St. Augustine, *De Civit. Dei,* XIV, 2 (PL 41, 404). [15] *Ibid.*

This suffices for the Reply to the Second Objection.

Reply Obj. 3. Even in the carnal sins there is a spiritual act, viz., the act of reason; but the end of these sins, from which they are named, is carnal pleasure.

Reply Obj. 4. As the *Gloss* says, *in the sin of fornication the soul is the body's slave in a special sense, because at the moment of sinning it can think of nothing else;*[16] whereas the pleasure of gluttony, although carnal, does not so utterly absorb the reason.—It may also be said that in this sin an injury is done to the body also, for it is defiled inordinately; and hence by this sin alone man is said especially to sin against his body. While covetousness, which is reckoned among the carnal sins, stands here for adultery, which is the unjust appropriation of another's wife.—Again, it may be said that the thing in which the covetous man takes pleasure is something bodily, and in this respect covetousness is numbered with the carnal sins; but the pleasure itself does not belong to the body, but to the spirit, and therefore Gregory says that it is a spiritual sin.

Third Article

WHETHER SINS DIFFER SPECIFICALLY IN REFERENCE TO THEIR CAUSES?

We proceed thus to the Third Article:—

Objection 1. It would seem that sins differ specifically in reference to their causes. For a thing takes its species from that whence it derives its being. Now sins derive their being from their causes. Therefore they take their species from them also. Therefore they differ specifically in reference to the diversity of their causes.

Obj. 2. Further, of all the causes the material cause seems to have least reference to the species. Now the object in a sin is like a material cause. Since, therefore, sins differ specifically according to their objects, it seems that much more do they differ in reference to their other causes.

Obj. 3. Further, Augustine, commenting on *Ps.* lxxix. 17 (*Things set on fire and dug down*), says that *every sin is due either to fear inducing false humility, or to love enkindling us to undue ardor.*[17] For it is written (*1 John* ii. 16) that *all that is in the world is the concupiscence of the flesh, or the concupiscence of the eyes, or the pride of life.* Now a thing is said to be in the world because of sin, inasmuch as the *world* denotes lovers of the world, as Augustine observes.[18] Gregory, too, distinguishes all sins according to the seven capital vices.[19] Now all these divisions refer to the causes of sins. Therefore, seemingly, sins differ specifically according to the diversity of their causes.

---

[16] Peter Lombard, *In I Cor.*, super VI, 18 (PL 191, 1584).   [17] *Enarr. in Psalm.*, super LXXIX, 17 (PL 36, 1027).   [18] *Tract.* II, super *Ioann.*, I, 10 (PL 35, 1393).
[19] *Moral.*, XXXI, 45 (PL 76, 621).

On the contrary, If this were the case, all sins would belong to one species, since they are due to one cause. For it is written (*Ecclus.* x. 15) that *pride is the beginning of all sin,* and (*1 Tim.* vi. 10) that *the desire of money is the root of all evils.* Now it is evident that there are various species of sins. Therefore sins do not differ specifically according to their different causes.

I answer that, Since there are four kinds of causes, they are attributed to various things in various ways. For the *formal* and the *material* cause regard properly the substance of a thing; and consequently substances differ, in respect of their matter and form, both in species and in genus.—The *agent* and the *end* regard directly movement and operation. Therefore movements and operations differ specifically in respect of these causes; in different ways, however, because the natural active principles are always determined to the same acts, so that the different species of natural acts are taken not only from the objects, which are the ends or terms of those acts, but also from their active principles. Thus, heating and cooling are specifically distinct with reference to hot and cold. On the other hand, the active principles in voluntary acts, such as the acts of sins, are not deter-mined of necessity to one act, and consequently from one active or motive principle diverse species of sins can proceed. Thus from fear, engendering false humility, man may proceed to theft, or murder, or to neglect the flock committed to his care; and these same things may proceed from love enkindling to undue ardor. Hence, it is evident that sins do not differ specifically according to their various active or motive causes, but only in respect of diversity in the final cause, which is the end and object of the will. For it has been shown above that human acts take their species from the end.[20]

Reply Obj. 1. The active principles in voluntary acts, not being deter-mined to one act, do not suffice for the production of human acts, unless the will be determined to one by the intention of the end, as the Philosopher proves.[21] Consequently sin derives both its being and its species from the end.

Reply Obj. 2. Objects, in relation to external acts, have the character of matter *about which,* but in relation to the interior act of the will, they have the character of end; and it is owing to this that they give the act its species. Nevertheless, even considered as the matter *about which,* they have the character of the termini from which movement takes its species.[22] But even the termini of movement specify movements, in so far as a ter-minus has the character of an end.

Reply Obj. 3. These distinctions of sins are given, not as distinct species of sins, but to show their various causes.

[20] Q. 1, a. 3; q. 18, a. 6.   [21] *Metaph.,* VIII, 5 (1048a 10).   [22] Aristotle, *Phys.,* V. 1 (224b 7); *Eth.,* X, 4 (1174b 4).

Fourth Article

WHETHER SIN IS FITTINGLY DIVIDED INTO SIN AGAINST GOD, AGAINST ONESELF, AND AGAINST ONE'S NEIGHBOR?

We proceed thus to the Fourth Article:—

Objection 1. It would seem that sin is unfittingly divided into sin against God, against one's neighbor and against oneself. For that which is common to all sins should not be reckoned as a part in the division of sin. But it is common to all sins to be against God, for it is stated in the definition of sin that it is *against God's law,* as was stated above.[23] Therefore sin against God should not be reckoned a part of the division of sin.

Obj. 2. Further, every division should consist of things in opposition to one another. But these three kinds of sin are not opposed to one another, for whoever sins against his neighbor sins against himself and against God. Therefore sin is not fittingly divided into these three.

Obj. 3. Further, specification is not taken from external things. But God and our neighbor are external to us. Therefore sins are not distinguished specifically with regard to them, and, consequently, sin is unfittingly divided according to these three.

On the contrary, Isidore, in giving the division of sins, says that *man is said to sin against himself, against God, and against his neighbor.*[24]

I answer that, As was stated above, sin is an inordinate act.[25] Now there should be a threefold order in man. One is in relation to the rule of reason, in so far as all our actions and passions should be commensurate with the rule of reason. Another order is in relation to the rule of the divine law, by which man should be directed in all things. Now if man were by nature a solitary animal, this twofold order would suffice. But since man is naturally a political and social animal, as is proved in *Politics* i.,[26] hence a third order is necessary, by which man is directed in relation to other men among whom he has to dwell. Of these orders the second contains the first and surpasses it. For whatever things are comprised under the order of reason, are comprised under the order of God Himself. Yet some things are comprised under the order of God which surpass the human reason; *e.g.,* matters of faith, and things due to God alone. Hence he that sins in such matters, for instance, by heresy, sacrilege, or blasphemy, is said to sin against God. In like manner, the first order includes the third and surpasses it, because in all things wherein we are directed in reference to our neighbor, we need to be directed according to the order of reason. Yet in some things we are directed according to reason in relation to ourselves only, and not in reference to our neighbor. Now when man sins in these matters, he is said to sin against himself, as is seen in the glutton, the lustful and

---

[23] Q. 71, a. 6.   [24] It is not Isidore. Cf. the anonymous *Summa Sententiarum,* III, 16 (PL 176, 113).   [25] Q. 71, a. 1.   [26] Aristotle, *Polit.,* I, 1 (1253a 2).

the prodigal. But when man sins in matters concerning his neighbor, he is said to sin against his neighbor, as appears in the thief and the murderer. Now the things whereby man is directed to God, his neighbor and himself are diverse. Therefore this distinction of sins is in respect of their objects, according to which the species of sins are diversified. Hence this distinction of sins is properly one of different species of sins, because the virtues also, to which sins are opposed, differ specifically in respect of these three. For it is evident from what has been said that by the theological virtues man is directed to God, by temperance and fortitude to himself, and by justice to his neighbor.[27]

Reply Obj. 1. To sin against God is common to all sins, in so far as the order to God includes every human order; but in so far as order to God surpasses the other two orders, sin against God is a special kind of sin.

Reply Obj. 2. When several things, of which one includes another, are distinct from one another, this distinction is understood to refer, not to the part contained in another, but to that in which one exceeds another. This may be seen in the division of numbers and figures. For a triangle is distinguished from a four-sided figure, not in respect of its being contained thereby, but in respect of that in which it is surpassed thereby; and the same applies to the numbers three and four.

Reply Obj. 3. Although God and our neighbor are external to the sinner himself, they are not external to the act of sin, but are related to it as its object.

Fifth Article

WHETHER THE DIVISION OF SINS ACCORDING TO THE DEBT
OF PUNISHMENT DIVERSIFIES THEIR SPECIES?

We proceed thus to the Fifth Article:—

Objection 1. It would seem that the division of sins according to the debt of punishment diversifies their species, for instance, when sin is divided into *mortal* and *venial*. For things which are infinitely apart cannot belong to the same species, nor even to the same genus. But venial and mortal sin are infinitely apart, since temporal punishment is due to venial sin, and eternal punishment to mortal sin. For the measure of the punishment corresponds to the gravity of the fault, according to *Deut.* xxv. 2: *According to the measure of the sin shall the measure also of the stripes be.* Therefore, venial and mortal sin are not in the same genus, nor can they be said to belong to the same species.

Obj. 2. Further, some sins are mortal in virtue of their species, as murder and adultery; and some are venial in virtue of their species, as an idle word and excessive laughter. Therefore venial and mortal sin differ specifically.

[27] Q. 62, a. 1; q. 66, a. 4 and 6.

Obj. 3. Further, as a virtuous act stands in relation to its reward, thus sin stands in relation to punishment. But reward is the end of the virtuous act. Therefore punishment is the end of sin. Now sins differ specifically in relation to their ends, as we have stated above. Therefore they are also specifically distinct according to the debt of punishment.

On the contrary, Those things that constitute a species are prior to the species, *e.g.,* specific differences. But punishment follows sin as its effect. Therefore sins do not differ specifically according to the debt of punishment.

I answer that, In things that differ specifically we find a twofold difference. The first causes the diversity of species, and is not to be found save in diverse species, *e.g., rational* and *irrational, animate* and *inanimate.* The other difference is consequent upon specific diversity; and though, in some cases, it may be consequent upon specific diversity, yet, in others, it may be found within the same species. Thus *white* and *black* are consequent upon the specific diversity of crow and swan, and yet this difference is found within the one species of man.

We must therefore say that the difference between venial and mortal sin, or any other difference in respect of the debt of punishment, cannot be a difference constituting specific diversity. For what is accidental never constitutes a species; and what is outside the agent's intention is accidental.[28] Now it is evident that punishment is outside the intention of the sinner, and therefore it is accidentally referred to sin on the part of the sinner. Nevertheless, it is referred to sin by an extrinsic principle, viz., the justice of the judge, who imposes various punishments according to the various manners of sin. Therefore, the difference derived from the debt of punishment may be consequent upon the specific diversity of sins, but cannot constitute it.

Now the difference between venial and mortal sin is consequent upon the diversity of that lack of order which constitutes the nature of sin. For lack of order is twofold, one that destroys the principle of order, and another which, without destroying the principle of order, causes lack of order in the things which follow the principle. Thus, in an animal's body, the frame may be so out of order that the vital principle is destroyed: this is death; while, on the other hand, though the vital principle remains, there may be disorder in the bodily humors: and then there is sickness. Now the principle of the entire moral order is the last end, which stands in the same relation to matters of action as an indemonstrable principle does to matters of speculation.[29] Therefore, when the soul is so disordered by sin as to turn away from its last end, viz., God, to Whom it is united by charity, there is mortal sin; but when it is disordered without turning away from God, then there is venial sin. For even as in the body, the disorder of death which results from the separation of the principle of life, is irreparable

---

[28] Aristotle, *Phys..* II, 5 (196b 23).   [29] Aristotle, *Eth.,* VII, 8 (1151a 16).

according to nature, while the disorder of sickness can be repaired because the vital principle itself remains, so it is in matters concerning the soul. Because, in speculative matters, it is impossible to convince one who errs concerning principles, whereas one who errs, but retains the principles, can be brought back to the truth by means of the principles. Likewise, in practical matters, he who by sinning turns away from his last end, if we consider the nature of his sin, falls irreparably, and therefore is said to sin mortally and to deserve eternal punishment. But when a man sins without turning away from God, by the very nature of his sin his disorder can be repaired, because the principle of the order is not destroyed; and therefore he is said to sin venially, because, namely, he does not sin so as to deserve to be punished eternally.

Reply Obj. 1. Mortal and venial sin are infinitely apart as regards what they *turn away from,* not as regards what they *turn to,* viz., the object which specifies them. Hence nothing hinders the same species from including mortal and venial sins. For instance, in the species *adultery* the first movement is a venial sin; while an idle word, which is, generally speaking, venial, may even be a mortal sin.

Reply Obj. 2. From the fact that one sin is mortal by reason of its species, and another venial by reason of its species, it follows that this difference is consequent upon the specific difference of sins, not that it is their cause. And this difference may be found even in things of the same species, as we have stated above.

Reply Obj. 3. The reward is intended by him that merits or acts virtually; whereas the punishment is not intended by the sinner, but, on the contrary, is against his will. Hence the comparison fails.

Sixth Article

WHETHER SINS OF COMMISSION AND OMISSION DIFFER SPECIFICALLY?

We proceed thus to the Sixth Article:—

Objection 1. It would seem that sins of commission and omission differ specifically. For *offense* and *sin* are co-divided against one another, according to *Ephes.* ii. 1, where it is written: *When you were dead in your offenses and sins,* which words the *Gloss* explains, saying: *"Offenses," by omitting to do what was commanded, and "sins," by doing what was forbidden.*[30] Whence it is evident that *offense* here denotes sins of omission; while *sin* denotes sins of commission. Therefore they differ specifically, since they are contrasted with one another as different species.

Obj. 2. Further, it is essential to sin to be against God's law, for this is part of its definition, as is clear from what has been said.[31] Now in God's

[30] *Glossa interl.* (VI, 91r); Peter Lombard, *In Ephes.,* super II, 1 (PL 192, 179).
[31] Q. 71, a. 6.

law, the affirmative precepts, against which is the sin of omission, are different from the negative precepts, against which is the sin of commission. Therefore, sins of omission and commission differ specifically.

Obj. 3. Further, omission and commission differ as affirmation and negation. Now affirmation and negation cannot be in the same species, since negation has no species; for *there is neither species nor difference of non-being,* as the Philosopher states.[32] Therefore omission and commission cannot belong to the same species.

On the contrary, Omission and commission are found in the same species of sin. For the covetous man both takes what belongs to others, which is a sin of commission, and gives not of his own to whom he should give, which is a sin of omission. Therefore omission and commission do not differ specifically.

I answer that, There is a twofold difference in sins, a material difference and a formal difference. The material difference is to be observed in the natural species of sinful acts, while the formal difference is gathered from their relation to one proper end, which is also their proper object. Hence we find certain acts differing from one another materially in species, which are, nevertheless, formally in the same species of sin, because they are directed to the one same end. Thus strangling, stoning and stabbing come under the one species of murder, although the actions themselves differ specifically according to the natural species.—Accordingly, if we refer to the species in sins of omission and commission materially, they differ specifically, using species in a broad sense, in so far as negation and privation may have a species. But if we refer to the species in sins of omission and commission formally, they do not differ specifically, because they are directed to the same end, and proceed from the same motive. For the covetous man, in order to hoard money, both robs and omits to give what he ought; and, in like manner, the glutton, to satiate his appetite, both eats too much and omits the prescribed fasts. The same applies to other sins, for negation in things is always founded on affirmation, which in a way is its cause. Hence in the physical order it comes under the same head that fire gives forth heat and that it does not give forth cold.

Reply Obj. 1. This division in terms of commission and omission is not according to formally different formal species, but only according to materially different species, as has been stated.

Reply Obj. 2. In God's law, the necessity for various affirmative and negative precepts was that men might be gradually led to virtue, first by abstaining from evil, to which we are induced by the negative precepts, and afterwards by doing good, to which we are induced by the affirmative precepts. Therefore the affirmative and negative precepts do not belong to different virtues, but to different degrees of virtue; and consequently they

---

[32] *Phys.,* IV, 8 (215a 10).

are not, of necessity, opposed to sins of different species. Moreover, sin is not specified by that from which it turns away, because in this respect it is a negation or privation, but by that to which it turns, in so far as sin is an act. Consequently, sins do not differ specifically according to the various precepts of the Law.

Reply Obj. 3. This objection considers the material diversity of sins. It must be observed, however, that although, properly speaking, negation is not in a species, yet it is allotted to a species by reduction to the affirmation on which it is based.

Seventh Article

WHETHER SINS ARE FITTINGLY DIVIDED INTO SINS OF
THOUGHT, WORD AND DEED?

We proceed thus to the Seventh Article:—

Objection 1. It would seem that sins are unfittingly divided into sins of thought, word and deed. For Augustine describes three stages of sin, of which the first is *when the carnal sense offers an enticement,* which is a sin of thought; the second stage is reached *when one is satisfied with the mere pleasure of the thought*; and the third stage, *when consent is given to the deed.*[33] Now these three belong to the sin of thought. Therefore it is unfitting to reckon sin of thought as one kind of sin.

Obj. 2. Further, Gregory reckons four degrees of sin, the first of which is *a fault hidden in the heart*; the second, *when it is done openly*; the third, *when it is formed into a habit*; and the fourth, *when man goes so far as to presume on God's mercy or to give himself up to despair.*[34] There is no distinction here between sins of deed and sins of word, and two other degrees of sin are added. Therefore the first division was unfitting.

Obj. 3. Further, there can be no sin of word or deed unless there precede sin of thought. Therefore these sins do not differ specifically. Therefore they should not be co-divided against one another.

On the contrary, Jerome, in commenting on *Ezech.* xliii. 23, says: *The human race is subject to three kinds of sin, for when we sin, it is either by thought, or word, or deed.*[35]

I answer that, Things differ specifically in two ways: first, when each has the complete species, and thus a horse and an ox differ specifically; secondly, when the diversity of species is derived from diversity of degree in generation or movement, and thus the building is the complete generation of a house, while the laying of the foundations and the setting up of the walls are incomplete species, as the Philosopher declares.[36] The same can apply to the generation of animals. Accordingly, sins are divided into these three (viz., into sins of thought, word and deed), not as into various

---

[33] *De Trin.,* XII, 12 (PL 42, 1008).   [34] *Moral.,* IV, 27 (PL 75, 661).   [35] *In Ezech.,* XIII, super XLIII. 23 (PL 25, 446).   [36] *Eth.,* X, 4 (1174a 19).

complete species, for the consummation of sin is in the deed, and therefore it is sins of deed that have the complete species. But the first beginning of sin is its foundation, as it were, in the sin of thought; the second degree is the sin of word, in so far as a man is ready to break out into a declaration of his thought; while the third degree consists in the consummation of the deed. Consequently, these three differ according to the various degrees of sin. Nevertheless, it is evident that these three belong to the one complete species of sin, since they proceed from the same motive. For the angry man, through desire of vengeance, is at first disturbed in thought, then he breaks out into words of abuse, and lastly he goes on to wrongful deeds. The same applies to lust and to any other sin.

Reply Obj. 1. All sins of thought have the common note of secrecy, in respect of which they form one degree, which is, however, divided into three stages, viz., of cogitation, pleasure and consent.

Reply Obj. 2. Sins of word and deed are both done openly, and for this reason Gregory reckons them under one head; whereas Jerome distinguishes between them because in sins of word there is nothing but manifestation which is principally intended, while in sins of deed, it is the consummation of the inward thought which is principally intended, and the outward manifestation is by way of sequel. Habit and despair are stages following the complete species of sin, even as boyhood and youth follow the complete generation of a man.

Reply Obj. 3. Sin of thought and sin of word are not distinguished from the sin of deed when they are united together with it, but when each is found by itself; even as one part of a movement is not distinguished from the whole movement when the movement is continuous, but only when there is a break in the movement.

Eighth Article

WHETHER EXCESS AND DEFICIENCY DIVERSIFY THE SPECIES OF SINS?

We proceed thus to the Eighth Article:—

Objection 1. It would seem that excess and deficiency do not diversify the species of sins. For excess and deficiency differ in respect of more and less. Now *more* and *less* do not diversify a species. Therefore excess and deficiency do not diversify the species of sins.

Obj. 2. Further, just as sin, in matters of action, is due to departing from the rectitude of reason, so falsehood, in speculative matters, is due to departing from the truth of a thing. Now the species of falsehood is not diversified by saying more or less than the thing. Therefore neither is the species of sin diversified by departing more or less from the rectitude of reason.

Obj. 3. Further, *one species cannot be made out of two,* as Porphyry declares.[37] Now excess and deficiency are united in one sin, for some are at once illiberal and wasteful, of which illiberality is a sin by deficiency, and prodigality, a sin by excess. Therefore excess and deficiency do not diversify the species of sins.

On the contrary, Contraries differ specifically, for *contrariety is a difference of form,* as is stated in *Metaph.* x.[38] Now vices that differ according to excess and deficiency are contrary to one another, as illiberality to wastefulness. Therefore they differ specifically.

I answer that, While there are two things in sin, viz., the act itself and its lack of order, in so far as sin is a departure from the order of reason and the divine law, the species of sin is gathered, not from its lack of order, which is outside the sinner's intention, as was stated above, but, on the contrary, from the act itself as terminating in the object to which the sinner's intention is directed. Consequently, wherever we find a different motive inclining the intention to sin, there will be a different species of sin. Now it is evident that the motive for sinning in sins by excess is not the same as the motive for sinning in sins by deficiency; in fact, they are contrary to one another, just as the motive in the sin of intemperance is love for bodily pleasures, while the motive in the sin of insensibility is hatred of the same. Therefore these sins not only differ specifically, but are contrary to one another.

Reply Obj. 1. Although *more* and *less* do not cause diversity of species, yet they are sometimes consequent upon specific difference, in so far as they are the result of a diversity of form. Such would be the case if we were to say that fire is lighter than air. Hence the Philosopher says that *those who held that there are no different species of friendship, by reason of its admitting of degree, were led by insufficient proof.*[39] In this way, to exceed reason or to fall short of it belongs to specifically different sins, in so far as they result from different motives.

Reply Obj. 2. It is not the sinner's intention to depart from reason; and so sins of excess and deficiency do not become of one kind through departing from the one rectitude of reason. On the other hand, sometimes he who utters a falsehood intends to hide the truth, and therefore, in this respect, it matters not whether he tells more or less. If, however, departure from the truth be not outside the intention, it is evident that then one is moved by different causes to tell more or less; and in this respect there are different kinds of falsehood, as is evident of the *boaster,* who exceeds in telling untruths for the sake of fame, and the *cheat,* who tells less than the truth in order to escape from paying his debts. This also explains how some false opinions are contrary to one another.

---

[37] *Isagoge,* trans. Boethius (PL 64, 150).   [38] Aristotle, *Metaph.,* IX, 4 (1055a 3).
[40] *Eth.,* VIII, 1 (1155b 13).

Reply Obj. 3. One may be prodigal and illiberal with regard to different objects. For instance, one may be illiberal in taking what one ought not, and prodigal in giving what one ought not. Now nothing hinders contraries from being in the same subject, in different respects.

Ninth Article

WHETHER SINS DIFFER SPECIFICALLY ACCORDING TO DIFFERENT CIRCUMSTANCES?

We proceed thus to the Ninth Article:—

Objection 1. It would seem that vices and sins differ specifically according to different circumstances. For, as Dionysius says, *evil results from each single defect.*[40] Now individual defects are corruptions of individual circumstances. Therefore from the corruption of each circumstance there results a corresponding species of sin.

Obj. 2. Further, sins are human acts. But human acts sometimes take their species from circumstances, as we have stated above.[41] Therefore sins differ specifically according as different circumstances are corrupted.

Obj. 3. Further, diverse species are assigned to gluttony, according to the words contained in the following verse:

Hastily, sumptuously, excessively, greedily, daintily.

Now these pertain to various circumstances, for *hastily* means sooner than is right; *excessively*, more than is right, and so on with the others. Therefore, the species of sin are diversified according to the various circumstances.

On the contrary, The Philosopher says that *every vice sins by doing more than one ought, and when one ought not;*[42] and in like manner as to the other circumstances. Therefore the species of sins are not diversified in this respect.

I answer that, As we have stated above, wherever there is a special motive for sinning, there is a different species of sin, because the motive for sinning is the end and object of sin. Now it happens sometimes that, although different circumstances are corrupted, there is but one motive. Thus the illiberal man, for the same motive, takes when he ought not, where he ought not, and more than he ought, and so on with the other circumstances, since he does this through an inordinate desire of hoarding money; and in such cases the corruption of different circumstances does not diversify the species of sins, but belongs to one and the same species.

Sometimes, however, the corruption of different circumstances arises from different motives. For instance, that a man eat hastily may be due to the fact that he cannot brook the delay in taking food, because of a rapid

---

[40] *De Div. Nom.,* IV, 30 (PG 3, 729).   [41] Q. 18, a. 10.   [42] *Eth.,* III, 7 (1115b 15); IV, 1 (1119b 22).

exhaustion of the digestive humors; that he desire too much food, may be due to a naturally strong digestion; and that he desire choice meats is due to his desire for pleasure in taking food. Hence, in such matters, the corruption of different circumstances entails different species of sins.

Reply Obj. 1. Evil, as such, is a privation, and so it has different species in respect of the things of which the subject is deprived, even as other privations. But sin does not take its species from privation or aversion, as was stated above, but from turning to the object of the act.

Reply Obj. 2. A circumstance never transfers an act from one species to another, save when there is another motive.

Reply Obj. 3. In the various species of gluttony there are various motives, as we have stated.

ON THE COMPARISON OF ONE SIN WITH ANOTHER

(*In Ten Articles*)

WE must now consider the comparison of one sin with another, under which head there are ten points of inquiry: (1) Whether all sins and vices are connected with one another? (2) Whether all are equal? (3) Whether the gravity of sin depends on its object? (4) Whether it depends on the excellence of the virtue to which it is opposed? (5) Whether carnal sins are more grievous than spiritual sins? (6) Whether the gravity of sins depends on their causes? (7) Whether it depends on their circumstances? (8) Whether it depends on how much harm ensues? (9) Whether on the position of the person sinned against? (10) Whether sin is aggravated by reason of the excellence of the person sinning?

First Article

WHETHER ALL SINS ARE CONNECTED WITH ONE ANOTHER?

We proceed thus to the First Article:—

Objection 1. It would seem that all sins are connected. For it is written (*Jas.* ii. 10): *Whosoever shall keep the whole Law, but offend in one point, is become guilty of all.* Now to be guilty of transgressing all the precepts of law is the same as to commit all sins, because, as Ambrose says, *sin is a transgression of the divine law, and disobedience of the heavenly commandments.*[1] Therefore, whoever commits one sin is guilty of all.

Obj. 2. Further, each sin banishes its opposite virtue. Now whoever lacks one virtue lacks them all, as was shown above.[2] Therefore whoever commits one sin is deprived of all the virtues. But whoever lacks a virtue has its opposite vice. Therefore whoever commits one sin is guilty of all sins.

Obj. 3. Further, all the virtues are connected which they have a principle in common, as was stated above.[3] Now just as the virtues have a common principle, so have sins, because, as the love of God, which builds the city of God, is the beginning and root of all the virtues, so self-love, which builds the city of Babylon, is the root of all sins, as Augustine declares.[4] Therefore all vices and sins are also connected, so that whoever has one has them all.

[1] *De Parad.*, VIII (PL 14, 309).   [2] Q. 65, a. 1.   [3] Q. 65, a. 1 and 2.   [4] *De Civit. Dei,* XIV, 28 (PL 41, 436).

On the contrary, Some vices are contrary to one another, as the Philosopher states.[5] But contraries cannot be together in the same subject. Therefore, it is impossible for all sins and vices to be connected with one another.

I answer that, The intention of the man who acts according to virtue in pursuance of his reason is different from the intention of the sinner in departing from the path of reason. For the intention of every man acting according to virtue is to follow the rule of reason, and hence the intention of all the virtues is directed to the same end, so that all the virtues are connected together in the right reason of things to be done, viz., prudence, as was stated above.[6] But the intention of the sinner is not directed towards departing from the path of reason; rather is it directed to tend to some appetible good whence it derives its species. Now these goods, to which the sinner's intention is directed when departing from reason, are of various kinds, having no mutual connection; in fact, they are sometimes contrary to one another. Since, therefore, vices and sins take their species from that to which they turn, it is evident that, in respect of that which completes a sin's species, sins are not connected with one another. For sin does not consist in passing from the many to the one, as is the case with virtues, which are connected, but rather in forsaking the one for the many.

Reply Obj. 1. James is speaking of sin, not as regards the thing to which it turns, and which causes the distinction of sins, as was stated above,[7] but as regards that from which sin turns away, inasmuch as man, by sinning, departs from a commandment of the Law. Now all the commandments of the Law are from one and the same, as he also says in the same passage, so that the same God is despised in every sin; and in this sense he says that whoever *offends in one point, is become guilty of all,* inasmuch as, by committing one sin, he incurs the debt of punishment through his contempt of God, which is the origin of all sins.

Reply Obj. 2. As we have stated above, the opposite virtue is not banished by every act of sin.[8] For venial sin does not destroy virtue, while mortal sin destroys infused virtue, by turning man away from God. Yet one act of sin, even of mortal sin, does not destroy the habit of acquired virtue. However, if such acts be repeated so as to engender a contrary habit, the habit of acquired virtue is destroyed, and its destruction entails the loss of prudence, since, when a man acts against any virtue whatever, he acts against prudence, without which no moral virtue is possible, as was stated above.[9] Consequently, all the moral virtues are destroyed as to the perfect and formal being of virtue, which they have in so far as they partake of prudence; yet there remain the inclinations to virtuous acts, which, however, are not virtues. Nevertheless, it does not follow that for this

---

[5] *Eth.,* II, 8 (1108b 27).   [6] Q. 65, a. 1.   [7] Q. 72, a. 1.   [8] Q. 71, a. 4.   [9] Q. 58, a. 4; q. 65, a. 1.

reason man contracts all vices or sins: first, because several vices are opposed to one virtue, so that a virtue can be destroyed by one of them, without the others being present; secondly, because sin is directly opposed to virtue, as regards the virtue's inclination to act, as was stated above.[10] Therefore, as long as any virtuous inclinations remain, it cannot be said that man has the opposite vices or sins.

Reply Obj. 3. The love of God is unitive, inasmuch as it draws man's affections from the many to the one; so that the virtues, which flow from the love of God, are connected together. But self-love disunites man's affections among different things, in so far as man loves himself, by desiring for himself temporal goods, which are various and of many kinds. Hence vices and sins, which arise from self-love, are not connected together.

Second Article

WHETHER ALL SINS ARE EQUAL?

We proceed thus to the Second Article:—

Objection 1. It would seem that all sins are equal. For sin is to do what is unlawful. Now to do what is unlawful is reproved in one and the same way in all things. Therefore sin is reproved in one and the same way. Therefore one sin is not graver than another.

Obj. 2. Further, every sin is a transgression of the rule of reason, which is to human acts what a linear rule is in corporeal things. Therefore to sin is the same as to pass over a line. But passing over a line occurs equally and in the same way, even if one go a long way from it or stay near it, since privations do not admit of more or less. Therefore all sins are equal.

Obj. 3. Further, sins are opposed to virtues. But all virtues are equal, as Cicero states.[11] Therefore all sins are equal.

On the contrary, Our Lord said to Pilate (*Jo.* xix. 11): *He that hath delivered me to thee, hath the greater sin,* and yet it is evident that Pilate was guilty of some sin. Therefore one sin is greater than another.

I answer that, The opinion of the Stoics, which Cicero adopts in the book on *Paradoxes*,[12] was that all sins are equal; and from this opinion arose the error of certain heretics, who not only hold all sins to be equal, but also maintain that all the pains of hell are equal.[13] So far as can be gathered from the words of Cicero, the Stoics arrived at their conclusion by looking at sin on the side of the privation only, in so far, namely, as it is a departure from reason. Hence, considering without reservation that no privation admits of more or less, they held that all sins are equal. Yet if we consider the matter carefully, we shall see that there are two kinds of

---

[10] Q. 71, a. 1.   [11] *Paradoxa Stoicorum*, III, 1 (p. 12).   [12] *Ibid.*   [13] Jovinian, in St. Jerome, *Adv. Iovin.*, II, 18; 31 (PL 23, 326; 342).—Cf. St. Augustine, *De Haeres.*, 82 (PL 42, 45).

privation. For there is a simple and pure privation, which consists, so to speak, in *being* corrupted. Thus, death is a privation of life, and darkness is a privation of light. Such privations do not admit of more or less, because nothing remains of the opposite habit; and hence a man is not less dead on the first day after his death, or on the third or fourth days, than after a year, when his corpse is already dissolved; and, in like manner, a house is no darker if the light be covered with several shades, than if it were covered by a single shade shutting out all the light.—There is, however, another privation which is not absolute, but retains something of the opposite habit. It consists in *becoming* corrupted rather than in *being* corrupted: *e.g.*, sickness, which is a privation of the due commensuration of the humors, yet so that something remains of that commensuration, or else the animal would cease to live. The same applies to deformity and the like. Such privations admit of more or less on the part of what remains of the contrary habit. For it matters much in sickness or deformity whether one departs more or less from the due commensuration of the humors or the members. The same applies to vices and sins, because in them the privation of the due commensuration of reason is such as not to destroy the order of reason altogether; or else evil, if total, destroys itself, as is stated in *Ethics* iv.[14] For the substance of the act or the affection of the agent could not remain, unless something remained of the order of reason. Therefore it matters much to the gravity of a sin whether one departs more or less from the rectitude of reason; and accordingly we must say that sins are not all equal.

Reply Obj. 1. To commit sins is unlawful because of some lack of order in them; and therefore those which contain a greater lack of order are more unlawful, and consequently graver sins.

Reply Obj. 2. This argument looks upon sin as though it were a pure privation.

Reply Obj. 3. Virtues are proportionately equal in one and the same subject. However, one virtue surpasses another in excellence according to its species; and, again, one man is more virtuous than another in the same species of virtue, as was stated above.[15] Moreover, even if the virtues were equal, it would not follow that vices are equal, since virtues are connected, and vices or sins are not.

Third Article

WHETHER THE GRAVITY OF SINS VARIES ACCORDING TO THEIR OBJECTS?

We proceed thus to the Third Article:—

Objection 1. It would seem that the gravity of sins does not vary accord-

---

[14] Aristotle, *Eth.*, IV, 5 (1126a 12).   [15] Q. 66, a. 1 and 2.

ing to their objects. For the gravity of a sin pertains to its mode or quality, whereas the object is the matter of the sin. Therefore the gravity of sins does not vary according to their various objects.

Obj. 2. Further, the gravity of a sin is the intensity of its malice. Now sin does not derive its malice from its turning to its object, and which is some appetible good, but rather from that from which it turns away. Therefore the gravity of sins does not vary according to their various objects.

Obj. 3. Further, sins that have different objects are of different genera. But things of different genera cannot be compared with one another, as is proved in *Physics* vii.[16] Therefore one sin is not graver than another by reason of the difference of objects.

On the contrary, Sins take their species from their objects, as was shown above.[17] But some sins are graver than others according to their species, as murder is graver than theft. Therefore the gravity of sins varies according to their objects.

I answer that, As is clear from what has been said, the gravity of sins varies in the same way as one sickness is graver than another.[18] For just as the good of health consists in a certain commensuration of the humors, in keeping with an animal's nature, so the good of virtue consists in a certain commensuration of the human act in accord with the rule of reason. Now it is evident that the higher the principle, the disorder of which causes the disorder in the humors, the graver is the sickness. Thus a sickness which comes on the human body from the heart, which is the principle of life, or from some neighboring part, is more dangerous. Therefore a sin must needs be so much the graver, as the disorder occurs in a principle which is higher in the order of reason. Now in matters of action the reason directs all things in view of the end, and therefore the higher the end which attaches to sins in human acts, the graver the sin. But the object of an act is its end, as was stated above,[19] and consequently the difference of gravity in sins depends on their objects. Thus it is clear that external things are directed to man as their end, while man is further directed to God as his end. Therefore a sin which is about the very substance of man, *e.g.,* murder, is graver than a sin which is about external things, *e.g.,* theft; and graver still is a sin committed directly against God, *e.g.,* unbelief, blasphemy, and the like. Furthermore, in each of these grades of sin, one sin will be graver than another according as it is about a higher or a lower principle. And since sins take their species from their objects, the difference of gravity, which is derived from the objects, first and foremost results, as it were, from the species.

Reply Obj. 1. Although the object is the matter about which an act is

---

[16] Aristotle, *Phys.,* VII, 4 (248b 6).   [17] Q. 72, a. 1.   [18] A. 2; q. 72, a. 5.   [19] Q. 72, a. 3, ad 2.

concerned, yet it has the character of an end, in so far as the intention of the agent is directed to it, as was stated above.[20] Now the form of a moral act depends on the end, as was shown above.[21]

Reply Obj. 2. From the very fact that a man turns unduly to some mutable good, it follows that he turns away from the immutable Good, which aversion stamps perfectly the nature of evil. Hence the various degrees of malice in sins must needs follow the diversity of those things to which man turns.

Reply Obj. 3. All the objects of human acts are related to one another, and therefore all human acts have in a way one genus, in so far as they are directed to the last end. Therefore, nothing prevents all sins from being comparable with one another.

Fourth Article

WHETHER THE GRAVITY OF SINS DEPENDS ON THE EXCEL-
LENCE OF THE VIRTUES TO WHICH THEY ARE OPPOSED?

We proceed thus to the Fourth Article:—

Objection 1. It would seem that the gravity of sins does not vary according to the excellence of the virtues to which they are opposed, so that, namely, the graver sin is opposed to the greater virtue. For, according to *Prov.* xv. 5, *in abundant justice there is the greatest strength.* Now, as Our Lord says (*Matt.* v. 20, *seqq.*), abundant justice restrains anger, that is a less grievous sin than murder, which a less abundant justice restrains. Therefore the least grievous sin is opposed to the greatest virtue.

Obj. 2. Further, it is stated in *Ethics* ii. that *virtue is about the difficult and the good,*[22] from which it seems to follow that the greater virtue is about what is more difficult. But it is a less grievous sin to fail in what is more difficult, than in what is less difficult. Therefore the less grievous sin is opposed to the greater virtue.

Obj. 3. Further, charity is a greater virtue than faith or hope (*1 Cor.* xiii. 13). Now hatred, which is opposed to charity, is a less grievous sin than unbelief or despair, which are opposed to faith and hope. Therefore the less grievous sin is opposed to the greater virtue.

On the contrary, The Philosopher says that the *worst is opposed to the best.*[23] Now in morals the best is the greatest virtue, and the worst is the most grievous sin. Therefore the most grievous sin is opposed to the greatest virtue.

I answer that, A sin is opposed to a virtue in two ways. First, principally and directly, and this is the sin which is about the same object as virtue; for contraries are about the same thing. In this way, the more grievous sin

---

[20] *Ibid.*   [21] Q. 18, a. 6; q. 72, a. 6.   [22] Aristotle, *Eth.,* II, 3 (1105a 9).   [23] *Op. cit.,* VIII, 10 (1160b 9).

must needs be opposed to the greater virtue, because, just as the degrees of gravity in a sin depend on the object, so also does the greatness of a virtue, since both sin and virtue take their species from the object, as was shown above.[24] Therefore the greatest sin must needs be directly opposed to the greatest virtue, as being most removed from it in the same genus.— Secondly, the opposition of virtue to sin may be considered according to a certain extension of the virtue in checking sin. For the greater a virtue is, the further it removes man from the contrary sin, so that it withdraws man not only from that sin, but also from whatever leads to it. And thus it is evident that the greater a virtue is, the more it withdraws man also from less grievous sins; just as the more perfect health is, the more does it ward off even minor ailments. And in this way the less grievous sin is opposed to the greater virtue, on the part of the latter's effect.

Reply Obj. 1. This argument considers the opposition which consists in restraining from sin; for thus abundant justice checks even minor sins.

Reply Obj. 2. The greater virtue, which is about a more difficult good, is opposed directly to the sin which is about a more difficult evil. For in each case there is a certain superiority, in that the will is shown to be more intent on good or evil, through not being overcome by the difficulty.

Reply Obj. 3. Charity is not any kind of love, but the love of God. Hence, not any kind of hatred is opposed to it directly, but the hatred of God, which is the most grievous of all sins.

Fifth Article

WHETHER CARNAL SINS ARE OF LESS GUILT THAN SPIRITUAL SINS?

We proceed thus to the Fifth Article:—

Objection 1. It would seem that carnal sins are not of less guilt than spiritual sins. Because adultery is a more grievous sin than theft, for it is written (*Prov.* vi. 30, 32): *The fault is not so great when a man has stolen,* . . . *but he that is an adulterer, for the folly of his heart shall destroy his own soul.* Now theft belongs to covetousness, which is a spiritual sin, while adultery pertains to lust, which is a carnal sin. Therefore carnal sins are of greater guilt than spiritual sins.

Obj. 2. Further, Augustine says in his commentary on *Leviticus* that *the devil rejoices chiefly in lust and idolatry.*[25] But he rejoices more in the greater sin. Therefore, since lust is a carnal sin, it seems that the carnal sins are of most guilt.

Obj. 3. Further, the Philosopher proves that *it is more shameful to be incontinent in lust than in anger.*[26] But anger is a spiritual sin, according

---

[24] Q. 60, a. 5; q. 72, a. 1.   [25] *De Civit. Dei*, II, 4; 26 (PL 41, 50; 74).   [26] *Eth.*, VII, 6 (1149b 2; b 24).

to Gregory,[27] while lust pertains to carnal sins. Therefore carnal sin is more grievous than spiritual sin.

On the contrary, Gregory says that carnal sins are of less guilt, but of more shame, than spiritual sins.[28]

I answer that, Spiritual sins are of greater guilt than carnal sins. Now this does not mean that each spiritual sin is of greater guilt than each carnal sin, but that, considering the sole difference between spiritual and carnal, spiritual sins are more grievous than carnal sins, other things being equal. Three reasons may be assigned for this. The first is on the part of the subject, for spiritual sins belong to the spirit, to which it is proper to turn to God, and to turn away from Him; whereas carnal sins are consummated in the carnal pleasure of the appetite, to which it chiefly belongs to turn to goods of the body. Hence carnal sin, as such, denotes more a *turning to* something, and for that reason implies a closer cleaving; whereas spiritual sin denotes more a *turning from* something, whence the notion of guilt arises, and for this reason it involves greater guilt.—A second reason may be taken on the part of the person against whom sin is committed. For carnal sin, as such, is against the sinner's own body, which he ought to love less, in the order of charity, than God and his neighbor, against whom he commits spiritual sins; and consequently spiritual sins, as such, are of greater guilt.—A third reason may be taken from the motive, since the stronger the impulse to sin, the less grievous the sin, as we shall state further on. Now carnal sins have a stronger impulse, viz., our innate concupiscence of the flesh. Therefore spiritual sins, as such, are of greater guilt.

Reply Obj. 1. Adultery belongs not only to the sin of lust, but also to the sin of injustice, and in this respect may be brought under the head of covetousness, as the *Gloss* observes on *Ephes.* v. 5 (*No fornicator, or unclean, or covetous person,* etc.)[29]; so that adultery is so much the more grievous than theft as a man loves his wife more than his chattels.

Reply Obj. 2. The devil is said to rejoice chiefly in the sin of lust because it is of the greatest adhesion, and man can with difficulty be withdrawn from it. *For the desire of pleasure is insatiable,* as the Philosopher states.[30]

Reply Obj. 3. As the Philosopher himself says, the reason why it is more shameful to be incontinent in lust than in anger is that lust partakes less of reason;[31] and in the same sense he says that *sins of intemperance are most worthy of reproach, because they are about those pleasures which are common to us and irrational animals.*[32] Hence, by these sins man is, so to

---

[27] *Moral.,* XXXI, 45 (PL 76, 62).   [28] *Op. cit.,* XXXIII, 12 (PL 76, 688).
[29] *Glossa ordin.* (VI, 95E); Peter Lombard, *In Ephes.,* super V, 5 (PL 192, 209).—
Cf. St. Jerome, *In Ephes.,* III, super V, 5 (PL 26, 554).   [30] *Eth.,* III, 12 (1119b 8)
[31] *Op. cit.,* VII, 6 (1149b 2; b 24).   [32] *Op. cit.,* III, 10 (1118b 2).

speak, brutalized; for which same reason Gregory says that they are more shameful.

Sixth Article

WHETHER THE GRAVITY OF A SIN DEPENDS ON ITS CAUSE?

We proceed thus to the Sixth Article:—

Objection 1. It would seem that the gravity of a sin does not depend on its cause. For the greater a sin's cause, the more forcibly it moves to sin, and so the more difficult is it to resist. But sin is lessened by the fact that it is difficult to resist. For it denotes weakness in the sinner, if he cannot easily resist sin; and a sin that is due to weakness is deemed less grievous. Therefore sin does not derive its gravity from its cause.

Obj. 2. Further, concupiscence is a general cause of sin, and therefore the *Gloss* on *Rom.* vii. 7 (*For I had not known concupiscence*) says: *The law is good, since by forbidding concupiscence, it forbids all evils.*[33] Now the greater the concupiscence by which man is overcome, the less grievous his sin. Therefore the gravity of a sin is diminished by the greatness of its cause.

Obj. 3. Further, just as rectitude of the reason is the cause of a virtuous act, so defect in the reason seems to be the cause of sin. Now the greater the defect in the reason, the less grievous the sin; so much so, that he who lacks the use of reason is altogether excused from sin, and he who sins through ignorance sins less grievously. Therefore the gravity of a sin is not increased by the greatness of its cause.

On the contrary, If the cause be increased, the effect is increased. Therefore the greater the cause of sin, the more grievous the sin.

I answer that, In the genus of sin, as in every other genus, two causes may be observed. The first is the direct and proper cause of sin, which is the will to sin; for it is compared to the sinful act as a tree to its fruit, as the *Gloss* observes on *Matt.* vii. 18 (*A good tree cannot bring forth evil fruit*).[34] And the greater this cause is, the more grievous will the sin be, since the greater the will to sin, the more grievously does man sin.

The other causes of sin are extrinsic and remote, as it were, being those by which the will is inclined to sin. Among these causes we must make a distinction, for some of them induce the will to sin in accord with the very nature of the will. Such is the end, which is the proper object of the will; and by such a cause sin is made more grievous, because a man sins more grievously if his will is induced to sin by the intention of a more evil end.— Other causes incline the will to sin against the nature and order of the will, whose natural inclination is to be moved freely of itself in accord with the

---

[33] *Glossa ordin.* (VI, 16E); *Glossa interl.* (VI, 16v); Peter Lombard, *In Rom.*, super VII. 7 (PL 191, 1416).   [34] *Glossa ordin.* (V, 29B).

judgment of reason. Therefore those causes which weaken the judgment of reason (*e.g.*, ignorance), or which weaken the free movement of the will (*e.g.*, weakness, violence, fear or the like), diminish the gravity of sin, even as they diminish its voluntariness; and so much so, that if the act be altogether involuntary, it is no longer sinful.

Reply Obj. 1. This argument considers the extrinsic moving cause, which diminishes voluntariness. The increase of such a cause diminishes the sin, as was stated.

Reply Obj. 2. If concupiscence be understood to include the movement of the will, then, where there is greater concupiscence, there is a greater sin. But if by concupiscence we understand a passion, which is a movement of the concupiscible power, then a greater concupiscence, forestalling the judgment of reason and the movement of the will, diminishes the sin, because the man who sins, being stimulated by a greater concupiscence, falls through a more grievous temptation, and therefore is less to be blamed. On the other hand, if concupiscence, taken in this sense, follows the judgment of reason and the movement of the will, then the greater the concupiscence, the graver the sin; because sometimes the movement of concupiscence is redoubled by the will tending unrestrainedly to its object.

Reply Obj. 3. This argument considers the cause which renders the act involuntary, and such a cause diminishes the gravity of sin, as was stated.

Seventh Article

WHETHER A CIRCUMSTANCE AGGRAVATES A SIN?

We proceed thus to the Seventh Article:—

Objection 1. It would seem that a circumstance does not aggravate a sin. For sin takes its gravity from its species. Now a circumstance does not specify a sin, for it is an accident thereof. Therefore the gravity of a sin is not taken from a circumstance.

Obj. 2. Further, a circumstance is either evil or not. If it is evil, it causes, of itself, a species of evil; and if it is not evil, it cannot make a thing worse. Therefore a circumstance in no way aggravates a sin.

Obj. 3. Further, the malice of a sin is derived from its turning away [from God]. But circumstances affect sin on the part of the object to which it turns. Therefore they do not add to the sin's malice.

On the contrary, Ignorance of a circumstance diminishes sin, for he who sins through ignorance of a circumstance deserves to be forgiven.[35] Now this would not be the case unless a circumstance aggravated a sin. Therefore a circumstance makes a sin more grievous.

I answer that, As the Philosopher says in speaking of the habits of virtue, *it is natural for a thing to be increased by that which causes it.*[36] Now it

---

[35] Aristotle, *Eth.*, III, 1 (1111a 1).   [36] *Op. cit.*, II, 2 (1104a 27).

is evident that a sin is caused by a defect in some circumstance, for the fact that a man departs from the order of reason is due to his not observing the due circumstances in his action. Therefore it is evident that it is natural for a sin to be aggravated by reason of its circumstances. This happens in three ways. First, in so far as a circumstance draws a sin from one genus to another. Thus, fornication is the intercourse of a man with one who is not his wife; but if to this be added the circumstance that the latter is the wife of another, the sin is drawn to another kind of sin, viz., injustice, in so far as he usurps another's property. And in this respect adultery is a more grievous sin than fornication.—Secondly, a circumstance aggravates a sin, not by drawing it into another genus, but only by multiplying the character of sin. Thus if a wasteful man gives both when he ought not, and to whom he ought not to give, he commits the same kind of sin in more ways than if he were merely to give to whom he ought not; and for that very reason his sin is more grievous, even as that sickness is the graver which affects more parts of the body. Hence Cicero says that *in taking his father's life a man commits many sins; for he outrages one who begot him, who fed him, who educated him, to whom he owes his lands, his house, his position in the republic.*[37]—Thirdly, a circumstance aggravates a sin by adding to the deformity which the sin derives from another circumstance. Thus, taking another's property constitutes the sin of theft, but if to this be added the circumstance that much is taken of another's property, the sin will be more grievous; although, in itself, to take much or little has not the character of a good or of an evil act.

Reply Obj. 1. Some circumstances do specify a moral act, as was stated above.[38] Nevertheless a circumstance which does not specify may aggravate a sin; because, just as the goodness of a thing is weighed not only in reference to its species, but also in reference to some accident, so the malice of an act is measured, not only according to the species of that act, but also according to a circumstance.

Reply Obj. 2. A circumstance may aggravate a sin either way. For if it is evil, it does not follow that it constitutes the sin's species; for it can multiply the character of evil within the same species, as was stated above. And if it be not evil, it can aggravate a sin in relation to the malice of another circumstance.

Reply Obj. 3. Reason should direct the action not only as regards the object, but also as regards every circumstance. Therefore one may turn aside from the rule of reason through corruption of any single circumstance, for instance, by doing something when one ought not or where one ought not. Now to depart thus from the rule of reason suffices to make the act evil. But this turning aside from the rule of reason results from man's turning away from God, to Whom man ought to be united by right reason.

---

[37] *Parad. Stoic.*, III, 2 (pp. 13-14).   [38] Q. 18. a. 10.

Eighth Article

WHETHER SIN IS AGGRAVATED BY REASON OF ITS CAUSING
MORE HARM?

We proceed thus to the Eighth Article:—
Objection 1. It would seem that a sin is not aggravated by reason of its causing more harm. For the harm done is an issue consequent upon the sinful act. But the issue of an act does not add to its goodness or malice, as was stated above.[39] Therefore a sin is not aggravated because of its causing more harm.

Obj. 2. Further, harm is inflicted chiefly by sins against our neighbor. For no one wishes to harm himself, and no one can harm God, according to *Job* xxxv. 6, 8: *If thy iniquities be multiplied, what shalt thou do against Him? . . . Thy wickedness may hurt a man that is like thee.* If, therefore, sins were aggravated through causing more harm, it would follow that sins against our neighbor are more grievous than sins against God or oneself.

Obj. 3. Further, greater harm is inflicted on a man by depriving him of the life of grace, than by taking away his natural life; because the life of grace is better than the life of nature, and so much so, that man ought to despise his natural life lest he lose the life of grace. Now, speaking absolutely, a man who leads a woman to commit fornication deprives her of the life of grace by leading her into mortal sin. If, therefore, a sin were more grievous because of its causing a greater harm, it would follow that fornication, absolutely speaking, is a more grievous sin than murder, which is evidently untrue. Therefore a sin is not more grievous because of its causing a greater harm.

On the contrary, Augustine says: *Since vice is contrary to nature, a vice is the more grievous according as it diminishes the integrity of a nature.*[40] Now the diminution of the integrity of a nature is a harm. Therefore a sin is graver according as it does more harm.

I answer that, Harm may bear a threefold relation to sin. For sometimes the harm resulting from a sin is foreseen and intended, as when a man does something with a mind to harm another, *e.g.,* a murderer or a thief. In this case the quantity of harm aggravates the sin directly, because then the harm is the direct object of the sin.—Sometimes the harm is foreseen, but not intended; for instance, when a man takes a short cut through a field, with the result that he knowingly injures the growing crops, although his intention is not to do this harm, but to commit fornication. In this case, again, the quantity of the harm done aggravates the sin; indirectly, however, in so far, namely, as it is because his will is strongly inclined to sin that a man does not forbear from doing, to himself or to another, a harm which he would not wish absolutely.—Sometimes, however, the

[39] Q. 20, a. 5.   [40] *De Lib. Arb.,* III, 14 (PL 32, 1291).

harm is neither foreseen nor intended, and then if this harm is connected with the sin accidentally, it does not aggravate the sin directly. But because he neglects to consider the harm that might ensue, a man is deemed punishable for the evil results of his action if it be unlawful. If, on the other hand, the harm follows directly from the sinful act, although it be neither foreseen nor intended, it aggravates the sin directly, because whatever is directly consequent upon a sin belongs, in a manner, to the very species of that sin. For instance, if a man is a notorious fornicator, the result is that many are scandalized; and although such was not his intention, nor was it perhaps foreseen by him, yet it aggravates his sin directly.

But this does not seem to apply to penal harm, which the sinner himself incurs. Such harm, if accidentally connected with the sinful act, and if neither foreseen nor intended, does not aggravate a sin, nor does it correspond with the gravity of the sin. Such would be the case of a man who, in running to kill someone, slips and hurts his foot. If, on the other hand, this harm is directly consequent upon the sinful act, although perhaps it be neither foreseen nor intended, then greater harm does not make greater sin, but, on the contrary, a graver sin calls for the infliction of a greater harm. Thus, an unbeliever who has heard nothing about the pains of hell, would suffer greater pain in hell for a sin of murder than for a sin of theft; but his sin is not aggravated because of his neither intending nor foreseeing this, as it would be in the case of a believer, who is seen to sin more grievously in the very fact that he despises a greater punishment, that he may satisfy his desire to sin; but the gravity of this harm is caused by the sole gravity of sin.

Reply Obj. 1. As we have already stated, in treating of the goodness and malice of external actions, the result of an action, if foreseen and intended, adds to the goodness and malice of an act.[41]

Reply Obj. 2. Although the harm done aggravates a sin, it does not follow that this alone renders a sin more grievous. In fact, it is lack of order which of itself aggravates a sin. Therefore the harm itself that ensues aggravates a sin, in so far only as it renders the act more inordinate. Hence it does not follow, supposing harm to be inflicted chiefly by sins against our neighbor, that such sins are the most grievous, since a much greater lack of order is to be found in sins which man commits against God, and in some which he commits against himself.—Moreover, we might say that although no man can do God any harm in His substance, yet he can endeavor to do so in things concerning Him, *e.g.*, by destroying faith, by outraging holy things, which are most grievous sins.—Again, a man sometimes knowingly and freely inflicts harm on himself, as in the case of suicide, though this be referred finally to some apparent good, for example, delivery from some anxiety.

---

[41] Q. 20, a. 5.

Reply Obj. 3. This argument does not hold, for two reasons. First, because the murderer intends directly to do harm to his neighbors, whereas the fornicator who solicits the woman intends not harm but pleasure; secondly, because murder is the direct and sufficient cause of bodily death, whereas no man can of himself be the sufficient cause of another's spiritual death, because no man dies spiritually except by sinning of his own will.

Ninth Article

WHETHER A SIN IS AGGRAVATED BY REASON OF THE CONDITION OF THE PERSON AGAINST WHOM IT IS COMMITTED?

We proceed thus to the Ninth Article:—

Objection 1. It would seem that sin is not aggravated by reason of the condition of the person against whom it is committed. For if this were the case, a sin would be aggravated chiefly by being committed against a just and holy man. But this does not aggravate a sin, because a virtuous man who bears a wrong with equanimity is less harmed by the wrong done him than others who, through being scandalized, are also hurt inwardly. Therefore the condition of the person against whom a sin is committed does not aggravate the sin.

Obj. 2. Further, if the condition of the person aggravated the sin, this would be still more the case if the person be near of kin; for, as Cicero says, *the man who kills his slave sins once; he that takes his father's life sins many times.*[42] But the kinship of a person sinned against does not seem to aggravate a sin, because every man is most akin to himself, and yet it is less grievous to harm oneself than another, *e.g.*, to kill one's own, than another's horse, as the Philosopher declares.[43] Therefore kinship of the person sinned against does not aggravate the sin.

Obj. 3. Further, the condition of the person who sins aggravates a sin chiefly because of his position or knowledge, according to *Wis.* vi. 7: *The mighty shall be mightily tormented*; and *Luke* xii. 47: *The servant who knew the will of his lord . . . and did it not . . . shall be beaten with many stripes.* Therefore, in like manner, on the part of the person sinned against, the sin is made more grievous by reason of his position and knowledge. But it does not seem to be a more grievous sin to inflict an injury on a rich and powerful person than on a poor man, since *there is no respect of persons with God* (*Rom.* ii. 11), according to Whose judgment the gravity of a sin is measured. Therefore the condition of the person sinned against does not aggravate the sin.

On the contrary, Holy Scripture censures especially those sins that are committed against the servants of God. Thus it is written (*3 Kings* xix. 14): *They have destroyed Thy altars. they have slain Thy prophets with*

---

[42] *Parad. Stoic.*, III, 2 (p. 13).   [43] *Eth.*, V, 11 (1138a 28).

the sword.—Moreover much blame is attached to the sin committed by a man against those who are akin to him, according to *Mich.* vii. 6: *The son dishonoreth the father, and the daughter riseth up against her mother.*— Furthermore, sins committed against persons of rank are expressly condemned. Thus it is written (*Job* xxxiv. 18): *Who saith to the king: "Thou art an apostate"; who calleth rulers ungodly.* Therefore the condition of the person sinned against aggravates the sin.

I answer that, The person sinned against is, in a manner, the object of the sin. Now it has been stated above that the primary gravity of a sin is derived from its object, so that a sin is deemed to be so much the more grave, as its object is a more principal end. But the principal ends of human acts are God, man himself and his neighbor. For whatever we do, it is because of one of these that we do it; although one of them is subordinate to the other. Therefore the greater or lesser gravity of a sin, in respect of the person sinned against, may be considered on the part of these three.

First, on the part of God, to Whom man is the more closely united, as he is more virtuous or more sacred to God; so that an injury inflicted on such a person redounds to God, according to *Zach.* ii. 8: *He that toucheth you, toucheth the apple of My eye.* Therefore a sin is the more grievous according as it is committed against a person more closely united to God by reason of personal sanctity, or official station.—On the part of man himself, it is evident that he sins all the more grievously according as the person against whom he sins is more united to him, either through natural affinity or kindness received or any other bond; because he seems to sin against himself rather than the other, and, for this very reason, sins all the more grievously, according to *Ecclus.* xiv. 5: *He that is evil to himself, to whom will he be good?*—On the part of his neighbor, a man sins the more grievously according as his sin affects more persons; so that a sin committed against a public personage, *e.g.,* a sovereign prince who stands in the place of the whole people, is more grievous than a sin committed against a private person. Hence it is expressly prohibited (*Exod.* xxii. 28): *The prince of thy people thou shalt not curse.* In like manner, it would seem that an injury done to a person of prominence is all the more grave because of the scandal and the disturbance it would cause among many people.

Reply Obj. 1. He who inflicts an injury on a virtuous person, so far as he is concerned, disturbs him internally and externally; but that the latter is not disturbed internally is due to his goodness, which does not extenuate the sin of the injurer.

Reply Obj. 2. The injury which a man inflicts on himself in those things which are subject to the dominion of his will, for instance, his possessions, is less sinful than if it were inflicted on another, because he does it of his own will; but in those things that are not subject to the dominion of his will, such as natural and spiritual goods, it is a graver sin to inflict an injury on oneself, for it is more grievous for a man to kill himself than another. Since, however, things belonging to our neighbor are not subject to the dominion of our will, the argument fails to prove, in respect of injuries done to such things, that it is less grievous to sin in their regard, unless indeed our neighbor be willing, or give his approval.

Reply Obj. 3. There is no respect for persons if God punishes more severely those who sin against a person of higher rank; for this is done because such an injury redounds to the harm of many.

Tenth Article

WHETHER THE EXCELLENCE OF THE PERSON SINNING AGGRAVATES THE SIN?

We proceed thus to the Tenth Article:—

Objection 1. It would seem that the excellence of the person sinning does not aggravate the sin. For man becomes great chiefly by cleaving to God, according to *Ecclus.* xxv. 13: *How great is he that findeth wisdom and knowledge! but there is none above him that feareth the Lord.* Now the more a man cleaves to God, the less is a sin imputed to him; for it is written (*2 Paral.* xxx. 18, 19): *The Lord Who is good will show mercy to all them, who with their whole heart seek the Lord the God of their fathers; and will not impute it to them that they are not sanctified.* Therefore a sin is not aggravated by the excellence of the person sinning.

Obj. 2. Further, *there is no respect of persons with God* (*Rom.* ii. 11). Therefore He does not punish one man more than another for one and the same sin. Therefore a sin is not aggravated by the excellence of the person sinning.

Obj. 3. Further, no one should reap disadvantage from good. But he would, if his action were the more blameworthy because of his goodness. Therefore a sin is not aggravated by reason of the excellence of the person sinning.

On the contrary, Isidore says: *A sin is deemed so much the more grievous, as the sinner is held to be a more excellent person.*[44]

I answer that, Sin is twofold. There is a sin which takes us unawares because of the weakness of human nature, and such sins are less imputable to one who is more virtuous, because he is less negligent in restraining such sins. However, human weakness does not allow us to escape them altogether.—But there are other sins which proceed from deliberation, and these sins are all the more imputed to a man according as he is more excellent. Four reasons may be assigned for this. First, because a more excellent person, *e.g.,* one who excels in knowledge and virtue, can more easily resist sin; and hence Our Lord said (*Luke* xii. 47) that the *servant who*

---

[44] *Sent.,* II, 18 (PL 83, 621).

knew the will of his lord, . . . and did it not . . . shall be beaten with many stripes.—Secondly, because of ingratitude, because every good in which a man excels is a gift of God, to Whom man is ungrateful when he sins; and in this respect any excellence, even in temporal goods, aggravates a sin, according to *Wis.* vi. 7: *The mighty shall be mightily tormented.*—Thirdly, because the sinful act is particularly inconsistent with the excellence of the person sinning. Such would be the case if a prince were to violate justice, whereas he is set up as the guardian of justice, or if a priest were to be a fornicator, whereas he has taken the vow of chastity. —Fourthly, because of example or scandal, because, as Gregory says: *Sin becomes much more scandalous, when the sinner is honored for his position.*[45] For the sins of the great are much more notorious and men are wont to bear them with more indignation.

Reply Obj. 1. The passage quoted alludes to those things which are done negligently when we are taken unawares through human weakness.

Reply Obj. 2. God does not respect persons in punishing the great more severely, because their excellence conduces to the gravity of their sin, as was stated.

Reply Obj. 3. The man who excels in anything reaps disadvantage, not from the good which he has, but from his abuse thereof.

[45] *Pastor.*, I, 2 (PL 77, 16).

ON THE SUBJECT OF SIN

(In Ten Articles)

WE must now consider the subject of vice or sin, under which head there are ten points of inquiry: (1) Whether the will can be the subject of sin? (2) Whether the will alone is the subject of sin? (3) Whether the sensuality can be the subject of sin? (4) Whether it can be the subject of mortal sin? (5) Whether the reason can be the subject of sin? (6) Whether lingering delectation [*delectatio morosa*], or non-lingering delectation, is in the lower reason as in its subject? (7) Whether the sin of consent to the act of sin is in the higher reason as in its subject? (8) Whether the lower reason can be the subject of mortal sin? (9) Whether the higher reason can be the subject of venial sin? (10) Whether there can be in the higher reason a venial sin directed to its proper object?

First Article

WHETHER THE WILL IS A SUBJECT OF SIN?

We proceed thus to the First Article:—

Objection 1. It would seem that the will cannot be a subject of sin. For Dionysius says that *evil is outside the will and the intention*.[1] But sin has the character of evil. Therefore sin cannot be in the will.

Obj. 2. Further, the will is directed either to the good or to what seems good. Now from the fact that the will wishes the good, it does not sin; and that it wishes what seems good, but is not truly good, points to a defect in the apprehensive power rather than in the will. Therefore sin is in no way in the will.

Obj. 3. Further, the same thing cannot be both subject and efficient cause of sin, because *the efficient and the material cause do not coincide*.[2] Now the will is the efficient cause of sin, because the first cause of sinning is the will, as Augustine states.[3] Therefore it is not the subject of sin.

On the contrary, Augustine says that *it is by the will that we sin, and by which we live righteously*.[4]

I answer that, Sin is an act, as was stated above.[5] Now some acts pass

---

[1] *De Div. Nom.*, IV, 32 (PG 3, 732).   [2] Aristotle, *Phys.*, II, 7 (198a 24).   [3] *De Duab. Anim.*, X; XI (PL 42, 104; 105); cf. *De Lib. Arb.*, III, 17 (PL 32, 1295).   [4] *Retract.*, I, 9 (PL 32, 596).   [5] Q. 21, a. 1; q. 71, a. 1 and 6.

into external matter, *e.g., to cut* and *to burn,* and such acts have for their matter and subject the thing into which the action passes. Hence the Philosopher states that *movement is the act of the thing moved, caused by a mover.*[6]—On the other hand, there are acts which do not pass into external matter, but remain in the agent, *e.g., to desire* and *to know;* and such are all moral acts, whether virtuous or sinful. Consequently, the proper subject of sin must needs be the power which is the principle of the act. Now since it is proper to moral acts that they be voluntary, as we have stated above,[7] it follows that the will, which is the principle of voluntary acts, both of good acts, and of evil acts or sins, is the principle of sins. Therefore it follows that sin is in the will as its subject.

Reply Obj. 1. Evil is said to be outside the will because the will does not tend to it under the aspect of evil. But since some evil is an apparent good, the will sometimes desires an evil, and in this sense sin is in the will.

Reply Obj. 2. If the defect in the apprehensive power were in no way subject to the will, there would be no sin, either in the will, or in the apprehensive power, as is evident in the case of those whose ignorance is invincible. It remains, therefore, that when there is in the apprehensive power a defect that is subject to the will, this defect also is deemed a sin.

Reply Obj. 3. This argument applies to those efficient causes whose actions pass into external matter, and which do not move themselves, but move other things; but it is the contrary of this that is to be observed in the will, and hence the argument does not hold.

Second Article

WHETHER THE WILL ALONE IS THE SUBJECT OF SIN?

We proceed thus to the Second Article:—

Objection 1. It would seem that the will alone is the subject of sin. For Augustine says that *no one sins except by the will.*[8] Now the subject of sin is the power by which we sin. Therefore the will alone is the subject of sin.

Obj. 2. Further, sin is an evil contrary to reason. Now good and evil pertaining to reason are the object of the will alone. Therefore the will alone is the subject of sin.

Obj. 3. Further, every sin is a voluntary act, because, as Augustine states, *so true is it that every sin is voluntary, that unless it be voluntary, it is no sin at all.*[9] Now the acts of the other powers are not voluntary, except in so far as those powers are moved by the will; nor does this suffice for them to be the subject of sin, because then even the external members of the body, which are moved by the will, would be a subject of sin, which is clearly untrue. Therefore the will alone is the subject of sin.

---

[6] *Phys.,* III, 3 (202a 13).   [7] Q. 1, a. 1; q. 18, a. 6 and 9.   [8] *De Duab. Anim.,* X (PL 42, 104).   [9] *De Lib. Arb.,* III, 18 (PL 32, 1295); *De Vera Relig.,* XIV (PL 34, 133).

On the contrary, Sin is contrary to virtue, and contraries are about one and the same thing. But the other powers of the soul, besides the will, are the subject of virtues, as was stated above.[10] Therefore the will is not the only subject of sin.

I answer that, As was shown above, whatever is a principle of a voluntary act is a subject of sin. Now voluntary acts are not only those which are elicited by the will, but also those which are commanded by the will, as we have stated above in treating of voluntariness.[11] Therefore not only the will can be a subject of sin, but also all those powers which can be moved to their acts, or restrained from their acts, by the will; and these same powers are the subjects of good and evil moral habits, because act and habit belong to the same subject.

Reply Obj. 1. We do not sin except by the will as first mover; but we sin by the other powers as moved by the will.

Reply Obj. 2. Good and evil pertain to the will as its proper objects; but the other powers have certain determinate goods and evils, by reason of which they can be the subject of virtue, vice and sin, in so far as they partake of will and reason.

Reply Obj. 3. The members of the body are not principles but merely organs of action, and hence they are compared to the soul which moves them as a slave who is moved but does not move. On the other hand, the internal appetitive powers are compared to reason as free agents, because they both act and are acted upon, as is made clear in *Politics* i.[12] Moreover, the acts of the external members are actions that pass into external matter, as may be seen in the blow that is inflicted in the sin of murder. Consequently there is no comparison.

Third Article

WHETHER THERE CAN BE SIN IN THE SENSUALITY?

We proceed thus to the Third Article:—

Objection 1. It would seem that there cannot be sin in the sensuality. For sin is proper to man, who is praised or blamed for his actions. Now the sensuality is common to us and irrational animals. Therefore sin cannot be in the sensuality.

Obj. 2. Further, *no man sins in what he cannot avoid,* as Augustine states.[13] But man cannot prevent the movement of the sensuality from being inordinate, since *the sensuality always remains corrupt, so long as we abide in this mortal life, and therefore it is signified by the serpent,* as Augustine declares.[14] Therefore the inordinate movement of the sensuality is not a sin.

---

[10] Q. 56, a. 3 and 4.   [11] Q. 6, a. 4.   [12] Aristotle, *Polit.,* I, 2 (1254b 4).   [13] *De Lib. Arb.,* III, 18 (PL 32, 1295).   [14] *De Trin.,* XII, 12; 13 (PL 42, 1007; 1009).

Obj. 3. Further, that which man himself does not do is not imputed to him as a sin. Now *that alone do we seem to do ourselves, which we do with the deliberation of reason,* as the Philosopher says.[15] Therefore the movement of the sensuality, which is without the deliberation of reason, is not imputed to a man as a sin.

On the contrary, It is written (*Rom.* vii. 19): *The good which I will I do not; but the evil which I will not, that I do;* which words Augustine explains as referring to the evil of concupiscence, which is clearly a movement of the sensuality.[16] Therefore there can be sin in the sensuality.

I answer that, As was stated above, sin may be found in any power whose act can be voluntary and inordinate, wherein consists the nature of sin. Now it is evident that the act of the sensuality can be voluntary, in so far as the sensuality, or sensitive appetite, is naturally able to be moved by the will. Therefore it follows that sin can be in the sensuality.

Reply Obj. 1. Although some of the powers of the sensitive part are common to us and irrational animals, nevertheless, in us, they have a certain excellence through being united to the reason. Thus we surpass other animals in the sensitive part inasmuch as we have the powers of cogitation and reminiscence, as was stated in the First Part.[17] In the same way, our sensitive appetite surpasses that of other animals by reason of a certain excellence consisting in its natural aptitude to obey the reason; and in this respect it can be the principle of a voluntary act and, consequently, the subject of sin.

Reply Obj. 2. The continual corruption of the sensuality is to be understood as referring to the 'fomes,' which is never completely destroyed in this life, since, though the stain of original sin passes, its effect remains. However, this corruption of the 'fomes' does not hinder man from using his rational will to check individual inordinate movements (if he be presentient of them), for instance by turning his thoughts to other things. Yet while he is turning his thoughts to something else, an inordinate movement may arise about this also. Thus when a man, in order to avoid the movements of concupiscence, turns his thoughts away from carnal pleasures to the considerations of science, sometimes an unpremeditated movement of vainglory will arise. Consequently, a man cannot avoid all such movements, because of the aforesaid corruption; but it is enough, for the conditions of a voluntary sin, that he be able to avoid each single one.

Reply Obj. 3. Man does not do perfectly what he does without the deliberation of reason, since the principal part of a man does nothing therein. Hence, this is not perfectly a human act, and consequently it cannot be a perfect act of virtue or of sin, but is something imperfect of that kind. Therefore such movement of the sensuality as forestalls the reason is a venial sin, which is something imperfect in the genus of sin.

---

[15] *Eth.,* IX, 8 (1168b 35).   [16] *Serm.* XXX, 2; 3 (PL 38, 188; 189).   [17] *S. T.,* I, q. 78, a. 4.

Fourth Article

WHETHER MORTAL SIN CAN BE IN THE SENSUALITY?

We proceed thus to the Fourth Article:—

Objection 1. It would seem that mortal sin can be in the sensuality. For an act is discerned by its object. Now it is possible to commit a mortal sin about the objects of the sensuality, *e.g.*, about carnal pleasures. Therefore the act of the sensuality can be a mortal sin, and hence mortal sin can be found in the sensuality.

Obj. 2. Further, mortal sin is opposed to virtue. But virtue can be in the sensuality, for temperance and fortitude are virtues of the irrational parts, as the Philosopher states.[18] Therefore, since it is natural to contraries to be about the same subject, sensuality can be the subject of mortal sin.

Obj. 3. Further, venial sin is a disposition to mortal sin. Now disposition and habit are in the same subject. Since, therefore, venial sin may be in the sensuality, as was stated above, mortal sin can be there also.

On the contrary, Augustine says, and the *Gloss* on *Rom.* vii. 14 repeats: *The inordinate movement of concupiscence, which is the sin of the sensuality, can even be in those who are in a state of grace,*[19] in whom, however, mortal sin is not to be found. Therefore the inordinate movement of the sensuality is not a mortal sin.

I answer that, Just as a disorder which destroys the principle of the body's life causes the body's death, so, too, a disorder which destroys the principle of spiritual life, viz., the last end, causes spiritual death, which is mortal sin, as was stated above.[20] Now it belongs to the reason alone, and not to the sensuality, to order anything to the end; and disorder in respect of the end can belong only to the power whose function it is to order others to the end. Therefore mortal sin cannot be in the sensuality, but only in the reason.

Reply Obj. 1. The act of the sensuality can concur towards a mortal sin; and yet the fact of its being a mortal sin is due, not to its being an act of the sensuality, but to its being an act of reason, to which the ordering to the end belongs. Consequently, mortal sin is imputed, not to the sensuality, but to reason.

Reply Obj. 2. An act of virtue is perfected not only in that it is an act of the sensuality, but still more in the fact of its being an act of reason and will, whose function it is to choose; for the act of moral virtue is not without the exercise of choice, and therefore the act of moral virtue, which perfects the appetitive power, is always accompanied by an act of

---

[18] *Eth.,* III, 10 (1117b 23).   [19] *Retract.,* I, 23 (PL 32, 621); *Glossa ordin.* (VI. 17E).   [20] Q. 72, a. 5.

prudence, which perfects the rational power. The same applies to mortal sin, as we have just stated.

Reply Obj. 3. A disposition may be related in three ways to that to which it disposes:—for sometimes it is the same thing and is in the same subject: thus, inchoate science is a disposition to perfect science;—sometimes it is in the same subject, but is not the same thing: thus, heat is a disposition to the form of fire;—sometimes it is neither the same thing, nor in the same subject, as in those things which are ordered to one another in such a way that we can arrive at one through the other: *e.g.,* goodness of the imagination is a disposition to science, which is in the intellect. In this way the venial sin, that is in the sensuality, may be a disposition to mortal sin, which is in the reason.

Fifth Article

WHETHER SIN CAN BE IN THE REASON?

We proceed thus to the Fifth Article:—

Objection 1. It would seem that sin cannot be in the reason. For the sin of any power is a defect in it. But the fault of the reason is not a sin; on the contrary, it excuses sin, for a man is excused from sin because of ignorance. Therefore sin cannot be in the reason.

Obj. 2. Further, the primary subject of sin is the will, as was stated above. Now reason precedes the will, since it directs it. Therefore sin cannot be in the reason.

Obj. 3. Further, there can be no sin except about things which are under our control. Now perfection and defect of reason are not among those things which are under our control, since by nature some are intellectually slow, and some are quick. Therefore no sin is in the reason.

On the contrary, Augustine says that sin is in the lower and in the higher reason.[21]

I answer that, The sin of any power is an act of that power, as we have clearly shown. Now reason has a twofold act: one is its proper act in relation to its proper object, and this is the act of knowing a truth; the other is the act of the reason as directing the other powers. Now in both of these ways there may be sin in the reason. First, in so far as it errs in the knowledge of truth, which error is imputed to the reason as a sin when it is in ignorance or error about what it is able and ought to know;—secondly, when it either commands the inordinate movements of the lower powers, or deliberately fails to check them.

Reply Obj. 1. This argument considers the defect in the proper act of the reason in relation to its proper object, and under circumstances when it is a defect of knowledge about something which one is unable to know;

---

[21] *De Trin.,* XII, 12 (PL 42, 1008).

for then this defect of reason is not a sin, and excuses from sin, as is evident with regard to the actions of madmen.—If, however, the defect of reason be about something which a man is able and ought to know, he is not altogether excused from sin, and the defect is imputed to him as a sin. —The defect which belongs only to the act of directing the other powers is always imputed to reason as a sin, because the reason can always obviate this defect by means of its proper act.

Reply Obj. 2. As was stated above, when we were treating of the acts of the will and the reason, the will moves and precedes the reason in one way, and the reason moves and precedes the will in another.[22] Hence both the movement of the will can be called rational, and the act of the reason, voluntary. Accordingly, sin is found in the reason, either through being a voluntary defect of the reason, or through the fact that the reason is the principle of the will's act.

The Reply to the Third Objection is evident from what has been said.

Sixth Article

WHETHER THE SIN OF LINGERING DELECTATION IS IN THE
REASON?

We proceed thus to the Sixth Article:—

Objection 1. It would seem that the sin of lingering delectation [*delectatio morosa*] is not in the reason.[23] For delectation denotes a movement of the appetitive power, as was stated above.[24] But the appetitive power is distinct from the reason, which is an apprehensive power. Therefore lingering delectation is not in the reason.

Obj. 2. Further, the object shows to which power an act belongs, since it is through the act that the power is directed to its object. Now lingering delectation is sometimes about sensible goods, and not about the goods of the reason. Therefore the sin of lingering delectation is not in the reason.

Obj. 3. Further, a thing is said to be lingering through taking a length of time. But length of time is no reason why an act should belong to a particular power. Therefore, lingering delectation does not belong to the reason.

On the contrary, Augustine says that *if the consent to a sensual delectation goes no further than the mere thought of the pleasure, I deem this to be like as though the woman alone had partaken of the forbidden fruit.*[25] Now *the woman* denotes the lower reason, as he himself explains. Therefore the sin of lingering delectation is in the reason.

I answer that, As has already been stated, sin may sometimes be in the

[22] Q. 17, a. 1.   [23] On this and the remaining problems in this question, cf. Peter Lombard, *Sent.*, II, xxiv, 5-13 (I, 422-428).   [24] Q. 31, a. 1.   [25] *De Trin.*, XII, 12 (PL 42, 1007).

reason considered as directing human actions. Now it is evident that reason directs not only external acts, but also internal passions. Consequently, when the reason fails in directing the internal passions, sin is said to be in the reason, as also when it fails in directing external actions. Now it fails, in two ways, in directing internal passions. First, when it commands unlawful passions: for instance, when a man deliberately provokes himself to a movement of anger, or of lust; secondly, when it fails to check the unlawful movement of a passion: for instance, when a man, having deliberately considered that a rising movement of passion is inordinate, continues, notwithstanding, to dwell upon it, and fails to drive it away. And in this sense the sin of lingering delectation is said to be in the reason.

Reply Obj. 1. Delectation is, indeed, in the appetitive power as its proximate principle; but it is in the reason as its first mover. This is in accordance with what has been stated above, viz., that actions which do not pass into external matter are in their principles as in their subjects.

Reply Obj. 2. Reason has its proper elicited act about its proper object, but it exercises the direction of all the objects of those lower powers that can be directed by the reason; and, accordingly, delectation about sensible objects comes also under the direction of reason.

Reply Obj. 3. Delectation is said to be lingering not from a delay of time, but because the reason in deliberating dwells thereon, and fails to drive it away, *deliberately holding and turning over what should have been cast aside as soon as it touched the mind,* as Augustine says.[26]

Seventh Article

WHETHER THE SIN OF CONSENT TO THE ACT IS IN THE HIGHER REASON?

We proceed thus to the Seventh Article:—

Objection 1. It would seem that the sin of consent to the act is not in the higher reason. For consent is an act of the appetitive power, as was stated above,[27] whereas the reason is an apprehensive power. Therefore the sin of consent to the act is not in the higher reason.

Obj. 2. Further, *the higher reason is intent on contemplating and consulting the eternal exemplars,* as Augustine states.[28] But sometimes consent is given to an act, without consulting the eternal exemplars, since man does not always think about divine things whenever he consents to an act. Therefore the sin of consent to the act is not always in the higher reason.

Obj. 3. Further, just as man can regulate his external actions according to the eternal exemplars, so he can regulate his internal pleasures or other passions. But *consent to a pleasure without deciding to fulfill it by deed be-*

[26] *Ibid.* (PL 42, 1008).   [27] Q. 15, a. 1.   [28] *De Trin.,* XII, 7 (PL 42, 1005).

longs to the lower reason, as Augustine states.[29] Therefore the consent to a sinful act likewise should sometimes be ascribed to the lower reason.

Obj. 4. Further, just as the higher reason excels the lower, so does the reason excel the imagination. Now sometimes man proceeds to act through the apprehension of the power of imagination, without any deliberation of his reason, as when, without premeditation, he moves his hand or foot. Therefore sometimes the lower reason likewise may consent to a sinful act, independently of the higher reason.

On the contrary, Augustine says: *If the consent to the evil use of things, that can be perceived by the bodily senses, so far approves of any sin as to point, if possible, to its consummation by deed, we are to understand that the woman has offered the forbidden fruit to her husband,*[30] who signifies the higher reason. Therefore it belongs to the higher reason to consent to the act of sin.

I answer that, Consent implies a judgment about the thing to which consent is given. For just as the speculative reason judges and delivers its sentence about intelligible matters, so the practical reason judges and pronounces sentence on matters of action. Now we must observe that in every case brought up for judgment, the final sentence belongs to the supreme tribunal, even as we see that in speculative matters the final sentence touching any proposition is delivered by referring it to the first principles. For, so long as there remains a yet higher principle, the question can still be submitted to it, and hence the judgment is still in suspense, since the final sentence has not as yet been pronounced. But it is evident that human acts can be regulated by the rule of human reason, which rule is derived from the created things that man knows naturally; and, further still, from the rule of the divine law, as was stated above.[31] Consequently, since the rule of the divine law is the higher rule, it follows that the ultimate sentence, whereby the judgment is finally pronounced, belongs to the higher reason which is intent on the eternal exemplars. Now when judgment has to be pronounced on several points, the final judgment deals with that which comes last. But in human acts the action itself comes last, and the delectation which is the inducement to the action is a preamble to it. Therefore the consent to an act belongs properly to the higher reason, while the preliminary judgment which is about the delectation belongs to the lower reason, which delivers judgment in a lower tribunal; although the higher reason can also judge of the delectation, since whatever is subject to the judgment of the lower tribunal is subject also to the judgment of the higher, but not conversely.

Reply Obj. 1. Consent is an act of the appetitive power, not absolutely, but in consequence of an act of reason deliberating and judging, as was stated above.[32] Because, that the consent is finally given to a thing is

[29] *Op. cit.,* XII, 12 (PL 42, 1008).   [30] *Ibid.*   [31] Q. 19, a. 4; q. 71, a. 6.   [32] Q. 15, a. 3.

due to the fact that the will tends to that upon which the reason has already passed its judgment. Hence consent may be ascribed both to the will and to the reason.

Reply Obj. 2. The higher reason is said to consent, from the very fact that it fails to direct the human act according to the divine law (which direction would impede the act of sin), whether or not it advert to the eternal law. For if it thinks of God's law, it holds it in actual contempt; and if not, it neglects it by a kind of omission. Therefore the consent to a sinful act always proceeds from the higher reason, because, as Augustine says, *the mind cannot effectively decide on the commission of a sin, unless by its consent, whereby it wields its sovereign power of moving the members to action, or of restraining them from action, it become the servant or slave of the evil deed.*[33]

Reply Obj. 3. The higher reason, by considering the eternal law, can direct or restrain the internal delectation, even as it can direct or restrain the external action. Nevertheless, before the judgment of the higher reason is pronounced, the lower reason, while deliberating the matter in reference to temporal principles, sometimes approves of this delectation; and then the consent to the delectation belongs to the lower reason. If, however, after considering the eternal exemplars, man persists in giving the same consent, such consent will then belong to the higher reason.

Reply Obj. 4. The apprehension of the imagination is sudden and indeliberate, and hence it can cause an act before the higher or lower reason has time to deliberate. But the judgment of the lower reason is deliberate, and so requires time during which the higher reason can also deliberate; and, consequently, if by its deliberation it does not check the sinful act, this will deservedly be imputed to it.

Eighth Article

WHETHER CONSENT TO DELECTATION IS A MORTAL SIN?

We proceed thus to the Eighth Article:—

Objection 1. It would seem that consent to delectation is not a mortal sin, for consent to delectation belongs to the lower reason, which does not consider the eternal exemplars, *i.e.*, the eternal law, and consequently does not turn away from them. Now every mortal sin consists in turning away from the divine law, as is evident from Augustine's definition of mortal sin, which was quoted above.[34] Therefore consent to delectation is not a mortal sin.

Obj. 2. Further, consent to a thing is not evil, unless the thing to which consent is given be evil. Now *the cause that anything is such is yet more so,* or at any rate not less. Consequently the thing to which a man consents

---

[33] *De Trin.*, XII, 12 (PL 42, 1008).   [34] Q. 71, a. 6.

cannot be a lesser evil than his consent. But delectation without deed is not a mortal sin, but only a venial sin. Therefore neither is the consent to the delectation a mortal sin.

Obj. 3. Further, delectations differ in goodness and malice according to the difference of the deeds, as the Philosopher states.[35] Now the inward thought is one thing, and the outward deed, *e.g.,* fornication, is another. Therefore the delectation consequent upon the act of inward thought differs in goodness and malice from the pleasure of fornication as much as the inward thought differs from the outward deed; and, consequently, there is a like difference of consent on either hand. But the inward thought is not a mortal sin, nor is the consent to that thought, and therefore neither is the consent to the delectation.

Obj. 4. Further, the external act of fornication or adultery is a mortal sin, not by reason of the delectation, since this is found also in the marriage act, but by reason of a lack of order in the act itself. Now he that consents to the delectation does not, for this reason, consent to the lack of order in the act. Therefore he does not seem to sin mortally.

Obj. 5. Further, the sin of murder is more grievous than simple fornication. Now it is not a mortal sin to consent to the delectation resulting from the thought of murder. Much less, therefore, is it a mortal sin to consent to the delectation resulting from the thought of fornication.

Obj. 6. Further, the Lord's Prayer is recited every day for the remission of venial sins, as Augustine asserts.[36] Now Augustine teaches that consent to delectation may be driven away by means of the Lord's Prayer; for he says that *this sin is much less grievous than if it be decided to fulfill it by deed, and hence we ought to ask pardon for such thoughts also, and we should strike our breasts and say: "Forgive us our trespasses."*[37] Therefore consent to delectation is a venial sin.

On the contrary, Augustine adds after a few words: *Man will be altogether lost unless, through the grace of the Mediator, he be forgiven those things which are deemed mere sins of thought, since without the will to do them, he desires nevertheless to enjoy them.*[38] But no man is lost except through mortal sin. Therefore consent to delectation is a mortal sin.

I answer that, There have been various opinions on this point. For some[39] have held that consent to delectation is not a mortal sin, but only a venial sin, while others[40] have held it to be a mortal sin, and this opinion is more common and more probable. For we must note that, since every delectation results from some action, as is stated in *Ethics* x.,[41] and again, that, since every delectation has an object, it follows that every delectation may be

---

[35] *Eth.,* X, 5 (1175b 26).   [36] *Enchir.,* LXXI (PL 40, 265).   [37] *De Trin.,* XII, 12 (PL 42, 1008).   [38] *Ibid.*   [39] The reference seems to be to St. Albert, *Summa de Creatur.,* I, tr. 4, q. 69, a. 3 (XXXIV, 713b); *In II Sent.,* d. xxiv, a. 13 (XXVII, 412a).   [40] Peter Lombard, *Sent.,* II, xxiv, 12 (I, 425-427).   [41] Aristotle, *Eth.,* X, 4 (1175a 5).

compared to two things, viz., to the operation from which it results, and to the object in which a person takes delight. Now it happens that an action, just as a thing, is an object of delectation, because the action itself can be considered as a good and an end in which the person, who delights in it, rests. Sometimes the action itself, which results in delectation, is the object of delectation, in so far as the appetitive power, to which it belongs to take delight in anything, is brought to bear on the action itself as a good: for instance, when a man thinks and delights in his thought, in so far as his thought pleases him. At other times, the delight consequent upon an action, e.g., a thought, has for its object another action, as being the object of his thought; and then his thought proceeds from the inclination of the appetite, not indeed to the thought, but to the action thought of. Accordingly, a man who is thinking of fornication may delight in either of two things: first, in the thought itself; secondly, in the fornication thought of. Now the delectation in the thought itself results from the inclination of the appetite to the thought. But the thought itself is not in itself a mortal sin. Sometimes, indeed, it is only a venial sin, as when a man thinks of such a thing for no purpose; and sometimes it is no sin at all, as when a man has a purpose in thinking of it: for instance, he may wish to preach or dispute about it. Consequently, such affection or delectation in respect of the thought of fornication is not a mortal sin in virtue of its genus, but is sometimes a venial sin and sometimes no sin at all; and hence neither is it a mortal sin to consent to such a thought. In this sense the first opinion is true.

But that a man, in thinking of fornication, takes pleasure in the act thought of, is due to the fact that his desire is inclined to this act. Therefore, the fact that a man consents to such a delectation amounts to nothing less than a consent to the inclination of his appetite to fornication; for no man takes pleasure except in that which is in conformity with his appetite. Now it is a mortal sin, if a man deliberately chooses that his appetite be conformed to what is in itself a mortal sin. Therefore, such a consent to delectation in a mortal sin is itself a mortal sin, as the second opinion maintains.

Reply Obj. 1. Consent to delectation may be not only in the lower reason, but also in the higher reason, as was stated above. Nevertheless, the lower reason may turn away from the eternal exemplars, for, though it is not intent on them as regulating according to them, which is proper to the higher reason, yet, it is intent on them as being regulated according to them. And it is thus that by turning from them it may sin mortally; for even the acts of the lower powers and of the external members may be mortal sins in so far as the direction of the higher reason fails in ruling them according to the eternal exemplars.

Reply Obj. 2. Consent to a sin that is venial in its genus is itself a venial sin, and accordingly one may conclude that the consent to take pleasure in a useless thought about fornication, is a venial sin. But delectation in the act itself of fornication is, in its genus, a mortal sin; and that it be a venial sin, before the consent is given, is accidental, viz., because of the incompleteness of the act. This incompleteness ceases when the deliberate consent has been given, so that, therefore, it has its complete nature and is a mortal sin.

Reply Obj. 3. This argument considers the delectation which has the thought for its object.

Reply Obj. 4. The delectation which has an external act for its object cannot be without pleasure in the external act as such, even though there be no decision to fulfill it because of the prohibition of some higher authority. Hence the act is inordinate, and consequently the delectation will also be inordinate.

Reply Obj. 5. The consent to delectation, resulting from taking pleasure in an act of murder thought of, is a mortal sin also; but not the consent to delectation resulting from pleasure taken in the thought of murder.

Reply Obj. 6. The Lord's Prayer is to be said in order that we may be preserved, not only from venial sin, but also from mortal sin.

Ninth Article

WHETHER THERE CAN BE VENIAL SIN IN THE HIGHER
REASON AS DIRECTING THE LOWER POWERS?

We proceed thus to the Ninth Article:—

Objection 1. It would seem that there cannot be venial sin in the higher reason as directing the lower powers, *i.e.*, as consenting to a sinful act. For Augustine says that the *higher reason is intent on considering and consulting the eternal exemplars.*[42] But mortal sin consists in turning away from the eternal exemplars. Therefore it seems that there can be only mortal sin in the higher reason.

Obj. 2. Further, the higher reason is the principle of the spiritual life, just as the heart is of the body's life. But the diseases of the heart are fatal. Therefore the sins of the higher reason are mortal.

Obj. 3. Further, a venial sin becomes a mortal sin if it be done out of contempt. But it would seem impossible deliberately to commit even a venial sin without contempt. Since, then, the consent of the higher reason is always accompanied by deliberate consideration of the eternal law, it seems that it cannot be without mortal sin, because of the contempt of the divine law.

On the contrary, Consent to a sinful act belongs to the higher reason, as was stated above. But consent to an act of venial sin is itself a venial sin. Therefore a venial sin can be in the higher reason.

[42] *De Trin.*, XII, 7 (PL 42, 1005).

I answer that, As Augustine says, the higher reason *is intent on contemplating or consulting the eternal exemplars.*[43] It contemplates the exemplars by considering their truth; it consults them by judging and directing other things according to them, and to this pertains the fact that, by deliberating through the eternal exemplars, it consents to an act or dissents from it. Now it may happen that the inordinateness of the act to which it consents is not contrary to the eternal exemplars in the same way as mortal sin is, because it does not imply aversion from the last end, but is outside them, as an act of venial sin is. Therefore, when the higher reason consents to an act of a venial sin, it does not turn away from the eternal exemplars; and therefore it sins, not mortally, but venially.

This suffices for the Reply to the First Objection.

Reply Obj. 2. Disease of the heart is twofold. One is in the very substance of the heart, and affects its natural equilibrium; such a disease is always mortal. The other is a disease of the heart consisting in some disorder either of the movement or of the parts surrounding the heart; such a disease is not always mortal. In like manner, there is mortal sin in the higher reason whenever the order itself of the higher reason to its proper object, namely, the eternal exemplars, is destroyed; but when the disorder leaves this untouched, the sin is not mortal but venial.

Reply Obj. 3. Deliberate consent to a sin does not always amount to contempt of the divine law, but only when the sin is contrary to the divine law.

Tenth Article

WHETHER VENIAL SIN CAN BE IN THE HIGHER REASON AS SUCH?

We proceed thus to the Tenth Article:—

Objection 1. It would seem that venial sin cannot be in the higher reason as such, *i.e.,* as considering the eternal exemplars. For the act of a power is not found to fail except it be inordinately disposed with regard to its object. Now the object of the higher reason is the eternal exemplars, in respect of which there can be no disorder without mortal sin. Therefore, there can be no venial sin in the higher reason as such.

Obj. 2. Further, since the reason is a deliberative power, there can be no act of reason without deliberation. Now every inordinate movement in things concerning God, if it be deliberate, is a mortal sin. Therefore venial sin is never in the higher reason as such.

Obj. 3. Further, it happens sometimes that a sin which takes us unawares is a venial sin. Now a deliberate sin is a mortal sin, because the reason, in deliberating, has recourse to some higher good, by acting against

[43] *Ibid.*

which man sins more grievously; just as when the reason, in deliberating about an inordinate pleasurable act, considers that it is contrary to the law of God, it sins more grievously in consenting than if it only considered that it is contrary to moral virtue. But the higher reason cannot have recourse to any higher tribunal than its own object. Therefore, if a movement that takes us unawares is not a mortal sin, neither will the subsequent deliberation make it a mortal sin; which is clearly false. Therefore there can be no venial sin in the higher reason as such.

On the contrary, A sudden movement of unbelief is a venial sin. But it belongs to the higher reason as such. Therefore, there can be a venial sin in the higher reason as such.

I answer that, The higher reason tends to its own object otherwise than to the objects of the lower powers that are directed by the higher reason. For it does not tend to the objects of the lower powers, except in so far as it consults the eternal exemplars about them, and so it does not regard them save by way of deliberation. Now deliberate consent to what is a mortal sin in its genus is itself a mortal sin; and consequently the higher reason always sins mortally if the acts of the lower powers to which it consents are mortal sins.

With regard to its own object it has a twofold act, viz. simple *intuition,* and *deliberation,* in respect of which it again consults the eternal exemplars about its own object. But in respect of simple intuition, it can have an inordinate movement about divine things, as when a man suffers a sudden movement of unbelief. And although unbelief, in its genus, is a mortal sin, yet a sudden movement of unbelief is a venial sin, because there is no mortal sin unless it be contrary to the law of God. Now it is possible for one of the doctrines of faith to present itself to the reason suddenly under some other aspect, before the eternal exemplar, *i.e.,* the law of God, is consulted, or can be consulted, on the matter; as, for instance, when a man suddenly apprehends the resurrection of the dead as impossible naturally, and rejects it as soon as he has thus apprehended it, before he has had time to deliberate and consider that this is proposed to our belief in accordance with the divine law. If, however, the movement of unbelief remains after this deliberation, it is a mortal sin. Therefore, in sudden movements, the higher reason may sin venially in respect of its proper object, even if it be a mortal sin in its genus, or it may sin mortally by giving a deliberate consent; but in things pertaining to the lower powers, it always sins mortally in things which are mortal sins in their genus, but not in those which are venial sins in their genus.

Reply Obj. 1. A sin which is against the eternal exemplars, though it be mortal in its genus, may nevertheless be venial, because of the incompleteness of a sudden action, as has been stated.

Reply Obj. 2. In matters of action, the simple intuition of the principles, from which deliberation proceeds, belongs to the reason, as well as does the act of deliberation: even as in speculative matters it belongs to the reason both to syllogize and to form propositions. Consequently, the reason also can have a sudden movement.

Reply Obj. 3. One and the same thing may be the subject of different considerations, of which one is higher than the other. Thus the existence of God may be considered either as capable of being known by the human reason, or as delivered to us by divine revelation, which is a higher consideration. Therefore, although the object of the higher reason is, in its nature, something sublime, yet it is reducible to some yet higher consideration; and in this way, that which in the sudden movement was not a mortal sin, becomes a mortal sin in virtue of the deliberation which brought it into the light of a higher consideration, as was explained above.

Question LXXV

THE CAUSES OF SIN, IN GENERAL

(*In Four Articles*)

WE must now consider the causes of sin: (1) in general; (2) in particular.[1] Under the first head there are four points of inquiry: (1) Whether sin has a cause? (2) Whether it has an internal cause? (3) Whether it has an external cause? (4) Whether one sin is the cause of another?

First Article

WHETHER SIN HAS A CAUSE?

We proceed thus to the First Article:—

Objection 1. It would seem that sin has no cause. For sin has the nature of evil, as was stated above.[2] But evil has no cause, as Dionysius says.[3] Therefore sin has no cause.

Obj. 2. Further, a cause is that from which something follows of necessity. Now that which is of necessity seems to be no sin, for every sin is voluntary. Therefore sin has no cause.

Obj. 3. Further, if sin has a cause, this cause is either good or evil. It is not a good, because good produces nothing but good, for *a good tree cannot bring forth evil fruit* (*Matt.* vii. 18). Likewise, neither can evil be the cause of sin, because the evil of punishment is a sequel to sin, and the evil of guilt is the same as sin. Therefore sin has no cause.

On the contrary, Whatever is done has a cause, for, according to *Job.* v. 6, *nothing upon earth is done without a cause.* But sin is something done, since it is a *word, deed or desire contrary to the law of God.*[4] Therefore sin has a cause.

I answer that, A sin is an inordinate act. Accordingly, in so far as it is an act, it can have a direct cause, even as any other act; but, in so far as it is inordinate, it has a cause in the same way as a negation or privation can have a cause. Now two causes may be assigned to a negation. First, the absence of the cause of affirmation: *i.e.,* the negation of the cause itself is the cause of the negation in itself, since the result of removing the cause is the removal of the effect. Thus, the absence of the sun is the cause of darkness. In the second place, the cause of an affirmation, of which a negation is a

[1] Q. 76.   [2] Q. 71, a. 6.   [3] *De Div. Nom.,* IV, 30 (PG 3, 732).   [4] St. Augustine, *Contra Faust.,* XXII, 27 (PL 42, 418).

sequel, is the accidental cause of the resulting negation. Thus fire, by causing heat in virtue of its principal tendency, consequently causes a privation of cold. The first of these suffices to cause a simple negation. But, since
the lack of order in sin and in every evil is not a simple negation, but the
privation of that which something ought naturally to have, such a lack of
order must needs have an accidental efficient cause. For that which naturally is and ought to be in a thing is never lacking except because of some
impeding cause. And, accordingly, we are wont to say that evil, which consists in a certain privation, has a deficient cause, or an accidental efficient
cause. Now every accidental cause is reducible to an essential cause. Since,
then, sin has, on the part of its lack of order, an accidental efficient cause,
and, on the part of the act, an essential efficient cause, it follows that the
lack of order in sin is a result of the cause of the act. Accordingly, then,
the will lacking the direction of the rule of reason and of the divine law,
and intent on some mutable good, causes the act of sin essentially, and the
lack of order in the act accidentally and without intention; for the lack of
order in the act results from the lack of direction in the will.

Reply Obj. 1. Sin signifies not only the privation of good, which privation is its lack of order, but also the act which is the subject of that privation, which has the nature of evil. How this evil has a cause, has been
explained.

Reply Obj 2. If this definition of cause is to be verified in all cases, it
must be understood as applying to a cause which is sufficient and not impeded. For it happens that a thing is the sufficient cause of something else,
and yet that the effect does not follow of necessity, because of some supervening impediment; or else it would follow that all things happen of necessity, as is proved in *Metaph.* vi.[5] Accordingly, though sin has a cause, it
does not follow that this is a necessary cause, since its effect can be impeded.

Reply Obj. 3. As was stated above, the will in failing to apply the rule of
reason or of the divine law is the cause of sin. Now the fact of not applying the rule of reason or of the divine law, has not in itself the nature of
evil, whether of punishment or of guilt, before it is applied to the act.
Accordingly, therefore, evil is not the cause of the first sin, but some good
lacking some other good.

Second Article

WHETHER SIN HAS AN INTERNAL CAUSE?

We proceed thus to the Second Article:—

Objection 1. It would seem that sin has no internal cause. For that which
is within a thing is always in it. If, therefore, sin had an internal cause,
man would always be sinning, since, given the cause, the effect follows.

[5] Aristotle, *Metaph.*, V, 3 (1027a 29).

Obj. 2. Further, a thing is not its own cause. But the internal movements of a man are sins. Therefore they are not the cause of sin.

Obj. 3. Further, whatever is within man is either natural or voluntary. Now that which is natural cannot be the cause of sin, for sin is contrary to nature, as Damascene states;[6] while that which is voluntary, if it be inordinate, is already a sin. Therefore nothing intrinsic can be the cause of the first sin.

On the contrary, Augustine says that *the will is the cause of sin.*[7]

I answer that, As we have stated above, the essential cause of sin must be considered on the part of the act. Now we may distinguish a twofold internal cause of human acts, one remote, the other proximate. The proximate internal cause of the human act is the reason and will, according to which man has free choice; while the remote cause is the apprehension of the sensitive part, and also the sensitive appetite. For just as it is due to the judgment of reason that the will is moved to something in accord with reason, so it is due to an apprehension of the senses that the sensitive appetite is inclined to something, which inclination sometimes influences the will and reason, as we shall explain further on.[8] Accordingly, a double interior cause of sin may be assigned: one proximate, on the part of the reason and will; the other remote, on the part of the imagination or sensitive appetite.

But since we have said above that the cause of sin is some apparent good as motive, yet lacking the due motive, viz., the rule of reason or the divine law, this motive, which is an apparent good, pertains to the apprehension of the senses and to the appetite; the lack of the due rule pertains to the reason, whose nature it is to consider this rule; and the completeness of the voluntary sinful act pertains to the will, so that the act of the will, given the conditions we have just mentioned, is already a sin.

Reply Obj. 1. That which is within a thing as its natural power is always in it; but that which is within it, as the internal act of the appetitive or apprehensive power, is not always in it. Now the power of the will is the potential cause of sin, but is made actual by the preceding movements, both of the sensitive part, in the first place, and afterwards, of the reason. For it is because a thing is proposed as appetible to the senses, and because the appetite is inclined, that the reason sometimes fails to consider the due rule, so that the will produces the act of sin. Since, therefore, the movements that precede it are not always actual, neither is man always actually sinning.

Reply Obj. 2. It is not true that all the internal movements belong to the substance of sin, for this consists principally in the act of the will; but some precede and some follow the sin itself.

---

[6] *De Fide Orth.,* II, 4; 30; IV, 20 (PG 94, 876; 976; 1196).   [7] *De Lib. Arb.,* III, 17 (PL 32, 1294); *De Duab. Anim.,* X; XI (PL 42, 104; 105).   [8] Q. 77, a. 1.

Reply Obj. 3. That which causes sin, as a power produces its act, is natural; and again, the movement of the sensitive part, from which sin follows, is sometimes natural, as, for instance, when anyone sins through appetite for food. Yet sin results in being unnatural from the very fact that the natural rule fails, which man, in accord with his nature, ought to observe.

Third Article

WHETHER SIN HAS AN EXTERNAL CAUSE?

We proceed thus to the Third Article:—

Objection 1. It would seem that sin has no external cause. For sin is a voluntary act. Now voluntary acts belong to principles that are within us, so that they have no external cause. Therefore sin has no external cause.

Obj. 2. Further, as nature is an internal principle, so is the will. Now in natural things sin can be due to none other than to an internal cause: for instance, the birth of a monster is due to the corruption of some internal principle. Therefore, in the moral order, sin can arise from none other than an internal cause. Therefore it has no external cause.

Obj. 3. Further, if the cause is multiplied, the effect is multiplied. Now the more numerous and weighty the external inducements to sin are, the less is a man's inordinate act imputed to him as a sin. Therefore nothing external is a cause of sin.

On the contrary, It is written (*Num.* xxxi. 16): *Are not these they, that deceived the children of Israel by the counsel of Balaam, and made you transgress against the Lord by the sin of Phogor?* Therefore something external can be a cause of sin.

I answer that, As we have stated above, the internal cause of sin is both the will, as completing the sinful act, and the reason, as lacking the due rule, and the sensitive appetite, as inclining to sin. Accordingly, something external might be a cause of sin in three ways, either by moving the will itself immediately, or by moving the reason, or by moving the sensitive appetite. Now, as was stated above, none can move the will inwardly save God alone,[9] Who cannot be a cause of sin, as we shall prove further on.[10] Hence it follows that nothing external can be a cause of sin, except by moving the reason, as a man or devil by enticing to sin; or by moving the sensitive appetite, as certain external sensibles move it. Yet neither does external enticement move the reason of necessity, in matters of action, nor do things proposed externally of necessity move the sensitive appetite, except perhaps it be disposed thereto in a certain way; and even the sensitive appetite does not, of necessity, move the reason and will. Therefore, something external can be a cause moving to sin, but not so as to be its suffi-

[9] Q. 9, a. 6.   [10] Q. 79, a. 1.

cient cause. But the sufficient accomplishing cause of sin is the will alone.

Reply Obj. 1. From the very fact that the external motive causes of sin do not lead to sin sufficiently and necessarily, it follows that it remains in our power to sin or not to sin.

Reply Obj. 2. The fact that sin has an internal cause does not prevent its having an external cause; for nothing external is a cause of sin, except through the medium of the internal cause, as was stated.

Reply Obj. 3. If the external causes inclining to sin be multiplied, the sinful acts are multiplied, because they incline to the sinful act in both greater numbers and greater frequency. Nevertheless, the character of guilt is lessened, since this depends on the fact that the act is voluntary and in our power.

Fourth Article

WHETHER ONE SIN IS A CAUSE OF ANOTHER?

We proceed thus to the Fourth Article:—

Objection 1. It would seem that one sin cannot be the cause of another. For there are four kinds of cause, none of which will fit in with one sin causing another. For the end has the character of good, and this is inconsistent with sin, which has the character of evil. In like manner, neither can a sin be an efficient cause, since *evil is not an efficient cause, but is weak and powerless,* as Dionysius declares.[11] The material and formal causes seem to have no place except in natural bodies, which are composed of matter and form. Therefore sin cannot have either a material or a formal cause.

Obj. 2. Further, *to produce its like belongs to a perfect thing,* as is stated in *Meteor.* iv.[12] But sin is essentially something imperfect. Therefore one sin cannot be a cause of another.

Obj. 3. Further, if one sin is the cause of a second sin, in the same way, yet another sin will be the cause of the first, and thus we go on indefinitely, which is absurd. Therefore one sin is not the cause of another.

On the contrary, Gregory says on *Ezechiel: A sin that is not quickly blotted out by repentance is both a sin and a cause of sin.*[13]

I answer that, Inasmuch as a sin has a cause on the part of the act of sin, it is possible for one sin to be the cause of another in the same way as one human act is the cause of another. Hence it happens that one sin may be the cause of another according to the four kinds of causes.—First, after the manner of an efficient or moving cause, both essentially and accidentally. Accidentally, as that which removes an impediment is called an accidental cause of movement; for when a man, by one sinful act, loses

---

[11] *De Div. Nom.,* IV, 31 (PG 3, 732).   [12] Aristotle, *Meteor.,* IV, 3 (380a 14).
[13] *In Ezech.,* I, hom. 11 (PL 76, 915).

grace, or charity, or shame, or anything else that withdraws him from sin, he thereby falls into another sin, so that the first sin is the accidental cause of the second. Essentially, as when by one sinful act a man is disposed to commit more readily another like act; because acts cause dispositions and habits inclining to like acts.—Secondly, after the manner of a material cause, one sin is the cause of another by preparing its matter. Thus covetousness prepares the matter for strife, which is often about the wealth a man has amassed together.—Thirdly, after the manner of a final cause, one sin causes another, in so far as a man commits one sin for the sake of another which is his end; as when a man is guilty of simony for the end of ambition, or fornication for the purpose of theft.—And since the end gives the form in moral matters, as was stated above,[14] it follows that one sin is also the formal cause of another; because in the act of fornication, committed for the purpose of theft, the former is as matter while the latter is as form.

Reply Obj. 1. Sin, in so far as it is inordinate, has the character of evil, but, in so far as it is an act, it has some good, at least apparent, as its end; so that, as an act, but not as being inordinate, it can be the cause, both final and efficient, of another sin.—A sin has matter, not *out of which,* but *about which* it is; and it has its form from its end. Consequently one sin can be the cause of another according to the four kinds of cause, as was stated above.

Reply Obj. 2. Sin is something imperfect because of the moral imperfection involved in its lack of order. Nevertheless, as an act it can have the perfection of a nature, and thus it can be the cause of another sin.

Reply Obj. 3. Not every cause of one sin is another sin. Hence, there is no need to go on to infinity, for one may come to one sin which is not caused by another sin.

[14] Q. 1, a. 3; q. 18, a. 6.

THE CAUSES OF SIN, IN PARTICULAR

(*In Four Articles*)

WE must now consider the causes of sin, in particular: (1) The internal causes of sin; (2) its external causes;[1] and (3) sins which are the causes of other sins.[2] In view of what has been said above, the first consideration will be threefold, so that in the first place we shall treat of ignorance, which is the cause of sin on the part of reason; secondly, of weakness or passion, which is the cause of sin on the part of the sensitive appetite;[3] thirdly, of malice, which is the cause of sin on the part of the will.[4]

Under the first head there are four points of inquiry: (1) Whether ignorance is a cause of sin? (2) Whether ignorance is a sin? (3) Whether it excuses from sin altogether? (4) Whether it diminishes sin?

First Article

WHETHER IGNORANCE CAN BE A CAUSE OF SIN?

We proceed thus to the First Article:—

Objection 1. It would seem that ignorance cannot be a cause of sin, because what does not exist is not the cause of anything. Now ignorance is a non-being, since it is a privation of knowledge. Therefore ignorance is not a cause of sin.

Obj. 2. Further, causes of sin should be reckoned according to the fact that sin is a *turning to* something, as was stated above.[5] Now ignorance seems to savor of *turning away* from something. Therefore it should not be reckoned a cause of sin.

Obj. 3. Further, every sin is seated in the will, as we have said above.[6] Now the will does not turn to that which is not known, because its object is the apprehended good. Therefore ignorance cannot be a cause of sin.

On the contrary, Augustine says *that some sin through ignorance.*[7]

I answer that, According to the Philosopher a moving cause is twofold, essential and accidental.[8] An essential cause is one that moves by its own power, as the generator is the moving cause of heavy and light things. An accidental cause is either the cause itself that removes an impediment, or the removal itself of an impediment. It is in this way that ignorance can be

---

[1] Q. 79. [2] Q. 84. [3] Q. 77. [4] Q. 78. [5] Q. 75, a. 1. [6] Q. 74, a. 1. [7] *De Nat. et Grat.,* LXVII (PL 44, 287); cf. *De Lib. Arb.,* III, 18 (PL 32, 1295). [8] *Phys.,* VIII, 4 (254b 7).

the cause of a sinful act, because it is a privation of the knowledge perfecting the reason that forbids the act of sin, in so far as it directs human acts.

Now we must observe that the reason directs human acts in accordance with a twofold knowledge, namely, universal and particular. For in conferring about what is to be done, it employs a syllogism, the conclusion of which is an act of judgment or of choice, or an operation. Now actions are about singulars, and therefore the conclusion of a practical syllogism is a singular proposition. But a singular proposition does not follow from a universal proposition, except through the medium of a particular proposition. Thus, a man is restrained from an act of parricide by the knowledge that it is wrong to kill one's father, and that this man is his father. Hence ignorance about either of these two propositions, viz., of the universal principle which is a rule of reason, or of the particular circumstance, could cause an act of parricide. Hence it is clear that not every kind of ignorance is the cause of a sin, but that alone which removes the knowledge which would prevent the sinful act. Consequently, if a man's will be so disposed that he would not be restrained from the act of parricide, even though he recognized his father, his ignorance about his father is not the cause of his committing the sin, but is concomitant with the sin. Hence such a man sins, not *through ignorance* but *in ignorance,* as the Philosopher states.[9]

Reply Obj. 1. Non-being cannot be the direct cause of anything, but it can be an accidental cause, as being the removal of an impediment.

Reply Obj. 2. As science, which is removed by ignorance, regards sin as turning towards something, so, too, ignorance of this respect of a sin is the cause of that sin, as removing its impediment.

Reply Obj. 3. The will cannot turn to that which is absolutely unknown; but if something be known in one respect, and unknown in another, the will can will it. It is thus that ignorance is the cause of sin: for instance, when a man knows that the being whom he is killing is a man, but not that it is his own father; or when one knows that a certain act is pleasurable, but not that it is a sin.

Second Article

WHETHER IGNORANCE IS A SIN?

We proceed thus to the Second Article:—

Objection 1. It would seem that ignorance is not a sin. For sin is *a word, deed or desire contrary to God's law,* as was stated above.[10] Now ignorance does not denote an act, either internal or external. Therefore ignorance is not a sin.

Obj. 2. Further, sin is more directly opposed to grace than to knowledge. Now privation of grace is not a sin, but a punishment resulting from sin. Therefore ignorance, which is privation of knowledge, is not a sin.

[9] *Eth.,* III, 1 (1110b 25).   [10] Q. 71, a. 6.

Obj. 3. Further, if ignorance is a sin, this can be only in so far as it is voluntary. But if ignorance is a sin through being voluntary, it seems that the sin will consist in the act itself of the will, rather than in the ignorance. Therefore, ignorance will not be a sin, but rather a result of sin.

Obj. 4. Further, every sin is taken away by repentance, nor does any sin, except only original sin, pass as to guilt yet remain in act. Now ignorance is not removed by repentance, but remains actually even when all guilt has been removed by repentance. Therefore, ignorance is not a sin, unless perchance it be original sin.

Obj. 5. Further, if ignorance be a sin, then a man will be sinning as long as he remains in ignorance. But ignorance is continual in the one who is ignorant. Therefore a person in ignorance would be continually sinning, which is clearly false; or else ignorance would be a most grievous sin. Therefore ignorance is not a sin.

On the contrary, Nothing but sin deserves punishment. But ignorance deserves punishment, according to *1 Cor.* xiv. 38: *If any man know not, he shall not be known.* Therefore ignorance is a sin.

I answer that, Ignorance differs from *nescience* in that nescience denotes mere absence of knowledge. Therefore whoever lacks knowledge about anything can be said to be nescient about it; in which sense Dionysius puts nescience in the angels.[11] On the other hand, ignorance denotes privation of knowledge, *i.e.,* lack of knowledge of those things that one has a natural aptitude to know. Some of these we are under an obligation to know, those, namely, without the knowledge of which we are unable to accomplish a due act rightly. Therefore, all are bound in common to know what belongs to faith, and the universal precepts of law; and each individual is bound to know matters regarding his duty or state. However, there are other things which a man may have a natural aptitude to know, yet he is not bound to know them: *e.g.,* the geometrical theorems, and contingent particulars, except in some individual case. Now it is evident that whoever neglects to have or do what he ought to have or do, commits a sin of omission. Therefore through negligence, ignorance of what one is bound to know is a sin; whereas it is not imputed as a sin to a man, if he fails to know what he is unable to know. Consequently, ignorance of such things is called *invincible,* because it cannot be overcome by study. For this reason such ignorance, not being voluntary, since it is not in our power to be rid of it, is not a sin. Hence it is evident that no invincible ignorance is a sin. On the other hand, vincible ignorance is a sin, if it be about matters one is bound to know; but not, if it be about things one is not bound to know.

Reply Obj. 1. As was stated above, when we say that sin is a *word, deed* or *desire,* we include the opposite negations, by reason of which omissions have the character of sin.[12] Hence negligence, through which ignorance is a

---

[11] *De Cael. Hier.,* VII, 3 (PG 3, 209); cf. *De Eccles. Hier.,* VI, pt. iii, 6 (PG 3, 537).
[12] Q. 71, a. 6, ad 1.

sin, is comprised in the above definition of sin, in so far as one omits to say what one ought, or to do what one ought, or to desire what one ought, in order to acquire the knowledge which we ought to have.

Reply Obj. 2. Although privation of grace is not a sin in itself, yet by reason of negligence in preparing oneself for grace it may have the character of sin, even as can ignorance. Nevertheless, there is a difference here, since man can acquire knowledge by his acts, whereas grace is not acquired by acts, but by God's favor.

Reply Obj. 3. Just as in a sin of transgression the sin consists not only in the act of the will, but also in the act willed, which is commanded by the will, so in a sin of omission, not only the act of the will is a sin, but also the omission, in so far as it is in some way voluntary; and, accordingly, the neglect to know, or even lack itself of consideration, is a sin.

Reply Obj. 4. Although when the guilt has passed away through repentance, the ignorance remains, according as it is a privation of knowledge, nevertheless, the negligence does not remain, by reason of which the ignorance is said to be a sin.

Reply Obj. 5. Just as in other sins of omission a man sins actually only at the time at which the affirmative precept is binding, so it is with the sin of ignorance. For the ignorant man sins actually indeed, not continually, but only at the time for acquiring the knowledge that he ought to have.

Third Article

WHETHER IGNORANCE EXCUSES FROM SIN ALTOGETHER?

We proceed thus to the Third Article:—

Objection 1. It would seem that ignorance excuses from sin altogether. For, as Augustine says, every sin is voluntary.[13] Now ignorance causes involuntariness, as was stated above.[14] Therefore ignorance excuses from sin altogether.

Obj. 2. Further, that which is done without intention is done accidentally. Now the intention cannot be about what is unknown. Therefore what a man does through ignorance is accidental in human acts. But what is accidental does not give the species. Therefore nothing that is done through ignorance in human acts should be deemed sinful or virtuous.

Obj. 3. Further, man is the subject of virtue and sin in so far as he is a partaker of reason. Now ignorance excludes knowledge, which perfects the reason. Therefore ignorance excuses from sin altogether.

On the contrary, Augustine says that *some things done through ignorance are rightly reproved.*[15] Now those things alone are rightly reproved which are sins. Therefore, some things done through ignorance are sins. Therefore, ignorance does not altogether excuse from sin.

[13] *De Vera Relig.,* XIV (PL 34, 133) ; *Retract.,* I, 9 (PL 32, 595).   [14] Q. 6, a. 8.
[15] *De Lib. Arb.,* III, 18 (PL 32, 1295).

I answer that, Ignorance, by its very nature, renders the act which it causes involuntary. Now it has already been stated that ignorance is said to cause the act which the contrary knowledge would have prevented; so that this act, if knowledge were present, would be contrary to the will, which is the meaning of the term *involuntary.* If, however, the knowledge which is removed by ignorance would not have prevented the act, because of the inclination of the will to it, the lack of this knowledge does not make that man unwilling, but not willing, as is stated in *Ethics* iii.[16] Now such ignorance, which is not the cause of the sinful act, as we have already stated, since it does not make the act to be involuntary, does not excuse from sin. The same applies to any ignorance that does not cause, but follows or accompanies, the sinful act.

On the other hand, ignorance which is the cause of the act, since it makes it to be involuntary, of its very nature excuses from sin because voluntariness is essential to sin.—But it may fail to excuse altogether from sin, and this for two reasons. First, on the part of the thing itself which is not known. For ignorance excuses from sin, in so far as something is not known to be a sin. Now it may happen that a person is ignorant of some circumstance of a sin, the knowledge of which would prevent him from sinning, whether it belong to the substance of the sin, or not; and nevertheless his knowledge is sufficient for him to be aware that the act is sinful: such is the case, for example, if a man strike someone, knowing that it is a man (which suffices for it to be sinful) and yet be ignorant of the fact that it is his father (which is a circumstance constituting another species of sin); or, suppose that he is unaware that this man will defend himself and strike him back, and that if he had known this he would not have struck him (which does not affect the sinfulness of the act). Therefore, though this man sins through ignorance, yet he is not altogether excused, because, notwithstanding, he has knowledge of the sin. Secondly, this may happen on the part of the ignorance itself, because, namely, this ignorance is voluntary, either directly, as when a man wishes of set purpose to be ignorant of certain things that he may sin the more freely; or indirectly, as when a man, through stress of work or other occupations, neglects to acquire the knowledge which would restrain him from sin. For such negligence renders the ignorance itself voluntary and sinful, provided it be about matters one is bound and able to know. Consequently, this ignorance does not altogether excuse from sin. If, however, the ignorance be such as to be entirely involuntary, either through being invincible or through being about matters one is not bound to know, then such ignorance excuses from sin altogether.

Reply Obj. 1. Not every ignorance causes involuntariness, as was stated above. Hence not every ignorance excuses from sin altogether.

Reply Obj. 2. So far as voluntariness remains in the ignorant person, the

---

[16] Aristotle, *Eth.,* III, 1 (1110b 23).

intention of sin remains in him; so that, in this respect, his sin is not accidental.

Reply Obj. 3. If the ignorance be such as to exclude the use of reason entirely, it excuses from sin altogether, as is the case with madmen and imbeciles; but such is not always the ignorance that causes the sin, and so it does not always excuse from sin altogether.

Fourth Article

WHETHER IGNORANCE DIMINISHES A SIN?

We proceed thus to the Fourth Article:—

Objection 1. It would seem that ignorance does not diminish a sin. For that which is common to all sins does not diminish sin. Now ignorance is common to all sins, for the Philosopher says[17] that *every evil man is ignorant.* Therefore ignorance does not diminish sin.

Obj. 2. Further, one sin added to another makes a greater sin. But ignorance is itself a sin, as was stated above. Therefore it does not diminish a sin.

Obj. 3. Further, the same thing does not both aggravate and diminish sin. Now ignorance aggravates sin, for Ambrose, commenting on *Rom.* ii. 4 (*Knowest thou not that the benignity of God leadeth thee to penance?*) says: *Thy sin is most grievous if thou knowest not.*[18] Therefore ignorance does not diminish sin.

Obj. 4. Further, if any kind of ignorance diminishes a sin, this would seem to be chiefly the case as regards the ignorance which removes the use of reason altogether. Now this kind of ignorance does not diminish sin, but increases it; for the Philosopher says that the *punishment is doubled for a drunken man.*[19] Therefore ignorance does not diminish sin.

On the contrary, Whatever is a reason for sin to be forgiven diminishes sin. Now such is ignorance, as is clear from *1 Tim.* i. 13: *I obtained . . . mercy . . . because I did it ignorantly.* Therefore ignorance diminishes or alleviates sin.

I answer that, Since every sin is voluntary, ignorance can diminish sin in so far as it diminishes its voluntariness; and if it does not render it less voluntary, in no way does it diminish the sin. Now it is evident that the ignorance which excuses from sin altogether (through making it altogether involuntary) does not diminish a sin, but does away with it altogether. On the other hand, ignorance which is not the cause of the commission of the sin, but is concomitant with it, neither diminishes nor increases the sin.

Therefore, sin cannot be diminished by any ignorance, but only by such as is a cause of the sin being committed, and yet does not excuse from the sin altogether. Now it happens sometimes that such ignorance is directly

---

[17] *Ibid.* (1110b 28).   [18] Cf. *Glossa ordin.* (VI, 6 F).   [19] *Eth.,* III, 5 (1113b 31).

and essentially voluntary, as when a man is purposely ignorant that he may sin more freely. Ignorance of this kind seems rather to make the act more voluntary and more sinful, since it is through the will's intention to sin that he is willing to bear the burden of ignorance for the sake of freedom in sinning. Sometimes, however, the ignorance which is the cause of a sin being committed, is not directly voluntary, but indirectly or accidentally, as when a man is unwilling to work hard at his studies, with the result that he is ignorant; or as when a man wilfully drinks too much wine, with the result that he becomes drunk and indiscreet. This ignorance diminishes voluntariness and, consequently, also the sin. For when a thing is not known to be a sin, the will cannot be said to consent to the sin directly, but only accidentally; and therefore in that case there is less contempt, and therefore less sin.

Reply Obj. 1. The ignorance whereby *every evil man is ignorant* is not the cause of sin being committed, but something resulting from that cause, viz., the passion or habit inclining to sin.

Reply Obj. 2. One sin added to another makes more sins, but it does not always make a greater sin, since, perchance, the two sins do not coincide, but remain separate sins. And so it may happen, if the first diminishes the second, that the two together have not the same gravity as one of them alone would have. Thus, murder is a more grievous sin if committed by a man when sober than if committed by a man when drunk, although in the latter case there are two sins; because drunkenness diminishes the sinfulness of the resulting sin beyond its own gravity.

Reply Obj. 3. The words of Ambrose may be understood as referring to simply affected ignorance; or they may have reference to a species of the sin of ingratitude, the highest degree of which is that man even ignores the benefits he has received; or, again, they may be an allusion to the ignorance of unbelief, which undermines the foundation of the spiritual edifice.

Reply Obj. 4. The drunken man deserves a *double punishment* for the two sins which he commits, viz., drunkenness, and the sin which results from his drunkenness; and yet drunkenness, because of the ignorance connected with it, diminishes the resulting sin, and more, perhaps, than the gravity of the drunkenness implies, as was stated above.—It might also be said that the words quoted refer to an ordinance of the legislator named Pittacus, who ordered drunkards to be more severely punished if they assaulted anyone, having an eye, not to the indulgence which the drunkard might claim, but to expediency, since more harm is done by the drunk than by the sober, as the Philosopher observes.[20]

[20] *Polit.,* II, 9 (1274b 18).

THE CAUSE OF SIN ON THE PART OF THE SENSITIVE APPETITE

(*In Eight Articles*)

WE must now consider the cause of sin, on the part of the sensitive appetite, as to whether a passion of the soul may be a cause of sin. Under this head there are eight points of inquiry: (1) Whether a passion of the sensitive appetite can move or incline the will? (2) Whether it can overcome the reason against the latter's knowledge? (3) Whether a sin resulting from a passion is a sin of weakness? (4) Whether the passion of self-love is the cause of every sin? (5) On the three causes of sin mentioned in *1 John* ii. 16: *Concupiscence of the eyes, Concupiscence of the flesh* and *Pride of life*. (6) Whether the passion which causes a sin diminishes it? (7) Whether passion excuses from sin altogether? (8) Whether a sin committed through passion can be mortal?

First Article

WHETHER THE WILL IS MOVED BY A PASSION OF THE SENSITIVE APPETITE?

We proceed thus to the First Article:—

Objection 1. It would seem that the will is not moved by a passion of the sensitive appetite. For no passive power is moved except by its object. Now the will is a power both passive and active, inasmuch as it is mover and moved, as the Philosopher says of the appetitive power in general.[1] Since, therefore, the object of the will is not a passion of the sensitive appetite, but rather the good defined by the reason, it seems that a passion of the sensitive appetite does not move the will.

Obj. 2. Further, the higher mover is not moved by the lower. Thus the soul is not moved by the body. Now the will, which is the rational appetite, is compared to the sensitive appetite as a higher mover to a lower; for the Philosopher says that *the rational appetite moves the sensitive appetite, even as, in the heavenly bodies, one sphere moves another.*[2] Therefore the will cannot be moved by a passion of the sensitive appetite.

Obj. 3. Further, nothing immaterial can be moved by that which is material. Now the will is an immaterial power, because it does not use a cor-

[1] *De An.,* III, 10 (433b 16).   [2] *Op. cit.,* III, 11 (434a 12).

poreal organ, since it is in the reason, as is stated in *De Anima* iii.;[3] whereas the sensitive appetite is a material power, since it is seated in an organ of the body. Therefore a passion of the sensitive appetite cannot move the intellective appetite.

On the contrary, It is written (*Dan.* xiii. 56): *Lust hath perverted thy heart.*

I answer that, A passion of the sensitive appetite cannot draw or move the will directly; but it can do so indirectly, and this in two ways. First, by a kind of distraction. For, since all the soul's powers are rooted in the one essence of the soul, it follows of necessity that, when one power is intent in its act, another power becomes relaxed in its operation, or is even altogether impeded, both because every power is weakened by being extended to many things (so that, on the contrary, through being concentrated on one thing, it is less able to be directed to several), and because, in the operations of the soul, a certain attention is requisite, and if this be closely fixed on one thing, less attention is given to another. In this way, by a kind of distraction, when the movement of the sensitive appetite is strengthened in respect of any passion whatever, the proper movement of the rational appetite or will must, of necessity, become relaxed or altogether impeded.

Secondly, this may happen on the part of the will's object, which is the good apprehended by reason. For the judgment and apprehension of reason is impeded because of a vehement and inordinate apprehension of the imagination and the judgment of the estimative power, as appears in those who are out of their mind. Now it is evident that the apprehension of the imagination and the judgment of the estimative power follow the passion of the sensitive appetite, even as the verdict of the taste follows the disposition of the tongue; and for this reason we observe that those who are in some kind of passion do not easily turn their imagination away from the object of their affections. The result is that the judgment of the reason often follows the passion of the sensitive appetite, and consequently the will's movement follows it also, since it has a natural inclination always to follow the judgment of the reason.

Reply Obj. 1. Although the passion of the sensitive appetite is not the direct object of the will, yet it occasions a certain change in the judgment about the object of the will, as we have stated.

Reply Obj. 2. The higher mover is not directly moved by the lower; but, in a manner, it can be moved by it indirectly, as has been stated.

The Third Objection is solved in like manner.

[3] *Op. cit.,* III, 9 (432b 5).

Second Article

WHETHER THE REASON CAN BE OVERCOME BY A PASSION,
AGAINST ITS KNOWLEDGE?

We proceed thus to the Second Article:—

Objection 1. It would seem that the reason cannot be overcome by a passion, against its knowledge. For the stronger is not overcome by the weaker. Now knowledge, because of its certitude, is the strongest thing in us. Therefore it cannot be overcome by a passion, which is weak and soon passes away.[4]

Obj. 2. Further, the will is not directed save to the good or the apparent good. Now when a passion draws the will to that which is really good, it does not influence the reason against its knowledge; and when it draws it to that which is good apparently, but not really, it draws it to that which appears good to the reason. But what appears to the reason is in the knowledge of the reason. Therefore a passion never influences the reason against its knowledge.

Obj. 3. Further, if it be said that it draws the reason from its knowledge of something in general to form a contrary judgment about a particular matter,—*on the contrary*, if a universal and a particular proposition be opposed, they are opposed by contradiction: *e.g., Every man,* and *Not every man.* Now if two opinions contradict one another, they are contrary to one another, as is stated in *De Interpretatione* ii.[5] If therefore anyone, while knowing something in general, were to pronounce an opposite judgment in a particular case, he would have two contrary opinions at the same time, which is impossible.

Obj. 4. Further, whoever knows the universal knows also the particular, which he knows to be contained in the universal. Thus who knows that every mule is sterile, knows that this particular animal is sterile, provided he knows it to be a mule, as is clear from *Posterior Analytics* i.[6] Now he who knows something in general, *e.g.,* that *no fornication is lawful,* knows this general proposition to contain, for example, the particular proposition, *This is an act of fornication.* Therefore it seems that his knowledge extends to the particular.

Obj. 5. Further, according to the Philosopher, *words express the thoughts of the soul.*[7] Now it often happens that man, while in a state of passion, confesses that what he has chosen is an evil, even in that particular case. Therefore he has knowledge, even in the particular.

Therefore it seems that the passions cannot draw the reason against its universal knowledge; because it is impossible for it to have universal knowledge together with an opposite particular judgment.

[4] Aristotle, *Cat.,* VIII (9b 28).   [5] Aristotle, *Perih.,* XIV (23b 40).   [6] Aristotle, *Post. Anal.,* I, 1 (71a 17).   [7] *Perih.,* I (16a 3).

On the contrary, The Apostle says (*Rom.* vii. 23): *I see another law in my members, fighting against the law of my mind, and captivating me in the law of sin.* Now the law that is in the members is concupiscence, of which he had been speaking previously. Since, then, concupiscence is a passion, it seems that a passion draws the reason counter to its knowledge.

I answer that, As the Philosopher states, the opinion of Socrates was that knowledge can never be overcome by passion.[8] Therefore he held every virtue to be a kind of knowledge, and every sin a kind of ignorance.[9] In this he was somewhat right, because, since the object of the will is a good or an apparent good, it is never moved to an evil, unless that which is not good appear good in some respect to the reason; so that the will would never tend to evil unless there were some ignorance or error in the reason. Hence it is written (*Prov.* xiv. 22): *They err that work evil.*

Experience, however, shows that many act contrary to the knowledge that they have, and this is confirmed by divine authority, according to the words of *Luke* xii. 47: *The servant who knew the will of his lord . . . and did not . . . shall be beaten with many stripes*; and the words of *James* iv. 17: *To him . . . who knoweth to do good, and doth it not, to him it is a sin.* Consequently Socrates was not altogether right, and it is necessary, with the Philosopher, to make a distinction.[10] Because, since man is directed to right action by a twofold knowledge, viz., universal and particular, a defect in either of them suffices to hinder the rectitude of the will and of the deed, as we have stated above.[11] It may happen, then, that a man has some knowledge in general, *e.g.,* that no fornication is lawful, and yet he does not know in particular that this act, which is fornication, must not be done; and this suffices for the will not to follow the universal knowledge of the reason. Again, it must be observed that nothing prevents a thing which is known habitually from not being considered actually. Hence, it is possible for a man to have correct knowledge not only in general but also in particular, and yet not to consider his knowledge actually; and in such a case it does not seem difficult for a man to act counter to what he does not actually consider.

Now, that a man sometimes fails to consider in particular what he knows habitually may happen through mere lack of attention. For instance, a man who knows geometry may not attend to the consideration of geometrical conclusions, which he is ready to consider at any moment. Sometimes a man fails to consider actually what he knows habitually, because of some supervening hindrance, *e.g.,* some external occupation, or some bodily infirmity; and, in this way, a man who is in a state of passion fails to consider in particular what he knows in general, in so far as the passions hinder him from considering it.

---

[8] *Eth.,* VII, 2 (1145b 23).   [9] *Ibid.;* cf. *op. cit.,* VI, 13 (1144b 19; b 28).   [10] *Op. cit.,* VII, 3 (1146b 31).   [11] Q. 76, a. 1.

Now it hinders him in three ways. First, by way of distraction, as was explained above. Secondly, by way of opposition, because a passion often inclines to something contrary to what man knows in the universal. Thirdly, by way of bodily transmutation, the result of which is that the reason is somehow fettered so as not to exercise its act freely; even as sleep or drunkenness, because of some change wrought on the body, fetters the use of reason. That this takes place in the passions is evident from the fact that sometimes, when the passions are very intense, man loses the use of reason altogether; for many have gone out of their minds through excess of love or anger. It is in this way that passion draws the reason to judge in the particular against the knowledge which it has in the universal.

Reply Obj. 1. Universal knowledge, which is most certain, does not hold the foremost place in action, but rather particular knowledge, since actions are about singulars; and therefore it is not astonishing that, in matters of action, passion acts counter to universal knowledge, if the consideration of particular knowledge be lacking.

Reply Obj. 2. The fact that something appears good in the particular to the reason, which yet is not good, is due to a passion; and yet this particular judgment is contrary to the universal knowledge of the reason.

Reply Obj. 3. It is impossible for anyone to have an actual knowledge or true opinion about a universal affirmative proposition, and at the same time a false opinion about a particular negative proposition, or *vice versa;* but it may well happen that a man has true habitual knowledge about a universal affirmative proposition, and actually a false opinion about a particular negative. For an act is directly opposed, not to a habit, but to an act.

Reply Obj. 4. He that has knowledge in the universal is hindered, because of a passion, from reasoning in the light of that universal, so as to draw the conclusion; but he reasons in the light of another universal proposition suggested by the inclination of the passion, and draws his conclusion accordingly. Hence the Philosopher says that the syllogism of an incontinent man has four propositions, including *two* universal, of which one comes from the reason, *e.g.,* No fornication is lawful, and the other, from passion, *e.g.,* Pleasure is to be pursued.[12] Hence passion fetters the reason, and hinders it from thinking and concluding under the first proposition; so that while the passion lasts, the reason argues and concludes under the second.

Reply Obj. 5. Even as a drunken man sometimes gives utterance to words of deep signification, of which, however, he is incompetent to judge, since his drunkenness hinders him, so a man who is in a state of passion may indeed say in words that he ought not to do so and so, yet his inner thought is that he must do it, as is stated in *Ethics* vii.[13]

---

[12] *Eth.,* VII, 3 (1147a 24).   [13] *Ibid.* (1147a 18).

Third Article

WHETHER A SIN COMMITTED THROUGH PASSION SHOULD BE
CALLED A SIN OF WEAKNESS?

We proceed thus to the Third Article:—

Objection 1. It would seem that a sin committed through passion should not be called a sin of weakness. For a passion is a vehement movement of the sensitive appetite, as was stated above. Now vehemence of movement is evidence of strength rather than of weakness. Therefore a sin committed through passion should not be called a sin of weakness.

Obj. 2. Further, weakness in man regards that which is most fragile in him. Now this is the flesh, and hence it is written (*Ps.* lxxvii. 39): *He remembered that they are flesh.* Therefore sins of weakness should be those which result from bodily defects, rather than those which are due to a passion.

Obj. 3. Further, man does not seem to be weak in respect of things which are subject to his will. Now it is subject to man's will, whether he shall do or do not the things to which his passions incline him, according to *Gen.* iv. 7: *Thy appetite shall be under thee, and thou shalt have dominion over it.* Therefore sin committed through passion is not a sin of weakness.

On the contrary, Cicero calls the passions diseases of the soul.[14] Now weakness is another name for disease. Therefore a sin that arises from passion should be called a sin of weakness.

I answer that, The cause of sin is on the part of the soul, in which sin chiefly resides. Now weakness may be attributed to the soul by way of a likeness to the weakness of the body. But man's body is said to be weak when it is disabled or hindered in the execution of its proper action. This takes place through some disorder of the body's parts, so that the humors and members of the human body cease to be subject to its governing and motive power. Hence a member is said to be weak when it cannot do the work of a healthy member, the eye, for instance, when it cannot see clearly, as the Philosopher states.[15] Therefore weakness is attributed to the soul when it is hindered from fulfilling its proper action because of a disorder in its parts. Now as the parts of the body are said to be out of order when they fail to comply with the order of nature, so too the parts of the soul are said to be inordinate when they are not subject to the order of reason; for the reason is the ruling power of the soul's parts. Accordingly, when the concupiscible or irascible power is affected by any passion contrary to the order of reason, with the result that an impediment arises in the aforesaid manner to the due action of man, it is said to be a sin of weakness. Hence the Philosopher compares the incontinent man to a paralytic whose members move in a manner contrary to his intention.[16]

---

[14] *Tusc. Disp.,* IV, 14 (p. 377).   [15] *De Hist. Anim.,* X, 1 (633b 20).   [16] *Eth.,* I, 13 (1102b 18).

Reply Obj. 1. Just as in the body the stronger the movement against the order of nature, the greater the weakness, so likewise, the stronger the movement of passion against the order of reason, the greater the weakness of the soul.

Reply Obj. 2. Sin consists chiefly in an act of the will, which is not hindered by weakness of the body; for he that is weak in body may have a will ready for action, and yet be hindered by a passion, as was stated above. Hence, when we speak of sins of weakness, we refer to weakness of soul rather than of body. And yet even weakness of soul is called weakness of the flesh, in so far as it is owing to a condition of the flesh that the passions of the soul arise in us, for the sensitive appetite is a power using a corporeal organ.

Reply Obj. 3. It is in the will's power to give or refuse its consent to what passion inclines us to do, and it is in this sense that our appetite is said to be under us; and yet this consent or dissent of the will is hindered by passion in the way already explained.

Fourth Article

WHETHER SELF-LOVE IS THE SOURCE OF EVERY SIN?

We proceed thus to the Fourth Article:—

Objection 1. It would seem that self-love is not the source of every sin. For that which is good and right in itself is not the proper cause of sin. Now love of self is a good and right thing in itself. Hence it is that man is commanded to love his neighbor as himself (*Levit.* xix. 18). Therefore self-love cannot be the proper cause of sin.

Obj. 2. Further, the Apostle says (*Rom.* vii. 8): *Sin taking occasion by the commandment wrought in me all manner of concupiscence*; on which words the *Gloss* says that *the law is good, since by forbidding concupiscence, it forbids all evils.*[17] The reason for this is that concupiscence is the cause of every sin. Now concupiscence is a distinct passion from love, as was stated above.[18] Therefore self-love is not the cause of every sin.

Obj. 3. Further, Augustine, in commenting on *Ps.* lxxix. 17 (*Things set on fire and dug down*), says that *every sin is due either to love arousing us to undue ardor or to fear inducing false humility.*[19] Therefore self-love is not the only cause of sin.

Obj. 4. Further, as man sins at times through inordinate love of self, so he sometimes sins through inordinate love of his neighbor. Therefore self-love is not the cause of every sin.

On the contrary, Augustine says that *self-love, amounting to contempt*

---

[17] *Glossa ordin.* (VI, 16 E); *Glossa interl.* (VI, 16v).—Cf. St. Augustine, *De Spir. et Litt.,* IV (PL 44, 204).   [18] Q. 23, a. 4; q. 30, a. 2.   [19] *Enarr. in Psalm.,* super LXXIX, 17 (PL 36, 1027).

of God, builds up the city of Babylon.[20] Now every sin makes man a citizen of Babylon. Therefore self-love is the cause of every sin.

I answer that, As we have stated above, the proper and essential cause of sin is to be considered on the part of the adherence to a mutable good.[21] In this respect, every sinful act proceeds from an inordinate desire for some temporal good. Now the fact that anyone desires a temporal good inordinately is due to the fact that he loves himself inordinately; for to wish anyone some good is to love him. Therefore it is evident that inordinate love of self is the cause of every sin.

Reply Obj. 1. Well ordered self-love, whereby man desires a fitting good for himself, is right and natural; but it is inordinate self-love, leading to the contempt of God, that Augustine reckons to be the cause of sin.

Reply Obj. 2. Concupiscence, whereby a man desires good for himself, is reduced to self-love as to its cause, as we have stated.

Reply Obj. 3. Man is said to love both the good he desires for himself, and himself for whom he desires it. Love, in so far as it is directed to the object of desire (*e.g.,* a man is said to love wine or money) admits fear as its cause, which pertains to the avoidance of evil; for every sin arises either from an inordinate desire for some good, or from an inordinate avoidance of some evil. But each of these is reduced to self-love, since it is through loving himself that a man either desires good things or avoids evil things.

Reply Obj. 4. A friend is like another self. Therefore the sin which is committed through love for a friend seems to be committed through self-love.

Fifth Article

WHETHER CONCUPISCENCE OF THE FLESH, CONCUPISCENCE OF THE EYES AND PRIDE OF LIFE ARE FITTINGLY DE-SCRIBED AS CAUSES OF SIN?

We proceed thus to the Fifth Article:—

Objection 1. It would seem that *concupiscence of the flesh, concupiscence of the eyes and pride of life* are unfittingly described as causes of sin. For according to the Apostle (*1 Tim.* vi. 10), *covetousness is the root of all evils.* Now pride of life is not included in covetousness. Therefore it should not be reckoned among the causes of sin.

Obj. 2. Further, concupiscence of the flesh is aroused chiefly by what is seen by the eyes, according to *Dan.* xiii. 56: *Beauty hath deceived thee.* Therefore concupiscence of the eyes should not be co-divided against concupiscence of the flesh.

Obj. 3. Further, concupiscence is desire for pleasure, as was stated above.[22] Now objects of pleasure are perceived not only by the sight, but

---

[20] *De Civit. Dei,* XIV, 28 (PL 41, 436).   [21] Q. 75, a. 1.   [22] Q. 30, a. 1.

also by the other senses. Therefore *concupiscence of the hearing* and of the other senses should also have been mentioned.

Obj. 4. Further, just as man is induced to sin through inordinate desire of good things, so is he also, through inordinate avoidance of evil things, as was stated above. But nothing is mentioned here pertaining to avoidance of evil. Therefore the causes of sin are insufficiently described.

On the contrary, It is written (*1 John* ii. 16): *All that is in the world is concupiscence of the flesh, or concupiscence of the eyes, or pride of life.* Now a thing is said to be *in the world* by reason of sin; and hence it is written (*ibid.* v. 19): *The whole world is seated in wickedness.* Therefore these three are causes of sin.

I answer that, As was stated above, inordinate self-love is the cause of every sin. Now self-love includes an inordinate desire of good, for a man desires good for the one he loves. Hence it is evident that an inordinate desire of good is the cause of every sin. Now good is, in two ways, the object of the sensitive appetite, wherein are the passions which are the cause of sin: first, absolutely, according as it is the object of the concupiscible part; secondly, under the aspect of something difficult, according as it is the object of the irascible part, as was stated above.[23]

But concupiscence is twofold, as we have stated above.[24] One is natural, and is directed to those things which sustain the nature of the body, whether as regards the preservation of the individual, such as food, drink and the like, or as regards the preservation of the species, such as sexual matters. The inordinate appetite of such things is called *concupiscence of the flesh.* The other is spiritual concupiscence, and is directed to those things which do not afford sustenance or pleasure by way of the senses of the flesh, but are delectable according to the apprehension of imagination, or some similar mode or perception. Such are money, apparel, and the like. This spiritual concupiscence is called *concupiscence of the eyes,* whether this be taken as referring to the sight itself, of which the eyes are the organ, so as to denote curiosity, according to Augustine's exposition;[25] or to the concupiscence of things which are proposed outwardly to the eyes, so as to denote covetous-ness, according to the explanation of others. The inordinate appetite of the arduous good pertains to the *pride of life*; for pride is the inordinate appetite of excellence, as we shall state further on.[26]

It is therefore evident that all passions that are a cause of sin can be reduced to these three. For all the passions of the concupiscible part can be reduced to the first two, and all the irascible passions to the third, which is not divided into two because all the irascible passions naturally conform to spiritual concupiscence.

Reply Obj. 1. *Pride of life* is included in covetousness according as the latter denotes any kind of appetite for any kind of good. How covetousness,

---

[23] Q. 23, a. 1.   [24] Q. 30, a. 3.   [25] *Confess.,* X, 35 (PL 32, 802).   [26] Q. 84, a. 2; II-II, q. 162, a. 1.

as a special vice, which goes by the name of *avarice,* is the root of all sins, shall be explained further on.[27]

Reply Obj. 2. *Concupiscence of the eyes* does not mean here the con- cupiscence for all things that can be seen by the eyes, but only for such things as afford, not carnal pleasure in respect of touch, but in respect of the eyes, *i.e.,* of any apprehensive power.

Reply Obj. 3. The sense of sight is the most excellent of all the senses, and covers a larger ground, as is stated in *Metaph.* i.[28] Hence its name is transferred to all the other senses, and even to the inner apprehensions, as Augustine states.[29]

Reply Obj. 4. Avoidance of evil is caused by the appetite for good, as was stated above,[30] and so those passions alone are mentioned which in- cline to good, as being the causes of those which cause inordinately the avoidance of evil.

Sixth Article

WHETHER SIN IS DIMINISHED BECAUSE OF PASSION?

We proceed thus to the Sixth Article:—

Objection 1. It would seem that sin is not diminished because of passion. For an increase in the cause adds to the effect. Thus, if a hot thing causes something to melt, a hotter will do so yet more. Now passion is a cause of sin, as was stated. Therefore, the more intense the passion, the greater the sin. Therefore passion does not diminish sin, but increases it.

Obj. 2. Further, a good passion stands in the same relation to merit as an evil passion does to sin. Now a good passion increases merit; for a man seems to merit the more, according as he is moved by a greater pity to help a poor man. Therefore an evil passion increases rather than diminishes a sin.

Obj. 3. Further, a man seems to sin the more grievously according as he sins with a more intense will. But the passion that impels the will makes it tend with greater intensity to the sinful act. Therefore passion aggravates a sin.

On the contrary, The passion of concupiscence is called a temptation of the flesh. But the greater the temptation that overcomes a man, the less grievous his sin, as Augustine states.[31] Therefore passion diminishes sin.

I answer that, Sin consists essentially in an act of free choice, which is an ability of the will and the reason;[32] while passion is a movement of the sensitive appetite. Now the sensitive appetite can be related to the free choice antecedently and consequently: antecedently, according as a passion

---

[27] Q. 84, a. 1.   [28] Aristotle, *Metaph.,* I, 1 (980a 23).   [29] *Serm.* CXII, 6 (PL 38, 646).   [30] Q. 25, a. 2; q. 29, a. 2.   [31] *De Civit. Dei,* XIV, 12 (PL 41, 420); *De Nat. et Grat.,* XXV (PL 44, 261).   [32] Cf. Peter Lombard, *Sent.,* II, xxiv, 3 (I, 421).

of the sensitive appetite draws or inclines the reason or the will, as we have stated above;[33] and consequently, in so far as the movements of the higher powers affect the lower, since it is not possible for the will to be moved to anything intensely without a passion being aroused in the sensitive appetite.

Accordingly, if we take passion as preceding the sinful act, it must needs diminish the sin, because the act is a sin in so far as it is voluntary, and under our control. Now a thing is said to be under our control through the reason and will; and therefore the more the reason and will do anything of their own accord, and not through the impulse of a passion, the more is it voluntary and under our control. In this respect passion diminishes sin, in so far as it diminishes its voluntariness.

On the other hand, a consequent passion does not diminish a sin, but increases it, or rather it is a sign of its gravity, in so far, namely, as it shows the intensity of the will towards the sinful act; and so it is true that the greater the pleasure or the concupiscence with which anyone sins, the greater the sin.

Reply Obj. 1. Passion is the cause of sin on the part of that to which the sinner turns. But the gravity of a sin is measured on the part of that from which he turns, which results accidentally from his turning to something else,—accidentally, *i.e.,* without intention. Now an effect is increased by the increase, not of its accidental cause, but of its essential cause.

Reply Obj. 2. A good passion consequent upon the judgment of reason increases merit; but if it precede, so that a man is moved to do well rather by his passion than by the judgment of his reason, such a passion diminishes the goodness and praiseworthiness of his action.

Reply Obj. 3. Although the movement of the will incited by the passion is more intense, yet it is not so much the will's own movement, as if it were moved to sin by the reason alone.

Seventh Article

WHETHER PASSION EXCUSES FROM SIN ALTOGETHER?

We proceed thus to the Seventh Article:—

Objection 1. It would seem that passion excuses from sin altogether. For whatever causes an act to be involuntary excuses from sin altogether. But concupiscence of the flesh, which is a passion, makes an act to be involuntary, according to *Gal.* v. 17: *The flesh lusteth against the spirit . . . so that you do not the things that you would.* Therefore passion excuses from sin altogether.

Obj. 2. Further, passion causes a certain ignorance in the particular, as we have stated above. But ignorance in the particular excuses from sin

[33] A. 1 and 2; q. 9, a. 2; q. 10, a. 3.

altogether, as was stated above.[34] Therefore passion excuses from sin altogether.

Obj. 3. Further, disease of the soul is graver than disease of the body. But bodily disease excuses from sin altogether, as in the case of mad people. Much more therefore does passion, which is a disease of the soul.

On the contrary, The Apostle (*Rom.* vii. 5) speaks of the passions as *passions of sins,* for no other reason than that they cause sin; which would not be the case if they excused from sin altogether. Therefore passion does not excuse from sin altogether.

I answer that, An act which is evil in its genus cannot be excused from sin altogether, unless it be rendered altogether involuntary. Consequently, if the passion be such that it renders the subsequent act wholly involuntary, it entirely excuses from sin; otherwise, it does not excuse entirely. Here two points should be observed: First, a thing may be voluntary either *in itself,* as when the will tends towards it directly, or *in its cause,* when the will tends towards that cause and not towards the effect (as is the case with one who wilfully gets drunk, for in that case he is considered to do voluntarily whatever he does through being drunk). Secondly, we must observe that a thing is said to be voluntary *directly* or *indirectly:* directly, if the will tends towards it; indirectly, if the will could have prevented it, but does not.

Accordingly, therefore, we must make a distinction. For a passion is sometimes so strong as to take away the use of reason altogether, as in the case of those who are mad through love or anger; and then, if such a passion were voluntary from the beginning, the act is reckoned a sin, because it is voluntary in its cause, as we have stated with regard to drunkenness. If, however, the cause be not voluntary but natural, for instance, if anyone through sickness or some such cause fall into such a passion as deprives him of the use of reason, his act is rendered wholly involuntary, and he is entirely excused from sin. Sometimes, however, the passion is not such as to take away the use of reason altogether. In that case reason can drive the passion away by turning to other thoughts, or it can prevent it from having its full effect, since the members are not put to work except by the consent of reason, as we have stated above.[35] Therefore such a passion does not excuse from sin altogether.

Reply Obj. 1 The words, *So that you do not the things that you would,* are not to be referred to outward deeds, but to the inner movement of concupiscence; for a man would wish never to desire evil. It is in this sense that we are to understand the words of *Rom.* vii. 19: *The evil which I will not, that I do.*—Or again they may be referred to the will as preceding the passion, as is the case with the incontinent who act counter to their resolution because of their concupiscence.

---

[34] Q. 19, a. 6.   [35] Q. 17, a. 9.

Reply Obj. 2. Ignorance in the particular, which excuses altogether, is ignorance of a circumstance which a man is unable to know even after taking due precautions. But passion causes an ignorance of law in the particular by preventing universal knowledge from being applied to a particular act; and this passion the reason is able to drive away, as was stated.

Reply Obj. 3. Bodily disease is involuntary. There would be a comparison, however, if it were voluntary, as we have stated about drunkenness, which is a kind of bodily disease.

Eighth Article

WHETHER A SIN COMMITTED THROUGH PASSION CAN BE MORTAL?

We proceed thus to the Eighth Article:—

Objection 1. It would seem that sin committed through passion cannot be mortal. For venial sin is co-divided against mortal sin. Now sin committed from weakness is *venial*, since it has in itself a motive for pardon [*venia*]. Since therefore sin committed through passion is a sin of weakness, it seems that it cannot be mortal.

Obj. 2. Further, the cause is more powerful than its effect. But passion cannot be a mortal sin, for there is no mortal sin in the sensuality, as was stated above.[36] Therefore a sin committed through passion cannot be mortal.

Obj. 3. Further, passion is a hindrance to reason, as we have explained above. Now it belongs to the reason to turn to God, or to turn away from Him, which is the essence of a mortal sin. Therefore a sin committed through passion cannot be mortal.

On the contrary, The Apostle says (*Rom.* vii. 5) that *the passions of the sins . . . work in our members to bring forth fruit unto death.* Now it is proper to mortal sin to bring forth fruit unto death. Therefore sin committed through passion may be mortal.

I answer that, Mortal sin, as was stated above, consists in turning away from our last end, which is God;[37] which aversion pertains to the deliberating reason, whose function it is also to direct towards the end. Therefore, that which is contrary to the last end can happen not to be a mortal sin only when the deliberating reason is unable to come to the rescue, which is the case in sudden movements. Now when anyone proceeds from passion to a sinful act, or to a deliberate consent, this does not happen suddenly; and so the deliberating reason can come to the rescue here, since it can drive the passion away, or at least prevent it from having its effect, as we have stated above.[38] Therefore, if it does not come to the rescue, there is a

[36] Q. 74, a. 4. [37] Q. 72, a. 5. [38] A. 7; q. 10, a. 3, ad 2.

mortal sin; and it is thus, as we see, that many murders and adulteries are committed through passion.

Reply Obj. 1. A sin may be venial in three ways. First, through its cause, *i.e.*, through having a cause to be forgiven, which cause lessens the sin; and thus a sin that is committed through weakness or ignorance is said to be venial. Secondly, through its issue; and thus every sin, through repentance, becomes venial, *i.e.*, receives pardon. Thirdly, in its genus, *e.g.*, an idle word. This is the only kind of venial sin that is opposed to mortal sin, whereas the objection regards the first kind.

Reply Obj. 2. Passion causes sin because of the adherence to something. But that this be a mortal sin is due to the aversion, which follows accidentally from the adherence, as was stated above. Hence the argument does not prove.

Reply Obj. 3. Passion does not always hinder the act of reason altogether. Consequently, the reason remains in possession of its free choice, so as to turn away from God, or turn to Him. If, however, the use of reason be taken away altogether, the sin is no longer either mortal or venial.

Question LXXVIII

ON THAT CAUSE OF SIN WHICH IS MALICE

(*In Four Articles*)

WE must now consider the cause of sin on the part of the will, viz. malice; and under this head there are four points of inquiry: (1) Whether it is possible for anyone to sin through certain malice, *i.e.*, purposely? (2) Whether everyone that sins through habit, sins through certain malice? (3) Whether every one that sins through certain malice, sins through habit? (4) Whether it is more grievous to sin through certain malice than through passion?

First Article

WHETHER ANYONE SINS THROUGH CERTAIN MALICE?

We proceed thus to the First Article:—

Objection 1. It would seem that no one sins purposely, or through certain malice. For ignorance is opposed to purpose or certain malice. Now *every evil man is ignorant,* according to the Philosopher.[1] And it is written (*Prov.* xiv. 22): *They err that work evil.* Therefore no one sins through certain malice.

Obj. 2. Further, Dionysius says that *no one works intending evil.*[2] Now to sin through malice [*malitia*] seems to denote the intention of doing evil [*malum*] in sinning, because an act is not denominated from that which is unintentional and accidental. Therefore no one sins through malice.

Obj. 3. Further, malice itself is a sin. If, therefore, malice is a cause of sin, it follows that sin goes on causing sin indefinitely, which is ridiculous. Therefore no one sins through malice.

On the contrary, it is written (*Job* xxxiv. 27): [*Who*] *as it were on purpose have revolted from God, and would not understand all His ways.* Now to revolt from God is to sin. Therefore some sin purposely or through certain malice.

I answer that, Man, like any other being, has naturally an appetite for the good, and so if his appetite incline away to evil, this is due to corruption or disorder in some one of the principles of man; for it is thus that sin occurs in the actions of natural things. Now the principles of human acts are the intellect and the appetite, both rational (*i.e.*, the will) and sensitive.

[1] *Eth.,* III, 1 (1110b 28).   [2] *De Div. Nom.,* IV, 19; 31 (PG 3, 716; 732).

644

Therefore even as sin occurs in human acts, sometimes through a defect of the intellect, as when anyone sins through ignorance, and sometimes through a defect in the sensitive appetite, as when anyone sins through passion, so too does it occur through a defect consisting in a disorder of the will. Now the will is out of order when it loves more the lesser good. But the consequence is that one chooses to suffer some disadvantage in relation to a good that is loved less, in order to obtain a good that one loves more; as when a man, even knowingly, suffers the loss of a bodily member that he may save his life, which he loves more. Accordingly, when an inordinate will loves some temporal good, *e.g.*, riches or pleasure, more than the order of reason or divine law, or divine charity, or some such thing, it follows that it is willing to suffer the loss of some spiritual good so that it may obtain possession of some temporal good. Now evil is merely the privation of some good, and so a man wishes knowingly a spiritual evil, which is evil absolutely, whereby he is deprived of a spiritual good, in order to possess a temporal good; and hence he is said to sin through certain malice, or on purpose, because he chooses evil knowingly.

Reply Obj. 1. Ignorance sometimes excludes the absolute knowledge that a particular action is evil, and then man is said to sin through ignorance; sometimes it excludes the knowledge that a particular action is evil at this particular moment, as when he sins through passion; and sometimes it excludes the knowledge that a particular evil is not to be suffered for the sake of possessing a particular good, but not the absolute knowledge that is an evil. It is thus that a man is ignorant when he sins through certain malice.

Reply Obj. 2. Evil cannot be intended by anyone for its own sake, but it can be intended for the sake of avoiding another evil, or obtaining another good, as was stated above. In such a case, anyone would choose to obtain a good intended for its own sake, without suffering loss of the other good, even as a lustful man would wish to enjoy a pleasure without offending God; but with the two set before him to choose from, he prefers sinning, and thereby incurring God's anger, to being deprived of the pleasure.

Reply Obj. 3. The malice through which anyone sins may be taken to denote habitual malice, in the sense in which the Philosopher calls an evil habit by the name of malice,[3] just as a good habit is called virtue; and in this way anyone is said to sin through malice when he sins through the inclination of a habit. It may also denote actual malice, whether by malice we mean the choice itself of evil (and thus anyone is said to sin through malice in so far as he sins through making a choice of evil), or whether by malice we mean some previous fault that gives rise to a subsequent fault, as when anyone impugns the grace of his brother through envy. Nor does this imply that a thing is its own cause, for the interior act is the cause of the

---

[3] *Eth.*, II, 5 (1105b 19).

exterior act, and one sin is the cause of another; not indefinitely, however, since we can trace it back to some previous sin, which is not caused by any previous sin, as was explained above.[4]

Second Article

WHETHER EVERYONE THAT SINS THROUGH HABIT, SINS THROUGH CERTAIN MALICE?

We proceed thus to the Second Article:—

Objection 1. It would seem that not everyone who sins through habit, sins through certain malice. For sin committed through certain malice seems to be most grievous. Now it happens sometimes that a man commits a slight sin through habit, as when he utters an idle word. Therefore sin committed from habit is not always committed through certain malice.

Obj. 2. Further, *Acts proceeding from habits are like the acts by which those habits are formed.*[5] But the acts which precede a vicious habit are not committed through certain malice. Therefore the sins that arise from habit are not committed through certain malice.

Obj. 3. Further, when a man commits a sin through certain malice, he is glad after having done it, according to *Prov.* ii. 14: *Who are glad when they have done evil, and rejoice in most wicked things*; and this because it is pleasant to obtain what we desire, and to do those actions which are connatural to us by reason of habit. But those who sin through habit are sorrowful after committing a sin, because *bad men, i.e.,* those who have a vicious habit, *are full of remorse.*[6] Therefore sins that arise from habit are not committed through certain malice.

On the contrary, A sin committed through certain malice is one that is done through choice of evil. Now we make choice of those things to which we are inclined by habit, as is stated in *Ethics* vi.[7] with regard to virtuous habits. Therefore a sin that arises from habit is committed through certain malice.

I answer that, There is a difference between a sin committed by one who has the habit, and a sin committed through habit; for it is not necessary to use a habit, since it is subject to the will of the person who has that habit. Hence habit is defined as being *something we use when we will,* as was stated above.[8] And thus, just as it may happen that one who has a vicious habit may break forth into a virtuous act (because a bad habit does not corrupt reason altogether, and something of it remains unimpaired, so that a sinner does some works which are generically good), so too it may happen sometimes that one who has a vicious habit acts, not from that habit, but through the uprising of a passion, or again through ig-

---

[4] Q. 75, a. 4, ad 3.   [5] Aristotle, *Eth.,* II, 2 (1104a 27; a 33).   [6] *Op. cit.,* IX, 4 (1156b 24).   [7] *Op. cit.,* VI, 2 (1139a 32).   [8] Q. 50, a. 1, obj. 1.

norance. But whenever he uses the vicious habit he must needs sin through certain malice; because, to anyone that has a habit, whatever is befitting to him according to that habit has the aspect of something lovable, since it thereby becomes, in a way, connatural to him, according as custom and habit are a sort of nature. Now the very thing which befits a man according to a vicious habit is something that excludes a spiritual good; and from this it follows that a man chooses a spiritual evil that he may obtain possession of what befits him in that habit. And this is to sin through certain malice. Therefore, it is evident that whoever sins through habit, sins through certain malice.

Reply Obj. 1. Venial sin does not exclude spiritual good, consisting in the grace of God or charity. Therefore it is an evil, not absolutely, but in a relative sense; and for that reason the habit thereof is not an absolute, but a relative, evil.

Reply Obj. 2. Acts proceeding from habits are of like species as the acts from which those habits were formed; but they differ from them as the perfect from the imperfect. Such is the difference between sin committed through certain malice and sin committed through passion.

Reply Obj. 3. He that sins through habit is always glad for what he does through habit, as long as he uses the habit. But since he is able not to use the habit, and to think of something else, by means of his reason which is not altogether corrupted, it may happen that while not using the habit he is sorry for what he has done through the habit. And so it often happens that such a man is sorry for his sin, not because sin in itself is displeasing to him, but because of his reaping some disadvantage from the sin.

Third Article

WHETHER ONE WHO SINS THROUGH CERTAIN MALICE, SINS THROUGH HABIT?

We proceed thus to the Third Article:—

Objection 1. It would seem that whoever sins through certain malice, sins through habit. For the Philosopher says that *an unjust action is not done as an unjust man does it, i.e.,* through choice, *unless it be done through habit.*[9] Now to sin through certain malice is to sin through making a choice of evil, as was stated above. Therefore no one sins through certain malice, unless he has the habit of sin.

Obj. 2. Further, Origen says that *a man is not suddenly ruined and lost, but must needs fall away little by little.*[10] But the greatest fall seems to be that of the man who sins through certain malice. Therefore a man comes to sin through certain malice, not from the outset, but from inveterate custom, which may engender a habit.

[9] *Op. cit.,* V, 6 (1134a 17; a 20).   [10] *Peri Archon,* I, 3 (PG 11, 155).

Obj. 3. Further, whenever a man sins through certain malice, his will must needs be inclined of itself to the evil he chooses. But by the nature of that power man is inclined, not to evil, but to good. Therefore, if he chooses evil, this must be due to something supervening, which is a passion or a habit. But when a man sins through passion, he sins, not through certain malice, but through weakness, as was stated.[11] Therefore whenever anyone sins through certain malice, he sins through habit.

Obj. 4. *On the contrary,* The good habit stands in the same relation to the choice of something good as the bad habit to the choice of something evil. But it happens sometimes that a man, without having the habit of a virtue, chooses that which is good according to that virtue. Therefore sometimes also a man, without having the habit of a vice, may choose evil, which is to sin through certain malice.

I answer that, The will is related differently to good and to evil. For from the very nature of the power it is inclined to the good of reason as to its proper object; and therefore every sin is said to be contrary to nature. Hence, if a will be inclined to some evil by its choice, this must be occasioned by something else. Sometimes, in fact, this is occasioned through some defect in the reason, as when anyone sins through ignorance; and sometimes this arises through the impulse of the sensitive appetite, as when anyone sins through passion. Yet neither of these amounts to a sin through certain malice, for then alone does anyone sin through certain malice when his will is moved to evil of its own accord. This may happen in two ways. First, through his having a corrupt disposition inclining him to evil, so that, according to that disposition, some evil is, as it were, suitable and similar to him; and to this thing, by reason of its suitableness, the will tends as to something good, because everything tends of its own accord to that which is suitable to it. Moreover, this corrupt disposition is either a habit acquired by custom, or a sickly condition on the part of the body, as in the case of a man who is naturally inclined to certain sins, by reason of some natural corruption in himself.—Secondly, the will, of its own accord, may tend to an evil through the removal of some obstacle. For instance, if a man be prevented from sinning, not because sin is in itself displeasing to him, but through hope of eternal life. or fear of hell, if hope give place to despair, or fear to presumption, he will end in sinning through certain malice, having been freed, as it were, from the bridle.

It is evident, therefore, that sin committed through certain malice always presupposes some lack of order in man, which, however, is not always a habit; so that it does not follow of necessity, if a man sins through certain malice, that he sins through habit.

Reply Obj. 1. To do an action as an unjust man does, may be not only to do unjust things through certain malice, but also to do them with pleas-

[11] Q. 77, a. 3.

ure, and without any notable resistance on the part of reason; and this occurs only in one who has a habit.

Reply Obj. 2. It is true that a man does not fall suddenly into sin from certain malice, and that something is presupposed; but this something is not always a habit, as we have stated above.

Reply Obj. 3. That which inclines the will to evil is not always a habit or a passion, but at times is something else, as we have said.

Reply Obj. 4. There is no comparison between choosing good and choosing evil, because evil is never without some good of nature, whereas good can be perfectly without the evil of fault.

Fourth Article

WHETHER IT IS MORE GRIEVOUS TO SIN THROUGH CERTAIN MALICE THAN THROUGH PASSION?

We proceed thus to the Fourth Article:—

Objection 1. It would seem that it is not more grievous to sin through certain malice than through passion. Because ignorance excuses from sin either altogether or in part. Now ignorance is greater in one who sins through certain malice than in one who sins through passion. For he that sins through certain malice suffers from the worst form of ignorance, which, according to the Philosopher, is ignorance of principle;[12] for he has a false estimation of the end, which is the principle in matters of action. Therefore, there is more excuse for one who sins through certain malice, than for one who sins through passion.

Obj. 2. Further, the more a man is impelled to sin, the less grievous his sin, as is clear with regard to a man who is thrown headlong into sin by a more impetuous passion. Now he that sins through certain malice is impelled by habit, the impulse of which is stronger than that of passion. Therefore to sin through habit is less grievous than to sin through passion.

Obj. 3. Further, to sin through certain malice is to sin through choosing evil. Now he that sins through passion also chooses evil. Therefore he does not sin less than the man who sins through certain malice.

On the contrary, A sin that is committed on purpose, for this very reason deserves heavier punishment, according to *Job* xxxiv. 26: *He hath struck them as being wicked, in open sight, who, as it were on purpose, have revolted from Him.* Now punishment is not increased except for a graver fault. Therefore a sin is aggravated through being done on purpose, *i.e.*, through certain malice.

I answer that, A sin committed through certain malice is more grievous than a sin committed through passion, for three reasons. First, because, as sin consists chiefly in an act of the will, it follows that, other things being

[12] *Eth.*, VII, 8 (1151a 16).

equal, a sin is all the more grievous according as the movement of the sin belongs more to the will. Now when a sin is committed through certain malice, the movement of sin belongs more to the will, which is then moved to evil of its own accord, than when a sin is committed through passion, when the will is impelled to sin by something extrinsic, as it were. Therefore a sin is aggravated by the very fact that it is committed through certain malice, and so much the more, as the malice is greater; whereas it is diminished by being committed through passion, and so much the more, as the passion is stronger.—Secondly, because the passion which incites the will to sin soon passes away, so that a man repents of his sin, and soon returns to his good intentions; whereas the habit, through which a man sins, is a permanent quality, so that he who sins through malice abides longer in his sin. For this reason the Philosopher compares the intemperate man, who sins through malice, to a sick man who suffers from a chronic disease, while he compares the incontinent man, who sins through passion, to one who suffers intermittently.[13]—Thirdly, because he who sins through certain malice is ill-disposed in relation to the end itself, which is the principle in matters of action; and so the defect is more dangerous than in the case of the man who sins through passion, whose purpose tends to a good end, although this purpose is interrupted, for the time being, because of the passion. Now the worst of all defects is a defect of principle. Therefore, it is evident that a sin committed through malice is more grievous than one committed through passion.

Reply Obj. 1. Ignorance of choice, to which the objection refers, neither excuses nor diminishes a sin, as was stated above.[14] Therefore neither does a greater ignorance of this kind make a sin to be less grave.

Reply Obj. 2. The impulse due to passion is, as it were, due to a defect which is outside the will; whereas, by a habit, the will is inclined from within. Hence the comparison fails.

Reply Obj. 3. It is one thing to sin while choosing, and another to sin through choosing. For he that sins through passion, sins while choosing, but not through choosing, because his choosing is not for him the first principle of his sin; for he is induced, through the passion, to choose what he would not choose, were it not for the passion. On the other hand, he that sins through certain malice, chooses evil of his own accord, in the way already explained; so that his choosing, of which he has full control, is the principle of his sin. That is why he is said to sin *through* choosing.

---

[13] *Ibid.* (1150b 32).   [14] Q. 76, a. 3 and 4.

Question LXXIX

ON THE EXTERNAL CAUSES OF SIN
(*In Four Articles*)

We must now consider the external causes of sin, and (1) on the part of God; (2) on the part of the devil;[1] (3) on the part of man.[2]

Under the first head there are four points of inquiry: (1) Whether God is a cause of sin? (2) Whether the act of sin is from God? (3) Whether God is the cause of spiritual blindness and hardness of heart? (4) Whether these things are directed to the salvation of those who are blinded or hardened?

First Article

WHETHER GOD IS A CAUSE OF SIN?

We proceed thus to the First Article:—

Objection 1. It would seem that God is a cause of sin. For the Apostle says of certain people (*Rom.* i. 28): *God delivered them up to a reprobate sense, to do those things which are not right;* and the Gloss comments on this by saying that *God works in men's hearts, by inclining their wills to whatever He wills, whether to good or to evil.*[3] Now sin consists in doing what is not right, and in having a will inclined to evil. Therefore God is to man a cause of sin.

Obj. 2. Further, it is written (*Wis.* xiv. 11): *The creatures of God are turned to an abomination, and a temptation to the souls of men.* But a temptation usually denotes a provocation to sin. Since therefore creatures were made by God alone, as was established in the First Part,[4] it seems that God is a cause of sin by provoking man to sin.

Obj. 3. Further, the cause of the cause is the cause of the effect. Now God is the cause of free choice, which itself is the cause of sin. Therefore God is the cause of sin.

Obj. 4. Further, every evil is opposed to good. But it is not contrary to God's goodness that He should cause the evil of punishment; since of this evil it is written (*Isa.* xlv. 7) that God creates evil, and (*Amos* iii. 6): *Shall there be evil in the city which God hath not done?* Therefore, it is not incompatible even with God's goodness that He should cause the evil of fault.

---

[1] Q. 80.   [2] Q. 81.   [3] *Glossa ordin.* (VI, 5 E).—cf. St. Augustine, *De Grat. et Lib. Arb.,* XXI (PL 44, 909).   [4] *S. T.,* I, q. 44, a. 1; q. 65, a. 1.

On the contrary, It is written (*Wis.* xi. 25): *Thou . . . hatest none of the things which Thou hast made.* Now God hates sin, according to *Wis.* xiv. 9: *To God the wicked and his wickedness are hateful.* Therefore God is not a cause of sin.

I answer that, Man is in two ways a cause either of his own or of another's sin. First, directly, namely, by inclining his or another's will to sin; secondly, indirectly, namely, by not preventing someone from sinning. Hence (*Ezech.* iii. 18) it is said to the watchman: *If thou say not to the wicked: 'Thou shalt surely die' . . . I will require his blood at thy hand.* Now God cannot be directly the cause of sin, either in Himself or in another, since every sin is a departure from the order directed towards God as the end; whereas God inclines and turns all things to Himself as to their last end, as Dionysius states.[5] Hence it is impossible that He should be either to Himself or to another the cause of departing from the order which is directed to Himself. Therefore, He cannot be directly the cause of sin.—In like manner, neither can He cause sin indirectly. For it happens that God does not give some the assistance by which they may avoid sin, which assistance were He to give, they would not sin. But He does all this according to the order of His wisdom and justice, since He Himself is Wisdom and Justice; so that if someone sin, it is not imputable to Him as though He were the cause of that sin. In the same way, a pilot is not said to cause the wrecking of the ship, because he is not steering the ship, unless he cease to steer it while he is able and bound to steer. It is therefore evident that God is in no way a cause of sin.

Reply Obj. 1. As to the words of the Apostle, the solution is clear from the text. For if God delivered some up to a reprobate sense, it follows that they already had a reprobate sense, so as to do what was not right. Accordingly, He is said to deliver them up to a reprobate sense, in so far as He does not hinder them from following that reprobate sense, even as we are said to expose a person to danger if we do not protect him.—The saying of Augustine, quoted by the *Gloss,* to the effect that *God inclines men's wills to good and evil,*[6] is to be understood as meaning that He inclines the will directly to good; and to evil, in so far as He does not hinder it, as was stated above. And yet even this is due as being deserved through a previous sin.

Reply Obj. 2. When it is said the *creatures of God are turned 'to' an abomination, and a temptation to the souls of men,* the preposition *to* does not denote causality but sequel. For God did not make creatures that they might be an evil to man; this was the result of man's folly, and therefore the text goes on to say, *and a snare to the feet of the unwise,* who, namely, in their folly, use creatures for a purpose other than that for which they were made.

---

[5] *De Div. Nom.,* I, 5 (PG 3, 593).   [6] *De Grat. et Lib. Arb.,* XXI (PL 44, 909); *Glossa ordin.* (VI, 5 E).

Reply Obj. 3. The effect which proceeds from an intermediate cause, according as it is subordinate to the first cause, is reduced to that first cause; but if it proceed from the intermediate cause according as it goes outside the order of the first cause, it is not reduced to that first cause. Thus, if a servant does any thing contrary to his master's orders, it is not ascribed to the master as though he were its cause. In like manner, sin, which our free choice commits against the commandment of God, is not attributed to God as being its cause.

Reply Obj. 4. *Punishment* is opposed to the good of the person punished, who is thereby deprived of some good or other; but *fault* is opposed to the good of subordination to God, and so is directly opposed to the divine goodness. Consequently, there is no comparison between fault and punishment.

Second Article

WHETHER THE ACT OF SIN IS FROM GOD?

We proceed thus to the Second Article:—
Objection 1. It would seem that the act of sin is not from God. For Augustine says that *the act of sin is not a thing.*[7] Now whatever is from God is a thing. Therefore the act of sin is not from God.

Obj. 2. Further, a man is not said to be the cause of sin, except because he is the cause of the sinful act; for *no one works, intending evil,* as Dionysius states.[8] Now God is not a cause of sin, as we have stated above. Therefore God is not the cause of the act of sin.

Obj. 3. Further, some acts are evil and sinful in their species, as was shown above.[9] Now whatever is the cause of a thing, causes whatever belongs to it according to its species. If therefore God caused the act of sin, He would be the cause of sin; which is false, as was proved above. Therefore God is not the cause of the act of sin.

On the contrary, The act of sin is a movement of free choice. Now *the will of God is the cause of every movement,* as Augustine declares.[10] Therefore God's will is the cause of the act of sin.

I answer that, The act of sin is both a being and an act, and in both respects it is from God. For every being, whatever the manner of its being, must be derived from the First Being, as Dionysius declares.[11] Again, every action is caused by something existing in act, since nothing produces an action save in so far as it is in act; and every being in act is reduced to the First Act, viz., God, as to its cause, Who is act by His Essence. Therefore God is the cause of every action, in so far as it is an action.—But sin denotes a being and an action with a defect. But this defect is from a created cause, viz., free choice, as falling away from the order of the First

---

[7] *De Perf. Iust.,* II (PL 44, 294).   [8] *De Div. Nom.,* IV, 19; 31 (PG 3, 716; 732).
[9] Q. 18, a. 5.   [10] *De Trin.,* III, 4 (PL 42, 873).   [11] *De Div. Nom.,* V, 4 (PG 3, 817).

Cause, viz., God. Consequently, this defect is not reduced to God as its cause, but to free choice; just as the defect of limping is reduced to a crooked leg as its cause, but not to the power of locomotion, which nevertheless causes whatever there is of movement in the limping. Accordingly, God is the cause of the act of sin; and yet He is not the cause of sin, because He does not cause the act to have a defect.

Reply Obj. 1. In this passage Augustine calls by the name of *thing* that which is a thing absolutely, viz., substance. But in this sense the act of sin is not a thing.

Reply Obj. 2. Not only the act, but also the defect, is reduced to man as its cause. For the defect consists in this, that man is not subject to Whom he ought to be, although he does not intend this principally. Therefore, man is the cause of the sin, while God is cause of the act, but in such a way, that He is in no way the cause of the defect accompanying the act; and hence He is not the cause of the sin.

Reply Obj. 3. As was stated above, acts and habits do not take their species from the privation itself, wherein consists the nature of evil, but from some object to which that privation is united.[12] Hence, this defect, which consists in not being from God, belongs to the species of the act consequently, and not as a specific difference.

Third Article

WHETHER GOD IS THE CAUSE OF SPIRITUAL BLINDNESS AND HARDNESS OF HEART?

We proceed thus to the Third Article:—

Objection 1. It would seem that God is not the cause of spiritual blindness and hardness of heart. For Augustine says that God is not the cause of that which makes man worse.[13] Now man is made worse by spiritual blindness and hardness of heart. Therefore God is not the cause of spiritual blindness and hardness of heart.

Obj. 2. Further, Fulgentius says: *God does not punish what He causes.*[14] Now God punishes the hardened heart, according to *Ecclus.* iii. 27: *A hard heart shall fear evil at the last.* Therefore God is not the cause of hardness of heart.

Obj. 3. Further, the same effect is not attributed to contrary causes. But the cause of spiritual blindness is said to be the malice of man, according to *Wis.* ii. 21: *For their own malice blinded them,* and again, according to 2 *Cor.* iv. 4: *The god of this world hath blinded the minds of unbelievers.* Now these causes seem to be opposed to God. Therefore God is not the cause of spiritual blindness and hardness of heart.

[12] Q. 18, a. 5, ad 2; q. 54, a. 3, ad 2.   [13] *Lib. 83 Quaest.,* q. 3 (PL 40, 11).
[14] *De duplici Praedest. Dei,* I, 19 (PL 65, 167).

On the contrary, It is written (*Isa.* vi. 10): *Blind the heart of this people, and make their ears heavy;* and *Rom.* ix. 18: *He hath mercy on whom He will, and whom He will He hardeneth.*

I answer that, Spiritual blindness and hardness of heart imply two things. One is the movement of the human mind in cleaving to evil, and turning away from the divine light. As regards this, God is not the cause of spiritual blindness and hardness of heart, just as He is not the cause of sin. The other thing is the withdrawal of grace, the result of which is that the mind is not illumined by God to see rightly, and man's heart is not softened to live rightly. As regards this, God is the cause of spiritual blindness and hardness of heart.

Now we must consider that God is the universal cause of the illumination of souls, according to *John* i. 9: *That was the true light which enlighteneth every man that cometh into this world,* even as the sun is the universal cause of the illumination of bodies, though not in the same way. For the sun illumines by necessity of nature, whereas God works freely through the order of His wisdom. Now, although the sun, so far as it is concerned, illumines all bodies, yet if it be encountered by an obstacle in a body, it leaves it in darkness. This is what happens to a house whose window-shutters are closed, although the sun is in no way the cause of the house being darkened, since it does not act of its own accord in failing to light up the interior of the house. The cause of this is the person who closed the shutters. On the other hand, God, of His own accord, withholds His grace from those in whom He finds an obstacle; so that the cause of the withholding of grace is not only the man who raises an obstacle to grace, but also God Who, of His own accord, withholds His grace. In this way, God is the cause of spiritual blindness, deafness of ear, and hardness of heart.

These differ from one another in respect of the effects of grace, which both perfects the intellect by the gift of wisdom, and softens the affections by the fire of charity. And since two of the senses excel in rendering service to the intellect, viz., sight and hearing, of which the former assists *discovery,* and the latter, *teaching,* hence it is that spiritual *blindness* corresponds to sight, *heaviness of the ears* to hearing, and *hardness of heart* to the affections.

Reply Obj. 1. Blindness and hardheartedness, as regards the withholding of grace, are punishments and, therefore, in this respect, they do not make a man worse. It is because he is already worsened by sin that he incurs them, even as other punishments.

Reply Obj. 2. This argument considers hardheartedness in so far as it is a sin.

Reply Obj. 3. Malice is the demeritorious cause of blindness, just as sin is the cause of punishment; and in this way, too, the devil is said to blind, in so far as he induces man to sin.

Fourth Article

WHETHER BLINDNESS AND HARDNESS OF HEART ARE DI-
RECTED TO THE SALVATION OF THOSE WHO ARE BLINDED
AND HARDENED?

We proceed thus to the Fourth Article:—

Objection 1. It would seem that blindness and hardness of heart are always directed to the salvation of those who are blinded and hardened. For Augustine says that *as God is supremely good, He would in no way allow evil to be done, unless He could draw some good from every evil.*[15] Much more, therefore, does He direct to some good the evil of which He Himself is the cause. Now God is the cause of blindness and hardness of heart, as was stated above. Therefore they are directed to the salvation of those who are blinded and hardened.

Obj. 2. Further, it is written (*Wis.* i. 13) that *God hath no pleasure in the destruction of the ungodly.* Now He would seem to take pleasure in their destruction, if He did not turn their blindness to their profit; just as a physician would seem to take pleasure in torturing the invalid, if he did not intend to heal the invalid when he prescribes a bitter medicine for him. Therefore God turns blindness to the profit of those who are blinded.

Obj. 3. Further, *God is not a respecter of persons (Acts* x. 34). Now He directs the blinding of some to their salvation, as in the case of some of the Jews, who were blinded so as not to believe in Christ, and, through not believing, to slay Him, and afterwards were seized with compunction, and converted, as is related by Augustine.[16] Therefore God turns all blindness to the spiritual welfare of those who are blinded.

Obj. 4. *On the other hand,* According to *Rom.* iii. 8, evil should not be done, that good may ensue. Now blindness is an evil. Therefore God does not blind some for the sake of their welfare.

I answer that, Blindness is a kind of preamble to sin. Now sin has a twofold relation,—to one thing directly, viz., to the sinner's damnation;—to another by reason of God's mercy or providence, viz., that the sinner may be healed, in so far as God permits some to fall into sin that by acknowledging their sin, they may be humbled and converted, as Augustine states.[17] Therefore blindness, of its very nature, is directed to the damnation of those who are blinded; and for this reason it is accounted an effect of reprobation. But, through God's mercy, temporary blindness is directed medicinally to the spiritual welfare of those who are blinded. This mercy, however, is not vouchsafed to all those who are blinded, but only to the predestined, to whom *all things work together unto good (Rom.* viii. 28).

---

[15] *Enchir.,* XI (PL 40, 236). [16] *Quaest. 17 in Matt.,* q. 14, super XIII, 15 (PL 35, 1372). [17] *De Nat. et Grat.,* XXVII (PL 44, 262).

Therefore, as regards some, blindness is directed to their healing; but as regards others, to their damnation, as Augustine says.[18]

Reply Obj. 1. Every evil that God does, or permits to be done, is directed to some good. But it is not always directed to the good of those in whom the evil is, but sometimes to the good of others, or of the whole universe. Thus He directs the sin of tyrants to the good of the martyrs, and the punishment of the lost to the glory of His justice.

Reply Obj. 2. God does not take pleasure in the loss of man, as regards the loss itself, but by reason of His justice, or of the good that ensues from the loss.

Reply Obj. 3. That God directs the blindness of some to their spiritual welfare is due to His mercy; but that the blindness of others is directed to their loss is due to His justice. As for the fact that He vouchsafes His mercy to some, and not to all, this does not make God a respecter of persons, as was explained in the First Part.[19]

Reply Obj. 4. Evil of fault must not be done that good may ensue; but evil of punishment must be inflicted for the sake of good.

[18] *Quaest. 17 in Matt.*, q. 14, super XIII, 15 (PL 35, 1372).   [19] *S. T.*, I, q. 23, a. 5, ad 3.

Question LXXX

ON THE CAUSE OF SIN, THE DEVIL

(*In Four Articles*)

WE must now consider the cause of sin, as regards the devil; and under this head there are four points of inquiry: (1) Whether the devil is directly the cause of sin? (2) Whether the devil induces us to sin by persuading us inwardly? (3) Whether he can make us sin of necessity? (4) Whether all sins are due to the devil's suggestion?

First Article

WHETHER THE DEVIL IS DIRECTLY THE CAUSE OF MAN'S SINNING?

We proceed thus to the First Article:—

Objection 1. It would seem that the devil is directly the cause of man's sinning. For sin consists directly in an act of the appetite. But Augustine says that *the devil inspires his friends with evil desires;*[1] and Bede, commenting on *Acts* v. 3, says that the devil *draws the mind to evil desires;*[2] and Isidore says that the devil *fills men's hearts with secret lusts.*[3] Therefore the devil is directly the cause of sin.

Obj. 2. Further, Jerome says that *as God is the perfecter of good, so is the devil the perfecter of evil.*[4] But God is directly the cause of our good. Therefore the devil is directly the cause of our sins.

Obj. 3. Further, the Philosopher says in a chapter of the *Eudemian Ethics: There must needs be some extrinsic principle of human counsel.*[5] Now human counsel is not only about good things but also about evil things. Therefore, as God moves man to take good counsel, and so directly is the cause of good, so the devil moves him to take evil counsel, and consequently is directly the cause of sin.

On the contrary, Augustine proves that *nothing else than his own will makes man's mind the slave of his desire.*[6] Now man does not become a slave to his desire except through sin. Therefore the cause of sin cannot be the devil, but man's own will alone.

I answer that, Sin is an action, and so a thing can be directly the cause of sin in the same way as anyone is directly the cause of an action; and

---

[1] *De Trin.,* IV, 12 (PL 42, 897).   [2] *In Act.,* super V, 3 (PL 92, 954).   [3] *Sent.,* II, 12 (PL 83, 647).   [4] *Adv. Iovin.,* II (PL 23, 299).   [5] *Eth. Eudem.,* VII, 14 (1248a 22).   [6] *De Lib. Arb.,* I, 11 (PL 32, 1233); III, 1 (PL 32, 1271).

this can happen only by moving that action's proper principle to act. Now the proper principle of a sinful action is the will, since every sin is voluntary. Consequently nothing can be directly the cause of sin, except that which can move the will to act.

Now the will, as we have stated above, can be moved by two things.[7] First, by its object, inasmuch as the apprehended appetible is said to move the appetite; secondly, by that agent which moves the will inwardly to will, and this is none other than either the will itself or God, as was shown above.[8] Now God cannot be the cause of sin, as was stated above.[9] Therefore it follows that, in this respect, a man's will alone is directly the cause of his sin.

As regards the object, a thing may be understood as moving the will in three ways. First, the object itself which is proposed to the will. Thus we say that food arouses man's desire to eat.—Secondly, he that proposes or offers this object.—Thirdly, he that persuades the will that the object proposed has the nature of a good, for he also, in a fashion, offers the will its proper object, which is a real or apparent good of reason.—Accordingly, in the first way sensible things, which we see outside us, move a man's will to sin.—In the second and third ways, either the devil or a man may incite to sin, either by offering an object of appetite to the senses, or by persuading the reason. But in none of these three ways can anything be the direct cause of sin, because the will is not, of necessity, moved by any object except the last end, as we have stated above.[10] Consequently, neither the thing offered to it externally nor he that proposes it, nor he that persuades, is the sufficient cause of sin. Therefore it follows that the devil is a cause of sin, neither directly nor sufficiently, but only by persuasion, or by proposing the object of appetite.

Reply Obj. 1. All these, and other like authorities that may be found, are to be understood as denoting that the devil induces man to affection for a sin either by suggesting to him or by offering him objects of appetite.

Reply Obj. 2. This comparison is true in so far as the devil is somewhat the cause of our sins, even as God is in a certain way the cause of our good actions, but does not bear on the way in which they are causes. For God causes good things in us by moving the will inwardly, whereas the devil cannot move us in this way.

Reply Obj. 3. God is the universal cause of all inward movements of man; but that the human will be determined to an evil counsel is directly due to the human will, and to the devil as persuading or offering the object of appetite.

[7] Q. 9, a. 1, 4 and 6; I, q. 105, a. 4.   [8] Q. 9, a. 3.   [9] Q. 79, a. 1.   [10] Q. 10, a. 2; I, q. 105, a. 4.

Second Article

WHETHER THE DEVIL CAN INDUCE MAN TO SIN BY INTERNAL INSTIGATIONS?

We proceed thus to the Second Article:—

Objection 1. It would seem that the devil cannot induce man to sin by internal instigations. For the internal movements of the soul are vital functions. Now no vital functions can be exercised except by an intrinsic principle, not even those of the vegetative soul, which are the lowest of vital functions. Therefore the devil cannot instigate man to evil through his internal movements.

Obj. 2. Further, all the internal movements arise from the external senses according to the order of nature. Now it belongs to God alone to do anything outside the order of nature, as was stated in the First Part.[11] Therefore the devil cannot effect anything in man's internal movements, except in respect of things which are perceived by the external senses.

Obj. 3. Further, the internal acts of the soul are to understand and to imagine. Now the devil can do nothing in connection with either of these, because, as was stated in the First Part, the devil does not act on the human intellect.[12] Nor does it seem possible for him to act on the imagination, since imaginary forms, being more spiritual, are more excellent than those which are in sensible matter; which, nevertheless, the devil is unable to produce, as is clear from what we have said in the First Part.[13] Therefore the devil cannot, through man's internal movements, induce him to sin.

On the contrary, In that case, the devil would never tempt man, unless he appeared visibly; which is evidently false.

I answer that, The interior part of the soul is intellective and sensitive, and the intellective part contains the intellect and the will. As regards the will, we have already stated the devil's relation to it. Now the intellect, of its very nature, is moved by that which illumines it for the knowledge of truth, and the devil has certainly no intention of exercising such an activity towards man. Rather does he darken man's reason so that it may consent to sin, and this darkness comes from the imagination and the sensitive appetite. Consequently, the whole interior operation of the devil seems to be confined to the imagination and the sensitive appetite, by moving either of which he can induce man to sin. For his operation may result in presenting certain forms to the imagination; and he is also able to incite the sensitive appetite to some passion or other.

The reason for this is that, as we have stated in the First Part, the corporeal nature has a natural aptitude to be moved locally by the spiritual nature.[14] Hence the devil can produce all those effects which can result

---

[11] *S. T.,* I, q. 110, a. 4.   [12] *S. T.,* I, q. 111, a. 2, ad 2.   [13] *S. T.,* I, q. 110, a. 2.
[14] *S. T.,* I, q. 110, a. 3.

from the local movement of bodies here below, except he be restrained by the divine power. Now the representation of forms to the imagination is due, sometimes, to local movement. For the Philosopher says that *when an animal sleeps, the blood descends in abundance to the sensitive principle, and the movements descend with it, viz., the impressions left by the action of sensible things, which impressions are preserved by means of sensible species, and continue to move the apprehensive principle, so that they appear just as though the sensitive principles were being affected by them at the time.*[15] Hence such a local movement of the vital spirits or humors can be procured by the demons, whether man sleep or wake; and so it happens that man's imagination is set to work.

In like manner, the sensitive appetite is incited to certain passions according to certain fixed movements of the heart and the vital spirits, and therefore the devil can co-operate in this also. And when certain passions have been aroused in the sensitive appetite, the result is that man more easily perceives the movement or sensible image which is brought, in the manner explained, before the apprehensive principle; since, as the Philosopher observes, *lovers are moved, by even a slight likeness, to an apprehension of the beloved.*[16] It also happens, through the rousing of a passion, that what is put before the imagination is judged as being something to be pursued, because to him who is held by a passion, whatever the passion inclines him to seems good. In this way the devil induces man inwardly to sin.

Reply Obj. 1. Although vital functions are always from an intrinsic principle, yet an extrinsic agent can co-operate with them, even as external heat co-operates with the functions of the vegetative soul, that food may be more easily digested.

Reply Obj. 2. This apparition of imaginary forms is not altogether outside the order of nature, nor is it due to a command alone, but according to local movement, as was explained above.

Consequently the Reply to the Third Objection is clear, because these forms are received originally from the senses.

Third Article

WHETHER THE DEVIL CAN INDUCE MAN TO SIN OF NECESSITY?

We proceed thus to the Third Article:—

Objection 1. It would seem that the devil can induce man to sin of necessity. For the greater can compel the lesser. Now it is said of the devil (*Job* xli. 24) that *there is no power on earth that can compare with him.* Therefore he can compel man to sin, while man dwells on the earth.

[15] *De Somno,* III (461b 11).   [16] *Op. cit.,* II (460b 5).

Obj. 2. Further, man's reason cannot be moved except in relation to things that are offered outwardly to the senses, or are represented to the imagination; because *all our knowledge arises from the senses, and we cannot understand without a phantasm.*[17] Now the devil can move man's imagination, as was stated above, and also the external senses, for Augustine says that *this evil,* of which, namely, the devil is the cause, *extends gradually through all the approaches to the senses, it adapts itself to shapes, blends with colors, mingles with sounds, seasons every flavor.*[18] Therefore it can incline man's reason to sin of necessity.

Obj. 3. Further, Augustine says that *there is some sin when the flesh lusteth against the spirit.*[19] Now the devil can cause concupiscence of the flesh, even as other passions, in the way explained above. Therefore he can induce man to sin of necessity.

On the contrary, It is written (*1 Pet.* v. 8): *Your adversary the devil, as a roaring lion, goeth about seeking whom he may devour.* Now it would be useless to admonish thus, if it were true that man were under the necessity of succumbing to the devil. Therefore he cannot induce man to sin of necessity.

Further, it is likewise written (*Jas.* iv. 7): *Be subject . . . to God, but resist the devil, and he will fly from you,* which would be said neither rightly nor truly, if the devil were able to compel us, in any way whatever, to sin; for then neither would it be possible to resist him, nor would he fly from those who do. Therefore he does not compel to sin.

I answer that, The devil, by his own power, unless he be restrained by God, can induce anyone to do an act which, in its genus, is a sin; but he cannot bring about the necessity of sinning. This is evident from the fact that man does not resist that which moves him to sin, except by his reason. Now the devil is able to impede the use of the reason altogether, by moving the imagination and the sensitive appetite; as is the case with one who is possessed. But then, when the reason is thus fettered, whatever man may do, it is not imputed to him as a sin. If, however, the reason is not altogether fettered, then, in so far as it is free, it can resist sin, as was stated above.[20] It is consequently evident that the devil can in no way compel a man to sin.

Reply Obj. 1. Not every power that is greater than man can move man's will; God alone can do this, as we have stated above.[21]

Reply Obj. 2. That which is apprehended by the senses or the imagination does not move the will of necessity, so long as man has the use of reason; nor does such an apprehension always fetter the reason.

Reply Obj. 3. The lusting of the flesh against the spirit, when the reason actually resists it, is not a sin, but is matter for the exercise of virtue. Now that reason does not resist is not in the devil's power, and therefore he cannot bring about the necessity of sinning.

[17] Aristotle, *De An.,* III, 7 (431a 16).   [18] *Lib. 83 Quaest.,* q. 12 (PL 40, 14). [19] *De Civit. Dei,* XIX, 4 (PL 41. 629).   [20] Q. 77, a. 7.   [21] Q. 9, a. 6.

Fourth Article

WHETHER ALL THE SINS OF MEN ARE DUE TO THE DEVIL'S
SUGGESTION?

We proceed thus to the Fourth Article:—

Objection 1. It would seem that all the sins of men are due to the devil's suggestions. For Dionysius says that the *crowd of demons is the cause of all evils, both to themselves and to others.*[22]

Obj. 2. Further, whoever sins mortally becomes the slave of the devil, according to *John* vii. 34: *Whosoever committeth sin is the slave of sin.* Now *by whom a man is overcome, of the same also he is the slave (2 Pet.* ii. 19). Therefore, whoever commits a sin has been overcome by the devil.

Obj. 3. Further, Gregory says that the sin of the devil is irreparable, because he sinned at no other's suggestion.[23] Therefore, if any men were to sin of their own free choice, and without suggestion from any other, their sin would be irremediable; which is clearly false. Therefore all the sins of men are due to the devil's suggestion.

On the contrary, It is written: *Not all our evil thoughts are incited by the devil; sometimes they are due to a movement of our free choice.*[24]

I answer that, The devil is the occasional and indirect cause of all our sins, in so far as he induced the first man to sin, by reason of whose sin human nature is so infected that we are all prone to sin; even as the burning of wood might be imputed to the man who dried the wood so as to make it easily inflammable.—He is not, however, the direct cause of all the sins of men, as though each were the result of his suggestion. Origen proves this from the fact that even if the devil did not exist, men would still have the desire for food, sexual pleasures and the like.[25] Now this desire might be inordinate, unless it were subordinate to reason, a matter that is subject to free choice.

Reply Obj. 1. The crowd of demons is the cause of all our evils, as regards their original cause, as we have stated.

Reply Obj. 2. A man becomes another's slave not only by being overcome by him, but also by subjecting himself to him spontaneously; and it is thus that one who sins of his own accord becomes the slave of the devil.

Reply Obj. 3. The devil's sin was irremediable, not only because he sinned without another's suggestion, but also because he was not already prone to sin, as the result of any previous sin; which can be said of no sin in man.

---

[22] *De Div. Nom.*, IV, 18 (PG 3, 716).   [23] *Moral.*, IV, 3 (PL 75, 642).   [24] Gennadius, *De Eccles. Dogm.*, LXXXII (PL 58, 999).   [25] *Peri Archon*, III, 3 (PG 11, 305).

Question LXXXI

ON THE CAUSE OF SIN, MAN
(*In Five Articles*)

WE must now consider the cause of sin, on the part of man. Now while man, like the devil, is the cause of another's sin by outward suggestion, he has a certain special manner of causing sin, by way of origin. Therefore we must speak about original sin, the consideration of which will be threefold: (1) Of its transmission; (2) of its essence;[1] (3) of its subject.[2]

Under the first head there are five points of inquiry: (1) Whether man's first sin is transmitted, by way of origin, to his descendants? (2) Whether all the other sins of our first parent, or of any other parents, are transmitted to their descendants, by way of origin? (3) Whether original sin is contracted by all those who are begotten of Adam by way of seminal generation? (4) Whether it would be contracted by anyone formed miraculously from some part of the human body? (5) Whether original sin would have been contracted if woman, and not man, had sinned?

First Article

WHETHER THE FIRST SIN OF OUR FIRST PARENT IS CONTRACTED BY HIS DESCENDANTS, BY WAY OF ORIGIN?

We proceed thus to the First Article:—

Objection 1. It would seem that the first sin of our first parent is not contracted by others, by way of origin. For it is written (*Ezech.* xviii. 20): *The son shall not bear the iniquity of the father.* But he would bear the iniquity if he contracted it from him. Therefore no one contracts any sin from one of his parents by way of origin.

Obj. 2. Further, an accident is not transmitted by way of origin, unless its subject be also transmitted, since accidents do not pass from one subject to another. Now the rational soul, which is the subject of sin, is not transmitted by way of origin, as was shown in the First Part.[3] Therefore neither can any sin be transmitted by way of origin.

Obj. 3. Further, whatever is transmitted by way of human origin is caused by the semen. But the semen cannot cause sin because it lacks the rational part of the soul, which alone can be a cause of sin. Therefore no sin can be contracted by way of origin.

Obj. 4. Further, that which is more perfect in nature is more powerful

[1] Q. 82.   [2] Q. 83.   [3] *S. T.,* I, q. 118, a. 2.

664

in action. Now perfect flesh cannot infect the soul united to it, or else the soul could not be cleansed of original sin so long as it is united to the body. Much less, therefore, can the semen infect the soul.

Obj. 5. Further, the Philosopher says: *No one finds fault with those who are ugly by nature, but only those who are so through want of exercise and through carelessness.*[4] Now those are said to be *naturally ugly* who are so from their origin. Therefore nothing which comes by way of origin is blameworthy or sinful.

On the contrary, The Apostle says (*Rom.* v. 12): *By one man sin entered into this world, and by sin death.* Nor can this be understood as denoting imitation or suggestion, since it is written (*Wis.* ii. 24): *By the envy of the devil, death came into the world.* It follows, therefore, that through origin from the first man sin entered into the world.

I answer that, According to the Catholic Faith, we are bound to hold that the first sin of the first man is transmitted to his descendants, by way of origin.[5] For this reason children are taken to be baptized soon after their birth, as having to be washed from some uncleanness. The contrary is part of the Pelagian heresy, as is clear from Augustine in many of his books.[6]

In endeavoring to explain how the sin of our first parent could be transmitted by way of origin to his descendants, various writers have gone about it in various ways. For some,[7] considering that the subject of sin is the rational soul, maintained that the rational soul is transmitted with the semen, so that thus an infected soul would seem to produce other infected souls. Others,[8] rejecting this as erroneous, endeavored to show how the guilt of the parent's soul can be transmitted to the children, even though the soul be not transmitted, from the fact that defects of the body are transmitted from parent to child. Thus a leper may beget a leper, or a gouty man may be the father of a gouty son, because of some seminal corruption, although this corruption is not leprosy or gout. Now since the body is proportioned to the soul, and since the soul's defects redound into the body, and *vice versa*, in like manner, say they, a culpable defect of the soul is passed on to the child through the transmission of the semen, although the semen itself is not the subject of guilt.

But all these explanations are insufficient. For granted that some bodily defects are transmitted by way of origin from parent to child, and granted that even some defects of the soul are transmitted, in consequence, because of a defect in a bodily disposition, as in the case of idiots begetting idiots, nevertheless, the fact of having a defect by the way of origin seems to exclude the notion of guilt, which is essentially something voluntary. There-

---

[4] *Eth.,* III, 5 (1114a 23).   [5] Cf. the Council of Carthage (418), can. 2 (Mansi, IV, 327).   [6] *Retract.,* I, 9 (PL 32, 598); *Contra Iulian.,* III, 1 (PL 44, 703); *De Dono Persev.,* II; XI (PL 45, 996; 1008).   [7] Anonymously reported by Peter Lombard, *Sent.,* II, xxxi, 2 (I, 468).—Cf. A. Gaudel, "Péché originel" (in *Dict. de théol. cath.,* vol. XII [1933]), col. 450.   [8] Peter Lombard, *Sent.,* II, xxxi, 3-6 (I, 469-472).

fore, granted that the rational soul were transmitted, from the very fact that the stain on the child's soul is not in its will, it would cease to be a guilty stain binding its subject to punishment; for, as the Philosopher says, *no one reproaches a man born blind; one rather takes pity on him.*[9]

Therefore we must explain the matter otherwise, by saying that all men born of Adam may be considered as one man inasmuch as they have one common nature, which they receive from their first parents;[10] even as in civil matters, all who are members of one community are reputed as one body, and the whole community as one man. Indeed, Porphyry says that *by sharing the same species, many men are one man.*[11] Accordingly, the multitude of men born of Adam are as so many members of one body. Now the action of one member of the body, of the hand, for instance, is voluntary, not by the will of that hand, but by the will of the soul, the first mover of the members. Therefore, a murder which the hand commits would not be imputed as a sin to the hand, considered by itself as apart from the body, but is imputed to it as something belonging to man and moved by man's first moving principle. In this way, then, the disorder which is in this man born of Adam is voluntary, not by his will, but by the will of his first parent, who, by the movement of generation, moves all who originate from him, even as the soul's will moves all the members to their actions. Hence the sin which is thus transmitted by the first parent to his descendants is called *original,* just as the sin which flows from the soul into the bodily members is called *actual.* And just as the actual sin that is committed by a member of the body is not the sin of that member, except inasmuch as that member is a part of the man (for which reason it is called a *human sin*), so original sin is not the sin of this person, except inasmuch as this person receives his nature from his first parent (for which reason it is called the *sin of nature,* according to *Ephes.* ii. 3: *We . . . were by nature children of wrath*).

Reply Obj. 1. The son is said not to bear the iniquity of his father, because he is not punished for his father's sin, unless he share in his guilt. It is thus in the case before us, because guilt is transmitted by the way of origin from father to son, even as actual sin is transmitted through being imitated.

Reply Obj. 2. Although the soul is not transmitted, because the power in the semen is not able to cause the rational soul, nevertheless the motion of the semen is a disposition to the transmission of the rational soul; so that the semen, by its own power, transmits the human nature from parent to child and, with that nature, the stain which infects it. For he that is born is associated with his first parent in his guilt, through the fact that

---

[9] *Eth.,* III, 5 (1114a 26).   [10] Cf. St. Augustine, *De Nupt. et Concupisc.,* II, 5 (PL 44, 444) ; A. Gaudel, *loc. cit.,* col. 395.   [11] *Isagoge,* trans. Boethius (PL 64, 111).

he inherits his nature from him by a kind of movement which is that of generation.

Reply Obj. 3. Although the guilt is not actually in the semen, yet human nature is there virtually, accompanied by that guilt.

Reply Obj. 4. The semen is the principle of generation, which is an act proper to nature, by helping it to propagate itself. Hence the soul is more infected by the semen than by the flesh which is already perfect, and already belonging to a certain person.

Reply Obj. 5. A man is not blamed for that which he has from his origin, if the man born be considered in himself. But if we consider him as referred to a principle, then he may be reproached for it; and thus a man may from his birth be under a family disgrace because of a crime committed by one of his forbears.

Second Article

WHETHER ALSO OTHER SINS OF THE FIRST PARENT OR OF NEARER ANCESTORS ARE TRANSMITTED TO THEIR DESCENDANTS?

We proceed thus to the Second Article:—

Objection 1. It would seem that also other sins, whether of the first parent or of nearer ancestors, are transmitted to their descendants. For punishment is never due unless for fault. Now some are punished by the judgment of God for the sins of their immediate parents, according to *Exod.* xx. 5: *I am . . . God, . . . jealous, visiting the iniquity of the fathers upon the children, unto the third and fourth generation.* Furthermore, according to human law, the children of those who are guilty of high treason are disinherited. Therefore the guilt of nearer ancestors is also transmitted to their descendants.

Obj. 2. Further, a man can better transmit to another that which he has of himself, than that which he has received from another. Thus, fire heats better than hot water does. Now a man transmits to his children, by the way of origin, the sin which he has from Adam. Much more therefore should he transmit the sin which he has contracted of himself.

Obj. 3. Further, the reason why we contract original sin from our first parent is because we were in him as in the principle of our nature, which he corrupted. But we were likewise in our nearer ancestors, as in principles of our nature, which, however it be corrupt, can be corrupted yet more by sin, according to *Apoc.* xxii. 11: *He that is filthy, let him be filthier still.* Therefore children contract, by way of origin, the sins of their nearer ancestors, even as they contract the sin of their first parent.

On the contrary, Good is more self-diffusive than evil. But the merits of the nearer ancestors are not transmitted to their descendants. Much less therefore are their sins.

I answer that, Augustine raises this question in the *Enchiridion,* and leaves it unsolved.[12] Yet if we look into the matter carefully we shall see that it is impossible for the sins of the nearer ancestors, or even any other but the first sin of our first parent, to be transmitted by way of origin. The reason is that a man begets his like in species but not in the individual. Consequently, those things that pertain directly to the individual, such as personal actions and matters affecting them, are not transmitted by parents to their children; for a grammarian does not transmit to his son the knowledge of grammar that he has acquired by his own studies. On the other hand, those things that concern the nature of the species are transmitted by parents to their children, unless there be a defect of nature. Thus a man with eyes begets a son having eyes, unless nature fails. And if nature be strong, even certain accidents of the individual pertaining to natural disposition are transmitted to the children, *e.g.,* fleetness of body, acuteness of intellect, and so forth; but in no way those that are purely personal, as was stated above.

Now just as something may belong to the person through himself, and also something through the gift of grace, so something may belong to nature through itself, viz., whatever is caused by the principles of nature, and something too through the gift of grace. In this way original justice, as was stated in the First Part, was a gift of grace, conferred by God on all human nature in our first parent.[13] This gift the first man lost by his first sin. Therefore, just as that original justice together with the nature was to have been transmitted to his posterity, so also was its disorder.— Other actual sins, however, whether of the first parent or of others, do not corrupt the nature as nature, but only as the nature of that person, *i.e.,* in respect of the proneness to sin; and consequently other sins are not transmitted.

Reply Obj. 1. According to Augustine, in his letter to Avitus,[14] children are never inflicted with spiritual punishment because of their parents, unless they share in their guilt, either in their origin or by imitation, because every soul is God's immediate possession, as is stated in *Ezech.* xviii. 4. Sometimes, however, by divine or human judgment, children receive bodily punishment because of their parents, inasmuch as the child, as to its body. is part of its father.

Reply Obj. 2. A man can more easily transmit that which he has of himself, provided it be transmissible. But the actual sins of our nearer ancestors are not transmissible, because they are purely personal, as we have stated above.

Reply Obj. 3. The first sin infects nature with a human corruption pertaining to nature; whereas other sins infect it with a corruption pertaining only to the person.

[12] *Enchir.,* XLVI; XLVII (PL 40, 254; 255).   [13] *S. T.,* I, q. 100, a. 1.   [14] *Epist.* CCL (PL 33, 1066).

Third Article

WHETHER THE SIN OF THE FIRST PARENT IS TRANSMITTED,
BY THE WAY OF ORIGIN, TO ALL MEN?

We proceed thus to the Third Article:—

Objection 1. It would seem that the sin of the first parent is not transmitted, by the way of origin, to all men. For death is a punishment consequent upon original sin. But not all those who are born of the seed of Adam will die, since those who will be still living at the coming of our Lord will never die, as may be gathered from *1 Thess.* iv. 14: *We who are alive . . . unto the coming of the Lord, shall not prevent them who have slept.* Therefore they do not contract original sin.

Obj. 2. Further, no one gives another what he has not himself. Now a man who has been baptized has not original sin. Therefore he does not transmit it to his children.

Obj. 3. Further, the gift of Christ is greater than the sin of Adam, as the Apostle declares (*Rom.* v. 15, *seqq.*). But the gift of Christ is not transmitted to all men; neither, therefore, is the sin of Adam.

On the contrary, The Apostle says (*Rom.* v. 12): *Death passed upon all men in whom all have sinned.*

I answer that, According to the Catholic Faith, we must firmly believe that, with the exception of Christ alone, all men descended from Adam contract original sin from him; or else all would not need redemption, which is through Christ; and this is erroneous. The reason for this may be gathered from what has been stated, viz., that original sin, in virtue of the sin of our first parent, is transmitted to his posterity; just as from the soul's will actual sin is transmitted to the members of the body, through their being moved by the will. Now it is evident that actual sin can be transmitted to all such members as have an inborn aptitude to be moved by the will. Therefore original sin is transmitted to all those who are moved by Adam by the movement of generation.

Reply Obj. 1. It is held with greater probability and more commonly that all those that are alive at the coming of our Lord will die, and rise again shortly, as we shall state more fully in the Third Part.[15] If, however, it be true, as others hold, that they will never die (an opinion which Jerome mentions, among others, in a letter to Minerius, on the Resurrection of the Body[16]), then we must say in reply to the objection that although they are not to die, the debt of death is none the less in them, and that the punishment of death will be remitted by God, since He can also forgive the punishment due for actual sins.

Reply Obj. 2. Original sin is taken away by Baptism as to the guilt, in so far as the soul recovers grace as regards the mind. Nevertheless original

---

[15] *S. T.,* III, Suppl., q. 78, a. 1, obj. 3.   [16] *Epist.* CXIX (PL 22, 971).

sin remains in its effect as regards the 'fomes,' which is the disorder of the lower parts of the soul and of the body itself (in respect of which, and not of the mind, man exercises his power of generation). Consequently, those who are baptized transmit original sin, since they do not beget as being renewed in Baptism, but as still retaining something of the oldness of the first sin.

Reply Obj. 3. Just as Adam's sin is transmitted to all who are born of Adam corporeally, so the grace of Christ is transmitted to all that are begotten of Him spiritually, by faith and Baptism; and this, not only in order to remove the sin of their first parent, but also to remove actual sins, and to lead them to glory.

Fourth Article

WHETHER ORIGINAL SIN WOULD BE CONTRACTED BY A PERSON FORMED MIRACULOUSLY FROM HUMAN FLESH?

We proceed thus to the Fourth Article:—

Objection 1. It would seem that original sin would be contracted by a person formed miraculously from human flesh. For the *Gloss* on *Gen.* iv. 1 says that *Adam's entire posterity was corrupted in his loins, because they were not severed from him in the place of life, before he sinned, but in the place of exile after he had sinned.*[17] But if a man were to be formed in the aforesaid manner, his flesh would be severed in the place of exile. Therefore it would contract original sin.

Obj. 2. Further, original sin is caused in us in so far as the soul is infected through the flesh. But man's flesh is entirely corrupted. Therefore a man's soul would contract the infection of original sin, from whatever part of the flesh it was formed.

Obj. 3. Further, original sin comes to all from our first parent in so far as we were all in him when he sinned. But those who might be formed out of human flesh would have been in Adam. Therefore they would contract original sin.

On the contrary, They would not have been in Adam *according to a seminal principle,* which alone is the cause of the transmission of original sin, as Augustine states.[18]

I answer that, As was stated above, original sin is transmitted from the first parent to his posterity inasmuch as they are moved by him through generation, even as the members are moved by the soul to actual sin. Now there is no movement to generation except by the active power of generation; so that those alone contract original sin who are descended from Adam through the active power of generation originally derived from

---

[17] *Glossa ordin.* (I, 44F); cf. St. Augustine, *De Genesi ad Litt.,* IX, 4 (PL 34, 396).
[18] *Op. cit.,* X, 18; 20 (PL 34, 422; 424).

Adam, *i.e.*, those who are descended from him through a seminal principle. For the *seminal principle* is nothing else than the active power of generation. But if anyone were to be formed by God out of human flesh, it is evident that the active power would not be derived from Adam. Consequently, he would not contract original sin, even as a hand would have no part in a human sin if it were moved, not by the man's will, but by some external mover.

Reply Obj. 1. Adam was not in the place of exile until after his sin. Consequently it is not because of the place of exile, but because of the sin, that original sin is transmitted to those to whom his active generation extends.

Reply Obj. 2. The flesh does not corrupt the soul, except in so far as it is the active principle in generation, as we have stated.

Reply Obj. 3. If a man were to be formed from human flesh, he would have been in Adam by way of bodily substance, but not according to a seminal principle, as was stated above. Therefore he would not contract original sin.

Fifth Article

WHETHER IF EVE, AND NOT ADAM, HAD SINNED, THEIR CHILDREN WOULD HAVE CONTRACTED ORIGINAL SIN?

We proceed thus to the Fifth Article:—

Objection 1. It would seem that if Eve, and not Adam, had sinned, their children would have contracted original sin. For we contract original sin from our parents, in so far as we were once in them, according to the word of the Apostle (*Rom.* v. 12): *In whom all have sinned*. Now a man pre-exists in his mother as well as in his father. Therefore a man would have contracted original sin from his mother's sin as well as from his father's.

Obj. 2. Further, if Eve, and not Adam, had sinned, their children would have been born liable to suffering and death, since it is *the mother* that *provides the matter in generation* as the Philosopher states[19]—and death and liability to suffering are the necessary results of matter. Now liability to suffering and the necessity of dying are punishments of original sin. Therefore if Eve, and not Adam, had sinned, their children would contract original sin.

Obj. 3. Further, Damascene says that *the Holy Ghost came upon the Virgin* (of whom Christ was to be born without original sin), *purifying her.*[20] But this purification would not have been necessary if the infection of original sin were not contracted from the mother. Therefore the infection of original sin is contracted from the mother; so that if Eve had sinned, her children would have contracted original sin, even if Adam had not sinned.

[19] *De Gener. Anim.*, II, 4 (738b 20).   [20] *De Fide Orth.*, III, 2 (PG 94, 985).

On the contrary, The Apostle says (*Rom.* v. 12): *By one man sin en-tered into this world.* Now, if woman would have transmitted original sin to her children, he should have said that it entered by two, since both of them sinned, or rather that it entered by a woman, since she sinned first. Therefore original sin is transmitted to the children, not by the mother, but by the father.

I answer that, The solution of this question is made clear by what has been said. For it has been stated that original sin is transmitted by the first parent in so far as he is the mover in the begetting of his children. And so it has been said that if anyone were begotten only materially of human flesh, they would not contract original sin. Now it is evident that, in the opinion of philosophers, the active principle of generation is from the father, while the mother provides the matter.[21] Therefore original sin is contracted, not from the mother, but from the father; so that if Eve, and not Adam, had sinned, their children would not contract original sin. Whereas, if Adam, and not Eve, had sinned, they would contract it.

Reply Obj. 1. The child pre-exists in its father as in its active principle, and in its mother as in its material and passive principle. Consequently the comparison fails.

Reply Obj. 2. Some hold that if Eve, and not Adam, had sinned, their children would be immune from the sin, but would have been subject to the necessity of dying and to other forms of suffering that are a necessary re-sult of the matter, which is provided by the mother, not as punishments, but as actual defects.[22]—This, however, seems unreasonable. For, as was stated in the First Part,[23] immortality and impassibility in the original state were a result, not of the condition of matter, but of original justice, whereby the body was subjected to the soul, so long as the soul remained subject to God. Now the privation of original justice is original sin. If, therefore, supposing Adam had not sinned, original sin would not have been transmitted to posterity because of Eve's sin, it is evident that the children would not have been deprived of original justice; and consequently they would not have been liable to suffer and subject to the necessity of dying.

Reply Obj. 3. This prevenient purification in the Blessed Virgin was not needed to hinder the transmission of original sin, but because it behoved the Mother of God to shine with the greatest purity. For nothing is worthy to receive God unless it be pure, according to *Ps.* xcii. 5: *Holiness becometh Thy House, O Lord.*

---

[21] Aristotle, *De Gener. Anim.,* II, 4 (738b 20); Avicenna, *De Nat. Anim.,* IX, 1 (411a); 3 (42r).   [22] St. Albert, *In IV Sent.,* d. i, a. 21 (XXIX, 37).   [23] *S. T.,* I, q. 97, a. 1; a. 2, ad 4.

Question LXXXII

ON ORIGINAL SIN, AS TO ITS ESSENCE
(In Four Articles)

WE must now consider original sin as to its essence, and under this head there are four points of inquiry: (1) Whether original sin is a habit? (2) Whether there is but one original sin in each man? (3) Whether original sin is concupiscence? (4) Whether original sin is equally in all?

First Article

WHETHER ORIGINAL SIN IS A HABIT?

We proceed thus to the First Article:—

Objection 1. It would seem that original sin is not a habit. For original sin is the absence of original justice, as Anselm states.[1] Hence original sin is a privation. But a privation is opposed to a habit. Therefore original sin is not a habit.

Obj. 2. Further, actual sin has the nature of fault more than does original sin, in so far as it is more voluntary. Now the habit of actual sin has not the nature of a fault, or else it would follow that a man, while asleep, would be guilty of sin. Therefore no original habit has the nature of a fault.

Obj. 3. Further, in wickedness act always precedes habit, because evil habits are not infused, but acquired. Now original sin is not preceded by an act. Therefore original sin is not a habit.

On the contrary, Augustine says in his book on the baptism of infants that because of original sin little children have the aptitude of concupiscence though they have not the act.[2] Now aptitude denotes some kind of habit. Therefore original sin is a habit.

I answer that, As was stated above, habit is twofold.[3] The first is a habit whereby power is inclined to an act; and thus science and virtue are called habits. In this way original sin is not a habit. The second kind of habit is the disposition of a nature composed of many principles—a disposition according to which that nature is well or ill disposed to something, and chiefly when such a disposition has become a sort of nature, as in the case of sickness or health. In this sense, original sin is a habit. For it is an inordinate disposition, arising from the destruction of the harmony which

---

[1] *De Conceptu Virg.,* II; III (PL 158, 434; 435). [2] *De Pecc. Meritis et Remiss.,* I, 39 (PL 44, 150).—Cf. Peter Lombard, *Sent.,* II, xxx, 9 (I, 465). [3] Q. 49, a. 4; q. 50, a. 1.

673

was essential to original justice, even as bodily sickness is an inordinate disposition of the body, by reason of the destruction of that equilibrium which is essential to health. Hence it is that original sin is called the *languor of nature*.[4]

Reply Obj. 1. As bodily sickness is partly a privation, in so far as it denotes the destruction of the equilibrium of health, and partly something positive, viz., the very humors that are inordinately disposed, so too original sin denotes the privation of original justice, and besides this, the inordinate disposition of the parts of the soul. Consequently it is not a pure privation, but a corrupt habit.

Reply Obj. 2. Actual sin is a lack of order in an act, whereas original sin, being the sin of nature, is an inordinate disposition of nature, and has the character of fault through being transmitted from our first parent, as was stated above.[5] Now this inordinate disposition of nature is a kind of habit, whereas the inordinate disposition of an act is not; and for this reason original sin can be a habit, whereas actual sin cannot.

Reply Obj. 3. This objection considers the habit which inclines a power to an act. But original sin is not this kind of habit. Nevertheless, a certain inclination to an inordinate act does follow from original sin, not directly, but indirectly, viz., by the removal of an obstacle, *i.e.*, original justice, which hindered inordinate movements; just as an inclination to inordinate bodily movements results indirectly from bodily sickness. Nor is it necessary to say that original sin is an *infused* habit, or an *acquired* habit, except by the act of our first parent, but not by our own act; but it is an *inborn* habit due to our corrupt origin.

Second Article

WHETHER THERE ARE SEVERAL ORIGINAL SINS IN ONE MAN?

We proceed thus to the Second Article:—

Objection 1. It would seem that there are many original sins in one man. For it is written (*Ps*. l. 7): *Behold I was conceived in iniquities, and in sins did my mother conceive me*. But the sin in which a man is conceived is original sin. Therefore there are several original sins in man.

Obj. 2. Further, one and the same habit does not incline its subject to contraries, since the inclination of a habit is like that of nature, which tends to one thing. Now original sin, even in one man, inclines to various and contrary sins. Therefore original sin is not one habit, but several.

Obj. 3. Further, original sin infects every part of the soul. Now the different parts of the soul are different subjects of sin, as was shown above.[6] Since, then, one sin cannot be in different subjects, it seems that original sin is not one but several.

---

[4] Peter Lombard, *Sent*., II, xxx, 8 (I, 464).   [5] Q. 81, a. 1.   [6] Q. 74.

On the contrary, It is written (*Jo.* i. 29): *Behold the Lamb of God, behold Him Who taketh away the sin of the world.* The reason for the employment of the singular is that the *sin of the world* is original sin, as the *Gloss* expounds this passage.[7]

I answer that, In one man there is one original sin. Two reasons may be assigned for this. The first is on the part of the cause of original sin. For it has been stated that the first sin alone of our first parent was transmitted to his posterity.[8] Therefore in one man original sin is one in number; and in all men, it is one in proportion, *i.e.,* in relation to its first principle.—The second reason may be taken from the very essence of original sin. For in every inordinate disposition, unity of species depends on the cause, while the unity of number is derived from the subject. For example, take bodily sickness. Various species of sickness proceed from diverse causes, *e.g.,* from excessive heat or cold, or from a lesion in the lung or liver; while one specific sickness in one man will be one in number. Now the cause of this corrupt disposition that is called original sin is one only, viz., the privation of original justice, removing the subjection of man's mind to God. Consequently, original sin is specifically one, and in one man can be only one in number; while in different men it is one in species and in proportion, but numerically many.

Reply Obj. 1. The employment of the plural, *in sins,* may be explained by the custom of the divine Scriptures which frequently use the plural for the singular, *e.g., They are dead that sought the life of the child* (*Matt.* ii. 20);—or by the fact that all actual sins pre-exist virtually in original sin as in a principle, so that it is virtually many;—or by the fact that there were many deformities in the sin of our first parent, viz., pride, disobedience, gluttony, and so forth;—or because the several parts of the soul are infected by original sin.

Reply Obj. 2. Of itself and directly, *i.e.,* by its own form, one habit cannot incline its subject to contraries. But there is no reason why it should not do so indirectly and accidentally, *i.e.,* by the removal of an obstacle. Thus, when the harmony of a mixed body is destroyed, the elements tend to contrary places. In like manner, when the harmony of original justice is destroyed, the various powers of the soul have various opposite tendencies.

Reply Obj. 3. Original sin infects the different parts of the soul, in so far as they are the parts of one whole; even as original justice held all the soul's parts together in one. Consequently, there is but one original sin, just as there is but one fever in one man, although the various parts of the body are affected.

[7] *Glossa ordin.* (V, 189F).   [8] Q. 81, a. 2.

Third Article

WHETHER ORIGINAL SIN IS CONCUPISCENCE?

We proceed thus to the Third Article:—

Objection 1. It would seem that original sin is not concupiscence. For every sin is contrary to nature, according to Damascene.[9] But concupiscence is in accordance with nature, since it is the proper act of the concupiscible part which is a natural power. Therefore concupiscence is not original sin.

Obj. 2. Further, through original sin *the passions of sins* are in us, according to the Apostle (*Rom.* vii. 5). Now there are several other passions besides concupiscence, as was stated above.[10] Therefore original sin is not concupiscence any more than another passion.

Obj. 3. Further, by original sin all the parts of the soul are disordered, as was stated above. But the intellect is the highest of the soul's parts, as the Philosopher states.[11] Therefore original sin is ignorance rather than concupiscence.

On the contrary, Augustine says: *Concupiscence is the guilt of original sin.*[12]

I answer that, Everything takes its species from its form, and we have said above that the species of original sin is taken from its cause. Consequently, the formal element of original sin must be considered in respect of the cause of original sin. But contraries have contrary causes. Therefore, the cause of original sin must be considered with respect to the cause of original justice, which is opposed to it. Now the whole order of original justice consists in man's will being subject to God. This subjection, first and chiefly, was in the will, whose function it is to move all the other parts to the end, as was stated above.[13] Hence, when the will was turned away from God, all the other powers of the soul became inordinate. Accordingly, the privation of original justice, whereby the will was made subject to God, is the formal element in original sin; while every other disorder of the soul's powers is a kind of material element in respect of original sin. Now the lack of order in the other powers of the soul consists chiefly in their turning inordinately to mutable good; and this lack of order may be called by the general name of concupiscence. Hence original sin is concupiscence *materially,* but the privation of original justice *formally.*

Reply Obj. 1. Since, in man, the concupiscible power is naturally governed by reason, the act of concupiscence is so far natural to man as it is in accord with the order of reason; while, in so far as it trespasses beyond the bounds of reason, it is, for a man, contrary to reason. Such is the concupiscence of original sin.

---

[9] *De Fide Orth.,* II, 4; 30; IV, 20 (PG 94, 876; 976; 1196).   [10] Q. 23, a. 4.
[11] *Eth.,* X, 7 (1177a 20).   [12] *Retract.,* I, 15 (PL 32, 608).   [13] Q. 9, a. 1.

Reply Obj. 2. As was stated above, all the irascible passions are reducible to the concupiscible passions as to more principle ones;[14] and of these, concupiscence is the most impetuous in moving, and is felt most, as was stated above.[15] Therefore original sin is ascribed to concupiscence both as being the chief passion and as including all the others, in a fashion.

Reply Obj. 3. As in good things the intellect and reason stand first, so, conversely, in evil things the lower part of the soul is found to take precedence, for it clouds and draws the reason, as was stated above.[16] Hence original sin is called concupiscence rather than ignorance,[17] although ignorance likewise is comprised among the material defects of original sin.

Fourth Article

WHETHER ORIGINAL SIN IS EQUALLY IN ALL?

We proceed thus to the Fourth Article:—

Objection 1. It would seem that original sin is not equally in all. For original sin is inordinate concupiscence, as was stated above. Now all are not equally prone to acts of concupiscence. Therefore original sin is not equally in all.

Obj. 2. Further, original sin is an inordinate disposition of the soul, just as sickness is an inordinate disposition of the body. But sickness is subject to degrees. Therefore original sin is subject to degrees.

Obj. 3. Further, Augustine says that *lust transmits original sin to the offspring.*[18] But the act of generation may be more lustful in one than in another. Therefore original sin may be greater in one than in another.

On the contrary, Original sin is a sin of nature, as was stated above.[19] But nature is equally in all. Therefore original sin is too.

I answer that, There are two things in original sin: one is the privation of original justice; the other is the relation of this privation to the sin of our first parent, from whom it is transmitted to man through his corrupt origin. As to the first, original sin has no degrees, since the gift of original justice is taken away entirely; and privations that remove something entirely, such as death and darkness, cannot be more or less, as was stated above.[20] In like manner, neither is this possible, as to the second, since all are related equally to the first principle of our corrupt origin, from which principle original sin takes the nature of guilt; for relations cannot be more or less. Consequently, it is evident that original sin cannot be more in one than in another.

Reply Obj. 1. When the bond of original justice, which held together all the powers of the soul in a certain order, is broken, each power of the soul

---

[14] Q. 25, a. 1.   [15] Q. 25, a. 2, ad 1.   [16] Q. 77, a. 1 and 2; q. 80, a. 2.   [17] Cf. Peter Lombard, *Sent.*, II, xxx, 8 (I, 464).—Cf. also Hugh of St. Victor, *De Sacram.*, I, pt. vii, 26 (PL 176, 298).   [18] *De Nupt. et Concupisc.*, I, 23; 24 (PL 44, 428; 429).—Cf. Fulgentius, *De Fide ad Petrum*, II (PL 65, 679).   [19] Q. 81, a. 1.   [20] Q. 73, a. 2.

tends to its own proper movement, and the more impetuously as it is stronger. Now it happens that some of the soul's powers are stronger in one man than in another because of the different bodily temperaments. Consequently, if one man is more prone than another to acts of concupiscence, this is not due to original sin, because the bond of original justice is equally broken in all, and the lower parts of the soul are, in all, left to themselves equally; but it is due to the various dispositions of the powers, as we have stated.

Reply Obj. 2. Sickness of the body, even sickness of the same species, has not an equal cause in all. For instance, if a fever be caused by corruption of the bile, the corruption may be greater or lesser, and nearer to or further from the principle of life. But the cause of original sin is equal in all, so that there is no comparison.

Reply Obj. 3. It is not actual lust that transmits original sin; for, supposing that God were to grant to a man to feel no inordinate lust in the act of generation, he would still transmit original sin. We must rather understand this to be habitual lust, whereby the sensitive appetite is not kept subject to reason by the bonds of original justice. This lust is equally in all.

ON THE SUBJECT OF ORIGINAL SIN

(*In Four Articles*)

WE must now consider the subject of original sin, under which head there are four points of inquiry: (1) Whether the subject of original sin is the flesh rather than the soul? (2) If it be the soul, whether this be through its essence, or through its powers? (3) Whether the will prior to the other powers is the subject of original sin? (4) Whether certain powers of the soul are specially infected, viz., the generative power, the concupiscible power and the sense of touch?

First Article

WHETHER ORIGINAL SIN IS MORE IN THE FLESH THAN IN THE SOUL?

We proceed thus to the First Article:—

Objection 1. It would seem that original sin is more in the flesh than in the soul. For the rebellion of the flesh against the mind arises from the corruption of original sin. Now the root of this rebellion is seated in the flesh, for the Apostle says (*Rom.* vii. 23): *I see another law in my members fighting against the law of my mind.* Therefore original sin is seated chiefly in the flesh.

Obj. 2. Further, a thing is more in its cause than in its effect. Thus heat is in the heating fire more than in the hot water. Now the soul is infected with the corruption of original sin by the carnal semen. Therefore original sin is in the flesh rather than in the soul.

Obj. 3. Further, we contract original sin from our first parent, in so far as we were in him according to a seminal principle. Now our souls were not in him thus, but only our flesh. Therefore original sin is not in the soul, but in the flesh.

Obj. 4. Further, the rational soul created by God is infused into the body. If therefore the soul were infected with original sin, it would follow that it is corrupted in its creation or infusion; and thus God would be the cause of sin, since He is the author of the soul's creation and infusion.

Obj. 5. Further, no wise man would pour a precious liquid into a vessel, knowing that the vessel will corrupt the liquid. But the rational soul is more precious than any liquid. If therefore the soul, by being united with the body, could be corrupted with the infection of original sin, God, Who is wisdom itself, would never infuse the soul into such a body. And yet He does. Therefore it is not corrupted by the flesh. Therefore original sin is not in the soul but in the flesh.

On the contrary, The same is the subject of a virtue and of the vice or sin contrary to that virtue. But the flesh cannot be the subject of virtue, for the Apostle says (*Rom.* vii. 18): *I know that there dwelleth not in me, that is to say, in my flesh, that which is good.* Therefore the flesh cannot be the subject of original sin, but only the soul.

I answer that, One thing can be in another in two ways. First, as in its cause, either principal, or instrumental; secondly, as in its subject. Accordingly, the original sin of all men was in Adam as in its principal cause, according to the words of the Apostle (*Rom.* v. 12): *In whom all have sinned;* whereas it is in the bodily semen as in its instrumental cause, since it is by the active power of the semen that original sin together with human nature is transmitted to the offspring. But original sin can in no way be in the flesh as its subject, but only in the soul.

The reason for this is that, as we have stated above, original sin is transmitted from the will of our first parent to his posterity by a certain movement of generation in the same way as actual sin is transmitted from any man's will to his other parts.[1] Now in this transmission, it is to be observed that whatever accrues, from the motion of the will consenting to sin, to any part of man that can in any way share in that guilt, either as its subject or as its instrument, has the character of sin. Thus, from the will consenting to gluttony, concupiscence of food accrues to the concupiscible power, and partaking of food accrues to the hand and the mouth, which, in so far as they are moved by the will to sin, are the instruments of sin. But that further action is evoked in the nutritive power and the internal members, which have no natural aptitude for being moved by the will, does not bear the character of guilt.

Accordingly, since the soul can be the subject of guilt, while the flesh, of itself, cannot be the subject of guilt, whatever accrues to the soul from the corruption of the first sin has the character of guilt, while whatever accrues to the flesh has the character, not of guilt, but of punishment; so that the soul is thus the subject of original sin, and not the flesh.

Reply Obj. 1. As Augustine says,[2] the Apostle is speaking, in that passage, of man already redeemed, who is delivered from guilt, but is still liable to punishment, by reason of which sin is stated to dwell *in the flesh.* Consequently it follows that the flesh is the subject, not of guilt, but of punishment.

Reply Obj. 2. Original sin is caused by the semen as by an instrumental cause. Now there is no need for anything to be more in the instrumental cause than in the effect, but only in the principal cause; and, in this way,

---

[1] Q. 81, a. 1.   [2] *Retract.*, I, 26 (PL 32, 629).

original sin was in Adam more fully, since in him it had the nature of actual sin.

Reply Obj. 3. The soul of any individual man was in Adam, according to a seminal principle, not indeed as in its effective principle, but as in a dispositive principle; because the bodily semen, which is transmitted from Adam, does not of its own power produce the rational soul, but disposes the matter for it.

Reply Obj. 4. The corruption of original sin is in no way caused by God, but by the sin alone of our first parent through carnal generation. And so, since creation implies a relation in the soul to God alone, it cannot be said that the soul is tainted through being created.—On the other hand, infusion implies relation both to God infusing and to the flesh into which the soul is infused. And so, with regard to God infusing, it cannot be said that the soul is stained through being infused; but only with regard to the body into which it is infused.

Reply Obj. 5. The common good takes precedence over private good. Therefore God, according to His wisdom, does not set aside the universal order of things, which is that such a soul be infused into such a body, so that this soul avoid its particular corruption; all the more so as the nature of the soul demands that it should not exist prior to its infusion into the body, as was stated in the First Part.[3] And it is better for the soul to be thus, according to its nature, than not to be at all, especially since it can avoid damnation by means of grace.

Second Article

WHETHER ORIGINAL SIN IS IN THE ESSENCE OF THE SOUL RATHER THAN IN THE POWERS?

We proceed thus to the Second Article:—

Objection 1. It would seem that original sin is not in the essence of the soul rather than in the powers. For the soul is naturally apt to be the subject of sin according to those parts which can be moved by the will. Now the soul is moved by the will, not as to its essence, but only as to the powers. Therefore original sin is in the soul, not according to its essence, but only according to the powers.

Obj. 2. Further, original sin is opposed to original justice. Now original justice was in a power of the soul, because power is the subject of virtue. Therefore original sin also is in a power of the soul, rather than in its essence.

Obj. 3. Further, just as original sin is derived by the soul from the flesh, so is it derived by the powers from the essence. But original sin is more in the soul than in the flesh. Therefore it is more in the powers than in the essence of the soul.

[3] *S. T.,* I, q. 90, a. 4; q. 118, a. 3.

Obj. 4. Further, original sin is said to be concupiscence, as was stated.[4] But concupiscence is in the powers of the soul. Therefore original sin is also.

On the contrary, Original sin is called a sin of nature, as was stated above.[5] Now the soul is the form and nature of the body according to its essence and not according to its powers, as was stated in the First Part.[6] Therefore the soul is the subject of original sin chiefly according to its essence.

I answer that, The subject of a sin is chiefly that part of the soul to which the moving cause of that sin primarily pertains. Thus, if the moving cause of a sin is sensual pleasure, which regards the concupiscible power through being its proper object, it follows that the concupiscible power is the proper subject of that sin. Now it is evident that original sin is caused through our origin. Consequently that part of the soul which is first reached by man's origin is the primary subject of original sin. Now the origin reaches the soul as the term of generation, according as it is the form of the body; and this belongs to the soul according to its own essence, as was proved in the First Part.[7] Therefore the soul is through its essence the primary subject of original sin.

Reply Obj. 1. As the motion of the will of an individual reaches to the soul's powers and not to its essence, so the motion of the will of the first generator, through the channel of generation, reaches first of all to the essence of the soul, as has been stated.

Reply Obj. 2. Even original justice pertained primarily to the essence of the soul, because it was God's gift to human nature, to which the essence of the soul is related before the powers. For the powers seem rather to regard the person, inasmuch as they are the principles of personal acts. Hence they are the proper subjects of actual sins, which are the sins of the person.

Reply Obj. 3. The body is related to the soul as matter to form, which, though it is subsequent in order of generation, nevertheless comes first in the order of perfection and nature. But the essence of the soul is related to the powers as a subject to its proper accidents, which are subsequent to their subject both in the order of generation and in that of perfection. Consequently the comparison fails.

Reply Obj. 4. Concupiscence, in relation to original sin, holds the position of matter and effect, as we have stated above.[8]

[4] Q. 82, a. 3.   [5] Q. 81, a. 1.   [6] *S. T.,* I, q. 76, a. 6.   [7] *Ibid.*   [8] Q. 82, a. 3.

Third Article

WHETHER ORIGINAL SIN INFECTS THE WILL BEFORE THE OTHER POWERS?

We proceed thus to the Third Article:—

Objection 1. It would seem that original sin does not infect the will before the other powers. For every sin belongs chiefly to that power by whose act it is caused. Now original sin is caused by an act of the generative power. Therefore it seems to belong to the generative power more than to the others.

Obj. 2. Further, original sin is transmitted through the carnal semen. But the other powers of the soul are more akin to the flesh than the will is, as is evident with regard to all the sensitive powers, which use a bodily organ. Therefore original sin is in them more than in the will.

Obj. 3. Further, the intellect precedes the will, for the object of the will is only the understood good. If, therefore, original sin infects all the powers of the soul, it seems that it must first of all infect the intellect, as preceding the others.

On the contrary, Original justice has a prior relation to the will, because it is *the rectitude of the will,* as Anselm states.[9] Therefore original sin, which is opposed to it, also has a prior relation to the will.

I answer that, Two things must be considered in the infection of original sin. First, its inherence to its subject, and in this respect it is related first to the essence of the soul, as was stated above. In the second place we must consider its inclination to act, and in this way it is related to the powers of the soul. It must therefore be related, first of all, to that power in which is seated the first inclination to commit a sin, and this is the will, as was stated above.[10] Therefore original sin is related, first of all, to the will.

Reply Obj. 1. Original sin, in man, is not caused by the generative power of the offspring, but by the act of the parental generative power. Consequently it does not follow that the child's generative power is the subject of original sin.

Reply Obj. 2. Original sin spreads in two ways: from the flesh to the soul, and from the essence of the soul to the powers. The former follows the order of generation, the latter follows the order of perfection. Therefore, although the other, viz., the sensitive powers, are more akin to the flesh, yet, since the will, being the higher power, is more akin to the essence of the soul, the infection of original sin reaches it first.

Reply Obj. 3. The intellect precedes the will, in one way, by proposing its object to it. In another way, the will precedes the intellect, in the order of motion to act,—which is the motion that pertains to sin.

---

[9] *De Conceptu Virg.,* III (PL 158, 436).   [10] Q. 74, a. 1 and 2.

Fourth Article

WHETHER THE AFORESAID POWERS ARE MORE INFECTED
THAN THE OTHERS?

We proceed thus to the Fourth Article:—
Objection 1. It would seem that the aforesaid powers are not more infected than the others. For the infection of original sin seems to pertain
more to that part of the soul which can be first the subject of sin. Now
this is the rational part, and chiefly the will. Therefore that power is most
infected by original sin.

Obj. 2. Further, no power of the soul is infected by guilt, except in so far
as it can obey reason. Now the generative power cannot obey reason, as
is stated in *Ethics* i.[11] Therefore the generative power is not the most infected by original sin.

Obj. 3. Further, of all the senses the sight is the most spiritual and the
nearest to reason, in so far as *it shows us how a number of things differ*.[12]
But the infection of guilt is first of all in the reason. Therefore the sight is
more infected than touch.

On the contrary, Augustine says that *the infection of original sin is most
apparent in the movements of the members of generation, which are not
subject to reason*.[13] Now those members serve the generative power in the
mingling of sexes, wherein there is the delectation of touch, which is the
most powerful incentive to concupiscence. Therefore the infection of original sin regards these three chiefly, viz., the generative power, the concupiscible power and the sense of touch.

I answer that, Those corruptions especially are said to be infectious
which are of such a nature as to be transmitted from one subject to another. Hence contagious diseases, such as leprosy and murrain and the
like, are said to be infectious. Now the corruption of original sin is transmitted by the act of generation, as we have stated above.[14] Therefore the
powers which concur in this act are chiefly said to be infected. Now this
act serves the generative power inasmuch as it is directed to generation;
and it includes delectation of the touch, which is the most potent object of
the concupiscible power. Consequently, while all the parts of the soul are
said to be corrupted by original sin, these three are specially said to be
corrupted and infected.

Reply Obj. 1. Original sin, in so far as it inclines to actual sins, belongs
chiefly to the will, as we have stated above. But in so far as it is transmitted to the offspring, it belongs to the aforesaid powers proximately, and
to the will, remotely.

Reply Obj. 2. The infection of actual sin belongs only to the powers

[11] Aristotle, *Eth.,* I, 13 (1102b 29).   [12] Aristotle, *Metaph.* I, 1 (980a 27).
[13] *De Civit. Dei,* XIV, 20 (PL 41, 428).   [14] Q. 81, a. 1.

which are moved by the will of the sinner. But the infection of original sin is not derived from the will of the contractor, but through the origin of his nature, which is effected by the generative power. Hence it is this power that is infected by original sin.

Reply Obj. 3. Sight is not related to the act of generation except in respect of remote disposition, in so far as the form of the concupiscible object is seen through the sight. But the delectation is completed in the touch. Therefore the aforesaid infection is ascribed to the touch rather than to the sight.

Question LXXXIV

ON THE CAUSE OF SIN, IN SO FAR AS ONE SIN
IS THE CAUSE OF ANOTHER

(*In Four Articles*)

WE must now consider the cause of sin, in so far as one sin is the cause of another. Under this head there are four points of inquiry: (1) Whether covetousness is the root of all sins? (2) Whether pride is the beginning of every sin? (3) Whether other special sins should be called capital vices, besides pride and covetousness? (4) How many capital vices there are, and which are they?

First Article

WHETHER COVETOUSNESS IS THE ROOT OF ALL SINS?

We proceed thus to the First Article:—

Objection 1. It would seem that covetousness is not the root of all sins. For covetousness, which is an immoderate desire for riches, is opposed to the virtue of liberality. But liberality is not the root of all virtues. Therefore covetousness is not the root of all sins.

Obj. 2. Further, the desire for the means proceeds from the desire for the end. Now riches, the desire for which is called covetousness, are not desired except as being useful for some end, as is stated in *Ethics* i.[1] Therefore covetousness is not the root of all sins, but proceeds from some deeper root.

Obj. 3. Further, it often happens that avarice, which is another name for covetousness, arises from other sins; as when a man desires money through ambition, or in order to sate his gluttony. Therefore it is not the root of all sins.

On the contrary, The Apostle says (*1 Tim.* vi. 10): *The desire of money is the root of all evil.*

I answer that, According to some, covetousness may be understood in three ways.[2] First, as denoting inordinate desire for riches; and thus it is a special sin. Secondly, as denoting inordinate desire for any temporal good; and thus it is a genus comprising all sins, because every sin includes an inordinate turning to a mutable good, as was stated above.[3] Thirdly, as denoting an inclination of a corrupt nature to desire corruptible

[1] Aristotle, *Eth.*, I, 5 (1096a 7).   [2] Cf. St. Albert, *In II Sent.*, d. xlii, a. 8 (XXVII, 668).   [3] Q. 72, a. 2.

686

goods inordinately; and they say that in this sense covetousness is the root of all sins, comparing it to the root of a tree, which draws its sustenance from the earth, just as every sin grows out of the love of temporal things.[4]

Now, though all this is true, it does not seem according to the mind of the Apostle when he states that covetousness is the root of all sins. For in that passage he clearly speaks against those who, because they *will become rich, fall into temptation, and into the snare of the devil* . . . *for covetousness is the root of all evils.* Hence it is evident that he is speaking of covetousness as denoting the inordinate desire for riches. Accordingly, we must say that covetousness, as denoting a special sin, is called the root of all sins, in likeness to the root of a tree, in furnishing sustenance to the whole tree. For we see that by riches a man acquires the means of committing any sin whatever, and of sating his desire for any sin whatever, since money helps a man to obtain all manner of temporal goods, according to *Eccles.* x. 19: *All things obey money.* Hence, in this sense the desire for riches is the root of all sins.

Reply Obj. 1. Virtue and sin do not arise from the same source. For sin arises from the desire of a mutable good; and consequently the desire of that good which helps one to obtain all temporal goods is called the root of all sins. But virtue arises from the desire for the immutable Good; and consequently charity, which is the love of God, is called the root of the virtues, according to *Ephes.* iii. 17: *Rooted and founded in charity.*

Reply Obj. 2. The desire for money is said to be the root of sins, not as though riches were sought for their own sake, as being the last end, but because they are much sought after as useful for any temporal end. And since a universal good is more desirable than a particular good, it moves the appetite more than any individual goods, which along with many others can be procured by means of money.

Reply Obj. 3. Just as in natural things we do not aim at knowing what always happens, but what happens most frequently, for the reason that the nature of corruptible things can be hindered so as not to act always in the same way, so also in moral matters we consider what happens in the majority of cases, not what happens invariably, for the reason that the will does not act of necessity. So when we say that covetousness is the root of all evils, we do not assert that no other evil can be its root, but that other evils more frequently arise from it, for the reason given.

Second Article

WHETHER PRIDE IS THE BEGINNING OF EVERY SIN?

We proceed thus to the Second Article:—

Objection 1. It would seem that pride is not the beginning of every sin.

---

[4] Cf. St. Albert, *In II Sent.*, d. xlii, a. 8 (XXVII, 667).

For the root is a beginning of a tree, so that the beginning of a sin seems to be the same as the root of sin. Now covetousness is the root of every sin, as was stated above. Therefore it is also the beginning of every sin, and not pride.

Obj. 2. Further, it is written (*Ecclus.* x. 14): *The beginning of the pride of man is apostasy from God.* But apostasy from God is a sin. Therefore another sin is the beginning of pride, so that the latter is not the beginning of every sin.

Obj. 3. Further, the beginning of every sin would seem to be that which causes all sins. Now this is inordinate self-love, which, according to Augustine, *builds up the city of Babylon.*[5] Therefore self-love, and not pride, is the beginning of every sin.

On the contrary, It is written (*Ecclus.* x. 15): *Pride is the beginning of all sin.*

I answer that, Some say that pride is to be taken in three ways.[6] First, as denoting inordinate desire to excel; and thus it is a special sin. Secondly, as denoting actual contempt of God, in so far as this means that they are not subject to His commandment; and thus, they say, it is a generic sin. Thirdly, as denoting an inclination to this contempt, owing to the corruption of nature; and in this sense they say that it is the beginning of every sin, and that it differs from covetousness, because covetousness regards sin as turning towards the mutable good by which sin is, as it were, nourished and fostered (for which reason covetousness is called the *root*), whereas pride regards sin as turning away from God, to Whose commandment man refuses to be subject (for which reason it is called the *beginning,* because the beginning of evil consists in turning away from God).

Now though all this is true, nevertheless, it is not according to the mind of the wise man who said, *Pride is the beginning of all sin.* For it is evident that he is speaking of pride as denoting inordinate desire to excel, as is clear from what follows (*verse* 17): *God hath overturned the thrones of proud princes*; indeed, this is the point of nearly the whole chapter. We must therefore say that pride, even as denoting a special sin, is the beginning of every sin. For we must note that, in voluntary actions, such as sins, there is a twofold order, namely, of intention, and of execution. In the former order, the principle is the end, as we have stated many times before.[7] Now man's end in acquiring all temporal goods is that, through their means, he may have some distinctive perfection and excellence. Therefore, from this point of view, pride, which is the desire to excel, is said to be the *beginning* of every sin.—On the other hand, in the order of execution, the first place belongs to that which, by furnishing the opportunity of fulfilling all desires of sin, has the character of a root; and such are riches. Hence,

---

from this point of view, covetousness is said to be the *root* of all evils, as we have stated above.

This suffices for the Reply to the First Objection.

Reply Obj. 2. Apostasy from God is stated to be the beginning of pride in so far as it denotes a turning away from God; because, from the fact that man wishes not to be subject to God, it follows that he desires inordinately his own excellence in temporal things. Therefore, in the passage quoted, apostasy from God does not denote the special sin, but rather that general condition of every sin, consisting in a turning away from the immutable good.—It may also be said that apostasy from God is said to be the beginning of pride because it is the first species of pride. For it is characteristic of pride to be unwilling to be subject to any superior, and especially to God; and from this it happens that a man is unduly lifted up in relation to the other species of pride.

Reply Obj. 3. In desiring to excel, man loves himself, for to love oneself is the same as to desire some good for oneself. Consequently, it amounts to the same whether we reckon pride or self-love as the beginning of every evil.

Third Article

WHETHER ANY OTHER SPECIAL SINS, BESIDES PRIDE AND AVARICE, SHOULD BE CALLED CAPITAL?

We proceed thus to the Third Article:—

Objection 1. It would seem that no other special sins, besides pride and avarice, should be called capital. For *the head seems to be to an animal, what the root is to a plant,* as is stated in *De Anima* ii.,[8] for the roots are like a mouth. If therefore covetousness is called the *root of all evils,* it seems that it alone. and no other sin, should be called a capital vice.

Obj. 2. Further, the head bears a certain relation of order to the other members, in so far as sensation and movement follow from the head. But sin implies privation of order. Therefore sin has not the character of head [*caput*]; so that no sins should be called *capital.*

Obj. 3. Further, capital crimes are those which receive capital punishment. But every kind of sin comprises some that are punished thus. Therefore the capital sins are not certain specific sins.

On the contrary, Gregory enumerates certain special vices under the name of capital.[9]

I answer that, Capital is derived from *caput* [*head*]. Now the head, properly speaking, is that part of an animal's body which is the principle and director of the whole animal. Hence, metaphorically speaking, every principle is called a head, and even men who direct and govern others are called heads. Accordingly, a capital vice is so called, in the first place, from

---

[8] Aristotle, *De An.,* II, 4 (416a 4).   [9] *Moral.,* XXXI, 45 (PL 76, 621).

head taken in the proper sense; and thus the name *capital* is given to a sin for which capital punishment is inflicted. It is not in this sense that we are now speaking of capital sins, but in another sense, in which the term *capital* is derived from head, taken metaphorically for a principle or director of others. In this way a capital vice is one from which other vices arise, chiefly by being their final cause; which origin is formal, as was stated above.[10] Therefore a capital vice is not only the principle of others, but is also their director and, in a way, their leader; because the art or habit, to which the end belongs, is always the principle and the commander in matters concerning the means. Hence Gregory compares these capital vices to the *leaders of an army*.[11]

Reply Obj. 1. The term *capital* is taken from *caput* and applied to something connected with, or partaking of, the head, as having some property thereof, but not as being the head taken literally. And therefore the capital vices are not only those which have the character of primary origin, as covetousness which is called the *root*, and pride which is called the *beginning*, but also those which have the character of proximate origin in respect of several sins.

Reply Obj. 2. Sin lacks order in so far as it turns away from God, for in this respect it is an evil; and evil, according to Augustine, is *the privation of mode, species and order.*[12] But in so far as sin implies a turning to something, it refers to some good, and therefore, in this respect, there can be order in sin.

Reply Obj. 3. This objection considers capital sin as so called from the punishment it deserves, in which sense we are not taking it here.

Fourth Article

WHETHER THE SEVEN CAPITAL VICES ARE SUITABLY RECKONED?

We proceed thus to the Fourth Article:—

Objection 1. It would seem that we ought not to reckon seven capital vices, viz., vainglory, envy, anger, covetousness, sloth, gluttony, lust. For sins are opposed to virtues. But there are four principal virtues, as was stated above.[13] Therefore there are only four principal or capital vices.

Obj. 2. Further, the passions of the soul are causes of sin, as was stated above.[14] But there are four principal passions of the soul, two of which, viz., hope and fear, are not mentioned among the above sins, whereas certain vices are mentioned to which pleasure and sadness belong, since pleasure belongs to gluttony and lust, and sadness to sloth and envy. Therefore the principal sins are unfittingly enumerated.

[10] Q. 72, a. 6.   [11] *Moral.,* XXXI, 45 (PL 76, 620).   [12] *De Nat. Boni,* IV (PL 42, 553).   [13] Q. 61, a. 2.   [14] Q. 77.

Obj. 3. Further, anger is not a principal passion. Therefore it should not be placed among the principal vices.

Obj. 4. Further, just as covetousness or avarice is the root of sin, so pride is the beginning of sin, as was stated above. But avarice is reckoned to be one of the capital vices. Therefore pride also should be placed among the capital vices.

Obj. 5. Further, some sins are committed which cannot be caused through any of these, as, for instance, when one sins through ignorance, or when one commits a sin with a good intention, *e.g.*, steals in order to give an alms. Therefore the capital vices are insufficiently enumerated.

On the contrary stands the authority of Gregory who enumerates them in this way.[15]

I answer that, As was stated above, the capital vices are those which give rise to others, especially in the manner of a final cause. Now this kind of origin may take place in two ways. First, because of the condition of the sinner, who is so disposed as to have a strong inclination for one particular end, with the result that he frequently goes forward to other sins. But this kind of origin does not come under the consideration of art, because man's particular dispositions are infinite in number.—Secondly, because of a natural relationship of the ends to one another; and it is in this way that most frequently one vice arises from another, so that this kind of origin can come under the consideration of art.

Accordingly, therefore, those vices are called capital whose ends have certain fundamental modes of moving the appetite; and it is in respect of these fundamental modes that the capital vices are differentiated. Now a thing moves the appetite in two ways. First, directly and of its very nature. Thus, good moves the appetite to seek it, while evil, for the same reason, moves the appetite to avoid it. Secondly, indirectly and because of something else, as it were. Thus one seeks an evil because of some attendant good, or avoids a good because of some attendant evil.

Now man's good is threefold. For, in the first place, there is a certain good of the soul, which derives its aspect of appetibility merely through being apprehended, viz., the excellence of honor and praise; and this good is sought inordinately by *vainglory*. Secondly, there is the good of the body, and this pertains either to the preservation of the individual, *e.g.*, meat and drink, which good is pursued inordinately by *gluttony,*—or the preservation of the species, *e.g.*, sexual intercourse, which good is sought inordinately by *lust*. Thirdly, there is external good, viz., riches, to which *covetousness* is directed. These same four vices avoid inordinately the contrary evils.

Or, again, the good moves the appetite chiefly through possessing some property of happiness, which all men seek naturally. Now, in the first place,

[15] *Moral.*, XXXI, 45 (PL 76, 621).

it is of the nature of happiness to contain perfection, since happiness is a perfect good, to which belongs excellence or renown, that is desired by *pride* or *vainglory*. Secondly, it is of the nature of happiness to contain satiety, which *covetousness* seeks in riches that give promise thereof. Thirdly, it is of its nature to contain pleasure, without which happiness is impossible, as is stated in *Ethics* i. and x.,[16] and this *gluttony* and *lust* pursue.

On the other hand, the avoidance of good because of an attendant evil occurs in two ways. For this happens either in respect of one's own good, and thus we have *sloth,* which is sadness about one's spiritual good because of the attendant bodily labor; or else it happens in respect of another's good, and this, if it be without recrimination, belongs to *envy*, which is sadness about another's good as being a hindrance to one's own excellence, while if it be with recrimination with a view to vengeance, it is *anger*. Furthermore, these same vices attack the contrary evils.

Reply Obj. 1. Virtue and vice do not originate in the same way, since virtue is caused by the subordination of the appetite to reason, or to the immutable good, which is God, whereas vice arises from the appetite for a mutable good. Therefore there is no need for the principal vices to be contrary to the principal virtues.

Reply Obj. 2. Fear and hope are irascible passions. Now all the passions of the irascible part arise from the passions of the concupiscible part; and these are all, in a way, directed to pleasure or sorrow. Hence pleasure and sorrow have a prominent place among the capital sins, as being the most important of the passions, as was stated above.[17]

Reply Obj. 3. Although anger is not a principal passion, yet it has a distinct place among the capital vices because it implies a special kind of movement in the appetite, in so far as one attacks the good of another as though to do so were a virtuous good, *i.e.,* as though to do so were a vindication of justice.

Reply Obj. 4. Pride is said to be the beginning of every sin according to the nature of an end, as was stated above; and it is according to the same nature of an end that we are to consider the capital sin as being principal. Therefore pride is not counted along with the others as a universal vice, but is reckoned as the *queen of them all,* as Gregory states.[18] But *covetousness is said to be the root from another point of view,* as we have stated above.

Reply Obj. 5. These vices are called capital because others arise from them most frequently; so that nothing prevents some sins from arising out of other causes.—Nevertheless, we might say that all the sins which are due to ignorance can be reduced to sloth, to which pertains the negligence

---

[16] Aristotle, *Eth.,* I, 8 (1099a 7); X, 7 (1177a 22).   [17] Q. 25, a. 4.   [18] *Moral.,* XXXI, 45 (PL 76, 620).

by which a man refuses to acquire spiritual goods because of the attendant labor; for the ignorance that can cause sin is due to negligence, as we have stated above.[19] As for the fact that a man commits a sin with a good intention, this seems to point to ignorance, in so far as he does not know that evils should not be done that good may come of them.

[19] Q. 76, a. 2.

ON THE EFFECTS OF SIN: CONCERNING THE CORRUPTION OF THE GOOD OF NATURE

(*In Six Articles*)

WE must now consider the effects of sin: (1) concerning the corruption of the good of nature; (2) the stain on the soul;[1] (3) the debt of punishment.[2]

Under the first head there are six points of inquiry: (1) Whether the good of nature is diminished by sin? (2) Whether it can be taken away altogether? (3) Of the four wounds, mentioned by Bede, with which human nature is stricken in consequence of sin. (4) Whether privation of mode, species and order is an effect of sin? (5) Whether death and other bodily defects are the result of sin? (6) Whether they are, in any way, natural to man?

First Article

WHETHER SIN DIMINISHES THE GOOD OF NATURE?

We proceed thus to the First Article:—

Objection 1. It would seem that sin does not diminish the good of nature. For man's sin is no worse than the devil's. But natural goods remain unimpaired in the demons after sin, as Dionysius states.[3] Therefore neither does sin diminish the good of human nature.

Obj. 2. Further, when that which is subsequent is changed, that which precedes remains unchanged, since substance remains the same when its accidents are changed. But nature exists before the voluntary action. Therefore, when sin has caused a disorder in a voluntary act, nature is not changed on that account, so that the good of nature be diminished.

Obj. 3. Further, sin is an action, while diminution is a passion. Now no agent is passive by the very reason of its acting, although it is possible for it to act on one thing, and to be passive as regards another. Therefore he who sins does not, by his sin, diminish the good of his nature.

Obj. 4. Further, no accident acts on its subject, because that which is patient is a potential being, while that which is subjected to an accident is already an actual being as regards that accident. But sin is in the good of nature as an accident in a subject. Therefore sin does not diminish the good of nature, since to diminish is to act.

[1] Q. 86. [2] Q. 87. [3] *De Div. Nom.*, IV, 23 (PG 3, 725).

On the contrary, A certain man going down from Jerusalem to Jericho (*Luke* x. 30), *i.e., to the corruption of sin, was stripped of his gifts, and wounded in his nature,* as Bede expounds the passage.[4] Therefore sin diminishes the good of nature.

I answer that, The good of human nature is threefold. First, there are the principles of which nature is constituted, and the properties that flow from them, such as the powers of the soul, and so forth. Secondly, since man has from nature an inclination to virtue, as was stated above,[5] this inclination to virtue is a good of nature. Thirdly, the gift of original justice, conferred on the whole human nature in the person of the first man, may be called a good of nature.

Accordingly, the first-mentioned good of nature is neither destroyed nor diminished by sin. The third good of nature was entirely destroyed through the sin of our first parent. But the second good of nature, viz., the natural inclination to virtue, is diminished by sin. For human acts produce an inclination to like acts, as was stated above.[6] Now from the very fact that a thing becomes inclined to one of two contraries, its inclination to the other contrary must needs be diminished. Therefore, as sin is opposed to virtue, from the very fact that a man sins there results a diminution of that good of nature which is the inclination to virtue.

Reply Obj. 1. Dionysius is speaking of the first-mentioned good of nature, which is *to be, to live and to understand,*[7] as anyone may see who reads the text.

Reply Obj. 2. Although nature precedes the voluntary action, yet it has an inclination to a certain voluntary action. Therefore, nature itself is not changed in itself through a change in the voluntary action; it is the inclination that is changed in so far as it is directed to its terminus.

Reply Obj. 3. A voluntary action proceeds from distinct powers, of which one is active and the other passive. The result is that, through voluntary actions, something is caused in the man who acts, or taken from him, as we have stated when treating of the production of habits.[8]

Reply Obj. 4. An accident does not act as an agent on its subject, but it acts on it formally, in the same sense as when we say that whiteness makes a thing white. In this way, there is nothing to hinder sin from diminishing the good of nature; but only in so far as sin is itself a diminution of the good of nature, because it belongs to the lack of order in our acts. But as regards the lack of order in the agent, we must say that such a lack of order is caused by the fact that, in the acts of the soul, there is an active and a passive element. Thus, the sensible object moves the sensitive appetite, and the sensitive appetite inclines the reason and will, as we have stated above.[9] Hence results the lack of order, not as though an accident

---

[4] *Glossa ordin.* (V, 153A).   [5] Q. 51, a. 1; q. 63, a. 1.   [6] Q. 50, a. 1.   [7] *De Div. Nom.,* IV, 23 (PG 3, 725).   [8] Q. 51, a. 2.   [9] Q. 77, a. 1 and 2.

acted on its own subject, but in so far as the object acts on the power, and one power acts on another and causes it to act without order.

Second Article

WHETHER THE ENTIRE GOOD OF HUMAN NATURE CAN BE DESTROYED BY SIN?

We proceed thus to the Second Article:—

Objection 1. It would seem that the entire good of human nature can be destroyed by sin. For the good of human nature is finite, since human nature itself is finite. Now any finite thing is entirely taken away, if the subtraction be continuous. Since, therefore, the good of nature can be continually diminished by sin, it seems that in the end it can be entirely taken away.

Obj. 2. Further, in a thing of one nature, the whole and the parts are uniform, as is evidently the case with air, water, flesh and all bodies with similar parts. But the good of nature is wholly uniform. Since, therefore, its part can be taken away by sin, it seems that the whole can also be taken away by sin.

Obj. 3. Further, that good of nature which is weakened by sin is aptitude for virtue. Now this aptitude is destroyed entirely in some because of sin. Thus the lost cannot be restored to virtue any more than the blind can to sight. Therefore sin can take away the good of nature entirely.

On the contrary, Augustine says that *evil does not exist except in some good.*[10] But the evil of sin cannot be in the good of virtue or of grace, because they are contrary to it. Therefore it must be in the good of nature, and consequently it does not destroy it entirely.

I answer that, As was stated above, the good of nature that is diminished by sin is the natural inclination to virtue, which is befitting to man from the very fact that he is a rational being; for it is due to this that he performs actions in accord with reason, which is to act virtuously. Now sin cannot entirely take away from man the fact that he is a rational being, for then he would no longer be capable of sin. Therefore it is not possible for this good of nature to be entirely destroyed.

Since, however, this same good of nature may be continually diminished by sin, some, in order to illustrate this, have made use of the example of a finite thing being diminished indefinitely, without being entirely destroyed.[11] For the Philosopher says that, if from a finite magnitude a continual subtraction be made in the same quantity, it will at last be entirely destroyed: *e.g.*, if from any finite length I were to subtract continuously the length of a span.[12] If, however, the subtraction be made each time in

<hr>

[10] *Enchir.,* XIV (PL 40, 238).   [11] Cf. William of Auxerre, *Summa Aurea,* II, tr. 26, q. 5 (fol. 87a).   [12] *Phys.,* III, 6 (206b 3).

the same proportion, and not in the same quantity, it may go on indefinitely; as, for instance, if a quantity be halved, and one half be diminished by half, it will be possible to go on thus indefinitely, provided that what is subtracted in each case be less than what was subtracted before.—But this does not apply to the question at issue, since a subsequent sin does not diminish the good of nature less than a previous sin, but possibly more, if it be a more grievous sin.

We must, therefore, explain the matter otherwise by saying that the aforesaid inclination is to be considered as intermediate between two terms; for it is based on the rational nature as in its root, and tends to the good of virtue as to its term and end. Consequently, its diminution may be understood in two ways: first, on the part of its root, secondly, on the part of its term. In the first way, it is not diminished by sin, because sin does not diminish nature, as we have stated above. But it is diminished in the second way, in so far as an obstacle is placed against its attaining its term. Now if it were diminished in the first way, it would needs be entirely destroyed at last by the complete destruction of the rational nature. Since, however, it is diminished on the part of the obstacle which is placed against its attaining its term, it is evident that it can be diminished indefinitely (because obstacles can be placed indefinitely, inasmuch as man can go on indefinitely adding sin to sin), and yet it cannot be destroyed entirely, because the root of this inclination always remains. An example of this may be seen in a transparent body, which has an inclination to receive light, from the very fact that it is transparent; yet this inclination or aptitude is diminished because of supervening clouds, although it always remains rooted in the nature of the body.

Reply Obj. 1. This objection holds when diminution is made by subtraction. But here the diminution is made by raising obstacles, and this neither diminishes nor destroys the root of the inclination, as we have stated above.

Reply Obj. 2. The natural inclination is indeed wholly uniform; nevertheless, it stands in relation both to its principle and to its term, and according to this diversity of relation, it is diminished in one way, and not in another.

Reply Obj. 3. Even in the lost the natural inclination to virtue remains, or else they would have no remorse of conscience. The fact, however, that it is not reduced to act is owing to their being deprived of grace according to divine justice. Thus, even in a blind man the aptitude to see remains in the very root of his nature, inasmuch as he is an animal naturally endowed with sight; and yet this aptitude is not reduced to act, for the lack of a cause capable of reducing it, by forming the organ requisite for sight.

Third Article

WHETHER WEAKNESS, IGNORANCE, MALICE AND CONCUPIS-
CENCE ARE SUITABLY RECKONED AS THE WOUNDS OF
NATURE CONSEQUENT UPON SIN?

We proceed thus to the Third Article:—
Objection 1. It would seem that weakness, ignorance, malice and concupiscence are not suitably reckoned as the wounds of nature consequent
upon sin. For one and the same thing is not both effect and cause of the
same thing. But these are reckoned to be causes of sin, as appears from
what has been said above.[13] Therefore, they should not be reckoned as
effects of sin.

Obj. 2. Further, malice is the name of a sin. Therefore it should have
no place among the effects of sin.

Obj. 3. Further, concupiscence is something natural, since it is the act
of the concupiscible power. But that which is natural should not be reckoned a wound of nature. Therefore concupiscence should not be reckoned
a wound of nature.

Obj. 4. Further, it has been stated that to sin from weakness is the same
as to sin from passion.[14] But concupiscence is a passion. Therefore it
should not be co-divided against weakness.

Obj. 5. Further, Augustine reckons *two things to be punishments inflicted on the soul of the sinner,* viz., *ignorance and difficulty,* from which
arise *error and vexation,*[15] which four do not coincide with the four in
question. Therefore it seems that one or the other reckoning is incomplete.

On the contrary, The authority of Bede suffices.[16]

I answer that, As a result of original justice, the reason had perfect hold
over the lower parts of the soul, while reason itself was perfected by God
in being subject to Him. Now this same original justice was forfeited
through the sin of our first parent, as we have already stated,[17] so that all
the powers of the soul are left, as it were, destitute of their proper order,
whereby they are naturally directed to virtue. Now destitution is called
a wounding of nature.

Furthermore, there are four of the soul's powers that can be the subject
of virtue, as was slated above,[18] viz., the reason, where prudence resides,
the will, where justice is, the irascible, the subject of fortitude, and the
concupiscible, the subject of temperance. Therefore, in so far as the reason
is deprived of its order to the true, there is the wound of ignorance; in
so far as the will is deprived of its order to the good, there is the wound of
malice; in so far as the irascible is deprived of its order to the arduous,

---

[13] Q. 76, a. 1; q. 77, a. 3 and 5; q. 78, a. 1.   [14] Q. 77, a. 3.   [15] *De Nat. et Grat.,*
LXVII (PL 44, 287); *De Lib. Arb.,* III, 18 (PL 32, 1296).   [16] Cf. *S. T.,* I, q. 101,
a. 1, obj. 2.   [17] Q. 81, a. 2.   [18] Q. 61, a. 2.

there is the wound of weakness; and in so far as the concupiscible is deprived of its order to the delectable as moderated by reason, there is the wound of concupiscence.

Accordingly, these are the four wounds inflicted on the whole of human nature as a result of our first parent's sin. But since the inclination to the good of virtue is diminished in each individual because of actual sin, as was explained above, these four wounds are also the result of other sins, in so far as, namely, through sin the reason is obscured, especially in practical matters, the will hardened against the good, good actions become more difficult, and concupiscence more inflamed.

Reply Obj. 1. There is no reason why the effect of one sin should not be the cause of another; for the soul, through sinning once, is more easily inclined to sin again.

Reply Obj. 2. Malice is not to be taken here as a sin, but as a certain proneness of the will to evil, according to the words of *Gen.* viii. 21: *Man's senses are prone to evil from his youth.*

Reply Obj. 3. As we have stated above, concupiscence is natural to man, in so far as it is subject to reason;[19] whereas, in so far as it goes beyond the bounds of reason, it is unnatural to man.

Reply Obj. 4. Speaking in a general way, every passion can be called a weakness, in so far as it weakens the soul's strength and impedes the reason. Bede, however, took weakness in the strict sense, as contrary to fortitude, which pertains to the irascible part.

Reply Obj. 5. The *difficulty* which is mentioned in this book of Augustine, includes the three wounds affecting the appetitive powers, viz., *malice, weakness* and *concupiscence;* for it is owing to these three that a man finds it difficult to tend to the good. *Error* and *vexation* are consequent wounds, since a man is vexed because he is weakened in relation to the objects of his concupiscence.

Fourth Article

WHETHER PRIVATION OF MODE, SPECIES AND ORDER IS THE EFFECT OF SIN?

We proceed thus to the Fourth Article:—

Objection 1. It would seem that privation of mode, species and order is not the effect of sin. For Augustine says that *where these three abound, the good is great; where they are less, there is less good; where they are not, there is no good at all.*[20] But sin does not destroy the good of nature. Therefore it does not destroy mode, species and order.

Obj. 2. Further, nothing is its own cause. But sin itself is the *privation*

[19] Q. 82, a. 3, ad 1.   [20] *De Nat. Boni,* III (PL 42, 553).

of mode, species and order, as Augustine states.[21] Therefore privation of mode, species and order is not the effect of sin.

Obj. 3. Further, diverse effects result from diverse sins. Now since mode, species and order are diverse, their corresponding privations must be diverse also, and, consequently, must be the result of sins that are diverse. Therefore privation of mode, species and order is not the effect of each sin.

On the contrary, Sin is to the soul what weakness is to the body, according to *Ps.* vi. *3, Have mercy on me, O Lord, for I am weak.* Now weakness deprives the body of mode, species and order. Therefore sin deprives the soul of mode, species and order.

I answer that, As we have stated in the First Part, mode, species and order belong to every created good, as such, and also every being.[22] For every being and every good as such depends on its form from which it derives its *species.* Again, any kind of form, whether substantial or accidental, of anything whatever, is according to some measure; and hence it is stated in *Metaph.* viii. that *the forms of things are like numbers,*[23] so that a form has a certain *mode* corresponding to its measure. Lastly, owing to its form, each thing has a relation of *order* to something else.

Accordingly, there are different grades of mode, species and order corresponding to the different degrees of good. There is therefore a good belonging to the very substance of nature, which good has its mode, species and order, and is neither destroyed nor diminished by sin. There is again the good of the natural inclination, which also has its mode, species and order; and this is diminished by sin, as was stated above, but is not entirely destroyed. Again, there is the good of virtue and grace; and this too has its mode, species and order, and is entirely taken away by sin. Lastly, there is a good consisting in the ordered act itself, which also has its mode, species and order; and the privation of this is essentially sin. Hence it is clear both how sin is privation of mode, species and order, and how it destroys or diminishes mode, species and order.

This suffices for the Replies to the first two Objections.

Reply Obj. 3. Mode, species and order follow one from the other, as we have explained above; and so they are destroyed or diminished together.

Fifth Article

WHETHER DEATH AND OTHER BODILY DEFECTS ARE THE RESULT OF SIN?

We proceed thus to the Fifth Article:—

Objection 1. It would seem that death and other bodily defects are not

---

[21] *Op. cit.,* IV (PL 42, 553).   [22] *S. T.,* I, q. 5, a. 5.   [23] Aristotle, *Metaph.,* VII, 3 (1043b 33).

the result of sin. For equal causes have equal effects. Now these defects are not equal in all, but abound in some more than in others; whereas original sin, from which especially these defects seem to result, is equal in all, as was stated above.[24] Therefore death and such defects are not the result of sin.

Obj. 2. Further, if the cause is removed, the effect is removed. But these defects are not removed when all sin is removed by baptism or penance. Therefore they are not the effect of sin.

Obj. 3. Further, actual sin has more of the character of guilt than original sin has. But actual sin does not change the nature of the body by subjecting it to some defect. Much less, therefore, does original sin. Therefore death and other bodily defects are not the result of sin.

On the contrary, The Apostle says (*Rom.* v. 12): *By one man sin entered into this world, and by sin death.*

I answer that, One thing causes another in two ways: first, essentially; secondly, accidentally. One thing is the cause of another essentially, if it produces its effect by reason of the power of its nature or form; and hence the effect is essentially intended by the cause. Consequently, since death and such defects are outside the intention of the sinner, it is evident that sin is not essentially the cause of these defects. Accidentally, one thing is the cause of another if it causes it by removing an obstacle. Thus it is stated in *Physics* viii. that by *displacing a pillar a man moves accidentally the stone resting thereon.*[25] In this way, the sin of our first parent is the cause of death and all such defects in human nature, in so far as by the sin of our first parent original justice was taken away, by which not only were the lower powers of the soul held together under the control of reason, without any disorder whatever, but also the whole body was held together in subjection to the soul, without any defect, as was stated in the First Part.[26] Therefore, when original justice was forfeited through the sin of our first parent, just as human nature was stricken in the soul by the disorder among the powers, as we have stated above,[27] so also it became subject to corruption, by reason of disorder in the body.

Now the withdrawal of original justice has the character of punishment, even as the withdrawal of grace has. Consequently, death and all consequent bodily defects are punishments of original sin. And although these defects are not intended by the sinner, nevertheless, they are ordered according to the justice of God, Who inflicts them as punishments.

Reply Obj. 1. Causes that produce their effects through themselves, if equal, produce equal effects; for if such causes be increased or diminished, the effect is increased or diminished. But equal causes of the removal of an obstacle do not point to equal effects. For, supposing a man employs

---

[24] Q. 82, a. 4.   [25] Aristotle, *Phys.*, VIII, 4 (255b 25).   [26] *S. T.*, I, q. 97, a. 1
[27] A. 3; q. 82, a. 3.

equal force in displacing two columns, it does not follow that the movements of the stones resting on them will be equal; rather, one will move with the greater velocity, which has the greater weight according to the property of its nature, to which it is left when the obstacle to its falling is removed. Accordingly, when original justice is removed, the nature of the human body is left to itself, so that according to diverse natural temperaments some men's bodies are subject to more defects, some to fewer, although original sin is equal in all.

Reply Obj. 2. Both original and actual sin are removed by the same cause that removes these defects, according to the Apostle (*Rom.* viii. 11): *He . . . shall quicken . . . your mortal bodies, because of His Spirit that dwelleth in you;* but each is done according to the order of divine wisdom, at a fitting time. For it is right that we should first of all be conformed to Christ's sufferings before attainging to the immortality and impassibility of glory, which was begun in Him, and by Him acquired for us. Hence it is necessary that our bodies should remain, for a time, subject to suffering, in order that we may merit the impassibility of glory, in conformity with Christ.

Reply Obj. 3. Two things may be considered in actual sin, the substance of the act, and the character of fault. As regards the substance of the act, actual sin can cause a bodily defect; and thus some sicken and die through eating too much. But as regards the fault, it deprives us of grace which is given to us that we may regulate the acts of the soul, but not that we may ward off defects of the body, as original justice did. Therefore actual sin does not cause those defects, as original sin does.

Sixth Article

WHETHER DEATH AND OTHER DEFECTS ARE NATURAL
TO MAN?

We proceed thus to the Sixth Article:—

Objection 1. It would seem that death and such defects are natural to man. For *the corruptible and the incorruptible differ generically.*[28] But man is of the same genus as other animals, which are naturally corruptible. Therefore man is naturally corruptible.

Obj. 2. Further, whatever is composed of contraries is naturally corruptible, as having within itself the cause of its corruption. But such is the human body. Therefore it is naturally corruptible.

Obj. 3. Further, a hot thing naturally consumes moisture. Now human life is preserved by hot and moist elements. Since, therefore, the vital functions are fulfilled by the action of natural heat, as is stated in *De Anima* ii.,[29] it seems that death and such defects are natural to man.

On the contrary, 1. God made in man whatever is natural to him. Now

---

[28] Aristotle, *Metaph.,* IX, 10 (1058b 28).   [29] Aristotle, *De An.,* II, 4 (416b 29).

God made not death (*Wis.* i. 13). Therefore death is not natural to man.

2. Further, that which is natural cannot be called either a punishment or an evil, since what is natural to a thing is suitable to it. But death and such defects are the punishment of original sin, as was stated above. Therefore they are not natural to man.

3. Further, matter is proportioned to form, and everything to its end. Now man's end is everlasting happiness, as was stated above,[30] and the form of the human body is the rational soul, which is incorruptible, as was proved in the First Part.[31] Therefore the human body is naturally incorruptible.

I answer that, We may speak of any corruptible thing in two ways: first, in respect of its universal nature, secondly, as regards its particular nature. A thing's particular nature is its own power of action and self-preservation; and in respect of this nature, *every corruption and defect is contrary to nature,* as is stated in *De Caelo* ii.,[32] since this power tends to the being and preservation of the thing to which it belongs.

On the other hand, the universal nature is an active power in some universal principle of nature, for instance, in some heavenly body; or again belonging to some superior substance, in which sense God is said by some to be *the Nature Who makes nature.*[33] This power intends the good and the preservation of the universe, for which alternate generation and corruption in things are requisite; and in this respect, corruption and defect in things are natural, not indeed as regards the inclination of the form which is the principle of being and perfection, but as regards the inclination of matter which is allotted proportionately to its particular form according to the allotment of the universal agent. And although every form intends perpetual being as far as it can, yet no form of a corruptible being can achieve its own perpetuity, except the rational soul, for the rational soul is not entirely subject to matter, as other forms are: indeed, it has an immaterial operation of its own, as was stated in the First Part.[34] Consequently, as regards his form, incorruption is more natural to man than to other corruptible things. But since the rational soul likewise is joined to a matter composed of contraries, from the inclination of that matter there results corruptibility in the whole man. In this respect, man is naturally corruptible as regards the nature of his matter, if it is left to its own inclination, but not as regards the nature of his form.

The first three objections argue on the side of the matter; while the other three argue on the side of the form. Therefore in order to solve them, we must observe that the form of man, which is the rational soul, is proportioned to its end, which is everlasting happiness, because of its incorruptibility; whereas the human body, which is corruptible, considered in

---

[30] Q. 2, a. 7; q. 5, a. 3 and 4.   [31] *S. T.,* I, q. 75, a. 6.   [32] Aristotle, *De Caelo,* II, 6 (288b 14).   [33] *Natura naturans:* cf. H. Siebeck in *Archiv für Geschichte der Philosophie,* III (1889-1890), pp. 370ff.   [34] *S. T.,* I, q. 75, a. 2.

respect of its nature, is in a way proportioned to its form and, in another way, not. For we may note a twofold condition in any matter, namely, one which the agent chooses, and another which is not chosen by the agent, and is a natural condition of matter. Thus, in order to make a knife, a smith chooses a matter both hard and flexible, which can be sharpened so as to be useful for cutting; and in respect of this condition iron is a matter adapted for a knife. But that iron be breakable and inclined to rust, results from the natural disposition of iron; nor does the workman choose this in the iron, indeed he would do without it if he could. Therefore this disposition of matter is not proportioned to the workman's intention, nor to the purpose of his art. In like manner, the human body is the matter chosen by nature in respect of its being of a mixed temperament, in order that it may be most suitable as an organ of touch and of the other sensitive and motive powers; whereas the fact that it is corruptible is due to a condition of matter, and is not chosen by nature. Indeed, nature would choose an incorruptible matter if it could. But God, to Whom every nature is subject, in forming man supplied the defect of nature, and by the gift of original justice gave the body a certain incorruptibility, as was stated in the First Part.[35] It is in this sense that it is said that *God made not death,* and that death is the punishment of sin.

This suffices for the Replies to the Objections.

[35] *S. T.,* I, q. 97, a. 1.

ON THE STAIN OF SIN

(*In Two Articles*)

WE must now consider the stain of sin, under which head there are two points of inquiry: (1) Whether an effect of sin is a stain on the soul? (2) Whether it remains in the soul after the act of sin?

First Article

WHETHER SIN CAUSES A STAIN ON THE SOUL?

We proceed thus to the First Article:—

Objection 1. It would seem that sin causes no stain on the soul. For a higher nature cannot be defiled by contact with a lower nature; and so the sun's ray is not defiled by contact with tainted bodies, as Augustine says.[1] Now the human soul is of a much higher nature than mutable things, to which it turns by sinning. Therefore it does not contract a stain from them by sinning.

Obj. 2. Further, sin is chiefly in the will, as was stated above.[2] *Now the will is in the reason,* as is stated in *De Anima* iii.[3] But the reason or intellect is not stained by considering anything whatever; rather is it perfected thereby. Therefore neither is the will stained by sin.

Obj. 3. Further, if sin causes a stain, this stain is either something positive, or a pure privation. If it be something positive, it can be only either a disposition or a habit; for it seems that nothing else can be caused by an act. But it is neither disposition nor habit. For it happens that a stain remains even after the removal of a disposition or habit; for instance, in a man who, after committing a mortal sin of prodigality, is so changed as to fall into a sin of the opposite vice. Therefore the stain does not denote anything positive in the soul.—Again, neither is it a pure privation. For all sins agree as concerns aversion and the privation of grace; and so it would follow that there is but one stain caused by all sins. Therefore stain is not the effect of sin.

On the contrary, It was said to Solomon (*Ecclus.* xlvii. 22): *Thou hast stained thy glory*; and it is written (*Ephes.* v. 27): *That He might present it to Himself a glorious church not having spot or wrinkle.* In each case it is question of the stain of sin. Therefore a stain is the effect of sin.

---

[1] St. Augustine (?), *Contra 5 Haeres.*, V (PL 42, 1107).   [2] Q. 74, a. 1 and 2.
[3] Aristotle, *De An.*, III, 9 (432b 5).

I answer that, A stain is properly ascribed to corporeal things, when a shiny body loses its sheen through contact with another body, *e.g.*, a garment, gold or silver, or the like. Accordingly, a stain is ascribed to spiritual things in like manner. Now man's soul has a twofold splendor: one from the refulgence of the natural light of reason, whereby man is directed in his actions; the other from the refulgence of the divine light, viz., of wisdom and grace, whereby man is also perfected for the purpose of doing good and fitting actions. Now, when the soul cleaves to things by love, there is a kind of contact in the soul; and when man sins, he cleaves to certain things against the light of reason and of the divine law, as was shown above.[4] Therefore the loss of splendor, occasioned by this contact, is metaphorically called a stain on the soul.

Reply Obj. 1. The soul is not defiled by inferior things, through their own power, as though they acted on the soul; on the contrary, the soul defiles itself by its own action, through cleaving to them inordinately, against the light of reason and of the divine law.

Reply Obj. 2. The action of the intellect is accomplished according as intelligible things are in the intellect according to the mode of the intellect; so that the intellect is not defiled, but perfected, by them. On the other hand, the act of the will consists in a movement towards things themselves, so that love attaches the soul to the thing loved. Thus it is that the soul is stained, when it cleaves inordinately, according to *Osee* ix. 10: *They . . . became abominable as those things were which they loved.*

Reply Obj. 3. The stain is neither something positive in the soul, nor does it denote a pure privation; it denotes a privation of the soul's splendor in relation to its cause, which is sin. Hence, diverse sins cause diverse stains. We may say that stain is like a shadow, which is the privation of light through the interposition of a body, and which varies according to the diversity of the interposed bodies.

Second Article

WHETHER THE STAIN REMAINS IN THE SOUL AFTER THE ACT OF SIN?

We proceed thus to the Second Article:—

Objection 1. It would seem that the stain does not remain in the soul after the act of sin. For after an act, nothing remains in the soul except habit or disposition. But the stain is not a habit or a disposition, as was stated above. Therefore the stain does not remain in the soul after the act of sin.

Obj. 2. Further, the stain is to the sin what the shadow is to the body, as was stated above. But the shadow does not remain when the body has

[4] Q. 71, a. 6.

passed by. Therefore the stain does not remain in the soul when the act of sin is past.

Obj. 3. Further, every effect depends on its cause. Now the cause of the stain is the act of sin. Therefore, when the act of sin is no longer there, neither is the stain in the soul.

On the contrary, It is written (*Jos.* xxii. 17): *Is it a small thing to you that you sinned with Beelphegor, and the stain of that crime remaineth in you to this day?*

I answer that, The stain of sin remains in the soul even when the act of sin is past. The reason for this is that the stain, as was stated above, denotes a blemish in the splendor of the soul, because of its withdrawing from the light of reason or of the divine law. Hence, so long as man remains out of this light, the stain of sin remains in him; but as soon as, moved by grace, he returns to the divine light and to the light of reason, the stain is removed. For although the act of sin, by which man withdrew from the light of reason and of the divine law, ceases, man does not at once return to the state in which he was before, but it is necessary that his will should have a movement contrary to the previous movement. Thus, if a man is separated from someone because of some sort of motion, he is not therefore brought any nearer when the motion ceases; it is still necessary for him to retrace his way by a contrary motion.

Reply Obj. 1. Nothing positive remains in the soul after the act of sin, except the disposition or habit; but there does remain something privative, viz., the privation of union with the divine light.

Reply Obj. 2. After the interposed body has passed by, the transparent body remains in the same position and relation towards the illuminating body, and so the shadow passes at once. But when the sin is past, the soul does not remain in the same relation to God; and so there is no comparison.

Reply Obj. 3. The act of sin parts man from God, which parting causes the loss of splendor, just as local movement causes local separation. Therefore, just as when movement ceases, local distance is not removed, so neither, when the act of sin ceases, is the stain removed.

ON THE DEBT OF PUNISHMENT

(*In Eight Articles*)

WE must now consider the debt of punishment. We shall consider (1) the debt itself; (2) mortal and venial sin, which differ in respect of the punishment due to them.[1]

Under the first head there are eight points of inquiry: (1) Whether the debt of punishment is an effect of sin? (2) Whether one sin can be the punishment of another? (3) Whether any sin incurs a debt of eternal punishment? (4) Whether sin incurs a debt of punishment that is infinite in quantity? (5) Whether every sin incurs a debt of eternal and infinite punishment? (6) Whether the debt of punishment can remain after sin? (7) Whether every punishment is inflicted for a sin? (8) Whether one person can incur punishment for another's sin?

First Article

WHETHER THE DEBT OF PUNISHMENT IS AN EFFECT OF SIN?

We proceed thus to the First Article:—

Objection 1. It would seem that the debt of punishment is not an effect of sin. For that which is accidentally related to a thing does not seem to be its proper effect. Now the debt of punishment is accidentally related to sin, for it is outside the intention of the sinner. Therefore the debt of punishment is not an effect of sin.

Obj. 2. Further, evil is not the cause of good. But punishment is good, since it is just, and is from God. Therefore it is not an effect of sin, which is evil.

Obj. 3. Further, Augustine says that *every inordinate affection is its own punishment.*[2] But punishment does not incur a further debt of punishment, because this would be to go on indefinitely. Therefore sin does not incur the debt of punishment.

On the contrary, It is written (*Rom.* ii. 9): *Tribulation and anguish upon every soul of man that worketh evil.* But to work evil is to sin. Therefore sin incurs a punishment, which is signified by the terms *tribulation and anguish.*

I answer that, It is by a transfer from natural things to human affairs that whenever one thing rises up against another, it suffers some detriment

[1] Q. 88.   [2] *Confess.,* I, 12 (PL 32, 670).

therefrom. For we observe in natural things that one contrary acts with greater intensity, when the other contrary supervenes; and for this reason *hot water freezes more rapidly*, as is stated in *Meteor*. i.[3] Therefore we find that the natural inclination of man is to repress those who rise up against him. Now it is evident that all things contained in an order are, in a manner, one in relation to the principle of that order. Consequently, whatever rises up against an order is put down by that order or by its principle. And because sin is an inordinate act, it is evident that whoever sins, commits an offense against some order. Hence he is put down, in consequence, by that same order; and this repression is punishment.

Accordingly, man can be punished with a threefold punishment, corresponding to the three orders to which the human will is subject. In the first place, a man's nature is subject to the order of his own reason; secondly, it is subject to the order of another man who governs him either in spiritual or in temporal matters, as a member either of the state or of the household; thirdly, it is subject to the universal order of the divine government. Now each of these orders is disturbed by sin, for the sinner acts against his reason, and against human and divine law. Therefore he incurs a threefold punishment: one, inflicted by himself, viz., remorse of conscience; another, inflicted by man; and a third, inflicted by God.

Reply Obj. 1. Punishment follows sin, inasmuch as this is an evil by reason of its inordinateness. Therefore, just as evil is accidental to the sinner's act, being outside his intention, so also is the debt of punishment.

Reply Obj. 2. Further, a just punishment may be inflicted either by God or by man; and hence the punishment itself is the effect of sin, not directly, but dispositively. Sin, however, makes man deserving of punishment, and that is an evil; for Dionysius says that *punishment is not an evil, but to deserve punishment is*.[4] Consequently the debt of punishment is considered to be directly the effect of sin.

Reply Obj. 3. This punishment of the inordinate affection is due to sin as overturning the order of reason. Nevertheless, sin incurs a further punishment, through disturbing the order of divine or human law.

Second Article

WHETHER SIN CAN BE THE PUNISHMENT OF SIN?

We proceed thus to the Second Article:—

Objection 1. It would seem that sin cannot be the punishment of sin. For the purpose of punishment is to bring man back to the good of virtue, as the Philosopher declares.[5] Now sin does not bring man back to the good

---

[3] Aristotle, *Meteor.*, I, 12 (348b 32).   [4] *De Div. Nom.*, IV, 22 (PG 3, 724).
[5] *Eth.*, X, 9 (1180a 4).

of virtue, but leads him in the opposite direction. Therefore sin is not the punishment of sin.

Obj. 2. Further, just punishments are from God, as Augustine says.[6] But sin is not from God, and is an injustice. Therefore sin cannot be the punishment of sin.

Obj. 3. Further, the nature of punishment is to be something against the will. But sin is something from the will, as was shown above.[7] Therefore sin cannot be the punishment of sin.

On the contrary, Gregory says that some sins are punishments of others.[8]

I answer that, We may speak of sin in two ways: first, in its essence; secondly, as to that which is accidental thereto. Sin, as such, can in no way be the punishment of another. For, considered in its essence, sin is something proceeding from the will, for it is from this that it derives the character of guilt; whereas punishment is essentially something against the will, as was stated in the First Part.[9] Consequently, it is evident that sin, regarded in its essence, can in no way be the punishment of sin.

On the other hand, sin can be the punishment of sin accidentally in three ways. First, when one sin is the cause of another, by removing an impediment thereto. For passions, temptations of the devil and the like are causes of sin, but are impeded by the help of divine grace which is withdrawn because of sin. Therefore, since the withdrawal of grace is a punishment, and is from God, as was stated above[10] the result is that the sin which ensues from this is also a punishment accidentally. It is in this sense that the Apostle speaks (*Rom.* i. 24) when he says: *Wherefore God gave them up to the desires of their heart, i.e.,* to their passions; because, namely, when men are deprived of the help of divine grace, they are overcome by their passions. In this way, sin is always said to be the punishment of a preceding sin.—Secondly, by reason of the substance of the act, which is such as to cause pain, whether it be an interior act, as is clearly the case with anger or envy, or an exterior act, as is the case with one who endures considerable trouble and loss in order to achieve a sinful act, according to *Wis.* v. 7: *We wearied ourselves in the way of iniquity.*—Thirdly, on the part of the effect, so that one sin is said to be a punishment by reason of its effect. In the last two ways, a sin is a punishment not only in respect of a preceding sin, but also with regard to itself.

Reply Obj. 1. Even when God punishes men by permitting them to fall into sin, this is directed to the good of virtue. Sometimes indeed it is for the good of those who are punished, when, namely, men arise from sin more humble and more cautious. But it is always for the amendment of others, who, seeing some men fall from sin to sin, are the more fearful of sinning.—With regard to the other two ways, it is evident that the punishment is intended for the sinner's amendment, since the very fact that a

---

[6] *Lib. 83 Quaest.,* q. 82 (PL 40, 98).   [7] Q. 74, a. 1 and 2.   [8] *In Ezech.,* I, hom. 11 (PL 76, 915).   [9] *S. T.,* I, q. 48, a. 5.   [10] Q. 79, a. 3.

man endures toil and loss in sinning is of a nature to withdraw man from sin.

Reply Obj. 2. This objection considers sin essentially as such; and the same answer applies to the Third Objection.

Third Article

WHETHER ANY SIN INCURS A DEBT OF ETERNAL PUNISHMENT?

We proceed thus to the Third Article:—

Objection. 1. It would seem that no sin incurs a debt of eternal punishment. For a just punishment is equal to the fault, since justice is equality; and hence it is written (*Isa.* xxvii. 8): *In measure against measure, when it shall be cast off, thou shalt judge it.* Now sin is temporal. Therefore it does not incur a debt of eternal punishment.

Obj. 2. Further, *punishments are a kind of medicine.*[11] But no medicine should be infinite, because it is directed to an end, and *what is directed to an end is not infinite,* as the Philosopher states.[12] Therefore no punishment should be infinite.

Obj. 3. Further, no one does a thing always unless he delights in it for its own sake. But *God hath not pleasure in the destruction of men.* Therefore He will not inflict eternal punishment on man.

Obj. 4. Further, nothing accidental is infinite. But punishment is accidental, for it is not natural to the one who is punished. Therefore it cannot be of infinite duration.

On the contrary, It is written (*Matt.* xxv. 46): *These shall go into everlasting punishment;* and (*Mark* iii. 29): *He that shall blaspheme against the Holy Ghost, shall never have forgiveness, but shall be guilty of an everlasting sin.*

I answer that, As we have stated above, sin incurs a debt of punishment through disturbing an order. But the effect remains so long as the cause remains. Therefore, so long as the disturbance of the order remains, the debt of punishment must needs remain also. Now disturbance of an order is sometimes reparable, sometimes irreparable, because a defect which destroys the principle is irreparable, whereas, if the principle be saved, defects can be repaired by virtue of that principle. For instance, if the principle of sight be destroyed, sight cannot be restored except by divine power; whereas, if the principle of sight be preserved, while there arise certain impediments to the use of sight, these can be remedied by nature or by art. Now in every order there is a principle by which one becomes a member of that order. Consequently, if a sin destroys the principle of the order by which man's will is subject to God, the disorder will be such as to be considered in itself irreparable, although it is possible to repair it by the

[11] Aristotle, *Eth.,* II, 3 (1104b 17).   [12] *Polit.,* I, 3 (1257b 27).

power of God. Now the principle of this order is the last end, to which man adheres by charity. Therefore whatever sins turn man away from God, so as to destroy charity, considered in themselves, incur a debt of eternal punishment.

Reply Obj. 1. Punishment is proportioned to sin in point of severity, both in divine and in human judgments. In no judgment, however, as Augustine says,[13] is it requisite for punishment to equal fault in point of duration. For the fact that adultery or murder is committed in a moment does not call for a momentary punishment; in fact, they are punished sometimes by imprisonment or banishment for life,—sometimes even by death. Now this does not take into consideration the time occupied in killing, but aims at removing a murderer from the society of the living; so that this punishment, in its own way, represents the eternity of punishment inflicted by God. Now, according to Gregory, it is just that he who has sinned against God in his own eternity should be punished in God's eternity.[14] A man is said to have sinned in his own eternity, not only because he sinned throughout his whole life, but also because, from the very fact that he fixes his end in sin, he has the will to sin everlastingly. Therefore Gregory says that the *wicked would wish to live without end, that they might abide in their sins for ever.*[15]

Reply Obj. 2. Even the punishment that is inflicted according to human laws is not always intended as a remedy for the one who is punished, but sometimes only for others. Thus when a thief is hanged, this is not for his own amendment, but for the sake of others, who at least may be deterred from crime through fear of the punishment, according to *Prov.* xix. 25: *The wicked man being scourged, the fool shall be wiser.* Accordingly, the eternal punishments inflicted by God on the reprobate are remedial punishments for those who refrain from sin through the thoughts of those punishments, according to *Ps.* lix. 6: *Thou hast given a warning to them that fear Thee, that they may flee from before the bow, that Thy beloved may be delivered.*

Reply Obj. 3. God does not delight in punishments for their own sake; but He does delight in the order of His justice, which requires them.

Reply Obj. 4. Although punishment is related indirectly to nature, nevertheless, it is essentially related to the disturbance of the order, and to God's justice. Therefore, so long as the disturbance lasts, the punishment endures.

Fourth Article

WHETHER SIN INCURS A DEBT OF PUNISHMENT INFINITE IN QUANTITY?

We proceed thus to the Fourth Article:—

Objection 1. It would seem that sin incurs a debt of punishment infinite

---

[13] *De Civit. Dei*, XXI, 11 (PL 41, 725).   [14] *Moral.*, XXXIV, 19 (PL 76, 738).
[15] *Ibid.*

in quantity. For it is written (*Jer.* x. 24): *Correct me, O Lord, but yet with judgment; and not in Thy fury, lest Thou bring me to nothing.* Now God's anger or fury signifies metaphorically the vengeance of divine justice; and to be brought to nothing is an infinite punishment, even as to make a thing out of nothing denotes infinite power. Therefore, according to God's vengeance, sin is awarded a punishment infinite in quantity.

Obj. 2. Further, the quantity of punishment corresponds to the quantity of fault, according to *Deut.* xxv. 2: *According to the measure of the sin shall the measure also of the stripes be.* Now a sin which is committed against God is infinite. For the gravity of a sin increases according to the greatness of the person sinned against (and, thus, it is a more grievous sin to strike the sovereign than a private individual); and God's greatness is infinite. Therefore an infinite punishment is due for a sin committed against God.

Obj. 3. Further, a thing may be infinite in two ways, in duration and in quantity. Now the punishment is infinite in duration. Therefore it is infinite in quantity also.

On the contrary, If this were the case, the punishments of all mortal sins would be equal, because one infinite is not greater than another.

I answer that, Punishment is proportioned to sin. Now sin comprises two things. First, there is the turning away from the immutable good, which is infinite; and therefore, in this respect, sin is infinite. Secondly, there is the inordinate turning to mutable good. In this respect sin is finite, both because the mutable good itself is finite, and because the movement of turning towards it is finite, since the acts of a creature cannot be infinite. Accordingly, in so far as sin consists in turning away from something, its corresponding punishment is the *pain of loss,* which also is infinite, because it is the loss of the infinite good, *i.e.,* God. But in so far as sin turns inordinately to something, its corresponding punishment is the *pain of sense,* which also is finite.

Reply Obj. 1. It would be inconsistent with divine justice for the sinner to be brought to nothing absolutely, because this would be incompatible with the perpetuity of punishment that the divine justice requires, as was stated above. However, the expression *to be brought to nothing* is applied to one who is deprived of spiritual goods, according to *1 Cor.* xiii. 2: *If I . . . have not charity, I am nothing.*

Reply Obj. 2. This argument considers sin as a turning away from something, for it is thus that man sins against God.

Reply Obj. 3. The duration of punishment corresponds to the duration of fault, not indeed on the part of the act, but on the part of the stain, for as long as this remains, the debt of punishment remains. But punishment corresponds to fault in the point of severity. Now a fault which is irreparable is such that, of itself, it lasts for ever; and hence it incurs an everlasting punishment. But it is not infinite as regards the thing it turns to; and hence, in this respect, it does not incur punishment of infinite quantity.

WHETHER EVERY SIN INCURS A DEBT OF ETERNAL PUNISHMENT?

We proceed thus to the Fifth Article:—

Objection 1. It would seem that every sin incurs a debt of eternal punishment. For punishment, as was stated above, is proportioned to the fault. Now eternal punishment differs infinitely from temporal punishment, whereas no sin seems to differ infinitely from another, since every sin is a human act, which cannot be infinite. Since, therefore, some sins incur a debt of everlasting punishment, as was stated above, it seems that no sin incurs a debt of mere temporal punishment.

Obj. 2. Further, original sin is the least of all sins, and therefore Augustine says that *the lightest punishment is incurred by those who are punished for original sin alone.*[16] But original sin incurs everlasting punishment, since children who have died in original sin, because they have not been baptized, will never see the kingdom of God, as is shown by our Lord's words (*Jo.* iii. 3): *Unless a man be born again, he cannot see the kingdom of God.* Much more, therefore, will the punishments of all other sins be everlasting.

Obj. 3. Further, a sin does not deserve greater punishment through being united to another sin, for divine justice has allotted its punishment to each sin. Now a venial sin deserves eternal punishment if it be united to a mortal sin in a lost soul, because in hell there is no remission of sins. Therefore venial sin by itself deserves eternal punishment. Therefore temporal punishment is not due for any sin.

On the contrary, Gregory says that certain slighter sins are remitted after this life.[17] Therefore all sins are not punished eternally.

I answer that, As was stated above, a sin incurs a debt of eternal punishment, in so far as it causes an irreparable breach in the order of divine justice by being opposed to the very principle of that order, viz., the last end. Now it is evident that in some sins there is disorder, but such as not to involve opposition to the last end, but only opposition to the things referable to the end. This takes place when one is too much or too little intent on them, without prejudicing the order to the last end; as, for instance, when a man is too fond of some temporal thing, yet would not offend God, for its sake, by breaking one of His commandments. Consequently, such sins do not incur everlasting, but only temporal, punishment.

Reply Obj. 1. Sins do not differ infinitely from one another in respect of their turning towards mutable good, which constitutes the substance

¹⁶ *Enchir.*, XCIII (PL 40, 275).   ¹⁷ *Dial.*, IV, 39 (PL 77, 396).

of the sinful act; but they do differ infinitely in respect of their turning away from something. For some sins consist in turning away from the last end, and some in a disorder affecting things which are means to the end. Now the last end differs infinitely from the things that are means to it.

Reply Obj. 2. Original sin incurs everlasting punishment, not because of its gravity, but by reason of the condition of the subject, viz., a human being deprived of grace, without which there is no remission of sin.

The same answer applies to the Third Objection about venial sin. For the eternity of punishment does not correspond to the quantity of the sin, but to its irremissibility, as we have stated above.

Sixth Article

WHETHER THE DEBT OF PUNISHMENT REMAINS AFTER SIN?

We proceed thus to the Sixth Article:—

Objection 1. It would seem that there remains no debt of punishment after sin. For if the cause be removed, the effect is removed. But sin is the cause of the debt of punishment. Therefore, when the sin is removed, the debt of punishment ceases also.

Obj. 2. Further, sin is removed when man returns to virtue. Now a virtuous man deserves, not punishment, but reward. Therefore, when sin is removed, the debt of punishment no longer remains.

Obj. 3. Further, *Punishments are a kind of medicine.*[18] But a man is not given medicine after being cured of his disease. Therefore, when sin is removed, the debt of punishment does not remain.

On the contrary, It is written (*2 Kings* xii. 13, 14): *David said to Nathan: I have sinned against the Lord. And Nathan said to David: The Lord also hath taken away thy sin; thou shalt not die. Nevertheless, because thou hast given occasion to the enemies of the Lord to blaspheme . . . the child that is born to thee shall die.* Therefore a man is punished by God even after his sin is forgiven; and so the debt of punishment remains when the sin has been removed.

I answer that, Two things may be considered in sin: the guilty act, and the consequent stain. Now it is evident that in all actual sins, when the act of sin has ceased, the guilt remains; for the act of sin makes man deserving of punishment, in so far as he transgresses the order of divine justice, to which he cannot return except he pay some sort of penal compensation which restores him to the equality of justice. Hence, according to the order of divine justice, he who has been too indulgent to his will, by transgressing God's commandment, suffers, either willingly or unwillingly, something contrary to what he would wish. This restoration of the equality of justice by penal compensation is also to be observed in injuries done to

[18] Aristotle, *Eth.,* II, 3 (1104b 17).

one's fellow men. Consequently, it is evident that when the sinful or injurious act has ceased, there still remains the debt of punishment.

But if we speak of the removal of sin as to the stain, it is evident that the stain of sin cannot be removed from the soul without the soul being united to God; since it was through being separated from Him that it suffered the loss of its splendor, in which the stain consists, as was stated above.[19] Now man is united to God by his will. Therefore the stain of sin cannot be removed from man unless his will accepts the order of divine justice, that is to say, unless either of his own accord he take upon himself the punishment of his past sin, or bear patiently the punishment which God inflicts on him; and in both ways punishment has the character of satisfaction. Now when punishment is satisfactory, it loses somewhat of the nature of punishment, for the nature of punishment is to be against the will; and although satisfactory punishment, absolutely speaking, is against the will, nevertheless, in this particular case and for this particular purpose it is voluntary. Consequently, it is voluntary absolutely, but involuntary in a certain respect, as we have explained when speaking of the voluntary and the involuntary.[20] We must therefore say that, wher the stain of sin has been removed, there may remain a debt of punishment, not indeed of punishment absolutely, but of satisfactory punishment.

Reply Obj. 1. Just as, after the act of sin has ceased, the stain remains, as was stated above,[21] so the debt of punishment also can remain. But when the stain has been removed, the debt of punishment does not remain in the same way, as we have stated.

Reply Obj. 2. The virtuous man does not deserve punishment absolutely, but he may deserve it as satisfactory, because his very virtue demands that he should do satisfaction for his offenses against God or man.

Reply Obj. 3. When the stain is removed, the wound of sin is healed as regards the will. But punishment is still requisite in order that the other powers of the soul be healed, since they were disordered by the sin committed. In other words, punishment is still requisite so that the disorder may be remedied by the contrary of that which caused it. Moreover, punishment is requisite in order to restore the equality of justice, and to remove the scandal given to others, so that those who were scandalized at the sin may be edified by the punishment, as may be seen in the example of David quoted above.

Seventh Article

WHETHER EVERY PUNISHMENT IS INFLICTED FOR A SIN?

We proceed thus to the Seventh Article:—

Objection 1. It would seem that not every punishment is inflicted for a sin. For it is written (*Jo.* ix. 2, 3) about the man born blind: *Neither hath*

[19] Q. 86, a. 1.   [20] Q. 6, a. 6.   [21] Q. 86, a. 2.

this man sinned, nor his parents . . . that he should be born blind. In like manner, we see that many children, those also who have been baptized, suffer grievous punishments, fevers, for instance, diabolical possession, and so forth, and yet there is no sin in them after they have been baptized. Moreover, before they are baptized, there is no more sin in them than in the other children who do not suffer such things. Therefore not every punishment is inflicted for a sin.

Obj. 2. Further, that sinners should thrive and that the innocent should be punished seem to come under the same head. Now each of these is frequently observed in human affairs; for it is written about the wicked (*Ps.* lxxii. 5): *They are not in the labor of men: neither shall they be scourged like other men;* and (*Job* xxi. 7): *the wicked live, are advanced, and strengthened with riches;* and (*Habac.* i. 13): *Why lookest Thou upon the contemptuous and holdest Thy peace, when the wicked man oppresseth the man that is more just than himself?* Therefore not every punishment is inflicted for a sin.

Obj. 3. Further, it is written of Christ (*1 Pet.* ii. 22) that *He did no sin, nor was guile found in His mouth.* And yet it is said (*ibid.,* 21) that He *suffered for us.* Therefore punishment is not always inflicted by God for sin.

On the contrary, It is written (*Job* iv. 7, seqq.): *Who ever perished innocent? Or when were the just destroyed? On the contrary, I have seen those who work iniquity . . . perishing by the blast of God;* and Augustine writes that *all punishment is just, and is inflicted for sin.*[22]

I answer that, As we have already stated, punishment can be considered in two ways, absolutely, and as being satisfactory. A satisfactory punishment is, in a way, voluntary. And since those who differ as to the debt of punishment may be one in will by the union of love, it happens that one who has not sinned bears willingly the punishment for another. Thus even in human affairs we see men take the debts of another upon themselves.— If, however, we speak of punishment absolutely, according as it has the nature of punishment, it has always a relation to a sin in the one punished. Sometimes this is a relation to actual sin, as when a man is punished by God or man for a sin committed by him. Sometimes it is a relation to original sin, and this either principally or consequently: principally, the punishment of original sin is that human nature is left to itself, and deprived of original justice; and consequently, there are all the penalties which result from this defect in human nature.

Nevertheless we must observe that sometimes a thing seems penal, and yet has not the nature of punishment absolutely. For punishment is a species of evil, as was stated in the First Part.[23] Now evil is a privation of good. And since a man's good is manifold, viz., the good of the soul, the good of the body, and external goods, it happens sometimes that a man

---

[22] *Retract.,* I, 9 (PL 32, 598); *De Lib. Arb.,* III, 18 (PL 32, 1296).   [23] *S. T.,* I, q. 48, a. 5.

suffers the loss of a lesser good that he may profit in a greater good; as when he suffers loss of money for the sake of bodily health, or loss of both of these for the sake of his soul's health and the glory of God. In such cases, the loss is an evil to a man, not absolutely, but relatively; and hence it does not answer to the name of punishment absolutely, but of medicinal punishment, because a doctor prescribes bitter potions to his patients, that he may restore them to health. And since such are not punishments properly speaking, they are not referred to sin as their cause, except in a restricted sense; because the very fact that human nature needs a treatment of penal medicines is due to the corruption of nature, which is itself the punishment of original sin. For there was no need, in the state of innocence, for penal exercises in order to make progress in virtue; so that whatever is penal in the exercise of virtue is reduced to original sin as its cause.

Reply Obj. 1. Such defects in those who are born with them, or from which children suffer, are the effects and the punishments of original sin, as we have stated above. Furthermore, they remain even after baptism, for the cause stated above.[24] As for the fact that they are not equally in all, this is due to the diversity of nature which is left to itself, as was stated above.[25] Nevertheless, they are directed by divine providence to the salvation of men, either of those who suffer, or of others who are admonished by their means—and also to the glory of God.

Reply Obj. 2. Temporal and bodily goods are indeed goods of man, but they are of small account; whereas spiritual goods are man's great goods. Consequently, it belongs to divine justice to give spiritual goods to the virtuous, and to award them as much of temporal goods or evils as suffices for virtue; for, as Dionysius says,[26] *divine justice does not enfeeble the fortitude of the virtuous man, by material gifts.* The very fact that others receive temporal goods is detrimental to their spiritual good; and hence the psalm quoted concludes (*verse* 6): *Therefore pride hath held them fast.*

Reply Obj. 3. Christ bore a satisfactory punishment, not for His sins, but for ours.

Eighth Article

WHETHER ANYONE IS PUNISHED FOR ANOTHER'S SIN?

We proceed thus to the Eighth Article:—

Objection 1. It would seem that one may be punished for another's sin. For it is written (*Exod.* xx. 5): *I am . . . God . . . jealous, visiting the iniquity of the fathers upon the children, unto the third and fourth generation of them that hate Me*; and (*Matt.* xxiii. 35): *That upon you may come all the just blood that hath been shed upon the earth.*

---

[24] Q. 85, a. 5, ad 2.   [25] Q. 85, a. 5, ad 1.   [26] *De Div. Nom.*, VIII, 8 (PG 3, 896).

Obj. 2. Further, human justice comes from divine justice. Now, according to human justice, children are sometimes punished for their parents, as in the case of high treason. Therefore also according to divine justice, one is punished for another's sin.

Obj. 3. Further, if it be replied that the son is punished, not for the father's sin, but for his own, inasmuch as he imitates his father's wickedness, this would not be said of the children rather than of outsiders, who are punished in like manner as those whose crimes they imitate. It seems, therefore, that children are punished, not for their own sins, but for those of their parents.

On the contrary, It is written (*Ezech.* xviii. 20): *The son shall not bear the iniquity of the father.*

I answer that, If we speak of that satisfactory punishment which one takes upon oneself voluntarily, one may bear another's punishment in so far as they are, in some way, one, as was stated above.—If, however, we speak of punishment inflicted because of sin, inasmuch as it has the nature of punishment, then each one is punished only for his own sin, because the sinful act is something personal.—But if we speak of a punishment that is remedial, in this way it does happen that one is punished for another's sin. For it has been stated that ills sustained in bodily goods, or even in the body itself, are remedial punishments intended for the health of the soul. Therefore, there is no reason why such punishments should not be inflicted on one for another's sin, either by God or by man: *e.g.,* on children for their parents, or on servants for their masters, inasmuch as they belong to them in some way. This must be in such a way, however, that, if the children or the servants take part in the sin, this penal ill has the character of punishment in regard to both the one punished and the one he is punished for. But if they do not take part in the sin, it has the character of punishment in regard to the one for whom the punishment is borne, while, in regard to the one who is punished, it is merely remedial (except accidentally, if he consent to the other's sin), since it is intended for the good of his soul, if he bears it patiently.

With regard to spiritual punishments, these are not merely remedial, because the good of the soul is not directed to a yet higher good. Consequently, no one suffers loss in the goods of the soul without some fault of his own. Therefore, as Augustine says,[27] such punishments are not inflicted on one for another's sin, because, as regards the soul, the son is not the father's property. Hence the Lord assigns the reason for this by saying (*Ezech.* xviii. 4): *All souls are mine.*

Reply Obj. 1. Both the passages quoted should be referred, apparently, to temporal or bodily punishments, in so far as children are the property of their parents, and descendants, of their forefathers.—Or, if they be referred to spiritual punishments, they must be understood in reference

---

[27] Cf. St. Augustine, *Epist. CCL* (PL 33, 1066).

to the imitation of sin; and so in *Exodus* these words are added, *Of them that hate Me,* and in the chapter quoted from *Matthew* (*verse* 32) we read: *Fill ye up then the measure of your fathers.*—The sins of the fathers are said to be punished in their children, because the latter are the more prone to sin through being brought up amid their parents' crimes, both by becoming accustomed to them, and by imitating their parents' example, conforming to their authority, as it were. Moreover, they deserve heavier punishment if, seeing the punishment of their parents, they fail to mend their ways.—The text adds, *to the third and fourth generation,* because men are wont to live long enough to see the third and fourth generation, so that both the children can witness their parents' sins so as to imitate them, and the parents can see their children's punishments so as to grieve for them.

Reply Obj. 2. The punishments which human justice inflicts on one for another's sin are bodily and temporal. They are also remedies or medicines against future sins, in order that either they who are punished, or others, may be restrained from similar faults.

Reply Obj. 3. Those who are near of kin are said to be punished for the sins of others, rather than outsiders, both because the punishment of kindred redounds somewhat upon those who sinned, as was stated above, in so far as the child is the father's property, and because the examples and the punishments that occur in one's own household are more moving. Consequently, when a man is brought up amid the sins of his parents, he follows them more intensely, and if he is not deterred by their punishments, he would seem to be the more obstinate and, therefore, to deserve more severe punishment.

ON VENIAL AND MORTAL SIN

(*In Six Articles*)

In the next place, since venial and mortal sins differ in respect of the debt of punishment, we must consider them. First, we shall consider venial sin as compared with mortal sin; secondly, we shall consider venial sin in itself.[1]

Under the first head there are six points of inquiry: (1) Whether venial sin is fittingly co-divided against mortal sin? (2) Whether they differ generically? (3) Whether venial sin is a disposition to mortal sin? (4) Whether a venial sin can become mortal? (5) Whether a venial sin can become mortal by reason of an aggravating circumstance? (6) Whether a mortal sin can become venial?

First Article

WHETHER VENIAL SIN IS FITTINGLY CO-DIVIDED AGAINST MORTAL SIN?

We proceed thus to the First Article:—

Objection 1. It would seem that venial sin is unfittingly co-divided against mortal sin. For Augustine says: *Sin is a word, deed or desire contrary to the eternal law.*[2] But the fact of being against the eternal law makes a sin to be mortal. Consequently every sin is mortal. Therefore venial sin is not co-divided against mortal sin.

Obj. 2. Further, the Apostle says (*1 Cor.* x. 31): *Whether you eat or drink, or whatever else you do, do all to the glory of God.* Now whoever sins breaks this commandment, because sin is not done for God's glory. Consequently, since to break a commandment is to commit a mortal sin, it seems that whoever sins, sins mortally.

Obj. 3. Further, whoever cleaves to a thing by love, cleaves either as enjoying it, or as using it, as Augustine states.[3] But no person, in sinning, cleaves to a mutable good as using it; for he does not refer it to that good which gives us happiness,—which, properly speaking, is *to use,* according to Augustine. Therefore, whoever sins enjoys a mutable good. Now *to enjoy what we should use is human perverseness,* as Augustine again says.[4] Therefore, since *perverseness* denotes a mortal sin, it seems that whoever sins, sins mortally.

[1] Q. 89. [2] *Contra Faust.,* XXII, 27 (PL 42, 418). [3] *De Doct. Christ.,* I, 3 (PL 34, 20). [4] *Lib. 83 Quaest.,* q. 30 (PL 40, 19).

Obj. 4. Further, whoever approaches one term, by that very fact turns away from the opposite. Now whoever sins, approaches a mutable good, and, consequently, turns away from the immutable good, so that he sins mortally. Therefore venial sin is unfittingly co-divided against mortal sin.

On the contrary, Augustine says, that *a crime is one that merits damnation, and a venial sin, one that does not.*[5] But a crime denotes a mortal sin. Therefore venial sin is fittingly co-divided against mortal sin.

I answer that, Certain terms do not appear to be mutually opposed, if taken in their proper sense, whereas they are opposed if taken metaphorically. Thus *to smile* is not opposed to *being dry*; but if we speak of the smiling meadows when they are decked with flowers and fresh with green hues, this is opposed to drought. In like manner, if mortal be taken literally as referring to the death of the body, it does not imply opposition to venial, nor belong to the same genus. But if mortal be taken metaphorically, as applied to sin, it is opposed to that which is venial.

For sin, being a sickness of the soul, as was stated above,[6] is said to be mortal by comparison with a disease, which is said to be mortal through causing an irreparable defect consisting in the loss of a principle, as we have stated above.[7] Now the principle of the spiritual life, which is a life in accord with virtue, is the order to the last end, as was stated above.[8] And if this order be lost, it cannot be restored by any intrinsic principle, but only by the power of God, as we have stated above.[9] For disorders in things referred to the end are restored through the end, even as an error about conclusions can be corrected through the truth of the principles. Hence the defect of order to the last end cannot be restored through something else as a higher principle, as neither can an error about principles. Therefore such sins are called mortal, as being irreparable. On the other hand, sins which imply a disorder in things referred to the end, but under the condition that the order to the end itself is preserved, are reparable. These sins are called venial, because a sin receives its acquittal [*veniam*] when the debt of punishment is taken away, and this ceases when the sin ceases, as was explained above.[10]

Accordingly, mortal and venial are mutually opposed as reparable and irreparable; and I say this with reference to the intrinsic principle, but not to the divine power, which can repair all diseases, whether of the body or of the soul. Therefore venial sin is fittingly co-divided against mortal sin.

Reply Obj. I. The division of sin into venial and mortal is not a division of a genus into its species which have an equal share of the generic nature; but it is the division of an analogous term into its members, of which it is predicated according to priority and posteriority. Consequently, the perfect notion of sin, which Augustine gives, applies to mortal sin. On

---

[5] *Tract.* XLI, super *Ioann.*, III, 35 (PL 35, 1697). [6] Q. 71, a. 1, ad 3; q. 72, a. 5; q. 74, a. 9, ad 2. [7] Q. 72, a. 5. [8] Q. 72, a. 5; q. 87, a. 3. [9] Q. 87, a. 3. [10] Q. 87, a. 6.

the other hand, venial sin is called a sin according to an imperfect notion of sin, and in relation to mortal sin; even as an accident is called a being in relation to substance, according to an imperfect notion of being. For it is not *against* the law, since he who sins venially neither does what the law forbids, nor omits what the law prescribes to be done; but he acts *outside* the law, through not observing the mode of reason, which the law intends.

Reply Obj. 2. This precept of the Apostle is affirmative, and so it does not bind for all times. Consequently, everyone who does not actually refer all his actions to the glory of God does not therefore act against this precept. In order, therefore, to avoid mortal sin each time that one fails actually to refer an action to God's glory, it is enough to refer oneself and all that one has to God habitually. Now venial sin excludes only actual reference of the human act to God's glory, and not habitual reference; because it does not exclude charity, which refers man to God habitually. Therefore it does not follow that he who sins venially, sins mortally.

Reply Obj. 3. He who sins venially cleaves to a temporal good, not as enjoying it, because he does not fix his end in it, but as using it, by referring it to God, not actually, but habitually.

Reply Obj. 4. Mutable good is considered to be a term in contraposition to the immutable good, unless one's end is fixed therein; because what is referred to the end has not the character of an end.

Second Article

WHETHER MORTAL AND VENIAL SIN DIFFER
GENERICALLY?

We proceed thus to the Second Article:—

Objection 1. It would seem that venial and mortal sin do not differ generically, so that some sins be generically mortal, and some generically venial. Because human acts are considered to be good or evil in their genus according to their matter or object, as was stated above.[11] Now either mortal or venial sin may be committed in regard to any object or matter, since a man can love any mutable good, either less than God, which may be a venial sin, or more than God, which is a mortal sin. Therefore venial and mortal sin do not differ generically.

Obj. 2. Further, as was stated above, a sin is called mortal when it is irreparable, venial when it can be repaired.[12] Now irreparability belongs to sin committed out of malice, which, according to some, is irremissible; whereas reparability belongs to sins committed through weakness or ignorance, which are remissible. Therefore mortal and venial sin differ as sin committed through malice differs from sin committed through weakness or ignorance. But, in this respect, sins differ, not in genus, but in cause, as

[11] Q. 18, a. 2.   [12] A. 1; q. 72, a. 5; q. 87, a. 3.

was stated above.[13] Therefore venial and mortal sin do not differ generically.

Obj. 3. Further, it was stated above that sudden movements both of the sensuality and of the reason are venial sins.[14] But sudden movements occur in every kind of sin. Therefore no sins are generically venial.

On the contrary, Augustine, in a sermon on purgatory enumerates certain genera of venial sins, and certain genera of mortal sins.[15]

I answer that, Venial sin is so called from *venia* [*pardon*]. Consequently, a sin may be called venial, first of all, because it has been pardoned; and thus Ambrose says that *penance makes every sin venial.*[16] This is called venial *from the result.* Secondly, a sin is called venial because it does not contain anything, either partially or totally, to prevent its being pardoned: partially, as when a sin contains something diminishing its guilt, *e.g.,* a sin committed through weakness or ignorance, and this is called venial *from the cause;* totally, through not destroying the order to the last end, and therefore it deserves temporal punishment, but not everlasting punishment. It is of this venial sin that we wish to speak now.

For as regards the first two, it is evident that they have no determinate genus; whereas venial sin, taken in the third sense, can have a determinate genus, so that one sin may be venial in genus, and another mortal in genus, according as the genus or species of an act is determined by its object. For when the will is directed to a thing that is in itself contrary to charity, by which man is directed to his last end, the sin is mortal by reason of its object. Consequently, it is a mortal sin in genus, whether it be contrary to the love of God, *e.g.,* blasphemy, perjury and the like, or against the love of one's neighbor, *e.g.,* murder, adultery and the like. Therefore, such sins are mortal by reason of their genus. Sometimes, however, the sinner's will is directed to a thing containing a certain inordinateness, but which is not contrary to the love of God and one's neighbor, *e.g.,* an idle word, excessive laughter, and so forth; and such sins are venial by reason of their genus.

Nevertheless, since moral acts derive their character of goodness and malice, not only from their objects, but also from some disposition of the agent, as was stated above,[17] it sometimes happens that a sin which is venial in genus, by reason of its object, becomes mortal on the part of the agent, either because he fixes his last end therein, or because he directs it to something that is a mortal sin in its own genus: *e.g.,* if a man direct an idle word to the commission of adultery. In like manner, it may happen, on the part of the agent, that a sin in genus mortal becomes venial because the act is imperfect, *i.e.,* not deliberated by reason, which is the proper principle of an evil act, as we have said above in reference to sudden movements of unbelief.[18]

---

[13] Q. 77, a. 8, ad 1.   [14] Q. 74, a. 3, ad 3; a. 10.   [15] St. Augustine (?), *Serm. CIV* (PL 39, 1946).   [16] *De Parad.,* XIV (PL 14, 327).   [17] Q. 18, a. 4 and 6.   [18] Q. 74, a. 10.

Reply Obj. 1. The very fact that anyone chooses something that is contrary to divine charity proves that he prefers it to the love of God and, consequently, that he loves it more than he loves God. Hence, that something is loved more than God belongs to the genus of sins which are of themselves contrary to charity; so that they are mortal by reason of their genus.

Reply Obj. 2. This argument considers those sins which are venial from their cause.

Reply Obj. 3. This argument considers those sins which are venial by reason of the imperfection of the act.

Third Article

WHETHER VENIAL SIN IS A DISPOSITION TO MORTAL SIN?

We proceed thus to the Third Article:—

Objection 1. It would seem that venial sin is not a disposition to mortal sin. For one contrary does not dispose to another. But venial and mortal sin are co-divided as contrary to one another, as was stated above. Therefore venial sin is not a disposition to mortal sin.

Obj. 2. Further, an act disposes to something of like species, and hence it is stated in *Ethics* ii. that *from like acts like dispositions and habits are engendered.*[19] But mortal and venial sin differ in genus or species, as was stated above. Therefore venial sin does not dispose to mortal sin.

Obj. 3. Further, if a sin is called venial because it disposes to mortal sin, it follows that whatever disposes to mortal sin is a venial sin. Now every good work disposes to mortal sin; and that is why Augustine says in his Rule that *pride lies in wait for good works that it may destroy them.*[20] Therefore even good works would be venial sins, which is absurd.

On the contrary, It is written (*Ecclus.* xix. 1): *He that contemneth small things shall fall by little and little.* Now he that sins venially seems to contemn small things. Therefore by little and little he is disposed to fall away altogether into mortal sin.

I answer that, A disposition is a kind of cause, and therefore, as there is a twofold manner of cause, so is there a twofold manner of disposition. For there is a cause which moves directly to the production of the effect, as a hot thing heats; and there is a cause which moves indirectly, by removing an obstacle, as he who displaces a pillar is said to displace the stone that rests on it. Accordingly, an act of sin disposes to something in two ways. First, directly, and thus it disposes to an act of like species. In this way, a sin venial in genus does not, primarily and of its nature, dispose to a sin mortal in genus, for they differ in species. Nevertheless, in this same way, a venial sin can dispose, by way of consequence, to a sin which is mortal on the part of the agent. For the disposition or habit may be so far strength-

---

[19] Aristotle, *Eth.*, II, 1 (1103a 26).   [20] *Epist. CCXI* (PL 33, 960).

ened by acts of venial sin, that the lust of sinning increases, and the sinner fixes his end in that venial sin; since the end for one who has a habit, as such, is to work according to that habit, and the consequence will be that, by sinning often venially, he becomes disposed to a mortal sin. Secondly, a human act disposes to something by removing an obstacle thereto. In this way a sin venial in genus can dispose to a sin mortal in genus. Because he that commits a sin venial in genus turns aside from some particular order; and through accustoming his will not to be subject to the due order in lesser matters, he is disposed not to subject his will even to the order of the last end, by choosing something that is a mortal sin in its genus.

Reply Obj. 1. Venial and mortal sin are not co-divided in contrariety to one another, as though they were species of one genus, as was stated above, but as an accident is co-divided against substance. Therefore, as an accident can be a disposition to a substantial form, so can a venial sin dispose to mortal sin.

Reply Obj. 2. Venial sin is not like mortal sin in species, but it is in genus, inasmuch as they both imply a defect of due order, although in different ways, as we have stated.

Reply Obj. 3. A good work is not, of itself, a disposition to mortal sin, but it can be the matter or occasion of mortal sin accidentally; whereas a venial sin, of its very nature, disposes to mortal sin, as we have stated.

Fourth Article

WHETHER A VENIAL SIN CAN BECOME MORTAL?

We proceed thus to the Fourth Article:—

Objection 1. It would seem that a venial sin can become a mortal sin. For Augustine, in explaining the words of *John* iii. 36 (*He that believeth not the Son, shall not see life*), says: *The slightest, i.e., venial, sins kill if we make little of them.*[21] Now a sin is called mortal through causing the spiritual death of the soul. Therefore a venial sin can become mortal.

Obj. 2. Further, a movement in the sensuality is a venial sin before the consent of reason, but after consent, it is a mortal sin, as was stated above.[22] Therefore a venial sin can become mortal.

Obj. 3. Further, venial and mortal sin differ as curable and incurable disease, as was stated above. But a curable disease may become incurable. Therefore a venial sin may become mortal.

Obj. 4. Further, a disposition may become a habit. Now venial sin is a disposition to mortal, as was stated. Therefore a venial sin can become mortal.

On the contrary, Things that differ infinitely are not changed into one another. Now venial and mortal sin differ infinitely, as is evident from

---

[21] *Tract.* XII, super *Ioann.*, III, 19 (PL 35, 1492).   [22] Q. 74, a. 8, ad 2.

what has been said above.[23] Therefore a venial sin cannot become mortal.

I answer that, For a venial sin to become a mortal sin may be understood in three ways. First, so that the same identical act be at first a venial sin, and then a mortal sin. This is impossible, because a sin, like any moral act, consists chiefly in an act of the will; so that an act is not one morally, if the will be changed, even though the act be continuous physically. If, however, the will be not changed, it is not possible for a venial sin to become mortal.

Secondly, this may be taken to mean that a sin generically venial becomes mortal. This is possible in so far as one may fix one's end in that venial sin, or direct it to some mortal sin as end, as was stated above.

Thirdly, this may be understood in the sense that many venial sins make up one mortal sin. If this be taken as meaning that many venial sins added together make one mortal sin, it is false, because all the venial sins in the world cannot incur a debt of punishment equal to that of one mortal sin. This is evident as regards the duration of the punishment, since mortal sin incurs a debt of eternal punishment, while venial sin incurs a debt of temporal punishment, as we have stated above.[24]—It is also evident as regards the pain of loss, because mortal sins deserve to be punished by the privation of seeing God, to which no other punishment is comparable, as Chrysostom states.[25]—It is likewise evident as regards the pain of sense, as to the remorse of conscience; although as to the pain of fire, the punishments may perhaps not be with proportion to one another.

If, however, this be taken as meaning that many venial sins make one mortal sin dispositively, it is true, as was shown above with regard to the two different manners of disposition, whereby venial sin disposes to mortal sin.

Reply Obj. 1. Augustine is referring to the fact of many venial sins making one mortal sin dispositively.

Reply Obj. 2. The very same movement of the sensuality which preceded the consent of reason can never become a mortal sin; but the movement of the reason in consenting is a mortal sin.

Reply Obj. 3. Disease of the body is not an act, but an abiding disposition; and, therefore, while remaining the same disease, it may undergo change. On the other hand, venial sin is a transient act, which cannot be taken up again; so that in this respect the comparison fails.

Reply Obj. 4. A disposition that becomes a habit is as something imperfect in the same species; and thus imperfect science, by being perfected, becomes a habit. On the other hand, venial sin is a disposition to something differing generically, like an accident which disposes to a substantial form, into which it is never changed.

[23] Q. 72, a. 5, ad 1; q. 87, a. 5, ad 1.   [24] Q. 87, a. 3 and 5.   [25] *In Matt.,* hom. XXIII (PG 57, 317).

Fifth Article

WHETHER A CIRCUMSTANCE CAN MAKE A VENIAL SIN TO BE
MORTAL?

We proceed thus to the Fifth Article:—

Objection 1. It would seem that a circumstance can make a venial sin
be mortal. For Augustine says in a sermon on purgatory that *if anger continue for a long time, or if drunkenness be frequent, they become mortal
sins.*[26] But anger and drunkenness are not mortal but venial sins in genus, or
else they would always be mortal sins. Therefore a circumstance makes a
venial sin to be mortal.

Obj. 2. Further, the Master of the Sentences says that delectation, if
lingering, is a mortal sin, but that if it be not lingering, it is a venial sin.[27]
Now lingering in delectation is a circumstance. Therefore a circumstance
makes a venial sin to be mortal.

Obj. 3. Further, evil and good differ more than venial and mortal sin,
both of which are in genus evil. But a circumstance makes a good act to be
evil, as when a man gives an alms for vainglory. Much more, therefore, can
it make a venial sin to be mortal.

On the contrary, Since a circumstance is an accident, its quantity cannot exceed that of the act itself, derived from the act's genus, because the
subject always excels its accident. If, therefore, an act be venial by reason
of its genus, it cannot become mortal by reason of an accident; since, in a
way, mortal sin infinitely surpasses the quantity of venial sin, as is evident from what has been said.[28]

I answer that, As was stated above, when we were treating of circumstances, a circumstance, as such, is an accident of the moral act;[29] and
yet a circumstance may happen to be taken as the specific difference of a
moral act, and then it loses its nature of circumstance, and constitutes
the species of the moral act. This happens in sins when a circumstance
adds the deformity of another genus. Thus when a man has knowledge of
another woman than his wife, the deformity of his act is opposed to chastity; but if this other be another man's wife, there is an additional deformity opposed to justice which forbids one to take what belongs to another. Accordingly, this circumstance constitutes a new species of sin
known as adultery.

It is, however, impossible for a circumstance to make a venial sin become mortal, unless it adds the deformity of another species. For it has
been stated above that the deformity of a venial sin consists in a disorder
affecting things that are referred to the end, whereas the deformity of a
mortal sin consists in a disorder about the last end. Consequently, it is

---

[26] St. Augustine (?), *Serm.* CIV (PL 39, 1946).　　[27] *Sent.,* II, xxiv, 12 (I, 425).
[28] Q. 72, a. 5, ad 1; q. 87, a. 5, ad 1.　　[29] Q. 7, a. 1; q. 18, a. 5, ad 4; a. 10 and 11.

evident that a circumstance cannot make a venial sin to be mortal, so long as it remains a circumstance, but only when it transfers the sin to another species, and becomes, as it were, the specific difference of the moral act.

Reply Obj. 1. Length of time is not a circumstance that draws a sin to another species, nor is frequency or custom, except perhaps by something accidental supervening. For an action does not acquire a new species through being repeated or prolonged, unless by chance something supervene in the repeated or prolonged act to change its species, *e.g.,* disobedience, contempt, or the like.

We must therefore say that, since anger is a movement of the soul tending to the injury of one's neighbor, if the angry movement tend to an injury which is a mortal sin in genus, such as murder or robbery, that anger will be a mortal sin in genus. And if it be a venial sin, this will be due to the imperfection of the act, in so far as it is a sudden movement of the sensuality; whereas, if it last a long time, it returns to its generic nature, through the consent of reason.—If, on the other hand, the injury to which the angry movement tends is a sin generically venial, for instance, if a man be angry with someone, so as to wish to say some trifling word in jest that would vex him a little, the anger will not be a mortal sin, however long it last, unless perhaps accidentally, *e.g.,* if it were to give rise to great scandal or something of the kind.

With regard to drunkenness, we reply that it is a mortal sin by reason of its genus. For, that a man, without necessity, and through the mere lust of wine, make himself unable to use his reason, by which he is directed to God and avoids committing many sins, is expressly contrary to virtue. But that it be a venial sin, is due to some sort of ignorance or weakness, as when a man is ignorant of the strength of the wine, or of his own weakness, so that he has no thought of getting drunk; for in that case the drunkenness is not imputed to him as a sin, but only the excessive drink. If, however, he gets drunk frequently, this ignorance no longer avails as an excuse, for his will seems to choose to give way to drunkenness rather than to refrain from excess of wine; and therefore the sin returns to its specific nature.

Reply Obj. 2. Lingering delectation is not a mortal sin except in those matters whic' are mortal sins in genus. In such matters, if the delectation be not lingering, there is a venial sin through the imperfection of the act, as we have said with regard to anger; because anger is said to be lasting, and delectation to be lingering, because of the approval of the deliberating reason.

Reply Obj. 3. A circumstance does not make a good act to be evil, unless it constitute the species of a sin, as we have stated above.[30]

[30] Q. 18, a. 5, ad 4.

Sixth Article

WHETHER A MORTAL SIN CAN BECOME VENIAL?

We proceed thus to the Sixth Article:—
Objection 1. It would seem that a mortal sin can become venial. For venial sin is equally distant from mortal, as mortal sin is from venial. But a venial sin can become mortal, as was stated above. Therefore, likewise, a mortal sin can become venial.

Obj. 2. Further, venial and mortal sin are said to differ in this, that he who sins mortally loves a creature more than God, while he who sins venially loves the creature less than God. Now it may happen that a person, in committing a sin in genus mortal, loves a creature less than God; for instance, if anyone being ignorant that simple fornication is a mortal sin, and contrary to the love of God, commits the sin of fornication, yet so as to be ready, for the love of God, to refrain from that sin if he knew that by committing it he was acting counter to the love of God. Therefore his sin will be a venial sin, and accordingly a mortal sin can become venial.

Obj. 3. Further, as was stated above, good is more distant from evil than venial from mortal sin. But an act which is evil in itself can become good; and thus to kill a man may be an act of justice, as when a judge condemns a thief to death. Much more therefore can a mortal sin become venial.

On the contrary, An eternal thing can never become temporal. But mortal sin deserves eternal punishment, whereas venial sin deserves temporal punishment. Therefore a mortal sin can never become venial.

I answer that, Venial and mortal differ as perfect and imperfect in the genus of sin, as we have stated above. Now the imperfect can become perfect by some sort of addition; and, consequently, a venial sin can become mortal by the addition of some deformity pertaining to the genus of mortal sin, as when a man utters an idle word for the purpose of fornication. On the other hand, the perfect cannot become imperfect by addition; and so a mortal sin cannot become venial, by the addition of a deformity pertaining to the genus of venial sin. For the sin is not diminished if a man commit fornication in order to utter an idle word; rather is it aggravated by the additional deformity.

Nevertheless, a sin which is in genus mortal can become venial by reason of the imperfection of the act, because then it does not completely fulfill the conditions of a moral act, since it is not a deliberate, but a sudden act, as is evident from what we have said above. This happens by a kind of subtraction, namely, of deliberate reason. And since a moral act takes its species from deliberate reason, the result is that by such a subtraction the species of the act is destroyed.

Reply Obj. 1. Venial differs from mortal as imperfect from perfect, even as a boy differs from a man. But the boy becomes a man, and not *vice versa*. Hence the argument does not hold.

Reply Obj. 2. If the ignorance be such as to excuse sin altogether, as the ignorance of a madman or a lunatic, then he that commits fornication in a state of such ignorance commits no sin, either mortal or venial. But if the ignorance be not invincible, then the ignorance itself is a sin, and contains within itself the lack of the love of God, in so far as a man neglects to learn those things by which he can safeguard himself in the love of God.

Reply Obj. 3. As Augustine says, *those things which are evil in themselves cannot be well done for any good end.*[31] Now murder is the slaying of the innocent, and this can in no way be well done. But, as Augustine states, *the judge who sentences a thief to death, or the soldier who slays the enemy of the state are not murderers.*[32]

[31] *Contra Mendacium*, I, 4; 5 (PL 32, 1226; 1227).   [32] *De Lib. Arb.*, I, 7 (PL 40, 528).

ON VENIAL SIN CONSIDERED IN ITSELF

(*In Six Articles*)

WE must now consider venial sin in itself, and under this head there are six points of inquiry: (1) Whether venial sin causes a stain in the soul? (2) Of the different kinds of venial sin, as symbolized by *wood, hay, stubble* (*1 Cor.* iii. 12). (3) Whether man could sin venially in the state of innocence? (4) Whether a good or a wicked angel can sin venially? (5) Whether the first movements of unbelievers are venial sins? (6) Whether venial sin can be in a man with original sin alone?

First Article

WHETHER VENIAL SIN CAUSES A STAIN IN THE SOUL?

We proceed thus to the First Article:—

Objection 1. It would seem that venial sin causes a stain in the soul. For Augustine says that if venial sins be multiplied, they destroy the beauty of our souls so as to deprive us of the embraces of our heavenly spouse.[1] But the stain of sin is nothing else but the loss of the soul's beauty. Therefore venial sins cause a stain in the soul.

Obj. 2. Further, mortal sin causes a stain in the soul, because of the lack of order in the act and affection of the sinner. But, in venial sin, there is a lack of order in the act and the affection. Therefore venial sin causes a stain in the soul.

Obj. 3. Further, the stain on the soul is caused by contact with a temporal thing, through love thereof, as was stated above.[2] But, in venial sin, the soul is in contact with a temporal thing through inordinate love. Therefore venial sin brings a stain on to the soul.

On the contrary, It is written (*Ephes.* v. 27): *That He might present it to Himself a glorious church, not having spot or wrinkle,* on which the *Gloss* says: *i.e., some grievous sin.*[3] Therefore it seems proper to mortal sin to cause a stain in the soul.

I answer that, As was stated above,[4] a stain denotes a loss of splendor due to contact with something, as may be seen in corporeal things, from which the term has been transferred to the soul, by way of likeness. Now just as in the body there is a twofold splendor, one resulting from the

---

[1] St. Augustine (?), *Serm.* CIV (PL 39, 1947).   [2] Q. 86, a. 1.   [3] Peter Lombard, *In Ephes.*, super V, 27 (PL 192, 214).   [4] Q. 86, a. 1.

inward disposition of the members and colors, the other resulting from an outward and added brightness, so, too, in the soul, there is a twofold splendor, one habitual, and, so to speak, intrinsic, the other, actual, like an outward brilliance. Now venial sin is a hindrance to actual splendor, but not to habitual splendor, because it neither destroys nor diminishes the habit of charity and of the other virtues, as we shall show further on,[5] but only hinders their acts. On the other hand, a stain denotes something permanent in the thing stained, and therefore it seems in the nature of a loss of habitual rather than of actual splendor. Therefore, properly speaking, venial sin does not cause a stain in the soul. If, however, we find it stated anywhere that it does induce a stain, this is in a restricted sense, in so far as it hinders the splendor that results from acts of virtue.

Reply Obj. 1. Augustine is speaking of the case in which many venial sins lead to mortal sin dispositively; because otherwise they would not sever the soul from the embrace of its heavenly spouse.

Reply Obj. 2. In mortal sin, the lack of order in the act destroys the habit of virtue, but not in venial sin.

Reply Obj. 3. In mortal sin, the soul comes into contact with a temporal thing as its end, so that the shedding of the light of grace, which comes to those who, by charity, cleave to God as their last end, is entirely cut off. On the contrary, in venial sin, man does not cleave to a creature as his last end. Hence there is no comparison.

Second Article

WHETHER VENIAL SINS ARE SUITABLY DESIGNATED AS *WOOD*, *HAY* AND *STUBBLE*

We proceed thus to the Second Article:—

Objection 1. It would seem that venial sins are unsuitably designated as *wood, hay* and *stubble* (*1 Cor.* iii. 12). For *wood, hay* and *stubble* are said to be built on a spiritual foundation. Now venial sins are something outside a spiritual foundation, even as false opinions are outside science. Therefore venial sins are not suitably designated as wood, hay and stubble.

Obj. 2. Further, he who builds wood, hay and stubble, *shall be saved yet so as by fire* (*verse* 15). But sometimes the man who commits a venial sin will not be saved, even by fire, *e.g.*, when a man dies in mortal sin to which venial sins are attached. Therefore venial sins are unsuitably designated by wood, hay and stubble.

Obj. 3. Further, according to the Apostle (*verse* 12) those who build *gold, silver, precious stones, i.e.,* the love of God and neighbor, and good works, are others from those who build wood, hay and stubble. But even those who love God and neighbor, and do good works, commit venial sins;

[5] *S. T.,* II-II, q. 24, a. 10; q. 133, a. 1, ad 2.

for it is written (*1 John* i. 8): *If we say that we have no sin we deceive our-selves.* Therefore venial sins are not suitably designated by these three.

Obj. 4. Further, there are many more than three differences and degrees of venial sins. Therefore they are unsuitably comprised under these three.

On the contrary, The Apostle says (*1 Cor.* iii. 15) that the man who builds up wood, hay and stubble, *shall be saved yet so as by fire,* so that he will suffer punishment, but not everlasting. Now the debt of temporal punishment belongs properly to venial sin, as was stated above.[6] Therefore these three signify venial sins.

I answer that, Some have understood the *foundation* to be unformed faith, upon which some build good works, signified by gold, silver and precious stones, while others build mortal sins, which according to them are designated by wood, hay and stubble. But Augustine disapproves of this explanation,[7] because, as the Apostle says (*Gal.* v. 21), he who does the works of the flesh, *shall not obtain the kingdom of God,* which signifies to be saved; whereas the Apostle says that he who builds wood, hay and stubble *shall be saved yet so as by fire.* Consequently wood, hay and stubble cannot be understood to denote mortal sins.

Others say that wood, hay, stubble designate good works, which are indeed built upon the spiritual edifice, but are mixed with venial sins.[8]

Thus, when a man is charged with the care of a family, which is a good thing, excessive love of his wife, or of his children or of his possessions insinuates itself into his life, under God however, so that, namely, for the sake of these things he would be unwilling to do anything in opposition to God.—But neither does this seem to be reasonable. For it is evident that all good works are referred to the love of God and one's neighbor, and therefore they are designated by *gold, silver* and *precious stones,* and con-sequently not by *wood, hay* and *stubble.*

We must therefore say that it is the very venial sins themselves, which insinuate themselves into those who have a care for earthly things, that are designated by wood, hay and stubble. For just as these are stored in a house, without belonging to the substance of the house, and can be burnt, while the house is saved, so also venial sins are multiplied in a man, while the spiritual edifice remains, and for them man suffers fire, either of temporal trials in this life, or of purgatory after this life, and yet he gains eternal salvation.

Reply Obj. 1. Venial sins are not said to be built upon the spiritual foundation, as though they were laid directly upon it, but because they are laid alongside it; in the same sense as it is written (*Ps.* cxxxvi. 1): *Upon the waters of Babylon, i.e.,* beside *the waters.* For venial sins do not destroy the spiritual edifice.

---

[6] Q. 87, a. 5.   [7] *De Fide et Oper.,* XV (PL 40, 213).   [8] Peter Lombard, *Sent.,* IV, xxi, 5 (II, 882); St. Augustine, *Enchir.,* LXVIII (PL 40, 264).

Reply Obj. 2. It is not said that everyone who builds wood, hay and stubble shall be saved as by fire, but only those who build *upon* the *foundation*. And this foundation is not unformed faith, as some have esteemed,[9] but faith quickened by charity, according to *Ephes.* iii. 17: *Rooted and founded in charity.* Accordingly, he that dies in mortal sin with venial sins has indeed wood, hay and stubble, but not built upon the spiritual edifice; and consequently he will not be saved so as by fire.

Reply Obj. 3. Although those who are withdrawn from the care of temporal things sometimes sin venially, yet they commit but slight venial sins, and in most cases they are cleansed by the fervor of charity. Hence, they do not build up venial sins, because these do not remain long in them. But the venial sins of those who are busy about earthly things remain longer, because they are unable to have such frequent recourse to the fervor of charity in order to remove them.

Reply Obj. 4. As the Philosopher says, *all things are comprised under three, the beginning, the middle, and the end.*[10] Accordingly, all degrees of venial sins are reduced to three, viz., to *wood,* which remains longer in the fire; *stubble,* which is burnt up at once; and *hay,* which is between these two; because venial sins are removed by fire quickly or slowly, according as man is more or less attached to them.

Third Article

WHETHER MAN COULD COMMIT A VENIAL SIN IN THE STATE OF INNOCENCE?

We proceed thus to the Third Article:—

Objection 1. It would seem that man could commit a venial sin in the state of innocence. For on *1 Tim.* ii. 14 (*Adam was not seduced*) the *Gloss* says: *Having had no experience of God's severity, it was possible for him to be so mistaken as to think that what he had done was a venial sin.*[11] But he would not have thought this unless he could have committed a venial sin. Therefore he could commit a venial sin without sinning mortally.

Obj. 2. Further, Augustine says: *We must not suppose that the tempter would have overcome man, unless first of all there had arisen in man's soul a movement of vainglory which should have been checked.*[12] Now the vainglory which preceded man's defeat, which was accomplished through his falling into mortal sin, could be nothing more than a venial sin.—In like manner, Augustine says that *man was allured by a certain desire of making the experiment, when he saw that the woman did not die when she had taken the forbidden fruit.*[13]—Again there seems to have

---

[9] Cf. St. Augustine, *De Fide et Oper.,* XV (PL 40, 213).   [10] *De Caelo,* I, 1 (268a 12).   [11] *Glossa ordin.* (VI, 119 B).—St. Augustine, *De Civit. Dei,* XIV, 11 (PL 41, 420).   [12] *De Genesi ad Litt.,* XI, 5 (PL 34, 432).   [13] *Op. cit.,* XI, 42 (PL 34, 454).

been a certain movement of unbelief in Eve, since she doubted what the Lord had said, as appears from her saying (*Gen.* iii. 3): *Lest perhaps we die*. Now these apparently were venial sins. Therefore man could commit a venial sin before he committed a mortal sin.

Obj. 3. Further, mortal sin is more opposed to the integrity of the original state than venial sin is. Now man could sin mortally notwithstanding the integrity of the original state. Therefore he could also sin venially.

On the contrary, Every sin deserves some punishment. But nothing penal was possible in the state of innocence, as Augustine declares.[14] Therefore he could not commit a sin that would not deprive him of that state of integrity. But venial sin does not change man's state. Therefore he could not sin venially.

I answer that, It is generally admitted that man could not commit a venial sin in the state of innocence.[15] This, however, is not to be understood as though, because of the perfection of his state, the sin which is venial for us would have been mortal for him, if he had committed it.[16] For the dignity of a person is a circumstance that aggravates a sin, but it does not transfer it to another species, unless there be an additional deformity by reason of disobedience, or of vow or the like, which does not apply to the question in point. Consequently, what is in itself venial could not be changed into mortal sin by reason of the excellence of the original state. We must therefore understand this to mean that he could not sin venially, because it was impossible for him to commit a sin which was in itself venial before losing the integrity of the original state by sinning mortally.

The reason for this is that venial sin occurs in us, either through the imperfection of the act, as in the case of sudden movements in the genus of mortal sin, or through some lack of order in respect of things referred to the end, when the due order to the end is safeguarded. Now each of these happens because of some defect of order, by reason of the fact that the lower powers are not checked by the higher. For the sudden rising of a movement of the sensuality in us is due to the fact that sensuality is not perfectly subject to reason; the sudden rising of a movement in the reason itself is due, in us, to the fact that the execution of the act of reason is not subject to the act of deliberation which proceeds from a higher good, as was stated above.[17] And that the human soul be out of order as regards things directed to the end, when the due order to the end is safeguarded, results from the fact that the things referred to the end are not infallibly contained under the ordination of the end, which holds the highest place, being the beginning, as it were, in matters concerning the appetite, as was stated above.[18] Now, in the state of innocence, as we have stated in the

---

[14] *De Civit. Dei,* XIV, 10 (PL 41, 417).   [15] Cf. St. Albert, *In II Sent.,* d. xxi, a. 10 (XXVII, 369).   [16] Cf. St. Bonaventure, *In II Sent.,* d. xxi, a. 3, q. 1 (II, 505).   [17] Q. 74, a. 10.   [18] Q. 10, a. 1; a. 2, ad 3; q. 72, a. 5.

First Part,[19] there was an unerring stability of order, so that the lower powers were always subjected to the higher, so long as man remained subject to God, as Augustine says.[20] Hence there could be no lack of order in man, unless first of all the highest part of man were not subject to God, which takes place through mortal sin. From this it is evident that, in the state of innocence, man could not commit a venial sin, before committing a mortal sin.

Reply Obj. 1. In the passage quoted, venial is not taken in the same sense as we take it now; but by venial sin we mean that which is easily forgiven.

Reply Obj. 2. This vainglory, which preceded man's downfall, was his first mortal sin, for it is stated to have preceded his downfall into the outward act of sin. This vainglory was followed, in the man, by the desire to make an experiment, and, in the woman, by doubt, for she gave way to vainglory merely through hearing the serpent mention the precept, as though she refused to be held in check by the precept.

Reply Obj. 3. Mortal sin is opposed to the integrity of the original state because it destroys that state; and this a venial sin cannot do. And because the integrity of the original state is incompatible with any lack of order whatever, the result is that the first man could not sin venially before committing a mortal sin.

Fourth Article

WHETHER A GOOD OR A WICKED ANGEL CAN SIN VENIALLY?

We proceed thus to the Fourth Article:—

Objection 1. It would seem that a good or a wicked angel can sin venially. Because man is like the angels in the higher part of his soul, which is called the mind, according to Gregory who says that *man understands in common with the angels.*[21] But man can commit a venial sin in the higher part of his soul. Therefore an angel can commit a venial sin also.

Obj. 2. Further, He that can do more, can do less. But an angel could love a created good more than God, and he did, by sinning mortally. Therefore he could also love a creature less than God inordinately, by sinning venially.

Obj. 3. Further, wicked angels seem to do certain things which are venial sins generically, by provoking man to laughter, and other like frivolities. But the circumstance of the person does not make a mortal sin to be venial, as was stated above, unless there be a special prohibition, which is not the case in point. Therefore an angel can sin venially.

---

[19] *S. T.,* I, q. 95, a. 1.   [20] *De Civit. Dei,* XIV, 17; 23; XIII, 13 (PL 41, 425; 431; 386).   [21] *In Evang.,* II, hom. 29 (PL 76, 1214).

On the contrary, The perfection of an angel is greater than that of man in his original state. But in his original state man could not sin venially; much less, therefore, can an angel.

I answer that, An angel's intellect, as we have stated in the First Part,[22] is not discursive, *i.e.,* it does not proceed from principles to conclusions, so as to understand both separately, as we do. Consequently, whenever the angelic intellect considers a conclusion, it must, of necessity, consider it in its principles. Now in matters of appetite, as we have often stated,[23] ends are like principles, while the means are like conclusions. Therefore, an angel's mind is not directed to the means, except as they stand under the order to the end. Consequently, from their very nature, they can have no lack of order in relation to the means, unless at the same time they have a lack of order in relation to the end, and this is a mortal sin. Now good angels are not moved to the means, except in subordination to the due end, which is God; and hence all their actions are acts of charity, so that no venial sin can be in them. On the other hand, wicked angels are moved to nothing except in subordination to the end which is their sin of pride. Therefore they sin mortally in everything that they do of their own will. —This does not apply to the *natural* desire for the good, which is in them, as we said in the First Part.[24]

Reply Obj. 1. Man is indeed like the angels in mind or intellect, but he differs in his mode of understanding, as we have stated above.

Reply Obj. 2. An angel could not love a creature less than God without, at the same time, either referring it to God as the last end, or to some inordinate end, for the reason given above.

Reply Obj. 3. The demons incite man to all such things which seem to be venial, that they may become intimate with him so as to lead him on to mortal sin. Consequently, in all such things they sin mortally because of the end they have in view.

Fifth Article

WHETHER THE FIRST MOVEMENTS OF THE SENSUALITY IN UNBELIEVERS ARE MORTAL SINS?

We proceed thus to the Fifth Article:—

Objection 1. It would seem that the first movements of the sensuality in unbelievers are mortal sins. For the Apostle says (*Rom.* viii. 1) that *there is . . . no condemnation to them that are in Christ Jesus, who walk not according to the flesh;* and he is speaking there of the concupiscence of the sensuality, as appears from the context (ch. vii.). Therefore the reason why concupiscence is not a matter of condemnation to those who walk not according to the flesh, *i.e.,* by consenting to concupiscence, is

[22] *S. T.,* I, q. 58, a. 3; q. 79, a. 8.   [23] Q. 8, a. 2; q. 10, a. 1; a. 2, ad 3; q. 72, a. 5.
[24] *S. T.,* I, q. 63, a. 4; q. 64, a. 2, ad 5.

because they are in Christ Jesus. But unbelievers are not in Christ Jesus. Therefore in unbelievers this is a matter of condemnation. Therefore the first movements of unbelievers are mortal sins.

Obj. 2. Further, Anselm says: *Those who are not in Christ, when they feel the sting of the flesh, follow the road of damnation, even if they walk not according to the flesh.*[25] But damnation is not due save to mortal sin. Therefore, since man feels the sting of the flesh in the first movements of concupiscence, it seems that the first movements of concupiscence in unbelievers are mortal sins.

Obj. 3. Further, Anselm says: *Man was so made that he should not have felt concupiscence.*[26] Now this liability seems to be remitted to man by the grace of baptism, which the unbeliever has not. Therefore every act of concupiscence in an unbeliever, even without his consent, is a mortal sin, because he acts against what he ought to do.

On the contrary, It is stated in *Acts* x. 34 that *God is not a respecter of persons.* Therefore He does not impute to one unto condemnation what He does not impute to another. But He does not impute first movements to believers, unto condemnation. Neither, therefore, does He impute them to unbelievers.

I answer that, It is senseless to say that the first movements of unbelievers are mortal sins, when they do not consent to them. This is evident for two reasons. First, because the sensuality itself cannot be the subject of mortal sin, as we have stated above.[27] Now the sensuality has the same nature in unbelievers as in believers. Therefore it is not possible for the mere movements of the sensuality in unbelievers to be mortal sins.

Secondly, from the state of the sinner. For the excellence of the person never diminishes sin but, on the contrary, increases it, as was stated above.[28] Therefore a sin is not less grievous in a believer than in an unbeliever, but much more so. For the sins of an unbeliever are more deserving of forgiveness because of his ignorance, according to *1 Tim.* i. 13: *I obtained the mercy of God, because I did it ignorantly in my unbelief;* whereas the sins of believers are more grievous because of the sacraments of grace, according to *Heb.* x. 29: *How much more, do you think, he deserveth worse punishments . . . who hath esteemed the blood of the testament unclean, by which he was sanctified?*

Reply Obj. 1. The Apostle is speaking of the condemnation due to original sin, which condemnation is remitted by the grace of Jesus Christ, although the *fomes* of concupiscence remain. Therefore the fact that believers are subject to concupiscence is not in them a sign of the condemnation due to original sin, as it is in unbelievers.

In this way also is to be understood the saying of Anselm. Therefore the Reply to the Second Objection is evident.

[25] *De Concord. Praesc. cum Lib. Arb.,* III, 7 (FL 158, 530).   [26] *Ibid.*   [27] Q. 74, a. 4.   [28] Q. 73, a. 10.

Reply Obj. 3. This freedom from liability to concupiscence was a result of original justice. Therefore that which is opposed to such liability pertains, not to actual sin, but to original sin.

Sixth Article

WHETHER VENIAL SIN CAN BE IN ANYONE WITH ORIGINAL SIN ALONE?

We proceed thus to the Sixth Article:—

Objection 1. It would seem that venial sin can be in a man with original sin alone. For disposition precedes habit. Now venial sin is a disposition to mortal sin, as stated above.[29] Therefore in an unbeliever, in whom original sin is not remitted, venial sin exists before mortal sin; and so at some time unbelievers have venial together with original sin, and without mortal sins.

Obj. 2. Further, venial sin has less in common and less connection with mortal sin than one mortal sin has with another. But an unbeliever in the state of original sin can commit one mortal sin without committing another. Therefore he can also commit a venial sin without committing a mortal sin.

Obj. 3. Further, it is possible to fix the time at which a child is first able to commit an actual sin; and when the child comes to that time, it can stay a short while, at least, without committing a mortal sin, because this happens even in the worst criminals. Now it is possible for the child to sin venially during that space of time, however short it may be. Therefore venial sin can be in anyone with original sin alone and without mortal sin.

On the contrary, Man is punished for original sin in the children's limbo, where there is no pain of sense, as we shall state further on;[30] whereas men are punished in hell for none other than mortal sin. Therefore there will be no place where a man can be punished for venial sin with no other than original sin.

I answer that, It is impossible for venial sin to be in anyone with original sin alone, and without mortal sin. The reason for this is because, before a man comes to the age of discretion, the lack of years hinders the use of reason and excuses him from mortal sin. Hence, much more does it excuse him from venial sin, if he does anything which is such generically. But when he begins to have the use of reason, he is not entirely excused from the guilt of venial or mortal sin. Now the first thing that occurs to a man to think about then is to deliberate about himself. And if he then direct himself to the due end, he will, by means of grace, receive the remission of original sin; whereas if he does not then direct himself to the due end, as far as he is capable of discretion at that particular age,

---

[29] Q. 88, a. 3.   [30] *S. T.*, III, Suppl., q. 69, a. 6.

he will sin mortally, through not doing that which is in his power to do. Accordingly, thenceforward there cannot be venial sin in him without mortal sin until after all sin shall have been remitted to him through grace.

Reply Obj. 1. Venial sin precedes mortal sin not as a necessary disposition, but as a contingent one, just as work sometimes disposes to fever, but not as heat disposes to the form of fire.

Reply Obj. 2. Venial sin is prevented from being with original sin alone, not because of its want of connection or likeness, but because of the lack of the use of reason, as we have stated above.

Reply Obj. 3. The child that is beginning to have the use of reason can refrain from other mortal sins for a time, but it is not free from the aforesaid sin of omission, unless it turn to God as soon as possible. For the first thing that occurs to a man who reaches the age of discretion is to think of himself, and to direct other things to himself as to their end, since the end is the first thing in the intention. Therefore this is the time when man is bound by God's affirmative precept, which the Lord expressed by saying (*Zach.* i. 3): *Turn ye to Me . . . and I will turn to you.*

TREATISE ON LAW

Question XC

ON THE ESSENCE OF LAW
(*In Four Articles*)

WE have now to consider the extrinsic principles of acts. Now the extrinsic principle inclining to evil is the devil, of whose temptations we have spoken in the First Part.[1] But the extrinsic principle moving to good is God, Who both instructs us by means of His Law, and assists us by His Grace. Therefore, in the first place, we must speak of law; in the second place, of grace.[2]

Concerning law, we must consider (1) law itself in general; (2) its parts.[3] Concerning law in general three points offer themselves for our consideration: (1) its essence; (2) the different kinds of law;[4] (3) the effects of law.[5]

Under the first head there are four points of inquiry: (1) Whether law is something pertaining to reason? (2) Concerning the end of law. (3) Its cause. (4) The promulgation of law.

First Article

WHETHER LAW IS SOMETHING PERTAINING TO REASON?

We proceed thus to the First Article:—

Objection 1. It would seem that law is not something pertaining to reason. For the Apostle says (*Rom.* vii. 23): *I see another law in my members,* etc. But nothing pertaining to reason is in the members, since the reason does not make use of a bodily organ. Therefore law is not something pertaining to reason.

Obj. 2. Further, in the reason there is nothing else but power, habit and act. But law is not the power itself of reason. In like manner, neither is it a habit of reason, because the habits of reason are the intellectual virtues, of which we have spoken above.[6] Nor again is it an act of reason, because then law would cease when the act of reason ceases, for instance. while we are asleep. Therefore law is nothing pertaining to reason.

Obj. 3. Further, the law moves those who are subject to it to act rightly. But it belongs properly to the will to move to act, as is evident from what

S. *T.,* I, q. 114. [2] Q. 109. [3] Q. 93. [4] Q. 91. [5] Q. 92. [6] Q. 57.

has been said above.[7] Therefore law pertains, not to the reason, but to the will, according to the words of the Jurist:[8] *Whatsoever pleaseth the sovereign has the force of law.*

On the contrary, It belongs to the law to command and to forbid. But it belongs to reason to command, as was stated above.[9] Therefore law is something pertaining to reason.

I answer that, Law is a rule and measure of acts, whereby man is induced to act or is restrained from acting; for *lex* [*law*] is derived from *ligare* [*to bind*], because it binds one to act. Now the rule and measure of human acts is the reason, which is the first principle of human acts, as is evident from what has been stated above.[10] For it belongs to the reason to direct to the end, which is the first principle in all matters of action, according to the Philosopher.[11] Now that which is the principle in any genus is the rule and measure of that genus: for instance, unity in the genus of numbers, and the first movement in the genus of movements. Consequently, it follows that law is something pertaining to reason.

Reply Obj. 1. Since law is a kind of rule and measure, it may be in something in two ways. First, as in that which measures and rules; and since this is proper to reason, it follows that, in this way, law is in the reason alone.—Secondly, as in that which is measured and ruled. In this way, law is in all those things that are inclined to something because of some law; so that any inclination arising from a law may be called a law, not essentially, but by participation as it were. And thus the inclination of the members to concupiscence is called *the law of the members.*[12]

Reply Obj. 2. Just as, in external acts, we may consider the work and the work done, for instance, the work of building and the house built, so in the acts of reason, we may consider the act itself of reason, *i.e.,* to understand and to reason, and something produced by this act. With regard to the speculative reason, this is first of all the definition; secondly, the proposition; thirdly, the syllogism or argument. And since the practical reason also makes use of the syllogism in operable matters, as we have stated above[13] and as the Philosopher teaches,[14] hence we find in the practical reason something that holds the same position in regard to operations as, in the speculative reason, the proposition holds in regard to conclusions. Such universal propositions of the practical reason that are directed to operations have the nature of law. And these propositions are sometimes under our actual consideration, while sometimes they are retained in the reason by means of a habit.

Reply Obj. 3. Reason has its power of moving from the will, as was stated above;[15] for it is due to the fact that one wills the end, that the

---

[7] Q. 9, a. 1.   [8] *Dig.,* I, iv, 1 (I, 35a).   [9] Q. 17, a. 1.   [10] Q. 1, a. 1, ad 3. [11] *Phys.,* II, 9 (200a 22); *Eth.,* VII, 8 (1151a 16).   [12] Peter Lombard, *Sent.,* II xxx, 8 (I, 464).   [13] Q. 13, a. 3; q. 76, a. 1; q. 77, a. 2, ad 4.   [14] *Eth.,* VII, 3 (1147a 24). [15] Q. 17, a. 1.

reason issues its commands as regards things ordained to the end. But in order that the volition of what is commanded may have the nature of law, it needs to be in accord with some rule of reason. And in this sense is to be understood the saying that the will of the sovereign has the force of law; or otherwise the sovereign's will would savor of lawlessness rather than of law.

Second Article

WHETHER LAW IS ALWAYS DIRECTED TO THE
COMMON GOOD?

We proceed thus to the Second Article:—
Objection 1. It would seem that law is not always directed to the common good as to its end. For it belongs to law to command and to forbid. But commands are directed to certain individual goods. Therefore the end of law is not always the common good.

Obj. 2. Further, law directs man in his actions. But human actions are concerned with particular matters. Therefore law is directed to some particular good.

Obj. 3. Further, Isidore says: *If law is based on reason, whatever is based on reason will be a law.*[16] But reason is the foundation not only of what is ordained to the common good, but also of that which is directed to private good. Therefore law is not directed only to the good of all, but also to the private good of an individual.

On the contrary, Isidore says that *laws are enacted for no private profit, but for the common benefit of the citizens.*[17]

I answer that, As we have stated above, law belongs to that which is a principle of human acts, because it is their rule and measure. Now as reason is a principle of human acts, so in reason itself there is something which is the principle in respect of all the rest. Hence to this principle chiefly and mainly law must needs be referred. Now the first principle in practical matters, which are the object of the practical reason, is the last end: and the last end of human life is happiness or beatitude, as we have stated above.[18] Consequently, law must needs concern itself mainly with the order that is in beatitude. Moreover, since every part is ordained to the whole as the imperfect to the perfect, and since one man is a part of the perfect community, law must needs concern itself properly with the order directed to universal happiness. Therefore the Philosopher, in the above definition of legal matters, mentions both happiness and the body politic, since he says that we call those legal matters *just which are adapted to produce and preserve happiness and its parts for the body politic.*[19] For the state is a perfect community, as he says in *Politics* i.[20]

---

[16] *Etymol.*, II, 10; V, 3 (PL 82, 130; 199).   [17] *Op. cit.*, V, 21 (PL 82, 203).   [18] Q. 2, a. 7; q. 3, a. 1; q. 69, a. 1.   [19] *Eth.*, V, 1 (1129b 17).   [20] Aristotle, *Polit.*, I, 1 (1252a 5).

Now, in every genus, that which belongs to it chiefly is the principle of the others, and the others belong to that genus according to some order towards that thing. Thus fire, which is chief among hot things, is the cause of heat in mixed bodies, and these are said to be hot in so far as they have a share of fire. Consequently, since law is chiefly ordained to the common good, any other precept in regard to some individual work must needs be devoid of the nature of a law, save in so far as it regards the common good. Therefore every law is ordained to the common good.

Reply Obj. 1. A command denotes the application of a law to matters regulated by law. Now the order to the common good, at which law aims, is applicable to particular ends. And in this way commands are given even concerning particular matters.

Reply Obj. 2. Actions are indeed concerned with particular matters, but those particular matters are referable to the common good, not as to a common genus or species, but as to a common final cause, according as the common good is said to be the common end.

Reply Obj. 3. Just as nothing stands firm with regard to the speculative reason except that which is traced back to the first indemonstrable principles, so nothing stands firm with regard to the practical reason, unless it be directed to the last end which is the common good. Now whatever stands to reason in this sense has the nature of a law.

Third Article

WHETHER THE REASON OF ANY MAN IS COMPETENT
TO MAKE LAWS?

We proceed thus to the Third Article:—

Objection 1. It would seem that the reason of any man is competent to make laws. For the Apostle says (*Rom.* ii. 14) that *when the Gentiles, who have not the law, do by nature those things that are of the law, . . . they are a law to themselves.* Now he says this of all in general. Therefore anyone can make a law for himself.

Obj. 2. Further, as the Philosopher says, *the intention of the lawgiver is to lead men to virtue.*[21] But every man can lead another to virtue. Therefore the reason of any man is competent to make laws.

Obj. 3. Further, just as the sovereign of a state governs the state, so every father of a family governs his household. But the sovereign of a state can make laws for the state. Therefore every father of a family can make laws for his household.

On the contrary, Isidore says, and the *Decretals* repeat: *A law is an ordinance of the people, whereby something is sanctioned by the Elders together with the Commonalty.*[22] Therefore not everyone can make laws.

[21] *Eth.,* II, 1 (1103b 3).   [22] *Etymol.,* V, 10 (PL 82, 200); Gratian, *Decretum,* I, ii, 1 (I, 3).

I answer that, A law, properly speaking, regards first and foremost the order to the common good. Now to order anything to the common good belongs either to the whole people, or to someone who is the vicegerent of the whole people. Hence the making of a law belongs either to the whole people or to a public personage who has care of the whole people; for in all other matters the directing of anything to the end concerns him to whom the end belongs.

Reply Obj. 1. As was stated above, a law is in a person not only as in one that rules, but also, by participation, as in one that is ruled. In the latter way, each one is a law to himself, in so far as he shares the direction that he receives from one who rules him. Hence the same text goes on: *Who show the work of the law written in their hearts (Rom.* ii. 15).

Reply Obj. 2. A private person cannot lead another to virtue efficaciously; for he can only advise, and if his advice be not taken, it has no coercive power, such as the law should have, in order to prove an efficacious inducement to virtue, as the Philosopher says.[23] But this coercive power is vested in the whole people or in some public personage, to whom it belongs to inflict penalties, as we shall state further on.[24] Therefore the framing of laws belongs to him alone.

Reply Obj. 3. As one man is a part of the household, so a household is a part of the state; and the state is a perfect community, according to *Politics* i.[25] Therefore, just as the good of one man is not the last end, but is ordained to the common good, so too the good of one household is ordained to the good of a single state, which is a perfect community. Consequently, he that governs a family can indeed make certain commands or ordinances, but not such as to have properly the nature of law.

Fourth Article

WHETHER PROMULGATION IS ESSENTIAL TO LAW?

We proceed thus to the Fourth Article:—

Objection 1. It would seem that promulgation is not essential to law. For the natural law, above all, has the character of law. But the natural law needs no promulgation. Therefore it is not essential to law that it be promulgated.

Obj. 2. Further, it belongs properly to law to bind one to do or not to do something. But the obligation of fulfilling a law touches not only those in whose presence it is promulgated, but also others. Therefore promulgation is not essential to law.

Obj. 3. Further, the binding force of law extends even to the future, since *laws are binding in matters of the future,* as the jurists say.[26] But

---

[23] *Eth.,* X, 9 (1180a 20).   [24] Q. 92, a. 2, ad 3; II-II, q. 64, a. 3.   [25] Aristotle, *Polit.,* I, 1 (1252a 5).   [26] *Codex Justinianus,* I, xiv, 7 (II, 68a).

promulgation concerns those who are present. Therefore it is not essential to law.

On the contrary, It is laid down in the *Decretals* that *laws are established when they are promulgated.*[27]

I answer that, As was stated above, a law is imposed on others as a rule and measure. Now a rule or measure is imposed by being applied to those who are to be ruled and measured by it. Therefore, in order that a law obtain the binding force which is proper to a law, it must needs be applied to the men who have to be ruled by it. But such application is made by its being made known to them by promulgation. Therefore promulgation is necessary for law to obtain its force.

Thus, from the four preceding articles, the definition of law may be gathered. Law is nothing else than an ordinance of reason for the common good, promulgated by him who has the care of the community.

Reply Obj. 1. The natural law is promulgated by the very fact that God instilled it into man's mind so as to be known by him naturally.

Reply Obj. 2. Those who are not present when a law is promulgated are bound to observe the law, in so far as it is made known or can be made known to them by others, after it has been promulgated.

Reply Obj. 3. The promulgation that takes place in the present extends to future time by reason of the durability of written characters, by which means it is continually promulgated. Hence Isidore says that *lex* [*law*] *is derived from legere* [*to read*] *because it is written.*[28]

---

[27] Gratian, *Decretum,* I, iv, 3 (I, 6).   [28] *Etymol.,* II, 10 (PL 82, 130).

ON THE VARIOUS KINDS OF LAW
(*In Six Articles*)

WE must now consider the various kinds of law, under which head there are six points of inquiry: (1) Whether there is an eternal law? (2) Whether there is a natural law? (3) Whether there is a human law? (4) Whether there is a divine law? (5) Whether there is one divine law, or several? (6) Whether there is a law of sin?

First Article

WHETHER THERE IS AN ETERNAL LAW?

We proceed thus to the First Article:—

Objection 1. It would seem that there is no eternal law. For every law is imposed on someone. But there was not someone from eternity on whom a law could be imposed, since God alone was from eternity. Therefore no law is eternal.

Obj. 2. Further, promulgation is essential to law. But promulgation could not be from eternity, because there was no one to whom it could be promulgated from eternity. Therefore no law can be eternal.

Obj. 3. Further, law implies order to an end. But nothing ordained to an end is eternal, for the last end alone is eternal. Therefore no law is eternal.

On the contrary, Augustine says: *That Law which is the Supreme Reason cannot be understood to be otherwise than unchangeable and eternal.*[1]

I answer that, As we have stated above, law is nothing else but a dictate of practical reason emanating from the ruler who governs a perfect community.[2] Now it is evident, granted that the world is ruled by divine providence, as was stated in the First Part,[3] that the whole community of the universe is governed by the divine reason. Therefore the very notion of the government of things in God, the ruler of the universe, has the nature of a law. And since the divine reason's conception of things is not subject to time, but is eternal, according to *Prov.* viii. 23, therefore it is that this kind of law must be called eternal.

Reply Obj. 1. Those things that do not exist in themselves exist in God, inasmuch as they are known and preordained by Him, according to *Rom.*

---

[1] *De Lib. Arb.,* I, 6 (PL 32, 1229).   [2] Q. 90, a. 1, ad 2; a. 3 and 4.   [3] *S. T.,* I, q. 22, a. 1, ad 2.

iv. 17: *Who calls those things that are not, as those that are*. Accordingly, the eternal concept of the divine law bears the character of an eternal law in so far as it is ordained by God to the government of things foreknown by Him.

Reply Obj. 2. Promulgation is made by word of mouth or in writing, and in both ways the eternal law is promulgated, because both the divine Word and the writing of the Book of Life are eternal. But the promulgation cannot be from eternity on the part of the creature that hears or reads.

Reply Obj. 3. Law implies order to the end actively, namely, in so far as it directs certain things to the end; but not passively,—that is to say, the law itself is not ordained to the end, except accidentally, in a governor whose end is extrinsic to him, and to which end his law must needs be ordained. But the end of the divine government is God Himself, and His law is not something other than Himself. Therefore the eternal law is not ordained to another end.

Second Article

WHETHER THERE IS IN US A NATURAL LAW?

We proceed thus to the Second Article:
Objection 1. It would seem that there is no natural law in us. For man is governed sufficiently by the eternal law, since Augustine says that *the eternal law is that by which it is right that all things should be most orderly*.[4] But nature does not abound in superfluities as neither does she fail in necessaries. Therefore man has no natural law.

Obj. 2. Further, by the law man is directed, in his acts, to the end, as was stated above.[5] But the directing of human acts to their end is not a function of nature, as is the case in irrational creatures, which act for an end solely by their natural appetite; whereas man acts for an end by his reason and will. Therefore man has no natural law.

Obj. 3. Further, the more a man is free, the less is he under the law. But man is freer than all the animals because of his free choice, with which he is endowed in distinction from all other animals. Since, therefore, other animals are not subject to a natural law, neither is man subject to a natural law.

On the contrary, the *Gloss* on *Rom.* ii. 14 (*When the Gentiles, who have not the law, do by nature those things that are of the law*) comments as follows: *Although they have no written law, yet they have the natural law, whereby each one knows, and is conscious of, what is good and what is evil.*[6]

I answer that, As we have stated above,[7] law, being a rule and measure, can be in a person in two ways: in one way, as in him that rules and

---

[4] *De Lib. Arb.,* I, 6 (PL 32, 1229).   [5] Q. 90, a. 2.   [6] *Glossa ordin.* (VI, 7E);
Peter Lombard, *In Rom.,* super II, 14 (PL 191, 1345).   [7] Q. 90, a. 1, ad 1.

measures; in another way, as in that which is ruled and measured, since a thing is ruled and measured in so far as it partakes of the rule or measure. Therefore, since all things subject to divine providence are ruled and measured by the eternal law, as was stated above, it is evident that all things partake in some way in the eternal law, in so far as, namely, from its being imprinted on them, they derive their respective inclinations to their proper acts and ends. Now among all others, the rational creature is subject to divine providence in a more excellent way, in so far as it itself partakes of a share of providence, by being provident both for itself and for others. Therefore it has a share of the eternal reason, whereby it has a natural inclination to its proper act and end; and this participation of the eternal law in the rational creature is called the natural law. Hence the Psalmist, after saying (*Ps.* iv. 6): *Offer up the sacrifice of justice*, as though someone asked what the works of justice are, adds: *Many say, Who showeth us good things?* in answer to which question he says: *The light of Thy countenance, O Lord, is signed upon us.* He thus implies that the light of natural reason, whereby we discern what is good and what is evil, which is the function of the natural law, is nothing else than an imprint on us of the divine light. It is therefore evident that the natural law is nothing else than the rational creature's participation of the eternal law.

Reply Obj. 1. This argument would hold if the natural law were something different from the eternal law; whereas it is nothing but a participation thereof, as we have stated above.

Reply Obj. 2. Every act of reason and will in us is based on that which is according to nature, as was stated above.[8] For every act of reasoning is based on principles that are known naturally, and every act of appetite in respect of the means is derived from the natural appetite in respect of the last end. Accordingly, the first direction of our acts to their end must needs be through the natural law.

Reply Obj. 3. Even irrational animals partake in their own way of the eternal reason, just as the rational creature does. But because the rational creature partakes thereof in an intellectual and rational manner, therefore the participation of the eternal law in the rational creature is properly called a law, since a law is something pertaining to reason, as was stated above.[9] Irrational creatures, however, do not partake thereof in a rational manner, and therefore there is no participation of the eternal law in them, except by way of likeness.

Third Article

WHETHER THERE IS A HUMAN LAW?

We proceed thus to the Third Article:—

Objection 1. It would seem that there is not a human law. For the

[8] Q. 10, a. 1.　　[9] Q. 90, a. 1.

natural law is a participation of the eternal law, as was stated above. Now through the eternal law *all things are most orderly*, as Augustine states.[10] Therefore the natural law suffices for the ordering of all human affairs. Consequently there is no need for a human law.

Obj. 2. Further, law has the character of a measure, as was stated above.[11] But human reason is not a measure of things, but *vice versa*, as is stated in *Metaph.* x.[12] Therefore no law can emanate from the human reason.

Obj. 3. Further, a measure should be most certain, as is stated in *Metaph.* x.[13] But the dictates of the human reason in matters of conduct are uncertain, according to *Wis.* ix. 14: *The thoughts of mortal men are fearful, and our counsels uncertain.* Therefore no law can emanate from the human reason.

On the contrary, Augustine distinguishes two kinds of law, the one eternal, the other temporal, which he calls human.[14]

I answer that, As we have stated above, a law is a dictate of the practical reason.[15] Now it is to be observed that the same procedure takes place in the practical and in the speculative reason, for each proceeds from principles to conclusions, as was stated above.[16] Accordingly, we conclude that, just as in the speculative reason, from naturally known indemonstrable principles we draw the conclusions of the various sciences, the knowledge of which is not imparted to us by nature, but acquired by the efforts of reason, so too it is that from the precepts of the natural law, as from common and indemonstrable principles, the human reason needs to proceed to the more particular determination of certain matters. These particular determinations, devised by human reason, are called human laws, provided that the other essential conditions of law be observed, as was stated above.[17] Therefore Tully says in his *Rhetoric* that *justice has its source in nature; thence certain things came into custom by reason of their utility; afterwards these things which emanated from nature, and were approved by custom, were sanctioned by fear and reverence for the law*.[18]

Reply Obj. 1. The human reason cannot have a full participation of the dictate of the divine reason, but according to its own mode, and imperfectly. Consequently, just as on the part of the speculative reason, by a natural participation of divine wisdom, there is in us the knowledge of certain common principles, but not a proper knowledge of each single truth, such as that contained in the divine wisdom, so, too, on the part of the practical reason, man has a natural participation of the eternal law, according to certain common principles, but not as regards the particular determinations of individual cases, which are, however, contained in the

---

[10] *De Lib. Arb.*, I, 6 (PL 32, 1229).   [11] Q. 90, a. 1.   [12] Aristotle, *Metaph.*, IX, 1 (1053a 31).   [13] *Ibid.*   [14] *De Lib. Arb.*, I, 6 (PL 32, 1229).   [15] Q. 90, a. 1, ad 2.   [16] *Ibid.*   [17] Q. 90.   [18] *De Invent.*, II, 53 (p. 148[b]).

eternal law. Hence the need for human reason to proceed further to sanction them by law.

Reply Obj. 2. Human reason is not, of itself, the rule of things. But the principles impressed on it by nature are the general rules and measures of all things relating to human conduct, of which the natural reason is the rule and measure, although it is not the measure of things that are from nature.

Reply Obj. 3. The practical reason is concerned with operable matters, which are singular and contingent, but not with necessary things, with which the speculative reason is concerned. Therefore human laws cannot have that inerrancy that belongs to the demonstrated conclusions of the sciences. Nor is it necessary for every measure to be altogether unerring and certain, but according as it is possible in its own particular genus.

Fourth Article

WHETHER THERE WAS ANY NEED FOR A DIVINE LAW?

We proceed thus to the Fourth Article:—

Objection 1. It would seem that there was no need for a divine law. For, as was stated above, the natural law is a participation in us of the eternal law. But the eternal law is the divine law, as was stated above. Therefore there is no need for a divine law in addition to the natural law and to human laws derived therefrom.

Obj. 2. Further, it is written (*Ecclus.* xv. 14) that *God left man in the hand of his own counsel.* Now counsel is an act of reason, as was stated above.[19] Therefore man was left to the direction of his reason. But a dictate of human reason is a human law, as was stated above. Therefore there is no need for man to be governed also by a divine law.

Obj. 3. Further, human nature is more self-sufficing than irrational creatures. But irrational creatures have no divine law besides the natural inclination impressed on them. Much less, therefore, should the rational creature have a divine law in addition to the natural law.

On the contrary, David prayed God to set His law before him, saying (*Ps.* cxviii. 33): *Set before me for a law the way of Thy justifications, O Lord.*

I answer that, Besides the natural and the human law it was necessary for the directing of human conduct to have a divine law. And this for four reasons. First, because it is by law that man is directed how to perform his proper acts in view of his last end. Now if man were ordained to no other end than that which is proportionate to his natural ability, there would be no need for man to have any further direction, on the part of his reason, in addition to the natural law and humanly devised law which is derived from it. But since man is ordained to an end of eternal happiness

[19] Q. 14, a. 1.

which exceeds man's natural ability, as we have stated above,[20] therefore it was necessary that, in addition to the natural and the human law, man should be directed to his end by a law given by God.

Secondly, because, by reason of the uncertainty of human judgment, especially on contingent and particular matters, different people form different judgments on human acts; whence also different and contrary laws result. In order, therefore, that man may know without any doubt what he ought to do and what he ought to avoid, it was necessary for man to be directed in his proper acts by a law given by God, for it is certain that such a law cannot err.

Thirdly, because man can make laws in those matters of which he is competent to judge. But man is not competent to judge of interior movements, that are hidden, but only of exterior acts which are observable; and yet for the perfection of virtue it is necessary for man to conduct himself rightly in both kinds of acts. Consequently, human law could not sufficiently curb and direct interior acts, and it was necessary for this purpose that a divine law should supervene.

Fourthly, because, as Augustine says,[21] human law cannot punish or forbid all evil deeds, since, while aiming at doing away with all evils, it would do away with many good things, and would hinder the advance of the common good, which is necessary for human living. In order, therefore, that no evil might remain unforbidden and unpunished, it was necessary for the divine law to supervene, whereby all sins are forbidden.

And these four causes are touched upon in *Ps.* cxviii. 8, where it is said: *The law of the Lord is unspotted, i.e.,* allowing no foulness of sin; *converting souls,* because it directs not only exterior, but also interior, acts; *the testimony of the Lord is faithful,* because of the certainty of what is true and right; *giving wisdom to little ones,* by directing man to an end supernatural and divine.

Reply Obj. 1. By the natural law the eternal law is participated proportionately to the capacity of human nature. But to his supernatural end man needs to be directed in a yet higher way. Hence the additional law given by God, whereby man shares more perfectly in the eternal law.

Reply Obj. 2. Counsel is a kind of inquiry, and hence must proceed from some principles. Nor is it enough for it to proceed from principles imparted by nature, which are the precepts of the natural law, for the reasons given above; but there is need for certain additional principles, namely, the precepts of the divine law.

Reply Obj. 3. Irrational creatures are not ordained to an end higher than that which is proportionate to their natural powers. Consequently the comparison fails.

[20] Q. 5, a. 5.   [21] *De Lib. Arb.,* I, 5 (PL 32, 1228).

Fifth Article

WHETHER THERE IS BUT ONE DIVINE LAW?

We proceed thus to the Fifth Article:—

Objection 1. It would seem that there is but one divine law. For, where there is one king in one kingdom, there is but one law. Now the whole of mankind is compared to God as to one king, according to *Ps.* xlvi. 8: *God is the King of all the earth.* Therefore there is but one divine law.

Obj. 2. Further, every law is directed to the end which the lawgiver intends for those for whom he makes the law. But God intends one and the same thing for all men, since according to *1 Tim.* ii. 4: *He will have all men to be saved, and to come to the knowledge of the truth.* Therefore there is but one divine law.

Obj. 3. Further, the divine law seems to be more akin to the eternal law, which is one, than the natural law, according as the revelation of grace is of a higher order than natural knowledge. But natural law is one for all men. Therefore much more is the divine law but one.

On the contrary, The Apostle says (*Heb.* vii. 12): *The priesthood being translated, it is necessary that a translation also be made of the law.* But the priesthood is twofold, as stated in the same passage, viz., the levitical priesthood, and the priesthood of Christ. Therefore the divine law is twofold, namely, the Old Law and the New Law.

I answer that, As we have stated in the First Part, distinction is the cause of number.[22] Now things may be distinguished in two ways. First, as those things that are altogether specifically different, *e.g.*, a horse and an ox. Secondly, as perfect and imperfect in the same species, *e.g.*, a boy and a man; and in this way the divine law is distinguished into Old and New. Hence the Apostle (*Gal.* iii. 24, 25) compares the state of man under the Old Law to that of a child *under a pedagogue;* but the state under the New Law, to that of a full grown man, who is *no longer under a pedagogue.*

Now the perfection and imperfection of these two laws is to be taken in connection with the three conditions pertaining to law, as was stated above. For, in the first place, it belongs to law to be directed to the common good as to its end, as was stated above.[23] This good may be twofold. It may be a sensible and earthly good, and to this man was directly ordained by the Old Law. Hence it is that, at the very outset of the Law, the people were invited to the earthly kingdom of the Chananæans (*Exod.* iii. 8, 17). Again it may be an intelligible and heavenly good, and to this, man is ordained by the New Law. Therefore, at the very beginning of His preaching, Christ invited men to the kingdom of heaven, saying (*Matt.* iv. 17): *Do penance, for the kingdom of heaven is at hand.* Hence Augus-

[22] *S. T.,* I, q. 30, a. 3. [23] Q. 90, a. 2.

tine says that *promises of temporal goods are contained in the Old Testament, for which reason it is called old; but the promise of eternal life belongs to the New Testament.*[24]

Secondly, it belongs to law to direct human acts according to the order of justice; wherein also the New Law surpasses the Old Law, since it directs our internal acts, according to *Matt.* v. 20: *Unless your justice abound more than that of the Scribes and Pharisees, you shall not enter into the kingdom of heaven.* Hence the saying that *the Old Law restrains the hand, but the New Law controls the soul.*[25]

Thirdly, it belongs to law to induce men to observe its commandments. This the Old Law did by the fear of punishment, but the New Law, by love, which is poured into our hearts by the grace of Christ, bestowed in the New Law, but foreshadowed in the Old. Hence Augustine says that *there is little difference between the Law and the Gospel—fear [timor] and love [amor].*[26]

Reply Obj. 1. As the father of a family issues different commands to the children and to the adults, so also the one King, God, in His one kingdom, gave one law to men while they were yet imperfect, and another more perfect law when, by the preceding law, they had been led to a greater capacity for divine things.

Reply Obj. 2. The salvation of man could not be achieved otherwise than through Christ, according to *Acts* iv. 12: *There is no other name . . . given to men, whereby we must be saved.* Consequently, the law that brings all to salvation could not be given until after the coming of Christ. But before His coming it was necessary to give to the people, of whom Christ was to be born, a law containing certain rudiments of justice unto salvation, in order to prepare them to receive Him.

Reply Obj. 3. The natural law directs man by way of certain general precepts, common to both the perfect and the imperfect. Hence it is one and the same for all. But the divine law directs man also in certain particular matters, to which the perfect and imperfect do not stand in the same relation. Hence the necessity for the divine law to be twofold, as we have already explained.

Sixth Article

WHETHER THERE IS A LAW IN THE *FOMES* OF SIN?

We proceed thus to the Sixth Article:—

Objection 1. It would seem that there is no law of the 'fomes' of sin.[27] For Isidore says that the *law is based on reason.*[28] But the 'fomes' of sin

---

[24] *Contra Faust.*, IV, 2 (PL 42, 217).   [25] Cf. Peter Lombard, *Sent.*, III, xl, 1 (II, 734).   [26] *Contra Adimant.*, XVII (PL 42, 159).   [27] Cf. Peter Lombard, *Sent.*, II, xxx, 8 (I, 464); St. John Damascene, *De Fide Orth.*, IV, 22 (PG 94, 1200).   [28] *Etymol.*, V, 3 (PL 82, 199).

is not based on reason, but deviates from it. Therefore the 'fomes' has not the nature of a law.

Obj. 2. Further, every law is binding, so that those who do not obey it are called transgressors. But man is not called a transgressor from not following the instigations of the 'fomes,' but rather from his following them. Therefore the 'fomes' has not the nature of a law.

Obj. 3. Further, law is ordained to the common good, as was stated above.[29] But the 'fomes' inclines us, not to the common good, but to our own private good. Therefore the 'fomes' has not the nature of law.

On the contrary, The Apostle says (*Rom.* vii. 23): *I see another law in my members, fighting against the law of my mind.*

I answer that, As we have stated above, law, as to its essence, resides in him that rules and measures, but, by way of participation, in that which is ruled and measured;[30] so that every inclination or ordination which may be found in things subject to law is called a law by participation, as was stated above.[31] Now those who are subject to law may receive a twofold inclination from the lawgiver. First, in so far as he directly inclines his subjects to something. According to this, he directs different subjects to different acts; and in this way we may say that there is a military law and a mercantile law. Secondly, indirectly, and thus by the very fact that a lawgiver deprives a subject of some dignity, the latter passes into another order, so as to be under another law, as it were. For example, if a soldier be turned out of the army, he will become a subject of rural or of mercantile legislation.

Accordingly, under the divine Lawgiver, various creatures have various natural inclinations, so that what is, as it were, a law for one, is against the law for another. Thus, I might say that fierceness is, in a way, the law of a dog, but against the law of a sheep or another meek animal. And so the law of man, which, by the divine ordinance, is allotted to him according to his proper natural condition, is that he should act in accordance with reason; and this law was so effective in man's first state, that nothing either outside or against reason could take man unawares. But when man turned his back on God, he fell under the influence of his sensual impulses. In fact, this happens to each one individually, according as he has the more departed from the path of reason; so that, after a fashion, he is likened to the beasts that are led by the impulse of sensuality, according to *Ps.* xlviii. 21: *Man, when he was in honor, did not understand: he hath been compared to senseless beasts, and made like to them.*

Accordingly, then, this very inclination of sensuality, which is called the 'fomes,' in other animals has absolutely the nature of law, yet only in so far as we may consider as law what is an inclination subject to law. But in man, it has not the nature of law in this way; rather is it a deviation from the law of reason. But since, by the just sentence of God, man

[29] Q. 90, a. 2.   [30] A. 2; q. 90, a. 1, ad 1.   [31] *Ibid.*

is deprived of original justice, and his reason bereft of its vigor, this impulse of sensuality, whereby he is led, has the nature of a law in so far as it is a penalty following from the divine law depriving man of his proper dignity.

Reply Obj. 1. This argument considers the 'fomes' in itself as an incentive to evil. It is not thus that it has the nature of a law, as we have stated above, but according as it results from the justice of the divine law; much as though we were to say that it is a law that a nobleman should be made subject to menial labor because of some misdeed.

Reply Obj. 2. This argument considers law in the light of a rule or measure; for it is in this sense that those who deviate from the law become transgressors. But the 'fomes' is not a law in this respect, but by a kind of participation, as was stated above.

Reply Obj. 3. This argument considers the 'fomes' as to its proper inclination, and not as to its origin. And yet if the inclination of sensuality be considered as it is in other animals, thus it is ordained to the common good, namely, to the preservation of nature in the species or in the individual. This is true in man also, in so far as sensuality is subject to reason. But it is called the 'fomes' in so far as it departs from the order of reason.

Question XCII

ON THE EFFECTS OF LAW
(*In Two Articles*)

WE must now consider the effects of law, under which head there are two points of inquiry: (1) Whether it is an effect of law to make men good? (2) Whether the *effects of law are to command, to forbid, to permit and to punish,* as the Jurist states?[1]

WHETHER IT IS AN EFFECT OF LAW TO MAKE MEN GOOD?

We proceed thus to the First Article:—

Objection 1. It seems that it is not an effect of law to make men good. For men are good through virtue, since virtue, as is stated in *Ethics* ii., is *that which makes its subject good.*[2] But virtue is in man from God alone, because He it is Who *works it in us without us,* as was stated above in the definition of virtue.[3] Therefore it does not belong to law to make men good.

Obj. 2. Further, Law does not profit a man unless he obeys it. But the very fact that a man obeys a law is due to his being good. Therefore in man goodness is presupposed to the law. Therefore the law does not make men good.

Obj. 3. Further, Law is ordained to the common good, as was stated above.[4] But some behave well in things regarding the community, who behave ill in things regarding themselves. Therefore it does not belong to law to make men good.

Obj. 4. Further, some laws are tyrannical, as the Philosopher says.[5] But a tyrant does not intend the good of his subjects, but considers only his own profit. Therefore law does not make men good.

On the contrary, The Philosopher says that the *intention of every law-giver is to make men good.*[6]

I answer that, As we have stated above, a law is nothing else than a dictate of reason in the ruler by whom his subjects are governed.[7] Now the virtue of any being that is a subject consists in its being well subordinated to that by which it is regulated; and thus we see that the virtue of

---

[1] *Dig.,* I, iii. 7 (I, 34a). [2] Aristotle, *Eth.,* II, 6 (1106a 15). [3] Q. 55, a. 4.
[4] Q. 90, a. 2. [5] *Polit.,* III, 6 (1282b 12). [6] *Eth.,* II, 1 (1103b 3). [7] Q. 90, a. 1, ad 2; a. 3 and 4.

the irascible and concupiscible powers consists in their being obedient to reason. In the same way, *the virtue of every subject consists in his being well subjected to his ruler,* as the Philosopher says.[8] But every law aims at being obeyed by those who are subject to it. Consequently it is evident that the proper effect of law is to lead its subjects to their proper virtue; and since virtue is *that which makes its subject good,* it follows that the proper effect of law is to make those, to whom it is given, good, either absolutely or in some particular respect. For if the intention of the lawgiver is fixed on a true good, which is the common good regulated according to divine justice, it follows that the effect of law is to make men good absolutely. If, however, the intention of the lawgiver is fixed on that which is not good absolutely, but useful or pleasurable to himself, or in opposition to divine justice, then law does not make men good absolutely, but in a relative way, namely, in relation to that particular government. In this way good is found even in things that are bad of themselves. Thus a man is called a good robber, because he works in a way that is adapted to his end.

Reply Obj. 1. Virtue is twofold, as was explained above, viz., acquired and infused.[9] Now the fact of being accustomed to an action contributes to both, but in different ways; for it causes the acquired virtue, while it disposes to infused virtue, and preserves and fosters it when it already exists. And since law is given for the purpose of directing human acts, insofar as human acts conduce to virtue, so far does law make men good. Therefore the Philosopher says in the second book of the *Politics* that *lawgivers make men good by habituating them to good works.*[10]

Reply Obj. 2. It is not always through the perfect goodness of virtue that one obeys the law, but sometimes it is through fear of punishment, and sometimes from the mere dictate of reason, which is a beginning of virtue, as we have stated above.[11]

Reply Obj. 3. The goodness of any part is considered in its relation with the whole; and hence Augustine says that *unseemly is the part that harmonizes not with the whole to which it belongs.*[12] Since, then, every man is a part of the state, it is impossible that a man be good, unless he be well ordered to the common good, nor can the whole be well ordered unless its parts be proportioned to it. Consequently, the common good of the state cannot flourish, unless the citizens be virtuous, at least those whose business it is to govern. But it is enough for the good of the community that the other citizens be so far virtuous that they obey the commands of their rulers. Hence the Philosopher says that *the virtue of a sovereign is the same as that of a good man, but the virtue of any common citizen is not the same as that of a good man.*[13]

---

[8] *Polit.,* I, 5 (1260a 20).   [9] Q. 63, a. 2.   [10] Cf. *Eth.,* II, 1 (1103b 3).   [11] Q. 63, a. 1.   [12] *Confess.,* III, 8 (PL 32, 689).   [13] *Polit.,* III, 2 (1277a 20).

Reply Obj. 4. A tyrannical law, through not being according to reason, is not a law, absolutely speaking, but rather a perversion of law; and yet in so far as it is something in the nature of a law, its aim is that the citizens be good. For it has the nature of law only in so far as it is an ordinance made by a superior to his subjects, and aims at being obeyed by them; and this is to make them good, not absolutely, but with respect to that particular government.

Second Article

WHETHER THE ACTS OF LAW ARE SUITABLY ASSIGNED?

We proceed thus to the Second Article:—

Objection 1. It would seem that the acts of law are not suitably assigned as consisting in *command, prohibition, permission* and *punishment.*[14] For *every law is a general precept*, as the Jurist states.[15] But command and precept are the same. Therefore the other three are superfluous.

Obj. 2. Further, the effect of law is to induce its subjects to be good, as was stated above. But counsel aims at a higher good than a command does. Therefore it belongs to law to counsel rather than to command.

Obj. 3. Further, just as punishment stirs a man to good deeds, so does reward. Therefore, if to punish is reckoned an effect of law, so also is to reward.

Obj. 4. Further, the intention of a lawgiver is to make men good, as was stated above. But he that obeys the law merely through fear of being punished is not good; because, *although a good deed may be done through servile fear, i.e., fear of punishment, it is not done well*, as Augustine says.[16] Therefore punishment is not a proper effect of law.

On the contrary, Isidore says: *Every law either permits something, as: 'A brave man may demand his reward"*; or forbids something, as: *'No man may ask a consecrated virgin in marriage'*; or punishes, as: *'Let him that commits a murder be put to death.'*[17]

I answer that, Just as an enunciation is a dictate of reason as asserting something, so a law is a dictate of reason as commanding something. Now it is proper to reason to lead from one thing to another. Therefore, just as, in the demonstrative sciences, the reason leads us from certain principles to assent to the conclusion, so it induces us by some means to assent to the precept of the law.

Now the precepts of law are concerned with human acts, in which the law directs, as stated above.[18] But there are three kinds of human acts. For, as was stated above, some acts are good of their nature, viz., acts of

---

[14] Gratian, *Decretum*, I, iii, 4 (I, 5).—Cf. St. Isidore, *Etymol.*, V, 19 (PL 82, 202). [15] *Dig.*, I, iii. 1 (I, 33b). [16] *Contra duas Epist. Pelag.*, II, 9 (PL 44, 586). [17] *Etymol.*, V, 19 (PL 82, 202). [18] Q. 90, a. 1 and 2; q. 91, a. 4.

virtue,[19] and in respect of these the act of the law is a precept or command, for *the law commands all acts of virtue*.[20] Other acts are evil of their nature, viz., acts of vice, and in respect of these the law forbids. And other acts are, of their nature, indifferent, and in respect of these the law permits. (We may add that all acts that are either not distinctly good or not distinctly bad may be called indifferent.) Furthermore, it is the fear of punishment that law makes use of in order to ensure obedience; and in this respect punishment is an effect of law.

Reply Obj. 1. Just as to cease from evil is a kind of good, so a prohibition is a kind of precept; and, accordingly, taking precept in a wide sense, every law is regularly called a precept.

Reply Obj. 2. To advise is not a proper act of law, but may be within the competence even of a private person, who cannot make a law. Hence, the Apostle, after giving a certain counsel (*1 Cor.* vii. 12) says: *I speak, not the Lord*. Consequently, it is not reckoned as an effect of law.

Reply Obj. 3. To reward may also pertain to anyone, but to punish pertains to none but the administrator of the law, by whose authority the pain is inflicted. Therefore to reward is not reckoned an effect of law, but only to punish.

Reply Obj. 4. From becoming accustomed to avoid evil and fulfill what is good, through fear of punishment, one is sometimes led on to do so likewise with pleasure and of one's own accord. Accordingly, law, even by punishing, leads men on to being good.

[19] Q. 18, a. 8.   [20] Aristotle, *Eth.*, V, 1 (1129b 19).

THE ETERNAL LAW

(*In Six Articles*)

WE must now consider each law by itself: (1) the eternal law; (2) the natural law;[1] (3) the human law;[2] (4) the Old Law;[3] (5) the New Law, which is the law of the Gospel.[4] Of the sixth law, which is the law of the 'fomes,' what we have said when treating of original sin must suffice.[5] Concerning the first there are six points of inquiry: (1) What is the eternal law? (2) Whether it is known to all? (3) Whether every law is derived from it? (4) Whether necessary things are subject to the eternal law? (5) Whether natural contingents are subject to the eternal law? (6) Whether all human things are subject to it?

First Article

WHETHER THE ETERNAL LAW IS A SUPREME EXEMPLAR EXISTING IN GOD?

We proceed thus to the First Article:—

Objection 1. It would seem that the eternal law is not a supreme exemplar existing in God. For there is only one eternal law. But there are many exemplars of things in the divine mind, for Augustine says that God *made each thing according to its exemplar.*[6] Therefore the eternal law does not seem to be the same as an exemplar existing in the divine mind.

Obj. 2. Further, it is of the nature of a law that it be promulgated by word, as was stated above.[7] But *Word* is a Personal name in God, as was stated in the First Part,[8] whereas *exemplar* refers to the essence. Therefore the eternal law is not the same as a divine exemplar.

Obj. 3. Further, Augustine says: *We see a law above our minds, which is called truth.*[9] But the law which is above our minds is the eternal law. Therefore truth is the eternal law. But the notion of truth is not the same as the notion of an exemplar. Therefore the eternal law is not the same as the supreme exemplar.

On the contrary, Augustine says that *the eternal law is the supreme exemplar to which we must always conform.*[10]

---

[1] Q. 94. [2] Q. 95. [3] Q. 98. [4] Q. 106. [5] Q. 81, 82, 83. [6] *Lib. 83 Quaest.,* q. 46 (PL 40, 30). [7] Q. 90, a. 4; q. 91, a. 1, ad 2. [8] *S. T.,* I, q. 34, a. 1. [9] *De Vera Relig.,* XXX (PL 34, 147). [10] *De Lib. Arb.,* I, 6 (PL 32, 1229).

I answer that, Just as in every artificer there pre-exists an exemplar of the things that are made by his art, so too in every governor there must pre-exist the exemplar of the order of those things that are to be done by those who are subject to his government. And just as the exemplar of the things yet to be made by an art is called the art or model of the products of that art, so, too, the exemplar in him who governs the acts of his subjects bears the character of a law, provided the other conditions be present which we have mentioned above as belonging to the nature of law.[11] Now God, by His wisdom, is the Creator of all things, in relation to which He stands as the artificer to the products of his art, as was stated in the First Part.[12] Moreover, He governs all the acts and movements that are to be found in each single creature, as was also stated in the First Part.[13] Therefore, just as the exemplar of the divine wisdom, inasmuch as all things are created by it, has the character of an art, a model or an idea, so the exemplar of divine wisdom, as moving all things to their due end, bears the character of law. Accordingly, the eternal law is nothing else than the exemplar of divine wisdom, as directing all actions and movements.

Reply Obj. 1. Augustine is speaking in that passage of the ideal exemplars which refer to the proper nature of each single thing; and consequently in them there is a certain distinction and plurality, according to their different relations to things, as was stated in the First Part.[14] But law is said to direct human acts by ordaining them to the common good, as was stated above.[15] Now things which are in themselves diverse may be considered as one, according as they are ordained to something common. Therefore the eternal law is one since it is the exemplar of this order.

Reply Obj. 2. With regard to any sort of word, two points may be considered: viz., the word itself, and that which is expressed by the word. For the spoken word is something uttered by the mouth of man, and expresses that which is signified by the human word. The same applies to the human mental word, which is nothing else than something conceived by the mind, by which man expresses mentally the things of which he is thinking. So, too, in God, therefore, the Word conceived by the intellect of the Father is the name of a Person; but all things that are in the Father's knowledge, whether they refer to the essence or to the Persons, or to the works of God, are expressed by this Word, as Augustine declares.[16] But among other things expressed by this Word, the eternal law itself is expressed thereby. Nor does it follow that the eternal law is a Personal name in God. Nevertheless, it is appropriated to the Son, because of the suitability of *exemplar* to *word.*

Reply Obj. 3. The exemplars of the divine intellect do not stand in the same relation to things as do the exemplars of the human intellect. For the human intellect is measured by things, so that a human concept is not true

---

[11] Q. 90.   [12] *S. T.,* I, q. 14, a. 8.   [13] *S. T.,* I, q. 103, a. 5.   [14] *S. T.,* I, q. 15, a. 2.
[15] Q. 90, a. 2.   [16] *De Trin.,* XV, 14 (PL 42, 1076).

by reason of itself, but by reason of its being consonant with things, since *an opinion is true or false according as things are or are not.* But the divine intellect is the measure of things, since each thing has truth in it in so far as it is like the divine intellect, as was stated in the First Part.[17] Consequently the divine intellect is true in itself, and its exemplar is truth itself.

Second Article

WHETHER THE ETERNAL LAW IS KNOWN TO ALL?

We proceed thus to the Second Article:—

Objection 1. It would seem that the eternal law is not known to all. For, as the Apostle says (*1 Cor.* ii. 11), *the things that are of God no man knoweth, but the Spirit of God.* But the eternal law is an exemplar existing in the divine mind. Therefore it is unknown to all save God alone.

Obj. 2. Further, as Augustine says, *the eternal law is that by which it is right that all things should be most orderly.*[18] But all do not know how all things are most orderly. Therefore all do not know the eternal law.

Obj. 3. Further, Augustine says that *the eternal law is not subject to the judgment of man.*[19] But according to *Ethics* i., *any man can judge well of what he knows.*[20] Therefore the eternal law is not known to us.

On the contrary, Augustine says that *knowledge of the eternal law is imprinted on us.*[21]

I answer that, A thing may be known in two ways: first, in itself; secondly, in its effect, in which some likeness of that thing is found: *e.g.,* someone, not seeing the sun in its substance, may know it by its rays. Hence we must say that no one can know the eternal law as it is in itself, except God and the blessed who see God in His essence. But every rational creature knows it according to some reflection, greater or less. For every knowledge of truth is a kind of reflection and participation of the eternal law, which is the unchangeable truth, as Augustine says.[22] Now all men know the truth to a certain extent, at least as to the common principles of the natural law. As to the other truths, they partake of the knowledge of truth, some more, some less; and in this respect they know the eternal law in a greater or lesser degree.

Reply Obj. 1. We cannot know the things that are of God as they are in themselves; but they are made known to us in their effects, according to *Rom.* i. 20: *The invisible things of God . . . are clearly seen, being understood by the things that are made.*

Reply Obj. 2. Although each one knows the eternal law according to his own capacity, in the way explained above, yet none can comprehend it,

---

[17] *S. T.,* I, q. 16, a. 1.   [18] *De Lib. Arb.,* I, 6 (PL 32, 1229).   [19] *De Vera Relig.,* XXXI (PL 34, 148).   [20] Aristotle, *Eth.,* I, 3 (1094b 27).   [21] *De Lib. Arb.,* I, 6 (PL 32, 1229).   [22] *De Vera Relig.,* XXXI (PL 34, 147).

for it cannot be made perfectly known by its effects. Therefore it does not follow that anyone who knows the eternal law, in the aforesaid way, knows also the whole order of things whereby they are most orderly.

Reply Obj. 3. To judge of a thing may be understood in two ways. First, as when a cognitive power judges of its proper object, according to *Job* xii. 11: *Doth not the ear discern words, and the palate of him that eateth, the taste?* It is to this kind of judgment that the Philosopher alludes when he says that *anyone judges well of what he knows*,[23] by judging, namely, whether what is put forward is true. In another way, we speak of a superior judging of a subordinate by a kind of practical judgment, as to whether he should be such and such or not. And thus none can judge of the eternal law.

Third Article

WHETHER EVERY LAW IS DERIVED FROM THE ETERNAL LAW?

We proceed thus to the Third Article:—

Objection 1. It would seem that not every law is derived from the eternal law. For there is a law of the 'fomes,' as was stated above,[24] which is not derived from that divine law which is the eternal law, since to it pertains the *prudence of the flesh,* of which the Apostle says (*Rom.* viii. 7) that *it cannot be subject to the law of God.* Therefore, not every law is derived from the eternal law.

Obj. 2. Further, nothing unjust can be derived from the eternal law, because, as was stated above, *the eternal law is that according to which it is right that all things should be most orderly.* But some laws are unjust, according to *Isa.* x. 1: *Woe to them that make wicked laws.* Therefore, not every law is derived from the eternal law.

Obj. 3. Further, Augustine says that *the law which is framed for ruling the people rightly permits many things which are punished by the divine providence.*[25] But the exemplar of the divine providence is the eternal law, as was stated above. Therefore not even every good law is derived from the eternal law.

On the contrary, divine Wisdom says (*Prov.* viii. 15): *By Me kings reign, and lawgivers decree just things.* But the exemplar of divine Wisdom is the eternal law, as was stated above. Therefore all laws proceed from the eternal law.

I answer that, As was stated above, law denotes a kind of plan directing acts towards an end.[26] Now wherever there are movers ordained to one another, the power of the second mover must needs be derived from the power of the first mover, since the second mover does not move except in so far as it is moved by the first. Therefore we observe the same in all those

[23] *Eth.,* I, 3 (1094b 27).   [24] Q. 91, a. 6.   [25] *De Lib. Arb.,* I, 5 (PL 32, 1228).
[26] Q. 90, a. 1 and 2.

who govern, namely, that the plan of government is derived by secondary governors from the governor in chief. Thus the plan of what is to be done in a state flows from the king's command to his inferior administrators; and again in things of art the plan of whatever is to be done by art flows from the chief craftsman to the under-craftsmen who work with their hands. Since, then, the eternal law is the plan of government in the Chief Governor, all the plans of government in the inferior governors must be derived from the eternal law. But these plans of inferior governors are all the other laws which are in addition to the eternal law. Therefore all laws, in so far as they partake of right reason, are derived from the eternal law. Hence Augustine says that *in temporal law there is nothing just and lawful but what man has drawn from the eternal law*.[27]

Reply Obj. 1. The 'fomes' has the nature of law in man in so far as it is a punishment resulting from the divine justice; and in this respect it is evident that it is derived from the eternal law. But in so far as it denotes a proneness to sin, it is contrary to the divine law, and has not the nature of law, as was stated above.[28]

Reply Obj. 2. Human law has the nature of law in so far as it partakes of right reason; and it is clear that, in this respect, it is derived from the eternal law. But in so far as it deviates from reason, it is called an unjust law, and has the nature, not of law, but of violence. Nevertheless, even an unjust law, in so far as it retains some appearance of law, through being framed by one who is in power, is derived from the eternal law; for all power is from the Lord God, according to *Rom*. xiii. 1.

Reply Obj. 3. Human law is said to permit certain things, not as approving of them, but as being unable to direct them. And many things are directed by the divine law, which human law is unable to direct, because more things are subject to a higher than to a lower cause. Hence the very fact that human law does not concern itself with matters it cannot direct comes under the ordination of the eternal law. It would be different, were human law to sanction what the eternal law condemns. Consequently, it does not follow that human law is not derived from the eternal law; what follows is rather that it is not on a perfect equality with it.

Fourth Article

WHETHER NECESSARY AND ETERNAL THINGS ARE SUBJECT TO THE ETERNAL LAW?

We proceed thus to the Fourth Article:—

Objection 1. It would seem that necessary and eternal things are subject to the eternal law. For whatever is reasonable is subject to reason. But the divine will is reasonable, for it is just. Therefore it is subject to reason. But the eternal law is the divine reason. Therefore God's will is subject to the

[27] *De Lib. Arb.*. I, 6 (PL 32, 1229).   [28] Q. 91, a. 6.

eternal law. But God's will is something eternal. Therefore eternal and necessary things are subject to the eternal law.

Obj. 2. Further, whatever is subject to a king is subject to the king's law. Now the Son, according to *1 Cor.* xv. 28, 24, *shall be subject . . . to God and the Father, . . . when He shall have delivered up the Kingdom to Him.* Therefore the Son, Who is eternal, is subject to the eternal law.

Obj. 3. Further, the eternal law is the exemplar of the divine providence. But many necessary things are subject to the divine providence: for instance, the stability of incorporeal substances and of the heavenly bodies. Therefore even necessary things are subject to the eternal law.

On the contrary, Things that are necessary cannot be otherwise than they are, and consequently need no restraining. But laws are imposed on men in order to restrain them from evil, as was explained above.[29] Therefore necessary things are not subject to law.

I answer that, As we have stated above, the eternal law is the exemplar of the divine government. Consequently, whatever is subject to the divine government is subject to the eternal law; while if anything is not subject to the divine government, neither is it subject to the eternal law. The application of this distinction may be gathered by looking around us. For those things are subject to human government which can be done by man; but what pertains to the nature of man (for instance, that he should have a soul, hands, or feet) is not subject to human government. Accordingly, all that is in things created by God, whether it be contingent or necessary, is subject to the eternal law; while things pertaining to the divine nature or essence are not subject to the eternal law, but are the eternal law itself.

Reply Obj. 1. We may speak of God's will in two ways. First, as to the will itself, and thus, since God's will is His very essence, it is subject neither to the divine government, nor to the eternal law, but is the same thing as the eternal law. Secondly, we may speak of God's will with reference to the things themselves that God wills about creatures. Now these things are subject to the eternal law in so far as their exemplar is in the divine wisdom. In reference to these things, God's will is said to be reasonable [*rationalis*], though regarded in itself it should rather be called their exemplar [*ratio*].

Reply Obj. 2. God the Son was not made by God, but was naturally born of God. Consequently, He is not subject to the divine providence or to the eternal law, but rather is Himself the eternal law by a kind of appropriation, as Augustine explains.[30] But He is said to be subject to the Father by reason of His human nature, in respect of which likewise the Father is said to be greater than He (*Jo.* xiv. 28).

The third objection we grant, because it deals with those necessary things that are created.

[29] Q. 92, a. 2. [30] *De Vera Relig.,* XXXI (PL 34, 147).

Reply Obj. 4. As the Philosopher says, some necessary things have a cause of their necessity, and therefore they derive from something else the fact that they cannot be otherwise.[31] And this is in itself a most effective part of restraint, for whatever is restrained is said to be restrained in so far as it cannot do otherwise than it is allowed to.

Fifth Article

WHETHER NATURAL CONTINGENTS ARE SUBJECT TO THE
ETERNAL LAW?

We proceed thus to the Fifth Article:—

Objection 1. It would seem that natural contingents are not subject to the eternal law. For promulgation is part of the nature of law, as was stated above.[32] But a law cannot be promulgated except to rational creatures, to whom it is possible to make an announcement. Therefore none but rational creatures are subject to the eternal law, and consequently natural contingents are not.

Obj. 2. Further, *Whatever obeys reason partakes somewhat of reason,* as is stated in *Ethics* i.[33] But the eternal law is the supreme exemplar, as was stated above. Since, then, natural contingents do not partake of reason in any way, but are altogether without reason, it seems that they are not subject to the eternal law.

Obj. 3. Further, the eternal law is most efficient. But in natural contingents defects occur. Therefore they are not subject to the eternal law.

On the contrary, It is written (*Prov.* viii. 29): *When He compassed the sea with its bounds, and set a law to the waters, that they should not pass their limits.*

I answer that, We must speak otherwise of the law of man than of the eternal law which is the law of God. For the law of man extends only to rational creatures subject to man. The reason for this is because law directs the actions of those that are subject to the government of someone. Hence, properly speaking, none imposes a law on his own actions. Now whatever is done regarding the use of irrational things subject to man is done by the act of man himself moving those things; for such irrational creatures do not move themselves, but are moved by others, as was stated above.[34] Consequently man cannot impose laws on irrational beings, however much they may be subject to him. But he can impose laws on rational beings subject to him, in so far as, by his command or pronouncement of any kind, he imprints on their minds a rule which is a principle of action.

Now just as man, by such pronouncement, impresses a kind of inward principle of action on the man that is subject to him, so God imprints on the whole of nature the principles of its proper actions. And so it is in this

---

[31] *Metaph.*, IV, 5 (1015b 10).   [32] Q. 90, a 4.   [33] Aristotle, *Eth.*, I, 13 (1102b 25; b 13).   [34] Q. 1, a. 2.

way that God is said to command the whole of nature, according to *Ps.*
cxlviii. 6: *He hath made a decree, and it shall not pass away.* And thus
all actions and movements of the whole of nature are subject to the eternal
law. Consequently, irrational creatures are subject to the eternal law,
through being moved by the divine providence; but not, as rational creatures are, through understanding the divine commandment.

Reply Obj. 1. The impression of an inward active principle is to natural
things what the promulgation of law is to men; because law, by being promulgated, imprints on man a directive principle of human actions, as was
stated above.

Reply Obj. 2. Irrational creatures neither partake of nor are obedient to
human reason, whereas they do partake of the divine reason by obeying it;
for the power of the divine reason extends over more things than the
power of the human reason does. And as the members of the human body
are moved at the command of reason, and yet do not partake of reason,
since they have no apprehension subject to reason, so too irrational creatures
are moved by God, without, for that reason, being rational.

Reply Obj. 3. Although the defects which occur in natural things are outside the order of particular causes, they are not outside the order of universal causes, especially the order of the First Cause, *i.e.*, God, from Whose
providence nothing can escape, as was stated in the First Part.[35] And since
the eternal law is the exemplar of the divine providence, as was stated
above, hence it is that the defects of natural things are subject to the eternal
law.

Sixth Article

WHETHER ALL HUMAN AFFAIRS ARE SUBJECT TO THE ETERNAL LAW?

We proceed thus to the Sixth Article:—

Objection 1. It would seem that not all human affairs are subject to the
eternal law. For the Apostle says (*Gal.* v. 18): *If you are led by the spirit,
you are not under the law.* But the just, who are the sons of God by adoption, are led by the spirit of God, according to *Rom.* viii. 14: *Whosoever
are led by the Spirit of God, they are the sons of God.* Therefore not all
men are under the eternal law.

Obj. 2. Further, the Apostle says (*Rom.* viii. 7): *The prudence of the
flesh is an enemy to God, for it is not subject to the law of God.* But many
are those in whom the prudence of the flesh dominates. Therefore all men
are not subject to the eternal law, which is the law of God.

Obj. 3. Further, Augustine says that *the eternal law is that by which the
wicked deserve misery, the good, a life of blessedness.*[36] But those who

---

[35] *S. T.*, I, q. 22, a. 2.   [36] *De Lib. Arb.*, I, 6 (PL 32, 1229).

are already blessed, and those who are already lost, are not in the state of merit. Therefore they are not under the eternal law.

On the contrary, Augustine says: *Nothing evades the laws of the most high Creator and Governor, for by Him the peace of the universe is administered.*[37]

I answer that, There are two ways in which a thing is subject to the eternal law, as we have explained above: first, by partaking of the eternal law by way of knowledge; secondly, by way of action and passion, *i.e.*, by partaking of the eternal law by way of an inward moving principle. In this second way, irrational creatures are subject to the eternal law, as was stated above. But since the rational nature, along with that which it has in common with all creatures, has something proper to itself inasmuch as it is rational, consequently it is subject to the eternal law in both ways. For each rational creature both has some knowledge of the eternal law, as was stated above, and it also has a natural inclination to that which is in harmony with the eternal law; for *we are naturally adapted to be the recipients of virtue,* as it is said in *Ethics* ii.[38]

Both ways, however, are imperfect and to a certain extent destroyed in the wicked; because in them the natural inclination to virtue is corrupted by vicious habits, and, moreover, the natural knowledge of what is good is darkened in them by passions and habits of sin. But in the good, both ways are found more perfect, because in them, besides the natural knowledge of what is good, there is the added knowledge of faith and wisdom; and, again, besides the natural inclination to what is good, there is the added interior motive of grace and virtue.

Accordingly, the good are perfectly subject to the eternal law, as always acting according to it. But the wicked are subject to the eternal law, imperfectly as to their actions, since both their knowledge of what is good and their inclination thereto are imperfect; but this imperfection on the part of action is supplied on the part of passion, in so far as they suffer what the eternal law decrees concerning them, according as they fail to act in harmony with that law. Hence Augustine says: *I esteem that the just act according to the eternal law;*[39] and: *Out of the just misery of the souls which deserted Him, God knew how to furnish the inferior parts of His creation with most suitable laws.*[40]

Reply Obj. 1. This saying of the Apostle may be understood in two ways. First, so that a man is said to be under the law because he is unwillingly subject to the binding power of the law, much as though this were a great burden. Hence, on the same passage the *Gloss* says that *he is under the law who refrains from evil deeds through fear of the punishment threatened by the law, and not from love of virtue.*[41] The spiritual man is not under the

---

[37] *De Civit. Dei*, XIX, 12 (PL 41, 640).   [38] Aristotle, *Eth.*, II, 1 (1103a 25). [39] *De Lib. Arb.*, I, 15 (PL 32, 1238).   [40] *De Catech. Rud.*, XVIII (PL 40, 333). [41] Peter Lombard, *In Gal.*, super V, 18 (PL 192, 158).

law in this way, for he fulfills the law willingly through charity, which is poured into his heart by the Holy Ghost. Secondly, it can be understood as meaning that the works of a man, who is led by the Holy Ghost, are said to be the works of the Holy Ghost rather than his own. Therefore, since the Holy Ghost is not under the law, as neither is the Son, as we have stated above, it follows that such works, in so far as they are of the Holy Ghost, are not under the law. The Apostle witnesses to this when he says (*2 Cor.* iii. 17): *Where the Spirit of the Lord is, there is liberty.*

Reply Obj. 2. The prudence of the flesh cannot be subject to the law of God as regards action, since it inclines to actions contrary to the divine law; yet it is subject to the law of God as regards passion, since it deserves to suffer punishment according to the law of divine justice. Nevertheless, in no man does the prudence of the flesh dominate so far as to destroy the whole good of his nature; and consequently there remains in man the inclination to do the things which belong to the eternal law. For we have seen above that sin does not destroy entirely the good of nature.[42]

Reply Obj. 3. A thing is maintained in the end and moved towards the end by one and the same cause. Thus heaviness, which makes a heavy body rest in the lower place, is also the cause of its being moved thither. We therefore reply that, just as it is according to the eternal law that some deserve happiness, others unhappiness, so is it by the eternal law that some are maintained in a happy state, others in an unhappy state. Accordingly, both the blessed and the damned are under the eternal law.

[42] Q. 85, a. 2.

THE NATURAL LAW
(*In Six Articles*)

WE must now consider the natural law, concerning which there are six points of inquiry: (1) What is the natural law? (2) What are the precepts of the natural law? (3) Whether all the acts of the virtues are prescribed by the natural law? (4) Whether the natural law is the same in all? (5) Whether it is changeable? (6) Whether it can be abolished from the mind of man?

First Article

WHETHER THE NATURAL LAW IS A HABIT?

We proceed thus to the First Article:—

Objection 1. It would seem that the natural law is a habit. For, as the Philosopher says, *there are three things in the soul, power, habit and passion.*[1] But the natural law is not one of the soul's powers, nor is it one of the passions, as we may see by going through them one by one. Therefore the natural law is a habit.

Obj. 2. Further, Basil says that the *conscience or synderesis is the law of our mind;*[2] which can apply only to the natural law. But *synderesis* is a habit, as was shown in the First Part.[3] Therefore the natural law is a habit.

Obj. 3. Further, the natural law abides in man always, as will be shown further on. But man's reason, which the law regards, does not always think about the natural law. Therefore the natural law is not an act, but a habit.

On the contrary, Augustine says that *a habit is that whereby something is done when necessary.*[4] But such is not the natural law, since it is in infants and in the damned who cannot act by it. Therefore the natural law is not a habit.

I answer that, A thing may be called a habit in two ways. First, properly and essentially, and thus the natural law is not a habit. For it has been stated above that the natural law is something appointed by reason, just as a proposition is a work of reason.[5] Now that which a man does is not the same as that whereby he does it, for he makes a becoming speech by the habit of grammar. Since, then, a habit is that by which we act, a law cannot be a habit properly and essentially.

---

[1] *Eth.,* II, 5 (1105b 20). [2] Cf. *In Hexaëm.,* hom. VII (PG 29, 158); St. John Damascene, *De Fide Orth.,* IV, 22 (PG 94, 1200). [3] *S. T.,* I, q. 79, a. 12. [4] *De Bono Coniug.,* XXI (PL 40, 390). [5] Q. 90, a. 1, ad 2.

Secondly, the term habit may be applied to that which we hold by a habit. Thus *faith* may mean *that which we hold by faith*. Accordingly, since the precepts of the natural law are sometimes considered by reason actually, while sometimes they are in the reason only habitually, in this way the natural law may be called a habit. So, too, in speculative matters, the indemonstrable principles are not the habit itself whereby we hold these principles; they are rather the principles of which we possess the habit.

Reply Obj. 1. The Philosopher proposes there to discover the genus of virtue;[6] and since it is evident that virtue is a principle of action, he mentions only those things which are principles of human acts, viz., powers, habits and passions. But there are other things in the soul besides th se three: *e.g.,* acts, as *to will* is in the one that wills; again, there are things known in the knower; moreover its own natural properties are in the soul, such as immortality and the like.

Reply Obj. 2. *Synderesis* is said to be the law of our intellect because it is a habit containing the precepts of the natural law, which are the first principles of human actions.

Reply Obj. 3. This argument proves that the natural law is held habitually; and this is granted.

To the argument advanced in the contrary sense we reply that sometimes a man is unable to make use of that which is in him habitually, because of some impediment. Thus, because of sleep, a man is unable to use the habit of science. In like manner, through the deficiency of his age, a child cannot use the habit of the understanding of principles, or the natural law, which is in him habitually.

Second Article

WHETHER THE NATURAL LAW CONTAINS SEVERAL PRECEPTS,
OR ONLY ONE?

We proceed thus to the Second Article:—

Objection 1. It would seem that the natural law contains, not several precepts, but only one. For law is a kind of precept, as was stated above.[7] If therefore there were many precepts of the natural law, it would follow that there are also many natural laws.

Obj. 2. Further, the natural law is consequent upon human nature. But human nature, as a whole, is one, though, as to its parts, it is manifold. Therefore, either there is but one precept of the law of nature because of the unity of nature as a whole, or there are many by reason of the number of parts of human nature. The result would be that even things relating to the inclination of the concupiscible power would belong to the natural law.

Obj. 3. Further, law is something pertaining to reason, as was stated

[6] *Eth.,* II, 5 (1105b 20).   [7] Q. 92, a. 2.

above.[8] Now reason is but one in man. Therefore there is only one precept of the natural law.

On the contrary, The precepts of the natural law in man stand in relation to operable matters as first principles do to matters of demonstration. But there are several first indemonstrable principles. Therefore there are also several precepts of the natural law.

I answer that, As was stated above, the precepts of the natural law are to the practical reason what the first principles of demonstrations are to the speculative reason, because both are self-evident principles.[9] Now a thing is said to be self-evident in two ways: first, in itself; secondly, in relation to us. Any proposition is said to be self-evident in itself, if its predicate is contained in the notion of the subject; even though it may happen that to one who does not know the definition of the subject, such a proposition is not self-evident. For instance, this proposition, *Man is a rational being,* is, in its very nature, self-evident, since he who says *man,* says *a rational being;* and yet to one who does not know what a man is, this proposition is not self-evident. Hence it is that, as Boethius says,[10] certain axioms or propositions are universally self-evident to all; and such are the propositions whose terms are known to all, as, *Every whole is greater than its part,* and, *Things equal to one and the same are equal to one another.* But some propositions are self-evident only to the wise, who understand the meaning of the terms of such propositions. Thus to one who understands that an angel is not a body, it is self-evident that an angel is not circumscriptively in a place. But this is not evident to the unlearned, for they cannot grasp it.

Now a certain order is to be found in those things that are apprehended by men. For that which first falls under apprehension is *being,* the understanding of which is included in all things whatsoever a man apprehends. Therefore the first indemonstrable principle is that *the same thing cannot be affirmed and denied at the same time,* which is based on the notion of *being* and *not-being:* and on this principle all others are based, as is stated in *Metaph.* iv.[11] Now as *being* is the first thing that falls under the apprehension absolutely, so *good* is the first thing that falls under the apprehension of the practical reason, which is directed to action (since every agent acts for an end, which has the nature of good). Consequently, the first principle in the practical reason is one founded on the nature of good, viz., that *good is that which all things seek after.* Hence this is the first precept of law, that *good is to be done and promoted, and evil is to be avoided.* All other precepts of the natural law are based upon this; so that all the things which the practical reason naturally apprehends as man's good belong to the precepts of the natural law under the form of things to be done or avoided.

Since, however, good has the nature of an end, and evil, the nature of the

---

[8] Q. 90, a. 1.   [9] Q. 91, a. 3.   [10] *De Hebdom.* (PL 64, 1311).   [11] Aristotle, *Metaph.,* III, 3 (1005b 29).

contrary, hence it is that all those things to which man has a natural inclination are naturally apprehended by reason as being good, and consequently as objects of pursuit, and their contraries as evil, and objects of avoidance. Therefore, the order of the precepts of the natural law is according to the order of natural inclinations. For there is in man, first of all, an inclination to good in accordance with the nature which he has in common with all substances, inasmuch, namely, as every substance seeks the preservation of its own being, according to its nature; and by reason of this inclination, whatever is a means of preserving human life, and of warding off its obstacles, belongs to the natural law. Secondly, there is in man an inclination to things that pertain to him more specially, according to that nature which he has in common with other animals; and in virtue of this inclination, those things are said to belong to the natural law *which nature has taught to all animals*,[12] such as sexual intercourse, the education of offspring and so forth. Thirdly, there is in man an inclination to good according to the nature of his reason, which nature is proper to him. Thus man has a natural inclination to know the truth about God, and to live in society; and in this respect, whatever pertains to this inclination belongs to the natural law: *e.g.*, to shun ignorance, to avoid offending those among whom one has to live, and other such things regarding the above inclination.

Reply Obj. 1. All these precepts of the law of nature have the character of one natural law, inasmuch as they flow from one first precept.

Reply Obj. 2. All the inclinations of any parts whatsoever of human nature, *e.g.*, of the concupiscible and irascible parts, in so far as they are ruled by reason, belong to the natural law, and are reduced to one first precept, as was stated above. And thus the precepts of the natural law are many in themselves, but they are based on one common foundation.

Reply Obj. 3. Although reason is one in itself, yet it directs all things regarding man; so that whatever can be ruled by reason is contained under the law of reason.

Third Article

WHETHER ALL THE ACTS OF THE VIRTUES ARE PRESCRIBED BY THE NATURAL LAW?

We proceed thus to the Third Article:—

Objection 1. It would seem that not all the acts of the virtues are prescribed by the natural law. For, as was stated above, it is of the nature of law that it be ordained to the common good.[13] But some acts of the virtues are ordained to the private good of the individual, as is evident especially in regard to acts of temperance. Therefore, not all the acts of the virtues are the subject of natural law.

---

[12] *Dig.*, I, i, 1 (I, 29a).—Cf. O. Lottin, *Le droit naturel*, pp. 34, 78.   [13] Q. 90, a. 2.

Obj. 2. Further, every sin is opposed to some virtuous act. If therefore all the acts of the virtues are prescribed by the natural law, it seems to follow that all sins are against nature; whereas this applies to certain special sins.

Obj. 3. Further, those things which are according to nature are common to all. But the acts of the virtues are not common to all, since a thing is virtuous in one, and vicious in another. Therefore, not all the acts of the virtues are prescribed by the natural law.

On the contrary, Damascene says that *virtues are natural.*[14] Therefore virtuous acts also are subject to the natural law.

I answer that, We may speak of virtuous acts in two ways: first, in so far as they are virtuous; secondly, as such and such acts considered in their proper species. If, then, we are speaking of the acts of the virtues in so far as they are virtuous, thus all virtuous acts belong to the natural law. For it has been stated that to the natural law belongs everything to which a man is inclined according to his nature. Now each thing is inclined naturally to an operation that is suitable to it according to its form: *e.g.,* fire is inclined to give heat. Therefore, since the rational soul is the proper form of man, there is in every man a natural inclination to act according to reason; and this is to act according to virtue. Consequently, considered thus, all the acts of the virtues are prescribed by the natural law, since each one's reason naturally dictates to him to act virtuously. But if we speak of virtuous acts, considered in themselves, *i.e.,* in their proper species, thus not all virtuous acts are prescribed by the natural law. For many things are done virtuously, to which nature does not primarily incline, but which, through the inquiry of reason, have been found by men to be conducive to well-living.

Reply Obj. 1. Temperance is about the natural concupiscences of food, drink and sexual matters, which are indeed ordained to the common good of nature, just as other matters of law are ordained to the moral common good.

Reply Obj. 2. By human nature we may mean either that which is proper to man, and in this sense all sins, as being against reason, are also against nature, as Damascene states;[15] or we may mean that nature which is common to man and other animals, and in this sense, certain special sins are said to be against nature: *e.g.* contrary to sexual intercourse, which is natural to all animals, is unisexual lust, which has received the special name of the unnatural crime.

Reply Obj. 3. This argument considers acts in themselves. For it is owing to the various conditions of men that certain acts are virtuous for some, as being proportioned and becoming to them, while they are vicious for others, as not being proportioned to them.

---

[14] *De Fide Orth.,* III. 14 (PG 94, 1045).   [15] *Op. cit.,* II, 4; 30; IV, 20 (PG 94, 876; 976; 1196).

Fourth Article

WHETHER THE NATURAL LAW IS THE SAME IN ALL MEN?

We proceed thus to the Fourth Article:—

Objection 1. It would seem that the natural law is not the same in all. For it is stated in the *Decretals* that *the natural law is that which is contained in the Law and the Gospel.*[16] But this is not common to all men, because, as it is written (*Rom.* x. 16), *all do not obey the gospel.* Therefore the natural law is not the same in all men.

Obj. 2. Further, *Things which are according to the law are said to be just,* as is stated in *Ethics* v.[17] But it is stated in the same book that nothing is so just for all as not to be subject to change in regard to some men.[18] Therefore even the natural law is not the same in all men.

Obj. 3. Further, as was stated above, to the natural law belongs everything to which a man is inclined according to his nature. Now different men are naturally inclined to different things,—some to the desire of pleasures, others to the desire of honors, and other men to other things. Therefore, there is not one natural law for all.

On the contrary, Isidore says: *The natural law is common to all nations.*[19]

I answer that, As we have stated above, to the natural law belong those things to which a man is inclined naturally; and among these it is proper to man to be inclined to act according to reason. Now it belongs to the reason to proceed from what is common to what is proper, as is stated in *Physics* i.[20] The speculative reason, however, is differently situated, in this matter, from the practical reason. For, since the speculative reason is concerned chiefly with necessary things, which cannot be otherwise than they are, its proper conclusions, like the universal principles, contain the truth without fail. The practical reason, on the other hand, is concerned with contingent matters, which is the domain of human actions; and, consequently, although there is necessity in the common principles, the more we descend towards the particular, the more frequently we encounter defects. Accordingly, then, in speculative matters truth is the same in all men, both as to principles and as to conclusions; although the truth is not known to all as regards the conclusions, but only as regards the principles which are called *common notions.*[21] But in matters of action, truth or practical rectitude is not the same for all as to what is particular, but only as to the common principles; and where there is the same rectitude in relation to particulars, it is not equally known to all.

It is therefore evident that, as regards the common principles whether of speculative or of practical reason, truth or rectitude is the same for all, and is equally known by all. But as to the proper conclusions of the speculative

[16] Gratian, *Decretum*, I, i. prol. (I, 1).   [17] Aristotle, *Eth.*, V, 1 (1129b 12). [18] *Op. cit.*, V, 7 (1134b 32).   [19] *Etymol.*, V, 4 (PL 82, 199).   [20] Aristotle, *Phys.*, I, 1 (184a 16).   [21] Boethius, *De Hebdom.* (PL 64, 1311).

reason, the truth is the same for all, but it is not equally known to all. Thus, it is true for all that the three angles of a triangle are together equal to two right angles, although it is not known to all. But as to the proper conclusions of the practical reason, neither is the truth or rectitude the same for all, nor, where it is the same, is it equally known by all. Thus, it is right and true for all to act according to reason, and from this principle it follows, as a proper conclusion, that goods entrusted to another should be restored to their owner. Now this is true for the majority of cases. But it may happen in a particular case that it would be injurious, and therefore unreasonable, to restore goods held in trust; for instance, if they are claimed for the purpose of fighting against one's country. And this principle will be found to fail the more, according as we descend further towards the particular, *e.g.*, if one were to say that goods held in trust should be restored with such and such a guarantee, or in such and such a way; because the greater the number of conditions added, the greater the number of ways in which the principle may fail, so that it be not right to restore or not to restore.

Consequently, we must say that the natural law, as to the first common principles, is the same for all, both as to rectitude and as to knowledge. But as to certain more particular aspects, which are conclusions, as it were, of those common principles, it is the same for all in the majority of cases, both as to rectitude and as to knowledge; and yet in some few cases it may fail, both as to rectitude, by reason of certain obstacles (just as natures subject to generation and corruption fail in some few cases because of some obstacle), and as to knowledge, since in some the reason is perverted by passion, or evil habit, or an evil disposition of nature. Thus at one time theft, although it is expressly contrary to the natural law, was not considered wrong among the Germans, as Julius Cæsar relates.[22]

Reply Obj. 1. The meaning of the sentence quoted is not that whatever is contained in the Law and the Gospel belongs to the natural law, since they contain many things that are above nature; but that whatever belongs to the natural law is fully contained in them. Therefore Gratian, after saying that *the natural law is what is contained in the Law and the Gospel,* adds at once, by way of example, *by which everyone is commanded to do to others as he would be done by.*[23]

Reply Obj. 2. The saying of the Philosopher is to be understood of things that are naturally just, not as common principles, but as conclusions drawn from them, having rectitude in the majority of cases, but failing in a few.[24]

Reply Obj. 3: Just as in man reason rules and commands the other powers, so all the natural inclinations belonging to the other powers must needs be directed according to reason. Therefore it is universally right for all men that all their inclinations should be directed according to reason.

[22] Caesar, *De Bello Gallico,* VI, 23 (I, 348).   [23] *Decretum,* I, i, prol. (I, 1).
[24] *Eth.,* V, 1 (1129b 12).

Fifth Article

WHETHER THE NATURAL LAW CAN BE CHANGED?

We proceed thus to the Fifth Article:—

Objection 1. It would seem that the natural law can be changed. For on *Ecclus.* xvii. 9 (*He gave them instructions, and the law of life*) the *Gloss* says: *He wished the law of the letter tc be written, in order to correct the law of nature.*[25] But that which is corrected is changed. Therefore the natural law can be changed.

Obj. 2. Further, the slaying of the innocent, adultery and theft are against the natural law. But we find these things changed by God: as when God commanded Abraham to slay his innocent son (*Gen.* xxii. 2); and when He ordered the Jews to borrow and purloin the vessels of the Egyptians (*Exod.* xii. 35); and when He commanded Osee to take to himself *a wife of fornications* (*Osee* i. 2). Therefore the natural law can be changed.

Obj. 3. Further, Isidore says that *the possession of all things in common, and universal freedom, are matters of natural law.*[26] But these things are seen to be changed by human laws. Therefore it seems that the natural law is subject to change.

On the contrary, It is said in the *Decretals: The natural law dates from the creation of the rational creature. It does not vary according to time, but remains unchangeable.*[27]

I answer that, A change in the natural law may be understood in two ways. First, by way of addition. In this sense, nothing hinders the natural law from being changed, since many things for the benefit of human life have been added over and above the natural law, both by the divine law and by human laws.

Secondly, a change in the natural law may be understood by way of subtraction, so that what previously was according to the natural law, ceases to be so. In this sense, the natural law is altogether unchangeable in its first principles. But in its secondary principles, which, as we have said, are certain detailed proximate conclusions drawn from the first principles, the natural law is not changed so that what it prescribes be not right in most cases. But it may be changed in some particular cases of rare occurrence, through some special causes hindering the observance of such precepts, as was stated above.

Reply Obj. 1. The written law is said to be given for the correction of the natural law, either because it supplies what was wanting to the natural law, or because the natural law was so perverted in the hearts of some men, as to certain matters, that they esteemed those things good which are naturally evil; which perversion stood in need of correction.

[25] *Glossa ordin.* (III, 403E).   [26] *Etymol.,* V, 4 (PL 82, 199).   [27] Gratian. *Decretum,* I, v, prol. (I, 7).

Reply Obj. 2. All men alike, both guilty and innocent, die the death of nature; which death of nature is inflicted by the power of God because of original sin, according to *1 Kings* ii. 6: *The Lord killeth and maketh alive.* Consequently, by the command of God, death can be inflicted on any man, guilty or innocent, without any injustice whatever.—In like manner, adultery is intercourse with another's wife; who is allotted to him by the law emanating from God. Consequently intercourse with any woman, by the command of God, is neither adultery nor fornication.—The same applies to theft, which is the taking of another's property. For whatever is taken by the command of God, to Whom all things belong, is not taken against the will of its owner, whereas it is in this that theft consists.—Nor is it only in human things that whatever is commanded by God is right; but also in natural things, whatever is done by God is, in some way, natural, as was stated in the First Part.[28]

Reply Obj. 3. A thing is said to belong to the natural law in two ways. First, because nature inclines thereto: *e.g.,* that one should not do harm to another. Secondly, because nature did not bring with it the contrary. Thus, we might say that for man to be naked is of the natural law, because nature did not give him clothes, but art invented them. In this sense, *the possession of all things in common and universal freedom* are said to be of the natural law, because, namely, the distinction of possessions and slavery were not brought in by nature, but devised by human reason for the benefit of human life. Accordingly, the law of nature was not changed in this respect, except by addition.

Sixth Article

WHETHER THE NATURAL LAW CAN BE ABOLISHED
FROM THE HEART OF MAN?

We proceed thus to the Sixth Article:—

Objection 1. It would seem that the natural law can be abolished from the heart of man. For on *Rom.* ii. 14 (*When the Gentiles who have not the law,* etc.) the *Gloss* says that *the law of justice, which sin had blotted out, is graven on the heart of man when he is restored by grace.*[29] But the law of justice is the law of nature. Therefore the law of nature can be blotted out.

Obj. 2. Further, the law of grace is more efficacious than the law of nature. But the law of grace is blotted out by sin. Much more, therefore, can the law of nature be blotted out.

Obj. 3. Further, that which is established by law is proposed as something just. But many things are enacted by men which are contrary to the law of nature. Therefore the law of nature can be abolished from the heart of man.

---

[28] *S. T.,* I, q. 105, a. 6, ad 1. [29] *Glossa ordin.* (VI, 7E); Peter Lombard, *In Rom.,* super II, 14 (PL 191, 1345).

On the contrary, Augustine says: *Thy law is written in the hearts of men, which iniquity itself effaces not.*[30] But the law which is written in men's hearts is the natural law. Therefore the natural law cannot be blotted out.

I answer that, As we have stated above, there belong to the natural law, first, certain most common precepts that are known to all; and secondly, certain secondary and more particular precepts, which are, as it were, conclusions following closely from first principles. As to the common principles, the natural law, in its universal meaning, cannot in any way be blotted out from men's hearts. But it is blotted out in the case of a particular action, in so far as reason is hindered from applying the common principle to the particular action because of concupiscence or some other passion, as was stated above.[31]—But as to the other, *i.e.,* the secondary precepts, the natural law can be blotted out from the human heart, either by evil persuasions, just as in speculative matters errors occur in respect of necessary conclusions; or by vicious customs and corrupt habits, as, among some men, theft, and even unnatural vices, as the Apostle states (*Rom.* i. 24), were not esteemed sinful.

Reply Obj. 1. Sin blots out the law of nature in particular cases, not universally, except perchance in regard to the secondary precepts of the natural law, in the way stated above.

Reply Obj. 2. Although grace is more efficacious than nature, yet nature is more essential to man, and therefore more enduring.

Reply Obj. 3. This argument is true of the secondary precepts of the natural law, against which some legislators have framed certain enactments which are unjust.

---

[30] *Confess.,* II, 4 (PL 32, 678).   [31] Q. 77, a. 2.

Question XCV

HUMAN LAW

(*In Four Articles*)

WE must now consider human law, and (1) concerning this law considered in itself; (2) its power;[1] (3) its mutability.[2] Under the first head there are four points of inquiry: (1) Its utility. (2) Its origin. (3) Its quality. (4) Its division.

First Article

WHETHER IT WAS USEFUL FOR LAWS TO BE FRAMED BY MEN?

We proceed thus to the First Article:—

Objection 1. It would seem that it was not useful for laws to be framed by men. For the purpose of every law is that man be made good thereby, as was stated above.[3] But men are more to be induced to be good willingly by means of admonitions, than against their will, by means of laws. Therefore there was no need to frame laws.

Obj. 2. Further, As the Philosopher says, *men have recourse to a judge as to animate justice.*[4] But animate justice is better than inanimate justice, which is contained in laws. Therefore it would have been better for the execution of justice to be entrusted to the decision of judges than to frame laws in addition.

Obj. 3. Further, every law is framed for the direction of human actions, as is evident from what has been stated above.[5] But since human actions are about singulars, which are infinite in number, matters pertaining to the direction of human actions cannot be taken into sufficient consideration except by a wise man, who looks into each one of them. Therefore it would have been better for human acts to be directed by the judgment of wise men, than by the framing of laws. Therefore there was no need of human laws.

On the contrary, Isidore says: *Laws were made that in fear thereof human audacity might be held in check, that innocence might be safeguarded in the midst of wickedness, and that the dread of punishment might prevent the wicked from doing harm.*[6] But these things are most necessary to mankind. Therefore it was necessary that human laws should be made.

[1] Q. 96.   [2] Q. 97.   [3] Q. 92, a. 1.   [4] *Eth.*, V, 4 (1132a 22).   [5] Q. 90, a. 1 and 2.
[6] *Etymol.*, V, 20 (PL 82, 202).

I answer that, As we have stated above, man has a natural aptitude for virtue; but the perfection of virtue must be acquired by man by means of some kind of training.[7] Thus we observe that a man is helped by diligence in his necessities, for instance, in food and clothing. Certain beginnings of these he has from nature, viz., his reason and his hands; but he has not the full complement, as other animals have, to whom nature has given sufficiently of clothing and food. Now it is difficult to see how man could suffice for himself in the matter of this training, since the perfection of virtue consists chiefly in withdrawing man from undue pleasures, to which above all man is inclined, and especially the young, who are more capable of being trained. Consequently a man needs to receive this training from another, whereby to arrive at the perfection of virtue. And as to those young people who are inclined to acts of virtue by their good natural disposition, or by custom, or rather by the gift of God, paternal training suffices, which is by admonitions. But since some are found to be dissolute and prone to vice, and not easily amenable to words, it was necessary for such to be restrained from evil by force and fear, in order that, at least, they might desist from evil-doing, and leave others in peace, and that they themselves, by being habituated in this way, might be brought to do willingly what hitherto they did from fear, and thus become virtuous. Now this kind of training, which compels through fear of punishment, is the discipline of laws. Therefore, in order that man might have peace and virtue, it was necessary for laws to be framed; for, as the Philosopher says, *as man is the most noble of animals if he be perfect in virtue, so he is the lowest of all, if he be severed from law and justice.*[8] For man can use his reason to devise means of satisfying his lusts and evil passions, which other animals are unable to do.

Reply Obj. 1. Men who are well disposed are led willingly to virtue by being admonished better than by coercion; but men whose disposition is evil are not led to virtue unless they are compelled.

Reply Obj. 2. As the Philosopher says, *it is better that all things be regulated by law, than left to be decided by judges.*[9] And this for three reasons. First, because it is easier to find a few wise men competent to frame right laws, than to find the many who would be necessary to judge rightly of each single case.—Secondly, because those who make laws consider long beforehand what laws to make, whereas judgment on each single case has to be pronounced as soon as it arises; and it is easier for man to see what is right, by taking many instances into consideration, than by considering one solitary instance.—Thirdly, because lawgivers judge universally and about future events, whereas those who sit in judgment judge of things present, towards which they are affected by love, hatred, or some kind of cupidity; and thus their judgment becomes perverted.

Since, then, the animated justice of the judge is not found in every man, and since it can be bent, therefore it was necessary, whenever possible, for

---

[7] Q. 63, a. 1; q. 94, a. 3.   [8] *Polit.*, I, 1 (1253a 31).   [9] *Rhetor.*, I, 1 (1354a 31).

the law to determine how to judge, and for very few matters to be left to the decision of men.

Reply Obj. 3. Certain individual facts which cannot be covered by the law *have necessarily to be committed to judges,* as the Philosopher says in the same passage: e.g., *concerning something that has happened or not happened,* and the like.[10]

Second Article

WHETHER EVERY HUMAN LAW IS DERIVED FROM THE NATURAL LAW?

We proceed thus to the Second Article:—

Objection 1. It would seem that not every human law is derived from the natural law. For the Philosopher says that *the legal just is that which originally was a matter of indifference.*[11] But those things which arise from the natural law are not matters of indifference. Therefore the enactments of human laws are not all derived from the natural law.

Obj. 2. Further, positive law is divided against natural law, as is stated by Isidore[12] and the Philosopher.[13] But those things which flow as conclusions from the common principles of the natural law belong to the natural law, as was stated above.[14] Therefore that which is established by human law is not derived from the natural law.

Obj. 3. Further, the law of nature is the same for all, since the Philosopher says that *the natural just is that which is equally valid everywhere.*[15] If therefore human laws were derived from the natural law, it would follow that they too are the same for all; which is clearly false.

Obj. 4. Further, it is possible to give a reason for things which are derived from the natural law. But *it is not possible to give the reason for all the legal enactments of the lawgivers,* as the Jurist says.[16] Therefore not all human laws are derived from the natural law.

On the contrary, Tully says: *Things which emanated from nature, and were approved by custom, were sanctioned by fear and reverence for the laws.*[17]

I answer that, As Augustine says, *that which is not just seems to be no law at all.*[18] Hence the force of a law depends on the extent of its justice. Now in human affairs a thing is said to be just from being right, according to the rule of reason. But the first rule of reason is the law of nature, as is clear from what has been stated above.[19] Consequently, every human law has just so much of the nature of law as it is derived from the law of nature. But if in any point it departs from the law of nature, it is no longer a law but a perversion of law.

---

[10] *Ibid.* (1354b 13).   [11] *Eth.,* V, 7 (1134b 20).   [12] *Etymol.,* V, 4 (PL 82, 199). [13] *Eth.,* V, 7 (1134b 18).   [14] Q. 94, a. 4.   [15] *Eth.,* V, 7 (1134b 19).   [16] *Dig.,* I, iii, 20 (I, 34a).   [17] *De Invent.,* II, 53 (p. 148b).   [18] *De Lib. Arb.,* I, 5 (PL 32, 1227). [19] Q. 91, a. 2, ad 2.

But it must be noted that something may be derived from the natural law in two ways: first, as a conclusion from principles; secondly, by way of a determination of certain common notions. The first way is like to that by which, in the sciences, demonstrated conclusions are drawn from the principles; while the second is likened to that whereby, in the arts, common forms are determined to some particular. Thus, the craftsman needs to determine the common form of a house to the shape of this or that particular house. Some things are therefore derived from the common principles of the natural law by way of conclusions: *e.g.*, that *one must not kill* may be derived as a conclusion from the principle that *one should do harm to no man;* while some are derived therefrom by way of determination: *e.g.*, the law of nature has it that the evil-doer should be punished, but that he be punished in this or that way is a determination of the law of nature.

Accordingly, both modes of derivation are found in the human law. But those things which are derived in the first way are contained in human law, not as emanating therefrom exclusively, but as having some force from the natural law also. But those things which are derived in the second way have no other force than that of human law.

Reply Obj. 1. The Philosopher is speaking of those enactments which are by way of determination or specification of the precepts of the natural law.

Reply Obj. 2. This argument holds for those things that are derived from the natural law by way of conclusion.

Reply Obj. 3. The common principles of the natural law cannot be applied to all men in the same way because of the great variety of human affairs; and hence arises the diversity of positive laws among various people.

Reply Obj. 4. These words of the Jurist are to be understood as referring to the decisions of rulers in determining particular points of the natural law; and to these determinations the judgment of expert and prudent men is related as to its principles, in so far, namely, as they see at once what is the best thing to decide. Hence the Philosopher says that, in such matters. *we ought to pay as much attention to the undemonstrated sayings and opinions of persons who surpass us in experience, age and prudence, as to their demonstrations.*[20]

Third Article

WHETHER ISIDORE'S DESCRIPTION OF THE QUALITY OF POSITIVE LAW IS APPROPRIATE?

We proceed thus to the Third Article:—

Objection 1. It would seem that Isidore's description of the quality of positive law is not appropriate, when he says: *Law shall be virtuous, just, possible to nature, according to the custom of the country, suitable to place and time, necessary, useful; clearly expressed, lest by its obscurity it lead*

---

[20] *Eth.*, VI, 11 (1143b 11).

to misunderstanding; framed for no private benefit, but for the common good.[21] For he had previously expressed the quality of law in three conditions, saying that *law is anything founded on reason, provided that it foster religion, be helpful to discipline, and further the common welfare.*[22] Therefore it was needless to add any further conditions to these.

Obj. 2. Further, Justice is included in virtue [*honestas*], as Tully says.[23] Therefore, after saying *virtuous,* it was superfluous to add *just.*

Obj. 3. Further, written law is co-divided against custom, according to Isidore.[24] Therefore it should not be stated in the definition of law that it is *according to the custom of the country.*

Obj. 4. Further, a thing may be necessary in two ways. It may be necessary absolutely, because it cannot be otherwise; and that which is necessary in this way is not subject to human judgment. Hence human law is not concerned with necessity of this kind. Again, a thing may be necessary for an end, and this necessity is the same as usefulness. Therefore it is superfluous to say both *necessary* and *useful.*

On the contrary stands the authority of Isidore.

I answer that, Whenever a thing is for an end, its form must be determined proportionately to that end; as the form of a saw is such as to be suitable for cutting.[25] Again, everything that is ruled and measured must have a form proportioned to its rule and measure. Now both these conditions are verified in human law, since it is both something ordained to an end, and it is also a rule or measure ruled or measured by a higher measure. Now this higher measure is twofold, viz., the divine law and the natural law, as was explained above.[26] But the end of human law is to be useful to man, as the Jurist states.[27] Therefore Isidore, in determining the nature of law, first lays down three conditions; viz., that it *foster religion,* inasmuch as it is proportioned to the divine law; that it be *helpful to discipline,* inasmuch as it is proportioned to the natural law; and that it *further the common welfare,* inasmuch as it is proportioned to the utility of mankind.

All the other conditions mentioned by him are reduced to these three. For it is called virtuous because it fosters religion. And when he goes on to say that it should be *just, possible to nature, according to the customs of the country, adapted to place and time,* he implies that it should be suitable to discipline. For human discipline depends, first, on the order of reason, to which he refers by saying *just.* Secondly, it depends on the ability of the agent, because discipline should be adapted to each one according to his ability, taking also into account the ability of nature (for the same burdens should not be laid on children as on adults); and it should be according to human customs, since man cannot live alone in society, paying no heed to others. Thirdly, it depends on certain circumstances, in respect

[21] *Etymol.,* V, 21 (PL 82, 203).   [22] *Op. cit.,* V, 3 (PL 82, 199).   [23] *De Off.,* I, 7 (p. 11).   [24] *Etymol.,* II, 10; V, 3 (PL 82, 131; 199).   [25] Aristotle, *Phys.,* II, 9 (200a 10; b 5).   [26] A. 2; q. 93, a. 3.   [27] *Dig.,* I, iii, 25 (I, 34b).

of which he says, *adapted to place and time.* The remaining words, *necessary, useful,* etc., mean that law should further the common welfare: so that *necessity* refers to the removal of evils, *usefulness,* to the attainment of good, *clearness of expression,* to the need of preventing any harm ensuing from the law itself. And since, as was stated above, law is ordained to the common good,[28] this is expressed in the last part of the description.

This suffices for the Replies to the Objections.

Fourth Article

WHETHER ISIDORE'S DIVISION OF HUMAN LAWS IS APPROPRIATE?

We proceed thus to the Fourth Article:—

Objection 1. It would seem that Isidore divided human statutes or human law wrongly. For under this law he includes the *law of nations,* so called, because, as he says, *nearly all nations use it.*[29] But, as he says, *natural law is that which is common to all nations.*[30] Therefore the law of nations is not contained under positive human law, but rather under natural law.

Obj. 2. Further, those laws which have the same force seem to differ, not formally, but only materially. But *statutes, decrees of the commonalty, senatorial decrees,* and the like which he mentions,[31] all have the same force. Therefore they do not differ, except materially. But art takes no notice of such a distinction, since it may go on to infinity. Therefore this division of human laws is not appropriate.

Obj. 3. Further, just as, in the state, there are princes, priests and soldiers, so there are other human offices. Therefore it seems that, as this division includes *military law,* and *public law,*[32] referring to priests and magistrates, so also it should include other laws pertaining to other offices of the state.

Obj. 4. Further, those things that are accidental should be passed over. But it is accidental to law that it be framed by this or that man. Therefore it is unreasonable to divide laws according to the names of lawgivers, so that one be called the *Cornelian* law, another the *Falcidian* law, etc.[33]

On the contrary, The authority of Isidore suffices.

I answer that, A thing can be divided essentially in respect of something contained in the notion of that thing. Thus a soul, either rational or irrational, is contained in the notion of animal; and therefore animal is divided properly and essentially in respect of its being rational or irrational, but not in the point of its being white or black, which are entirely outside the notion of animal. Now, in the notion of human law, many things are con-

---

[28] Q. 90, a. 2.   [29] *Etymol.,* V, 6 (PL 82, 200).   [30] *Op. cit.,* V, 4 (PL 82, 199). [31] *Op. cit.,* V, 9 (PL 82, 200).   [32] *Op. cit.,* V, 7; 8 (PL 82, 200).   [33] *Op. cit.,* V, 15 (PL 82, 201).

tained, in respect of any of which human law can be divided properly and essentially. For, in the first place, it belongs to the notion of human law to be derived from the law of nature, as was explained above. In this respect positive law is divided into the *law of nations* and *civil law*, according to the two ways in which something may be derived from the law of nature, as was stated above. For to the law of nations belong those things which are derived from the law of nature as conclusions from principles, *e.g.*, just buyings and sellings, and the like, without which men cannot live together; and this belongs to the law of nature, since man is by nature a social animal, as is proved in *Politics* i.[34] But those things which are derived from the law of nature by way of particular determination belong to the civil law, according as each state decides on what is best for itself.

Secondly, it belongs to the notion of human law to be ordained to the common good of the state. In this respect, human law may be divided according to the different kinds of men who work in a special way for the common good: *e.g.*, priests, by praying to God for the people; princes, by governing the people; soldiers, by fighting for the safety of the people. Therefore certain special kinds of law are adapted to these men.

Thirdly, it belongs to the notion of human law to be framed by the one who governs the community of the state, as was shown above.[35] In this respect, there are various human laws according to the various forms of government. Of these, according to the Philosopher,[36] one is *monarchy*, *i.e.*, when the state is governed by one; and then we have *Royal Ordinances*. Another form is *aristocracy*, *i.e.*, government by the best men or men of highest rank; and then we have the *Authoritative legal opinions* [*Responsa Prudentum*] and *Decrees of the Senate* [*Senatus consulta*]. Another form is *oligarchy*, *i.e.*, government by a few rich and powerful men; and then we have *Prætorian*, also called *Honorary*, law. Another form of government is that of the people, which is called democracy, and there we have *Decrees of the commonalty* [*Plebiscita*]. There is also tyrannical government, which is altogether corrupt, which, therefore, has no corresponding law. Finally, there is a form of government made up of all these, and which is the best; and in this respect we have *law sanctioned by the Lords and Commons*, as is stated by Isidore.[37]

Fourthly, it belongs to the notion of human law to direct human actions. In this respect, according to the various matters of which the law treats, there are various kinds of laws, which are sometimes named after their authors. Thus we have the *Lex Julia* about adultery,[38] the *Lex Cornelia* concerning assassins,[39] and so on, differentiated in this way, not because of the authors, but because of the matters to which they refer.

Reply Obj. 1. The law of nations is indeed, in some way, natural to man,

---

[34] Aristotle, *Polit.*, I, 1 (1253a 2).   [35] Q. 90, a. 3.   [36] *Polit.*, III, 7 (1279a 26). [37] *Etymol.*, V, 10; II, 10 (PL 82, 200; 130).   [38] *Dig.*, XLVIII, v (I, 845a).   [39] *Op. cit.*, XLVIII, viii (I, 852b).

in so far as he is a reasonable being, because it is derived from the natural law by way of a conclusion that is not very remote from its principles. Therefore men easily agreed thereto. Nevertheless, it is distinct from the natural law, especially from that natural law which is common to all animals.

The Replies to the other Objections are evident from what has been said.

ON THE POWER OF HUMAN LAW

(In Six Articles)

We must now consider the power of human law. Under this head there are six points of inquiry: (1) Whether human law should be framed in a common way? (2) Whether human law should repress all vices? (3) Whether human law is competent to direct the acts of all the virtues? (4) Whether it binds man in conscience? (5) Whether all men are subject to human law? (6) Whether those who are under the law may act outside the letter of the law?

First Article

WHETHER HUMAN LAW SHOULD BE FRAMED IN A COMMON WAY RATHER THAN IN THE PARTICULAR?

We proceed thus to the First Article:—

Objection 1. It would seem that human law should be framed, not in a common way, but rather in the particular. For the Philosopher says that *the legal just . . . includes all particular acts of legislation . . . and all those matters which are the subject of decrees,*[1] which are also individual matters, since decrees are framed about individual actions. Therefore law is framed not only in a common way, but also in the particular.

Obj. 2. Further, law is the director of human acts, as was stated above.[2] But human acts are about individual matters. Therefore human laws should be framed, not in a common way, but rather in the particular.

Obj. 3. Further, law is a rule and measure of human acts, as was stated above.[3] But a measure should be most certain, as is stated in *Metaph.* x.[4] Since, therefore, in human acts no universal proposition can be so certain as not to fail in some individual cases, it seems that laws should be framed, not in a common way, but in the particular.

On the contrary, The Jurist says that *laws should be made to suit the majority of instances; and they are not framed according to what may possibly happen in an individual case.*[5]

I answer that, Whatever is for an end should be proportioned to that end. Now the end of law is the common good, because, as Isidore says, *law should be framed, not for any private benefit, but for the common good of*

---

[1] *Eth.,* V, 7 (1134b 23).   [2] Q. 90, a. 1 and 2.   [3] *Ibid.*   [4] Aristotle, *Metaph.,* IX, 1 (1053a 1).   [5] *Dig.,* I, iii, 3; 4 (I, 34a).

all the citizens.[6] Hence human laws should be proportioned to the common good. Now the common good comprises many things. Therefore law should take account of many things, as to persons, as to matters, and as to times. For the community of the state is composed of many persons, and its good is procured by many actions; nor is it established to endure for only a short time, but to last for all time by the citizens succeeding one another, as Augustine says.[7]

Reply Obj. 1. The Philosopher divides the legal just, *i.e.,* positive law, into three parts.[8] For some things are laid down absolutely in a common way, and these are the common laws. Of these he says that *the legal is that which originally was a matter of indifference, but which, when enacted, is so no longer: e.g.,* the fixing of the ransom of a captive.—Some things affect the community in one respect, and individuals in another. These are called *privileges, i.e., private laws,*[9] as it were, because they regard private persons, although their power extends to many matters; and in regard to these, he adds, *and further, all particular acts of legislation.*—Other matters are legal, not through being laws, but through being applications of common laws to particular cases. Such are decrees which have the force of law; and in regard to these he adds, *all matters subject to decrees.*

Reply Obj. 2. A principle of direction should be applicable to many. Hence the Philosopher says that all things belonging to one genus are measured by one, which is the principle in that genus.[10] For if there were as many rules or measures as there are things measured or ruled, they would cease to be of use, since their use consists in being applicable to many things. Hence law would be of no use, if it did not extend further than to one single act. For the decrees of prudent men are made for the purpose of directing individual actions, whereas law is a *common precept,* as was stated above.[11]

Reply Obj. 3. *We must not seek the same degree of certainty in all things.*[12] Consequently, in contingent matters, such as natural and human things, it is enough for a thing to be certain, as being true in the greater number of instances, though at times, and less frequently, it fail.

Second Article

WHETHER IT BELONGS TO HUMAN LAW TO REPRESS ALL VICES?

We proceed thus to the Second Article:—

Objection 1. It would seem that it belongs to human law to repress all vices. For Isidore says that *laws were made in order that, in fear thereof,*

---

[6] *Etymol.,* II, 10; V, 21 (PL 82, 131; 203).   [7] *De Civit. Dei,* XXII, 6 (PL 41, 759).
[8] *Eth.,* V, 7 (1134b 20).   [9] Cf. Gratian, *Decretum,* I, iii, 3 (I, 5); St. Isidore, *Etymol.,* V, 18 (PL 82, 202).   [10] *Metaph.,* IX, 1 (1052b 18).   [11] Q. 92, a. 2, obj. 1.
[12] Aristotle, *Eth.,* I, 3 (1094b 13).

man's audacity might be held in check.[13] But it would not be held in check sufficiently unless all evils were repressed by law. Therefore human law should repress all evils.

Obj. 2. Further, the intention of the lawgiver is to make the citizens virtuous. But a man cannot be virtuous unless he forbear from all kinds of vice. Therefore it belongs to human law to repress all vices.

Obj. 3. Further, human law is derived from the natural law, as was stated above.[14] But all vices are contrary to the law of nature. Therefore human law should repress all vices.

On the contrary, We read in *De Libero Arbitrio,* i: *It seems to me that the law which is written for the governing of the people rightly permits these things, and that divine providence punishes them.*[15] But divine providence punishes nothing but vices. Therefore human law rightly allows some vices, by not repressing them.

I answer that, As was stated above, law is framed as a rule or measure of human acts.[16] Now a measure should be homogeneous with that which it measures, as is stated in *Metaph.* x.,[17] since different things are measured by different measures. Therefore laws imposed on men should also be in keeping with their condition, for, as Isidore says, law should be *possible both according to nature, and according to the customs of the country.*[18] Now the ability or facility of action is due to an interior habit or disposition, since the same thing is not possible to one who has not a virtuous habit, as is possible to one who has. Thus the same thing is not possible to a child as to a full-grown man, and for which reason the law for children is not the same as for adults, since many things are permitted to children, which in an adult are punished by law or at any rate are open to blame. In like manner, many things are permissible to men not perfect in virtue, which would be intolerable in a virtuous man.

Now human law is framed for the multitude of human beings, the majority of whom are not perfect in virtue. Therefore human laws do not forbid all vices, from which the virtuous abstain, but only the more grievous vices, from which it is possible for the majority to abstain; and chiefly those that are injurious to others, without the prohibition of which human society could not be maintained. Thus human law prohibits murder, theft and the like.

Reply Obj. 1. Audacity seems to refer to the assailing of others. Consequently, it belongs to those sins chiefly whereby one's neighbor is injured. These sins are forbidden by human law, as was stated.

Reply Obj. 2. The purpose of human law is to lead men to virtue, not suddenly, but gradually. Therefore it does not lay upon the multitude of imperfect men the burdens of those who are already virtuous, viz., that

---

[13] *Etymol.,* V, 20 (PL 82, 202). Q. 95, a. 2. [15] St. Augustine, *De Lib. Arb.,* I, 5 (PL 32, 1228). [16] Q. 90, a. 1 and 2. [17] Aristotle, *Metaph.,* IX, 1 (1053a 24). [18] *Etymol.,* II, 10; V, 21 (PL 82, 131, 203).

they should abstain from all evil. Otherwise these imperfect ones, being unable to bear such precepts, would break out into yet greater evils. As it is written (*Prov.* xxx. 33): *He that violently bloweth his nose, bringeth out blood*; again (*Matt.* ix. 17): if *new wine, i.e.*, precepts of a perfect life, is *put into old bottles, i.e.*, into imperfect men, *the bottles break, and the wine runneth out, i.e.*, the precepts are despised, and those men, from contempt, break out into evils worse still.

Reply Obj. 3. The natural law is a participation in us of the eternal law, while human law falls short of the eternal law. For Augustine says: *The law which is framed for the government of states allows and leaves unpunished many things that are punished by divine providence. Nor, if this law does not attempt to do everything, is this a reason why it should be blamed for what it does.*[19] Therefore, human law likewise does not prohibit everything that is forbidden by the natural law.

Third Article

WHETHER HUMAN LAW PRESCRIBES THE ACTS OF ALL THE VIRTUES?

We proceed thus to the Third Article:—

Objection 1. It would seem that human law does not prescribe the acts of all the virtues. For vicious acts are contrary to acts of virtue. But human law does not prohibit all vices, as was stated above. Therefore neither does it prescribe all acts of virtue.

Obj. 2. Further, a virtuous act proceeds from a virtue. But virtue is the end of law, so that whatever is from a virtue cannot come under a precept of law. Therefore human law does not prescribe all acts of virtue.

Obj. 3. Further, law is ordained to the common good, as was stated above.[20] But some acts of virtue are ordained, not to the common good, but to private good. Therefore law does not prescribe all acts of virtue.

On the contrary, The Philosopher says that law *prescribes the performance of the acts of a brave man, . . . and the acts of the temperate man, . . . and the acts of the meek man; and in like manner as regards the other virtues and vices, prescribing the former, forbidding the latter.*[21]

I answer that, The species of virtues are distinguished by their objects, as was explained above.[22] Now all the objects of the virtues can be referred either to the private good of an individual, or to the common good of the multitude. Thus, matters of fortitude may be achieved either for the safety of the state, or for upholding the rights of a friend; and in like manner with the other virtues. But law, as was stated above, is ordained to the common good.[23] Therefore, there is no virtue whose acts cannot be prescribed by the law. Nevertheless, human law does not prescribe concern-

---

[19] *De Lib. Arb.,* I, 5 (PL 32, 1228).   [20] Q. 90, a. 2.   [21] *Eth.,* V, 1 (1129b 19).
[22] Q. 54, a. 2; q. 60, a. 1; q. 62, a. 2.   [23] Q. 90, a. 2.

ing all the acts of every virtue, but only in regard to those that are ordainable to the common good,—either immediately, as when certain things are done directly for the common good,—or mediately, as when a lawgiver prescribes certain things pertaining to good order, whereby the citizens are directed in the upholding of the common good of justice and peace.

Reply Obj. 1. Human law does not forbid all vicious acts, by the obligation of a precept, as neither does it prescribe all acts of virtue. But it forbids certain acts of each vice, just as it prescribes some acts of each virtue.

Reply Obj. 2. An act is said to be an act of virtue in two ways. First, from the fact that a man does something virtuous; and thus the act of justice is to do what is right, and an act of fortitude is to do brave things. In this way law prescribes certain acts of virtue.—Secondly, an act of virtue is so called when a man does a virtuous thing in a way in which a virtuous man does it. Such an act always proceeds from virtue. Nor does it come under a precept of law, but is the end at which every lawgiver aims.

Reply Obj. 3. There is no virtue whose act is not ordainable to the common good, as was stated above, either mediately or immediately.

Fourth Article

WHETHER HUMAN LAW BINDS A MAN IN CONSCIENCE?

We proceed thus to the Fourth Article:—

Objection 1. It would seem that human law does not bind a man in conscience. For an inferior power cannot impose its law on the judgment of a higher power. But the power of man, which frames human law, is beneath the divine power. Therefore human law cannot impose its precept on a divine judgment, such as is the judgment of conscience.

Obj. 2. Further, the judgment of conscience depends chiefly on the commandments of God. But sometimes God's commandments are made void by human laws, according to *Matt.* xv. 6: *You have made void the commandment of God for your tradition.* Therefore human law does not bind a man in conscience.

Obj. 3. Further, human laws often bring loss of character and injury on man, according to *Isa.* x. 1, 2: *Woe to them that make wicked laws, and when they write, write injustice; to oppress the poor in judgment, and do violence to the cause of the humble of My people.* But it is lawful for anyone to avoid oppression and violence. Therefore human laws do not bind man in conscience.

On the contrary, It is written (*1 Pet.* ii. 19): *This is thanksworthy, if for conscience . . . a man endure sorrows, suffering wrongfully.*

I answer that, Laws framed by man are either just or unjust. If they be just, they have the power of binding in conscience from the eternal law whence they are derived, according to *Prov.* viii. 15: *By Me kings reign, and lawgivers decree just things.* Now laws are said to be just, both from the end (when, namely, they are ordained to the common good), from their author (that is to say, when the law that is made does not exceed the power of the lawgiver), and from their form (when, namely, burdens are laid on the subjects according to an equality of proportion and with a view to the common good). For, since one man is a part of the community, each man, in all that he is and has, belongs to the community; just as a part, in all that it is, belongs to the whole. So, too, nature inflicts a loss on the part in order to save the whole; so that for this reason such laws as these, which impose proportionate burdens, are just and binding in conscience, and are legal laws.

On the other hand, laws may be unjust in two ways: first, by being contrary to human good, through being opposed to the things mentioned above:—either in respect of the end, as when an authority imposes on his subjects burdensome laws, conducive, not to the common good, but rather to his own cupidity or vainglory; or in respect of the author, as when a man makes a law that goes beyond the power committed to him; or in respect of the form, as when burdens are imposed unequally on the community, although with a view to the common good. Such are acts of violence rather than laws, because, as Augustine says, *a law that is not just seems to be no law at all.*[24] Therefore, such laws do not bind in conscience, except perhaps in order to avoid scandal or disturbance, for which cause a man should even yield his right, according to *Matt.* v. 40, 41: *If a man . . . take away thy coat, let go thy cloak also unto him; and whosoever will force thee one mile, go with him other two.*

Secondly, laws may be unjust through being opposed to the divine good. Such are the laws of tyrants inducing to idolatry, or to anything else contrary to the divine law. Laws of this kind must in no way be observed, because, as is stated in *Acts* v. 29, *we ought to obey God rather than men.*

Reply Obj. 1. As the Apostle says (*Rom.* xiii. 1, 2), all human power is from God . . . *therefore he that resisteth the power,* in matters that are within its scope, *resisteth the ordinance of God;* so that he becomes guilty in conscience.

Reply Obj. 2. This argument is true of laws that are contrary to the commandments of God, which is beyond the scope of [human] power. Therefore in such matters human law should not be obeyed.

Reply Obj. 3. This argument is true of a law that inflicts an unjust burden on its subjects. Furthermore, the power that man holds from God does not extend to this. Hence neither in such matters is man bound to obey the law, provided he avoid giving scandal or inflicting a more grievous injury.

[24] *De Lib. Arb.,* I, 5 (PL 32, 1227).

Fifth Article

WHETHER ALL ARE SUBJECT TO LAW?

We proceed thus to the Fifth Article:—

Objection 1. It would seem that not all are subject to the law. For those alone are subject to a law for whom a law is made. But the Apostle says (*1 Tim.* i. 9): *The law is not made for the just man.* Therefore the just are not subject to human law.

Obj. 2. Further, Pope Urban says (this is also found in the *Decretals*): *He that is guided by a private law need not for any reason be bound by the public law.*[25] Now all spiritual men are led by the private law of the Holy Ghost, for they are the sons of God, of whom it is said (*Rom.* viii. 14): *Whosoever are led by the Spirit of God, they are the sons of God.* Therefore not all men are subject to human law.

Obj. 3. Further, the Jurist says that *the sovereign is exempt from the laws.*[26] But he that is exempt from the law is not bound thereby. Therefore not all are subject to law.

On the contrary, The Apostle says (*Rom.* xiii. 1): *Let every soul be subject to the higher powers.* But subjection to a power seems to imply subjection to the laws framed by that power. Therefore all men should be subject to law.

I answer that, As was stated above, the notion of law contains two things: first, that it is a rule of human acts; secondly, that it has coercive power.[27] Therefore a man may be subject to law in two ways. First, as the regulated is subject to the regulator; and whoever is subject to a power in this way is subject to the law framed by that power. But it may happen in two ways that one is not subject to a power. In one way, by being altogether free from its authority. And so it happens that the subjects of one city or kingdom are not bound by the laws of the sovereign of another city or kingdom, since they are not subject to his authority. In another way, by being under a yet higher law. Thus the subject of a proconsul should be ruled by his command, but not in those matters in which the subject receives his orders from the emperor; for in these matters he is not bound by the mandate of the lower authority, since he is directed by that of a higher. In this way, one who is subject absolutely to a law may not be subject thereto in certain matters, in respect of which he is ruled by a higher law.

Secondly, a man is said to be subject to a law as the coerced is subject to the coercer. In this way the virtuous and righteous are not subject to law, but only the wicked. For coercion and violence are contrary to the will; but the will of the good is in harmony with law, whereas the will of the wicked is discordant from it. Therefore in this sense the good are not subject to law, but only the wicked.

[25] Gratian, *Decretum*, II, xix, q. 2, can. 2 (I, 840).   [26] *Dig.*, I, iii. 31 (I, 34b).
[27] Q. 90, a. 1 and 2; a. 3, ad 2.

Reply Obj. 1. This argument is true of subjection by way of coercion, for, in this way, *the law is not made for the just men,* because *they are a law to themselves,* since they *show the work of the law written in their hearts,* as the Apostle says (*Rom.* ii. 14, 15). Consequently law does not coerce them in the way that it does the wicked.

Reply Obj. 2. The law of the Holy Ghost is above all law framed by man, and therefore spiritual men, in so far as they are led by the law of the Holy Ghost, are not subject to the law in those matters that are inconsistent with the guidance of the Holy Ghost. Nevertheless, it is an effect of the guidance of the Holy Ghost that spiritual men are subject to human laws, according to *1 Pet.* ii. 13: *Be ye subject . . . to every human creature for God's sake.*

Reply Obj. 3. The sovereign is said to be *exempt from the law,* as to its coercive power, since, properly speaking, no man is coerced by himself, and law has no coercive power save from the authority of the sovereign. Thus is the sovereign said to be exempt from the law because none is competent to pass sentence on him, if he acts against the law. Therefore on *Ps.* l. 6 (*To Thee only have I sinned*) the *Gloss* says that *there is no man who can judge the deeds of a king.*[28] But as to the directive force of law, the sovereign is subject to the law by his own will, according to the statement that *whatever law a man makes for another, he should keep himself.*[29] And the authority of a wise man says: *Obey the law that thou makest thyself.*[30] Moreover the Lord reproaches those who *say and do not;* and who *bind heavy burdens and lay them on men's shoulders, but with a finger of their own they will not move them* (*Matt.* xxiii. 3, 4). Hence, in the judgment of God, the sovereign is not exempt from the law, as to its directive force; but he should fulfill it voluntarily, and not of constraint. Again, the sovereign is above the law, in so far as, when it is expedient, he can change the law, and rule within it according to time and place.

Sixth Article

WHETHER HE WHO IS UNDER A LAW MAY ACT OUTSIDE
THE LETTER OF THE LAW?

We proceed thus to the Sixth Article:—

Objection 1. It seems that he who is subject to a law may not act outside the letter of the law. For Augustine says: *Although men judge about temporal laws when they make them, yet when once they are made they must pass judgment, not on them, but according to them.*[31] But if anyone disregard the letter of the law, saying that he observes the intention of the

---

[28] Peter Lombard, *In Psalm.*, super. I, 6 (PL 191, 486).—Cf. *Glossa ordin.* (III, 157E). [29] *Decretal. Greg.* IX, I, ii, 6 (II, 8). [30] Pseudo-Ausonius, *Septem Sapientum Sententiae,* II, Pittacus (*Ausonius,* ed. H. G. E. White, New York: G. P. Putnam's Sons, 1921. vol. II, p. 272). [31] *De Vera Relig.*, XXXI (PL 34, 148).

lawgiver, he seems to pass judgment on the law. Therefore it is not right for one who is under a law to disregard the letter of the law, in order to observe the intention of the lawgiver.

Obj. 2. Further, he alone is competent to interpret the law who can make the law. But those who are subject to the law cannot make the law. Therefore they have no right to interpret the intention of the lawgiver, but should always act according to the letter of the law.

Obj. 3. Further, every wise man knows how to explain his intention by words. But those who framed the laws should be reckoned wise, for Wisdom says (*Prov.* viii. 15): *By Me kings reign, and lawgivers decree just things.* Therefore we should not judge of the intention of the lawgiver otherwise than by the words of the law.

On the contrary, Hilary says: *The meaning of what is said is according to the motive for saying it; because things are not subject to speech, but speech to things.*[32] Therefore we should take account of the motive of the lawgiver, rather than of his very words.

I answer that, As was stated above, every law is directed to the common welfare of men, and derives the force and nature of law accordingly; but in so far as it fails of this common welfare, it is without binding power. Hence the Jurist says: *By no reason of law, or favor of equity, is it allowable for us to interpret harshly, and render burdensome, those useful measures which have been enacted for the welfare of man.*[33] Now it often happens that the observance of some point of law conduces to the common welfare in the majority of instances, and yet, in some cases, is very injurious. Since, then, the lawgiver cannot have in view every single case, he shapes the law according to what happens most frequently, by directing his attention to the common good. Hence, if a case arise wherein the observance of that law would be injurious to the general welfare, it should not be observed. For instance, suppose that in a besieged city it be an established law that the gates of the city are to be kept closed, this is good for public welfare as a general rule; but if it were to happen that the enemy are in pursuit of certain citizens, who are defenders of the city, it would be a great calamity for the city if the gates were not opened to them; and so in that case the gates ought to be opened, contrary to the letter of the law, in order to maintain the common welfare, which the lawgiver had in view.

Nevertheless, it must be noted that if the observance of the law according to the letter does not involve any sudden risk, needing instant remedy, it is not permissible for everyone to expound what is useful and what is not useful to the state; rather those alone can do this who are in authority, and who, in the event of such cases, have the power to dispense from the laws. If, however, the peril be so sudden as not to allow the delay involved in referring the matter to authority, the necessity itself carries with it a dispensation, since necessity knows no law.

---

[32] *De Trin.,* IV (PL 10, 107).   [33] *Dig.,* I, iii, 25 (I, 34b).

Reply Obj. 1. He who in a case of necessity acts outside the letter of the law does not judge of the law; but he judges of a particular case in which he sees that the letter of the law is not to be observed.

Reply Obj. 2. He who follows the intention of the lawgiver does not interpret the law absolutely; but he interprets the law in a case in which it is evident, by reason of the manifest harm, that the lawgiver intended otherwise. For if it be a matter of doubt, he must either act according to the letter of the law, or consult those in power.

Reply Obj. 3. No man is so wise as to be able to consider every single case; and therefore he is not able sufficiently to express in words all those things that are suitable for the end he has in view. And even if a lawgiver were able to take all the cases into consideration, he ought not to mention them all, in order to avoid confusion; but he should frame the law according to that which is of most common occurrence.

ON CHANGE IN LAWS

(In Four Articles)

WE must now consider change in laws, under which head there are four points of inquiry: (1) Whether human law is changeable? (2) Whether it should be always changed, whenever anything better occurs? (3) Whether it is abolished by custom, and whether custom obtains the force of law? (4) Whether the application of human law should be changed by the dispensation of those in authority?

First Article

WHETHER HUMAN LAW SHOULD BE CHANGED IN ANY WAY?

We proceed thus to the First Article:—

Objection 1. It would seem that human law should not be changed in any way at all. For human law is derived from the natural law, as was stated above.[1] But the natural law endures unchangeably. Therefore human law should also remain without any change.

Obj. 2. Further, as the Philosopher says, a measure should be absolutely stable.[2] But human law is the measure of human acts, as was stated above.[3] Therefore it should remain without change.

Obj. 3. Further, it is of the nature of law to be just and right, as was stated above.[4] But that which is right once is right always. Therefore that which is law once should always be law.

On the contrary, Augustine says: *A temporal law, however just, may be justly changed in the course of time.*[5]

I answer that, As was stated above, human law is a dictate of reason, whereby human acts are directed.[6] Thus there may be two causes for the just change of human law: one on the part of reason, the other on the part of the men whose acts are regulated by law. The cause on the part of reason is that it seems natural to human reason to advance gradually from the imperfect to the perfect. Hence, in the speculative sciences, we see that the teaching of the early philosophers was imperfect, and that it was afterwards perfected by those who succeeded them. So also in practical matters, for those who first endeavored to discover something useful for the human community, not being able by themselves to take everything into consider-

---

[1] Q. 95, a. 2. [2] *Eth.*, V, 5 (1133a 25). [3] Q. 90, a. 1 and 2. [4] Q. 95, a. 2.
[5] *De Lib.* Arb., I, 6 (PL 32, 1229). [6] Q. 91, a. 3.

ation, set up certain institutions which were deficient in many ways; and these were changed by subsequent lawgivers who made institutions that might prove less frequently deficient in relation to the common welfare.

On the part of man, whose acts are regulated by law, the law can be rightfully changed because of changed condition among men, to whom different things are expedient according to the difference of their conditions. An example is proposed by Augustine: *If a people have a sense of moderation and responsibility, and are most careful guardians of the common welfare, it is right to enact a law allowing such a people to choose their own magistrates for the government of the commonwealth. But if, as time goes on, the same people become so corrupt as to sell their votes, and entrust the government to scoundrels and criminals, then the right of appointing their public officials is rightly forfeit to such a people, and the choice devolves to a few good men.*[7]

Reply Obj. 1. The natural law is a participation of the eternal law, as was stated above,[8] and therefore endures without change, owing to the unchangeableness and perfection of the divine reason, the author of nature. But the reason of man is changeable and imperfect, and so his law is subject to change. Moreover, the natural law contains certain universal precepts which are everlasting; whereas human law contains certain particular precepts, according to various circumstances.

Reply Obj. 2. A measure should be as enduring as possible. But nothing can be absolutely unchangeable in things that are subject to change. And therefore human law cannot be altogether unchangeable.

Reply Obj. 3. In corporeal things, *right* is predicated absolutely, and therefore, as far as it itself is concerned, always remains right. But rectitude is predicated of law with reference to the common welfare, to which one and the same thing is not always adapted, as was stated above; and hence rectitude of this kind is subject to change.

Second Article

WHETHER HUMAN LAW SHOULD ALWAYS BE CHANGED
WHENEVER SOMETHING BETTER OCCURS?

We proceed thus to the Second Article:—

Objection 1. It would seem that human law should be changed whenever something better occurs. For human laws are devised by human reason, like the other arts. But in the other arts, the tenets of former times give place to others, if something better occurs. Therefore the same should apply to human laws.

Obj. 2. Further, by taking note of the past we can provide for the future. Now unless human laws had been changed when it was found possible to improve them, considerable inconvenience would have ensued, because the

---

[7] *De Lib. Arb.,* I, 6 (PL 32, 1229).   [8] Q. 91, a. 2; q. 96, a. 2, ad 3.

laws of old were crude in many points. Therefore it seems that laws should be changed whenever anything better occurs to be enacted.

Obj. 3. Further, human laws are enacted about single acts of man. But we cannot acquire perfect knowledge in singular matters, except by experience, which *requires time,* as is stated in *Ethics* ii.[9] Therefore it seems that as time goes on it is possible for something better to occur for legislation.

On the contrary, It is stated in the *Decretals: It is absurd, and a detestable shame, that we should suffer those traditions to be changed which we have received from the fathers of old.*[10]

I answer that, As was stated above, human law is rightly changed in so far as such change is conducive to the common welfare. But, to a certain extent, the mere change of law is of itself prejudicial to the common welfare, because custom avails much for the observance of laws, seeing that what is done contrary to general custom, even in slight matters, is looked upon as a rather serious offense. Consequently, when a law is changed, the binding power of law is diminished, in so far as custom is abolished. Therefore human law should never be changed, unless, in some way or other, the common welfare be compensated according to the extent of the harm done in this respect. Such compensation may arise either from some very great and very evident benefit conferred by the new enactment; or from the extreme urgency of the case, due to the fact that either the existing law is clearly unjust, or its observance extremely harmful. Therefore the Jurist says that *in establishing new laws, there should be evidence of the benefit to be derived, before departing from a law which has long been considered just.*[11]

Reply Obj. 1. Rules of art derive their force from reason alone, and therefore whenever something better occurs, the rule followed hitherto should be changed. But *laws derive the greatest force from custom,* as the Philosopher states,[12] and consequently they should not be easily changed.

Reply Obj. 2. This argument proves that laws ought to be changed, not in view of any improvement, but for the sake of a great benefit, or in a case of great urgency, as was stated above. This answer applies also to the Third Objection.

Third Article

WHETHER CUSTOM CAN OBTAIN THE FORCE OF LAW?

We proceed thus to the Third Article:—

Objection 1. It would seem that custom cannot obtain the force of law, nor abolish a law. For human law is derived from the natural law and from

---

[9] Aristotle, *Eth.*, II, 1 (1103a 16).   [10] Gratian, *Decretum,* I, xii, 5 (I, 28).   [11] *Dig.*, i, iv, 2 (I, 35a).   [12] *Polit.*, II, 5 (1269a 20).

the divine law, as was stated above.[13] But human custom cannot change either the law of nature or the divine law. Therefore neither can it change human law.

Obj. 2. Further, many evils cannot make one good. But he who first acted against the law did evil. Therefore by multiplying such acts, nothing good is the result. Now a law is something good, since it is a rule of human acts. Therefore law is not abolished by custom, so that custom itself should obtain the force of law.

Obj. 3. Further, the framing of laws belongs to those public men whose business it is to govern the community; and that is why private individuals cannot make laws. But custom grows by the acts of private individuals. Therefore custom cannot obtain the force of law, so as to abolish the law.

On the contrary, Augustine says: *The customs of God's people and the institutions of our ancestors are to be considered as laws. And those who throw contempt on the customs of the Church ought to be punished as those who disobey the law of God.*[14]

I answer that, All law proceeds from the reason and will of the lawgiver, —the divine and natural laws from the reasonable will of God, the human law from the will of man as regulated by reason. Now just as the human reason and will, in practical matters, may be made manifest by speech, so they may be made known by deeds; for evidently a man chooses as good that which he carries into execution. But it is evident that, by human speech, law can be both changed and set forth, in so far as it manifests the interior movement and thought of human reason. Therefore by actions also, especially if they be repeated, so as to make a custom, law can be changed and set forth; and furthermore something can be established which obtains the force of law, in so far as, by repeated external actions, the inward movement of the will and the conceptions of the reason are most revealingly declared. For when a thing is done again and again, it seems to proceed from a deliberate judgment of reason. Accordingly, custom has the force of a law, abolishes law, and is the interpreter of law.

Reply Obj. 1. The natural and divine laws proceed from the divine will, as was stated above. Therefore they cannot be changed by a custom proceeding from the will of man, but only by divine authority. Hence it is that no custom can prevail over the divine or natural laws; for Isidore says: *Let custom yield to authority, and let evil customs be eradicated by law and reason.*[15]

Reply Obj. 2. As was stated above, human laws fail in some cases.[16] Hence it is possible sometimes to act outside the law, namely, in a case where the law fails; and yet the act will not be evil. And when such cases are multiplied, by reason of some change in man, then custom shows that

---

[13] Q. 93, a. 3; q. 95, a. 2.   [14] Cf. Gratian, *Decretum*, I, xi, 7 (I, 25).—St. Augustine, *Epist.* XXXVI, 1 (PL 33, 136).   [15] *Synonym.*, II, 80 (PL 83, 863).   [16] Q. 96, a. 6

the law is no longer useful; just as it might be declared by the verbal promulgation of a law to the contrary. If, however, the same reason remains, for which the law was hitherto useful, then it is not the custom that prevails against the law, but the law that overcomes the custom; unless perhaps the sole reason why the law seems useless is that it is not *possible according to the custom of the country,* which has been stated to be one of the conditions of law.[17] For it is not easy to set aside the custom of a whole people.

Reply Obj. 3. The people among whom a custom is introduced may be of two conditions. For if they are free, and able to make their own laws, the consent of the whole people expressed by a custom counts far more in favor of a particular observance than does the authority of the sovereign, who has not the power to frame laws, except as representing the people. Therefore, although each individual cannot make laws, yet the whole people can. If, however, the people have not the free power to make their own laws, or to abolish a law made by a higher authority, nevertheless, among such a people a prevailing custom obtains the force of law in so far as it is tolerated by those to whom it belongs to make laws for that people; because, by the very fact that they tolerate it, they seem to approve of that which is introduced by custom.

Fourth Article

WHETHER THE RULERS OF THE PEOPLE CAN DISPENSE FROM
HUMAN LAWS?

We proceed thus to the Fourth Article:—

Objection 1. It would seem that the rulers of the people cannot dispense from human laws. For law is established for the *common welfare,* as Isidore says.[18] But the common good should not be set aside for the private convenience of an individual, because, as the Philosopher says, *the good of the nation is more godlike than the good of one man.*[19] Therefore it seems that a man should not be dispensed from acting in compliance with the common law.

Obj. 2. Further, those who are placed over others are commanded as follows *(Deut.* i. 17): *You shall hear the little as well as the great; neither shall you respect any man's person, because it is the judgment of God.* But to allow one man to do that which is equally forbidden to all seems to be respect of persons. Therefore the rulers of a community cannot grant such dispensations, since this is against a precept of the divine law.

Obj. 3. Further, human law, in order to be just, should accord with the natural and divine laws, or else it would not *foster religion,* nor be *helpful to discipline,* which is requisite to the nature of law, as is laid down by

---

[17] St. Isidore, *Etymol.,* V, 21 (PL 82, 203).   [18] *Op. cit.,* II, 10; V, 21 (PL 82, 131; 203).   [19] *Eth.,* I, 2 (1094b 10).

Isidore.[20] But no man can dispense from the divine and natural laws. Neither, therefore, can he dispense from human law.

On the contrary, The Apostle says (*1 Cor.* ix. 17): *A dispensation is committed to me.*

I answer that, Dispensation, properly speaking, denotes a measuring out to individuals of some common goods. Thus the head of a household is called a dispenser, because to each member of the household he distributes work and the necessaries of life in due weight and measure. Accordingly, in every community a man is said to dispense, from the very fact that he directs how some common precept is to be fulfilled by each individual. Now it happens at times that a precept, which is conducive to the common weal as a general rule, is not good for a particular individual, or in some particular case, either because it would hinder some greater good, or because it would be the occasion of some evil, as we have explained above.[21] But it would be dangerous to leave this to the discretion of each individual, except perhaps by reason of an evident and sudden emergency, as was stated above.[22] Consequently, he who is placed over a community is empowered to dispense from a human law that rests upon his authority, so that, when the law fails in its application to persons or circumstances, he may allow the precept of the law not to be observed. If, however, he grant this permission without any such reason, and of his mere will, he will be an unfaithful or an imprudent dispenser: unfaithful, if he has not the common good in view, imprudent, if he ignores the nature and function of granting dispensations. Hence Our Lord says (*Luke* xii. 42): *Who, thinkest thou, is the faithful and wise dispenser whom his lord setteth over his family?*

Reply Obj. 1. When a person is dispensed from observing the common law, this should not be done to the prejudice of, but with the intention of benefiting, the common good.

Reply Obj. 2. It is not respect of persons if unequal measures are served out to those who are themselves unequal. Therefore, when the condition of any person requires that he should reasonably receive special treatment, it is not respect of persons if he be the object of special favor.

Reply Obj. 3. Natural law, so far as it contains common precepts which never fail, does not allow of dispensation. In the other precepts, however, which are as conclusions of the common precepts, man sometimes grants a dispensation: for instance, that a loan should not be paid back to the betrayer of his country, or something similar. But to the divine law each man stands as a private person to the public law to which he is subject. Therefore, just as none can dispense from public human law, except the man from whom the law derives its authority, or his delegate, so, in the precepts of the divine law, which are from God, none can dispense but God, or the man to whom He may give special power for that purpose.

---

[20] *Etymol.,* II, 10; V, 3 (PL 82, 131; 199).　　[21] Q. 96, a. 6.　　[22] *Ibid.*

ON THE OLD LAW

(*In Six Articles*)

WE must consequently now consider the Old Law. And (1) the Law itself: (2) its precepts.[1] Under the first head there are six points of inquiry: (1) Whether the Old Law was good? (2) Whether it was from God? (3) Whether it came from Him through the angels? (4) Whether it was given to all? (5) Whether it is binding on all? (6) Whether it was given at a suitable time?

First Article

WHETHER THE OLD LAW WAS GOOD?

We proceed thus to the First Article:—

Objection 1. It would seem that the Old Law was not good. For it is written (*Ezech.* xx. 25): *I gave them statutes that were not good, and judgments in which they shall not live.* But a law is not said to be good except because of the goodness of the precepts that it contains. Therefore the Old Law was not good.

Obj. 2. Further, it belongs to the goodness of a law that it conduce to the common welfare, as Isidore says.[2] But the Old Law was not salutary; rather was it deadly and injurious. For the Apostle says (*Rom.* vii. 8, *seq.*): *Without the law sin was dead. And I lived some time without the law. But when the commandment came, sin revived, and I died.* Again he says (*Rom.* v. 20): *Law entered in that sin might abound.* Therefore the Old Law was not good.

Obj. 3. Further, it belongs to the goodness of law that it should be possible to obey it, both according to nature, and according to human custom. But such the Old Law was not, since Peter says (*Acts* xv. 10): *Why tempt you [God] to put a yoke on the necks of the disciples, which neither our fathers nor we have been able to bear?* Therefore it seems that the Old Law was not good.

On the contrary, The Apostle says (*Rom.* vii. 12): *Wherefore the law indeed is holy, and the commandment holy, and just, and good.*

I answer that, Without any doubt, the Old Law was good. For just as a doctrine is shown to be true by the fact that it accords with right reason, so a law is proved to be good by the fact that it accords with reason. Now

[1] Q. 99.   [2] *Etymol.,* II, 10; V, 21 (PL 82, 131; 203).

the Old Law was in accordance with reason. For it repressed concupiscence, which is in conflict with reason, as evidenced by the commandment, *Thou shalt not covet thy neighbor's goods (Exod.* xx. 17). Moreover, the same law forbade all kinds of sin; and these too are contrary to reason. Consequently it is evident that it was a good law. The Apostle argues in the same way (*Rom.* vii.): *I am delighted,* says he (*verse* 22), *with the law of God, according to the inward man*; and again (*verse* 16): *I consent to the law, that is good.*

But it must be noted that the good has various degrees, as Dionysius states.[3] For there is a perfect good, and an imperfect good. In things ordained to an end, there is perfect goodness when a thing is such that it is sufficient in itself to conduce to the end; while there is imperfect goodness when a thing is of some assistance in attaining the end, but is not sufficient for the realization thereof. Thus a medicine is perfectly good, if it gives health to a man; but it is imperfect, if it helps to cure him, without being able to bring him back to health. Now it must be observed that the end of human law is different from the end of divine law. For the end of human law is the temporal tranquillity of the state, and this end law effects by directing external actions, as regards those evils which might disturb the peaceful condition of the state. On the other hand, the end of the divine law is to bring man to that end which is everlasting happiness; and this end is hindered by any sin, not only of external action, but also of internal action. Consequently, that which suffices for the perfection of human law, viz., the prohibition and punishment of sin, does not suffice for the perfection of the divine law; but it is requisite that it should make man altogether fit to partake of everlasting happiness. Now this cannot be done save by the grace of the Holy Ghost, whereby *charity,* which fulfills the law, . . . *is spread abroad in our hearts (Rom.* v. 5); for *the grace of God is life everlasting (ibid.* vi. 23). But the Old Law could not confer this grace, for this was reserved to Christ; because, as it is written (*Jo.* i. 17), the law was given *by Moses, grace and truth came by Jesus Christ.* Consequently the Old Law was good indeed, but imperfect, according to *Heb.* vii. 19: *The law brought nothing to perfection.*

Reply Obj. 1. The Lord refers there to the ceremonial precepts; and these are said not to be good, because they did not confer grace unto the remission of sins, although by fulfilling these precepts man confessed himself a sinner. Hence it is said pointedly, *and judgments in which they shall not live; i.e.,* whereby they are unable to obtain life; and so the text goes on: *And I polluted them, i.e.,* showed them to be polluted, *in their own gifts, when they offered all that opened the womb, for their offenses.*

Reply Obj. 2. The law is said to have been deadly, as being, not the cause, but the occasion of death, because of its imperfection, and this in so far as it did not confer grace enabling man to fulfill what it prescribed, and

---

[3] *De Div. Nom.,* IV, 20 (PG 3, 720).

to avoid what it forbade. Hence this occasion was not given to men, but taken by them. Therefore the Apostle says (*ibid.* 11): *Sin, taking occasion by the commandment, seduced me, and by it killed me.* In the same sense, when it is said that *the law entered in that sin might abound,* the conjunction *that* must be taken as consecutive and not final: namely, in so far as men, taking occasion from the law, sinned all the more, both because a sin became more grievous after law had forbidden it, and because concupiscence increased, since we desire a thing the more when it is forbidden.

Reply Obj. 3. The yoke of the law could not be borne without the help of grace, which the law did not confer; for it is written (*Rom.* ix. 16): *It is not of him that willeth, nor of him that runneth,* viz., that he wills and runs in the commandments of God, *but of God that showeth mercy.* Therefore it is written (*Ps.* cxviii. 32): *I have run the way of Thy commandments, when Thou didst enlarge my heart, i.e.,* by giving me grace and charity.

Second Article

WHETHER THE OLD LAW WAS FROM GOD?

We proceed thus to the Second Article:—

Objection 1. It would seem that the Old Law was not from God. For it is written (*Deut.* xxxii. 4): *The works of God are perfect.* But the Law was imperfect, as was stated above.[4] Therefore the Old Law was not from God.

Obj. 2. Further, it is written (*Eccles.* iii. 14): *I have learned that all the works which God hath made continue forever.* But the Old Law does not continue forever, since the Apostle says (*Heb.* vii. 18): *There is indeed a setting aside of the former commandment, because of the weakness and unprofitableness thereof.* Therefore the Old Law was not from God.

Obj. 3. Further, a wise lawgiver should remove not only evil, but also the occasions of evil. But the Old Law was an occasion of sin, as was stated above. Therefore the giving of such a law does not pertain to God, to Whom *none is like among the lawgivers* (*Job* xxxvi. 22).

Obj. 4. Further, it is written (*1 Tim.* ii. 4) that God *will have all men to be saved.* But the Old Law did not suffice to save men, as was stated above.[5] Therefore the giving of such a law did not pertain to God. Therefore the Old Law was not from God.

On the contrary, Our Lord said (*Matt.* xv. 6), while speaking to the Jews, to whom the Law was given: *You have made void the commandment of God for your tradition.* And shortly before (*verse* 4) He had said: *Honor thy father and mother,* which is contained expressly in the Old Law (*Exod.* xx. 12; *Deut.* v. 16). Therefore the Old Law was from God.

[4] A. 1: q. 91, a. 5.   [5] A. 1; q. 91, a. 5, ad 2.

I answer that, The Old Law was given by the good God, Who is the Father of Our Lord Jesus Christ. For the Old Law ordained men to Christ in two ways. First, by bearing witness to Christ; and so He Himself says (*Luke* xxiv. 44): *All things must needs be fulfilled, which are written in the law . . . , and in the prophets, and in the psalms, concerning Me*; and (*Jo.* v. 46): *If you did believe Moses, you would perhaps believe Me also; for he wrote of Me.*—Secondly, as a kind of disposition, since by withdrawing men from idolatrous worship it directed them to the worship of one God, by Whom the human race was to be saved through Christ. Therefore the Apostle says (*Gal.* iii. 23): *Before the faith came, we were kept under the law shut up unto that faith which was to be revealed.* Now it is evident that it is the same thing which gives a disposition to the end, and which brings to the end; and when I say *the same,* I mean that it does so either by itself or through its subjects. For the devil would not have made a law whereby men would be led to Christ, Who was to cast him out, according to *Matt.* xii. 26: *If Satan cast out Satan, his kingdom is divided.* Therefore the Old Law was given by the same God from Whom came salvation to man, through the grace of Christ.

Reply Obj. 1. Nothing prevents a thing from being not perfect absolutely, and yet perfect according to a certain time. Thus a boy is said to be perfect, not absolutely, but with regard to the condition of time. So, too, precepts that are given to children are perfect in comparison with the condition of those to whom they are given, although they are not perfect absolutely. And such were the precepts of the Law. Hence the Apostle says (*Gal.* iii. 24): *The law was our pedagogue in Christ.*

Reply Obj. 2. Those works of God endure forever which God so made that they would endure forever; and these are His perfect works. But the Old Law was set aside when there came the perfection of grace, not as though it were evil, but as being weak and useless for this time; because, as the Apostle goes on to say, *the law brought nothing to perfection (Heb.* vii. 19). Hence he says (*Gal.* iii. 25): *After the faith is come, we are no longer under a pedagogue.*

Reply Obj. 3. As was stated above, God sometimes permits certain ones to fall into sin, that they may thereby be humbled.⁶ So also did He wish to give such a law as men by their own forces could not fulfill, so that, while presuming on their own powers, they might find themselves to be sinners, and, being humbled, might have recourse to the help of grace.

Reply Obj. 4. Although the Old Law did not suffice to save men, yet another help for salvation from God besides the Law was available for men, viz., faith in the Mediator, by which the fathers of old were justified even as we are. Accordingly, God did not fail men by giving them insufficient aids to salvation.

⁶ Q. 79, a. 4.

Third Article

WHETHER THE OLD LAW WAS GIVEN THROUGH THE ANGELS?

We proceed thus to the Third Article:—

Objection 1. It seems that the Old Law was not given through the angels, but immediately by God. For an angel means a *messenger,* so that the word *angel* denotes ministry, not lordship, according to *Ps.* cii. 20, 21: *Bless the Lord all ye His angels . . . you ministers of His.* But the Old Law is related to have been given by the Lord, for it is written (*Exod.* xx. 1): *And the Lord spoke . . . these words,* and further on: *I am the Lord Thy God.* Moreover, the same expression is often repeated in *Exodus,* and in the books following the Law. Therefore the Law was given by God immediately.

Obj. 2. Further, according to *Jo.* i. 17, *the Law was given by Moses.* But Moses received it from God immediately, for it is written (*Exod.* xxxiii. 11): *The Lord spoke to Moses face to face, as a man is wont to speak to his friend.* Therefore the Old Law was given by God immediately.

Obj. 3. Further, it belongs to the sovereign alone to make a law, as was stated above.[7] But God alone is Sovereign as regards the salvation of souls, while the angels are the *ministering spirits,* as is stated in *Heb.* i. 14. Therefore it was not meet for the Law to be given through the angels, since it is ordained to the salvation of souls.

On the contrary, The Apostle said (*Gal.* iii. 19) that the Law was *given by angels in the hand of a Mediator.* And Stephen said (*Acts* vii. 53): *[Who] have received the Law by the disposition of angels.*

I answer that, The Law was given by God through the angels. And besides the general reason given by Dionysius, viz., that *the gifts of God should be brought to men by means of the angels,*[8] there is a special reason why the Old Law should have been given through them. For it has been stated that the Old Law was imperfect, and yet disposed man to that perfect salvation of the human race which was to come through Christ. Now it is to be observed that wherever there is an order of powers or arts, he that holds the highest place exercises the principal and perfect acts; while those things which dispose to the ultimate perfection are effected by him through his subordinates. Thus, the ship-builder himself rivets the planks together, but prepares the material by means of the workmen who assist him under his direction. Consequently, it was fitting that the perfect law of the New Testament should be given by the incarnate God immediately; but that the Old Law should be given to men by the ministers of God, *i.e.,* by the angels. It is thus that the Apostle at the beginning of his epistle to the *Hebrews* (i. 2) proves the excellence of the New Law over the Old; because in the New Testament *God . . . hath spoken to us by His Son,* whereas in the Old Testament *the word* was *spoken by angels* (ii. 2).

[7] Q. 90, a. 3.   [8] *De Cael. Hier.,* IV, 2 (PG 3, 180).

Reply Obj. 1. As Gregory says at the beginning of his *Moralia, the angel who is described to have appeared to Moses is sometimes mentioned as an angel, sometimes as the Lord: an angel, in truth, in so far as he performed the service of exterior speech; and the Lord, because He was the Master within Who supplied the power of speaking.*[9] Hence also it is that the angel spoke in the name of the Lord.

Reply Obj. 2. As Augustine says,[10] it is stated in *Exodus* (xxxiii. 11) that *the Lord spoke to Moses face to face;* and shortly afterwards we read (xxxiii. 18): '*Show me Thy glory.' Therefore he perceived what he saw and he desired what he saw not.* Hence he did not see the very essence of God, and consequently he was not taught by God immediately. Accordingly, when Scripture states that *He spoke to him face to face,* this is to be understood as expressing the opinion of the people, who thought that Moses was speaking with God mouth to mouth, although God spoke and appeared to him by means of a subordinate creature, *i.e.,* an angel and a cloud.—Again, we may say that this vision *face to face* means some kind of sublime and familiar contemplation, inferior to the vision of the divine essence.

Reply Obj. 3. It is for the sovereign alone to make a law by his own authority; but sometimes, after making a law, he promulgates it through others. Thus, God made the Law by His own authority, but He promulgated it through the angels.

Fourth Article

WHETHER THE OLD LAW SHOULD HAVE BEEN GIVEN TO THE JEWS ALONE?

We proceed thus to the Fourth Article:—

Objection 1. It would seem that the Old Law should not have been given to the Jews alone. For the Old Law disposed men for the salvation which was to come through Christ, as was stated above. But that salvation was to come, not to the Jews alone, but to all nations, according to *Isa.* xlix. 6: *It is a small thing that thou shouldst be my servant to raise up the tribes of Jacob, and to convert the dregs of Israel. Behold I have given thee to be the light of the Gentiles, that thou mayest be My salvation, even to the farthest part of the earth.* Therefore the Old Law should have been given to all nations, and not to one people only.

Obj. 2. Further, according to *Acts* x. 34, 35, *God is not a respecter of persons; but in every nation, he that feareth Him, and worketh justice, is acceptable to Him.* Therefore the way of salvation should not have been opened to one people more than to another.

Obj. 3. Further, the law was given through the angels, as was stated above. But God always vouchsafed the ministrations of the angels, not to

---

[9] *Moral.,* Praef., 1 (PL 75, 517).   [10] *De Genesi ad Litt.,* XII, 27 (PL 34, 477).

the Jews alone, but to all nations; for it is written (*Ecclus.* xvii. 14): *Over every nation He set a ruler.* Furthermore, on all nations He bestows temporal goods, which are of less account with God than spiritual goods. Therefore He should likewise have given the Law to all peoples.

On the contrary, It is written (*Rom.* iii. 1, 2): *What advantage then hath the Jew? . . . Much every way. First, indeed, because the words of God were committed to them;* and (*Ps.* cxlvii. 9): *He hath not done in like manner to every nation; and His judgments He hath not made manifest unto them.*

I answer that, It might be assigned as a reason for the Law being given to the Jews, rather than to other peoples, that the Jewish people alone remained faithful to the worship of one God, while the others turned away to idolatry; and so the latter were unworthy to receive the Law, lest a holy thing should be given to dogs.

But this reason does not seem fitting, because that people turned to idolatry, even after the Law had been made; and this was more grievous, as is clear from *Exod.* xxxii. and from *Amos* v. 25, 26: *Did you offer victims and sacrifices to Me in the desert for forty years, O house of Israel? But you carried a tabernacle for your Moloch, and the image of your idols, the star of your god, which you made to yourselves.* Moreover it is stated expressly (*Deut.* ix. 6): *Know therefore that the Lord thy God giveth thee not this excellent land in possession for thy justices, for thou art a very stiff-necked people.* But the real reason is given in the preceding verse: *That the Lord might accomplish His word, which He promised by oath to thy fathers Abraham, Isaac and Jacob.*

What this promise was is shown by the Apostle, who says (*Gal.* iii. 16) that *to Abraham were the promises made and to his seed. He saith not, 'And to his seeds,' as of many: but as of one, 'And to thy seed, which is Christ.'* And so God vouchsafed both the Law and other special benefits to that people because of the promise made to their fathers that Christ should be born of them. For it was fitting that the people of whom Christ was to be born should be signalized by a special sanctification, according to the words of *Levit.* xix. 2: *Be ye holy, because I . . . am holy.* Nor again was it because of the merit of Abraham himself that this promise was made to him, viz., that Christ should be born of his seed; but it was because of gratuitous election and vocation. Hence it is written (*Isa.* xli. 2): *Who hath raised up the just one from the east, hath called him to follow him?*

It is therefore evident that it was merely from gratuitous election that the patriarchs received the promise, and that the people sprung from them received the law, according to *Deut.* iv. 36, 37: *Ye did hear His words out of the midst of the fire, because He loved thy fathers, and chose their seed after them.* And if again it be asked why He chose this people, and not another, that Christ might be born thereof, a fitting answer is given by Augustine: *Why He draweth one and draweth not another, seek not thou to judge, if thou wish not to err.*[11]

Reply Obj. 1. Although the salvation, which was to come through Christ, was prepared for all nations, yet it was necessary that Christ should be born of one people, which, for this reason, was privileged above other peoples, according to *Rom.* ix. 4: *To whom,* namely, the Jews, *belongeth the adoption as of children of God,* . . . *and the testament, and the giving of the Law;* . . . *whose are the fathers, and of whom is Christ according to the flesh.*

Reply Obj. 2. Respect of persons takes place in those things which are given according to what is due; but it has no place in those things which are bestowed gratuitously. For he who, out of generosity, gives of his own to one and not to another is not a respecter of persons; but if he were a dispenser of goods held in common, and were not to distribute them according to personal merits, he would be a respecter of persons. Now God bestows the benefits of salvation on the human race gratuitously; and so He is not a respecter of persons, if He gives them to some rather than to others. Hence Augustine says: *All whom God teaches, He teaches out of pity; but whom He teaches not, out of justice He teaches not;*[12] for this is due to the condemnation of the human race for the sin of the first parent.

Reply Obj. 3. The benefits of grace are forfeited by man because of sin, but not the benefits of nature. Among the latter are the ministries of the angels, which the very order of various natures demands, viz., that the lowest beings be governed through the intermediate beings; and also bodily aids, which God vouchsafes not only to men, but also to beasts, according to *Ps.* xxxv. 7: *Men and beasts Thou wilt preserve, O Lord.*

Fifth Article

WHETHER ALL MEN WERE BOUND TO OBSERVE THE OLD LAW?

We proceed thus to the Fifth Article:—

Objection 1. It would seem that all men were bound to observe the Old Law. For whoever is subject to the king must needs be subject to his law. But the Old Law was given by God, Who is *King of all the earth* (*Ps.* xlvi. 8). Therefore all the inhabitants of the earth were bound to observe the Law.

Obj. 2. Further, the Jews could not be saved without observing the Old Law; for it is written (*Deut.* xxvii. 26): *Cursed be he that abideth not in the words of this law, and fulfilleth them not in work.* If, therefore, other men could be saved without the observance of the Old Law, the Jews would be in a worse plight than other men.

Obj. 3. Further, the Gentiles were admitted to the Jewish ritual and to

[11] *Tract.* XXVI, super *Ioann.,* VI, 44 (PL 35, 1607).   [12] *De Praedest. Sanct.,* VIII (PL 44, 971).

the observances of the Law; for it is written (*Exod.* xii. 48): *If any stranger be willing to dwell among you, and to keep the Phase of the Lord, all his males shall first be circumcised, and then shall he celebrate it according to the manner; and he shall be as he that is born in the land.* But it would have been useless to admit strangers to the legal observances according to the divine ordinance, if they could have been saved without the observance of the Law. Therefore none could be saved without observing the Law.

On the contrary, Dionysius says that many of the Gentiles were brought back to God by the angels.[13] But it is clear that the Gentiles did not observe the Law. Therefore some could have been saved without observing the Law.

I answer that, The Old Law showed forth the precepts of the natural law, and added certain precepts of its own. Accordingly, as to those precepts of the natural law contained in the Old Law, all were bound to observe the Old Law, not because they belonged to the Old Law, but because they belonged to the natural law. But as to those precepts which were added by the Old Law, they were not binding on any save the Jewish people alone.

The reason for this is because the Old Law, as was stated above, was given to the Jewish people that it might receive a prerogative of holiness, in reverence for Christ Who was to be born of that people. Now when any laws are enacted for the special sanctification of certain ones, these are binding on them alone; and thus clerics who are set aside for the service of God are bound to certain obligations to which the laity are not bound, and religious likewise are bound by their profession to certain works of perfection, to which the secular clergy is not bound. In like manner, this people was bound to certain special observances, to which other peoples **were not** bound. Therefore it is written (*Deut.* xviii. 13): *Thou shalt be perfect and without spot before the Lord thy God*; and for this reason they used a kind of form of profession, as appears from *Deut.* xxvi. 3: *I profess this day before the Lord thy God,* etc.

Reply Obj. 1. Whoever are subject to a king are bound to observe his law, which he makes for all in general. But if he orders certain things to be observed by the servants of his household, others are not bound thereto.

Reply Obj. 2. The more a man is united to God, the better his state becomes; and so the more the Jewish people were bound to the worship of God, the greater their excellence over other peoples. Hence it is written (*Deut.* iv. 8): *What other nation is there so renowned that hath ceremonies and just judgments, and all the law?* In like manner, from this point of view, the state of clerics is better than that of the laity, and the state of religious than that of the secular clergy.

Reply Obj. 3. The Gentiles obtained salvation more perfectly and more

[13] *De Cael. Hier.,* IX, 4 (PG 3, 261).

securely under the observances of the Law than under the mere natural law; and for this reason they were admitted to them. So, too, the laity are now admitted to the ranks of the clergy, and secular priests to those of the religious, although they can be saved without this.

Sixth Article

WHETHER THE OLD LAW WAS SUITABLY GIVEN AT THE TIME OF MOSES?

We proceed thus to the Sixth Article:—

Objection 1. It would seem that the Old Law was not suitably given at the time of Moses. For the Old Law disposed man for the salvation which was to come through Christ, as was stated above. But man needed this salutary remedy immediately after he had sinned. Therefore the Law should have been given immediately after sin.

Obj. 2. Further, the Old Law was given for the sanctification of those from whom Christ was to be born. Now the promise concerning the *seed, which is Christ (Gal.* iii. 16), was first made to Abraham, as is related in *Gen.* xii. 7. Therefore the Law should have been given at once at the time of Abraham.

Obj. 3. Further, as Christ was born of those alone who descended from Noe through Abraham, to whom the promise was made, so was He born of no other of the descendants of Abraham but David, to whom the promise was renewed, according to *2 Kings* xxiii. 1: *The man to whom it was appointed concerning the Christ of the God of Jacob . . . said.* Therefore the Old Law should have been given after David, just as it was given after Abraham.

On the contrary, The Apostle says (*Gal.* iii. 19) that the Law *was set because of transgressions, until the seed should come, to whom He made the promise, being ordained by angels in the hand of a Mediator:*—ordained, *i.e., given in an orderly fashion,* as the *Gloss* explains.[14] Therefore it was fitting that the Old Law should be given in this order of time.

I answer that, It was most fitting for the Law to be given at the time of Moses. The reason for this may be taken from two things in respect of which every law is imposed on two kinds of men. For it is imposed on some men who are hard-hearted and proud, whom the law restrains and tames; and it is imposed on good men, who, through being instructed by the law, are helped to fulfill what they desire to do. Hence it was fitting that the Law should be given at such a time as would be appropriate for overcoming man's pride. For man was proud of two things, viz., of knowledge and of power. He was proud of his knowledge, as though his natural reason could suffice him for salvation; and, accordingly, in order that his pride might be overcome in this matter, man was left to the guidance of

---

[14] Peter Lombard, *In Gal.,* super III, 19 (PL 192, 127).—Cf. *Glossa ordin.* (VI, 83B).

his reason without the help of a written law. And so man was able to learn from experience that his reason was deficient, since about the time of Abraham man had fallen headlong into idolatry and the most shameful vices. Therefore, after those times, it was necessary for a written law to be given as a remedy for human ignorance, because *by the Law is the knowledge of sin* (*Rom.* iii. 20). But after man had been instructed by the Law, his pride was convinced of weakness, since he was unable to fulfill what he knew. Hence, as the Apostle concludes (*Rom.* viii. 3, 4), *what the Law could not do in that it was weak through the flesh, God sent His own Son, . . . that the justification of the Law might be fulfilled in us.*

With regard to good men, the Law was given to them as a help. Now this was most needed by the people at the time when the natural law began to be obscured because of the exuberance of sin; for it was fitting that this help should be bestowed on men in an orderly manner, so that they might be led from imperfection to perfection. And so it was becoming that the Old Law should be given between the law of nature and the law of grace.

Reply Obj. 1. It was not fitting for the Old Law to be given at once after the sin of the first man, both because man was so confident in his own reason, that he did not acknowledge his need of the Old Law, and because as yet the dictate of the natural law was not darkened by habitual sinning.

Reply Obj. 2. A law should not be given save to the people, since it is a common precept, as was stated above.[15] Hence at the time of Abraham God gave men certain familiar and, as it were, household precepts; but when Abraham's descendants had multiplied, so as to form a people, and when they had been freed from slavery, it was fitting that they should be given a law. For *slaves are not that part of the people or state to which it is fitting for the law to be directed,* as the Philosopher says.[16]

Reply Obj. 3. Since the Law had to be given to a certain people, not only those of whom Christ was born received the Law, but the whole people who were marked with the seal of circumcision, which was the sign of the promise made to Abraham, and in which he believed, according to *Rom.* iv. 11. Hence, even before David, the Law had to be given to that people as soon as they were collected together.

[15] Q. 96, a. 1.   [16] *Polit.*, III, 5 (1280a 32); cf. *op. cit.*, IV, 4 (1291a 9).

ON THE PRECEPTS OF THE OLD LAW
(*In Six Articles*)

WE must now consider the precepts of the Old Law. And (1) how they are distinguished from one another; (2) each kind of precept.[1] Under the first head there are six points of inquiry: (1) Whether the Old Law contains several precepts or only one? (2) Whether the Old Law contains any moral precepts? (3) Whether it contains ceremonial precepts in addition to the moral precepts? (4) Whether besides these it contains judicial precepts? (5) Whether it contains any others besides these three? (6) How the Old Law induced men to keep its precepts.

First Article

WHETHER THE OLD LAW CONTAINS ONLY ONE PRECEPT?

We proceed thus to the First Article:—

Objection 1. It would seem that the Old Law contains but one precept. For a law is nothing else than a precept, as was stated above.[2] Now there is but one Old Law. Therefore it contains but one precept.

Obj. 2. Further, the Apostle says (*Rom.* xiii. 9): *If there be any other commandment, it is comprised in this word: Thou shalt love thy neighbor as thyself.* But this is only one commandment. Therefore the Old Law contains but one commandment.

Obj. 3. Further, it is written (*Matt.* vii. 12): *All things . . . whatsoever you would that men should do to you, do you also to them. For this is the Law and the prophets.* But the whole of the Old Law is comprised in the Law and the prophets. Therefore the whole of the Old Law contains but one precept.

On the contrary, The Apostle says (*Ephes.* ii. 15): *Making void the Law of commandments contained in decrees*; where he is referring to the Old Law, as the *Gloss* comments on the passage.[3] Therefore the Old Law comprises many commandments.

I answer that, Since a precept of law is binding, it is about something which must be done; and that a thing must be done arises from the necessity of some end. Hence it is evident that a precept implies, in its very notion, a relation to an end, in so far as a thing is commanded as being

---

[1] Q. 100.   [2] Q. 92, a. 2, ad 1.   [3] *Glossa ordin.* (VI, 91F).—Cf. Ambrosiaster, *In Ephes.*, super II, 15 (PL 17, 401).

necessary or expedient to an end. Now many things may happen to be necessary or expedient to an end; and, accordingly, precepts may be given about various things as being ordained to one end. Consequently, we must say that all the precepts of the Old Law are one as being related to one end; and yet they are many according to the diversity of the things that are ordained to that end.

Reply Obj. 1. The Old Law is said to be one as being ordained to one end; but it comprises various precepts, according to the distinction of the things which it directs to the end. So, too, the art of building is one according to the unity of its end, because it aims at the building of a house; and yet it contains various rules, according to the variety of acts ordained thereto.

Reply Obj. 2. As the Apostle says (*1 Tim.* i. 5), *the end of the commandment is charity,* since every law aims at establishing friendship either between man and man, or between man and God. Therefore the whole Law is fulfilled in this one commandment, *Thou shalt love thy neighbor as thyself,* as expressing the end of all the commandments; for the love of one's neighbor includes love of God, when we love our neighbor for God's sake. Hence the Apostle put this commandment in place of the two which are about the love of God and of one's neighbor, and of which Our Lord said (*Matt.* xxii. 40): *On these two commandments dependeth the whole Law and the prophets.*

Reply Obj. 3. As is stated in *Ethics* ix., *friendship towards another arises from friendship towards oneself,*[4] in so far as a man looks on another as on himself. Hence, when it is said, *All things whatsoever you would that men should do to you, do you also to them,* this is an explanation of the rule of neighborly love contained implicitly in the words, *Thou shalt love thy neighbor as thyself;* so that it is an explanation of this commandment.

Second Article

WHETHER THE OLD LAW CONTAINS MORAL PRECEPTS?

We proceed thus to the Second Article:—

Objection 1. It would seem that the Old Law contains no moral precepts. For the Old Law is distinguished from the law of nature, as was stated above.[5] But the moral precepts belong to the law of nature. Therefore they do not belong to the Old Law.

Obj. 2. Further, the divine law should have come to man's assistance where human reason fails him; as is evident in regard to things that are of faith, which are above reason. But man's reason seems to suffice for the moral precepts. Therefore the moral precepts do not belong to the Old Law, which is a divine law.

---

[4] Aristotle, *Eth.,* IX, 4 (1166a 1).   [5] Q. 91, a. 4 and 5; q. 98, a. 5.

Obj. 3. Further, the Old Law is said to be *the letter* that *killeth* (*2 Cor.* iii. 6). But the moral precepts do not kill, but quicken, according to *Ps.* cxviii. 93: *Thy justifications I will never forget, for by them Thou hast given me life.* Therefore the moral precepts do not belong to the Old Law.

On the contrary, It is written (*Ecclus.* xvii. 9): *Moreover, He gave them discipline and the law of life for an inheritance.* Now discipline belongs to morals; for the *Gloss* on *Heb.* xii. 11 (*Now all chastisement* [*disciplina*], etc.) says: *Discipline is an exercise in morals by means of difficulties.*[6] Therefore the Law which was given by God comprised moral precepts.

I answer that, The Old Law contained some moral precepts, as is evident from *Exod.* xx. 13, 15: *Thou shalt not kill, Thou shalt not steal.* And this was reasonable, because, just as the principal intention of human law is to create friendship between man and man, so the chief intention of the divine law is to establish man in friendship with God. Now since likeness is the principle of love, according to *Ecclus.* xiii. 19: *Every beast loveth its like,* there cannot possibly be any friendship of man to God, Who is supremely good, unless men become good; and so it is written (*Levit.* xix. 2; *cf.* xi. 45): *You shall be holy, for I am holy.* But the goodness of man is virtue, which makes its possessor good. Therefore it was necessary for the Old Law to include precepts about acts of virtue; and these are the moral precepts of the Law.

Reply Obj. 1. The Old Law is distinguished from the natural law, not as being altogether foreign to it, but as something added thereto. For just as grace presupposes nature, so the divine law must presuppose the natural law.

Reply Obj. 2. It was fitting that the divine law should come to man's assistance not only in those things for which reason is insufficient, but also in those things in which human reason may happen to be impeded. Now as to the most common principles of the natural law, the human reason could not err universally in moral matters; but through being habituated to sin, it became darkened as to what ought to be done in the particular. But with regard to the other moral precepts, which are like conclusions drawn from the common principles of the natural law, the reason of many men went astray, to the extent of judging to be lawful things that are evil in themselves. Hence there was need for the authority of the divine law to rescue man from both these defects. Thus, among the articles of faith, not only are those things set forth to which reason cannot reach, such as the Trinity of the Godhead, but also those to which right reason can attain, such as that God is one; and this in order to remove the manifold errors to which reason is liable.

Reply Obj. 3. As Augustine proves,[7] even the letter of the law is said

---

[6] *Glossa ordin.* (VI, 159B); Peter Lombard, *In Hebr.,* super XII, 11 (PL 192, 503).
[7] *De Spir. et Litt.,* XIV (PL 44, 216).

to be the occasion of death, as to the moral precepts; that is to say, it prescribes what is good without furnishing the aid of grace for its fulfillment.

Third Article

WHETHER THE OLD LAW COMPRISES CEREMONIAL PRECEPTS BESIDES MORAL PRECEPTS?

We proceed thus to the Third Article:—

Objection 1. It would seem that the Old Law does not comprise ceremonial precepts besides moral precepts. For every law that is given to man is for the purpose of directing human acts. Now human acts are called moral, as was stated above.[8] Therefore it seems that the Old Law given to men should not comprise other than moral precepts.

Obj. 2. Further, those precepts that are styled ceremonial seem to refer to the divine worship. But divine worship is the act of a virtue, viz., religion, which, as Tully says, *offers worship and ceremony to the divine nature.*[9] Since, then, the moral precepts are about acts of virtue, as was stated above, it seems that the ceremonial precepts should not be distinguished from the moral precepts.

Obj. 3. Further, the ceremonial precepts seem to be those which signify something figuratively. But, as Augustine observes, *of all signs employed by men words hold the first place.*[10] Therefore there was no need for the Law to contain ceremonial precepts about certain figurative actions.

On the contrary, It is written (*Deut.* iv. 13, 14): *Ten words . . . He wrote in two tables of stone; and He commanded me at that time that I should teach you the ceremonies and judgments which you shall do.* But the ten commandments of the Law are moral precepts. Therefore besides the moral precepts there are others which are ceremonial.

I answer that, As was stated above, the divine law is instituted chiefly in order to direct men to God, while human law is instituted chiefly in order to direct men in relation to one another. Hence human laws have not concerned themselves with the institution of anything relating to divine worship except as affecting the common good of mankind; and for this reason they have devised many institutions relating to divine matters, according as it seemed expedient for the formation of human morals, as may be seen in the rites of the Gentiles. On the other hand, the divine law directed men to one another according to the demands of that order whereby man is directed to God, which order was the chief aim of that law. Now man is directed to God not only by the interior acts of the mind, which are to believe, to hope and to love, but also by certain external works, whereby man makes profession of his subjection to God; and it is these works that are said to belong to the divine worship. This worship is called *ceremony*,

---

[8] Q. 1, a. 3.   [9] *De Invent.*, II, 53 (p. 148[b]).   [10] *De Doct. Christ.*, II, 3 (PL 34, 37).

—as meaning the *munia, i.e.,* gifts, of *Ceres* (who was the goddess of fruits), as some say,[11] because, at first, offerings were made to God from the fruits;—or because, as Valerius Maximus states,[12] the word *ceremony* was introduced among the Latins to signify the divine worship, being derived from a town near Rome called *Caere;* since, when Rome was taken by the Gauls, the sacred chattels of the Romans were taken thither and most carefully preserved. Accordingly, those precepts of the Law which refer to the divine worship are specially called ceremonial.

Reply Obj. 1. Human acts extend also to the divine worship, and therefore the Old Law given to man contains precepts about these matters also.

Reply Obj. 2. As was stated above, the precepts of the natural law are common and require to be determined.[13] Now they are determined both by human law and by divine law. And just as these very determinations which are made by human law are said to be, not of natural, but of positive, law, so the determinations of the precepts of the natural law effected by the divine law are distinct from the moral precepts which belong to the natural law. Therefore, to worship God, since it is an act of virtue, belongs to a moral precept; but the determination of this precept, namely, that He is to be worshipped by such and such sacrifices and such and such offerings, belongs to the ceremonial precepts. Consequently, the ceremonial precepts are distinct from the moral precepts.

Reply Obj. 3. As Dionysius says, the things of God cannot be manifested to men except by means of sensible likenesses.[14] Now these likenesses move the soul more when they are not only expressed in words, but also offered to the senses. Therefore the things of God are set forth in the Scriptures not only by likenesses expressed in words, as in the case of metaphorical expressions, but also by likenesses of things set before the eyes; and this pertains to the ceremonial precepts.

Fourth Article

WHETHER, BESIDES THE MORAL AND CEREMONIAL PRECEPTS, THERE ARE ALSO JUDICIAL PRECEPTS?

We proceed thus to the Fourth Article:—

Objection 1. It would seem that there are no judicial precepts in addition to the moral and ceremonial precepts in the Old Law. For Augustine says that in the Old Law there are *precepts concerning the life we have to lead, and precepts regarding the life that is foreshadowed.*[15] Now the precepts of the life we have to lead are moral precepts, and the precepts of the life that is foreshadowed are ceremonial. Therefore, besides these two kinds of precepts, we should not put any judicial precepts in the Law.

---

[11] St. Albert, *In IV Sent.,* d. i, a. 7 (XXIX, 19).   [12] *Factorum et Dictorum Memorabilium Libri Novem,* I, 1. 10 (ed. C. Kempf, Leipsig: B. G. Teubner, 1888), p. 6. [13] Q. 91, a. 3.   [14] *De Cael. Hier.,* I, 3 (PG 3, 121).   [15] *Contra Faust.,* VI, 2; X, 2 (PL 42, 228; 243).

Obj. 2. Further, the *Gloss* on *Ps.* cxviii. 102 (*I have not declined from Thy judgments*) says,—*i.e., from the rule of life Thou hast set for me.*[16] But a rule of life belongs to the moral precepts. Therefore the judicial precepts should not be considered as distinct from the moral precepts.

Obj. 3. Further, judgment seems to be an act of justice, according to *Ps.* xciii. 15: *Until justice be turned into judgment.* But acts of justice, like the acts of the other virtues, belong to the moral precepts. Therefore the moral precepts include the judicial precepts, and consequently should not be held as distinct from them.

On the contrary, It is written (*Deut.* vi. 1): *These are the precepts, and ceremonies, and judgments;* where *precepts* stands for *moral precepts* antonomastically. Therefore there are judicial precepts besides moral and ceremonial precepts.

I answer that, As we have stated above, it belongs to the divine law to direct men to one another and to God. Now each of these belongs, from a universal point of view, to the dictates of the natural law, to which dictates the moral precepts are to be referred; yet each of them has to be determined by divine or human law, because naturally known principles are common, both in speculative and in practical matters. Accordingly, just as the determination of the common principle about divine worship is effected by the ceremonial precepts, so the determination of the common precepts of that justice which is to be observed among men is effected by the judicial precepts.

We must therefore distinguish three kinds of precept in the Old Law, viz., *moral* precepts, which are dictated by the natural law; *ceremonial* precepts, which are determinations of the divine worship; and *judicial* precepts, which are determinations of the justice to be maintained among men. Therefore the Apostle (*Rom.* vii. 12), after saying that the *Law is holy,* adds that *the commandment is just, and holy, and good: just,* in respect of the judicial precepts; *holy,* with regard to the ceremonial precepts (since that is holy which is consecrated to God); and *good, i.e.,* conducive to virtue, as to the moral precepts.

Reply Obj. 1. Both the moral and the judicial precepts aim at the ordering of human life; and consequently they are both comprised under one of the heads mentioned by Augustine, viz., under the precepts of the life we have to lead.

Reply Obj. 2. Judgment denotes the execution of justice, by an application of the reason to individual cases in a determinate way. Hence the judicial precepts have something in common with the moral precepts, in that they are derived from reason, and something in common with the ceremonial precepts, in that they are determinations of common precepts. This explains why sometimes *judgments* comprise both judicial and moral pre-

---

[16] *Glossa ordin.* (III, 269A).—Cf. Cassiodorus, *Expos. in Psalt.,* super *Ps.* CXVIII, 102 (PL 70, 870).

cepts, as in *Deut.* v. 1: *Hear, O Israel, the ceremonies and judgments*; and sometimes judicial and ceremonial precepts, as in *Levit.* xviii. 4: *You shall do My judgments, and shall observe My precepts*, where *precepts* denotes moral precepts, while *judgments* refers to judicial and ceremonial precepts.

Reply Obj. 3. The act of justice, in general, belongs to the moral precepts; but its determination to some special kind of act belongs to the judicial precepts.

Fifth Article

WHETHER THE OLD LAW CONTAINS ANY OTHERS BESIDES THE MORAL, JUDICIAL AND CEREMONIAL PRECEPTS?

We proceed thus to the Fifth Article:—

Objection 1. It would seem that the Old Law contains other precepts besides the moral, judicial and ceremonial precepts. For the judicial precepts belong to the act of justice, which is between man and man, while the ceremonial precepts belong to the act of religion, whereby God is worshipped. Now besides these there are many other virtues, viz., temperance, fortitude, liberality, and several others, as was stated above.[17] Therefore, besides the aforesaid precepts, the Old Law should comprise others.

Obj. 2. Further, it is written (*Deut.* xi. 1): *Love the Lord thy God, and observe His precepts and ceremonies, His judgments and commandments.* Now precepts concern moral matters, as was stated above. Therefore, besides the moral, judicial and ceremonial precepts, the Law contains others which are called *commandments*.

Obj. 3. Further, it is written (*Deut.* vi. 17): *Keep the precepts of the Lord thy God, and the testimonies and ceremonies which I have commanded thee.* Therefore, in addition to the above, the Law comprises *testimonies*.

Obj. 4. Further, it is written (*Ps.* cxviii. 93): *Thy justifications (i.e., Thy Law*, according to the *Gloss*[18]) *I will never forget.* Therefore in the Old Law there are not only moral, ceremonial and judicial precepts, but also others, called *justifications*.

On the contrary, It is written (*Deut.* vi. 1): *These are the precepts and ceremonies and judgments which the Lord your God commanded . . . you.* And these words are placed at the beginning of the Law. Therefore all the precepts of the Law are included under them.

I answer that, Some things are included in the Law by way of precept; other things, as being ordained to the fulfillment of the precepts. Now the precepts refer to things which have to be done. To their fulfillment man is induced by two considerations: viz., the authority of the lawgiver, and the benefit derived from the fulfillment, which benefit consists in the at-

---

[17] Q. 60, a. 5.   [18] *Glossa interl.* (III, 268v); Peter Lombard, *In Psalm.*, super CXVIII, 93 (PL 191, 1090).

tainment of some good, useful, pleasurable or virtuous, or in the avoidance of some contrary evil. Hence it was necessary that in the Old Law certain things should be set forth to indicate the authority of God the lawgiver: *e.g., Deut.* vi. 4: *Hear, O Israel, the Lord our God is one Lord*; and *Gen.* i. 1: *In the beginning God created heaven and earth*; and these are called *testimonies.*—Again, it was necessary that in the Law certain rewards should be appointed for those who observe the Law, and punishments for those who transgress, as may be seen in *Deut.* xxviii. 1: *If thou wilt hear the voice of the Lord Thy God . . . He will make thee higher than all the nations,* etc.; and these are called *justifications,* according as God punishes or rewards certain persons justly.

The things that have to be done do not come under the precept except in so far as they have the character of a duty. Now a duty is twofold, namely, one according to the rule of reason, the other according to the rule of a law which prescribes that duty. And, in the same way, the Philosopher distinguishes a twofold just—moral and legal.[19] Moral duty is twofold, because reason dictates that something must be done, either as being so necessary that without it the order of virtue would be destroyed, or as being useful for the better maintaining of the order of virtue. According to this, some of the moral precepts are expressed by way of absolute command or prohibition, as *Thou shalt not kill, thou shalt not steal*; and these are properly called *precepts.* Other things are prescribed or forbidden, not as an absolute duty, but as something better to be done. These may be called *commandments,* because they are expressed by way of inducement and persuasion. An example is found in *Exod.* xxii. 26: *If thou take of thy neighbor a garment in pledge, thou shalt give it him again before sunset*; and there are other like cases. Therefore Jerome says that *justice is in the precepts, charity in the commandments.*[20]—Duty as fixed by the Law belongs to the *judicial* precepts, as regards human affairs; to the *ceremonial* precepts, as regards divine matters.

Nevertheless, those ordinances also which refer to punishments and rewards may be called *testimonies,* in so far as they testify to the divine justice. Again all the precepts of the Law may be styled *justifications,* as being executions of legal justice. Furthermore, the commandments may be distinguished from the precepts, so that those things be called *precepts* which God Himself prescribed, and those things *commandments* which He enjoined [*mandavit*] through others, as the very word seems to denote.

From this it is clear that all the precepts of the Law are either moral, ceremonial or judicial; and that other ordinances have not the character of a precept, but are directed to the observance of the precepts, as was stated above.

Reply Obj. 1. Justice alone, of all the virtues, implies the notion of duty. Consequently, moral matters are determinable by law in so far as

---

[19] *Eth.,* V, 7 (1134b 18).   [20] Cf. Pelagius, *In Marc.,* proem. (PL 30, 610).

they belong to justice: of which religion is likewise a part, as Tully says.[21] Therefore the legal just cannot be anything foreign to the ceremonial and judicial precepts.

The Replies to the other Objections are clear from what has been said.

Sixth Article

WHETHER THE OLD LAW SHOULD HAVE INDUCED MEN TO THE OBSERVANCE OF ITS PRECEPTS BY MEANS OF TEMPORAL PROMISES AND THREATS?

We proceed thus to the Sixth Article:—

Objection 1. It would seem that the Old Law should not have induced men to the observance of its precepts by means of temporal promises and threats. For the purpose of the divine law is to subject man to God by fear and love, and hence it is written (*Deut.* x. 12): *And now, Israel, what doth the Lord thy God require of thee, but that thou fear the Lord thy God, and walk in His ways, and love Him?* But the desire for temporal goods leads man away from God, for Augustine says that *covetousness is the bane of charity.*[22] Therefore temporal promises and threats seem to be contrary to the intention of a lawgiver; and this makes a law worthy of rejection, as the Philosopher declares.[23]

Obj. 2. Further, the divine law is more excellent than human law. Now, in the sciences, we notice that the loftier the science, the higher the means that it employs. Therefore, since human law employs temporal threats and promises as means of persuading man, the divine law should have used, not these, but more lofty means.

Obj. 3. Further, the reward of justice and the punishment of guilt cannot be that which befalls equally the good and the wicked. But as stated in *Eccles.* ix. 2, *all* temporal *things equally happen to the just and to the wicked, to the good and to the evil, to the clean and to the unclean, to him that offereth victims, and to him that despiseth sacrifices.* Therefore temporal goods or evils are not suitably set forth as punishments or rewards of the commandments of the divine law.

On the contrary, It is written (*Isa.* i. 19, 20): *If you be willing, and will hearken to Me, you shall eat the good things of the land. But if you will not, and will provoke Me to wrath, the sword shall devour you.*

I answer that, Just as in the speculative sciences men are led to assent to the conclusions by syllogistic means, so, too, in every law, men are led to observe its precepts by means of punishments and rewards. Now it is to be observed that, in the speculative sciences, the means are adapted to the conditions of the recipient; and so the mode of procedure must be an orderly one, so that the instruction is based on principles more generally

---

[21] *De Invent.,* II, 53 (p. 148ᵇ).   [22] *Lib. 83 Quaest.,* q. 36 (PL 40, 25).   [23] *Polit.,* VII, 2 (1324b 23).

known. So, likewise, he who would persuade a man to the observance of any precepts needs to move him at first by things for which he has an affection; just as children are induced to do something by means of little childish gifts. Now it has been said above that the Old Law disposed men to Christ, as the imperfect disposes to the perfect;[24] and therefore it was given to a people as yet imperfect in comparison to the perfection which was to result from Christ's coming. For this reason, that people is compared to a child that is still under a pedagogue (*Gal.* iii. 24). But the perfection of man consists in his despising temporal things and cleaving to things spiritual, as is clear from the words of the Apostle (*Phil.* iii. 13, 15): *Forgetting the things that are behind, I stretch forth myself to those that are before. . . . Let us therefore, as many as are perfect, be thus minded.* Those who are yet imperfect desire temporal goods, albeit in subordination to God; whereas the perverse place their end in temporal goods. It was therefore fitting that the Old Law should conduct men to God by means of temporal goods for which the imperfect have an affection.

Reply Obj. 1. Covetousness, whereby man places his end in temporal goods, is the bane of charity. But the attainment of temporal goods which man desires in subordination to God is a road leading the imperfect to the love of God, according to *Ps.* xlviii. 19: *He will praise Thee, when Thou shalt do well to him.*

Reply Obj. 2. Human law persuades men by means of temporal rewards or by punishments to be inflicted by men; whereas the divine law persuades men by means of rewards or punishments to be received from God. In this respect it employs higher means.

Reply Obj. 3. As anyone can see, who reads carefully the story of the Old Testament, the common condition of the people prospered under the Law as long as they obeyed it; and as soon as they departed from the precepts of the Law, they were overtaken by many calamities. But certain individuals, although they observed the justice of the Law, met with misfortunes, either because they had already become spiritual (so that misfortune might withdraw them all the more from attachment to temporal things, and that their virtue might be tried), or because, while outwardly fulfilling the works of the Law, their heart was altogether fixed on temporal goods, and far removed from God, according to *Isa.* xxix. 13 [*Matt.* xv. 8]: *This people honoreth Me with their lips; but their heart is far from Me.*

---

[24] Q. 91, a. 5, ad 2; q. 98, a. 1, 2 and 3.

ON THE MORAL PRECEPTS OF THE OLD LAW

(In Twelve Articles)

WE must now consider each kind of precept in the Old Law. And (1) the moral precepts, (2) the ceremonial precepts,[1] (3) the judicial precepts.[2] Under the first head there are twelve points of inquiry: (1) Whether all the moral precepts of the Old Law belong to the law of nature? (2) Whether the moral precepts of the Old Law are about the acts of all the virtues? (3) Whether all the moral precepts of the Old Law are reducible to the ten precepts of the decalogue? (4) How the precepts of the decalogue are distinguished from one another. (5) Their number. (6) Their order. (7) The manner in which they were given. (8) Whether they are dispensable? (9) Whether the mode of observing a virtue comes under the precept of the Law? (10) Whether the mode of charity comes under the precept? (11) The distinction of other moral precepts. (12) Whether the moral precepts of the Old Law justify man?

First Article

WHETHER ALL THE MORAL PRECEPTS OF THE OLD LAW BELONG TO THE LAW OF NATURE?

We proceed thus to the First Article:—

Objection 1. It would seem that not all the moral precepts belong to the law of nature. For it is written (*Ecclus*. xvii. 9): *Moreover He gave them instructions, and the law of life for an inheritance.* But instruction is in contradistinction to the law of nature, since the law of nature is not learned, but possessed by natural instinct. Therefore not all the moral precepts belong to the natural law.

Obj. 2. Further, the divine law is more perfect than human law. But human law adds certain things concerning good morals to those that belong to the law of nature; as is evidenced by the fact that the natural law is the same in all men, while these moral institutions are various for various people. Much more reason therefore was there why the divine law should add to the law of nature ordinances pertaining to good morals.

Obj. 3. Further, just as natural reason leads to good morals in certain matters, so does faith. Hence it is written (*Gal.* v. 6) that faith *worketh by charity*. But faith is not included in the law of nature, since that which

---

[1] Q. 101.   [2] Q. 104.

is of faith is above nature. Therefore not all the moral precepts of the divine law belong to the law of nature.

On the contrary, The Apostle says (*Rom.* ii. 14) that *the Gentiles, who have not the Law, do by nature those things that are of the Law;* which must be understood of things pertaining to good morals. Therefore all the moral precepts of the Law belong to the law of nature.

I answer that, The moral precepts are distinct from the ceremonial and judicial precepts, for they are about things pertaining of their very nature to good morals. Now since human morals depend on their relation to reason, which is the proper principle of human acts, those morals are called good which accord with reason, and those are called bad which are discordant from reason. And as every judgment of the speculative reason proceeds from the natural knowledge of first principles, so every judgment of the practical reason proceeds from naturally known principles, as was stated above.[3] From these principles one may proceed in various ways to judge of various matters. For some matters connected with human actions are so evident, that after very little consideration one is able at once to approve or disapprove of them by means of these common first principles; while other matters cannot be the subject of judgment without much consideration of the various circumstances. Not all are able to do this carefully, but only those who are wise; just as it is not possible for all to consider the particular conclusions of the sciences, but only for those who are philosophers. Lastly, there are some matters of which man cannot judge unless he be helped by divine instruction: *e.g.,* matters of faith.

It is therefore evident that since the moral precepts are about matters which concern good morals; and since good morals are such as are in accord with reason; and since every judgment of human reason must needs be derived in some way from natural reason,—it follows, of necessity, that all the moral precepts belong to the law of nature, but not all in the same way. For there are certain things which the natural reason of every man, of its own accord and at once, judges to be done or not to be done: *e.g., Honor thy father and thy mother,* and, *Thou shalt not kill, Thou shalt not steal* (*Exod.* xx. 12, 13, 15); and these belong to the law of nature absolutely. And there are certain things which, after a more careful consideration, wise men deem obligatory. Such belong to the law of nature, yet so that they need to be inculcated, the wiser teaching the less wise: *e.g., Rise up before the hoary head, and honor the person of the aged man* (*Levit.* xix. 32), and the like.—And there are some things, to judge of which human reason needs divine instruction, whereby we are taught about the things of God: *e.g., Thou shalt not make to thyself a graven thing, nor the likeness of anything; Thou shalt not take the name of the Lord thy God in vain* (*Exod.* xx. 4, 7).

This suffices for the Replies to the Objections.

[3] Q. 94, a. 2 and 4.

Second Article

WHETHER THE MORAL PRECEPTS OF THE LAW ARE ABOUT ALL THE ACTS OF THE VIRTUES?

We proceed thus to the Second Article:—

Objection 1. It would seem that the moral precepts of the Law are not about all the acts of the virtues. For the observance of the precepts of the Old Law is called justification, according to *Ps.* cxviii. 8: *I will keep Thy justifications.* But justification is the execution of justice. Therefore the moral precepts are only about acts of justice.

Obj. 2. Further, that which comes under a precept has the character of a duty. But the character of duty belongs to justice alone and to none of the other virtues, for the proper act of justice consists in rendering to each one his due. Therefore the precepts of the moral law are not about the acts of the other virtues, but only about the acts of justice.

Obj. 3. Further, every law is made for the common good, as Isidore says.[4] But of all the virtues justice alone regards the common good, as the Philosopher says.[5] Therefore the moral precepts are only about the acts of justice.

On the contrary, Ambrose says that *a sin is a transgression of the divine law, and a disobedience to the commandments of heaven.*[6] But there are sins contrary to all the acts of virtue. Therefore it belongs to the divine law to direct all the acts of virtue.

I answer that, Since the precepts of the Law are ordained to the common good, as was stated above,[7] the precepts of the Law must needs be diversified according to the various kinds of community. Hence the Philosopher teaches that the laws which are made in a state that is ruled by a king must be different from the laws of a state that is ruled by the people, or by a few powerful men in the state.[8] Now human law is ordained for one kind of community, and the divine law for another kind. For human law is ordained for the civil community, which men have in relation to one another; and men are ordained to one another by outward acts, whereby men live in communion with one another. This life in common of man with man pertains to justice, whose proper function consists in directing the human community. Therefore human law makes precepts only about acts of justice; and if it commands acts of the other virtues, this is only in so far as they assume the nature of justice, as the Philosopher explains.[9]

But the community for which the divine law is ordained is that of men in relation to God, either in this life or in the life to come. Therefore the divine law proposes precepts about all those matters whereby men are well

---

[4] *Etymol.*, II, 10; V, 21 (PL 82, 131; 203).   [5] *Eth.*, V, 1 (1130a 4).   [6] *De Parad.*, VIII (PL 14, 309).   [7] Q. 90, a. 2.   [8] *Polit.*, IV, 1 (1289a 11; a. 22).   [9] *Eth.*, V, 1 (1129b 23).

ordered in their relations to God. Now man is united to God by his reason or mind, in which is God's image. Therefore the divine law proposes precepts about all those matters whereby human reason is well ordered. But this is effected by the acts of all the virtues, since the intellectual virtues set in good order the acts of the reason in themselves, while the moral virtues set in good order the acts of the reason in reference to interior passions and exterior actions. It is therefore evident that the divine law fittingly proposes precepts about the acts of all the virtues, and yet in such a way that certain matters, without which the order of virtue, which is the order of reason, cannot even exist, come under an obligation of precept, while other matters, which pertain to the well-being of perfect virtue, come under an admonition of counsel.

Reply Obj. 1. The fulfillment of the commandments of the Law, even of those which are about the acts of the other virtues, has the character of justification, inasmuch as it is just that man should obey God; or, again, inasmuch as it is just that all that belongs to man should be subject to reason.

Reply Obj. 2. Justice, properly so called, regards the duty of one man to another; but all the other virtues regard the duty of the lower powers to reason. It is in relation to this latter duty that the Philosopher speaks of a kind of metaphorical justice.[10]

The Reply to the Third Objection is clear from what has been said about the different kinds of community.

Third Article

WHETHER ALL THE MORAL PRECEPTS OF THE OLD LAW ARE REDUCIBLE TO THE TEN PRECEPTS OF THE DECALOGUE?

We proceed thus to the Third Article:—

Objection 1. It would seem that not all the moral precepts of the Old Law are reducible to the ten precepts of the decalogue. For the first and principal precepts of the Law are, *Thou shalt love the Lord thy God,* and, *Thou shalt love thy neighbor,* as is stated in *Matt.* xxii. 37, 39. But these two are not contained in the precepts of the decalogue. Therefore not all the moral precepts are contained in the precepts of the decalogue.

Obj. 2. Further, the moral precepts are not reducible to the ceremonial precepts, but rather *vice versa.* But among the precepts of the decalogue, one is ceremonial, viz., *Remember that thou keep holy the Sabbath-day* (*Exod.* xx. 8). Therefore the moral precepts are not reducible to all the precepts of the decalogue.

Obj. 3. Further, the moral precepts are about all the acts of the virtues. But among the precepts of the decalogue are only such as regard acts of

---

[10] *Eth.,* V, 11 (1138b 5).

justice, as may be seen by going through them all. Therefore the precepts of the decalogue do not include all the moral precepts.

On the contrary, The *Gloss* on *Matt.* v. 11 (*Blessed are ye when they shall revile you,* etc.) says that *Moses, after propounding the ten precepts, set them out in detail.*[11] Therefore all the precepts of the Law are so many parts of the precepts of the decalogue.

I answer that, The precepts of the decalogue differ from the other precepts of the Law in the fact that God Himself is said to have given the precepts of the decalogue; whereas He gave the other precepts to the people through Moses. Therefore the decalogue includes those precepts the knowledge of which man has immediately from God. Such are those which, with but slight reflection, can be gathered at once from the first common principles, and those also which become known to man immediately through divinely infused faith. Consequently, two kinds of precepts are not reckoned among the precepts of the decalogue: viz., the first common principles, for they need no further promulgation after being once imprinted on the natural reason to which they are self-evident, as, for instance, that one should do evil to no man, and other similar principles;—and again those which the careful reflection of wise men shows to be in accord with reason, for the people receive these principles from God, through the teaching of wise men. Nevertheless, both kinds of precepts are contained in the precepts of the decalogue, but in different ways. For the first common principles are contained in them, as principles in their proximate conclusions; while those which are known through wise men are contained, conversely, as conclusions in their principles.

Reply Obj. 1. These two principles are the first common principles of the natural law, and are self-evident to human reason, either through nature or through faith. Therefore all the precepts of the decalogue are referred to these as conclusions to common principles.

Reply Obj. 2. The precept of the Sabbath observance is moral in one respect, in so far as it commands man to give some time to the things of God, according to *Ps.* xlv. 11: *Be still and see that I am God.* In this respect it is placed among the precepts of the decalogue; but not as to the fixing of the time, in which respect it is a ceremonial precept.

Reply Obj. 3. The notion of duty is not so patent in the other virtues as it is in justice. Hence the precepts about the acts of the other virtues are not so well known to the people as are the precepts about acts of justice. Therefore the acts of justice especially come under the precepts of the decalogue, which are the primary elements of the Law.

[11] *Glossa ordin.* (V, 19B).

Fourth Article

WHETHER THE PRECEPTS OF THE DECALOGUE ARE SUITABLY
DISTINGUISHED FROM ONE ANOTHER?

We proceed thus to the Fourth Article:—

Objection 1. It would seem that the precepts of the decalogue are unsuitably distinguished from one another (*Exod.* xx.). For worship is a virtue distinct from faith. Now the precepts are about the acts of the virtues. But that which is said at the beginning of the decalogue, *Thou shalt not have strange gods before Me,* belongs to faith; and that which is added, *Thou shalt not make . . . any graven thing,* etc., belongs to worship. Therefore these are not one precept, as Augustine asserts,[12] but two.

Obj. 2. Further, the affirmative precepts in the Law are distinct from the negative precepts; *e.g., Honor thy father and thy mother,* and, *Thou shalt not kill.* But this, *I am the Lord thy God,* is affirmative; and that which follows, *Thou shalt not have strange gods before Me,* is negative. Therefore these are two precepts, and do not, as Augustine says, make one.

Obj. 3. Further, the Apostle says (*Rom.* vii. 7): *I had not known concupiscence, if the Law did not say: 'Thou shalt not covet.'* Hence it seems that this precept, *Thou shalt not covet,* is one precept, and, therefore, should not be divided into two.

On the contrary stands the authority of Augustine who, in commenting on *Exodus,* distinguishes three precepts as referring to God, and seven as referring to our neighbor.[13]

I answer that, The precepts of the decalogue are differently divided by different authorities. For Hesychius, commenting on *Levit.* xxvi. 26 (*Ten women shall bake your bread in one oven*) says that the precept of the Sabbath-day observance is not one of the ten precepts, because its observance, in the letter, is not binding for all time.[14] But he distinguishes four precepts pertaining to God, of which the first is *I am the Lord thy God;* the second, *Thou shalt not have strange gods before Me* (thus also Jerome distinguishes these two precepts, in his commentary on *Osee* x. 10, *On thy two iniquities*[15]); the third precept, according to him, is, *Thou shalt not make to thyself any graven thing;* and the fourth, *Thou shalt not take the name of the Lord thy God in vain.* He states that there are six precepts pertaining to our neighbor: the first, *Honor thy father and thy mother;* the second, *Thou shalt not kill;* the third, *Thou shalt not commit adultery;* the fourth, *Thou shalt not steal;* the fifth, *Thou shalt not bear false witness;* the sixth, *Thou shalt not covet.*

But, in the first place, it seems unbecoming for the precept of the Sabbath-day observance to be put among the precepts of the decalogue, if it in

---

[12] *Quaest. in Heptat.,* II, q. 71, super *Exod.,* XX, 3 (PL 34, 621).   [13] *Ibid.* (PL 34, 620).   [14] *In Levit.,* VII, super XXVI, 26 (PG 93, 1150).   [15] *In Osee,* III, super X, 10 (PL 25, 952).

no way belonged to the decalogue. Secondly, because, since it is written (*Matt.* vi. 24), *No man can serve two masters,* the two statements, *I am the Lord thy God,* and, *Thou shalt not have strange gods before Me* seem to be of the same nature and to form one precept. Hence Origen, who also distinguishes four precepts as referring to God, unites these two under one precept, and reckons in the second place, *Thou shalt not make . . . any graven thing*; as third,*Thou shalt not take the name of the Lord thy God in vain*; and as fourth, *Remember that thou keep holy the Sabbath-day.*[16] The other six he reckons in the same way as Hesychius.

Since, however, the making of graven things or the likeness of anything is not forbidden except as to the point of their being worshipped as gods—for God commanded an image of the Seraphim to be made and placed in the tabernacle, as is related in *Exod.* xxv. 18—Augustine more fittingly unites these two, *Thou shalt not have strange gods before Me,* and, *Thou shalt not make . . . any graven thing,* into one precept. Likewise, to covet another's wife, for the purpose of carnal union, belongs to the concupiscence of the flesh; whereas, to covet other things, which are desired for the purpose of possession, belongs to the concupiscence of the eyes. And so Augustine reckons as distinct precepts that which forbids the coveting of another's goods, and that which prohibits the coveting of another's wife.[17] Thus he distinguishes three precepts as referring to God, and seven as referring to our neighbor. And this is better.

Reply Obj. 1. Worship is merely a declaration of faith, and therefore the precepts about worship should not be reckoned as distinct from those about faith. Nevertheless, precepts should be given about worship rather than about faith, because the precept about faith is presupposed to the precepts of the decalogue, as is also the precept of charity. For just as the first common precepts of the natural law are self-evident to one having natural reason, and need no promulgation, so also to believe in God is a first and self-evident principle to one possessed of faith; *for he that cometh to God must believe that He is* (*Heb.* xi. 6). Hence it needs no other promulgation than the infusion of faith.

Reply Obj. 2. The affirmative precepts are distinct from the negative when one is not comprised in the other. Thus that a man should honor his parents does not include that he should not kill another man; nor does the latter include the former. But when an affirmative precept is included in a negative, or *vice versa,* we do not find that two distinct precepts are given. Thus, there is not one precept saying that *Thou shalt not steal,* and another binding one to keep another's property intact, or to give it back to its owner. In the same way, there are not different precepts about believing in God, and about not believing in strange gods.

Reply Obj. 3. All covetousness has one common notion, and therefore

---

[16] *In Exod.,* hom. VII (PG 12. 351).   [17] *Quaest. in Heptat.,* II, q. 71 super *Exod.,* XX, 17 (PL 34, 621).

the Apostle speaks of the commandment about covetousness as though it were one. But because there are various special kinds of covetousness, therefore Augustine distinguishes different prohibitions against coveting; for covetousness differs specifically in respect of the diversity of actions or the things coveted, as the Philosopher says.[18]

Fifth Article

WHETHER THE PRECEPTS OF THE DECALOGUE ARE SUITABLY SET FORTH?

We proceed thus to the Fifth Article:—

Objection 1. It would seem that the precepts of the decalogue are unsuitably set forth. For sin, as is stated by Ambrose, is *a transgression of the divine law and a disobedience to the commandments of heaven.*[19] But sins are distinguished according as man sins against God, or his neighbor, or himself. Since, then, the decalogue does not include any precepts directing man in his relations to himself, but only such as direct him in his relations to God and his neighbor, it seems that the precepts of the decalogue are insufficiently enumerated.

Obj. 2. Further, just as the Sabbath-day observance pertained to the worship of God, so also did the observance of other solemnities, and the offering of sacrifices. But the decalogue contains a precept about the Sabbath-day observance. Therefore it should contain others also, pertaining to the other solemnities, and to the sacrificial rite.

Obj. 3. Further, as sins against God include the sin of perjury, so also do they include blasphemy, or other ways of lying against the teaching of God. But there is a precept forbidding perjury: *Thou shalt not take the name of the Lord thy God in vain.* Therefore there should be also a precept of the decalogue forbidding blasphemy and false doctrine.

Obj. 4. Further, just as man has a natural affection for his parents, so has he also for his children. Moreover the commandment of charity extends to all our neighbors. But the precepts of the decalogue are ordained unto charity, according to *1 Tim.* i. 5: *The end of the commandment is charity.* Therefore, as there is a precept referring to parents, so there should have been some precepts referring to children and other neighbors.

Obj. 5. Further, in every kind of sin, it is possible to sin in thought or in deed. But in some kinds of sin, namely in theft and adultery, the prohibition of sins of deed, that is, when it is said, *Thou shalt not commit adultery, Thou shalt not steal,* is distinct from the prohibition of the sin of thought, that is, when it is said, *Thou shalt not covet thy neighbor's goods,* and, *Thou shalt not covet thy neighbor's wife.* Therefore the same should have been done in regard to the sins of homicide and false witness.

[18] *Eth.,* X, 5 (1175b 28).   [19] *De Parad.,* VIII (PL 14, 309).

Obj. 6. Further, just as sin happens through disorder of the concupiscible part, so does it arise through disorder of the irascible part. But some precepts forbid inordinate concupiscence, as when it is said, *Thou shalt not covet.* Therefore the decalogue should have included some precepts forbidding the disorders of the irascible part. Therefore it seems that the ten precepts of the decalogue are unfittingly enumerated.

On the contrary, It is written (*Deut.* iv. 13): *He shewed you His covenant, which He commanded you to do, and the ten words that He wrote in two tables of stone.*

I answer that, As we have stated above, just as the precepts of human law direct man in his relations to the human community, so the precepts of the divine law direct man in his relations to a community or commonwealth of men under God. Now in order that any man may dwell rightly in a community, two things are required: the first is that he behave well towards the head of the community; the other is that he behave well towards those who are his fellows and partners in the community. It is therefore necessary that the divine law should contain, in the first place, precepts ordering man in his relations to God, and, in the second place, other precepts ordering man in his relations to other men who are his neighbors and live with him under God.

Now man owes three things to the head of the community: first, fidelity; secondly, reverence; thirdly, service. Fidelity to his master consists in his not giving sovereign honor to another; and this is the sense of the first commandment, in the words, *Thou shalt not have strange gods.* Reverence to his master requires that he should do nothing injurious to him; and this is conveyed by the second commandment, *Thou shalt not take the name of the Lord thy God in vain.* Service is due to the master in return for the benefits which his subjects receive from him; and to this belongs the third commandment on the sanctification of the Sabbath in remembrance of the creation of all things.

To his neighbors a man behaves himself well both in particular and in general: in particular, as to those to whom he is indebted, by paying his debts: and in this sense is to be taken the commandment about honoring one's parents; in general, as to all men, by doing harm to none, either by deed, or by word, or by thought. By deed, harm is done to one's neighbor,—sometimes in his person, *i.e.,* as to his personal existence, and this is forbidden by the words, *Thou shalt not kill;*—sometimes in a person united to him, as to the propagation of offspring, and this is prohibited by the words, *Thou shalt not commit adultery;*—sometimes in his possessions, which are directed to both the aforesaid, and with regard to this it is said, *Thou shalt not steal.*—Harm done by word is forbidden when it is said, *Thou shalt not bear false witness against thy neighbor;* and harm done by thought is forbidden in the words, *Thou shalt not covet.*

The three precepts that direct man in his behavior towards God may also be differentiated in this same way. For the first refers to deeds, and hence it is said, *Thou shalt not make . . . a graven thing*; the second, to words, and hence it is said, *Thou shalt not take the name of the Lord thy God in vain*; the third, to thoughts, because the sanctification of the Sabbath, in so far as it is the subject of a moral precept, requires repose of the heart in God.—Or, according to Augustine, by the first commandment we reverence the unity of the First Principle; by the second, the divine truth; by the third, His goodness, whereby we are sanctified, and wherein we rest as in our last end.[20]

Reply Obj. 1. This objection may be answered in two ways. First, because the precepts of the decalogue can be reduced to the precepts of charity. Now there was need for man to receive a precept about loving God and his neighbor, because in this respect the natural law had become obscured because of sin; but not about the duty of loving oneself, because in this respect the natural law retained its vigor (or because love of oneself is contained in the love of God and of one's neighbor; since true self-love consists in directing oneself to God). And for this reason the decalogue includes only those precepts which refer to our neighbor and to God.

Secondly, it may be answered that the precepts of the decalogue are those which the people received from God immediately; and so it is written (*Deut.* x. 4): *He wrote in the tables, according as He had written before, the ten words, which the Lord spoke to you.* Hence the precepts of the decalogue need to be such as the people can understand at once. Now a precept has the nature of a duty. But it is easy for a man, especially for a believer, to understand that, of necessity, he owes certain duties to God and to his neighbor. But that, in matters which regard himself and not another, man has, of necessity, certain duties to himself, is not so evident; for, at first glance, it seems that everyone is free in matters that concern himself. And therefore the precepts which prohibit the disorders of a man with regard to himself reach the people through the instruction of men who are versed in such matters; and, consequently, they are not contained in the decalogue.

Reply Obj. 2. All the solemnities of the Old Law were instituted in celebration of some divine favor, either in memory of past favors, or in sign of some favor to come; and in like manner, all the sacrifices were offered up with the same purpose. Now of all the divine favors to be commemorated, the chief was that of the creation, which was called to mind by the sanctification of the Sabbath; and so the reason for this precept is given in *Exod.* xx. 11: *In six days the Lord made heaven and earth,* etc. And of all future blessings, the chief and final was the repose of the mind in God, either, in the present life, by grace, or, in the future life, by glory. This repose was also foreshadowed in the Sabbath-day observance; and consequently it is written (*Isa.* lviii. 13): *If thou turn away thy foot from the*

[20] *Enarr. in Psalm.*, super XXXII, 2 (PL 36, 281).

Sabbath, from doing thy own will in My holy day, and call the Sabbath delightful, and the holy of the Lord glorious. For these favors first and chiefly are borne in mind by men, especially by the faithful.—But other solemnities were celebrated because of certain particular temporal and transitory favors, such as the celebration of the Passover in memory of the past favor of the delivery from Egypt, and as a sign of the future Passion of Christ, which, though temporal and transitory, brought us to the repose of the spiritual Sabbath. Consequently, the Sabbath alone, and none of the other solemnities and sacrifices, is mentioned in the precepts of the decalogue.

Reply Obj. 3. As the Apostle says (*Heb.* vi. 16), *men swear by one greater than themselves; and an oath for confirmation is the end of all their controversy.* Hence, since oaths are common to all, inordinate swearing is the matter of a special prohibition by a precept of the decalogue. But the sin of false doctrine applies only to a few, and therefore it was not necessary that it should be mentioned among the precepts of the decalogue. According to one interpretation, however, the words, *Thou shalt not take the name of the Lord thy God in vain,* are a prohibition of false doctrine, for one *Gloss* expounds them thus: *Thou shalt not say that Christ is a creature.*[21]

Reply Obj. 4. That a man should not do harm to anyone is an immediate dictate of his natural reason, and therefore the precepts of the decalogue that forbid the doing of harm are binding on all men. But it is not an immediate dictate of the natural reason that a man should do one thing in return for another, unless he happen to be indebted to someone. Now a son's debt to his father is so evident that one cannot get away from it by denying it; for the father is the principle of generation and being, and also of upbringing and teaching. Hence the decalogue does not prescribe deeds of kindness or service to be done to anyone except to one's parents. On the other hand, parents do not seem to be indebted to their children for any favors received, but rather the reverse is the case. Furthermore, a child is a part of his father, and *parents love their children as being a part of themselves,* as the Philosopher states.[22] Hence, just as the decalogue contains no ordinance as to man's behavior towards himself, so, for the same reason, it includes no precept about loving one's children.

Reply Obj. 5. The pleasure of adultery and the usefulness of wealth, in so far as they have the character of pleasurable or useful good, are, of themselves, objects of appetite; and for this reason they needed to be forbidden not only in the deed but also in the desire. But murder and falsehood are, of themselves, objects of repulsion (since it is natural for man to love his neighbor and the truth), and are desired only for the sake of some-

---

[21] *Glossa ordin.,* super *Deut.,* V, 11 (I, 337A); St. Isidore, *Quaest. in Vet. Test., In Exod.,* XXIX, super XX, 7 (PL 83, 301). [22] *Eth.,* VIII, 12 (1161b 19).

thing else. Consequently, with regard to sins of murder and false witness, it was necessary to proscribe, not sins of thought, but only sins of deed.

Reply Obj. 6. As was stated above, all the passions of the irascible part arise from the passions of the concupiscible part.[23] Hence, as the precepts of the decalogue are, as it were, the first elements of the Law, there was no need for mention of the irascible passions, but only of the concupiscible passions.

Sixth Article

WHETHER THE TEN PRECEPTS OF THE DECALOGUE ARE GIVEN IN THE PROPER ORDER?

We proceed thus to the Sixth Article:—

Objection 1. It would seem that the ten precepts of the decalogue are not given in the proper order. For love of one's neighbor is seemingly prior to love of God, since our neighbor is better known to us than God is. This is according to *1 John* iv. 20: *He that loveth not his brother, whom he seeth, how can he love God, Whom he seeth not?* But the first three precepts belong to the love of God, while the other seven pertain to the love of our neighbor. Therefore the precepts of the decalogue are not given in the proper order.

Obj. 2. Further, acts of virtue are prescribed by the affirmative precepts, and acts of vice are forbidden by the negative precepts. But according to Boethius, in his commentary on the *Categories,* vices should be uprooted before virtues are sown.[24] Therefore, among the precepts concerning our neighbor, the negative precepts should have preceded the affirmative.

Obj. 3. Further, the precepts of the Law are about men's actions. But actions of thought precede actions of word or outward deed. Therefore the precepts about not coveting, which regard our thoughts, are unsuitably placed last in order.

On the contrary, The Apostle says (*Rom.* xiii. 1): *The things that are of God, are well ordered.* But the precepts of the decalogue were given immediately by God, as was stated above. Therefore they are arranged in a becoming order.

I answer that, As we have stated above, the precepts of the decalogue are such as the mind of man is ready to grasp at once. Now it is evident that a thing is so much the more easily grasped by the reason as its contrary is more grievous and repugnant to reason. But since the order of reason begins with the end, it is clear that for a man to be inordinately disposed towards his end is supremely contrary to reason. Now the end of human life and society is God. Consequently, it was necessary for the precepts of the decalogue, first of all, to direct man to God, since the contrary to this is most grievous. So, too, in an army, which is ordained to the

---

[23] Q. 25, a. 1.   [24] *In Cat. Arist.,* IV (PL 64, 277).

commander as to its end, it is requisite, first, that the soldier should be subject to the commander, and the opposite of this is most grievous; and, secondly, it is requisite that he should be in co-ordination with the other soldiers.

Now among those things whereby we are ordained to God, the first is that man should be subjected to Him faithfully, by having nothing in common with His enemies. The second is that he should show Him reverence. And the third is that he should offer Him his service. Thus, in an army, it is a greater sin for a soldier to act treacherously and make a compact with the foe than to be insolent to his commander; and this last is more grievous than if he be found wanting in some point of service to him.

As to the precepts that direct man in his behavior towards his neighbor, it is evident that it is more repugnant to reason, and a more grievous sin, if man does not observe the due order as to those persons to whom he is most indebted. Consequently, among those precepts that direct man in his relations to his neighbor, the first place is given to that one which regards his parents. Among the other precepts we again find the order to be according to the gravity of sin. For it is more grave and more repugnant to reason to sin by deed than by word, and by word than by thought. And among sins of deed, murder which destroys life in one already living is more grievous than adultery, which imperils the life of the unborn child; and adultery is more grave than theft, which regards external goods.

Reply Obj. 1. Although our neighbor is better known than God by the way of the senses, nevertheless, the love of God is the reason for the love of our neighbor, as will be made clear later on.[25] Hence the precepts ordaining man to God demanded priority over the others.

Reply Obj. 2. Just as God is the universal principle of being for all things, so is a father a principle of being for his son. Therefore the precept regarding parents was fittingly placed after the precepts regarding God. The argument holds in respect of affirmative and negative precepts about the same kind of deed; although even then it is not altogether cogent. For although, in the order of execution, vices should be uprooted before virtues are sown (according to *Ps.* xxxiii. 15: *Turn away from evil, and do good*; and *Isa.* i. 16, 17: *Cease to do perversely; learn to do well*), yet in the order of knowledge virtue precedes vice, because *the crooked line is known by the straight*,[26] and *by the law is the knowledge of sin* (*Rom.* iii. 20). Therefore the affirmative precept demanded the first place. However, this is not the reason for the order, but that which was given above. For in the precepts regarding God, which belong to the first table, an affirmative precept is placed last, since its transgression implies a less grievous sin.

Reply Obj. 3. Although sin of thought stands first in the order of execution, yet its prohibition holds a later position in the order of reason.

---

[25] *S. T.*, II-II, q. 25, a. 1; q. 26, a. 2.   [26] Aristotle, *De An.*, I, 5 (411a 5).

Seventh Article

WHETHER THE PRECEPTS OF THE DECALOGUE ARE SUITABLY
FORMULATED?

We proceed thus to the Seventh Article:—
Objection 1. It would seem that the precepts of the decalogue are unsuitably formulated. For the affirmative precepts direct man to acts of virtue, while the negative precepts withdraw him from acts of vice. But in every matter there are virtues and vices opposed to one another. Therefore, in whatever matter there is an ordinance of a precept of the decalogue, there should have been an affirmative and a negative precept. Therefore it was unfitting that affirmative precepts should be framed in some matters, and negative precepts in others.

Obj. 2. Further, Isidore says that every law is based on reason.[27] But all the precepts of the decalogue belong to the divine law. Therefore the reason should have been pointed out in each precept, and not only in the first and third.

Obj. 3. Further, by observing the precepts, man deserves to be rewarded by God. But the divine promises concern the rewards of the precepts. Therefore the promise should have been included in each precept, and not only in the first and fourth.

Obj. 4. Further, the Old Law is called *the law of fear*,[28] in so far as it induced men to observe the precepts by means of the threat of punishments. But all the precepts of the decalogue belong to the Old Law. Therefore a threat of punishment should have been included in each, and not only in the first and second.

Obj. 5. Further, all the commandments of God should be retained in the memory, for it is written (*Prov.* iii. 3): *Write them in the tables of thy heart.* Therefore it was not fitting that mention of the memory should be made in the third commandment only. Consequently, it seems that the precepts of the decalogue are unsuitably formulated.

On the contrary, It is written (*Wis.* xi. 21) that *God made all things in measure, number and weight.* Much more therefore did He observe a suitable manner in formulating His Law.

I answer that, The highest wisdom is contained in the precepts of the divine law, and hence it is written (*Deut.* iv. 6): *This is your wisdom and understanding in the sight of nations.* Now it belongs to wisdom to arrange all things in due manner and order. Therefore it must be evident that the precepts of the Law are suitably set forth.

Reply Obj. 1. Affirmation of one thing always leads to the denial of its opposite; but the denial of one opposite does not always lead to the

[27] *Etymol.*, II, 10; V, 3 (PL 82, 130; 199). [28] Cf. St. Augustine, *De Mor. Eccl.*, I, 28 (PL 32, 1334).

affirmation of the other. For it follows that, if a thing is white, it is not black; but it does not follow that, if it is not black, it is white, because negation extends further than affirmation. And hence, too, that one ought not to do harm to another, which pertains to the negative precepts, extends to more persons, as a primary dictate of reason, than that one ought to do someone a service or kindness. Nevertheless, it is a primary dictate of reason that man is a debtor in the point of rendering a service or kindness to those from whom he has received kindness, if he has not yet repaid the debt. Now there are two whose favors no man can sufficiently repay, viz., God and man's father, as is stated in *Ethics* viii.[29] Therefore it is that there are only two affirmative precepts, one about the honor due to parents, the other about the celebration of the Sabbath in remembrance of the divine favor.

Reply Obj. 2. The reasons for the purely moral precepts are manifest, and so there was no need to add a reason. But some of the precepts include ceremonial matters, or a determination of a common moral precept. Thus, the first precept includes the determination, *Thou shalt not make a graven thing*; and in the third precept the Sabbath-day is fixed. Consequently, there was need to state the reason in each case.

Reply Obj. 3. Generally speaking, men direct their actions to something useful. Consequently in those precepts in which it seemed that there would be no useful result, or that some utility might be hindered, it was necessary to add a promise of reward. And since parents are already on the way to depart from us, no benefit is expected from them; and so a promise of reward is added to the precept about honoring one's parents. The same applies to the precept forbidding idolatry, since thereby it seemed that men were hindered from receiving the apparent benefit which they think they can get by entering into a compact with the demons.

Reply Obj. 4. Punishments are especially necessary against those who are prone to evil, as is stated in *Ethics* x.[30] Therefore a threat of punishment is affixed only to those precepts of the law which forbade evils to which men were prone. Now men were prone to idolatry by reason of the general custom of the nations. Likewise men are prone to perjury because of the frequent use of oaths. Hence it is that a threat is affixed to the first two precepts.

Reply Obj. 5. The commandment about the Sabbath was made in remembrance of a past blessing. Therefore special mention of the memory is made therein.—Or again, the commandment about the Sabbath has a determination affixed to it that does not belong to the natural law, and so this precept needed a special admonition.

---

[29] Aristotle, *Eth.*, VIII, 14 (1163b 15).   [30] *Op. cit.*, X, 9 (1180a 4).

Eighth Article

WHETHER THE PRECEPTS OF THE DECALOGUE ARE
DISPENSABLE?

We proceed thus to the Eighth Article:—
Objection 1. It would seem that the precepts of the decalogue are dispensable. For the precepts of the decalogue belong to the natural law. But the natural law fails in some cases and is changeable, as does human nature, as the Philosopher says.[31] Now the failure of law to apply in certain particular cases is a reason for dispensation, as was stated above.[32] Therefore a dispensation can be granted in the precepts of the decalogue.

Obj. 2. Further, man stands in the same relation to human law as God does to divine law. But man can dispense from the precepts of a law made by man. Therefore, since the precepts of the decalogue are ordained by God, it seems that God can dispense from them. Now our superiors are God's vicegerents on earth, for the Apostle says (*2 Cor.* ii. 10): *For what I have pardoned, if I have pardoned anything, for your sakes have I done it in the person of Christ.* Therefore superiors can dispense from the precepts of the decalogue.

Obj. 3. Further, among the precepts of the decalogue is one forbidding murder. But it seems that a dispensation is given by men in this precept: *e.g.*, when according to the prescription of human law men such as evildoers or enemies are lawfully slain. Therefore the precepts of the decalogue are dispensable.

Obj. 4. Further, the observance of the Sabbath is ordained by a precept of the decalogue. But a dispensation was granted in this precept, for it is written (*1 Machab.* ii. 41): *And they determined in that day, saying: Whosoever shall come up to fight against us on the Sabbath-day, we will fight against him.* Therefore the precepts of the decalogue are dispensable.

On the contrary are the words of *Isa.* xxiv. 5, where some are reproved because *they have changed the ordinance, they have broken the everlasting covenant*; which words, seemingly, apply principally to the precepts of the decalogue. Therefore the precepts of the decalogue cannot be changed by dispensation.

I answer that, As we have stated above, precepts admit of dispensation when there occurs a particular case in which, if the letter of the law be observed, the intention of the lawgiver is frustrated.[33] Now the intention of every lawgiver is directed first and chiefly to the common good; secondly, to the order of justice and virtue, whereby the common good is preserved and attained. If, therefore, there be any precepts which contain the very preservation of the common good, or the very order of justice and virtue, such precepts contain the intention of the lawgiver, and therefore are indis-

---

[31] *Op. cit.,* V, 7 (1134b 29).   [32] Q. 96, a. 6; q. 97, a. 4.   [33] *Ibid.*

pensable. For instance, if in some community a law were enacted, such as this, that no man should work for the destruction of the commonwealth, or betray the state to its enemies, or that no man should do anything unjust or evil, such precepts would not admit of dispensation. But if other precepts were enacted, subordinate to the above, and determining certain special modes of procedure, these latter precepts would admit of dispensation, in so far as the omission of these precepts in certain cases would not be prejudicial to the former precepts which contain the intention of the lawgiver. For instance, if, for the safeguarding of the commonwealth, it were enacted in some city that from each ward some men should keep watch as sentries in case of siege, some might be dispensed from this because of some greater utility.

Now the precepts of the decalogue contain the very intention of the lawgiver, Who is God. For the precepts of the first table, which direct us to God, contain the very order to the common and final good, which is God; while the precepts of the second table contain the order of justice to be observed among men, namely, that nothing undue be done to anyone, and that each one be given his due; for it is in this sense that we are to take the precepts of the decalogue. Consequently, the precepts of the decalogue admit of no dispensation whatever.

Reply Obj. 1. The Philosopher is not speaking of the natural law which contains the very order of justice; for it is a never-failing principle that *justice should be preserved.* But he is speaking in reference to certain fixed modes of observing justice, which fail to apply in certain cases.

Reply Obj. 2. As the Apostle says (*2 Tim.* ii. 13), God *continueth faithful, He cannot deny Himself.* But He would deny Himself if He were to do away with the very order of His own justice, since He is justice itself. Therefore God cannot dispense a man so that it be lawful for him not to direct himself to God, or not to be subject to His justice, even in those matters in which men are directed to one another.

Reply Obj. 3. The slaying of a man is forbidden in the decalogue, in so far as it bears the character of something undue; for in this sense the precept contains the very notion of justice. Human law, however, cannot make it lawful for a man to be slain without due cause. But it is not undue for evil-doers or foes of the common weal to be slain; and so this is not contrary to the precept of the decalogue, and such killing is not murder as forbidden by that precept, as Augustine observes.[34] In like manner, when a man's property is taken from him, if it be due that he should lose it, this is not theft or robbery as forbidden by the decalogue.

Consequently when the children of Israel, by God's command, took away the spoils of the Egyptians (*Exod.* xii. 35), this was not theft, since it was due to them by the sentence of God.—Likewise, when Abraham consented to slay his son (*Gen.* xxii), he did not consent to murder, because his son

[34] *De Lib. Arb.,* I, 4 (PL 32, 1226).

was due to be slain by the command of God, Who is Lord of life and death; for He it is Who inflicts the punishment of death on all men, both the just and the unjust because of the sin of our first parent, and if a man be the executor of that sentence by divine authority, he will be no murderer any more than God would be.—Again Osee, by taking unto himself a wife of fornications, or an adulterous woman (*Osee* i. 2), was not guilty either of adultery or of fornication; for he took unto himself one who was his by command of God, Who is the Author of the institution of marriage.

Accordingly, therefore, the precepts of the decalogue, as to the notion of justice which they contain, are unchangeable; but as to any determination by application to individual actions,—for instance, that this or that be murder, theft, or adultery, or not—in this point, they admit of change. Sometimes this takes place by divine authority alone, namely, in such matters as are exclusively of divine institution, as marriage and the like; sometimes also by human authority, namely, in such matters as are subject to human jurisdiction; for in *this* respect men stand in the place of God, though not in all respects.

Reply Obj. 4. This determination was an interpretation rather than a dispensation. For a man is not taken to break the Sabbath if he does something necessary for human welfare, as Our Lord proves (*Matt.* xii. 3 *seq.*).

Ninth Article

WHETHER THE MODE OF VIRTUE FALLS UNDER THE PRECEPT OF THE LAW?

We proceed thus to the Ninth Article:—

Objection 1. It would seem that the mode of virtue falls under the precept of the law. For the mode of virtue is that deeds of justice should be done justly, that deeds of fortitude should be done bravely, and in like manner as to the other virtues. But it is commanded (*Deut.* xvi. 20) that *thou shalt follow justly after that which is just.* Therefore the mode of virtue falls under the precept.

Obj. 2. Further, that which belongs to the intention of the lawgiver comes chiefly under the precept. But the intention of the lawgiver is directed chiefly to make men virtuous, as is stated in *Ethics* ii.[35] Now it belongs to a virtuous man to act virtuously. Therefore the mode of virtue falls under the precept.

Obj. 3. Further, the mode of virtue seems to consist properly in working willingly and with pleasure. But this falls under a precept of the divine law, for it is written (*Ps.* xciv. 2): *Serve ye the Lord with gladness*; and (*2 Cor.* ix. 7): *Not with sadness or necessity: for God loveth a cheerful giver.* On this the *Gloss* says: *Whatever good ye do, do gladly, and then*

---

[35] Aristotle, *Eth.*, II, 1 (1103b 3).

you will do it well; whereas if you do it sorrowfully, it is done in thee, not by thee.[36] Therefore the mode of virtue falls under the precept of the law.

On the contrary, No man can act as a virtuous man acts unless he has the habit of virtue, as the Philosopher explains.[37] Now whoever transgresses a precept of the law deserves to be punished. Hence it would follow that a man who has not the habit of virtue would deserve to be punished, whatever he does. But this is contrary to the intention of law, which aims at leading man to virtue, by habituating him to good works. Therefore the mode of virtue does not fall under the precept.

I answer that, As was stated above, a precept of law has compulsory power.[38] Hence that on which the compulsion of the law is brought to bear, falls directly under the precept of the law. Now the law compels through fear of punishment, as is stated in *Ethics* x.,[39] because that properly falls under the precept of the law for which the penalty of the law is inflicted. But divine law and human law are differently situated as to the appointment of penalties, since the penalty of the law is inflicted only for those things which come under the judgment of the lawgiver; for the law punishes in accordance with the verdict given. Now man, the framer of human law, is competent to judge only of outward acts, because *man seeth those things that appear,* according to *1 Kings* xvi. 7; while God alone, the framer of the divine law, is competent to judge of the inward movements of wills, according to *Ps.* vii. 10: *The searcher of hearts and reins is God.*

Accordingly, therefore, we must say that the mode of virtue is in some respect regarded both by human and by divine law; in some respect it is regarded by the divine, but not by the human law; and in another way, it is regarded neither by the human nor by the divine law. Now the mode of virtue consists in three things, as the Philosopher states in *Ethics* ii.[40] The first is that man should act *knowingly,* and this is subject to the judgment of both divine and human law, because what a man does in ignorance, he does accidentally. Hence, according to both human and divine law, certain things are judged according to ignorance to be punishable or pardonable.

The second point is that a man should act *deliberately, i.e., from choice, choosing that particular action for its own sake;* wherein a twofold internal movement is implied, of volition and of intention, about which we have spoken above.[41] And concerning these two, divine law alone, and not human law, is competent to judge. For human law does not punish the man who wishes to slay, but slays not; whereas the divine law does, according to *Matt.* v. 22: *Whosoever is angry with his brother, shall be in danger of the judgment.*

The third point is that he should *act from a firm and immovable prin-*

---

[36] *Glossa ordin.* (III, 226A; VI, 72A); St. Augustine, *Enarr. in Psalm.,* super XCI, 4 (PL 37, 1174).   [37] *Eth.,* II, 4 (1105a 17); V, 8 (1135b 24).   [38] Q. 90, a. 3, ad 2.   [39] Aristotle, *Eth.,* X, 9 (1179b 11; 1180a 3; a 21).   [40] *Eth.,* II, 4 (1105a 31).   [41] Q. 8 and 12.

ciple, which firmness belongs properly to a habit, and implies that the action proceeds from a rooted habit. In this respect, the mode of virtue does not fall under the precept either of divine or of human law, since neither by man nor by God is he punished as breaking the law who gives due honor to his parents and yet has not the habit of filial piety.

Reply Obj. 1. The mode of doing an act of justice, which falls under the precept, is that it be done in accordance with the order of what is right, but not that they be done from the habit of justice.

Reply Obj. 2. The intention of the lawgiver bears on two things. His aim, in the first place, is to lead men to something by the precepts of the law; and this is virtue. Secondly, his intention is brought to bear on the matter itself of the precept; and this is something leading or disposing to virtue, viz., an act of virtue. For the end of the precept and the matter of the precept are not the same; just as neither in other things is the end the same as that which conduces to the end.

Reply Obj. 3. That works of virtue should be done without sadness falls under the precept of the divine law, for whoever works with sadness works unwillingly. But to work with pleasure, *i.e.,* joyfully or cheerfully, in one respect falls under the precept, viz., in so far as pleasure ensues from the love of God and one's neighbor (which love falls under the precept), and since love is the cause of pleasure. In another respect, to work with pleasure does not fall under the precept, in so far as pleasure ensues from a habit; for *pleasure taken in a work proves the existence of a habit,* as is stated in *Ethics* ii.[42] For an act may give pleasure either because of its end or through its proceeding from a becoming habit.

Tenth Article

WHETHER THE MODE OF CHARITY FALLS UNDER THE PRECEPT
OF THE DIVINE LAW?

We proceed thus to the Tenth Article:—

Objection 1. It would seem that the mode of charity falls under the precept of the divine law. For it is written (*Matt.* xix. 17): *If thou wilt enter into life, keep the commandments;* whence it seems to follow that the observance of the commandments suffices for entrance into life. But good works do not suffice for entrance into life, except they be done from charity; for it is written (*1 Cor.* xiii. 3): *If I should distribute all my goods to feed the poor, and if I should deliver my body to be burned, and have not charity, it profiteth me nothing.* Therefore the mode of charity is included in the commandment.

Obj. 2. Further, the mode of charity consists, properly speaking, in doing all things for God. But this falls under the precept, for the Apostle

[42] Aristotle, *Eth.,* II, 3 (1104b 3).

says (*1 Cor.* x. 31): *Do all to the glory of God.* Therefore the mode of charity falls under the precept.

Obj. 3. Further, if the mode of charity does not fall under the precept, it follows that one can fulfill the precepts of the law without having charity. Now what can be done without charity can be done without grace, which is always united with charity. Therefore one can fulfill the precepts of the law without grace. But this is the error of Pelagius, as Augustine declares.[43] Therefore the mode of charity is included in the commandment.

On the contrary, Whoever breaks a commandment sins mortally. If, therefore, the mode of charity falls under the precept, it follows that whoever acts otherwise than from charity sins mortally. But whoever has not charity acts otherwise than from charity. Therefore it follows that whoever has not charity sins mortally in whatever he does, however good this may be in itself; which is absurd.

I answer that, Opinions have been opposed on this question.[44] For some have said absolutely that the mode of charity comes under the precept; and yet that it is possible for one not having charity to fulfill this precept, because he can dispose himself to receive charity from God. Nor (say they) does it follow that a man not having charity sins mortally whenever he does something good of its kind; because it is an affirmative precept that binds one to act from charity, and is binding not for all time, but only for such time as one possesses charity.—On the other hand, some have said that the mode of charity is altogether outside the precept.

Both these opinions are true up to a certain point. For the act of charity can be considered in two ways. First, as an act by itself, and thus it falls under the precept of the law which specially prescribes it, viz., *Thou shalt love the Lord thy God (Deut.* vi. 5), and *Thou shalt love thy neighbor (Levit.* xix. 18). In this sense, the first opinion is true. For it is not impossible to observe this precept which regards the act of charity, since a man can dispose himself to possess charity, and when he possesses it, he can use it. Secondly, the act of charity can be considered as being the mode of the acts of the other virtues, *i.e.,* inasmuch as the acts of the other virtues are ordained to charity, which is *the end of the commandment,* as is stated in *1 Tim.* i. 5; for it has been said above that the intention of the end is a formal mode of the act ordained to the end.[45] In this sense, the second opinion is true in saying that the mode of charity does not fall under the precept, that is to say, that this commandment, *Honor thy father,* does not mean that a man must honor his father from charity, but merely that he must honor him. Therefore he that honors his father, yet has not charity, does not break this precept; although he does break the precept concerning the act of charity, for which reason he deserves to be punished.

Reply Obj. 1. Our Lord did not say, *If thou wilt enter into life, keep one*

---

[43] *De Haeres.,* 88 (PL 42, 47).   [44] Cf. St. Albert, *In III Sent.,* d. xxxvi, a. 6 (XXVIII, 677).   [45] Q. 8, a. 2.

commandment; but *keep* all *the commandments,* among which is also included the commandment concerning the love of God and our neighbor.

Reply Obj. 2. The precept of charity contains the injunction that God should be loved from our whole heart, which means that all things should be referred to God. Consequently, man cannot fulfill the precept of charity, unless he also refer all things to God. Therefore he that honors his father and mother is bound to honor them from charity, not in virtue of the precept, *Honor thy father and mother,* but in virtue of the precept, *Thou shalt love the Lord thy God with thy whole heart.* And since these are two affirmative precepts that do not bind for all times, they can be binding, each one at a different time; so that it may happen that a man fulfills the precept of honoring his father and mother, without at the same time breaking the precept concerning the omission of the mode of charity.

Reply Obj. 3. Man cannot fulfill all the precepts of the law, unless he fulfill the precept of charity, which is impossible without grace. Consequently it is not possible, as Pelagius maintained, for man to fulfill the law without grace.

Eleventh Article

WHETHER IT IS RIGHT TO DISTINGUISH OTHER MORAL PRECEPTS OF THE LAW BESIDES THE DECALOGUE?

We proceed thus to the Eleventh Article:—

Objection 1. It would seem that it is wrong to distinguish other moral precepts of the law besides the decalogue. For, as Our Lord declared (*Matt.* xxii. 40), *on these two commandments* of charity *dependeth the whole law and the prophets.* But these two commandments are explained by the ten commandments of the decalogue. Therefore there is no need for other moral precepts.

Obj. 2. Further, the moral precepts are distinguished from the judicial and ceremonial precepts, as was stated above.[46] But the determinations of the common moral precepts belong to the judicial and ceremonial precepts; and the common moral precepts are contained in the decalogue, or are even presupposed to the decalogue, as was stated above. Therefore it was unsuitable to lay down other moral precepts besides the decalogue.

Obj. 3. Further, the moral precepts are about the acts of all the virtues, as was stated above. Therefore, as the Law contains, besides the decalogue, moral precepts pertaining to religion, liberality, mercy and chastity, so there should have been added some precepts pertaining to the other virtues, for instance, fortitude, sobriety and so forth. And yet such is not the case. It is therefore unbecoming to distinguish other moral precepts in the Law besides those of the decalogue.

[46] Q. 99, a. 3.

On the contrary, It is written (*Ps.* xviii. 8): *The law of the Lord is unspotted, converting souls.* But man is preserved from the stain of sin and his soul is converted to God by other moral precepts besides those of the decalogue. Therefore it was right for the Law to include other moral precepts.

I answer that, As is evident from what has been stated, the judicial and ceremonial precepts derive their force from their institution alone,[47] since, before they were instituted, it seemed of no consequence whether things were done in this or that way. But the moral precepts derive their efficacy from the very dictate of natural reason, even if they were never included in the Law. Now of these there are three grades. For some are most certain, and so evident as to need no promulgation. Such are the commandments of the love of God and our neighbor, and others like these, as was stated above, which are, as it were, the ends of the commandments; and so no man can have an erroneous judgment about them. Some precepts are more particular, the reason of which even an uneducated man can easily grasp; and yet they need to be promulgated, because human judgment, in a few instances, happens to be led astray concerning them. These are the precepts of the decalogue. Again, there are some precepts the reason for which is not so evident to everyone, but only to the wise; and these are moral precepts added to the decalogue, and given to the people by God through Moses and Aaron.

But since the things that are evident are the principles whereby we know those that are not evident, the other moral precepts added to the decalogue are reducible to the precepts of the decalogue as so many corollaries. Thus, the first commandment of the decalogue forbids the worship of strange gods, and to this are added other precepts forbidding things relating to the worship of idols. Thus it is written (*Deut.* xviii. 10, 11): *Neither let there be found among you anyone that shall expiate his son or daughter, making them to pass through the fire: . . . neither let there be any wizard nor charmer, nor anyone that consulteth pythonic spirits, or fortune-tellers, or that seeketh the truth from the dead.* The second commandment forbids perjury. To this is added the prohibition of blasphemy (*Levit.* xxiv. 15 *seq.*) and the prohibition of false doctrine (*Deut.* xiii.). To the third commandment are added all the ceremonial precepts. To the fourth commandment, prescribing the honor due to parents, is added the precept about honoring the aged, according to *Levit.* xix. 32: *Rise up before the hoary head, and honor the person of the aged man;* and likewise all precepts prescribing the reverence to be observed towards our betters, or kindliness towards our equals or inferiors. To the fifth commandment, which forbids murder, is added the prohibition of hatred and of any kind of violence inflicted on our neighbor, according to *Levit.* xix. 16: *Thou shalt not stand against the blood of thy neighbor;* and likewise the prohibition

[47] *Ibid.*

against hating one's brother (*ibid.* 17): *Thou shalt not hate thy brother in thy heart*. To the sixth commandment, which forbids adultery, is added the prohibition about whoredom, according to *Deut.* xxiii. 17: *There shall be no whore among the daughters of Israel, nor whoremonger among the sons of Israel*; and the prohibition against unnatural sins, according to *Levit.* xviii. 22, 23: *Thou shalt not lie with mankind . . . thou shalt not copulate with any beast*. To the seventh commandment, which prohibits theft, is added the precept forbidding usury, according to *Deut.* xxiii. 19: *Thou shalt not lend to thy brother money to usury*; and the prohibition against fraud, according to *Deut.* xxv. 13: *Thou shalt not have divers weights in thy bag*; and, universally, all prohibitions relating to peculations and larceny. To the eighth commandment, forbidding false testimony, is added the prohibition against false judgment, according to *Exod.* xxiii. 2: *Neither shalt thou yield in judgment, to the opinion of the most part, to stray from the truth*; and the prohibition against lying (*ibid.* 7): *Thou shalt fly lying*; and the prohibition against detraction, according to *Levit.* xix. 16: *Thou shalt not be a detractor, nor a whisperer among the people*. To the other two commandments no further precepts are added, because all evil desires are forbidden by them.

Reply Obj. 1. The precepts of the decalogue are ordained to the love of God and our neighbor as pertaining evidently to our duty towards them; but the other precepts are so ordained as pertaining thereto less evidently.

Reply Obj. 2. It is in virtue of their institution that the ceremonial and judicial precepts *are determinations of the precepts of the decalogue,* not by reason of a natural instinct, as in the case of the superadded moral precepts.

Reply Obj. 3. The precepts of a law are ordained for the common good, as was stated above.[48] And since those virtues which direct our conduct towards others pertain directly to the common good, as also does the virtue of chastity, in so far as the generative act conduces to the common good of the species, hence precepts bearing directly on these virtues are given both in the decalogue and in addition thereto. As to the act of fortitude, there are the orders to be given by the commanders in the war, which is undertaken for the common good; as is clear from *Deut.* xx. 3, where the priest is commanded [to speak thus]: *Be not afraid, do not give back*. In like manner, the prohibition of acts of gluttony is left to paternal admonition, since it is contrary to the good of the household; and so it is said (*Deut.* xxi. 20) in the person of parents: *He slighteth hearing our admonitions, he giveth himself to revelling, and to debauchery and banquetings*.

[48] Q. 90, a. 2.

Twelfth Article

WHETHER THE MORAL PRECEPTS OF THE OLD LAW
JUSTIFIED MAN?

We proceed thus to the Twelfth Article:—
Objection 1. It would seem that the moral precepts of the Old Law justified man. For the Apostle says (*Rom.* ii. 13): *For not the hearers of the Law are justified before God, but the doers of the Law shall be justified.* But the doers of the Law are those who fulfill the precepts of the Law. Therefore the fulfilling of the precepts of the Law was a cause of justification.

Obj. 2. Further, it is written (*Levit.* xviii. 5): *Keep My laws and My judgments, which if a man do, he shall live in them.* But the spiritual life of man is through justice. Therefore the fulfilling of the precepts of the Law was a cause of justification.

Obj. 3. Further, the divine law is more efficacious than human law. But human law justifies man, since there is a kind of justice consisting in fulfilling the precepts of law. Therefore the precepts of the Law justified man.

On the contrary, The Apostle says (*2 Cor.* iii. 6): *The letter killeth,* which, according to Augustine, refers even to the moral precepts.[49] Therefore the moral precepts did not cause justice.

I answer that, Just as *healthy* is said properly and first of that which is possessed of health, and secondarily of that which is a sign or a safeguard of health, so justification means first and properly the causing of justice, while secondarily and improperly, as it were, it may denote a sign of justice or a disposition thereto. If justice be taken in the last two ways, it is evident that it was conferred by the precepts of the Law; in so far, namely, as they disposed men to the justifying grace of Christ, which they also signified. For, as Augustine says, *even the life of that people foretold and foreshadowed Christ.*[50]

But if we speak of justification properly so called, then we must notice that it can be considered as it is found in the habit or as in the act; so that, accordingly, justification may be taken in two ways. First, according as man is made just by becoming possessed of the habit of justice; secondly, according as he does works of justice, so that in this sense justification is nothing else than the execution of justice. Now justice, like the other virtues, may denote either the acquired or the infused virtue, as is clear from what has been stated.[51] The acquired virtue is caused by works, but the infused virtue is caused by God Himself through His grace. The latter is true justice, of which we are speaking now, and in respect of which a man is said to be just before God, according to *Rom.* iv. 2: *If Abraham were*

---

[49] *De Spir. et Litt.*, XIV (PL 44, 215).   [50] *Contra Faust.*, XXII, 24 (PL 42, 417).
[51] Q. 63, a. 4.

justified by works, he hath whereof to glory, but not before God. Hence this justice could not be caused by the moral precepts, which are about human actions; and therefore the moral precepts could not justify man by causing justice.

If, on the other hand, by justification we understand the execution of justice, thus all the precepts of the Law justified man, but in various ways. For the ceremonial precepts, taken as a whole, contained something just in itself, in so far as they aimed at offering worship to God; whereas, taken individually, they contained that which is just, not in itself, but by being a determination of the divine law. Hence it is said of these precepts that they did not justify man save through the devotion and obedience of those who complied with them. On the other hand, the moral and judicial precepts, either in general or also in particular, contained that which is just in itself; but the moral precepts contained that which is just in itself according to that *general justice* which is *every virtue,* according to *Ethics* v.;[52] whereas the judicial precepts belonged to *special justice,* which is about contracts connected with the human mode of life, between one man and another.

Reply Obj. 1. The Apostle takes justification for the execution of justice.

Reply Obj. 2. The man who fulfills the precepts of the Law is said to live in them because he did not incur the penalty of death, which the Law inflicted on its transgressors. It is in this sense that the Apostle quotes this passage (*Gal.* iii. 12).

Reply Obj. 3. The precepts of human law justify man by acquired justice; but it is not about this that we are inquiring now, but only about that justice which is before God.

[52] Aristotle, *Eth.*, V, 1 (1129b 30).

ON THE CEREMONIAL PRECEPTS IN THEMSELVES

(*In Four Articles*)

WE must now consider the ceremonial precepts, and first we must consider them in themselves; secondly, their cause;[1] thirdly, their duration.[2] Under the first head there are four points of inquiry: (1) The nature of the ceremonial precepts. (2) Whether they are figurative? (3) Whether there should have been many of them? (4) Of their various kinds.

First Article

WHETHER THE NATURE OF THE CEREMONIAL PRECEPTS CONSISTS IN THEIR PERTAINING TO THE WORSHIP OF GOD?

We proceed thus to the First Article:—

Objection 1. It would seem that the nature of the ceremonial precepts does not consist in their pertaining to the worship of God.[3] For, in the Old Law, the Jews were given certain precepts about abstinence from food (*Levit.* xi. 19); and about refraining from certain kinds of clothes, *e.g.* (*Levit.* xix. 19): *Thou shalt not wear a garment that is woven of two sorts*; and again (*Num.* xv. 38): *To make to themselves fringes in the corners of their garments*. But these are not moral precepts, since they do not remain in the New Law. Nor are they judicial precepts, since they do not pertain to the pronouncing of judgment between man and man. Therefore they are ceremonial precepts. Yet they seem in no way to pertain to the worship of God. Therefore the nature of the ceremonial precepts does not consist in their pertaining to divine worship.

Obj. 2. Further, some state that the ceremonial precepts are those which pertain to solemnities; as though they were so called from the *cerei* [candles] which are lit up on those occasions.[4] But many other things besides solemnities pertain to the worship of God. Therefore it does not seem that the ceremonial precepts are so called from their pertaining to the divine worship.

Obj. 3. Further, some say that the ceremonial precepts are patterns, *i.e.*, rules, of salvation, because the Greek χαῖρε is the same as the Latin *salve*.[5] But all the precepts of the Law are rules of salvation, and not only those

---

[1] Q. 102. [2] Q. 103. [3] Cf. St. Albert, *In IV Sent.*, d. i, a. 7 (XXIX, 19); Cicero, *De Nat. Deor.*, II, 28 (p. 78). [4] St. Albert, *In IV Sent.*, d. i, a. 7 (XXIX, 18). [5] Unknown.

that pertain to the worship of God. Therefore not only those precepts which pertain to the divine worship are called ceremonial.

Obj. 4. Further, Rabbi Moses says that the ceremonial precepts are those for which there is no evident reason.[6] But there is evident reason for many things pertaining to the worship of God: *e.g.*, the observance of the Sabbath, the feasts of the Passover and of the Tabernacles, and many other things, the reason for which is set down in the Law. Therefore the ceremonial precepts are not those which pertain to the worship of God.

On the contrary, It is written (*Exod.* xviii. 19, 20): *Be thou to the people in those things that pertain to God . . . and . . . shew the people the ceremonies and the manner of worshipping.*

I answer that, As was stated above, the ceremonial precepts are determinations of the moral precepts whereby man is directed to God, just as the judicial precepts are determinations of the moral precepts whereby he is directed to his neighbor.[7] Now man is directed to God by the worship due to Him. Therefore those precepts are properly called ceremonial which pertain to the divine worship.—The reason for their being so called was given above when we established the distinction between the ceremonial and the other precepts.[8]

Reply Obj. 1. The divine worship includes not only sacrifices and the like, which seem to be directed to God immediately, but also those things whereby His worshippers are duly prepared to worship Him. Thus, too, in other matters, whatever is preparatory to the end comes under the science whose object is the end. Accordingly, those precepts of the Law which regard the clothing and food of God's worshippers, and other such matters, pertain to a certain preparation of the ministers, with a view to fitting them for the divine worship; just as those who administer to a king make use of certain special observances. Consequently, such are contained under the ceremonial precepts.

Reply Obj. 2. The alleged explanation of the name does not seem very probable, especially as the Law does not contain many instances of the lighting of candles in solemnities, since even the lamps of the Candlestick were furnished with *oil of olives,* as is stated in *Levit.* xxiv. 2. Nevertheless, we may say that all things pertaining to the divine worship were more carefully observed on solemn festivals; so that all ceremonial precepts may be included under the observance of solemnities.

Reply Obj. 3. Neither does this explanation of the name appear to be very much to the point, since the word *ceremony* is not Greek but Latin. We may say, however, that, since man's salvation is from God, those precepts above all seem to be rules of salvation which direct man to God; and accordingly those which refer to divine worship are called ceremonial precepts.

Reply Obj. 4. This explanation of the ceremonial precepts has a certain

---

[6] *Guide,* III, 28 (p. 314).   [7] Q. 99, a. 4.   [8] Q. 99, a. 3.

amount of probability. Not that they are called ceremonial precisely because there is no evident reason for them; rather this is a kind of consequence. For, since the precepts referring to the divine worship must needs be figurative, as we shall state further on, the consequence is that the reason for them is not so very evident.

Second Article

WHETHER THE CEREMONIAL PRECEPTS ARE FIGURATIVE?

We proceed thus to the Second Article:—

Objection 1. It would seem that the ceremonial precepts are not figurative. For it is the duty of every teacher to express himself in such a way as to be easily understood, as Augustine states.[9] Now this seems very necessary in the framing of a law, because precepts of law are proposed to the populace; for which reason *a law should be manifest*, as Isidore declares.[10] If, therefore, the precepts of the Law were given as figures of something, it seems unbecoming that Moses should have delivered these precepts without explaining what they signified.

Obj. 2. Further, whatever is done for the worship of God should be entirely free from unfittingness. But the performance of actions in representation of others seems to savor of the theatre or of the drama; because formerly the actions performed in theatres were done to represent the actions of others. Therefore it seems that such things should not be done for the worship of God. But the ceremonial precepts are ordained to the divine worship, as was stated above. Therefore they should not be figurative.

Obj. 3. Further, Augustine says that *God is worshipped chiefly by faith, hope and charity.*[11] But the precepts of faith, hope and charity are not figurative. Therefore the ceremonial precepts should not be figurative.

Obj. 4. Further, Our Lord says (*Jo.* iv. 24): *God is a spirit, and they that adore Him must adore Him in spirit and in truth.* But a figure is not the very truth; in fact, one is co-divided against the other. Therefore the ceremonial precepts, which refer to the divine worship, should not be figurative.

On the contrary, The Apostle says (*Coloss.* ii. 16, 17): *Let no man . . . judge you in meat or in drink, or in respect of a festival day, or of the new moon, or of the sabbaths, which are a shadow of things to come.*

I answer that, As was stated above, the ceremonial precepts are those which refer to the worship of God.[12] Now the divine worship is twofold: interior, and exterior. For since man is composed of soul and body, each of these should be applied to the worship of God, the soul by an interior worship, and the body by an outward worship. Hence it is written (*Ps.* lxxxiii. 3): *My heart and my flesh have rejoiced in the living God.* And just as the body is ordained to God through the soul, so the exterior worship is or-

---

[9] *De Doct. Christ.,* IV, 8; 10 (PL 34, 98; 99).   [10] *Etymol.,* II, 10; V, 21 (PL 82, 131; 203).   [11] *Enchir.,* III; IV (PL 40, 232; 233).   [12] A. 1; q. 99, a. 3 and 4.

dained to the interior worship. Now interior worship consists in the soul being united to God by the intellect and by affection. Therefore, according to the various ways in which the intellect and the affection of the man who worships God are rightly united to God, his exterior actions are applied in various ways to the divine worship.

For in the state of future beatitude, the human intellect will gaze on the divine truth in itself. Therefore the exterior worship will not consist in anything figurative, but solely in the praise of God, proceeding from the inward knowledge and affection, according to *Isa.* li. 3: *Joy and gladness shall be found therein, thanksgiving and the voice of praise.*

But in the present state of life, we are unable to gaze upon the divine truth in itself, and we need the ray of the divine light to shine upon us under the form of certain sensible figures, as Dionysius states; in various ways, however, according to the various states of human knowledge. For under the Old Law, neither was the divine truth manifest in itself, nor was the way leading to that manifestation as yet opened out, as the Apostle declares (*Heb.* ix. 8). Hence the exterior worship of the Old Law needed to be figurative not only of the future truth to be manifested in our heavenly country, but also of Christ, Who is the way leading to that heavenly manifestation. But under the New Law this way is already revealed, and therefore it needs no longer to be foreshadowed as something future, but to be brought to our minds as something past or present; and the truth of the glory to come, which is not yet revealed, alone needs to be foreshadowed. This is what the Apostle says (*Heb.* x. 1): *The Law has a shadow of the good things to come, not the very image of the things;* for a shadow is less than an image, so that the image belongs to the New Law, but the shadow to the Old.

Reply Obj. 1. The things of God are not to be revealed to man except in proportion to his capacity, or else he would be in danger of a downfall, were he to despise what he cannot grasp. Hence it was more beneficial that the divine mysteries should be revealed to an uncultivated people under a veil of figures, that thus they might know them at least implicitly by using those figures to the honor of God.

Reply Obj. 2. Just as human reason fails to grasp poetical expressions because of their being lacking in truth, so does it fail to grasp divine things perfectly, because of the sublimity of the truth they contain; and therefore in both cases there is need of signs by means of sensible figures.

Reply Obj. 3. Augustine is speaking there of interior worship; to which, however, exterior worship should be ordained, as we stated above.

The same answer applies to the Fourth Objection, because men were taught by Christ to practise more perfectly the spiritual worship of God.

Third Article

WHETHER THERE SHOULD HAVE BEEN MANY CEREMONIAL PRECEPTS?

We proceed thus to the Third Article:—

Objection 1. It would seem that there should not have been many ceremonial precepts. For those things which conduce to an end should be proportioned to that end. But the ceremonial precepts, as was stated above, are ordained to the worship of God and to the foreshadowing of Christ. Now *there is but one God, of Whom are all things, . . . and one Lord Jesus Christ, by Whom are all things (1 Cor.* viii. 6). Therefore there should not have been many ceremonial precepts.

Obj. 2. Further, the great number of the ceremonial precepts was an occasion of transgression, according to the words of Peter *(Acts* xv. 10): *Why tempt you God to put a yoke upon the necks of the disciples, which neither our fathers nor we have been able to bear?* Now the transgression of the divine precepts is an obstacle to man's salvation. Since, therefore, every law should conduce to man's salvation, as Isidore says,[13] it seems that the ceremonial precepts should not have been given in great number.

Obj. 3 Further, the ceremonial precepts referred to the exterior and bodily worship of God, as was stated above. But the Law should have lessened this bodily worship, since it directed men to Christ, Who taught them to worship God *in spirit and in truth,* as is stated in *John* iv. 23. Therefore there should not have been many ceremonial precepts.

On the contrary, It is written *(Osee* viii. 12): *I shall write to them My manifold laws;* and *(Job* xi. 6): *That He might show thee the secrets of His wisdom, and that His Law is manifold.*

I answer that, As we have stated above, every law is given to a people.[14] Now a people contains two kinds of men: some, prone to evil, who have to be coerced by the precepts of the law, as was stated above;[15] others, inclined to good, either from nature or from custom, or even from grace, and these have to be taught and improved by means of the precepts of law. Accordingly, with regard to both kinds of men, it was expedient that the Old Law should contain many ceremonial precepts. For in that people there were many prone to idolatry, and so it was necessary to recall them by means of ceremonial precepts from the worship of idols to the worship of God. And since men served idols in many ways, it was necessary, on the other hand, to devise many means of repressing every single one; and, again, to lay many obligations on such men, in order that being burdened, as it were, by their duties to the divine worship, they might have no time for the service of idols. As to those who were inclined to good, it was likewise necessary that there should be many ceremonial precepts, both because

---

[13] *Etymol.,* II, 10; V, 3 (PL 82, 131; 199).   [14] Q. 96, a. 1.   [15] Q. 95, a. 1.

their mind was thus turned to God in many ways, and more continually, and because the mystery of Christ, which was foreshadowed by these ceremonial precepts, brought many useful things to the world, and afforded men many considerations, which needed to be signified by various ceremonies.

Reply Obj. 1. When that which conduces to an end is sufficient to conduce thereto, then one such thing suffices for one end. Thus one remedy, if it be efficacious, suffices sometimes to restore man to health, and then the remedies need not to be multiplied. But when that which conduces to an end is weak and imperfect, it needs to be multiplied; and thus many remedies are given to a sick man, when one is not enough to heal him. Now the ceremonies of the Old Law were weak and imperfect, both for representing the mystery of Christ, because of its surpassing excellence, and for subjugating men's minds to God. Hence the Apostle says (*Heb.* vii. 18, 19): *There is a setting aside of the former commandment because of the weakness and unprofitableness thereof, for the law brought nothing to perfection.* Consequently, these ceremonies needed to be in great number.

Reply Obj. 2. A wise lawgiver should suffer lesser transgressions that the greater may be avoided. And, therefore, in order to avoid the sin of idolatry, and the pride which would arise in the hearts of the Jews, if they were to fulfill all the precepts of the Law, the fact that they would in consequence find many occasions of disobedience did not prevent God from giving them many ceremonial precepts.

Reply Obj. 3. The Old Law lessened bodily worship in many ways. Thus it forbade sacrifices to be offered in every place and by any person. Many such things it enacted for the lessening of bodily worship, as Rabbi Moses the Egyptian testifies.[16] Nevertheless, it was necessary not to attenuate the bodily worship of God so much as to allow men to fall away into the worship of idols.

Fourth Article

WHETHER THE CEREMONIES OF THE OLD LAW ARE SUITABLY DIVIDED INTO SACRIFICES, SACRED THINGS, SACRAMENTS AND OBSERVANCES?

We proceed thus to the Fourth Article:—

Objection 1. It would seem that the ceremonies of the Old Law are unsuitably divided into *sacrifices, sacred things, sacraments and observances.*[17] For the ceremonies of the Old Law foreshadowed Christ. But this was done only by the sacrifices, which foreshadowed the sacrifice in which Christ *delivered Himself an oblation and a sacrifice to God* (*Ephes.* v. 2). Therefore none but the sacrifices were ceremonies.

---

[16] *Guide*, III, 32 (p. 325).   [17] Cf. Peter Lombard, *Sent.*, IV, i, 6; 4 (II, 748; 746).

Obj. 2. Further, the Old Law was ordained to the New. But in the New Law the sacrifice is the Sacrament of the Altar. Therefore in the Old Law there should not have been a distinction between *sacrifices* and *sacraments*.

Obj. 3. Further, a *sacred thing* is something dedicated to God; in which sense the tabernacle and its vessels were said to be consecrated. But all the ceremonial precepts were ordained to the worship of God, as was stated above. Therefore all ceremonies were sacred things. Therefore *sacred things* should not be taken as a part of the ceremonies.

Obj. 4. Further, *Observances* are so called from having to be observed. But all the precepts of the Law had to be observed. For it is written (*Deut.* viii. 11): *Observe and beware lest at any time thou forget the Lord thy God, and neglect His commandments and judgments and ceremonies.* Therefore the *observances* should not be considered as a part of the ceremonies.

Obj. 5. Further, the solemn festivals are reckoned as part of the ceremonial, since they were a shadow of things to come (*Coloss.* ii. 16, 17); and the same may be said of the oblations and gifts, as appears from the words of the Apostle (*Heb.* ix. 9). And yet these do not seem to be included in any of those mentioned above. Therefore the above division of ceremonies is unsuitable.

On the contrary, In the Old Law each of the above is called a ceremony. For the sacrifices are called ceremonies (*Num.* xv. 24): *They shall offer a calf . . . and the sacrifices and libations thereof, as the ceremonies require.* Of the sacrament of Order it is written (*Levit.* vii. 35): *This is the anointing of Aaron and his sons in the ceremonies.* Of sacred things also it is written (*Exod.* xxxviii. 21): *These are the instruments of the tabernacle of the testimony . . . in the ceremonies of the Levites.* And again of the observances it is written (*3 Kings* ix. 6): *If you . . . shall turn away from following Me, and will not observe My . . . ceremonies which I have set before you.*

I answer that, As was stated above, the ceremonial precepts are ordained to the divine worship. Now in this worship we may consider the worship itself, the worshippers, and the instruments of worship. The worship consists especially in *sacrifices,* which are offered up in honor of God. The instruments of worship refer to the *sacred things,* such as the tabernacle, the vessels and so forth. With regard to the worshippers, two points may be considered. The first point is their preparation for divine worship, which is effected by a sort of consecration either of the people or of the ministers; and to this the *sacraments* refer. The second point is their particular mode of life, whereby they are distinguished from those who do not worship God; and to this pertain the *observances,* for instance, in matters of food, clothing, and so forth.

Reply Obj. 1. It was necessary for the sacrifices to be offered both in some certain place and by some certain men; and all this pertained to the worship of God. Therefore, just as their sacrifices signified Christ the victim, so too their sacraments and sacred things foreshadowed the sacraments and sacred things of the New Law, while their observances foreshadowed the mode of life of the people under the New Law. All of these things pertain to Christ.

Reply Obj. 2. The sacrifice of the New Law, viz., the Eucharist, contains Christ Himself, the Author of our Sanctification; for *He* sanctified *the people by His own blood* (*Heb.* xiii. 12). Hence this Sacrifice is also a sacrament. But the sacrifices of the Old Law did not contain Christ, but foreshadowed Him; and hence they are not called sacraments. In order to signify this there were certain sacraments, apart from the sacrifices of the Old Law, which sacraments were figures of the sanctification to come. Nevertheless to certain consecrations certain sacrifices were united.

Reply Obj. 3. The sacrifices and sacraments were, of course, sacred things. But certain things were sacred through being dedicated to the divine worship, and yet were not sacrifices or sacraments; and so they retained the common designation of sacred things.

Reply Obj. 4. Those things which pertained to the mode of life of the people who worshipped God retained the common designation of observances, in so far as they fell short of the above. For they were not called sacred things because they had no immediate connection with the worship of God, such as the tabernacle and its vessels had. But by a sort of consequence, they were matters of ceremony, in so far as they affected the fitness of the people who worshipped God.

Reply Obj. 5. Just as the sacrifices were offered in a fixed place, so they were offered at fixed times; and for this reason the solemn festivals seem to be reckoned among the sacred things. But the oblations and gifts are counted together with the sacrifices because they were offered to God, and hence the Apostle says (*Heb.* v. 1): *Every high-priest taken from among men is ordained for men in things that appertain to God, that he may offer up gifts and sacrifices.*

Question CII

ON THE CAUSES OF THE CEREMONIAL PRECEPTS

(*In Six Articles*)

WE must now consider the causes of the ceremonial precepts, under which head there are six points of inquiry: (1) Whether there was any cause for the ceremonial precepts? (2) Whether the cause of the ceremonial precepts was literal or figurative? (3) The causes of the sacrifices. (4) The causes of the sacraments. (5) The causes of the sacred things. (6) The causes of the observances.

First Article

WHETHER THERE WAS ANY CAUSE FOR THE CEREMONIAL PRECEPTS?

We proceed thus to the First Article:—

Objection 1. It would seem that there was no cause for the ceremonial precepts. For on *Ephes.* ii. 15 (*Making void the law of the commandments*) the *Gloss* says, *i.e., making void the Old Law as to the carnal observances, by substituting decrees, i.e., evangelical precepts, which are based on reason.*[1] But if the observances of the Old Law were based on reason, it would have been useless to void them by the reasonable decrees of the New Law. Therefore there was no reason for the ceremonial observances of the Old Law.

Obj. 2. Further, the Old Law succeeded the law of nature. But in the law of nature there was a precept for which there was no reason save that man's obedience might be tested, as Augustine says concerning the prohibition about the tree of life.[2] Therefore in the Old Law there should have been some precepts for the purpose of testing man's obedience, having no reason in themselves.

Obj. 3. Further, man's works are called moral according as they proceed from reason. If, therefore, there is any reason for the ceremonial precepts, they would not differ from the moral precepts. It seems, therefore, that there was no cause for the ceremonial precepts; for the reason of a precept is taken from some cause.

On the contrary, It is written (*Ps.* xviii. 9): *The commandment of the Lord is lightsome, enlightening the eyes.* But the ceremonial precepts are

---

[1] *Glossa interl.* (VI, 91v); Peter Lombard, *In Ephes.,* super II, 15 (PL 192, 185).
[2] *De Genesi ad Litt.,* VIII, 6; 13 (PL 34, 377; 383).

commandments of God. Therefore they are lightsome; and yet they would not be so, if they had no reasonable cause. Therefore the ceremonial precepts have a reasonable cause.

I answer that, Since, according to the Philosopher, it is the function of a *wise man to dispose everything in order,*[3] those things which proceed from the divine wisdom must needs be well ordered, as the Apostle states (*Rom.* xiii. 1). Now there are two conditions required for things to be well ordered. First, that they be ordained to their due end, which is the principle of the whole order in matters of action; for those things that happen by chance, outside the intention of the end, or which are not done seriously but for fun, are said to be inordinate. Secondly, that which is done in view of the end should be proportioned to the end. From this it follows that the reason for whatever conduces to the end is taken from the end. Thus the reason for the disposition of a saw is taken from cutting, which is its end, as is stated in *Physics* ii.[4] Now it is evident that the ceremonial precepts, like all the other precepts of the Law, were institutions of divine wisdom; and so it is written (*Deut.* iv. 6): *This is your wisdom and understanding in the sight of nations.* Consequently, we must needs say that the ceremonial precepts were ordained to a certain end, from which their reasonable causes can be gathered.

Reply Obj. 1. It may be said that there was no reason for the observances of the Old Law, in the sense that there was no reason in the very nature of the thing done: for instance, that a garment should not be made of wool and linen. But there could be a reason for them in their relation to something else, namely, in so far as something was signified or excluded thereby. On the other hand, the decrees of the New Law, which consist chiefly in faith and the love of God, are reasonable from the very nature of the act.

Reply Obj. 2. The reason for the prohibition concerning the tree of the knowledge of good and evil was not that this tree was naturally evil; and yet this prohibition was reasonable in its relation to something else, inasmuch as it signified something. And so, too, the ceremonial precepts of the Old Law were reasonable because of their relation to something else.

Reply Obj. 3. The moral precepts in their very nature have reasonable causes: e.g., *Thou shalt not kill, Thou shalt not steal.* But the ceremonial precepts have a reasonable cause in their relation to something else, as was stated above.

Second Article

WHETHER THE CEREMONIAL PRECEPTS HAVE A LITERAL
CAUSE OR MERELY A FIGURATIVE CAUSE?

We proceed thus to the Second Article:—

Objection 1. It would seem that the ceremonial precepts have not a lit-

---

[3] *Metaph.,* I, 2 (982a 18).   [4] Aristotle, *Phys.,* II, 9 (200a 10; b 5).

eral, but merely a figurative, cause. For among the ceremonial precepts, the chief were circumcision and the sacrifice of the paschal lamb. But neither of these had any but a figurative cause, because each was given as a sign. For it is written (*Gen.* xvii. 11): *You shall circumcise the flesh of your foreskin, that it may be for a sign of the covenant between Me and you*; and of the celebration of the Passover it is written (*Exod.* xiii. 9): *It shall be as a sign in thy hand, and as a memorial before thy eyes.* Therefore much more did the other ceremonial precepts have none but a figurative reason.

Obj. 2. Further, an effect is proportioned to its cause. But all the ceremonial precepts are figurative, as was stated above.[5] Therefore they have only a figurative cause.

Obj. 3. Further, if it be a matter of indifference whether a certain thing, considered in itself, be done in a particular way or not, it seems that it has not a literal cause. Now there are certain points in the ceremonial precepts which appear to be a matter of indifference, as to whether they be done in one way or in another: for instance, the number of animals to be offered, and other such particular circumstances. Therefore there is no literal cause for the precepts of the Old Law.

On the contrary, Just as the ceremonial precepts foreshadowed Christ, so did the stories of the Old Testament; for it is written (*1 Cor.* x. 11) that *all [these things] happened to them in figure.* Now in the stories of the Old Testament, besides the mystical or figurative, there is the literal sense. Therefore the ceremonial precepts had also literal, besides their figurative, causes.

I answer that, As was stated above, the reason for whatever conduces to an end must be taken from that end. Now the end of the ceremonial precepts was twofold, for they were ordained to the divine worship for that particular time, and to the foreshadowing of Christ; just as the words of the prophet regarded the time being in such a way as to be utterances figurative of the time to come, as Jerome says on *Osee* i. 3.[6] Accordingly, the reasons for the ceremonial precepts of the Old Law can be taken in two ways. First, in respect of the divine worship which was to be observed for that particular time; and these reasons are literal, whether they refer to the shunning of idolatry, or recall certain divine benefits, or remind men of the divine excellence, or point out the disposition of mind which was then required in those who worshipped God.—Secondly, their reasons can be gathered from the point of view of their being ordained to foreshadow Christ; and thus their reasons are figurative and mystical, whether they refer to Christ Himself and the Church, which pertains to the allegorical sense, or to the morals of the Christian people, which pertains to the moral sense, or to the state of future glory, inasmuch as we are brought thereto by Christ, which pertains to the anagogical sense.

[5] Q. 101, a. 2.   [6] *In Osee,* I, super I, 3 (PL 25, 364).

Reply Obj. 1. Just as the use of metaphorical expressions in Scripture belongs to the literal sense, because the words are employed in order to convey that particular meaning, so also the meaning of those legal ceremonies which commemorated certain divine benefits, because of which they were instituted, and of others similar which belonged to that time, does not go beyond the order of literal causes. Consequently, when we assert that the cause of the celebration of the Passover was its signification of the delivery from Egypt, or that circumcision was a sign of God's covenant with Abraham, we assign the literal cause.

Reply Obj. 2. This argument would avail, if the ceremonial precepts had been given merely as figures of things to come, and not for the purpose of worshipping God then and there.

Reply Obj. 3. As we stated when speaking of human laws, there is a reason for them in the universal, but not in regard to the particular conditions, which depend on the judgment of those who frame them.[7] So, too, many particular determinations in the ceremonies of the Old Law have no literal cause, but only a figurative cause; whereas, considered universally, they have a literal cause.

Third Article

WHETHER A SUITABLE CAUSE CAN BE ASSIGNED FOR THE CEREMONIES WHICH PERTAINED TO SACRIFICES?

We proceed thus to the Third Article:—

Objection 1. It would seem that no suitable cause can be assigned for the ceremonies pertaining to sacrifices. For those things which were offered in sacrifice are such as are necessary for sustaining human life: *e.g.*, animals and certain loaves. But God needs no such sustenance, according to *Ps.* xlix. 13: *Shall I eat the flesh of bullocks? Or shall I drink the blood of goats?* Therefore such sacrifices were unfittingly offered to God.

Obj. 2. Further, only three kinds of quadrupeds were offered in sacrifice to God, viz., oxen, sheep and goats; of birds, generally the turtledove and the dove; but especially, in the cleansing of a leper, an offering was made of sparrows. Now many other animals are more noble than these. Since, therefore, whatever is best should be offered to God, it seems that not only of these three should sacrifices have been offered to Him.

Obj. 3. Further, just as man has received from God the dominion over birds and beasts, so also has he received dominion over fishes. Consequently, it was unfitting for fishes to be excluded from the divine sacrifices.

Obj. 4. Further, turtledoves and doves indifferently are commanded to be offered up. Since, then, the young of the dove are commanded to be offered, so also should the young of the turtledove.

Obj. 5. Further, God is the Author of life, not only of men, but also of

[7] Q. 96, a. 1 and 6.

animals, as is clear from *Gen.* i. 20, *seqq.* Now death is opposed to life. Therefore it was fitting that living animals rather than slain animals should be offered to God, especially as the Apostle admonishes us (*Rom.* xii. 1) to present our bodies *a living sacrifice, holy, pleasing unto God.*

Obj. 6. Further, if none but slain animals were offered in sacrifice to God, it seems that it mattered not how they were slain. Therefore it was unfitting that the manner of immolation should be determined, especially as regards birds (*Levit.* i. 15, *seqq.*).

Obj. 7. Further, every defect in an animal is a step towards corruption and death. If therefore slain animals were offered to God, it was unreasonable to forbid the offering of an imperfect animal, *e.g.,* a lame, or a blind, or otherwise defective animal.

Obj. 8. Further, those who offer victims to God should partake thereof, according to the words of the Apostle (*1 Cor.* x. 18): *Are not they that eat of the sacrifices partakers of the altar?* It was therefore unbecoming for the offerers to be denied certain parts of the victims, namely, the blood, the fat, the breast-bone and the right shoulder.

Obj. 9. Further, just as holocausts were offered up in honor of God, so also were the peace-offerings and sin-offerings. But no female animal was offered up to God as a holocaust, although holocausts were offered of both quadrupeds and birds. Therefore it was inconsistent that female animals should be offered up in peace-offerings and sin-offerings, and that nevertheless birds should not be offered up in peace-offerings.

Obj. 10. Further, all the peace-offerings seem to be of one kind. Therefore it was unfitting to make a distinction among them, so that it was forbidden to eat the flesh of certain peace-offerings on the following day, while it was allowed to eat the flesh of other peace-offerings, as is laid down in *Levit.* vii. 15, *seqq.*

Obj. 11. Further, all sins agree in turning us from God. Therefore, in order to reconcile us to God, one kind of sacrifice should have been offered up for all sins.

Obj. 12. Further, all animals that were offered up in sacrifice were offered up in one way, viz., slain. Therefore it does not seem to be suitable that products of the soil should be offered up in various ways. For sometimes an offering was made of ears of corn, sometimes of flour, sometimes of bread; and sometimes the bread was baked in an oven, sometimes in a pan, sometimes on a gridiron.

Obj. 13. Further, whatever things are serviceable to us should be recognized as coming from God. It was therefore unbecoming that besides animals nothing but bread, wine, oil, incense and salt should be offered to God.

Obj. 14. Further, bodily sacrifices denote the inward sacrifice of the heart, whereby man offers his soul to God. But in the inward sacrifice the sweetness, which is denoted by honey, surpasses the pungency which salt represents; for it is written (*Ecclus*. xxiv. 27): *My spirit is sweet above honey*. Therefore it was unbecoming that the use of honey, and of leaven, which makes bread savory, should be forbidden in a sacrifice; while the use was prescribed, of salt which is pungent, and of incense which has a bitter taste. Consequently, it seems that things pertaining to the ceremonies of the sacrifices have no reasonable cause.

On the contrary, It is written (*Levit*. i. 13): *The priest shall offer it all and burn it all upon the altar for a holocaust and most sweet savor to the Lord*. Now according to *Wis*. vii. 28, *God loveth none but him that dwelleth with wisdom*; whence it seems to follow that whatever is acceptable to God is wisely done. Therefore these ceremonies of the sacrifices were wisely done, as having reasonable causes.

I answer that, As was stated above, the ceremonies of the Old Law had a twofold cause, viz., a literal cause, according as they were intended for divine worship, and a figurative or mystical cause, according as they were intended to foreshadow Christ; and in either case the ceremonies pertaining to the sacrifices can be assigned to a fitting cause.

For according as the ceremonies of the sacrifices were intended for the divine worship, the causes of the sacrifices can be taken in two ways. First, in so far as the sacrifice represented the directing of the mind to God, to which the offerer of the sacrifice was stimulated. Now in order to direct his mind to God rightly, man must recognize that whatever he has is from God as from its first principle, and direct it to God as its last end. This was denoted in the offerings and sacrifices by the fact that man offered some of his own belongings in honor of God, as though in recognition of his having received them from God, according to the saying of David (*1 Paral*. xxix. 14): *All things are Thine; and we have given Thee what we received of Thy hand*. Therefore, in offering up sacrifices, man made protestation that God is the first principle of the creation of all things, and their last end, to which all things must be directed.

And since, for the human mind to be directed to God rightly, it must recognize no first author of things other than God, nor place its end in any other, for this reason it was forbidden in the Law to offer sacrifice to any other but God, according to *Exod*. xxii. 20: *He that sacrificeth to gods shall be put to death, save only to the Lord*. Therefore another reasonable cause may be assigned to the ceremonies of the sacrifices, from the fact that thereby men were withdrawn from offering sacrifices to idols. Hence, too, it is that the precepts about the sacrifices were not given to the Jewish people until after they had fallen into idolatry by worshipping the molten calf; as though such sacrifices were instituted that the people, being ready to offer sacrifices, might offer those sacrifices to God rather than to idols. Thus it is written (*Jer*. vii. 22): *I spake not to your fathers and I commanded them not, in the day that I brought them out of the land of Egypt, concerning the matter of burnt-offerings and sacrifices*.

Now of all the gifts which God vouchsafed to mankind after they had fallen away by sin, the chief is that He gave His Son; and so it is written (*Jo.* iii. 16): *God so loved the world, as to give His only-begotten Son, that whosoever believeth in Him may not perish, but may have life everlasting.* Consequently the chief sacrifice is that whereby Christ Himself *delivered Himself . . . to God for an odor of sweetness* (*Ephes.* v. 2). And for this reason all the other sacrifices of the Old Law were offered up in order to foreshadow this one individual and paramount sacrifice—the imperfect forecasting the perfect. Hence the Apostle says (*Heb.* x. 11) that the priest of the Old Law *often* offered *the same sacrifices, which can never take away sins; but* Christ offered *one sacrifice for sins, forever.* And since the reason for a figure is taken from that which the figure represents, therefore, the reasons for the figurative sacrifices of the Old Law should be taken from the true sacrifice of Christ.

Reply Obj. 1. God did not wish these sacrifices to be offered to Him because of the things themselves that were offered, as though He stood in need of them; and so it is written (*Isa.* i. 11): *I desire not holocausts of rams, and fat of fatlings, and blood of calves and lambs and buck-goats.* But, as was stated above, He wished them to be offered to Him in order to prevent idolatry;—in order to signify the right ordering of man's mind to God;—and in order to represent the mystery of the Redemption of man by Christ.

Reply Obj. 2. In all the respects mentioned above, there was a suitable reason for these animals, rather than others, being offered up in sacrifice to God. First, in order to prevent idolatry. For idolaters offered all other animals to their gods, or made use of them in their sorceries; on the other hand, the Egyptians (among whom the people had been dwelling) considered it abominable to slay these animals, and so they did not offer them in sacrifice to their gods. Hence it is written (*Exod.* viii. 26): *We shall sacrifice the abominations of the Egyptians to the Lord our God.* For they worshipped the sheep; they reverenced the ram (because demons appeared under the form thereof); while they employed oxen for agriculture, which was reckoned by them as something sacred.

Secondly, this was suitable for the aforesaid right ordering of man's mind to God; and in two ways. First, because it is chiefly by means of these animals that human life is sustained, and moreover they are most clean and partake of a most clean food; whereas other animals are either wild, and not deputed to ordinary use among men, or, if they be tame, they have unclean food, as pigs and geese. Now nothing but what is clean should be offered to God. These birds especially were offered in sacrifice, because there were plenty of them in the land of promise.—Secondly, because the sacrificing of these animals represented purity of heart. For, as the *Gloss* says on *Levit.* i., *We offer a calf when we overcome the pride of the flesh; a lamb, when we restrain our unreasonable motions; a goat, when we con-*

quer our wantonness; a turtledove, when we keep chaste; unleavened bread, when we feast on the unleavened bread of sincerity.[8] And it is evident that the dove denotes charity and simplicity of heart.

Thirdly, it was fitting that these animals should be offered, that they might foreshadow Christ. For, as the same *Gloss* observes, *Christ is offered in the calf to denote the strength of the cross; in the lamb, to signify His innocence; in the ram, to foreshadow His headship; in the goat, to signify the likeness of sinful flesh. The turtledove and dove denoted the union of the two natures*; or else the turtledove signified chastity, while the dove was a figure of charity. *The wheat-flour foreshadowed the sprinkling of believers with the water of Baptism.*[9]

Reply Obj. 3. Fish, through living in water, are further removed from man than other animals, which, like man, live in the air. Again, fish die as soon as they are taken out of water, and so they could not be offered in the temple like other animals.

Reply Obj. 4. Among turtledoves the older ones are better than the young, while with doves the case is the reverse. *Therefore,* as Rabbi Moses observes,[10] *turtledoves and young doves are commanded to be offered because nothing should be offered to God but what is best.*

Reply Obj. 5. The animals which were offered in sacrifice were slain, because it is by being killed that they become useful to man, inasmuch as God gave them to man for food. So, too, they were burnt with fire, because it is by being cooked that they are made fit for human consumption. Moreover, the slaying of the animals signified the destruction of sins, and also that man deserved death because of his sins; as though these animals were slain in man's stead, in order to betoken the expiation of sins.—Again, the slaying of these animals signified the slaying of Christ.

Reply Obj. 6. The Law fixed the special manner of slaying the sacrificial animals in order to exclude other ways of killing, whereby idolaters sacrificed animals to idols.—Or again, as Rabbi Moses says, *the Law chose that manner of slaying which was least painful to the slain animal.*[11] This excluded cruelty on the part of the offerers, and any mangling of the animals slain.

Reply Obj. 7. It is because unclean animals are wont to be held in contempt among men that it was forbidden to offer them in sacrifice to God; and for this reason, too, they were forbidden (*Deut.* xxiii. 18) to offer *the hire of a strumpet or the price of a dog in the house of . . . God.* For the same reason they did not offer animals before the seventh day, because such were abortive, as it were, since the flesh was not yet firm because of its exceeding softness.

Reply Obj. 8. There were three kinds of sacrifices. There was one in which the victim was entirely consumed by fire: this was called *a holo-*

[8] *Glossa ordin.* (I, 214B); St. Isidore, *Quaest. in Vet. Test., In Levit.,* I (PL 83, 321). [9] *Ibid.* [10] *Guide,* III, 46 (p. 360). [11] *Op. cit.,* III, 48 (p. 371).

caust, i.e., *all burnt.* For this kind of sacrifice was offered to God especially to show reverence to His majesty, and love of His goodness; and it typified the state of perfection as regards the fulfillment of the counsels. Therefore the whole was burnt up, so that as the whole animal, by being dissolved into vapor, soared aloft, so it might denote that the whole man, and whatever belongs to him, are subject to the authority of God, and should be offered to Him.

Another sacrifice was the *sin-offering,* which was offered to God because of man's need for the forgiveness of sin; and this typifies the state of penitents in satisfying for sins. It was divided into two parts, for one part was burnt, while the other was granted to the use of the priests to signify that the remission of sins is granted by God through the ministry of His priests. When, however, this sacrifice was offered for the sins of the whole people, or especially for the sin of the priest, the whole victim was burnt up. For it was not fitting that the priests should have the use of that which was offered for their own sins, to signify that nothing sinful should remain in them. Moreover, this would not be satisfaction for sin; for if the offering were granted to the use of those for whose sins it was offered, it would seem to be the same as if it had not been offered.

The third kind of sacrifice was called the *peace-offering,* which was offered to God, either in thanksgiving, or for the welfare and prosperity of the offerers, in acknowledgment of benefits already received or yet to be received; and this typifies the state of those who are proficient in the observance of the commandments. These sacrifices were divided into three parts, for one part was burnt in honor of God, another part was allotted to the use of the priests, and the third part to the use of the offerers, in order to signify that man's salvation is from God, by the direction of God's ministers, and through the co-operation of those who are saved.

But it was the universal rule that the blood and fat were not allotted to the use either of the priests or of the offerers; but the blood was poured out at the foot of the altar, in honor of God, while the fat was burnt upon the altar (*Levit.* ix. 9, 10). The reason for this was, first, in order to prevent idolatry, for idolaters used to drink the blood and eat the fat of the victims, according to *Deut.* xxxii. 38: *Of whose victims they ate the fat, and drank the wine of their drink-offerings.*—Secondly, in order to form them to a right way of living. For they were forbidden the use of the blood that they might abhor the shedding of human blood; and so it is written (*Gen.* ix. 4, 5): *Flesh with blood you shall not eat, for I will require the blood of your lives.* And they were forbidden to eat the fat, in order to withdraw them from lasciviousness, and hence it is written (*Ezech.* xxxiv. 3): *You have killed that which was fat.*—Thirdly, because of the reverence due to God. For blood is most necessary for life, for which reason *life* is said to be *in the blood* (*Levit.* xvii. 11, 14); while fat is a sign of abundant nourishment. Therefore, in order to show that to God we owe both life and a sufficiency of all good things, the blood was poured out, and the fat burnt up in His honor.—Fourthly, in order to foreshadow the shedding of Christ's blood, and the abundance of His charity, whereby He offered Himself to God for us.

In the peace-offerings, the breast-bone and the right shoulder were allotted to the use of the priest, in order to prevent a certain kind of divination which is known as *spatulamantia*, so called because it was customary in divining to use the shoulder-blade [*spatula*] and the breast-bone of the animals offered in sacrifice; and so these things were taken away from the offerers. This also denoted the priest's need of wisdom in the heart, to instruct the people (signified by the breast-bone, which covers the heart), and his need of fortitude, in order to bear with human frailty (signified by the right shoulder).

Reply Obj. 9. Because the holocaust was the most perfect kind of sacrifice, therefore none but a male was offered for a holocaust; for the female is an imperfect animal.—The offering of turtledoves and doves was because of the poverty of the offerers, who were unable to offer bigger animals. And since peace-victims were offered freely, and no one was bound to offer them against his will, hence these birds were offered, not among the peace-victims, but among the holocausts and victims for sin, which man was obliged to offer at times. Moreover these birds, because of their lofty flight, were befitting the perfection of the holocausts; and they were suitable for sin-offerings, because their song is doleful.

Reply Obj. 10. The holocaust was the chief of all the sacrifices, because all was burnt in honor of God, and nothing of it was eaten. The second place in holiness belongs to the sacrifice for sins, which was eaten in the court only, and on the very day of the sacrifice (*Levit.* vii. 6, 15). The third place must be given to the peace-offerings of thanksgiving, which were eaten on the same day, but anywhere in Jerusalem. Fourth in order were the *ex-voto* peace-offerings, the flesh of which could be eaten even on the morrow. The reason for this order is that man is bound to God, chiefly because of His majesty; secondly, because of the sins he has committed; thirdly, because of the benefits he has already received from Him; fourthly, by reason of the benefits he hopes to receive from Him.

Reply Obj. 11. Sins are more grievous by reason of the state of the sinner, as was stated above;[12] and so different victims are commanded to be offered for the sin of a priest, or of a prince, or of some other private individual. *But, as Rabbi Moses says, we must take note that the more grievous the sin, the lower the species of animal offered for it. Therefore the goat, which is a very base animal, was offered for idolatry; while a calf was offered for a priest's ignorance, and a ram for the negligence of a prince.*[13]

Reply Obj. 12. In the matter of sacrifices, the Law had in view the poverty of the offerers, so that those who could not have a four-footed animal

[12] Q. 73, a. 10.   [13] *Guide*, III, 46 (p. 363).

at their disposal might at least offer a bird; and that he who could not have a bird might at least offer bread; and that if a man had not even bread he might offer flour or ears of corn.

The figurative cause is that the bread signifies Christ Who is the *living bread (Jo.* vi. 41, 51). He was indeed an ear of corn, as it were, during the state of the law of nature, in the faith of the patriarchs; He was like flour in the doctrine of the Law of the prophets; and He was like perfect bread after He had taken human nature; baked in the fire, *i.e.,* formed by the Holy Ghost in the oven of the virginal womb; baked again in a pan by the toils which He suffered in the world; and consumed by fire on the cross as on a gridiron.

Reply Obj. 13. The products of the soil are useful to man, either as food, and of these bread was offered; or as drink, and of these wine was offered; or as seasoning, and of these oil and salt were offered; or as healing, and of these they offered incense, which both smells sweetly and binds easily together.

Now the bread foreshadowed the flesh of Christ; and the wine, His blood, whereby we were redeemed; oil betokens the grace of Christ; salt, His knowledge; incense, His prayer.

Reply Obj. 14. Honey was not offered in the sacrifices to God, both because it was wont to be offered in the sacrifices to idols, and in order to denote the absence of all carnal sweetness and pleasure from those who intend to sacrifice to God.—Leaven was not offered, to denote the exclusion of corruption. Perhaps, too, it was wont to be offered in the sacrifices to idols.

Salt, however, was offered, because it wards off the corruption of putrefaction; for sacrifices offered to God should be incorrupt. Moreover, salt signifies the discretion of wisdom, or again, mortification of the flesh.

Incense was offered to denote devotion of the heart, which is necessary in the offerer; and, again, to signify the odor of a good name, for incense is composed of matter both rich and fragrant. And since the sacrifice *of jealousy* did not proceed from devotion, but rather from suspicion, therefore incense was not offered therein (*Num.* v. 15).

Fourth Article

WHETHER A SUFFICIENT REASON CAN BE ASSIGNED FOR THE CEREMONIES PERTAINING TO HOLY THINGS?

We proceed thus to the Fourth Article:—

Objection 1. It would seem that no sufficient reason can be assigned for the ceremonies of the Old Law that pertain to holy things. For Paul said (*Acts* xvii. 24): *God, Who made the world and all things therein, He being Lord of heaven and earth, dwelleth not in temples made by hands.* It was therefore unfitting that in the Old Law a tabernacle or temple should be set up for the worship of God.

Obj. 2. Further, the state of the Old Law was not changed except by Christ. But the tabernacle denoted the state of the Old Law. Therefore it should not have been changed by the building of a temple.

Obj. 3. Further, the divine law, more than any other indeed, should lead man to the worship of God. But an increase of divine worship requires multiplication of altars and temples, as is evident in regard to the New Law. Therefore it seems that, also under the Old Law, there should have been not only one tabernacle or temple, but many.

Obj. 4. Further, the tabernacle or temple was ordained to the worship of God. But in God we should worship above all His unity and simplicity. Therefore it seems unbecoming for the tabernacle or temple to be divided by means of veils.

Obj. 5. Further, the power of the First Mover, *i.e.,* God, appears first of all in the east, for it is in that quarter that the first movement begins. But the tabernacle was set up for the worship of God. Therefore it should have been built so as to point to the east rather than the west.

Obj. 6. Further, the Lord commanded (*Exod.* xx. 4) that they should *not make . . . a graven thing, nor the likeness of anything.* It was therefore unfitting for graven images of the cherubim to be set up in the tabernacle or temple. In like manner the ark, the propitiatory, the candlestick, the table, the two altars, seem to have been placed there without reasonable cause.

Obj. 7. Further, the Lord commanded (*Exod.* xx. 24): *You shall make an altar of earth unto Me*; and again (*ibid.,* 26): *Thou shalt not go up by steps unto My altar.* It was therefore unfitting that subsequently they should be commanded to make an altar of wood laid over with gold or brass, and of such a height that it was impossible to go up to it except by steps. For it is written (*Exod.* xxvii. 1, 2): *Thou shalt make also an altar of setim wood, which shall be five cubits long, and as many broad, . . . and three cubits high . . . and thou shalt cover it with brass*; and (*Exod.* xxx. 1, 3): *Thou shalt make . . . an altar to burn incense, of setim wood . . . and thou shalt overlay it with the purest gold.*

Obj. 8. Further, in God's works nothing should be superfluous, for neither in the works of nature is anything superfluous to be found. But one cover suffices for one tabernacle or house. Therefore it was unbecoming to furnish the tabernacle with many coverings, viz., curtains, curtains of goats' hair, rams' skins dyed red, and violet-colored skins (*Exod.* xxvi.).

Obj. 9. Further, exterior consecration signifies interior holiness, the subject of which is the soul. It was therefore unsuitable for the tabernacle and its vessels to be consecrated, since they were inanimate things.

Obj. 10. Further, it is written (*Ps.* xxxiii. 2): *I will bless the Lord at all times, His praise shall always be in my mouth.* But the solemn festivals were instituted for the praise of God. Therefore it was not fitting that certain days should be fixed for keeping solemn festivals; so that it seems that there was no suitable cause for the ceremonies relating to holy things.

On the contrary, The Apostle says (*Heb.* viii. 4) that those who *offer gifts according to the law . . . serve unto the example and shadow of heavenly things. As it was answered to Moses, when he was to finish the tabernacle: See, says He, that thou make all things according to the pattern which was shown thee on the mount.* But that is most reasonable, which presents a likeness to heavenly things. Therefore the ceremonies relating to holy things had a reasonable cause.

I answer that, The chief purpose of the whole external worship of God is that man may hold God in reverence. Now man's tendency is to reverence less those things which are common, and indistinct from other things; whereas he admires and reveres those things which are distinct from others in some point of excellence.[14] Hence, too, it is customary among men for kings and princes, who ought to be reverenced by their subjects, to be clothed in more precious garments, and to possess vaster and more beautiful abodes. And for this reason it behoved special times, a special abode, special vessels, and special ministers to be appointed for the divine worship, so that thereby the soul of man might be brought to greater reverence for God.

In like manner, the state of the Old Law, as was observed above, was instituted that it might foreshadow the mystery of Christ.[15] Now that which foreshadows something should be determinate, so that it may present some likeness thereto. Consequently, certain special points had to be observed in matters pertaining to the worship of God.

Reply Obj. 1. The divine worship regards two things, namely, God Who is worshipped, and the persons who worship Him. Accordingly God, Who is worshipped, is confined to no bodily place, and so there was no need, on His part, for a tabernacle or temple to be set up. But men, who worship Him, are corporeal beings, and for their sake there was need for a special tabernacle or temple to be set up for the worship of God, for two reasons. First, that through coming together with the thought that the place was set aside for the worship of God, they might approach thither with greater reverence. Secondly, that certain things relating to the excellence of Christ's divine or human nature might be signified by the arrangement of various details in such temple or tabernacle.

To this Solomon refers (*3 Kings* viii. 27) when he says: *If heaven and the heavens of heavens cannot contain Thee, how much less this house which I have built* for *Thee?* And further on (*ibid.* 29, 30) he adds: *That Thy eyes may be open upon this house . . . of which Thou hast said: My name shall be there; . . . that Thou mayest hearken to the supplication of Thy servant and of Thy people Israel.* From this it is evident that

---

[14] Cf. Moses Maimonides, *Guide,* III, 45 (p. 357).   [15] A. 2; q. 100, a. 12; q. 101, a. 2.

the house of the sanctuary was set up, not in order to contain God, as abiding therein locally, but that God's name might dwell there, *i.e.*, that God might be made known there by means of things done and said there; and that those who prayed there might, through reverence for the place, pray more devoutly, so as to be heard more readily.

Reply Obj. 2. Before the coming of Christ, the state of the Old Law was not changed as regards the fulfillment of the Law, which was effected in Christ alone; but it was changed as regards the condition of the people that were under the Law. For, at first, the people were in the desert, having no fixed abode; afterwards they were engaged in various wars with the neighboring nations; and lastly, at the time of David and Solomon, the state of that people was one of great peace. And then for the first time the temple was built in the place which Abraham, instructed by God, had chosen for the purpose of sacrifice. For it is written (*Gen.* xxii. 2) that the Lord commanded Abraham to *offer* his son *for a holocaust upon one of the mountains which I will show thee*; and it is related further on (*ibid.* 14) that *he called the name of that place, The Lord seeth*, as though, according to the divine prevision, that place were chosen for the worship of God. Hence it is written (*Deut.* xii. 5, 6): *You shall come to the place which the Lord your God shall choose . . . and you shall offer . . . your holocausts and victims.*

Now it was not meet for that place to be pointed out by the building of the temple before the aforesaid time; and this for three reasons assigned by Rabbi Moses.[16] First, lest the Gentiles might seize hold of that place. Secondly, lest the Gentiles might destroy it. The third reason is lest each tribe might wish that place to fall to their lot, and strifes and quarrels be the result. Hence the temple was not built until they had a king who would be able to quell such quarrels. Until that time a portable tabernacle was employed for divine worship, as though no place was as yet fixed for the worship of God. This is the literal reason for the distinction between the tabernacle and the temple.

The figurative reason may be assigned to the fact that they signify a twofold state. For the tabernacle, which was changeable, signifies the state of the present changeable life; whereas the temple, which was fixed and stable, signifies the state of future life which is altogether unchangeable. For this reason it is said that in the building of the temple no sound was heard of hammer or saw, to signify that all movements of disturbance will be far removed from the future state.—Or else the tabernacle signifies the state of the Old Law, while the temple built by Solomon betokens the state of the New Law. Hence the Jews alone worked at the building of the tabernacle, whereas the temple was built with the co-operation of the Gentiles, viz., the Tyrians and Sidonians.

[16] *Guide*, III, 45 (p. 355).

Reply Obj. 3. The reason for the unity of the temple or tabernacle may be either literal or figurative. The literal reason was the exclusion of idolatry. For the Gentiles put up various temples to various gods; and so, to strengthen in the minds of men their belief in the divine unity, God wished sacrifices to be offered to Him in one place only.—Another reason was in order to show that bodily worship was not accepted for its own sake; and so they were restrained from offering sacrifices anywhere and everywhere. But the worship of the New Law, in the sacrifice whereof spiritual grace is contained, is of itself acceptable to God; and consequently the multiplication of altars and temples is permitted in the New Law.

As to those matters that regarded the spiritual worship of God, consisting in the teaching of the Law and the Prophets, there were, even under the Old Law, various places, called *synagogues,* appointed for the people to gather together for the praise of God; just as now there are places called *churches* in which the Christian people gather together for the divine worship. Thus our church takes the place of both temple and synagogue, since the very sacrifice of the Church is spiritual; and so with us the place of sacrifice is not distinct from the place of teaching. The figurative reason may be that hereby is signified the unity of the Church, whether militant or triumphant.

Reply Obj. 4. Just as the unity of the temple or tabernacle betokened the unity of God, or the unity of the Church, so also the division of the tabernacle or temple signified the distinction of those things that are subject to God, and from which we arise to the worship of God. Now the tabernacle was divided into two parts: one was called the *Holy of Holies,* and was placed to the west; the other was called the *Holy Place,* which was situated to the east. Moreover there was a court facing the tabernacle. Accordingly, there are two reasons for this distinction. One is according as the tabernacle is ordained to the worship of God. For the different parts of the world are thus betokened by the division of the tabernacle. For that part which was called the Holy of Holies signified the higher world, which is that of spiritual substances; while that part which is called the Holy Place signified the corporeal world. Hence the Holy Place was separated from the Holy of Holies by a veil, which was of four different colors (denoting the four elements), viz., of linen, signifying earth, because linen, *i.e.,* flax, grows out of the earth; purple, signifying water, because the purple tint was made from certain shells found in the sea; violet, signifying air, because it has the color of the air; and scarlet twice dyed, signifying fire;—and this because matter composed of the four elements is a veil between us and incorporeal substances. Hence the high-priest alone, and that once a year, entered into the inner tabernacle, *i.e.,* the Holy of Holies; whereby we are taught that man's final perfection consists in his entering into that world. But into the outward tabernacle, *i.e.,* the Holy Place, the priests entered every day, whereas the people were admitted only to the court; for the people are able to perceive material things, the inner nature of which only wise men by dint of study are able to discover.

But with regard to the figurative reason, the outward tabernacle, which was called the Holy Place, betokened the state of the Old Law, as the Apostle says (*Heb.* ix. 6, *seq.*); because into that tabernacle *the priests always entered accomplishing the offices of sacrifices.* But the inner tabernacle, which was called the Holy of Holies, signified either the glory of heaven or the spiritual state of the New Law, which is a kind of beginning of the glory to come. To the latter state Christ brought us; and this was signified by the high-priest entering alone, once a year, into the Holy of Holies.—The veil betokened the concealing of the spiritual sacrifices under the sacrifices of old. This veil was adorned with four colors: viz., that of linen, to designate purity of the flesh; purple, to denote the sufferings which the saints underwent for God; scarlet twice dyed, signifying the twofold love of God and our neighbor; and violet, in token of heavenly contemplation.—With regard to the state of the Old Law, the people and the priests were situated differently from one another. For the people saw the mere corporeal sacrifices which were offered in the court, whereas the priests were intent on the inner meaning of the sacrifices, because their faith in the mysteries of Christ was more explicit. Hence they entered into the outer tabernacle. This outer tabernacle was divided from the court by a veil, because some matters relating to the mystery of Christ were hidden from the people, while they were known to the priests; though they were not fully revealed to them, as they were subsequently in the New Testament, as it is said in *Ephes.* iii. 5.

Reply Obj. 5. Worship towards the west was introduced in the Law for the exclusion of idolatry, because all the Gentiles, in reverence to the sun, worshipped towards the east.[17] Hence it is written (*Ezech.* viii. 16) that certain men *had their backs towards the temple of the Lord, and their faces to the east, and they adored towards the rising of the sun.* Accordingly, in order to exclude this, the tabernacle had the Holy of Holies to westward, that they might adore toward the west. A figurative reason may also be found in the fact that the whole state of the first tabernacle was ordained to foreshadow the death of Christ, which is signified by the west, according to *Ps.* lxvii. 5: *Who ascendeth unto the west; the Lord is His name.*

Reply Obj. 6. Both literal and figurative reasons may be assigned for the things contained in the tabernacle. The literal reason is in connection with the divine worship. And because, as was already observed, the inner tabernacle, called the Holy of Holies, signified the higher world of spiritual substances, hence that tabernacle contained three things, viz., *the ark of the testament in which was a golden pot that had manna, and the rod of Aaron that had blossomed, and the tables* (*Heb.* ix. 4) on which were

---

[17] Cf. Moses Maimonides, *Guide,* III, 45 (p. 355).

written the ten commandments of the Law. Now the ark stood between two *cherubim* that looked one towards the other, and over the ark was a stone table, called the *propitiatory,* raised above the wings of the cherubim, as though it were held up by them, and appearing, to the imagination, to be the very seat of God. For this reason it was called the *propitiatory,* as though the people received thence propitiation at the prayers of the high-priest. And so it was held up, so to speak, by the cherubim, in obedience, as it were, to God; while the ark of the testament was like the foot-stool to Him that sat on the propitiatory.—These three things denote three things in that higher world. And first, God Who is above all, and incomprehensible to any creature. Hence no likeness of Him was used, in order thus to denote His invisibility. But there was something to represent His seat, since, namely, the creature, which is beneath God, as the seat is beneath its occupant, is comprehensible.—Again in that higher world there are spiritual substances called angels. These are signified by the two cherubim, looking one towards the other, to show that they are at peace with one another, according to *Job* xxv. 2: *Who maketh peace in . . . high places.* For this reason, too, there was more than one cherub, to betoken the multitude of heavenly spirits, and to prevent their receiving worship from those who had been commanded to worship but one God. —Moreover there are, enclosed as it were in that spiritual world, the intelligible exemplars of whatsoever takes place in this world, just as the likenesses of effects are included in their causes, and the models of works of art in the artisan. This was betokened by the ark, which represented, by means of the three things it contained, the three things of greatest import in human affairs. These are wisdom, signified by the tables of the testament; the power of governing, betokened by the rod of Aaron; and life, denoted by the manna which was the means of sustenance. Or else these three signified three divine attributes, viz., wisdom, in the tables; power, in the rod; goodness, in the manna,—both by reason of its sweetness, and because it was through the goodness of God that it was granted to man (and that is why it was preserved as a memorial of the divine mercy).—Again, these three things were represented in Isaias' vision. For he *saw the Lord sitting upon a throne high and elevated,* and the seraphim standing by, and he saw that the house was filled with the glory of the Lord; and so the seraphim cried out: *All the earth is full of His glory* (*Isa.* vi. 1, 3).—And thus, the images of the seraphim were set up, not to be worshipped, for this was forbidden by the first commandment, but as a sign of their function, as was stated above.

The outer tabernacle, which denotes this present world, also contained three things, viz., the *altar of incense,* which was directly opposite the ark; the *table of proposition,* with the twelve loaves of proposition on it, which stood on the northern side; and the *candlestick,* which was placed towards the south. These three things seem to correspond to the three which were enclosed in the ark, and they represented the same things as the latter, but more clearly; because, in order that wise men, denoted by the priests entering the temple, might grasp the exemplars of things, it was necessary to express them more manifestly than they are in the divine or the angelic mind. Accordingly, the candlestick betokened, as a sensible sign thereof, the wisdom which was expressed on the tables in intelligible words. The altar of incense signified the office of the priests, whose duty it was to bring the people to God; and this was signified also by the rod. For on that altar the sweet-smelling incense was burnt, signifying the holiness of the people acceptable to God. For it is written (*Apoc.* viii. 3) that the smoke of the sweet-smelling spices signifies the *justifications of the saints* [*cf. ibid.* xix. 8]. Moreover it was fitting that the dignity of the priesthood should be denoted, in the ark, by the rod, and, in the outer tabernacle, by the altar of incense; for the priest is the mediator between God and the people, governing the people by divine power, denoted by the rod, and offering to God the fruit of His government, *i.e.*, the holiness of the people, on the altar of incense, so to speak.—The table signified the sustenance of life, just as the manna did; but the former, a more general and a coarser kind of nourishment; the latter, a sweeter and more delicate. —Again, the candlestick was fittingly placed on the southern side, while the table was placed to the north, because the south is the right-hand side of the world, while the north is the left-hand side, as is stated in *De Caelo et Mundo* ii.;[18] and wisdom, like other spiritual goods, belongs to the right hand, while temporal nourishment belongs to the left, according to *Prov.* iii. 16: *In her left hand riches and glory.* Now priestly power is midway between temporal goods and spiritual wisdom, because thereby both spiritual wisdom and temporal goods are dispensed.

A more literal signification may be assigned. For the ark contained the tables of the Law, in order to prevent forgetfulness of the Law; and so it is written (*Exod.* xxiv. 12): *I will give thee two tables of stone, and the Law, and the commandments which I have written, that thou mayest teach them* to the children of Israel.—The rod of Aaron was placed there to restrain the people from insubordination to the priesthood of Aaron; and hence it is written (*Num.* xvii. 10): *Carry back the rod of Aaron into the tabernacle of the testimony, that it may be kept there for a token of the rebellious children of Israel.*—The manna was kept in the ark to remind them of the benefit conferred by God on the children of Israel in the desert; and hence it is written (*Exod.* xvi. 32): *Fill a gomor of it, and let it be kept unto generations to come hereafter, that they may know the bread wherewith I fed you in the wilderness.*—The candlestick was set up to enhance the beauty of the temple; for the magnificence of a house depends on its being well lighted. Now the candlestick had seven branches, as Josephus observes,[19] to signify the seven planets, wherewith the whole

---

[18] *De Caelo*, II, 2 (285b 16).   [19] *Antiquities*, III, 7 (IV, 404).

world is illuminated. Hence the candlestick was placed towards the south, because for us the course of the planets is from that quarter.—The altar of incense was instituted that there might always be in the tabernacle a sweet-smelling smoke; and this both out of reverence for the tabernacle, and as a remedy for the stenches arising from the shedding of blood and the slaying of animals. For men despise evil-smelling things as being vile, whereas sweet-smelling things are more appreciated.—The table was placed there to signify that the priests who served the temple should take their food in the temple; and so, as is stated in *Matt.* xii. 4, it was lawful for none but the priests to eat the twelve loaves which were put on the table in remembrance of the twelve tribes. And the table was not placed in the middle directly in front of the propitiatory, in order to exclude an idolatrous rite. For the Gentiles, on the feasts of the moon, set up a table in front of the idol of the moon; and that is why it is written (*Jerem.* vii. 18): *The women knead the dough, to make cakes to the queen of heaven.*

In the court outside the tabernacle was the altar of holocausts, on which sacrifices of those things which the people possessed were offered to God; and consequently the people who offered these sacrifices to God by the hands of the priest could be present in the court. But the priests alone, whose function it was to offer the people to God, could approach the inner altar, whereon the very devotion and holiness of the people was offered to God. Now this altar was put up outside the tabernacle and in the court, to exclude idolatrous worship; for the Gentiles placed altars inside the temples to offer up sacrifices thereon to idols.

The figurative reason for all these things may be taken from the relation of the tabernacle to Christ, Who was foreshadowed therein. Now it must be observed that to show the imperfection of the figures of the Law, various figures were instituted in the temple to betoken Christ. For He was foreshadowed by the *propitiatory,* since He is *a propitiation for our sins* (*1 John* ii. 2). So, too, this propitiatory was fittingly carried by cherubim, since of Him it is written (*Heb.* i. 6): *Let all the angels of God adore Him.*—He is also signified by the ark, because, just as the ark was made of setim wood, so was Christ's body composed of most pure members. Moreover, it was gilded, for Christ was full of wisdom and charity, which are betokened by gold. And in the ark was a golden pot, *i.e.,* His holy soul, having manna, *i.e., all the fullness of the Godhead* (*Coloss.* ii. 9). Also there was a rod in the ark, *i.e.,* His priestly power; for *He was made a . . . priest forever* (*Heb.* vi. 20). And therein were the tables of the Testament, to denote that Christ Himself is the giver of the Law.—Again, Christ was signified by the candlestick, for He said Himself (*Jo.* viii. 12): *I am the Light of the world;* while the seven lamps denoted the seven gifts of the Holy Ghost. He is also betokened in the table, because He is our spiritual food, according to *Jo.* vi. 41, 51: *I am the living bread*; and the twelve loaves signified the twelve apostles, or their teaching. Or, again, the candlestick and table may signify the Church's teaching and faith, which also give enlightenment and spiritual refreshment.—Again, Christ is signified by the two altars of holocausts and incense. For all works of virtue must be offered by us to God through Him, both those whereby we afflict the body (which are offered, as it were, on the altar of holocausts), and those which, with greater perfection of mind, are offered to God in Christ by the spiritual desires of the perfect (on the altar of incense, as it were, according to *Heb.* xiii. 15: *By Him therefore let us offer the sacrifice of praise always to God*).

Reply Obj. 7. The Lord commanded an altar to be made for the offering of sacrifices and gifts, in honor of God, and for the upkeep of the ministers who served the tabernacle. Now concerning the construction of the altar the Lord issued a twofold precept. One was at the beginning of the Law (*Exod.* xx. 24, ff), when the Lord commanded them to make *an altar of earth,* or at least *not of hewn stones;* and again, not to make the altar high, so as to make it necessary to *go up* to it *by steps.* This was in detestation of idolatrous worship, for the Gentiles made their altars ornate and high, thinking that there was something holy and divine in such things. For this reason, too, the Lord commanded (*Deut.* xvi. 21): *Thou shalt plant no grove, nor any tree near the altar of the Lord thy God*; since idolaters were wont to offer sacrifices beneath trees, because of the pleasantness and shade afforded by them.—There was also a figurative reason for these precepts. Because we must confess that in Christ, Who is our altar, there is the true nature of flesh, as regards His humanity (and this is to make an altar of earth), and again, in regard to His divinity, we must confess His equality with the Father (and this is *not to go up* to the altar by steps). Moreover we should not couple the doctrine of Christ to that of the Gentiles, which provokes men to lewdness.

But when once the tabernacle had been constructed to the honor of God, there was no longer reason to fear these occasions of idolatry. Therefore the Lord commanded the altar of holocausts to be made of brass, for this would make it conspicuous to all the people; and the altar of incense of gold, which was visible to none but the priests. Nor was brass so precious as to give the people an occasion for idolatry.

Since, however, the reasons for the precept, *Thou shalt not go up by steps unto My altar,* is stated to have been *lest thy nakedness be discovered* (*Exod.* xx. 26), it should be observed that this too was instituted with the purpose of preventing idolatry; for in the feasts of Priapus the Gentiles uncovered their nakedness before the people.[20] But later on the priests were prescribed the use of loin-cloths for the sake of decency; and so without any danger the altar could be placed so high that the priests, when offering sacrifices, would go up by steps of wood, not fixed but movable.

[20] Cf. Maimonides, *Guide,* III, 45 (p. 357).

Reply Obj. 8. The body of the tabernacle consisted of boards placed on end, and covered on the inside with curtains of four different colors, viz., twisted linen, violet, purple and scarlet twice dyed. These curtains, however, covered the sides only of the tabernacle, while the roof of the tabernacle was covered with violet-colored skins, and over this there was another covering of rams' skins dyed red, and over this a third made of goats' hair, which not only covered the roof of the tabernacle, but also reached to the ground and covered the boards of the tabernacle on the outside. The literal reason for these coverings taken altogether was the adornment and protection of the tabernacle, that it might be held in reverence. Taken singly, according to some, *the curtains denoted the sidereal heavens, which is adorned with various stars; the curtain of goats' skin signified the waters which are above the firmament; the skins dyed red denoted the empyrean heavens, where the angels are; the violet skins, the heaven of the Blessed Trinity.*[21]

The figurative meaning of these things is that the boards of which the tabernacle was constructed signify the faithful of Christ, who compose the Church. The boards were covered on the inner side by curtains of four colors, because the faithful are inwardly adorned with the four virtues: for *the twisted linen,* as the *Gloss* observes, *signifies the flesh refulgent with purity; violet signifies the mind desirous of heavenly things; purple denotes the flesh subject to passions; the twice dyed scarlet betokens the mind in the midst of the passions shining forth with the love of God and our neighbor.*[22] The coverings of the building designate prelates and doctors, who ought to be conspicuous for their heavenly manner of life (signified by the violet-colored skins); who should also be ready to suffer martyrdom (denoted by the skins dyed red); and who should be austere of life and patient in adversity (betokened by the curtains of goats' hair, which were exposed to wind and rain), as the *Gloss* observes.[23]

Reply Obj. 9. The literal reason for the sanctification of the tabernacle and vessels was that they might be treated with greater reverence, being deputed, as it were, to the divine worship by this consecration.—The figurative reason is that this sanctification signified the sanctification of the living tabernacle, *i.e.,* the faithful, of whom the Church of Christ is composed.

Reply Obj. 10. Under the Old Law, there were seven temporal solemnities, and one continual solemnity, as may be gathered from *Num.* xxviii. and xxix. There was a continual feast, since the lamb was sacrificed every day, morning and evening; and this continual feast of an abiding sacrifice signified the perpetuity of divine beatitude.

Of the temporal feasts, the first was that which was repeated every week. This was the solemnity of the *Sabbath,* celebrated in remembrance of the

---

[21] Peter Comestor, *Hist. Scholast., Exod.,* cap. 58 (PL 198, 1179).   [22] *Glossa ordin.* (I, 180F).—St. Bede, *De Tabernaculo,* II, 2 (PL 91, 425).   [23] *Glossa ordin.* (I, 181C; 182E).—Cf. St. Bede, *De Tabernaculo,* II, 3; 4 (PL 91, 430; 435).

work of the creation of the universe as we have said above.[24]—Another solemnity, viz., the *New Moon*, was repeated every month, and was observed in remembrance of the work of the divine government. For the things of this lower world owe their variety chiefly to the movement of the moon, and hence this feast was kept at the new moon; but not at the full moon, to avoid the worship of idolaters who used to offer sacrifices to the moon at that particular time.—And these two blessings are bestowed in common on the whole human race, and hence the feasts were repeated more frequently.

The other five feasts were celebrated once a year, and commemorated the benefits which had been conferred especially on that people. For there was the feast of the *Passover,* in the first month, to commemorate the blessing of being delivered out of Egypt. The feast of *Pentecost* was celebrated fifty days later, to recall the blessing of the giving of the Law.—The other three feasts were kept in the seventh month, nearly the whole of which was solemnized by them, just as the seventh day. For on the first of the seventh month was the feast of *Trumpets,* in remembrance of the delivery of Isaac, when Abraham found the ram caught by its horns, which they represented by the horns which they blew.—The feast of Trumpets was a kind of invitation that they prepare themselves to keep the following feast, which was kept on the tenth day. This was the feast of *Expiation,* in remembrance of the blessing whereby, at the prayer of Moses, God forgave the people's sin of worshipping the calf. After this was the feast of *Scenopegia* or of *Tents,* which was kept for seven days, to commemorate the blessing of being protected and led by God through the desert, where they lived in tents. Hence, during this feast, they had to take *the fruits of the fairest tree, i.e.,* the citron, *and trees of dense foliage, i.e.,* the myrtle, which is fragrant, *and branches of palm-trees, and willows of the brook,* which retain their greenness a long time; and these are to be found in the Land of promise, to signify that God had brought them through the arid land of the wilderness to a land of delights.—On the eighth day another feast was observed, of *Assembly and Congregation,* on which the people collected the expenses necessary for the divine worship; and it signified the uniting of the people and the peace granted to them in the Land of promise.

The figurative reason for these feasts was that the continual sacrifice of the lamb foreshadowed the perpetuity of Christ, Who is the *Lamb of God,* according to *Heb.* xiii. 8: *Jesus Christ yesterday and to-day, and the same forever.*—The *Sabbath* signified the spiritual rest given to us by Christ, as is stated in *Heb.* iv. The *Neomenia,* which is the beginning of the new moon, signified the enlightening of the primitive Church by Christ's preaching and miracles. The feast of *Pentecost* signified the descent of the Holy Ghost on the apostles. The feast of *Trumpets* signified the preaching of

[24] Q. 100, a. 5.

the apostles. The feast of *Expiation* signified the cleansing of the Christian people from sins. The feast of *Tents* signified their pilgrimage in this world, wherein they walk by advancing in virtue.—The feast of *Assembly and Congregation* foreshadowed the assembly of the faithful in the kingdom of heaven, and so this feast is described as *most holy* (*Levit.* xxiii. 36). These three feasts followed immediately on one another, because those who expiate their vices should advance in virtue, until they come to see God, as is stated in *Ps.* lxxxiii. 8.

Fifth Article

WHETHER THERE CAN BE ANY SUITABLE CAUSE FOR THE SACRAMENTS OF THE OLD LAW?

We proceed thus to the Fifth Article:—

Objection 1. It would seem that there can be no suitable cause for the sacraments of the Old Law. For those things that are done for the purpose of divine worship should not be like the observances of idolaters, since it is written (*Deut.* xii. 31): *Thou shalt not do in like manner to the Lord thy God; for they have done to their gods all the abominations which the Lord abhorreth.* Now worshippers of idols used to knive themselves to the shedding of blood; for it is related (*3 Kings* xviii. 28) that they *cut themselves after their manner with knives and lancets, till they were all covered with blood.* For this reason the Lord commanded (*Deut.* xiv. 1): *You shall not cut yourselves nor make any baldness for the dead.* Therefore it was unfitting for circumcision to be prescribed by the Law (*Levit.* xii. 3).

Obj. 2. Further, those things which are done for the worship of God should be marked with decorum and gravity, according to *Ps.* xxxiv. 18: *I will praise Thee in a grave people.* But it seems to savor of levity for a man to eat with haste. Therefore it was unfittingly commanded (*Exod.* xii. 11) that they should eat the Paschal lamb *in haste.* Other things, too, relative to the eating of the lamb, were prescribed, which seem altogether unreasonable.

Obj. 3. Further, the sacraments of the Old Law were figures of the sacraments of the New Law. Now the Paschal lamb signified the sacrament of the Eucharist, according to *1 Cor.* v. 7: *Christ our Pasch is sacrificed.* Therefore there should also have been some sacraments in the Old Law to foreshadow the other sacraments of the New Law, such as Confirmation, Extreme Unction, Matrimony and so forth.

Obj. 4. Further, purification can scarcely be done except by removing something impure. But as far as God is concerned, no bodily thing is reputed impure, because all bodies are God's creatures; and *every creature of God is good, and nothing to be rejected that is received with thanks-*

giving (*1 Tim.* iv. 4). It was therefore unfitting for them to be purified after contact with a corpse, or any similar corporeal infection.

Obj. 5. Further, it is written (*Ecclus.* xxxiv. 4): *What can be made clean by the unclean?* But the ashes of the red heifer, which was burnt, were unclean, since they made a man unclean; for it is stated (*Num.* xix. 7 *seq.*) that the priest who immolated her was rendered unclean *until the evening*; and likewise he that burnt her, and he that gathered up her ashes. Therefore it was unfittingly prescribed there that the unclean should be purified by being sprinkled with those cinders.

Obj. 6. Further, sins are not something corporeal that can be carried from one place to another; nor can man be cleansed from sin by means of something unclean. It was therefore unfitting for the purpose of expiating the sins of the people that the priest should confess the sins of the children of Israel on one of the buck-goats, that it might carry them away into the wilderness; while they were rendered unclean by the other, which they used for the purpose of purification, by burning it together with the calf outside the camp; so that they had to wash their clothes and their bodies with water (*Levit.* xvi.).

Obj. 7. Further, what is already cleansed should not be cleansed again. It was therefore unfitting to apply a second purification to a man cleansed from leprosy, or to a house, as is laid down in *Levit.* xiv.

Obj. 8. Further, spiritual uncleanness cannot be cleansed by material water or by shaving the hair. Therefore it seems unreasonable that the Lord ordered (*Exod.* xxx. 18 *seq.*) the making of a brazen laver with its foot, that the priests might wash their hands and feet before entering the temple; and that He commanded (*Num.* viii. 7) the Levites to be sprinkled with the water of purification, and to shave all the hairs of their flesh.

Obj. 9. Further, that which is greater cannot be cleansed by that which is less. Therefore it was unfitting that, in the Law, the higher and lower priests, as is stated in *Levit.* viii., and the Levites, according to *Num.* viii. 5, should be consecrated with any bodily anointing, bodily sacrifices and bodily oblations.

Obj. 10. Further, as is stated in *1 Kings* xvi. 7, *Man seeth those things that appear, but the Lord beholdeth the heart.* But those things that appear outwardly in man are the disposition of his body and his clothes.[25] Therefore it was unfitting for certain special garments to be appointed to the higher and lower priests, as is related in *Exod.* xxviii. It seems, moreover, unreasonable that anyone should be debarred from the priesthood because of defects in the body, as stated in *Levit.* xxi. 17, *seq.*: *Whosoever of thy seed throughout their families hath a blemish, he shall not offer bread to his God . . . if he be blind, if he be lame,* etc. It seems, therefore, that the sacraments of the Old Law were unreasonable.

On the contrary, It is written (*Levit.* xx. 8): *I am the Lord that sanctify*

[25] Moses Maimonides, *Guide,* III, 45 (p. 357).

you. But nothing unreasonable is done by God, for it is written (*Ps.* ciii. 24): *Thou hast made all things in wisdom*. Therefore there was nothing without a reasonable cause in the sacraments of the Old Law, which were ordained to the sanctification of man.

I answer that, As we have stated above, the sacraments are, properly speaking, things applied to the worshippers of God for their consecration so as, in some way, to depute them to the worship of God.[26] Now the worship of God belonged in a general way to the whole people; but in a special way, it belonged to the priests and Levites, who were the ministers of divine worship. Consequently, in these sacraments of the Old Law, certain things concerned the whole people in general, while others belonged to the ministers in a distinctive way.

In regard to both, three things were necessary. The first was establishment in the state of worshipping God; and this establishment was brought about,—for all in general, by circumcision, without which no one was admitted to any of the legal observances,—and for the priests, by their consecration. The second thing required was the use of those things that pertain to divine worship. And thus, as to the people, there was the partaking of the paschal banquet, to which no uncircumcised man was admitted, as is clear from *Exod.* xii. 43, *seq.*; and, as to the priests, the offering of the victims, and the eating of the loaves of proposition and of other things that were allotted to the use of the priests. The third thing required was the removal of all impediments to divine worship, viz., of uncleannesses. And then, as to the people, certain purifications were instituted for the removal of certain external uncleannesses, and also expiations from sins; while, as to the priests and Levites, the washing of hands and feet and the shaving of the hair were instituted.

And all these things had reasonable causes, both literal, in so far as they were ordained to the worship of God according to that time, and figurative, in so far as they were ordained to foreshadow Christ (as we shall see by taking them one by one).

Reply Obj. 1. The chief literal reason for circumcision was in order that man might profess his belief in one God. And because Abraham was the first to sever himself from the infidels, by going out from his house and kindred, for this reason he was the first to receive circumcision. This reason is set forth by the Apostle (*Rom.* iv. 9, *seq.*) thus: *He received the sign of circumcision, a seal of the justice of the faith which he had, being uncircumcised,* because, namely, we are told that *unto Abraham faith was reputed to justice,* for the reason that *against hope he believed in hope, i.e.,* against the hope that is of nature he believed in the hope that is of grace, *that he might be made the father of many nations,* when he was an old man, and his wife an old and barren woman. And in order that this declaration and imitation of Abraham's faith might be fixed firmly

[26] Q. 101, a. 4.

in the hearts of the Jews, they received in their flesh such a sign as they could not forget; and so it is written (*Gen.* xvii. 13): *My covenant shall be in your flesh for a perpetual covenant.* This was done on the eighth day, because until then a child is very tender, and so might be seriously injured, and is considered as something not yet firmly knit; and hence neither are animals offered before the eighth day. And it was not delayed after that time, lest some might refuse the sign of circumcision because of the pain; and also lest the parents, whose love for their children increases as they become used to their presence and as they grow older, should withdraw their children from circumcision.—A second reason may have been the weakening of concupiscence in that member.—A third motive may have been to revile the worship of Venus and Priapus, which gave honor to that part of the body.—The Lord's prohibition extended only to the cutting of oneself in honor of idols; and such was not the circumcision of which we have been speaking.

The figurative reason for circumcision was that it foreshadowed the removal of corruption, which was to be brought about by Christ, and will be perfectly fulfilled in the eighth age, which is the age of those who rise from the dead. And since all corruption of guilt and punishment comes to us, through our carnal origin, from the sin of our first parent, therefore circumcision was applied to the generative member. Hence the Apostle says (*Coloss.* ii. 11): *You are circumcised* in Christ *with circumcision not made by hand in despoiling of the body of the flesh, but in the circumcision of* Our Lord Jesus *Christ.*

Reply Obj. 2. The literal reason for the paschal banquet was to commemorate the blessing of being led by God out of Egypt. Hence, by celebrating this banquet, they declared that they belonged to that people which God had taken to Himself out of Egypt. For when they were delivered from Egypt, they were commanded to sprinkle the lamb's blood on the transoms of their house doors, as though declaring that they were departing from the rites of the Egyptians who worshipped the ram. Hence, by the sprinkling or rubbing of the blood of the lamb on the door-posts, they were delivered from the danger of extermination which threatened the Egyptians.

Now two things are to be observed in their departure from Egypt: namely, their haste in going, for the Egyptians pressed them to go forth speedily, as is related in *Exod.* xii. 33; and there was the danger that anyone who did not hasten to go with the crowd might be slain by the Egyptians. Their haste was shown in two ways. First, by what they ate. For they were commanded to eat unleavened bread, as a sign *that it could not be leavened, the Egyptians pressing them to depart* (*Exod.* xii. 39); and to eat roast meat, for this took less time to prepare; and that they should not break a bone thereof, because in their haste there was no time to break bones. Secondly, as to the manner of eating. For it is written: *You shall gird your reins, and you shall have shoes on your feet, holding staves in your hands, and you shall eat in haste* (*Exod.* xii. 11); which clearly designates men at the point of starting on a journey. To this also is to be referred the command: *In one house shall it be eaten, neither shall you carry forth of the flesh thereof out of the house* (*Exod.* xii. 46); because, namely, through their haste, they could not send any gifts of it.

The stress they suffered while in Egypt was denoted by the wild lettuces. The figurative reason is evident, for the sacrifice of the paschal lamb signified the sacrifice of Christ, according to *1 Cor.* v. 7: *Christ our pasch is sacrificed.* The blood of the lamb, which ensured deliverance from the destroyer, by being sprinkled on the transoms, signified faith in Christ's Passion in the hearts and on the lips of the faithful, by which same Passion we are delivered from sin and death, according to *1 Pet.* i. 18: *You were . . . redeemed . . . with the precious blood . . . of a lamb unspotted.* The partaking of its flesh signified the eating of Christ's body in the Sacrament; and the flesh was roasted at the fire to signify Christ's Passion or charity. And it was eaten with unleavened bread to signify the blameless life of the faithful who partake of Christ's body, according to *1 Cor.* v. 8: *Let us feast . . . with the unleavened bread of sincerity and truth.* The wild lettuces were added to denote repentance for sins, which is required of those who receive the body of Christ. Their loins were girt in sign of chastity, and the shoes of their feet are the examples of our dead ancestors. The staves they were to hold in their hands denoted pastoral authority: and it was commanded that the paschal lamb should be eaten in one house, *i.e.*, in the Catholic Church, and not in the conventicles of heretics.

Reply Obj. 3. Some of the sacraments of the New Law had corresponding figurative sacraments in the Old Law. For Baptism, which is a sacrament of Faith, corresponds to circumcision. Hence it is written (*Col.* ii. 11, 12): *You are circumcised . . . in the circumcision of Our Lord Jesus Christ; buried with Him in Baptism.* In the New Law the sacrament of the Eucharist corresponds to the banquet of the paschal lamb. The sacrament of Penance in the New Law corresponds to all the purifications of the Old Law. The sacrament of Orders corresponds to the consecration of the pontiff and of the priests. To the sacrament of Confirmation, which is the sacrament of the fullness of grace, there would be no corresponding sacrament of the Old Law, because the time of fullness had not yet come, since *the Law brought no man to perfection* (*Heb.* vii. 19). The same applies to the sacrament of Extreme Unction, which is an immediate preparation for entrance into glory, to which the way was not yet opened out in the Old Law, since the price had not yet been paid. Matrimony did indeed exist under the Old Law, as a function of nature, but not as the sacrament of the union of Christ with the Church, for that union was not as yet brought about. Hence, under the Old Law, it was allowable to give a bill of divorce, which is contrary to the nature of a sacrament.

Reply Obj. 4. As was already stated, the purifications of the Old Law were ordained for the removal of impediments to the divine worship, which is twofold, viz., spiritual, consisting in devotion of the mind to God, and corporeal, consisting in sacrifices, oblations and so forth. Now men are hindered in spiritual worship by sins, whereby men were said to be polluted, for instance, by idolatry, murder, adultery or incest. From such pollutions men were purified by certain sacrifices, offered either for the whole community in general, or also for the sins of individuals; not that those carnal sacrifices had of themselves the power of expiating sin, but that they signified that expiation of sins which was to be effected by Christ, and of which those of old became partakers by protesting their faith in the Redeemer, while taking part in the figurative sacrifices.

The impediments to external worship consisted in certain bodily uncleannesses, which were considered in the first place as existing in man, and consequently in other animals also, and in man's clothes, dwelling-place and vessels. In man himself, uncleanness was considered as arising partly from himself, and partly from contact with unclean things. Anything proceeding from man was reputed unclean that was already subject to corruption, or exposed thereto; and consequently, since death is a kind of corruption, the human corpse was considered unclean. In like manner, since leprosy arises from corruption of the humors, which break out externally and infect other persons, therefore, lepers also were considered unclean; again, so were women suffering from a flow of blood, whether from weakness, or from nature (either at the monthly course or at the time of conception); and, for the same reason, men were reputed unclean if they suffered from a flow of seed, whether due to weakness, to nocturnal pollution or to sexual intercourse. For every humor issuing from man in the aforesaid ways involves some unclean infection. Again, man contracted uncleanness by touching any unclean thing whatever.

Now there was both a literal and a figurative reason for these uncleannesses. The literal reason was taken from the reverence due to those things that belong to the divine worship, both because men are not wont, when unclean, to touch precious things, and in order that by rarely approaching sacred things they might have greater respect for them. For since man could seldom avoid all the aforesaid uncleannesses, the result was that men could seldom approach to touch things belonging to the worship of God, so that when they did approach, they did so with greater reverence and humility.[27] Moreover, in some of these, the literal reason was that men should not be kept away from worshipping God through fear of coming in contact with lepers and others similarly afflicted with loathsome and contagious diseases. In others, again, the reason was to avoid idolatrous worship, because in their sacrificial rites the Gentiles sometimes employed

[27] Moses Maimonides, *Guide*, III, 47 (p. 367).

human blood and seed. All these bodily uncleannesses were purified either by the mere sprinkling of water, or, in the case of those which were more grievous, by some sacrifice of expiation for the sin which was the occasion of the uncleanness in question.

The figurative reason for these uncleannesses was that they were figures of various sins. For the uncleanness of any corpse signifies the uncleanness of sin, which is the death of the soul. The uncleanness of leprosy betokened the uncleanness of heretical doctrine, both because heretical doctrine is contagious just as leprosy is, and because no doctrine is so false as not to have some truth mingled with error, just as on the surface of a leprous body one may distinguish the healthy parts from those that are infected. The uncleanness of a woman suffering from a flow of blood denotes the uncleanness of idolatry, because of the blood which is offered up. The uncleanness of the man who has suffered seminal loss signifies the uncleanness of empty words, for *the seed is the word of God* (*Luke* viii. 11). The uncleanness of sexual intercourse and of the woman in childbirth signifies the uncleanness of original sin. The uncleanness of the woman in her periods signifies the uncleanness of a mind that is sensualized by pleasure. Speaking generally, the uncleanness contracted by touching an unclean thing denotes the uncleanness arising from consent in another's sin, according to *2 Cor.* vi. 17: *Go out from among them, and be ye separate . . . and touch not the unclean thing.*

Moreover, this uncleanness arising from the touch was contracted even by inanimate objects; for whatever was touched in any way by an unclean man became itself unclean. Wherein the Law attenuated the superstition of the Gentiles, who held that uncleanness was contracted not only by touch, but also by speech or look, as Rabbi Moses states of a woman in her periods.[28] The mystical sense of this was that *to God the wicked and his wickedness are hateful alike* (*Wis.* xiv. 9).

There was also an uncleanness of inanimate things considered in themselves, such as the uncleanness of leprosy in a house or in clothes. For just as leprosy occurs in men through a corrupt humor causing putrefaction and corruption in the flesh, so, too, through some corruption and excess of humidity or dryness there arises sometimes a kind of corruption in the stones with which a house is built, or in clothes. Hence the Law called this corruption by the name of leprosy, whereby a house or a garment was deemed to be unclean; and this both because all corruption savored of uncleanness, as was stated above, and because the Gentiles worshipped their household gods as a preservative against this corruption. Hence the Law prescribed such houses, where this kind of corruption was of a lasting nature, to be destroyed; and such garments to be burnt, in order to avoid all occasion of idolatry. There was also an uncleanness of vessels, of which it is written (*Num.* xix. 15): *The vessel that hath no*

[28] *Ibid.* (p. 368).

cover, and binding over it, shall be unclean. The cause of this uncleanness was that anything unclean might easily drop into such vessels, so
as to render them unclean. Moreover, this command aimed at the pre-
vention of idolatry. For idolaters believed that if mice, lizards or the like,
which they used to sacrifice to the idols, fell into the vessels or into the
water, these became more pleasing to the gods. Even now some women let
down uncovered vessels in honor of the nocturnal deities which they call
Janæ.

The figurative reason for these uncleannesses is that the leprosy of a
house signified the uncleanness of the assembly of heretics; the leprosy
of a linen garment signified an evil life arising from bitterness of mind;
the leprosy of a woollen garment denoted the wickedness of flatterers;
leprosy in the warp signified the vices of the soul; leprosy on the woof
denoted sins of the flesh, for as the warp is in the woof, so is the soul in
the body. The vessel that has neither cover nor binding betokens a man
who lacks the veil of taciturnity, and who is unrestrained by any severity
of discipline.

Reply Obj. 5. As was stated above, there was a twofold uncleanness in
the Law: one by way of corruption in the mind or in the body, and this
was the graver uncleanness; the other was by mere contact with an unclean thing, and this was less grave, and was more easily expiated. For
the former uncleanness was expiated by sacrifices for sins, since all corruption is due to sin, and signifies sin; whereas the latter uncleanness was
expiated by the mere sprinkling of a certain water, of which water we
read in *Num.* xix. For there God commanded them to take a red cow in
memory of the sin they had committed in worshipping a calf. And a cow
is mentioned rather than a calf, because it was thus that the Lord was
wont to designate the synagogue, according to *Osee* iv. 16: *Israel hath
gone astray like a wanton heifer*; and this was, perhaps, because they
worshipped heifers after the custom of Egypt, according to *Osee* x. 5:
[They] have worshipped the kine of Bethaven. And in detestation of the
sin of idolatry it was sacrificed outside the camp; in fact, whenever sacrifice was offered up in expiation of the multitude, of sins, it was all burnt
outside the camp. Moreover, in order to show that this sacrifice cleansed
the people from all their sins, *the priest* dipped *his finger in her blood,*
and sprinkled *it over against the door of the tabernacle seven times*; for
the number seven signifies a complete totality. Further, the very sprinkling of blood pertained to the detestation of idolatry, in which the blood
that was offered up was not poured out, but was collected together, and
men gathered round it to eat in honor of the idols. Likewise, it was burnt
by fire, either because God appeared to Moses in a fire, and the Law was
given from the midst of fire, or to denote that idolatry, together with all
that was connected therewith, was to be extirpated altogether; just as the
cow was burnt *with her skin and her flesh, her blood and dung being de-*

livered to the flames. To this burning were added *cedar-wood, and hyssop, and scarlet twice dyed,* to signify that, just as cedar-wood is not liable to putrefaction, and scarlet twice dyed does not easily lose its color, and hyssop retains its odor after it has been dried, so also was this sacrifice for the preservation of the whole people, and for their good behavior and devotion. Hence it is said of the ashes of the cow: *That they may be reserved for the multitude of the children of Israel* (*Num.* xix. 9). Or, according to Josephus, the four elements are indicated here.[29] For *cedar-wood* was added to the fire, to signify the earth, because of its earthiness; *hyssop,* to signify the air, because of its smell; *scarlet twice dyed,* to signify water, for the same reason as purple, because of the dyes which are taken out of the water:—thus denoting the fact that this sacrifice was offered to the Creator of the four elements. And since this sacrifice was offered for the sin of idolatry, both *he that burned her,* and *he that gathered up the ashes,* and *he that sprinkled the water* in which the ashes were placed, were deemed unclean in detestation of that sin, in order to show that whatever was in any way connected with idolatry should be cast aside as being unclean. From this uncleanness they were purified by the mere washing of their clothes; nor did they need to be sprinkled with the water because of this kind of uncleanness, for otherwise the process would have been unending, since he that sprinkled the water became unclean, so that if he were to sprinkle himself he would remain unclean; and if another were to sprinkle him, that one would have become unclean, and in like manner, whoever might sprinkle him, and so on indefinitely.

The figurative reason for this sacrifice was that the red cow signified Christ in respect of his assumed weakness, denoted by the female sex; while the color of the cow designated the blood of His Passion. And the *red cow was of full age,* because all Christ's works are perfect, *in which there* was *no blemish; and which* had *not carried the yoke,* because Christ was innocent, nor did He carry the yoke of sin. It was commanded to be taken to Moses, because they blamed Christ for transgressing the law of Moses by breaking the Sabbath. And it was commanded to be delivered *to Eleazar the priest,* because Christ was delivered into the hands of the priests to be slain. It was immolated *without the camp,* because Christ *suffered outside the gate* (*Heb.* xiii. 12). And the priest dipped *his finger in her blood,* because by the separation [*i.e.,* of the blood from the red heifer], symbolized by the finger, the mystery of Christ's Passion should be considered and imitated.

It was sprinkled *over against . . . the tabernacle,* which denotes the synagogue, to signify either the condemnation of the unbelieving Jews, or the purification of believers; and this *seven times,* in token either of the seven gifts of the Holy Ghost, or of the seven days wherein all time is comprised. Again, all things that pertain to the Incarnation of Christ

[29] *The Jewish War,* V, 5, 4 (III, 264).

should be burnt with fire, *i.e.*, they should be understood spiritually; for the *skin* and *flesh* signified Christ's outward works, the *blood* denoted the subtle inward force which quickened His external deeds, and the *dung* betokened His weariness, His thirst, and all such things pertaining to His weakness. Three things were added, viz., *cedar-wood*, which denotes the height of hope or contemplation; *hyssop*, in token of humility or faith; *scarlet twice dyed*, which denotes twofold charity; for it is by these three that we should cling to Christ suffering. The ashes of this burning were gathered by *a man that is clean*, because the relics of the Passion came into the possession of the Gentiles, who were not guilty of Christ's death. The ashes were put into water for the purpose of expiation, because Baptism receives from Christ's Passion the power of washing away sins. The priest who immolated and burned the cow, and he who burned, and he who gathered together the ashes, were unclean, as also he that sprinkled the water. This was the case either because the Jews became unclean through putting Christ to death (whereby our sins are expiated), and this, until the evening, *i.e.*, until the end of the world, when the remnants of Israel will be converted; or else because they who handle sacred things with a view to the cleansing of others contract certain uncleannesses, as Gregory says,[30] and this until the evening, *i.e.*, until the end of this life.

Reply Obj. 6. As was stated above, an uncleanness which was caused by corruption either of mind or of body was expiated by sin-offerings. Now special sacrifices were wont to be offered for the sins of individuals; but since some were neglectful about expiating such sins and uncleannesses, or, through ignorance, failed to offer this expiation, it was laid down that once a year, on the tenth day of the seventh month, a sacrifice of expiation should be offered for the whole people. And because, as the Apostle says (*Heb.* vii. 28), *the Law maketh men priests, who have infirmity*, it behooved the priest first of all to offer a calf for his own sins, in memory of Aaron's sin in fashioning the molten calf; and besides, to offer a ram for a holocaust, which signified that the priestly sovereignty denoted by the ram, who is the head of the flock, was to be ordained to the glory of God.— Then he offered two he-goats for the people, one of which was offered in expiation of the sins of the multitude. For the he-goat is an evil-smelling animal, and from its skin clothes are made having a pungent odor, so as to signify the stench, uncleanness and the sting of sin. After this he-goat had been immolated, its blood was taken, together with the blood of the calf, into the Holy of Holies, and the entire sanctuary was sprinkled with it, so as to signify that the tabernacle was cleansed from the uncleannesses of the children of Israel. But the corpses of the he-goat and calf which had been offered up for sin had to be burnt, to denote the destruction of sins. They were not, however, burnt on the altar, since none but holocausts were burnt thereon, but it was prescribed that they should be burnt outside the

[30] *Pastor.*, II, 5 (PL 77, 34).

camp, in detestation of sin; for this was done whenever sacrifice was offered for a grievous sin, or for a multitude of sins. The other goat was let loose into the wilderness, not indeed to offer it to the demons (whom the Gentiles worshipped in desert places), because it was unlawful to offer aught to them, but in order to point out the effect of the sacrifice which had been offered up. Hence the priest put his hand on its head, while confessing the sins of the children of Israel: as though that goat were to carry them away into the wilderness, where it would be devoured by wild beasts, because it bore the punishment of the people's sins. And it was said to bear the sins of the people, either because the forgiveness of the people's sins was signified by its being let loose, or because on its head written lists of sins were fastened.

The figurative reason of these things was that Christ was foreshadowed both by the calf, because of His power, by the ram, because He is the Head of the faithful, and by the he-goat, because of *the likeness of sinful flesh* (*Rom.* viii. 3). Moreover, Christ was sacrificed for the sins of both priests and people, since both those of high and those of low degree are cleansed from sin by His Passion. The blood of the calf and of the goat was brought into the Holies by the priest, because the entrance to the kingdom of heaven was opened to us by the blood of Christ's Passion. Their bodies were burnt outside the camp, because *Christ suffered without the gate,* as the Apostle declares (*Heb.* xiii. 12). The scape-goat may denote either Christ's divinity which went away into solitude when the Man Christ suffered, not by going to another place, but by restraining His power; or it may signify the base concupiscence which we ought to cast away from ourselves, while we offer up to Our Lord acts of virtue.

With regard to the uncleanness contracted by those who burnt these sacrifices, the reason is the same as that which we assigned to the sacrifice of the red heifer.

Reply Obj. 7. The legal rite did not cleanse the leper of his deformity, but declared him to be cleansed. This is shown by the words of *Levit.* xiv. 3, *seq.,* where it is said that the priest, *when he shall find that the leprosy is cleansed,* shall command *him that is to be purified.* Consequently, the leper was already healed; but he was said to be purified in so far as the verdict of the priest restored him to the society of men and to the worship of God. It happened sometimes, however, that bodily leprosy was miraculously cured by the legal rite, when the priest erred in his judgment.

Now this purification of a leper was twofold. For, in the first place, he was declared to be clean, and, secondly, he was restored, as clean, to the society of men and to the worship of God, that is, after seven days. At the first purification, the leper who sought to be cleansed offered for himself *two living sparrows, . . . cedar-wood, and scarlet, and hyssop,* in such wise that a sparrow and the hyssop should be tied to the cedar-wood with a scarlet thread, so that the cedar-wood was like the handle of an aspersory:

while the hyssop and sparrow were that part of the aspersory which was dipped into the blood of the other sparrow which was *immolated . . . over living waters*. These four things he offered as an antidote to the four defects of leprosy. For cedar-wood, which is not subject to putrefaction, was offered against the putrefaction; hyssop, which is a sweet-smelling herb, was offered up against the stench; a living sparrow was offered up against numbness; and scarlet, which has a vivid color, was offered up against the repulsive color of leprosy. The living sparrow was let loose to fly away into the plain, because the leper was restored to his former liberty.

On the eighth day he was admitted to divine worship, and was restored to the society of men, but only after having shaved all the hair of his body, and washed his clothes, because leprosy rots the hair, infects the clothes, and gives them an evil smell. Afterwards a sacrifice was offered for his sin, since leprosy was frequently a result of sin. Some of the blood of the sacrifice was put on the tip of the ear of the man that was to be cleansed, *and on the thumb of his right hand, and the great toe of his right foot*; because it is in these parts that leprosy is first diagnosed and felt. In this rite, moreover, three liquids were employed: viz., blood, against the corruption of the blood; oil, to denote the healing of the disease; and living waters, to wash away the filth.

The figurative reason was that the divine and human natures in Christ were denoted by the two sparrows, one of which, in likeness to His human nature, was offered up in an earthen vessel over living waters, because the waters of Baptism are sanctified by Christ's Passion. The other sparrow, in token of His impassible divinity, remained living, because divinity cannot die; and hence it flew away, for it could not be encompassed by the Passion. Now this living sparrow, together with the cedar-wood and scarlet or cochineal and hyssop, *i.e.*, faith, hope and charity, as was stated above, was put into the water for the purpose of sprinkling, because we are baptized in the faith of the God-Man. By the waters of Baptism or of his tears man washes his clothes, *i.e.*, his works, and all his hair, *i.e.*, his thoughts. The tip of the right ear of the man to be cleansed is moistened with some of the blood and oil, in order to strengthen his hearing against harmful words; and the thumb and toe of his right hand and foot are moistened that his deeds may be holy. Other matters pertaining to this purification, or to that also of any other uncleannesses, call for no special remark, beyond what applies to other sacrifices, whether for sins or for trespasses.

Reply Objs. 8 and 9. Just as the people were initiated by circumcision to the divine worship, so were the ministers by some special purification or consecration; and so they are commanded to be separated from other men, as being specially deputed, rather than others, to the ministry of the divine worship. And all that was done touching them in their consecration or institution was with a view to show that they were in possession of a prerogative of purity, power and dignity. Hence three things were done in the institution of ministers. For first, they were purified; secondly, they were adorned and consecrated; thirdly, they were employed in the ministry. All in general used to be purified by washing in water, and by certain sacrifices; but the Levites in particular shaved all the hair of their bodies, as is stated in *Levit.* viii [*cf. Num.* viii. 7].

With regard to the high-priests and priests, the consecration was performed as follows. First, when they had been washed, they were clothed with certain special garments in designation of their dignity. In particular, the high-priest was anointed on the head with the oil of unction, to denote that the power of consecration was poured forth by him on to others, just as oil flows from the head on to the lower parts of the body (according to *Ps.* cxxxii. 2: *Like the precious ointment on the head that ran down upon the beard, the beard of Aaron*). But the Levites received no other consecration besides being offered to the Lord by the children of Israel through the hands of the high-priest, who prayed for them. The lesser priests were consecrated on the hands only, which were to be employed in the sacrifices. The tip of their right ear and the thumb of their right hand, and the great toe of their right foot were tinged with the blood of the sacrificial animal, to denote that they should be obedient to God's law in offering the sacrifices (this is denoted by touching their right ear); and that they should be careful and ready in performing the sacrifices (this is signified by the moistening of the right foot and hand). They themselves and their garments were sprinkled with the blood of the animal that had been sacrificed, in remembrance of the blood of the lamb by which they had been delivered in Egypt. At their consecration, the following sacrifices were offered: a calf, for sin, in remembrance of Aaron's sin in fashioning the molten calf; a ram, for a holocaust, in remembrance of the sacrifice of Abraham, whose obedience it behooved the high-priest to imitate; again, a ram of consecration, which was as a peace-offering, in remembrance of the delivery from Egypt through the blood of the lamb; and a basket of bread, in remembrance of the manna vouchsafed to the people.

In reference to their being destined to the ministry, the fat of the ram, one roll of bread, and the right shoulder were placed on their hands, to show that they received the power of offering these things to the Lord; while the Levites were initiated to the ministry by being brought into the tabernacle of the covenant, as being destined to the ministry touching the vessels of the sanctuary.

The figurative reason of these things was that those who are to be consecrated to the spiritual ministry of Christ should be first of all purified by the waters of Baptism, and by the waters of tears, in their faith in Christ's Passion, which is a sacrifice both of expiation and of purification. They have also to shave all the hair of their body, *i.e.*, all evil thoughts. They should, moreover, be decked with virtues, and be consecrated with the oil of the Holy Ghost, and with the sprinkling of Christ's blood. And thus they should be intent on the fulfillment of their spiritual ministry.

Reply Obj. 10. As was already stated, the purpose of the Law was to induce men to have reverence for the divine worship, and this in two ways: first, by excluding from the worship of God whatever might be an object of contempt; secondly, by introducing into the divine worship all that seemed to savor of reverence. And, indeed, if this was observed in regard to the tabernacle and its vessels, and in the animals to be sacrificed, much more was it to be observed in the very ministers. Therefore, in order to obviate contempt for the ministers, it was prescribed that they should have no bodily stain or defect, since men so deformed are wont to be despised by others. For the same reason, it was also commanded that the choice of those who were to be destined to the service of God was not to be made in an indiscriminate way from any family, but according to their descent from one particular stock, thus giving them distinction and nobility.

In order that they might be revered, special ornate vestments were appointed for their use, and a special form of consecration. This indeed is the general reason of ornate garments. But the high-priest in particular had eight vestments. First, he had a linen tunic. Secondly, he had a purple tunic, round the bottom of which were placed *little bells* and *pomegranates of violet, and purple, and scarlet twice dyed*. Thirdly, he had the ephod, which covered his shoulders and his breast down to the girdle; and it was made of gold and violet and purple, and scarlet twice dyed and twisted linen; and on his shoulders he bore two onyx stones, on which were graven the names of the children of Israel. Fourthly, he had the rational, made of the same material; it was square in shape, and was worn on the breast, and was fastened to the ephod. On this rational there were twelve precious stones set in four rows, on which also were graven the names of the children of Israel, in token that the priest bore the burden of the whole people, since he bore their names on his shoulders; and that it was his duty ever to think of their welfare, since he wore them on his breast, bearing them in his heart, so to speak. And the Lord commanded the *Doctrine and Truth* to be put in the rational; for certain matters pertaining to the truth of justice and doctrine were written on it. The Jews indeed pretend that on the rational was placed a stone which changed color according to the various things which were about to happen to the children of Israel; and this they call the *Truth and Doctrine*. Fifthly, he wore a belt or girdle made of the four colors mentioned above. Sixthly, there was the tiara or mitre which was made of linen. Seventhly, there was the golden plate which hung over his forehead, on which was inscribed the Lord's name. Eighthly, there were *the linen breeches to cover the flesh of their nakedness*, when they went up to the sanctuary or altar. Of these eight vestments the lesser priests had four, viz., the linen tunic and breeches, the belt and the tiara.

According to some,[31] the literal reason for these vestments was that they denoted the disposition of the terrestrial globe, as though the high-priest confessed himself to be the minister of the Creator of the world; and so it is written (*Wis.* xviii. 24): *In the robe* of Aaron *was the whole world* described. For the linen breeches signified the earth out of which the flax grows. The surrounding belt signified the ocean which surrounds the earth. The violet tunic denoted the air by its color; its little bells betoken the thunder; the pomegranates, the lightning. The ephod, by its many colors, signified the sidereal heavens; the two onyx stones denoted the two hemispheres, or the sun and moon. The twelve precious stones on the breast are the twelve signs of the zodiac; and they are said to have been placed on the rational because in heaven are the exemplars of earthly things, according to *Job* xxxviii. 33: *Dost thou know the order of heaven, and canst thou set down the reason [rationem] thereof on the earth?* The turban or tiara signified the empyrean, and the golden plate was a token of God, the governor of the universe.

The figurative reason is evident. For bodily stains or defects, wherefrom the priests had to be immune, signify the various vices and sins from which they should be free. Thus it is forbidden that he should be blind, *i.e.*, he ought not to be ignorant; he must not be lame, *i.e.*, vacillating and uncertain of purpose; he must not have *a little, or a great, or a crooked nose, i.e.*, that he should not, from lack of discretion, exceed in one direction or in another, or even exercise some base occupation, for the nose signifies discretion, because it discerns odors. It is forbidden that he should have *a broken foot* or *hand, i.e.*, he should not lose the power of doing good works or of advancing in virtue. He is rejected, too, if he have a swelling either in front or behind, by which is signified too much love of earthly things; —if he be blear-eyed, *i.e.*, if his mind is darkened by carnal affections, for running of the eyes is caused by a flow of matter. He is also rejected if he have *a pearl in his eye, i.e.*, if he presumes in his own estimation that he is clothed in the white robe of righteousness. Again, he is rejected *if he have a continued scab, i.e.*, lustfulness of the flesh; also, if he have *a dry scurf,* which covers the body without giving pain, and is a blemish on the comeliness of the members, which denotes avarice. Lastly, he is rejected *if he have a rupture* or hernia, through baseness rending his heart, though it appear not in his deeds.

The vestments denote the virtues of God's ministers. Now there are four things that are necessary to all His ministers, viz., chastity denoted by the breeches; a pure life, signified by the linen tunic; the moderation of discretion, betokened by the girdle; and rectitude of purpose, denoted by the mitre covering the head. But the high-priests needed four other things in addition to these. First, a continual recollection of God in their thoughts,

[31] *Glossa ordin.* (III, 385E) ; Rhabanus Maurus, *In Sap.,* III, 17, super XVIII, 24 (PL 109, 758).

and this was signified by the golden plate worn over the forehead, with the name of God engraved thereon. Secondly, they had to bear with the shortcomings of the people; this was denoted by the ephod which they bore on their shoulders. Thirdly, they had to carry the people in their mind and heart by the solicitude of charity, in token of which they wore the rational. Fourthly, they had to lead a godly life by performing works of perfection; and this was signified by the violet tunic. Hence little golden bells were fixed to the bottom of the violet tunic, which bells signified the teaching of divine things united in the high-priest to his godly mode of life. In addition to these were the pomegranates, signifying unity of faith and concord in good morals; because his doctrine should hold together in such a way that it should not rend asunder the unity of faith and peace.

Sixth Article

WHETHER THERE WAS ANY REASONABLE CAUSE FOR THE CEREMONIAL OBSERVANCES?

We proceed thus to the Sixth Article:—
Objection 1. It would seem that there was no reasonable cause for the ceremonial observances. For, as the Apostle says (*1 Tim.* iv. 4), *every creature of God is good, and nothing to be rejected that is received with thanksgiving.* It was therefore unfitting that they should be forbidden to eat certain foods, as being unclean, according to *Levit.* xi.

Obj. 2. Further, just as animals are given to man for food, so also are herbs; and so it is written (*Gen.* ix. 3): *As the green herbs have I delivered all* flesh *to you.* But the Law did not distinguish any herbs from the rest as being unclean, although some are most harmful, for instance, those that are poisonous. Therefore it seems that neither should any animals have been prohibited as being unclean.

Obj. 3. Further, if the matter from which a thing is generated be unclean, it seems that likewise the thing generated therefrom is unclean. But flesh is generated from blood. Since therefore all flesh was not prohibited as unclean, it seems that in like manner neither should blood have been forbidden as unclean; nor the fat which is engendered from blood.

Obj. 4. Further, Our Lord said (*Matt.* x. 28; [*cf. Luke* xii. 4]) that those should not be feared *that kill the body,* since after death they *have no more that they can do*; which would not be true if after death harm might come to man through anything done with his body. Much less therefore does it matter to an animal already dead how its flesh is cooked. Consequently, there seems to be no reason in what is said, *Exod.* xxiii. 19: *Thou shalt not boil a kid in the milk of its dam.*

Obj. 5. Further, all that is first brought forth of man and beast, as being most perfect, is commanded to be offered to the Lord (*Exod.* xiii). Therefore it is an unfitting command that is set forth in *Levit.* xix. 23: *When you shall be come into the land, and shall have planted in it fruit trees, you shall take away the uncircumcision of them, i.e.,* the first crops, and they *shall be unclean to you, neither shall you eat of them.*

Obj. 6. Further, clothing is something extraneous to man's body. Therefore certain kinds of garments should not have been forbidden to the Jews: for instance (*Levit.* xix. 19): *Thou shalt not wear a garment that is woven of two sorts;* and (*Deut.* xxii. 5): *A woman shall not be clothed with man's apparel, neither shall a man use woman's apparel;* and further on (verse 11): *Thou shalt not wear a garment that is woven of woollen and linen together.*

Obj. 7. Further, to be mindful of God's commandments concerns not the body but the heart. Therefore it is unsuitably prescribed (*Deut.* vi. 8, seq.) that they should *bind* the commandments of God *as a sign* on their hands; that they should *write them in the entry;* and (*Num.* xv. 38, *seq.*) that they should *make to themselves fringes in the corners of their garments, putting in them ribands of blue, that . . . they may remember . . . the commandments of the Lord.*

Obj. 8. Further, the Apostle says (*1 Cor.* ix. 9) that God doth not *take care for oxen,* and, therefore, neither of other irrational animals. Therefore without reason is it commanded (*Deut.* xxii. 6): *If thou find, as thou walkest by the way, a bird's nest in a tree . . . thou shalt not take the dam with her young;* and (*Deut.* xxv. 4): *Thou shalt not muzzle the ox that treadeth out thy corn;* and (*Levit.* xix. 19): *Thou shalt not make thy cattle to gender with beasts of any other kind.*

Obj. 9. Further, no distinction was made between clean and unclean plants. Much less, therefore, should any distinction have been made about the cultivation of plants. Therefore it was unfittingly prescribed (*Levit.* xix. 19): *Thou shalt not sow thy field with different seeds;* and (*Deut.* xxii. 9, *seq.*): *Thou shalt sow thy vineyard with divers seeds;* and: *Thou shalt not plough with an ox and an ass together.*

Obj. 10. Further, it is apparent that inanimate things are most of all subject to the power of man. Therefore it was unfitting to debar man from taking the silver and gold of which idols were made, or anything they found in the houses of idols, as expressed in the commandment of the Law (*Deut.* vii. 25, *seq.*). It also seems an absurd commandment set forth in *Deut.* xxiii. 13, that they should *dig round about and . . . cover with earth that which they were eased of.*

Obj. 11. Further, piety is required especially in priests. But it seems to be an act of piety to assist at the burial of one's friends; and so Tobias is commended for so doing (*Tob.* i. 20, *seqq.*). In like manner, it is sometimes an act of piety to marry a loose woman, because she is thereby delivered from sin and infamy. Therefore it seems inconsistent for these things to be forbidden to priests (*Levit.* xxi.).

On the contrary, It is written (*Deut.* xviii. 14): *But thou art otherwise instructed by the Lord thy God*; from which words we may gather that these observances were instituted by God to be a special prerogative of that people. Therefore they are not without reason or cause.

I answer that, The Jewish people, as we have stated above, were especially chosen for the worship of God, and among them the priests themselves were specially set apart for that purpose. And just as other things that are applied to the divine worship need to be marked in some particular way so that they be worthy of the worship of God, so too in that people's, and especially the priests', mode of life, there needed to be certain special things befitting the divine worship, whether spiritual or corporeal. Now the worship prescribed by the Law foreshadowed the mystery of Christ, so that whatever they did was a figure of things pertaining to Christ, according to *1 Cor.* x. 11: *All these things happened to them in figures.* Consequently, the reasons for these observances may be taken in two ways: first, according to their fittingness to the worship of God; secondly, according as they foreshadow something touching the Christian mode of life.

Reply Obj. 1. As was stated above, the Law distinguished a twofold pollution or uncleanness: one, that of sin, whereby the soul was defiled; and another consisting in some kind of corruption, whereby the body was in some way infected. Speaking, then, of the first-mentioned uncleanness, no kind of food is unclean, or can defile a man, by reason of its nature; and so we read (*Matt.* xv. 11): *Not that which goeth into the mouth defileth a man; but what cometh out of the mouth, this defileth a man.* These words are explained [verse 17] as referring to sins. Yet certain foods can defile the soul accidentally, in so far as man partakes of them against obedience or a vow, or from excessive concupiscence, or through their being an incentive to lust, for which reason some refrain from wine and flesh-meat.

If, however, we speak of bodily uncleanness, consisting in some kind of corruption, the flesh of certain animals is unclean either because, like the pig, they feed on unclean things, or because their life is among unclean surroundings (thus certain animals, like moles and mice and such live underground, whence they contract a certain unpleasant smell), or because their flesh, through being too moist or too dry, engenders corrupt humors in the human body.[32] Hence they were forbidden to eat the flesh of flat-footed animals, *i.e.*, animals having an uncloven hoof, because of their earthiness; and, in like manner, they were forbidden to eat the flesh of animals that have many clefts in their feet, because such are very fierce and their flesh is very dry (*e.g.*, the flesh of lions and the like). For the same reason they were forbidden to eat certain birds of prey the flesh of which is very dry, and certain water-fowl because of their exceeding humidity. In like manner, certain fish lacking fins and scales were prohibited because of their excessive moisture, such as eels and the like. They were, however, allowed to eat ruminants and animals with a divided hoof, be-

[32] Moses Maimonides, *Guide*, III, 48 (p. 370).

cause in such animals the humors are well absorbed, and their nature well balanced; for neither are they too moist, as is indicated by the hoof, nor are they too earthy, which is shown by their not having a flat but a cloven hoof. Of fishes they were allowed to partake of the drier kinds, of which the fins and scales are an indication, because thereby the moist nature of the fish is tempered. Of birds they were allowed to eat the tamer kinds, such as hens, partridges, and the like.—Another reason was detestation of idolatry, because the Gentiles, and especially the Egyptians, among whom they had grown up, offered up these forbidden animals to their idols, or employed them for the purpose of sorcery; whereas they did not eat those animals which the Jews were allowed to eat, but worshipped them as gods, or abstained, for some other motive, from eating them, as was stated above. The third reason was to prevent excessive care about food; and so they were allowed to eat those animals which could be procured easily and promptly.

With regard to blood and fat, they were forbidden to partake of those of any animal whatever without exception. Blood was forbidden, both in order to avoid cruelty, that they might abhor the shedding of human blood, as was stated above, and in order to shun the idolatrous rite whereby it was customary for men to collect the blood and to gather together around it for a banquet in honor of the idols, to whom they held the blood to be most acceptable. Hence the Lord commanded the blood to be poured out and to be covered with earth (*Levit.* xvii. 13). For the same reason they were forbidden to eat animals that had been suffocated or strangled, because the blood of these animals would not be separated from the body, or because this form of death is very painful to the victim, and the Lord wished to withdraw them from cruelty even in regard to irrational animals, so that they should be less inclined to be cruel to other men, through being accustomed to being kind to beasts. They were forbidden to eat the fat, both because idolaters ate it in honor of their gods, and because it used to be burnt in honor of God, and, again, because blood and fat are not nutritious, which is the cause assigned by Rabbi Moses.[33] The reason why they were forbidden to eat the sinews is given in *Gen.* xxxii. 32, where it is stated that *the children of Israel . . . eat not the sinew . . . because he touched the sinew of* Jacob's *thigh and it shrank.*

The figurative reason for these things is that all these animals signified certain sins, in token of which those animals were prohibited. Hence Augustine says: *If the swine and lamb be called in question, both are clean by nature, because all God's creatures are good; yet the lamb is clean, and the pig is unclean in a certain signification. Thus, if you speak of a foolish, and of a wise man, each of these expressions is clean considered in the nature of the sound, letters and syllables of which it is composed;*

[33] *Ibid.* (p. 371).

but in signification, the one is clean, the other unclean.[34] The animal that chews the cud and has a divided hoof is clean in signification. For division of the hoof is a figure of the two Testaments, or of the Father and Son, or of the two natures in Christ, or of the distinction of good and evil. For chewing the cud signifies meditation on the Scriptures and a sound understanding thereof, and whoever lacks either of these is spiritually unclean. In like manner, those fish that have scales and fins are clean in signification. For fins signify the heavenly or contemplative life, while scales signify a life of trials, each of which is required for spiritual cleanness.—Of birds certain special kinds were forbidden.[35] In the eagle, which flies at a great height, pride is forbidden; in the griffon, which is hostile to horses and men, cruelty of powerful men is prohibited. The osprey, which feeds on very small birds, signifies those who oppress the poor. The kite, which is full of cunning, denotes those who are fraudulent in their dealings. The vulture, which follows an army, expecting to feed on the carcasses of the slain, signifies those who like others to die or to fight among themselves that they may gain thereby. Birds that are ravens signify those who are blackened by their lusts, or those who lack kindly feelings, for the raven did not return when once it had been let loose from the ark. The ostrich which, though a bird, cannot fly, and is always on the ground, signifies those who fight for God's cause, and at the same time are taken up with worldly business. The owl, which sees clearly at night, but cannot see in daytime, denotes those who are clever in temporal affairs, but dull in spiritual matters. The gull, which both flies in the air and swims in the water, signifies those who are partial both to Circumcision and to Baptism; or else it denotes those who would fly by contemplation, yet dwell in the waters of sensual delights. The hawk, which helps men to seize the prey, is a figure of those who assist the strong to prey on the poor.[36] The screech-owl, which seeks its food by night but hides by day, signifies the lustful man who seeks to lie hidden in his deeds of darkness.[37] The cormorant, so constituted that it can stay a long time under water, denotes the glutton who plunges into the waters of pleasure. The ibis is an African bird with a long beak, and feeds on snakes; and perhaps it is the same as the stork.[38] It signifies the envious man, who refreshes himself with the ills of others, as with snakes. The swan is bright in color, and by the aid of its long neck extracts its food from deep places on land or water; it may denote those who seek earthly profit through an external brightness of virtue. The bittern is a bird of the East; it has a long beak, and its jaws are furnished with follicules, wherein it stores its food at first, after a time proceeding to digest it;[39] it is a figure of the miser, who is excessively

---

[34] *Contra Faust.*, VI, 7 (PL 42, 233).   [35] Cf. Rhabanus Maurus, *De Univ.*, VIII, 1; 6 (PL 111, 222; 240-255); St. Isidore, *Etymol.*, XII, 2; 17 (PL 82, 436; 459).   [36] St. Albert, *In De Anim.*, XXIII, tr. 1, ch. 22 (XII, 482).   [37] *Op. cit.*, XXIII, tr. 1, ch. 22 (XII, 493).   [38] *Op. cit.*, VIII, tr. 1, ch. 2 (XI, 427).   [39] *Op. cit.*, XXIII, tr. 1, ch. 24 (XII, 497).

careful in hoarding up the necessities of life. The coot has this peculiarity apart from other birds, that it has a webbed foot for swimming, and a cloven foot for walking, for it swims like a duck in the water, and walks like a partridge on land;[40] it drinks only when it bites, since it dips all its food in water; it is a figure of the man who will not take advice, and does nothing but what is soaked in the water of his own will. The heron, commonly called a falcon, signifies those whose *feet are swift to shed blood* (*Ps.* xiii. 3). The plover, which is a garrulous bird, signifies the gossip. The hoopoe, which builds its nest on dung, feeds on fœtid ordure, and whose song is like a groan, denotes worldly grief which works death in those who are unclean. The bat, which flies near the ground, signifies those who, being gifted with worldly knowledge, seek none but earthly things.—Of fowls and quadrupeds, those alone were permitted which have the hind-legs longer than the fore-legs, so that they can leap, whereas those were forbidden which cling rather to the earth; because those who abuse the doctrine of the four Evangelists, so that they are not lifted up thereby, are reputed unclean.—By the prohibition of blood, fat and nerves, we are to understand the forbidding of cruelty, lust and boldness in committing sin.

Reply Obj. 2. Men were wont to eat plants and other products of the soil even before the deluge, but the eating of flesh seems to have been introduced after the deluge; for it is written (*Gen.* ix. 3): *Even as the green herbs have I delivered . . . all* flesh *to you*. The reason for this was that the eating of the products of the soil savors rather of a simple life, whereas the eating of flesh savors of delicate and overcareful living. For the soil gives birth to the herb of its own accord, and such products of the earth may be had in great quantities with very little effort; whereas no small trouble is necessary either to rear or to catch an animal. Consequently God, being wishful to bring His people back to a more simple way of living, forbade them to eat many kinds of animals, but not those things that are produced by the soil.—Another reason may be that animals were offered to idols, while the products of the soil were not.

The Reply to the Third Objection is clear from what has been said.

Reply Obj. 4. Although the kid that is slain has no perception of the manner in which its flesh is cooked, yet it would seem to savor of heartlessness if the dam's milk, which was intended for the nourishment of her offspring, were served up on the same dish.—It might also be said that the Gentiles, in celebrating the feasts of their idols, prepared the flesh of kids in this manner, for the purpose of sacrifice or banquet; and so (*Exod.* xxiii.), after the solemnities to be celebrated under the Law had been foretold, it is added: *Thou shalt not boil a kid in the milk of its dam*. The figurative reason for this prohibition is this:—the kid, signifying Christ, because of *the likeness of sinful flesh* (*Rom.* viii. 3), was not to be

---

[40] *Ibid.* (XII, 501).

seethed, *i.e.,* slain, by the Jews, *in the milk of its dam, i.e.,* during His infancy.—Or else it signifies that the kid, *i.e.,* the sinner, should not be boiled in the milk of its dam, *i.e.,* should not be cajoled by flattery.

Reply Obj. 5. The Gentiles offered their gods the first-fruits, which they held to bring them good luck; or they burnt them for the purpose of sorcery.[41] Consequently [the Israelites] were commanded to look upon the fruits of the first three years as unclean. For in that country nearly all trees bear fruit in three years' time, those trees, namely, that are cultivated either from seed, or from a graft or from a cutting; but it seldom happens that the fruit-stones or seeds encased in a pod are sown, since it would take a longer time for these to bear fruit, and the Law considered what happened most frequently. The fruits, however, of the fourth year, as being the firstlings of clean fruits, were offered to God; and from the fifth year onward they were eaten.

The figurative reason was that this foreshadowed the fact that, after the three states of the Law (the first lasting from Abraham to David, the second, until they were carried away to Babylon, the third until the time of Christ), the Fruit of the Law, *i.e.,* Christ, was to be offered to God. —Or again, that we should mistrust our first efforts, because of their imperfection.

Reply Obj. 6. It is said of a man in *Ecclus.* xix. 27, that *the attire of the body . . .* shows *what he is.* Hence the Lord wished His people to be distinguished from other nations, not only by the sign of circumcision, which was in the flesh, but also by a certain difference of attire. Therefore they were forbidden to wear garments woven of woolen and linen together, and for a woman to be clothed with man's apparel, or *vice versa,* for two reasons. First, to avoid idolatrous worship. For the Gentiles, in their religious rites, used garments of this sort, made of various materials. Moreover, in the worship of Mars, women put on men's armor; while, conversely, in the worship of Venus men donned women's attire.[42]—The second reason was to preserve them from lust, because the employment of various materials in the making of garments signified inordinate union of sexes, while the use of male attire by a woman, or *vice versa,* has an incentive to evil desires, and offers an occasion of lust. The figurative reason is that the prohibition of wearing a garment woven of woolen and linen signified that it was forbidden to unite the simplicity of innocence, denoted by wool, with the duplicity of malice, betokened by linen.—It also signifies that woman is forbidden to presume to teach, or perform other duties of men; or that man should not adopt the effeminate manners of a woman.

Reply Obj. 7. As Jerome says on *Matt.* xxiii. 6, *the Lord commanded them to make violet-colored fringes in the four corners of their garments*

---

[41] Cf. Moses Maimonides, *Guide,* III, 37 (p. 334).   [42] Cf. *op. cit.,* III, 37 (p. 335)

so that the Israelites might be distinguished from other nations.[43] Hence, in this way, they professed to be Jews; and consequently the very sight of this sign reminded them of their Law.

When we read: *Thou shalt bind them on thy hand, and they shall be ever before thy eyes,* the Pharisees gave a false interpretation to these words, and wrote the decalogue of Moses on a parchment, and tied it on their foreheads like a wreath, so that it moved in front of their eyes;[44] whereas the intention of the Lord in giving this commandment was that they should be bound in their hands, *i.e.,* in their works, and that they should be before their eyes, *i.e.,* in their thoughts. The violet-colored fillets which were inserted in their cloaks signify the godly intention which should accompany our every deed.—It may, however, be said that, because they were a carnal-minded and stiff-necked people, it was necessary for them to be stirred by these sensible things to the observance of the Law.

Reply Obj. 8. Affection in man is twofold: it may be an affection of reason, or it may be an affection of passion. If a man's affection be one of reason, it matters not how man behaves to animals, because God has subjected all things to man's power, according to *Ps.* viii. 8: *Thou hast subjected all things under his feet*; and it is in this sense that the Apostle says that *God has no care for oxen,* because God does not ask of man what he does with oxen or other animals.

But if man's affection be one of passion, then it is moved also in regard to other animals, for since the passion of pity is caused by the afflictions of others, and since it happens that even irrational animals are sensible to pain, it is possible for the affection of pity to arise in a man with regard to the sufferings of animals. Now it is evident that if a man practise a pitying affection for animals, he is all the more disposed to take pity on his fellow-men; and so it is written (*Prov.* xii. 10): *The just regardeth the lives of his beasts; but the bowels of the wicked are cruel.* Consequently the Lord, in order to inculcate pity in the Jewish people, who were prone to cruelty, wished them to practise pity even with regard to brute animals, and forbade them to do certain things savoring of cruelty to animals. Hence He prohibited them to *boil a kid in the milk of its dam*; and to *muzzle the ox that treadeth out the corn*; and to slay *the dam with her young.*—It may, nevertheless, be also said that these prohibitions were made in hatred of idolatry. For the Egyptians held it to be wicked to allow the ox to eat of the grain while threshing the corn. Moreover, certain sorcerers were wont to ensnare the mother bird with her young during incubation, and to employ them for the purpose of securing fruitfulness and good luck in bringing up children. Another reason was because it was held to be a good omen to find the mother sitting on her young.

As to the mingling of animals of diverse species, the literal reason may have been threefold. The first was to show detestation for the idolatry of

---

[43] *In Matt.,* IV, super XXIII, 6 (PL 26, 175).   [44] *Ibid.* (PL 26, 174).

the Egyptians,[45] who employed various mixtures in worshipping the planets, which produce various effects, and on various kinds of things according to their various conjunctions.—The second reason was in condemnation of unnatural sins.—The third reason was the entire removal of all occasions of concupiscence. For animals of different species do not easily breed, unless this be brought about by man; and movements of lust are aroused by seeing such things. Therefore in the Jewish traditions we find it prescribed, as is stated by Rabbi Moses,[46] that men shall turn away their eyes from such sights.

The figurative reason for these things is that the necessities of life should not be withdrawn from the ox that treadeth the corn, *i.e.,* from the preacher bearing the sheaves of doctrine, as the Apostle states (*1 Cor.* ix. 4, *seqq.*). —Again, we should not take the dam with her young, because in certain things we have to keep the spiritual senses, *i.e.,* the offspring, and set aside the observance of the letter, *i.e.,* the mother, for instance in all the ceremonies of the Law. It is also forbidden that beasts of burden, *i.e.,* any of the common people, should be allowed to engender, *i.e.,* to have any connection, with animals of another kind, *i.e.,* with Gentiles or Jews.

Reply Obj. 9. All these minglings were forbidden in agriculture; literally, in detestation of idolatry. For the Egyptians, in worshipping the stars, employed various combinations of seeds, animals and garments; in order to represent the various conjunctions of the stars.[47]—Or else all these minglings were forbidden in detestation of the unnatural vice.

They have, however, a figurative reason. For the prohibition: *Thou shalt not sow thy field with different seeds,* is to be understood, in the spiritual sense, of the prohibition to sow strange doctrine in the Church, which is a spiritual vineyard.—Likewise *the field, i.e.,* the Church, must not be sown *with different seeds, i.e.,* with Catholic and heretical doctrines. —Neither is it allowed to plough *with an ox and an ass together*; and thus a fool should not accompany a wise man in preaching, for one would hinder the other.

Reply Obj. 11.[48] Sorcerers and idolatrous priests made use, in their rites, of the bones and flesh of dead men. Therefore, in order to extirpate the customs of idolatrous worship, the Lord commanded that the priests of inferior degree, who at fixed times served in the temple, should not *incur an uncleanness at the death* of anyone except of those who were closely related to them, viz., their father or mother, and others thus near of kin to them. But the high-priest had always to be ready for the service of the sanctuary, and so he was absolutely forbidden to approach the dead, however nearly related to him.—They were also forbidden to marry *a harlot* or *one that has been put away,* or any other than a virgin, and this both because of the reverence due to the priesthood, the honor of which

---

[45] Cf. Maimonides, *Guide,* III, 37 (p. 337).   [46] *Op. cit.,* III, 49 (p. 377).   [47] Cf. *op. cit.,* III, 37 (p. 337).   [48] The answer to Obj. 10 is lacking in the mss.

would seem to be tarnished by such a marriage, and for the sake of the children who would be disgraced by the mother's shame, which was most of all to be avoided when the priestly dignity was passed on from father to son.—Again, they were commanded to shave neither head nor beard, and not to make incisions in their flesh, in order to exclude the rites of idolatry. For the priests of the Gentiles shaved both head and beard; and so it is written (*Baruch* vi. 30): *Priests sit in their temples having their garments rent, and their heads and beards shaven.* Moreover, in worshipping their idols, *they cut themselves with knives and lancets* (*3 Kings* xviii. 28). For this reason the priests of the Old Law were commanded to do the contrary.

The spiritual reason for these things is that priests should be entirely free from dead works, *i.e.*, sins. And they should not shave their heads, *i.e.*, set wisdom aside; nor should they shave their beards, *i.e.*, set aside the perfection of wisdom; nor rend their garments or cut their flesh, *i.e.*, they should not incur the sin of schism.

ON THE DURATION OF THE CEREMONIAL PRECEPTS

(*In Four Articles*)

WE must now consider the duration of the ceremonial precepts, under which head there are four points of inquiry: (1) Whether the ceremonial precepts were in existence before the Law? (2) Whether at the time of the Law the ceremonies of the Old Law had any power of justification? (3) Whether they ceased at the coming of Christ? (4) Whether it is a mortal sin to observe them after the coming of Christ?

First Article

WHETHER THE CEREMONIES OF THE LAW WERE IN EXISTENCE BEFORE THE LAW?

We proceed thus to the First Article:—

Objection 1. It would seem that the ceremonies of the Law were in existence before the Law. For sacrifices and holocausts were ceremonies of the Old Law, as was stated above.[1] But sacrifices and holocausts preceded the law, for it is written (*Gen.* iv. 3, 4) that *Cain offered, of the fruits of the earth, gifts to the Lord,* and that *Abel offered of the firstlings of his flock, and of their fat.* Noe also *offered holocausts* to the Lord (*Gen.* viii. 20), and Abraham did in like manner (*Gen.* xxii. 13). Therefore the ceremonies of the Old Law preceded the Law.

Obj. 2. Further, the erecting and consecrating of the altar were part of the ceremonies relating to holy things. But these preceded the Law. For we read (*Gen.* xiii. 18) that *Abraham . . . built . . . an altar to the Lord;* and (*Gen.* xxviii. 18) that *Jacob . . . took the stone . . . and set it up for a title, pouring oil upon the top of it.* Therefore the legal ceremonies preceded the Law.

Obj. 3. Further, the first of the legal sacraments seems to have been circumcision. But circumcision preceded the Law, as appears from *Gen.* xvii. 10. In like manner, the priesthood preceded the Law, for it is written (*Gen.* xiv. 18) that *Melchisedech . . . was the priest of the most high God.* Therefore the sacramental ceremonies preceded the Law.

Obj. 4. Further, the distinction of clean from unclean animals belongs to the ceremonies of observances, as was stated above.[2] But this distinction preceded the Law, for it is written (*Gen.* vii. 2, 3): *Of all clean beasts*

<hr />

[1] Q. 102, a. 3. [2] Q. 102, a. 6, ad 1.

take seven and seven . . . but of the beasts that are unclean, two and two. Therefore the legal ceremonies preceded the Law.

On the contrary, It is written (*Deut.* vi. 1): *These are the precepts and ceremonies . . . which the Lord your God commanded that I should teach you.* But they would not have needed to be taught about these things if the aforesaid ceremonies had been already in existence. Therefore the legal ceremonies did not precede the Law.

I answer that, As is clear from what has been said, the legal ceremonies were ordained for a double purpose,[3] namely, the worship of God, and the foreshadowing of Christ. Now whoever worships God must needs worship Him by means of certain fixed things pertaining to exterior worship. But the fixing of the divine worship belongs to the ceremonies, just as the determining of our relations with our neighbor is a matter belonging to the judicial precepts, as was stated above.[4] Consequently, as among men in general there were certain judicial precepts, not indeed established by the authority of divine law, but ordained by human reason, so also there were some ceremonies fixed, not by the authority of any law, but according to the will and devotion of those that worship God. Since, however, even before the Law some of the leading men were gifted with the spirit of prophecy, it is to be believed that a heavenly instigation, like a private law, prompted them to worship God in a certain definite way, which would be both in keeping with the interior worship, and a suitable token of Christ's mysteries, which were foreshadowed also by other things that they did, according to *1 Cor.* x. 11: *All . . . things happened to them in figure.* Therefore there were some ceremonies before the Law, but they were not legal ceremonies, because they were not as yet established by legislation.

Reply Obj. 1. The patriarchs offered up these oblations, sacrifices and holocausts previously to the Law, out of a certain devotion of their own will, according as it seemed proper to them to offer up in honor of God those things which they had received from Him, and thus to testify that they worshipped God Who is the beginning and end of all.

Reply Obj. 2. They also established certain sacred things because they thought that the honor due to God demanded that certain places should be set apart from others for the purpose of divine worship.

Reply Obj. 3. The sacrament of circumcision was established by command of God before the Law. Hence it cannot be called a sacrament of the Law as though it were an institution of the Law, but only as an observance included in the Law. Hence Our Lord said (*Jo.* vii. 22) that circumcision was *not of Moses, but of his fathers.*—Again, among those who worshipped God, the priesthood was in existence before the Law by human appointment, for the Law allotted the priestly dignity to the firstborn.

Reply Obj. 4. The distinction of clean from unclean animals was in

[3] Q. 101, a. 2; q. 102, a. 2.   [4] Q. 99, a. 4.

vogue before the Law, not with regard to eating them, since it is written (*Gen.* ix. 3): *Everything that moveth and liveth shall be meat for you*; but only as to the offering of sacrifices, because they used only certain animals for that purpose. If, however, they did make any distinction in regard to eating, it was not that it was considered illegal to eat such animals, since this was not forbidden by any law, but from dislike or custom; and thus even now we see that certain foods are looked upon with disgust in some countries, while people partake of them in others.

Second Article

WHETHER, AT THE TIME OF THE LAW, THE CEREMONIES OF THE OLD LAW HAD ANY POWER OF JUSTIFICATION?

We proceed thus to the Second Article:—

Objection 1. It would seem that the ceremonies of the Old Law had the power of justification at the time of the Law. For expiation for sin and consecration pertain to justification. But it is written (*Exod.* xxix. 21) that the priests and their apparel were consecrated by the sprinkling of blood and the anointing of oil; and (*Levit.* xvi. 16) that, by sprinkling the blood of the calf, the priest expiated *the sanctuary from the uncleanness of the children of Israel, and from their transgressions and . . . their sins.* Therefore the ceremonies of the Old Law had the power of justification.

Obj. 2. Further, that by which man pleases God pertains to justification, according to *Ps.* x. 8: *The Lord is just and hath loved justice.* But some pleased God by means of ceremonies, according to *Levit.* x. 19: *How could I . . . please the Lord in the ceremonies, having a sorrowful heart?* Therefore the ceremonies of the Old Law had the power of justification.

Obj. 3. Further, things relating to the divine worship pertain to the soul rather than to the body, according to *Ps.* xviii. 8: *The Law of the Lord is unspotted, converting souls.* But the leper was cleansed by means of the ceremonies of the Old Law, as is stated in *Levit.* xiv. Much more therefore could the ceremonies of the Old Law cleanse the soul by justifying it.

On the contrary, The Apostle says (*Gal.* ii. 21): *If there had been a law given which could justify, Christ died in vain, i.e.,* without cause. But this is inadmissible. Therefore the ceremonies of the Old Law did not confer justice.

I answer that, As we have stated above, a twofold uncleanness was distinguished in the Old Law.[5] One was spiritual and is the uncleanness of sin. The other was bodily, which rendered a man unfit for divine worship. Thus a leper, or anyone that touched carrion, was said to be unclean; and so uncleanness was nothing but a kind of irregularity. From this uncleanness, then, the ceremonies of the Old Law had the power to

[5] Q. 102, a. 5, ad 4.

cleanse, because they were ordered by the Law to be employed as remedies for the removal of the aforesaid uncleannesses which were contracted in consequence of the prescription of the Law. Hence the Apostle says (*Heb.* ix. 13) that *the blood of goats and of oxen, and the ashes of a heifer, being sprinkled, sanctify such as are defiled, to the cleansing of the flesh.* And just as this uncleanness, which was washed away by such ceremonies, affected the flesh rather than the soul, so also the ceremonies themselves are called by the Apostle shortly before [verse 10] justices of the flesh: *justices of the flesh,* says he, *being laid on them until the time of correction.*

On the other hand, they had no power of cleansing from uncleanness of the soul, *i.e.,* from the uncleanness of sin. The reason for this was that at no time could there be expiation from sin, except through Christ, *Who taketh away the sins of the world* (*Jo.* i. 29). And since the mystery of Christ's Incarnation and Passion had not yet really taken place, those ceremonies of the Old Law could not really contain in themselves a power flowing from Christ already incarnate and crucified, such as the sacraments of the New Law contain. Consequently, they could not cleanse from sin. Thus the Apostle says (*Heb.* x. 4) that *it is impossible that with the blood of oxen and goats sin should be taken away*; and for this reason he calls them (*Gal.* iv. 9) *weak and needy elements*: weak indeed, because they cannot take away sin; but this weakness results from their being needy, *i.e.,* from the fact that they do not contain grace within themselves.

However, it was possible, at the time of the Law, for the minds of the faithful to be united, by faith, to Christ incarnate and crucified; so that they were justified by faith in Christ, of which faith the observance of these ceremonies was a sort of profession, inasmuch as they foreshadowed Christ. Hence in the Old Law certain sacrifices were offered up for sins, not as though the sacrifices themselves washed sins away, but because they were professions of faith which cleansed from sin. In fact, the Law itself implies this in the terms employed, for it is written (*Levit.* iv. 26; v. 16) that in offering the sacrifice for sin *the priest shall pray for him . . . and it shall be forgiven him,* as though the sin were forgiven, not in virtue of the sacrifices, but through the faith and devotion of those who offered them.—It must be observed, however, that the very fact that the ceremonies of the Old Law washed away uncleanness of the body was a figure of that expiation from sins which is effected by Christ.

It is therefore evident that under the state of the Old Law the ceremonies had no power of justification.

Reply Obj. 1. That sanctification of priests and their sons, and of their apparel or of anything else belonging to them, by sprinkling them with blood, had no other effect but to appoint them to the divine worship, and to remove impediments from them, *to the cleansing of the flesh,* as the Apostle states (*Heb.* ix. 13), in token of that sanctification whereby *Jesus* sanctified *the people by His own blood* (*ibid.* xiii. 12).—Moreover, the expiation must be understood as referring to the removal of these bodily uncleannesses, not to the forgiveness of sin. Hence, even the sanctuary, which could not be the subject of sin, is stated to be expiated.

Reply Obj. 2. The priests pleased God in the ceremonies by their obedience and devotion, and by their faith in the reality foreshadowed; not by reason of the things considered in themselves.

Reply Obj. 3. Those ceremonies, which were prescribed in the cleansing of a leper, were not ordained for the purpose of taking away the defilement of leprosy. This is clear from the fact that these ceremonies were not applied to a man until he was already healed. Hence it is written (*Levit.* xiv. 3, 4) that the priest, *going out of the camp, when he shall find that the leprosy is cleansed, shall command him that is to be purified to offer,* etc.; whence it is evident that the priest was appointed the judge of leprosy, not before, but after cleansing. But these ceremonies were employed for the purpose of taking away the uncleanness of irregularity.— They do say, however, that if a priest were to err in his judgment, the leper would be cleansed miraculously by the power of God, but not in virtue of the sacrifice. Thus also it was by miracle that the thigh of the adulterous woman rotted, when she had drunk the water *on which* the priest had *heaped curses,* as is stated in *Num.* v. 19-27.

Third Article

WHETHER THE CEREMONIES OF THE OLD LAW CEASED AT THE COMING OF CHRIST?

We proceed thus to the Third Article:—

Objection 1. It would seem that the ceremonies of the Old Law did not cease at the coming of Christ. For it is written (*Baruch* iv. 1): *This is the book of the commandments of God, and the law that is forever.* But the legal ceremonies were part of the Law. Therefore the legal ceremonies were to last forever.

Obj. 2. Further, the offering made by a leper after being cleansed was a ceremony of the Law. But the Gospel commands the leper, who has been cleansed, to make this offering (*Matt.* viii. 4). Therefore the ceremonies of the Old Law did not cease at Christ's coming.

Obj. 3. Further, as long as the cause remains, the effect remains. But the ceremonies of the Old Law had certain reasonable causes, inasmuch as they were ordained to the worship of God, over and above the fact that they were intended to be figures of Christ. Therefore the ceremonies of the Old Law should not have ceased.

Obj. 4. Further, circumcision was instituted as a sign of Abraham's faith; the observance of the sabbath, to recall the blessing of creation; and other solemnities, in remembrance of other divine favors, as was stated above.[6] But Abraham's faith is always to be imitated even by us, and the blessing of creation and other divine favors should never be forgotten. Therefore, at least circumcision and the other legal solemnities should not have ceased.

On the contrary, The Apostle says (*Coloss.* ii. 16, 17): *Let no man . . . judge you in meat or in drink, or in respect of a festival day, or of the new moon, or of the sabbaths, which are a shadow of things to come*; and (*Heb.* viii. 13): *In saying a new [testament], he hath made the former old, and that which decayeth and groweth old is near its end.*

I answer that, All the ceremonial precepts of the Old Law were ordained to the worship of God, as was stated above.[7] Now exterior worship should be in proportion to the interior worship, which consists in faith, hope and charity. Consequently exterior worship had to be subject to variations according to the variations in the interior worship, in which a threefold state may be distinguished. One state was in respect of faith and hope both in heavenly goods and in the means of obtaining them, and in both of these considered as things to come. Such was the state of faith and hope in the Old Law.—Another state of the interior worship is that in which we have faith and hope in heavenly goods as things to come, but in the means of obtaining heavenly goods as in things present or past. Such is the state of the New Law.—The third state is that in which both are possessed as present, wherein nothing is believed in as lacking, nothing hoped for as being yet to come. Such is the state of the Blessed.

In this state of the Blessed, then, nothing in regard to the worship of God will be figurative; there will be nought but *thanksgiving and voice of praise* (*Isa.* li. 3). Hence it is written concerning the city of the Blessed (*Apoc.* xxi. 22): *I saw no temple therein: for the Lord God Almighty is the temple thereof, and the Lamb.* Proportionately, therefore, the ceremonies of the first-mentioned state, which foreshadowed the second and third states, had need to cease at the advent of the second state; and other ceremonies had to be introduced which would be in keeping with the state of divine worship for that particular time, wherein heavenly goods are a thing of the future, but the divine favors whereby we obtain the heavenly goods are a thing of the present.

Reply Obj. 1. The Old Law is said to be *forever* unqualifiedly and absolutely as regards its moral precepts; but as regards the ceremonial precepts it lasts forever in respect of the reality which those ceremonies foreshadowed.

Reply Obj. 2. The mystery of the redemption of the human race was fulfilled in Christ's Passion. Hence Our Lord said then: *It is consummated* (*Jo.* xix. 30). Consequently the prescriptions of the Law must have ceased then altogether because their reality was fulfilled. As a sign of this we read that at the Passion of Christ *the veil of the temple was rent* (*Matt*

---

[6] Q. 102, a. 4, ad 10; a. 5, ad 1.   [7] Q. 101, a. 1 and 2.

xxvii. 51). Hence, before Christ's Passion, while Christ was preaching and working miracles, the Law and the Gospel were concurrent, since the mystery of Christ had already begun, but was not as yet consummated. And for this reason Our Lord, before His Passion, commanded the leper to observe the legal ceremonies.

Reply Obj. 3. The literal reasons, already given,[8] for the ceremonies refer to the divine worship which was founded on faith in that which was to come. Hence, at the advent of Him Who was to come, both that worship ceased, and all the reasons referring thereto.

Reply Obj. 4. The faith of Abraham was commended in that he believed in God's promise concerning his seed to come, in which all nations were to be blessed. Therefore, as long as this seed was yet to come, it was necessary to make profession of Abraham's faith by means of circumcision. But now that it is consummated, the same thing needs to be declared by means of another sign, viz., Baptism, which, in this respect, took the place of circumcision, according to the saying of the Apostle (*Coloss.* ii. 11, 12): *You are circumcised with circumcision not made by hand, in despoiling of the body of the flesh, but in the circumcision of Christ, buried with Him in Baptism.*

As to the Sabbath, which was a sign recalling the first creation, its place is taken by the *Lord's Day,* which recalls the beginning of the new creature in the Resurrection of Christ.—In like manner, other solemnities of the Old Law are supplanted by new solemnities, because the blessings vouchsafed to that people foreshadowed the favors granted us by Christ. Hence the feast of the Passover gave place to the feast of Christ's Passion and Resurrection; the feast of Pentecost, when the Old Law was given, to the feast of Pentecost on which was given the Law of the living spirit; the feast of the New Moon, to Lady Day, when appeared the first rays of the sun, *i.e.,* Christ, by the fullness of grace; the feast of Trumpets, to the feasts of the Apostles; the feast of Expiation, to the feasts of Martyrs and Confessors; the feast of Tabernacles, to the feast of the Church Dedication; the feast of the Assembly and Collection, to the feast of the Angels, or even to the feast of All Saints.

Fourth Article

WHETHER, AFTER CHRIST'S PASSION, THE LEGAL CEREMONIES CAN BE OBSERVED WITHOUT COMMITTING MORTAL SIN?

We proceed thus to the Fourth Article:—

Objection 1. It would seem that since Christ's Passion the legal ceremonies can be observed without committing mortal sin. For we must not believe that the apostles committed mortal sin after receiving the Holy Ghost, since by His fullness they were *endued with power from on high*

[8] Q. 102.

(*Luke* xxiv. 49). But the apostles observed the legal ceremonies after the coming of the Holy Ghost, for it is stated (*Acts* xvi. 3) that Paul circumcised Timothy, and (*Acts* xxi. 26) that Paul, at the advice of James, *took the men, and . . . being purified with them, entered into the temple, giving notice of the accomplishment of the days of purification, until an oblation should be offered for every one of them.* Therefore the legal ceremonies can be observed after the Passion of Christ without committing mortal sin.

Obj. 2. Further, one of the legal ceremonies consisted in shunning the fellowship of Gentiles. But the first Pastor of the Church complied with this observance, for it is stated (*Gal.* ii. 12) that, *when* certain men *had come* to Antioch, Peter *withdrew and separated himself* from the Gentiles. Therefore the legal ceremonies can be observed after Christ's Passion without committing mortal sin.

Obj. 3. Further, the commands of the apostles did not lead men into sin. But it was commanded by apostolic decree that the Gentiles should observe certain ceremonies of the Law; for it is written (*Acts* xv. 28, 29): *It hath seemed good to the Holy Ghost and to us, to lay no further burden upon you than these necessary things: that you abstain from things sacrificed to idols, and from blood, and from things strangled, and from fornication.* Therefore the legal ceremonies can be observed after Christ's Passion without committing mortal sin.

On the contrary, The Apostle says (*Gal.* v. 2): *If you be circumcised, Christ shall profit you nothing.* But nothing save mortal sin hinders us from receiving Christ's fruit. Therefore, after Christ's Passion, it is a mortal sin to be circumcised, or to observe the other legal ceremonies.

I answer that, All ceremonies are professions of faith, in which the interior worship of God consists. Now man can make profession of his inward faith by deeds as well as by words; and in either profession, if he make a false declaration, he sins mortally. Now, though our faith in Christ is the same as that of the fathers of old, yet, since they came before Christ, whereas we come after Him, the same faith is expressed in different words, by us and by them. For by them was it said: *Behold a virgin shall conceive and bear a son* (*Isa.* vii. 14), where the verbs are in the future tense; whereas we express the same by means of verbs in the past tense, and say that she *conceived and bore.* In like manner, the ceremonies of the Old Law betokened Christ as having yet to be born and to suffer, whereas our sacraments signify Him as already born and having suffered. Consequently, just as it would be a mortal sin now for anyone, in making a profession of faith, to say that Christ is yet to be born, which the fathers of old said devoutly and truthfully, so too it would be a mortal sin now to observe those ceremonies which the fathers of old fulfilled with devotion and fidelity. Such is the teaching of Augustine, who says: *It is no longer promised that He shall be born, shall suffer and rise again, truths of which their sacraments were a kind of image; but it is declared that He is already born, has suffered and risen again, of which our sacraments, in which Christians share, are the actual representation.*[9]

Reply Obj. 1. On this point there seems to have been a difference of opinion between Jerome and Augustine. For Jerome distinguished two periods of time.[10] One was the time previous to Christ's Passion, during which the legal ceremonies were neither dead, since they were obligatory, and did expiate in their own fashion; nor deadly, because it was not sinful to observe them. But immediately after Christ's Passion, they began to be, not only dead, so as no longer to be either effectual or binding, but also deadly, so that whoever observed them was guilty of mortal sin. Hence he maintained that after the Passion the apostles never observed the legal ceremonies in real earnest, but only by a kind of pious pretence, lest, namely, they should scandalize the Jews and hinder their conversion. This pretence, however, is to be understood, not as though they did not in reality perform those actions, but in the sense that they performed them without the mind to observe the ceremonies of the Law; and thus a man might cut away his foreskin for health's sake, not with the intention of observing legal circumcision.

But since it seems unbecoming that the apostles, in order to avoid scandal, should have hidden things pertaining to the truth of life and doctrine, and that they should have made use of pretense in things pertaining to the salvation of the faithful, therefore, Augustine more fittingly distinguished three periods of time.[11] One was the time that preceded the Passion of Christ, during which the legal ceremonies were neither deadly nor dead; another period was after the publication of the Gospel, during which the legal ceremonies are both dead and deadly. The third is a middle period, viz., from the Passion of Christ until the publication of the Gospel, during which the legal ceremonies were dead, indeed, because they had neither effect nor binding force; but were not deadly, because it was lawful for the Jewish converts to Christianity to observe them, provided they did not put their trust in them so as to hold them to be necessary unto salvation, as though faith in Christ could not justify without the legal observances. On the other hand, there was no reason why those who were converted from paganism to Christianity should observe them. Hence Paul circumcised Timothy, who was born of a Jewish mother; but he was unwilling to circumcise Titus, who had been born a Gentile.

The reason why the Holy Ghost did not wish the converted Jews to be debarred at once from observing the legal ceremonies, while converted pagans were forbidden to observe the rites of paganism, was in order to show that there is a difference between these rites. For pagan ceremonial was rejected as absolutely unlawful, and as prohibited by God for all time;

[9] *Contra Faust.*, XIX, 16 (PL 42, 357).   [10] *Epist.* CXII (PL 22, 921).—Cf. *In Gal.*, I, super II, 11 (PL 26, 364).   [11] *Epist.* LXXXII, 2 (PL 33, 280).

whereas the legal ceremonial ceased as being fulfilled through Christ's Passion, being instituted by God as a figure of Christ.

Reply Obj. 2. According to Jerome, Peter withdrew himself from the Gentiles by pretense, in order to avoid giving scandal to the Jews, of whom he was the Apostle.[12] Hence he did not sin at all in acting thus. On the other hand, Paul in like manner made a pretense of blaming him, in order to avoid scandalizing the Gentiles, whose Apostle he was.—But Augustine disapproves of this solution.[13] For in the canonical Scripture (viz., *Gal.* ii. 11), wherein we must not hold anything to be false, Paul says that Peter *was to be blamed.* Consequently it is true that Peter was at fault, and Paul blamed him in very truth and not with pretense. Peter, however, did not sin by observing the legal ceremonial for the time being, because this was lawful for him who was a converted Jew. But he did sin by excessive minuteness in the observance of the legal rites lest he should scandalize the Jews, with the result that he gave scandal to the Gentiles.

Reply Obj. 3. Some have held that this prohibition of the Apostles is not to be taken literally, but spiritually,[14] namely, that the prohibition of blood signifies the prohibition of murder; the prohibition of things strangled, that of violence and rapine; the prohibition of things offered to idols, that of idolatry; while fornication is forbidden as being evil in itself. This opinion they gather from certain glosses, which expound these prohibitions in a mystical sense.—Since, however, murder and rapine were held to be unlawful even by the Gentiles, there would have been no need to give this special commandment to those who were converted to Christ from paganism. Hence others maintain that those foods were forbidden literally, not to prevent the observance of legal ceremonies, but in order to prevent gluttony. Thus Jerome says on *Ezech.* xliv. 31 (*The priest shall not eat of anything that is dead*): *He condemns those priests who from gluttony did not keep these precepts.*[15]

But since certain foods are more delicate than these and more conducive to gluttony, there seems no reason why these should have been forbidden more than the others.

We must therefore follow a third opinion,[16] and hold that these foods were forbidden literally, not with the purpose of enforcing compliance with the legal ceremonies, but in order to further the union of Gentiles and Jews living side by side. For blood and things strangled were loathsome to the Jews by ancient custom, and the Jews might have suspected the Gentiles of relapse into idolatry if the latter had partaken of things offered to idols. Hence these things were prohibited for the time being, during which the Gentiles and Jews were to become united together. But as time went on, with the lapse of the cause, the effect lapsed also, when the truth

---

[12] *In Gal.*, I, super II, 14 (PL 26, 367).   [13] *Epist.* LXXXII, 2 (PL 33, 280). [14] William of Auxerre, *Summa Aurea*, IV, tr. 1, q. 2 (244vb).   [15] *In Ezech.*, XIII (PL 25, 464).   [16] Uncertain reference; but cf. note 11.

of the Gospel teaching was divulged, wherein Our Lord taught that *not that which entereth into the mouth defileth a man (Matt.* xv. 11); and that *nothing is to be rejected that is received with thanksgiving (1 Tim.* iv. 4).—With regard to fornication, a special prohibition was made, because the Gentiles did not hold it to be sinful.

ON THE JUDICIAL PRECEPTS

(*In Four Articles*)

WE must now consider the judicial precepts, and first of all we shall consider them in general; in the second place, we shall consider their reasons.[1] Under the first head there are four points of inquiry: (1) What is meant by the judicial precepts? (2) Whether they are figurative? (3) Their duration. (4) Their division.

First Article

WHETHER THE JUDICIAL PRECEPTS WERE THOSE WHICH DIRECTED MAN IN RELATION TO HIS NEIGHBOR?

We proceed thus to the First Article:—

Objection 1. It would seem that the judicial precepts were not those which directed man in his relations to his neighbor. For the judicial precepts take their name from *judgment*. But there are many things that direct man as to his neighbor, which are not subject to judgment. Therefore the judicial precepts were not those which directed man in his relations to his neighbor.

Obj. 2. Further, the judicial precepts are distinct from the moral precepts, as was stated above.[2] But there are many moral precepts which direct man as to his neighbor, as is evidently the case with the seven precepts of the second table. Therefore the judicial precepts are not so called from directing man as to his neighbor.

Obj. 3. Further, as the ceremonial precepts relate to God, so do the judicial precepts relate to one's neighbor, as is stated above.[3] But among the ceremonial precepts, there are some which concern man himself, such as observances in matter of food and apparel, of which we have already spoken.[4] Therefore the judicial precepts are not so called from directing man as to his neighbor.

On the contrary, It is reckoned (*Ezech.* xviii. 8) among other works of a good and just man that *he hath executed true judgment between man and man.* But the judicial precepts are so called from *judgment.* Therefore it seems that the judicial precepts were those which directed the relations between man and man.

[1] Q. 105.　[2] Q. 99, a. 4.　[3] Q. 99, a. 4; q. 101, a. 1.　[4] Q. 102, a. 6, ad 1 and 6.

I answer that, As is evident from what we have stated above, in every law some precepts derive their binding force from the dictate of reason itself, because natural reason dictates that something ought to be done or to be avoided.[5] These are called *moral* precepts, since human morals are based on reason.—At the same time, there are other precepts which derive their binding force, not from the very dictate of reason (because, considered in themselves, they do not imply an obligation of something due or undue), but from some institution, divine or human: and such are certain determinations of the moral precepts. When, therefore, the moral precepts are fixed by divine institution in matters relating to man's subordination to God, they are called *ceremonial* precepts; but when they refer to man's relations to other men, they are called *judicial* precepts. Hence, there are two conditions attached to the judicial precepts: viz., first, that they refer to man's relations to other men; secondly, that they derive their binding force, not from reason alone, but in virtue of their institution.

Reply Obj. 1. Judgments emanate through the official pronouncement of certain men who are at the head of affairs, and in whom the judicial power is vested. Now it belongs to those who are at the head of affairs to regulate not only litigious matters, but also voluntary contracts which are concluded between man and man, and whatever matters concern the community at large and the government thereof. Consequently, the judicial precepts are not only those which concern actions at law, but also all those that are directed to the ordering of one man in relation to another, which ordering is subject to the direction of the sovereign as supreme judge.

Reply Obj. 2. This argument holds in respect of those precepts which direct man in his relations to his neighbor, and derive their binding force from the sole dictate of reason.

Reply Obj. 3. Even in those precepts which direct us to God, some are moral precepts, which the reason itself dictates when it is quickened by faith: *e.g.,* that God is to be loved and worshipped. There are also ceremonial precepts, which have no binding force except in virtue of their divine institution. Now God is concerned not only with the sacrifices that are offered to Him, but also with whatever relates to the fitness of those who offer sacrifices to Him and worship Him. For men are ordained to God as to their end, and hence it concerns God and, consequently, is a matter of ceremonial precept, that man should show some fitness for the divine worship. On the other hand, man is not ordained to his neighbor as to his end, so as to need to be disposed in himself with regard to his neighbor, for such is the relationship of a slave to his master, since a slave *is his master's in all that he is,* as the Philosopher says.[6] Hence there are no judicial precepts ordaining man in himself. All such precepts are moral, because the reason, which is the principle in moral matters, holds the same

[5] Q. 95, a. 2; q. 99, a. 4.   [6] *Polit.,* I, 2 (1254a 12).

position in man, with regard to things that concern him, as a prince or judge holds in the state.—Nevertheless, we must take note that, since the relations of man to his neighbor are more subject to reason than the relations of man to God, there are more precepts whereby man is directed in his relations to his neighbor, than whereby he is directed to God. For the same reason, there had to be more ceremonial than judicial precepts in the Law.

Second Article

WHETHER THE JUDICIAL PRECEPTS WERE FIGURATIVE?

We proceed thus to the Second Article:—
Objection 1. It would seem that the judicial precepts were not figurative. For it seems proper to the ceremonial precepts to be instituted as figures of something else. Therefore, if the judicial precepts are figurative, there will be no difference between the judicial and the ceremonial precepts.

Obj. 2. Further, just as certain judicial precepts were given to the Jewish people, so also were some given to other and pagan peoples. But the judicial precepts given to other peoples were not figurative, but stated what had to be done. Therefore it seems that neither were the judicial precepts of the Old Law figures of anything.

Obj. 3. Further, those things which relate to the divine worship had to be taught under certain figures, because the things of God are above our reason, as was stated above.[7] But things concerning our neighbor are not above our reason. Therefore the judicial precepts, which direct us in relation to our neighbor, should not have been figurative.

On the contrary, The judicial precepts are expounded both in the allegorical and in the moral sense in *Exodus* xxi.

I answer that, A precept may be figurative in two ways. First, primarily and essentially, because, namely, it is instituted principally that it may be the figure of something. In this way the ceremonial precepts are figurative, since they were instituted for the very purpose that they might foreshadow something relating to the worship of God and the mystery of Christ.—But some precepts are figurative, not primarily and essentially, but consequently. In this way the judicial precepts of the Old Law are figurative. For they were not instituted for the purpose of being figurative, but in order that they might regulate the state of that people according to justice and equity. Nevertheless, they did foreshadow something consequently, since, namely, the entire state of that people, who were directed by these precepts, was figurative, according to *1 Cor.* x. 11: *All . . . things happened to them in figure.*

Reply Obj. 1. The ceremonial precepts are not figurative in the same way as the judicial precepts, as was explained above.

[7] Q. 101, a. 1, ad 2.

Reply Obj. 2. The Jewish people were chosen by God that Christ might be born of them. Consequently, the entire state of that people had to be prophetic and figurative, as Augustine states.[8] For this reason, even the judicial precepts that were given to this people were more figurative than those which were given to other nations. Thus, too, the wars and deeds of this people are expounded in the mystical sense, but not the wars and deeds of the Assyrians or Romans, although the latter are more famous in the eyes of men.

Reply Obj. 3. In this people the direction of man in regard to his neighbor, considered in itself, was evident to reason. But in so far as it was referred to the worship of God, it was above reason, and in this respect it was figurative.

Third Article

WHETHER THE JUDICIAL PRECEPTS OF THE OLD LAW BIND FOREVER?

We proceed thus to the Third Article:—

Objection 1. It would seem that the judicial precepts of the Old Law bind forever. For the judicial precepts relate to the virtue of justice, since a judgment is an execution of the virtue of justice. Now *justice is perpetual and immortal* (*Wis.* i. 15). Therefore the judicial precepts bind forever.

Obj. 2. Further, divine institutions are more enduring than human institutions. But the judicial precepts of human laws bind forever. Therefore much more do the judicial precepts of the divine Law.

Obj. 3. Further, the Apostle says (*Heb.* vii. 18) that *there is a setting aside of the former commandment, because of the weakness and unprofitableness thereof.* Now this is true of a ceremonial precept, which *could not, as to the conscience, make him perfect that serveth only in meats and in drinks, and divers washings and justices of the flesh,* as the Apostle declares (*Heb.* ix. 9, 10). On the other hand, the judicial precepts were useful and efficacious in respect of the purpose for which they were instituted, viz., to establish justice and equity among men. Therefore the judicial precepts of the Old Law are not set aside, but still retain their efficacy.

On the contrary, The Apostle says (*Heb.* vii. 12) that *the priesthood being translated it is necessary that a translation also be made of the Law.* But the priesthood was transferred from Aaron to Christ. Therefore the entire Law was also transferred. Therefore the judicial precepts are no longer in force.

I answer that, The judicial precepts did not bind forever, but were annulled by the coming of Christ; yet not in the same way as the ceremonial precepts. For the ceremonial precepts were annulled so far as to

---

[8] *Contra Faust.,* XXII, 24 (PL 42, 417).

be not only *dead,* but also *deadly*[9] to those who observe them after the coming of Christ, especially after the promulgation of the Gospel. On the other hand, the judicial precepts are dead, indeed, because they have no binding force; but they are not deadly. For if a sovereign were to order these judicial precepts to be observed in his kingdom, he would not sin, unless perchance they were observed, or ordered to be observed, as though they derived their binding force through being institutions of the Old Law; for it would be a deadly sin to intend to observe them thus.

The reason for this difference may be gathered from what has been said above. For it has been stated that the ceremonial precepts are figurative primarily and essentially, as being instituted chiefly for the purpose of foreshadowing the mysteries of Christ to come.—On the other hand, the judicial precepts were not instituted that they might be figures, but that they might shape the state of that people who were directed to Christ. Consequently, when the state of that people changed with the coming of Christ, the judicial precepts lost their binding force; for the Law was a pedagogue, leading men to Christ, as is stated in *Gal.* iii. 24. Since, however, these judicial precepts are instituted, not for the purpose of being figures, but for the performance of certain deeds, the observance thereof is not prejudicial to the truth of faith. But the intention of observing them, as though one were bound by the Law, is prejudicial to the truth of faith; for it would follow that the former state of the people still lasts, and that Christ has not yet come.

Reply Obj. 1. The obligation of observing justice is certainly perpetual. But the determination of those things that are just, according to human or divine institution, must needs be different, according to the different states of mankind.

Reply Obj. 2. The judicial precepts established by men retain their binding force forever, so long as the state of government remains the same. But if the state or nation pass to another form of government, the laws must needs be changed. For democracy, which is government by the people, demands different laws from those of oligarchy, which is government by the rich, as the Philosopher shows.[10] Consequently, when the state of that people changed, the judicial precepts had to be changed also.

Reply Obj. 3. Those judicial precepts directed the people to justice and equity, in keeping with the demands of that state. But after the coming of Christ, there had to be a change in the state of that people, so that in Christ there was no distinction between Gentile and Jew, as there had been before. For this reason the judicial precepts needed to be changed also.

[9] Cf. St. Augustine, *Epist.* LXXXII, 2 (PL 33, 283); St. Albert, *In IV Sent.,* d. iii, a. 6 (XXIX, 73).   [10] *Polit.,* IV, 1 (1289a 11; a 22).

Fourth Article

WHETHER IT IS POSSIBLE TO ASSIGN A DEFINITE DIVISION
OF THE JUDICIAL PRECEPTS?

We proceed thus to the Fourth Article:—

Objection 1. It would seem that it is impossible to assign a definite division of the judicial precepts. For the judicial precepts direct men in their relations to one another. But those things which need to be directed, as pertaining to the relationship between man and man, and which are used by men, are not subject to division, since they are infinite in number. Therefore it is not possible to assign a definite division of the judicial precepts.

Obj. 2. Further, the judicial precepts are decisions on moral matters. But moral precepts do not seem to be capable of division, except in so far as they are reducible to the precepts of the decalogue. Therefore there is no definite division of the judicial precepts.

Obj. 3. Further, because there is a definite division of the ceremonial precepts, the Law alludes to this division by describing some as *sacrifices*, others as *observances*. But the Law contains no allusion to a division of the judicial precepts. Therefore it seems that they have no definite division.

On the contrary, Wherever there is order there must needs be division. But the notion of order is chiefly applicable to the judicial precepts, since thereby that people was ordered. Therefore it is most necessary that they should have a definite division.

I answer that, Since law is the art, as it were, of directing or ordering the life of man, just as in every art there is a definite division in the rules of the art, so in every law there must be a definite division of precepts, or else the law would be rendered useless by confusion. We must therefore say that the judicial precepts of the Old Law, whereby men were directed in their relations to one another, are subject to division according to the diverse ways in which man is directed.

Now in every people a fourfold order is to be found: one, of the people's sovereign to his subjects; a second, of the subjects among themselves; a third, of the citizens to foreigners; a fourth, of members of the same household, such as the order of the father to his son, of the wife to her husband, of the master to his servant; and according to these four orders we may distinguish different kinds of judicial precepts in the Old Law. For certain precepts are laid down concerning the institution of the sovereign and relating to his office, and about the respect due to him; and this is one part of the judicial precepts.—Again, certain precepts are given for the relations of citizens to one another: *e.g.,* about buying and selling, judgments and penalties; and this is the second part of the judicial precepts.—Again, certain precepts are enjoined with regard to foreigners: *e.g.,* about wars waged against their foes, and about the way to receive travelers and strangers; and this is the third part of the judicial precepts.—Lastly, certain precepts are given relating to home life: *e.g.*, about servants, wives and children; and this is the fourth part of the judicial precepts.

Reply Obj. 1. Things pertaining to the ordering of relations between one man and another are indeed infinite in number; and yet they are reducible to certain distinct heads, according to the different relations in which one man stands to another, as was stated above.

Reply Obj. 2. The precepts of the decalogue hold the first place in the moral order, as was stated above,[11] and consequently it is fitting that other moral precepts should be distinguished in relation to them. But the judicial and ceremonial precepts have a different binding force, derived, not from natural reason, but from their institution alone. Hence there is a distinct reason for distinguishing them.

Reply Obj. 3. The Law alludes to the division of the judicial precepts in the very things themselves which are prescribed by the judicial precepts of the Law.

[11] Q. 100, a. 3.

ON THE REASON FOR THE JUDICIAL PRECEPTS

(*In Four Articles*)

WE must now consider the reason for the judicial precepts, under which head there are four points of inquiry: (1) Concerning the reason for the judicial precepts relating to the rulers. (2) Concerning precepts relating to the fellowship of one man with another. (3) Concerning those relating to foreigners. (4) Concerning those relating to domestic matters.

First Article

WHETHER THE OLD LAW ENJOINED FITTING PRECEPTS CONCERNING RULERS?

We proceed thus to the First Article:—

Objection 1. It would seem that the Old Law made unfitting precepts concerning rulers. For as the Philosopher says, *the ordering of the people depends mostly on the highest rule.*[1] But the Law contains no precept relating to the institution of the chief ruler, and yet we find therein prescriptions concerning the inferior rulers. Thus (*Exod.* xviii. 21): *Provide out of all the people wise men*, etc.; again (*Num.* xi. 16): *Gather unto Me seventy men of the ancients of Israel*; and again (*Deut.* i. 13): *Let Me have from among you wise and understanding men*, etc. Therefore the Law provided insufficiently in regard to the rulers of the people.

Obj. 2. Further, *The best gives of the best*, as Plato states.[2] Now the best ordering of a state or of any nation is to be ruled by a king, because this kind of government approaches nearest in resemblance to the divine government, whereby God rules the world from the beginning. Therefore the Law should have set a king over the people, and they should not have been allowed a choice in the matter, as indeed they were allowed (*Deut.* xvii. 14, 15): *When thou . . . shalt say: I will set a king over me . . . thou shalt set him*, etc.

Obj. 3. Further, according to *Matt.* xii. 25: *Every kingdom divided against itself shall be made desolate*, a saying which was verified in the Jewish people, whose destruction was brought about by the division of the kingdom. But the Law should aim chiefly at things pertaining to the general well-being of the people. Therefore it should have forbidden the king-

---

[1] *Polit.,* III, 6 (1278b 10).　　[2] *Timaeus,* trans. Chalcidius, IX (p. 157) ; X (p. 158).— Cf. *Timaeus* (29A; 29E).

dom to be divided under two kings, nor should this have been introduced even by divine authority, as we read of its being introduced by the authority of the prophet Ahias the Silonite (*3 Kings* xi. 29 *seq.*).

Obj. 4. Further, just as priests are instituted for the benefit of the people in things concerning God, as is stated in *Heb.* v. 1, so rulers are set up for the benefit of the people in human affairs. But certain things were allotted as a means of livelihood for the priests and Levites of the Law: *e.g.*, the tithes and first-fruits, and many like things. Therefore, in like manner, certain things should have been determined for the livelihood of the rulers of the people, especially since they were forbidden to accept presents, as is clearly stated in *Exod.* xxiii. 8: *You shall not take bribes, which even blind the wise, and pervert the words of the just.*

Obj. 5. Further, as a kingdom is the best form of government, so is tyranny the most corrupt. But when the Lord appointed the king, He established a tyrannical law, for it is written (*1 Kings* viii. 11): *This will be the right of the king, that shall reign over you: He will take your sons,* etc. Therefore the Law made unfitting provision with regard to the institution of rulers.

On the contrary, The people of Israel is commended for the beauty of its order (*Num.* xxiv. 5): *How beautiful are thy tabernacles, O Jacob, and thy tents, O Israel.* But the beautiful ordering of a people depends on the right establishment of its rulers. Therefore the Law made right provision for the people with regard to its rulers.

I answer that, Two points are to be observed concerning the right ordering of rulers in a state or nation. One is that all should take some share in the government, for this form of constitution ensures peace among the people, commends itself to all, and is most enduring, as is stated in *Politics* ii.[3] The other point is to be observed in respect of the kinds of government, or the different ways in which the constitutions are established. For whereas these differ in kind, as the Philosopher states,[4] nevertheless, the first place is held by the *kingdom,* where the power of government is vested in one, and *aristocracy,* which signifies government by the best, where the power of government is vested in a few. Accordingly, the best form of government is in a state or kingdom, wherein one is given the power to preside over all, while under him are others having governing powers. And yet a government of this kind is shared by all, both because all are eligible to govern, and because the rulers are chosen by all. For this is the best form of polity, being partly kingdom, since there is one at the head of all; partly aristocracy, in so far as a number of persons are set in authority; partly democracy, *i.e.*, government by the people, in so far as the rulers can be chosen from the people, and the people have the right to choose their rulers.

Such was the form of government established by the divine Law. For Moses and his successors governed the people in such a way that each of

---

[3] Aristotle, *Polit.*, II, 6 (1270b 17).   [4] *Op. cit.*, III. 5 (1279a 32; b 4).

them was ruler over all; so that there was a kind of kingdom. Moreover, seventy-two men were chosen, who were elders in virtue, for it is written (*Deut.* i. 15): *I took out of your tribes men wise and honorable, and appointed them rulers*; so that there was an element of aristocracy. But it was a democratic government in so far as the rulers were chosen from all the people, for it is written (*Exod.* xviii. 21): *Provide out of all the people wise men*, etc.; and, again, in so far as they were chosen by the people. Hence it is written (*Deut.* i. 13): *Let me have from among you wise men,* etc. Consequently, it is evident that the ordering of the rulers was well provided for by the Law.

Reply Obj. 1. This people was governed under the special care of God, and so it is written (*Deut.* vii. 6): *The Lord thy God hath chosen thee to be His peculiar people*; and this is why the Lord reserved to Himself the institution of the chief ruler. For this too did Moses pray (*Num.* xxvii. 16): *May the Lord the God of the spirits of all the flesh provide a man, that may be over this multitude.* Thus by God's order Josue was set at the head in place of Moses; and we read about each of the judges who succeeded Josue that God *raised . . . up a savior* for the people, and that *the spirit of the Lord was* in them (*Judges* iii. 9, 10, 15). Hence the Lord did not leave even the choice of a king to the people, but reserved this to Himself, as appears from *Deut.* xvii. 15: *Thou shalt set him whom the Lord thy God shall choose.*

Reply Obj. 2. A kingdom is the best form of government of the people, so long as it is not corrupt. But since the power granted to a king is so great, it easily degenerates into tyranny, unless he to whom this power is given be a very virtuous man; for it is only the virtuous man that conducts himself well in the midst of prosperity, as the Philosopher observes.[5] Now perfect virtue is to be found in few. And, what is more, the Jews were inclined to cruelty and avarice, which vices above all turn men into tyrants. Hence from the very first the Lord did not set up the kingly authority with full power, but gave them judges and governors to rule them. But afterwards when the people asked Him to do so, being indignant with them, so to speak, He granted them a king, as is clear from His words to Samuel (*1 Kings* viii. 7): *They have not rejected thee, but Me, that I should not reign over them.*

Nevertheless, as regards the appointment of a king, He did establish the manner of election from the very beginning (*Deut.* xvii. 14, *seqq.*). He then determined two points: first, that in choosing a king they should wait for the Lord's decision; and that they should not make a man of another nation king, because such kings are wont to take little interest in the people they are set over, and consequently to have no care for their welfare. Secondly, He prescribed how the king after his appointment should behave, in regard to himself, namely, that he should not accumulate chariots

[5] *Eth.,* IV, 3 (1124a 30).

and horses, or wives, or immense wealth, because through craving for such things princes become tyrants and forsake justice.—He also appointed the manner in which they were to conduct themselves towards God, namely, that they should continually read and ponder on God's Law, and should ever fear and obey God.—Moreover, He decided how they should behave towards their subjects, namely, that they should not proudly despise them, or ill-treat them, and that they should not depart from the paths of justice.

Reply Obj. 3. The division of the kingdom, and the multitude of kings, was rather a punishment inflicted on that people for their many dissensions, especially against the just rule of David, than a benefit conferred on them for their profit. Hence it is written (*Osee* xiii. 11): *I will give thee a king in My wrath*; and (*ibid.* viii. 4): *They have reigned, but not by Me: they have been princes, and I knew not.*

Reply Obj. 4. The priestly office was bequeathed by succession from father to son, and this, in order that it might be held in greater respect, if not any man from the people could become a priest; for honor was given to them out of reverence for the divine worship. Hence it was necessary to put aside certain things for them both as to tithes and as to first-fruits, and, again, as to oblations and sacrifices, that they might be afforded a means of livelihood. On the other hand, the rulers, as was stated above, were chosen from the whole people, and hence had their own possessions, from which to derive a living; and so much the more, since the Lord forbade even a king to have superabundant wealth, or to make too much show of magnificence, both because he could scarcely avoid the excesses of pride and tyranny arising from such things, and because, if the rulers were not very rich, and if their office involved much work and anxiety, it would not tempt the ambition of the common people, and would not thus become an occasion of sedition.

Reply Obj. 5. That right was not given to the king by divine institution; rather was it foretold that kings would usurp that right, by framing unjust laws, and by degenerating into tyrants who preyed on their subjects. This is clear from what follows: *And you shall be his slaves* (*1 Kings* viii. 17), which is significative of tyranny, since a tyrant rules his subjects as though they were his slaves. Hence Samuel spoke these words to deter them from asking for a king; for the narrative continues: *But the people would not hear the voice of Samuel.*—It may happen, however, that even a good king, without being a tyrant, may take away the sons, and make them tribunes and centurions, and may take many things from his subjects in order to secure the common weal.

Second Article

WHETHER THE JUDICIAL PRECEPTS WERE SUITABLY FRAMED
AS TO THE RELATIONS OF ONE MAN WITH ANOTHER?

We proceed thus to the Second Article:—

Objection 1. It would seem that the judicial precepts were not suitably framed as regards the relations of one man with another. For men cannot live together in peace, if one man takes what belongs to another. But this seems to have been approved by the Law, since it is written (*Deut.* xxiii. 24): *Going into thy neighbor's vineyard, thou mayst eat as many grapes as thou pleasest.* Therefore the Old Law did not make suitable provisions for man's peace.

Obj. 2. Further, one of the chief causes of the downfall of states has been the holding of property by women, as the Philosopher says.[6] But this was introduced by the Old Law, for it is written (*Num.* xxvii. 8): *When a man dieth without a son, his inheritance shall pass to his daughter.* Therefore the Law made unsuitable provision for the welfare of the people.

Obj. 3. Further, it is most conducive to the preservation of human society that men may provide themselves with necessaries by buying and selling, as is stated in *Politics* i.[7] But the Old Law took away the force of sales, since it prescribes that in the 50th year of the jubilee all that is sold shall return to the vendor (*Levit.* xxv. 28). Therefore in this matter the Law gave the people an unfitting command.

Obj. 4. Further, man's needs require that men should be ready to lend, which readiness ceases if the creditors do not return the pledges. Hence it is written (*Ecclus.* xxix. 10): *Many have refused to lend, not out of wickedness, but they were afraid to be defrauded without cause.* And yet this was encouraged by the Law. First, because it prescribed (*Deut.* xv. 2): *He to whom any thing is owing from his friend or neighbor or brother, cannot demand it again, because it is the year of remission of the Lord;* and (*Exod.* xxii. 15) it is stated that if a borrowed animal should die while the owner is present, the borrower is not bound to make restitution. Secondly, because the security acquired through the pledge is lost. For it is written (*Deut.* xxiv. 10): *When thou shalt demand of thy neighbor any thing that he oweth thee, thou shalt not go into his house to take away a pledge;* and again (verses 12, 13): *The pledge shall not lodge with thee that night, but thou shalt restore it to him presently.* Therefore the Law made insufficient provision in the matter of loans.

Obj. 5. Further, considerable risk attaches to goods deposited with a fraudulent depositary, and so great caution should be observed in such matters. Hence it is stated in *2 Mach.* iii. 15 that *the priests . . . called upon Him from heaven, Who made the law concerning things given to be*

---

⁵ *Polit.,* II, 6 (1270a 23).   ⁷ *Op. cit.,* I, 3 (1257a 14).

kept, that He would preserve them safe, for them that had deposited them. But the precepts of the Old Law observed little caution in regard to deposits, since it is prescribed (*Exod.* xxii. 10, 11) that when goods deposited are lost, the owner is to stand by the oath of the depositary. Therefore the Law made unsuitable provision in this matter.

Obj. 6. Further, just as a workman offers his work for hire, so do men let houses and so forth. But there is no need for the tenant to pay his rent as soon as he takes a house. Therefore it seems an unnecessarily hard prescription (*Levit.* xix. 13) that *the wages of him that hath been hired by thee shall not abide with thee until the morning.*

Obj. 7. Further, since there is often pressing need for a judge, it should be easy to gain access to one. It was therefore unfitting that the Law (*Deut.* xvii. 8, 9) should command them to go to one fixed place to ask for judgment on doubtful matters.

Obj. 8. Further, it is possible that not only two, but three or more, should agree to tell a lie. Therefore it is unreasonably stated (*Deut.* xix. 15) that *in the mouth of two or three witnesses every word shall stand.*

Obj. 9. Further, punishment should be fixed according to the gravity of the fault; for which reason also it is written (*Deut.* xxv. 2): *According to the measure of the sin, shall the measure also of the stripes be.* Yet the Law fixed unequal punishments for certain faults, for it is written (*Exod.* xxii. 1) that the thief *shall restore five oxen for one ox, and four sheep for one sheep.* Moreover, certain slight offenses are severely punished. Thus (*Num.* xv. 32, *seqq.*) a man is stoned for gathering sticks on the Sabbath day; and (*Deut.* xxi. 18, *seqq.*) the unruly son is commanded to be stoned because of certain small transgressions, viz., because *he gave himself to revelling . . . and banquetings.* Therefore the Law prescribed punishments in an unreasonable manner.

Obj. 10. Further, as Augustine says, *Tully writes that the laws recognize eight forms of punishment: indemnity, prison, stripes, retaliation, public disgrace, exile, death, slavery.*[8] Now some of these were prescribed by the Law. *Indemnity,* as when a thief was condemned to make restitution fivefold or fourfold. *Prison,* as when (*Num.* xv. 34) a certain man is ordered to be imprisoned. *Stripes,* as when it is said (*Deut.* xxv. 2), *if they see that the offender be worthy of stripes, they shall lay him down, and shall cause him to be beaten before them.* *Public disgrace* was brought on him who refused to take to himself the wife of his deceased brother, for she took off *his shoe from his foot, and did spit in his face* (*ibid.* 9). It prescribed the *death* penalty, as is clear from *Levit.* xx. 9: *He that curseth his father, or mother, dying let him die.* The Law also recognized the *lex talionis,* by prescribing (*Exod.* xxi. 24): *Eye for eye, tooth for tooth.* Therefore it seems unreasonable that the Law should not have inflicted the two other punishments, viz., *exile* and *slavery.*

[8] *De Civit. Dei,* XXI, 11 (PL 41, 725).

Obj. 11. Further, no punishment is due except for a fault. But brute animals cannot commit a fault. Therefore the Law is unreasonable in punishing them (*Exod.* xxi. 29): *If the ox . . . shall kill a man or a woman, it shall be stoned;* and (*Levit.* xx. 16): *The woman that shall lie under any beast shall be killed together with the same.* Therefore it seems that matters pertaining to the relations of one man with another were unsuitably regulated by the Law.

Obj. 12. Further, the Lord commanded (*Exod.* xxi. 12) a murderer to be punished with death. But the death of a brute animal is reckoned of much less account than the slaying of a man. Hence murder cannot be sufficiently punished by the slaying of a brute animal. Therefore it is unfittingly prescribed (*Deut.* xxi. 1, 4) that *when there shall be found . . . the corpse of a man slain, and it is not known who is guilty of the murder . . . the ancients* of the nearest city *shall take a heifer of the herd, that hath not drawn in the yoke, nor ploughed the ground, and they shall bring her into a rough and stony valley, that never was ploughed, nor sown; and there they shall strike off the head of the heifer.*

On the contrary, It is recalled as a special blessing (*Ps.* cxlvii. 20) that *He hath not done in like manner to every nation; and His judgments He hath not made manifest to them.*

I answer that, As Augustine says, quoting Tully, *a nation is a body of men united together by consent to the law and by community of welfare.*[9] Consequently it is of the essence of a nation that the mutual relations of the citizens be ordered by just laws. Now the relations of one man with another are twofold: some are effected under the guidance of those in authority, while others are effected by the will of private individuals. And since whatever is subject to the power of an individual can be disposed according to his will, hence it is that the decision of matters between one man and another and the punishment of evildoers depend on the direction of those in authority, to whom men are subject. On the other hand, the power of private persons is exercised over the things they possess, and consequently their dealings with one another, as regards such things, depend on their own will, for instance in buying, selling, giving and so forth. Now the Law provided sufficiently in respect of each of these relations between one man and another. For it established judges, as is clearly indicated in *Deut.* xvi. 18: *Thou shalt appoint judges and magistrates in all its gates, . . . that they may judge the people with just judgment.* It also directed the manner of pronouncing just judgments, according to *Deut.* i. 16, 17: *Judge that which is just, whether he be one of your own country or a stranger: there shall be no difference of persons.* It also removed an occasion of pronouncing unjust judgment, by forbidding judges to accept bribes (*Exod.* xxiii. 8; *Deut.* xvi. 19). It likewise prescribed the number of

[9] *Op. cit.,* II, 21 (PL 41, 67).—Cicero, *De Re Publica,* I, 25 (p. 24).

witnesses, viz., two or three (*Deut.* xvii. 6; xix. 15); and it appointed certain punishments for certain crimes, as we shall state farther on.

But with regard to possessions, it is a very good thing, says the Philosopher, that the things possessed should be distinct, and that the use thereof should be partly common, and partly granted to others by the will of the possessors.[10] These three points were provided for by the Law. For, in the first place, the possessions themselves were divided among individuals; for it is written (*Num.* xxxiii. 53, 54): *I have given you the land for a possession, and you shall divide it among you by lot.* And since many states have been ruined through want of regulations in the matter of possessions, as the Philosopher observes,[11] therefore, the Law provided a threefold remedy against the irregularity of possessions. The first was that they should be divided equally; and so it is written (*Num.* xxxiii. 54): *To the more you shall give a larger part, and to the fewer, a lesser.* A second remedy was that possessions could not be alienated forever, but after a certain lapse of time should return to their former owner, so as to avoid confusion of possessions. The third remedy aimed at the removal of this confusion, and provided that the dead should be succeeded by their next of kin: in the first place, the son; secondly, the daughter; thirdly, the brother; fourthly, the father's brother; fifthly, any other next of kin. Furthermore, in order to preserve the distinction of property, the Law enacted that heiresses should marry within their own tribe, as is recorded in *Num.* xxxvi. 6.

Secondly, the Law commanded that, in some respects, the use of things should belong to all in common. First, as regards the care of them, for it was prescribed (*Deut.* xxii. 1-4): *Thou shalt not pass by, if thou seest thy brother's ox or his sheep go astray; but thou shalt bring them back to thy brother.* And in like manner as to other things. Secondly, as regards fruits. For all alike were allowed, on entering a friend's vineyard, to eat of the fruit, but not to take any away. And, especially, with respect to the poor, it was prescribed that the forgotten sheaves, and the bunches of grapes and fruit, should be left behind for them (*Levit.* xix. 9; *Deut.* xxiv. 19). Moreover, whatever grew in the seventh year was common property, as is stated in *Exod.* xxiii. 11 and *Levit.* xxv. 4.

Thirdly, the law recognized the transference of goods by the owner. There was a purely gratuitous transfer. Thus it is written (*Deut.* xiv. 28, 29): *The third day thou shalt separate another tithe . . . and the Levite . . . and the stranger, and the fatherless, and the widow . . . shall come and shall eat and be filled.* And there was a transfer for a consideration, for instance, by selling and buying, by letting out and hiring, by loan and also by deposit, concerning all of which we find that the Law made ample provision. Consequently, it is clear that the Old Law provided sufficiently concerning the mutual relations of one man with another.

[10] *Polit.*, II, 2 (1263a 25).   [11] *Op. cit.*, II, 6 (1270a 23).

Reply Obj. 1. As the Apostle says (*Rom.* xiii. 8), *he that loveth his neighbor hath fulfilled the Law,* because, namely, all the precepts of the Law, chiefly those concerning our neighbor, seem to aim at the end that men should love one another. Now it is an effect of love that men give their own goods to others, because, as is stated in *1 John* iii. 17: *He that . . . shall see his brother in need, and shall shut up his bowels from him, how doth the charity of God abide in him?* Hence the purpose of the Law was to accustom men to give of their own to others readily. Thus the Apostle (*1 Tim.* vi. 18) commands the rich *to give easily and to communicate to others.* Now a man does not give easily to others if he will not suffer another man to take some little thing from him without any great injury to him. And so the Law laid down that it should be lawful for a man, on entering his neighbor's vineyard, to eat of the fruit there, but not to carry any away, lest this should lead to the infliction of a grievous harm, and cause a disturbance of the peace; for among cultivated people the taking of a little does not disturb the peace, in fact, it rather strengthens friendship and accustoms men to give to one another.

Reply Obj. 2. The Law did not prescribe that women should succeed to their father's estate except in default of male issue, failing which it was necessary that succession should be granted to the female line in order to comfort the father, who would have been sad to think that his estate would pass to strangers. Nevertheless, the Law observed due caution in the matter, by providing that those women who succeeded to their father's estate should marry within their own tribe, in order to avoid confusion of tribal possessions, as is stated in *Num.* xxxvi. 7, 8.

Reply Obj. 3. As the Philosopher says, the regulation of possessions conduces much to the preservation of a state or nation.[12] Consequently, as he himself observes, it was forbidden by the law in some of the pagan states *that anyone should sell his possessions, except to avoid a manifest loss.* For if possessions were to be sold indiscriminately, they might happen to come into the hands of a few, so that it might become necessary for a state or country to become void of inhabitants. Hence the Old Law, in order to remove this danger, ordered things in such a way that, while provision was made for men's needs by allowing the sale of possessions to avail for a certain period, at the same time the said danger was removed by prescribing the return of those possessions after that period had elapsed. The reason for this law was to prevent confusion of possessions, and to ensure the continuance of a definite distinction among the tribes.

But as the town houses were not allotted to distinct estates, therefore the Law allowed them to be sold in perpetuity, like movable goods. For the number of houses in a town was not fixed, whereas there was a fixed limit to the amount of possessions, which could not be exceeded, while the number of houses in a town could be increased. On the other hand, houses

---

[12] *Op. cit.,* II, 4 (1266b 14).

situated, not in a town, but *in a village that hath no walls,* could not be sold in perpetuity, because such houses are built merely with a view to the cultivation and care of possessions; and so the Law rightly made the same prescription in regard to both (*Levit.* xxv.).

Reply Obj. 4. As was stated above, the purpose of the Law was to accustom men to its precepts, so as to be ready to come to one another's assistance, because this is a very great incentive to friendship. The Law granted these facilities for helping others in the matter not only of gratuitous and absolute donations, but also of mutual transfers, for the latter kind of succor is more frequent and benefits the greater number. Now it granted facilities for this purpose in many ways. First of all by prescribing that men should be ready to lend, and that they should not be less inclined to do so as the year of remission drew nigh, as is stated in *Deut.* xv. 7, *seqq.*—Secondly, by forbidding them to burden a man to whom they might grant a loan, either by exacting usury, or by accepting necessities of life in security; and by prescribing that, when this had been done, they should be restored at once. For it is written (*Deut.* xxiii. 19): *Thou shalt not lend to thy brother money to usury*; and (xxiv. 6): *Thou shalt not take the nether nor the upper millstone to pledge, for he hath pledged his life to thee*; and (*Exod.* xxii. 26): *If thou take of thy neighbor a garment in pledge, thou shalt give it him again before sunset.*—Thirdly, by forbidding them to be importunate in exacting payment. Hence it is written (*Exod.* xxii. 25): *If thou lend money to any of my people that is poor that dwelleth with thee, thou shalt not be hard upon them as an extortioner.* For this reason, too, it is enacted (*Deut.* xxiv. 10, 11): *When thou shalt demand of thy neighbor anything that he oweth thee, thou shalt not go into his house to take away a pledge, but thou shalt stand without, and he shall bring out to thee what he hath*; and this both because a man's house is his surest refuge, and so it is offensive to a man to be set upon in his own house, and because the Law does not allow the creditor to take away whatever he likes in security, but rather permits the debtor to give what he needs least.—Fourthly, the Law prescribed that debts should cease altogether after the lapse of seven years. For it was probable that those who could conveniently pay their debts would do so before the seventh year, and would not defraud the lender without cause. But if they were altogether insolvent, there was the same reason for remitting the debt from love for them, as there was for renewing the loan because of their need.

As regards animals granted in loan, the Law enacted that if, through the neglect of the person to whom they were lent, they perished or deteriorated in his absence, he was bound to make restitution. But if they perished or deteriorated while he was present and taking proper care of them, he was not bound to make restitution, especially if they were hired for a consideration; for they might have died or deteriorated in the same way if they had remained in possession of the lender, so that if the animal had been saved through being lent, the lender would have gained something by the loan which would no longer have been gratuitous. And especially was this to be observed when animals were hired for a consideration, because then the owner received a certain price for the use of the animals, and hence he had no right to any profit, by receiving indemnity for the animal, unless the person who had charge of it were negligent. In the case, however, of animals not hired for a consideration, equity demanded that he should receive something by way of restitution at least to the value of the hire of the animal that had perished or deteriorated.

Reply Obj. 5. The difference between a loan and a deposit is that a loan is in respect of goods transferred for the use of the person to whom they are transferred, whereas a deposit is for the benefit of the depositor. Hence in certain cases there was a stricter obligation of returning a loan than of restoring goods held in deposit. For the latter might be lost in two ways. First, unavoidably: *i.e.,* either through a natural cause, for instance, if an animal held in deposit were to die or depreciate in value; or through an extrinsic cause, for instance, if it were taken by an enemy, or devoured by a beast (in which case, however, a man was bound to restore to the owner whatever was left of the animal thus slain). But in the other cases mentioned above, he was not bound to make restitution, but only to take an oath in order to clear himself of suspicion of fraud. Secondly, the goods deposited might be lost through an avoidable cause, for instance, by theft, and then the depositary was bound to restitution because of his neglect. But, as was stated above, he who held an animal on loan was bound to restitution, even if he were absent when it depreciated or died, because he was held responsible for less negligence than a depositary, who was only held responsible in case of theft.

Reply Obj. 6. Workmen who offer their labor for hire are poor men who toil for their daily bread; and therefore the Law commanded wisely that they should be paid at once, lest they should lack food. But they who offer other commodities for hire are wont to be rich, nor are they in such need of their price in order to gain a livelihood; and consequently the comparison does not hold.

Reply Obj. 7. The purpose for which judges are appointed among men is that they may decide doubtful points in matters of justice. Now a matter may be doubtful in two ways. First, among people in general; and in order to remove doubts of this kind, it was prescribed (*Deut.* xvi. 18) that *judges and magistrates* should be appointed in each tribe, *to judge the people with just judgment.*—Secondly, a matter may be doubtful even among experts, and therefore, in order to remove doubts of this kind, the Law prescribed that all should foregather in some chief place chosen by God, where there would be both the High-Priest, who would decide doubtful matters relating to the ceremonies of divine worship, and the chief judge of the people, who would decide matters relating to the judgments of men; just as even now cases are taken from a lower to a higher court either by appeal or by consultation. Hence it is written (*Deut.* xvii. 8, 9): *If thou perceive that there be among you a hard and doubtful matter in judgment, . . . and thou see that the words of the judges within thy gates do vary, arise and go up to the place, which the Lord thy God shall choose; and thou shalt come to the priests of the Levitical race, and to the judge that shall be at that time.* But such doubtful matters did not often occur for judgment; and so the people were not burdened on this account.

Reply Obj. 8. In the business affairs of men, there is no such thing as demonstrative and infallible proof, and we must be content with a certain conjectural probability, such as that which an orator employs to persuade. Consequently, although it is quite possible for two or three witnesses to agree to a falsehood, yet it is neither easy nor probable that they succeed in so doing; and hence their testimony is taken as being true, especially if they do not waver in giving it, or are not otherwise suspect. Moreover, in order that witnesses might not easily depart from the truth, the Law commanded that they should be most carefully examined, and that those who were found untruthful should be severely punished, as is stated in *Deut.* xix. 16, *seqq.*

There was, however, a reason for fixing on this particular number, in token of the unerring truth of the divine Persons, Who are sometimes mentioned as two, because the Holy Ghost is the bond of the other two Persons, and sometimes as three. As Augustine observes on *Jo.* viii. 17, *In your law it is written that the testimony of two men is true.*[13]

Reply Obj. 9. A severe punishment is inflicted not only because of the gravity of a fault, but also for other reasons. First, because of the greatness of the sin, because a greater sin, other things being equal, deserves a greater punishment. Secondly, because of a habitual sin, since men are not easily cured of habitual sin except by severe punishments. Thirdly, because of a great desire for or a great pleasure in the sin; for men are not easily deterred from such sins unless they be severely punished. Fourthly, because of the facility of committing a sin and of concealing it; for such sins, when discovered, should be more severely punished in order to deter others from committing them.

Again, with regard to the greatness of a sin, four degrees may be observed, even in respect of one single deed. The first is when a sin is committed unwillingly, because then, if the sin be altogether involuntary, man is altogether excused from punishment; for it is written (*Deut.* xxii. 25, *seqq.*) that a girl who suffers violence in a field is not guilty of death, because *she cried, and there was no man to help her.* But if a man sinned in any way voluntarily, and yet through weakness, as, for instance, when a man sins from passion, the sin is diminished; and the punishment, according to true judgment, should be diminished also, unless perchance the

[13] *Tract.* XXXVI (PL 35, 1669).

common weal requires that the sin be severely punished in order to deter others from committing such sins, as was stated above.—The second degree is when a man sins through ignorance, and then he was held to be guilty to a certain extent, because of his negligence in acquiring knowledge; yet he was not punished by the judges but expiated his sin by sacrifices. Hence it is written (*Levit.* iv. 2): *The soul that sinneth through ignorance,* etc. This is, however, to be taken as applying to ignorance of fact, and not to ignorance of the divine precept, which all were bound to know.—The third degree was when a man sinned from pride, *i.e.,* through deliberate choice or malice; and then he was punished according to the greatness of the sin. —The fourth degree was when a man sinned from stubbornness or obstinacy; and then he was to be utterly cut off as a rebel and a destroyer of the commandment of the Law.

Accordingly, we must say that, in appointing the punishment for theft, the Law considered what would be likely to happen most frequently (*Exod.* xxii. 1-9). Hence, as regards theft of other things which can easily be safeguarded from a thief, the thief restored only twice their value. But sheep cannot be easily safeguarded from a thief, because they graze in the fields; and so it happened more frequently that sheep were stolen in the fields. Consequently, the Law inflicted a heavier penalty, by ordering four sheep to be restored for the theft of one. As to cattle, they were yet more difficult to safeguard, because they are kept in the fields, and do not graze in flocks as sheep do; and so a yet more heavy penalty was inflicted in their regard, so that five oxen were to be restored for one ox. And this holds unless perchance the animal itself were discovered in the thief's possession; because in that case he had to restore only twice the number, as in the case of other thefts. For there was reason to presume that he intended to restore the animal, since he kept it alive. Or, we might say, according to the *Gloss,* that *a cow is useful in five ways: it may be used for sacrifice, for ploughing, for food, for milk, and its hide is employed for various purposes.*[14] Therefore for one cow five had to be restored. But the sheep was useful in four ways: *for sacrifice, for meat, for milk, and for its wool.*[15]— The unruly son was slain, not because he ate and drank, but because of his stubbornness and rebellion, which were always punished by death, as was stated above.—As to the man who gathered sticks on the Sabbath, he was stoned as a breaker of the Law, which commanded the Sabbath to be observed, as a witness to the belief in the newness of the world, as was stated above.[16] And so he was slain as an unbeliever.

Reply Obj. 10. The Old Law inflicted the death penalty for the more grievous crimes, viz., for those which are committed against God, and for murder, for stealing a man, irreverence towards one's parents, adultery and incest. In the case of theft of other things, it inflicted punishment by

---

[14] *Glossa ordin.,* super *Exod.,* XXII, 1 (I, 169F).   [15] *Ibid.* (I, 170A).   [16] Q. 100, a. 5.

indemnification, while in the case of blows and mutilation it authorized punishment by retaliation; and likewise for the sin of bearing false witness. In other faults of less degree, it prescribed the punishment of stripes or of public disgrace.

The punishment of slavery was prescribed by the Law in two cases. First, in the case of a slave who was unwilling to avail himself of the privilege granted by the Law, whereby he was free to depart in the seventh year of remission; and so he was punished by remaining a slave forever.— Secondly, in the case of a thief, who had not wherewith to make restitution, as is stated in *Exod.* xxii. 3.

The punishment of absolute exile was not prescribed by the Law, because God was worshipped by that people alone, whereas all other nations were given to idolatry; and so if any man were exiled from that people absolutely, he would be in danger of falling into idolatry. For this reason it is related (*1 Kings* xxvi. 19) that David said to Saul: *They are cursed in the sight of the Lord, who have cast me out this day, that I should not dwell in the inheritance of the Lord, saying: Go, serve strange gods.* There was, however, a restricted sort of exile; for it is written in *Deut.* xix. 4 that *he that striketh his neighbor ignorantly, and is proved to have had no hatred against him, shall flee to one of the cities* of refuge and *abide there until the death of the high-priest.* For then it became lawful for him to return home, because, when the whole people thus suffered a loss, they forgot their private quarrels, so that the next of kin of the slain were not so eager to kill the slayer.

Reply Obj. 11. Brute animals were ordered to be slain, not because of any fault of theirs, but as a punishment to their owners, who had not safeguarded their beasts from these offenses. Hence the owner was more severely punished if his ox had butted anyone *yesterday or the day before* (in which case steps might have been taken to avoid the danger) than if it had taken to butting suddenly.—Or again, the animal was slain in detestation of the sin, and lest men should be made subject to horror at the sight thereof.

Reply Obj. 12. The literal reason for this commandment, as Rabbi Moses declares, was because the slayer was frequently from the nearest city;[17] and so the slaying of the calf was a means of investigating the hidden murder. This was brought about in three ways. In the first place, the elders of the city swore that they had taken every measure for safeguarding the roads. Secondly, the owner of the heifer was indemnified for the slaying of his beast, and if the murder were previously discovered, the beast was not slain. Thirdly, the place where the heifer was slain remained uncultivated. Therefore, in order to avoid this twofold loss, the men of that city would readily make known the murderer, if they knew who he was; and it would seldom happen but that some word or sign would escape about

[17] *Guide*, III, 40 (p. 343).

the matter.—Or again, this was done in order to frighten people, in detestation of murder. For the slaying of a heifer, which is a useful animal and full of strength, especially before it has been put under the yoke, signified that whoever committed murder, however useful and strong he might be, was to forfeit his life, and that by a cruel death, which was implied by the striking off of its head; and that the murderer, as vile and abject, was to be cut off from the fellowship of men, which was betokened by the fact that the heifer, after being slain, was left to rot in a rough and uncultivated place.

Mystically, the heifer taken from the herd signifies *the flesh of Christ, which had not drawn a yoke, since it had done no sin; nor did it plough the ground, i.e., it never knew the stain of revolt.*[18] The fact of the heifer being killed in an uncultivated valley signified the despised death of Christ, whereby all sins are washed away, and the devil is shown to be the arch-murderer.

Third Article

WHETHER THE JUDICIAL PRECEPTS REGARDING FOREIGNERS WERE FRAMED IN A SUITABLE MANNER?

We proceed thus to the Third Article:—

Objection 1. It would seem that the judicial precepts regarding foreigners were not suitably framed. For Peter said (*Acts* x. 34, 35): *In very deed I perceive that God is not a respecter of persons, but in every nation, he that feareth Him and worketh justice is acceptable to Him.* But those who are acceptable to God should not be excluded from the Church of God. Therefore it is unsuitably commanded (*Deut.* xxiii. 3) that *the Ammonite and the Moabite, even after the tenth generation, shall not enter into the church of the Lord forever*; whereas, on the other hand, it is prescribed (*ibid.* 7) to be observed with regard to certain other nations: *Thou shalt not abhor the Edomite, because he is thy brother, nor the Egyptian, because thou wast a stranger in his land.*

Obj. 2. Further, we do not deserve to be punished for those things which are not in our power. But it is not a man's fault if he is a eunuch, or if he is born of a prostitute. Therefore it is unsuitably commanded (*Deut.* xxiii. 1, 2) that *an eunuch and one born of a prostitute shall not enter into the church of the Lord.*

Obj. 3. Further, the Old Law mercifully forbade strangers to be molested; for it is written (*Exod.* xxii. 21): *Thou shalt not molest a stranger, nor afflict him, for yourselves also were strangers in the land of Egypt*; and (xxiii. 9): *Thou shalt not molest a stranger, for you know the hearts of strangers, for you also were strangers in the land of Egypt.* But it is an affliction to be burdened with usury. Therefore the Law unsuitably per-

[18] *Glossa ordin.,* super *Deut.* XXI, 1 (I, 354A).

mitted them (*Deut.* xxiii. 19, 20) to lend money to strangers for usury.

Obj. 4. Further, men are much more akin to us than trees. But we should show greater care and love for those things that are nearest to us, according to *Ecclus.* xiii. 19: *Every beast loveth its like; so also every man him that is nearest to himself.* Therefore the Lord unsuitably commanded (*Deut.* xx. 13-19) that all the inhabitants of a captured hostile city were to be slain, but that the fruit-trees should not be cut down.

Obj. 5. Further, every one should prefer the common good of virtue to the good of the individual. But the common good is sought in a war which men fight against their enemies. Therefore it is unsuitably commanded (*Deut.* xx. 5-7) that certain men should be sent home, for instance, a man that had built a new house, or who had planted a vineyard, or who had married a wife.

Obj. 6. Further, no man should profit by his own fault. But it is a man's fault if he be timid or faint-hearted, since this is contrary to the virtue of fortitude. Therefore the timid and faint-hearted are unfittingly excused from the toil of battle (*Deut.* xx. 8).

On the contrary, Divine Wisdom declares (*Prov.* viii. 8): *All my words are just; there is nothing wicked nor perverse in them.*

I answer that, Man's relations with foreigners are twofold, peaceful and hostile, and in directing both kinds of relation the Law contained suitable precepts. For the Jews were offered three opportunities of peaceful relations with foreigners. First, when foreigners passed through their land as travelers. Secondly, when they came to dwell in their land as new-comers. And in both these respects the Law made kind provision in its precepts; for it is written (*Exod.* xxii. 21): *Thou shalt not molest a stranger [advenam]*; and again (*ibid.* xxiii. 9): *Thou shalt not molest a stranger [peregrino].* Thirdly, when any foreigners wished to be admitted entirely to their fellowship and mode of worship. With regard to these a certain order was observed. For they were not at once admitted to citizenship; just as it was the law with some nations that no one was deemed a citizen except after two or three generations, as the Philosopher says.[19] The reason for this was that if foreigners were allowed to meddle with the affairs of a nation as soon as they settled down in its midst, many dangers might occur, since the foreigners, not yet having the common good firmly at heart, might attempt something injurious to the people. Hence it was that the Law prescribed in respect of certain nations that had close relations with the Jews (viz., the Egyptians among whom they were born and educated, and the Idumeans, the children of Esau, Jacob's brother), that they should be admitted to the fellowship of the people after the third generation; whereas others (with whom their relations had been hostile, such as the Ammonites and Moabites) were never to be admitted to citizenship; while the Amalekites, who were yet more hostile to them, and had no fellowship of kindred

[19] *Polit.,* III, 1 (1275b 23).

with them, were to be held as foes in perpetuity; for it is written (*Exod.* xvii. 16): *The war of the Lord shall be against Amalec from generation to generation.*

In like manner, with regard to hostile relations with foreigners, the Law contained suitable precepts. For, in the first place, it commanded that war should be declared for a just cause. Thus it is commanded (*Deut.* xx. 10) that when they advanced to besiege a city, they should at first make an offer of peace.—Secondly, it enjoined that when once they had entered on a war they should undauntedly persevere in it, putting their trust in God. And in order that they might be the more heedful of this command, it ordered that on the approach of battle the priest should hearten them by promising them God's aid.—Thirdly, it prescribed the removal of whatever might prove an obstacle to the fight, and that certain men, who might be in the way, should be sent home.—Fourthly, it enjoined that they should use moderation in pursuing the advantage of victory, by sparing women and children, and by not cutting down the fruit-trees of that country.

Reply Obj. 1. The Law excluded the men of no nation from the worship of God and from things pertaining to the welfare of the soul; for it is written (*Exod.* xii. 48): *If any stranger be willing to dwell among you, and to keep the Phase of the Lord, all his males shall first be circumcised, and then shall he celebrate it according to the manner, and he shall be as that which is born in the land.* But in temporal matters concerning the public life of the people, admission was not granted to everyone at once, for the reason given above, but to some, *i.e.*, the Egyptians and Idumeans, in the third generation; while others were excluded in perpetuity, in detestation of their past offense, *i.e.*, the peoples of Moab, Ammon, and Amalec. For just as one man is punished for a sin committed by him, in order that others seeing this may be deterred and refrain from sinning, so too may one nation or city be punished for a crime, that others may refrain from similar crimes.

Nevertheless, it was possible by dispensation for a man to be admitted to citizenship because of some act of virtue. Thus it is related (*Judith* xiv. 6) that Achior, the captain of the children of Ammon, *was joined to the people of Israel, with all the succession of his kindred.*—The same applies to Ruth the Moabite, who was *a virtuous woman* (*Ruth* iii. 11); although it may be said that this prohibition regarded men and not women, who are not competent to be citizens, absolutely speaking.

Reply Obj. 2. As the Philosopher says, a man is said to be a citizen in two ways: first, absolutely; secondly, in a restricted sense.[20] A man is a citizen absolutely if he has all the rights of citizenship, for instance, the right of debating or voting in the popular assembly. On the other hand, any man may be called citizen only in a restricted sense if he dwells within the state, even lowly people, or children, or old men, who are not fit to

[20] *Op. cit.*, III, 3 (1278a 2).

enjoy power in matters pertaining to the common welfare. For this reason bastards, by reason of their base origin, were excluded from the *ecclesia, i.e.,* from the popular assembly, down to the tenth generation. The same applies to eunuchs, who were not competent to receive the honor due to a father, especially among the Jews, where the divine worship was continued through carnal generation; for even among the pagans, those who had many children were marked with special honor, as the Philosopher remarks.[21]— Nevertheless, in matters pertaining to the grace of God, eunuchs were not discriminated from others, as neither were strangers, as we have already stated; for it is written *(Isa.* lvi. 3): *Let not the son of the stranger that adhereth to the Lord speak, saying: The Lord will divide and separate me from His people. And let not the eunuch say: Behold I am a dry tree.*

Reply Obj. 3. It was not the intention of the Law to sanction the acceptance of usury from strangers, but only to tolerate it because of the proneness of the Jews to avarice, and in order to promote an amicable feeling towards those out of whom they made a profit.

Reply Obj. 4. A distinction was observed with regard to hostile cities. For some of them were far distant, and were not among those which had been promised to them. When they had taken these cities, they killed all the men who had fought against God's people, whereas the women and children were spared. But in the neighboring cities, which had been promised to them, all were ordered to be slain, because of their former crimes, to punish which God sent the Israelites as executors of divine justice; for it is written *(Deut.* ix. 5): *Because they have done wickedly, they are destroyed at thy coming in.*—The fruit-trees were commanded to be left untouched for the use of the people themselves, to whom the city with its territory was destined to be subjected.

Reply Obj. 5. The builder of a new house, the planter of a vineyard, the newly married husband, were excluded from fighting for two reasons. First, because man is wont to give all his affection to those things which he has lately acquired, or is on the point of having, and consequently he is apt to dread the loss of these above other things. Therefore it was likely enough that because of this affection they would fear death all the more, and be so much the less brave in battle.—Secondly, because, as the Philosopher says, *it is a misfortune for a man if he is prevented from obtaining something good when it is within his grasp.*[22] And so, lest the surviving relations should be the more grieved at the death of these men who had not entered into the possession of the good things prepared for them, and also lest the people should be horror-stricken at the sight of their misfortune, these men were taken away from the danger of death by being removed from the battle.

Reply Obj. 6. The timid were sent back home, not that they might be the gainers thereby, but lest the people might be the losers by their

[21] *Polit.,* II, 6 (1270b 1).   [22] *Phys.,* II, 5 (197a 27).

presence, since their timidity and flight might cause others to be afraid and run away.

Fourth Article

WHETHER THE OLD LAW SET FORTH SUITABLE PRECEPTS ABOUT THE MEMBERS OF THE HOUSEHOLD?

We proceed thus to the Fourth Article:—

Objection 1. It would seem that the Old Law set forth unsuitable precepts about the members of the household. For a slave *is in every respect his master's property*, as the Philosopher states.[23] But that which is a man's property should be his always. Therefore it was unfitting for the Law to command (*Exod.* xxi. 2) that slaves should *go out free* in the seventh year.

Obj. 2. Further, a slave is his master's property, just as an animal, *e.g.*, an ass or an ox. But it is commanded (*Deut.* xxii. 1-3) with regard to animals, that they should be brought back to the owner if they be found going astray. Therefore it was unsuitably commanded (*Deut.* xxiii. 15): *Thou shalt not deliver to his master the servant that is fled to thee.*

Obj. 3. Further, the divine Law should encourage mercy more even than the human law. But according to human laws, those who ill-treat their servants and maidservants are severely punished; and the worse treatment of all seems to be that which results in death. Therefore it is unfittingly commanded (*Exod.* xxi. 20, 21) that *he that striketh his bondman or bondwoman with a rod, and they die under his hands . . . if the party remain alive a day . . . he shall not be subject to the punishment, because it is his money.*

Obj. 4. Further, the dominion of a master over his slave differs from that of the father over his son.[24] But the dominion of master over slave gives the former the right to sell his slave or maidservant. Therefore it was unfitting for the Law to allow a man to sell his daughter to be a servant or handmaid (*Exod.* xxi. 7).

Obj. 5. Further, a father has power over his son. But he who has power over the sinner has the right to punish him for his offenses. Therefore it is unfittingly commanded (*Deut.* xxi. 18 *seqq.*) that a father should bring his son to the ancients of the city for punishment.

Obj. 6. Further, the Lord forbade them (*Deut.* vii. 3, *seqq.*) to make marriages with strange nations, and commanded the dissolution of such as had been contracted (*1 Esdras* x.). Therefore it was unfitting to allow them to marry captive women from strange nations (*Deut.* xxi. 10 *seqq.*).

Obj. 7. Further, the Lord forbade them to marry within certain degrees of consanguinity and affinity, according to *Levit.* xviii. Therefore it was unsuitably commanded (*Deut.* xxv. 5) that if any man died without issue, his brother should marry his wife.

---

[23] *Polit.*, I, 2 (1254a 12).   [24] Aristotle, *Polit.*, I, 5 (1259a 37); 2 (1253b 8); III, 4 (1278b 32).

Obj. 8. Further, as there is the greatest familiarity between man and wife, so should there be the staunchest fidelity. But this is impossible if the marriage bond can be sundered. Therefore it was unfitting for the Lord to allow (*Deut.* xxiv. 1-4) a man to put his wife away, by writing a bill of divorce; and, besides, that he could not take her again to wife.

Obj. 9. Further, just as a wife can be faithless to her husband, so can a slave be to his master, and a son to his father. But the Law did not command any sacrifice to be offered in order to investigate the injury done by a servant to his master, or by a son to his father. Therefore it seems to have been superfluous for the Law to prescribe the *sacrifice of jealousy* in order to investigate a wife's adultery (*Num.* v. 12 *seqq.*). Consequently, it seems that the Law put forth unsuitable judicial precepts about the members of the household.

On the contrary, It is written (*Ps.* xviii. 10): *The judgments of the Lord are true, justified in themselves.*

I answer that, The mutual relations of the members of a household regard every-day actions directed to the necessities of life, as the Philosopher states.[25] Now the preservation of man's life may be considered from two points of view. First, from the point of view of the individual, *i.e.*, in so far as man preserves his individual life. Now for the purpose of the preservation of life, considered from this standpoint, man has at his service external goods, by means of which he provides himself with food and clothing and other such necessaries of life, in the handling of which he has need of servants. Secondly, man's life is preserved from the point of view of the species, by means of generation, for which purpose man needs a wife, that she may bear him children. Accordingly, the mutual relations of the members of a household admit of a threefold combination: viz., that of master and servant, that of husband and wife, and that of father and son; and in respect of all these relationships the Old Law contained fitting precepts. Thus, with regard to servants, it commanded them to be treated with moderation—both as to their work, namely, lest they should be burdened with excessive labor, and so the Lord commanded (*Deut.* v. 14) that on the Sabbath day *thy manservant and thy maidservant* should *rest even as thyself*;—and also as to the infliction of punishment, for it ordered those who maimed their servants to set them free (*Exod.* xxi. 26, 27). Similar provision was made in favor of a maidservant when married to anyone (*ibid.* 7, *seqq.*). Moreover, with regard to those servants in particular who were taken from among the people, the Law prescribed that they should go out free in the seventh year, taking whatever they brought with them, even their clothes (*ibid.* 2, *seqq.*); and furthermore it was commanded (*Deut.* xv. 13) that they should be given provision for the journey.

With regard to wives, the Law made certain prescriptions as to the taking of wives in marriage: for instance, that they should marry a

[25] *Op. cit.,* I, 1 (1252b 13).

wife from their own tribe (*Num.* xxxvi. 6), and this lest confusion should ensue in the property of various tribes. Also, that a man should marry the wife of his deceased brother when the latter died without issue, as is prescribed in *Deut.* xxv. 5, 6, and this in order that he who could not have successors according to carnal origin might at least have them by a kind of adoption, and that thus the deceased might not be entirely forgotten. It also forbade them to marry certain women, namely, women of strange nations, through fear of their losing their faith, and those of their near kindred, because of the natural respect due to them.—Furthermore it prescribed in what way wives were to be treated after marriage. Thus, it was prescribed that they should not be slandered without grave reason: wherefore it ordered punishment to be inflicted on the man who falsely accused his wife of a crime (*Deut.* xxii. 13, *seqq.*). Also that a man's hatred of his wife should not be detrimental to his son (*Deut.* xxi. 15, *seqq.*). Again, that a man should not ill-use his wife through hatred of her, but rather that he should write a bill of divorce and send her away (*Deut.* xxiv. 1). Furthermore, in order to foster conjugal love from the very outset, it was prescribed that no public duties should be laid on a recently married man, so that he might be free to rejoice with his wife.

With regard to children, the Law commanded parents to educate them by instructing them in the faith. Hence it is written (*Exod.* xii. 26 *seqq.*): *When your children shall say to you: What is the meaning of this service? you shall say to them: It is the victim of the passage of the Lord.* Moreover, they are commanded to teach them the rules of right conduct; and so it is written (*Deut.* xxi. 20) that the parents had to say: *He slighteth hearing our admonitions, he giveth himself to revelling and to debauchery.*

Reply Obj. 1. As the children of Israel had been delivered by the Lord from slavery, and for this reason were bound to the service of God, He did not wish them to be slaves in perpetuity. Hence it is written (*Levit.* xxv. 39, *seqq.*): *If thy brother, constrained by poverty, sell himself to thee, thou shalt not oppress him with the service of bondservants, but he shall be as a hireling and a sojourner . . . for they are My servants, and I brought them out of the land of Egypt: let them not be sold as bondmen*; and consequently, since they were slaves, not absolutely, but in a restricted sense, after a lapse of time they were set free.

Reply Obj. 2. This commandment is to be understood as referring to a servant whom his master seeks to kill, or to help him in committing some sin.

Reply Obj. 3. With regard to the ill-treatment of servants, the Law seems to have taken into consideration whether it was certain or not. For if it were certain, the Law fixed a penalty: for maiming, the penalty was forfeiture of the servant, who was ordered to be given his liberty; while for slaying, the punishment was that of a murderer, when the servant died under the blow of his master.—If, however, the injury were not certain, but only probable, the Law did not impose any penalty as regards a man's own servant: *e.g.*, if the servant did not die at once after being struck, but after some days; for it would be uncertain whether he died as a result of the blows he received. For when a man struck a free man, yet so that he did not die at once, but *walked abroad again upon his staff,* he that struck him was quit of murder, even though afterwards he died. Nevertheless, he was bound to pay the doctor's fees incurred by the victim of his assault. But this was not the case if a man killed his own servant, because whatever the servant had, even his very person, was the property of his master. Hence the reason for his not being subject to a pecuniary penalty is set down as being *because it is his money.*

Reply Obj. 4. As was stated above, no Jew could own a Jew as a slave absolutely, but only in a restricted sense, as a hireling for a fixed time. And in this way the Law permitted that through stress of poverty a man might sell his son or daughter. This is shown by the very words of the Law, where we read: *If any man sell his daughter to be a servant, she shall not go out as bondwomen are wont to go out.* Moreover, in this way a man might sell not only his son, but even himself, rather as a hireling than as a slave, according to *Levit.* xxv. 39, 40: *If thy brother, constrained by poverty, sell himself to thee, thou shalt not oppress him with the service of bondservants; but he shall be as a hireling and a sojourner.*

Reply Obj. 5. As the Philosopher says, paternal authority has the power only of admonition,[26] but not that of coercion, whereby rebellious and headstrong persons can be compelled. Hence in this case the Lord commanded the stubborn son to be punished by the rulers of the city.

Reply Obj. 6. The Lord forbade them to marry strange women because of the danger of seduction, lest they should be led astray into idolatry. And specially did this prohibition apply with respect to those nations who dwelt near them, because it was more probable that they would adopt their religious practices. When, however, the woman was willing to renounce idolatry and become an adherent of the Law, it was lawful to take her in marriage; as was the case with Ruth whom Booz married. Therefore she said to her mother-in-law (*Ruth* i. 16): *Thy people shall be my people, and thy God my God.* Accordingly, it was not permitted to marry a captive woman unless she first shaved her hair, and pared her nails, and put off the raiment wherein she was taken, and mourned for her father and mother, in token that she renounced idolatry forever.

Reply Obj. 7. As Chrysostom says, *because death was an unmitigated evil for the Jews, who did everything with a view to the present life, it was ordained that children should be born to the dead man through his brother, thus affording a certain mitigation to his death. It was not, however, ordained that any other than his brother or one next of kin should marry the wife of the deceased, because* the offspring of this union *would*

[26] *Eth.,* X, 9 (1180a 18)

not be looked upon as that of the deceased; and, moreover, a stranger would not be under the obligation to support the household of the deceased, as his brother would be bound to do from motives of justice because of his relationship.[27] Hence it is evident that, in marrying the wife of his dead brother, he took his dead brother's place.

Reply Obj. 8. The Law permitted a wife to be divorced, not as though it were just absolutely speaking, but because of the Jews' hardness of heart, as Our Lord declared (*Matt.* xix. 8). Of this, however, we must speak more fully in the treatise on Matrimony.[28]

Reply Obj. 9. Wives break their conjugal faith by adultery, both easily, for motives of pleasure, and hiddenly, since *the eye of the adulterer observeth darkness* (*Job* xxiv. 15). But this does not apply to a son in respect of his father, or to a servant in respect of his master, because the latter infidelity is not the result of the lust of pleasure, but rather of malice; nor can it remain hidden like the infidelity of an adulterous woman.

[27] *In Matt.*, hom. XLVIII (PG 58, 489). [28] *S. T.*, III, Suppl., q. 67.

ON THE LAW OF THE GOSPEL, CALLED THE NEW LAW, CONSIDERED IN ITSELF

(In Four Articles)

IN proper sequence we have to consider now the Law of the Gospel which is called the New Law, and in the first place we must consider it in itself; secondly, in comparison with the Old Law;[1] thirdly, we shall treat of those things that are contained in the New Law.[2] Under the first head there are four points of inquiry: (1) What kind of law is it? *i.e.,* is it a written law or is it instilled in the heart? (2) On its efficacy, *i.e.,* does it justify? (3) On its beginning, *i.e.,* should it have been given at the beginning of the world? (4) On its end, *i.e.,* whether it will last until the end, or will another law take its place?

First Article

WHETHER THE NEW LAW IS A WRITTEN LAW?

We proceed thus to the First Article:—

Objection 1. It would seem that the New Law is a written law. For the New Law is just the same as the Gospel. But the Gospel is set forth in writing, according to *John* xx. 31: *But these are written that you may believe.* Therefore the New Law is a written law.

Obj. 2. Further, the law that is instilled in the heart is the natural law, according to *Rom.* ii. 14, 15: *[The Gentiles] do by nature those things that are of the law . . . who have the work of the law written in their hearts.* If therefore the law of the Gospel were instilled in our hearts, it would not be distinct from the law of nature.

Obj. 3. Further, the law of the Gospel is proper to those who are in the state of the New Testament. But the law that is instilled in the heart is common to those who are in the New Testament and to those who are in the Old Testament; for it is written (*Wis.* vii. 27) that divine wisdom *through nations conveyeth herself into holy souls, she maketh the friends of God and prophets.* Therefore the New Law is not instilled in our hearts.

On the contrary, The New Law is the law of the New Testament. But the law of the New Testament is instilled in our hearts. For the Apostle, quoting the authority of *Jeremias* xxxi. 31, 33 (*Behold the days shall come, saith the Lord, and I will perfect unto the house of Israel, and unto*

---

[1] Q. 107.　　[2] Q. 108.

the house of Juda, a new testament) says, explaining what this testament is (*Heb.* viii. 8, 10): *For this is the testament which I will make to the house of Israel . . . by giving My laws into their mind, and in their heart will I write them.* Therefore the New Law is instilled in our hearts.

I answer that, Each thing appears to be that which preponderates in it, as the Philosopher states.[3] Now that which is preponderant in the law of the New Testament, and whereon all its efficacy is based, is the grace of the Holy Ghost, which is given through faith in Christ. Consequently, the New Law is chiefly the grace itself of the Holy Ghost, which is given to those who believe in Christ. This is manifestly stated by the Apostle who says (*Rom.* iii. 27): *Where is . . . thy boasting? It is excluded. By what law? Of works? No, but by the law of faith*; for he calls the grace itself of faith *a law.* And still more clearly it is written (*Rom.* viii. 2): *The law of the spirit of life, in Christ Jesus, hath delivered me from the law of sin and of death.* Hence Augustine says that, *just as the law of deeds was written on tables of stone, so is the law of faith inscribed on the hearts of the faithful*;[4] and elsewhere in the same book: *What else are the divine laws written by God Himself on our hearts but the very presence of His Holy Spirit?*[5]

Nevertheless, the New Law contains certain things that dispose us to receive the grace of the Holy Ghost, and pertaining to the use of that grace. Such things are of secondary importance, so to speak, in the New Law, and the faithful needed to be instructed concerning them, by word and by writing, both as to what they should believe and as to what they should do. Consequently, we must say that the New Law is in the first place a law that is inscribed on our hearts, but that secondarily it is a written law.

Reply Obj. 1. The Gospel writings contain only such things as pertain to the grace of the Holy Ghost, either by disposing us thereto, or by directing us to the use thereof. Thus, with regard to the intellect, the Gospel contains certain matters pertaining to the manifestation of Christ's divinity or humanity, which dispose us by means of faith, through which we receive the grace of the Holy Ghost; and with regard to the affections, it contains matters touching the contempt of the world, whereby man is rendered fit to receive the grace of the Holy Ghost, for *the world, i.e.,* worldly men, *cannot receive* the Holy Ghost (*Jo.* xiv. 17). As to the use of spiritual grace, this consists in works of virtue to which the writings of the New Testament exhort men in diverse ways.

Reply Obj. 2. There are two ways in which a thing may be instilled into man. First, through being part of his nature; and thus the natural law is instilled into man. Secondly, a thing is instilled into man by being, as it were, added to his nature by a gift of grace. In this way the New

[3] *Eth.,* IX, 8 (1169a 2).   [4] *De Spir. et Litt.,* XXIV (PL 44, 225).   [5] *Op. cit.,* XXI (PL 44, 222).

Law is instilled into man, not only by indicating to him what he should do, but also by helping him to accomplish it.

Reply Obj. 3. No man ever had the grace of the Holy Ghost except through faith in Christ, either explicit or implicit. Now by faith in Christ man belongs to the New Testament. Consequently, whoever had the law of grace instilled into them belonged to the New Testament.

Second Article

WHETHER THE NEW LAW JUSTIFIES?

We proceed thus to the Second Article:—

Objection 1. It would seem that the New Law does not justify. For no man is justified unless he obey God's law, according to *Heb.* v. 9: *He, i.e.,* Christ, *became to all that obey Him the cause of eternal salvation.* But the Gospel does not always cause men to believe in it, for it is written (*Rom.* x. 16): *All do not obey the Gospel.* Therefore the New Law does not justify.

Obj. 2. Further, the Apostle proves in his epistle to the Romans that the Old Law did not justify, because transgression increased at its advent; for it is stated (*Rom.* iv. 15): *The Law worketh wrath, for where there is no law, neither is there transgression.* But much more did the New Law increase transgression, since he who sins after the giving of the New Law deserves greater punishment, according to *Heb.* x. 28, 29: *A man making void the Law of Moses dieth without any mercy under two or three witnesses. How much more, do you think, he deserveth worse punishments, who hath trodden under-foot the Son of God,* etc.? Therefore the New Law, like the Old Law, does not justify.

Obj. 3. Further, justification is an effect proper to God, according to *Rom.* viii. 33: *God that justifieth.* But the Old Law was from God just as the New Law. Therefore the New Law does not justify any more than the Old Law did.

On the contrary, The Apostle says (*Rom.* i. 16): *I am not ashamed of the Gospel, for it is the power of God unto salvation to everyone that believeth.* But there is no salvation but to those who are justified. Therefore the Law of the Gospel justifies.

I answer that, As we have stated above, there is a twofold element in the Law of the Gospel. There is the chief element, viz., the grace of the Holy Ghost bestowed inwardly. And as to this, the New Law justifies. Hence Augustine says: *There, i.e.,* in the Old Testament, *the Law was set forth in an outward fashion, that the unjust might be afraid; here, i.e.,* in the New Testament, *it is given in an inward manner, that they may be justified.*[6]—The other element of the Evangelical Law is secondary, namely, the teachings of faith, and those commandments which direct

---

[6] *Op. cit.,* XVII (PL 44. 218).

human affections and human actions. And as to this, the New Law does not justify. Hence the Apostle says (*2 Cor.* iii. 6): *The letter killeth, but the spirit quickeneth,* which Augustine explains by saying that the letter denotes any writing that is external to man, even that of the moral precepts such as are contained in the Gospel.[7] Therefore the letter even of the Gospel would kill, unless there were the inward presence of the healing grace of faith.

Reply Obj. 1. This argument is true of the New Law, not as to its prin·cipal, but as to its secondary, element, *i.e.,* as to the dogmas and precepts outwardly put before man either in words or in writing.

Reply Obj. 2. Although the grace of the New Testament helps man to avoid sin, yet it does not so confirm man in good that he cannot sin; for this belongs to the state of glory. Hence if a man sin after receiving the grace of the New Testament, he deserves greater punishment, as being ungrateful for greater benefits, and as not using the help given to him. And this is why the New Law is not said to *work wrath,* namely, because as far as it is concerned, it gives man sufficient help to avoid sin.

Reply Obj. 3. The same God gave both the New and the Old Law, but in different ways. For He gave the Old Law written on tables of stone, whereas He gave the New Law written *in the fleshly tables of the heart,* as the Apostle expresses it (*2 Cor.* iii. 3). Therefore, as Augustine says, *the Apostle calls this letter, which is written outside man, a ministration of death and a ministration of condemnation, whereas he calls the other letter, i.e., the Law of the New Testament, the ministration of the spirit and the ministration of justice; because through the gift of the Spirit we work justice, and are delivered from the condemnation due to transgression.*[8]

Third Article

WHETHER THE NEW LAW SHOULD HAVE BEEN GIVEN FROM THE BEGINNING OF THE WORLD?

We proceed thus to the Third Article:—

Objection 1. It would seem that the New Law should have been given from the beginning of the world. *For there is no respect of persons with God* (*Rom.* ii. 11). But *all* men *have sinned and do need the glory of God* (*ibid.* iii. 23). Therefore the Law of the Gospel should have been given from the beginning of the world, in order that it might bring succor to all.

Obj. 2. Further, as men dwell in various places, so do they live in various times. But God, *Who will have all men to be saved* (*1 Tim.* ii. 4), commanded the Gospel to be preached in all places, as may be seen in the last chapters of Matthew and Mark. Therefore the Law of the Gospel

---

[7] *Op. cit.,* XIV; XVII (PL 44, 215; 219).   [8] *Op. cit.,* XVIII (PL 44, 219).

should have been at hand for all times, so as to be given from the beginning of the world.

Obj. 3. Further, man needs to save his soul, which is for all eternity, more than to save his body, which is a temporal matter. But God provided man from the beginning of the world with things that are necessary for the health of his body, by subjecting to his power whatever was created for the sake of man (*Gen.* i. 26-29). Therefore the New Law also, which is very necessary for the health of the soul, should have been given to man from the beginning of the world.

On the contrary, The Apostle says (*1 Cor.* xv. 46): *That was not first which is spiritual, but that which is natural.* But the New Law is most spiritual. Therefore it was not fitting for it to be given from the beginning of the world.

I answer that, Three reasons may be assigned why it was not fitting for the New Law to be given from the beginning of the world. The first is because the New Law, as was stated above, consists chiefly in the grace of the Holy Ghost, which it behoved not to be given abundantly until sin, which is an obstacle to grace, had been cast out of man through the accomplishment of his redemption by Christ. Hence it is written (*Jo.* vii. 39): *As yet the Spirit was not given, because Jesus was not yet glorified.* This reason the Apostle states clearly (*Rom.* viii. 2, *seqq.*) where, after speaking of *the Law of the Spirit of life,* he adds: *God sending His own Son, in the likeness of sinful flesh, of sin hath condemned sin in the flesh, that the justification of the Law might be fulfilled in us.*

A second reason may be taken from the perfection of the New Law. For a thing is not brought to perfection at once from the outset, but through an orderly succession of time; and thus one is at first a boy, and then a man. And this reason is stated by the Apostle (*Gal.* iii. 24, 25): *The Law was our pedagogue in Christ that we might be justified by faith. But after the faith is come, we are no longer under a pedagogue.*

The third reason is found in the fact that the New Law is the law of grace, and so it behoved man first of all to be left to himself under the state of the Old Law, so that, through falling into sin, he might realize his weakness, and acknowledge his need of grace. This reason is set down by the Apostle (*Rom.* v. 20): *The Law entered in, that sin might abound, and when sin abounded grace did more abound.*

Reply Obj. 1. Because of the sin of our first parents, mankind deserved to be deprived of the aid of grace; and so *from whom it is withheld it is justly withheld, and to whom it is given, it is mercifully given,* as Augustine states.[9] Consequently, it does not follow that there is respect of persons with God, from the fact that He did not offer the Law of grace to all from the beginning of the world, which Law was to be published in due course of time, as was stated above.

[9] Cf. *Epist.* CCVII, 5 (PL 33, 984).

Reply Obj. 2. The state of mankind does not vary according to diversity of place, but according to succession of time. Hence the New Law avails for all places, but not for all times; although at all times there have been some persons belonging to the New Testament, as was stated above.

Reply Obj. 3. Things pertaining to the health of the body are of service to man as regards his nature, which sin does not destroy; whereas things pertaining to the health of the soul are ordained to grace, which is lost through sin. Consequently the comparison will not hold.

Fourth Article

WHETHER THE NEW LAW WILL LAST TILL THE END OF THE WORLD?

We proceed thus to the Fourth Article:—

Objection 1. It would seem that the New Law will not last till the end of the world. For, as the Apostle says (*1 Cor.* xiii. 10), *when that which is perfect is come, that which is in part shall be done away.* But the New Law is *in part,* since the Apostle says (*ibid.* 9): *We know in part and we prophesy in part.* Therefore the New Law is to be done away, and will be succeeded by a more perfect state.[10]

Obj. 2. Further, Our Lord (*Jo.* xvi. 13) promised His disciples the knowledge of all truth when the Holy Ghost, the Comforter, should come. But the Church does not yet know all truth in the state of the New Testament. Therefore we must look forward to another state, wherein all truth will be revealed by the Holy Ghost.[11]

Obj. 3. Further, just as the Father is distinct from the Son and the Son from the Father, so is the Holy Ghost distinct from the Father and the Son. But there was a state corresponding with the Person of the Father, viz., the state of the Old Law, wherein men were intent on begetting children; and likewise there is a state corresponding to the Person of the Son, viz., the state of the New Law, wherein the clergy who are intent on wisdom (which is appropriated to the Son) hold a prominent place. Therefore, there will be a third state corresponding to the Holy Ghost, wherein spiritual men will hold the first place.[12]

Obj. 4. Further, Our Lord said (*Matt.* xxiv. 14): *This Gospel of the kingdom shall be preached in the whole world . . . and then shall the consummation come.* But the Gospel of Christ is already preached throughout the whole world, and yet the consummation has not yet come. Therefore the Gospel of Christ is not the Gospel of the kingdom, but another Gospel, that of the Holy Ghost, is yet to come, as another Law.[13]

On the contrary, Our Lord said (*Matt.* xxiv. 34): *I say to you that this generation shall not pass till all [these] things be done;* which passage

---

[10] Cf. H. Denifle, *Chartularium,* no. 243 (I, 272). [11] Cf. *ibid.* (I, 274). [12] Cf. *ibid.* [13] Cf. *ibid.* (I, 272).

Chrysostom explains as referring to *the generation of those that believe in Christ*.[14] Therefore the state of those who believe in Christ will last until the consummation of the world.

I answer that, The state of the world may change in two ways. In one way, according to a change of law, and thus no other state will succeed this state of the New Law. For the state of the New Law succeeded the state of the Old Law, as a more perfect law a less perfect one. Now no state of the present life can be more perfect than the state of the New Law, since nothing can approach nearer to the last end than that which is the immediate cause of our being brought to the last end. But the New Law does this, and so the Apostle says (*Heb.* x. 19-22): *Having therefore, brethren, a confidence in the entering into the Holies by the blood of Christ, a new . . . way which He hath dedicated for us . . . let us draw near.* Therefore no state of the present life can be more perfect than that of the New Law, since the nearer a thing is to the last end, the more perfect it is.

In another way, the state of mankind may change according as man stands in relation to one and the same law more or less perfectly. And thus the state of the Old Law underwent frequent changes, since at times the laws were very well kept, and at other times were altogether unheeded. Thus, too, the state of the New Law is subject to change with regard to various places, times and persons, according as the grace of the Holy Ghost dwells in man more or less perfectly. Nevertheless, we are not to look forward to a state wherein man is to possess the grace of the Holy Ghost more perfectly than he has possessed it hitherto, and especially the apostles who *received the first-fruits of the Spirit, i.e., sooner and more abundantly than others,* as the *Gloss* expounds on *Rom.* viii. 23.[15]

Reply Obj. 1. As Dionysius says, there is a threefold state of mankind.[16] The first was under the Old Law, the second is that of the New Law, the third will take place, not in this life, but in heaven. But, just as the first state is figurative and imperfect in comparison with the state of the Gospel, so the present state is figurative and imperfect in comparison with the heavenly state, with the advent of which the present state will be done away, as it is said in that very passage (*verse* 12): *We see now through a glass in a dark manner, but then face to face.*

Reply Obj. 2. As Augustine says, Montanus and Priscilla pretended that Our Lord's promise to give the Holy Ghost was fulfilled, not in the apostles, but in themselves.[17] In like manner, the Manicheans maintained that it was fulfilled in Manes whom they held to be the Paraclete.[18] Hence none of the above accepted the *Acts of the Apostles*, where it is clearly shown that the aforesaid promise was fulfilled in the apostles, just as Our

---

[14] *In Matt.,* hom. LXXVIII (PG 58, 702). [15] *Glossa interl.* (VI, 19r) ; Peter Lombard, *In Rom.,* super VIII, 23 (PL 191, 1444). [16] *De Eccles. Hier.,* V (PG 3, 501). [17] Cf. St. Augustine, *De Haeres.,* 26 (PL 42, 30). [18] *Op. cit.,* 46 (PL 42, 38).

Lord promised them a second time (*Acts* i. 5): *You shall be baptized with the Holy Ghost, not many days hence* (which we read as having been fulfilled in *Acts* ii). However, these foolish notions are refuted by the statement (*Jo.* vii. 39) that *as yet the Spirit was not given, because Jesus was not yet glorified*; from which we gather that the Holy Ghost was given as soon as Christ was glorified in His Resurrection and Ascension. Moreover, this excludes the senseless idea that the Holy Ghost is to be expected to come at some other time.[19]

Now the Holy Ghost taught the apostles all truth in respect of matters necessary for salvation, those things, namely, that we are bound to believe and to do. But He did not teach them about all future events, for this did not concern them, according to *Acts* i. 7: *It is not for you to know the times or moments which the Father hath put in His own power.*

Reply Obj. 3. The Old Law corresponded not only to the Father, but also to the Son, because Christ was foreshadowed in the Old Law. Hence Our Lord said (*Jo.* v. 46): *If you did believe Moses, you would perhaps believe Me also, for he wrote of Me.* In like manner, the New Law corresponds not only to Christ, but also to the Holy Ghost, according to *Rom.* viii. 2: *The law of the Spirit of life in Christ Jesus*, etc. Hence we are not to look forward to another law corresponding to the Holy Ghost.

Reply Obj. 4. Since Christ said at the very outset of the preaching of the Gospel: *The kingdom of heaven is at hand* (*Matt.* iv. 17), it is most absurd to say that the Gospel of Christ is not the Gospel of the kingdom. However, the preaching of the Gospel of Christ may be understood in two ways. First, as denoting the spreading abroad of the knowledge of Christ; and thus the Gospel was preached throughout the whole world even at the time of the apostles, as Chrysostom states.[20] And in this sense the words that follow—*and then shall the consummation come* (*Matt.* xxiv. 14)—refer to the destruction of Jerusalem, of which He was speaking literally.—Secondly, the preaching of the Gospel may be understood as extending throughout the world and producing its full effect, so that, namely, the Church would be founded in every nation. And in this sense, as Augustine writes to Hesychius,[21] the Gospel is not preached to the whole world yet, but when it is, the consummation of the world will come.

---

[19] *E.g.*, the idea of the Abbot Joachim. Cf. above, the notes to objections 1-4.   [20] *In Matt.*, hom. LXXV (PG 58, 688).   [21] *Epist.* CXCIX, 12 (PL 33, 923).

ON THE NEW LAW AS COMPARED WITH THE OLD
(*In Four Articles*)

WE must now consider the New Law as compared with the Old, under which head there are four points of inquiry: (1) Whether the New Law is distinct from the Old Law? (2) Whether the New Law fulfills the Old? (3) Whether the New Law is contained in the Old? (4) Which is the more burdensome, the New or the Old Law?

First Article

WHETHER THE NEW LAW IS DISTINCT FROM THE OLD LAW?

We proceed thus to the First Article:—

Objection 1. It would seem that the New Law is not distinct from the Old. For both these laws were given to those who believe in God, since *without faith it is impossible to please God,* according to *Heb.* xi. 6. But the faith of olden times and of nowadays is the same, as the *Gloss* says on *Matt.* xxi. 9.[1] Therefore the law is the same also.

Obj. 2. Further, Augustine says that *there is little difference between the Law and Gospel,—fear and love.*[2] But the New and Old Laws cannot be differentiated in respect of these two things, since even the Old Law comprised precepts of charity: *Thou shalt love thy neighbor* (*Levit.* xix. 18), and: *Thou shalt love the Lord thy God* (*Deut.* vi. 5).—In like manner, neither can they differ according to the other difference which Augustine assigns, viz., that *the Old Testament contained temporal promises, whereas the New Testament contains spiritual and eternal promises,*[3] since even the New Testament contains temporal promises, according to *Mark* x. 30: He shall receive *a hundred times as much . . . in this time, houses and brethren,* etc., while in the Old Testament they hoped in promises spiritual and eternal, according to *Heb.* xi. 16: *But now they desire a better, that is to say, a heavenly country,* which is said of the patriarchs. Therefore it seems that the New Law is not distinct from the Old.

Obj. 3. Further, the Apostle seems to distinguish both laws by calling the Old Law *a law of works,* and the New Law *a law of faith* (*Rom.* iii. 27). But the Old Law was also a law of faith, according to *Heb.* xi. 39:

---

[1] *Glossa ordin.,* super *II Cor.,* IV, 13 (VI, 66A).—Cf. St. Augustine, *Enarr. in Psalm.,* super I, 14 (PL 36, 596).   [2] *Contra Adimant.,* XVII (PL 42, 159).   [3] *Contra Faust.,* IV, 2 (PL 42, 217).

All were approved by the testimony of faith, which he says of the patriarchs of the Old Testament. In like manner, the New Law is a law of works, since it is written (*Matt.* v. 44): *Do good to them that hate you;* and (*Luke* xxii. 19): *Do this for a commemoration of Me.* Therefore the New Law is not distinct from the Old.

On the contrary, the Apostle says (*Heb.* vii. 12): *The priesthood being translated it is necessary that a translation also be made of the Law.* But the priesthood of the New Testament is distinct from that of the Old, as the Apostle shows in the same place. Therefore the Law is also distinct.

I answer that, As was stated above, every law ordains human conduct to some end.[4] Now things ordained to an end may be divided in two ways, considered from the point of view of the end. First, through being ordained to diverse ends, and this diversity will be specific, especially if such ends are proximate. Secondly, by reason of being closely or remotely connected with the end. Thus it is clear that movements differ in species through being directed to diverse terms, while according as one part of a movement is nearer to the term than another part, the diversity of perfect and imperfect movement follows.

Accordingly, then, two laws may be distinguished from one another in two ways. First, through being altogether diverse, from the fact that they are ordained to diverse ends. Thus a state-law, ordained to democratic government, would differ specifically from a law ordained to government by the aristocracy. Secondly, two laws may be distinguished from one another through one of them being more closely connected with the end, and the other more remotely. Thus, in one and the same state there is one law enjoined on men of mature age, who can forthwith accomplish that which pertains to the common good; and another law regulating the education of children who need to be taught how they are to achieve manly deeds later on.

We must therefore say that, according to the first way, the New Law is not distinct from the Old Law, because they both have the same end, namely, man's subjection to God; and there is but one God of the New and of the Old Testament, according to *Rom.* iii. 30: *It is one God that justifieth circumcision by faith, and uncircumcision through faith.*—According to the second way, the New Law is distinct from the Old Law, because the Old Law is like a pedagogue of children, as the Apostle says (*Gal.* iii. 24), whereas the New Law is the law of perfection, since it is the law of charity, of which the Apostle says (*Coloss.* iii. 14) that it is *the bond of perfection.*

Reply Obj. 1. The unity of faith under both Testaments witnesses to the unity of end, for it has been stated above that the object of the theological virtues, among which is faith, is the last end.[5] Yet faith had a

---

[4] Q. 90, a. 2; q. 91, a. 4.   [5] Q. 62, a. 2.

different state in the Old and in the New Law, since what they believed as future, we believe as fact.

Reply Obj. 2. All the differences assigned between the Old and New Laws are gathered from their relative perfection and imperfection. For the precepts of every law prescribe acts of virtue. Now the imperfect, who as yet are not possessed of a virtuous habit, are directed in one way to perform virtuous acts, while those who are perfected by the possession of virtuous habits are directed in another way. For those who as yet are not endowed with virtuous habits are directed to the performance of virtuous acts by reason of some outward cause, for instance, by the threat of punishment, or the promise of some extrinsic rewards, such as honor, riches, or the like. Hence the Old Law, which was given to men who were imperfect, that is, who had not yet received spiritual grace, was called the *Law of fear,* inasmuch as it induced men to observe its commandments by threatening them with penalties; and it is likewise spoken of as containing temporal promises.—On the other hand, those who are possessed of virtue are inclined to do virtuous deeds through love of virtue, not because of some extrinsic punishment or reward. Hence the New Law, which derives its pre-eminence from the spiritual grace instilled into our hearts, is called the *Law of love;* and it is described as containing spiritual and eternal promises, which are objects of the virtues, chiefly of charity. Accordingly, such persons are inclined of themselves to those objects, not as to something foreign, but as to something of their own.—For this reason, too, the Old Law is described as *restraining the hand, not the will,*[6] since when a man refrains from some sins through fear of being punished, his will does not shrink absolutely from sin, as does the will of a man who refrains from sin through love of righteousness. Hence the New Law, which is the Law of love, is said to restrain the will.

Nevertheless, there were some in the state of the Old Testament who, having charity and the grace of the Holy Ghost, looked chiefly to spiritual and eternal promises; and in this respect they belonged to the New Law. —In like manner, in the New Testament there are some carnal men who have not yet attained to the perfection of the New Law; and these it was necessary, even under the New Testament, to lead to virtuous acts by the fear of punishment and by temporal promises.

But although the Old Law contained precepts of charity, nevertheless, it did not confer the Holy Ghost, by Whom *charity . . . is spread abroad in our hearts* (*Rom.* v. 5).

Reply Obj. 3. As was stated above, the New Law is called the law of faith, in so far as its pre-eminence is derived from that very grace which is given inwardly to believers; and for this reason it is called the grace of faith.[7] Nevertheless, it consists secondarily in certain deeds, moral and sacramental; but the New Law does not consist chiefly in these latter

---

[6] Cf. Peter Lombard, *Sent.,* III, xl, 1 (II, 734).   [7] Q. 106, a. 1 and 2.

things, as did the Old Law. As to those under the Old Testament who through faith were acceptable to God, in this respect they belonged to the New Testament; for they were not justified except through faith in Christ, Who is the Author of the New Testament. Hence of Moses the Apostle says (*Heb.* xi. 26) that he esteemed *the reproach of Christ greater riches than the treasure of the Egyptians.*

Second Article

WHETHER THE NEW LAW FULFILLS THE OLD?

We proceed thus to the Second Article:—

Objection 1. It would seem that the New Law does not fulfill the Old. For to fulfill and to void are contrary. But the New Law voids or excludes the observances of the Old Law, for the Apostle says (*Gal.* v. 2): *If you be circumcised, Christ shall profit you nothing.* Therefore the New Law is not a fulfillment of the Old.

Obj. 2. Further, one contrary is not the fulfillment of another. But Our Lord propounded in the New Law precepts that were contrary to precepts of the Old Law. For we read (*Matt.* v 27-32): *You have heard that it was said to them of old: . . . Whosoever shall put away his wife, let him give her a bill of divorce. But I say to you that whosoever shall put away his wife . . . maketh her to commit adultery.* Furthermore, the same evidently applies to the prohibition against swearing, against retaliation, and against hating one's enemies. In like manner, Our Lord seems to have done away with the precepts of the Old Law relating to the different kinds of foods (*Matt.* xv. 11): *Not that which goeth into the mouth defileth a man, but what cometh out of the mouth, this defileth a man.* Therefore the New Law is not a fulfillment of the Old.

Obj. 3. Further, whoever acts against a law does not fulfill the law. But Christ in certain cases acted against the Law. For He touched the leper (*Matt.* viii. 3), which was contrary to the Law. Likewise, He seems to have broken the Sabbath frequently, since the Jews used to say of Him (*Jo.* ix. 16): *This man is not of God, who keepeth not the sabbath.* There-fore Christ did not fulfill the Law, and so the New Law given by Christ is not a fulfillment of the Old.

Obj. 4. Further, the Old Law contained precepts, moral, ceremonial and judicial, as was stated above.[8] But Our Lord (*Matt.* v.) fulfilled the Law in some respects, but without mentioning the judicial and ceremonial precepts. Therefore it seems that the New Law is not a complete fulfillment of the Old.

On the contrary, Our Lord said (*Matt.* v. 17): *I am not come to de-stroy, but to fulfill*; and He went on to say (*verse* 18): *One jot or one tittle shall not pass of the Law till all be fulfilled.*

[8] Q. 99, a. 4.

I answer that, As was stated above, the New Law is compared to the Old as the perfect to the imperfect. Now everything perfect fulfills that which is lacking in the imperfect. Accordingly, the New Law fulfills the Old by supplying that which was lacking in the Old Law.

Now two things in the Old Law offer themselves to our consideration, viz., the end, and the precepts contained in the Law.

The end of every law is to make men just and virtuous, as was stated above.[9] Consequently, the end of the Old Law was the justification of men. The Law, however, could not accomplish this, but foreshadowed it by certain ceremonial actions, and promised it in words. And in this respect, the New Law fulfills the Old by justifying men through the power of Christ's Passion. This is what the Apostle says (*Rom.* viii. 3, 4): *What the Law could not do . . . God sending His own Son in the likeness of sinful flesh . . . hath condemned sin in the flesh, that the justification of the Law might be fulfilled in us.*—And in this respect, the New Law gives what the Old Law promised, according to *2 Cor.* i. 20: *Whatever are the promises of God, in Him, i.e.,* in Christ, *they are 'Yea.'*—Again, in this respect, it also fulfills what the Old Law foreshadowed. Hence it is written (*Coloss.* ii. 17) concerning the ceremonial precepts that they were *a shadow of things to come, but the body is of Christ*; in other words, the reality is found in Christ. Therefore the New Law is called the law of reality, whereas the Old Law is called the law of shadow or of figure.

Now Christ fulfilled the precepts of the Old Law both in His works and in His doctrine. In His works, because He was willing to be circumcised and to fulfill the other legal observances, which were binding for the time being, according to *Gal.* iv. 4: *Made under the Law.*—In His doctrine He fulfilled the precepts of the Law in three ways. First, by explaining the true sense of the Law. This is clear in the case of murder and adultery, the prohibition of which the Scribes and Pharisees thought to refer only to the exterior act; and so Our Lord fulfilled the Law by showing that the prohibition extended also to the interior acts of sins. Secondly, Our Lord fulfilled the precepts of the Law by prescribing the safest way of complying with the statutes of the Old Law. Thus the Old Law forbade perjury, and this is more safely avoided by abstaining altogether from swearing, save in cases of urgency. Thirdly, Our Lord fulfilled the precepts of the Law by adding some counsels of perfection; and this is clearly seen in *Matt.* xix. 21, where Our Lord said to the man who affirmed that he had kept all the precepts of the Old Law: *One thing is wanting to thee: If thou wilt be perfect, go, sell whatsoever thou hast,* etc.

Reply Obj. 1. The New Law does not void the observance of the Old Law except in the point of ceremonial precepts, as was stated above.[10] Now the latter were figurative of something to come. Therefore, from the very fact that the ceremonial precepts were fulfilled when those things

---

[9] Q. 92, a. 1.   [10] Q. 103, a. 3 and 4.

were accomplished which they foreshadowed, it follows that they are no longer to be observed; for if they were to be observed, this would mean that something is still to be accomplished and is not yet fulfilled. Thus the promise of a future gift holds no longer when it has been fulfilled by the presentation of the gift. In this way, the legal ceremonies are abolished by being fulfilled.

Reply Obj. 2. As Augustine says, those precepts of Our Lord are not contrary to the precepts of the Old Law.[11] For what Our Lord commanded about a man not putting away his wife is not contrary to what the Law prescribed. *For the Law did not say: 'Let him that wills, put his wife away,' the contrary of which would be not to put her away. On the contrary, the Law was unwilling that a man should put away his wife, since it prescribed a delay, so that excessive eagerness for divorce might cease through being weakened during the writing of the bill. Hence Our Lord, in order to impress the fact that a wife ought not easily to be put away, allowed no exception save in the case of fornication.*[12] The same applies to the prohibition about swearing, as was stated above. The same is also clear with respect to the prohibition of retaliation. For the Law fixed a limit to revenge, by forbidding men to seek vengeance unreasonably; whereas Our Lord deprived them of vengeance more completely by commanding them to abstain from it altogether. With regard to the hatred of one's enemies, He dispelled the false interpretation of the Pharisees, by admonishing us to hate, not the person, but his sin.—As to discriminating among various foods, which was a ceremonial matter,—Our Lord did not forbid this to be observed; but He showed that no foods are naturally unclean, but only in token of something else, as was stated above.[13]

Reply Obj. 3. It was forbidden by the Law to touch a leper because, by doing so, man incurred a certain uncleanness of irregularity, as also by touching the dead, as was stated above.[14] But Our Lord, Who healed the leper, could not contract an uncleanness.—By those things which He did on the Sabbath, He did not break the Sabbath in reality, as the Master Himself shows in the Gospel; and this both because He worked miracles by His divine power, which is ever active among things, and because His works were concerned with the salvation of man, while the Pharisees were concerned for the well-being of animals even on the Sabbath; and again because through urgency He excused His disciples for gathering the ears of corn on the Sabbath. But He did seem to break the Sabbath according to the superstitious interpretation of the Pharisees, who thought that man ought to abstain from doing even works of kindness on the Sabbath; which was contrary to the intention of the Law.

Reply Obj. 4. The reason why the ceremonial precepts of the Law are not mentioned in *Matt.* v. is because, as was stated above, their observance

---

[11] *Contra Faust.*, XIX, 26 (PL 42, 364).   [12] Cf. St. Augustine, *De Serm. Dom.*, I, 14 (PL 34, 1248).   [13] Q. 102, a. 6, ad 1.   [14] *Ibid.*; a. 5, ad 4.

was abolished by their fulfillment.—But of the judicial percepts He mentioned that of retaliation; so that what He said about it should refer to all the others. With regard to this precept, He taught that the intention of the Law was that retaliation should be sought out of love of justice, and not as a punishment out of revengeful spite, which He forbade, admonishing man to be ready to suffer yet greater insults; and this remains still in the New Law.

Third Article

WHETHER THE NEW LAW IS CONTAINED IN THE OLD?

We proceed thus to the Third Article:—

Objection 1. It would seem that the New Law is not contained in the Old. For the New Law consists chiefly in faith, and so it is called the *law of faith* (*Rom.* iii. 27). But many points of faith are set forth in the New Law which are not contained in the Old. Therefore the New Law is not contained in the Old.

Obj. 2. Further, a *Gloss* says on *Matt.* v. 19 (*He that shall break one of these least commandments*) that the lesser commandments are those of the Law, and the greater commandments, those contained in the Gospel.[15] Now the greater cannot be contained in the lesser. Therefore the New Law is not contained in the Old.

Obj. 3. Further, who holds the container holds the contents. If, therefore, the New Law is contained in the Old, it follows that whoever had the Old Law had the New; so that it was superfluous to give men a New Law when once they had the Old. Therefore the New Law is not contained in the Old.

On the contrary, According to the saying in *Ezech.* i. 16, there was *a wheel in the midst of a wheel,* i.e., *the New Testament within the Old,* according to Gregory's exposition.[16]

I answer that, One thing may be contained in another in two ways. First, actually, as a located thing is in a place. Secondly, virtually, as an effect in its cause, or as the complement in that which is incomplete; and thus a genus contains its species, and a seed contains the whole tree, virtually. It is in this way that the New Law is contained in the Old, for it has been stated that the New Law is compared to the Old as perfect to imperfect. Hence Chrysostom, expounding *Mark* iv. 28 (*The earth of itself bringeth forth fruit, first the blade, then the ear, afterwards the full corn in the ear*) expresses himself as follows: *He brought forth first the blade, i.e., the Law of Nature; then the ear, i.e., the Law of Moses; lastly, the full corn, i.e., the Law of the Gospel.*[17] In this way, the New Law is in the Old as the corn in the ear.

---

[15] Cf. St. Augustine, *De Serm. Dom.,* I, i (PL 34, 1231).   [16] *In Ezech.,* I, hom. 6 (PL 76, 834).   [17] Apparently not in St. John Chrysostom.

Reply Obj. 1. Whatsoever is set down in the New Testament explicitly and openly as a point of faith is contained in the Old Testament as a matter of belief, but implicitly, under a figure. Accordingly, even as to those things which we are bound to believe, the New Law is contained in the Old.

Reply Obj. 2. The precepts of the New Law are said to be greater than those of the Old Law in so far as they are set forth explicitly. But as to the substance itself of the precepts of the New Testament, they are all contained in the Old. Hence Augustine says that *nearly all Our Lord's admonitions or precepts, where He expressed Himself by saying: 'But I say unto you,' are to be found also in those ancient books.*[18] Yet, *since they thought that murder was only the slaying of the human body, Our Lord declared to them that every wicked impulse to injure our brother is to be looked on as a kind of murder.*[19] And it is with reference to declarations of this kind that the precepts of the New Law are said to be greater than those of the Old. Nothing, however, prevents the greater from being contained in the lesser virtually; just as a tree is contained in the seed.

Reply Obj. 3. What is set forth implicitly needs to be declared explicitly. Hence, after the publishing of the Old Law, a New Law also had to be given.

Fourth Article

WHETHER THE NEW LAW IS MORE BURDENSOME THAN THE OLD?

We proceed thus to the Fourth Article:—

Objection 1. It would seem that the New Law is more burdensome than the Old. For Chrysostom says: *The commandments given to Moses are easy to obey: Thou shalt not kill, Thou shalt not commit adultery; but the commandments of Christ are difficult to accomplish, for instance: Thou shalt not give way to anger, or to lust.*[20] Therefore the New Law is more burdensome than the Old.

Obj. 2. Further, it is easier to make use of earthly prosperity than to suffer tribulations. But in the Old Testament observance of the Law was followed by temporal prosperity, as may be gathered from *Deut.* xxviii. 1-14; whereas many kinds of trouble befall those who observe the New Law, as is stated in 2 *Cor.* vi. 4-10: *Let us exhibit ourselves as the ministers of God, in much patience, in tribulation, in necessities, in distresses,* etc. Therefore the New Law is more burdensome than the Old.

Obj. 3. Something added is an added burden. But the New Law is something added to the Old. For the Old Law forbade perjury, while the New Law proscribed even swearing; the Old Law forbade a man to cast off his

---

[18] *Contra Faust.*, XIX, 28 (PL 42, 366). [19] *Op. cit.*, XIX, 23 (PL 42, 361).
[20] Cf. Pseudo-Chrysostom, *Op. Imperf. in Matt.*, hom. X, super V, 19 (PG 56, 687).

wife without a bill of divorce, while the New Law forbade divorce altogether, as is clearly stated in *Matt.* v. 31 *seqq.*, according to Augustine's exposition.[21] Therefore the New Law is more burdensome than the Old.

On the contrary, It is written (*Matt.* xi. 28): *Come to Me, all you that labor and are burdened*; which words are expounded by Hilary thus: *He calls to Himself all those that labor under the difficulty of observing the Law, and are burdened with the sins of this world.*[22] And further on He says of the yoke of the Gospel: *For My yoke is sweet and My burden light* (*Matt.* xi. 30). Therefore the New Law is a lighter burden than the Old.

I answer that, A twofold difficulty may attach to works of virtue with which the precepts of the Law are concerned. One is on the part of the outward works, which of themselves are, in a way, difficult and burdensome. And in this respect the Old Law is a much heavier burden than the New, since the Old Law by its numerous ceremonies prescribed many more outward acts than the New Law, which, in the teaching of Christ and the apostles, added very few precepts to those of the natural law; although afterwards some were added, through being instituted by the holy Fathers. Even in these Augustine says that moderation should be observed, lest good conduct should become a burden to the faithful. For he says, in reply to the queries of Januarius, that, *whereas God in His mercy wished religion to be a free service rendered by the public solemnization of a small number of most manifest sacraments, certain persons make it a slave's burden; so much so, that the state of the Jews who were subject to the sacraments of the Law, and not to the presumptuous devices of man, was more tolerable.*[23]

The other difficulty attaches to works of virtue as to interior acts; *e.g.*, that a virtuous deed be done with promptitude and pleasure. It is this difficulty that virtue solves, because to act thus is difficult for a man without virtue, but through virtue it becomes easy to him. In this respect the precepts of the New Law are more burdensome than those of the Old, because the New Law prohibits certain interior movements of the soul, which were not expressly forbidden in the Old Law in all cases, although they were forbidden in some, without, however, any punishment being attached to the prohibition. Now this is very difficult to a man without virtue. And so the Philosopher also states that it is easy to do what a just man does, but that to do it in the same way, viz., with pleasure and promptitude, is difficult to a man who is not just.[24] Accordingly, we read likewise (*1 John* v. 3) that *His commandments are not heavy*; which words Augustine expounds by saying that *they are not heavy to the man that loveth; whereas they are a burden to him that loveth not.*[25]

---

[21] *De Serm. Dom.*, I, 14 (PL 34, 1248); *Contra Faust.*, XIX, 23; 26 (PL 42, 361; 364). [22] *In Matt.*, super XI, 28 (PL 9, 984). [23] *Epist.* LV, 19 (PL 33, 221). [24] *Eth.*, V, 9 (1137a 5). [25] *De Nat. et Grat.*, LXIX (PL 44, 289); *De Perfect. Iust.*, X (PL 44, 302).

Reply Obj. 1. The passage quoted speaks expressly of the difficulty of the New Law as to the deliberate curbing of interior movements.

Reply Obj. 2. The tribulations suffered by those who observe the New Law are not imposed by the Law itself. Moreover, they are easily borne because of the love in which the same Law consists; since, as Augustine says, *love makes light and nothing of things that seem arduous and beyond our power.*[26]

Reply Obj. 3. The object of these additions to the precepts of the Old Law was to render it easier to do what it prescribed, as Augustine states.[27] Accordingly, this does not prove that the New Law is more burdensome, but rather that it is a lighter burden.

[26] *Serm.* LXX, 3 (PL 38, 444). [27] *De Serm. Dom.,* I, 17; 21 (PL 34, 1256; 1265); *Contra Faust.,* XIX, 23; 26 (PL 42, 362; 365).

ON THOSE THINGS THAT ARE CONTAINED IN THE NEW LAW
(*In Four Articles*)

WE must now consider those things that are contained in the New Law, under which head there are four points of inquiry: (1) Whether the New Law ought to prescribe or to forbid any outward works? (2) Whether the New Law makes sufficient provision in prescribing and forbidding external acts? (3) Whether in the matter of internal acts it directs man sufficiently? (4) Whether it adds counsels to precepts in a fitting way?

First Article

WHETHER THE NEW LAW OUGHT TO PRESCRIBE OR PROHIBIT ANY EXTERNAL ACTS?

We proceed thus to the First Article:—

Objection 1. It would seem that the New Law should not prescribe or prohibit any external acts. For the New Law is the Gospel of the kingdom, according to *Matt.* xxiv. 14: *This Gospel of the kingdom shall be preached in the whole world.* But the kingdom of God consists, not in exterior, but only in interior acts, according to *Luke* xvii. 21: *The kingdom of God is within you;* and *Rom.* xiv. 17: *The kingdom of God is not meat and drink, but justice and peace and joy in the Holy Ghost.* Therefore the New Law should not prescribe or forbid any external acts.

Obj. 2. Further, the New Law is *the law of the Spirit* (*Rom.* viii. 2). But *where the Spirit of the Lord is, there is liberty* (*2 Cor.* iii. 17). Now there is no liberty when man is bound to do or avoid certain external acts. Therefore the New Law does not prescribe or forbid any external acts.

Obj. 3. Further, all external acts are understood as referable to the hand, just as interior acts belong to the soul. But this is assigned as the difference between the New and Old Laws, that the *Old Law restrains the hand, whereas the New Law restrains the soul.*[1] Therefore the New Law should not contain prohibitions and commands about external acts, but only about interior acts.

On the contrary, Through the New Law, men are made *children of light;* and so it is written (*Jo.* xii. 36): *Believe in the light that you may be the children of light.* Now it is becoming that children of light should do deeds of light and cast aside deeds of darkness, according to *Ephes.*

---

[1] Cf. Peter Lombard, *Sent.*, III, xl, 1 (II, 734).

v. 8: *You were heretofore darkness, but now light in the Lord. Walk . . . as children of the light.* Therefore the New Law had to forbid certain external acts and prescribe others.

I answer that, As we have stated above, the New Law consists chiefly in the grace of the Holy Ghost, which is shown forth by faith that worketh through love.[2] Now men become receivers of this grace through God's Son made man, Whose humanity grace filled first, and thence flowed forth to us. Hence it is written (*Jo.* i. 14): *The Word was made flesh,* and afterwards: *full of grace and truth*; and further on: *Of His fullness we all have received, and grace for grace.* Hence it is added that *grace and truth came by Jesus Christ.* Consequently, it was becoming that the grace which flows from the incarnate Word should be given to us by means of certain external sensible objects; and that from this inward grace, whereby the flesh is subjected to the Spirit, certain external works should ensue.

Accordingly, external acts may have a twofold connection with grace. In the first place, as leading in some way to grace. Such are the sacramental acts which are instituted in the New Law, *e.g.,* Baptism, the Eucharist, and the like.

In the second place, there are those external acts which ensue from the promptings of grace; and in these we must observe a difference. For there are some which are necessarily in keeping with, or in opposition to, inward grace, which consists in faith that works through love. Such external works are prescribed or forbidden in the New Law. Thus confession of faith is prescribed, and denial of faith is forbidden; for it is written (*Matt.* x. 32, 33): *[Every one] that shall confess Me before men, I will also confess him before My Father. . . . But he that shall deny Me before men, I will also deny him before My Father.*—On the other hand, there are works which are not necessarily opposed to, or in keeping with, faith that works through love. Such works are not prescribed or forbidden in the New Law by virtue of its primitive institution; they have been left by the Lawgiver, *i.e.,* Christ, to the discretion of each individual. And so to each one it is free to decide what he should do or avoid; and to each superior, to direct his subjects in such matters as regards what they must do or avoid. Therefore, in this respect also the Gospel is called the *law of liberty,* since the Old Law decided many points and left few to man to decide as he chose.

Reply Obj. 1. The kingdom of God consists chiefly in interior acts, but as a consequence all things that are essential to interior acts belong also to the kingdom of God. Thus, if the kingdom of God is interior justice, peace and spiritual joy, all external acts that are incompatible with justice, peace and spiritual joy are in opposition to the kingdom of God, and consequently should be forbidden in the Gospel of the kingdom. On the other hand, those things that are indifferent as regards the aforesaid, for

---

[2] Q. 106, a. 1 and 2.

instance, to eat of this or that food, are not part of the kingdom of God; and so the Apostle says before the words quoted: *The kingdom of God is not meat and drink.*

Reply Obj. 2. According to the Philosopher, what is *free is for the sake of itself.*[3] Therefore he acts freely, who acts of his own accord. Now man does of his own accord that which he does from a habit that is suitable to his nature, since a habit inclines after the manner of a nature. If, however, a habit be in opposition to nature, man would not act according to his nature, but according to some corruption affecting that nature. Since, then, the grace of the Holy Ghost is like an interior habit bestowed on us and inclining us to act rightly, it makes us do freely those things that are becoming to grace, and shun what is opposed to it.

Accordingly, the New Law is called the law of liberty in two respects. First, because it does not bind us to do or avoid certain things, except such as are of themselves necessary or opposed to salvation, and come under the prescription or prohibition of the law. Secondly, because it also makes us comply freely with these precepts and prohibitions, inasmuch as we do so through the promptings of grace. It is for these two reasons that the New Law is called *the law of perfect liberty* (*Jas.* i. 25).

Reply Obj. 3. The New Law, by restraining the soul from inordinate movements, must needs also restrain the hand from inordinate acts, which ensue from inward movements.

Second Article

WHETHER THE NEW LAW MADE SUFFICIENT ORDINATIONS
ABOUT EXTERNAL ACTS?

We proceed thus to the Second Article:—

Objection 1. It would seem that the New Law made insufficient ordinations about external acts. For faith that works through charity seems chiefly to belong to the New Law, according to *Gal.* v. 6: *In Christ Jesus neither circumcision availeth anything, nor uncircumcision, but faith that worketh through charity.* But the New Law declared explicitly certain points of faith which were not set forth explicitly in the Old Law: *e.g.*, belief in the Trinity. Therefore it should also have added certain outward moral deeds, which were not fixed in the Old Law.

Obj. 2. Further, in the Old Law not only sacraments were instituted, but also certain sacred things, as was stated above.[4] But in the New Law, although certain sacraments are instituted, yet no sacred things seem to have been instituted by Our Lord (pertaining, for instance, either to the sanctification of a temple or of the vessels, or to the celebration of some particular feast). Therefore the New Law made insufficient ordinations about external matters.

[3] *Metaph.*, I, 2 (982b 26).   [4] Q. 101, a. 4; q. 102, a. 4.

Obj. 3. Further, in the Old Law, just as there were certain observances pertaining to God's ministers, so also were there certain observances pertaining to the people, as was stated above when we were treating of the ceremonial of the Old Law.[5] Now in the New Law certain observances seem to have been prescribed for the ministers of God, as may be gathered from *Matt.* x. 9: *Do not possess gold, nor silver, nor money in your purses,* nor other things which are mentioned here and *Luke* ix. and x. Therefore certain observances pertaining to the faithful should also have been instituted in the New Law.

Obj. 4. Further, in the Old Law, besides moral and ceremonial precepts, there were certain judicial precepts. But in the New Law there are no judicial precepts. Therefore the New Law made insufficient ordinations about external works.

On the contrary, Our Lord said (*Matt.* vii. 24): *Every one . . . that heareth these My words, and doth them, shall be likened to a wise man that built his house upon a rock.* But a wise builder leaves out nothing that is necessary to the building. Therefore Christ's words contain all things necessary for man's salvation.

I answer that, As we have stated above, the New Law had to make such prescriptions or prohibitions alone as are essential for the reception or the right use of grace. And since we cannot of ourselves obtain grace, but through Christ alone, hence Christ of Himself instituted the sacraments whereby we obtain grace: viz., Baptism, Eucharist, Orders of the ministers of the New Law (by the institution of the apostles and seventy-two disciples), Penance, and indissoluble Matrimony. He promised Confirmation through the sending of the Holy Ghost, and we read that by His institution the apostles healed the sick by anointing them with oil (*Mark* vi. 13). These are the sacraments of the New Law.

The right use of grace is by means of works of charity. These, in so far as they are essential to virtue, pertain to the moral precepts, which also formed part of the Old Law. Hence, in this respect, the New Law had nothing to add as regards external action.—The determination of these works in their relation to divine worship belongs to the ceremonial precepts of the Law; and, in relation to our neighbor, to the judicial precepts, as was stated above.[6] Therefore, since these determinations are not in themselves necessarily connected with inward grace, wherein the Law consists, they do not come under a precept of the New Law, but are left to the decision of man. Some of these determinations relate to subjects, as when a precept is given to an individual; others, to superiors, temporal or spiritual, those, namely, that pertain to the common good.

Accordingly, the New Law had no other external works to determine, by prescribing or forbidding, except the sacraments and those moral precepts

[5] Q. 101, a. 4; q. 102, a. 6.   [6] Q. 99, a. 4.

which pertain to the nature of virtue, for instance, that one must not kill, or steal, and so forth.

Reply Obj. 1. Matters of faith are above human reason, and so we cannot attain to them except through grace. Consequently, when grace came to be bestowed more abundantly, the result was an increase in the number of explicit points of faith. On the other hand, it is through human reason that we are directed to works of virtue, for it is a rule of human action, as was stated above.[7] Therefore, in such matters as these, there was no need for any precepts to be given beyond the moral precepts of the Law, which proceed from the dictate of reason.

Reply Obj. 2. In the sacraments of the New Law, grace is bestowed, which cannot be received except through Christ. Consequently, they had to be instituted by Him. But in the sacred things no grace is given: for instance, in the consecration of a temple, an altar or the like, or, again, in the celebration of the feasts. Therefore our Lord left the institution of such things to the discretion of the faithful, since they have not, of themselves, any necessary connection with inward grace.

Reply Obj. 3. Our Lord gave the apostles those precepts, not as ceremonial observances, but as moral statutes. Now they can be understood in two ways. First, following Augustine, as being, not commands, but permissions.[8] For He permitted them to set forth to preach without scrip or stick, and the like, as being empowered to accept their livelihood from those to whom they preached; and so He goes on to say: *For the laborer is worthy of his hire* (*Luke* x. 7). Nor is it a sin, but a work of supererogation, for a preacher to take the means of livelihood with him, without accepting payment from those to whom he preaches, as Paul did (*1 Cor.* ix. 4, *seqq.*).

Secondly, according to the explanation of other holy men,[9] they may be considered as temporal commands laid upon the apostles for the time during which they were sent to preach in Judea before Christ's Passion. For the disciples, being yet as little children under Christ's care, needed to receive some special commands from Christ, such as all subjects receive from their superiors; and especially so, since they were to be accustomed little by little to renounce the care of temporal things, so as to become fitted for the preaching of the Gospel throughout the whole world. Nor must we wonder if He established certain fixed modes of life, as long as the state of the Old Law endured and the people had not as yet achieved the perfect liberty of the Spirit. These statutes He abolished shortly before His Passion, as though the disciples had by their means become sufficiently practised. Hence He said (*Luke* xxii. 35, 26): *When I sent you without purse and scrip and shoes, did you want anything? But they said: Noth-*

---

[7] Q. 19, a. 3; q. 63, a. 2.   [8] *De Consensu Evang.*, XXX (PL 34, 1114).   [9] Cf. St. John Chrysostom, *Hom. II, In Rom.* XVI, 3, hom. 2 (PG 51, 199); St. Bede, *In Luc.*, VI, super XXII, 35 (PL 92, 601).

ing. Then said He unto them: But now, he that hath a purse, let him take it, and likewise a scrip. For the time of perfect liberty was already at hand, when they would be left entirely to their own judgment in matters not necessarily connected with virtue.

Reply Obj. 4. Considered in themselves, judicial precepts likewise are not essential to virtue in respect of any particular determination, but only in regard to the common notion of justice. Consequently, Our Lord left the judicial precepts to the discretion of those who were to have spiritual or temporal charge of others. But as regards the judicial precepts of the Old Law, some of them He explained, because they were misunderstood by the Pharisees, as we shall state later on.

Third Article

WHETHER THE NEW LAW DIRECTED MAN SUFFICIENTLY AS REGARDS INTERIOR ACTIONS?

We proceed thus to the Third Article:—

Objection 1. It would seem that the New Law directed man insufficiently as regards interior actions. For there are ten commandments of the decalogue directing man to God and his neighbor. But Our Lord partly fulfilled only three of them, namely, with reference to the prohibition of murder, of adultery and of perjury. Therefore it seems that, by omitting to fulfill the other precepts, He directed man insufficiently.

Obj. 2. Further, as regards the judicial precepts, our Lord ordained nothing in the Gospel, except in the matter of divorcing a wife, of punishment by retaliation and of persecuting one's enemies. But there are many other judicial precepts of the Old Law, as was stated above.[10] Therefore, in this respect, He directed human life insufficiently.

Obj. 3. Further, in the Old Law, besides moral and judicial precepts, there were ceremonial precepts, about which Our Lord made no ordination. Therefore it seems that He ordained insufficiently.

Obj. 4. Further, in order that the mind be inwardly well disposed, man should do no good deed for any temporal end whatever. But there are many other temporal goods besides the favor of man, and there are many other good works besides fasting, alms-giving and prayer. Therefore Our Lord unbecomingly taught that only in respect of these three works, and of no other earthly goods, ought we to shun the glory of human favor.

Obj. 5. Further, solicitude for the necessary means of livelihood is instilled into man by nature, and this solicitude even other animals share with man; and so it is written (*Prov.* vi. 6, 8): *Go to the ant, O sluggard, and consider her ways . . . she provideth her meat for herself in the summer, and gathereth her food in the harvest.* But every command issued against the inclination of nature is an unjust command, inasmuch as it is contrary

[10] Q. 104, a. 4; q. 105.

to the law of nature. Therefore it seems that Our Lord unbecomingly forbade solicitude about food and raiment.

Obj. 6. Further, no act of virtue should be the subject of a prohibition. Now judgment is an act of justice, according to *Ps.* xciii. 15: *Until justice be turned into judgment.* Therefore it seems that Our Lord unbecomingly forbade judgment, and consequently that the New Law directed man insufficiently in the matter of interior acts.

On the contrary, Augustine says: *We should take note that, when He said: 'He that heareth these My words,' He indicates clearly that this sermon of the Lord is replete with all the precepts whereby a Christian's life is formed.*[11]

I answer that, As is evident from Augustine's words just quoted, the sermon which Our Lord delivered on the mountain contains the whole formation of the life of a Christian. Therein man's interior movements are ordered. For after declaring that his end is beatitude, and after commending the authority of the apostles, through whom the teaching of the Gospel was to be promulgated, He orders man's interior movements, first, in regard to man himself, secondly, in regard to his neighbor.

This he does in regard to man himself in two ways, corresponding to man's two interior movements in relation to any prospective action, viz., the volition of what has to be done, and the intention of the end. Therefore, in the first place, He orders man's will in relation to the various precepts of the Law, by prescribing that man should refrain not merely from those external works that are evil in themselves, but also from internal acts, and from the occasions of evil deeds. In the second place, He orders man's intention by teaching that, in our good works, we should seek neither human praise, nor worldly riches, which is to lay up treasures on earth.

Afterwards, He orders man's interior movement in relation to his neighbor, by forbidding us, on the one hand, to judge him rashly, unjustly, or presumptuously; and, on the other, to entrust him too readily with sacred things if he be unworthy.

Lastly, He teaches us how to fulfill the teaching of the Gospel, viz., by imploring the help of God, by striving to enter by the narrow door of perfect virtue, and by being wary lest we be led astray by evil influences. Moreover, He declares that we must observe His commandments, and that it is not enough to make profession of faith, or to work miracles, or merely to hear His words.

Reply Obj. 1. Our Lord explained the manner of fulfilling those precepts which the Scribes and Pharisees did not rightly understand; and this affected chiefly those three precepts of the decalogue. For they thought that the prohibition of adultery and murder covered the external act only, and not the internal desire. And they held this opinion about murder and adultery rather than about theft and false witness, because the movement

[11] *De Serm. Dom.,* I, 1 (PL 34, 1231).

of anger tending to murder, and the movement of desire tending to adultery, seem to be in us to some extent from nature, but not the desire of stealing or of bearing false witness.—They held a false opinion about perjury, for they thought that perjury indeed was a sin, but that oaths were of themselves to be desired and to be taken frequently, since they seem to proceed from reverence to God. Hence our Lord shows that an oath is not desirable as a good thing; and that it is better to speak without oaths, unless necessity forces us to have recourse to them.

Reply Obj. 2. The Scribes and Pharisees erred about the judicial precepts in two ways. First, because they considered certain matters, contained in the Law of Moses by way of permission, to be right in themselves: namely, divorce of a wife, and the taking of usury from strangers. Therefore our Lord forbade a man to divorce his wife (*Matt.* v. 32); and to receive usury (*Luke* vi. 35), when He said: *Lend, hoping for nothing thereby.*

In another way they erred by thinking that certain things, which the Old Law commanded to be done for justice's sake, should be done out of desire for revenge, or out of lust for temporal goods, or out of hatred of one's enemies; and this in respect of three precepts. For they thought that desire for revenge was lawful because of the precept concerning punishment by retaliation; whereas this precept was given that justice might be safeguarded, not that man might seek revenge. Therefore, in order to do away with this, Our Lord teaches that man should be prepared in his mind to suffer yet more if necessary.—They thought, too, that movements of covetousness were lawful, because of those judicial precepts which prescribed restitution of what had been purloined, together with something added thereto, as was stated above;[12] whereas the Law commanded this to be done in order to safeguard justice, not to encourage covetousness. Therefore Our Lord teaches that we should not demand our goods from motives of cupidity, and that we should be ready to give yet more if necessary.—They thought that the movement of hatred was lawful, because of the commandments of the Law about the slaying of one's enemies; whereas the Law ordered this for the fulfillment of justice, as was stated above,[13] not to satisfy hatred. Therefore Our Lord teaches us that we ought to love our enemies, and to be ready to do good to them if necessary. For these precepts are to be taken as binding *the mind to be prepared to fulfill them,* as Augustine says.[14]

Reply Obj. 3. The moral precepts necessarily retained their force under the New Law, because they belong of themselves to the nature of virtue; whereas the judicial precepts did not necessarily continue to bind in exactly the same way as had been fixed by the Law, but this was left to man to decide in one way or another. Hence Our Lord directed us becomingly with regard to these two kinds of precepts. On the other hand, the

[12] Q. 105, a. 2, ad 9.   [13] Q. 105, a. 3, ad 4.   [14] *De Serm. Dom.,* I, 19 (PL 34, 1260).

observance of the ceremonial precepts was totally abolished by the advent of the reality; and so, in regard to these precepts, He commanded nothing on this occasion when He was giving the general points of His doctrine. Elsewhere, however, He makes it clear that the entire bodily worship which was fixed by the Law was to be changed into a spiritual worship, as is evident from *John* iv. 21, 23, where He says: *The hour cometh when you shall neither on this mountain, nor in Jerusalem, adore the Father . . . but . . . the true adorers shall adore the Father in spirit and in truth.*

Reply Obj. 4. All worldly goods may be reduced to three, namely, honors, riches and pleasures, according to *1 John* ii. 16: *All that is in the world is the concupiscence of the flesh,* which refers to pleasures of the flesh, *and the concupiscence of the eyes,* which refers to riches, *and the pride of life,* which refers to ambition for renown and honor. Now the Law did not promise an abundance of carnal pleasures; on the contrary, it forbade them. But it did promise exalted honors and abundant riches; for it is written in reference to the former (*Deut.* xxviii. 1): *If thou wilt hear the voice of the Lord thy God, . . .* He *will make thee higher than all the nations*; and in reference to the latter, we read a little further on (*verse* 11): He *will make thee abound with all goods.* But the Jews so distorted the true meaning of these promises, as to think that we ought to serve God with these things as the end in view. Therefore Our Lord set this aside by teaching, first of all, that works of virtue should not be done for human glory. And He mentions three works to which all others may be reduced, since whatever a man does in order to curb his desires comes under the head of fasting; and whatever a man does for the love of his neighbor comes under the head of alms-giving; and whatever a man does for the worship of God comes under the head of prayer. He mentions these three especially, as they hold the principal place, and are most often used by men in order to gain glory.—In the second place, He taught us that we must not place our end in riches, when He said: *Lay not up to yourselves treasures on earth* (*Matt.* vi. 19).

Reply Obj. 5. Our Lord forbade, not necessary, but inordinate solicitude. Now there is a fourfold solicitude to be avoided in temporal matters. First, we must not place our end in them, nor serve God for the sake of the necessities of food and raiment. Therefore He says: *Lay not up for yourselves,* etc. Secondly, we must not be so anxious about temporal things as to despair of God's help; and so Our Lord says (*ibid.* 32): *Your Father knoweth that you have need of all these things.* Thirdly, we must not add presumption to our solicitude; in other words, we must not be confident of getting the necessaries of life by our own efforts without God's help. Such solicitude Our Lord sets aside by saying that a man cannot add anything to his stature (*ibid.* 27). Fourthly, we must not anticipate the time of anxiety, namely, by being solicitous now for the needs, not of the

present, but of a future time; and so He says (*ibid.* 34): *Be not . . .
solicitous for to-morrow.*

Reply Obj. 6. Our Lord did not forbid the judgment of justice, without
which holy things could not be withdrawn from the unworthy. But he
forbade inordinate judgment, as was stated above.

Fourth Article

WHETHER CERTAIN DEFINITE COUNSELS ARE FITTINGLY
PROPOSED IN THE NEW LAW?

We proceed thus to the Fourth Article:—

Objection 1. It would seem that certain definite counsels are not fittingly proposed in the New Law. For counsels are given about that which
is expedient for an end, as we stated above, when treating of counsel.[15]
But the same things are not expedient for all. Therefore certain definite
counsels should not be proposed to all.

Obj. 2. Further, counsels regard a greater good. But there are no definite
degrees of the greater good. Therefore definite counsels should not be given.

Obj. 3. Further, counsels pertain to the perfection of life. But obedience
pertains to the perfection of life. Therefore it was unfitting that no counsel
of obedience should be contained in the Gospel.

Obj. 4. Further, many matters pertaining to the perfection of life are
found among the commandments, as, for instance, *Love your enemies*
(*Matt.* v. 44), and those precepts which Our Lord gave His apostles (*ibid.*
x.). Therefore the counsels are unfittingly given in the New Law, both
because they are not all mentioned, and because they are not distinguished
from the commandments.

On the contrary, The counsels of a wise friend are of great use, according to *Prov.* xxvii. 9: *Ointment and perfumes rejoice the heart; and the
good counsels of a friend rejoice the soul.* But Christ is our wisest and
greatest friend. Therefore His counsels are supremely useful and becoming.

I answer that, The difference between a counsel and a commandment is
that a commandment implies obligation, whereas a counsel is left to the
option of the one to whom it is given. So in the New Law, which is the law of
liberty, counsels are fittingly added to the commandments, but not in the
Old Law, which is the law of bondage. We must therefore understand the
commandments of the New Law to have been given about matters that are
necessary to gain the end of eternal beatitude, to which end the New Law
brings us forthwith; but that the counsels are about matters that render the
gaining of this end more assured and expeditious.

Now man is placed between the things of this world and spiritual goods,
wherein eternal happiness consists; so that the more he cleaves to the one,
the more he withdraws from the other, and conversely. Therefore he that

[15] Q. 14, a. 2.

cleaves wholly to the things of this world, so as to make them his end, and to look upon them as the reason and rule of all he does, falls away altogether from spiritual goods. Hence this disorder is removed by the commandments. Nevertheless, for man to gain the aforesaid end, he does not need to renounce the things of the world altogether, since he can, while using the things of this world, attain to eternal happiness, provided he does not place his end in them. But he will attain more speedily thereto by giving up the goods of this world entirely; and that is why the evangelical counsels are given.

Now the goods of this world, which come into use in human life, consist in three things, viz., in external wealth, pertaining to the *concupiscence of the eyes,* in carnal pleasures, pertaining to the *concupiscence of the flesh,* and in honors, which pertain to the *pride of life,* according to *1 John* ii. 16; and it is in renouncing these three altogether, as far as possible, that the evangelical counsels consist. Moreover, every form of the religious life that professes the state of perfection is based on these three; for riches are renounced by poverty, carnal pleasures by perpetual chastity, and the pride of life by the bondage of obedience.

Now if a man observe these absolutely, this is in accordance with the counsels as they stand. But if a man observe any one of them in a particular case, this is taking that counsel in a restricted sense, namely, as applying to that particular case. For instance, when anyone gives an alms to a poor man, not being bound so to do, he follows the counsels in that particular case. In like manner, when a man for some fixed time refrains from carnal pleasures that he may give himself to prayer, he follows the counsel for that particular time. And again, when a man follows not his will as to some deed which he might do lawfully, he follows the counsel in that particular case: for instance, if he does good to his enemies when he is not bound to, or if he forgives an injury of which he might justly seek to be avenged. In this way, too, all particular counsels may be reduced to these three general and perfect counsels.

Reply Obj. 1. The aforesaid counsels, considered in themselves, are expedient to all, but because some people are ill-disposed, it happens that they are inexpedient to some of them, because their disposition is not inclined to such things. Hence Our Lord, in proposing the evangelical counsels, always makes mention of man's fitness for observing the counsels. For in giving the counsel of perpetual poverty (*Matt.* xix. 21), He begins with the words: *If thou wilt be perfect,* and then He adds: *Go, sell all thou hast.* In like manner, when He gave the counsel of perpetual chastity, saying (*ibid.,* 12): *There are eunuchs who have made themselves eunuchs for the kingdom of heaven,* He added straightway: *He that can take, let him take it.* And, again, the Apostle (*1 Cor.* vii. 35), after giving the counsel of virginity, says: *And this I speak for your profit, not to cast a snare upon you.*

Reply Obj. 2. The greater goods are not definitely fixed in the particular, but the goods which are unqualifiedly and absolutely greater in the universal, are fixed; and to these all the above particular goods may be reduced, as was stated above.

Reply Obj. 3. Even the counsel of obedience is understood to have been given by Our Lord in the words: *And* [let him] *follow Me* (*Matt.* xvi. 24). For we follow Him not only by imitating His works, but also by obeying His commandments, according to *John* x. 27: *My sheep hear My voice . . . and they follow Me.*

Reply Obj. 4. Those things which Our Lord prescribed about the true love of our enemies, and other similar sayings (*Matt.* v. and *Luke* vi.), may be referred to the preparation of the mind, and then they are necessary for salvation; for instance, that man be prepared to do good to his enemies, and other similar actions, when there is need. Hence these things are placed among the precepts. But that anyone should actually and promptly behave thus towards an enemy when there is no special need, is to be referred to the particular counsels, as was stated above.—As to those matters which are set down in *Matt.* x. and *Luke* ix. and x., they were either disciplinary commands for that particular time, or concessions, as was stated above. Hence they are not set down among the counsels.

TREATISE ON GRACE

Question CIX

ON THE EXTERIOR PRINCIPLE OF HUMAN ACTS, NAMELY, THE GRACE OF GOD

(*In Ten Articles*)

WE must now consider the exterior principle of human acts, *i.e.*, God, in so far as, through grace, we are helped by Him to do the right. First, we must consider the grace of God; secondly, its cause;[1] thirdly, its effects.[2]

The first point of consideration will be threefold, for we shall consider (1) the necessity of grace; (2) grace itself, as to its essence;[3] (3) its division.[4]

Under the first head there are ten points of inquiry (1) Whether without grace man can know any truth? (2) Whether without God's grace man can do or will any good? (3) Whether without grace man can love God above all things? (4) Whether without grace man can keep the commandments of the Law through his natural powers? (5) Whether without grace he can merit eternal life? (6) Whether without grace man can prepare himself for grace? (7) Whether without grace he can rise from sin? (8) Whether without grace man can avoid sin? (9) Whether man, having received grace, can do good and avoid sin without any further divine help? (10) Whether he can of himself persevere in good?

First Article

WHETHER WITHOUT GRACE MAN CAN KNOW ANY TRUTH?

We proceed thus to the First Article:—

Objection 1. It would seem that without grace man can know no truth. For on *1 Cor.* xii. 3 (*No man can say, the Lord Jesus, but by the Holy Ghost*) the *Gloss* of Ambrose says: *Every truth, by whomsoever spoken, is from the Holy Ghost.*[5] Now the Holy Ghost dwells in us by grace. Therefore we cannot know truth without grace.

Obj. 2. Further, Augustine says that *the most certain sciences are like things lit up by the sun so as to be seen.* Now God Himself is He Who *illumines, while reason is in the mind as sight is in the eye, and the eyes*

---

[1] Q. 112.   [2] Q. 113.   [3] Q. 110.   [4] Q. 111.   [5] Peter Lombard, *In I Cor.*, super XII, 3 (PL 191, 1651); cf. *Glossa ordin.* (VI, 52A).

of the mind are the senses of the soul.[6] Now the bodily senses, however pure, cannot see any visible thing without the sun's light. Therefore the human mind, however perfect, cannot, by reasoning, know any truth without divine light; and this pertains to the aid of grace.

Obj. 3. Further, the human mind can understand truth only by thinking, as is clear from Augustine.[7] But the Apostle says (*2 Cor.* iii. 5): *Not that we are sufficient to think anything of ourselves, as of ourselves; but our sufficiency is from God.* Therefore man cannot, of himself, know truth without the help of grace.

On the contrary, Augustine says *I do not approve having said in the prayer: O God, Who dost wish the sinless alone to know the truth; for it may be answered that many who are not sinless know many truths.*[8] Now man is cleansed from sin by grace, according to *Ps.* l. 12: *Create a clean heart in me, O God, and renew a right spirit within my bowels.* Therefore without grace man of himself can know truth.

I answer that, To know truth is a certain use or act of intellectual light, since, according to the Apostle (*Ephes.* v. 13): *All that is made manifest is light.* Now every use implies some movement, taking movement broadly, so as to call thinking and willing movements, as is clear from the Philosopher.[9] But in corporeal things we see that for movement there is required not merely the form which is the principle of the movement or action, but also the motion of the first mover. Now the first mover in the order of corporeal things is the body of the heavens. Hence no matter how perfectly fire has heat, it would not bring about alteration, except by the motion of the body of the heavens. But it is clear that, just as all corporeal movements are reduced to the motion of the body of the heavens as to the first corporeal mover, so all movements, both corporeal and spiritual, are reduced to the absolutely First Mover, Who is God. And hence no matter how perfect a corporeal or spiritual nature is supposed to be, it cannot proceed to its act unless it be moved by God. Now this motion is according to the plan of His providence, and not by a necessity of nature, as the motion of the body of the heavens. But not only is every motion from God as from the First Mover, but all formal perfection is from Him as from the First Act. Hence the action of the intellect, or of any created being whatsoever, depends upon God in two ways: first, inasmuch as it is from Him that it has the form whereby it acts; secondly, inasmuch as it is moved by Him to act.

Now every form bestowed on created things by God has power for a determined act, which it can effect in proportion to its own proper endowment; and beyond this act it is powerless, except by a superadded form, as water can heat only when heated by the fire. And thus, the human understanding has a form, viz., intelligible light itself, which of itself is

---

[6] *Solil.,* I, 6 (PL 32, 875).   [7] *De Trin.,* XIV, 7 (PL 42, 1043).   [8] *Retract.,* I, 4 (PL 32, 589).   [9] *De An.,* III, 4 (429b 25) ; 7 (431a 4).

sufficient for knowing certain intelligible truths, viz., those we can come to know through sensible things. Higher intelligible truths the human intellect cannot know, unless it be perfected by a stronger light, viz., the light of faith or of prophecy, which is called the *light of grace,* inasmuch as it is added to nature.

Hence we must say that for the knowledge of any truth whatsoever man needs divine help in order that the intellect may be moved by God to its act. But he does not need a new illumination added to his natural light in order to know the truth in all things, but only in those that surpass his natural knowledge. And yet at times God miraculously instructs some by His grace in things that can be known by natural reason, even as He sometimes brings about miraculously what nature can do.

Reply Obj. 1. Every truth, by whomsoever spoken, is from the Holy Ghost as bestowing the natural light, and moving us to understand and to speak the truth; but not as dwelling in us by sanctifying grace, or as bestowing any habitual gift superadded to nature. For this takes place only with regard to knowing and speaking certain truths, and especially in regard to such as pertain to faith, of which the Apostle was speaking.

Reply Obj. 2. The material sun sheds its light outside us, but the intelligible Sun, Who is God, shines within us. Hence the natural light bestowed upon the soul is God's illumination, whereby we are illumined to see what pertains to natural knowledge; and for this there is required no further illumination, but only for such things as surpass natural knowledge.

Reply Obj. 3. We always need God's help for every thought, inasmuch as He moves the intellect to act; for to understand anything actually is to think, as is clear from Augustine.[10]

Second Article

WHETHER MAN CAN WILL OR DO ANY GOOD WITHOUT GRACE?

We proceed thus to the Second Article:—

Objection 1. It would seem that man can will and do good without grace. For that is in man's power of which he is master. Now man is master of his acts, and especially of his willing, as was stated above.[11] Hence man, of himself, can will and do good without the help of grace.

Obj. 2. Further, any being has more power over what is according to its nature than over what is beyond its nature. Now sin is against nature, as Damascene says;[12] whereas the work of virtue is according to the nature of men, as was stated above.[13] Therefore, since man can sin of himself, much more would it seem that of himself he can will and do good.

---

[10] *De Trin.,* XIV, 7 (PL 42, 1043).   [11] Q. 1, a. 1; q. 13, a. 6.   [12] *De Fide Orth.,* II, 4; 30 (PG 94, 876; 976); cf. *op. cit.,* IV, 20 (PG 94, 1196).   [13] Q. 71, a. 1.

Obj. 3. Further, the good of the intellect is truth, as the Philosopher says.[14] Now the intellect can of itself know truth, even as every other thing can perform its natural operation of itself. Therefore, much more can man, of himself, do and will good.

On the contrary, The Apostle says (*Rom.* ix. 16): *It is not of him that willeth,* namely, to will, *nor of him that runneth,* namely, to run, *but of God that showeth mercy.* And Augustine says that *without grace men do nothing good when they either think or will or love or act.*[15]

I answer that, Man's nature may be looked at in two ways: first, in its integrity, as it was in our first parent before sin; secondly, as it is corrupted in us after the sin of our first parent. Now in both states human nature needs the help of God, as First Mover, to do or will any good whatsoever, as was stated above. But in the state of integrity of nature, as regards the sufficiency of operative power, man by his natural endowments could will and do the good proportioned to his nature, which is the good of acquired virtue; but he could not do the good that exceeded his nature, which is the good of infused virtue. But in the state of corrupted nature, man falls short even of what he can do by his nature, so that he is unable to fulfill all of it by his own natural powers. Yet because human nature is not altogether corrupted by sin, namely, so as to be shorn of every good of nature, even in the state of corrupted nature it can, by virtue of its natural endowments, perform some particular good, such as to build dwellings, plant vineyards, and the like; yet it cannot do all the good natural to it, so as to fall short in nothing. In the same way, a sick man can of himself make some movements, yet he cannot be perfectly moved with the movement of one in health, unless by the help of medicine he be cured.

Hence in the state of the integrity of nature, man needs a gratuitous strength superadded to natural strength for one reason, viz., in order to do and will supernatural good; but in the state of corrupted nature he needs it for two reasons, viz., in order to be healed and, furthermore, in order to carry out works of supernatural virtue, which are meritorious. Beyond this, in both states man needs the divine help that he may be moved to act well.

Reply Obj. 1. Man is master of his acts, both of his willing and not willing, because of the deliberation of reason, which can be bent to one side or another. And although he is master of his deliberating or not deliberating, yet this can only be by a previous deliberation; and since this cannot go on to infinity, we must come at length to this, that man's free choice is moved by an extrinsic principle, which is above the human mind, namely, by God, as the Philosopher proves in the chapter on *Good Fortune.*[16] Hence the mind even of an uncorrupted man is not so mas-

---

[14] *Eth.*, VI, 2 (1139a 27). [15] *De Corrept. et Grat.*, II (PL 44, 917). [16] Cf. *Eth. Eudem.*, VII, 14 (1248a 14).

ter of its act that it does not need to be moved by God; and much more needy is the free choice of man weakened by sin, whereby it is hindered from good by the corruption of its nature.

Reply Obj. 2. To sin is nothing else than to fail in the good which belongs to any being according to its nature. Now, as every created thing has its being from another, and, considered in itself, is nothing, so does it need to be conserved by another in the good which pertains to its nature. For it can of itself fail in good, even as of itself it can fall into non-existence, unless it is conserved by God.

Reply Obj. 3. Man cannot even know truth without divine help, as was stated above. And yet human nature is more corrupted by sin in regard to the desire for good, than in regard to the knowledge of truth.

Third Article

WHETHER BY HIS OWN NATURAL POWERS AND WITHOUT GRACE MAN CAN LOVE GOD ABOVE ALL THINGS?

We proceed thus to the Third Article:—

Objection 1. It would seem that without grace man cannot love God above all things by his own natural powers. For to love God above all things is the proper and principal act of charity. Now of himself man cannot possess charity, since the *charity of God is poured forth in our hearts by the Holy Ghost Who is given to us,* as it is said *Rom.* v. 5. Therefore man by his natural powers alone cannot love God above all things.

Obj. 2. Further, no nature can rise above itself. But to love anything more than itself is to tend to something above itself. Therefore without the help of grace no created nature can love God above itself.

Obj. 3. Further, to God, Who is the Highest Good, is due the highest love, which is that He be loved above all things. Now without grace man is not capable of giving God the highest love, which is His due; otherwise it would be useless to add grace. Hence man, without grace, cannot love God above all things through his natural powers alone.

On the contrary, As some maintain, man was first made with only natural endowments.[17] In that state it is manifest that he loved God to some extent. But he did not love God equally with himself, or less than himself, or otherwise he would have sinned. Therefore he loved God above himself. Therefore man, by his natural powers alone, can love God more than himself and above all things.

I answer that, As was said above in the First Part, where the various opinions concerning the natural love of the angels were set forth, in the state of integral nature man could, by his natural power, do his connatural good without the addition of any gratuitous gift, though not with-

---

[17] Cf. above, *S. T.,* I, q. 95, a. 1.

out the help of God moving him.[18] Now to love God above all things is natural to man and to every nature, not only rational but irrational, and even inanimate, according to the manner of love which can belong to each creature. The reason for this is that it is natural to all to seek and love things according as they are naturally fit [to be sought and loved] since *all things act according as they are naturally fit,* as is stated in *Physics* ii.[19] Now it is manifest that the good of the part is for the good of the whole. Hence everything, by its natural appetite and love, loves its own proper good because of the common good of the whole universe, which is God. Hence Dionysius says that *God leads everything to the love of Himself.*[20] Hence in the state of integral nature man referred the love of himself and of all other things to the love of God as to its end; and thus he loved God more than himself and above all things. But in the state of corrupted nature man falls short of this in the appetite of his rational will, which, unless it be cured by God's grace, follows its private good, because of the corruption of nature. And so we must say that in the state of integral nature man did not need the gift of grace added to his natural endowments in order to love God above all things naturally, although he needed God's help moving him to it; but in the state of corrupted nature, man needs, even for this, the help of grace healing his nature.

Reply Obj. 1. Charity loves God above all things in a higher way than nature does. For nature loves God above all things inasmuch as He is the beginning and the end of natural good; whereas charity loves Him according as He is the object of beatitude, and inasmuch as man has a spiritual fellowship with God. Moreover, charity adds to the natural love of God a certain quickness and joy, in the same way that every habit of virtue adds to the good act which is done merely by the natural reason of a man who has not the habit of virtue.

Reply Obj. 2. When it is said that no nature can rise above itself, we must not understand this as if it could not be directed to any object above itself; for it is clear that our intellect by its natural knowledge can know things above itself, as is shown in our natural knowledge of God. But we are to understand that nature cannot rise to an act exceeding the proportion of its strength. Now to love God above all things is not such an act, for it is natural to every creature, as was said above.

Reply Obj. 3. Love is said to be highest not only with regard to the degree of love, but also with regard to the motive of loving, and the mode of love. And thus the highest degree of love is that whereby charity loves God as the giver of beatitude, as was said above.

[18] *S. T.,* I, q. 60, a. 5.   [19] Aristotle, *Phys.,* II, 8 (199a 10).   [20] *De Div. Nom.,* IV, 10 (PG 3, 708).

Fourth Article

WHETHER MAN, WITHOUT GRACE AND BY HIS OWN NATURAL
POWERS, CAN FULFILL THE COMMANDMENTS OF THE LAW?

We proceed thus to the Fourth Article:—

Objection 1. It would seem that man without grace, and by his own natural powers, can fulfill the commandments of the Law. For the Apostle says (*Rom.* ii. 14) that *the Gentiles, who have not the law, do by nature those things that are of the Law.* Now what a man does naturally he can do of himself without grace. Hence a man can fulfill the commandments of the Law without grace.

Obj. 2. Further, Jerome says that *they are anathema who say God has laid impossibilities upon man.*[21] Now what a man cannot fulfill by himself is impossible to him. Therefore a man can fulfill all the commandments of himself.

Obj. 3. Further, of all the commandments of the Law, the greatest is this, *Thou shalt love the Lord thy God with thy whole heart* (*Matt.* xxii. 37). Now man can fulfill this command by his natural powers, by loving God above all things, as was stated above. Therefore man can fulfill all the commandments of the Law without grace.

On the contrary, Augustine says that it is part of the heresy of the Pelagians that *they believe that without grace man can fulfill all the divine commandments.*[22]

I answer that, There are two ways of fulfilling the commandments of the Law.—The first regards the substance of works, as when a man does works of justice, fortitude, and of other virtues. And in this way man in the state of integral nature could fulfill all the commandments of the Law; or otherwise he would have been unable not to sin in that state, since to sin is nothing else than to transgress the divine commandments. But in the state of corrupted nature man cannot fulfill all the divine commandments without healing grace. Secondly, the commandments of the Law can be fulfilled not merely as regards the substance of the act, but also as regards the mode of acting, *i.e.,* their being done out of charity. And in this way, neither in the state of integral nature, nor in the state of corrupted nature can man fulfill the commandments of the Law without grace. Hence, Augustine, having stated that *without grace men can do no good whatever,* adds: *Not only do they know by its light what to do, but by its help they do lovingly what they know.*[23] Beyond this, in both states they need the help of God's motion in order to fulfill the commandments, as was stated above.

Reply Obj. 1. As Augustine says, *do not be disturbed at his saying that*

---

[21] Cf. Pelagius, *Epist.* I, 16 (PL 30, 32).   [22] *De Haeres.*, 88 (PL 42, 47).   [23] *De Corrept. et Grat.*, II (PL 44, 917).

they do by nature those things that are of the Law; for the Spirit of grace works this, in order to restore in us the image of God, after which we were naturally made.[24]

Reply Obj. 2. What we can do with the divine assistance is not altogether impossible to us; for according to the Philosopher: *What we can do through our friends, we can do, in some sense, by ourselves.*[25] Hence Jerome concedes that *our will is in such a way free that we must confess we still always require God's help.*[26]

Reply Obj. 3. Man cannot, with his purely natural endowments, fulfill the precept of the love of God according as it is fulfilled through charity, as was stated above.

Fifth Article

WHETHER MAN CAN MERIT ETERNAL LIFE WITHOUT GRACE?

We proceed thus to the Fifth Article:—

Objection 1. It would seem that man can merit eternal life without grace. For our Lord says (*Matt.* xix. 17): *If thou wilt enter into life, keep the commandments;* from which it would seem that to enter into eternal life rests with man's will. But what rests with our will, we can do of ourselves. Hence it seems that man can merit eternal life of himself.

Obj. 2. Further, eternal life is the wage or reward bestowed by God on men, according to *Matt.* v. 12: *Your reward is very great in heaven.* But wage or reward is meted by God to everyone according to his works, according to *Ps.* lxi. 13: *Thou wilt render to every man according to his works.* Hence, since man is master of his works, it seems that it is within his power to reach eternal life.

Obj. 3. Further, eternal life is the last end of human life. Now every natural thing by its natural endowments can attain its end. Much more, therefore, can man attain to eternal life by his natural endowments, without grace.

On the contrary, The Apostle says (*Rom.* vi. 23): *The grace of God is life everlasting.* And, as the *Gloss* says, this is said *that we may understand that God, of His own mercy, leads us to everlasting life.*[27]

I answer that, Acts leading to an end must be proportioned to the end. But no act exceeds the proportion of its active principle; and hence we see in natural things that nothing can by its operation bring about an effect which exceeds its active power, but only such as is proportioned to its power. Now eternal life is an end exceeding the proportion of human nature, as is clear from what we have said above.[28] Hence man, by his

---

[24] *De Spir. et Litt.*, XXVII (PL 44, 229).   [25] *Eth.*, III, 3 (1112b 27).   [26] Cf. Pelagius, *Libellus Fidei ad Innocentium* (PL 45, 1718).   [27] *Glossa ordin.* (VI, 15F); Peter Lombard, *In Rom.*, super VI, 23 (PL 191, 1412).—Cf. St. Augustine, *Enchir.* CVII (PL 40, 282).   [28] Q. 5, a. 5.

natural powers, cannot produce meritorious works proportioned to eternal life; but for this a higher power is needed, viz., the power of grace. And thus, without grace, man cannot merit eternal life; yet he can perform works leading to a good which is connatural to man, as *to toil in the fields, to drink, to eat, or to have friends,* and the like, as Augustine says in his third *Reply to the Pelagians.*[29]

Reply Obj. 1. Man, by his will, does works meritorious of eternal life; but, as Augustine says in the same book, for this it is necessary that the will of man should be prepared with grace by God.[30]

Reply Obj. 2. As the *Gloss* says upon *Rom.* vi. 23 (*The grace of God is life everlasting*): *It is certain that everlasting life is meted to good works; but the works to which it is meted belong to God's grace.*[31] What is more, it has been said that to fulfill the commandments of the Law, in their due way, whereby their fulfillment may be meritorious, requires grace.

Reply Obj. 3. This objection has to do with the natural end of man. Now human nature, since it is nobler, can be raised by the help of grace to a higher end, which lower natures can in no way reach; even as a man who can recover his health by the help of medicines is better disposed to health than one who can in no way recover it, as the Philosopher observes.[32]

Sixth Article

WHETHER A MAN, BY HIMSELF AND WITHOUT THE EXTERNAL AID OF GRACE, CAN PREPARE HIMSELF FOR GRACE?

We proceed thus to the Sixth Article:—

Objection 1. It would seem that man, by himself and without the external help of grace, can prepare himself for grace. For nothing impossible is laid upon man, as was stated above. But it is written (*Zach.* i. 3): *Turn ye to Me . . . and I will turn to you.* Now to prepare for grace is nothing more than to turn to God. Therefore it seems that man of himself, and without the external help of grace, can prepare himself for grace.

Obj. 2. Further, man prepares himself for grace by doing what is in him to do, since, if man does what is in him to do, God will not deny him grace; for it is written (*Matt.* vii. 11) that God gives His good Spirit *to them that ask Him.* But what is in our power, is in us to do. Therefore it seems to be in our power to prepare ourselves for grace.

Obj. 3. Further, if a man needs grace in order to prepare for grace, with equal reason will he need grace to prepare himself for the first grace; and thus to infinity, which is impossible. Hence it seems that we must not go beyond what was said first, viz., that man, of himself and without grace, can prepare himself for grace.

[29] Pseudo-Augustine, *Hypognost.,* III, 4 (PL 45, 1624).   [30] *Ibid.*   [31] Peter Lombard, *In Rom.,* super VI, 23 (PL 191, 1412).   [32] *De Caelo,* II, 12 (292b 13).

Obj. 4. Further, it is written (*Prov.* xvi. 1) that *it is the part of man to prepare the soul.* Now an action is said to be the part of a man when he can do it by himself. Hence it seems that man by himself can prepare himself for grace.

On the contrary, It is written (*Jo.* vi. 44): *No man can come to Me except the Father, Who hath sent Me, draw him.* But if man could prepare himself, he would not need to be drawn by another. Hence man cannot prepare himself without the help of grace.

I answer that, The preparation of the human will for good is twofold: —the first, whereby it is prepared to operate rightly and to enjoy God; and this preparation of the will cannot take place without the habitual gift of grace, which is the principle of meritorious works, as was stated above. There is a second way in which the human will may be taken to be prepared for the gift of habitual grace itself. Now in order that man prepare himself to receive this gift, it is not necessary to presuppose any further habitual gift in the soul, otherwise we should go on to infinity. But we must presuppose a gratuitous gift of God, Who moves the soul inwardly or inspires the good wish. For it is in these two ways that we need the divine assistance, as was stated above. Now that we need the help of God to move us, is manifest. For since every agent acts for an end, every cause must direct its effect to its end; and hence since the order of ends is according to the order of agents or movers, man must be directed to the last end by the motion of the first mover, and to the proximate end by the motion of any of the subordinate movers. So, too, the spirit of the soldier is bent towards seeking the victory by the motion of the leader of the army—and towards following the standard of a regiment by the motion of the standard-bearer. And thus, since God is absolutely the First Mover, it is by His motion that everything seeks Him under the common notion of good, whereby everything seeks to be likened to God in its own way. Hence Dionysius says that *God turns all to Himself*.[33] But He directs just men to Himself as to a special end, which they seek and to which they wish to cling, according to *Ps.* lxxii. 28, *it is good for Me to adhere to my God.* And that they are *turned* to God can only spring from God's having *turned* them. Now to prepare oneself for grace is, as it were, to be turned to God; just as whoever has his eyes turned away from the light of the sun prepares himself to receive the sun's light, by turning his eyes towards the sun. Hence it is clear that man cannot prepare himself to receive the light of grace except by the gratuitous help of God moving him inwardly.

Reply Obj. 1. Man's turning to God is by free choice, and thus man is bidden to turn himself to God. But free choice can be turned to God only when God turns it, according to *Jer.* xxxi. 18: *Convert me and I shall be converted, for Thou art the Lord, my God*; and *Lament.* v 21: *Convert us, O Lord, to Thee, and we shall be converted.*

---

[33] *De Div. Nom.,* IV, 10 (PG 3, 708).

Reply Obj. 2. Man can do nothing unless moved by God, according to *John* xv. 5: *Without Me, you can do nothing.* Hence when a man is said to do what is in him to do, this is said to be in his power according as he is moved by God.

Reply Obj. 3. This objection regards habitual grace, for which some preparation is required, since every form requires a disposition in that which is to be its subject. But in order that man should be moved by God, no further motion is presupposed, since God is the First Mover. Hence we need not go to infinity.

Reply Obj. 4. It is the part of man to prepare his soul, since he does this by his free choice. And yet he does not do this without the help of God moving him, and drawing him to Himself, as was said above.

Seventh Article

WHETHER MAN CAN RISE FROM SIN WITHOUT THE HELP OF GRACE?

We proceed thus to the Seventh Article:—

Objection 1. It would seem that man can rise from sin without the help of grace. For what is presupposed to grace takes place without grace. But to rise from sin is presupposed to the illumination of grace, since it is written (*Ephes.* v. 14): *Arise from the dead and Christ shall enlighten thee.* Therefore man can rise from sin without grace.

Obj. 2. Further, sin is opposed to virtue as illness to health, as was stated above.[34] Now man, by force of his nature, can rise from illness to health, without the external help of medicine, since there still remains in him the principle of life, from which natural operation proceeds. Hence it seems that, with equal reason, man may be restored by himself, and return from the state of sin to the state of justice without the help of external grace.

Obj. 3. Further, every natural thing can return by itself to the act befitting its nature, as hot water returns by itself to its natural coldness, and a stone cast upwards returns by itself to its natural movement. Now sin is an act against nature, as is clear from Damascene.[35] Hence it seems that man by himself can return from sin to the state of justice.

On the contrary, The Apostle says (*Gal.* ii. 21 [cf. iii. 21]): *For if there had been a law given which could give life, then Christ died in vain, i.e.,* to no purpose. Hence with equal reason, if man has a nature whereby he can be justified, *Christ died in vain, i.e.,* to no purpose. But this cannot fittingly be said. Therefore he cannot be justified by himself, *i.e.,* he cannot return from a state of sin to a state of justice.

---

[34] Q. 71, a. 1, ad 3.   [35] *De Fide Orth.,* II, 4; 30 (PG 94, 876; 976); cf. *op. cit.,* IV, 20 (PG 94, 1196).

I answer that, Man by himself can in no way rise from sin without the help of grace. For since sin is transient as to the act and abiding in its guilt, as was stated above,[36] to rise from sin is not the same as to cease from the act of sin; but to rise from sin means that man has restored to him what he lost by sinning. Now man incurs a triple loss by sinning, as was shown above,[37] viz., stain, corruption of natural good, and debt of punishment. He incurs a stain, inasmuch as he forfeits the adornment of grace through the deformity of sin. Natural good is corrupted, inasmuch as man's nature is disordered because man's will is not subject to God's; and when this order is overthrown, the consequence is that the whole nature of sinful man remains disordered. Lastly, there is the debt of punishment, inasmuch as by sinning man deserves eternal damnation.

Now it is manifest that none of these three can be restored except by God. For since the adornment of grace comes from the illumination of the divine light, this adornment cannot be brought back, except God give His light anew. Hence a habitual gift is necessary; and this is the light of grace. Likewise, the order of nature can be restored, *i.e.,* man's will can be subject to God, only when God draws man's will to Himself, as was stated above. So, too, the guilt of eternal punishment can be remitted by God alone, against Whom the offense was committed and Who is man's Judge. And thus, in order that man rise from sin there is required the help of grace, both as regards a habitual gift and as regards the internal motion of God.

Reply Obj. 1. To man is bidden that which pertains to the act of free choice, as this act is required in order that man should rise from sin. Hence when it is said, *Arise, and Christ shall enlighten thee,* we are not to think that the complete rising from sin precedes the illumination of grace; but that when man by his free choice, moved by God, strives to rise from sin, he receives the light of justifying grace.

Reply Obj. 2. The natural reason is not the sufficient principle of the health that is in man by justifying grace. The principle of this health is grace, which is taken away by sin. Hence man cannot be restored by himself, but requires the light of grace to be poured upon him anew, as if the soul were infused into a dead body for its resurrection.

Reply Obj. 3. When nature is integral, it can be restored by itself to what is befitting and proportioned to it; but without exterior help it cannot be restored to what surpasses its limits. And thus human nature, undone by reason of the act of sin, remains no longer integral, but corrupted, as was stated above; nor can it be restored, by itself, even to its connatural good, and much less to the good of supernatural justice.

[36] Q. 87, a. 6.   [37] Q. 85, a. 1; q. 86, a. 1; q. 87, a. 1.

Eighth Article

WHETHER MAN WITHOUT GRACE CAN AVOID SIN?

We proceed thus to the Eighth Article:—

Objection 1. It would seem that without grace man can avoid sin. For *no one sins in what he cannot avoid,* as Augustine says.[38] Hence, if a man in mortal sin cannot avoid sin, it would seem that in sinning he does not sin, which is impossible.

Obj. 2. Further, men are corrected that they may not sin. If, therefore, a man in mortal sin cannot avoid sin, correction would seem to be given to no purpose; which is absurd.

Obj. 3. Further, it is written (*Ecclus.* xv. 18): *Before man is life and death, good and evil; that which he shall choose shall be given him.* But by sinning no one ceases to be a man. Hence it is still in his power to choose good or evil; and thus man can avoid sin without grace.

On the contrary, Augustine says: *Whoever denies that we ought to say the prayer 'Lead us not into temptation' (and they deny it who maintain that the help of God's grace is not necessary to man for salvation, but that the gift of the law is enough for the human will) ought without doubt to be removed beyond all hearing, and to be anathematized by the tongues of all.*[39]

I answer that, We may speak of man in two ways: first, in the state of integral nature; secondly, in the state of corrupted nature. Now in the state of integral nature, man, even without habitual grace, could avoid sinning either mortally or venially, since to sin is nothing else than to stray from what is according to our nature—and in the state of integral nature man could avoid this. Nevertheless, he could not have done it without God's help upholding him in good, since if this had been withdrawn, even his nature would have fallen back into nothingness.

But in the state of corrupted nature man needs grace to heal his nature in order that he may entirely abstain from sin. And in the present life this healing is wrought first in the mind, since the carnal appetite is not yet entirely healed. Hence the Apostle (*Rom.* vii. 25) says in the person of one who is healed: *I myself, with the mind, serve the law of God, but with the flesh, the law of sin.* And in this state man can abstain from all mortal sin, whose source is in the reason, as was stated above;[40] but man cannot abstain from all venial sin because of the corruption of his lower appetite of sensuality. For man can, indeed, repress each of its movements (and hence they are sinful and voluntary), but not all, because, while he is resisting one, another may arise, and also because the reason is not always alert to avoid these movements, as was said above.[41]

---

[38] *De Duab. Anim.,* X; XI (PL 42, 103; 105); *De Lib. Arb.,* III, 18 (PL 32, 1295).
[39] *De Perfect. Iust.,* XXI (PL 44, 317).   [40] Q. 74, a. 4.   [41] Q. 74, a. 3, ad 2.

So, too, before man's reason, wherein is mortal sin, is restored by justifying grace, he can avoid each mortal sin, and for a time, since it is not necessary that he should always be actually sinning. But it cannot be that he remains for a long time without mortal sin. Hence Gregory says that *a sin not at once taken away by repentance, by its weight drags us down to other sins,*[42] and this because, as the lower appetite ought to be subject to the reason, so should the reason be subject to God, and should place in Him the end of its will. Now it is by the end that all human acts ought to be regulated, even as it is by the judgment of the reason that the movements of the lower appetite should be regulated. And thus, even as inordinate movements of the sensitive appetite cannot help occurring since the lower appetite is not subject to reason, so likewise, since man's reason is not entirely subject to God, the consequence is that many disorders occur in the acts itself of the reason. For when man's heart is not so fixed on God as to be unwilling to be parted from Him for the sake of finding any good or avoiding any evil, many things happen for the achieving or avoiding of which a man strays from God and breaks His commandments, and thus sins mortally; especially since, when surprised, a man acts according to his preconceived end and his pre-existing habits, as the Philosopher says,[43] although with the premeditation of his reason a man may do something outside the order of his preconceived end and the inclination of his habit. But because a man cannot always have this premeditation, it cannot help occurring that he acts in accordance with his will turned aside from God, unless, by grace, he is quickly brought back to the due order.

Reply Obj. 1. Man can avoid each but not every act of sin, except by grace, as was stated above. Nevertheless, since it is by his own shortcoming that he does not prepare himself to have grace, the fact that he cannot avoid sin without grace does not excuse him from sin.

Reply Obj. 2. Correction is useful *in order that out of the sorrow of correction may spring the wish to be regenerate; if indeed he who is corrected is a son of promise, in such sort that while the noise of correction is outwardly resounding and punishing, God by hidden inspirations is inwardly also causing him to will,* as Augustine says.[44] Correction is therefore necessary, from the fact that man's will is required in order to abstain from sin; and yet it is not sufficient without God's help. Hence it is written (*Eccles.* vii. 14): *Consider the works of God that no man can correct whom He hath despised.*

Reply Obj. 3. As Augustine says, this saying is to be understood of man in the state of integral nature, when as yet he was not a slave of sin.[45] Hence he was able to sin and not to sin. Now, too, whatever a man wills, is given to him; but his willing good, he has by God's assistance.

---

[42] *In Ezech.,* I, hom. 2 (PL 76, 915).   [43] *Eth.,* III, 8 (1117a 18).   [44] *De Corrept. et Grat.,* I (PL 44, 921).   [45] Pseudo-Augustine, *Hypognost.,* III, 2 (PL 45, 1621).

Ninth Article

WHETHER ONE WHO HAS ALREADY OBTAINED GRACE CAN, OF HIMSELF AND WITHOUT FURTHER HELP OF GRACE, DO GOOD AND AVOID SIN?

We proceed thus to the Ninth Article:—

Objection 1. It would seem that whoever has already obtained grace can, by himself and without further help of grace, do good and avoid sin. For a thing is useless or imperfect, if it does not fulfill what it was given for. Now grace is given to us that we may do good and keep from sin. Hence if with grace man cannot do this, it seems that grace is either useless or imperfect.

Obj. 2. Further, by grace the Holy Spirit dwells in us, according to *1 Cor.* iii. 16: *Know you not that you are the temple of God, and that the Spirit of God dwelleth in you?* Now since the Spirit of God is omnipotent, He is sufficient to ensure our doing good and to keep us from sin. Hence a man who has obtained grace can do the above two things without any further assistance of grace.

Obj. 3. Further, if a man who has obtained grace needs further aid of grace in order to live righteously and to keep free from sin, with equal reason he will need yet another grace, even though he has obtained this first help of grace. Therefore we must go on to infinity; which is impossible. Hence, whoever is in grace needs no further help of grace in order to work righteously and to keep free from sin.

On the contrary, Augustine says that *as the eye of the body, though most healthy, cannot see unless it is helped by the brightness of light, so neither can a man, even if he is most perfectly justified, live righteously unless he be helped by the eternal light of justice.*[46] But justification is by grace, according to *Rom.* iii. 24: *Being justified freely by His grace.* Hence, even a man who already possesses grace needs a further assistance of grace in order to live righteously.

I answer that, As was stated above, in order to live righteously a man needs a twofold help of God—first, a habitual gift whereby corrupted human nature is healed, and after being healed is lifted up so as to work deeds meritorious of eternal life, which exceed the capability of nature. Secondly, man needs the help of grace in order to be moved by God to act.

Now with regard to the first kind of help, man does not need a further help of grace, that is, a further infused habit. Yet he needs the help of grace in another way, *i.e.*, in order to be moved by God to act righteously; and this for two reasons: first, for the general reason that no created thing can put forth any act, unless by virtue of the divine motion; secondly, for this special reason—the condition of the state of human nature. For, although

[46] *De Nat. et Grat.,* XXVI (PL 44, 261).

healed by grace as to the mind, yet it remains corrupted and poisoned in the flesh, whereby it serves *the law of sin* (*Rom.* vii. 25). In the intellect, too, there remains the darkness of ignorance, whereby, as is written (*Rom.* viii. 26): *We know not what we should pray for as we ought*; since, because of the various turns of circumstances, and because we do not know ourselves perfectly, we cannot fully know what is for our good, according to *Wis.* ix. 14: *For the thoughts of mortal men are fearful and our counsels uncertain.* Hence we must be guided and guarded by God, Who knows and can do all things. For this reason also it is becoming in those who have been born again as sons of God to say: *Lead us not into temptation,* and *Thy Will be done on earth as it is in heaven,* and whatever else is contained in the Lord's Prayer pertaining to this.

Reply Obj. 1. The gift of habitual grace is not therefore given to us that we may no longer need the divine help; for every creature needs to be preserved in the good received from Him. Hence, if after having received grace man still needs the divine help, it cannot be concluded that grace is given to no purpose, or that it is imperfect, since man will need the divine help even in the state of glory, when grace shall be fully perfected. But here grace is to some extent imperfect, inasmuch as it does not completely heal man, as was stated above.

Reply Obj. 2. The operation of the Holy Ghost, which moves and protects, is not circumscribed by the effect of habitual grace which it causes in us; but beyond this effect He, together with the Father and the Son, moves and protects us.

Reply Obj. 3. This argument merely proves that man needs no further habitual grace.

Tenth Article

WHETHER MAN POSSESSED OF GRACE NEEDS THE HELP OF
GRACE IN ORDER TO PERSEVERE?

We proceed thus to the Tenth Article:—

Objection 1. It would seem that man possessed of grace needs no help of grace to persevere. For perseverance is something less than virtue, even as continence is, as is clear from the Philosopher.[47] Now since man is justified by grace, he needs no further help of grace in order to have the virtues. Much less, therefore, does he need the help of grace to have perseverance.

Obj. 2. Further, all the virtues are infused together. But perseverance is put down as a virtue. Hence it seems that, together with grace, perseverance is given when the other virtues are infused.

Obj. 3. Further, as the Apostle says (*Rom.* v. 20), more was restored to man by Christ's gift than he had lost by Adam's sin. But Adam received

---

[47] *Eth.,* VII, 1 (1145b 1); 9 (1151b 32).

what enabled him to persevere. Therefore, all the more is there restored in us by the grace of Christ the ability to persevere. And thus man does not need grace in order to persevere.

On the contrary, Augustine says: *Why is perseverance besought of God, if it is not bestowed by God? For is it not a mocking request to seek what we know He does not give, and what is in our power without His giving it?*[48] Now perseverance is besought even by those who are sanctified by grace; and this is seen when we say *Hallowed be Thy name,* which Augustine confirms by the words of Cyprian.[49] Hence man, even when possessed of grace, needs perseverance to be given to him by God.

I answer that, Perseverance is taken in three ways. First, to signify a habit of the mind whereby a man stands steadfastly, lest he be moved by the assault of sadness from what is virtuous. And thus perseverance is to sadness as continence is to concupiscence and pleasure, as the Philosopher says.[50] Secondly, perseverance may be called a habit whereby a man has the purpose of persevering in good until the end. And in both these ways perseverance is infused together with grace, even as are continence and the other virtues. Thirdly, perseverance is called the abiding in good to the end of life. And in order to have this perseverance man does not, indeed, need another habitual grace, but he needs the divine assistance guiding and guarding him against the attacks of the passions, as appears from the preceding article. And hence after anyone has been justified by grace, he still needs to beseech God for the aforesaid gift of perseverance, that he may be kept from evil till the end of his life. For grace is given to many to whom perseverance in grace is not given.

Reply Obj. 1. This objection regards the first mode of perseverance, as the second objection regards the second.

Hence the solution of the second objection is clear.

Reply Obj. 3. As Augustine says, *in the original state man received a gift whereby he could persevere, but to persevere was not given him. But now, by the grace of Christ, many receive both the gift of grace whereby they may persevere, and the further gift of persevering.*[51] And thus, Christ's gift is greater than Adam's fault. Nevertheless, it was easier for man to persevere through the gift of grace in the state of innocence, in which the flesh was not rebellious against the spirit, than it is now. For the restoration by Christ's grace, although it is already begun in the mind, is not yet completed in the flesh, as it will be in heaven, where man will not merely be able to persevere, but will be unable to sin.

[48] *De Dono Persev.,* II (PL 45, 996).   [49] *Ibid.*—Cf. also *De Corrept. et Grat.,* VI, 10 (PL 44, 922).   [50] *Eth.,* VII, 7 (1150a 13).   [51] Cf. *De Corrept. et Grat.,* XII, 34 (PL 44, 937).

ON THE GRACE OF GOD, AS REGARDS ITS ESSENCE
(*In Four Articles*)

WE must now consider the grace of God as regards its essence; and under this head there are four points of inquiry: (1) Whether grace posits something in the soul? (2) Whether grace is a quality? (3) Whether grace differs from infused virtue? (4) The subject of grace.

First Article

WHETHER GRACE POSITS ANYTHING IN THE SOUL?

We proceed thus to the First Article:—

Objection 1. It would seem that grace does not posit anything in the soul. For man is said to have the grace of God even as the grace of man. Hence it is written (*Gen.* xxxix. 21) that the Lord gave to Joseph *grace in the sight of the chief keeper of the prison.* Now when we say that a man has the favor [*gratiam*] of another, nothing is posited in him who has the favor of the other, but an acceptance is posited in him whose favor he has. Hence, when we say that a man has the grace of God, nothing is posited in his soul; but we merely signify the divine acceptance.

Obj. 2. Further, as the soul quickens the body, so does God quicken the soul; and hence it is written (*Deut.* xxx. 20): *He is thy life.* Now the soul quickens the body immediately. Therefore, likewise, nothing can come as a medium between God and the soul. Hence grace posits nothing created in the soul.

Obj. 3. Further, on *Rom.* i. 7 (*Grace to you and peace*) the *Gloss* says: *Grace, i.e., the remission of sins.*[1] Now the remission of sins posits nothing in the soul, but only in God, Who does not impute sin, according to *Ps.* xxxi. 2: *Blessed is the man to whom the Lord hath not imputed sin.* Hence neither does grace posit anything in the soul.

On the contrary, Light posits something in what is illumined. But grace is a light of the soul, and hence Augustine says: *The light of truth rightly deserts the prevaricator of the law, and he who has been thus deserted becomes blind.*[2] Therefore grace posits something in the soul.

I answer that, According to the common manner of speech, *grace* is usually taken in three ways, First, for anyone's love, as we are accustomed to

---

[1] *Glossa interl.* (VI, 4r); Peter Lombard, *In Rom.*, super I, 7 (PL 191, 1316).   [2] *De Nat. et Grat.*, XXII (PL 44, 258).

say that the soldier is in the good graces of the king, *i.e.*, that the king looks on him with favor. Secondly, it is taken for any gift freely bestowed, as we are accustomed to say: I do you this act of grace. Thirdly, it is taken for the recompense of a gift given *gratis*, according to which we are said to be *grateful* for benefits. Of these three, the second depends on the first, since one bestows something on another *gratis* from the love wherewith he receives him into his good *graces*. And from the second proceeds the third, since from benefits bestowed *gratis* arises *gratitude*.

Now as regards the last two, it is clear that grace posits something in him who receives grace: first, the gift given gratis; secondly, the acknowledgment of the gift. But as regards the first, a difference must be noted between the grace of God and the grace of man. For since the creature's good springs from the divine will, it is from the love by which God wills the good of the creature that some good comes in the creature. On the other hand, the will of man is moved by the good pre-existing in things; and hence man's love does not wholly cause the good of the thing, but presupposes it either in part or wholly. Therefore it is clear that every love of God is followed at some time by a good caused in the creature, but not co-eternal with the eternal love. And according to this difference of good the love of God towards the creature is looked at differently. For one is common, whereby He loves *all things that are* (*Wis.* xi. 25), and thereby gives things their natural being. But the second is a special love, whereby He draws the rational creature above the condition of its nature to a participation of the divine good; and according to this love He is said to love anyone absolutely, since it is by this love that God wills absolutely the eternal good, which is Himself, for the creature.

Accordingly, when a man is said to have the grace of God, there is signified something supernatural bestowed on man by God. Nevertheless, the grace of God sometimes signifies God's eternal love, in which sense it is also called the grace of predestination, inasmuch as God gratuitously, and not from merits, predestines or elects some; for it is written (*Ephes.* i. 5): *He hath predestinated us into the adoption of children . . . unto the praise of the glory of His grace.*

Reply Obj. 1. Even when a man is said to be in another's good graces, it is understood that there is something in him pleasing to the other, even as anyone is said to have God's grace; with this difference, however, that what is pleasing to a man in another is presupposed to his love, but whatever is pleasing to God in a man is caused by the divine love, as was said above.

Reply Obj. 2. God is the life of the soul after the manner of an efficient cause; but the soul is the life of the body after the manner of a formal cause. Now there is no medium between form and matter, since the form, of itself, informs the matter or subject; whereas the agent informs the subject, not by its substance, but by the form which it causes in the matter.

Reply Obj. 3. Augustine says: *When I said that grace was for the remis-*

siun of sins, and peace for our reconciliation with God, you must not take it to mean that peace and reconciliation do not pertain to general grace, but that the special name of grace signifies the remission of sins.[3] Not only grace, therefore, but many other of God's gifts pertain to grace. Furthermore, the remission of sins does not take place without some effect divinely caused in us, as will appear later.[4]

Second Article

WHETHER GRACE IS A QUALITY OF THE SOUL?

We proceed thus to the Second Article:—

Objection 1. It would seem that grace is not a quality of the soul. For no quality acts on its subject, since the action of a quality is not without the action of its subject, and thus the subject would necessarily act upon itself. But grace acts upon the soul, by justifying it. Therefore grace is not a quality.

Obj. 2. Furthermore, substance is nobler than quality. But grace is nobler than the nature of the soul, since we can do many things by grace to which nature is not equal, as was stated above.[5] Therefore grace is not a quality.

Obj. 3. Furthermore, no quality remains after it has ceased to be in its subject. But grace remains, since it is not corrupted; for in that case it would be reduced to nothing, just as it was created from nothing (hence it is called a *new creature* [*Gal.* vi. 15]). Therefore grace is not a quality.

On the contrary, on *Ps.* ciii. 15 (*That he may make the face cheerful with oil*) the *Gloss* says: *Grace is a certain splendor of soul, which wins the divine love.*[6] But splendor of soul is a quality, even as beauty of body. Therefore grace is a quality.

I answer that, As we have stated above, there is understood to be an effect of God's gratuitous will in whoever is said to have God's grace. Now it was stated that man is aided by God's gratuitous will in two ways.[7] First, inasmuch as man's soul is moved by God to know or will or do something, and in this way the gratuitous effect in man is not a quality, but a movement of the soul; for *motion is the act of the mover in the moved,* as it is said in *Physics* iii.[8] Secondly, man is helped by God's gratuitous will inasmuch as a habitual gift is infused by God into the soul; and this for the reason that it is not fitting that God should provide less for those He loves, that they may acquire supernatural good, than for creatures whom He loves that they may acquire natural good. Now He so provides for natural creatures, that not merely does He move them to their natural acts, but He bestows upon them certain forms and powers, which are the principles of

---

[3] *Retract.,* XXV (PL 32, 624).   [4] Q. 113, a. 2.   [5] Q. 109.   [6] *Glossa ordin.* (III, 240E).—Cf. St. Augustine, *Enarr. in Psalm.,* super CIII, 15 (PL 37, 1369).   [7] Q. 109, a. 1, 2 and 5.   [8] Aristotle, *Phys.,* III, 3 (202a 13).

acts, in order that they may of themselves be inclined to these movements. And thus it is that the movements whereby they are moved by God become connatural and easy for creatures, according to *Wis.* viii. 1: *she . . . ordereth all things sweetly.* Much more, therefore, does He infuse into those whom He moves towards the acquisition of supernatural good certain supernatural forms or qualities, whereby they may be moved by Him sweetly and promptly to acquire eternal good. Hence the gift of grace is a quality.

Reply Obj. 1. Grace, as a quality, is said to act upon the soul, not after the manner of an efficient cause, but after the manner of a formal cause, as whiteness makes a thing white, and justice, just.

Reply Obj. 2. Every substance is either the nature of the thing of which it is the substance, or it is a part of the nature, in which sense matter and form are called substance. And because grace is above human nature, it cannot be a substance or a substantial form; it is rather an accidental form of the soul. Now what is in God substantially comes to be accidentally in the soul participating in the divine goodness, as is clear in the case of knowledge. And thus, because the soul participates in the divine goodness imperfectly, the participation of the divine goodness, which is grace, has its being in the soul in a less perfect way than the soul subsists in itself. Nevertheless, inasmuch as it is an expression or participation of the divine goodness, it is nobler than the nature of the soul, though not in its mode of being.

Reply Obj. 3. As Boethius says, *the being of an accident is to inhere.*[9] Hence no accident is called being as if it had being, but because by it something is; and hence it is said to belong to a being rather than to be a being.[10] And because to become and to be corrupted belong to what is, properly speaking no accident comes into being or is corrupted, but is said to come into being and to be corrupted inasmuch as its subject begins or ceases to be actually with this accident. In this sense, grace is also said to be created, inasmuch as men are created with reference to it, *i.e.,* are given a new being out of nothing, *i.e.,* not from merits, according to *Ephes.* ii. 10, *created in Jesus Christ in good works.*

Third Article

WHETHER GRACE IS THE SAME AS VIRTUE?

We proceed thus to the Third Article:—

Objection 1. It would seem that grace is the same as virtue. For Augustine says that *operating grace is faith that worketh by charity.*[11] But faith that works by charity is a virtue. Therefore grace is a virtue.

---

[9] Cf. Pseudo-Bede, *Sent.,* I, A (PL 90, 968).   [10] Aristotle, *Metaph.,* VI, i (1028a 18).
[11] *De Spir. et Litt.,* XIV, XXXII (PL 44, 217; 237).

Obj. 2. Further, what fits the definition fits the defined. But the definitions of virtue given by saints and philosophers fit grace, since *it makes its subject good, and his work good,*[12] and *it is a good quality of the mind, whereby we live righteously,* etc.[13] Therefore grace is a virtue.

Obj. 3. Further, grace is a quality. Now it is clearly not in the *fourth* species of quality, viz., *form,* which is the *abiding figure of things,* since it does not belong to bodies. Nor is it in the *third,* since it is not a *passion nor a passion-like quality,* which is in the sensitive part of the soul, as is proved in *Physics* vii.;[14] whereas grace is principally in the mind. Nor is it in the *second* species, which is *natural power* or *impotence;* for grace is above nature and is not concerned with good and evil, as is a natural power. Therefore it must be in the *first* species, which is *habit* or *disposition.* Now the habits of the mind are virtues; since even science itself is a virtue, after a manner, as was stated above.[15] Therefore grace is the same as virtue.

On the contrary, If grace is a virtue, it would seem before all to be one of the three theological virtues. But grace is neither faith nor hope, for these can be without sanctifying grace. Nor is it charity, since *grace foreruns charity,* as Augustine says in his book *On The Predestination of the Saints.*[16] Therefore grace is not a virtue.

I answer that, Some held that grace and virtue were identical in essence, and differed only logically; so that it would be *grace* according to which a man is pleasing to God, or which is given gratuitously, and it would be *virtue* inasmuch as it empowers us to act rightly. The Master of the *Sentences* seems to have thought this.[17]

But if anyone rightly considers the nature of virtue, this cannot hold, since, as the Philosopher says, *virtue is a disposition of what is perfect,— and I call perfect what is disposed according to its nature.*[18] Now from this it is clear that the virtue of a thing is spoken of in relation to an already existing nature, for everything is disposed with reference to what befits its nature. But it is manifest that the virtues acquired by human acts, of which we spoke above,[19] are dispositions by which a man is fittingly disposed with reference to the nature by which he is a man; whereas infused virtues dispose man in a higher manner and towards a higher end, and consequently in relation to some higher nature, *i.e.,* in relation to a participation of the divine nature, which is called the light of grace, according to 2 Pet. i. 4: *He hath given us most great and most precious promises, that by these you may be made partakers of the divine nature.* And it is in respect of receiving this nature that we are said to be born again sons of God.

And thus, just as the natural light of reason is something different from the acquired virtues, which are ordained to this natural light, so also the

---

[12] Cf. Aristotle, *Eth.,* II, 6 (1106a 15).   [13] Cf. above, q. 55, a. 4.   [14] Aristotle, *Phys.,* VII, 3 (245b 3).   [15] Q. 56, a. 3; q. 57, a. 1 and 2.   [16] Cf. *De Dono Persev.,* XVI (PL 45, 1018).   [17] Peter Lombard, *Sent.,* II, xxvii, 6 (I, 447).   [18] *Phys.,* VII, 3 (246a 13).   [19] Q. 55.

light of grace, which is a participation of the divine nature, is something different from the infused virtues which are derived from and are ordained to this light; and hence the Apostle says (*Ephes.* v. 8): *For you were heretofore darkness, but now light in the Lord. Walk then as children of the light.* For as the acquired virtues enable a man to walk in accordance with the natural light of reason, so the infused virtues enable a man to walk as befits the light of grace.

Reply Obj. 1. Augustine calls *faith that worketh by charity* grace, since the act of faith of him that worketh by charity is the first act by which sanctifying grace is manifested.

Reply Obj. 2. *Good* is placed in the definition of virtue with reference to its suitableness for some pre-existing nature, essential or participated. Now good is not attributed to grace in this manner, but as to the root of goodness in man, as was stated above.

Reply Obj. 3. Grace is reduced to the first species of quality; and yet it is not the same as virtue, but rather a certain disposition which is presupposed to the infused virtues, as their principle and root.

Fourth Article

WHETHER GRACE IS IN THE ESSENCE OF THE SOUL AS IN A SUBJECT, OR IN ONE OF THE POWERS?

We proceed thus to the Fourth Article:—

Objection 1. It would seem that grace is not in the essence of the soul as in a subject, but in one of the powers. For Augustine says that grace is related to the will or to free choice *as a rider to his horse.*[20] Now the will or free choice is a power, as was stated above.[21] Hence grace is in a power of the soul as in a subject.

Obj. 2. Further, *Man's merit springs from grace,* as Augustine says.[22] Now merit consists in acts, which proceed from a power. Hence it seems that grace is a perfection of a power of the soul.

Obj. 3. Further, if the essence of the soul is the proper subject of grace, the soul, inasmuch as it has an essence, must be capable of grace. But this is false, since it would follow that every soul would be capable of grace. Therefore the essence of the soul is not the proper subject of grace.

Obj. 4. Further, the essence of the soul is prior to its powers. Now what is prior may be understood without what is posterior. Hence it follows that grace may be taken to be in the soul, although we suppose no part or power of the soul, viz., neither the will, nor the intellect, nor anything else; which is unreasonable.

On the contrary, By grace we are born again sons of God. But genera-

---

[20] Pseudo-Augustine, *Hypognost.,* III, 11 (PL 45, 1632).   [21] *S. T.,* I, q. 83, a. 2.
[22] *De Grat. et Lib. Arb.,* XI (PL 44, 889).

tion terminates at the essence prior to the powers. Therefore grace is in the soul's essence prior to being in the powers.

I answer that, This question depends on the preceding. For if grace is the same as virtue, it must necessarily be in the powers of the soul as in a subject; for the soul's powers are the proper subject of virtue, as was stated above.[23] But if grace differs from virtue, it cannot be said that a power of the soul is the subject of grace, since every perfection of the soul's powers has the nature of virtue, as was stated above.[24] Hence it remains that grace, being prior to virtue, has therefore a subject prior to the powers of the soul, so that it is in the essence of the soul. For just as man through his intellectual power participates in the divine knowledge through the virtue of faith, and through his power of will participates in the divine love through the virtue of charity, so also through the nature of the soul does he participate in the divine nature, after the manner of a likeness, through a certain regeneration or re-creation.

Reply Obj. 1. Just as from the essence of the soul flow its powers, which are the principles of operations, so likewise the virtues, whereby the powers are moved to act, flow into the powers of the soul from grace. And thus grace is compared to the will as the mover to the moved, which is the same comparison as that of a horseman to the horse—but not as an accident to a subject.

And thereby is made clear the Reply to the second objection. For grace is the principle of meritorious works through the medium of the virtues, just as the essence of the soul is the principle of vital operations through the medium of the powers.

Reply Obj. 3. The soul is the subject of grace, as being in the species of intellectual or rational nature. But the soul is not classed in a species by any of its powers, since the powers are natural properties of the soul following upon the species. Hence the soul differs specifically in its essence from other souls, viz., of brute animals and of plants. Consequently, it does not follow that, if the essence of the human soul is the subject of grace, every soul may be the subject of grace; for this belongs to the essence of the soul inasmuch as it is of such a species.

Reply Obj. 4. Since the powers of the soul are natural properties following upon the species, the soul cannot be without them. Yet, granted that it were without them, the soul would still be called intellectual or rational in its species; not that it would actually have these powers, but because of the species of such an essence, from which these powers naturally flow.

[23] Q. 56, a. 1.   [24] Q. 55, a. 1; q. 56, a. 1.

ON THE DIVISION OF GRACE
(*In Five Articles*)

WE must now consider the division of grace, under which head there are five points of inquiry: (1) Whether grace is fittingly divided into gratuitous grace and sanctifying grace? (2) The division of sanctifying grace into operating and co-operating grace. (3) Its division into prevenient and subsequent grace. (4) The division of gratuitous grace. (5) On the comparison between sanctifying and gratuitous grace.

First Article

WHETHER GRACE IS FITTINGLY DIVIDED INTO SANCTIFYING GRACE AND GRATUITOUS GRACE?

We proceed thus to the First Article:—

Objection 1. It would seem that grace is not fittingly divided into sanctifying grace and gratuitous grace. For grace is a gift of God, as is clear from what has been already stated.[1] But man is not therefore pleasing to God because something is given him by God, but rather on the contrary; for something is freely given by God because man is pleasing to Him. Hence there is no sanctifying grace.

Obj. 2. Further, whatever is not given because of preceding merits is given gratis. Now even natural good is given to man without preceding merit, since nature is presupposed to merit. Therefore nature itself is given gratuitously by God. But nature is co-divided against grace. Therefore to be gratuitously given is not fittingly set down as a difference of grace, since it is found also outside the genus of grace.

Obj. 3. Further, members of a division are mutually opposed. But even sanctifying grace, whereby we are justified, is given to us gratuitously, according to *Rom.* iii. 24: *Being justified freely* [*gratis*] *by His grace.* Hence sanctifying grace ought not to be divided against gratuitous grace.

On the contrary, The Apostle attributes both to grace, viz., to sanctify and to be gratuitously given. For with regard to the first he says (*Ephes.* i. 6): *He hath graced us in His beloved Son.* And with regard to the second (*Rom.* xi. 6): *And if by grace, it is not now by works, otherwise grace is no more grace.* Therefore grace can be distinguished by its having one only or both.

[1] Q. 110, a. 1.

I answer that, As the Apostle says (*Rom.* xiii. 1), *those things that are of God are well ordered.* Now the order of things consists in this, that some things are led to God by others, as Dionysius says.[2] And hence, since grace is ordained to lead men to God, this takes place in a certain order, so that some are led to God by others.

According to this, consequently, there is a twofold grace: one, whereby man himself is united to God, and this is called *sanctifying grace*; the other is that whereby one man co-operates with another in leading him to God, and this gift is called *gratuitous grace,* since it is bestowed on a man beyond the capability of nature, and beyond the merit of the person. But since it is bestowed on a man, not to justify him, but rather that he may co-operate in the justification of another, it is not called sanctifying grace. And it is of this that the Apostle says (*1 Cor.* xii. 7): *And the manifestation of the Spirit is given to every man unto utility, i.e.,* of others.

Reply Obj. 1. Grace is said to make pleasing, not efficiently, but formally, *i.e.,* because thereby a man is justified, and is made worthy to be called pleasing to God, according to *Col.* i. 21. He *hath made us worthy to be made partakers of the lot of the saints in light.*

Reply Obj. 2. Grace, inasmuch as it is gratuitously given, excludes the notion of debt. Now debt may be taken in two ways. First, as arising from merit; and this is referred to the person to whom it belongs to do meritorious works, according to *Rom.* iv. 4: *Now to him that worketh, the reward is not reckoned according to grace, but according to debt.* The second debt concerns the condition of nature. Thus we say it is due to a man to have reason, and whatever else belongs to human nature. Yet in neither way is debt taken to mean that God is under an obligation to His creature, but rather that the creature ought to be subject to God, so that the divine ordination may be fulfilled in it, which is that a certain nature should have certain conditions or properties, and that by doing certain works it should attain to something further. Hence natural endowments are not a debt in the first sense, but in the second. But supernatural gifts are due in neither sense. Hence they especially merit the name of grace.

Reply Obj. 3. Sanctifying grace adds to the notion of gratuitous grace something which also belongs to the nature of grace, since it makes man pleasing to God. And hence gratuitous grace, which does not do this, keeps the common name, as happens in many other cases; and thus the two parts of the division are opposed as sanctifying and non-sanctifying grace.

[2] *De Cael. Hier.,* IV, 3 (PG 3, 181).

Second Article

WHETHER GRACE IS FITTINGLY DIVIDED INTO OPERATING
AND CO-OPERATING GRACE?

We proceed thus to the Second Article:—

Objection 1. It would seem that grace is not fittingly divided into operating and co-operating grace. For grace is an accident, as was stated above.[3] Now no accident can act upon its subject. Therefore no grace can be called operating.

Obj. 2. Further, if grace operates anything in us, it assuredly brings about justification. But not only grace works this. For Augustine says on *John* xiv. 12 (*the works that I do he also shall do*) *He Who created thee without thyself, will not justify thee without thyself.*[4] Therefore no grace ought to be called unqualifiedly operating.

Obj. 3. Further, to co-operate seems to pertain to the inferior agent, and not to the principal agent. But grace works in us more than does free choice, according to *Rom.* ix. 16: *It is not of him that willeth, nor of him that runneth, but of God that sheweth mercy.* Therefore no grace ought to be called co-operating.

Obj. 4. Further, division ought to rest on opposition. But to operate and to co-operate are not opposed, for one and the same thing can both operate and co-operate. Therefore grace is not fittingly divided into operating and co-operating.

On the contrary, Augustine says: *God, by co-operating with us, perfects what He began by operating in us, since He who perfects by co-operation with such as are willing, begins by operating that they may will.*[5] But the operations of God whereby He moves us to good pertain to grace. Therefore grace is fittingly divided into operating and co-operating.

I answer that, As was stated above, grace may be taken in two ways.[6] First, as a divine help, whereby God moves us to will and to act; secondly, as a habitual gift divinely bestowed on us. Now in both these ways grace is fittingly divided into operating and co-operating. For the operation of an effect is not attributed to the thing moved but to the mover. Hence, in that effect in which our mind is moved and does not move, but in which God is the sole mover, the operation is attributed to God; and it is with reference to this that we speak of *operating grace.* But in that effect in which our mind both moves and is moved, the operation is not attributed only to God, but also to the soul; and it is with reference to this that we speak of *co-operating grace.*

Now there is a double act in us. First, there is the interior act of the will, and with regard to this act the will is as something moved, and God is the

---

[3] Q. 110, a. 2, ad 2.   [4] *Serm.* CLXIX, 11 (PL 38, 923).   [5] *De Grat. et Lib. Arb.,*
XVII (PL 44, 901).   [6] Q. 109, a. 2, 3, 6 and 9; q. 110, a. 2.

mover; and especially so when the will, which hitherto willed evil, begins to will good. And hence, inasmuch as God moves the human mind to this act, we speak of operating grace. But there is another act, namely, the exterior act. Now since this act is commanded by the will, as was shown above,[7] the operation of this act is attributed to the will. And because God assists us in this act, both by strengthening our will interiorly so as to attain to the act, and by granting outwardly the capability of operating, it is with respect to this that we speak of co-operating grace. Hence after the aforesaid words Augustine subjoins: *He operates that we may will; and when we will, He co-operates that we may accomplish.* And thus, if grace is taken for God's gratuitous motion, whereby He moves us to meritorious good, it is fittingly divided into operating and co-operating grace.

But if grace is taken for the habitual gift, then again there is a double effect of grace, even as of every other form, the first of which is *being,* and the second, *operation.* Thus, the work of heat is to make its subject hot, and to give heat outwardly. In this way, habitual grace, inasmuch as it heals and justifies the soul, or makes it pleasing to God, is called operating grace; but inasmuch as it is the principle of meritorious works, which proceed from free choice, it is called co-operating grace.

Reply Obj. 1. Inasmuch as grace is a certain accidental quality, it does not act upon the soul efficiently, but formally, even as whiteness makes a surface white.

Reply Obj. 2. God does not justify us without ourselves, because while we are being justified we consent to God's justice by a movement of our free choice. Nevertheless this movement is not the cause of grace, but the effect; and hence the whole operation pertains to grace.

Reply Obj. 3. One thing is said to co-operate with another not merely when it is a secondary agent under a principal agent, but when it helps to the end intended. Now man is helped by God to will the good, through the means of operating grace. And hence, under the presupposition of the end, grace co-operates with us.

Reply Obj. 4. Operating and co-operating grace are the same grace, but they are distinguished by their different effects, as is plain from what has been said.

Third Article

WHETHER GRACE IS FITTINGLY DIVIDED INTO PREVENIENT AND SUBSEQUENT GRACE?

We proceed thus to the Third Article:—

Objection 1. It would seem that grace is not fittingly divided into prevenient and subsequent. For grace is an effect of the divine love. But God's love is never subsequent, but always prevenient, according to *1 John* iv. 10:

[7] Q. 17, a. 9.

Not as though we had loved God, but because He hath first loved us.
Therefore grace ought not to be divided into prevenient and subsequent.

Obj. 2. Further, there is but one sanctifying grace in man, since it is
sufficient, according to *2 Cor.* xii. 9: *My grace is sufficient for thee.* But the
same thing cannot be before and after. Therefore grace is not fittingly divided into prevenient and subsequent.

Obj. 3. Further, grace is known by its effects. Now there are an infinite
number of effects—one preceding another. Hence if it is with regard to
these that grace must be divided into prevenient and subsequent, it would
seem that there are infinite species of grace. Now no art takes note of the
infinite in number. Hence grace is not fittingly divided into prevenient
and subsequent.

On the contrary, God's grace is the outcome of His mercy. Now both are
found in *Ps.* lviii. 11: *His mercy shall prevent me,* and again, *Ps.* xxii. 6:
Thy mercy will follow me. Therefore grace is fittingly divided into prevenient and subsequent.

I answer that, Just as grace is divided into operating and co-operating,
according to its diverse effects, so also is it divided into prevenient and
subsequent, however we consider grace. Now there are five effects of grace
in us. Of these, the first is, to heal the soul; the second, to desire good; the
third, to carry into effect the good proposed; the fourth, to persevere in
good; the fifth, to reach glory. And hence grace, inasmuch as it causes the
first effect in us, is called prevenient with respect to the second, and inasmuch as it causes the second, it is called subsequent with respect to the
first effect. And as one effect is posterior to this effect, and prior to that,
so grace may be called prevenient and subsequent because of the same effect
viewed in relation to other and different effects. And this is what Augustine
says: *It is prevenient, inasmuch as it heals, and subsequent, inasmuch as,
being healed, we are strengthened; it is prevenient, inasmuch as we are
called, and subsequent, inasmuch as we are glorified.*[8]

Reply Obj. 1. God's love signifies something eternal, and hence can never
be called anything but prevenient. But grace signifies a temporal effect,
which can precede and follow another; and thus grace may be both prevenient and subsequent.

Reply Obj. 2. The division into prevenient and subsequent grace does not
divide grace in its essence, but only in its effects, as was already said of operating and co-operating grace. For subsequent grace, inasmuch as it pertains to glory, is not numerically distinct from prevenient grace whereby
we are at present justified. For even as the charity of earth is not voided
in heaven, so must the same be said of the light of grace, since the notion
of neither implies imperfection.

Reply Obj. 3. Although the effects of grace may be infinite in number,

[8] *De Nat. et. Grat.,* XXXI (PL 44, 264).

even as human acts are infinite, nevertheless, all are reduced to some things determinate in species, and moreover all coincide in this, that one precedes another.

Fourth Article

WHETHER GRATUITOUS GRACE IS RIGHTLY DIVIDED BY THE APOSTLE?

We proceed thus to the Fourth Article:—

Objection 1. It would seem that gratuitous grace is not rightly divided by the Apostle. For every gift vouchsafed to us by God may be called a gratuitous grace. Now there are an infinite number of gifts freely bestowed on us by God as regards both the good of the soul and the good of the body; and yet they do not make us pleasing to God. Hence gratuitous graces cannot be contained under any certain division.

Obj. 2. Further, gratuitous grace is distinguished from sanctifying grace. But faith pertains to sanctifying grace, since we are justified by it, according to *Rom.* v. 1: *Being justified therefore by faith.* Hence it is not right to place faith among the gratuitous graces, especially since the other virtues, *e.g.*, hope and charity, are not so placed.

Obj. 3. Further, the operation of healing, and speaking diverse tongues are miracles. For the interpretation of speeches pertains either to wisdom or to science, according to *Dan.* i. 17: *And to these children God gave knowledge and understanding in every book and wisdom.* Hence it is not correct to divide the grace of healing and the kinds of tongues against the working of miracles; and the interpretation of speeches against the word of wisdom and science.

Obj. 4. Further, as wisdom and science are gifts of the Holy Ghost, so also are understanding, counsel, piety, fortitude and fear, as was stated above.[9] Therefore these also ought to be placed among the gratuitous graces.

On the contrary, The Apostle says (*1 Cor.* xii. 8, 9, 10): *To one indeed by the Spirit is given the word of wisdom; and to another the word of knowledge, according to the same Spirit; to another, the working of miracles; to another, prophecy; to another, the discerning of spirits; to another divers kinds of tongues; to another interpretation of speeches.*

I answer that, As was said above, gratuitous grace is ordained to this, viz., that a man may help another to be led to God. Now no man can help in this by moving interiorly (for this belongs to God alone), but only exteriorly by teaching or persuading. Hence gratuitous grace embraces whatever a man needs in order to instruct another in divine things which are above reason. Now for this three things are required. First, a man must possess the fullness of knowledge of divine things, so as to be capable of teaching others. Secondly, he must be able to confirm or prove what he says, or

[9] Q. 68, a. 4.

otherwise his words would have no weight. Thirdly, he must be capable of presenting fittingly to his hearers what he knows.

Now as regards the first, three things are necessary, as may be seen in human teaching. For whoever would teach another in any science must first be certain of the principles of that science; and with regard to this there is *faith,* which is certitude of invisible things, the principles of Catholic doctrine. Secondly, it behooves the teacher to know the principal conclusions of the science; and hence we have the word of *wisdom,* which is the knowledge of divine things. Thirdly, he ought to abound with examples and a knowledge of effects, whereby at times he needs to manifest causes; and thus we have the word of *science,* which is the knowledge of human things, since *the invisible things of Him . . . are clearly seen, being understood by the things that are made (Rom.* i. 20).

Now the confirmation of such things as are within reason rests upon arguments; but the confirmation of what is above reason rests on what is proper to the divine power, and this in two ways. First, when the teacher of sacred doctrine does what God alone can do in miraculous deeds, whether with respect to bodily health—and thus there is the *grace of healing,* or merely for the purpose of manifesting the divine power; for instance, that the sun should stand still or darken, or that the sea should be divided—and thus there is the *working of miracles.* Secondly, when he can manifest what God alone can know, and these are either future contingents—and thus there is *prophecy,* or also the secrets of hearts, and thus there is the *discerning of spirits.*

But the capability of speaking can concern either the idiom in which a person can be understood, and thus there is *kinds of tongues*; or it can concern the sense of what is said, and thus there is the *interpretation of speeches.*

Reply Obj. 1. As was stated above, not all the benefits divinely conferred upon us are called gratuitous graces, but only those that surpass the power of nature—*e.g.,* that a fisherman should be replete with the word of wisdom and of science, and the like; and such as these are here set down as gratuitous graces.

Reply Obj. 2. Faith is enumerated here under the gratuitous graces, not as a virtue justifying man in himself, but as implying a super-eminent certitude of faith, whereby a man is fitted for instructing others concerning such things as belong to faith. With regard to hope and charity, they belong to the appetitive power, according as man is ordained thereby to God.

Reply Obj. 3. The grace of healing is distinguished from the general working of miracles because it has a special reason for inducing one to the faith, since a man is all the more ready to believe when he has received the gift of bodily health through the virtue of faith. So, too, to speak with divers tongues and to interpret speeches have special efficacy in bestowing faith. Hence they are set down as special gratuitous graces.

Reply Obj. 4. Wisdom and science are not numbered among the gratuitous graces in the same way as they are reckoned among the gifts of the Holy Ghost, *i.e.,* inasmuch as man's mind is rendered easily movable by the Holy Ghost to the things of wisdom and science; for thus they are gifts of the Holy Ghost, as was stated above.[10] But they are numbered among the gratuitous graces, inasmuch as they imply such a fullness of science and wisdom that a man can not only think rightly of divine things, but can instruct others and overpower adversaries. Hence it is significant that it is the *word* of wisdom and the *word* of science that are placed in the gratuitous graces, since, as Augustine says: *It is one thing merely to know what a man must believe in order to reach everlasting life, and another thing to know how this may benefit the godly and may be defended against the ungodly.*[11]

Fifth Article

WHETHER GRATUITOUS GRACE IS NOBLER THAN SANCTIFYING GRACE?

We proceed thus to the Fifth Article:—

Objection 1. It would seem that gratuitous grace is nobler than sanctifying grace. For *the people's good is better than the individual good,* as the Philosopher says.[12] Now sanctifying grace is ordained to the good of one man alone, whereas gratuitous grace is ordained to the common good of the whole Church, as was stated above. Hence gratuitous grace is nobler than sanctifying grace.

Obj. 2. Further, it is a greater power that is able to act upon another, than that which is confined to itself, even as greater is the brightness of the body that can illuminate other bodies, than of that which can only shine but cannot illuminate; and hence the Philosopher says that *justice is the most excellent of the virtues,*[13] since by it a man bears himself rightly also towards others. But by sanctifying grace a man is perfected only in himself, whereas by gratuitous grace a man works for the perfection of others. Hence gratuitous grace is nobler than sanctifying grace.

Obj. 3. Further, what is proper to the best is nobler than what is common to all; and thus *to reason,* which is proper to man, is nobler than *to sense,* which is common to all animals. Now sanctifying grace is common to all the members of the Church, but gratuitous grace is the proper gift of the more exalted members of the Church. Hence gratuitous grace is nobler than sanctifying grace.

On the contrary, The Apostle (*1 Cor.* xii. 31), having enumerated the gratuitous graces, adds: *And I shew unto you yet a more excellent way;* and as the sequel proves, he is speaking of charity, which pertains to sancti-

[10] Q. 68, a. 1 and 4.   [11] *De Trin.,* XIV, 1 (PL 42, 1037).   [12] *Eth.,* I, 2 (1094b 8).
[13] *Op. cit.,* V, 1 (1129b 27; b 32).

fying grace. Hence sanctifying grace is more noble than gratuitous grace.

I answer that, The higher the good to which a virtue is ordained, the more excellent is the virtue. Now the end is always greater than the means. But sanctifying grace ordains a man immediately to a union with his last end, whereas gratuitous grace ordains a man to what is preparatory to the end; and thus by prophecy and miracles and so forth, men are induced to unite themselves to their last end. Hence sanctifying grace is nobler than gratuitous grace.

Reply Obj. 1. As the Philosopher says, a multitude, *e.g.,* an army, has a double good.[14] The first is in the multitude itself, viz., the order of the army; the second is separate from the multitude, viz., the good of the leader, and this is the better good, since the other is ordained to it. Now gratuitous grace is ordained to the common good of the Church, which is ecclesiastical order, whereas sanctifying grace is ordained to the separate common good, which is God. Hence sanctifying grace is the nobler.

Reply Obj. 2. If gratuitous grace could cause a man to have sanctifying grace, it would follow that gratuitous grace was the nobler; even as the brightness of the sun that illumines is more excellent than that of some body that is lit up. But by gratuitous grace a man cannot cause another to be united to God, which he himself has by sanctifying grace; but he causes certain dispositions towards it. Hence gratuitous grace needs not to be the more excellent, even as in fire, the heat, which manifests the species by which it acts to produce heat in other things, is not more noble than the substantial form of the fire.

Reply Obj. 3. To sense is ordained to reason as to an end, and hence to reason is nobler. But here it is the contrary; for what is proper is ordained to what is common as to an end. Hence there is no comparison.

[14] *Metaph.,* XI, 10 (1075a 11).

ON THE CAUSE OF GRACE

(*In Five Articles*)

WE must now consider the cause of grace, and under this head there are five points of inquiry: (1) Whether God alone is the efficient cause of grace? (2) Whether any disposition towards grace is needed on the part of the recipient, by an act of free choice? (3) Whether such a disposition can make grace follow of necessity? (4) Whether grace is equal in all? (5) Whether anyone can know that he has grace?

First Article

WHETHER GOD ALONE IS THE CAUSE OF GRACE?

We proceed thus to the First Article:—

Objection 1. It would seem that God alone is not the cause of grace. For it is written (*Jo.* i. 17): *Grace and truth came by Jesus Christ.* Now, by the name Jesus Christ is understood not merely the divine nature assuming, but the created nature assumed. Therefore a creature may be the cause of grace.

Obj. 2. Further, there is this difference between the sacraments of the New Law and those of the Old, that the sacraments of the New Law cause grace, whereas the sacraments of the Old Law merely signify it. Now the sacraments of the New Law are certain visible elements. Therefore God is not the only cause of grace.

Obj. 3. Further, according to Dionysius, *Angels cleanse, enlighten and perfect both lesser angels and men.*[1] Now the rational creature is cleansed, enlightened and perfected by grace. Therefore God is not the only cause of grace.

On the contrary, It is written (*Ps.* lxxxiii. 12): *The Lord will give grace and glory.*

I answer that, Nothing can act beyond its species, since the cause must always be more powerful than its effect. Now the gift of grace surpasses every capability of created nature, since it is nothing short of a partaking of the divine nature, which exceeds every other nature. And thus it is impossible that any creature should cause grace. For it is as necessary that God alone should deify, by bestowing a partaking of the divine nature through a participated likeness, as it is impossible that anything save fire should enkindle.

[1] *De Cael. Hier.,* III, 2; IV, 2; VII, 3; VIII, 2 (PG 3, 165; 180; 209; 240).

Reply Obj. 1. Christ's humanity is an *organ of His divinity,* as Dama-scene says.[2] Now an instrument does not bring forth the action of the prin-cipal agent by its own power, but in virtue of the principal agent. Hence Christ's humanity does not cause grace by its own power, but by the power of the divine nature joined to it, whereby the actions of Christ's humanity are saving actions.

Reply Obj. 2. Just as in the person of Christ the humanity causes our salvation by grace, under the principal agency of the divine power, so like-wise in the sacraments of the New Law, which are derived from Christ, grace is instrumentally caused by the sacraments, and principally by the power of the Holy Ghost working in the sacraments, according to *John* iii. 5: *Unless a man be born again of water and the Holy Ghost he cannot enter into the kingdom of God.*

Reply Obj. 3. Angels cleanse, enlighten and perfect angels or men, by instruction, and not by justifying them through grace. Hence Dionysius says that *this cleansing and enlightenment and perfecting is nothing else than the assumption of divine science.*[3]

Second Article

WHETHER ANY PREPARATION AND DISPOSITION FOR GRACE
IS REQUIRED ON MAN'S PART?

We proceed thus to the Second Article:—

Objection 1. It would seem that no preparation or disposition for grace is required on man's part, since, as the Apostle says (*Rom.* iv. 4), *To him that worketh, the reward is not reckoned according to grace, but according to debt.* Now a man's preparation by free choice can be only through some operation. Hence it would do away with the notion of grace.

Obj. 2. Further, whoever continues sinning is not preparing himself to have grace. But to some who continue sinning grace is given, as is clear in the case of Paul, who received grace while he was *breathing out threat-enings and slaughter against the disciples of the Lord* (*Acts* ix. 1). Hence no preparation for grace is required on man's part.

Obj. 3. Further, an agent of infinite power needs no disposition in mat-ter, since it does not even require matter, as appears in creation, to which grace is compared, for it is called *a new creature* (*Gal.* vi. 15). But only God, Who has infinite power, causes grace, as was stated above. Hence no prep-aration is required on man's part to obtain grace.

On the contrary, It is written (*Amos* iv. 12): *Be prepared to meet thy God, O Israel;* and (*1 Kings* vii. 3): *Prepare your hearts unto the Lord.*

I answer that, As was stated above, grace is taken in two ways.[4] First, as a habitual gift of God. Secondly, as a help from God, Who moves the soul

---

[2] *De Fide Orth.,* III, 19 (PG 94, 1080).   [3] Cf. *De Cael. Hier.,* VII, 3 (PG 3, 209).
[4] Q. 109, a. 2, 3, 6 and 9; q. 110, a. 2; q. 111, a. 2.

to good. Now taking grace in the first sense, a certain preparation of grace is required for it, since a form can be only in disposed matter. But if we speak of grace as it signifies a help from God moving us to good, no preparation is required on man's part, anticipating, as it were, the divine help, but rather, every preparation in man must be by the help of God moving the soul to good. And thus even the good movement of free choice, whereby anyone is prepared for receiving the gift of grace, is an act of free choice moved by God. And it is thus that man is said to prepare himself, according to *Prov.* xvi. 1: *It is the part of man to prepare the soul;* yet it is principally from God, Who moves the free choice. Hence it is said that man's will is prepared by God (*Prov.* viii. 35), and that man's steps are guided by God (*Prov.* xxxvi. 23).

Reply Obj. 1. A certain preparation of man for grace is simultaneous with the infusion of grace; and this operation is meritorious, not indeed of grace, which is already possessed, but of glory, which is not yet possessed. But there is another imperfect preparation, which sometimes precedes the gift of sanctifying grace, which yet is from God's motion. But it does not suffice for merit, since man is not yet justified by grace, and merit can only arise from grace, as will be seen farther on.[5]

Reply Obj. 2. Since a man cannot prepare himself for grace unless God prevent and move him to good, it is of no account whether anyone arrive at perfect preparation instantaneously, or step by step. For it is written (*Ecclus.* xi. 23): *It is easy in the eyes of God on a sudden to make the poor man rich.* Now it sometimes happens that God moves a man to good, but not perfect good, and this preparation precedes grace. But He sometimes moves him suddenly and perfectly to good, and man receives grace suddenly, according to *John* vi. 45: *Every one that hath heard of the Father, and hath learned, cometh to Me.* And thus it happened to Paul, since, suddenly when he was in the midst of sin, his heart was perfectly moved by God to hear, to learn, to come; and hence he received grace suddenly.

Reply Obj. 3. An agent of infinite power needs no matter or disposition of matter, brought about by the action of some other cause; and yet, looking to the condition of the thing caused, it must cause, in the thing caused, both the matter and the due disposition for the form. So, likewise, when God infuses grace into a soul, no preparation is required which He Himself does not bring about.

Third Article

WHETHER GRACE IS NECESSARILY GIVEN TO WHOEVER PREPARES HIMSELF FOR IT, OR TO WHOEVER DOES WHAT HE CAN?

We proceed thus to the Third Article:—

Objection 1. It would seem that grace is necessarily given to whoever

[5] Q. 114, a. 2.

prepares himself for grace, or to whoever does what he can, because, on *Rom.* v. 1 (*Being justified . . . by faith, let us have peace,* etc.) the *Gloss* says: *God welcomes whoever flies to Him, otherwise there would be injustice with Him.*[6] But it is impossible for injustice to be with God. Therefore it is impossible for God not to welcome whoever flies to Him. Hence he receives grace of necessity.

Obj. 2. Further, Anselm says that the reason why God does not bestow grace on the devil is that he did not wish, nor was he prepared, to receive it.[7] But if the cause be removed, the effect must needs be removed also. Therefore, if anyone is willing to receive grace it is bestowed on him of necessity.

Obj. 3. Further, good is diffusive of itself, as appears from Dionysius.[8] But the good of grace is better than the good of nature. Hence, since natural forms necessarily come to disposed matter, much more does it seem that grace is necessarily bestowed on whoever prepares himself for grace.

On the contrary, Man is compared to God as clay to the potter, according to *Jer.* xviii. 6: *As clay is in the hand of the potter, so are you in My hand.* But however much the clay is prepared, it does not necessarily receive its shape from the potter. Hence, however much a man prepares himself, he does not necessarily receive grace from God.

I answer that, As was stated above, man's preparation for grace is from God, as mover, and from free choice, as moved. Hence the preparation may be looked at in two ways. First, as it is from free choice, and thus there is no necessity that it should obtain grace, since the gift of grace exceeds every preparation of human power. But it may be considered, secondly, as it is from God the mover, and thus it has a necessity—not indeed of coercion, but of infallibility—as regards what it is ordained to by God, since God's intention cannot fail, according to the saying of Augustine, in his book *On the Predestination of the Saints,* that *by God's good gifts whoever is liberated, is most certainly liberated.*[9] Hence if God intends, while moving, that the one whose heart He moves should attain to grace, he will infallibly attain to it, according to *John* vi. 45: *Every one that hath heard of the Father, and hath learned, cometh to Me.*

Reply Obj. 1. This *Gloss* is speaking of such as fly to God by a meritorious act of their free choice, already *informed* with grace; for if they did not receive grace, it would be against the justice which He Himself established.—Or if it refers to the movement of free choice before grace, it is speaking in the sense that man's flight to God is by a divine motion, which ought not, in justice, to fail.

Reply Obj. 2. The first cause of the defect of grace is on our part; but

---

[6] Peter Lombard, *In Rom.,* super III, 21 (PL 191, 1360).   [7] *De Casu Diab.,* III (PL 158, 328).   [8] *De Div. Nom.,* IV, 20 (PG 3, 719).   [9] Cf. *De Dono Persev.,* XIV (PL 45, 1014).

the first cause of the bestowal of grace is on God's, according to *Osee* xiii. 9: *Destruction is thy own, O Israel; thy help is only in Me.*

Reply Obj. 3. Even in natural things, the form does not necessarily follow the disposition of the matter, except by the power of the agent that causes the disposition.

Fourth Article

WHETHER GRACE IS GREATER IN ONE THAN IN ANOTHER?

We proceed thus to the Fourth Article:—

Objection 1. It would seem that grace is not greater in one than in another. For grace is caused in us by the divine love, as was stated above.[10] Now it is written (*Wis.* vi. 8): *He made the little and the great and He hath equally care of all.* Therefore all obtain grace from Him equally.

Obj. 2. Further, whatever is a maximum cannot be more or less. But grace is a maximum since it joins us with our last end. Therefore there is no greater or less in it. Hence it is not greater in one than in another.

Obj. 3. Further, grace is the soul's life, as was stated above.[11] But there is no greater or less in life. Hence, neither is there in grace.

On the contrary, It is written (Ephes. iv. 7): *But to every one of us is given grace according to the measure of the giving of Christ.* Now what is given in measure is not given to all equally. Hence all have not an equal grace.

I answer that, As was stated above, habits can have a double magnitude.[12] One concerns the end or object, as when a virtue is said to be more noble through being ordained to a greater good; the other is on the part of the subject, which participates more or less in the habit inhering to it.

Now as regards the first magnitude, sanctifying grace cannot be greater or less, since, of its nature, grace joins man to the highest good, which is God. But as regards the subject, grace can receive more or less, inasmuch as one may be more perfectly illumined by the light of grace than another. And a certain reason for this is on the part of him who prepares himself for grace; since he who is better prepared for grace receives more grace. Yet it is not here that we must seek the first cause of this diversity, since man prepares himself only inasmuch as his free choice is prepared by God. Hence the first cause of this diversity is to be sought on the part of God, Who dispenses His gifts of grace variously, in order that the beauty and perfection of the Church may result from these various degrees; even as He instituted the various conditions of things, that the universe might be perfect. Hence, after the Apostle had said (*Ephes.* iv. 7): *To every one of us is given grace according to the measure of the giving of Christ,* having enumerated the various graces, he adds (*verse* 12): *For the perfecting of the saints . . . for the edifying of the body of Christ.*

---

[10] Q. 110, a. 1. [11] Q. 110, a. 1, ad 2. [12] Q. 52, a. 1 and 2; q. 66, a. 1 and 2.

Reply Obj. 1. The divine care may be looked at in two ways. First, as regards the divine act, which is simple and uniform; and thus His care looks equally to all, since by one simple act He administers great things and little. But, secondly, it may be considered in those things which come to creatures by the divine care; and thus, inequality is found, inasmuch as God by His care provides greater gifts for some, and lesser gifts for others.

Reply Obj. 2. This objection is based on the first kind of magnitude in grace; since grace cannot be greater by ordaining to a greater good, but inasmuch as it ordains more or less to a greater or lesser participation of the same good. For there may be diversity of intensity and remission both in grace and in final glory as regards the subjects' participation.

Reply Obj. 3. Natural life pertains to man's substance, and hence cannot be more or less; but man partakes of the life of grace accidentally, and hence man may possess it more or less.

Fifth Article

WHETHER MAN CAN KNOW THAT HE HAS GRACE?

We proceed thus to the Fifth Article:—

Objection 1. It would seem that man can know that he has grace. For grace is in the soul by its essence. Now the soul has most certain knowledge of those things that are in it by their essence, as appears from Augustine.[13] Hence grace may be known most certainly by one who has grace.

Obj. 2. Further, as science is a gift of God, so is grace. But whoever receives science from God, knows that he has science, according to *Wis.* vii. 17: The Lord *hath given me the true knowledge of the things that are.* Hence, with equal reason, whoever receives grace from God, knows that he has grace.

Obj. 3. Further, light is more knowable than darkness, since, according to the Apostle (*Ephes.* v. 13), *all that is made manifest is light.* Now sin, which is spiritual darkness, may be known with certainty by one that is in sin. Much more, therefore, may grace, which is spiritual light, be known.

Obj. 4. Further, the Apostle says (*1 Cor.* ii. 12): *Now we have received not the Spirit of this world, but the Spirit that is of God; that we may know the things that are given us from God.* Now grace is God's first gift. Hence, the man who receives grace by the Holy Spirit, by the same Holy Spirit knows the grace given to him.

Obj. 5. Further, it was said by the Lord to Abraham (*Gen.* xxii. 12): *Now I know that thou fearest God, i.e.,* I have made thee know. But He is speaking there of chaste fear, which is not apart from grace. Hence a man may know that he has grace.

---

[13] *De Genesi ad Litt.,* XII, 25; 31 (PL 34, 475; 479).

On the contrary, It is written (*Eccles.* ix. 1): *Man knoweth not whether he be worthy of love or hatred.* Now sanctifying grace maketh a man worthy of God's love. Therefore no one can know whether he has sanctifying grace.

I answer that, There are three ways of knowing a thing. First, by revelation, and thus anyone may know that he has grace, for God by a special privilege reveals this at times to some, in order that the joy of safety may begin in them even in this life, and that they may carry on toilsome works with greater trust and greater energy, and may bear the evils of this present life, as when it was said to Paul (*2 Cor.* xii. 9): *My grace is sufficient for thee.*

Secondly, a man may, of himself, know something, and with certainty; and in this way no one can know that he has grace. For certitude about a thing can be had only when we may judge of it by its proper principle. Thus it is by indemonstrable universal principles that certitude is obtained concerning demonstrative conclusions. Now no one can know he has the science of a conclusion if he does not know its principle. But the principle of grace and its object is God, Who by reason of His very excellence is unknown to us, according to *Job* xxxvi. 26: *Behold God is great, exceeding our knowledge.* And hence His presence in us and His absence cannot be known with certainty, according to *Job* ix. 11: *If He come to me, I shall not see Him; if He depart, I shall not understand.* And hence man cannot judge with certainty that he has grace, according to *1 Cor.* iv. 3, 4: *But neither do I judge my own self . . . but He that judgeth me is the Lord.*

Thirdly, things are known conjecturally by signs; and thus anyone may know he has grace, when he is conscious of delighting in God and of despising worldly things, and inasmuch as a man is not conscious of any mortal sin. In this sense it is written (*Apoc.* ii. 17): *To him that overcometh I will give the hidden manna . . . which no man knoweth, but he that receiveth it,* because whoever receives it knows, by experiencing a certain sweetness, which he who does not receive does not experience. Yet this knowledge is imperfect, and hence the Apostle says (*1 Cor.* iv. 4): *I am not conscious to myself of anything, yet am I not hereby justified,* since, according to *Ps.* xviii. 13: *Who can understand sins? From my secret ones cleanse me, O Lord, and from those of others spare Thy servant.*

Reply Obj. 1. Those things which are in the soul by their essence are known through experimental knowledge, in so far as through his acts man has experience of his inward principles. For example, we perceive our will by willing, and by exercising the functions of life, we observe that there is life in us.

Reply Obj. 2. It belongs to the nature of science that a man should have certitude of the objects of science; so, too, it belongs to the nature of faith that a man should be certain of the things of faith, and this, because certitude belongs to the perfection of the intellect, wherein these gifts exist. Hence, whoever has science or faith is certain that he has them. But it is otherwise with grace and charity and the like, which perfect the appetitive power.

Reply Obj. 3. Sin has for its principal and object a mutable good, which is known to us. But the object or end of grace is unknown to us because of the greatness of its light, according to *1 Tim.* vi. 16: *Who . . . inhabiteth light inaccessible.*

Reply Obj. 4. The Apostle is here speaking of the gifts of glory (*1 Cor.* ii. 10), which have been given to us in hope, and these we know most certainly by faith, although we do not know for certain that we have grace to enable us to merit them.—Or it may be said that he is speaking of the privileged knowledge, which comes of revelation. Hence he adds (*verse* 10): *But to us God hath revealed them by His Spirit.*

Reply Obj. 5. What was said to Abraham may refer to the experimental knowledge which we have through our deeds. For in the deed that Abraham had just wrought, he could know experimentally that he had the fear of God.—Or it may refer to a revelation.

ON THE EFFECTS OF GRACE
(*In Ten Articles*)

WE have now to consider the effects of grace: (1) concerning the justifica-tion of the ungodly, which is the effect of operating grace; and (2) concerning merit, which is the effect of co-operating grace.[1] Under the first head there are ten points of inquiry: (1) What is the justification of the ungodly? (2) Whether grace is required for it? (3) Whether any movement of free choice is required for it? (4) Whether a movement of faith is required for the justification of the ungodly? (5) Whether a movement of free choice against sin is required for it? (6) Whether the remission of sins is to be reckoned with the foregoing? (7) Whether the justification of the ungodly is a work of time or is sudden? (8) Of the natural order of the things concurring to justification. (9) Whether the justification of the ungodly is God's greatest work? (10) Whether the justification of the ungodly is miraculous?

First Article

WHETHER THE JUSTIFICATION OF THE UNGODLY IS THE REMISSION OF SINS?

We proceed thus to the First Article:—

Objection 1. It would seem that the justification of the ungodly is not the remission of sins. For sin is opposed not only to justice, but to all the other virtues, as was stated above.[2] Now justification signifies a certain movement towards justice. Therefore not every remission of sin is justification, since every movement is from one contrary to the other.

Obj. 2. Further, everything ought to be named from what is predominant in it, according to *De Anima* ii.[3] Now the remission of sins is brought about chiefly by faith, according to *Acts* xv. 9: *Purifying their hearts by faith*; and by charity, according to *Prov.* x. 12: *Charity covereth all sins.* Therefore the remission of sins ought to be named from faith or charity rather than justice.

Obj. 3. Further, the remission of sins seems to be the same as being called, for whoever is called is afar off, and we are afar off from God by sin. But one is called before being justified, according to *Rom.* viii. 30: *And*

[1] Q. 114. [2] Q. 71, a. 1. [3] Aristotle, *De An.*, II, 4 (416b 23).

whom He called, them He also justified. Therefore justification is not the remission of sins.

On the contrary, On *Rom.* viii. 30 (*Whom He called, them He also justified*) the *Gloss* says, *i.e., by the remission of sins.*[4] Therefore the remission of sins is justification.

I answer that, Justification, taken passively, implies a movement towards justice, as heating implies a movement towards heat. But since justice, by its nature, signifies a certain rectitude of order, it may be taken in two ways. First, inasmuch as it signifies a right order in man's act, and thus justice is placed among the virtues—either as particular justice, which directs a man's acts by regulating them in relation to his fellow-man—or as legal justice, which directs a man's acts by regulating them in their relation to the common good of society, as appears from *Ethics* v.[5]

Secondly, justice is so called inasmuch as it signifies a certain rectitude of order in the interior disposition of a man, in so far as what is highest in man is subject to God, and the inferior powers of the soul are subject to the superior, *i.e.,* to the reason; and this disposition the Philosopher calls *justice metaphorically speaking.*[6] Now this justice may be in man in two ways: First, by simple generation, which is from privation to form; and thus justification may belong even to such as are not in sin, when they receive this justice from God, as Adam is said to have received original justice. Secondly, this justice may be brought about in man by a movement from one contrary to the other, and thus justification implies a transmutation from the state of injustice to the aforesaid state of justice. And it is thus we are now speaking of the justification of the ungodly, according to the Apostle (*Rom.* iv. 5): *But to him that worketh not, yet believeth in Him that justifieth the ungodly,* etc. And because movement is named from its term *whereto* rather than from its term *whence,* the transmutation whereby anyone is changed by the remission of sins from the state of ungodliness to the state of justice borrows its name from its term *whereto,* and is called the *justification of the ungodly.*

Reply Obj. 1. Every sin, inasmuch as it signifies the disorder of a mind not subject to God, may be called injustice, as being contrary to the aforesaid justice, according to *1 John* iii. 4: *Whosoever committeth sin, committeth also iniquity; and sin is iniquity.* And thus the removal of any sin is called the justification of the ungodly.

Reply Obj. 2. Faith and charity express a special ordering of the human mind to God by the intellect and will; whereas justice expresses a general rectitude of order. Hence this transmutation is named from justice rather than from charity or faith.

Reply Obj. 3. *Being called* refers to God's help moving and exciting our

---

[4] *Glossa interl.* (VI, 20r); Peter Lombard, *In Rom.,* super VIII, 30 (PL 191, 1450)
[5] Aristotle, *Eth.,* V, 1 (1129b 13); 2 (1130a 14).   [6] *Op. cit.,* V, 11 (1138b 5).

mind to give up sin; and this motion of God is not the remission of sin, but its cause.

Second Article

WHETHER THE INFUSION OF GRACE IS REQUIRED FOR THE REMISSION OF GUILT, *I.E.*, FOR THE JUSTIFICATION OF THE UNGODLY?

We proceed thus to the Second Article:—

Objection 1. It would seem that for the remission of guilt, which is the justification of the ungodly, no infusion of grace is required. For anyone may be moved from one contrary without being led to the other, if the contraries are not immediate. Now the state of guilt and the state of grace are not immediate contraries, for there is the middle state of innocence wherein a man has neither grace nor guilt. Hence a man may be pardoned his guilt without his being brought to a state of grace.

Obj. 2. Further, the remission of guilt consists in the divine imputation, according to *Ps.* xxxi. 2: *Blessed is the man to whom the Lord hath not imputed sin.* Now the infusion of grace puts something into our soul, as was stated above.[7] Hence the infusion of grace is not required for the remission of guilt.

Obj. 3. Further, no one can be subject to two contraries at once. Now some sins are contraries, as wastefulness and miserliness. Hence, whoever is subject to the sin of wastefulness is not simultaneously subject to the sin of miserliness; yet it may happen that he has been subject to it previously. Hence by sinning with the vice of wastefulness he is freed from the sin of miserliness. And thus a sin is remitted without grace.

On the contrary, It is written (*Rom.* iii. 24): *Justified freely by His grace.*

I answer that, By sinning a man offends God, as was stated above.[8] Now an offense is remitted to anyone, only when the soul of the offender is at peace with the offended. Hence sin is remitted to us when God is at peace with us, and this peace consists in the love whereby God loves us. Now God's love, considered on the part of the divine act, is eternal and unchangeable; whereas, as regards the effect it imprints on us, it is sometimes interrupted, inasmuch as we sometimes fall short of it and once more regain it. Now the effect of the divine love in us, which is taken away by sin, is grace, whereby a man is made worthy of eternal life, from which sin shuts him out. Hence we could not conceive the remission of guilt, without the infusion of grace.

Reply Obj. 1. More is required for an offender to be pardoned an offense, than for one who has committed no offense, not to be hated. For it may happen among men that one man neither hates nor loves another. But if the

---

[7] Q. 110, a. 1.   [8] Q. 71, a. 6, ad 5; q. 87, a. 3.

other offends him, then the forgiveness of the offense can spring only from a special good-will. Now God's good-will is said to be restored to man by the gift of grace; and hence, although a man before sinning may be without grace and without guilt, yet that he is without guilt after sinning can be only because he has grace.

Reply Obj. 2. Just as God's love does not merely consist in the act of the divine will but also signifies a certain effect of grace, as was stated above,[9] so likewise, when God does not impute sin to a man, there is signified a certain effect in him to whom the sin is not imputed; for it proceeds from the divine love that sin is not imputed to a man by God.

Reply Obj. 3. As Augustine says, *if to leave off sinning were the same as to have no sin, it would be enough if Scripture warned us thus: 'My son, hast thou sinned? do so no more'* (*Ecclus.* xxi. 1). *Now this is not enough, but it is added: 'But for thy former sins also pray that they may be forgiven thee.'* [10] For the act of sin passes, but the guilt remains, as was stated above.[11] Hence, when anyone passes from the sin of one vice to the sin of a contrary vice, he ceases to have the act of the former sin, but he does not cease to have the guilt; and so he has the guilt of both sins at once. For sins are not contrary to each other on the part of their turning from God, wherein sin has its guilt.

Third Article

WHETHER FOR THE JUSTIFICATION OF THE UNGODLY THERE IS REQUIRED A MOVEMENT OF FREE CHOICE?

We proceed thus to the Third Article:—

Objection 1. It would seem that no movement of free choice is required for the justification of the ungodly. For we see that by the sacrament of Baptism infants and sometimes adults are justified without a movement of free choice; and hence Augustine says that when one of his friends was taken with a fever, *he lay for a long time senseless and in a deadly sweat, and when he was despaired of, he was baptized without his knowing, and was regenerated;* [12] which is effected by justifying grace. Now God does not confine His power to the sacraments. Hence He can justify a man without the sacraments, and without any movement of free choice.

Obj. 2. Further, a man has not the use of reason when asleep, and without it there can be no movement of free choice. But Solomon received from God the gift of wisdom when asleep, as is related in *3 Kings* iii. 5, and *2 Paral.* i. 7. Hence with equal reason the gift of justifying grace is sometimes bestowed by God on man without the movement of his free choice.

Obj. 3. Further, grace is preserved by the same cause that brings it into being; for Augustine says that *so ought man to turn to God that he be ever*

---

[9] Q. 110, a. 1.   [10] *De Nupt. et Concupisc.*, I, 26 (PL 44, 430).   [11] Q. 87, a. 6.
[12] *Confess.*, IV, 4 (PL 32, 696).

made just by Him.[13] Now grace is preserved in man without a movement of his free choice. Hence it can be infused in the beginning without a movement of free choice.

On the contrary, It is written (*Jo.* vi. 45): *Every one that hath heard of the Father, and hath learned, cometh to Me.* Now to learn cannot be without a movement of free choice, since the learner assents to the teacher. Hence no one comes to the Father by justifying grace without a movement of free choice.

I answer that, The justification of the ungodly is brought about by God moving man to justice. For He it is *that justifieth the ungodly,* according to *Rom.* iv. 5. Now God moves everything in its own manner, just as we see that in natural things what is heavy and what is light are moved differently, because of their diverse natures. Hence He moves man to justice according to the condition of his human nature. But it is proper to man's nature to have free choice. Hence in him who has the use of free choice God's motion to justice does not take place without a movement of the free choice; but He so infuses the gift of justifying grace that at the same time He moves free choice to accept the gift of grace, in such as are capable of being moved thus.

Reply Obj. 1. Infants are not capable of the movement of free choice, and so it is by the sole information of their souls that God moves them to justice. Now this cannot be brought about without a sacrament; because, just as original sin, from which they are justified, does not come to them from their own will, but by carnal generation, so also grace is given them by Christ through spiritual regeneration. And the same reason holds good with madmen and idiots, that have never had the use of free choice. But in the case of one who has had the use of free choice, and afterwards has lost it either through sickness or sleep, he does not obtain justifying grace by the exterior rite of Baptism, or of any other sacrament, unless he intended to make use of this sacrament, and this can be only by the use of free choice. And it was in this way that he of whom Augustine speaks was regenerated, because both previously and afterwards he assented to the Baptism.[14]

Reply Obj. 2. Solomon neither merited nor received wisdom while asleep; but it was declared to him in his sleep that because of his previous desire wisdom would be infused into him by God. Hence it is said in his person (*Wis.* vii. 7): *I wished, and understanding was given unto me.*

Or it may be said that his sleep was not natural, but was the sleep of prophecy, according to *Num.* xii. 6: *If there be among you a prophet of the Lord, I will appear to him in a vision, or I will speak to him in a dream.* In such cases the use of free choice remains.

And yet it must be observed that the comparison between the gift of wisdom and the gift of justifying grace does not hold. For the gift of

---

[13] *De Genesi ad Litt.,* VIII, 12 (PL 34, 382).   [14] *Confess.,* IV, 4 (PL 32, 696).

justifying grace especially ordains a man to good, which is the object of the will; and hence a man is moved to it by a movement of the will which is a movement of free choice. But wisdom perfects the intellect, which precedes the will; and hence, without any complete movement of the free choice, the intellect can be illumined with the gift of wisdom, even as we see that things are revealed to men in sleep, according to *Job* xxxiii. 15, 16: *When deep sleep falleth upon men and they are sleeping in their beds, then He openeth the ears of men, and teaching, instructeth them in what they are to learn.*

Reply Obj. 3. In the infusion of justifying grace there is a certain transmutation of the human soul, and hence the movement of the human soul itself is required in order that the soul may be moved in its own manner. But the conservation of grace is without transmutation; and so no movement on the part of the soul is required, but only a continuation of the divine causality.

Fourth Article

WHETHER A MOVEMENT OF FAITH IS REQUIRED FOR THE JUSTIFICATION OF THE UNGODLY?

We proceed thus to the Fourth Article:—

Objection 1. It would seem that no movement of faith is required for the justification of the ungodly. For just as a man is justified by faith, so also by other things, viz., by fear, of which it is written (*Ecclus.* i. 27): *The fear of the Lord driveth out sin, for he that is without fear cannot be justified*; and again by charity, according to *Luke* vii. 47: *Many sins are forgiven her because she hath loved much*; and again by humility, according to *James* iv. 6: *God resisteth the proud and giveth grace to the humble*; and again by mercy, according to *Prov.* xv. 27: *By mercy and faith sins are purged away.* Hence the movement of faith is no more required for the justification of the ungodly, than the movements of the aforesaid virtues.

Obj. 2. Further, the act of faith is required for justification only inasmuch as a man knows God by faith. But a man may know God in other ways, viz., by natural knowledge, and by the gift of wisdom. Hence no act of faith is required for the justification of the ungodly.

Obj. 3. Further, there are several articles of faith. Therefore, if the act of faith is required for the justification of the ungodly, it would seem that a man ought to think on every article of faith when he is first justified. But this seems unbefitting, since such thought would require a long delay of time. Hence it seems that an act of faith is not required for the justification of the ungodly.

On the contrary, It is written (*Rom.* v. 1): *Being justified therefore by faith, let us have peace with God.*

I answer that, As we have stated above, a movement of free choice is required for the justification of the ungodly, inasmuch as man's mind is
moved by God. Now God moves man's soul by turning it to Himself, according to *Ps.* lxxxiv. 7, in the other version: *Thou wilt turn us, O God, and
bring us to life.* Hence for the justification of the ungodly a movement of
the mind is required, by which it is turned to God. Now the first turning to
God is by faith, according to *Heb.* xi. 6: *He that cometh to God must believe that He is.* Hence a movement of faith is required for the justification
of the ungodly.

Reply Obj. 1. The movement of faith is not perfect unless it is quickened
by charity, and so in the justification of the ungodly, a movement of charity
is infused together with the movement of faith. Now free choice is moved to
God by being subject to Him, and hence an act of filial fear and an act of
humility also concur. For it may happen that one and the same act of free
choice springs from different virtues, when one commands and another is
commanded, inasmuch as the act may be ordained to various ends. Now
the act of mercy counteracts sin either by way of satisfying for it, and thus
it follows justification; or by way of preparation, inasmuch as the *merciful
obtain mercy* (*Matt.* v. 7), and thus it can either precede justification, or
concur with the other virtues towards justification, inasmuch as mercy is
included in the love of our neighbor.

Reply Obj. 2. By natural knowledge a man is not turned to God according as He is the object of beatitude and the cause of justification. Hence
such knowledge does not suffice for justification. On the other hand, the
gift of wisdom presupposes the knowledge of faith, as was stated above.[15]

Reply Obj. 3. As the Apostle says (*Rom.* iv. 5), *to him that . . . believeth in Him that justifieth the ungodly his faith is reputed to justice, according to the purpose of the grace of God.* Hence it is clear that in the
justification of the ungodly an act of faith is required in order that a man
may believe that God justifies man through the mystery of Christ.

Fifth Article

WHETHER FOR THE JUSTIFICATION OF THE UNGODLY THERE
IS REQUIRED A MOVEMENT OF FREE CHOICE AGAINST SIN?

We proceed thus to the Fifth Article:—

Objection 1. It would seem that no movement of free choice against sin
is required for the justification of the ungodly. For charity alone suffices
to take away sin, according to *Prov.* x. 12: *Charity covereth all sins.* Now
the object of charity is not sin. Therefore for this justification of the ungodly no movement of free choice against sin is required.

Obj. 2. Further, whoever is tending onward ought not to look back, according to *Philip.* iii. 13, 14: *Forgetting the things that are behind, and*

---

[15] Q. 68, a. 2; a. 4, ad 3.

stretching forth myself to those that are before, I press towards the mark, to the prize of the supernal vocation. But whoever is stretching forth to justice has his sins behind him. Hence he ought to forget them, and not stretch forth to them by a movement of free choice.

Obj. 3. Further, in the justification of the ungodly one sin is not remitted without another, for *it is irreverent to expect half a pardon from God.* Hence, in the justification of the ungodly, if man's free choice must move against sin, he ought to think of all his sins. But this is unfitting both because a great space of time would be required for such thought, and because a man could not obtain the forgiveness of such sins as he had forgotten. Hence for the justification of the ungodly no movement of free choice against sin is required.

On the contrary, It is written (*Ps.* xxxi. 5): *I will confess against myself my injustice to the Lord; and Thou hast forgiven the wickedness of my sin.*

I answer that, As we have stated above, the justification of the ungodly is a certain movement whereby the human mind is moved by God from the state of sin to the state of justice. Hence it is necessary for the human mind to be related to both extremes by an act of free choice, as a body in local movement is related to both terms of the movement. Now it is clear that in local movement the moving body leaves the term *whence* and nears the term *whereto.* Hence the human mind, while it is being justified, must, by a movement of free choice, withdraw from sin and draw near to justice. Now to withdraw from sin and to draw near to justice, in a movement of free choice, means detestation and desire. For Augustine says on the words *the hireling fleeth,* etc. (*Jo.* x. 12): *Our affections are the movements of our soul; joy is the soul's outpouring; fear is the soul's flight; your soul goes forward when you seek; your soul flees, when you are afraid.*[16] Hence in the justification of the ungodly there must be two movements of the free choice, one, whereby it tends to God's justice, the other whereby it hates sin.

Reply Obj. 1. It belongs to the same virtue to seek one contrary and to avoid the other; and hence, as it belongs to charity to love God, so likewise, does it to detest sin whereby the soul is separated from God.

Reply Obj. 2. A man ought not to return to those things that are behind, by loving them; but, in this sense, he ought to forget them, lest he be drawn to them. Yet he ought to recall them to mind, in order to detest them; for this is to fly from them.

Reply Obj. 3. Before justification, a man must detest each sin he remembers to have committed, and from this remembrance the soul goes on to have a general movement of detestation with regard to all sins committed, in which are included such sins as have been forgotten. For a man is then

---

[16] *Tract.* XLVI, super *Ioann.,* X, 12 (PL 35, 1732).

in such a frame of mind that he would be sorry even for those he does not remember, if they were present to his memory; and this movement co-operates in his justification.

WHETHER THE REMISSION OF SINS OUGHT TO BE RECKONED AMONG THE THINGS REQUIRED FOR JUSTIFICATION?

We proceed thus to the Sixth Article:—

Objection 1. It would seem that the remission of sins ought not to be reckoned among the things required for justification. For the substance of a thing is not reckoned together with those that are required for a thing; and thus a man is not reckoned together with his body and soul. But the justification of the ungodly is itself the remission of sins, as was stated above. Therefore the remission of sins ought not to be reckoned among the things required for the justification of the ungodly.

Obj. 2. Further, infusion of grace and remission of sins are the same; just as illumination and the expulsion of darkness are the same. But a thing ought not to be reckoned together with itself, for unity is opposed to multitude. Therefore the remission of sins ought not to be reckoned with the infusion of grace.

Obj. 3. Further, the remission of sin follows, as effect from cause, from the movement of free choice towards God and sin; since it is by faith and contrition that sin is forgiven. But an effect ought not to be reckoned with its cause, since things thus enumerated together, and, as it were, co-divided, are by nature simultaneous. Hence the remission of sins ought not to be reckoned with the things required for the justification of the ungodly.

On the contrary, In reckoning what is required for a thing, we ought not to pass over the end, which is the chief part of everything. Now the remission of sins is the end of the justification of the ungodly; for it is written (*Isa.* xxvii. 9): *This is all the fruit, that the sin thereof should be taken away.* Hence the remission of sins ought to be reckoned among the things required for justification.

I answer that, There are four things which are accounted to be necessary for the justification of the ungodly,[17] viz., the infusion of grace, the movement of free choice towards God by faith, the movement of free choice against sin, and the remission of guilt. The reason for this is that, as was stated above, the justification of the ungodly is a movement whereby the soul is moved by God from a state of sin to a state of justice. Now in the movement whereby one thing is moved by another, three things are required:—first, the motion of the mover; secondly, the movement of the moved; thirdly, the consummation of the movement, or the attainment of

[17] Cf. St. Albert, *In IV Sent.,* d. xvii, a. 10-11 (XXIX, 673-679); St. Bonaventure. *In IV Sent.,* d. xvii, pt. 1, a. 1, q. 1-4 (IV, 418-424).

the end. On the part of the divine motion, there is the infusion of grace; on the part of the free choice which is moved, there are two movements,— of departure from the term *whence*, and of approach to the term *whereto*; while the consummation of the movement or the attainment of the end of the movement is signified in the remission of guilt; for in this is the justification of the ungodly completed.

Reply Obj. 1. The justification of the ungodly is called the remission of sins, according as every movement has its species from its term. Nevertheless, many other things are required in order to reach the term, as was stated above.

Reply Obj. 2. The infusion of grace and the remission of sin may be considered in two ways. First, with respect to the substance of the act, and thus they are the same; for by the same act God bestows grace and remits guilt. Secondly, they may be considered on the part of the objects, and thus they differ by the difference between guilt, which is taken away, and grace, which is infused; just as in natural things generation and corruption differ, although the generation of one thing is the corruption of another.

Reply Obj. 3. This enumeration is not the division of a genus into its species, in which the things enumerated must be simultaneous, but it is a division of the things required for the completion of anything; and in this enumeration we may have what precedes and what follows, since some of the principles and parts of a composite thing may precede and some follow.

Seventh Article

WHETHER THE JUSTIFICATION OF THE UNGODLY TAKES PLACE IN AN INSTANT OR SUCCESSIVELY?

We proceed thus to the Seventh Article:—

Objection 1. It would seem that the justification of the ungodly does not take place in an instant, but successively, since, as was already stated, for the justification of the ungodly there is required a movement of free choice. Now the act of free choice is election, which requires the deliberation of counsel, as was stated above.[18] Hence, since deliberation implies a certain reasoning process, and this implies succession, the justification of the ungodly would seem to be successive.

Obj. 2. Further, the movement of free choice is not without actual consideration. But it is impossible to understand at once things that are actually many, as was stated above.[19] Hence, since for the justification of the ungodly there is required a movement of free choice towards several things, viz., towards God and towards sin, it would seem impossible for the justification of the ungodly to be in an instant.

Obj. 3. Further, a form that may be greater or less, *e.g.*, blackness or

[18] Q. 14, a. 1.   [19] *S. T.*, I, q. 85, a. 4.

whiteness, is received successively by its subject. Now grace may be greater or less, as was stated above.[20] Hence it is not received suddenly by its subject. Therefore, seeing that the infusion of grace is required for the justification of the ungodly, it would seem that the justification of the ungodly cannot be in an instant.

Obj. 4. Further, the movement of free choice, which co-operates in justification, is meritorious; and hence it must proceed from grace, without which there is no merit, as we shall state further on.[21] Now a thing receives its form before operating by this form. Hence grace is first infused, and then free choice is moved towards God and to detest sin. Hence justification is not all at once.

Obj. 5. Further, if grace is infused into the soul, there must be an instant when it first dwells in the soul; so, too, if sin is forgiven, there must be a last instant that man is in sin. But it cannot be the same instant, or otherwise opposites would be in the same subject simultaneously. Hence they must be two successive instants, between which there must be time, as the Philosopher says.[22] Therefore the justification of the ungodly takes place, not all at once, but successively.

On the contrary, The justification of the ungodly is caused by the justifying grace of the Holy Spirit. Now the Holy Spirit comes to men's minds suddenly, according to *Acts* ii. 2: *And suddenly there came a sound from heaven as of a mighty wind coming*; upon which the *Gloss* says that *the grace of the Holy Spirit knows no tardy efforts.*[23] Hence the justification of the ungodly is not successive, but instantaneous.

I answer that, The entire justification of the ungodly consists, as to its origin, in the infusion of grace. For it is by grace that free choice is moved and guilt is remitted. Now the infusion of grace takes place in an instant and without succession. And the reason for this is that if a form be not suddenly impressed upon its subject, this is either because that subject is not disposed, or because the agent needs time to dispose the subject. Hence we see that immediately the matter is disposed by a preceding alteration, the substantial form enters the matter. Thus, because the atmosphere of itself is disposed to receive light, it is suddenly illuminated by a body actually luminous. Now it was stated that in order to infuse grace into the soul God needs no disposition, save what He Himself has made.[24] And sometimes this sufficient disposition for the reception of grace He makes suddenly, sometimes gradually and successively, as was stated above.[25] For the reason why a natural agent cannot suddenly dispose matter is that in the matter there is a resistant which has some disproportion to the power of the agent; and hence we see that the stronger the agent, the more speedily is the matter disposed. Therefore, since the divine power is infinite, it can instantaneously dispose any created matter to its form; and much more

---

[20] Q. 112, a. 4.   [21] Q. 114, a. 2.   [22] *Phys.,* VI, 1 (231b 6).   [23] *Glossa interl.* (VI, 166v).   [24] Q. 112, a. 2.   [25] Q. 112, a. 2, ad 2.

man's free choice, whose movement is by nature instantaneous. Therefore the justification of the ungodly by God takes place in an instant.

Reply Obj. 1. The movement of free choice, which concurs in the justification of the ungodly, is a consent to detest sin, and to draw near to God; and this consent takes place suddenly. Sometimes, indeed, it happens that deliberation precedes, yet this is not of the substance of justification, but a way to justification; just as local movement is a way to illumination, and alteration to generation.

Reply Obj. 2. As was stated above, there is nothing to prevent two things from being understood at once, in so far as they are somehow one.[26] Thus, we understand the subject and predicate together, inasmuch as they are united in relation to one affirmation. And in the same manner, free choice can be moved to two things at once in so far as one is ordained to the other. Now the movement of free choice against sin is ordained to the movement of free choice towards God, since a man detests sin as contrary to God, to Whom he wishes to cling. Hence, in the justification of the ungodly, free choice simultaneously detests sin and turns to God, even as a body approaches one point and withdraws from another simultaneously.

Reply Obj. 3. The reason why a form is not received instantaneously in matter is not the fact that it can inhere more or less; for thus the light would not be suddenly received in the air, which can be illumined more and less. But the reason is to be sought on the part of the disposition of the matter or subject, as was stated above.

Reply Obj. 4. The same instant the form is acquired, the thing begins to operate with the form. Thus, the instant it is generated, fire moves upwards, and if its movement were instantaneous, it would be terminated in the same instant. Now to will and not to will—the movements of free choice —are not successive, but instantaneous. Hence the justification of the ungodly need not be successive.

Reply Obj. 5. The succession of opposites in the same subject must be looked at differently in the things that are subject to time and in those that are above time. For in those that are in time, there is no last instant in which the previous form inheres in the subject, but there is the last time, and the first instant when the subsequent form inheres in the matter or subject; and this for the reason, that in time we are not to consider one instant as immediately preceding another instant, since neither do instants succeed each other immediately in time, nor points in a line, as is proved in *Physics* vi.[27] But time is terminated by an instant. Hence in the whole of the previous time wherein anything is moving towards its form, it is under the opposite form; but in the last instant of this time, which is the first instant of the subsequent time, it has the form which is the term of the movement.

[26] *S. T.*, I, q. 85, a. 4; q. 58, a. 2.   [27] Aristotle, *Phys.*, VI, 1 (231b 6).

But in those beings that are above time, it is otherwise. For if there be any succession of affections or intellectual conceptions in them (*e.g.*, in the angels), such succession is not measured by continuous time, but by discrete time, even as the things measured are not continuous, as was stated above.[28] In these, therefore, there is a last instant in which the preceding is, and a first instant in which the subsequent is. Nor must there be time in between, since there is no continuity of time, which would necessitate this.

Now the human mind, which is justified, is, in itself, above time, but is subject to time accidentally, inasmuch as it understands with continuity and time, in keeping with the phantasms in which it considers the intelligible species, as was stated above.[29] We must, therefore, decide from this about its change as regards the condition of temporal movements, *i.e.*, we must say that there is no last instant that sin inheres, but a last time; whereas there is a first instant that grace inheres, but in all the time previous sin inhered.

Eighth Article

WHETHER THE INFUSION OF GRACE IS NATURALLY THE FIRST OF THE THINGS REQUIRED FOR THE JUSTIFICATION OF THE UNGODLY?

We proceed thus to the Eighth Article:—

Objection 1. It would seem that the infusion of grace is not what is naturally required first for the justification of the ungodly. For we withdraw from evil before drawing near to good, according to *Ps.* xxxvi. 27: *Turn away from evil, and do good.* Now the remission of guilt concerns the turning away from evil, and the infusion of grace concerns the turning to good. Hence the remission of guilt is naturally before the infusion of grace.

Obj. 2. Further, the disposition naturally precedes the form to which it disposes. Now the movement of free choice is a disposition for the reception of grace. Therefore it naturally precedes the infusion of grace.

Obj. 3. Further, sin hinders the soul from tending freely to God. Now a hindrance to movement must be removed before the movement takes place. Hence the remission of guilt and the movement of free choice against sin are naturally before the movement of free choice towards God and before the infusion of grace.

On the contrary, The cause is naturally prior to its effect. Now the infusion of grace is the cause of whatever is required for the justification of the ungodly, as was stated above. Therefore it is naturally prior to it.

I answer that, The aforesaid four things required for the justification of the ungodly are simultaneous in time, since the justification of the ungodly is not successive, as was stated above; but in the order of nature, one is

---

[28] *S. T.,* I, q. 53, a. 3.   [29] *S. T.,* I, q. 84, a. 7.—Cf. Aristotle, *De Memor.,* I (450a 8); St. Thomas, *In II Sent.,* d. iii, q. 1, a. 2 and 6; *In B. de Trinitate,* q. 6, a. 4.

prior to another. According to the order that is natural among them, the first is the infusion of grace; the second, the movement of free choice towards God; the third, the movement of free choice against sin; the fourth, the remission of guilt.

The reason for this is that in every movement the motion of the mover is naturally first; the disposition of the matter, or the movement of the moved, is second; the end or term of the movement in which the motion of the mover rests, is last. Now the motion of God the mover is the infusion of grace, as was stated above; the movement or disposition of the moved is the double movement of free choice; and the term or end of the movement is the remission of sin, as was stated above. Hence, in their natural order, the first in the justification of the ungodly is the infusion of grace; the second is the movement of free choice towards God; the third is the movement of free choice against sin, for he who is being justified detests sin because it is against God, and thus the movement of free choice towards God naturally precedes the movement of free choice against sin, since it is its cause and reason; the fourth and last is the remission of guilt, to which this transmutation is ordained as to an end, as was stated above.

Reply Obj. 1. The withdrawal from one term and approach to another may be looked at in two ways. First, on the part of the thing moved, and thus the withdrawal from a term naturally precedes the approach to a term, since in the subject of movement the opposite which is put away is prior to the opposite which the subject moved attains to by its movement. But on the part of the agent, it is the other way about, since the agent, by the form pre-existing in it, acts for the removal of the opposite form. And thus, the sun by its light acts for the removal of darkness, and hence, on the part of the sun, illumination is prior to the removal of darkness; but on the part of the atmosphere to be illuminated, to be freed from darkness is, in the order of nature, prior to being illuminated, although both are simultaneous in time. And since the infusion of grace and the remission of guilt are referred to God Who justifies, hence in the order of nature the infusion of grace is prior to the remission of guilt. But if we look at what takes place on the part of the man justified, it is the other way about, since in the order of nature liberation from guilt is prior to the obtaining of justifying grace.—Or it may be said that the term *whence* of justification is guilt, and the term *whereto* is justice, and that grace is the cause of the forgiveness of sin and of the obtaining of justice.

Reply Obj. 2. The disposition of the subject precedes the reception of the form in the order of nature; and yet it is subsequent to the action of the agent, whereby the subject is disposed. Hence the movement of free choice precedes the reception of grace in the order of nature, but follows the infusion of grace.

Reply Obj. 3. As the Philosopher says,[30] in movements of the soul the

[30] *Phys.,* II, 9 (200a 19).

movement towards the principle of speculation or the end of action is the very first; but in exterior movements the removal of the impediment precedes the attainment of the end. And since the movement of free choice is a movement of the soul, in the order of nature it moves towards God as to its end, before removing the impediment of sin.

Ninth Article

WHETHER THE JUSTIFICATION OF THE UNGODLY IS GOD'S GREATEST WORK?

We proceed thus to the Ninth Article:—

Objection 1. It would seem that the justification of the ungodly is not God's greatest work. For it is by the justification of the ungodly that we attain the grace of a wayfarer. Now by glorification we receive the grace of heaven, which is greater. Hence the glorification of angels and of men is a greater work than the justification of the ungodly.

Obj. 2. Further, the justification of the ungodly is ordained to the particular good of one man. But the good of the universe is greater than the good of one man, as is plain from *Ethics* i.[31] Hence the creation of heaven and earth is a greater work than the justification of the ungodly.

Obj. 3. Further, to make something from nothing, in which case there is nothing to co-operate with the agent, is greater than to make something with the co-operation of the recipient. Now in the work of creation something is made from nothing, and hence nothing can co-operate with the agent. But in the justification of the ungodly God makes something from something, *i.e.*, a just man from a sinner, and there is a co-operation on man's part, since there is a movement of free choice, as was stated above. Hence the justification of the ungodly is not God's greatest work.

On the contrary, It is written (*Ps.* cxliv. 9): *His tender mercies are over all His works,* and in a Collect we say: *O God, Who dost show forth Thine all-mightiness most by pardoning and having mercy.*[32] And Augustine, expounding the words, *greater than these shall he do* (*Jo.* xiv. 12), says that *for a just man to be made from a sinner is greater than to create heaven and earth.*[33]

I answer that, A work may be called great in two ways. First, on the part of the mode of action, and thus the work of creation is the greatest work, wherein something is made from nothing; secondly, a work may be called great because of the magnitude of what is made, and thus the justification of the ungodly, which terminates at the eternal good of a participation in God, is greater than the creation of heaven and earth, which terminates at the good of mutable nature. Hence, Augustine, after saying that *for a just man to be made from a sinner is greater than to*

---

[31] Aristotle, *Eth.*, I, 2 (1094b 10).   [32] Collect of the Tenth Sunday after Pentecost.
[33] *Tract.* LXXII, super *Ioann.*, XIV, 12 (PL 35, 1823).

create heaven and earth, adds, *for heaven and earth shall pass away, but the salvation and the justification of the predestined shall endure.*[34]

Again, we must bear in mind that a thing is called great in two ways. First, in absolute quantity, and thus the gift of glory is greater than the gift of grace that justifies the ungodly; and in this respect the glorification of the just is greater than the justification of the ungodly. Secondly, a thing may be said to be great in proportionate quantity. In this sense we speak of a *small* mountain and a *large* millet. And thus the gift of grace that justifies the ungodly is greater than the gift of glory that beatifies the just, for the gift of grace exceeds the worthiness of the ungodly, who are worthy of punishment, more than the gift of glory exceeds the worthiness of the just, who by the fact of their justification are worthy of glory. Hence Augustine says in the same reference: *Let him that can judge whether it is greater to create the angels just, than to justify the ungodly. Certainly, if they both betoken equal power, the latter betokens greater mercy.*

And thus the reply to the first is clear.

Reply Obj. 2. The good of the universe is greater than the particular good of one, if we consider both in the same genus. But the good of grace in one is greater than the good of nature in the whole universe.

Reply Obj. 3. This objection rests on the manner of acting, in which way creation is God's greatest work.

Tenth Article

WHETHER THE JUSTIFICATION OF THE UNGODLY IS A MIRACULOUS WORK?

We proceed thus to the Tenth Article:—

Objection 1. It would seem that the justification of the ungodly is a miraculous work. For miraculous works are greater than the non-miraculous. Now the justification of the ungodly is greater than the other miraculous works, as is clear from the quotation from Augustine. Hence the justification of the ungodly is a miraculous work.

Obj. 2. Further, the movement of the will in the soul is like the natural inclination in natural things. But when God works in natural things against the inclination of their nature, it is a miraculous work, as when He gave sight to the blind or raised the dead. Now the will of the ungodly is bent on evil. Hence, since God, in justifying a man, moves him to good, it would seem that the justification of the ungodly is miraculous.

Obj. 3. Further, as wisdom is a gift of God, so also is justice. Now it is miraculous that anyone should suddenly obtain wisdom from God without study. Therefore it is miraculous that the ungodly should be justified by God.

[34] *Ibid.*

On the contrary, Miraculous works are beyond natural power. Now the justification of the ungodly is not beyond natural power; for Augustine says that *to be capable of having faith and to be capable of having charity belongs to man's nature; but to have faith and charity belongs to the grace of the faithful.*[35] Therefore the justification of the ungodly is not miraculous.

I answer that, In miraculous works it is usual to find three things.[36] The first is on the part of the active power, because they can be performed only by divine power. That is why they are absolutely wondrous, since their cause is hidden, as we have stated above.[37] And in this sense, both the justification of the ungodly and the creation of the world, and, generally speaking, every work that can be done by God alone, is miraculous.

Secondly, in certain miraculous works it is found that the form introduced is beyond the natural power of such matter, just as in the resurrection of the dead, life is above the natural power of such a body. In this sense, the justification of the ungodly is not miraculous, because the soul is naturally capable of grace; since, by the fact of having been made to the likeness of God, it is fit to receive God by grace, as Augustine says.[38]

Thirdly, in miraculous works something is found outside the usual and customary order of causing an effect, as when a sick man suddenly, and beyond the wonted course of healing by nature or art, receives perfect health. And in this sense the justification of the ungodly is sometimes miraculous and sometimes not. For the common and wonted course of justification is that God moves the soul interiorly and that man is converted to God, first by an imperfect conversion, and afterwards reaches a perfect conversion; because *charity begun merits increase, so that when increased it may merit perfection,* as Augustine says.[39] Yet God sometimes moves the soul so vehemently that it reaches the perfection of justice at once, as took place in the conversion of Paul, which was accompanied at the same time by a miraculous external prostration. Hence the conversion of Paul is commemorated in the Church as miraculous.

Reply Obj. 1. Certain miraculous works, although they are less than the justification of the ungodly, as regards the good caused, are yet beyond the wonted order of such effects, and thus have more of the nature of a miracle.

Reply Obj. 2. It is not a miraculous work whenever a natural thing is moved contrary to its inclination, or otherwise it would be miraculous for water to be heated, or for a stone to be thrown upwards; but only whenever this takes place beyond the order of the proper cause which naturally does this. Now no other cause save God can justify the ungodly,

---

[35] *De Praedest. Sanct.,* V (PL 44, 968). [36] Cf. St. Albert, *In IV Sent.,* d. xvii, a. 12 (XXIX, 679). [37] *S. T.,* I, q. 105, a. 7. [38] *De Trin.,* XIV, 8 (PL 42, 1044). [39] *Epist.* CLXXXVI, 3 (PL 33, 819).—Cf. *In Epist. Ioann.,* V (PL 35, 2014).

even as nothing save fire can heat water. Hence the justification of the ungodly by God is not miraculous in this respect.

Reply Obj. 3. A man naturally acquires wisdom and science from God by his own talent and study. Hence it is miraculous when a man comes to possess wisdom or science outside this order. But a man does not naturally acquire justifying grace by his own action, but by God's. Hence there is no parity.

ON MERIT, WHICH IS THE EFFECT OF CO-OPERATING GRACE
(*In Ten Articles*)

WE must now consider merit, which is the effect of co-operating grace, and under this head there are ten points of inquiry: (1) Whether man can merit anything from God? (2) Whether without grace anyone can merit eternal life? (3) Whether anyone with grace can merit eternal life condignly? (4) Whether it is chiefly through the instrumentality of charity that grace is the principle of merit? (5) Whether a man can merit the first grace for himself? (6) Whether he can merit it for someone else? (7) Whether anyone can merit restoration after sin? (8) Whether he can merit for himself an increase of grace or of charity? (9) Whether he can merit final perseverance? (10) Whether temporal goods fall under merit?

First Article

WHETHER A MAN CAN MERIT ANYTHING FROM GOD?

We proceed thus to the First Article:—

Objection 1. It would seem that a man can merit nothing from God. For no one, it would seem, merits by giving another his due. But by all the good we do, we cannot make sufficient return to God, since yet more is His due, as also the Philosopher says.[1] Hence it is written (*Luke* xvii. 10): *When you have done all these things that are commanded you, say: We are unprofitable servants; we have done that which we ought to do.* Therefore a man can merit nothing from God.

Obj. 2. Further, it would seem that a man merits nothing from God by what profits himself only, and profits God nothing. Now by acting well, a man profits himself or another man, but not God, for it is written (*Job* xxxv. 7): *If thou do justly, what shalt thou give Him, or what shall He receive of thy hand?* Hence a man can merit nothing from God.

Obj. 3. Further, whoever merits anything from another makes him his debtor; for a man's wage is a debt due to him. Now God is no one's debtor, and hence it is written (*Rom.* xi. 35): *Who hath first given to Him, and recompense shall be made him?* Hence no one can merit anything from God.

On the contrary, It is written (*Jer.* xxxi. 16): *There is a reward for thy work.* Now a reward means something bestowed by reason of merit. Hence it would seem that a man may merit from God.

[1] *Eth.,* VIII, 14 (1163b 15).

I answer that, Merit and reward refer to the same, for a reward means something given anyone in return for work or toil, as a sort of price for it. Hence, just as it is an act of justice to give a just price for anything received from another, so also is it an act of justice to make a return for work or toil. *Now justice is a kind of equality,* as is clear from the Philosopher,[2] and hence justice exists absolutely between those that are absolutely equal; but where there is no absolute equality between them, neither is there absolute justice, but there may be a certain manner of justice, as when we speak of a father's or a master's right, as the Philosopher says.[3] And hence where there is justice absolutely, there is the character of merit and reward absolutely. But where there is nothing absolutely just, but only relatively, there is no character of merit absolutely, but only relatively, in so far as the character of justice is preserved there; since the child merits something from his father and the slave from his lord.

Now it is clear that between God and man there is the greatest inequality; for they are infinitely apart, and all man's good is from God. Hence there can be no justice of absolute equality between man and God, but only of a certain proportion, inasmuch as both operate after their own manner. Now the manner and measure of human virtue is in man from God. Hence man's merit with God exists only on the presupposition of the divine ordination, so that, namely, man obtains from God, as a sort of reward of his operation, what God gave him the power of operation for, even as natural things by their proper movements and operations obtain that to which they were ordained by God. There is a difference, however, since the rational creature moves itself to act by its free choice; and so its action has the character of merit, which is not the case in other creatures.

Reply Obj. 1. Man merits, inasmuch as by his own will he does what he ought; or otherwise the act of justice whereby anyone discharges a debt would not be meritorious.

Reply Obj. 2. God seeks from our goods not profit, but glory, *i.e.,* the manifestation of His goodness; even as He seeks it also in His own works. Now nothing accrues to Him, but only to ourselves, by our worship of Him. Hence we merit from God, not that by our works anything accrues to Him, but inasmuch as we work for His glory.

Reply Obj. 3. Since our action has the character of merit only on the presupposition of the divine ordination, it does not follow that God is made our debtor absolutely, but His own, inasmuch as it is owing that His will should be carried out.

---

[2] *Eth.,* V, 3 (1131a 12).   [3] *Op. cit.,* V, 6 (1134a 25; b. 8).

Second Article

WHETHER ANYONE WITHOUT GRACE CAN MERIT ETERNAL LIFE?

We proceed thus to the Second Article:—

Objection 1. It would seem that without grace anyone can merit eternal life. For man merits from God what he is divinely ordained to, as was stated above. Now man by his nature is ordained to beatitude as his end; and so it is likewise natural for him to wish to be blessed. Hence man, by his natural endowments and without grace, can merit beatitude, which is eternal life.

Obj. 2. Further, the less a work is due, the more meritorious it is. Now, less due is that work which is done by one who has received fewer benefits. Hence, since he who has only natural endowments has received fewer gifts from God than he who has gratuitous gifts as well as those of nature, it would seem that his works are more meritorious with God. And thus, if he who has grace can merit eternal life to some extent, much more can he who has no grace.

Obj. 3. Further, God's mercy and liberality infinitely surpass human mercy and liberality. Now a man may merit from another, even though he has not hitherto had his grace. Much more, therefore, would it seem that a man without grace can merit eternal life.

On the contrary, The Apostle says (*Rom.* vi. 23): *The grace of God, life everlasting.*

I answer that, Man without grace may be looked at in two states, as was said above.[4] The first is the state of integral nature, in which Adam was before his sin; the second is the state of corrupted nature, in which we are before being restored by grace. Therefore, if we speak of man in the first state, there is only one reason why man cannot merit eternal life without grace by his purely natural endowments, viz., because man's merit depends on the divine pre-ordination. Now no act of anything whatsoever is divinely ordained to anything exceeding the proportion of the powers which are the principles of its act; for it is a law of divine providence that nothing shall act beyond its powers. But eternal life is a good exceeding the proportion of created nature, since it exceeds its knowledge and desire, according to *1 Cor.* ii. 9: *Eye hath not seen, nor ear heard, neither hath it entered into the heart of man.* And hence it is that no created nature is a sufficient principle of an act meritorious of eternal life, unless there is added a supernatural gift, which we call grace. But if we speak of man as existing in sin, a second reason is added to this, viz., the impediment of sin. For since sin is an offense against God, excluding us from eternal life, as is clear from what has been said above,[5] no one existing in a state of mortal sin can merit eternal life unless first he be reconciled to God,

[4] Q. 109, a. 2.   [5] Q. 87, a. 3; q. 113, a. 2.

through the forgiveness of his sin, which is brought about by grace. For the sinner deserves, not life, but death, according to *Rom.* vi. 23: *The wages of sin is death.*

Reply Obj. 1. God ordained human nature to attain the end of eternal life, not by its own power, but by the help of grace; and in this way its act can be meritorious of eternal life.

Reply Obj. 2. Without grace, a man cannot have a work equal to a work proceeding from grace, since the more perfect the principle, the more perfect the action. But the objection would hold good, if we supposed the operations equal in both cases.

Reply Obj. 3. With regard to the first reason adduced, the case is different in God and in man. For a man receives all his power of well-doing from God, and not from man. Hence a man can merit nothing from God except by His gift, which the Apostle expresses aptly saying (*Rom.* xi. 35): *Who hath first given to Him, and recompense shall be made to him?* But man may merit from man, before he has received anything from him, by what he has received from God

But as regards the second proof, taken from the impediment of sin, the case is similar with man and God, since one man cannot merit from another whom he has offended, unless he first makes satisfaction to him and is reconciled.

Third Article

WHETHER A MAN IN GRACE CAN MERIT ETERNAL LIFE
CONDIGNLY?

We proceed thus to the Third Article:—

Objection 1. It would seem that a man in grace cannot merit eternal life condignly, for the Apostle says (*Rom.* viii. 18): *The sufferings of this time are not worthy [condignae] to be compared with the glory to come, that shall be revealed in us.* But of all meritorious works, the sufferings of the saints would seem the most meritorious. Therefore no works of men are meritorious of eternal life condignly.

Obj. 2. Further, on *Rom.* vi. 23 (*The grace of God, life everlasting*) the *Gloss* says: *He might have truly said: 'The wages of justice, life everlasting'; but He preferred to say 'The grace of God, life everlasting,' that we may know that God leads us to life everlasting of His own mercy and not by our merits.*[6] Now when anyone merits something condignly he receives it, not from mercy, but from merit. Hence it would seem that a man with grace cannot merit eternal life condignly.

Obj. 3. Further, merit that equals the reward would seem to be condign. Now no act of the present life can equal eternal life, which surpasses our knowledge and our desire, and, moreover, surpasses the charity or

---

[6] *Glossa ordin.* (VI, 15F).—Cf. St. Augustine, *Enchir.*, CVII (PL 40, 282).

love of the wayfarer, even as it exceeds nature. Therefore with grace a man cannot merit eternal life condignly.

On the contrary, What is granted in accordance with a just judgment would seem a condign reward. But eternal life is granted by God in accordance with the judgment of justice, according to *2 Tim.* iv. 8: *As to the rest, there is laid up for me a crown of justice, which the Lord, the just judge, will render to me in that day.* Therefore man merits eternal life condignly.

I answer that, Man's meritorious work may be considered in two ways. First, as it proceeds from free choice; secondly, as it proceeds from the grace of the Holy Ghost. If it is considered as regards the substance of the work, and inasmuch as it proceeds from free choice, there can be no condignity because of the very great inequality. But there is congruity, because of an equality of proportion; for it would seem congruous that, if a man does what he can, God should reward him according to the excellence of His power.

If, however, we speak of a meritorious work inasmuch as it proceeds from the grace of the Holy Ghost moving us to eternal life, it is meritorious of eternal life condignly. For thus the value of its merit depends upon the power of the Holy Ghost moving us to eternal life, according to *John* iv. 14: *Shall become in him a fount of water springing up into life everlasting.* Furthermore, the worth of the work depends on the dignity of grace, whereby man, being made a partaker of the divine nature, is adopted as a son of God, to whom the inheritance is due by right of adoption, according to *Rom.* viii. 17: *If sons, heirs also.*

Reply Obj. 1. The Apostle is speaking of the substance of the sufferings of the saints.

Reply Obj. 2. This saying is to be understood of the first cause of our reaching eternal life, viz., God's mercy. But our merit is a subsequent cause.

Reply Obj. 3. The grace of the Holy Ghost which we have at present, although unequal to glory in act, is equal to it virtually, like the seed of a tree, wherein the whole tree is virtually. So likewise by grace the Holy Ghost dwells in man; and He is a sufficient cause of life everlasting. Hence He is called the *pledge* of our inheritance (*2 Cor.* i. 22).

Fourth Article

WHETHER GRACE IS THE PRINCIPLE OF MERIT THROUGH CHARITY MORE THAN THROUGH THE OTHER VIRTUES?

We proceed thus to the Fourth Article:—

Objection 1. It would seem that grace is not the principle of merit through charity more than through the other virtues. For wages are due to work, according to *Matt.* xx. 8: *Call the laborers and pay them their hire.* Now every virtue is a principle of some operation, since virtue is an operative habit, as was stated above.[7] Hence every virtue is equally a principle of merit.

Obj. 2. Further, the Apostle says (*1 Cor.* iii. 8): *Every man shall receive his own reward according to his labor.* Now charity lessens rather than increases the labor, because, as Augustine says, *love makes all hard and repulsive tasks easy and next to nothing.*[8] Hence charity is no greater principle of merit than any other virtue.

Obj. 3. Further, the greatest principle of merit would seem to be the one whose acts are most meritorious. But the acts of faith and patience or fortitude would seem to be the most meritorious, as appears in the martyrs, who strove for the faith patiently and bravely even till death. Hence other virtues are a greater principle of merit than charity.

On the contrary, Our Lord said (*Jo.* xiv. 21): *He that loveth Me, shall be loved of My Father; and I will love him and will manifest Myself to him.* Now eternal life consists in the manifest knowledge of God, according to *John* xvii. 3: *This is eternal life, that they may know Thee, the only true and living God.* Hence the merit of eternal life rests chiefly with charity.

I answer that, As we may gather from what has been stated above, human acts have the character of merit from two causes. First and chiefly from the divine ordination, inasmuch as acts are said to merit that good to which man is divinely ordained. Secondly, on the part of free choice, inasmuch as man, beyond other creatures, has the power of voluntary acts by acting of himself. And in both these ways does merit chiefly rest with charity. For we must first bear in mind that eternal life consists in the fruition of God. Now the human mind's movement to the fruition of the divine good is the proper act of charity, by which all the acts of the other virtues are ordained to this end, since all the other virtues are commanded by charity. Hence the merit of eternal life pertains first to charity, and secondly, to the other virtues, inasmuch as their acts are commanded by charity. It is likewise manifest that what we do out of love we do most willingly. Hence, even inasmuch as merit depends on voluntariness, merit is chiefly attributed to charity.

Reply Obj. 1. Charity, inasmuch as it has the last end for its object, moves the other virtues to act. For the habit to which the end pertains always commands the habits to which the means pertain, as was said above.[9]

Reply Obj. 2. A work can be toilsome and difficult in two ways. First, from the greatness of the work, and thus the greatness of the labor pertains to the increase of merit; and thus charity does not lessen the labor— rather, it makes us undertake the greatest toils, *for it does great things, if it exists,* as Gregory says.[10] Secondly, from the defect of the operator;

---

[7] Q. 55, a. 2.   [8] *Serm.* LXX, 3 (PL 38, 444).   [9] Q. 9, a. 1.   [10] *In Evang.,* II, hom. 30 (PL 76, 1221).

for what is not done with a ready will is hard and difficult to all of us, and such labor lessens merit and is removed by charity.

Reply Obj. 3. The act of faith is not meritorious unless *faith . . . worketh by charity* (*Gal.* v. 6). So, too, the acts of patience and fortitude are not meritorious unless a man does them out of charity, according to *1 Cor.* xiii. 3: *If I should deliver my body to be burned, and have not charity, it profiteth me nothing.*

Fifth Article

WHETHER A MAN CAN MERIT FOR HIMSELF THE FIRST GRACE?

We proceed thus to the Fifth Article:—

Objection 1. It would seem that a man can merit for himself the first grace, because, as Augustine says, *faith merits justification.*[11] Now a man is justified by the first grace. Therefore a man can merit the first grace.

Obj. 2. Further, God gives grace only to the worthy. Now, no one is said to be worthy of some good, unless he has merited it condignly. Therefore we may merit the first grace condignly.

Obj. 3. Further, with men we may merit a gift already received. Thus if a man receives a horse from his master, he merits it by a good use of it in his master's service. Now God is much more bountiful than man. Much more, therefore, can a man merit by subsequent works the first grace already received from God.

On the contrary, The nature of grace is repugnant to reward of works, according to *Rom.* iv. 4: *Now to him that worketh, the reward is not reckoned according to grace but according to debt.* Now a man merits what is reckoned to him according to debt as the reward of his works. Hence a man cannot merit the first grace.

I answer that, The gift of grace can be considered in two ways. First, in the nature of a gratuitous gift, and thus it is manifest that all merit is repugnant to grace, since, as the Apostle says (*Rom.* xi. 6), *if by grace, it is not now by works.*—Secondly, it may be considered according to the nature of the thing given, and thus, also, it cannot come under the merit of him who has not grace, both because it exceeds the proportion of nature, and because prior to grace a man in the state of sin has an obstacle to his meriting grace, viz., sin. But when anyone has grace, the grace already possessed cannot come under merit, since reward is the term of work, whereas grace is the principle of all our good works, as was stated above.[12] But if anyone merits a further gratuitous gift by virtue of the preceding grace, it would not be the first grace. Hence it is manifest that no one can merit for himself the first grace.

Reply Obj. 1. As Augustine says, he was deceived on this point for a

---

[11] *Epist.* CLXXXVI, 3 (PL 33, 818).   [12] Q. 109.

time, believing the beginning of faith to be from us, and its consummation to be granted us by God; and this he here retracts.[13] And it seems to be in this sense that he speaks of faith as meriting justification. But if we suppose, as the truth of faith holds, that the beginning of faith is in us from God, even the first act must flow from grace, and thus cannot be meritorious of the first grace. Therefore man is justified by faith, not as though man, by believing, were to merit justification, but that, he believes while he is being justified; inasmuch as a movement of faith is required for the justification of the ungodly, as was stated above.[14]

Reply Obj. 2. God gives grace to none but to the worthy, not that they were previously worthy, but that by His grace He makes them worthy, Who alone *can make him clean that is conceived of unclean seed* (*Job* xiv. 4).

Reply Obj. 3. Man's every good work proceeds from the first grace as from its principle; but not from any gift of man. Consequently, there is no comparison between gifts of grace and gifts of men.

Sixth Article

WHETHER A MAN CAN MERIT THE FIRST GRACE FOR ANOTHER?

We proceed thus to the Sixth Article:—

Objection 1. It would seem that a man can merit the first grace for another. For on *Matt.* ix. 2 (*Jesus seeing their faith,* etc.) the *Gloss* says: *How much is our personal faith worth with God, Who set such a price on another's faith, as to heal the man both inwardly and outwardly!*[15] Now inward healing is brought about by grace. Hence a man can merit the first grace for another.

Obj. 2. Further, the prayers of the just are not empty, but efficacious, according to *James* v. 16: *The continued prayer of a just man availeth much.* Now he had previously said: *Pray one for another, that you may be saved.* Hence, since man's salvation can be brought about only by grace, it seems that one man can merit for another his first grace.

Obj. 3. Further, it is written (*Luke* xvi. 9): *Make unto you friends of the mammon of iniquity, that when you shall fail they may receive you into everlasting dwellings.* Now it is through grace alone that anyone is received into everlasting dwellings, for by it alone does anyone merit eternal life, as was stated above.[16] Hence one man may by merit obtain for another his first grace.

On the contrary, It is written (*Jer.* xv. 1): *If Moses and Samuel shall stand before Me, My soul is not towards this people*; and yet they had great merit with God. Hence it seems that no one can merit the first grace for another.

[13] *Retract.,* I, 23 (PL 32, 621).   [14] Q. 113, a. 4.   [15] *Glossa ordin.* (V, 32 E). [16] A. 2; q. 109, a. 5.

I answer that, As was shown above, our works are meritorious from two causes. First, by virtue of the divine motion, and thus we merit condignly; secondly, according as they proceed from free choice, in so far as we do them willingly, and thus they have congruous merit, since it is congruous that when a man makes good use of his power, God should by His super-excellent power work still higher things. And therefore it is clear that no one can merit condignly for another his first grace, save Christ alone; for each one of us is moved by God to reach eternal life through the gift of grace, and hence condign merit does not reach beyond this motion. But Christ's soul is moved by God through grace not only so as to reach the glory of eternal life, but also so as to lead others to it, inasmuch as He is the Head of the Church, and the Author of human salvation, according to *Heb.* ii. 10: *Who hath brought many children into glory, the Author of their salvation.*

But one may merit the first grace for another congruously, because a man in grace fulfills God's will, and it is congruous and in harmony with friendship that God should fulfill man's desire for the salvation of another, although sometimes there may be an impediment on the part of him whose salvation the just man desires. And it is in this sense that the passage from *Jeremias* speaks.

Reply Obj. 1. A man's faith avails for another's salvation by congruous, and not by condign, merit.

Reply Obj. 2. The impetration of prayer rests on mercy, whereas condign merit rests on justice; and hence a man may impetrate many things from the divine mercy in prayer, which he does not merit in justice, according to *Dan.* ix. 18: *For it is not for our justifications that we present our prayers before Thy face, but for the multitude of Thy tender mercies.*

Reply Obj. 3. The poor who receive alms are said to receive others into everlasting dwellings, either by impetrating their forgiveness in prayer, or by meriting congruously by other good works, or, materially speaking, inasmuch as by these works of mercy, exercised towards the poor, we merit to be received into everlasting dwellings.

Seventh Article

WHETHER A MAN CAN MERIT RESTORATION AFTER A FALL?

We proceed thus to the Seventh Article:—

Objection 1. It would seem that anyone can merit for himself restoration after a fall. For what a man can justly ask of God, he can justly merit. Now, as Augustine says, nothing can more justly be besought of God than to be restored after a fall, according to *Ps.* lxx. 9: *When my strength shall fail, do not Thou forsake me.* Hence a man can merit to be restored after a fall.

Obj. 2. Further, a man's works benefit himself more than another.

Now a man can, to some extent, merit for another his restoration after a fall, even as his first grace. Much more, therefore, can he merit for himself restoration after a fall.

Obj. 3. Further, when a man is once in grace, he merits eternal life by the good works he does, as was shown above.[17] Now no one can attain eternal life unless he is restored by grace. Hence it would seem that he merits for himself restoration.

On the contrary, It is written (*Ezech.* xviii. 24): *If the just man turn himself away from his justice and do iniquity . . . all his justices which he hath done shall not be remembered.* Therefore his previous merits will in no way help him to rise again. Hence no one can merit for himself restoration after a fall.

I answer that, No one can merit for himself restoration after a future fall, either condignly or congruously. He cannot merit this for himself condignly, since the nature of this merit depends on the motion of divine grace, and this motion is interrupted by the subsequent sin; and hence all benefits which he afterwards obtains from God, whereby he is restored, do not fall under merit, for the motion of the preceding grace does not extend to them. Again, congruous merit, whereby one merits the first grace for another, is prevented from having its effect because of the impediment of sin in the one for whom it is merited. Much more, therefore, is the efficacy of such merit impeded by the obstacle which is in him who merits, and in him for whom it is merited; for both of these are in the same person. And therefore a man can in no way merit for himself restoration after a fall.

Reply Obj. 1. The desire whereby we seek for restoration after a fall is called just, and likewise the prayer whereby this restoration is besought is called just, because it tends to justice; but not in such a way that it depends on justice by way of merit, but only on mercy.

Reply Obj. 2. Anyone may congruously merit for another his first grace, because there is no impediment (at least, on the part of him who merits) such as is found when anyone recedes from justice after the merit of grace.

Reply Obj. 3. Some have said that no one *absolutely* merits eternal life except by the act of final grace, but only *conditionally, i.e.,* if he *perseveres*.[18] But it is unreasonable to say this, for sometimes the act of the last grace is not more, but less, meritorious than preceding acts, because of the prostration of illness. Hence it must be said that every act of charity merits eternal life absolutely; but by subsequent sin, there arises an impediment to the preceding merit, so that it does not obtain its effect, just as natural causes fail of their effects because of a supervening impediment.

---

[17] A. 2; q. 109, a. 5.   [18] St. Bonaventure, *In II Sent.,* d. xxviii, dub. 2 (II, 691); *In III Sent.,* d. xxiv, a. 1, q. 1 (III, 511); *In IV Sent.,* d. xiv, pt. 2, a. 2, q. 1 (IV, 336).

Eighth Article

WHETHER A MAN CAN MERIT THE INCREASE OF GRACE OR
CHARITY?

We proceed thus to the Eighth Article:—

Objection 1. It would seem that a man cannot merit an increase of grace or of charity. For when anyone receives the reward he merited, no other reward is due to him; and thus it was said of some (*Matt.* vi. 2): *They have received their reward.* Hence, if anyone were to merit the increase of charity or of grace, it would follow that, when his grace has been increased, he could not expect any further reward, which is unfitting.

Obj. 2. Further, nothing acts beyond its species. But the principle of merit is grace or charity, as was shown above. Therefore no one can merit greater grace or charity than he has.

Obj. 3. Further, what falls under merit a man merits by every act flowing from grace or charity, just as by every such act a man merits eternal life. If, therefore, the increase of grace or charity falls under merit, it would seem that by every act quickened by charity a man would merit an increase of charity. But what a man merits, he infallibly receives from God, unless hindered by subsequent sin; for it is written (*2 Tim.* i. 12): *I know Whom I have believed, and I am certain that He is able to keep that which I have committed unto Him.* Hence it would follow that grace or charity is increased by every meritorious act; and this would seem impossible since at times meritorious acts are not very fervent, and would not suffice for the increase of charity. Therefore, the increase of charity does not come under merit.

On the contrary, Augustine says that *charity merits increase, so that, being increased, it merits to be perfected.*[19] Hence the increase of grace or charity falls under merit.

I answer that, As was stated above, whatever the motion of grace reaches to falls under condign merit. Now the motion of a mover extends not merely to the last term of the movement, but to the whole progress of the movement. But the term of the movement of grace is eternal life; and the progress in this movement is by the increase of charity or of grace, according to *Prov.* iv. 18: *But the path of the just, as a shining light, goeth forward and increaseth even to perfect day,* which is the day of glory. And thus the increase of grace falls under condign merit.

Reply Obj. 1. Reward is the term of merit. But there is a double term of movement, viz., the last, and the intermediate, which is both beginning and term; and this term is the reward of increase. Now the reward of human favor is as the last end to those who place their end in it; and hence such as these receive no other reward.

---

[19] Cf. *Epist.* CLXXXVI, 3 (PL 33, 819).—Cf. also *In Epist. Ioann.,* V (PL 35, 2014).

Reply Obj. 2. The increase of grace is not above the power of the pre-existing grace, although it is above its quantity, even as a tree is not above the power of the seed, although above its quantity.

Reply Obj. 3. By every meritorious act a man merits the increase of grace, even as he merits the consummation of grace, which is eternal life. But just as eternal life is not given at once, but in its own time, so neither is grace increased at once, but in its own time, viz., when a man is sufficiently disposed for the increase of grace.

Ninth Article

WHETHER A MAN CAN MERIT PERSEVERANCE?

We proceed thus to the Ninth Article:—

Objection 1. It would seem that anyone can merit perseverance. For what a man obtains by asking can come under the merit of anyone that is in grace. Now men obtain perseverance by asking it of God, or otherwise it would be useless to ask it of God in the petitions of the Lord's Prayer, as Augustine says.[20] Therefore perseverance can come under the merit of whoever has grace.

Obj. 2. Further, it is more not to be able to sin, than not to sin. But not to be able to sin comes under merit, for we merit eternal life, of which impeccability is an essential part. Much more, therefore, can we merit not to sin, which is to persevere.

Obj. 3. Further, increase of grace is greater than perseverance in the grace we already possess. But a man can merit an increase of grace, as was stated above. Much more, therefore, can he merit perseverance in the grace he has already.

On the contrary, What we merit, we obtain from God, unless it is hindered by sin. Now many have meritorious works, who do not obtain perseverance. Nor can it be urged that this takes place because of the impediment of sin, since to sin is itself opposed to perseverance; and thus if anyone were to merit perseverance, God would not permit him to fall into sin. Hence perseverance does not come under merit.

I answer that, Since man's free choice is naturally flexible towards good and evil, there are two ways of obtaining from God perseverance in good. First, inasmuch as free choice is determined to good by consummate grace, which will be in glory; secondly, on the part of the divine motion, which inclines man to good unto the end. Now, as we have explained above, that which is related as a term to the movement of free choice directed by God as mover falls under human merit; but not what is related to the aforesaid movement as principle. Hence it is clear that the perseverance of glory, which is the term of the aforesaid movement, falls under merit; but the

[20] *De Dono Persev.,* II (PL 45, 996); *De Corrept. et Grat.,* VI (PL 44, 922).

perseverance of the wayfarer does not fall under merit, since it depends solely on the divine motion, which is the principle of all merit. Now God bestows the good of perseverance freely, on whomsoever He bestows it.

Reply Obj. 1. We impetrate in prayer even things that we do not merit, since God hears sinners who beseech the pardon of their sins, which they do not merit, as appears from Augustine on *John* ix. 31: *Now we know that God doth not hear sinners.*[21] Otherwise it would have been useless for the publican to say: *O God, be merciful to me a sinner (Luke* xviii. 13). So too we can impetrate of God in prayer the grace of perseverance either for ourselves or for others, although it does not fall under merit.

Reply Obj. 2. The perseverance of glory is compared as term to the movement of free choice; not so the perseverance of the wayfarer, for the reason given in the body of the article.

In the same way we may answer the third objection which concerns the increase of grace, as was explained above.

Tenth Article

WHETHER TEMPORAL GOODS FALL UNDER MERIT?

We proceed thus to the Tenth Article:—

Objection 1. It would seem that temporal goods fall under merit. For what is promised to some as a reward of justice falls under merit. Now, temporal goods were promised in the Old Law as the reward of justice, as appears from *Deut.* xxviii. Hence it seems that temporal goods fall under merit.

Obj. 2. Further, that would seem to fall under merit which God bestows on anyone for a service done. But God sometimes bestows temporal goods on men for services done for Him. For it is written (*Exod.* i. 21): *And because the midwives feared God, He built them houses;* on which the *Gloss* of Gregory says that *life everlasting might have been awarded them as the fruit of their good-will, but because of their sin of falsehood they received an earthly reward.*[22] And it is written (*Ezech.* xxix. 18): *The King of Babylon hath made his army to undergo hard service against Tyre . . . and there hath been no reward given him;* and further on: *And it shall be wages for his army. . . . I have given him the land of Egypt because he hath labored for me.* Therefore temporal goods fall under merit.

Obj. 3. Further, as good is to merit so is evil to demerit. But because of the demerit of sin some are punished by God with temporal punishments, as appears from the Sodomites (*Gen.* xix). Hence temporal goods fall under merit.

---

[21] *Tract.* XLIV, super *Ioann.*, IX, 31 (PL 35, 1718).   [22] *Moral.*, XVIII, 3 (PL 76, 41).—Cf. *Glossa ordin.*, super *Exod.*, I, 19 (I, 124E).

Obj. 4. On the contrary, What falls under merit is not related in a like way to all. But temporal goods are related to the good and the wicked alike, according to *Eccles.* ix. 2: *All things equally happen to the just and the wicked, to the good and to the evil, to the clean and to the unclean, to him that offereth victims and to him that despiseth sacrifices.* Therefore temporal goods do not fall under merit.

I answer that, What falls under merit is a reward or wage, which has the nature of some good. Now man's good is twofold, the first, absolutely, the second, relatively. Now man's good absolutely is his last end (according to *Ps.* lxxii. 27: *But it is good for me to adhere to my God*), and consequently what is ordained and leads to this end; and these fall absolutely under merit. But the relative good, and not the absolute good, of man is what is good to him now, or what is a good to him in some respect; and this does not fall under merit absolutely, but relatively.

Hence we must say that if temporal goods are considered as they are useful for virtuous works, whereby we are led to eternal life, they fall directly and absolutely under merit, even as increase of grace, and everything whereby a man is helped to attain beatitude after the first grace. For God gives men, both just and wicked, enough temporal goods to enable them to attain to eternal life; and to this extent these temporal goods are absolutely good. Hence it is written (*Ps.* xxxiii. 10): *For there is no want to them that fear Him*; and again (*Ps.* xxxvi. 25): *I have not seen the just forsaken,* etc.

But if these temporal goods are considered in themselves, they are not man's good absolutely, but relatively, and thus they do not fall under merit absolutely, but relatively, inasmuch as men are moved by God to do temporal works, in which with God's help they reach their purpose. And thus, just as eternal life is absolutely the reward of the works of justice in relation to the divine motion, as was stated above, so have temporal goods, considered in themselves, the nature of reward, given the relation to the divine motion, whereby men's wills are moved to undertake these works, even though, sometimes, men have not a right intention in them.

Reply Obj. 1. As Augustine says, *in these temporal promises were figures of spiritual things to come, which are fulfilled in us. For the carnal people were adhering to the promises of the present life; and not merely their speech but even their life was prophetic.*[23]

Reply Obj. 2. These retributions are said to have been divinely brought about in relation to the divine motion, and not in relation to the malice of their wills, especially as regards the King of Babylon, since he did not besiege Tyre as if wishing to serve God, but rather in order to usurp dominion. So, too, although the midwives had a good will with regard to

---

[26] *Contra Faust.,* IV, 2 (PL 42, 218).

saving the children, yet their will was not right, inasmuch as they made up falsehoods.

Reply Obj. 3. Temporal evils are imposed as a punishment on the wicked, inasmuch as they are not thereby helped to reach eternal life. But to the just, who are aided by these evils, they are not punishments but medicines, as was stated above.[24]

Reply Obj. 4. All things happen equally to the good and the wicked, as regards the substance of temporal good or evil; but not as regards the end, since the good and not the wicked are led to beatitude by them.

And now enough has been said regarding morals in general.

[24] Q. 87, a. 7.

SECOND PART OF THE SECOND PART

PROLOGUE

AFTER the general treatment on virtues and vices, and of other matters con-nected with the subject of morals, we must now consider each of these things in particular. For there is little use in speaking about moral matters in general, since actions are in the order of the particular. Now moral matters can be considered in particular from two points of view: first, from the point of view of the moral matter itself, for instance, by considering a particular virtue or a particular vice; secondly, from the point of view of the various states of man, for instance, by considering subjects and superiors, the active life and the contemplative life, or any other differences among men.

Accordingly, we shall treat first in a special way of those matters which regard all the states of man; secondly, in a special way, of those matters which regard particular states.[1]

As to the first, we must observe that if we were to treat of each virtue, gift, vice and precept separately, we should have to say the same thing over and over again. For if one wished to treat adequately of this precept: *Thou shalt not commit adultery,* he would have to inquire about adultery which is a sin, the knowledge about which depends on his knowledge of the opposite virtue. The shorter and quicker method, therefore, will be if we include the consideration of each virtue, together with its corresponding gift, opposite vice, and affirmative and negative precepts, in the same treatise. Moreover this method will be suitable to the vices according to their proper species. For it has been shown above that vices and sins differ in species according to the matter or object, and not according to other differences of sins,[2] for instance, in respect of being sins of thought, word and deed, or committed through weakness, ignorance or malice, and other like differences. Now it is one and the same matter about which a virtue acts rightly and the opposite vice deviates from the right. Accordingly, we may reduce the whole of moral matters to the consideration of the virtues.

The virtues themselves may be reduced to seven in number, three of which are theological, and of these we must treat first; while the other four are the cardinal virtues, of which we shall treat afterwards.[3] Of the intellectual

[1] Q. 171. [2] *S. T.,* I-II, q. 72. [3] Q. 47.

virtues there is one, prudence, which is included and reckoned among the cardinal virtues; whereas art does not pertain to moral science which is concerned with things to be done, for art is *right reason about things to be made,* as was stated above.[4] The other three intellectual virtues, namely, wisdom, understanding and science agree, even in name, with some of the gifts of the Holy Ghost. Therefore we shall consider them while considering the gifts corresponding to those virtues. The other moral virtues are all in some way reducible to the cardinal virtues, as was explained above.[5] Hence, in treating about each cardinal virtue we shall treat also of all the virtues which, in any way whatever, belong to that virtue, as also of the opposite vices. In this way no matter pertaining to morals will be overlooked.

[4] *S. T.,* I-II, q. 57, a. 3 and 4.   [5] *S. T.,* I-II, q. 61, a. 3.

ON FAITH

(*In Ten Articles*)

HAVING to treat now of the theological virtues, we shall begin with Faith, secondly we shall speak of Hope,[1] and thirdly, of Charity.[2]

The treatise on Faith will be fourfold: (1) of faith itself; (2) of the corresponding gifts, science and understanding;[3] (3) of the opposite vices;[4] (4) of the precepts pertaining to this virtue.[5]

About faith itself we shall consider: (1) its object; (2) its act;[6] (3) the habit of faith.[7]

Under the first head there are ten points of inquiry: (1) Whether the object of faith is the First Truth? (2) Whether the object of faith is something complex or incomplex, *i.e.*, whether it is a thing or a proposition? (3) Whether anything false can come under faith? (4) Whether the object of faith can be anything seen? (5) Whether it can be anything known? (6) Whether the things to be believed should be divided into a certain number of articles? (7) Whether the same articles are of faith for all times? (8) Of the number of articles. (9) Of the manner of embodying the articles in a symbol. (10) Who has the right to propose a symbol of faith?

First Article

WHETHER THE OBJECT OF FAITH IS THE FIRST TRUTH?

We proceed thus to the First Article:—

Objection 1. It would seem that the object of faith is not the First Truth. For it seems that the object of faith is that which is proposed to us to be believed. Now not only things pertaining to the Godhead, *i.e.* the First Truth, are proposed to us to be believed, but also things concerning Christ's human nature, the sacraments of the Church, and the condition of creatures. Therefore the object of faith is not only the First Truth.

Obj. 2. Further, Faith and unbelief have the same object since they are opposed to one another. Now unbelief can be about all things contained in Holy Scripture, for whichever one of them a man denies, he is considered an unbeliever. Therefore faith also is about all things contained in Holy Scripture. But there are many things therein concerning man and other creatures. Therefore the object of faith is not only the First Truth, but also created truth.

[1] Q. 17.   [2] Q. 23.   [3] Q. 8.   [4] Q. 10.   [5] Q. 16.   [6] Q. 2.   [7] Q. 4.

Obj. 3. Further, Faith is co-divided against charity, as stated above.[8] Now by charity we love not only God, Who is the highest Good, but also our neighbor. Therefore the object of faith is not only the First Truth.

On the contrary, Dionysius says that *faith is about the simple and ever-lasting truth.*[9] Now this is the First Truth. Therefore the object of faith is the First Truth.

I answer that, The object of every cognitive habit includes two things: first, that which is known materially, and is the material object, so to speak, and, secondly, that whereby it is known, which is the formal aspect of the object. Thus, in the science of geometry, the conclusions are what is known materially, while the formal aspect of the science consists in the means of demonstration, through which the conclusions are known.

Accordingly, if in faith we consider the formal aspect of the object, it is nothing else than the First Truth. For the faith of which we are speaking does not assent to anything, except because it is revealed by God. Hence faith bases itself on the divine Truth as on its means. If, however, we consider materially the things to which faith assents, they include not only God, but also many other things, which, nevertheless, do not come under the assent of faith except as bearing some relation to God, inasmuch as, namely, through certain effects of the divine operation man is helped on his journey towards the enjoyment of God. Consequently, from this point of view also the object of faith is, in a way, the First Truth, inasmuch as nothing comes under faith except in relation to God; even as the object of the medical art is health, for it considers nothing save in relation to health.

Reply Obj. 1. Things concerning Christ's human nature, the sacraments of the Church, or any creatures whatever, come under faith in so far as by them we are directed to God, and inasmuch as we assent to them because of the divine Truth.

The same answer applies to the Second Objection, as regards all things contained in Holy Scripture.

Reply Obj. 3. Charity also loves our neighbor because of God, so that its object, properly speaking, is God, as we shall show further on.[10]

Second Article

WHETHER THE OBJECT OF FAITH IS SOMETHING COMPLEX, SUCH AS A PROPOSITION?

We proceed thus to the Second Article:—

Objection 1. It would seem that the object of faith is not something complex such as a proposition. For the object of faith is the First Truth, as was stated above. Now the First Truth is something simple. Therefore the object of faith is not something complex.

Obj. 2. Further, The exposition of faith is contained in the symbol. Now

[8] *S. T.,* I-II, q. 62, a. 3. [9] *De Div. Nom.,* VII, 4 (PG 3, 872). [10] Q. 25, a. 1.

the symbol does not contain propositions, but things; for it is not stated therein that God is almighty, but: *I believe in God . . . almighty.* Therefore the object of faith is not a proposition but a thing.

Obj. 3. Further, Faith is succeeded by vision, according to *1 Cor.* xiii. 12: *We see now through a glass in a dark manner, but then face to face. Now I know in part, but then I shall know even as I am known.* But the object of the heavenly vision is something simple, for it is the divine essence. Therefore the faith of the wayfarer is also.

On the contrary, Faith is a mean between science and opinion. Now the mean is in the same genus as the extremes. Since, then, science and opinion are about propositions, it seems that faith is likewise about propositions; so that its object is something complex.

I answer that, The thing known is in the knower according to the mode of the knower. Now the mode proper to the human intellect is to know the truth by composition and division, as was stated in the First Part.[11] Hence things that are simple in themselves are known by the intellect with a certain complexity, just as on the other hand the divine intellect knows, without any complexity, things that are complex in themselves.

Accordingly, the object of faith may be considered in two ways. First, as regards the thing itself which is believed, and thus the object of faith is something simple, namely, the thing itself about which we have faith; secondly, on the part of the believer, and in this respect the object of faith is something complex, such as a proposition.

Hence in the past both opinions have been held with a certain amount of truth.[12]

Reply Obj 1. This argument considers the object of faith on the part of the thing believed.

Reply Obj. 2. The symbol mentions the things about which faith is, in so far as the act of the believer is terminated in them, as is evident from the manner of speaking about them. Now the act of the believer does not terminate in a proposition, but in a thing. For we do not form propositions, except in order to have knowledge about things through their means; and this is true of faith as well as of science.

Reply Obj. 3. The object of the heavenly vision will be the First Truth seen in itself, according to *1 John* iii. 2: *We know that when He shall appear, we shall be like to Him: because we shall see Him as He is.* Hence that vision will not be by way of a proposition, but by way of simple under-standing. On the other hand, by faith, we do not apprehend the First Truth as it is in itself. Hence the comparison fails.

---

[11] *S. T.,* I, q. 85, a. 5.   [12] Cf. Philip the Chancellor and William of Auxerre in M.-D. Chenu, "Contribution à l'histoire du traité de la foi. Commentaire historique de la IIa IIae, q. 1, a. 2" in *Mélanges thomistes* (*Bibliothèque Thomiste,* III; Le Saulchoir, Kain, 1923) p. 132.

Third Article

WHETHER ANYTHING FALSE CAN COME UNDER FAITH?

We proceed thus to the Third Article:—

Objection 1. It would seem that something false can come under faith. For faith is co-divided against hope and charity. Now something false can come under hope, since many hope to have eternal life, who will not obtain it. The same may be said of charity, for many are loved as being good, who, nevertheless, are not good. Therefore something false can be the object of faith.

Obj. 2. Further, Abraham believed that Christ would be born, according to *John* viii. 56: *Abraham your father rejoiced that he might see My day; he saw it, and was glad.* But after the time of Abraham, God might not have taken flesh, for it was merely because He willed that He did; so that what Abraham believed about Christ would have been false. Therefore the object of faith can be something false.

Obj. 3. Further, The ancients believed in the future birth of Christ, and many continued so to believe, until they heard the preaching of the Gospel. Now, when once Christ was born, even before He began to preach, it was false that Christ was yet to be born. Therefore something false can come under faith.

Obj. 4. Further, It is a matter of faith that one should believe that the true Body of Christ is contained in the Sacrament of the altar. But it might happen that the bread was not rightly consecrated, and that there was not Christ's true Body there, but only bread. Therefore something false can come under faith.

On the contrary, No virtue that perfects the intellect is related to what is false, considered as the evil of the intellect, as the Philosopher declares.[13] Now faith is a virtue that perfects the intellect, as we shall show further on.[14] Therefore nothing false can come under it.

I answer that, Nothing comes under any power, habit or act, except by means of the formal aspect of the object. Thus color cannot be seen except by means of light, and a conclusion cannot be known save through the means of demonstration. Now it has been stated that the formal aspect of the object of faith is the First Truth. Hence nothing can come under faith, save in so far as it stands under the First Truth, under which nothing false can stand; just as neither can non-being stand under being, nor evil under goodness. It follows therefore that nothing false can come under faith.

Reply Obj. 1. Since the true is the good of the intellect, but not of the appetitive power, it follows that all the virtues which perfect the intellect exclude the false altogether, because it belongs to the nature of a virtue to be related to the good alone. On the other hand, those virtues which per-

---

[13] *Eth.,* VI, 2 (1139b 13; a. 27).   [14] Q. 4, a. 2 and 5.

fect the appetitive part do not entirely exclude the false, for it is possible to act in accordance with justice or temperance, while having a false opinion about what one is doing. Therefore, since faith perfects the intellect, whereas hope and charity perfect the appetitive part, the comparison between them fails.

Nevertheless, neither can anything false come under hope, for a man hopes to obtain eternal life, not by his own power (since this would be an act of presumption), but with the help of grace; and if he perseveres therein, he will obtain eternal life surely and infallibly.

In like manner, it belongs to charity to love God, wherever He may be; so that it matters not to charity whether God be in the individual whom we love for God's sake.

Reply Obj. 2. That *God would not take flesh,* considered in itself, was possible even after Abraham's time; but in so far as it stands in God's foreknowledge, it has a certain necessity of infallibility, as was explained in the First Part,[15] and in this way it comes under faith. Hence, in so far as it comes under faith, it cannot be false.

Reply Obj. 3. After Christ's birth, to believe in Him was to believe in Christ's birth at some time or other. The fixing of the time, however, wherein some were deceived, was not due to their faith, but to a human conjecture. For it is possible for a believer to have a false opinion through a human conjecture, but it is quite impossible for a false opinion to be the outcome of faith.

Reply Obj. 4. The faith of the believer is not directed to such and such species of bread, but to the fact that the true Body of Christ is under the species of sensible bread when it is rightly consecrated. Hence, if it be not rightly consecrated, it does not follow that anything false comes under faith.

Fourth Article

WHETHER THE OBJECT OF FAITH CAN BE SOMETHING SEEN?

We proceed thus to the Fourth Article:—

Objection 1. It would seem that the object of faith is something seen. For our Lord said to Thomas (*Jo.* xx. 29): *Because thou hast seen Me, Thomas, thou hast believed.* Therefore vision and faith regard the same object.

Obj. 2. Further, The Apostle, while speaking of the knowledge of faith, says (*1 Cor.* xiii. 12): *We see now through a glass in a dark manner.* Therefore what is believed is seen.

Obj. 3. Further, Faith is a spiritual light. Now something is seen under every light. Therefore faith is about things seen.

[15] *S. T.,* I, q. 14, a. 13.

Obj. 4. Further, *Every sense is a kind of sight,* as Augustine states.[16] But faith is of things heard, according to *Rom.* x. 17: *Faith . . . cometh by hearing.* Therefore faith is about things seen.

On the contrary, The Apostle says (*Heb.* xi. 1) that *faith is the evidence of things that appear not.*

I answer that, Faith signifies the assent of the intellect to that which is believed. Now the intellect assents to a thing in two ways. First, through being moved to assent by its very object, which is known either by itself (as in the case of first principles, which are held by the habit of understanding), or through something else already known (as in the case of conclusions which are held by the habit of science). Secondly, the intellect assents to something, not through being sufficiently moved to this assent by its proper object, but through an act of choice, whereby it turns voluntarily to one side rather than to the other. Now if this be accompanied by doubt and fear of the opposite side, there will be opinion; while, if there be certainty and no fear of the other side, there will be faith.

Now those things are said to be seen which, of themselves, move the intellect or the senses to knowledge of them. Therefore it is evident that neither faith nor opinion can be of things seen either by the senses or by the intellect.

Reply Obj. 1. Thomas *saw one thing, and believed another.* He saw the Man and, believing Him to be God, he made profession of his faith, saying: *My Lord and my God.*[17]

Reply Obj. 2. Those things which come under faith can be considered in two ways. First, in particular, and in this way they cannot be seen and believed at the same time, as was shown above. Secondly, in general, that is, under the common aspect of credibility; and in this way they are seen by the believer. For he would not believe unless, on the evidence of signs, or of something similar, he saw that they ought to be believed.

Reply Obj. 3. The light of faith makes us see what we believe. For just as, by the habits of the other virtues, man sees what is becoming to him in respect of that habit, so, by the habit of faith, the human mind is inclined to assent to such things as are becoming to a right faith, and not to assent to others.

Reply Obj. 4. Hearing is of words signifying what is of faith, but not of the things themselves that are believed. Hence it does not follow that these things are seen.

[16] *Serm.* CXII, 6 (PL 38, 646). [17] St. Gregory, *In Evang.,* II, hom. 26 (PL 76, 1202).

Fifth Article

WHETHER THOSE THINGS THAT ARE OF FAITH CAN BE AN OBJECT OF SCIENCE?

We proceed thus to the Fifth Article:—

Objection 1. It would seem that those things that are of faith can be an object of science. For where science is lacking there is ignorance, since ignorance is the opposite of science. Now we are not in ignorance of those things we have to believe, since ignorance of such things belongs to unbelief, according to *1 Tim.* i. 13: *I did it ignorantly in unbelief.* Therefore things that are of faith can be an object of science.

Obj. 2. Further, Science is acquired by arguments. Now sacred writers employ arguments to inculcate things that are of faith. Therefore such things can be an object of science.

Obj. 3. Further, Things which are demonstrated are an object of science, since a *demonstration is a syllogism that produces science.* Now certain matters of faith have been demonstrated by the philosophers, such as the existence and unity of God, and so forth. Therefore things that are of faith can be an object of science.

Obj. 4. Further, Opinion is further from science than faith is, since faith is said to stand between opinion and science. Now opinion and science can, in a way, be about the same object, as is stated in *Posterior Analytics* i.[18] Therefore faith and science can be about the same object also.

On the contrary, Gregory says that *when a thing is manifest, it is the object, not of faith, but of perception.*[19] Therefore things that are of faith are not the object of perception, whereas what is an object of science is the object of perception. Therefore there can be no faith about things which are an object of science.

I answer that, All science is derived from self-evident and therefore *seen* principles; and so all objects of science must needs be, in a fashion, seen.

Now, as was stated above, it is impossible that one and the same thing should be believed and seen by the same person. Hence it is equally impossible for one and the same thing to be an object of science and of belief for the same person. It may happen, however, that a thing which is an object of vision or science for one, is believed by another; for we hope to see some day what we now believe about the Trinity, according to *1 Cor.* xiii. 12: *We see now through a glass in a dark manner; but then face to face.* And this vision the angels possess already, so that what we believe, they see. In like manner, it may also happen that what is an object of vision or scientific knowledge for one man, even in the state of a wayfarer, is, for another man, an object of faith, because he does not know it by demonstration.

[18] Aristotle, *Post. Anal,* I, 33 (89a 25).   [19] *In Evang.,* II, hom. 26 (PL 76, 1202).

Nevertheless, that which is proposed to be believed equally by all is equally unknown by all as an object of science. Such are the things which are of faith absolutely. Consequently, faith and science are not about the same things.

Reply Obj. 1. Unbelievers are in ignorance of things that are of faith, for neither do they see or know them in themselves, nor do they know them to be credible. The faithful, on the other hand, know them, not as by demonstration, but by the light of faith which makes them see that they ought to believe them, as was stated above.

Reply Obj. 2. The arguments employed by holy men to prove things that are of faith are not demonstrations; they are either persuasive arguments showing that what is proposed to our faith is not impossible, or else they are proofs drawn from the principles of faith, *i.e.*, from the authority of Holy Scripture, as Dionysius declares.[20] Whatever is based on these principles is as well proved in the eyes of the faithful as a conclusion drawn from self-evident principles is in the eyes of all. Hence, again, theology is a science, as we stated at the outset of this work.[21]

Reply Obj. 3. Things which can be proved by demonstration are reckoned among what is of faith, not because they are believed absolutely by all, but because they are a necessary presupposition to matters of faith; so that those who do not know them by demonstration must possess them at least by faith.

Reply Obj. 4. As the Philosopher says, *science and opinion about the same object can certainly be in different men,*[22] as we have stated above about science and faith; yet it is possible for one and the same man to have science and faith about the same thing relatively, *i.e.* in relation to the object, but not in the same respect. For it is possible for the same person, about one and the same object, to know one thing and to have an opinion about another; and, in like manner, one may know by demonstration the unity of God, and believe that there are three Persons in God. On the other hand, in one and the same man, about the same object, and in the same respect, science is incompatible with either opinion or faith, but for different reasons. For science is incompatible with opinion about the same object absolutely, for the reason that science demands that its object should be deemed impossible to be otherwise, whereas it is essential to opinion that its object should be deemed possible to be otherwise. But that which is the object of faith, because of the certainty of faith, is also deemed impossible to be otherwise; and the reason why science and faith cannot be about the same object, and in the same respect, is because the object of science is something seen, whereas the object of faith is the unseen, as was stated above.

---

[20] *De Div. Nom.*, II, 2 (PG 3, 640).   [21] *S. T.*, I, q. 1, a. 2.   [22] *Post. Anal.*, I, 33 (89b 2).

Sixth Article

WHETHER THOSE THINGS THAT ARE OF FAITH SHOULD BE DIVIDED INTO CERTAIN ARTICLES?

We proceed thus to the Sixth Article:—

Objection 1. It would seem that those things that are of faith should not be divided into certain articles. For all things contained in Holy Scripture are matters of faith. But these, by reason of their multitude, cannot be reduced to a certain number. Therefore it seems superfluous to distinguish certain articles of faith.

Obj. 2. Further, Material differences can be multiplied indefinitely, and therefore art should take no notice of them. Now the formal aspect of the object of faith is one and indivisible, as was stated above, viz. the First Truth; so that matters of faith cannot be distinguished in respect of their formal object. Therefore no notice should be taken of a material division of matters of faith into articles.

Obj. 3. Further, It has been said by some that *an article is an indivisible truth concerning God, exacting our belief.*[23] Now belief is a voluntary act, since, as Augustine says, *no man believes against his will.*[24] Therefore it seems that matters of faith should not be divided into articles.

On the contrary, Isidore says: *An article is a glimpse of divine truth, tending thereto.*[25] Now we can get a glimpse of divine truth only by way of some distinction, since things which in God are one, are manifold in our intellect. Therefore matters of faith should be divided into articles.

I answer that, The term *article* is apparently derived from the Greek, for the Greek ἄρθρον, which the Latin renders *articulus,* signifies a fitting together of distinct parts; and so the small parts of the body which fit together are called the articulations of the members. Likewise, in the Greek grammar, articles are parts of speech which are affixed to words to show their gender, number or case. Again, in rhetoric, articles are parts that fit together in a sentence, for Tully says that an article is composed of words each pronounced singly and separately, *e.g., Your passion, your voice, your look, have struck terror into your foes.*[26]

Hence matters of Christian faith are said to contain distinct articles in so far as they are divided into parts which fit together. Now the object of faith is something unseen concerning God, as was stated above. Consequently, any matter that, for a special reason, is unseen, is a special article;

---

[23] Cf. J.-M. Parent, "La notion du dogme au XIIIe siècle" (*Études d'histoire littéraire et doctrinale du XIIIe siècle,* 1932) p. 149.   [24] *Tract.* XXVI, super *Ioann.,* VI, 44 (PL 35, 1607).   [25] St. Albert, *In III Sent.,* d. xxiv, a. 4 (XXVIII, 449), and St. Bonaventure, *In III Sent.,* d. xxiv, a. 3, q. 2 (III, 527), mention St. Isidore. But Philip the Chancellor refers to the same definition without mentioning the author of it.—Cf. J.-M. Parent, "La notion du dogme . . . ," p. 149.   [26] Pseudo-Cicero, *Rhetor. ad Herenn.,* IV, 19 (p. 135).

whereas when there are several matters unknown under the same aspect, we are not to distinguish various articles. Thus one encounters one difficulty in seeing that God suffered, and another in seeing that He rose again from the dead, and so the article of the Resurrection is distinguished from the article of the Passion. But that He suffered, died and was buried, present the same difficulty, so that if one be accepted, it is not difficult to accept the others; and hence all these belong to one article.

Reply Obj. 1. Some things proposed to our belief are in themselves of faith, while others are of faith, not in themselves, but only in relation to others; even as in the sciences certain propositions are put forward on their own account, while others are put forward in order to manifest others. Now, since the chief object of faith consists in those things which we hope to see in heaven, according to *Heb.* xi. 1: *Faith is the substance of things to be hoped for,* it follows that those things are in themselves of faith, which order us directly to eternal life. Such are the Trinity of Persons in Almighty God, the mystery of Christ's Incarnation, and the like; and these are distinct articles of faith. On the other hand, certain things in Holy Scripture are proposed to our belief, not chiefly on their own account, but for the manifestation of those mentioned above: *e.g.,* that Abraham had two sons, that a dead man rose again at the touch of Eliseus' bones, and the like, which are related in Holy Scripture for the purpose of manifesting the divine majesty or the Incarnation of Christ; and such things should not form distinct articles.

Reply Obj. 2. The formal aspect of the object of faith can be taken in two ways: first, on the part of the thing believed, and thus there is one formal aspect of all matters of faith, viz. the First Truth; and from this point of view there is no distinction of articles. Secondly, the formal aspect of matters of faith can be considered from our point of view, and thus the formal aspect of a matter of faith is that it is something unseen; and from this point of view there are various distinct articles of faith, as we saw above.

Reply Obj. 3. This definition of an article is taken from an etymology of the word as derived from the Latin, rather than in accordance with its real meaning, as derived from the Greek. Hence it does not carry much weight. Yet even then it could be said that, although faith is exacted of no man by a necessity of coercion, since belief is a voluntary act, yet it is exacted of him by a necessity of the end, since *he that cometh to God must believe that He is,* and *without faith it is impossible to please God,* as the Apostle declares (*Heb.* xi. 6).

Seventh Article

WHETHER THE ARTICLES OF FAITH HAVE INCREASED IN THE COURSE OF TIME?

We proceed thus to the Seventh Article:—

Objection 1. It would seem that the articles of faith have not increased in the course of time. For, as the Apostle says (*Heb.* xi. 1), *faith is the substance of things to be hoped for.* Now the same things are to be hoped for at all times. Therefore, at all times, the same things are to be believed.

Obj. 2. Further, Development has taken place in the sciences devised by man, because of defects in the knowledge of those who discovered them, as the Philosopher observes.[27] Now the doctrine of faith was not devised by man, but was delivered to us by God, as is stated in *Ephes.* ii. 8: *It is the gift of God.* Since, then, there can be no lack of knowledge in God, it seems that knowledge of matters of faith was perfect from the beginning, and did not increase as time went on.

Obj. 3. Further, The operation of grace proceeds in an orderly fashion no less than the operation of nature. Now nature always makes a beginning with perfect things, as Boethius states.[28] Therefore it seems that the operation of grace also began with perfect things, so that those who were the first to deliver the faith knew it most perfectly.

Obj. 4. Further, Just as the faith of Christ has reached us through the Apostles, so too, in the Old Testament, the knowledge of faith was delivered by the early patriarchs to those who came later, according to *Deut.* xxxii. 7: *Ask thy father, and he will declare to thee.* Now the Apostles were most fully instructed about the mysteries, for *they received them more fully than others, even as they received them earlier,* as the *Gloss* says on *Rom.* viii. 23: *Ourselves also who have the first-fruits of the Spirit.*[29] Therefore it seems that knowledge of matters of faith has not increased as time went on.

On the contrary, Gregory says that *the knowledge of the holy fathers increased as time went on . . . ; and the nearer they were to Our Savior's coming, the more fully did they receive the mysteries of salvation.*[30]

I answer that, The articles of faith stand in the same relation to the doctrine of faith, as self-evident principles to teaching based on natural reason. Among these principles there is a certain order, so that some are contained implicitly in others; and thus all principles are reduced, as to their first principle, to this one: *The same thing cannot be affirmed and denied at the same time,* as the Philosopher states.[30a] In like manner, all the articles are contained implicitly in certain primary truths of faith, such as

---

[27] *Metaph.,* I a, 1 (993a 30; b 11).　　[28] *De Consol.,* III, prose 10 (PL 63, 764).
[29] *Glossa interl.* (VI, 19r); Peter Lombard, *In Rom.,* super VIII, 23 (PL 191, 1444).
[30] *In Ezech.,* II, hom. 16 (PL 76, 980).　　[30a] *Metaph.,* III, 6 (1011b 20).

God's existence, and His providence over the salvation of man, according to *Heb.* xi.: *He that cometh to God, must believe that He is, and is a rewarder to them that seek Him.* For the being of God includes all that we believe to exist in God eternally, and in these our happiness consists, while belief in His providence includes all those things which God dispenses in time for man's salvation, and which are the way to that happiness; and in this way, again, some of those articles which follow from these are contained in others. Thus faith in the Redemption of mankind includes implicitly the Incarnation of Christ, His Passion and so forth.

Accordingly, we must conclude that, as regards the substance of the articles of faith, they have not received any increase as time went on; since whatever those who lived later have believed, was contained, albeit implicitly, in the faith of those Fathers who preceded them. But there was an increase in the number of articles believed explicitly, since to those who lived in later times some were known explicitly which were not known explicitly by those who lived before them. Hence the Lord said to Moses (*Exod.* vi. 2, 3): *I am the God of Abraham, the God of Isaac, the God of Jacob . . . and My name Adonai I did not show them.* David also said (*Ps.* cxviii. 100): *I have had understanding above ancients*; and the Apostle says (*Ephes.* iii. 5) that the mystery of Christ, *in other generations was not known, as it is now revealed to His holy apostles and prophets.*

Reply Obj. 1. Among all men the same things were always to be hoped for. But as they did not acquire this hope save through Christ, the further they were removed from Christ in point of time, the further they were from obtaining what they hoped for. Hence the Apostle says (*Heb.* xi. 13): *All these died according to faith, not having received the promises, but beholding them afar off.* Now the further off a thing is, the less distinctly is it seen; and so those who were near Christ's advent had a more distinct knowledge of the good things to be hoped for.

Reply Obj. 2. Progress in knowledge occurs in two ways. First, on the part of the teacher, be he one or many, who makes progress in knowledge as time goes on; and this is the kind of progress that takes place in the sciences devised by man. Secondly, on the part of the learner. Thus the master, who has perfect knowledge of an art, does not deliver it all at once to his disciple from the very outset, for he would not be able to take it all in, but he suits his teaching to the disciple's capacity and instructs him little by little. It is in this way that men made progress in the knowledge of faith as time went on. Hence the Apostle (*Gal.* iii. 24) compares the state of the Old Testament to childhood.

Reply Obj. 3. Two causes are requisite before actual generation can take place, namely, an agent and matter. In the order of the active cause, the more perfect is naturally first; and in this way nature makes a beginning with perfect things, since the imperfect is not brought to perfection, except by something perfect already in existence. On the other hand, in the order of the material cause, the imperfect comes first, and in this way nature proceeds from the imperfect to the perfect. Now in the manifestation of faith, God is as the active cause, having perfect knowledge from all eternity; while man is likened to matter in receiving the influx of God's action. Hence, among men, the knowledge of faith had to proceed from imperfection to perfection; and, although some men have functioned as active causes, through being teachers of the faith, nevertheless, *the manifestation of the Spirit is given* to such men for the common good, according to *1 Cor.* xii. 7. Hence the knowledge of faith was imparted to the Fathers, who were instructors in the faith, so far as was necessary at the time for the instruction of the people, either openly or in figures.

Reply Obj. 4. The ultimate consummation of grace was effected by Christ, and so the time of His coming is called the *time of fullness* (*Gal.* iv. 4). Hence those who were nearest to Christ, whether before, like John the Baptist, or after, like the Apostles, had a fuller knowledge of the mysteries of faith; for even with regard to man's state we find that the perfection of manhood comes in youth, and that a man's state is all the more perfect, whether before or after, the nearer it is to the time of his youth.

Eighth Article

WHETHER THE ARTICLES OF FAITH ARE SUITABLY FORMULATED?

We proceed thus to the Eighth Article:—

Objection 1. It would seem that the articles of faith are unsuitably formulated. For those things which can be known by demonstration do not belong to faith in such a way as to be objects of belief among men, as was stated above. Now it can be known by demonstration that there is one God; and hence the Philosopher proves this,[31] and many other philosophers demonstrated the same truth. Therefore that *there is one God* should not be set down as an article of faith.

Obj. 2. Further, Just as it is necessary to faith that we should believe God to be almighty, so is it too that we should believe Him to be *all-knowing* and *provident for all,* about both of which points some have erred.[32] Therefore, among the articles of faith, mention should have been made of God's wisdom and providence, even as of His omnipotence.

Obj. 3. Further, To know the Father is the same thing as to know the Son, according to *John* xiv. 9: *He that seeth Me, seeth the Father also.* Therefore there ought to be but one article about the Father and Son, and, for the same reason, about the Holy Ghost.

Obj. 4. Further, The Person of the Father is not lesser than the Person of the Son, and of the Holy Ghost. Now there are several articles about

---

[31] *Metaph.,* XI, 10 (1076a 4).   [32] Cf. *S. T.,* I, q. 14, a. 6; q. 22, a. 2.

the Person of the Holy Ghost, and likewise about the Person of the Son. Therefore there should be several articles about the Person of the Father.

Obj. 5. Further, Just as certain things are said, by appropriation, of the Person of the Father and of the Person of the Holy Ghost, so too is something appropriated to the Person of the Son, in respect of His Godhead. Now, among the articles of faith, a place is given to a work appropriated to the Father, viz. the creation, and likewise, a work appropriated to the Holy Ghost, viz., that *He spoke by the prophets.* Therefore the articles of faith should contain some work appropriated to the Son in respect of His Godhead.

Obj. 6. Further, The sacrament of the Eucharist presents a special difficulty over and above the other articles. Therefore, it should have been mentioned in a special article; and consequently it seems that there is not a sufficient number of articles.

On the contrary stands the authority of the Church which formulates the articles thus.[33]

I answer that, As was stated above, to faith those things belong essentially, the sight of which we shall enjoy in eternal life, and by which we are brought to eternal life. Now two things are proposed to us to be seen in eternal life, viz., the secret of the Godhead, to see which is to possess happiness, and the mystery of Christ's Incarnation, *by Whom we have access* to the glory of the sons of God, according to *Rom.* v. 2. Hence it is written (*Jo.* xvii. 3): *This is eternal life, that they may know Thee, the . . . true God, and Jesus Christ Whom Thou hast sent.* Therefore the first distinction in matters of faith is that some concern the majesty of the Godhead, while others pertain to the mystery of Christ's human nature, which is the *mystery of godliness* (*1 Tim.* iii. 16).

Now with regard to the majesty of the Godhead, three things are proposed to our belief: first, the unity of the Godhead, to which the first article refers; secondly, the trinity of the Persons, to which three articles refer, corresponding to the three Persons; and thirdly, the works proper to the Godhead. The first of these refers to the order of nature, in relation to which the article about the creation is proposed to us; the second refers to the order of grace, in relation to which all matters concerning the sanctification of man are included in one article; while the third refers to the order of glory, and in relation to this another article is proposed to us concerning the resurrection of the body and life everlasting. Thus there are seven articles referring to the Godhead.

In like manner, with regard to Christ's human nature, there are seven articles, the first of which refers to Christ's incarnation or conception; the second, to His virginal birth; the third, to His Passion, death and burial; the fourth, to His descent into hell; the fifth, to His resurrection; the sixth,

---

[33] *Symb. Nicaeno-Constantinopolitanum* (Denzinger, no. 86).

to His ascension; the seventh, to His coming for the judgment. And thus there are fourteen articles in all.

Some, however, distinguish twelve articles, six pertaining to the Godhead, and six to the humanity.[34] For they include in one article the three articles about the three Persons, because we have one knowledge of the three Persons; while they divide the article referring to the work of glorification into two, viz., the resurrection of the body, and the glory of the soul. Likewise they unite the conception and nativity into one article.

Reply Obj. 1. By faith we hold many truths about God which the philosophers were unable to discover by natural reason, *e.g.*, about His providence and omnipotence, and that He alone is to be worshipped, all of which are contained in the one article of the unity of God.

Reply Obj. 2. The very name of the Godhead implies a kind of watching over things, as was stated in the First Part.[35] Now in beings having an intellect, power does not work save by the will and knowledge. Hence God's omnipotence includes, in a way, universal knowledge and providence. For He would not be able to do all He wills in things here below, unless He knew them, and exercised His providence over them.

Reply Obj. 3. We have but one knowledge of the Father, Son and Holy Ghost, as to the unity of the essence, to which the first article refers. But as to the distinction of the Persons, which is by the relations of origin, knowledge of the Father does indeed, in a way, include knowledge of the Son, for He would not be Father, had he not a Son; and between them the bond is the Holy Ghost. From this point of view, there was a sufficient motive for those who referred one article to the three Persons. Since, however, with regard to each Person, certain points have to be observed, about which some happen to fall into error, looking at it in this way, we may distinguish three articles about the three Persons. For Arius believed in the omnipotence and eternity of the Father, but he did not believe the Son to be co-equal and consubstantial with the Father; hence the need for an article about the Person of the Son in order to settle this point. In like manner, it was necessary to appoint a third article about the Person of the Holy Ghost, against Macedonius. In the same way, Christ's conception and birth, like the resurrection and life everlasting, can from one point of view be united together in one article, in so far as they are ordained to one end; while, from another point of view, they can be distinct articles, inasmuch as each one separately presents a special difficulty.

Reply Obj. 4. It belongs to the Son and Holy Ghost to be sent to sanctify the creature; and about this several things have to be believed. Hence it is that there are more articles about the Persons of the Son and Holy Ghost than about the Person of the Father, Who is never sent, as we stated in the First Part.[36]

[34] Cf. St. Bonaventure, *In Hexaëm.*, coll. VIII (V, 371).   [35] *S. T.*, I, q. 13, a. 8.
[36] *S. T.*, I, q. 43, a. 4.

Reply Obj. 5. The sanctification of a creature by grace, and its consummation by glory, is also effected by the gift of charity, which is appropriated to the Holy Ghost, and by the gift of wisdom, which is appropriated to the Son; so that each work belongs by appropriation, but under different aspects, both to the Son and to the Holy Ghost.

Reply Obj. 6. Two things may be considered in the sacrament of the Eucharist. One is the fact that it is a sacrament, and in this respect it is like the other effects of sanctifying grace. The other is that Christ's body is miraculously contained therein, and thus it is included under God's omnipotence, like all other miracles which are ascribed to God's almighty power.

Ninth Article

WHETHER IT IS SUITABLE FOR THE ARTICLES OF FAITH TO
BE EMBODIED IN A SYMBOL?

We proceed thus to the Ninth Article:—

Objection 1. It would seem that it is unsuitable for the articles of faith to be embodied in a symbol. For Holy Scripture is the rule of faith, to which no addition or subtraction can lawfully be made, since it is written (*Deut.* iv. 2): *You shall not add to the word that I speak to you, neither shall you take away from it.* Therefore it was unlawful to make a symbol as a rule of faith, after Holy Scripture had once been published.

Obj. 2. Further, According to the Apostle (*Ephes.* iv. 5) there is but *one faith.* Now the symbol is a profession of faith. Therefore it is not fitting that there should be many symbols.

Obj. 3. Further, The confession of faith, which is contained in the symbol, concerns all the faithful. But the faithful are not all competent to believe in God, but only those who have formed faith. Therefore it is unfitting for the symbol of faith to be expressed in the words: *I believe in one God.*

Obj. 4. Further, The descent into hell is one of the articles of faith, as was stated above. But the descent into hell is not mentioned in the symbol of the ancient Fathers. Therefore the latter is formulated inadequately.

Obj. 5. Further, Augustine, expounding the passage, *You believe in God, believe also in Me* (*Jo.* xiv. 1), says: *We believe Peter or Paul, but we speak only of believing 'in' God.*[37] Since then the Catholic Church is merely a created being, it seems unfitting to say: *In the One, Holy, Catholic and Apostolic Church.*

Obj. 6. Further, A symbol is drawn up that it may be a rule of faith. Now a rule of faith ought to be proposed to all, and that publicly. Therefore every symbol, besides the symbol of the Fathers, should be sung at Mass. Therefore it seems unfitting to publish the articles of faith in a symbol.

[37] *Tract.* XXIX, super *Ioann.*, VII, 17 (PL 35, 1631).

On the contrary, The universal Church cannot err, since she is governed by the Holy Ghost Who is the Spirit of truth; for such was Our Lord's promise to His disciples (*Jo.* xvi. 13): *When He, the Spirit of truth, is come, He will teach you all truth.* Now the symbol is published by the authority of the universal Church. Therefore it contains nothing defective.

I answer that, As the Apostle says (*Heb.* xi. 6), *he that cometh to God, must believe that He is.* Now a man cannot believe, unless the truth be proposed to him that he may believe it. Hence the need for the truth of faith to be collected together, so that it might the more easily be proposed to all, lest through ignorance anyone might stray from the truth of faith. It is from being such a collection of the truths of faith that the symbol takes its name.

Reply Obj. 1. The truth of faith is contained in Holy Scripture diffusely, under various modes of expression, and sometimes obscurely, so that, in order to gather the truth of faith from Holy Scripture, one needs long study and practice; and these are unattainable by all those who require to know the truth of faith, many of whom have no time for study, being busy with other affairs. And so it was necessary to gather together a clear summary from the sayings of Holy Scripture, to be proposed to the belief of all. This indeed was no addition to Holy Scripture, but something derived from it.

Reply Obj. 2. The same doctrine of faith is taught in all the symbols. Nevertheless, the people need more careful instruction about the truth of faith when errors arise, lest the faith of simple believers be corrupted by heretics. It was this that gave rise to the necessity of formulating several symbols, which in no way differ from one another, save that, because of the obstinacy of heretics, one contains more explicitly what another contains implicitly.

Reply Obj. 3. The confession of faith is drawn up in a symbol, in the person, as it were, of the whole Church, which is united together by faith. Now the faith of the Church is formed faith; since such is the faith to be found in all those who are of the Church not only outwardly but also by merit. Hence the confession of faith is expressed in a symbol, in a manner that is in keeping with formed faith, so that even if some of the faithful lack formed faith, they should endeavor to acquire it.

Reply Obj. 4. No error about the descent into hell had arisen among the heretics, so that there was no need to be more explicit on that point. For this reason it is not repeated in the symbol of the Fathers, but is supposed as already settled in the symbol of the Apostles. For a subsequent symbol does not cancel a preceding one; rather does it expound it, as was stated above.

Reply Obj. 5. If we say: '*In*' the holy Catholic Church, this must be taken as verified in so far as our faith is directed to the Holy Ghost, Who sanctifies the Church; so that the sense is: *I believe in the Holy Ghost sanctifying the Church.* But it is better and more in keeping with the common use to omit the *in,* and say simply, *the holy Catholic Church,* as Pope Leo observes.[38]

Reply Obj. 6. Since the symbol of the Fathers is an explanation of the symbol of the Apostles, and was drawn up after the faith was already spread abroad, and when the Church was already at peace, it is sung publicly in the Mass. On the other hand, the symbol of the Apostles, which was drawn up at the time of persecution, before the faith was made public, is said secretly at Prime and Compline, as though it were against the darkness of past and future errors.

Tenth Article

WHETHER IT BELONGS TO THE SOVEREIGN PONTIFF TO DRAW UP A SYMBOL OF FAITH?

We proceed thus to the Tenth Article:—

Objection 1. It would seem that it does not belong to the Sovereign Pontiff to draw up a symbol of faith. For a new edition of the symbol becomes necessary in order to explain the articles of faith, as was stated above. Now, in the Old Testament, the articles of faith were more and more explained as time went on, because the truth of faith became clearer through greater nearness to Christ, as was stated above. Since, then, this reason ceased with the advent of the New Law, there is no need for the articles of faith to be more and more explicit. Therefore it does not seem to belong to the authority of the Sovereign Pontiff to draw up a new edition of the symbol.

Obj. 2. Further, No man has the power to do what is forbidden under pain of anathema by the universal Church. Now it was forbidden under pain of anathema by the universal Church to make a new edition of the symbol. For it is stated in the acts of the first council of Ephesus that after the symbol of the Nicene council had been read through, *the holy synod decreed that it was unlawful to utter, write or draw up any other creed than that which was defined by the Fathers assembled at Nicaea together with the Holy Ghost,*[39] and this under pain of anathema. The same was repeated in the acts of the council of Chalcedon.[40] Therefore it seems that the Sovereign Pontiff has no authority to publish a new edition of the symbol.

Obj. 3. Further, Athanasius was not a Sovereign Pontiff, but patriarch of Alexandria, and yet he published a symbol which is sung in the Church. Therefore it does not seem to belong to the Sovereign Pontiff, any more than to other bishops, to publish a new edition of the symbol.

---

[38] Cf. Rufinus, *In Symb. Apost.* (PL 21, 373). [39] *Conc. Ephes.,* actio VI (Denzinger, no. 125). [40] *Conc. Chalced.,* actio V (Mansi, VII, 109).

On the contrary, The symbol was drawn up by a general council. Now such a council cannot be convoked otherwise than by the authority of the Sovereign Pontiff, as is stated in the *Decretals.*[41] Therefore it belongs to the authority of the Sovereign Pontiff to draw up a symbol.

I answer that, As was stated above, a new edition of the symbol becomes necessary in order to set aside the errors that may arise. Consequently to publish a new edition of the symbol belongs to that authority which is empowered to decide matters of faith definitely, so that all may hold them with unshaken faith. Now this belongs to the authority of the Sovereign Pontiff, *to whom the more important and more difficult questions that arise in the Church are referred,* as is stated in the *Decretals.*[42] Hence Our Lord said to Peter whom he made Sovereign Pontiff (*Luke* xxii. 32): *I have prayed for thee,* Peter, *that thy faith fail not, and thou, being once converted, confirm thy brethren.* The reason for this is that there should be but one faith in the whole Church, according to *1 Cor.* i. 10: *That you all speak the same thing, and that there be no schisms among you*; and this could not be secured unless any question of faith that may arise be decided by him who presides over the whole Church, so that the whole Church may hold firmly to his decision. Consequently it belongs to the sole authority of the Sovereign Pontiff to publish a new edition of the symbol, as do all other matters which concern the whole Church, such as to convoke a general council, and so forth.

Reply Obj. 1. The truth of faith is sufficiently explicit in the teaching of Christ and the Apostles. But since, according to *2 Pet.* iii. 16, some men are so evil-minded as to pervert the apostolic teaching and other doctrines and Scriptures to their own destruction, it was necessary as time went on to express the faith more explicitly against the errors which arose.

Reply Obj. 2. This prohibition and sentence of the council was intended for private individuals, who have no business to decide matters of faith; for this decision of the general council did not take away from a subsequent council the power of drawing up a new edition of the symbol, containing, not indeed a new faith, but the same faith with greater explicitness. For every council has taken into account that a subsequent council would expound matters more fully than the preceding council, if this became necessary through the rise of some heresy. Consequently, this belongs to the Sovereign Pontiff, by whose authority the council is convoked, and its decision confirmed.

Reply Obj. 3. Athanasius drew up a declaration of faith, not under the form of a symbol, but rather by way of an exposition of doctrine, as appears from his way of speaking. But since it contained briefly the whole truth of faith, it was accepted by the authority of the Sovereign Pontiff, so as to be considered as a rule of faith.

---

[41] Gratian, *Decretum,* I, xvii, 4 (I, 51).   [42] *Ibid.,* 5 (I, 52).

ON THE INTERIOR ACT OF FAITH
(In Ten Articles)

WE must now consider the act of faith, and (1) the interior act; (2) the exterior act.[1]

Under the first head there are ten points of inquiry: (1) What is *to believe*, which is the interior act of faith? (2) In how many ways is it expressed? (3) Whether it is necessary for salvation to believe in anything above natural reason? (4) Whether it is necessary to believe those things that are attainable by natural reason? (5) Whether it is necessary for salvation to believe certain things explicitly? (6) Whether all are equally bound to explicit faith? (7) Whether explicit faith in Christ is always necessary for salvation? (8) Whether it is necessary for salvation to believe in the Trinity explicitly? (9) Whether the act of faith is meritorious? (10) Whether human reason diminishes the merit of faith?

First Article

WHETHER TO BELIEVE IS TO THINK WITH ASSENT?

We proceed thus to the First Article:—

Objection 1. It would seem that to believe is not to think with assent. Because the Latin word *cogitatio* [*thought*] implies an inquiry, for *cogitare* [*to think*] seems to be equivalent to *coagitare, i.e., to discuss together*. Now Damascene says that faith is *an assent without inquiry*.[2] Therefore thinking has no place in the act of faith.

Obj. 2. Further, Faith resides in the reason, as we shall show further on.[3] Now to think is an act of the cogitative power, which belongs to the sensitive part, as was stated in the First Part.[4] Therefore thought has nothing to do with faith.

Obj. 3. Further, To believe is an act of the intellect, since its object is truth. But assent seems to be an act, not of the intellect, but of the will, even as consent is, as was stated above.[5] Therefore to believe is not to think with assent.

On the contrary, This is how *to believe* is defined by Augustine.[6]

I answer that, To think can be taken in three ways. First, in a general way for any kind of actual consideration of the intellect, as Augustine ob-

---

[1] Q. 3.   [2] *De Fide Orth.,* IV, 11 (PG 94, 1128).   [3] Q. 4, a. 2.   [4] *S. T.,* I, q. 78, a. 4.   [5] Q. 1, a. 4; I-II, q. 15, a. 1.   [6] *De Praedest. Sanct.,* II (PL 44, 963).

serves: *By understanding I mean now the power whereby we understand when thinking.*[7] Secondly, *to think* is more strictly taken for that consideration of the intellect which is accompanied by some kind of inquiry, and which precedes the intellect's arrival at the stage of perfection that comes with the certitude of vision. In this sense Augustine says that *the Son of God is not called the Thought, but the Word of God. When our thought realizes what we know and takes form therefrom, it becomes our word. Hence the Word of God must be understood without any thinking on the part of God, for there is nothing there that can take form, or be unformed.*[8] In this way thought is, properly speaking, the movement of the soul while yet deliberating, and not yet perfected by the clear vision of truth. Since, however, such a movement of the soul may be one of deliberation either about universal intentions, which belongs to the intellectual part, or about particular intentions, which belongs to the sensitive part, hence it is that *to think* is taken secondly for an act of the deliberating intellect, and thirdly for an act of the cogitative power.

Accordingly, if *to think* be understood broadly according to the first sense, then *to think with assent* does not express completely what is meant by *to believe;* for, in this way, a man thinks with assent even when he considers what he knows by science or what he understands. If, on the other hand, *to think* be understood in the second way, then this expresses completely the nature of the act of believing. For among the acts belonging to the intellect, some have a firm assent without any such kind of thinking, as when a man considers the things that he knows by science or what he understands, for this consideration is already formed. But some acts of the intellect have unformed thought devoid of a firm assent, whether they incline to neither side, as in one who *doubts;* or incline to one side rather than the other, but because of some slight motive, as in one who *suspects;* or incline to one side, yet with fear of the other, as in one who *opines.* But this act, *to believe,* cleaves firmly to one side, in which respect belief has something in common with science and understanding; yet its knowledge does not attain the perfection of clear vision, wherein it agrees with doubt, suspicion and opinion. Hence it is proper to the believer to think with assent; so that the act of believing is distinguished from all the other acts of the intellect which are about the true or the false.

Reply Obj. 1. Faith has not that inquiry of natural reason which demonstrates what is believed, but an inquiry into those things whereby a man is induced to believe, for instance, that such things have been uttered by God and confirmed by miracles.

Reply Obj. 2. *To think* is not taken here for the act of the cogitative power, but for an act of the intellect, as was explained above.

Reply Obj. 3. The intellect of the believer is determined to one object,

---

[7] *De Trin.,* XIV, 7 (PL 42, 1044).   [8] *Op. cit.,* XV, 16 (PL 42, 1079).

not by the reason, but by the will, and so assent is taken here for an act of the intellect as determined to one object by the will.

Second Article

WHETHER THE ACT OF FAITH IS SUITABLY DISTINGUISHED AS BELIEVING GOD, BELIEVING IN A GOD, AND BELIEVING IN GOD?

We proceed thus to the Second Article:—

Objection 1. It would seem that the act of faith is unsuitably distinguished as believing God, believing in a God, and believing in God. For one habit has but one act. Now faith is one habit since it is one virtue. Therefore it is unreasonable to say that there are several acts of faith.

Obj. 2. Further, That which is common to all acts of faith should not be reckoned as a particular kind of act of faith. Now *to believe God* is common to all acts of faith, since faith is founded on the First Truth. Therefore it seems unreasonable to distinguish it from certain other acts of faith.

Obj. 3. Further, That which can be said of unbelievers cannot be called an act of faith. Now unbelievers can be said to believe that there is a God. Therefore it should not be reckoned an act of faith.

Obj. 4. Further, Movement towards the end belongs to the will, whose object is the good and the end. Now to believe is an act, not of the will, but of the intellect. Therefore *to believe in God,* which implies movement towards an end, should not be reckoned as a species of that act.

On the contrary is the authority of Augustine who makes this distinction.[9]

I answer that, The act of any power or habit depends on the relation of that power or habit to its object. Now the object of faith can be considered in three ways. For, since *to believe* is an act of the intellect, in so far as the will moves it to assent, as was stated above, the object of faith can be considered either on the part of the intellect, or on the part of the will that moves the intellect.

If it be considered on the part of the intellect, then two things can be observed in the object of faith, as was stated above.[10] One of these is the material object of faith, and in this way an act of faith is *to believe in a God,* because, as was stated above, nothing is proposed to our belief except inasmuch as it is referred to God.[11] The other is the formal aspect of the object, for it is the medium because of which we assent to such and such a point of faith; and thus an act of faith is *to believe God,* since, as was stated above, the formal object of faith is the First Truth,[12] to Which man gives his adhesion, so as to assent for Its sake to whatever he believes.

[9] *Serm.* CXLIV, 2 (PL 38, 788); *Tract.* XXIX, super *Ioann.,* VII, 17 (PL 35, 1631).
[10] Q. 1, a. 1.   [11] *Ibid.*   [12] *Ibid.*

Thirdly, if the object of faith be considered in so far as the intellect is moved by the will, an act of faith is *to believe in God*. For the First Truth is referred to the will, through having the nature of an end.

Reply Obj. 1. These three do not denote different acts of faith, but one and the same act having different relations to the object of faith.

This suffices for the *Reply* to the *Second Objection*.

Reply Obj. 3. Unbelievers cannot be said *to believe in a God* as we understand it in relation to the act of faith. For they do not believe that God exists under the conditions that faith determines; and hence they do not truly believe in a God, since, as the Philosopher observes, *to know simple things defectively is not to know them at all.*[13]

Reply Obj. 4. As was stated above, the will moves the intellect and the other powers of the soul to the end;[14] and in this respect an act of faith is *to believe in God*.

Third Article

WHETHER IT IS NECESSARY FOR SALVATION TO BELIEVE ANYTHING ABOVE THE NATURAL REASON?

We proceed thus to the Third Article:—

Objection 1. It would seem unnecessary for salvation to believe anything above the natural reason. For the salvation and perfection of a thing seem to be sufficiently insured by its natural endowments. Now matters of faith surpass man's natural reason, since they are things unseen, as was stated above.[15] Therefore to believe seems unnecessary for salvation.

Obj. 2. Further, it is dangerous for man to assent to matters wherein he cannot judge whether that which is proposed to him be true or false, according to *Job* xii. 11: *Doth not the ear discern words?* Now a man cannot form a judgment of this kind in matters of faith, since he cannot reduce them back to first principles, by which all our judgments are guided. Therefore it is dangerous to believe in such matters. Therefore to believe is not necessary for salvation.

Obj. 3. Further, Man's salvation rests on God, according to *Ps.* xxxvi. 39: *But the salvation of the just is from the Lord.* Now *the invisible things* of God *are clearly seen, being understood by the things that are made; His eternal power also and divinity*, according to *Rom.* i. 20. But those things which are clearly seen by the understanding are not an object of belief. Therefore it is not necessary for man's salvation that he should believe certain things.

On the contrary, It is written (*Heb.* xi. 6): *Without faith it is impossible to please God.*

---

[13] *Metaph.*, VIII, 10 (1051b 25).   [14] *S. T.*, I, q. 82, a. 4; I-II, q. 9, a. 1.   [15] Q. 1, a. 4

I answer that, Wherever one nature is subordinate to another, we find that two things concur towards the perfection of the lower nature, one of which is in terms of that nature's proper movement, while the other is in terms of the movement of the higher nature. Thus water by its proper movement moves towards the center, while according to the movement of the moon, it moves round the center by ebb and flow. In like manner, the spheres of the planets have their proper movements from west to east, while in accordance with the movement of the first heaven, they have a movement from east to west. Now the created rational nature alone is immediately ordered to God, since other creatures do not attain to the universal, but only to something particular, for they partake of the divine goodness either in *being* only, as inanimate things, or also in *living,* and in *knowing singulars,* as plants and animals; whereas the rational nature, inasmuch as it apprehends the universal notion of good and being, is immediately related to the universal principle of being.

Consequently the perfection of the rational creature consists not only in what belongs to it according to its nature, but also in that which it acquires through a supernatural participation of the divine goodness. Hence it was said above that man's ultimate happiness consists in a supernatural vision of God.[16] To this vision man cannot attain unless he be taught by God, according to *John* vi. 45: *Every one that hath heard of the Father and hath learned cometh to Me.* Now man acquires a share of this learning, not all at once, but a little at a time, according to the mode of his nature; and every one who learns thus must needs believe, in order that he may acquire science in a perfect degree. And so the Philosopher likewise remarks that *it behooves a learner to believe.*[17]

Hence, in order that a man arrive at the perfect vision of heavenly happiness, he must first of all believe God, as a disciple believes the master who is teaching him.

Reply Obj. 1. Since man's nature is dependent on a higher nature, natural knowledge does not suffice for its perfection, and some supernatural knowledge is necessary, as was stated above.

Reply Obj. 2. Just as man assents to first principles by the natural light of his intellect, so does a virtuous man, by the habit of virtue, judge rightly of things concerning that virtue; and in this way, by the light of faith which God bestows on him, a man assents to matters of faith and not to those which are against faith. Consequently, *there is no* danger or *condemnation to them that are in Christ Jesus,* and whom He has enlightened by faith.

Reply Obj. 3. In many respects, faith perceives the invisible things of God in a higher way than natural reason does in proceeding to God from His creatures. Hence it is written (*Ecclus.* iii. 25): *Many things are shown to thee above the understanding of man.*

---

[16] *S. T.,* I, q. 12, a. 1; I-II, q. 3, a. 8.   [17] *Soph. Elench.,* II (161b 3).

Fourth Article

WHETHER IT IS NECESSARY TO BELIEVE THOSE THINGS
WHICH CAN BE PROVED BY NATURAL REASON?

We proceed thus to the Fourth Article:—

Objection 1. It would seem unnecessary to believe those things which can be proved by natural reason. For nothing is superfluous in God's works, much less even than in the works of nature. Now it is superfluous to employ other means, where one already suffices. Therefore it would be superfluous to receive by faith things that can be known by natural reason.

Obj. 2. Further, Those things must be believed which are the object of faith. Now science and faith are not about the same object, as was stated above.[18] Since, therefore, all things that can be known by natural reason are an object of science, it seems that there is no need to believe what can be proved by natural reason.

Obj. 3. Further, All things knowable by science would seem to have one nature; so that if some of them are proposed to man as objects of faith, in like manner the others should also be believed. But this is not true. Therefore it is not necessary to believe those things which can be proved by natural reason.

On the contrary, It is necessary to believe that God is one and incorporeal; which things philosophers prove by natural reason.

I answer that, It is necessary for man to receive by faith not only things which are above reason, but also those which can be known by reason; and this for three motives. First, in order that man may arrive more quickly at the knowledge of divine truth. For the science to whose province it belongs to prove the existence of God and many other such truths is the last of all to offer itself to human inquiry, since it presupposes many other sciences; so that it would be far along in life that man would arrive at the knowledge of God. The second reason is, in order that the knowledge of God may be more widespread. For many are unable to make progress in the study of science, either through dullness of ability, or through having a number of occupations and temporal needs, or even through laziness in learning; and all these persons would be altogether deprived of the knowledge of God, unless divine things were brought to their knowledge by way of faith. The third reason is for the sake of certitude. For human reason is very deficient in things concerning God. A sign of this is that philosophers, in their inquiry into human affairs by natural investigation, have fallen into many errors, and have disagreed among themselves. And consequently, in order that men might have knowledge of God, free of doubt and uncertainty, it was necessary for divine truths to be delivered to them by way of faith, being told to them, as it were, by God Himself Who cannot lie.

[18] Q. 1, a. 5.

Reply Obj. 1. The inquiry of natural reason does not suffice mankind for the knowledge of divine truths, even of those that can be proved by reason; and so it is not superfluous if these be believed.

Reply Obj. 2. Science and faith cannot be in the same subject and about the same object; but what is an object of science for one can be an object of faith for another, as was stated above.[19]

Reply Obj. 3. Although all things that can be known by science have the notion of science in common, they do not all alike lead man to beatitude; and hence they are not all equally proposed to our belief.

Fifth Article

WHETHER MAN IS BOUND TO BELIEVE ANYTHING EXPLICITLY?

We proceed thus to the Fifth Article:—

Objection 1. It would seem that man is not bound to believe anything explicitly. For no man is bound to do what is not in his power. Now it is not in man's power to believe a thing explicitly, for it is written (*Rom.* x. 14, 15): *How shall they believe Him, of whom they have not heard? And how shall they hear without a preacher? And how shall they preach unless they be sent?* Therefore man is not bound to believe anything explicitly.

Obj. 2. Further, Just as we are directed to God by faith, so also are we by charity. Now man is not bound to keep the precepts of charity, but it is enough if he be ready to fulfill them. This is evidenced by the precept of Our Lord (*Matt.* v. 39): *If one strike thee on one cheek, turn to him also the other*; and by others of the same kind, according to Augustine's exposition.[20] Therefore neither is man bound to believe anything explicitly, but it is enough if he be ready to believe whatever God proposes to be believed.

Obj. 3. Further, The good of faith consists in a certain obedience, according to *Rom.* i. 5: *For obedience to the faith in all nations.* Now the virtue of obedience does not require man to keep certain fixed precepts, but it is enough that his mind be ready to obey, according to *Ps.* cxviii. 60: *I am ready and am not troubled, that I may keep Thy commandments.* Therefore it seems enough for faith, too, that man should be ready to believe whatever God may propose, without believing anything explicitly.

On the contrary, It is written (*Heb.* xi. 6): *He that cometh to God must believe that He is, and is a rewarder to them that seek Him.*

I answer that, The precepts of the Law, which man is bound to fulfill, concern acts of virtue which are the means of attaining salvation. Now an act of virtue, as was stated above, depends on the relation of the habit to its object.[21] But two things may be considered in the object of any virtue, namely, that which is the proper and direct object of that virtue, which is

---

[19] *Ibid.*   [20] *De Serm. Dom.,* I, 19 (PL 34, 1260).   [21] Q. 2, a. 2.

necessarily in every act of virtue, and that which is accidental and consequent to the object properly so called. Thus, it belongs properly and directly to the object of fortitude to face the dangers of death, and to charge at the foe with danger to oneself, for the sake of the common good; and yet that, in a just war, a man be armed, or strike another with his sword, and so forth, is reduced to the object of fortitude, but indirectly.

Accordingly, just as a virtuous act is required for the fulfillment of a precept, so is it necessary that the virtuous act should terminate in its proper and direct object; but, on the other hand, the fulfillment of the precept does not require that a virtuous act should terminate in those things which have an accidental or secondary relation to the proper and direct object of that virtue, except in certain places and at certain times.

We must, therefore, say that the direct object of faith is that whereby man is made one of the Blessed, as was stated above;[22] while the indirect and secondary object comprises all things delivered by God to us in Holy Scripture, for instance, that Abraham had two sons, that David was the son of Jesse, and so forth. Therefore, as regards the primary points or articles of faith, man must believe them explicitly, just as he must have faith; but as to other points of faith, man is not bound to believe them explicitly, but only implicitly, or to be ready to believe them, in so far as he is prepared to believe whatever is contained in the divine Scriptures. Then alone is he bound to believe such things explicitly, when it is clear to him that they are contained in the doctrine of faith.

Reply Obj. 1. If we understand those things alone to be in a man's power, which we can do without the help of grace, then we are bound to do many things which we cannot do without the aid of healing grace, such as to love God and our neighbor, and likewise to believe the articles of faith. But with the help of grace we can do this, for this help *to whomsoever it is given from above it is mercifully given; and from whom it is withheld it is justly withheld, as a punishment of a previous, or at least of original, sin,* as Augustine states.[23]

Reply Obj. 2. Man is bound to love definitely those lovable things which are properly and directly the objects of charity, namely, God and neighbor. The objection refers to those precepts of charity which belong, as by a consequence, to the object of charity.

Reply Obj. 3. The virtue of obedience is seated, properly speaking, in the will; and hence the promptness of the will, which is subject to authority, suffices for the act of obedience, because it is the proper and direct object of obedience. But this or that precept is accidental or consequent to that proper and direct object.

[22] Q. 1, a. 6, ad 1.   [23] Cf. *Epist.* CXC, 3 (PL 33, 860); *De Praedest. Sanct.*, VIII (PL 44, 971).

Sixth Article

WHETHER ALL ARE EQUALLY BOUND TO HAVE EXPLICIT
FAITH?

We proceed thus to the Sixth Article:—

Objection 1. It would seem that all are equally bound to have explicit faith. For all are bound to those things which are necessary for salvation, as is evident concerning the precepts of charity. Now it is necessary for salvation that certain things should be believed explicitly, as we have said. Therefore all are equally bound to have explicit faith.

Obj. 2. Further, No one should be put to a test in matters that he is not bound to believe explicitly. But simple persons are sometimes tested in reference to the slightest articles of faith. Therefore all are bound to believe everything explicitly.

Obj. 3. Further, If the simple are bound to have, not explicit, but only implicit faith, their faith must needs be implied in the faith of the learned. But this seems unsafe, since it is possible for the learned to err. Therefore it seems that the simple should also have explicit faith; so that all are, therefore, equally bound to have explicit faith.

On the contrary, It is written (*Job* i. 14): *The oxen were ploughing, and the asses feeding beside them,* because, as Gregory expounds this passage, the simple, who are signified by the asses, ought, in matters of faith, to stay by the learned, who are denoted by the oxen.[24]

I answer that, The unfolding of matters of faith is the result of divine revelation, for matters of faith surpass natural reason. Now divine revelation reaches those of lower degree through those who are over them, in a certain order; to men, for instance, through the angels, and to the lower angels through the higher, as Dionysius explains.[25] In like manner, therefore, the unfolding of faith must needs reach men of lower degree through those of higher degree. Consequently, just as the higher angels, who illumine those who are below them, have a fuller knowledge of divine things than the lower angels, as Dionysius states,[26] so too, men of higher degree, whose business it is to teach others, are under obligation to have fuller knowledge of matters of faith, and to believe them more explicitly.

Reply Obj. 1. The unfolding of the articles of faith is not equally necessary for the salvation of all, since those of higher degree, whose duty it is to teach others, are bound to believe explicitly more things than others are.

Reply Obj. 2. Simple persons should not be put to the test about subtle questions of faith, unless they be suspected of having been corrupted by heretics, who are wont to corrupt the faith of simple people in such questions. If, however, it is found that they are free from obstinacy in their

---

[24] *Moral.*, II, 30 (PL 75, 578).   [25] *De Cael. Hier.*, IV, 3; VII, 3; VIII, 2 (PG 3, 180· 209; 240).   [26] *Op. cit.*, XII, 2 (PG 3, 292).

heterodox sentiments, and that it is due to their simplicity, it is no fault of theirs.

Reply Obj. 3. The simple have no faith implied in that of the learned, except in so far as the latter adhere to the divine teaching. Hence the Apostle says (*1 Cor.* iv. 16): *Be ye followers of me, as I also am of Christ.* Hence it is not human knowledge, but the divine truth, that is the rule of faith; and if any of the learned stray from this rule, he does not harm the faith of the simple ones, who think that the learned believe rightly—unless the simple hold obstinately to their individual errors, against the faith of the universal Church, which cannot err, since Our Lord said: (*Luke* xxii. 32): *I have prayed for thee,* Peter, *that thy faith fail not.*

Seventh Article

WHETHER IT IS NECESSARY FOR THE SALVATION OF ALL THAT THEY SHOULD BELIEVE EXPLICITLY IN THE MYSTERY OF CHRIST?

We proceed thus to the Seventh Article:—

Objection 1. It would seem that it is not necessary for the salvation of all that they should believe explicitly in the mystery of Christ. For man is not bound to believe explicitly what the angels do not know; for the unfolding of faith is the result of divine revelation, which reaches man by means of the angels, as was stated above.[27] Now even the angels were in ignorance of the mystery of the Incarnation; and so, according to the commentary of Dionysius,[28] it is they who ask (*Ps.* xxiii. 8): *Who is this king of glory?* and (*Isa.* lxiii. 1): *Who is this that cometh from Edom?* Therefore men were not bound to believe explicitly in the mystery of Christ's Incarnation.

Obj. 2. Further, It is evident that John the Baptist was one of the learned, and most nigh to Christ, Who said of him (*Matt.* xi. 11) that *there hath not risen among them that are born of women, a greater than* he. Now John the Baptist does not appear to have known the mystery of the Incarnation of Christ explicitly, since he asked Christ (*Matt.* xi. 3): *Art Thou He that art to come, or look we for another?* Therefore even the learned were not bound to explicit faith in Christ.

Obj. 3. Further, Many gentiles obtained salvation through the ministry of the angels, as Dionysius states.[29] Now it would seem that the gentiles had neither explicit nor implicit faith in Christ, since they received no revelation. Therefore it seems that it was not necessary for the salvation of all to believe explicitly in the mystery of Christ.

On the contrary, Augustine says: *Our faith is sound if we believe that no*

---

[27] *S. T.*, I, q. 111, a. 1.   [28] *De Cael. Hier.*, VII, 3 (PG 3, 209).   [29] *Op. cit.*, IX, 4 (PG 3, 261).

man, old or young, is delivered from the contagion of death and the bonds of sin, except by the one Mediator of God and men, Jesus Christ.[30]

I answer that, As was stated above, the object of faith includes, properly and directly, that thing through which man obtains beatitude.[31] Now the mystery of Christ's Incarnation and Passion is the way by which men obtain beatitude; for it is written (*Acts* iv. 12): *There is no other name under heaven given to men, whereby we must be saved.* Therefore belief of some kind in the mystery of Christ's Incarnation was necessary at all times and for all persons, but this belief differed according to differences of times and persons. The reason for this is that before the state of sin, man believed explicitly in Christ's Incarnation, in so far as it was intended for the consummation of glory, but not as it was intended to deliver man from sin by the Passion and Resurrection, since man had no foreknowledge of his future sin. He does, however, seem to have had foreknowledge of the Incarnation of Christ, from the fact that he said (*Gen.* ii. 24): *Wherefore a man shall leave father and mother, and shall cleave to his wife,* of which the Apostle says (*Ephes.* v. 32) that *this is a great sacrament . . . in Christ and the Church;* and it is incredible that the first man was ignorant about this sacrament.

But after sin, men believed explicitly in Christ, not only as to the Incarnation, but also as to the Passion and Resurrection, by which the human race is delivered from sin and death: for otherwise they would not have foreshadowed Christ's Passion by certain sacrifices both before and after the Law. The meaning of these sacrifices was known by the learned explicitly, while the simple folk knew it under the veil of the sacrifices, believing them to be directed by God to Christ's coming, and thus their knowledge was covered with a veil, so to speak. And, as was stated above, the farther they were from Christ, the more difficult they found it to know Christ's mysteries; and the nearer they were to Christ, the more distinct was their knowledge of Christ's mysteries.[32]

After grace had been revealed, both learned and simple folk are bound to explicit faith in the mysteries of Christ, chiefly as regards those which are observed throughout the Church, and publicly proclaimed, such as the articles that refer to the Incarnation, of which we have spoken above.[33] As to other minute points in reference to the articles of the Incarnation, men have been bound to believe them more or less explicitly according to each one's state and office.

Reply Obj. 1. The mystery of the Kingdom of God was not entirely hidden from the angels, as Augustine observes,[34] yet certain aspects thereof were better known to them when Christ revealed them to them.

Reply Obj. 2. It was not through ignorance that John the Baptist inquired of Christ's advent in the flesh, since he had clearly professed his

---

[30] Cf. *Epist.* CXC, 2 (PL 33, 858).   [31] A. 5; q. 1, a. 6, ad 1.   [32] Q. 1, a. 7.   [33] Q. 1, a. 8.   [34] *De Genesi ad Litt.,* V, 19 (PL 34, 334).

belief therein, saying: *I saw, and I gave testimony, that this is the Son of God (Jo.* i. 34). Hence he did not say: *Art Thou He that hast come?* but *Art Thou He that art to come?* thus asking about the future, not about the past. Likewise it is not to be believed that he was ignorant of Christ's future Passion, for he had already said (*ibid.* 29): *Behold the Lamb of God, behold Him who taketh away the sins of the world,* thus foretelling His future immolation; and since other prophets had foretold it, as may be seen especially in *Isaias* liii. We may therefore say with Gregory that he asked this question, being in ignorance as to whether Christ would descend into hell in His own Person.[35] But he was not ignorant of the fact that the power of Christ's Passion would be extended to those who were detained in Limbo, according to *Zach.* ix. 11: *Thou also, by the blood of Thy testament, hast sent forth Thy prisoners out of the pit, wherein is no water;* nor was he bound to believe explicitly, before its fulfillment, that Christ was to descend thither Himself.

It may also be replied that, as Ambrose observes in his commentary on *Luke* vii. 19, he made this inquiry, not from doubt or ignorance, but from devotion;[36] or again, with Chrysostom, that he inquired, not as though ignorant himself, but because he wished his disciples to be satisfied, on that point, by Christ;[37] and so the latter framed His answer so as to instruct the disciples, by pointing to the signs of His works.

Reply Obj. 3. Many of the gentiles received revelations of Christ, as is clear from their predictions. Thus we read (*Job* xix. 25): *I know that my Redeemer liveth.* The Sibyl too foretold certain things about Christ, as Augustine relates.[38] Moreover we read in the history of the Romans, that at the time of Constantine Augustus and his mother Helen a tomb was discovered, wherein lay a man on whose breast was a golden plate with the inscription: *Christ shall be born of a virgin, and in Him I believe. O sun, during the lifetime of Helen and Constantine, thou shalt see me again.*[39] If, however, some were saved without receiving any revelation, they were not saved without faith in a Mediator, for, though they did not believe in Him explicitly, they did, nevertheless, have implicit faith through believing in divine providence, since they believed that God would deliver mankind in whatever way was pleasing to Him, and according to the revelation of the Spirit to those who knew the truth, as is stated in *Job* xxxv. 11: *Who teacheth us more than the beasts of the earth.*

---

[35] *In Evang.,* I, hom. 6 (PL 76, 1095).   [36] *In Luc.,* V, super VII, 19 (PL 15, 1748).
[37] *In Matt.,* hom. XXXVI (PG 57, 418).   [38] *Contra Faust.,* XIII, 15 (PL 42, 290).
[39] Cf. Theophanes, *Chronographia,* A.C. 773 (PG 108, 917).

Eighth Article

WHETHER IT IS NECESSARY FOR SALVATION TO BELIEVE EXPLICITLY IN THE TRINITY?

We proceed thus to the Eighth Article:—

Objection 1. It would seem that it was not necessary for salvation to believe explicitly in the Trinity. For the Apostle says (*Heb.* xi. 6): *He that cometh to God must believe that He is, and is a rewarder to them that seek Him.* Now one can believe this without believing in the Trinity. Therefore it was not necessary to believe explicitly in the Trinity.

Obj. 2. Further, Our Lord said (*Jo.* xvii. 5, 6): *Father, . . . I have manifested Thy name to men,* which words Augustine expounds as follows: *Not the name by which Thou art called God, but the name whereby Thou art called My Father*;[40] and further on he adds: *In that He made this world, God is known to all nations; in that He is not to be worshipped together with false gods, 'God is known in Judea'; but, in that He is the Father of this Christ, through Whom He takes away the sin of the world, He now makes known to men this name of His, which hitherto they knew not.* Therefore before the coming of Christ it was not known that Paternity and Filiation were in the Godhead; and so the Trinity was not believed explicitly.

Obj. 3. Further, That which we are bound to believe explicitly of God is the object of heavenly happiness. Now the object of heavenly happiness is the highest good, which can be understood to be in God, without any distinction of Persons. Therefore it was not necessary to believe explicitly in the Trinity.

On the contrary, In the Old Testament the Trinity of Persons is expressed in many ways. Thus at the very outset of *Genesis* it is written in manifestation of the Trinity: *Let us make man to Our image and likeness* (*Gen.* i. 26). Therefore from the very beginning it was necessary for salvation to believe in the Trinity.

I answer that, It is impossible to believe explicitly in the mystery of Christ, without faith in the Trinity, since the mystery of Christ includes that the Son of God took flesh; that He renewed the world through the grace of the Holy Ghost; and, again, that He was conceived by the Holy Ghost. Therefore just as, before Christ, the mystery of Christ was believed explicitly by the learned, but implicitly and under a veil, so to speak, by the simple, so too was it with the mystery of the Trinity. And consequently, when once grace had been revealed, all were bound to explicit faith in the mystery of the Trinity; and all who are born again in Christ have this bestowed on them by the invocation of the Trinity, according to *Matt.* xxviii.

[40] *Tract.* CVI, super *Ioann,* XVII, 6 (PL 35, 1909).

19: *Going therefore teach ye all nations, baptizing them in the name of the Father, and of the Son and of the Holy Ghost.*

Reply Obj. 1. Explicit faith in those two things was necessary at all times and for all people; but it was not sufficient at all times and for all people.

Reply Obj. 2. Before Christ's coming, faith in the Trinity lay hidden in the faith of the learned, but through Christ and the Apostles it was shown to the world.

Reply Obj. 3. God's highest goodness, as we understand it now through its effects, can be understood without the Trinity of Persons; but as understood in itself, and as seen by the Blessed, it cannot be understood without the Trinity of Persons. Moreover, the mission of the divine Persons brings us to heavenly happiness.

Ninth Article

WHETHER TO BELIEVE IS MERITORIOUS?

We proceed thus to the Ninth Article:—

Objection 1. It would seem that to believe is not meritorious. For the principle of all merit is charity, as was stated above.[41] Now faith, like nature, is a preamble to charity. Therefore, just as an act of nature is not meritorious, since we do not merit by our natural gifts, so neither is an act of faith.

Obj. 2. Further, Belief is intermediate between opinion and scientific knowledge or the consideration of things known by science. Now the considerations of science are not meritorious, nor on the other hand is opinion. Therefore belief is not meritorious.

Obj. 3. Further, He who assents to a point of faith either has a sufficient motive for believing, or he has not. If he has a sufficient motive for his belief, this does not seem to imply any merit on his part, since he is no longer free to believe or not to believe; whereas if he has not a sufficient motive for believing, this is a mark of levity, according to *Ecclus.* xix. 4: *He that is hasty to give credit, is light of heart,* so that, seemingly, he gains no merit thereby. Therefore to believe is by no means meritorious.

On the contrary, It is written (*Heb.* xi. 33) that the saints *by faith . . . obtained promises,* which would not be the case if they did not merit by believing. Therefore to believe is meritorious.

I answer that, As was stated above, our actions are meritorious in so far as they proceed from free choice moved with grace by God.[42] Therefore every human act proceeding from free choice, if it be referred to God, can be meritorious. Now the act of believing is an act of the intellect assenting to divine truth at the command of the will moved by the grace of God,

---

[41] *S. T.,* I-II, q. 114, a. 4.   [42] *S. T.,* I-II, q. 114, a. 3 and 4.

so that it is subject to free choice in relation to God; and consequently the act of faith can be meritorious.

Reply Obj. 1. Nature is compared to charity, which is the principle of merit, as matter to form; whereas faith is compared to charity as the disposition which precedes the ultimate form. Now it is evident that the subject or the matter cannot act by virtue of the form, nor can a preceding disposition, before the advent of the form; but after the advent of the form, both the subject and the preceding disposition act by virtue of the form, which is the chief principle of action, even as the heat of fire acts by virtue of the substantial form of fire. Accordingly, neither nature nor faith can, without charity, produce a meritorious act; but, when accompanied by charity, the act of faith is made meritorious thereby, even as an act of nature, and a natural act of free choice.

Reply Obj. 2. Two things may be considered in science, namely, the assent of the one who has science to the thing that he knows, and his consideration of that thing. Now the assent of science is not subject to free choice, because the knower is obliged to assent by the force of the demonstration; and so scientific assent is not meritorious. But the actual consideration of what a man knows by science is subject to his free choice, for it is in his power to consider or not to consider. Hence consideration of science may be meritorious if it be referred to the end of charity, *i.e.*, to the honor of God or the good of our neighbor. On the other hand, in the case of faith, both these things are subject to free choice, so that in both respects the act of faith can be meritorious. But in the case of opinion, there is no firm assent, since it is weak and infirm, as the Philosopher observes,[43] so that it does not seem to proceed from a perfect act of the will; and for this reason, as regards the assent, it does not appear to be very meritorious, though it can be as regards the actual consideration.

Reply Obj. 3. The believer has sufficient motive for believing, for he is moved by the authority of divine teaching confirmed by miracles, and, what is more, by the inward instigation of the divine invitation; and so he does not believe lightly. He has not, however, sufficient reason for scientific knowledge, and hence he does not lose the merit.

Tenth Article

WHETHER REASONS IN SUPPORT OF WHAT WE BELIEVE LESSEN THE MERIT OF FAITH?

We proceed thus to the Tenth Article:—

Objection 1. It would seem that reasons in support of what we believe lessen the merit of faith. For Gregory says that *there is no merit in believing what is shown by reason.*[44] If, therefore, human reason provides

---

[43] *Post. Anal.,* I, 33 (89a 5).   [44] *In Evang.,* II, hom. 26 (PL 76, 1197).

sufficient proof, the merit of faith is altogether taken away. Therefore it seems that any kind of human reasoning in support of matters of faith diminishes the merit of believing.

Obj. 2. Further, Whatever lessens the measure of virtue, lessens the amount of merit, since *happiness is the reward of virtue*, as the Philosopher states.[45] Now human reasoning seems to diminish the measure of the virtue of faith, since it is essential to faith to be about the unseen, as was stated above.[46] Now the more a thing is supported by reasons, the less it is unseen. Therefore human reasons in support of matters of faith diminish the merit of faith.

Obj. 3. Further, Contrary things have contrary causes. Now an inducement in opposition to faith increases the merit of faith, whether it consist in persecution inflicted by one who endeavors to force a man to renounce his faith, or in an argument persuading him to do so. Therefore reasons in support of faith diminish the merit of faith.

On the contrary, It is written (*1 Pet.* iii. 15): *Being ready always to satisfy every one that asketh you a reason of that faith and hope which is in you.* Now the Apostle would not give this advice, if it would imply a diminution in the merit of faith. Therefore reason does not diminish the merit of faith.

I answer that, As we have stated above, the act of faith can be meritori-ous in so far as it is subject to the will, not only as to the use, but also as to the assent. Now human reasoning in support of what we believe may stand in a twofold relation to the will of the believer.—First, as preceding the act of the will, as, for instance, when a man either has not the will, or not a prompt will, to believe, unless he be moved by human reasons; and in this way human reasoning diminishes the merit of faith. In this sense it has been said above that, in moral virtues, a passion which precedes choice makes the virtuous act less praiseworthy.[47] For just as a man ought to perform acts of moral virtue because of the judgment of his reason, and not because of a passion, so he ought to believe matters of faith, not because of human reasoning, but because of the divine authority.—Secondly, human reasons may be consequent to the will of the believer. For when a man has a will ready to believe, he loves the truth he believes, he thinks out and takes to heart whatever reasons he can find in support thereof; and in this way, human reasoning does not exclude the merit of faith, but is a sign of greater merit. Thus, again, in moral virtues, a consequent passion is the sign of a more prompt will, as was stated above.[48] We have an indication of this in the words of the Samaritans to the woman, who is a type of human reason: *We now believe, not for thy saying* (*Jo.* iv. 42).

Reply Obj. 1. Gregory is referring to the case of a man who has no will

---

[45] *Eth.,* I, 9 (1099b 16).   [46] Q. 1, a. 4 and 5.   [47] *S. T.,* I-II, q. 24, a. 3, ad 1; q. 77, a. 6, ad 2.   [48] *S. T.,* I-II, q. 24, a. 3, ad 1.

to believe what is of faith, unless he be induced by reasons. But when a man has the will to believe what is of faith, on the authority of God alone, although he may have reasons in demonstration of some of them, *e.g.*, of the existence of God, the merit of his faith is not, for that reason, lost or diminished.

Reply Obj. 2. The reasons which are brought forward in support of the authority of faith are not demonstrations which can bring intellectual vision to the human intellect; and so the unseen is not removed. But they remove obstacles to faith, by showing that what faith proposes is not impossible; and hence such reasons do not diminish the merit or the measure of faith. On the other hand, though demonstrative reasons in support of the preambles of faith, but not of the articles of faith, diminish the measure of faith, since they make the thing believed to be seen; yet they do not diminish the measure of charity, which makes the will ready to believe them, even if they were unseen. And so the measure of merit is not diminished.

Reply Obj. 3. Whatever is in opposition to faith, whether it consist in a man's thoughts, or in outward persecution, increases the merit of faith in so far as the will is shown to be more prompt and firm in believing. Hence the martyrs had more merit of faith, through not renouncing faith because of persecution; and even the wise have greater merit of faith, through not renouncing their faith because of the reasons brought forward by philosophers or heretics in opposition to faith. On the other hand, things that are favorable to faith do not always diminish the promptness of the will to believe, and therefore they do not always diminish the merit of faith.

Question III

ON THE EXTERIOR ACT OF FAITH
(*In Two Articles*)

WE must now consider the exterior act, viz., the confession of faith, under which head there are two points of inquiry: (1) Whether confession is an act of faith? (2) Whether confession of faith is necessary for salvation?

First Article

WHETHER CONFESSION IS AN ACT OF FAITH?

We proceed thus to the First Article:—

Objection 1. It would seem that confession is not an act of faith. For the same act does not belong to different virtues. Now confession belongs to penance, of which it is a part. Therefore it is not an act of faith.

Obj. 2. Further, Man is sometimes deterred by fear, or some kind of confusion, from confessing his faith; and so the Apostle (*Ephes.* vi. 19) asks for prayers that it may be granted him *with confidence, to make known the mystery of the gospel.* Now it belongs to fortitude, which moderates daring and fear, not to be deterred from doing good because of confusion or fear. Therefore it seems that confession is not an act of faith, but rather of fortitude or constancy.

Obj. 3. Further, Just as the ardor of faith makes one confess one's faith outwardly, so does it make one do other external good works; for it is written (*Gal.* v. 6) that *faith . . . worketh by charity.* But other external works are not reckoned as acts of faith. Therefore neither is confession an act of faith.

On the contrary, The *Gloss* explains the words of *2 Thess.* i. 11 (*and the work of faith in power*) as referring to *confession, which is a work proper to faith.*[1]

I answer that, Exterior acts belong properly to that virtue to whose end they are specifically referred; and thus fasting is referred specifically to the end of abstinence, which is to curb the flesh, and consequently it is an act of abstinence.

Now confession of those things that are of faith is referred specifically, as to its end, to that which concerns faith, according to *2 Cor.* iv. 13: *Having the same spirit of faith, . . . we believe, and therefore we speak also.* For the exterior utterance is intended to signify the interior thought. There-

[1] *Glossa ordin.* (VI, 114B).

fore, just as the interior thought of matters of faith is properly an act of faith, so too is the exterior confession of them.

Reply Obj. 1. A threefold confession is commended by the Scriptures. One is the confession of what belongs to faith, and this is a proper act of faith, since it is referred to the end of faith, as was stated above. Another is the confession of thanksgiving or praise, and this is an act of adoration [*latria*], for its purpose is to give outward honor to God, which is the end of adoration. The third is the confession of sins, which is ordained to the blotting out of sins, which is the end of penance, to which virtue it therefore belongs.

Reply Obj. 2. That which removes an obstacle is not an essential cause, but an accidental one, as the Philosopher proves.[2] Hence fortitude, which removes an obstacle to the confession of faith, viz., fear or shame, is not the proper and essential cause of confession, but an accidental one, so to speak.

Reply Obj. 3. Interior faith, with the aid of charity, causes all exterior acts of virtue by means of the other virtues, by commanding, but not eliciting them; whereas it produces the act of confession as its proper act, without the help of any other virtue.

Second Article

WHETHER CONFESSION OF FAITH IS NECESSARY FOR SALVATION?

We proceed thus to the Second Article:—

Objection 1. It would seem that confession of faith is not necessary for salvation. For a thing seems to be sufficient for salvation, if it is a means of attaining the end of virtue. Now the proper end of faith is the union of the human mind with divine truth, and this can be realized without any exterior confession. Therefore confession of faith is not necessary for salvation.

Obj. 2. Further, By outward confession of faith, a man reveals his faith to another man. But this is unnecessary save for those who have to instruct others in the faith. Therefore it seems that the simple folk are not bound to confession of faith.

Obj. 3. Further, Whatever may tend to scandalize and disturb others, is not necessary for salvation; for the Apostle says (*1 Cor.* x. 32): *Be without offence to the Jews and to the gentiles, and to the Church of God.* Now confession of the faith sometimes causes a disturbance among unbelievers. Therefore it is not necessary for salvation.

On the contrary, The Apostle says (*Rom.* x. 10): *With the heart we believe unto justice; but with the mouth, confession is made unto salvation.*

I answer that, Things that are necessary for salvation come under the

---

[2] *Phys.*, VIII, 4 (255b 24).

precepts of the divine law. Now since confession of faith is something affirmative, it can only fall under an affirmative precept. Hence its necessity for salvation depends on how it falls under an affirmative precept of the divine law. Now affirmative precepts, as was stated above, do not bind for always, although they are always binding;[3] but they bind as to place and time and according to other due circumstances, in respect of which human acts have to be regulated in order to be acts of virtue.

Thus, then, it is not necessary for salvation to confess one's faith at all times and in all places, but in certain places and at certain times, when, namely, by omitting to do so, we would deprive God of due honor, or our neighbor of a service that we ought to render him. Such would be the case of a man who, on being asked about his faith, were to remain silent, so as to make people believe either that he is without faith, or that the faith is false, or so as to turn others away from the faith; for in such cases as these, confession of faith is necessary for salvation.

Reply Obj. 1. The end of faith, even as of the other virtues, must be referred to the end of charity, which is the love of God and neighbor. Consequently, when God's honor and our neighbor's good demand, man should not be contented with being united by faith to God's truth, but ought to confess his faith outwardly.

Reply Obj. 2. In cases of necessity, where faith is in danger, every one is bound to proclaim his faith to others, either to give good example and encouragement to the rest of the faithful, or to check the attacks of unbelievers; but at other times it is not the duty of all the faithful to instruct others in the faith.

Reply Obj. 3. There is nothing commendable in making a public confession of one's faith, if it cause a disturbance among unbelievers, without any profit either to the faith or to the faithful. Hence Our Lord said (*Matt.* vii. 6): *Give not that which is holy to dogs, neither cast ye your pearls before swine . . . lest turning upon you, they tear you.* Yet, if there is hope of profit to the faith, or if there be urgency, a man should disregard the disturbance of unbelievers, and confess his faith in public. Hence it is written (*Matt.* xv. 12, 14) that when the disciples had said to Our Lord that *the Pharisees, when they heard this word, were scandalized,* He answered: *Let them alone, they are blind, and leaders of the blind.*

---

[3] *S. T.,* I-II, q. 71, a. 5, ad 3; q. 100, a. 10.

Question IV

ON THE VIRTUE ITSELF OF FAITH
(*In Eight Articles*)

WE must now consider the virtue itself of faith, and, in the first place, faith itself; secondly, those who have faith;[1] thirdly, the cause of faith;[2] fourthly, its effects.[3]

Under the first head there are eight points of inquiry: (1) What is faith? (2) In what power of the soul does it reside? (3) Whether its form is charity? (4) Whether formed [*formata*] faith and formless [*informis*] faith are one identically? (5) Whether faith is a virtue? (6) Whether it is one virtue? (7) Of its relation to the other virtues. (8) Of its certitude as compared with the certitude of the intellectual virtues.

First Article

THETHER THIS IS A FITTING DEFINITION OF FAITH: *FAITH IS THE SUBSTANCE OF THINGS TO BE HOPED FOR, THE EVIDENCE OF THINGS THAT APPEAR NOT?*

We proceed thus to the First Article:—

Objection 1. It would seem that the Apostle gives an unfitting definition of faith when he says (*Heb.* xi. 1): *Faith is the substance of things to be hoped for, the evidence of things that appear not.* For no quality is a substance, whereas faith is a quality, since it is a theological virtue, as was stated above.[4] Therefore it is not a substance.

Obj. 2. Further, Different virtues have different objects. Now things to be hoped for are the object of hope. Therefore they should not be included in a definition of faith, as though they were its object.

Obj. 3. Further, Faith is perfected by charity rather than by hope, since charity is the form of faith, as we shall state further on. Therefore the definition of faith should have included the thing to be loved rather than the thing to be hoped for.

Obj. 4. Further, The same thing should not be placed in different genera. Now *substance* and *evidence* are different genera, and neither is subalternate to the other. Therefore it is unfitting to state that faith is both *substance* and *evidence*. Therefore faith is unfittingly defined.

Obj. 5. Further, Evidence manifests the truth of the matter for which it is adduced. Now a thing is said to be apparent when its truth is made

[1] Q. 5. [2] Q. 6. [3] Q. 7. [4] *S. T.,* I-II, q. 62, a. 3.

manifest. Therefore it seems to imply a contradiction to speak of the *evidence of things that appear not*, for an argument makes a previously obscure thing to be apparent. And so faith is unfittingly defined.

On the contrary, The authority of the Apostle suffices.

I answer that, Though some say that the above words of the Apostle are not a definition of faith,[5] because the definition reveals the quiddity and essence of a thing, as it is said in *Metaph*. vii.,[6] yet if we consider the matter rightly, this definition overlooks none of the points in reference to which faith can be defined, although the words themselves are not arranged in the form of a definition, just as the philosophers touch on the principles of the syllogism without employing the syllogistic form.

In order to make this clear, we must observe that since habits are known by their acts, and acts by their objects, faith, being a habit, should be defined by its proper act in relation to its proper object. Now the act of faith is to believe, as was stated above,[7] which is an act of the intellect determined to one object by the will's command. Hence an act of faith is related both to the object of the will, *i.e.*, to the good and the end, and to the object of the intellect, *i.e.*, to the true. And since faith, through being a theological virtue, as was stated above,[8] has one and the same thing for object and end, its object and end must, of necessity, be in proportion to one another. Now it has been already stated that the object of faith is the First Truth, as unseen, and whatever we hold because of it;[9] so that it must needs be under the aspect of something unseen that the First Truth is the end of the act of faith, which aspect is that of a thing hoped for, according to the Apostle (*Rom*. viii. 25): *We hope for that which we see not*. For to see the truth is to possess it, and no one hopes for what one has already, but for what one has not, as was stated above.[10]

Accordingly, the relation of the act of faith to its end, which is the object of the will, is indicated by the words: *Faith is the substance of things to be hoped for*. For we are wont to call by the name of substance the first beginning of a thing, especially when the whole subsequent thing is virtually contained in the first beginning. For instance, we might say that the first self-evident principles are the substance of science, because, namely, these principles are in us the first beginnings of science, the whole of which is itself contained in them virtually. In this way, then, faith is said to be the *substance of things to be hoped for*, for the reason that in us the first beginning of things to be hoped for is brought about by the assent of faith, which contains virtually all things to be hoped for. For we hope to be made happy through seeing the unveiled truth to which our faith cleaves, as was made evident when we were speaking of happiness.[11]

---

[5] Cf. Hugh of St. Victor, *De Sacram.*, I, x, 2 (PL 176, 330).   [6] Aristotle, *Metaph.*, VI, 4 (1030a 6); 5 (1031a 12); 12 (1037b 25).   [7] Q. 2, a. 1, ad 3; a. 2 and 9.   [8] *S. T.*, I-II, q. 62, a. 3.   [9] Q. 1, a. 1 and 4.   [10] *S. T.*, I-II, q. 67, a. 4.   [11] *S. T.*, I-II, q. 3, a. 8; q. 4, a. 3.

The relationship of the act of faith to the object of the intellect, considered as the object of faith, is indicated by the words, *evidence of things that appear not,* where *evidence* is taken for the result of evidence. For evidence induces the intellect to adhere to a truth, and so the firm adhesion of the intellect to the non-apparent truth of faith is called *evidence* here. Hence another reading has *conviction,* because, namely, the intellect of the believer is convinced by divine authority, so as to assent to what it sees not.

Accordingly, if anyone would reduce the foregoing words to the form of a definition, he may say that *faith is a habit of the mind, whereby eternal life is begun in us, making the intellect assent to what is non-apparent.* In this way faith is distinguished from all other things pertaining to the intellect. For when we describe it as *evidence,* we distinguish it from opinion, suspicion and doubt, which do not make the intellect adhere to anything firmly; when we go on to say, *of things that appear not,* we distinguish it from science and understanding, the object of which is something apparent; and when we say that it is *the substance of things to be hoped for,* we distinguish the virtue of faith from faith commonly so called, which has no reference to the beatitude we hope for.

Whatever other definitions are given of faith are explanations of this one given by the Apostle. For when Augustine says that *faith is a virtue whereby we believe what we do not see,*[12] and when Damascene says that *faith is an assent without inquiry,*[13] and when others say that *faith is that certainty of the mind about absent things which surpasses opinion but falls short of science,*[14] these all amount to the same as the Apostle's words: *Evidence of things that appear not*; and when Dionysius says that *faith is the solid foundation of the believer, establishing him in the truth, and showing forth the truth in him,*[15] this comes to the same as *substance of things to be hoped for.*

Reply Obj. 1. *Substance,* here, does not stand for the supreme genus codivided against the other genera, but for that likeness to substance which is found in each genus, namely, inasmuch as the first thing in a genus contains the others virtually and is said to be the substance thereof.

Reply Obj. 2. Since faith pertains to the intellect as commanded by the will, it must needs be directed, as to its end, to the objects of those virtues which perfect the will, among which is hope, as we shall prove further on.[16] For this reason the definition of faith includes the object of hope.

Reply Obj. 3. Love may be of the seen and of the unseen, of the present and of the absent. Consequently a thing to be loved is not so adapted to

---

[12] *Tract.* XL, super *Ioann.,* VIII, 32 (PL 35, 1690); *Quaest. Evang.,* II, 39, super *Luc.* XVII, 5 (PL 35, 1352).   [13] *De Fide Orth.,* IV, 11 (PG 94, 1128).   [14] Cf. Hugh of St. Victor, *De Sacram.,* I, x, 1 (PL 176, 330).   [15] *De Div. Nom.,* VII, 4 (PG 3, 872). [16] Q. 18, a 1.

faith, as a thing to be hoped for, since hope is always of the absent and the unseen.

Reply Obj. 4. Substance and *evidence,* as included in the definition of faith, do not denote various genera of faith, nor different acts, but different relationships of one act to different objects, as is clear from what has been said.

Reply Obj. 5. Evidence taken from the proper principles of a thing makes it apparent, whereas evidence taken from divine authority does not make a thing apparent in itself; and such is the evidence referred to in the definition of faith.

Second Article

WHETHER FAITH RESIDES IN THE INTELLECT?

We proceed thus to the Second Article:—

Objection 1. It would seem that faith does not reside in the intellect as in its subject. For Augustine says that *faith resides in the believer's will.*[17] Now the will is a power distinct from the intellect. Therefore faith does not reside in the intellect.

Obj. 2. Further, The assent of faith to believe anything proceeds from the will obeying God. Therefore it seems that faith owes all its praise to obedience. But obedience is in the will. Therefore faith is in the will, and not in the intellect.

Obj. 3. Further, The intellect is either speculative or practical. Now faith is not in the speculative intellect, since this is not concerned with things to be sought or avoided, as is stated in *De Anima* iii.,[18] so that it is not a principle of operation, whereas *faith . . . worketh by charity (Gal.* v. 6). Likewise, neither is it in the practical intellect, the object of which is some true, contingent thing that can be made or done. For the object of faith is the eternal truth, as was shown above.[19] Therefore faith does not reside in the intellect.

On the contrary, Faith is succeeded by the heavenly vision, according to *1 Cor.* xiii. 12: *We see now through a glass in a dark manner; but then face to face.* Now vision is in the intellect. Therefore faith is likewise.

I answer that, Since faith is a virtue, its act must needs be perfect. Now for the perfection of an act proceeding from two active principles each of these principles must be perfect; for it is not possible for a thing to be sawn well, unless the sawyer possess the art, and the saw be well fitted for sawing. Now, in a power of the soul, which is related to opposite objects, a disposition to act well is a habit, as was stated above.[20] Therefore an act that proceeds from two such powers must be perfected by a habit residing in each of them. But it has been stated above that to believe is an act of

[17] *De Praedest. Sanct.,* V (PL 44, 968).   [18] Aristotle, *De An.,* III, 9 (432b 28).
[19] Q. 1, a. 1.   [20] *S. T.,* I-II, q. 49, a. 4, ad 1; a. 2 and 3.

the intellect, inasmuch as the will moves it to assent.[21] And this act proceeds from the will and the intellect, both of which have a natural aptitude to be perfected by a habit, as we said above.[22] Consequently, if the act of faith is to be perfect, there needs to be a habit in the will as well as in the intellect: even as there needs to be the habit of prudence in the reason, besides the habit of temperance in the concupiscible part, in order that the act of that part be perfect. Now, to believe is immediately an act of the intellect, because the object of that act is *the true,* which pertains properly to the intellect. Consequently faith, which is the proper principle of that act, must needs reside in the intellect.

Reply Obj. 1. Augustine takes faith for the act of faith, which is said to depend on the believer's will in so far as his intellect assents to matters of faith at the command of the will.

Reply Obj. 2. Not only does the will need to be ready to obey, but also the intellect needs to be well disposed to follow the command of the will, even as the concupiscible part needs to be well disposed in order to follow the command of reason; and hence there needs to be a habit of virtue not only in the will commanding, but also in the intellect assenting.

Reply Obj. 3. Faith resides in the speculative intellect, as is clear from its object. But since this object, which is the First Truth, is the end of all our desires and actions, as Augustine proves,[23] it follows that faith worketh by charity just as *the speculative intellect becomes practical by extension.*[24]

Third Article

WHETHER CHARITY IS THE FORM OF FAITH?

We proceed thus to the Third Article:—

Objection 1. It would seem that charity is not the form of faith. For each thing derives its species from its form. When, therefore, two things are opposite members of a division, one cannot be the form of the other. Now faith and charity are stated to be opposite members of a division, as different species of virtue (*1 Cor.* xiii. 13). Therefore charity is not the form of faith.

Obj. 2. Further, A form and the thing of which it is the form are in one subject, since out of them is produced what is one absolutely. Now faith is in the intellect, while charity is in the will. Therefore charity is not the form of faith.

Obj. 3. Further, The form of a thing is a principle thereof. Now obedience, rather than charity, seems to be the principle of believing on the part of the will, according to *Rom.* i. 5: *For obedience to the faith in all nations.* Therefore obedience, rather than charity, is the form of faith.

<hr>

[21] A. 1; q. 2, a. 1, ad 3; a. 2 and 9.   [22] *S. T.,* I-II, q. 50, a. 4 and 5.   [23] *De Trin.,* I, 8; 10 (PL 42, 831; 834).   [24] Aristotle, *De An.,* III, 10 (433a 15).

On the contrary, Each thing works through its form. Now faith works through charity. Therefore the love of charity is the form of faith.

I answer that, As appears from what has been said above, voluntary acts take their species from their end, which is the will's object.[25] Now that which gives a thing its species functions as a form in natural things. Therefore the form of any voluntary act is, in a manner, the end to which that act is directed, both because it takes its species from it, and because the mode of an action should correspond proportionately to the end. Now it is evident from what has been said that the act of faith is directed to the object of the will, *i.e.,* the good, as to its end; and this good which is the end of faith, viz., the divine Good, is the proper object of charity. Therefore charity is called the form of faith, in so far as the act of faith is perfected and formed by charity.

Reply Obj. 1. Charity is called the form of faith because it quickens the act of faith. Now nothing hinders one act from being quickened by different habits, and thus to be reduced to various species in a certain order, as was stated above when we were treating of human acts in general.[26]

Reply Obj. 2. This objection is true of an intrinsic form. But it is not thus that charity is the form of faith, but in the sense that it quickens the act of faith, as was explained above.

Reply Obj. 3. Even obedience, and hope likewise, and whatever other virtue might precede the act of faith, is quickened by charity, as we shall show further on.[27] Consequently, charity is spoken of as the form of faith.

Fourth Article

WHETHER FORMLESS FAITH CAN BECOME FORMED, OR FORMED FAITH, FORMLESS?

We proceed thus to the Fourth Article:—

Objection 1. It would seem that formless faith does not become formed, or formed faith formless. For, according to *1 Cor.* xiii. 10, *when that which is perfect is come, that which is in part shall be done away.* Now formless faith is imperfect in comparison with formed faith. Therefore when formed faith comes, formless faith is done away, so that they are not one identical habit.

Obj. 2. Further, A dead thing does not become a living thing. Now formless faith is dead, according to *James* ii. 20: *Faith without works is dead.* Therefore formless faith cannot become formed.

Obj. 3. Further, God's grace, by its advent, has no less effect in a believer than in an unbeliever. Now by coming to an unbeliever it causes the habit of faith. Therefore when it comes to a believer, who hitherto had the habit of formless faith, it causes another habit of faith in him.

[25] *S. T.,* I-II, q. 1, a. 3; q. 18, a. 6.   [26] *S. T.,* I-II, q. 18, a. 7, ad 1.   [27] Q. 23, a. 8.

Obj. 4. Further, As Boethius says, *accidents cannot be altered.*[28] Now faith is an accident. Therefore the same faith cannot be at one time formed, and at another formless.

On the contrary, On the words, *Faith without works is dead (Jas.* ii. 20), the *Gloss* adds, *by which it lives once more.*[29] Therefore faith which was dead and formless becomes formed and living.

I answer that, There have been various opinions on this question. For some have said that formed and formless faith are distinct habits, but that when formed faith comes, formless faith is done away, and that, in like manner, when a man sins mortally, after having formed faith, a new habit of formless faith is infused into him by God.[30] But it seems unfitting that grace should deprive man of a gift of God by coming to him, and that a gift of God should be infused into man because of a mortal sin.

Consequently others have said that formed and formless faith are indeed distinct habits, but that, all the same, when formed faith comes, the habit of formless faith is not taken away, and that it remains together with the habit of formed faith in the same subject.[31] Yet again it seems unreasonable that the habit of formless faith should remain inactive in a person having formed faith.

We must therefore hold a different view, and say that formed and formless faith are one and the same habit. The reason is that a habit is diversified by that which pertains essentially to that habit. Now since faith is a perfection of the intellect, that pertains essentially to faith which pertains to the intellect. Now what pertains to the will does not pertain directly to faith, so as to be able to diversify the habit of faith. But the distinction of formed from formless faith is in respect of something pertaining to the will, *i.e.*, charity, and not in respect of something pertaining to the intellect. Therefore formed and formless faith are not distinct habits.

Reply Obj. 1. The saying of the Apostle refers to those imperfect things from which imperfection is inseparable, for then, when the perfect comes, the imperfect must needs be done away. Thus with the advent of clear vision, faith is done away, because it is essentially *of the things that appear not.* When, however, imperfection is not inseparable from the imperfect thing, the same identical thing which was imperfect becomes perfect. Thus, childhood is not essential to man, and consequently the same identical subject, who was a child, becomes a man. Now formlessness is not essential to faith, but is accidental thereto, as was stated above. Therefore formless faith itself becomes formed.

Reply Obj. 2. That which makes an animal live is inseparable from an animal, because it is a form essential to it, viz., the soul; and consequently a dead thing cannot become a living thing, and a living and a dead thing

---

[28] *In Cat. Arist.,* I (PL 64, 198).   [29] *Glossa interl.* (VI, 212v).   [30] William of Auxerre, *Summa Aurea,* III, tr. 15, q. 2 (208vb); q. 3 (209ra).   [31] Cf.. St. Bonaventure, *In III Sent.,* d. xxiii, a. 2, q. 4 (III, 496).

differ specifically. On the other hand, that which gives faith its form, or makes it live, is not of the essence of faith. Hence there is no comparison.

Reply Obj. 3. Grace causes faith not only when faith begins anew to be in a man, but also as long as faith lasts. For it has been said above that God is always working man's justification, even as the sun is always lighting up the air.[32] Hence grace is not less effective when it comes to a believer than when it comes to an unbeliever; since it causes faith in both, in the former by confirming and perfecting it, in the latter by creating it anew.

We might also reply that it is accidental, namely, because of the disposition of the subject, that grace does not cause faith in one who has it already; just as, on the other hand, a second mortal sin does not take away grace from one who has already lost it through a previous mortal sin.

Reply Obj. 4. When formed faith becomes formless, faith is not changed, but its subject, the soul, which at one time has faith without charity, and at another time, with charity, is changed.

Fifth Article

WHETHER FAITH IS A VIRTUE?

We proceed thus to the Fifth Article:—

Objection 1. It would seem that faith is not a virtue. For virtue is directed to the good, since *it is virtue that makes its subject good,* as the Philosopher states.[33] But faith is directed to the true. Therefore faith is not a virtue.

Obj. 2. Further, Infused virtue is more perfect than acquired virtue. Now faith, because of its imperfection, is not placed among the acquired intellectual virtues, as the Philosopher states.[34] Much less, therefore, can it be considered an infused virtue.

Obj. 3. Further, formed and formless faith are of the same species, as was stated above. Now formless faith is not a virtue, since it is not connected with the other virtues. Therefore neither is formed faith a virtue.

Obj. 4. Further, The gratuitous graces and the fruits are distinct from the virtues. But faith is numbered among the gratuitous graces (*1 Cor.* xii. 9) and likewise among the fruits (*Gal.* v. 23). Therefore faith is not a virtue.

On the contrary, Man is justified by the virtues, since *justice is the whole of virtue* as the Philosopher states.[35] Now man is justified by faith, according to *Rom.* v. 1: *Being justified therefore by faith let us have peace,* etc. Therefore faith is a virtue.

I answer that, As was shown above, human virtue is the virtue by which human acts are rendered good.[36] Hence, any habit that is always the prin-

---

[32] *S. T.,* I, q. 104, a. 1; I-II, q. 109, a. 9.   [33] *Eth.,* II, 6 (1106a 15; a 22).   [34] *Op. cit.,* VI, 3 (1139b 15).   [35] *Op. cit.,* V, 1 (1130a 9).   [36] *S. T.,* I-II, q. 56, a. 3.

ciple of a good act may be called a human virtue. Such a habit is formed faith. For since to believe is an act of the intellect assenting to the truth at the command of the will, two things are required that this act may be perfect. One is that the intellect should infallibly tend to its object, which is the true, while the other is that the act should be infallibly directed to the last end, because of which the will assents to the true; and both of these are to be found in the act of formed faith. For it belongs to the very nature of faith that the intellect should ever tend to the true, since nothing false can be the object of faith, as was proved above,[37] while the effect of charity, which is the form of faith, is that the soul always has its will directed to a good end. Therefore formed faith is a virtue.

On the other hand, formless faith is not a virtue, because, though the act of formless faith is duly perfect on the part of the intellect, it has not its due perfection on the part of the will. So, too, if temperance be in the concupiscible part without prudence being in the rational part, temperance is not a virtue, as was stated above,[38] because the act of temperance requires both an act of reason, and an act of the concupiscible part; even as the act of faith requires an act of the will, and an act of the intellect.

Reply Obj. 1. The true is itself the good of the intellect, since it is its perfection, and consequently faith has a relation to some good in so far as it directs the intellect to the true. Furthermore, it has a relation to the good considered as the object of the will, inasmuch as it is formed by charity.

Reply Obj. 2. The faith of which the Philosopher speaks is based on human reasoning in a conclusion which does not follow of necessity from its premises, and which is subject to be false. Hence such a faith is not a virtue. On the other hand, the faith of which we are speaking is based on the divine truth, which is infallible, and consequently its object cannot be anything false; so that faith of this kind can be a virtue.

Reply Obj. 3. Formed and formless faith do not differ specifically, as though they belonged to different species. But they differ as perfect and imperfect within the same species. Hence formless faith, being imperfect, does not satisfy the conditions of a perfect virtue, for *virtue is a kind of perfection.*[39]

Reply Obj. 4. Some say that the faith which is numbered among the gratuitous graces is formless faith.[40] But this is said without reason, since the gratuitous graces, which are mentioned in that passage, are not common to all the members of the Church. Hence the Apostle there says: *There are diversities of graces*; and again: *To one is given* this grace and *to another* that. Now formless faith is common to all the members of the Church, because its formlessness is not part of its substance, if we consider it as a gratuitous gift. We must therefore say that, in that passage, faith denotes a

---

[37] Q. 1, a. 3.   [38] *S. T.,* I-II, q. 65, a. 1.   [39] Aristotle, *Phys.,* VII, 3 (246a 13; 247a 2). [40] St. Bonaventure, *In III Sent.,* d. xxiii, a. 2, q. 4 (III, 494); St. Albert, *In III Sent.,* d. xxiii, a. 5, ad 5; a. 9 (XXVIII, 414; 421).

certain excellency of faith, for instance, *constancy in faith,* according to the *Gloss,* or the *word of faith.*[41]

Faith is numbered among the fruits in so far as it gives a certain pleasure in its act by reason of its certainty; and so the *Gloss* on the fifth chapter to the *Galatians,* where the fruits are enumerated, explains faith as being *certainty about the unseen.*[42]

Sixth Article

WHETHER FAITH IS ONE VIRTUE?

We proceed thus to the Sixth Article:—

Objection 1. It would seem that faith is not one. For just as faith is a gift of God, according to *Ephes.* ii. 8, so also wisdom and science are numbered among God's gifts, according to *Isa.* xi. 2. Now wisdom and science differ in this, that wisdom is about eternal things, and science about temporal things, as Augustine states.[43] Since, then, faith is about eternal things, and also about some temporal things, it seems that faith is not one virtue, but divided into several parts.

Obj. 2. Further, Confession is an act of faith, as was stated above.[44] Now confession of faith is not one and the same for all, since what we confess as past the fathers of old confessed as yet to come, as appears from *Isa.* vii. 14: *Behold a virgin shall conceive.* Therefore faith is not one.

Obj. 3. Further, Faith is common to all believers in Christ. But one accident cannot be in many subjects. Therefore all cannot have one faith.

On the contrary, The Apostle says (*Ephes.* iv. 5): *One Lord, one faith.*

I answer that, If we take faith as a habit, we can consider it in two ways. First, on the part of the object, and thus there is one faith. For the formal object of faith is the First Truth, by adhering to which we believe whatever is contained in faith. Secondly, on the part of the subject, and thus faith is diversified according as it is in various subjects. Now it is evident that faith, like any other habit, takes its species from the formal aspect of its object, but is individuated by its subject. Hence if we take faith for the habit by which we believe, it is one specifically, but differs numerically according to its various subjects. If, on the other hand, we take faith for that which is believed, then, again, there is one faith, since what is believed by all is one and the same thing; for though the things believed, which all agree in believing, be diverse from one another, yet they are all reduced to one.

Reply Obj. 1. Temporal matters, which are proposed to be believed, do not belong to the object of faith, except in relation to something eternal, viz., the First Truth, as was stated above.[45] Hence there is one faith of

---

[41] *Glossa interl.,* super *I Cor.,* XII, 9 (VI, 52v).   [42] *Glossa interl.,* super *Gal.,* V, 22 (VI, 87v); Peter Lombard, *In Gal.,* super V, 22 (PL 192, 160).   [43] *De Trin.,* XII, 14; 15 (PL 42, 1009; 1012).   [44] Q. 3, a. 1.   [45] Q. 1, a. 1.

things both temporal and eternal. It is different with wisdom and science, which consider temporal and eternal matters under their proper natures.

Reply Obj. 2. This difference of past and future arises, not from any difference in the thing believed, but from the different relationships of believers to the one thing believed, as we have likewise mentioned above.[46]

Reply Obj. 3. This objection considers the numerical diversity of faith.

Seventh Article

WHETHER FAITH IS THE FIRST OF THE VIRTUES?

We proceed thus to the Seventh Article:—

Objection 1. It would seem that faith is not the first of the virtues. For the *Gloss* on *Luke* xii. 4 (*I say to you My friends*) says that *fortitude is the foundation of faith.*[47] Now the foundation precedes that which is founded thereon. Therefore faith is not the first of the virtues.

Obj. 2. Further, The *Gloss* on *Psalm* xxxvi. 3 (*Be not emulous*) says that hope *leads on to faith.*[48] Now hope is a virtue, as we shall state further on.[49] Therefore faith is not the first of the virtues.

Obj. 3. Further, It was stated above that the intellect of the believer is moved, out of obedience to God, to assent to what belongs to faith. Now obedience also is a virtue. Therefore faith is not the first virtue.

Obj. 4. Further, Not formless but formed faith is the foundation, as the *Gloss* remarks on *1 Cor.* iii. 11.[50] Now faith is formed by charity, as was stated above. Therefore it is owing to charity that faith is the foundation; so that charity is the foundation even more than faith is (for the foundation is the first part of a building), and consequently it seems to precede faith.

Obj. 5. Further, The order of habits is taken from the order of acts. Now in the act of faith, the act of the will, which is perfected by charity, precedes the act of the intellect, which is perfected by faith, as the cause which precedes its effect. Therefore charity precedes faith. Therefore faith is not the first of the virtues.

On the contrary, The Apostle says (*Heb.* xi. 1) that *faith is the substance of things to be hoped for.* Now the substance of a thing has the nature of that which is first. Therefore faith is first among the virtues.

I answer that, One thing can precede another in two ways: first, essentially; secondly, by accident. Essentially faith precedes all other virtues. For since the end is the principle in matters of action, as was stated above,[51] the theological virtues, the object of which is the last end, must needs precede all the others. Now the last end must of necessity be present in the intellect before it is present in the will, since the will has no inclination for

---

[46] *S. T.,* I-II, q. 103, a. 4.　　[47] *Glossa ordin.* (V. 157A).—St. Ambrose, *In Luc.,* super XII, 4 (PL 15, 1817).　　[48] *Glossa interl.,* (III, 136v).　　[49] Q. 17, a. 1.　　[50] *Glossa ordin.* (VI, 37E).—Cf. St. Augustine, *De Fide et Oper.,* XVI (PL 40, 215).　　[51] *S. T.,* I-II, q. 13, a. 3; q. 34, a. 4, ad 1; q. 57, a. 4.

anything except in so far as it is apprehended by the intellect. Hence, since the last end is present in the will by hope and charity, and in the intellect, by faith, the first of all the virtues must, of necessity, be faith, because natural knowledge cannot reach God as the object of heavenly beatitude, which is the aspect under which hope and charity tend towards Him.

On the other hand, some virtues can precede faith accidentally. For an accidental cause precedes its effect accidentally. Now that which removes an obstacle is a kind of accidental cause, according to the Philosopher;[52] and in this sense certain virtues may be said to precede faith accidentally, in so far as they remove obstacles to belief. Thus fortitude removes the inordinate fear that hinders faith; humility removes pride, whereby a man refuses to submit himself to the truth of faith. The same may be said of some other virtues, although there are no real virtues, unless faith be presupposed, as Augustine states.[53]

This suffices for the *Reply* to the *First Objection*.

Reply Obj. 2. Hope cannot lead to faith absolutely. For one cannot hope to obtain eternal happiness, unless one believes this possible, since hope does not tend to the impossible, as was stated above.[54] It is, however, possible for one to be led by hope to persevere in faith, or to hold firmly to faith; and it is in this sense that hope is said to lead to faith.

Reply Obj. 3. Obedience is twofold. For sometimes it denotes the inclination of the will to fulfill God's commandments. In this way, it is not a special virtue, but a general condition of every virtue, since all acts of virtue come under the precepts of the divine law, as was stated above.[55] In this sense, obedience is requisite for faith. In another way, obedience denotes an inclination to fulfill the commandments considered as a duty. In this way, it is a special virtue, and a part of justice; for a man does his duty towards his superior when he obeys him. In this sense, obedience follows faith, whereby man knows that God is his superior, Whom he must obey.

Reply Obj. 4. To be a foundation, a thing requires not only to come first, but also to be connected with the other parts of the building; since the building would not be founded on it unless the other parts adhered to it. Now the connecting bond of the spiritual edifice is charity, according to *Coloss.* iii. 14: *Above all . . . things have charity which is the bond of perfection.* Consequently, faith without charity cannot be the foundation; and yet it does not follow that charity precedes faith.

Reply Obj. 5. Some act of the will is required before faith, but not an act of the will quickened by charity. This latter act presupposes faith, because the will cannot tend to God with perfect love unless the intellect possesses a right faith about Him.

---

[52] *Phys.* VIII, 4 (255b 24). [53] *Contra Julian.,* IV, 3 (PL 44, 750). [54] *S. T.,* I-II, q. 40, a. 1. [55] *S. T.,* I-II, q. 100, a. 2.

Eighth Article

WHETHER FAITH IS MORE CERTAIN THAN SCIENCE AND THE OTHER INTELLECTUAL VIRTUES?

We proceed thus to the Eighth Article:—

Objection 1. It would seem that faith is not more certain than science and the other intellectual virtues. For doubt is opposed to certitude, and so a thing would seem to be the more certain, through being less doubtful, just as a thing is the whiter, the less it has of an admixture of black. Now understanding, science and also wisdom are free of any doubt about their objects; whereas the believer may sometimes suffer a movement of doubt, and doubt about matters of faith. Therefore faith is no more certain than the intellectual virtues.

Obj. 2. Further, Sight is more certain than hearing. But *faith is through hearing* according to *Rom.* x. 17; whereas understanding, science and wisdom include some kind of intellectual vision. Therefore science and understanding are more certain than faith.

Obj. 3. Further, In matters concerning the intellect, the more perfect is the more certain. Now understanding is more perfect than faith, since faith is the way to understanding, according to another version of *Isa.* vii. 9: *If you will not believe, you shall not understand;*[56] and Augustine says that *faith is strengthened by science.*[57] Therefore it seems that science or understanding is more certain than faith.

On the contrary, The Apostle says (*1 Thess.* ii. 15): *When you had received of us the word of the hearing, i.e.,* by faith, . . . *you received it not as the word of men, but, as it is indeed, the word of God.* Now nothing is more certain than the word of God. Therefore science is not more certain than faith, nor is anything else.

I answer that, As was stated above, two of the intellectual virtues are about contingent matter, viz., prudence and art;[58] and to these faith is preferable in point of certitude by reason of its matter, since it is about eternal things, which never change. But the other three intellectual virtues, viz., wisdom, science and understanding, are about necessary things, as was stated above.[59] But it must be observed that wisdom, science and understanding may be taken in two ways: first, as intellectual virtues, according to the Philosopher;[60] secondly, for gifts of the Holy Ghost. If we consider them in the first way, we must note that certitude can be looked at in two ways. First, on the part of its cause, and thus a thing which has a more certain cause is itself more certain. In this way, faith is more certain than these three virtues because it is founded on the divine truth, whereas the aforesaid three virtues are based on human reason. Secondly, certitude may

[56] The Septuagint.　　[57] *De Trin.*, XIV, 1 (PL 42, 1037).　　[58] *S. T.*, I-II, q. 57, a. 4, ad 2; a. 5, ad 3.　　[59] *S. T.*, I-II, q. 57, a. 5, ad 3.　　[60] *Eth.*, VI, 3 (1139b 15).

be considered on the part of the subject, and thus the more a man's intellect lays hold of a thing, the more certain it is. In this way, faith is less certain, because matters of faith are above the human intellect, whereas the objects of the aforesaid three virtues are not. Since, however, a thing is judged absolutely according to its cause, but relatively, according to a disposition on the part of the subject, it follows that faith is more certain absolutely, while the others are more certain relatively, *i.e.,* for us. Likewise, if these three be taken as gifts received in this present life, they are related to faith as to their principle, which they presuppose; so that in this way also faith is more certain.

Reply Obj. 1. This doubt is not on the side of the cause of faith, but on our side, in so far as we do not fully grasp with our intellect what belongs to faith.

Reply Obj. 2. Other things being equal, sight is more certain than hearing; but if the person from whom we hear surpasses greatly the seer's sight, hearing is more certain than sight. Thus a man of little science is more certain about what he hears on the authority of an expert in science, than about what is apparent to him according to his own reason; and much more is a man certain about what he hears from God, Who cannot be mistaken, than about what he sees with his own reason, which can be mistaken.

Reply Obj. 3. The gifts of understanding and science are more perfect than the knowledge of faith in the point of their greater clearness, but not in regard to more certain adhesion. For the whole certitude of the gifts of understanding and science arises from the certitude of faith, even as the certitude of the knowledge of conclusions arises from the certitude of the principles. But in so far as science, wisdom and understanding are intellectual virtues, they are based upon the natural light of reason, which falls short of the certitude of God's word, on which faith is founded.

CONCERNING THOSE WHO HAVE FAITH

(*In Four Articles*)

WE must now consider those who have faith, under which head there are four points of inquiry: (1) Whether there was faith in the angels, or in man, in their original state? (2) Whether the demons have faith? (3) Whether those heretics who err in one article have faith in the others? (4) Whether, among those who have faith, one has it more than another?

First Article

WHETHER THERE WAS FAITH IN THE ANGELS, OR IN MAN, IN THEIR ORIGINAL STATE?

We proceed thus to the First Article:—

Objection 1. It would seem that there was no faith, either in the angels or in man, in their original state. For Hugh of S. Victor says in his *Sentences* that *man cannot see God or things that are in God, because the eye of contemplation is closed in him.*[1] Now the angels, in their original state, before they were either confirmed in grace, or had fallen from it, had their eye opened to contemplation, since *they saw things in the Word,* according to Augustine.[2] Likewise, the first man, while in the state of innocence, appears to have had his eye open to contemplation; for Hugh of S. Victor says that *in his original state man knew his Creator, not by the mere outward perception of hearing, but by inward inspiration, not as believers now seek an absent God by faith, but by seeing Him clearly present to his contemplation.*[3] Therefore there was no faith in the angels and man in their original state.

Obj. 2. Further, The knowledge of faith is dark and obscure, according to *1 Cor.* xiii. 12: *We see now through a glass in a dark manner.* Now in their original state there was no obscurity either in the angels or in man, because obscurity is a punishment of sin. Therefore there could be no faith in the angels or in man, in their original state.

Obj. 3. Further, The Apostle says (*Rom.* x. 17) that *faith . . . cometh by hearing, and hearing by the word of God.* Now this could not apply to the angels and man in their original state, for then there was no hearing from

---

[1] *De Sacram.,* I, x, 2 (PL 176, 330).   [2] *De Genesi ad Litt.,* II, 8 (PL 34, 270).
[3] *De Sacram.,* I, vi, 14 (PL 176, 271).

another. Therefore, in that state, there was no faith either in man or in the angels.

On the contrary, It is written (*Heb.* xi. 6): *He that cometh to God must believe that He is, and is a rewarder to them that seek Him.* Now the original state of the angels and of man was one of approach to God. Therefore they had need of faith.

I answer that, Some say that there was no faith in the angels before they were confirmed in grace or fell from it, and in man before he sinned, by reason of the manifest contemplation that they had of divine things.[4] Since, however, *faith is the evidence of things that appear not,* according to the Apostle (*Heb.* xi. 1), and since *by faith we believe what we see not,* according to Augustine,[5] that manifestation alone excludes faith which renders apparent or seen the principal object of faith. Now the principal object of faith is the First Truth, the vision of which gives the happiness of heaven and takes the place of faith. Consequently, since the angels before their confirmation in grace, and man before sin, did not possess the happiness whereby God is seen in His essence, it is evident that the knowledge they possessed was not such as to exclude faith.

It follows, then, that the absence of faith in them could be explained only by their being altogether ignorant of the object of faith. And if man and the angels were created in a purely natural state, as some hold,[6] perhaps one might hold that there was no faith in the angels before their confirmation in grace, or in man before sin, because the knowledge of faith surpasses not only a man's, but even an angel's natural knowledge about God. Since, however, we have stated in the First Part that man and the angels were created with the gift of grace,[7] we must needs say that there was in them a certain beginning of hoped-for happiness, by reason of grace received but not yet consummated, which happiness was begun in their will by hope and charity, and in the intellect by faith, as stated above.[8] Consequently we must hold that the angels had faith before they were confirmed, and man, before he sinned.

Nevertheless we must observe that, in the object of faith, there is something formal, as it were, namely, the First Truth, surpassing all the natural knowledge of a creature, and something material, namely, the thing to which we assent while adhering to the First Truth. With regard to the former, before obtaining the happiness to come, faith is common to all who have knowledge of God, by adhering to the First Truth; whereas with regard to the things which are proposed as the material object of faith, some are believed by one, and known manifestly by another, even in the

---

[4] *Ibid.*—Cf. Peter Lombard, *Sent.,* IV, i, 5 (II, 747).   [5] *Tract.* XL, super *Ioann.* VIII, 32 (PL 35, 1690); *Quaest. Evang.,* II, 39, super *Luc.* XVII, 5 (PL 35, 1352). [6] William of Auxerre, *Summa Aurea,* II, tr. 1, ch. 1 (fol. 35rb); St. Bonaventure, *In II Sent.,* d. xxix, a. 2, q. 2 (II, 703).—Cf. *S. T.,* I, q. 95, a. 1.   [7] *S. T.,* I, q. 62, a. 3; q. 95, a. 1.   [8] Q. 4, a. 7.

present state, as we have shown above.[9] In this respect, too, it may be said that the angels before being confirmed, and man, before sin, possessed manifest knowledge about certain points in the divine mysteries, which now we cannot know except by believing them.

Reply Obj. 1. Although the words of Hugh of S. Victor are those of a master, and have the force of an authority, yet it may be said that the contemplation which removes the need of faith is heavenly contemplation, whereby the supernatural truth is seen in its essence. Now the angels did not possess this contemplation before they were confirmed, nor did man before he sinned; and yet their contemplation was of a higher order than ours, for by its means they approached nearer to God, and had manifest knowledge of more of the divine effects and mysteries than we can have knowledge of. Hence faith was not in them so that they sought an absent God as we seek Him, since by the light of wisdom He was more present to them than He is to us; although He was not so present to them as He is to the Blessed by the light of glory.

Reply Obj. 2. There was no obscurity of sin or punishment in the original state of man and the angels, but there was a certain natural obscurity in the human and angelic intellect in so far as every creature is darkness in comparison with the immensity of the divine light; and this obscurity suffices for the notion of faith.

Reply Obj. 3. In the original state there was no hearing anything from man speaking outwardly, but there was from God inspiring inwardly; and thus the prophets heard, according to the *Psalm* (lxxxiv. 9): *I will hear what the Lord God will speak in me.*

Second Article

WHETHER IN THE DEMONS THERE IS FAITH?

We proceed thus to the Second Article:—

Objection 1. It would seem that the demons have no faith. For Augustine says that *faith depends on the believer's will;*[10] and this is a good will, since by it man wishes to believe in God. Since then no deliberate will of the demons is good, as was stated above,[11] it seems that in the demons there is no faith.

Obj. 2. Further, Faith is a gift of divine grace, according to *Ephes.* ii. 8: *By grace you are saved through faith, . . . for it is the gift of God.* Now according to the *Gloss* on *Osee* iii. 1 (*They look to strange gods, and love the husks of the grapes*), the demons lost their gifts of grace by sinning.[12] Therefore faith did not remain in the demons after they sinned.

Obj. 3. Further, Unbelief would seem to be graver than other sins, as Augustine observes on *John* xv. 22 (*If I had not come and spoken to them,*

[9] Q. 1, a. 5.   [10] *De Praedest. Sanct.*, V (PL 44, 968).   [11] *S. T.*, I, q. 64, a. 2, ad 5.
[12] *Glossa ordin.* (IV, 336E).—St. Jerome, *In Osee*, super III, 1 (PL 25, 883).

they would not have sin; but now they have no excuse for their sin).[13] Now the sin of unbelief is in some men. Consequently, if the demons have faith, some men would be guilty of a sin graver than that of the demons, which seems unreasonable. Therefore in the demons there is no faith.

On the contrary, It is written (*Jas.* ii. 19): *The devils . . . believe and tremble.*

I answer that, As we have stated above, the believer's intellect assents to that which he believes, not because he sees it either in itself, or by resolving it to first self-evident principles, but because his will commands his intellect to assent.[14] Now, that the will moves the intellect to assent may be due to two causes. First, by the fact that the will is ordered towards the good; and in this way, to believe is a praiseworthy action. Secondly, because the intellect is convinced that it ought to believe what is said, though that conviction is not based on the evidence in the thing said. Thus, if a prophet, while preaching the word of God, were to foretell something, and were to give a sign, by raising a dead person to life, the intellect of a witness would be convinced so as to recognize clearly that God, Who lieth not, was speaking, although the thing itself foretold would not be evident in itself and consequently the notion of faith would not be removed.

Accordingly, we must say that faith is commended in the first sense in the faithful of Christ. And in this way faith is not in the demons, but only in the second way, for they see many evident signs, whereby they recognize that the teaching of the Church is from God, although they do not see the things themselves that the Church teaches, for instance, that there are three Persons in God, and so forth.

Reply Obj. 1. The demons are, in a way, compelled to believe by the evidence of signs, and so their will deserves no praise for their belief.

Reply Obj. 2. Faith, which is a gift of grace, inclines man to believe by giving him a certain affection for the good, even when that faith is formless. Consequently, the faith which the demons have is not a gift of grace. Rather are they compelled to believe through their natural intellectual acumen.

Reply Obj. 3. The very fact that the signs of faith are so evident, that the demons are compelled to believe, is displeasing to them, so that their malice is by no means diminished by their belief.

Third Article

WHETHER A MAN WHO DISBELIEVES ONE ARTICLE OF FAITH CAN HAVE FORMLESS FAITH IN THE OTHER ARTICLES?

We proceed thus to the Third Article:—

Objection 1. It would seem that a heretic who disbelieves one article of

---

[13] *Tract.* LXXXIX, super *Ioann.* XV, 22 (PL 35, 1856).   [14] Q. 1, a. 4; q. 2, a. 1, ad 3; q. 4, a. 1 and 2.

faith can have formless faith in the other articles. For the natural intellect of a heretic is not more able than that of a Catholic. Now a Catholic's intellect needs the aid of the gift of faith in order to believe any article whatever of faith. Therefore it seems that heretics cannot believe any articles of faith without the gift of formless faith.

Obj. 2. Further, Just as faith contains many articles, so does one science, viz., geometry, contain many conclusions. Now a man may possess the science of geometry as to some geometrical conclusions, and yet be ignorant of other conclusions. Therefore a man can believe some articles of faith, without believing the others.

Obj. 3. Further, Just as man obeys God in believing the articles of faith, so does he also in keeping the commandments of the Law. Now a man can obey some commandments, and disobey others. Therefore he can believe some articles, and disbelieve others.

On the contrary, Just as mortal sin is contrary to charity, so is disbelief in one article of faith contrary to faith. Now charity does not remain in a man after one mortal sin. Therefore neither does faith, after a man disbelieves one article.

I answer that, Neither formed nor formless faith remains in a heretic who disbelieves one article of faith. The reason for this is that the species of every habit depends on the formal nature of the object, without which the species of the habit cannot remain. Now the formal object of faith is the First Truth, as manifested in Holy Scripture and the teaching of the Church, which proceeds from the First Truth. Consequently, whoever does not adhere, as to an infallible and divine rule, to the teaching of the Church, which proceeds from the First Truth manifested in Holy Scripture, has not the habit of faith, but holds that which is of faith otherwise than by faith. So, too, it is evident that a man whose mind holds a conclusion, without knowing how it is proved, has not scientific knowledge, but merely an opinion about it. Now it is manifest that he who adheres to the teaching of the Church, as to an infallible rule, assents to whatever the Church teaches. Otherwise, if, of the things taught by the Church, he holds what he chooses to hold, and rejects what he chooses to reject, he no longer adheres to the teaching of the Church as to an infallible rule, but to his own will. Hence it is evident that a heretic, who obstinately disbelieves one article of faith, is not prepared to follow the teaching of the Church in all things; but if he is not obstinate, he is no longer in heresy but only in error. Therefore it is clear that such a heretic with regard to one article has no faith in the other articles, but only a kind of opinion in accordance with his own will.

Reply Obj. 1. A heretic does not hold the other articles of faith, about which he does not err, in the same way as one of the faithful does, namely, by adhering absolutely to the divine truth, because in order to do so a man needs the help of the habit of faith; but he holds the things that are of faith by his own will and judgment.

Reply Obj. 2. The various conclusions of a science have their respective means of demonstration, one of which may be known without another, so that we may know some conclusions of a science without knowing the others. On the other hand, faith adheres to all the articles of faith by reason of one means, viz., because of the First Truth proposed to us in the Scriptures understood correctly according to the teaching of the Church. Hence whoever abandons this means is altogether lacking in faith.

Reply Obj. 3. The various precepts of the Law may be referred either to their respective proximate motives, and thus one can be kept without another; or to their primary motive, which is perfect obedience to God, in which a man fails whenever he breaks one commandment, according to *James* ii. 10: *Whosoever shall . . . offend in one point is become guilty of all.*

Fourth Article

WHETHER FAITH CAN BE GREATER IN ONE MAN THAN IN ANOTHER?

We proceed thus to the Fourth Article:—

Objection 1. It would seem that faith cannot be greater in one man than in another. For the quantity of a habit is taken from its object. Now whoever has faith believes everything that is of faith, since by failing in one point a man loses his faith altogether, as was stated above. Therefore it seems that faith cannot be greater in one than in another.

Obj. 2. Further, Those things which consist in a maximum cannot be *more* or *less*. Now the notion of faith consists in a maximum because it requires that man should adhere to the First Truth above all things. Therefore faith cannot be *more* or *less*.

Obj. 3. Further, Faith is to knowledge by grace as the understanding of principles is to natural knowledge, since the articles of faith are the first principles of knowledge by grace, as was shown above.[15] Now the understanding of principles is possessed in equal degree by all men. Therefore faith is possessed in equal degree by all the faithful.

On the contrary, Wherever we find great and little, there we find more and less. Now in faith we find great and little, for Our Lord said to Peter (*Matt.* xiv. 31): *O thou of little faith, why didst thou doubt?* And to the woman he said (*Matt.* xv. 28): *O woman, great is thy faith!* Therefore faith can be greater in one than in another.

I answer that, As was stated above, the quantity of a habit may be considered from two points of view:[16] first, on the part of the object; secondly, on the part of its participation by the subject. The object of faith may

---

[15] Q. 1, a. 7.   [16] *S. T.,* I-II, q. 52, a. 1 and 2; q. 112, a. 4.

be considered in two ways: first, according to its formal aspect; secondly, according to the material object which is proposed to be believed. Now the formal object of faith is one and simple, namely the First Truth, as was stated above.[17] Hence in this respect there is no diversity of faith among believers, but it is specifically one in all, as was stated above.[18] But the things which are proposed as the matter of our belief are many and can be received more or less explicitly; and in this respect one man can believe explicitly more things than another, so that faith can be greater in one man because of the greater explicitness of faith.

If, on the other hand, we consider faith from the point of view of its participation by the subject, this happens in two ways, since the act of faith proceeds both from the intellect and from the will, as was stated above.[19] Consequently a man's faith may be described as being greater, in one way, on the part of his intellect, because of its greater certitude and firmness, and, in another way, on the part of his will, because of his greater promptitude, devotion or confidence.

Reply Obj. 1. A man who obstinately disbelieves a thing that is of faith has not the habit of faith, and yet he who does not explicitly believe all, while he is prepared to believe all, has that habit. In this respect, one man has greater faith than another, on the part of the object, in so far as he believes more things, as was stated above.

Reply Obj. 2. It is of the nature of faith that one should give the first place to the First Truth. But among those who do this, some submit to it with greater certitude and devotion than others; and in this way faith is greater in one than in another.

Reply Obj. 3. The understanding of principles follows from man's very nature, which is equally shared by all; whereas faith follows from the gift of grace, which is not equally in all, as was explained above.[20] Hence the comparison fails.

Nevertheless, the virtual power of principles is more known to one than to another, according to the greater capacity of intellect.

[17] Q. 1, a. 1.   [18] Q. 4, a. 6.   [19] A. 2; q. 1, a. 4; q. 2, a. 1, ad 3; a. 9; q. 4, a. 1 and 2. [20] *S. T.*, I-II, q. 112, a. 4.

Question VI

ON THE CAUSE OF FAITH

(In Two Articles)

WE must now consider the cause of faith, under which head there are two points of inquiry: (1) Whether faith is infused into man by God? (2) Whether formless faith is a gift of God?

First Article

WHETHER FAITH IS INFUSED INTO MAN BY GOD?

We proceed thus to the First Article:—

Objection 1. It would seem that faith is not infused into man by God. For Augustine says that *science begets faith in us, and nourishes, defends and strengthens it.*[1] Now those things which science begets in us seem to be acquired rather than infused. Therefore faith does not seem to be in us by divine infusion.

Obj. 2. Further, That to which man attains by hearing and seeing seems to be acquired by him. Now man attains to belief both by seeing miracles and by hearing the teachings of faith; for it is written (*Jo.* iv. 53): *The father . . . knew that it was at the same hour, that Jesus said to him, Thy son liveth; and himself believed, and his whole house*; and (*Rom.* x. 17) it is said that *faith is through hearing.* Therefore man attains to faith by acquiring it.

Obj. 3. Further, That which depends on a man's will can be acquired by him. But *faith depends on the believer's will*, according to Augustine.[2] Therefore faith can be acquired by man.

On the contrary, It is written (*Ephes.* ii. 8, 9): *By grace you are saved through faith, and that not of yourselves . . . that no man may glory . . . for it is the gift of God.*

I answer that, Two things are requisite for faith. First, that the things which are of faith should be proposed to man; and this is necessary in order that man believe something explicitly. The second thing requisite for faith is the assent of the believer to the things which are proposed to him. Accordingly, as regards the first of these, faith must needs be from God. For the things which are of faith surpass human reason, and hence they do not come to man's knowledge, unless God reveal them. To some, indeed, they are revealed by God immediately, as those things which were revealed

[1] *De Trin.*, XIV, 1 (PL 42, 1037).　　[2] *De Praedest. Sanct.*, V (PL 44, 968).

to the Apostles and prophets, while to some they are proposed by God in sending preachers of the faith, according to *Rom.* x. 15: *How shall they preach, unless they be sent?*

As regards the second, viz., man's assent to the things which are of faith, we may observe a twofold cause, one of external inducement, such as seeing a miracle, or being persuaded by someone to embrace the faith; neither of which is a sufficient cause, since of those who see the same miracle, or who hear the same sermon, some believe, and some do not. Hence we must assert another and internal cause, which moves man inwardly to assent to what belongs to faith.

The Pelagians held that this cause was nothing else than man's free choice,[3] and consequently they said that the beginning of faith is from ourselves, inasmuch as, namely, it is in our power to be ready to assent to the things which are of faith, but that the consummation of faith is from God, Who proposes to us the things we have to believe. But this is false, for since, by assenting to what belongs to faith, man is raised above his nature, this must needs come to him from some supernatural principle moving him inwardly; and this is God. Therefore faith, as regards the assent which is the chief act of faith, is from God moving man inwardly by grace.

Reply Obj. 1. Science begets and nourishes faith by way of external persuasion afforded by some science; but the chief and proper cause of faith is that which moves man inwardly to assent.

Reply Obj. 2. This argument likewise refers to the cause that proposes outwardly the things that are of faith, or persuades man to believe by words or deeds.

Reply Obj. 3. To believe does indeed depend on the will of the believer; but man's will needs to be prepared by God with grace, in order that he may be raised to things which are above his nature, as was stated above.

Second Article

WHETHER FORMLESS FAITH IS A GIFT OF GOD?

We proceed thus to the Second Article:—

Objection 1. It would seem that formless faith is not a gift of God. For it is written (*Deut.* xxxii. 4) that *the works of God are perfect.* Now formless faith is something imperfect. Therefore it is not the work of God.

Obj. 2. Further, Just as an act is said to be deformed through lacking its due form, so too faith is called formless when it lacks the form due to it. Now the deformed act of sin is not from God, as was stated above.[4] Therefore neither is formless faith from God.

Obj. 3. Further, Whomsoever God heals, He heals wholly; for it is written (*Jo.* vii. 23): *If a man receives circumcision on the Sabbath-day,*

[3] Cf. *Conc. Arausic.*, II (529), can. 5 (Denzinger, no. 178).   [4] *S. T.*, I-II, q. 79, a. 2.

that the law of Moses may not be broken, are you angry at Me because I have healed the whole man on the Sabbath-day? Now faith heals man from unbelief. Therefore whoever receives from God the gift of faith is at the same time healed from all his sins. But this is not done except by formed faith. Therefore formed faith alone is a gift of God, and consequently formless faith is not from God.

On the contrary, A *Gloss* on *1 Cor.* xiii. 2 says that *the faith which lacks charity is a gift of God.*[5] Now this is formless faith. Therefore formless faith is a gift of God.

I answer that, Formlessness is a privation. Now it must be noted that privation sometimes belongs to the notion of a species, whereas sometimes it does not, but supervenes in a thing already possessed of its proper species. Thus privation of the due equilibrium of the humors belongs to the nature of the species of sickness, while darkness does not belong to the nature of the species of a diaphanous body, but supervenes in it. Since, therefore, when we assign the cause of a thing, we intend to assign the cause of that thing as existing in its proper species, it follows that what is not the cause of a privation cannot be assigned as the cause of the thing to which that privation belongs as belonging to the nature of its species. For we cannot assign, as the cause of a sickness, something which is not the cause of a disturbance in the humors; though we can assign, as cause of a diaphanous body, something which is not the cause of the darkness, which does not belong to the nature of the diaphanous body. Now the formlessness of faith does not belong to the nature of the species of faith, since faith is said to be formless through lack of an extrinsic form, as was stated above.[6] Consequently, the cause of formless faith is that which is the cause of faith absolutely so called; and this is God, as was stated above. It follows, therefore, that formless faith is a gift of God.

Reply Obj. 1. Formless faith, though it is not absolutely perfect with the perfection of a virtue, is, nevertheless, perfect with a perfection that suffices for the nature of faith.

Reply Obj. 2. The deformity of an act belongs to the nature of the species of an act, considered as a moral act, as was stated above;[7] for an act is said to be deformed through being deprived of an intrinsic form, viz., the due commensuration of the act's circumstances. Hence we cannot say that God is the cause of a deformed act, for He is not the cause of its deformity, though He is the cause of the act as an act.

We may also reply that deformity denotes not only the privation of a due form, but also a contrary disposition; and so deformity is compared to the act as falsehood is to faith. Hence, just as the deformed act is not from God, so neither is a false faith; and as formless faith is from God, so, too,

---

[5] Peter Lombard, *Sent.,* III, xxiii, 4 (II, 657); *In I Cor.,* super XIII, 2 (PL 191, 1659). —Cf. *Glossa ordin.* (VI, 54A).   [6] Q. 4, a. 4.   [7] *S. T.,* I, q. 48, a. 1, ad 2; I-II, q. 18, a. 5.

acts that are good of their very nature, though not quickened by charity, as is frequently the case in sinners, are from God.

Reply Obj. 3. He who receives faith from God, without charity, is healed from unbelief, not entirely (because the sin of his previous unbelief is not removed) but in part, namely, in that he ceases from committing such and such a sin. Thus it happens frequently that a man desists from one act of sin, through God causing him thus to desist, without desisting from another act of sin, through the instigation of his own malice. And in this way sometimes it is granted by God to a man to believe, and yet he is not granted the gift of charity; so, too, the gift of prophecy, or the like, is given to some without charity.

Question VII

ON THE EFFECTS OF FAITH

(*In Two Articles*)

WE must now consider the effects of faith, under which head there are two points of inquiry: (1) Whether fear is an effect of faith? (2) Whether the heart is purified by faith?

First Article

WHETHER FEAR IS AN EFFECT OF FAITH?

We proceed thus to the First Article:—

Objection 1. It would seem that fear is not an effect of faith. For an effect does not precede its cause. Now fear precedes faith, for it is written (*Ecclus.* ii. 8): *Ye that fear the Lord, believe in Him.* Therefore fear is not an effect of faith.

Obj. 2. Further, The same thing is not the cause of contraries. Now fear and hope are contraries, as was stated above,[1] and faith begets hope, as the *Gloss* observes on *Matt.* i. 2.[2] Therefore fear is not an effect of faith.

Obj. 3. Further, One contrary does not cause another. Now the object of faith is a good, which is the First Truth, while the object of fear is an evil, as was stated above.[3] But acts take their species from the object, according to what was stated above.[4] Therefore faith is not a cause of fear.

On the contrary, It is written (*Jas.* ii. 19): *The devils . . . believe and tremble.*

I answer that, Fear is a movement of the appetitive power, as was stated above.[5] Now the principle of all appetitive movements is apprehended good or evil, and consequently the principle of fear and of every appetitive movement must be an apprehension. But through faith there arises in us an apprehension of certain penal evils, which are inflicted in accordance with the divine judgment. In this way, then, faith is a cause of the fear whereby one dreads to be punished by God; and this is servile fear.

It is also a cause of filial fear, whereby one dreads to be separated from God, or whereby one shrinks from equalling oneself to Him, and holds Him in reverence, inasmuch as faith makes us appreciate God as an unfathomable and supreme good, separation from which is the greatest evil, and to which it is wicked to wish to be equalled. Of the first fear, viz., servile fear,

---

[1] *S. T.,* I-II, q. 23, a. 2; q. 40, a. 4, ad 1.　　[2] *Glossa interl.* (V, 5r).　　[3] *S. T.,* I-II, q. 42, a. 1.　　[4] *S. T.,* I-II, q. 18, a. 2.　　[5] *S. T.,* I-II, q. 41, a. 1; q. 42, a. 1.

formless faith is the cause, while formed faith is the cause of the second, viz., filial fear, because through charity it makes man to adhere to God and to be subject to Him.

Reply Obj. 1. Fear of God cannot altogether precede faith, because if we knew nothing at all about Him, with regard to rewards and punishments, concerning which faith teaches us, we should in no way fear Him. If, however, faith be presupposed in reference to certain articles of faith, for example the divine excellence, then reverential fear follows, the result of which is that man submits his intellect to God, so as to believe in all the divine promises. Hence the text quoted continues: *And your reward shall not be made void.*

Reply Obj. 2. The same thing in respect of contraries can be the cause of contraries, but not under the same aspect. Now faith begets hope in so far as it enables us to appreciate the prize which God awards to the just, while it is the cause of fear in so far as it makes us appreciate the punishments which He intends to inflict on sinners.

Reply Obj. 3. The primary and formal object of faith is the good which is the First Truth; but the material object of faith includes also certain evils, for instance, that it is an evil either not to submit to God, or to be separated from Him, and that sinners will suffer penal evils from God; and in this way faith can be the cause of fear.

Second Article

WHETHER FAITH HAS THE EFFECT OF PURIFYING THE HEART?

We proceed thus to the Second Article:—

Objection 1. It would seem that faith does not purify the heart. For purity of the heart pertains chiefly to the affections, whereas faith is in the intellect. Therefore faith has not the effect of purifying the heart.

Obj. 2. Further, That which purifies the heart is incompatible with impurity. But faith is compatible with the impurity of sin, as may be seen in those who have formless faith. Therefore faith does not purify the heart.

Obj. 3. Further, If faith were to purify the human heart in any way, it would chiefly purify the intellect of man. Now it does not purify the intellect from obscurity, since it is a veiled knowledge. Therefore faith in no way purifies the heart.

On the contrary, Peter said (*Acts* xv. 9): *Purifying their hearts by faith.*

I answer that, A thing is impure through being mixed with baser things. For silver is not called impure when mixed with gold, which betters it, but when mixed with lead or tin. Now it is evident that the rational creature is more excellent than all temporal and corporeal creatures; so that it becomes impure through subjecting itself to temporal things by loving them. From this impurity the rational creature is purified by means of a contrary movement, namely, by tending to that which is above it, viz., God. The first beginning of this movement is faith, since *he that cometh to God must believe that He is,* according to *Heb.* xi. 6. Hence the first principle of the purification of the heart is faith; and if this be perfected through being quickened by charity, the heart will be perfectly purified thereby.

Reply Obj. 1. Things that are in the intellect are the principles of those which are in the appetite, in so far as it is the apprehended good that moves the appetite.

Reply Obj. 2. Even formless faith excludes a certain impurity which is contrary to it, viz., that of error, and which consists in this, that the human intellect adheres inordinately to things below itself, through wishing to measure divine things by the rule of sensible things. But when it is quickened by charity, then it is incompatible with any kind of impurity, because *charity covereth all sins (Prov.* x. 12).

Reply Obj. 3. The obscurity of faith does not pertain to the impurity of sin, but rather to the natural defect of the human intellect, according to the present state of life.

BIBLIOGRAPHY [1]

The following list of books does not pretend to be a bibliography either of St. Thomas himself or of all the literature on which the *Summa Theologica* depends. Such a bibliography is scarcely necessary, since there are in existence excellent and exhaustive Thomistic bibliographical monographs. For the years down to 1920, one may consult the *Bibliographie Thomiste* of P. Mandonnet and J. Destrez (*Bibliothèque Thomiste*, vol. I, Kain: Le Saulchoir, 1921). The years 1920 to 1940 are covered by the recent work of V. Bourke (*Thomistic Bibliography*, St. Louis: St. Louis University Press, 1945). On the writings of St. Thomas Aquinas himself, their authenticity, chronology, etc., there are the well known works of Mandonnet and Grabmann (cf. P. Mandonnet, *Des écrits authentiques de s. Thomas d'Aquin*, 2nd ed. [Fribourg: Imprimérie de l'Oeuvre de Saint-Paul, 1910]; M. Grabmann, *Die Werke des Hl. Thomas von Aquin*, 2nd ed. [*Beiträge zur Geschichte der Philosophie und Theologie des Mittelalters*, Band XX, 1-2, Münster: Aschendorff, 1931]).

These ample works of reference dispense with the need of reproducing here any general bibliography on St. Thomas Aquinas. I have therefore restricted myself to including in the following list only such primary sources, collections of documents and secondary works which have been used in the annotations to the text of St. Thomas Aquinas.

I

Abelard, Peter:
Introductio ad Theologiam, PL 178, coll. 987-1114.
Alain of Lille:
Theologicae Regulae, PL 210, coll. 621-684.
Albert the Great, St.:
Opera Omnia, 38 vols., ed. A. Borgnet (Paris: Vivès, 1890-1899).
De Quindecim Problematibus (in P. Mandonnet, *Siger de Brabant et l'Averroisme Latin au XIIIme Siècle*, Louvain: Institut Supérieur de Philosophie de l'Université, Pt. II, 1908, pp. 29-52).
De Animalibus Libri XXVI, nach der Cölner Urschrift, ed. H. Stadler (in *Beiträge zur Geschichte der Philosophie und Theologie des Mittelalters*, Bände XV-XVI, Münster, Aschendorff, 1916-1921).
Summa de Bono (cf., below, O. Lottin, *Le droit naturel*).
Alcher of Clairvaux (Pseudo-Augustine):
De Spiritu et Anima Liber Unus, PL 40, coll. 779-832.
Alexander of Aphrodisias:
De Intellectu et Intellecto (in G. Théry, *Alexandre d'Aphrodise [Autour du décret de 1210, II] Bibliothèque Thomiste*, vol. VII, Kain: Le Saulchoir, 1926, pp. 74-82).
Alexander of Hales:
Summa Theologica, 3 vols. (Quaracchi: Ex Typographia Collegii S. Bonaventurae, 1924-1930).
Alfred of Sareshel (Alfredus Anglicus):
De Motu Cordis, ed. Cl. Baeumker (in *Beiträge zur Geschichte der Philosophie und Theologie des Mittelalters*, Band XXIII, 1-2, Münster, Aschendorff, 1923).
Ambrose, St.:
Opera Omnia, PL 14-17.

[1] The only abbreviations which may require explanation are two: PL stands for *Patrologia Latina* (*i.e.*, J. P. Migne, *Patrologiae Cursus Completus*, Series II, 221 vols., Paris, 1844-1864, with later reprints); PG stands for *Patrologia Graeca* (*i.e.*, J. P. Migne, *Patrologiae Cursus Completus*, Series I, 162 vols., Paris, 1857-1866, with later reprints).

Ambrosiaster:
Commentaria in XII Epistolas Beati Pauli, PL 17, coll. 47-536. (Pseudo-Ambrose)
Quaestiones Veteris et Novi Testamenti, PL 35, coll. 2215-2422. (Pseudo-Augustine)
Anonymous (Pseudo-Hugh of St. Victor):
Summa Sententiarum septem Tractatibus Distincta, PL 176, coll. 41-174.
Anselm of Canterbury, St.:
Opera Omnia, PL 158-159.
S. Anselmi Opera Omnia, I (continens opera quae Prior et Abbas Beccensis composuit), ed. F. S. Schmitt (Secovii: Ex officina Abbatiae Secoviensis in Styria, 1938).
Aristotle:
Aristotelis Opera, 5 vols., edidit Academia Regia Borussica, ex recognitione I. Bekker (Berlin: G. Reimer, 1831).
The Works of Aristotle, 11 vols., ed. W. D. Ross (Oxford: Clarendon Press, 1928-1931).
The Basic Works of Aristotle, ed. and with an introduction by R. McKeon (New York: Random House, 1941).
Augustine, St.:
Opera Omnia, PL 32-47.
Averroes:
Aristotelis Stagiritae Libri Omnes . . . cum Averrois Cordubensis variis in eosdem Commentariis, 11 vols., Venetiis apud Juntas, 1550-1552.
Avicebron:
Avencebrolis (Ibn Gebirol) Fons Vitae. Ex Arabico in latinum translatus ab Johanne Hispano et Dominic Gundissalino, ed. Cl. Baeumker (in *Beiträge zur Geschichte der Philosophie und Theologie des Mittelalters,* Band I, 2-4, Münster, Aschendorff, 1892-1895).
Avicenna:
Opera in lucem redacta ac nuper quantum ars niti potuit per canonicos emendata, Venetiis, 1508.

Basil the Great, St.:
Opera Omnia, PG 29-32.
Bede the Venerable, St.:
Opera Omnia, PL 90-95.
Bernard of Clairvaux, St.:
Opera Omnia, PL 182-184.
Boethius:
Opera Omnia, PL 63-64.
Bonaventure, St.:
Opera Omnia, 10 vols. (Quaracchi: Ex Typographia Collegii S. Bonaventurae, 1882-1902).

Cassiodorus:
Opera Omnia, PL 69-70.
Chalcidius:
Timaeus . . . translatus et in eundem Commentarius (in *Fragmenta Philosophorum Graecorum,* ed. G. A. Mullach, Paris: Firmin-Didot, 1867, vol. II, pp. 147-258).
Cicero, Marcus Tullius:
Scripta Quae Manserunt Omnia:
Fasc. 1: (Anonymous) *Rhetorica ad Herennium,* ed. F. Marx (Leipsig: B. G. Teubner, 1923).
Fasc. 2: Rhetorici Libri Duo (De Inventione), ed. E. Stroebel (Leipsig: B. G. Teubner, 1915).
Fasc. 39: De Re Publica, ed. K. Ziegler (Leipsig: B. G. Teubner, 1929).
Fasc. 42: Academicorum Reliquiae cum Lucullo, ed. O. Plasberg (Leipzig: B. G. Teubner, 1922).
Fasc. 43: De Finibus Bonorum et Malorum, ed. Th. Schiche (Leipsig: B. G. Teubner, 1915).
Fasc. 44: Tusculanae Disputationes, ed. M. Pohlenz (Leipsig: B. G. Teubner, 1918).
Fasc. 45: De Natura Deorum, ed. W. Ax (Leipsig: B. G. Teubner, 1933).

Fasc. 46: De Divinatione, De Fato, Timaeus, ed. O. Plasberg—W. Ax (B. G. Teubner, 1938).
Fasc. 48: De Officiis, ed. C. Atzert (Leipsig: B. G. Teubner, 1932).
Topica (in *M. Tullii Ciceronis Opera Rhetorica,* vol. II, Leipsig: B. G. Teubner, 1893).
Costa-Ben-Luca:
Liber de Differentia Animae et Spiritus, trans. by John of Spain, ed. C. S. Barach (in *Excerpta e Libro Alfredi Anglici De Motu Cordis item Costa-Ben-Lucae De Differentia Animae et Spiritus Liber,* Bibliotheca Philosophorum Mediae Aetatis, vol. II, Innsbruck, 1878, pp. 115-139).

Dionysius the Pseudo-Areopagite:
Opera Omnia, PG 3-4.

Fulgentius:
De Fide ad Petrum, sive De Regula Verae Fidei Liber unus, PL 40, coll. 753-780.
(Pseudo-Augustine)
Liber de duplici Praedestinatione Dei, Una Bonorum ad Gloriam, Altera Malorum ad Poenam, PL 65, coll. 153-178.

Gennadius:
Liber de Ecclesiasticis Dogmatibus, PL 42, coll. 1213-1222; PL 58, coll. 979-1000.
Gilbert de la Porrée:
Commentaria in Boethium, PL 64.
(?) *Liber de sex Principiis Gilberto Porretano Ascriptus,* ed. A. Heysse (in *Opuscula et Textus,* Series Scholastica, fasc. VII, Münster: Aschendorff, 1929).
Giles of Rome:
De Erroribus Philosophorum Aristotelis, Averrois, Avicennae, Algazelis, Alkindi et Rabbi Moysis (in P. Mandonnet, *Siger de Brabant et l'Averroisme Latin au XIIIme Siècle,* Louvain: Institut Supérieur de Philosophie de l'Université, Pt. II, 1908, pp. 3-25).
De Erroribus Philosophorum..., ed. J. Koch and trans. J. O. Riedl (Milwaukee: Marquette University Press, 1944).
Glossa Ordinaria..., 6 vols. (Basileae, 1506-1508).
Gratian:
Decretum. Cf. *Corpus Iuris Canonici.*
Gregory of Nyssa, St.:
De Hominis Opificio, PG 44, coll. 123-256.
Gregory the Great, St.:
Opera Omnia, PL 75-79.
Grosseteste, Robert:
Die philosophischen Werke des Robert Grosseteste Bischofs von Lincoln, ed. L. Baur (in *Beiträge zur Geschichte der Philosophie und Theologie des Mittelalters,* Band IX, Münster: Aschendorff, 1912).
"An unedited text of Robert Grosseteste on the Subject-matter of Theology," ed. G. B. Phelan (*Revue néo-scolastique de philosophie,* vol. XXXVI, *Mélanges de Wulf,* Feb. 1934, pp. 172-179).
Gundissalinus, Dominicus:
De Anima, ed. J. T. Muckle (*Mediaeval Studies,* II, 1940, pp. 23-103, with an introduction by E. Gilson).

Hermes Trismegistus, Pseudo-:
Liber XXIV Philosophorum, ed. Cl. Baeumker (in *Abhandlungen aus den Gebiete der Philosophie und ihrer Geschichte,* Festgabe Hertling, Freiburg, 1913, pp. 17-40).
Hilary, St.:
Opera Omnia, PL 9-10.
Hugh of St. Victor:
Opera Omnia, PL 175-177.

Isaac Israeli:
Liber de Definicionibus, ed. J. T. Muckle (*Archives d'histoire doctrinale et littéraire du moyen-âge,* vol. XII-XIII, 1937-1938, pp. 299-340).

Isidore of Seville, St.:
Opera Omnia, PL 81-84.

Jerome, St.:
Opera Omnia, PL 22-30.
John Chrysostom, St.:
Opera Omnia, PG 47-64.
John Damascene, St.:
Expositio Accurata Fidei Orthodoxae, PG 94, coll. 789-1228.
Josephus:
Josephus, ed. and trans. H. Thackeray and R. Marcus (Cambridge, Mass.: Harvard University Press, 1926-).
Justinian:
Institutiones; Digesta; Codex. Cf. *Corpus Iuris Civilis.*

Kilwardby, Robert:
De Natura Theologiae, ed. F. Stegmüller (in *Opuscula et Textus,* Series Scholastica, fasc. XVII, Münster: Aschendorff, 1935).
Liber de Causis, ed. R. Steele (in *Opera hactenus inedita Rogeri Baconi,* fasc. XII, Oxford: Clarendon Press, 1935).

Macrobius:
Macrobius, ed. F. Eyssenhardt (Leipsig: B. G. Teubner, 1893).
Moses Maimonides:
The Guide for the Perplexed, trans. from the original Arabic text by M. Friedländer, 2nd ed. (London: G. Routledge, 1936).

Nemesius (Pseudo-Gregory of Nyssa):
De Natura Hominis, PG 40, coll. 503-818.

Origen:
Opera Omnia, PG 11-17.

Peter Lombard:
Libri IV Sententiarum, 2 vols. (Quaracchi: Ex Typographia Collegii S. Bonaventurae, 1916).
Collectanea in omnes Divi Pauli Epistolas, Rom., I Cor., PL 191, coll. 1297-1696; others, PL 192, coll. 9-520.
Peter of Poitiers:
Sententiarum Libri quinque, PL 211, coll. 783-1280.
Peter of Spain:
Summulae Logicales (Cologne, 1489).
Plato:
Platonis Opera, 5 vols. in 6, ed. J. Burnet (Oxford: Clarendon Press, 1905-1913).
The Dialogues of Plato, 5 vols., trans. B. Jowett (Oxford: Clarendon Press, 1871).
The Dialogues of Plato, 2 vols., trans. B. Jowett with an introduction by R. Demos (New York: Random House, 1937).
Plotinus:
Enneads, 6 vols., ed. and trans. into French by E. Bréhier (Paris: Société d'Edition "Les Belles Lettres," 1924-1938).
Enneads, 5 vols., trans. by S. McKenna (London and Boston: The Medici Society, 1917-1930).
Porphyry:
Isagoge, trans. into Latin by Boethius, PL 64, coll. 77-158.
The Introduction of Porphyry (in *The Organon or Logical Treatises of Aristotle,* trans. by O. F. Owen, vol. II, London: G. Bell, 1887, pp. 609-633).
Proclus:
The Elements of Theology, ed. E. R. Dodds (Oxford: Clarendon Press, 1933).
Prosper of Aquitaine:
Opera Omnia, PL 51.

Ptolemy:
Liber Ptholemei quattuor tractatuum (Quadripartitum) cum Centiloquio ... (Venetiis, 1484).
Syntaxis Mathematica, 2 vols., ed. J. L. Heiberg (Leipsig: B. G. Teubner, 1898-1903).

Rhabanus Maurus:
Opera Omnia, PL 107-112.
Richard of St. Victor:
Opera Omnia, PL 196.

Simplicius:
In Aristotelis Categorias Commentarium, ed. C. Kalbfleisch (in *Commentaria in Aristotelem Graeca,* edita consilio et auctoritate Academiae Litterarum Regiae Borussicae, vol. VIII, Berlin: G. Reimer, 1907).

Themistius:
Paraphrases Aristotelis, 2 vols., ed. L. Spengel (Leipsig: B. G. Teubner, 1866).
Thomas Aquinas, St.:
Opera Omnia, ed. E. Fretté and P. Maré, 34 vols. (Paris: Vivès, 1872-1880).
S. Thomae de Aquino Ordinis Praedicatorum Summa Theologiae, cura et studio Instituti Studiorum Medievalium Ottaviensis ad textum S. Pii Pp. V iussu confectum recognita. Vols. 1-4, 1941-1944 (Ottawa: Impensis Studii Generalis O. Pr.).
S. Thomae de Aquino Doctoris Angelici Summa Contra Gentiles. Editio Leonina Manualis (Romae: Apud Sedem Commissionis Leoninae, 1934).
Le "De Ente et Essentia" de s. Thomas d'Aquin, ed. M.-D. Roland-Gosselin (*Bibliothèque Thomiste,* vol. VIII, Kain: Le Saulchoir, 1926).
S. Thomae Aquinatis Opuscula Omnia, 5 vols., ed. P. Mandonnet (Paris: P. Lethielleux, 1927).

William of Auvergne:
Opera Omnia, 2 vols. (Paris, 1674).
William of Auxerre:
Summa Aurea in quattuor Libros Sententiarum (Paris, 1500).
William of Sherwood:
Introductiones in Logicam, ed. M. Grabmann (Sitzungsberichte der Bayerischen Akademie der Wissenschaften, Philosophisch-historische Abteilung, München, 1937, Heft 10).

II

Arnou, R.:
"Platonisme des pères" (*Dictionnaire de théologie catholique,* vol. XII, 2, 1935, coll. 2258-2392).

Baeumker, Cl.:
Witelo, ein Philosoph und Naturforscher des XIII Jahrhunderts (in *Beiträge zur Geschichte der Philosophie und Theologie des Mittelalters,* Band III, 2, Münster: Aschendorff, 1908).

Bareille, G.:
"Anges, II" (*Dictionnaire de théologie catholique,* vol. I, 1909, coll. 1192-1222).

Bergeron, M.:
"La structure du concept latin de personne" (*Études d'histoire littéraire et doctrinale du XIIIe siècle,* deuxième série, 1932, Ottawa: Institut d'Études Médiévales, pp. 121-162).

Capelle, G. C.:
Amaury de Bène. Étude sur son panthéisme formel (*Autour du décret de 1210,* III [*Bibliothèque Thomiste,* vol. XVI], Paris: J. Vrin, 1932).

Chenu, M.-D.:
"Contribution à l'histoire du traité de la foi. Commentaire historique de II-II, q. 1, a.2" (*Mélanges Thomistes* [*Bibliothèque Thomiste*, vol. III], Kain: Le Saulchoir, 1923, pp. 123-140).
"Grammaire et théologie aux XIIe et XIIIe siècles" (*Archives d'histoire doctrinale et littéraire du moyen age*, vol. X, 1935-1936, pp. 5-28).
Corpus Iuris Canonici, 2 vols., ed. E. L. Richter- E. Friedberg (Leipsig: B. Tauchnitz, 1922).
Vol. I. *Decretum Gratiani.*
Vol. II. *Decretalium Collectiones.*
Corpus Iuris Civilis, 2 vols. (Berlin: Weidmann. Vol. I, 15th ed., 1928; Vol. II, 9th ed., 1915).
Vol. I. *Institutiones,* ed. Paul Krueger; *Digesta,* ed. Theodore Mommsen, revised by Paul Krueger.
Vol. II. *Codex Justinianus,* ed. and revised by Paul Krueger.

Denifle, H., and Chatelain, E.:
Chartularium Universitatis Parisiensis, 4 vols. (Paris: Delalain, 1889-1897).
Denzinger, H., and Bannwart, C.:
Enchiridion Symbolorum Definitionum et Declarationum de Rebus Fidei et Morum, 16th-17th ed. by J. P. Umberg (Freiburg: Herder and Co., 1928).
De Vaux, R.:
Notes et textes sur l'avicennisme latin aux confins des XIIe-XIIIe siècles (Bibliothèque Thomiste, vol. XX, Paris: J. Vrin, 1934).
Duhem, P.:
Le Système du Monde, 5 vols. (Paris: Hermann, 1913-1917).

Gaudel, A.:
"Péché originel" (*Dictionnaire de théologie catholique,* vol. XII, 1930, coll. 275-606).
Gilson, E.:
"Pourquoi saint Thomas a critiqué saint Augustin" (*Archives d'histoire doctrinale et littéraire du moyen-âge,* vol. I, 1926, pp. 1-127).
"Les sources gréco-arabes de l'augustinisme avicennisant" (*Archives d'histoire doctrinale et littéraire du moyen-âge,* vol. IV, 1929, pp. 5-149).

Kleineidam, E.:
Das Problem der hylomorphen Zusammensetzung der geistigen Substanzen im 13. Jahrhundert, behandelt bis Thomas von Aquin (Breslau, 1930).
Kors, J. B.:
La justice primitive et le péché originel d'après s. Thomas (Bibliothèque Thomiste, vol. II, Kain: Le Saulchoir, 1922).

Landgraf, A.:
"Studien zur Theologie des Zwölften Jahrhunderts" (*Traditio,* vol. I, 1943, New York: Cosmopolitan Science and Art Service Co., pp. 183-222).
Lottin, O.:
"Les dons du Saint-Esprit chez les théologiens depuis P. Lombard jusqu'à S. Thomas d'Aquin" (*Recherches de théologie ancienne et médiévale,* vol. I, 1929, pp. 41-97).
Le Droit Naturel chez Saint Thomas d'Aquin et ses prédécesseurs, 2nd ed. (Bruges: Ch. Beyaert, 1931).
"La composition hylémorphique des substances spirituelles. Les débuts de la controverse" (*Revue néo-scolastique de philosophie,* vol. XXXIV, 1932, pp. 21-41).

Mansi, J. D.:
Sacrorum Conciliorum Nova et Amplissima Collectio, 54 vols. (Paris and Leipsig: H. Welter, 1901-1927).
Muckle, J. T.:
"The *De Officiis Ministrorum* of Saint Ambrose" (*Mediaeval Studies,* vol. I, 1939, pp. 63-80).

"Isaac Israeli's Definition of Truth" (*Archives d'histoire doctrinale et littéraire du moyen âge,* 1933; vol. VIII, pp. 5-8).

Parent, J.-M.:
"La notion de dogme au XIIIe siècle" (*Études d'histoire littéraire et doctrinale du XIIIe siècle,* première série, 1932, Ottawa: Institut d'Études Médiévales, pp. 141-163).

Von Arnim, H.:
Stoicorum Veterum Fragmenta, 4 vols. (Leipsig: B. G. Teubner, 1921-1924).

BIBLIOGRAPHY.

INDEX OF AUTHORS

The purpose of this Index is to bring together in some sort of organized form the various notions which St. Thomas Aquinas either quotes from or attributes to the writers whom he is citing. Such a task should not be misunderstood. I do not wish to hold that St. Thomas Aquinas had a direct knowledge of all the authors whom he cites and of all their works. It is perfectly clear, for example, that St. Thomas often cites St. Augustine from indirect sources and collections, and not directly. This is true of other writers as well. Unfortunately, we do not always know the exact historical channels through which St. Thomas' quotations came to him. Hence, both the Notes and the Index must be used with caution.

A further caution is necessary. The summary under each author in the Index is based on not only what St. Thomas quotes from his predecessors and contemporaries, but also on how he himself interprets these references. Primarily, therefore, the Index is a doctrinal picture as seen by the eyes of St. Thomas Aquinas. This picture does not include more than that. In other words, the faithfulness of St. Thomas' historical vision would have to be checked and verified by reading the sources, in the various authors, on which the Index is based. Nor, on the other hand, does the Index include St. Thomas' estimate, whether favorable or unfavorable, of the writers referred to or quoted. In short, this Index includes merely the historical materials upon which the work of verification and interpretation might be based.

Finally, it ought to be clear that any large compilation of references from widely scattered works by one and the same author is bound to be somewhat artificial. This is the case with the references from the works of Aristotle and St. Augustine. The divisions and subdivisions which I have introduced under these authors in the Index are intended merely as devices to facilitate the location of texts. Very often there is no more than the most general continuity among the texts brought together under one heading. Often, too, the same text could appear under more than one heading. These are necessary and inevitable limitations. But if, in spite of them, the Index facilitates the location of St. Thomas' quotations from the authors whom he cites (this point applies especially to Aristotle, St. Augustine and the Pseudo-Dionysius), then my main purpose has been achieved.

(The abbreviation *O.t.c.* = *On the contrary*.)

Abelard
Alain of Lille
Albert the Great, St.
Albumasar
Alcher of Clairvaux
Alexander of Aphrodisias
Alexander of Hales
Algazel
Amaury of Bène
Ambrose, St.
Ambrosiaster
Andronicus of Rhodes
Anonymous
Anselm of Canterbury, St.
Aristotle
Athanasius, St.
Athanasius, Pseudo-
Augustine, St.
Ausonius, Pseudo-

Averroes
Avicebron
Avicenna

Basil the Great, St.
Bede the Venerable, St.
Benedict, St.
Bernard of Clairvaux, St.
Boethius
Bonaventure, St.
Book of Causes:
    cf. *Liber de Causis*

Caesar, Julius
Candidus the Arian
Cassiodorus
Chalcidius
Cicero

* * * * *

ABELARD,
    That God must do what He does (I, 25, 5).
    That time does not affect the truth of a proposition (I, 14, 15, ad 3).

ALAIN OF LILLE,
    That the names affirmed of God are intended to signify His relation to creatures (I, 13, 2). Cf. I, 13, 6.

God and future contingents: I, 14, 13, ad 2.
    That the name *God*, according to the mode of signification, can stand for a person (I, 39, 4).
    That it is improper to say that the Father and the Son are one principle of the Holy Ghost (I, 36, 4).
    Definition of person: I, 29, 3, ad 2.

ALBERT THE GREAT, ST.,

That the local motion of the angels is instantaneous (I, 53, 3).—That the angels were created in grace (I, 62, 3).

That the empyrean heaven is the place of contemplation (I, 66, 3, obj. 3; ad 2).

That the first creation was fourfold, including the angelic nature, the empyrean heaven, formless corporeal matter and time (I, 66, 4).

That the watery heaven, which is above the sidereal heaven, is so called merely because of its transparency (I, 68, 2). That it is the primum mobile, and moves the whole heaven with a diurnal motion in order to produce the continuity of generation (I, 68, 2, ad 3).

That the intellectual soul is not the form of the body (I, 76, 1).

On the difference of the *potential whole,* in relation to its parts, from the *universal whole* and the *integral whole*: I, 77, 1, ad 1.

That the external senses are distinguished on the basis of their organs (I, 78, 3).

That free choice is a power (I, 83, 2); and that it is a power distinct from the will (I, 83, 4, obj. 1).

That the first man was created in grace (I, 95, 1). [?]

That the terrestrial paradise was on the equator (I, 102, 2, obj. 4).

That the soul is in the body as God is in the world (I-II, 17, 8, obj. 2).

That first principles are known naturally (I-II, 51, 1, *O.t.c.*).—That the principles of common law are called the seeds of the virtues (*ibid.*, Resp.).

That in the sin of omission no act is required (I-II, 71, 5).—That covetousness is the root of all sins (I-II, 84, 1).

ALBUMASAR,

That the movement of the heavens is the cause of our acts of will and choice (*C.G.*, III, 87).

ALCHER OF CLAIRVAUX [PSEUDO-AUGUSTINE],

That the soul is united to the body by means of a corporeal spirit (I, 76, 7).—That the separated soul retains all its powers (I, 77, 8, obj. 1); and that the acts of these powers are also retained by the separated soul (*ibid.*, Resp.).—That *intellect* and *reason* are distinct powers (I, 79, 8, obj. 1); so, too, with *intellect* and *intelligence* (I, 79, 10, obj. 1).—That

the soul has the irascible, concupiscible and rational powers before being united to the body (I, 82, 5, obj. 3).—That the soul becomes forgetful and asleep through its union with the body (I, 84, 4).—That the separated soul knows singulars by abstraction from sensible things (I, 89, 7).—That the soul is in the body as God is in the world (I-II, 17, 8, obj. 2).

ALEXANDER OF APHRODISIAS,

That the agent intellect is substantially separate from man, and one for all men (I, 79, 4-5).

ALEXANDER OF HALES,

That time and eternity differ in that time has a beginning and an end, while eternity has neither (I, 10, 4); and that aeviternity differs from both in that it has a beginning but no end (I, 10, 5). That there is only one aeviternity (I, 10, 6), and that time takes its unity from the unity of eternity, which is the source of all duration (*ibid.*).—That the beginning of the world in time can be demonstrated (I, 46, 2, obj. 1; 2; 5).—That angels are composed of matter and form (I, 50, 2, obj. 1).—That the angels were created in the state of nature (I, 62, 3).—That the first man was not created in grace (I, 95, 1).—That the soul is joined to the body, not as its form, but as its mover (I, 76, 4).—That synderesis is the reason, not as reason, but as nature (I, 79, 12).—That free choice is a power with a habit (I, 83, 2).

ALGAZEL,

That there can be actually an infinity of souls, since such an infinity is accidental (I, 46, 2, ad 8).

AMAURY OF BÈNE,

That no created intellect can see the essence of God (I, 12, 1).

AMBROSE, ST.,

That it is of the nature of light that it was created without limit, species and order (I, 5, 5, obj. 5).—That to be everywhere and in all things is proper to God (I, 8, 4, *O.t.c.*).—That there are some divine names which point to what is proper to God, while there are others which are said of Him metaphorically (I, 13, 3, *O.t.c.*).—That the name *Lord* is a name expressing power (I, 13, 7, obj. 1).—That *God* is a name expressing a nature (I, 13, 8, *O.t.c.*). Cf. I, 67, 1, *O.t.c.*—That to say *God is one* does not point a quality in God, but excludes a plurality of gods (I, 30, 3, *O.t.c.*).—That there is one divinity in the Father and the Son (I, 31, 2).—That the informity of matter preceded its formation temporally (I, 66, 1).—That in the beginning animals were produced in their actuality by the divine Word (I, 71, ad 1).—That the seven days were, not one, but distinct (I, 74, 2).—That there are four cardinal virtues: temperance, justice, prudence and fortitude (I-II, 61, 1, *O.t.c.*). Cf. also I-II, 61, 3; 4, obj. 2; 69, 3, ad 3.—That the virtues are connected, so that he who has one has several (I, 65, 1, *O.t.c.*).—On the beatitudes and virtues, cf. I-II, 69, *passim.*—On the virtues and fruits, cf. I-II, 70, 1, ad 2.—That sin is a transgression of the divine law and a disobedience of the heavenly commandments (I-II, 73, 1, obj. 1; 100, 2, *O.t.c.*; 100, 5, obj. 1).—That every sin becomes venial through penance (I-II, 88, 2).

AMBROSIASTER [PSEUDO-AUGUSTINE],
Cf. I, 63, 3, *O.t.c.*; 95, 1, obj. 2 and ad 2; 97, 1; 97, 3, ad 1; 97, 4.

ANDRONICUS OF RHODES,
Definition of perseverance: I-II, 58, 2, obj. 2.

ANONYMOUS,
Summa Sententiarum: cf. I, 29, 4; I-II, 72, 4, *O.t.c.*

ANSELM OF CANTERBURY, ST.,
That truth is related to true things as time to temporal things (I, 16, 6, obj. 2).—That truth is a sort of rectitude (I, 16, 8, obj. 3).—That God works justice according to His wisdom and goodness (I, 21, 1, ad 3).—That justice is the rectitude of the will (I, 21, 2, obj. 1). Cf. also I-II, 83, 3, *O.t.c.*—That for the Highest Spirit to speak is to behold by thinking (I, 34, 1, obj. 2).—For St. Thomas' criticism, cf. *ibid.*, ad 2.—That the devil desired that which, had he not fallen, he would have reached (I, 63, 3).—That original sin is the deprivation of original justice (I-II, 82, 1, obj. 1).—That man was so made that he should not have felt concupiscence (I-II, 89, 5, obj. 3).

ARISTOTLE,
General Divisions:
  I. Logic.
  II. Physics.
  III. Metaphysics.
  IV. Psychology.
  V. Ethics and Politics.
  VI. Aristotle as a Historical Source.
I. Logic.
That names are the signs of concepts (I, 13, 1; I-II, 7, 1; 77, 2, obj. 5). Cf. I, 34, 1; 85, 2, obj. 3; 85, 5, *O.t.c.*—On equivocal terms: I, 13, 10, ad 4.—That the universal is everywhere and always (I, 8, 4, obj. 1; 46, 2).

On habit as a category: I-II, 49, 1, obj. 2.—That one species of quality is habit and disposition (I-II, 49, 2, *O.t.c.*).—That habit is a quality difficult to remove (I, 89, 5, obj. 4; I-II, 49, 1, *O.t.c.*; 49, 2, obj. 3).—That habit is a disposition and that disposition is an order in one having parts (I-II, 49, 1 with obj. 3; 49, 4; 50, 6, ad 3).—On the threefold mode of this order: I-II, 49, 1, ad 3.—On the twofold meaning of disposition: I-II, 49, 2, ad 3.—On heat, cold, sickness and health as dispositions or habits: I-II, 49, 2, obj. 2. Cf. I-II, 49, 3, ad 3; 50, 1 and *O.t.c.*

That the principle of contrariety is privation and habit (I, 75, 7).—That the first contrariety is between habit and privation (I, 48, 1, ad 1).—That affirmation and negation are contraries (I-II, 64, 3, ad 3).—On contrary propositions: I-II, 53, 1.—That contraries differ in species since contrariety is a difference in form (I-II, 72, 8, *O.t.c.*).—On *distance* and contraries: I, 67, 2, ad 3; I-II, 7, 1.—That a mean is properly between contraries (I-II, 64, 3, obj. 3).—That two contradictory opinions are contrary (I-II, 77, 2, obj. 3).—That of the same subject of which there is affirmation there can also be negation (I, 39, 4, ad 5).—On good and evil as genera of contraries: *C.G.*, III, 8.—That good and evil are not in a genus (I, 48, 1, obj. 1).—That between good and evil there is nothing intermediate (I, 48, 1, obj. 3).—That the good cannot be taken as the difference of any species (I-II, 54, 3, obj. 2).

On the self-evidence of first principles: I, 2, 1, obj. 2.—That no one can think the opposite of that which is self-evident (I, 2, 1, *O.t.c.*).

On the truth of propositions: I, 14, 15.—That since science is a habit, it is a quality difficult to remove (I-II, 67, 2, obj. 2).—That in each science it is necessary to presuppose the essence of the subject (I, 1, 7, obj. 1).—That one science is of one subject matter (I, 1, 3, obj. 1).—On essence as a principle of demonstration: *C.G.*, III, 56.—On inquiry and demonstration: *C.G.*, III, 50.—That a demonstration is a syllogism producing science (I, 117, 1; I-II, 54, 2, ad 2).—That we have science when we know that a thing cannot be otherwise (*C.G.*, III, 39).— That from necessary principles only a necessary conclusion follows (I, 14, 13, obj. 2).—That opinion and science can, in a manner, be about the same thing (II-II, 1, 5, obj. 4 and ad 4).—That opinion is weak and uncertain assent (II-II, 2, 9, ad 2).—That opinion and speech are true or false according as things are or are not (I, 16, 1, obj. 3).—That he who learns must believe (II-II, 2, 3).

II. Physics:
1. The Natural.
2. Form and Finality.
3. Matter.
4. Bodies and Motion.
5. Time.
6. Place.
7. The Infinite.
8. The Production of Bodies.
9. The Order of Motion.
10. Motion and Movers.
11. Accidental Causality.
12. The Heavens.
13. The Prime Movers.
14. Some Definitions.

1. The Natural.

On the manifold meaning of nature: I-II, 10, 1.—That the name *nature* was first used to signify the generation of living things (I, 29, 1, ad 4; 115, 2).—That nature is a principle of motion (I-II, 58, 1, ad 3).—That the natural philosopher and the astronomer both demonstrate the roundness of the earth (I-II, 54, 2, obj. 2).—That even in beings without knowledge, nature seeks the end (I-II, 12, 5, obj. 1).—That intellect and nature act for an end (I, 19, 4).—That a natural agent is distinguished from a voluntary agent (I-II, 10, 1, obj. 1).—That there is order in things moved according to nature, as in things moved according to reason (I-II, 13, 2, ad 3).—That no one is moved towards the impossible (I-II, 14, 6, *O.t.c.*). —That as a thing is done naturally, so is it naturally suitable to be done (I, 60, 5). —That nature does nothing in vain (*C.G.*, III, 49).—That unless impeded, nature always acts in the same way (I, 19, 8, obj. 2).—That there is no new act in an animal which is not preceded by an external

motion (I-II, 6, 1, obj. 2).—That the movement of an animal, though against the natural inclination of the body, is natural to the animal since it is natural to it to be moved according to appetite (I-II, 6, 5, ad 3).—That a stone never becomes accustomed to being borne upward (I-II, 71, 2, obj. 2).—On the definition of the violent: *C.G.*, III, 88; I-II, 9, 4, obj. 2.—That motion is a kind of life for all natural things (I, 18, 1, obj. 1).—That local motion is more perfect than, and prior to, augmentation and diminution (I, 18, 1, obj. 2).—That every corruption and defect is against nature (I-II, 85, 6). —That sins in nature are monsters (I-II, 21, 1, obj. 1).—That there are sins in nature and art (I-II, 21, 1, obj. 2; 21, 2, obj. 1 and 2).—That the sins of nature are neither praiseworthy nor blameworthy (I-II, 21, 2, obj. 1).—That in its operation, art imitates nature (*C.G.*, III, 10).—

2. Form and Finality.

That each thing acts according to the aptitude it has by nature (I-II, 109, 3).— That that for the sake of which a thing is is as the end and good of other things (I, 5, 4, *O.t.c.*).—That what is directed to an end is not infinite (I-II, 87, 3, obj. 2).— That the form of a saw is such as befits cutting (I-II, 95, 3; 102, 1).—That the form and nature of a thing is an end (I-II, 49, 2).—That when a thing receives form and figure it is not said to be altered but to come to be (I-II, 52, 1).

3. Matter.

That prime matter cannot be moved (I, 76, 4, obj. 2).—That there is matter in everything that is moved (I, 9, 2, obj. 1). —That things that are one in genus are one in matter (I, 66, 2, obj. 2).—That the intellect knows matter only according to its proportion to form (I, 87, 1).—That matter and the heavens are ungenerated (I, 46, 1, obj. 3 and ad 3).

4. Bodies and Motion.

That nothing indivisible is moved (I, 53, 1, obj. 1 and ad 1).—That no body acts except through motion (*C.G.*, III, 84).—That no body acts unless it is moved (*C.G.*, III, 65).—That only a body is moved (I, 50, 1, obj. 2; *C.G.*, III, 84).—On the motion of light and heavy bodies: *C.G.*, III, 23.—That things that agree in matter are mutually changeable (I, 66, 2, *O.t.c.*).—That action and passion are the same as to the substance of motion and differ only according to different relations (I, 45, 2, ad 2).— That that which comes to be is composed of a subject and of something else

(I, 44, 2, obj. 1 and ad 1).—That everything that changes was changing (I, 46, 3, obj. 2).—That a continuous motion is one (I-II, 20, 6, obj. 1).—That some things are corruptible because of their great distance from God (I, 65, 3, obj. 2; C.G., III, 62).

5. Time.

That time is continuous (I, 63, 6, ad 4). —That time is the number of the first heavenly movement (C.G., III, 84).— That things which sometimes are and sometimes are not are measured by time (I, 86, 3, obj. 2; C.G., III, 62).—That those things are said to be measured by time which have their beginning and end in time (I, 10, 1; 10, 4).—That the now of time is the same in all time (I, 10, 4, obj. 2).—That the measure of the first motion is the measure of all other motions (I, 10, 4, obj. 3). Cf. I, 10, 6. —That before and after in the measure are derived from the change in the measured (I, 10, 5).—That before and after are in time according as they are found in motion (I, 46, 1, ad 7).—On the now and time: I, 46, 1, ad 7.—That motion and time have quantity and continuity from the magnitude through which the motion takes place (I, 7, 3, obj. 4; 53, 1; 53, 2; 53, 3).—On the relation of instants in time and of points in a line: I-II, 113, 7, ad 5.—That there is time between two successive instants (I-II, 113, 7, obj. 5).— That time is the cause of forgetting (I-II, 53, 3, ad 3).

6. Place.

That not everything that is is in a place, but only a movable body (I, 52, 1, obj. 1).—That to be in a place is to be measured and contained by it (I, 51, 1, obj. 3).—That every place is filled with a sensible body (I, 52, 3, obj. 2).—That nothing is in itself (I, 40, 1, obj. 2).

7. The Infinite.

That the infinite cannot be traversed either by the finite or the infinite (I, 14, 12, obj. 2; C.G., III, 2).—That the infinite, as infinite, is unknown (I, 86, 2, O.t.c.; C.G., III, 54).—That the notion of the infinite pertains to quantity (I, 14, 12, ad 1).—That in material things the infinite is found only potentially (I, 86, 2).— That every infinite is imperfect (I, 25, 2, obj. 1).—That the infinite cannot be derived from some principle (I, 7, 2, O.t.c.). —That the continuous is that which is infinitely divisible (I, 7, 3, obj. 3).—That if the same amount were continually taken from a finite magnitude, it would

finally be completely consumed (I-II, 85, 2).

8. The Production of Bodies.

That only the form which is in matter can produce form in this matter (I, 105, 1, obj. 1).—That it is against the nature of sensible things for their forms to subsist without matter (I, 84, 4).—That the forms of physical things do not subsist without matter (I, 79, 3).—That the forms which are in matter are not from separate forms but from forms in matter (I, 91, 2; C.G., III, 103).—That not forms but composites are generated (I, 91, 2; I-II, 52, 2).—That it is the composite which is properly said to become (I, 65, 4; 110, 2).—That the generation of one thing is the corruption of another (I, 98, 1, obj. 1; C.G., III, 104).

9. The Order of Motion.

On objects as specifying termini of motion: I-II, 72, 3, ad 2.—That potency is prior to act in the order of generation and time (I-II, 50, 2, ad 3).—That nothing is moved by itself (I, 77, 6, obj. 3).— That action and passion are one act (I-II, 20, 6, obj. 2).—That local motion is naturally the first motion (I, 67, 2, ad 3).— That local motion is more perfect than, and naturally prior to, alteration (I, 78, 3).—That local motion is the first motion; that it is more perfect than all other corporeal motions (I, 110, 3, with obj. 2). —That local motion can alone be perpetual (C.G., III, 82).—That in alterations more and less are taken as contraries (I-II, 67, 3).—That rarefaction consists in having the same matter receive greater dimensions (I, 92, 3, ad 1). Cf. I-II, 52, 2, ad 1.—That augmentation takes place in relation to quantity (I-II, 52, 1, obj. 1; 52, 2, obj. 1).

10. Motion and Movers.

That a thing is perfect when it can produce its like (I, 5, 4; 45, 5, obj. 1; 90, 3, obj. 3).—That the agent is nobler than the recipient (I, 79, 2, obj. 3; 79, 5, ad 1; 82, 4, obj. 1; 84, 6).—That he who has the power has the action (I, 51, 3; 77, 5). —On the two ways of being a mover: I-II, 53, 3.—That a moving cause is twofold, namely, essential or accidental (I-II, 76, 1).—That every motion is the act of the movable by the mover (I, 103, 5, ad 2; I-II, 13, 2, ad 3; 74, 1; 110, 2).—That the act of the mover and the moved is the same (I-II, 17, 4, ad 1).—That it is the agent which makes matter to be in act (I, 76, 7).—That the mover is not moved by what it moves (I-II, 9, 2, obj. 3).—

That the mover and the moved must be simultaneous (I, 8, 1; 105, 2, obj. 1; C.G., III, 68, 87).—That the form of the generating cause is the end of generation (C.G., III, 19).—That the efficient and the material cause do not coincide (I-II, 74, 1, obj. 3).—That the end of generation, the form of the generated and the agent are not one in number (I, 44, 4, obj. 2).—That the same thing can move itself but in different respects (I-II, 51, 2, ad 2).—That, if possible, it is better for a thing to come to be through one than through many (I, 103, 6, obj. 2).— On the necessity of an active principle of generation and corruption: I, 115, 3, ad 2.—On the oblique circle as the cause of generation and change: I, 44, 2; 69, 1, ad 4; C.G., III, 76.—That man and the sun generate man (I, 91, 2, ad 2; 115, 3, ad 2; 118, 1, ad 3; C.G., III, 69, 104).— That the father is the efficient cause of the son (I, 46, 2, obj. 7).

11. Accidental Causality.

On generation per accidens: I, 45, 5, ad 2.—That an accidental cause is subsequent to a substantial cause (I, 49, 3).— That a form is corrupted in a twofold way, essentially (by its contrary) and accidentally (by the corruption of its subject) (1, 89, 5).—That being is generated and corrupted accidentally in so far as this or that being is corrupted and generated (I, 16, 8, ad 2).—That a cause which removes an obstacle is an accidental cause (II-II, 3, 1, ad 2; 4, 7).— On how a thing can be the accidental cause of another: I-II, 85, 5.—That what is accidental is subsequent to what is essential (C.G., III, 15).—That the accidental is that which is unintentional (I-II, 71, 5; 72, 5).—That privation is an accidental principle in changeable things (C.G., III, 14).—That one opposite is not the cause of the other except accidentally (C.G., III, 10).—That things which happen always or frequently are not by chance or fortuitous (C.G., III, 3).

12. The Heavens.

That the first motion, namely, the diurnal motion, is the cause of the continuity of generation (I, 104, 2).—That multiform motions are reduced to the uniform motion of the heavens as to their cause (I-II, 9, 5, obj. 1).—That the heavens is composed of all its matter (I, 68, 4, obj. 2).—That the movements of the heavens and the heavenly bodies are natural (I, 70, 3, obj. 4).—That the fixed stars are

in spheres and move only with the motion of the spheres (I, 70, 1, ad 3).—On some uncertainties concerning the heavenly bodies and their movers: C.G., III, 44.—That the matter of the heavens is in potency only to place (I, 66, 2).— That the heavens is not like the four elements, but is a distinct fifth kind of body (I, 68, 1).—That there can be no evil in the heavenly bodies (I, 63, 1, obj. 2).— On the heavenly bodies and the knowledge of the future: I, 86, 4, ad 2.—On the knowledge of heavenly bodies by remotion: I, 88, 2, ad 2.—That the heavenly bodies are moved by spiritual substances (I, 110, 1, ad 2).—That these spiritual substances have not a direct providence over corporeal singulars (ibid., ad 3).—That the world is eternal because incorruptible substances always exist (I, 46, 1, ob. 2 and ad 2); because time is eternal (I, 46, 1, obj. 7).—That there are some dialectical problems, e.g., whether the world is eternal (I, 46, 1).—That the whole universe is a perfect body (I, 8, 4, obj. 3).—On the east as the right part of the heavens: I, 102, 1.—On the right and left parts of the world: I-II, 102, 4, ad 6.—That the power of the mover of the heavens is applied in the east (I, 52, 2).

13. The Prime Movers.

That we have perfect knowledge when we know the first cause (C.G., III, 25).— That in the genus of movable things the first is that which moves itself (I, 70, 3, obj. 5).—That it belongs to a perfect thing to produce its like (I-II, 75, 4, obj. 2).—That an unmoved mover causes an eternal and uniform motion (I, 75, 1, obj. 1 and ad 1).—On the relation of parts in the first self-moved mover: I, 70, 3.—On the two parts of a moved mover: I, 76, 4, obj. 2.—That the power of the prime mover is infinite because it can move in an infinite time (I, 105, 2, ad 3).—That the power of the prime mover is not in a magnitude (I, 105, 2, ad 3).—That an infinite power moves instantaneously (I, 105, 2, obj. 3).—That a finite power cannot move in an infinite time (I, 104, 4, obj. 2).—That if the power of any body were infinite, it would move in null time (I, 25, 2, obj. 3 and ad 3).—That separate substances are related to sensible things as efficient and final causes (I, 50, 3 with obj. 3 and ad 3).—That as universal causes are related to the universal, so particular causes are to the particular (I, 76, 2, O.t.c.).—That

God is the first mover unmoved (I, 19, 1, obj. 3).

14. Some Definitions.

Definitions: The Infinite (I, 14, 12, obj. 1; 86, 1).—Nature (I, 29, 1, obj. 4 and ad 4; C.G., III, 23).—Vacuum (I, 46, 1, ad 4).—Motion (I, 53, 1, obj. 2; 58, 1, obj. 1; C.G., III, 20; I-II, 9, 3, obj. 1; 10, 1, ad 2).

III. Metaphysics:

1. Wonder and Ignorance.
2. Wisdom.
3-4. Principles and Causes.
5. Unity, Truth, Goodness.
6. Substance and Accident.
7. Definition, Genus and Species.
8. Potency and Power.
9. God.

1. Wonder and Ignorance.

That ignorance of the cause produces admiration at the sight of the eclipse of the sun (I, 105, 7).—On human progress in the knowledge of truth: C.G., III, 48. —That there was progress in the sciences discovered by man because of the defects in the knowledge of those who first discovered the sciences (II-II, 1, 7, obj. 2).— That the intellect is related to what is most manifest in nature as the eye of the owl to the light of the sun (I, 1, 5; C.G., III, 25, 45, 54).

2. Wisdom.

That wisdom considers the highest cause, God (I-II, 57, 2; 65, 5).—That the intellectual virtue wisdom considers the divine so far as this can be investigated by the human reason (I-II, 62, 2, ad 2).—That the humblest knowledge of the highest realities is more desirable than the most certain knowledge of the lowest realities (I, 1, 5; I-II, 66, 5, ad 3).— That it is a great thing to be able to know something concerning heavenly beings even by means of a weak and dialectical argument (I-II, 66, 5, ad 3).—On the name *divine science* for metaphysics: C.G., III, 25.—On theology as part of philosophy: I, 1, 1, obj. 2.—That to order belongs to the wise man (I, 65, 3, obj. 1; C.G., III, 77; I-II, 102, 1).—That it belongs to the wise man to rule, not to be ruled (I, 1, 6, obj. 1).—That wisdom is called the head of the other sciences (I, 1, 6, obj. 2; 88, 1; C.G., III, 44).—That it belongs to wisdom to judge (I, 79, 10, ad 3).—That a speculative science is nobler than a practical science (I, 14, 16, O.t.c.).

3-4. Principles and Causes.

That the first indemonstrable principle is founded on the notion of being and non-being, and that all other principles are founded on it (I-II, 94, 2).—That of non-being there are no species or differences (I-II, 72, 6, obj. 3).—That it is impossible to affirm and to deny simultaneously (II-II, 1, 7).—That a measure ought to be most certain (I-II, 91, 3, obj. 3; 96, 1, obj. 3).—That a measure is homogeneous with the thing measured (I, 13, 5, obj. 3; I-II, 19, 4, obj. 2; 96, 2). That the first principle must be most perfect (I, 44, 2, ad 2).—That the things which are the most true are the most being (I, 2, 3).—That that which is most such in any genus is the cause of all that are in that genus (I, 2, 3; C.G., III, 16). Cf. I, 10, 6; C.G., III, 24.—That that because of which a thing is such is yet more so (I, 16, 1, obj. 3; C.G., III, 17).— That what is through itself is prior to that which is through another (C.G., III, 46).—That what is through itself is the cause of what is through another (C.G., III, 52).—That that which is most being and most true is the cause of every being and of every truth (I, 44, 1).—On infinite regress in efficient causes: I, 46, 2, obj. 7.—That the necessity of the effect depends upon the necessity of the cause (I, 46, 1).—That an effect which has a *per se* cause from which it follows necessarily, necessarily comes to be if that cause exists or has existed (I, 22, 4, obj. 1; C.G., III, 94).—That there are some necessary things which have a cause of their necessity (I, 44, 1, ad 2; I-II, 93, 4, ad 4).—That a sufficient cause can be impeded, or otherwise all things would happen of necessity (I-II, 75, 1, ad 2).—That all things do not happen of necessity (I, 115, 6).—That in mathematics there is no demonstration through the efficient cause (I, 44, 1, obj. 3).—That *good* is not found in mathematics (I, 5, 3, obj. 4).

5. Unity, Truth, Goodness.

That *one* has the nature of a first measure and that number is multitude measured by one (I, 11, 2).—That what is one has no contrary (I-II, 71, 1, obj. 1).—That if any substance is a form without matter, it is through itself a being and one, and does not have a cause which makes it to be being and one (I, 61, 1, obj. 2; 75, 5, obj. 3 and ad 3).—That number is multitude measured by unity (I, 85, 8, obj. 2).—That every being is one through its essence (I, 6, 3, obj. 1; 11, 4, obj. 3).—That equality is according to unity in quantity (I, 42, 1, obj. 1). Cf. I, 47, 2, obj. 2.—That it is expressed by a denial of the lesser and the greater (I,

will, can be found in God if they befit His nature (I, 19, 3, obj. 3).—That the life of God is most perfect and eternal because His intellect is most perfect and always in act (I, 18, 3).—That God has one simple operation (I, 20, 1, ad 1).— That God is one (II-II, 1, 8, obj. 1).— That from the unity of order in things we may conclude the unity of God as governor of things (I, 47, 3, ad 1).—That beings resist an unsuitable disposition, and that a plurality of rules is not good: hence the governor of the world is one (I, 103, 3).—On the best disposition of a multitude: I, 108, obj. 1 and ad 1.—That the good of a multitude is twofold, immanent and transcendent (I-II, 111, 5, ad 1).—That things are not said relatively because they are referred to other things but because other things are referred to them (I, 13, 7).—That God is named relatively to the creature because the creature is referred to Him (I, 13, 7, ad 4).—That God is the end of creatures as the general is the end of the army (I, 108, 6). Cf. I, 103, 2, ad 3.—That what is best in things is the good of the order of the universe (I, 15, 2; C.G., III, 64).— That when many are directed to one end, one is found to head and rule them (I, 96, 4).—On desire in the cause of the motion of the heavens: I, 70, 3, obj. 4.— On magnifying God: I, 32, 1, obj. 1 and ad 1.

IV. Psychology:
1. The Soul (soul and body; powers; organs).
2. Living Operations.
3-4. The Intellect (immateriality; man as a microcosm).
5. The Agent Intellect.
6. The Possible Intellect and Knowledge.
7-11. The Nature and Order of Knowledge.
12. Appetite.
13. Biology.

1. The Soul (soul and body; powers; organs).

On the definition of the soul: I, 76, 4, obj. 1 and ad 1; 76, 5, O.t.c.; 77, 1.— That the soul is the cause and the principle of the living body (I, 18, 3, obj. 2). —That the first principle by which we understand is the form of the body (I, 76, 1).—That that by which we first sense and understand is the soul (I, 77, 1, obj. 4; 77, 5, obj. 2).—On the soul as first act: I, 77, 1.—That the intellectual principle is the form of man (I, 76, 1).—On whether the soul is in the body: I, 76, 8,

obj. 1.—On soul and body as one: I, 76, 7, O.t.c.—That when the soul has departed, the parts of the body are said to be human equivocally (1, 76, 8).—That the soul can move, not any body, but only its own (I, 117, 4, O.t.c.).—That as a part of the soul is related to a part of the body, so the whole soul is related to the whole body (I, 76, 8, obj. 3).—That the soul rules the body with a despotic rule, and the intellect the appetite with a political and royal rule (I, 81, 3, ad 2; I-II, 58, 2).—That the body is compared to the soul as the slave to the master (I-II, 17, 2, obj. 2).—That those who are of keen minds are of soft flesh (I, 76, 5; 85, 7; C.G., III, 84; I-II, 50, 4, obj. 3).— That souls are like different figures one of which contains the other (I, 76, 3) Cf. I, 77, 4, O.t.c.—On the manifold meaning of to live: I, 78, 1, obj. 2.— That to live is for living things to be (I, 18, 2, O.t.c.; 54, 1, obj. 2; 54, 2, obj. 1; C.G., III, 104).—That the first principle of life in the sublunary world is the vegetative soul (I, 97, 3).—On the parts of the vegetative soul: I, 78, 2 with obj. 4 and O.t.c.—That an animal cannot be without the sense of touch (C.G., III, 109).—That the sense of touch is one genus, but is divided into many senses according to species (I, 78, 3, ad 3).— That the sense of taste is a species of the sense of touch, residing only in the tongue (I, 78, 3, ad 4).—That the soul has many powers (I, 77, 2, O.t.c.).—That acts and operations are prior to powers and are themselves preceded by objects (I, 77, 3, O.t.c.; 79, 10, obj. 3; 87, 2, O.t.c.; 87, 3). —On the five powers of the soul: I, 78, 1, O.t.c.—That apprehensive and motor powers belong to different genera (I, 79, 11, obj. 1).—That the appetitive and the intellective are different genera of powers in the soul (I, 79, 1, obj. 2).—That the appetitive is distinguished from the other powers (I, 80, 1, O.t.c.).—That memory is a power of the sensitive soul (I, 77, 8, obj. 4).—That imagination and memory are passions of the first sensitive (I, 78, 4, obj. 3).—On the passive intellect as the particular reason: I-II, 51, 3.—That there are only five external senses (I, 78, 3, O.t.c.).—That the same power of the soul is concerned with one contrariety, as sight with white and black (I, 81, 2, obj. 1).— That if an old man receives the eye of a youth he will see as a youth (I, 77, 8, obj. 3).—That among the senses sight is more spiritual and nearer to the reason because it points out more differences in things

(I-II, 83, 4, obj. 3).—That the sense of sight is more excellent than the other sense and extends to more things (I-II, 77, 5, ad 3).—On the tongue as ordered to taste and speech: I-II, 12, 3, *O.t.c.*—That those who lack one sense are missing in one science (I, 78, 4, obj. 4).—That in sleep the sense is fettered (I, 84, 8, obj. 2). —On why this is so: I, 84, 8, ad 2.—On the cause of dreams: I, 111, 3.—On dreams in animals: I-II, 80, 2.—On prophetic dreams: *C.G.*, III, 86.—That the sense is corrupted or weakened by strong sensibles (*C.G.*, III, 59).

2. Living Operations.

That life is manifest in animals (I, 18, 1).—That life is divided into four operations (I, 18, 2, obj. 1).—That the operations of life are carried on through the act of natural heat (I-II, 85, 6, obj. 3).— On heat as the instrument of the power of the soul and also of the nutritive power: I, 118, 1, ad 3.—That processive motion is one of the operations of life (I, 51, 3, obj. 3).—That to live is principally to sense and to understand (I, 18, 2 and ad 1).—That to say that the soul senses or understands is as if one were to say that it weaves or builds (I, 75, 2, obj. 2).—That to sense is not proper either to the soul or to the body (I, 77, 5, *O.t.c.*).—That to sense is not an act of the soul alone (I, 84, 6).—That the operations of man are common to soul and body (I-II, 50, 4, obj. 1; 50, 4, ad 1).— That understanding is said to be common to soul and body because of the phantasms, which are related to the possible intellect as its object (I-II, 50, 4, ad 1). —That the act of the external sense is perceived by the common sense (I, 87, 3, obj. 3).—That the sensible in act is the sense in act (I, 14, 2; 55, 1, ad 2).—That common sensibles are not accidental sensibles (I, 78, 3, obj. 2 and ad 2).—That custom helps good memory (I-II, 50, 3, ad 3).—That meditation strengthens memory (I-II, 51, 3).—That the action of the imaginative power belongs to the composite (I, 84, 6, ad 2).—That a phantasm cannot be without the body (I, 75, 6, obj. 3).—That a phantasm is a motion produced by the sense in act (I, 12, 3, obj. 3; 84, 6, ad 2; 111, 3, obj. 1).—On understanding and sensing as motions: I, 105, 3, obj. 2.—That to understand, to sense and to will are acts of that which is perfect, *i.e.*, of that which exists in act (I, 18, 3, ad 1).—That in the large sense of the word, understanding and willing are *motions* (I-II, 109, 1).—That in the

motions of the soul the absolutely first motion is towards the principle of speculation or towards the principle of action (I-II, 113, 8, ad 3).—That intellect and will are the two moving principles in man (I-II, 58, 4).—That the soul is not moved (I, 77, 6, obj. 3).

3-4. The Intellect (immateriality; man as a microcosm).

That the highest form to which the consideration of the natural philosopher extends, namely the soul, is separate but yet in matter (I, 76, 1, ad 1).—That if the soul does not have a proper operation, it cannot exist separately (I, 89, 1, *O.t.c.*). —On when a form is separable:I-II, 53, 2, obj. 2.—That in the soul, as in nature, there is something by which it becomes all things and something by which it makes all things (I, 54, 4, obj. 1 and ad 1; 79, 3, *O.t.c.; C.G.*, III, 43, 45). Cf. I, 79, 4, *O.t.c.*; 85, 1, obj. 4; 88, 1.—That the intellect is a part or a power of the soul which is the form of man (I, 76, 2; 79, 1, *O.t.c.*).—That the intellect is the highest part of the soul (I-II, 82, 3, obj. 3).— That among the activities of the soul, only understanding takes place without a bodily organ (I, 75, 3).—That the intellect is not the act of a body (I-II, 50, 4, obj. 1).—On the comparison of intellect and sense: I, 85, 6.—That reason is of universals, sense of particulars (I, 14, 11, obj. 1; 57, 2, obj. 1). Cf. I, 86, 1, *O.t.c.* —That the intellect is a substance that is not corrupted (I-II, 53, 1, obj. 2).— That the intellect is a certain substance (I, 79, 1, ad 1).—That the intellect is separate and unmixed (I, 14, 1; 76, 1, obj. 1 and ad 1).—That the intellect comes from the outside (I, 118, 2, ad 2).—That the intellect is simple (I, 85, 8, obj. 3).—That the action of the intellect is not transitive (I, 105, 3, obj. 1).

4. That the soul is in a manner all things (I, 14, 1; 16, 3; 84, 2, obj. 2). —That if the intellect had a determinate sensible nature this would prevent the knowability of other natures to it (I, 56, 2, obj. 1).—That man is a miniature world (I, 91, 1; I-II, 17, 8, obj. 2).—That rational powers are related to opposites (I, 62, 8, obj. 2; 79, 12, *O.t.c.*; 82, 1, obj 2; *C.G.*, III, 31; I-II, 10, 2; 13, 6, *O.t.c.*). —That things are related to the intellect according as they are separable from matter (I, 85, 1, *O.t.c.*).—That the excellence of intelligibles does not corrupt the intellect (I, 88, 1, obj. 3).—That because of their materiality plants do not have knowledge (I, 14, 1).—That beings such

the scientific part of the soul is different from the ratiocinative part (I, 79, 9, obj. 3 and ad 3).

9. That what is subsequently known according to us is prior and more known (or knowable) according to nature (I-II, 57, 2).—That the intellect, as proceeding from the imperfect to the perfect, first knows the universal (I, 14, 6).—That we must proceed from universals to particulars (I, 85, 3, O.t.c.).—That the defined falls within our knowledge before the parts of the definition do (I, 85, 3, obj. 3).—That our first knowledge is confused, but later we arrive at a distinct knowledge of the principles of things (I, 85, 2).—That in the beginning children call all men father, but later acquire a more distinct knowledge of each (I, 85, 3).

10. That the intellect is in potency in a twofold way, namely, as before learning and discovery and as before actual consideration (I, 58, 1). Cf. I, 79, 6.—On habitual knowledge as potential: I-II, 49, 3, obj. 1; 50, 4.—That we can know many things; but we understand one (I, 12, 10, obj. 1; 58, 2, obj. 1; 85, 4, O.t.c.).—That we can have a habitual knowledge of many but an actual knowledge of one (I, 14, 7, obj. 1).—That we cannot understand many things together (I-II, 12, 3, obj. 3).—That we cannot know the difference between two things unless we apprehend them together (I, 85, 4, obj. 4).

11. That all teaching and learning is from pre-existing knowledge (I, 117, 1).—That the teacher causes science in the learner by reducing him from potency to act (I, 117, 1).—That knowledge is lost in two ways, by forgetting and by deception (I, 89, 5; I-II, 53, 1 with O.t.c.; 53, 3, O.t.c.).

12. Appetite.
That in beings in which there is sense, there is appetite (I, 78, 1).—That appetite is twofold and that the higher moves the lower (I, 80, 2, O.t.c.; 81, 3; 106, 2, obj. 3).—That it is the nature of the sensitive appetite to be moved by rational appetite (I-II, 50, 3, ad 3).—That the sensitive appetite is rational by participation because it obeys reason (I, 79, 2, ad 2).—That, in us, the universal reason moves through the particular reason (I, 20, 1, ad 1; I-II, 10, 3, obj. 3).—That a universal opinion does not move except through a particular one (I, 80, 2, ad 3; 86, 1, ad 2; 105, 1, obj. 2).—That the will is contained within appetite (I, 59, 1, obj. 2).—That voluntary motion is natural to a living being as living (I, 70, 3, ad 5).—That the will is in the reason (I, 59, 1, obj. 1; 79, 1, ad 2; 82, 1, obj. 2; 82, 5, O.t.c.; 87, 4; I-II, 6, 2, obj. 1; 8, 1, obj. 2; 9, 5; 10, 2, O.t.c.; 15, 1, ad 1; 56, 6, obj. 1; 77, 1, obj. 3; 86, 1, obj. 2).—That the apprehended good is the object of the will (C.G., III, 85).—That the object of the will moves the will as an appetible moving the appetite (I, 19, 2, obj. 2).—That the apprehended appetible is an unmoved mover, and appetite a moved mover (I, 80, 2; I-II, 6, 1, obj. 1; 9, 1, O.t.c.).—That the object of the will is related to the will as the mover to its movable subject (I-II, 10, 2, obj. 1).—That the will is a moved mover (I, 19, 1, obj. 3; 59, 1, obj. 3; I-II, 6, 4, obj. 2; 50, 5, ad 2; 77, 1, obj. 1).—On willing as the act of what is perfect: I, 59, 1, ad 3.—On imagination and appetite: I-II, 9, 1, obj. 2.—That vision is a cause of love (I-II, 67, 6, ad 3).—That lovers are moved, even by a slight likeness, to an apprehension of the thing they love (I-II, 80, 2).—That when the body is corrupted the soul neither remembers nor loves (I, 89, 6, obj. 1).

13. Biology.
That the living is prior to animal, and animal is prior to man, in generation (I, 67, 4). Cf. I, 76, 3, obj. 3; 85, 3, ad 4.—That man and animal do not come to be together, but that the animal having a sensitive soul comes to be first (I, 118, 2, obj. 2).—That the moving principle in animals is sense or intellect or appetite (I, 78, 1, obj. 4).—That the head is to an animal what the roots are to the plant (I-II, 84, 3, obj. 1).—That the brain is the most moist part of the body (I, 115, 5, ad 1).—That food nourishes in so far as it is potentially flesh (I, 119, 1).—On the distinction between flesh according to species and flesh considered materially: I, 119, 1, obj. 2 and ad 2.—That the semen is superfluous food (I, 119, 2, O.t.c.).—On animals and self-preservation: I, 81, 2.—That in generation the active principle is from the father, while the mother gives the matter (I-II, 81, 5 with obj. 2).—On what the father and the mother supply in generation: I, 118, 1, ad 4.—That woman is a misbegotten male (I, 92, 1, obj. 1; 99, 2, obj. 1).—On why woman is generated: I, 92, 1, ad 1; 99, 2, ad 1.—On why man and woman are joined together: I, 92, 2.—On digestion and heat: I, 78, 1.

V. Ethics and Politics:
1. The End.
2. Happiness.
3. The Will and Voluntariness.
4. Sensitive Appetite and Passion.
5. Habits.
6. Virtue.
7. Evil and Vice.
8. The Intellectual Virtues.
9. The Practical Intellect.
10. The Moral Virtues.
11. Prudence and Art.
12. Justice.
13. Law, Society and Government.

1. The End.

That things seek being naturally (*C.G.*, III, 19).—That the end is the first principle of operation (I-II, 90, 1).—That the good is that which all things desire (I, 5, 1; 6, 2, obj. 2).—That the good is that which all seek (I, 80, 1, obj. 1; *C.G.*, III, 3, 16; I-II, 8, 1).—That the end is an apparent good (I-II, 8, 1).—That the good is in things themselves (I-II, 64, 2, obj. 1).—That the good is to be found both in substance and in accident (I, 60, 3).—That an end is twofold, namely, a reality and its use (I, 26, 3, ad 2).—That some ends are operations, while some are works (I, 103, 2, obj. 2 and ad 2).—That some human operations are ends (I-II, 14, 2, obj. 2).—That a good action is an end, although a production is never an end (I-II, 19, 1, obj. 2).—That the useful is a relational good (I-II, 7, 2, ad 1; 8, 2, obj. 2).

2. Happiness.

That the highest felicity of man concerns speculation on the highest object (*C.G.*, III, 25, 44).—That beatitude consists not in habit but in act (I, 58, 1; 62, 7, obj. 3).—That happiness is an operation according to virtue (I, 88, 1).—That it is a common good open to all capable of virtue (I, 88, 1; *C.G.*, III, 39, 44).—That happiness consists in perfect operation according to perfect virtue (*C.G.*, III, 48; I-II, 51, 2, *O.t.c.*).—That the highest happiness of man is operation according to wisdom which is the highest of the intellectual virtues (*C.G.*, III, 44).—That beatitude has the nature of an end and is the reward of virtue (I, 26, 1, obj. 2; 62, 4).—That happiness is the reward of virtue (I-II, 57, 1, obj. 2; II-II, 2, 10, obj. 2).—That beatitude contains a sufficiency of all goods (*C.G.*, III, 63).—That in this life, man cannot reach his last end (*C.G.*, III, 48).—That man reaches, not perfect happiness, but human happiness (*C.G.*,

III, 48).—That one swallow does not make a spring nor one day a happy man (I-II, 51, 3, *O.t.c.*).—That it belongs to man to draw himself as much as possible towards the divine (I-II, 61, 5).—That the most perfect contemplation, by which the highest intelligible, namely, God, can be contemplated in this life, is the highest happiness of man (I, 62, 1; 76, 1).—That the wise man is happy (*C.G.*, III, 44).—That happiness cannot be without pleasure (I-II, 84, 4).—That the appetite for pleasure is insatiable (I-II, 73, 5, ad 2).—That all pleasure is an accompaniment of operation (I-II, 74, 8).—That enjoyment perfects operation as beauty perfects youth (*C.G.*, III, 26; I-II, 15, 4).—That pleasures differ in goodness and wickedness according to the difference of our operations (I-II, 74, 8, obj. 3).—That the acts of the virtues are praiseworthy because they are directed to happiness (*C.G.*, III, 27).—That riches are not desired except as useful to some end (I-II, 84, 1, obj. 2).—That to philosophize is better than to make money (I-II, 66, 3).—On honor and happiness: *C.G.*, III, 28-29.—That the highest good of man is not subject to fortune (*C.G.*, III, 30).—That the goods of fortune are undetermined (*C.G.*, III, 92).—That a good is fortuitous when it is outside our intention (*C.G.*, III, 92).—On fortune and the heavenly bodies: *C.G.*, III, 92.

3. The Will and Voluntariness.

On the definition of the voluntary: I-II, 6, 1.—On that which is absolutely voluntary: I, 113, 7.—That that is voluntary whose principle is in itself (I-II, 6, 1, obj. 1).—That a thing is voluntary not only because the will is brought to bear on it, but also because its being or non-being lies in our power (I-II, 71, 5, ad 2).—That children and brute animals share in the voluntary (I-II, 6, 2, *O.t.c.*).—That that being is free which is its own master (I, 83, 1, obj. 3; 96, 4; *C.G.*, III, 112; I-II, 108, 1, ad 2).—That an intelligible form produces a determinate effect because it is determined to one effect by appetite (I, 14, 8).—That for the production of human acts the will must be determined to one thing through the intention of the end (I-II, 72, 3, ad 1).—That the will tends to its first motion through the impulse of some external mover (I-II, 9, 4).

That the free choice of man must be moved by some external principle which is above the human mind (I-II, 109, 2, ad 1).—That there is a principle of motion external to man, namely, God (I-II, 68, 1).—That we seem to do only that which we do with the deliberation of reason (I-II, 74, 3, obj. 3).—That will is of the end and election of the means to the end (I, 82, 1, ad 3; 83, 4, obj. 2; I-II, 8, 2, obj. 1; 13, 2, obj. 1; 13, 3, *O.t.c.*).— That we choose only the things that we think are done by us (I-II, 13, 4, *O.t.c.*). —That will is of the possible and the impossible (I-II, 13, 5, obj. 1).—That election is not of the impossible (I-II, 13, 5, *O.t.c.*).—That the end is related to the objects of choice as principles are to conclusions (I-II, 13, 6, obj. 1).—That the means are not only acts but also instruments (I-II, 13, 4, obj. 1).—That election is the desire of those things which are in our power (I, 83, 3, *O.t.c.*; I-II, 13, 1, *O.t.c.*).—That election is either an appetitive intellect or an intellective appetite (I, 83, 3; I-II, 13, 1; 14, 1, ad 1).—That there is an ignorance which belongs to election (I-II, 13, 1, obj. 3).—That election is the appetite of that on which one has taken counsel, and that counsel is a certain inquiry (I, 59, 3, obj. 1; 60, 2, obj. 1; 83, 3 with ad 2; I-II, 14, 1).—On election and virtue: I-II, 13, 3, obj. 1.— That there cannot be wrongness in choice unless the judgment of the intellect fails in the particular (*C.G.*, III, 85).—On erring reason: I-II, 19, 5.

That wickedness is voluntary (*C.G.*, III, 5).—That he who injures himself sins less than if he were to injure another (I-II, 73, 9, obj. 2).—That a drunkard deserves twice the punishment (I-II, 76, 4, obj. 4 and ad 4).—On the miseries of the wicked: I-II, 69, 2, ad 2.—That every wicked person is ignorant (I-II, 76, 4, obj. 1; 78, 1, obj. 1).—That ignorance of a principle is the greatest ignorance (I-II, 78, 4, obj. 1).—That the involuntary is accompanied by sadness (I-II, 6, 5, obj. 2).—That some involuntary acts are caused by violence (I-II, 6, 5, *O.t.c.*).— That some are caused by ignorance (I-II, 6, 8, *O.t.c.*).—On ignorance, the involuntary and the non-voluntary: I-II, 6, 8; 76, 3.—On circumstances: I-II, 7, 3.— That circumstances are the particular conditions of our individual acts (I-II, 7, 1, *O.t.c.*).—That the principle circumstances are *why* and *in what the act consists* (I-II, 7, 4, obj. 1 and ad 1).—On sinning *through* ignorance and *in* ignorance: I-II, 76, 1.—That he who sins through ignorance of a circumstance deserves pardon (I-II, 73, 7, *O.t.c.*).

4. Sensitive Appetite and Passion.

That the will is compared to the sensitive appetite as a higher mover to the lower (I-II, 77, 1, obj. 2).—That universally all appetite is rational by participation (I-II, 56, 6, ad 2; 60, 1).—That appetite obeys reason (I-II, 17, 1, *O.t.c.*). —That those things which obey reason participate somewhat in reason (I-II, 93, 5, obj. 2).—That the lower part of the soul participates somewhat in reason, in the manner of one obeying a commander (I, 57, 4, ad 3).—That the sensitive powers, according as they obey reason, are in a manner called rational (I-II, 50, 3, ad 1). Cf. I-II, 50, 4; 55, 4, ad 3.— That the power whose act is commanded by reason is reason by participation (I-II, 17, 6, obj. 2).—That reason rules the appetitive power with a political rule (I-II, 58, 2).—That reason rules the irascible and concupiscible powers with a political rule (I-II, 56, 4, ad 3).—That reason moves the irascible and concupiscible powers by a royal or political rule (I-II, 9, 2, ad 3).—That concupiscence is divided into many species according to the diversity of acts or objects (I-II, 100, 4, ad 3).—That the generative power of the soul is incapable of obedience (I-II, 83, 4, obj. 2).—That the interior appetitive powers in a man act and are also acted upon (I-II, 74, 2, ad 3).— That anger, joy and the like are passions of the composite (I, 3, 2, obj. 2).—That passions are neither virtues nor vices (I-II, 59, 1, *O.t.c.*).—That passion is weak and transitory (I-II, 77, 2, obj. 1).

5. Habits.

That we are naturally intended for the possession of virtue (I-II, 93, 6).—That habits are certain perfections (I-II, 49, 4, *O.t.c.*; 52, 1, obj. 2).—That habit is a quality difficult to remove (I-II, 68, 3, obj. 1).—That habit is like a nature (I-II, 53, 1, ad 1).—On habit as an action between that which has and what is had: I-II, 49, 1.—That the habits of soul and body are dispositions of the perfect in relation to what is best (I-II, 49, 2).— That habit is a disposition according to which one is well or ill disposed in nature or in relation to an end (I-II, 49, 3). Cf. I-II, 50, 4, obj. 3; 52, 1.—That habits are said to dispose us well or ill towards passions or actions (I, 83, 2; I-II, 49, 2). —That as a man is, such does the end seem to him (I, 83, 1, obj. 5; I-II, 9, 2; 10, 3, obj. 2; 58, 5).—That men prefer that to which they are inclined by habit (I-II, 78, 2, *O.t.c.*).—That like habits produce like acts (I-II, 18, 5, *O.t.c.*; 18,

9, obj. 2; 50, 1; 51, 4, obj. 3; 52, 3, with obj. 2).—That acts proceeding from a habit are like the acts from which the habit is generated (I-II, 78, 2, obj. 2).—That habits are like the acts from which they are acquired (I, 89, 5; 89, 6, obj. 2).—That an act disposes towards something like it in species (I-II, 88, 3, obj. 2).—That the habits of virtues and vices are caused by acts (I-II, 51, 2, *O.t.c.*).—That only he who has the habit can perform unjust acts as the unjust man would perform them, namely, from choice (I-II, 78, 3, obj. 1).—That enjoyment of operation is the sign of a habit (I-II, 65, 3, obj. 2; 100, 9, ad 3).—That in what happens suddenly man acts according to a preconceived end and a pre-existing habit (I-II, 109, 8).—That some acts diminish a habit (I-II, 52, 3, *O.t.c.*).—On whether habits receive more and less: I-II, 52, 1.—On increase in habits without addition: I-II, 52, 2, *O.t.c.*—That there is no alteration in habits (I-II, 52, 1, obj. 3).—But cf. *ibid.*, ad 3.—That physical things cannot acquire or lose customs (I-II, 51, 2).—That there are different habits in different parts of the soul (I-II, 50, 2, *O.t.c.*).—That temperance and fortitude are in the irrational part of the soul (I-II, 50, 3, *O.t.c.*; 56, 4, *O.t.c.*; 67, 1, obj. 3; 74, 4, obj. 2).

6. Virtue.

That virtue is a certain perfection (II-II, 4, 5, ad 3).—That virtue is the peak of power (I-II, 55, 1, obj. 1; 55, 3; 56, 1, *O.t.c.*; 64, 1, obj. 1; 66, 1, obj. 2).—That virtue is the disposition of what is perfect towards what is best; and that the perfect is that which is disposed according to nature (I-II, 55, 2, obj. 3; 62, 1, obj. 1; 66, 5, obj. 2; 71, 1; 110, 3).—That virtue makes its possessor and his work good (I-II, 20, 3, obj. 2; 20, 5, obj. 1; 21, 2, *O.t.c.*; 55, 2, *O.t.c.*; 55, 3, *O.t.c.*; 56, 1, obj. 2; 56, 3, obj. 3; 92, 1, obj. 1; 110, 3, obj. 2; II-II, 4, 5, obj. 1).—That it pertains to the nature of virtue not only that we do something good according to it, but also that we do it well (I-II, 65, 4).—That virtue, like art, is concerned with the difficult (I-II, 60, 5).—That virtue is concerned with the difficult and the good (I-II, 73, 4, obj. 2).—That three things are required for virtue: knowledge, will and immobility of operation (I-II, 56, 2, obj. 2; 61, 4, obj. 3; 100, 9).—That different virtues can concern the same object (I-II, 54, 3, obj. 3).—That science and virtue are distinguished as genera one of which is not subalternate

to the other (I-II, 57, 1, obj. 3).—That sciences and virtues are in us by nature aptitudinally (I-II, 63, 1).—That science and virtue are habits (I-II, 55, 1, *O.t.c.*).—That in physical things, there is virtue not only for operation but also for being (I-II, 55, 2, obj. 2).—That virtue is a right disposition of the soul, as health is of the body (I-II, 59, 2, obj. 2).—That health is some sort of virtue (I-II, 71, 1, ad 3).—That virtues are generated and corrupted from contrary acts (I-II, 53, 1, *O.t.c.*; 71, 4, *O.t.c.*).

7. Evil and Vice.

That to lack a good is evil (I-II, 70, 3).—That in matters of good and evil act is greater than power (I-II, 71, 3).—That a perfect evil would destroy itself (I, 49, 3; I-II, 73, 2).—That some vices are contraries (I-II, 73, 1, *O.t.c.*).—That the worst is contrary to the best (I-II, 73, 4, *O.t.c.*).—That good happens in one way but evil in many (I, 19, 12, obj. 4; 63, 9, obj. 1).—On wickedness as a habit: I-II, 78, 1, ad 3.—On remorse and those who sin from habit: I-II, 78, 2, obj. 3.—On the use of *good* in *good thief*: I-II, 55, 3, ad 1.

8. The Intellectual Virtues.

That there are three things in the soul, namely, power, habit and passion (I-II, 94, 1, obj. 1 and ad 1).—That the intellect is the highest power of the soul (I, 82, 3, *O.t.c.*).—That each thing appears to be that which is best in it (I-II, 106, 1).—That in a way man is said to be what is best in him (I, 75, 4, ad 1).—That the action of the intellect is a life (*C.G.*, III, 61).—That we become knowing from the exercise of understanding (I, 86, 2).—That all virtues are either intellectual or moral (I-II, 56, 5, *O.t.c.*; 56, 6, obj. 2; 58, 2, *O.t.c.*).—That moral virtues are in the appetitive part, and intellectual virtues in the intellect or reason (I-II, 56, 5, *O.t.c.*).—That some virtues are intellectual and reside in the reason (I-II, 53, 1).—That moral virtue is in that which is rational by participation; intellectual virtue is in that which is rational essentially (I-II, 66, 3, *O.t.c.*).—That the good of intellectual virtue is the true absolutely (I-II, 64, 3).—That the true is the end and the good of the intellect (*C.G.*, III, 25; I-II, 109, 2, obj. 3).—That as the true is the good of the intellect, so the false is its evil (I, 94, 4).—That no virtue perfecting the intellect is related to the false in so far as this is the evil of the intellect (II-II, 1, 3, *O.t.c.*).—That *science, wisdom, intellect* and likewise *art* are intellectual virtues (I-II, 56, 3; II-II, 4, 8).—On wisdom, science and intellect as the only intellectual virtues: I-II, 57, 2, *O.t.c.*—That intellect, wisdom and science are of necessary things (I, 86, 3, obj. 1).—That wisdom, science and the intellect of first principles are in the intellectual part of the soul (I-II, 50, 4, *O.t.c.*).—That wisdom is as the head among the intellectual virtues (I-II, 66, 5, *O.t.c.*).—That wisdom is a science (I-II, 57, 2, obj. 1).—On the habit called the intellect of principles: I, 79, 12.—That the habit of the first intelligibles is called *intellect* (*C.G.*, III, 43).—On the intellect of first principles as natural: I-II, 51, 1, *O.t.c.*—That the knowledge of principles comes to us from sense (I-II, 5, 1).—That some intellectual virtues are in the part of the soul which considers the necessary (I-II, 57, 1, *O.t.c.*).—That opinion and surmise are not intellectual virtues (I-II, 57, 2, ad 3).—That because of its imperfection faith is not placed among the acquired intellectual virtues (II-II, 4, 5, obj. 2).

9. The Practical Intellect.

That the speculative intellect is not concerned with things to be sought and avoided (II-II, 4, 2, obj. 3).—That the speculative intellect becomes by extension practical (I, 79, 11, *O.t.c.*; II-II, 4, 2, ad 3).—That the practical intellect differs from the speculative by its end (I, 14, 16; 79, 11).—That it is the practical intellect which moves (I-II, 9, 1, ad 2).—That in operable matters, the end functions as a principle does in demonstrative matters (I, 82, 1; I-II, 8, 2; 54, 2, ad 3; 72, 5).—That in operable matters, the end is as a principle, not as a conclusion (I-II, 13, 3).—That in human acts, ends are as principles in speculative matters (I-II, 57, 4).—That in the will the end is what a principle is in the intellect (I, 60, 2).—That the true of the practical intellect differs from the true of the speculative intellect (I-II, 57, 5, ad 3).—That the good of the practical intellect is the true that is in conformity with right appetite (I-II, 19, 3, obj. 2).—That in the active life knowledge is sought, not for itself, but for operation (I-II, 69, 3, ad 2).—That the end of a practical science is a practical operation (I, 1, 4, obj. 1).—That the practical reason uses a syllogism in operable matters (I-II, 90, 1, ad 2).—That the choice of a particular operable is as the conclusion of a syllogism of the practical intellect (I, 86, 1, ad 2).—That among particulars we can acquire perfect knowledge only through experience, which requires time (I-II, 97, 2, obj. 3).—That each one judges well what he knows (I-II, 93, 2, obj. 3 and ad 3).

10. The Moral Virtues.

That virtue consists in a mean determined by reason, as the wise man would determine it (*C.G.*, III, 48; I-II, 64, 3, obj. 2).—That moral virtue consists in a mean with reference to us, as determined by reason (I-II, 64, 2, *O.t.c.*).—That moral virtue must be with right reason (I-II, 58, 4, ad 3).—That moral virtue is an elective habit fixed on the mean of reason (I-II, 58, 1, obj. 2; 58, 2, obj. 4; 59, 1; 64, 1, *O.t.c.*).—That the virtuous man is the measure and rule of human acts (I, 1, 6, ad 3; 109, 4, ad 3).—That only he who has the habit of virtue can act as a virtuous man does (I-II, 100, 9, *O.t.c.*).—That the virtuous man acts as and when he ought (I-II, 18, 3, *O.t.c.*).—That only the virtuous man bears good fortune well (I-II, 105, 1, ad 2).—That the good man has shame in the sense that he would be ashamed if he committed something shameful (I, 95, 3).—That it is as difficult to act according to virtue as it is to reach the center of a circle (*C.G.*, III, 5).—That it is enough to approximate the mean of right reason in virtue (I-II, 66, 1).—That we must not look for the same certitude in all things (I-II, 96, 1, ad 3).—That in its essence virtue is a mean, while in its goodness it is an extreme (I-II, 64, 1, ad 1).—That the moral virtues are directed to operation by the practical reason and by right appetite (I-II, 61, 2, obj. 2).—That election is the principle act of moral virtue (I-II, 56, 4, obj. 4).—That moral virtues are sometimes caused by the exercise of acts (I-II, 65, 1, obj. 1).—That moral virtues can be acquired from human acts (I-II, 65, 2, obj. 2).—That virtue is concerned with the difficult and the good (I, 95, 4, obj. 2).—That praiseworthy works are works of virtue, blameworthy works works of vice (I-II, 21, 2, *O.t.c.*).—That moral virtue is concerned with pleasure and sadness (I-II, 59, 4, obj. 1).—That moral virtue does what is best in relation to pleasure and sorrow (I-II, 60, 2, obj. 1).—That it belongs to virtue to sorrow moderately when one ought (I-II, 59, 3).—That virtues are not without passion (I-II, 59, 2, ad 1).

That the subject of the moral virtues is rational by participation (I-II, 59, 4, obj. 2).—That there are virtues even in the irrational part of the soul (I-II, 55, 4, obj. 3).—That it is ridiculous to place moral virtues in angels (I-II, 67, 1, obj. 1 and ad 1).—On heroic or divine virtue: I-II, 68, 1, ad 1.—On the principle of the connection of the cardinal virtues: I-II, 65, 1.—That it is ridiculous to attribute the cardinal virtues to God (I-II, 61, 5, obj. 1).—That it is the greatest of the virtues which are the most honored (I-II, 66, 4). —On the objects of fortitude, temperance and justice: I-II, 60, 4, *O.t.c.*—That truth is a species of virtue (I, 16, 4, obj. 3).—That truth is a virtue distinct from justice (I, 21, 2, obj. 2).—That temperance participates in reason less than does fortitude (I-II, 66, 1).—That the temperate man desires as and what he ought (I, 95, 2, ad 3).—That some virtues, such as fortitude and temperance, are concerned with passions (I-II, 59, 4, obj. 3).—That justice which is a moral virtue is not concerned with passions (I-II, 59, 4, *O.t.c.*).—On the ten moral virtues concerned with the passions: I-II, 60, 5.—On *friendship, truthfulness* and *wittiness* as virtues: I-II, 60, 5.—On friendship and love: I-II, 65, 5.—On friendship and self-love: I, 60, 3, *O.t.c.*; 60, 4, obj. 2; I-II, 99, 1, ad 3.—That there cannot be a love of friendship towards irrational beings (I, 20, 2, obj. 3).—That what we can do through our friends we can, in a manner, do through ourselves (I-II, 109, 4, ad 2).—That a gift is an unreturnable giving (I, 38, 2; 68, 1, obj. 3).—On magnanimity: I-II, 61, 3, obj. 1.—On magnanimity and magnificence: I-II, 64, 1, obj. 2 and ad 2. Cf. I-II, 65, 1, obj. 2. —That magnanimity exists only on the presupposition of other virtues (I-II, 66, 4, ad 3).—That liberality consists in giving what is one's own (I-II, 66, 4, ad 1). —On the difference between the gentle and the patient man: I-II, 59, 2, obj. 1.— That perseverance is related to sadness continence to concupiscence and pleasure (I-II, 109, 10).—That perseverance and continence are something less than virtues (I-II, 109, 10, obj. 1). Cf. I-II, 58, 3, ad 2.—That incontinence in relation to concupiscence is more shameful than incontinence in relation to anger (I-II, 73, 5, obj. 3 and ad 3).—On the incontinent man as a paralytic: I-II, 77, 3.—That virtues are more permanent than disciplines (I-II, 53, 1, obj. 3 and ad 3; 66, 3, obj. 1).

11. Prudence and Art.

That prudence is numbered among the intellectual virtues (I-II, 58, 3, obj. 1).—

That prudence is the right reason of operable matters (I-II, 56, 2, obj. 3; 57, 5, obj. 1).—That it is not compatible with a perverse will (I-II, 56, 2, obj. 3).— That the moral virtues are directed to the very acts of the virtues, which acts are themselves as ends, while prudence is directed to the means to the end (I-II, 20, 3, ad 2).—That moral virtue causes the right intention of the end, while prudence causes the right election of the means (I-II, 66, 3, obj. 3).—That prudence disposes a man well in the choice of means (*C.G.*, III, 35; I-II, 13, 2, obj. 3; 56, 4, ad 4).—That it is proper to prudence to order other things to the end (I, 22, 1 and ad 1).—That prudence presupposes the moral virtues by which the appetite is ordered to the good (I, 22, 1, ad 3).—That the mean in the case of each virtue is determined according to the right reason of prudence (I-II, 66, 3, ad 3).—That prudence would be greater than wisdom if man were the highest reality in the world (I-II, 66, 5, ad 1).—That prudence is concerned with contingent operations (*C.G.*, III, 35).— That the soul becomes prudent and knowing through rest from motion (*C.G.*, III, 84).—On the object of political prudence: I-II, 66, 5, obj. 1.—That pleasures corrupt the judgment of prudence (I-II, 59, 2, obj. 3).—That to sin willingly is opposed to prudence (I-II, 58, 5, *O.t.c.*). —That it is better to sin willingly in art; not so in prudence (I-II, 21, 2, ad 2).— That prudence cannot be lost by forgetting (I-II, 53, 1).—That some animals participate somewhat in prudence, although no irrational animals participate in happiness (*C.G.*, III, 35).—On prudence and bees: I-II, 13, 2, obj. 3.

On counsel: I-II, 14, 4 with obj. 3.— That counsel is only of what is possible (I-II, 14, 5, obj. 3).—That those who take counsel seem to inquire and to decide (I-II, 14, 5, *O.t.c.*).—That prudence is of good counsel (I, 22, 1, obj. 1; 22, 2, obj. 3; 57, 4, obj. 3; 57, 5, obj. 2; 58, 5, obj. 3).—That counsel has no place except in difficult matters (I-II, 68, 7, ad 3).—That there must be an external principle of human counsel (I-II, 80, 1, obj. 3).—On eubulia: I-II, 57, 6, obj. 1. —On eubulia, synesis and gnome as virtues joined to prudence: I-II, 57, 6, *O.t.c.*

That art is a virtue (I-II, 57, 3, obj. 2 and *O.t.c.*).—That prudence is distinguished from art (I-II, 57, 4, *O.t.c.*).— That prudence and art are concerned with what can be otherwise (I-II, 57, 3, obj.

2).—That science and art are sometimes called virtues (I-II, 56, 3).—That art is the right reason of things to be made, not of things to be done (I-II, 68, 4, ad 1).— That making and doing differ (I-II, 57, 4).—That art is an intellectual virtue and has a mean (I-II, 64, 3, *O.t.c.*).— That the more architectonic art governs the less (I-II, 9, 1).

12. Justice.

On justice as a habit: I-II, 19, 1, *O.t.c.*; 50, 5, *O.t.c.*—That justice is the whole of virtue (II-II, 4, 5, *O.t.c.*).—On general justice as being every virtue: I-II, 100, 12.—That justice is the noblest of virtues (I-II, 66, 4, and *O.t.c.*; 115, 5, obj. 2).—On the mean of justice as a real mean: I-II, 64, 2, obj. 3.—On the domain of justice: I-II, 60, 3, obj. 3.— That to do the works of a just man is easy; but to do them as a just man does, joyously and promptly, is difficult to one not having justice (I-II, 107, 4).—That no just man fails to take pleasure in a just operation (I-II, 59, 5, *O.t.c.*).—That justice is a kind of equality (I-II, 114, 1).—On justice between those who are not equal: *ibid.*—On metaphorical justice: I-II, 100, 2, ad 2; 113, 1.—That justice concerns operations, while temperance, fortitude and gentleness concern the passions (I-II, 60, 2, *O.t.c.*).

On the twofold just, namely, the moral and the legal: I-II, 99, 5.—That there is only a distinction of reason between the legal justice which directs the acts of men to the common good and the virtue which directs the acts of a man in relation to one man (I-II, 60, 3, obj. 2).— That only justice is concerned with the common good (I-II, 100, 2, obj. 3).—On legal justice: I-II, 95, 2, obj. 1.—That only legal justice is directed to the common good (I-II, 61, 5, obj. 4). Cf. *ibid.*, ad 4.—On legal justice as ordering the act of man in relation to the common good of the multitude: I-II, 113, 1.—That the precepts of human law concern acts of justice, and the acts of the other virtues only in so far as these have the character of justice (I-II, 100, 2).

13. Law, Society and Government.

That natural law is the law which has the same power everywhere (I-II, 95, 2, obj. 3).—That the natural law, like human nature, fails in some respects and is mutable (I-II, 100, 8, obj. 1 and ad 1).— On the value of the opinions of wise men in the particularization of natural law: I-II, 95, 2, ad 4.—That nothing is so just for all as not to be subject to change in some respects (I-II, 94, 4, obj. 2 and ad 2).—On what is included in human law: I-II, 96, 1, obj. 1 and ad 1.—That what is according to law is said to be just (I-II, 94, 4, obj. 2).—That those legal matters are just which make and preserve happiness and what belongs to it (I-II, 90, 2).—That positive law is distinguished from natural law (I-II, 95, 2, obj. 2).

That the common good is better (greater, more divine) than the good of the individual (*C.G.*, III, 17, 69, 80; I-II, 111, 5, obj. 1; 113, 9, obj. 2).— That man is naturally a political or social animal (*C.G.*, III, 85; I-II, 72, 4; 95, 4). —That the state is a perfect community (I-II, 90, 2; 90, 3, ad 3).—That states which are ruled differently have different kinds of law (I-II, 100, 2). Cf. I-II, 104, 3, ad 2.—On a kingdom as one form of government: I-II, 95, 4.—That the ordering of a people depends mostly on the highest rule (I-II, 105, 1, obj. 1).—That the virtue of any subject is to be properly subordinated to the ruler (I-II, 92, 1).— That the virtue of the ruler and of the good man is the same (I-II, 92, 1. ad 3).

That the intention of the lawgiver is principally directed towards making men virtuous (I-II, 100, 9, 2).—That the purpose of the law maker is to direct man towards virtue (I-II, 90, 3, obj. 2 and ad 2).—That there is a difference in the rule of a master over his slave and of a father over his son (I-II, 105, 4, obj. 4). Cf. *ibid.*, ad 5.—That law commands all the acts of the virtues (I-II, 92, 2).—That the will of any legislator is to make men good (I-II, 92, 1, *O.t.c.*).—That legislators make men good by habituation (I-II, 92, 1, ad 1).—That political virtues and vices do not come from nature but from customary use (*C.G.*, III, 85).—That it is necessary to leave some particular matters to judges (I-II, 95, 1, ad 3).—That it is better to determine all things by law than to leave them to the judgment of judges (I-II, 95, 1, ad 2).—That men turn to a judge as to justice personified (I-II, 95, 1, obj. 2).—On *minister* as an animate instrument: *C.G.*, III, 79.—On what law commands and prohibits: I-II, 96, 3, *O.t.c.*—On law and temporal promises and threats: I-II, 99, 6, obj. 1.— That law commands with respect to all the acts of the virtues (I-II, 65, 3, *O.t.c.*). —That law coerces through fear of punishment (I-II, 100, 9).—That punishments are inflicted to lead men back to the good of virtue (I-II, 87, 2, obj. 1).— That punishments are a sort of medicine

(I-II, 87, 3, obj. 2; 87, 6, obj. 3).—That punishments are especially necessary against those who are prone to evil (I-II, 100, 7, ad 4).—That a measure must especially be permanent (I-II, 97, 1, obj. 2).—That laws have a very great strength from custom (I-II, 97, 2, ad 1). —That some laws are tyrannical (I-II, 92, 1, obj. 4).—On the twofold meaning of citizen: I-II, 105, 3, ad 2.—That the virtues of citizens vary according as they are well related to different kinds of government (I-II, 63, 4).—That community of possessions is an occasion of discord (I, 98, 1, ad 3).—On how to obtain good government: I-II, 105, 1.—That human society is especially preserved because men exchange with one another, by means of buying and selling, the things they need (I-II, 105, 2, obj. 3).—That states and kingdoms are especially destroyed because women acquire possessions (I-II, 105, 2, obj. 2).—On property and the stability of the state: I-II, 105, 2, ad 3.—On the basis of domestic community: I-II, 105, 4.—That fathers love their sons as something belonging to them (I-II, 100, 5, ad 4).—That there are two beings whom a man cannot sufficiently repay for all that they have done, namely, God and his own father (I-II, 100, 7, ad 1).—That we cannot, by means of all our good deeds, sufficiently repay God what we owe Him (I-II, 114, 1, obj. 1).

On slaves: C.G., III, 81.—That, in what they are, slaves belong to their masters (I-II, 104, 1, ad 3; 105, 4, obj. 1).— That slaves are not part of a people or a state to which it is fitting to give a law (I-II, 98, 6, ad 2).—That man has a natural dominion over all animals (C.G., III, 22).—That if man is perfect in virtue he is the best of animals; but if he is without law and justice he is the worst of all (I-II, 95, 1).

VI. Aristotle as a Historical Source.

On the ancient [Pre-Attic] philosophers: I, 7, 1; 9, 1; 14, 12, ad 3; 16, 1, ad 2; 22, 2, ad 3; 44, 1, ad 2; 44, 2; 45, 2, obj. 1; 46, 1, ad 3 and 7; 46, 2, ad 8; 50, 1; 66, 1, O.t.c.; 66, 1; 66, 1, ad 2; 66, 2; 75, 1 and ad 1-2; 76, 4; 84, 2; 84, 6; 85, 2; 115, 1; 115, 3, ad 2; 115, 4; C.G., III, 2, 84, 86, 90; I-II, 9, 5; 90, 1. On Thales: I, 68, 3.—On Pythagoras and Pythagoreans: I, 4, 1; 11, 1; 48, 1, ad 1; 74, 1; C.G., III, 9.—On Heraclitus: I, 84, 1; 85, 2.—On Empedocles: I, 14, 11; 46, 1, ad 5; 50, 2, ad 2; 75, 3; 84, 2; 85, 2; C.G., III, 84, 85.—On Anaxagoras: I, 46, 1, ad 5; 46, 2, obj. 3 and ad 3; 47,

1; 66, 1, ad 2.—On Protagoras: I, 16, 1, obj. 2; 85, 2.—On Socrates: I-II, 58, 2; 58, 4, ad 3; 77, 2.

On Plato: I, 6, 4; 9, 1, ad 1; 11, 1; 15, 3; 18, 4, ad 3; 44, 2; 50, 3; 65, 4; 66, 1, ad 4; 66, 2; 76, 1; 79, 3; 84, 1; 84, 3; 84, 4; 85, 2; 115, 1; C.G., III, 24, 69.—Criticism of Plato: I, 6, 4; 15, 1, ad 1; 76, 3; 84, 1; 85, 3, ad 4; C.G., III, 41. —On the Platonists: I, 5, 2; I-II, 58, 4, ad 3.—On Speusippus: I, 4, 1.

On Democritus: I, 16, 1, obj. 2; 22, 2, ad 3; 47, 1 and 3; 84, 6; 115, 1; C.G., III, 84.

ATHANASIUS, ST.,
As a Historical Source: I, 42, 2, ad 4; I-II, 63, 1, obj. 1.

ATHANASIUS, PSEUDO-,
Citations: I, 10, 2; 27, 4, O.t.c.; 29, 3, O.t.c.; 30, 1, O.t.c.; 30, 2, obj. 5; 31, 1, O.t.c.; 33, 1, obj. 3; 36, 2, O.t.c.; 39, 3; 41, 6; 42, 1, O.t.c.; 42, 2, O.t.c.; 42, 3, obj. 2; 42, 3, O.t.c.; 42, 4.

AUGUSTINE, ST.,
General Divisions:
    I. Faith.
   II. God.
  III. Creation.
   IV. The Angels; the Demons.
    V. Creation and Order.
   VI. Law.
  VII. Grace.
 VIII. Man.
   IX. Scriptural Interpretations.
    X. St. Augustine as a Historical Source.
I. Faith.
    1. Definition of belief.
    2. Scripture.
    1. Definition of belief.
That faith is to believe what is not seen (I-II, 70, 1, obj. 3).—That no one believes except willingly (I, 111, 1, ad 1; I-II, 56, 3; 65, 4, obj. 2; II-II, 1, 6, obj. 3).—That to be able to have faith and charity belongs to the nature of man; but to have faith and the charity of grace belongs to believers (I-II, 113, O.t.c.).— That to believe is to think with assent (II-II, 2, 1, O.t.c.).—On believing God, believing in a God, and believing in God: II-II, 2, 2, O.t.c.—That we believe Peter and Paul, but we believe only *in* God (II-II, 1, 9, obj. 5).—That faith is the virtue

(I, 39, 8, obj. 2).—On power as appropriated to the Father, wisdom to the Son, goodness to the Holy Spirit: I, 39, 7; 39, 8, obj. 3.

On the Person of the Father: I, 29, 4, obj. 1.—That the Father is the principle of the whole Godhead (I, 33, 1, O.t.c.).—On the meaning of unbegotten: I, 33, 4, ad 1.—On whether *unbegotten* is the same as Father: I, 40, 3, obj. 3.—That the Father is not wise with a generated wisdom (I, 37, 2, obj. 1; 39, 7, ad 2).—That if God the Father could not generate a Son equal to Him, where is His omnipotence? (I, 44, 4, O.t.c.; 42, 6, obj. 3).

That Father and Son are one wisdom because one essence (I, 39, 5, obj. 1).—That everything that is included in the knowledge of the Father is expressed by the Word (I-II, 93, 1, ad 2).—That there is nothing lesser in the Word of God than in the knowledge of God (I, 34, 3, ad 5). —That only the Son is the Word (I, 34, 2, O.t.c.).—That the name *Word* signifies not only a reference to the Father but also a reference to all those things which were made by the Word (I, 34, 3, O.t.c.). —That the divine Word cannot properly be called a *thought* (I, 34, 1, ad 1; II-II, 2, 1).—That *word* is knowledge with love (I, 24, 1, obj. 2; 43, 5, ad 2).—On intellectual conception as a likeness of the divine Word: I, 34, 1.—On *Word* as a personal name: I, 34, 1, O.t.c.—That the Word of God is a form that has not been formed (I, 3, 8, obj. 2).—On *image* as a personal name in God: I, 35, 1, O.t.c.—On image as an express likeness: I, 35, 1; 35, 2, obj. 2.—That if an image is perfect, it is equal to that of which it is the image, not vice versa (I, 42, 1, obj. 3).— That the Son alone is the image of the Father (I, 35, 2, O.t.c.; 93, 5, obj. 4).— That the Son did not generate a Creator; not that He could not, but that it was not fitting (I, 41, 6, obj. 2 and ad 2).

That Father and Son are one principle of the Holy Spirit (I, 36, 4, O.t.c.).—On the name Holy Spirit: I, 36, 1.—That the Holy Spirit is He whereby the Begotten is loved by, and loves, His Begetter (I, 37, 2, O.t.c.).—That the Holy Spirit proceeds temporally for the sanctification of the creature (I, 43, 3, O.t.c.).—On the Holy Spirit as *Gift*: I, 38, 1, obj. 1 and O.t.c.; 38, 2 with O.t.c.—On the name *Love*: I, 37, 1, obj. 1.

On the use of *to be sent* and *to send* in relation to the divine Persons: I, 43, 8.— That the Father alone is never said to be sent (I, 43, 4, O.t.c.). Cf. *ibid.*, ad 2; 43,

7, obj. 1.—On mission and the Son: I, 43, 3, obj. 3; 43, 5, ad 1-2; 43, 6. ad 1-2. —That an invisible mission takes place for the sanctification of creatures (I, 43, 6, O.t.c.).—On the purpose of visible missions: I, 43, 7, ad 6.—On the participation of the angels in visible mission: I, 43, 7, obj. 5.

On the Sibyl on Christ: II-II, 2, 7, ad 3.

III. Creation.

That nothing comes to be unless the Omnipotent wills it to come, either by allowing it or by making it (I, 19, 12).— On the meaning of *to make* and *to create*: I, 45, 1, obj. 1 and ad 1.—That it is unfitting to say that God created things without reason (I, 47, 3, obj. 1).—That God did not create things without reason (I, 19, 5, obj. 1).—That because God is good we are (I, 5, 4, obj. 3 and ad 3; 13, 2; 19, 4, obj. 3; 104, 3, obj. 2).—That God's benefits are unfailing (I-II, 112, 3).— That the creating Spirit does not move Himself through time or through place (I, 9, 1, obj. 1).—On the work of propagation as distinguished from the work of creation: I, 45, 8, O.t.c.—That neither good nor bad angels can be the creators of anything (I, 45, 5, O.t.c.).—That the work of creation pertains to the production of formless matter and of a formless spiritual nature; and that these two are outside time and hence the creation of both is said to be before all days (I, 74, 1, ad 1).—That the formlessness of the corporeal and spiritual creature did not precede its formation in time (I, 62, 1, obj. 2; 63, 5, obj. 2; 66, 1; 69, 1).—That God made two things, one near Himself (the angels) and the other near nothing (prime matter) (I, 44, 2, O.t.c.; 54, 3, obj. 3).—That there are two creatures of God without time (I, 66, 4, obj. 1).—That the spiritual and corporeal creature was created in the beginning of time (I, 66, 4, O.t.c.).—That the two first creatures were the angelic nature and corporeal matter (I, 66, 4).—That God made two things, one of which was formed and the other (namely, the matter of corporeal things) was formless (I, 66, 2, obj. 1).

That names which signify relation to creatures are said of God temporally (I, 13, 7, O.t.c.).

IV. The Angels; the Demons.

That the angels are included in the first creation of things and are designated by the name *heaven* or *light* (I, 61, 1, ad 1). —That the angels were created in the upper part of the air (I, 61, 4, obj. 2).—

That the angels were created in grace (I, 62, 3, *O.t.c.*; 95, 1, *O.t.c.*).—That the angelic nature was created unformed and called *heaven*; then it was formed and called *light* (I, 62, 3, obj. 1).—That from their creation the angels enjoy the contemplation of the Word (I, 58, 1, *O.t.c.*).—That the love of charity is infused in the angels by the Holy Spirit (I, 60, 5, obj. 4).—That in the angels there is life which understands and senses (I, 54, 5, obj. 1).—That the angel knows himself (I, 56, 1, *O.t.c.*).—On the morning and evening knowledge of the angels: I, 58, 6 with *O.t.c.*; 58, 7 with *O.t.c.* and ad 2.— That things have a threefold being, namely, in the Word, in themselves and in the angelic understanding (I, 58, 6, obj. 3).—That the things which exist in the Word of God have proceeded in a twofold way, namely, into the angelic intellect and into their proper being (I, 56, 2; 89, 3).—That beings below the angels are so caused that they first come to be in the knowledge of the rational creature and then in themselves (I, 55, 2 with ad 1; *C.G.*, III, 59).—That the angelic mind can easily comprehend together all that it wishes (I, 58, 2, *O.t.c.*).—That the angels knew the mystery of the kingdom of God from the beginning (I, 64, 1, obj. 4 and ad 4; II-II, 2, 7, ad 1).—On whether the angels knew the mystery of the Incarnation: I, 57, 5, obj. 1.—On the angels and the thoughts of the heart: I, 57, 4.—On angels and assumed bodies: I, 51, 3, *O.t.c.*; 51, 3, ad 6.—That there are no passions in the angels (I, 59, 4, ad 2).— That before the confirmation or the fall of the angels, an angel saw things in the Word (II-II, 5, 1, obj. 1).—On whether the angel fell in the first moment of his creation: I, 63, 5 with ad 1; 63, 6, *O.t.c.* and ad 4.

That the wicked angels are ruled by the good (I, 109, 4, *O.t.c.*; *C.G.*, III, 83).— That corporeal matter does not obey the angels but rather God (I, 65, 4, *O.t.c.*; 110, 2, *O.t.c.*; 117, 3, *O.t.c.*).—That the good angels were separated from the wicked as light from darkness (I, 64, 1, obj. 5).—That demons are said to be aerial animals (I, 51, 1, obj. 1 and ad 1; *C.G.*, III, 109).—That the angels have no carnal sins; but they have spiritual sins: pride and envy (I, 63, 2, *O.t.c.*).—That the demons take pleasure even in the obscenities of carnal pleasures (I, 63, 2, obj. 1).—That the devil has power against those who despise the commandments of God, and he takes joy in this

unhappy power (I, 64, 3, obj. 1).—That in the angels there is a nature that cannot sin (I, 62, 8, *O.t.c.*).—That the cloudy atmosphere is as a prison for demons until the day of judgment (I, 64, 4, *O.t.c.*).

V. Creation and Order.
1. The Work of the Six Days.
2. Providence.
3. Order and Goodness.
4. Evil.

1. The Work of the Six Days.

On the order of creation in the six days: I, 74, 2.—That the seven days are one day represented under a sevenfold aspect (I, 74, 2).—On the meaning of the repose of the seventh day: I, 73, 2; 74, 1, ad 5.— On the Holy Spirit as moving over the formlessness of matter: I, 74, 3, ad 4.— On whether the heavens are animated: I, 70, 3.—On the formation of the body of woman: I, 92, 4, obj. 2-3 with *O.t.c.* and ad 2-3.—That we existed in Adam not only according to a seminal principle, but also corporeally (I, 119, 2, obj. 4 and ad 4).—That light holds the first place among bodies (I, 67, 2, obj. 1).—On the production of light as the formation of the formless spiritual and corporeal nature: I, 67, 4.—On the *heaven* which was made on the first and second day: I, 68, 1, ad 1.—On the waters above the firmament: I, 68, 2.—On the work of the third day: I, 69, 1 with ad 1-5.—On the production of the luminaries: I, 70, 1 with obj. 1 and ad 1.—On the production of fish and birds on the fifth day potentially: I, 71, 1.—That all things were created together (I, 62, 3; 70, 1, obj. 3).—On seminal principles: I, 62, 3; 70, 2, ad 5; 102, 1, ad 5; 115, 2 with *O.t.c.* and ad 4; I-II, 81, 4, *O.t.c.*—That as to his body man was made, in the work of the six days, according to the causal principles which God inserted into the corporeal creature (I, 91, 2, obj. 4).—That on the third day plants were produced, not actually, but according to their seminal principle (I, 69, 2; 74, 2, ad 1; 102, 1, ad 5).—That the germination of plants was not included in the work of the sixth day (I, 62, 1, ad 2).—That angels cannot change bodies to any form without the use of seminal principles (I, 91, 2; 110, 3, *O.t.c.*; 115, 2, obj. 2).

2. Providence.

That the will of God is the cause of all things that happen (I, 116, 4, obj. 2).— That the will of God is the cause of all motions (I-II, 79, 2, *O.t.c.*).—That the will or power of God is called by the name fate (I, 116, 2, obj. 1; 116, 4, obj.

2).—That the will of God is the first cause of health and sickness, rewards and punishments, grace and retribution (*C.G.*, III, 97).—That if a man wishes to call the will or power of God by the name *fate*, let him hold the doctrine but correct his language (I, 116, 1; *C.G.*, III, 93).—On the origin of the name *fate*: I, 116, 1, obj. 2.—On the ordering of second causes as a *series of causes*: I, 116, 2, ad 1.—On the influence of the stars on the human body: *C.G.*, III, 84.—On the magic arts, demons and miracles: I, 110, 4, obj. 2; 114, 4 with obj. 2, *O.t.c.* and ad 1-3; 115, 5, ad 3; 117, 4, ad 2; I-II, 9, 5, ad 3.—That nothing happens by chance in the world (I, 103, 7, ad 2; 116, 1, ad 2).

3. Order and Goodness.

That God loves His creature for two purposes, namely, that it should be and that it should endure (I, 74, 3, ad 3).—That God uses us for our own gain and for His own goodness (I, 62, 9, obj. 2).—That God is not the author of evil because He is not the cause of tending towards non-being (I, 49, 2, *O.t.c.*; 104, 3, obj. 1).—That if the power of God ceased to rule created things, their form and nature would all perish (I, 104, 1; *C.G.*, III, 65).—That if God did not conserve things they would be reduced to nothing (I, 9, 2).—On how God rules things: I, 103, 6, *O.t.c.*—That in the establishment of natural things we are not concerned with what God can do but with what suits the nature of things (I, 76, 5, ad 1).—That God leaves nothing without suitable parts (I, 103, 5, *O.t.c.*). —That individual creatures are good, but that the universe taken together is very good (I, 25, 6, obj. 3).—On the fittingness of all things in the universe: 1, 72, 1, ad 6.

That peace is the tranquillity of order (I, 103, 2, obj. 3).—That order pertains to the notion of the good (I, 109, 1, obj. 1).—That the nature of the good consists in measure, species and order (I-II, 63, 2).—That measure, species and order are the three universal goods in the things made by God (I, 5, 5, *O.t.c.*; 45, 7).—That measure, species and order are good; and that they are evil either because they are less than they ought to be or because they do not fit the things to which they are applied (I, 5, 5, ad 4).— That where these three [*i.e.*, measure, species and order] are great, there is a great good; where they are small, the good is small; where they are not at all,

there is no good (I-II, 85, 4, obj. 1).— That in so far as we are we are good (I, 5, 1, *O.t.c.*).—On the contribution of number, weight and measure to things: I, 5, 5, obj. 1.—That order is that disposition among equal and unequal things which gives to each thing its place (I, 96, 3, *O.t.c.*).—That God does not love all beings equally (I, 20, 3, *O.t.c.*).—That inequality in things comes from God and is not due to sin (I, 47, 2).—That according to the order of nature a living substance is higher than a non-living substance (I, 18, 4, obj. 3; 70, 3, obj. 2).— That in beings that are great without magnitude to be greater is to be better (I, 42, 1, ad 1; I-II, 52, 1).—That the whole corporeal creature is administered by God through the angels (I, 63, 7; 91, 2, obj. 1; 102, 2, ad 1).—That all bodies are administered by God through the spirit of life (I, 70, 3; 110, 1, *O.t.c.*; *C.G.*, III, 83).—That the lower things are ruled by the higher according to a certain order (I, 65, 3, obj. 1; 66, 3, obj. 2; 108, 6; 115, 3, *O.t.c.*; *C.G.*, III, 83; I-II, 9, 5, obj. 2).—That God moves the spiritual creature in time, and the corporeal creature in place and time (I, 10, 5, obj. 1; 12, 10, obj. 2; 25, 2, obj. 3; 57, 3, ad 2; 61, 2, ad 2; 85, 4, ad 1).—That bodies are acted upon and not agents; that God is an agent and not acted upon; that spiritual substances are agents and acted upon (I, 115, 1, obj. 1).—That an agent is nobler than a recipient (I, 79, 2, obj. 3; 82, 4, obj. 1; 92, 1, obj. 2; 115, 5, *O.t.c.*; I-II, 9, 2, obj. 1).

On miracles: I, 105, 7, obj. 2 and *O.t.c.*; 105, 8, obj. 1.—That God, the Creator of all natures, does nothing against nature (I, 105, 6, obj. 1; *C.G.*, III, 100).—That God sometimes acts against the customary course of nature, but never against the highest law because He does not act against Himself (I, 105, 6 with *O.t.c.*).— That that is natural to each thing which He made from Whom is all measure, number and order in nature (I, 105, 2, ad 1; *C.G.*, III, 100; I-II, 10, 4, obj. 2).

4. Evil.

That every part which is not in harmony with its whole is shameful (I-II, 92, 1, ad 3).—That evil could not possibly originate elsewhere than from good (I, 49, 1, *O.t.c.*).—That evil exists only in good (I, 48, 3, *O.t.c.*; I-II, 85, 2, *O.t.c.*). —That evil is so called because it injures (I, 48, 5, *O.t.c.*; *C.G.*, III, 11).—That evil is a privation of good (I, 14, 10, obj. 1). —That evil is the privation of measure

species and order (I-II, 84, 3, ad 2).—
That evil injures inasmuch as it takes
away good (I, 49, 4, obj. 2).—That evil
cannot entirely consume good (I, 48, 4,
O.t.c.).—On evil and the rule of the dia-
lecticians on contraries: I, 48, 3, ad 3.—
On the place of evil in the beauty of
world order: I, 19, 9, obj. 2.—That
though evils as evils are not good, yet
it is good that there should be not only
goods but also evils (I, 19, 9, obj. 1).

VI. Law.

1. The Eternal Law; Temporal Law.
2. The Old Law and the New Law.
3. Predestination.

1. The Eternal Law; Temporal Law.

That in no way is a thing withdrawn
from the law of the highest Creator and
Governor, by Whom the peace of the
universe is administered (I-II, 93, 6,
O.t.c.).—That just as the law of deeds
was written on table of stone, so the law
of faith is inscribed in the hearts of the
faithful (I-II, 106, 1).—That the law
of God is written in the hearts of men,
and no iniquity erases it (I-II, 94, 6,
O.t.c.).—That the laws of God written
by God in the hearts of the faithful are
the very presence of the Holy Spirit (I-
II, 106, 1; 106, 2, ad 3).—That in the
law of nature a precept could be found
which existed only to test man's obedience
(I-II, 102, 1, obj. 2).

That there are two laws, the one
eternal and the other temporal or human
(I-II, 91, 3, *O.t.c.*).—That the eternal law
is the law by which it is just that all
things be most ordered (I-II, 91, 2, obj.
1; 91, 3, obj. 1; 93, 2, obj. 2).—That the
notion of the eternal law is impressed
upon us (I-II, 93, 2, *O.t.c.*).—That the
eternal law is the highest reason to which
we must always submit (I-II, 93, 1,
O.t.c.).—That the law which is called
the highest reason cannot but appear
immutable and eternal (I-II, 91, 1, *O.t.c.*).
—That the eternal law is the law of
which men cannot judge (I-II, 93, 2, obj.
3).—That there evidently exists above
our mind a law which is called truth (I-
II, 93, 1, obj. 3).—That all knowledge of
truth is an irradiation and a participation
of the eternal law, which is immutable
truth (I-II, 93, 2).—That the eternal
law is the law by which the wicked merit
misery, and the good, eternal life (I-II,
93, 6, obj. 3).—That the Son of God is
not subject to divine providence or to
the eternal law; but He Himself is rather
the eternal law by a kind of appropriation (I-II, 93, 4, ad 2).—That the just

act under the eternal law (I-II, 93, 6).—
On the eternal law and the souls that
have deserted God: I-II, 93, 6.

That there is nothing just and lawful
in temporal law that man has not drawn
from the eternal law (I-II, 93, 3).—That
a law is not a law if it is not just (I-II,
95, 2; 96, 4).—That the community of
the state is established to last, not for
a short time, but for all time through
the succession of citizens (I-II, 96, 1).—
That though men judge temporal laws
when they establish them, nevertheless,
when these laws have been established
and confirmed, it is not permissible to
judge them but according to them (I-II,
96, 6, obj. 1).—That though temporal
law is just, it can in the course of time
be changed (I-II, 97, 1, *O.t.c.*).—On the
value of custom as law: I-II, 97, 3, *O.t.c.*
—An example of a just change in law:
I-II, 97, 1.—That human law cannot
punish or prohibit all evils (I-II, 91, 4).
—That the law which is written for the
government of people rightly permits
many things which are punished by the
divine providence (I-II, 93, 3, obj. 3;
96, 2, *O.t.c.* and ad 3).

2. The Old Law and the New Law.

On the precepts of the Decalogue:
I-II, 100, 4 with obj. 1 and *O.t.c.*; 100,
5; 100, 8, ad 3.

That in the Old Law there were
precepts both of the life to be led and of
the life that was foreshadowed (I-II,
99, 4, obj. 1).—That the promises of
temporal things are contained in the Old
Testament, and that is why it is called
Old; but the promise of eternal life pertains to the New Testament (I-II, 91,
5; 107, 1, ad 2).—That the letter of the
law is sometimes said to kill even with
respect to moral precepts because it prescribes what is good but does not furnish
the aid of grace for its fulfillment (I-II,
99, 2, ad 3; 100, 12, *O.t.c.*; 106, 2).—
That there is a small difference between
the Law and the Gospel, namely, that
between fear [*ti*mor] and love [*amor*]
(I-II, 91, 5; 107, 1, obj. 2).—That the
Sermon on the Mount contains all the
precepts by which the Christian life is
formed (I-II, 108, 3, *O.t.c.*).—That almost all the precepts of our Lord are
found in the Old Testament (I-II, 107,
3, ad 2).—On the coming of Christ in
the Jewish law: I-II, 103, 4.—That the
life of the Jewish people was prophetic
and figurative of Christ (I-II, 100, 12;
104, 2, ad 2; 114, 10, ad 1).—On the
permissions of our Lord to the Apostles:

I-II, 108, 2, ad 3.—On the guilt of St. Peter in relation to the Jewish law: I-II, 103, 4, ad 2.—On the New Law in relation to the judicial precepts of the Old: I-II, 108, 3, ad 2.—That the New Law forbade divorce altogether (I-II, 107, 4, obj. 3).

3. Predestination.

That the number of the predestined is certain (I, 23, 7, *O.t.c.*).—On the nature of predestination: I, 23, 1, obj. 3; 23, 2, obj. 2-3 and *O.t.c.*—That no one is saved whom God does not will to be saved (I, 19, 6, ad 1; 19, 8, obj. 1).—On the mystery of the divine election: I, 23, 5, ad 3; I-II, 98, 4 with ad 2; 106, 3, ad 1. Cf. I, 23, 4, ad 2.—That He Who created you without you will not justify you without you (I-II, 55, 4, obj. 6; 111, 2, obj. 2).—On the Book of Life: I, 24, 1, obj. 2; 24, 3, obj. 1.—On God in relation to all men, to the Jews and to Christians: II-II, 2, 8, obj. 2.

VII. Grace.

That grace not only shows what ought to be done, but also offers the means whereby men may do with love what they know they ought to do (I-II, 109, 4).—That there is no good that men do without grace, whether by thinking or willing or loving or acting (I-II, 109, 2, *O.t.c.*).—That man cannot live rightly unless God aids him with the eternal light of justice (I-II, 109, 9, *O.t.c.*).— That by co-operating God perfects in us what He begins by operating (I-II, 111, 2, *O.t.c.*).—On grace as prevenient and subsequent: I-II, 111, 3.—That operating grace is the faith that works through love (I-II, 110, 3, obj. 1).—That grace precedes charity (I-II, 110, 3, *O.t.c.*).— That when grace is given it is out of mercy; when it is not given, this is with justice (II-II, 2, 5, ad 1).—That man's merits begin from grace (I-II, 110, 4, obj. 2).—That one may obtain through prayers of petition what one does not merit (I-II, 114, 9, obj. 1 and ad 1).— That faith merits justification (I-II, 114, 5, obj. 1). But cf. *ibid.*, ad 1.—That it is a greater work to justify the ungodly than to create heaven and earth (I-II, 113, 9, *O.t.c.*).—That a man ought so to turn to God that he may always be made just by Him (I-II, 113, 3, obj. 3).—That those who are in grace need to receive the grace of preservance (I-II, 109, 10, *O.t.c.* and ad 3).—That inchoate charity merits increase, so that, having been increased, it may merit to be perfected (I-II, 113, 10; 114, 8, *O.t.c.*).—On grace

as specially signifying the remission of sins: I-II, 110, 1, ad 3.

VIII. Man.

1. The First Man.
2. The Image of God.
3. Soul; the Higher and Lower Reason.
4. Understanding; Certitude; Sensation.
5. Truth; Illumination; Wisdom and Vision.
6. Beatitude; *Use* and *Enjoyment*.
7. Habit; Virtue; the Virtues; Theological Virtues and Gifts.
8. Voluntariness and Sin; Sensuality; Vice and Sin; Original Sin; Sin and Punishment.
9. The Two Cities.

1. The First Man.

That the rectitude of man consists in the perfect subjection of the body to the soul (I, 99, 1).—On the unfailing reign of order in the state of innocence: I-II, 89, 3.—That nothing penal could exist in the state of innocence (I-II, 89, 3, *O.t.c.*). —That in the state of innocence nothing was lacking which a good will could desire (I, 96, 4, obj. 3).—On whether in the state of innocence God intended man to be ruled by man: I, 96, 4 with obj. 1. —On the tree of life and immortality: I, 97, 4.—On paradise: I, 102, 1 with *O.t.c.* and ad 2.—On the beatitude of the first man: I, 94, 1, obj. 1-2 and ad 1.— That only some passions were in the first man (I, 95, 2 with *O.t.c.*).—On generation in the state of innocence: I, 98, 2 with ad 2, 4.—On the state of original justice and evil: I, 94, 4.—On the disobedience of the flesh as a consequent punishment of man's transgression: I, 95, 1.—On pride and the seduction of Eve: I, 94, 4, ad 1.

2. The Image of God.

That intellectual creatures are so near God in likeness that nothing is nearer (I, 93, 2).—That God granted to man, and to no other creature, to be in His image (I, 93, 3, obj. 1).—That man is to the image of God in such a way that he is immediately formed by God (I, 93, 3, obj. 2; 106, 1, obj. 3).—That man excels other things not in the fact that God made him but in the fact that he was made to the image of God (I, 91, 4, ad 1).—That this is man's excellence, that God made him to His image in that He gave him an intellectual nature by which to rule over animals (I, 93, 2, *O.t.c.*).— That it is according to our minds that we are in the image of God (I, 14, 2, obj. 3).—That the image of the Trinity is found in the mind according to memory, understanding and will (I, 59, 1, *O.t.c.*).—That the image of God in the mind is for the remembering, the understanding and the love of God (I, 93, 8, *O.t.c.*).—On the image of the Trinity as found in the soul according to its acts: I, 93, 7, *passim.*—That the trinity which is in us we see rather than believe; the divine Trinity we believe rather than see (I, 93, 5, ad 3).—That when we seek a trinity in the soul, we seek it in the whole soul without separating the temporal activity of the soul from the contemplation of the eternal (I, 93, 8, obj. 2).—That when we know God a likeness of God comes to be in us (I, 12, 2, obj. 2).—On the image of God and the natural knowledge and love of God: I, 93, 8, ad 3.—That by the fact of being in the image of God the soul is fit to receive God through grace (I-II, 113, 10).—On the image of God in man as the image of a king on a silver coin: I, 93, 1, ad 2.— On image and likeness: I, 93, 1; 93, 9 with obj. 1.

3. Soul; the Higher and Lower Reason.

On Varro, who rightly held that man is neither the soul alone nor the body alone but soul and body together: I, 75, 4, *O.t.c.*—That it is evidently perverse and opposed to the Catholic Faith to say that God made the soul, not from the nothing, but from Himself (I, 90, 1, *O.t.c.*).—That there are not several [*i.e.*, several kinds of] human souls (I, 76, 2, obj. 6 and ad 6).—That the soul is not made either of corporeal or spiritual matter (I, 75, 5, *O.t.c.*).—On the error of those who think that the human mind is a body: I, 75, 2, *O.t.c.*—That the soul is called simple in comparison with the body because it does not occupy place (I, 75, 1, *O.t.c.*).—On the incorruptibility of the soul as based on the capacity of the intellect for truth: I, 61, 2, obj. 3.— On understanding and will as in the mind: I, 79, 1, obj. 2.—That mind, knowledge and love are in the soul substantially (I, 77, 1, obj. 1).—That memory, understanding and will are one life, one mind and one essence (I, 77, 1, obj. 1; 79, 6, *O.t.c.*; 79, 7, obj. 1).— That memory, intelligence and will are one essence, one life (I, 54, 1, ad 2).—On memory as in the mind: I, 54, 5, ad 2.— On the affections as movements of the soul: I-II, 113, 5.—On how the affections are known: I, 87, 4, obj. 3.—That the powers of the soul are not accidents (I,

77, 1, obj. 5).—That the soul is wholly in the whole body and wholly in each part of the body (I, 8, 4, obj. 5; 52, 2, obj. 1; 76, 8, *O.t.c.*).—That the soul administers the body through light and air, which are more like a spirit (I, 76, 7, obj. 1).

On the higher and lower reason: I, 79, 9 with obj. 3.—That the higher and lower reason are distinguished only by their functions (I, 79, 9, *O.t.c.*).—That to the superior part of the soul belongs what man has not in common with the beasts (I, 79, 6, obj. 1; 79, 8, *O.t.c.*; I-II, 55, 4, obj. 3).—That the higher reason aims at seeing and consulting the eternal (I-II, 16, 4, obj. 3; 74, 7, obj. 2; 74, 9 with obj. 1).—That the image of the Trinity is in the higher part of the reason, not in the lower (I, 79, 9, obj. 1). —That mind and spirit refer to an essence (I, 79, 1, obj. 1).—That the mind is a spirit or an essence (I, 79, 1, ad 1).— That the mind always remembers itself, always knows and loves itself (I, 93, 7, ad 4; 93, 8).—That memory, understanding and will are not three powers (I, 79, 7, ad 1).—That consent belongs to the higher reason (I-II, 15, 1, obj. 1). —That consent to pleasure belongs to the lower reason (I-II, 15, 4, obj. 1).

4. Understanding; Certitude; Sensation.

That to think is to have actual understanding (I-II, 109, 1, ad 3).—That the human mind cannot understand truth except by thinking (I-II, 109, 1, obj. 3). —That whatever is comprehended by knowledge is bounded by the comprehension of the knower (I, 14, 12, obj. 1).— That what comprehends itself is finite to itself (I, 14, 3, obj. 1).—That man understands that he understands (I, 87, 3, *O.t.c.*).—On the three kinds of vision, namely, corporeal (through the senses), spiritual (through the imagination) and intellectual (through the intellect): I, 78, 4, obj. 6; 79, 13, obj. 1.—On trinities in vision: I, 93, 6, ad 4.—That the mind does not seek to see itse[f as though it were absent; it seeks to distinguish itself as though it were present (I, 87, 1; *C.G.*, III, 46).—That the mind knows itself through itself because it is incorporeal (I, 87, 1, obj. 1; *C.G.*, III, 46).—That as the mind gathers the knowledge of corporeal things through the senses of the body, so it gathers the knowledge of incorporeal things through itself (I, 88, 1, obj. 1; 89, 2; *C.G.*, III, 46).—That the soul senses some things without the body.

and some through the body (I, 77, 5, obj. 3).—That those things which are in the soul by their essence are seen by intellectual vision (I, 12, 11, obj. 4).—On the intelligible as in the intellect according to memory: I, 107, 1.—That the intention of the will joins the seen body to the sight, and likewise the species in the memory to the sight of the soul thinking within (I-II, 12, 1, O.t.c.).—That of all signs employed by men words hold the first place (I-II, 99, 3, obj. 3).—That it is the duty of every teacher so to express himself as to be easily understood (I-II, 101, 2, obj. 1).—That one man cannot know one thing better than another can (I, 12, 6, obj. 2).—On whether the soul knows the future: I, 86, 4, ad 2.—On whether the angel can change man's imagination: I, 111, 3, obj. 3.

That that is comprehended which is so wholly seen that no part of it escapes the seer (I, 12, 7, obj. 2; 14, 3, ad 1).—That everything that understands itself comprehends itself (I, 14, 3, O.t.c.).—That the soul has a most certain knowledge of the things that are in it by their essence (I-II, 112, 5, obj. 1).—That to consider what is true as false is not natural to man as created, but is a punishment of man condemned (I, 94, 4, O.t.c.).—That in sleep the soul adheres to a likeness as to the reality itself (I, 94, 4, obj. 4).—That he who understands a thing otherwise than as it is does not understand it (I, 85, 7, obj. 1).—That he who is deceived does not understand that in which he is deceived (I, 17, 3, obj. 1; 85, 6, O.t.c.).

That the name of the sense of sight is transferred to all the other senses and even to all interior apprehension (I-II, 77, 5, ad 3; II-II, 1, 4, obj. 4).—That the body does not sense, but the soul through the body (I, 84, 6).—That body does not act on spirit (I, 84, 6, obj. 2).—That where the soul sees there it senses; where it senses there it lives; where it lives there it is (I, 8, 4, obj. 6).—That if all the senses of the body report according as they are affected, nothing else can be demanded of them (I, 17, 2, obj. 1).—That we must not expect pure truth from the senses of the body (I, 84, 6, obj. 1).—That the senses entrap us in error by their deceptive similitudes (I, 17, 2, O.t.c.).—On the survival of sensitive powers after death: I, 77, 8, obj. 6.—That God has never been seen by corporeal vision (I, 12, 3, O.t.c.).

5. Truth; Illumination; Wisdom and Vision.

That truth is not equal to the mind because then it would be as mutable as the mind (I, 16, 8, obj. 1).—That nothing is more eternal than the nature of a circle and that two and three are five (I, 16, 7, obj. 2).—That truth is a likeness of a principle, without any unlikeness (I, 16, 1; 16, 5, obj. 2; 39, 8, O.t.c.). —That truth is that by which is revealed that which is (I, 16, 1).—That truth is that which is seen (I, 16, 1, obj. 1).— That the true is that which is (I, 17, 4, obj. 1).—That if the true is that which is, then the false does not exist anywhere (I, 17, 1, obj. 1).—That only that which is true is understood (I, 58, 5, O.t.c.).—That things show nothing else than their form (I, 17, 1, obj. 2).—That every body is a true body and a false unity (I, 17, 1, O.t.c.).—On the tragedian as a false Hector: I, 17, 1; 17, 4, obj. 2.

That nothing is above the human mind except God (I, 16, 6, obj. 1).—That it belongs to the reason to judge of corporeal things according to the incorporeal and eternal exemplars which would not be immutable unless they were above the mind (C.G., III, 47).—That God illumines; that the reason is in the mind as sight in the eyes; and that the eyes of the mind are the senses of the soul (I-II, 109, 1, obj. 2).—On vision in the divine truth: C.G., III, 47.—That when we both see something is true, we see it in the immutable truth above our minds (I, 12, 11, obj. 3; 84, 5, O.t.c.; C.G., III, 47).— That we behold the inviolable truth from which we define as perfectly as we can what the mind of man ought to be in the light of the eternal exemplars (I, 87, 1). —That we know all things in the light of the first truth and judge of all through it (I, 88, 3, obj. 1; C.G., III, 47).—That as the air becomes bright when light is present, so man is illumined when God is present to him, but is in darkness so long as God is absent (I, 104, 1).—That the immutable rules of truth pertain to the reason according to its higher part (I, 79, 12, obj. 3).—That knowledge in the eternal exemplars does not mean that the divine ideas themselves are seen (I, 84, 5).—That in addition to the divine illumination we must derive our knowledge from things (I, 84, 5).—That there are many impure persons who know many truths (I-II, 109, 1, O.t.c.).— That the wicked as well as the good know many truths (I, 12, 12, ad 3).—On the need of divine illumination for learning: I, 12, 11, ad 3.—On *light* as used properly among spiritual realities and figuratively among corporeal realities: I, 67, 1, obj. 1. —That according as we perceive something eternal by the mind we are not in this world (I, 66, 3, obj. 3; 112, 1, ad 1).

That wisdom is concerned with eternal things, and science with temporal things (II-II, 4, 6, obj. 1).—That wisdom is said to be the knowledge of divine things (I, 1, 6).—On the kingdom of heaven as the beginning of perfect wisdom: I-II, 69, 2, ad 3.—That in the vision of God all that the mind will see it will see immutably (I, 93, 8, ad 4).—That no one is wise unless he understands the divine ideas (I, 15, 1, *O.t.c.*).—On the raising of St. Paul and Moses to the vision of God: I, 12, 11, ad 2.—On the manifold meaning of *caelum*: I, 68, 4.—On prophetic vision: I, 43, 7, ad 2.—That vision is the whole reward (I, 26, 2, *O.t.c.*).

6. Beatitude; *Use* and *Enjoyment.*

That all seek beatitude with one will (I, 82, 1, *O.t.c.*).—That the first truth is the end of all our desires and actions (II-II, 4, 2, ad 3).—That the Father, Son and Holy Ghost are the reality we must enjoy (I, 39, 3, obj. 3 and ad 3).— That happy is the man who knows God even if he does not know other things (I, 12, 8, ad 4; 26, 3).—That to reach God by the mind in any way whatsoever is a great beatitude (I, 12, 7).—That in the beatific vision we shall behold with one glance all that we shall see (I, 12, 10, *O.t.c.*; 58, 2; *C.G.*, III, 60).—That the souls of the blessed desire the glorification of the body (I-II, 67, 4, obj. 3). —That the kingdom of heaven, which is the reward of the poor, is heavenly beatitude (I-II, 69, 2, obj. 3).—That the rewards of the beatitudes can be fulfilled in this life (I-II, 69, 2 with *O.t.c.*).

That it is given to men to enjoy and to use (I-II, 11, 2, obj. 1).—That whoever clings to a thing with love clings to it either as enjoying it or as using it (I-II, 88, 1, obj. 3).—That to enjoy is to cling to a thing for its own sake with love (I-II, 11, 1, *O.t.c.*; 11, 4, *O.t.c.*).—That he who enjoys uses (I-II, 16, 3, obj. 1 and ad 1).—That it is the will through which we enjoy (I-II, 11, 3, obj. 3).—That we enjoy those things we know in which the will rests with delight (I-II, 11, 3; 70, 1, obj. 2).—That to enjoy is to use a reality itself with joy (I-II, 11, 4, obj. 1).—That

if a thing is for the sake of something else, we do not enjoy it (I-II, 11, 3, *O.t.c.*).—That use consists in directing the things we use to obtaining something else (I-II, 16, 1, obj. 1; 16, 2, obj. 1).—That all the things that were made were made for man's use (I-II, 16, 1, obj. 3).—That to use is to apply something to the purpose of the will (I-II, 16, 1, *O.t.c.*; 16, 3, obj. 2).—That only a rational animal can exercise use (I-II, 16, 2, *O.t.c.*).— That no one rightly uses God (I-II, 16, 3, *O.t.c.*).—That animals enjoy food and any bodily pleasure (I-II, 11, 2, *O.t.c.*). But cf. *ibid.*, ad 4.

7. Habit; Virtue; the Virtues; Theological Virtues and Gifts.

That the name *habit* is taken from the verb *to have* (I-II, 49, 1, obj. 1).—That habit is that by which a thing is done when there is need (I-II, 49, 3, *O.t.c.*; 94, 1, *O.t.c.*).—On habits in animals: I-II, 50, 3, ad 2.

That virtues are very great goods which no one can use badly (I-II, 57, 3, obj. 1; 66, 1, obj. 2; 68, 8, obj. 3).—That virtue is in the soul, not in the body, because the soul is ruled by the body; hence if one uses the body well, this is attributed to the soul (I-II, 56, 4, obj. 3).—That virtue is a good quality of the mind (I, 16, 4, obj. 3).—That all virtue is love (I-II, 56, 3, obj. 1).—That virtue is the order of love (I-II, 55, 1, obj. 4).— That virtue is right and perfect reason (I-II, 58, 2, obj. 3).—That virtue is the art of living rightly (I-II, 58, 2, obj. 1). —That virtue is the good use of free choice (I-II, 55, 1, obj. 2).—That it is virtue by which we live rightly (I-II, 56, 1, obj. 1; 65, 2, *O.t.c.*).—That virtue makes the soul to be best (I-II, 55, 3, *O.t.c.*).—That the ordering which is called virtue consists in enjoying what is to be enjoyed and in using what is to be used (I-II, 55, 1, obj. 4).—That the soul must pursue something in order that virtue might be able to be born in it; and this is God, for if we follow Him, we live well (I-II, 61, 5).—That God is the highest object to which a man ought to be disposed by virtue (I-II, 55, 2, obj. 3).— That we are conformed to God according to virtue (I-II, 59, 5, obj. 3).

That virtue is fourfold, as a result of the diverse affection of love itself (I-II, 61, 4, *O.t.c.*).—That the four cardinal virtues are the order of love (I-II, 62, 2, obj. 3).—That the virtues in the human soul are connected with one another (I-II,

65, 1, *O.t.c.*).—That those who are equal in fortitude are equal in prudence and temperance (I-II, 66, 2 with *O.t.c.*).— That the moral virtues remain after this life (I-II, 67, 4, obj. 1).—That pity is an act of virtue when it is subject to reason so that justice is preserved (I-II, 59, 1, ad 3).

That God is especially worshipped by faith, hope and charity (I-II, 101, 2, obj. 3).—On true virtues as presupposing faith: II-II, 4, 7.—That love makes the burdens of faith easy to bear (I-II, 107, 4, ad 3; 114, 4, obj. 2).—On the excellence of the virtue of charity: I-II, 68, 8, obj. 1.—That charity is a movement of the soul towards loving God and neighbor (I-II, 70, 1, ad 3).—That charity includes within itself all the cardinal virtues (I-II, 65, 3, *O.t.c.*).—That cupidity is the poison of charity (I-II, 99, 6, obj. 1).—That hope cannot be without love (I-II, 65, 4, obj. 3).—That hope presupposes love (I-II, 66, 6, obj. 2).—On wisdom and science: I-II, 66, 5, obj. 3.— That since God is the father of all, the worship of God likewise is called piety (I-II, 68, 4, ad 2).—On the motives of the beatitudes: I-II, 69, 3, ad 3.

9. The Two Cities.

On the two loves and the two cities: I, 60, 5, obj. 5; 108, 1; 108, 8.—That as the love of God, which makes the city of God, is the principle and root of all the virtues, so self-love, which makes the city of Babylon, is the root of all sins (I-II, 73, 1, obj. 3).—That self-love even to the contempt of God makes the city of Babylon (I-II, 77, 4, *O.t.c.*; 84, 2, obj. 3).— That the devil inspires evil affections upon his society (I-II, 80, 1, obj. 1).—That the devil rejoices especially in the sins of lust and idolatry (I-II, 73, 5, obj. 2).— On *world* as meaning the lovers of the world: I-II, 72, 3, obj. 3.

8. Voluntariness and Sin; Sensuality; Vice and Sin; Original Sin; Sin and Punishment.

That if something is necessary it is not voluntary (I, 82, 1, obj. 1).—That nothing is loved except what is known (I, 60, 1, *O.t.c.*).—That the intellect does not move the will necessarily (I-II, 9, 1, obj. 1; 58, 2).—That the will is the power by which we sin and also by which we live rightly (I, 82, 2, *O.t.c.*; I-II, 9, 6, obj. 3; 20, 1, *O.t.c.*; 74, 1, *O.t.c.*).—That God inclines the will of man to good and to evil (I-II, 79, 1, ad 1).—That it is not due to God that a man becomes more wicked (I, 19, 9, *O.t.c.*; I-II, 79, 3, obj. 1).—

That the first cause of sinning is the will (I-II, 74, 1, obj. 3; 75, 2, *O.t.c.*). Cf. I-II, 74, 2, obj. 1.—That every sin is so voluntary that it is not a sin unless it is voluntary (I-II, 71, 5, obj. 2; 74, 2, obj. 3). Cf. I-II, 6, 8, obj. 2; 76, 3, obj. 1.— That by a bad use of his free choice a man loses both himself and it (I, 83, 2, obj. 3).—That there cannot be sin unless the intention of the mind yields to and serves the evil action (I-II, 15, 4, *O.t.c.*; 74, 7, ad 2).—That the mind of man becomes the servant of lust only by its own will (I-II, 80, 1, *O.t.c.*).—That evil is not in things but in the use of sinners (I-II, 18, 2, obj. 1).—That there is sadness and grief only in the case of those things which are opposed to the will (I, 113, 7 with obj. 2).—That the greater the temptation, the lesser the sin (I-II, 77, 6, *O.t.c.*).—That what we do while sleeping is not imputed as sin (I, 84, 8, *O.t.c.*).

On the origin of the name *sensuality*: I, 81, 1.—That sensuality is distinguished from the higher and lower reason which are concerned with knowledge (I, 81, 1, obj. 2).—On sensuality as signified by the serpent: I, 79, 12, obj. 2; 81, 3, obj. 1; I-II, 74, 3, obj. 2.—That if the will is perverse, the movements of the passions are perverse; but if the will is right, then, far from being blameworthy, the movements of the passions are praiseworthy (I-II, 59, 2, *O.t.c.*).—That the inordinate movement of concupiscence, which is a sin of sensuality, can be also in those who are in grace (I-II, 74, 4, *O.t.c.*).— That the movement of the members does not always obey reason (I-II, 17, 9, obj. 3 and ad 3).

That all natures owe their being natures to God; and they are vicious in so far as they depart from the art by which they were made (I-II, 71, 2, ad 4).—That when the light of truth rightly deserts the transgressor of the law, he becomes blind (I-II, 110, 1, *O.t.c.*).—That every vice, in that it is a vice, is against nature (I-II, 71, 2, *O.t.c.*).—That vice is a quality according to which the wicked soul is disposed (I-II, 71, 1, *O.t.c.*).—That vice is what is lacking to the perfection of nature (I-II, 71, 1).—That since vice is opposed to nature, the malice of vices increases according as the integrity of natures is diminished (I-II, 73, 8, *O.t.c.*).

That a sin is a deed, a word or a desire against the eternal law (I-II, 19, 4, *O.t.c.*; 21, 1, *O.t.c.*; 71, 2, obj. 4; 71, 6, obj. 1; 72, 1, *O.t.c.*; 75, 1, *O.t.c.*; 88, 1, obj. 1).—

That in that which he cannot avoid no
one sins (I-II, 74, 3, obj. 2; 109, 8, obj.
1).—That sin is nothing else than to
neglect eternal things and to pursue temporal things (I-II, 71, 6, obj. 3).—That
sin is the will to hold or to acquire what
justice forbids (I-II, 71, 6, obj. 2).—
That sin is the privation of measure,
species and order (I-II, 85, 4, obj. 2).—
That sin is in the lower and in the higher
reason (I-II, 74, 5, O.t.c.).—That to consent to the accomplishment of sin belongs
to the higher reason (I-II, 74, 7, O.t.c.).—
On the three degrees of sin: I-II, 72, 7,
obj. 1. Cf. I-II, 74, 8, obj. 6.—On the
source of all sin: I-II, 72, 3, obj. 3; 77,
4, obj. 3.—On the four consequences of
sin: I-II, 85, 3, obj. 5.—That the act of
sin is not a reality (I-II, 79, 2, obj. 1).—
That some sin through ignorance (I-II,
76, 1, O.t.c.).—That some things done
through ignorance are rightly reproved
(I-II, 76, 3, O.t.c.).—That to turn from
sin is not the same as not to have sin
(I-II, 113, 2, ad 3).—That if the smallest sins are neglected, they kill (I-II, 88,
4, obj. 1).—That it is a crime [i.e., mortal
sin] which deserves damnation, while
venial sin does not (I-II, 88, 1, O.t.c.).
On lingering delectation: I-II, 74, 6,
ad 3.—On the sin of lingering delectation
as in the lower reason: I-II, 74, 6, O.t.c.
—That consent to delectation without the
determination to fulfill the act belongs to
the lower reason (I-II, 74, 6, obj. 3).—
That man will be damned unless sins of
consent to delectation are remitted
through the grace of Christ (I-II, 74, 8,
O.t.c.).—On concupiscence of the eyes
and curiosity: I-II, 77, 5.—That pride insinuates itself even into good works so
that they perish (I-II, 55, 4, obj. 5; 88,
3, obj. 3).—That it is a sin when the flesh
lusts against the spirit (I-II, 80, 3, obj. 3).
—That evil insinuates itself through all
the sensible approaches to the mind (I-II,
80, 3, obj. 3).
That all posterity was corrupted in
Adam (I-II, 81, 4, obj. 1).—That a
seminal principle alone causes the transmission of original sin (I-II, 81, 4, O.t.c.).
—That concupiscence is the guilt of original sin (I-II, 82, 3, O.t.c.).—That lust
transmits original sin to the offspring (I-
II, 82, 4, obj. 3).—That those who are
punished only for original sin receive a
most gentle punishment (I-II, 87, 5, obj.
2).—That in no sentence is it required
that punishment be equal to the guilt in
duration (I-II, 87, 3, ad 1).—That children are not punished for their parents

unless they share in the guilt either by
origin or by imitation (I-II, 81, 2, ad 1).
That punishment is just and given for
some sin (I-II, 87, 7, O.t.c.).—That just
punishments are from God (I-II, 87, 2,
obj. 2).—That the unjust suffer spiritual
punishments in this life (I-II, 69, 2, ad 2).
—That God allows some men to fall into
sin in order that by recognizing their sin
they may become humble and converted
(I-II, 79, 4).—That sorrow for a good
lost by punishment is the witness to a
good nature (I, 64, 3, ad 3).—That the
Lord's Prayer is said daily for the remission of venial sins (I-II, 74, 8, obj. 6).—
That whoever denies that we should pray
lest we enter temptation should be removed from the hearing of men (I-II,
109, 8, O.t.c.).

IX. Scriptural Interpretations.
Scriptural Interpretations: Gen., i. 2 (I,
66, 1, obj. 1 and ad 1). Gen., ii. 15 (I, 102,
3). Exod., xxxiii. 11 (I-II, 98, 3, ad 2).
Isaias, xi. 2 and Matt., v. 3 (I-II, 68, 7,
O.t.c.; 69, 1, obj. 1). Matt., vi. 22-23 (I-
II, 12, 1, obj. 1-2). Matt., xii. 45 (I-II,
68, 1, obj. 2). Matt., xxvi. 39 (I-II, 19, 9,
O.t.c.). John, vi. 2 (I, 92, 3, ad 1). John,
viii. 17 (I-II, 105, 2, ad 8). John, xxi. 20
(I, 20, 4, obj. 3 and ad 3). Rom., ii. 14
(I-II, 109, 4, ad 1). Rom., vii. 15 (I-II,
74, 3, O.t.c.). Rom., vii. 23 (I-II, 83, 1,
obj. 1 and ad 1). I Cor., iii. 12 (I-II,
89, 2). I Cor., xiii. 12 (I, 12, 2, O.t.c.).
II Cor., vii. 4 (I, 12, 9, obj. 3). Gal., v.
22 (I-II, 11, 3, ad 1; 70, 3, ad 4; 70, 4).
Ephes., iii. 10 (I, 117, 2, ad 1).

X. St. Augustine as a Historical Source.
On the ancient naturalists: I, 2, 1, ad
2; 44, 2; C.G., III, 84.—On Anaxagoras:
I, 70, 3.—On Plato: I, 6, 4; 15, 3, obj. 4;
44, 1; 66, 1, ad 2 in contr.; 66, 2.—On the
Platonists: I, 32, 1, obj. 1 and ad 1; 63, 7;
C.G., III, 109.—On the Peripatetics: I-II,
59, 2.—On Democritus and the Epicureans: I, 22, 2; 84, 6.—On the Stoics:
I-II, 59, 2; 59, 3; 66, 1.—On Posidonius:
I, 116, 1.—On Varro: I, 90, 1.—On Cicero: I, 116, 1; I-II, 59, 1, obj. 3; 67, 1;
105, 2 with obj. 10.—On Hermes: C.G.,
III, 104.—On Apuleius: I, 115, 5.—On
Porphyry: I, 63, 4, obj. 1; 66, 3; 115, 5
with obj. 3; C.G., III, 106, 107.—On
Aulus Gellius: I-II, 59, 2.
On the twofold opinion of the philosophers who held the eternity of the
world: I, 46, 2, ad 1; 46, 3.—On the divine will in the philosophers: I, 19, 5,
ad 2.—On the world soul: I, 3, 8; 51,
1, ad 1.—On the Manicheans: I, 8, 3;
90, 1; C.G., III, 15; I-II, 106, 4, ad 2

On Arius: I, 27, 1; 42, 1, ad 2.—On the Chiliastae: *C.G.*, III, 27.—On Eunomius: I, 42, 1, ad 2.—On Montanus and Priscilla: I-II, 106, 4, ad 2.—On the Priscillianists: *C.G.*, III, 85.—On Pelagianism: I-II, 81, 1; 100, 10, obj. 3; 109, 4, *O.t.c.*—On Sabellius: I, 27, 1.—On Valentine: I, 34, 2, obj. 2 and ad 2.

On St. Hilary: I-II, 16, 3, ad 3.

AUGUSTINE, PSEUDO-,
Cf. I, 110, 4; 114, 4; I-II, 109, 5; 109, 8, ad 3; 110, 4, obj. 1. Cf. also Alcher of Clairvaux, Ambrosiaster and Fulgentius.

AUSONIUS, PSEUDO-,
Cf. I-II, 96, 5, ad 3.

AVERROES [THE COMMENTATOR],
That God is the measure of all substances (I, 3, 5, obj. 2).—That God lacks no perfection found in any genus (I, 4, 2).—That only incorruptible substances are subject to providence, while those that are corruptible are subject to providence in their species (I, 22, 2).—That it is contrary to the nobility of God to exercise providence over material things (*C.G.*, III, 76).—That the world did not begin to be, or otherwise there would have existed a vacuum before it (I, 46, 1, obj. 4).—That time never began, nor will end, and hence neither will motion (*ibid.*, obj. 7). Cf. also *ibid.*, obj. 1, 2, 5, 6.—That the substance of the agent intellect is its own operation (I, 54, 1, obj. 1).—That separate substances have no other powers but intellect and will (I, 54, 5).—That only the form belongs to the essence of the species, while matter is part of the individual, not of the species (I, 75, 4). Cf. also I, 85, 1, ad 2.—That the possible intellect is joined to this or that particular body by means of an intelligible species (I, 76, 1).—That there is one intellect in all men and that a diversity in phantasms causes the diversity in the intellectual operations of men (I, 76, 2).—That there is one possible intellect in all men (I, 117, 1).—That the agent intellect is substantially separate from the soul (I, 79, 4).—That in this life man can finally come to know separate substances (I, 88, 1).—How this takes place (*ibid.* and *C.G.*, III, 41; 43).—That the teacher does not cause knowledge in the student accord-

ing to the manner of a natural agent (I, 117, 1, ad 2).—That food is truly changed into true human nature (I, 119. 1).—That a habit is that whereby one acts when he wills to do so (I, 107, 1; I-II, 49, 3, *O.t.c.*; 50, 1, obj. 1; 51, 1, obj. 1).—On the sensitive powers as the subject of habits, cf. I-II, 50, 4.—Averroes as a Historical Source: Cf. I, 7, 4; 9, 1; 10, 6; 11, 1; 13, 7; 14, 11; 76, 3; 76, 4, ad 3; 79, 2, ad 2; 79, 3, ad 2; 88, 1; 88, 2; 104, 2; 105, 5; 118, 1; *C.G.*, III, 42; 44; 69.

AVICEBRON,
That what the intellect distinguishes is also distinct in reality (I, 50, 2).—That angels are composed of matter and form (I, 50, 2, obj. 2; 4).—That the matter of spiritual and corporeal substances is the same (I, 50, 2). (For St. Thomas' criticisms, cf. *ibid.*)—That the matter of all bodies is the same (I, 66, 2).—That things proceeded from God hierarchically (I, 65, 3).—That no corporeal substance is active (I, 115, 1, obj. 2-4).—That all actions which seem to be the actions of bodies are the work of a spiritual power penetrating through them (I, 115, 1).— That a corporeal form is impeded by quantity from acting on another body (*ibid.*). Cf. also *C.G.*, III, 69.

AVICENNA,
That the *one* which is convertible with being adds something to being (I, 11, 1, ad 1).—That God precedes the world only in nature (I, 46, 1, obj. 8).—That the world is from eternity since God, Who is its author, is eternal (*ibid.*, obj. 9).— That the world proceeds from God necessarily, and, consequently, that all things happen of necessity (I, 115, 6; *C.G.*, III, 86-87).—That the world proceeded from God mediately (I, 47, 1). (Cf. *ibid.* for St. Thomas' criticism; cf. also I, 65, 3).— That the angels, acting in the power of God, produced souls (I, 90, 3).—(According to St. Thomas, Avicenna does not repudiate the term *creation*: cf. I, 46, 2, ad 2).—That angels have a universal knowledge of singulars (I, 57, 2).—That the forms of bodies do not subsist separately, as Plato said, but in the intellects of separate substances, from which they come to bodies (I, 65, 4). (On how Avicenna and Plato agree and disagree in this problem, according to St. Thomas.

cf. I, 84, 4; 110, 2.) For a criticism, cf. *C.G.*, III, 69; 103.—That the agent intellect is substantially separate from the soul (I, 79, 4).—On the division of intellects, cf. I, 79, 10.—That the soul is joined to the body as its mover (I, 76, 1).—That there are five interior sensitive powers (I, 78, 4, *O.t.c.*).—That the intelligible species cannot be preserved in the possible intellect (I, 79, 6; cf. also I, 89, 5 and I-II, 67, 2).—That the senses are necessary to the soul in order to rouse it to turn to the agent intellect (I, 84, 4). (For St. Thomas' criticism, cf. *ibid*. For St. Thomas' criticism of the notion that the body is an impediment to knowledge, cf. I, 89, 1).—That science and virtue are from the outside (I-II, 63, 1).—On Avicenna and Plato on the question of providence, cf. I, 110, 1, ad 3.

BASIL THE GREAT, ST.,

Most of the references to St. Basil occur in the treatise on the work of the six days: Cf. I, 66, 1; 3; *ibid.*, ad 3-4; 67, 4, and ad 4; 68, 1; 2, and ad 2-3; 4; 69, 1, ad 1 and 5; 70, 1, ad 4; 70, 3; 71, and ad 1; 72, and ad 1; 74, 1-2; 74, 3, ad 1, 2, 4, 6, 7.—Conscience as meaning synderesis: I, 79, 13; I-II, 94, 1, obj. 2.—Some trinitarian opinions: I, 33, 3, obj. 2 and ad 2; 34, 2, obj. 5 and ad 5.

BEDE THE VENERABLE, ST.,

On the work of the six days, cf. I, 66, 3; 68, 1, ad 1; 68, 4; 69, 1, ad 1; 69, 2; 70, 1; 71, and ad 1; 72. Cf. also, I, 96, 1, ad 2.—On the precepts given by Christ to the Apostles: cf. I-II, 108, 2, ad 3.

BENEDICT, ST.,

Cited: I-II, 13, 5, obj. 3.

BERNARD OF CLAIRVAUX, ST.,

That among all things called *one*, the unity of the divine Trinity holds the first place (I, 11, 4, *O.t.c.*).—Bernard's report of Gilbert de la Porrée: I, 28, 2.—That all spirits need a corporeal instrument (I, 51, 1, obj. 1). Cf. St. Thomas' interpretation: *ibid.*, ad 1.—That free choice is "a faculty of the will and the reason", and "the habit of a soul that is master of itself" (I, 83, 2, obj. 2). For St. Thomas' interpretation of *faculty* and *habit*, cf. *ibid.*, ad 2.

BOETHIUS,

Definitions cited: Eternity (I, 10, 1, obj. 1; 10, 4; *C.G.*, III, 61); providence (I, 22, 1); fate (I, 116, 1-2, *O.t.c.*; 116, 3, obj. 2; 116, 4, obj. 3; *C.G.*, III, 93); person (I, 29, 1, obj. 1); beatitude (I, 26, 1, obj. 1; *C.G.*, III, 63); liberty (I-II, 17, 1, ad 2).—Trinitarian citations: I, 28, 1, obj. 1-2; 28, 3, *O.t.c.*; 36, 1, obj. 2; 39, 1; 40, 2, *O.t.c.*; 41, 1, obj. 1.—That an argument from authority is weakest (I, 1, 8, obj. 2).—That some propositions are known by all in common; others are known only to the learned (I-II, 94, 2). Cf. also I, 2, 1; 51, 1, obj. 1; I-II, 94, 4.—That a simple form cannot be a subject (I, 3, 6, *O.t.c.*; 29, 2, ad 5; 50, 2, obj. 2; 54, 3, obj. 2; 77, 1, obj. 6).—That the reason cannot grasp a simple form (I, 12, 12, obj. 1).—That the flowing now produces time; the fixed now, eternity (I, 10, 2, obj. 1).—On eternity and time, cf. also the comparisons (I, 79, 8, obj. 2; 116, 3, obj. 1).—That God carries the world in His mind, forming it to His image (I, 93, 2, obj. 2).—That God governs all things through Himself (*C.G.*, III, 83).—That the Highest Good rules all things strongly, and disposes them sweetly (I, 103, 8, *O.t.c.*).—That in God *that which is* [*quod est*] and *that by which it is* [*quo est*] do not differ (I, 40, 1, *O.t.c.*).—That beings other than God are good by participation (I, 6, 3, *O.t.c.*).—That for things to be good is not the same as for them to be (I, 5, 1, obj. 1 and ad 1).—That unity belongs to the essence of goodness because things desire unity in the same way that they desire goodness (I, 103, 3).—That that is truly one which does not admit of number (I, 30, 1, obj. 3).—That *good* refers to the essence; *just*, to the act (I, 21, 1, obj. 4). Cf. I, 27, 5, ad 2.—That the forms which are in matter come from the forms which are without matter (I, 65, 4, obj. 1; *C.G.*, III, 24).—That genera and species subsist; individuals subsist and also substand (I, 29, 2, *O.t.c.*).—That nature begins from what is perfect (II-II, 1, 7, obj. 3). —On *nature* as having many meanings: I-II, 10, 1.—That sense, imagination, reason and intelligence behold the same man differently (I, 79, 10, ad 2).—That reason belongs only to mankind, intelligence alone to God (I, 79, 10, ad 2).—On intellectual knowledge according to the Stoics, cf. *C.G.*, III, 84.—That that whose end is good is likewise good (I-II, 18, 4, *O.t.c.*).—That vices must be uprooted before virtues are sown (I-II, 100, 6, obj. 2).

—That incorporeal beings are not in place
(I, 8, 2, obj. 1).—That accidents cannot
be changed (II-II, 4, 4, obj. 4).—On
faith as a mean between contrary heresies: I-II, 64, 4, obj. 3.—On the origin
of the name *person*: I, 29, 3, obj. 2.—
On how some things transcend fate: I,
116, 4.—On evil: *C.G.*, III, 71.—On
things as formed according to the nature
of numbers: *C.G.*, III, 97.

BONAVENTURE, ST.,
On the difference between eternity, time
and aeviternity: I, 10, 5.—On future contingents: I, 14, 13, ad 2.—Trinitarian
opinions: I, 30, 3; 32, 1, obj. 2; 35, 2;
36, 4, ad 7; 40, 2; 41, 5; 43, 8.—That
angels are composed of matter and form
because everything in a genus is composed of matter and form (I, 50, 2, obj.
1); because everything having the properties of matter, viz., to be a subject and
a recipient, contains matter (*ibid.*, obj.
2); because they are not pure act (*ibid.*,
obj. 3); because, as creatures, they are
limited forms (*ibid.*, obj. 4).—That the
angels were not created in grace (I, 62,
3). Cf. I, 63, 5; II-II, 5, 1.—That the
soul is composed of matter and form, because where the properties of matter are
found, it also is found (I, 75, 5, obj. 2);
because it is not a pure form (*ibid.*, obj.
4).—That the soul is in the body as God
is in the world (I-II, 17, 8, obj. 2).—On
the mediation of light in the union of
soul and body: I, 76, 7.—On the distinction of the external senses: I, 78,
3.—That *free choice* is the name of a
habit (I, 83, 2).—On intellectual knowledge in the eternal exemplars: I, 84, 5.—
On some opinions on the first man: I, 89,
3; 95, 1; 96, 1, ad 2; 98, 2, ad 3; 102, 2,
obj. 4.—On the conditions of justification:
I-II, 113, 6.—On merit and eternal life: I-
II, 114, 7, ad 3.—That human acts are
divided into good, evil and indifferent (I-
II, 19, 5).—That there are twelve articles
of faith (II-II, 1, 8).—On formed and
formless faith: II-II, 4, 4; 5, ad 4.

Book of Causes,
Cf. *Liber de Causis*

CAESAR, JULIUS,
That at one time among the Germans
it was not thought wrong to rob (I-II,
94, 4).

CANDIDUS THE ARIAN,
On twelve modes of generation: I, 42,
2, obj. 1.

CASSIODORUS,
That the separated soul knows singulars by abstracting from sensible things
(I, 89, 7).—Commentary on *Psalm* cxviii.
102 (I-II, 94, 4, obj. 2).

CHALCIDIUS,
Quotes some unnamed authors according to whom Plato held matter to be
uncreated (I, 15, 3, ad 3).

CICERO,
That the fixed order of the world reveals its government, as does a well-ordered house (I, 103, 1).—That human affairs are not subject to the divine providence (I, 22, 2, ad 4; cf. also *C.G.*, III,
94, [4]).—That virtue is a habit after the
manner of a nature, in accord with reason
(I-II, 56, 5; 56, 6, obj. 1; 58, 1, obj. 3;
58, 4, obj. 1; 71, 2, ad 3).—That what
health is to the body virtue is to the soul
(I-II, 55, 1, obj. 1).—That the virtues are
the health of the soul (I-II, 59, 2, obj. 2;
71, 1, obj. 3).—That the passions are diseases of the soul (I-II, 59, 2, obj. 2; 59, 3,
obj. 3; 71, 1, ad 3; 77, 3, *O.t.c.*).—That
he who has not one virtue has none (I-
II, 65, 1, *O.t.c.*).—On the interconnection
of the virtues: I-II, 61, 4, ad 1.—That all
the virtues are equal (I-II, 73, 2, obj. 3).
—That the cardinal virtues are the principal virtues (I-II, 61, 3, *O.t.c.*).—On the
parts of prudence: I-II, 57, 6, obj. 4.—On
providence as part of prudence: I, 22, 1,
obj. 1.—On the several parts in fortitude,
justice and the other virtues: I-II, 54, 4,
obj. 2.—On religion as part of justice: I-
II, 99, 5, ad 1.—On justice as part of vir-
tuousness [*honestas*]: I-II, 95, 3, obj. 3.
—On piety as a special virtue which directs one to the good of one's country: I-
II, 60, 3, ad 2.—On those who say that
they despise power and public office: I-
II, 61, 5, obj. 3. But cf. *ibid.*, ad 3.—That
he who kills his servant sins once, but he
who kills his father commits many sins
(I-II, 73, 9, obj. 2; 73, 7).—On human
custom and the development of law: I-
II, 91, 3; 90, 2, *O.t.c.*—On the problem
of the division of the good: I, 5, 6, obj.
2.—Oratorical citations: I-II, 7, 1, obj. 1;
7, 3; II-II, 1, 6.—Definition of glory:
C.G., III, 29.—Cicero as a Historical

Source: I, 88, 1; 89, 1; 103, 1; I-II, 59, 2, ad 1; 70, 3.

CLEMENT OF ROME, PSEUDO-,
On Simon Magus and the magic arts: I, 117, 4, obj. 2.

CORPUS IURIS CIVILIS,
Digesta: cf. I-II, 90, 1, obj. 3; 92, *Introd.*; 92, 2, obj. 1; 94, 2; 95, 2, obj. 4; 95, 4; 96, 1, *O.t.c.*; 96, 5, obj. 3; 96, 6; 97, 2.—*Codex*: cf. I-II, 90, 4, obj. 3.

COSTA-BEN-LUCA,
That the soul is joined to the body by means of a corporeal spirit (I, 76, 7).

DIONYSIUS THE PSEUDO-AREOPAGITE,
Divisions:
   I. Faith.
   II. God; Creation; the Divine Names.
   III. Providence; Order (hierarchy); Good; Evil.
   IV. The Angels; the Demons.
   V. Man.
   VI. Dionysius as an Interpreter and a Source.
   I. Faith.
That faith is the enduring foundation of believers, rooting them in truth and giving evidence of the truth in them (II-II, 4, 1).—That faith is concerned with the simple and ever-existing truth (II-II, 1, 1, *O.t.c.*).—That the arguments of the saints in proof of what belongs to faith proceed from the authority of Sacred Scripture (II-II, 1, 6, ad 2).—That we should not in any way say or think anything of the supersubstantial hidden divinity except what is divinely revealed to us in sacred writings (I, 29, 3, obj. 1; 32, 2, obj. 1; 36, 2, obj. 1; 39, 2, obj. 2). —That Hierotheus is taught not only by learning, but also by suffering divine things (I, 1, 6, ad 3).—That the ray of the divine revelation is not destroyed because of the sensible figures in which it is veiled (I, 1, 9, ad 2).—That it is more fitting that divine things should be taught in Scripture under the figures of lowly bodies rather than those of noble bodies (I, 1, 9, ad 3).—That the New Law is a figure of future glory (I, 1, 10).
   II. God; Creation; the Divine Names.
That God does not exist in a certain way, but absolutely and unlimitedly pre-possesses all being in Himself (I, 4, 2; 75, 5, ad 1).—That God is above existing things (I, 12, 1, obj. 3).—That God does not enter into composition with things (I, 3, 8, *O.t.c.*).—That God is above all substance and life (I, 13, 3, ad 2).—That God cannot be comprehended by anything (I, 12, 1, ad 1).—That the being of God alone is absolutely infinite, comprehending all things in itself (I, 54, 2).— That God pre-possesses unitedly all existing things (I, 4, 2, *O.t.c.*; 91, 1).— That the being of all things is the Godhead, Who is above being (I, 3, 8, obj. 1). —That things pre-exist in God according to their simple being (I, 57, 1).—That all things pre-exist in God (I, 80, 1).— That God is all things, as being their cause (I, 4, 2).—That God knows what is dark through His own light (I, 14, 10). —That God does not know things according to an idea (I, 15, 1, obj. 1).
That as the sun illumines all things without preference, so the divine good sends forth the rays of its goodness to all existing things (I, 19, 4, obj. 1; 23, 4, obj. 1).—That the ray of the sun has a great likeness to the divine goodness (I, 93, 2, obj. 2).—That every procession of a divine manifestation comes to us from the movement of the Father of lights (I, 9, 1, ad 2).—That to create is common to the whole Godhead (I, 45, 6, *O.t.c.*).— That the divine goodness is in a way moved and proceeds to things, in so far as it communicates itself to them (I, 73, 2).—That every being, in whatever manner it be, must be derived from the first being (I-II, 79, 2).—That all things are good, beings and living things by participation in God (I, 75, 5, obj. 1).—That life participates in being itself, as does every form (I, 75, 5, ad 4).—That things are like God according as they imitate Him, and unlike Him according as they fall short of their cause (I, 4, 3, ad 1).
That we name God from creatures, as a cause from its effects (I, 5, 2, ad 1; 13, 2, obj. 2; 13, 6, obj. 2-3).—That the name *good* reveals excellently all God's effects (I, 13, 11, obj. 2).—On *good* as prior to *being* among divine names: I, 5, 2, obj. 1.—On *light* as one of the intelligible names of God: I, 67, 1, obj. 2.— That negations are true of God, but affirmations are vague (I, 13, 12, obj. 1). (On *vague*, cf. *ibid.*, ad 1).—That names like *good*, *wise*, etc., are more truly denied of God than affirmed (I, 13, 3, obj. 2).— That God is incomprehensible and above all celestial minds (I, 56, 3, obj. 1).—

That the material likenesses of immaterial things are very unlike (I, 88, 2, ad 1).—That higher things cannot in any way be known through the likenesses of a lower order of things (I, 12, 2).—That we cannot apprehend God either by sense or imagination or opinion or reason or science (I, 12, 1, obj. 1; 13, 1, obj. 1).—That when Scripture says that someone has seen God, the meaning is that certain figures, sensible or imaginary, representing something divine are formed in him (I, 12, 11, ad 1).—That it is impossible to apprehend the intelligible by the sensible, the simple by the composite and the incorporeal by the corporeal (I, 88, 2, *O.t.c.*).—That it is impossible to touch God (I, 105, 2, obj. 1 and ad 1).

III. Providence: Order (hierarchy); Good; Evil.

That the Godhead is He Who sees all things with perfect providence and goodness (I, 13, 8).—That the cause of all things is, by the abundance of His loving goodness, outside Himself as a providence over all things (I, 20, 2, ad 1).—That God contains all things in a perfect providence and goodness and accomplishes all things by Himself (I, 103, 4, *O.t.c.*).—That God gathers all things in all things (I, 55, 1, obj. 3).—That the true justice of God consists in this, that He gives to all things what is proper to their dignity and preserves the nature of each thing in its proper order and power (I, 21, 1).—That it does not belong to the divine providence to corrupt nature but to preserve it (I, 22, 4, *O.t.c.*; 48, 2, ad 3; I-II, 10, 4; 51, 4, obj. 2).—That it belongs to divine justice not to weaken the strength of the virtuous by means of material gifts (I-II, 87, 7, ad 2).—That God directs all things to the love of Himself (I-II, 109, 3; 109, 6).—That God inclines and turns all things to Himself as to the last end (I-II, 79, 1).

That nothing exists which does not participate in unity (I, 11, 1, *O.t.c.*).—That there is no multitude which does not participate in unity (I, 11, 1, ad 2; I-II, 17, 4).—That it is an immovable and divine law that the lower should be returned to God through the higher (I, 106, 3, *O.t.c.*; I-II, 63, 3, obj. 1).—That divine wisdom joins the end of what is first to the beginning of what is second (I, 110, 3; *C.G.*, III, 97).—That the highest part of a lower nature reaches to the lowest part of a higher nature (I, 78, 2).—That the order of things consists in this, that some are returned to God through others

(I-II, 111, 1).—That the lowest things are led back to their source by the first (I, 90, 3, obj. 2).—That in beings of one order there is a mutual likeness, but not between a cause and that which is caused (I, 4, 3, ad 4; 42, 1, ad 3).—That caused things have imperfect images of their causes (I, 93, 2, obj. 1).—That though being is more perfect than life, and life more perfect than wisdom, yet a living being is more perfect than a being, and a wise being more perfect than a living being (I, 4, 2, ad 3). Cf. I, 44, 3, obj. 4 and ad 4.—That plants have the lowest grade of life (I, 18, 1, *O.t.c.*).—That the lower exists in the higher in a more eminent way than in itself (I, 84, 2, obj. 2).—That lower bodies are produced by the higher (I, 90, 3, obj. 1).—That the light of the sun aids in the generation of sensible bodies, moves them to life, and nourishes, increases and perfects them (I, 115, 3, *O.t.c.; C.G.*, III, 83).—On the active power of corporeal fire: I, 115, 1, *O.t.c.*—That the light of the sun was formless in the first three days, and was afterwards formed on the fourth (I, 67, 4, ad 2; 68, 1; 70, 1, ad 2).

That all things seek the good (*C.G.*, III, 3; I-II, 8, 1, *O.t.c.*).—That the good is praised as beautiful (I, 5, 4, obj. 1).—That the good is self-diffusive and communicative (I, 73, 3, obj. 2; *C.G.*, III, 24; I-II, 112, 3, obj. 3).—That the good is that from which all things subsist and are (I, 5, 4, obj. 2; 6, 1).—That the good has diverse grades (I-II, 98, 1).—That *good* extends to existing and non-existing things, while being extends only to existing things (I, 5, 2, obj. 2 and ad 1; *C.G.*, III, 20).—That good happens in one way, while evil happens in many (I, 19, 12, obj. 4; I-II, 70, 4, ad 2).—That good is more powerful than evil (I-II, 63, 2, *O.t.c.*).—That each particular defect causes evil, while good is caused by an integral cause (I-II, 18, 4, ad 3; 18, 11, obj. 3; 19, 6, ad 1; 71, 5, ad 1; 72, 9, obj. 1).—That love is a certain unitive force (I, 37, 1, obj. 3; 60, 3, obj. 2).—That love places the lover outside himself and somehow transforms him into the object of his love (I, 20, 2, obj. 1).—On the distinction between natural and intellectual love: I, 60, 1, obj. 1.—On the distinction between rational and intellectual love: I, 60, 2, obj. 1.

That evil is removed from being and, even more, from non-being (I, 48, 2, obj. 1).—That evil is not an existing thing, nor something in existing things (I, 48,

ferior (I, 45, 5, ad 1).—That the angels purify, illumine and perfect both inferior angels and even men (I-II, 112, 1, obj. 3).—That the angels of the second hierarchy are purged and illumined and perfected by the angels of the first (I, 106, 1, *O.t.c.*).—That the angels of the second hierarchy are illumined by those in the first (I, 112, 4, obj. 1).—That angelic purgation, illumination and perfection is nothing other than the acquisition of divine knowledge (I-II, 112, 1, ad 3).— That purgation among the angels is an illumination of what is unknown leading to more perfect knowledge (I, 106, 2, ad 1).—On the higher angels teaching the lower: I, 106, 1; 106, 4, *O.t.c.*; 107, 5, obj. 3.—That the prophets are taught by the angels (I, 57, 5, obj. 3).—That many gentiles were brought to God through the angels (I-II, 98, 5, *O.t.c.*; II-II, 2, 7, obj. 3).—On the angels as learning the mysteries of grace from Christ: I, 57, 5, *O.t.c.* —On the existence of nescience in the angels: I, 101, 1, ad 2; I-II, 76, 2.—That lower angels are purged of their nescience by higher angels (I, 12, 8, *O.t.c.*).

That the multitude of the demons is the cause of all evils to themselves and to others (I, 114, 3, obj. 1; I-II, 80, 4, obj. 1).—That the demons seek what is good and best, namely, to be, to live and to understand (I, 64, 2 obj. 5).—That the demons have received some gifts which are in no way changed but remain complete and most brilliant (I, 64, 1, *O.t.c.*). —That after the Fall the natural gifts remained in the demons (I, 95, 1; 109, 1; I-II, 63, 1, *O.t.c.*; 85, 1, obj. 1 and ad 1).—That the demons are not naturally wicked (I, 63, 4, *O.t.c.*).—That in the angels there is an irrational madness and a mad concupiscence (I, 59, 4, obj. 1).—That in the demons there is a perverted phantasy (I, 54, 5, obj. 3; 58, 5, obj. 1).—On nescience and error in the demons: I, 58, 5, obj. 2-3.

V. Man.

That human souls owe to the divine goodness that they are intellectual and that they have an incorruptible substantial life (I, 75, 6, *O.t.c.*).—That a threefold motion is found in the soul (I, 94, 2).—That men reach the knowledge of intelligible truth by proceeding from one thing to another (I, 79, 8).—That human souls must gather their knowledge from divisible things by way of sense (I, 76, 5; 84, 4, ad 1).—That the human mind cannot rise to the immaterial contemplation of the celestial hierarchies unless it uses the guidance of material things (I, 88, 2, obj. 1).—That divine things cannot be manifested to men except under sensible likenesses (I-II, 99, 3, ad 3).—That men receive the divine illuminations under the likenesses of sensible things (I, 108, 1).— That the divine ray can shine upon us only by being covered by the variety of sacred veils (I, 1, 9; 12, 13, obj. 2; 111, 1).—That the divine revelations come to men through the angels (I, 111, 1, *O.t.c.*; 117, 2, *O.t.c.*; I-II, 98, 3).—That man's intellect is reduced to act not only by God but also by angelic illuminations (I-II, 9, 6, obj. 2).—That the good of man consists in being in accord with reason, while his evil consists in violating reason (I-II, 18, 5; 55, 4, ad 2; 58, 1, obj. 3; 71, 2; 71, 6, obj. 5).—That man has a threefold state, namely, that of the Old Law, that of the New, and that of future glory (I-II, 106, 4, ad 1).—That he is better united to God in this life who is united to Him as to the absolutely unknown (I, 12, 13, obj. 1).—That in the present state of life the soul is joined to God as to the unknown (I, 84, 5, obj. 1; *C.G.*, III, 49).—That more divine than any thing else is to become a co-worker of God (*C.G.*, III, 21).—On illumination and baptism: I, 111, 1, obj. 1.

VI. Dionysius as an Interpreter and a Source.—Scriptural Interpretations: *Job*, xi. 8 (I, 3, 1, ad 1). *Psalm* xxiii. 8 (I, 106, 4, obj. 2; 107, 2, *O.t.c.*; II-II, 2, 7, obj. 1). —Dionysius as a Historical Source: I, 84, 5.

EADMER [PSEUDO-ANSELM],
That the will moves the intellect and all the other powers of the soul as an efficient cause (I, 82, 4).

EUCLID,
Definitions of line and point: I, 85, 8; *ibid.*, obj. 2 and ad 2.

EUSTRATIUS,
That men can in no way be raised to equality with the angels (I, 108, 8).

FISHACRE, ROBERT,
Historical Source on I, 29, 4.

FULGENTIUS,
That God does not punish that of which He is the author (I-II, 79, 3, obj.

2).—On lust and the transmission of original sin: I-II, 82, 4, obj. 3.

FULGENTIUS [PSEUDO-AUGUSTINE],
Trinitarian citations: I, 31, 2, *O.t.c.*; 35, 1, obj. 1 and ad 1; 39, 6, *O.t.c.*; 41, 1, *O.t.c.*; 42, 1, ad 1; 93, 5, obj. 1.

GENNADIUS OF MARSEILLES,
Cited anonymously. On the beatitude in which the angels were created: I, 62, 1, obj. 1.—That only men have a substantive soul; animals do not (I, 75, 3, *O.t.c.*).—That there are not two souls in man, one animal and the other spiritual, obeying the reason; but that one and the same soul vivifies the body and orders itself by its own reason (I, 76, 3, *O.t.c.*).—That man is composed of only two substances, the soul with its reason and the flesh with its senses (I, 77, 8, *O.t.c.*).—That the human soul is created simultaneously with the body (I, 118, 3, *O.t.c.*).—That it is not generated (I, 118, 2, *O.t.c.*).—That some of our thoughts arise, not because of the devil, but through the movement of our choice (I, 114, 3, *O.t.c.*; I-II, 80, 4, *O.t.c.*).— On the image of God in the soul: I, 93, 5, obj. 2.

GILBERT DE LA PORRÉE,
That form consists of a simple and invariable essence (I, 9, 2, obj. 3). [?]— On relations in God: I, 28, 2.—On the name God in relation to nature and person: I, 39, 4.

GRATIAN,
Definition of law: I-II, 90, 3, *O.t.c.*; the function of law: I-II, 92, 2, obj. 1; the immutability of natural law: I-II, 94, 5, *O.t.c.*—That the natural law is what is contained in the Law and the Gospel (I-II, 94, 4, obj. 1; for St. Thomas' interpretation of Gratian, cf. *ibid.*, ad 1).— On privilege and private law: I-II, 96, 1, ad 1; 96, 5, obj. 2.—On law and tradition: I-II, 97, 2, *O.t.c.*; law and custom: I-II, 97, 3, *O.t.c.*—On the Pope and the summoning of a general council: II-II, 1, 10, *O.t.c.*—On the Pope and the more difficult issues of the Church: II-II, 1, 10.

GREGORY OF NAZIANZUS, ST.,
(Quoted from St. John Damascene)

That the angels were created before all other beings (I, 61, 3, with obj. 1).

GREGORY OF NYSSA, ST.,
That, since the divinity is the plenitude of goodness, for man to be made to the image of God is for human nature to be made a partaker of all good (I, 93, 5, obj. 2).—On the multiplication of mankind in paradise: I, 98, 2.

GREGORY THE GREAT, ST.,
That where human reason offers evidence faith has no merit (I, 1, 8, obj. 2; II-II, 2, 10, obj. 1).—That of things that are not seen there is faith, not knowledge (I, 12, 13, obj. 3); and of things seen there is knowledge, not faith (II-II, 1, 5, *O.t.c.*).—That by its very manner of speech sacred Scripture transcends all the sciences (I, 1, 10, *O.t.c.*).—That we express the perfections of God as best we can, stammeringly (I, 4, 1, ad 1).—That he is blessed who, in enjoying himself, needs no added glory (I, 26, 2, *O.t.c.*).— That those who see God see all things (I, 12, 8, obj. 1 and ad 1). Cf. also I, 89, 8; *C.G.*, III, 59.—That the sentence of God changes, but not His counsel (I, 19, 7, ad 2; *C.G.*, III, 96).—That it is better to say of the Son that He is always born (I, 42, 2, ad 4).—That in being generated the Son is sent (I, 43, 2, obj. 1).—That the Holy Ghost is Love (I, 37, 1, *O.t.c.*). —That He Who made the world through Himself, rules it through Himself (I, 22, 3, *O.t.c.*; *C.G.*, III, 83).—That the world would sink to nothingness if God did not conserve it in being (I, 104, 1).—That the faithful ought not consider fate to be anything (I, 116, 1, obj. 1; *C.G.*, III, 93).—That, as concerns the substance of matter, all things were created together; but not as concerns form (I, 119, 2).— That an angel is a rational animal (I, 51, 1, obj. 2).—On the ordering of the angels: I, 108, 5-6; 109, 4, *O.t.c.*; 113, 2; 113, 3, obj. 3; *C.G.*, III, 80.—On the angels as administrators of corporeal creatures: I, 110, 1; *C.G.*, III, 83; their mission: I, 112, 1-4.—How the angels speak to God: I, 107, 3; 107, 4, ad 2.—That some men are assumed into the highest orders of angels (I, 117, 2, obj. 3).—That man has sense in common with brute animals and understanding in common with the angels (I, 54, 5, *O.t.c.*). Cf. also I, 79, 1, obj. 3; 84, 3, obj. 1; I-II, 89, 4, obj. 1.—That in paradise man had a knowledge which

was like that of the angels in eminence (I, 94, 2, with obj. 1).—That after the resurrection one will be able to read another's thoughts (I, 57, 4, obj. 1). Cf. I, 107, 1, obj. 1 and ad 1.—That the contemplative life is of greater merit than the active life (I-II, 57, 1).—That the whole fabric of good works rises from four virtues (I-II, 61, 2, O.t.c.).—That without humility the other virtues are like straws in the wind (I-II, 61, 3, obj. 2).—On the interconnection of the four cardinal virtues: I-II, 61, 4, obj. 1. Cf. I-II, 65, 1.—That one virtue without the others is absolutely nothing, or imperfect (I-II, 65, 1, O.t.c.).—That charity does great works if it is present (I-II, 114, 4, ad 2).—On the gifts of the Holy Ghost: I-II, 68, passim.—That the first angel who sinned was from the highest order (I, 63, 7, O.t.c.; 63, 9, ad 3; 64, 2, O.t.c.—That the sin of the devil is irreparable (I-II, 80, 4, obj. 3).—That, without sin, we are all equal (I, 92, 1, obj. 2; 96, 3, obj. 1.—That pride is the queen of sins (I-II, 84, 4, ad 4).—That many sins are born from pride and envy (I, 63, 2, obj. 3).—That pride is found both in spiritual and corporeal matters (I-II, 72, 1, obj. 3).—That of the seven capital sins five are spiritual and two carnal (I-II, 72, 2, O.t.c.). Cf. I-II, 72, 3, obj. 3; 84, 3-4.—That the carnal sins are lesser than the spiritual (I-II, 73, 5, O.t.c.).—On the grades of sin: I-II, 72, 7, obj. 2.—That anger is a spiritual sin (I-II, 73, 5, obj. 3).—That the eminence of a person increases sin because of scandal (I-II, 73, 10).—That the sin which is not quickly removed is both sin and the cause of sin (I-II, 75, 4, O.t.c.; 109, 8).—That some sins are a punishment of sin (I-II, 87, 2, O.t.c.).—On the justice of eternal punishment: I-II, 87, 3, ad 1.—That certain less grave sins will be remitted after this life (I-II, 87, 5, O.t.c.).—That the evils which oppress us in this life compel us to go to God (I, 21, 4, ad 3).—That in battle a general loves that soldier more who, having fled, returns to fight bravely than him who has never fled and never fought bravely (I, 20, 4, ad 4).—On idle words: I-II, 18, 9, O.t.c.—On John the Baptist: II-II, 2, 7, ad 2.—Scriptural interpretations cited: Gen. i. 1 (I, 46, 2, O.t.c.); Exod. i, 31 (I-II, 114, 10, obj. 2); Exod. xxxiii. 11 (I-II, 98, 3, ad 1); Num. xix. 7 (I-II, 102, 5, ad 5); Job i. 14 (II-II, 2, 6, O.t.c.); Job iii. 13 (I, 100, 2, obj. 1); Ezech. i. 16 (I-II, 107, 3, O.t.c.); Dan. x. 13 (I. 113, 8).

GROSSETESTE, ROBERT,
On the subject matter of theology: I, 1, 7.—That the antecedent of the conditional proposition, If God knew that this thing would be, it will be, is contingent (I, 14, 13, ad 2).

GUNDISSALINUS, DOMINICUS,
On matter and form in the angels: I, 50, 2, obj. 4.—That with the destruction of the body the habit of science acquired in this life is lost (I, 89, 5).

HERMES TRISMEGISTUS, PSEUDO-,
That unity begot unity, and reflected upon itself its own desire (I, 32, 1, obj. 1). Cf. St. Thomas' interpretation: ibid., ad 1.

HESYCHIUS,
Interpretation of Levit. xxvi. 26 (I-II, 100, 4).

HILARY OF POITIERS, ST.,
That in God being is not an accident but subsistent truth (I, 3, 4, O.t.c.).—That God, being power, is not made up of things weak; and, being light, He is not made up of things dark (I, 3, 7).—That God is of immense power (I, 25, 2, O.t.c.).—That the admission of companionship or plurality excludes the notion of oneness or solitude (I, 30, 3, O.t.c.; 31, 2).—That among the divine Persons nothing is diverse, foreign or separable (I, 31, 2, obj. 3; 41, 3, obj. 1; 43, 1, obj. 2).—That neither is God solitary, nor has He diversity (I, 31, 2).—That man should not think that he can reach an understanding of the mystery of generation (I, 32, 1).—That, though the Father as principle is greater, the Son is not lesser (I, 33, 1, ad 2; 42, 4, ad 1).—That it is proper to the Father to be unbegotten (I, 33, 4).—That, since God is one, there can be only one unbegotten being (I, 33, 4, ad 4).—That an image is the unvaried likeness of its model (I, 35, 1, obj. 2; 93, 1, obj. 3).—On likeness cf. also I, 14, 2, obj. 2.—That Father, Son and Holy Ghost are three in substance, though one in harmony (I, 39, 2, obj. 1).—On the difficulty of predicating one substance of Father and Son: I, 39, 2, obj. 6 and ad 6).—That the Son has nothing else than birth (I, 40, 3, O.t.c.).—That the Father did not generate the Son by natural ne-

cessity or compulsion (I, 41, 2, obj. 1 and ad 1).—That the Son did not proceed as a creature from the will of God (I, 41, 2).—On generation and the divine essence: I, 41, 5.—That, as being the likeness of his nature, every son is equal to his father (I, 42, 4). Cf. *ibid.*, ad 1.—That in accord with His nature an immutable God generates an immutable God (I, 42, 5).—That the unity of the divine nature is such that what the Son does through Himself He does not do by Himself (I, 42, 6, ad 1).—That *Spirit* in God sometimes means the Father, sometimes the Son and sometimes the Holy Ghost (I, 36, 1, obj. 1).—That the Holy Ghost is from the Father and the Son as authors (I, 36, 4, obj. 7).—That *eternity* is in the Father, *likeness* in the Image, and *use* in the Gift (I-II, 16, 3, obj. 3).—That man is in the common image of the Trinity (I, 93, 5, obj. 1).—That man reveals the plurality of the divine Persons in being said to be made to the image of God (I, 95, 5, *O.t.c.*).—That when the will is not subject to the reason, its persistence in its acts is unruly (I-II, 19, 3, *O.t.c.*).—St. Hilary as a Historical Source: I, 34, 2, ad 2; 41, 2.—Exposition of *Matt.* xxi. 28: I-II, 107, 4, *O.t.c.*

HILDEBERT OF LAVARDIN,
"Your fates lead you": I, 116, 2, ad 3.

HOMER,
Odyssey, XVIII, 136, cited: I, 115, 4; *C.G.*, III, 84; I-II, 9, 5.

HUGH OF ST. VICTOR,
On the works of salvation as the subject-matter of theology: I, 1, 7.—On the senses of Scripture: I, 1, 10.—That though God does not will evil, He yet wills it to be, because it is a good that evils be or come to be (I, 19, 9, ad 1). Cf. St. Thomas' criticism, *ibid.*—On power as appropriated to the Father: I, 39, 7; 39, 8, obj. 3.—On the formation of Eve's body: I, 92, 3, ad 1.—On the children of the first man and sin: I, 100, 1, obj. 1.—That the words of St. Paul (*Heb.* xi. 1) are not a definition of faith (II-II, 4, 1).—That faith is a certitude of the soul, about things absent, located above opinion and below knowledge (*ibid.*).—On the eye of contemplation, closed in man now, open in the state of innocence: II-II, 5, 1, obj. 1.

ISAAC ISRAELI,
Cf. I, 57, 2.

ISIDORE OF SEVILLE, ST.,
That the angels know many things by experience (I, 54, 5, obj. 1). Cf. I, 58, 3, obj. 3; 89, 3, *O.t.c.*—That *paradise* is the name of a place in the east, and may be rendered in Latin by *garden* (I, 102, 1).—That men are deceived now by the same blandishments as were our first parents (I, 114, 3).—That the more excellent the person sinning, the graver the sin (I-II, 73, 10, *O.t.c.*).—That the devil fills the hearts of men with secret desires (I-II, 80, 1, obj. 1).—That law is enacted, not for a private good, but for the common good of the citizens (I-II, 90, 2, *O.t.c.*). Cf. I-II, 95, 1; 97, 4, obj. 1; 98, 1, obj. 1; 100, 2, obj. 3.—That law is an ordinance of the people, whereby something is sanctioned by the Elders together with the people (I-II, 90, 3, *O.t.c.*). Cf. I-II, 95, 4.—On the purpose of law: I-II, 95, 1, *O.t.c.*; 96, 2, obj. 1.—That *lex* [*law*] is derived from *legere* [to *read*] because it is written (I-II, 90, 4, ad 3). —That if law is based on reason, whatever is based on reason is a law (I-II, 90, 2, obj. 3). Cf. I-II, 91, 6, obj. 1; 100, 7, obj. 2.—That whatever is based on reason is a law provided it is in harmony with religion, helps discipline and promotes salvation (I-II, 95, 3, obj. 1). Cf. I-II, 97, 4, obj. 3; 101, 3, obj. 2.—That the natural law is common to all nations (I-II, 94, 4, *O.t.c.*). Cf. I-II, 95, 4, obj. 1.—That according to the natural law all things are possessed in common (I, 98, 1, obj. 3).—That the possession of all things in common, and universal freedom, are matters of natural law (I-II, 94, 5, obj. 3).—That positive law is distinguished from natural law (I-II, 95, 2, obj. 2).—Characteristics of [positive] law: I-II, 95, 3, obj. 1; 96, 2; 97, 3, ad 2; 100, 2, obj. 1.—That the law of nations is so varied because almost all nations use it (I-II, 95, 4, obj. 1).—That written law is distinguished from custom (I-II, 95, 3, obj. 3).—That custom should yield to authority, and that law and reason should eradicate evil customs (I-II, 97, 3, ad 1).—On the *Lex Julia* and the *Lex Cornelia*, cf. I-II, 95, 4. Cf. also: I-II, 95, 4, obj. 2, 3, 5.

JEROME, ST.,
That the old Doctors of the Church

gan of His divinity (I-II, 112, 1, ad 1).

That providence is of existing things, which are not eternal (I, 22, 1, obj. 2).— That God foreknows all things, but He does not predetermine all things (I, 23, 1, obj. 1; *C.G.*, III, 90).

That in created intellectual substances there is mutability from good to evil, through choice (I, 9, 2).—That the angel is an ever movable intellectual substance (I, 50, 1, obj. 2 and ad 2).—That the angel is an intellectual substance whose immortality is by grace, not by nature (I, 50, 5, obj. 1). Cf. *ibid.*, ad 1.—That an angel is where he acts (I, 52, 2, obj. 3). —That an angel acts where he is (I, 107, 4, obj. 1).—That while an angel is in heaven, he is not on earth (I, 52, 2, *O.t.c.*).—That when the angels are with us, they are not in heaven (I, 113, 6, obj. 3).—That those angels who fell were among the lower angels (I, 63, 7; 110, 1, ad 3).—That what the Fall was to the angels, this death is to men (I, 64, 2).— That all sins are from the devil (I, 114, 3, obj. 1).

That light is a quality (I, 67, 3, *O.t.c.*). —That the heaven which was said to be made on the first day is a spherical heaven without stars (I, 68, 1, ad 1).— That there are many heavens (I, 68, 4). —That the heavens and the luminaries are inanimate and insensible (I, 70, 3, *O.t.c.*).—That the heavenly bodies are not the cause of generation and corruption (I, 115, 3, obj. 1; *C.G.*, III, 86).— That the heavenly bodies are by no means the cause of human acts (I, 115, 4, *O.t.c.*; I-II, 9, 5, *O.t.c.*).—On the heavenly bodies, cf. also *C.G.*, III, 84.—That generation is the work of nature producing from the substance of the generator that which is generated (I, 119, 2, obj. 2).

On the meaning of man as in the image of God: I, 93, 5, obj. 2; 93, 9.—That the first man, living in paradise, led a life which was blessed and rich with all things (I, 94, 1, obj. 1).—That paradise is a divine place and a worthy dwelling of him who was in the image of God (I, 102, 2, *O.t.c.*).

On the superior reason or *mens*: I, 79, 9, obj. 4.—On the meaning of intelligence (*intelligentia*): I, 79, 10, obj. 3 and ad 3.—On conscience: I, 79, 13.

On the distinction of the appetitive from the knowing powers: I, 80, 1, *O.t.c.* —On the distinction of the irascible and concupiscible powers: I, 81, 2, *O.t.c.*; 82, 5, *O.t.c.*—That these powers are subject to the authority and the persuasion of reason (I, 81, 3, *O.t.c.*).—On the will moving the intellect: I, 82, 4, *O.t.c.*— That free choice accompanies reason (I, 83, 3, obj. 1).—That through free choice man inquires, examines, judges and disposes (I-II, 17, 6, *O.t.c.*).—On *thelesis* and *bulesis*: I, 83, 4, obj. 1.—That free choice is nothing else than the will (I, 83, 4, *O.t.c.*).—That that is voluntary whose principle is in itself (I-II, 6, 1, obj. 1).—That the voluntary is an act which is a rational operation (I-II, 6, 1, *O.t.c.*).—That praise or blame accompanies voluntary acts (I-II, 6, 2, obj. 3). —That children and brute animals share in the voluntary (I-II, 6, 2, *O.t.c.*).— That brute animals do not act; they are rather acted upon (I-II, 6, 2, obj. 2).— That impulse to action is found in brute animals (I-II, 17, 2, obj. 3).—That what is involuntary is accompanied by sorrow (I-II, 6, 5, obj. 2; 6, 7, obj. 3).—That the involuntary can be such through violence (I-II, 6, 5, *O.t.c.*).—That the involuntary is worthy of compassion and pardon (I-II, 6, 7, *O.t.c.*; 6, 7, obj. 1).— That some involuntary acts are caused by ignorance (I-II, 6, 7, *O.t.c.*; 7, 2, *O.t.c.*). —That counsel is an appetite (I-II, 14, 1, obj. 1 and ad 1).—That consent requires appetite (I-II, 15, 1, *O.t.c.*).—That after judgment a man disposes and loves what he has joined through counsel, and this is called consent (I-II, 15, 2, *O.t.c.*). Cf. I-II, 15, 3, *O.t.c.*—On the use of the will: I-II, 16, 1, obj. 2; 16, 4, *O.t.c.*; 17, 3, *O.t.c.*

That virtues are natural and equally present in all (I-II, 63, 1, obj. 1; 94, 3, *O.t.c.*).—That mercy is a kind of sadness (I, 21, 3, obj. 1).

That the movement of the will to sin is against nature (I-II, 6, 4, obj. 3).— That sin is against nature (I-II, 75, 2, obj. 3; 94, 3, ad 2, 109, 2, obj. 2; 109, 7, obj. 3).

Scriptural Interpretation: *I Tim.* ii, 4 (I, 19, 6, ad 1).

Damascene as a Historical Source: I, 61, 3, obj. 1.

JOHN OF ROCHELLE,
That angels and souls are without matter (I, 9, 2, obj. 1).

JOSEPHUS,
Cf. *C.G.*, III, 85; I-II, 102, 4, ad 6; 102, 5, ad 5.

NEMESIUS OF EMESA [PSEUDO-GREGORY OF NYSSA],

That it is God's will through which all things receive a fitting end (*C.G.*, III, 73).—That providence is of those things that do not lie in our power, but not of those things that do (*C.G.*, III, 90).

On Plato's opinion concerning the threefold division of providence: I, 103, 6, obj. 1.

That the irrational part of the soul is divided into the desiderative and the irascible (I, 82, 5, *O.t.c.*; I-II, 17, 7, *O.t.c.*).

That the appetite obeys the reason (I-II, 17, 1, *O.t.c.*).—That the nutritive and the generative powers are not subject to the persuasion of reason (I-II, 117, 8, *O.t.c.*).—That the pulse is not subject to the persuasion of the reason (I-II, 17, 9, obj. 2 and ad 2).

That the voluntary is that whose principle is in itself (I-II, 6, 1, obj. 1).— That children and brute animals share in the voluntary (I-II, 6, 2, *O.t.c.*).—That children and brute animals act voluntarily but not freely (I-II, 13, 2, *O.t.c.*).—That what is done through fear is mixed of the voluntary and the involuntary (I-II, 6, 6).—That what is done through fear is voluntary rather than involuntary (I-II, 6, 6, *O.t.c.*).—That the violent is that whose principle lies outside the recipient, who does not concur in the action (I-II, 6, 6, ad 1).—That the ignorance of circumstances causes involuntariness (I-II, 7, 2, *O.t.c.*).—That the most important circumstances of an act are *why it is done* and *what is it* (I-II, 7, 4, *O.t.c.*).—That all counsel is a question, but not every question is a counsel (I-II, 14, 1, *O.t.c.*). —That we take counsel not of the end but of the means to the end (I-II, 14, 2, *O.t.c.*).—That counsel has no place in what is done through science or art (I-II, 114, 4, *O.t.c.*), except in conjectural matters (I-II, 114, 4).

Nemesius as a Historical Source: I, 22, 2; 22, 3; 23, 8; 66, 2; 66, 2, ad 1; 75, 1; 75, 3; 75, 4; 84, 2; 91, 1; 116, 4; *C.G.*, III, 73, 76.

ORIGEN,

That it is not because God knows a thing as future that it will be; it is because it will be that God knows it before it comes to be (I, 14, 8, obj. 1 and ad 1).

That *word* is said metaphorically in God (I, 34, 1, obj. 1).—That the Son is always born (I, 42, 2, ad 4).

That predestination is of him who does not exist; destination is of him who does (I, 23, 2, obj. 2).—That the effect of predestination is preordained for one because of matter pre-existing in another life; and that human souls, having been created from the beginning of the world, have in this world in their union with bodies received a diversity of states according to the diversity of their works (I, 23, 5; 90, 4).

That it is proper to the nature of God alone that it should exist without any material substance and without the accompaniment of any bodily addition (I, 51, 1, obj. 1).—That all created spiritual substances are joined to bodies (I, 51, 1, ad 1).

That in the beginning all things were created equal, and that inequality arose in the first creatures, which were all rational substances, through the diverse use of free choice (I, 47, 2). Cf. *ibid.*, ad 3.— That all spiritual substances proceeded from God in a certain equality (I, 10, 6). —That all of them, including human souls, are of one species (I, 50, 4; 75, 7; 118, 3).

On the interval between creation and the angelic fall: I, 63, 6, obj. 2 and ad 2. —That souls and angels, having achieved beatitude, can again fall into wretchedness (*C.G.*, III, 62).

That every created will, with the exception of the soul of Christ, can, because of the liberty of choice, be turned both to good and to evil (I, 64, 2).—That God gives us the power to will, but not in such a way that He makes us will this or that thing (*C.G.*, III, 89).—That man does not fall into sin suddenly but gradually (I-II, 78, 3, obj. 2).—That directly the devil is not the cause of all our sins (I, 114, 3; I-II, 80, 4).—That a demon who has been overcome cannot again tempt the same man concerning the same or another sin (I, 114, 5).—That angels are brought to trial, testing whether men have fallen through their own indolence or through the angels' neglect (I, 113, 7, obj. 4).—That angels are deputed to the administration of animals and plants (I, 110, 1, ad 3).

That conscience is a correcting spirit and teacher joined to the soul, by means of which the soul may be separated from evil and adhere to the good (I, 79, 13, obj. 1).

On the distinction of the precepts of the Decalogue: I-II, 100, 4.

That the heavenly bodies are **animated**

(I, 70, 3).—That the corporeal creature was not made as having been first intended by God, but as a punishment for spiritual creatures because of their sins (I, 65, 2).

PELAGIUS,
Cf. I-II, 99, 5; 109, 4, obj. 2 and ad 2.

PETER COMESTOR,
On the meaning of some of the sacred things in the Old Law: I-II, 102, 4, ad 8.

PETER LOMBARD [MAGISTER SENTENTIARUM],
That even the faith which is without charity is a gift of God (II-II, 6, 2, O.t.c.).—On the subject-matter of theology: I, 1, 7.—That numeral terms do not posit anything in God (I, 30, 3).—That the Father always exists because He always generates the Son (I, 40, 4, obj. 1 and ad 1).—That generation and nativity are called by other names paternity and filiation (I, 41, 1, ad 2).—That when the Son is said to be born of the essence of the Father, there is designated the relation of a principle which is, as it were, active (I, 41, 3, ad 2).—That the power of generating signifies principally the divine essence (I, 41, 5).

That just as from one countenance in man there result many reflections in a mirror, so from one divine truth there result many truths (I, 16, 6).—That every truth, by whomever said, is from the Holy Spirit (I-II, 109, 1, obj. 1).

That God can communicate the power of creating to a creature (I, 45, 5).—That it is quite probable that the light made on the first day was a corporeal light (I, 70, 1, ad 2).

That God is in all things by His essence, power and presence (I, 8, 3, obj. 1).—On predestination: I, 23, 6, O.t.c.—That predestination is the preparation of grace in this life and of glory in the future life (I, 23, 2, obj. 4).

That the angels who were created with a more perfect nature and were endowed with greater wisdom likewise received greater gifts of grace (I, 62, 2, O.t.c.).—That the angels are like one another by gifts of grace and nature (I, 108, 4, O.t.c.).

That memory, intelligence and will are natural powers of the soul (I, 93, 7, obj. 3).—That *image* consists in the knowledge of truth, while *likeness* consists in the love of virtue (I, 93, 9, obj. 4).—That likeness is in the essence of the soul because it is immortal and indivisible; whereas *image* is in the rest (I, 93, 9, obj. 2).—That image is understood according to memory, intelligence and will; whereas likeness is understood according to innocence and justice (I, 93, 9, ad 3).—That intellectual vision is of those things which are in the soul by their essence (I, 57, 1, obj. 2).—That in the state of innocence man saw God without a medium (I, 94, 1, obj. 3).—That free choice is a faculty of will and reason (I, 83, 2, obj. 2; I-II, 77, 6).—That sensuality is the appetite of things pertaining to the body (I, 81, 1, O.t.c.).

On the definition of virtue: I-II, 55, 4, obj. 1.—That he has a right heart who wills what God wills (I-II, 19, 10, O.t.c.).—On the term *bonum ex genere*: I-II, 18, 2.—That discipline is the training of morals by means of difficult works (I-II, 99, 2, O.t.c.).—On the gifts and the virtues: I-II, 68, 1.—On whether grace and virtue differ: I-II, 110, 3.—That the first man would not have merited by resisting temptation; whereas now he who resists temptation merits (I, 95, 4, obj. 3).—That eternal life is the reward for good works; but the good works themselves pertain to the grace of God (I-II, 109, 5, ad 2).

On original sin as a *sickness of nature*: I-II, 82, 1.—On original sin as being more concupiscence than ignorance: I-II, 82, 3, ad 3.—On the transmission of original sin: I-II, 81, 1.—That temptation is not a sin but the matter for the exercise of virtue (I, 48, 5, obj. 3).—On the inclination of the members to concupiscence as the *law of the members*: I-II, 90, 1, ad 1.—On whether consent to delectation is a mortal sin: I-II, 74, 8; 88, 5, obj. 2.—On the sin of omission: I-II, 71, 5.—That every fornicator is either impure or covetous (I-II, 73, 5, ad 1).

That the Old Law restrains the hand, while the New restrains the soul (I-II, 91, 5; 107, 1, ad 2; 108, 1, obj. 3).—On the law of justice as written in the interior man: I-II, 94, 6, obj. 1.—That those who have not a written law have nevertheless a natural law, by which each one understands and is aware of what is good and what is evil (I-II, 91, 2, O.t.c.).—That that law is good which, while prohibiting concupiscence, prohibits all evil (I-II, 73. 6, obj. 2).—That he is under the law who abstains from an evil deed through fear of the punishment